484   CHAPTER 13 Rediscovering the Student in Teaching

ing them be aware of their own role in constructing knowledge (Cunningham, 1992). The assumptions we make, our beliefs, and experiences shape what each of us comes to "know" about the world. Different assumptions and different experiences lead to different knowledge. Constructivists stress the importance of understanding the knowledge construction process so that students will be aware of the influences that shape their thinking; thus they will be able to choose, develop, and defend positions in a self-critical way while respecting the positions of others. This is consistent with APA Principles 1, 3, 9, and 12.

The last characteristic of constructivist teaching listed by Driscoll (1994) is student-centered instruction. Because student-centered teaching is the focus of this chapter, we will spend several pages discussing this topic.

Student-Centered Teaching Methods

In this section we will examine examples of student-centered teaching practices

Grouping: Cooperation and Competition   375

teacher could praise the same work by saying, "Good for you! Your understanding of the author's use of metaphors has improved tremendously. You earned an A." This statement provides information about the student's growing competence and should increase intrinsic motivation. But if the information is negative, as in "You still have not grasped the concept of metaphor and your grade shows it," then motivation is likely to diminish.

Autonomy Supporting Class Climates

What can teachers do to support student autonomy? An obvious first step is to limit their controlling messages to their students and make sure the information they provide highlights students' growing competence. Unfortunately, when teachers are under pressure and "controlled" by the school administration, they are likely to treat students the same way. In one study, teachers told to "make sure" their students performed well in solving problems were more critical and gave students more hints and less time for independent work than teachers who were told that their job was to "help" the students learn how to solve the problems themselves. And the students of the pressured teachers actually performed worse (Boggiano, Flink, Shields, Seelbach, & Barrett, in press). Table 10.2 on page 376 lists five essential elements that support student autonomy.

Recognizing Accomplishment

The third TARGETT area is *recognition*. How should students' accomplishments be acknowledged and rewarded? In chapter 6 we discussed the importance of authentic praise that focuses on progress, growing competence, and independence. We have also seen that giving students rewards for activities that they already enjoy can undermine intrinsic motivation. Students should be recognized for improving on their own personal best, for tackling difficult tasks, for persistence, and for creativity— not just for performing better than others. The next section explains one way to use personal progress as a basis for recognition in classrooms.

Focus on . . .

Supporting Autonomy and Recognizing Accomplishment

■ Name three characteristics of a classroom environment that supports students' autonomy.
■ How can recognition undermine motivation and a sense of self-efficacy?
■ Why would providing rationales for class rules help students feel more autonomous?

Grouping: Cooperation and Competition

You may remember a teacher who made you want to work hard—someone who made a subject come alive. Or you may remember how many hours you spent practicing as a member of a team, orchestra, choir, or theater troupe. If you do, then you know the motivational power of relationships with other people. David Johnson and Roger Johnson (1985) describe the power this way:

Motivation to learn is inherently interpersonal. It is through interaction with other people that students learn to value learning for its own sake, enjoy the process that students learn to value learning for its own sake, enjoy the process of learning, and take pride in their acquisition of knowledge and development of skill. Of the interpersonal relationships available in the classroom, peers may be the most influential on motivation to learn. (p. 250)

...mpletely new chapter, "Rediscovering the Student in Teaching" (Ch.13), focuses on what is known about how to encourage and support students' learning as it considers the teaching and learning process from emerging constructivist perspectives. Topics include...

- APA's learner-centered psychological principles
- Complex learning environments
- Student-centered teaching methods

In addition, new coverage of constructivism appears throughout the text, and is also especially evident in chapters 7, 10.

UNPARALLELED IN INCORPORATING APPLICATIONS AS PART OF EVERY DISCUSSION

Only Woolfolk makes the discussion of applications so much a part of the text narrative that students come away from their reading with the feeling that they've been visiting a classroom. Special features such as *Guidelines* and *Teacher's Casebook* focus even more attention on the practical aspects of educational psychology.

USERS AGREE. NO TEXT DOES IT BETTER.

INCREASED EMPHASIS ON COGNITIVE PERSPECTIVES

This clear, readable, well-organized revision incorporates the most recent thinking on cognitive development, self-regulated learning and constructivist approaches to teaching, teacher thinking, student thinking, and assessment. Over 200 new references have been added.

Chapters 7 and 8 have been revised to incorporate contemporary perspectives and challenges to traditional cognitive theories of learning. Chapter 7 discusses constructivist viewpoints on the development and content of knowledge and alternative perspectives on memory (connectionism). Chapter 8 discusses new ideas about expert problem solving and developing thinking skills in the classroom.

New topics include...
- assisted learning and scaffolding
- instructional conversations
- the brain cortex
- connectionist models of memory
- the ACT model of developing expertise and problem-solving skills
- studies of children's expert knowledge
- expert classroom managers
- constructivist approaches to teaching
- cooperative learning
- self-efficacy
- autonomy and motivation
- self-determination
- problem-based learning
- motivation to learn
- authentic assessment
- portfolios
- judging test items

Check for the newest thinking on cognition!

Check for the latest on motivation!

TABLE 10.1 The TARGETT Model for Supporting Student Motivation to Learn

Teachers make decisions in many areas that can influence motivation to learn. The TARGETT acronym highlights task, autonomy, recognition, grouping, evaluation, time, and teacher expectations.

Tasks for Learning 369

TARGETT Area	Focus	Objectives	Examples of Possible Strategies
Task	How learning tasks are structured—what the student is asked to do	Enhance intrinsic attractiveness of learning tasks Make learning meaningful	Encourage instruction that relates to students' backgrounds and experience Avoid payment (monetary or other) for attendance, grades, or achievement Foster goal setting and self-regulation
Autonomy/Responsibility	Student participation in learning/school decisions	Provide optimal freedom for students to make choices and take responsibility	Give alternatives in making assignments Ask for student comments on school life—and take them seriously Encourage students to take initiatives and evaluate their own learning Establish leadership opportunities for *all* students
Recognition	The nature and use of recognition and reward in the school setting	Provide opportunities for *all* students to be recognized for learning Recognize progress in goal	Foster "personal best" awards Reduce emphasis on "honor rolls" Recognize and publicize a wide range of school-related activities of students
Group			
Evalua			
Time			
Teache Expec			

Source:
Journal

Women and Men: Differences in the Classroom 171

Americans face prejudice and discrimination in subtle or blatant ways every day. One of the most discouraging findings I encountered while writing this chapter is that only 4 percent of the scientists, engineers, and mathematicians in the United States are either African American or Hispanic American—whereas more than 20 percent of the total population is from one of these groups. Even though their attitudes toward science and math are more favorable than the attitudes of white students, black and Hispanic students begin to lose out in science and math as early as elementary school. They are chosen less often for gifted classes and acceleration or enrichment programs. They are more likely to be tracked into "basic skills" classes. As they progress through junior high, high school, and college, their paths take them farther and farther out of the pipeline that produces our scientists. If they do persist and become scientists or engineers, they, along with women, will still be paid less than whites for the same work (National Science Foundation, 1988; Oakes, 1990).

Focus on... Ethnic and Racial Differences

■ Explain how prejudice might develop.
■ What is meant by ethnic pride?
■ Distinguish between prejudice and discrimination.

Women and Men: Differences in the Classroom

While I was proofreading this very page for the last edition, riding cross-country on a train, the conductor stopped beside my seat. He said, "I'm sorry, dear, for interrupting your homework, but do you have a ticket?" I had to smile at his (I'm sure unintended) sexism. I doubt that he made the same comment to the man across the aisle writing on his legal pad. Like racial discrimination, messages of sexism can be subtle. In this section we will examine how men and women are socialized and the role of teachers in providing an equitable education for both sexes.

Gender-Role Identity

The word *gender* usually refers to judgments about masculinity and femininity, judgments that are influenced by culture and context. In contrast, *sex* refers to biological differences (Deaux, 1993). **Gender-role identity** is the image each of us has of ourselves as masculine or feminine in characteristics—a part of our self-concept. People with a "feminine" identity would rate themselves high on characteristics usually associated with females, such as "sensitive" or "warm," and low on characteristics traditionally associated with males, such as "forceful" and "competitive." Most people see themselves in gender-typed terms, as high on *either* masculine or feminine characteristics. Some children and adults, however, are more **androgynous**—they rate themselves high on *both* masculine and feminine traits. They can be assertive or sensitive, depending on the situation. Having either a masculine or an androgynous identity is associated with higher self-esteem than having a feminine identity, possibly because feminine characteristics are not as valued (Bem, 1974; Boldizar, 1991).

Gender-Role Identity Beliefs about characteristics and behaviors associated with one sex as opposed to the other.

Androgynous Having some typically male and some typically female characteristics apparent in one individual.

REORGANIZED COVERAGE OF MOTIVATION

Chapters 9 and 10 have been reorganized to provide a streamlined presentation of both the issues and explanations pertaining to motivation (Ch.9) and the action of motivation in the classroom (Ch.10). Information is based on the most recent research in real classrooms.

New topics covered include...
• Self-regulated learning
• Autonomy support
• Authentic tasks
• Problem-based learning

STRONG COVERAGE OF MULTICULTURAL AND GENDER ISSUES

An entire chapter on the impact of culture and community discusses the important issue of diversity, including cultural differences in the classroom. In addition, multicultural and gender issues are integrated throughout the textbook.
Some new topics include...
• changes in laws about individuals with disabilities
• collaborative consultation in serving students with special needs
• the development of prejudice
• multicultural education
• effective teaching for students placed at risk
• gender-role identity and gender schemas

Special annotations in the Annotated Instructor's Edition help build awareness of multicultural issues.

Check for sensitivity to culture and individual differences throughout the text material!

1

First to provide all the study aids students need to become successful learners.

NO OTHER TEXTBOOK DOES SUCH A MASTERFUL JOB OF USING THE PRINCIPLES OF EDUCATIONAL PSYCHOLOGY TO ACTUALLY TEACH STUDENTS ABOUT THE SUBJECT. FROM "GUIDELINES" AND "WHAT WOULD YOU DO?" QUESTIONS TO "FOCUS ON LEARNING" QUESTIONS, THERE ARE MANY BUILT-IN FEATURES TO HELP STUDENTS LEARN TO ANALYZE PROBLEMS AND DEVELOP WORKABLE CLASSROOM SOLUTIONS.

Check for relevance to today's classrooms!

WHAT DO YOU THINK?

Have you ever had the experience of being the only one in a group who had trouble doing something? The first time you tried to skate, throw a football, play tennis, or bowl, perhaps you were the only one who didn't know how. How would you feel if every day in school you faced the same kind of difficulty, while everyone else seemed to find the work easier than you? What kind of support and teaching would you need to keep trying?

Language and Labeling

Every child is a distinctive collection of talents, abilities, and limitations. In that sense we all are "exceptional." But some students are called exceptional because they have learning abilities or problems and require special education or other services to reach their potential. Exceptional students may have men-

WHAT WOULD YOU DO?

Preschool and Kindergarten
A little girl in your kindergarten class seldom speaks. When she does, she usually says only a word or two. She seems to understand when others talk, but almost never responds verbally. How would you approach this situation?

Elementary and Middle School
The school psychologist tells you that one of your students is going to start taking medication designed to "calm him down." What would you want to know? How would you respond?

The principal tells you that she is assigning two more students to your class because you are "new, and have more training in mainstreaming than the older teachers." One student is mildly retarded and has problems making friends. The other is blind. How would you prepare your class and modify your teaching for these students?

Junior High and High School
A student in your fifth-period class is failing. When you look at your grade book, you see that it is the written

work that is giving the student trouble. Multiple-choice test scores and class participation are fine. How would you identify the source of the problem?

Your school has just received the results of the fall testing, including scores for all your students on a group test of intelligence. What would you do with the results?

How would you adapt your teaching to accommodate a hearing-impaired student in your biology lab class?

Cooperative Learning Activity
Assume the faculty at your school has decided to reconsider how students are assigned to classes. The traditional way in the school has been between-class ability grouping, because your school serves a very wide range of students. Work with four or five members of your educational psychology class to design a system, then present your recommendations to the entire class. Be prepared to justify your recommendations and explain how you would implement them.

What Would You Do? **149**

108

Exception
have abil
nificant
special e
to reach

Check for critical thinking questions!

This market leader continues to be written with the problems of teachers and the needs of today's students in mind.

As in previous editions, the author explains concepts and theories with examples and analogies, then explores the implications for practice. As a result, students understand what they read, can visualize applications, and can transfer what they learn to new situations.

"What Do You Think?" Questions

at the beginning of every chapter help students examine their own ideas and prepare them to relate their experiences to the material in the chapter.

"What Would You Do?" Questions

at the end of every chapter help students to think through the use of the information they've just learned to solve real problems. There are questions for each level: preschool/kindergarten; elementary/middle; and junior high/high as well as a cooperative learning activity.

Together, these two learning devices make the value and relevance of the material obvious to students.

USERS AGREE. NO TEXT DOES IT BETTER.

Check for realistic, current examples.

"Point/Counterpoint" Sections

in each chapter present two perspectives on a controversial, professional, or research issue. Many of the topics considered have "made the news" recently and are central to the discussions of educational reform. Topics include: paying students to learn, gender issues in math and science, and nontraditional learner-based curricula.

CNN Connection

Each "Point/Counterpoint" feature is tied to a Cable News Network videotape segment that adds to the students' knowledge and broadens their perspective on each issue.

REVISED
Teachers' Casebook Sections

This popular feature from previous editions poses relevant questions based on real situations. Students get to read the responses of expert teachers around the country, including many who have been chosen *Teacher of the Year*. These sections at the end of each chapter show readers how application of educational psychology can address common, real-life teaching challenges.

Check for multiple perspectives!

Check for relevant examples of practical applications!

these are the ways most real people use to solve their problems (Huessmann, Eron, Klein, Brice, & Fischer, 1983).

Many popular films and video games are also filled with graphic depictions of violence, sometimes performed by the "hero." Students growing up in the inner cities see street gangs and drug deals. Newspapers, magazines, and the radio are filled with stories of murders, rapes, and robberies. In some preschools the children don't play "Mommy" and "Daddy"; they pretend to sell "nickel bags" of heroin to their playmates. This description appeared in the *Washington Post* (June 2, 1988):

As children huddle, drug games begin. From one child's pocket comes chalk, crushed to resemble cocaine, inside plastic sandwich bags smuggled from home. Soon another child passes cash—thick knots of Monopoly money, or notebook paper, wrapped with rubber bands and dubbed "bankroll."

Socialization: The Home and the School 87

Focus on . . .   Moral Development

- Distinguish the key differences among the preconventional, conventional, and postconventional levels of moral reasoning.
- Describe Gilligan's levels of moral reasoning.
- How can teachers encourage moral behavior?

---

86 CHAPTER 3 Personal, Social, and Emotional Development

Guidelines

Dealing with Aggression and Encouraging Cooperation

Present yourself as a nonaggressive model.
Examples
1. Do not use threats of aggression to win obedience.
2. When problems arise, model nonviolent conflict-resolution strategies.

Ensure that your classroom has enough space and appropriate materials for every student.
Examples
1. Prevent overcrowding.
2. Make sure prized toys or resources are plentiful.
3. Remove or confiscate materials that encourage personal aggression, such as toy guns.

Make sure students do not profit from aggressive behaviors.
Examples
1. Comfort the victim of aggression and ignore the aggressor.
2. Use reasonable punishment, especially with older students.

Teach directly about positive social behaviors.
Examples
1. Incorporate lessons on social ethics/morality through reading selections and discussions.
2. Discuss the effects of antisocial actions such as stealing, bullying, and spreading rumors.

Provide opportunities for learning tolerance and cooperation.
Examples
1. Emphasize the similarities among people rather than the differences.
2. Set up group projects that encourage cooperation.

Aggression. Aggression is not to be confused with assertiveness, which means affirming or maintaining a legitimate right. Helen Bee (1981) gives this example of the difference between the two types of behavior: "A child who says, 'That's my toy!' is showing assertiveness. If he bashes his playmate over the head to reclaim it, he has shown aggression" (p. 350).

Modeling plays an important role in the expression of aggression (Bandura, Ross, & Ross, 1963). Children who grow up in homes filled with harsh punishment and family violence are more likely to use aggression to solve their own problems (Emery, 1989; Holden & Ritchie, 1991).

One very real source of aggressive models is found in almost every home in America—television. Most children spend more time watching television than they do in any other activity except sleep (Timmer, Eccles, & O'Brien, 1988). You can reduce the negative effects of TV violence by stressing three points with your students: most people do not behave in the aggressive ways shown on television; the violent acts on TV are not real, but are created by special effects and stunts; and there are better ways to resolve conflicts, and

"SCOTT, YOU'VE BEEN WATCHING TOO MUCH TV."

(© Stan Fine—Phi Delta Kappan)

Aggression Bold, direct action that is intended to hurt someone else or take property; unprovoked attack.

NEW
"Focus on Learning" Questions
at the end of each major section of the chapters provide students with an opportunity for critical, on-going review of the material.

Guidelines
Not cookbook applications, but research-based principles with specific examples of their use in practice, the Guidelines are found throughout each chapter. These guidelines, so popular in previous editions, help readers understand concepts, visualize applications, and transfer this information to new situations.

A Margin Glossary
defines terms in the margins of the text to provide easy access to the terms and their relevant examples as the student studies.

An Appendix on Research
This "minichapter" discusses key terms, methods, and concepts as the readers go through the processes of planning and evaluating a study. It stands on its own and is completely optional.

Check for excellent student study aids!

1

First to provide a supplements package that makes excellent use of today's hottest technology.

No other textbook package makes it so easy to keep your course dynamic and exciting. From news video segments on educational issues, classroom footage, and a special "Classroom Insights" laserdisc, to the exciting new CD-ROM of interactive classroom management cases, Allyn & Bacon has pulled it all together for you.

Check for an Annotated Instructor's Edition with Chapter-at-a-Glance planning charts that help you use all your resources!

The Annotated Instructor's Edition (AIE) includes all the material from the student edition, marginal annotations throughout, and an instructor's section up front. It is a guide to coordinating all the supplements so that all resources can be considered in planning the class.

• **Extended Teaching Outlines & Chapter-at-a-Glance charts** located at the front of the AIE.

• **Annotated Text** Annotations appear only in the AIE — not in the student edition.

Annotation headings include the following:

- Planning Tips
- Teaching Tips
- Examples
- Objectives
- Handouts
- Background
- Critical Thinking
- Cooperative Learning
- Reflection/ Journal Writing
- Multicultural Awareness
- Field Experiences
- Research
- Casebook
- Applications
- Discussions
- Connections
- Film/Video
- CNN Video
- Transparency
- Study Guide
- Test Bank

The Instructor's Resource Manual (IRM)

by Lynne Díaz-Rico & Ruth Sandlin, both of California State San Bernardino.

This 400+ page manual provides extra teaching ideas — additional class activities, summaries of the latest research, over 100 handout masters, many with activities for classroom use, transparency and master guide, objectives, teaching ideas keyed to annotations, discussion questions, background material on the videos program, and many other resources for teaching each chapter. All the IRM elements for teaching each chapter are referenced in the AIE annotations.

NEW Instructor's Resource Manual on Disk

Provided as an ASCII file, this disk allows you the convenience of incorporating your own teaching materials into those provided within the published IRM.

NEW Media Guide

provides summaries of the CNN *Connections* video and the *Classroom Insights* video segments, and illuminates the underlying principles in action.

Student Study Guide

by Lynne Díaz-Rico & Ruth Sandlin, both of California State San Bernardino.

Contains chapter objectives and outlines, lists of key concepts, sample test items, maps of key concepts, and case studies to extend your students' understanding and ensure that they can meet chapter objectives.

Educational Psychology Transparencies II

Over 130 color acetate transparencies updated and expanded from the previous edition — keyed to the text and ready to use.

Some restrictions may apply. See your Allyn & Bacon representative for details.

All information is accurate as of date of printing.

Test Bank

by Steven Ross, Memphis State University & Kathryn Linden, Purdue University

Substantially revised, improved, and reviewed. Graphic items, case study items, and essay and short answer items have been added. In addition to multiple choice questions, the test-bank includes case study items, essay questions, and short answer items. Answer Feedback explains why each answer is correct. Item validation information is provided for many questions. Sample tests for each chapter, plus a mid-term and final are included for busy professors. Over 1500 questions in all.

Computerized Test Bank

Choose either *Test Manager,* an easy-to-use testing program with a grading component, for the IBM or Macintosh.

Call-In Testing

allows instructors to call a toll-free number, indicate their choices for test items, and receive a master copy of the test in less than a week. Or request a FAX test for next-day rush situations.

NEW Classroom Insights II

An all new set of classroom footage segments that illustrate key concepts from the text through classroom examples. Available on VHS videotape, this 2-hour video features a variety of segments that illustrate some of the most important principles of Educational Psychology.

"Classroom Insights" Videodisc

illustrates key concepts from the text through live classroom examples.

CNN "Connections" Videotape Series

features segments from recent Cable News Network broadcasts focusing on issues in educational psychology. Each segment is keyed to the Point/Counterpoint feature in every chapter. Over 45 clips, 75% of which are new to this edition.

Additional supplements for purchase:

NEW Interactive Cases in Education: Classroom Management

by Peter Desberg, Joel Colbert & Kim Trimble.

A Macintosh-based CD-ROM program that provides 6 different classroom management situations via QuickTime movies and encourages interactive participation by students. For sale to students; demo is available.

"Teaching Worlds" Classroom Simulation Software

This disk of 12 realistic classroom simulations and brief manual with exercises and activities allows instructors to provide individualized learning experiences through interactive software — even for large classes. For IBM only.

Readings and Cases in Educational Psychology

by Anita Woolfolk

This collection of articles from professional journals was developed to expand the usual textbook coverage of current topics in the field. It provides a closer examination of many of the most important and widely debated questions in teaching today — questions about multiculturalism, whole language, self-esteem, testing, classroom management, and motivation. Also included are 5 in-depth cases that reflect the use of educational psychology in the content areas. The articles, written by educational psychology professors, span the age levels from pre-school through secondary grades.

USERS AGREE. NO TEXT DOES IT BETTER.

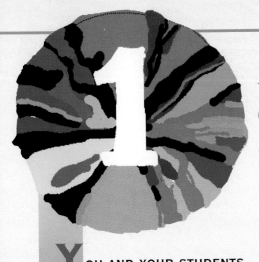

First to provide you with access to the wonderful world of AMERICA ONLINE!

YOU AND YOUR STUDENTS WILL GAIN A WHOLE NEW MEANS OF COMMUNICATION WHEN YOU START TO EXPERIENCE AMERICA ONLINE. ITS AWARD-WINNING INTERFACE MAKES NAVIGATING EASY. YOU'LL JUST POINT AND CLICK TO DOWNLOAD ANY OF THOUSANDS OF PROGRAMS; ATTEND REAL-TIME, ONLINE CONFERENCES AND FORUMS; KEEP IN TOUCH THROUGH ELECTRONIC MAIL; AND GET THE LATEST NEWS AND INFORMATION FROM LEADING MAGAZINES AND NEWS WIRES.

CONNECT TO A WHOLE NEW WORLD OF TEACHING AND LEARNING!

AMERICA Online

Here's your key to the wonderful world of AMERICA ONLINE!

We'll help you get started! Adopt this Allyn & Bacon textbook for your educational psychology course, and we'll waive the America Online membership fee for the first two months! Use this introductory membership to access a wide range of interactive services and educational information including a fast and easy gateway to the Internet. All you need is a computer and a modem! We'll make it easy for your students to get started too! What's more, Allyn & Bacon, as a leader in educational publishing, will be developing online services specifically for college and univesity faculty and student use!

Ask your local Allyn & Bacon Representative for more details. Or, if you have already selected this textbook for your course adoption, please give us a call at 1-800-827-6364 ext. 4314 and we'll send you a FREE America Online Faculty Starter Kit!

Annotated Instructor's Edition

Educational Psychology

S I X T H   E D I T I O N

Anita E. Woolfolk
The Ohio State University

Instructor's Section Prepared by

Ruth A. Sandlin
Lynne T. Díaz-Rico
California State University, San Bernardino

Allyn and Bacon

Boston ▪ London ▪ Toronto ▪ Sydney ▪ Tokyo ▪ Singapore

Vice President, Education: Nancy Forsyth
Developmental Editor: Alicia Reilly
Series Editorial Assistant: Christine Nelson
Production Administrator: Susan McIntyre
Editorial Production Service: Kathy Smith
Photo Research: Susan Duane
Cover Administrator: Linda Dickinson
Composition Buyer: Linda Cox
Manufacturing Buyer: Megan Cochran
Marketing Manager: Ellen Mann

 This textbook is printed on
recycled, acid-free paper.

Printed in the United States of America
10 9 8 7 6 5 4 3 2 1   99 98 97 96 95 94

ISBN 0-205-16211-8

Instructor's Section Contents

(Contents of the student text appears on page iv.)

INSTRUCTOR'S SECTION

ACKNOWLEDGMENTS

During the years I have worked on this book, from initial draft to this most recent revision, many people have supported the project. Without their help, this text simply could not have been written.

Many educators contributed to this project. Carol Weinstein wrote the section in chapter 11 on spaces for learning. Angela O'Donnell generously shared her insights about educational psychology with me and created the concept maps for the *Study Guide.* Steve Ross of Memphis State University and Kathryn Linden of Purdue University are responsible for the *Test Bank* and the answer feedback material that accompanies each item. The *Instructor's Resource Manual,* the *Study Guide,* and the Instructor's Section that accompanies the *Annotated Instructor's Edition* were written by Lynne Díaz-Rico and Ruth Sandlin, of the California State University, San Bernardino. They continue to bring creative thinking and exceptional dedication to the project. Their ideas have improved my teaching. The research summaries for the *Instructor's Resource Manual* were written by Wayne K. Hoy II, now Vice President of Advanced Software Products. Chapters 9 and 10 on motivation were redesigned by Johnmarshall Reeve of the University of Wisconsin, Milwaukee. He is responsible for the new organization and material in those chapters. Hermine Marshall, San Francisco State University, Asghar Iran-Najad, University of Alabama, and Kay Bull, Oklahoma State University, contributed ideas, information and insights to the cognitive and constructivist sections of the text.

My writing was guided by extensive and thoughtful reviews from the following individuals:

Joyce Alexander,
Indiana University

Kay Bull,
Oklahoma State University

Maureen Sherry Carr,
Oregon State University

Peggy Dettmer,
Kansas State University

Carlos Diaz,
Florida Atlantic University

Lynne Díaz-Rico,
*California State University
San Bernardino*

Miranda D'Amico,
McGill University

Roberta Dimord,
Delaware Valley College

Kathy Farber,
Bowling Green State University

Ricardo Garcia,
University of Idaho

Karl Haberlandt,
Trinity College

Daniel P. Hallahan,
University of Virginia

Sharon Lee Hiett,
University of Central Florida

Robert L. Hohn,
University of Kansas

Dianne Horgan,
The University of Memphis

Ali Iran-Nejad,
The University of Alabama

Sharon Lamb,
Bryn Mawr College

Kathryn Linden,
Purdue University

Hermine Marshall,
University of California, Berkeley

Marion Mason,
Bloomsburg University

Suzanne Morin,
Shippensburg University

Stephen A. Parker,
Chicago State University

Suzanne H. Pasch,
University of Wisconsin

Michael Piechowski,
Northland College

Johnmarshall Reeve,
University of Wisconsin

Leslie Rescorla,
Bryn Mawr College

Steven Richman,
Nassau Community College

Dianne Rivera,
Florida Atlantic University

Harry Robinson,
Muskegon Community College

Barak Rosenshine,
University of Illinois

Ruth Sandlin,
*California State University
San Bernardino*

Julie Turner,
Pennsylvania State University

Jerry Willis,
University of Houston

James Young,
Brigham Young University

As I made decisions about how to revise this edition, I benefited from the ideas of professors around the country who took the time to complete surveys and answer my questions. Thanks to: Jeanne Callihan, University of Texas, San Antonio; D. G. Underwood, Clemson University; Kathryn W. Linden, Purdue University; James M. Boland, Indiana University Northwest; David S. Bender, Pennsylvania State University, Berks; Keith W. Allred, Brigham Young University; Wensan Yan, Gonzaga University; George Vrhel, Sauk Valley College; Henri Groenheim, Towson State University; Dan G. Holt, Purdue University; William L. Franzen, University of Missouri, St. Louis; Norma Y. Stevens, Belmont University; Richard H. Blake, Weber State University; Perry Castelli, Troy State University; John Wheeler, Southwest Baptist University; John Baer, Rider College; Melva M. Burke, Pfeiffer College; Sheila Drake, Kansas Wesleyan University; Jackson F. Lee, Jr., Francis Marion College; Joseph McCloskey, Gloucester County College; Linda Metzke, Lyndon State College; Arthur Hernandez, University of Texas, San Antonio; Robert R. Hayden, Siena College; Mary Ann Chapko, Indiana University Northwest; Tony Williams, Marshall University; Joe Bordeaux, Lindenwood College; Arthur Landry, Carthage College; Ron J. Sjoerdsma, Calvin College; Paula Hillman, University of Wisconsin, Waukesha; Brenna Beedle, Eastern Washington University; Ruth Anne Niles, Radford University; Gail C. Delicio, Clemson University; Daniel Fasko, Sr., Morehead State University; Mary R. Sudzina, University of Dayton; Stacey Neuharth-Pritchitt, Purdue University; Lynne Díaz-Rico, California State University, San Bernardino; Hagop S. Pambookian, Shawnee State University; Roberta Ralston Dimord, Delaware Valley College; Paul Berghoff, Pembroke State University; Marcia Salner, Sangamon State University.

Many classroom teachers across the country contributed their experience, creativity, and expertise to the *Teachers' Casebook*. I have thoroughly enjoyed my association with these master teachers and I am grateful for the perspective they brought to the book. Thanks to: Julie Addison (Roxborough Elementary School, Littleton, Colorado); Eileen D. Akers (Jackson-Via Elementary School, Charlottesville, Virginia); Kathy Andrews (Lane Center School for Exceptional Children, Houston, Texas); Laura Atkinson (Chapel Hill, North Carolina); Harriet Chipley (Lookout Mountain Elementary School, Lookout Mountain, Tennessee); Carolyn R. Cook (Ramona Elementary School, Ramona, California); Karen Beechy Creider (Central High School, Philadelphia, Pennsylvania); Kathryn Daniels (Fredericktown Elementary School, Fredericktown, Ohio); Rugth Ann Dearth (Fredericktown Junior High School, Fredericktown, Ohio); Jane Dusell (Medford Area Senior High School, Medford, Wisconsin); Stephen C. Ellwood IV (St. Francis Elementary School, St. Francis, Maine); Donald Falk (Fredericktown Intermediate School, Fredericktown, Ohio); Bruce Fisher (Fortuna Elementary School, Fortuna, California); Candice J. Gallagher (Fredericktown Intermediate School, Fredericktown, Ohio); Betty Garner (Pattonville I.D.E.A.L. Center, Maryland Heights, Missouri); Carol Gibbs (Happy Valley School, Rossville, Georgia); Nancy R. Gonzalez (Robert Frost School, Mount Prospect, Illinois); Marc Gray (Highland Middle School, Louisville, Kentucky); Joanne S. Groseclose (Marion Intermediate School, Marion, Virginia); Sarah Gustafsen (The Okeechobee Center, Okeechobee, Florida); K. Janice Hill (Dillingham School, Dillingham, Alabama); Bonnie Hettman (Lima Central Catholic High School, Lima, Ohio); Dori Hoffman-Latter (Walker Middle School, Charlottesville, Virginia); Malcolm Jarrell (Jackson-Via Elementary School, Charlottesville, Virginia); Don Knies (Brooklyn Friends School, Brooklyn, New York); Sharon Klotz (Kiel Middle School, Kiel, Wisconsin); James D. Kraft (Wausau West High School, Wausau, Wisconsin); Karen B. Kreider (Central High School, Philadelphia, Pennsylvania); Lawrence Leebens (Forest Hills Elementary School, Eden Prairie, Minnesota); Brenda M. Lloyd (St. Anne's-Belfield, Charlottesville, Virginia); Joan H. Lowe (Russell Elementary School, Hazelwood, Missouri); Phyllis N. Marshall (Hoech Middle School, St. Ann, Missouri); Louise Harrold Melucci (Greenwood School, Warwick, Rhode Island); Marcia E. Miller (Walker Elementary School, Charlottesville, Virginia); Kathy A. Minniear (LaVeta Bauer Elementary School, Dayton, Ohio); Deborah H. Platt (Eugene Field Elementary School, Mitchell, South Dakota); Ida Pofahl (Denison Elementary School, Denison, Iowa); Jan Reynolds (Fredericktown Intermediate School, Fredericktown, Ohio); R. Chris Rohde (Chippewa Falls Senior High School, Chippewa Falls, Wisconsin); Linda Stahl (Ponca City Senior High School, Ponca City, Oklahoma); Kay Toliver (East Harlem Tech Middle School, New York City, New York); Marie Vachon (St. Paul School, Ramsey, New Jersey); Darlene A. Walsh (Greenbush Elementary School, West Warwick, Rhode Island); Simone Wharton (New York, New York); Cynthia Newman Wisdom (Trace Crossings Elementary School, Hoover, Alabama).

In a project of this size, so many people make essential contributions. Laurie Frankenthaler, Permissions Coordinator, worked diligently to obtain permissions for the material reproduced in this text and the supplements. Susan Duane guided the collection of photographs. The text designer, Debbie Schneck, and cover coordinator, Linda Knowles, made the look of this book my favorite yet. Kathy Smith, Production Coordinator, Susan McIntyre, Production Administrator, and Elaine Ober, Production Manager coordinated all aspects of the project, including the *Annotated Instructor's Edition,* with amazing skill and grace. Somehow they brought order to what could have been chaos. Now the book is in the able hands of Sandi Kirshner, Director of Marketing, Ellen Mann, Marketing Manager, Lou Kennedy, Director of Advertising, and their staff. I can't wait to see what they are planning for me now! What a talented and creative group of women—I am honored to work with them all.

On this edition, I was privileged to work with an outstanding editorial group. Bill Barke, President of Allyn and Bacon, brought his distinctive style and leadership to the project, making the effort a pleasure. Nancy Forsyth, the Editor in Chief for Education, brought her intelligence, creativity, sound judgment, and style to all our work. She will always have my deepest respect and enduring friendship. Christine Nelson, editorial assistant, kept everything running smoothly and kept my fax machine humming. On this edition I was fortunate to have the help of Alicia Reilly, an outstanding developmental editor with just the right combination of knowledge and organizational ability. She guided this revision in all its many aspects, always staying just ahead of whatever had to happen next—remarkable! The supplements package and the excellent pedagogical supports would not exist without her tireless efforts.

Finally, I want to thank my family and friends for their kindness and support during the long days and nights that I worked on this book. Again, to my daughter, Liz, thanks for your insights about teachers and students, shared over the years. You have been my greatest teacher—my continuing source of pride and humility. To my family, Anita Wieckert; Marion, Charlie, Bob, Lucas, Geoffrey, Eric, and Suzie Pratt; Claudia Casser; and Wayne C., Elsie, Wayne K., and Kelly Hoy—you are the greatest.

And finally, to Wayne Hoy, my friend, colleague, inspiration, passion, husband—the best is yet to be, thanks to you. Who would have thought life could be so good?

Anita Woolfolk Hoy

INSTRUCTOR'S SECTION

Instructor's Section

Educational Psychology

Teachers, Teaching, and Educational Psychology

Content Changes in the Sixth Edition

- New section, "What about the Students?"
- New Figure (1.2—Correlations Do Not Show Causation)
- Focus Questions for each major heading

Main Headings in Chapter 1

- What Is Good Teaching?
- Teaching: Artistry, Technique, and a Lot of Work
- The Role of Educational Psychology
- The Contents of This Book

Chapter Objectives

After completing chapter 1, the student should be able to:

1. Describe elements of good teaching.
2. Compare and contrast characteristics and methods of expert and novice teachers.
3. Describe Shulman's (1987) seven areas of professional knowledge of expert teachers.
4. Compare and contrast teaching as an art and a science.
5. Describe how teaching requires a balance of reflection and technique.
6. Identify the concerns of beginning teachers and describe how these concerns change developmentally.
7. Define educational psychology and the areas of study that it includes.
8. Compare and contrast descriptive studies versus experimental research studies.
9. Justify the importance of theory in educational practice.
10. Preview the general organization of information in the textbook and explain how it will be useful to teachers.

CHAPTER 1 AT A GLANCE

Acetate Transparencies

T1   Components of Good Teaching
T2   Three Types of Correlation
T3   Correlations Do Not Show Causation

In the Instructor's Resource Manual

Learning Activities and Related Research

1.1   Teaching Tip: Team Building Activity
1.2   Reflection/Journal Writing: Characteristics of Your Best Teacher
1.3   Teaching Tip: A Day in the Life of a Teacher
1.4   Field Experience: Survey on Teaching Roles
1.5   Cooperative Learning: Advantages/ Disadvantages of Teaching
1.6   Teaching Tip: Decision Making
1.7   Critical Thinking: Teaching: Art or Science—Technology or Reflection?
1.8   Background: Restructuring the Education of Teachers
1.9   Field Experience: Expert Teacher Knowledge
1.10   Multicultural Awareness: Teacher Demographics versus Student Demographics
1.11   Teaching Tip: What Do You Know about Educational Psychology?
1.12   Teaching Tip: Experimental versus Correlational Research

Discussion Questions

Additional Resources for Teaching This Chapter

Recommended Films, Videotapes, and Audiocassettes

Guide to CNN Videotape

Handout Masters

1.0   Lecture Outline: Teachers, Teaching, and Educational Psychology
1.1   Name Tags
1.2   A Day in the Life of an Elementary School Teacher
1.3   A Day in the Life of a Secondary School Teacher
1.4   Survey on Teaching Roles
1.5   Stress Test
1.6   Journals in Educational Psychology
1.7   Concept Map: Expert Teachers

In Other Supplements

Test Bank **Items 1.1–1.77**
   Answer Feedback

CNN Videotape **Segment 1: Today's Classroom Teacher**   4:19 min.

CHAPTER

2

Cognitive Development and Language

Content Changes in the Sixth Edition

- New section, "Assisted Learning" and Scaffolding
- New section, "Instructional Conversations"
- New section on constraints in language learning and universal grammar
- Expanded discussion of Vygotsky
- New Figure (2.1—The Brain Cortex)
- New Table (2.3—Elements of the Instructional Conversation)
- Focus Questions for each major heading

Main Headings in Chapter 2

- A Definition of Development
- Piaget's Theory of Cognitive Development
- Implications of Piaget's Theory for Teachers
- Vygotsky's Alternative to Piaget
- The Development of Language

Chapter Objectives

After reading chapter 2, the student should be able to:

1. Describe development and give examples of four kinds of development.
2. Describe three principles of how development takes place.
3. Explain how children's thinking differs at each stage of development.
4. Describe the processes of organization and adaptation and their relation to schemes, assimilation, accommodation, and equilibration.
5. Name each of Piaget's four stages of cognitive development, and give one major accomplishment of children during each stage.
6. Describe the implications for teachers of Piaget's theory, stating the importance of understanding students' thinking and matching teaching strategies to abilities.
7. Explain three criticisms or limitations of Piaget's theory.
8. Discuss Vygotsky's theory of cognitive development, including his concept of a "zone of proximal development."
9. Trace the development of language through the beginning of the school years, using the following terms: holophrases, overextension, telegraphic speech, and overregulation.
10. Describe strategies that teachers can use to help students develop language abilities and knowledge.

CHAPTER 2 AT A GLANCE

Acetate Transparencies

T4   Central Issues in Development
T5   Piaget's Stages of Intellectual Development
T6   Schemes of Learning
T7   Assimilation and Accommodation in Cognitive Development
T8   Children's Perception of Conservation of Liquid
T9   Children's Perception of Conservation of Mass
T10 Centration
T11 Reversible Thinking
T12 Vocabulary Changes in Childhood
T13 Knowledge Needed to Produce Meaningful Speech
T14 Teaching Model Based on Vygotsky's Theory

In the Instructor's Resource Manual

Learning Activities and Related Research

2.1 **Field Experience:** Four Tasks That Assess Children's Thinking
2.2 **Teaching Tip:** The Piagetian Concept of Schemes
2.3 **Reflection/Journal Writing:** Cognitive Disequilibrium
2.4 **Cooperative Learning:** Assessing Cognitive Development: Piagetian Tasks
2.5 **Cooperative Learning:** Children's Understanding of Humor
2.6 **Inquiry:** Children's Conception of Death
2.7 **Field Experience:** Academic versus Developmentally Appropriate Kindergartens
2.8 **Field Experience:** Four Tasks That Assess Children's Thinking

2.9 **Cooperative Learning:** Piagetian Theory: What Does It Mean to Teachers?
2.10 **Issues:** Speeding Up Cognitive Development: Pro and Con
2.11 **Inquiry:** Simplifying Instructions
2.12 **Critical Thinking:** Comparison of Piaget and Vygotsky
2.13 **Background:** Are Humans Born with a Special Language Capacity?

Discussion Questions

Additional Resources for Teaching This Chapter

Recommended Films, Videotapes, and Audiocassettes

Guide to CNN Videotape

Handout Masters

2.0 Lecture Outline: Cognitive Development and Language
2.1 Four Tasks That Assess Children's Thinking
2.2 Children's Humor
2.3 Piagetian Stages
2.4 Children's Conception of Death
2.5 Concept Map: Piaget's Theory of Cognitive Development

In Other Supplements

Test Bank Items 2.1–2.109
   Answer Feedback

CNN Videotape Segment 2:
Accelerating Development   7:55 min.

Personal, Social, and Emotional Development

Content Changes in the Sixth Edition

- Expanded coverage of Ethnic Pride and Identity
- Expanded coverage of Self-Concept
- New section, "Intention"
- Morality of Caring section expanded to include more on Gilligan and other researchers
- Updates to Child Abuse section
- New section, "Taking the Perspective of Others"
- New Table (3.4—"Selman's Five Stages of Perspective Taking")
- New Table (3.6—"Indicators of Child Abuse")
- New Point/Counterpoint—"Should Schools Teach Values?"
- Focus Questions for each major heading

Main Headings in Chapter 3

- The Work of Erikson
- Understanding Ourselves and Others
- Moral Development
- Socialization: The Home and the School
- The Preschool Years
- The Elementary-School Years
- Issues Affecting Adolescents

Chapter Objectives

After completing chapter 3, the student should be able to:

1. State the general characteristics of Erikson's theory of psychosocial development.
2. Name Erikson's eight developmental crises and environmental conditions that encourage positive resolution of the crises.
3. Suggest how teachers can foster self-esteem in their students.
4. Describe Kohlberg's stages of moral reasoning and give an example of each.
5. Evaluate alternatives to Kohlberg's theory of moral development.
6. Explain the factors that encourage cheating and aggression in classrooms and discuss possible responses to each.

7. Take a stand on affective and moral education.
8. Describe developmentally appropriate education for students of different ages.
9. Describe the child's changing view of friendship.
10. List the problems of early and late maturers.
11. Suggest ways to help adolescents make responsible decisions about sex and drugs.

CHAPTER 3 AT A GLANCE

Acetate Transparencies

T15 Erikson's Stages of Psychosocial Development
T16 Comparing Erikson and Piaget
T17 The Structure of Self-Concept
T18 Projected Number of Children Not Living with Both Parents
T19 Stages of Moral Development
T20 The Cortex
T21 Lateralization of Brain Function
T22 Beware of Simplified Views of the Brain
T23 The Effects of Media Violence

In the Instructor's Resource Manual

Learning Activities and Related Research

3.1 **Multicultural Awareness:** Culture and Morality
3.2 **Background:** Caring Kids: The Role of the School
3.3 **Background:** Cheating and Plagiarism
3.4 **Application:** Moral Dilemma
3.5 **Cooperative Learning:** Issues of Socialization
3.6 **Field Experience:** Estimating Social Relations
3.7 **Field Experience:** Interviewing Children about Friendship
3.8 **Application:** Unpopular Children

Discussion Questions

Additional Resources for Teaching This Chapter

Recommended Films, Videotapes, and Audiocassettes

Guide to CNN Videotape

Handout Masters

3.0 Lecture Outline: Personal, Social, and Emotional Development
3.1 Conditions That Encourage Positive Resolutions of Erikson's Developmental Crises
3.2 Resolving Developmental Crises
3.3 Sociogram
3.4 Culture and Moral Development: Twelve Offenses
3.5 Self-Esteem Index
3.6 Eisenberg's Levels of Prosocial Moral Reasoning
3.7 Concept Map: Erikson's Theory of Psychosocial Development

In Other Supplements

Test Bank Items 3.1–3.114
  Answer Feedback

CNN Videotape Segment 3: Education and Morality   9:43 min.

INSTRUCTOR'S SECTION

Learning Abilities and Learning Problems

Content Changes in the Sixth Edition

- New Section, "Changes in the Law," detailing recent legislation affecting students with disabilities
- Expanded discussion of Learning Disabilities
- New research on within-class grouping
- New section, "Resource Rooms, Collaborative Consultation, and Cooperative Teaching"
- New Table (4.3—"The Eight Gripes of Gifted Students")
- New Table (4.4—"Learning Disabilities across the Lifespan")
- New Point/Counterpoint—"Is Full Inclusion a Reasonable Approach to Teaching?"
- Focus Questions for each major heading

Main Headings in Chapter 4

- Language and Labeling
- Individual Differences in Intelligence
- Ability Differences and Teaching
- Cognitive and Learning Styles
- Students with Learning Challenges
- Mainstreaming

Chapter Objectives

After completing chapter 4, the student should be able to:
1. Discuss the potential problems in categorizing and labeling students.
2. Begin to develop a personal concept of intelligence to aid in teaching.
3. Trace the development of IQ tests, and interpret the meaning of an IQ test score.
4. Identify the methods, common practices, and implications of ability grouping.
5. Discuss how one might recognize and teach students who are mildly retarded or who are gifted.
6. Critically analyze the concepts of cognitive-style and learning-style preference, describing any implications for teachers.

7. Adapt lessons to make them appropriate for students with varying learning styles.
8. List indicators of hearing, vision, language, and behavior problems, as well as indicators of specific learning disabilities.
9. Adapt teaching methods to meet the needs of exceptional students.
10. Discuss the implications for teaching of Public Laws 94-142, 99-457, and 101-476.
11. Explain the concept of "least restrictive placement," and discuss the challenges associated with its application.

CHAPTER 4 AT A GLANCE

Acetate Transparencies

T24 Guilford's Faces of Intellect
T25 Sternberg's Triarchic Theory
T26 The Modern Stanford-Binet Intelligence Scale
T27 Distribution of Intelligence Scores
T28 Illustration of Items Used in Intelligence Testing
T29 A Test of Cognitive Style
T30 Examples of Instructional Enrichment
T31 Defining Mental Retardation
T32 Percentage of Children Served in Education Programs for the Handicapped
T33 Least Restrictive Environment
T34 Considerations for Individualized Determination of LRE
T35 Models of Special Ed Services
T36 LD is Fastest Growing Category
T37 Flowchart for Individualized Program Process

In the Instructor's Resource Manual

Learning Activities and Related Research

4.1 Research: Definitions of Intelligence
4.2 Application: Taking an Intelligence Test
4.3 Critical Thinking: Interview on IQ Testing
4.4 Teaching Tip: Thoughts about Being Gifted
4.5 Application: Communication Disorders
4.6 Field Experience: Early Interventions
4.7 Field Experience: Examination of Special Education Services
4.8 Critical Thinking: Mainstreaming

4.9 Background: Effects of Handicapped Students Tutoring Regular Students
4.10 Background: Caring Kids: The Role of the School

Discussion Questions

Additional Resources for Teaching This Chapter

Recommended Films, Videotapes, and Audiocassettes

Guide to CNN Videotape

Handout Masters

4.0 Lecture Outline: Learning Abilities and Learning Problems
4.1 Myths and Facts about Special Education
4.2 Myths and Facts about Mental Retardation
4.3 Indicators of Giftedness
4.4 Guidelines for Teaching the Hearing-Impaired Student
4.5 Myths and Facts about Vision Impairment
4.6 Indicators of Learning Problems
4.7A and 4.7B   An Educational Plan
4.8A and 4.8B   Individualized Education Program
4.9 Concept Map: Adapting Instruction for Learner Differences
4.10 Learning Styles: The Crucial Differences

In Other Supplements

Test Bank Items 4.1–4.124
    Answer Feedback

CNN Videotape Segment 4:
Supported Inclusion   8:52 min.

The Impact of Culture and Community

Content Changes in the Sixth Edition

- New section, "The Development of Prejudice"
- New information on gender differences and mathematics
- New section on Gender Role Identity and Gender Schemas
- New Figure (5.1—"The Dimension of Multicultural Education")
- New Figure (5.4—"Gender Schema Theory")
- Focus Questions for each major heading

Main Headings for Chapter 5

- Today's Multicultural Classrooms
- Social Class Differences
- Ethnic and Racial Differences
- Women and Men: Differences in the Classroom
- Language Differences in the Classroom
- Creating Culturally Compatible Classrooms

Chapter Objectives

After completing chapter 5, the student will be able to:

1. Compare the old notion of the melting pot with current views about multicultural education.
2. Define culture and list the various groups that make up each individual's cultural identity.
3. Explain why the school achievement of low-income students often falls below that of middle- and upper-class students.
4. Give examples of conflicts and compatibilities between home and school cultures.
5. Describe the school's role in the development of gender differences.
6. Summarize the arguments for and against bilingual education.
7. Incorporate multicultural concepts into classroom teaching.

CHAPTER 5 AT A GLANCE

Acetate Transparencies

T38 The Dimension of Multicultural Education
T39 Individuals Belong to Many Different Groups
T40 Projected Number of Children in Poverty
T41 Projected Number of Children in U.S. by Ethnic Group
T42 Could You Pass This Test?
T43 Prejudice and the Processing of Social Information
T44 Two Approaches to Balanced Bilingual Instruction
T45 Gender Schema Theory
T46 Student-Teacher Interaction Differences in Diverse Classrooms

In the Instructor's Resource Manual

Learning Activities and Related Research

5.1 **Cooperative Learning:** Clarifying the Goals of a Multicultural Curriculum
5.2 **Field Experience:** Observing Diversity in the Classroom
5.3 **Reflection/Journal Writing:** Cultural Identity
5.4 **Field Experience:** Experiencing Social Class Differences
5.5 **Cooperative Learning:** Cultural Differences: Possible Sources of Conflict
5.6 **Critical Thinking:** Historical Perspectives and Cultural Consciousness
5.7 **Teaching Tip:** Cultural Differences
5.8 **Application:** Racial Attitudes
5.9 **Critical Thinking:** Racism

5.10 **Field Experience:** Gender Equity
5.11 **Application:** Immigrant Student Project
5.12 **Multicultural Awareness:** Promoting Success for Language-Minority Students
5.13 **Application:** Beyond Learning Styles

Discussion Questions

Additional Resources for Teaching This Chapter

Recommended Films, Videotapes, and Audiocassettes

Guide to CNN Videotape

Handout Masters

5.0 Lecture Outline: The Impact of Culture and Community
5.1 Goals of Education in a Multicultural Society
5.2 Cultural Differences: Possible Sources of Conflict
5.3 Multicultural Societies: A Definition Guide
5.4 Goals of a Multicultural Approach to Teaching
5.5 Vasquez's Model for Adapting Instruction
5.6 Concept Map: Culturally Compatible Classrooms

In Other Supplements

Test Bank Items 5.1–5.82
   Answer Feedback

CNN Videotape Segment 5:
Multicultural Education   12:00 min.

Behavioral Views of Learning

Content Changes in the Sixth Edition

- New section on Task Analysis
- New Point/Counterpoint—"Should Students Be Rewarded for Learning?"
- Focus Questions for each major heading

Main Headings in Chapter 6

- Understanding Learning
- Early Explanations of Learning: Contiguity and Classical Conditioning
- Operant Conditioning: Trying New Responses
- Applied Behavior Analysis
- Social Learning Theory
- Self-Regulation and Cognitive Behavior Modification
- Problems and Issues

Chapter Objectives

After completing chapter 6, the student should be able to:

1. Give a complete definition of learning.
2. Contrast the behavioral and cognitive views of learning.
3. Define the terms "stimulus" and "response" and give several examples of each.
4. Explain the process of contiguity learning.
5. Draw a diagram of classical conditioning learning, explaining how a child can become afraid of school. Include the concepts of generalization and discrimination in this explanation.
6. Use the classical conditioning diagram to suggest how to prevent and extinguish a child's fear of animals.
7. Define the following terms: operant, behavior, antecedents. consequences, and cueing.
8. State the basic principle of operant conditioning.
9. Identify the four forms consequences can take and the effect of each on the behavior that it follows. Give an example of each.
10. Define continuous and intermittent reinforcement. State the purpose for which each should be used.
11. Contrast the effects of the four schedules of reinforcement.
12. Discuss the use of teacher attention as reinforcement, including components of effective praise and mistakes teachers often make in using praise.

13. Give two ways of selecting effective reinforcers and illustrate how they would be used according to the Premack principle.
14. Describe three methods for developing new behaviors in students.
15. Identify three methods for dealing with undesirable behavior, and give a classroom example of each.
16. Identify negative side effects of punishment and explain how punishment can be used appropriately.
17. Define observational learning. Include its five effects in the definition.
18. Describe the processes of self-regulation and cognitive behavior modification.
19. Compare self-management and cognitive behavior modification.
20. Discuss the ethical issues involved in a behavior change program.
21. Name two potential drawbacks to the use of behavioral methods and explain how they can be counteracted in the classroom.

CHAPTER 6 AT A GLANCE

Acetate Transparencies

T47 Three Stages of Classical Conditioning
T48 Kinds of Reinforcement and Punishment
T49 Schedules of Intermittent Reinforcement
T50 Effects of Praise
T51 Key Factors in Observational Learning
T52 Six Examples of Learning
T53 Classical Conditioning in Advertising

In the Instructor's Resource Manual

Learning Activities and Related Research

6.1 **Reflection/Journal Writing:** Positive and Negative Reinforcement
6.2 **Application:** Schedules of Reinforcement
6.3 **Field Experience:** What Is Rewarding
6.4 **Multicultural Awareness:** Reinforcer Preferences Questionnaire
6.5 **Application:** The Case of Bobby Richard
6.6 **Application:** Positive Practice
6.7 **Cooperative Learning:** Behavior Problem Scenarios
6.8 **Cooperative Learning:** Reinforcement versus Punishment
6.9 **Field Experience:** Interview on Behavioral Methods
6.10 **Background:** Peer Modeling

6.11 **Background:** Peer Modeling
6.12 **Background:** Self-Management
6.13 **Background:** Extrinsic versus Intrinsic Rewards

Discussion Questions

Additional Resources for Teaching This Chapter

Recommended Films, Videotapes, and Audiocassettes

Guide to CNN Videotape

Handout Masters

6.0 Lecture Outline: Behavioral Views of Learning
6.1 Survey of Reinforcer Preferences
6.2 Intervention Techniques
6.3 Behavior Problem Scenarios
6.4 Concept Map: Applied Behavior Analysis
6.5 Behavior Analysis Chart

In Other Supplements

Test Bank Items 6.1–6.128
   Answer Feedback

CNN Videotape Segment 6:
Paying Kids to Learn   6:42 min.

Cognitive Views of Learning

Content Changes in the Sixth Edition

- Reorganized and updated treatment of information processing
- New section on Images
- Expanded coverage of Retrieval
- New information in section on "Becoming Knowledgeable"
- New information in section on "Rote Memorization"
- New section, "Connectionism: Another Alternative to the Three-Store Model"
- New section, "Development of Declarative Knowledge"
- New section, "Becoming an Expert: Development of Procedural Knowledge"
- New section, "Becoming an Expert Student: Learning Strategies and Study Skills"
- New section, "Contructivism: Challenging Symbolic Processing Models"
- New Table (7.5—Four Views of Learning)
- New Figure (7.7—Connectionism Model)
- New Point/Counterpoint—"What's Wrong with Memorization?"
- Focus Questions for each major heading

Main Headings in Chapter 7

- Elements of the Cognitive Perspective
- The Information Processing Model of Memory
- Metacognition, Self-Regulation, and Individual Differences
- Becoming Knowledgeable: Some Basic Principles
- Contructivism: Challenging Symbolic Processing Models

Chapter Objectives

After studying chapter 7, the student should be able to do the following:

1. Descibe the cognitive view of learning, listing the topics studied by cognitivists.
2. Contrast behavioral views of the learning process with those of cognitivists.

3. Give examples of the roles of perception and attention in learning.
4. Diagram the sequence of information processing from sensory input to long-term memory.
5. Define declarative, procedural, and conditional knowledge.
6. Compare top-down and bottom-up perceptual processing.
7. Describe the role of attention in learning and identify the implications for teaching.
8. Explain how various types of information and knowledge may be stored in memory. Use the concepts of propositional networks, images, and schemas in the explanation.
9. Contrast the short-term and long-term memory systems.
10. Give examples of how information may be processed to enhance long-term storage.
11. Name three possible reasons for "forgetting" information.
12. Integrate the stages of information processing theory with the levels of processing theory.
13. Compare older children's metacognitive abilities with those of younger children.
14. Discuss individual differences in short-term and long-term memory.
15. Define "mnemonics" and explain four mnemonics strategies for helping students to remember information. Give examples of each.
16. Identify four principles of learning strategy instruction for students.

CHAPTER 7 AT A GLANCE

Acetate Transparencies

T54 Types of Learning
T55 The Information Processing System
T56 The Information Processing System I
T57 The Information Processing System II
T58 Three Types of Memory
T59 Memory and Meaning
T60 Short-Term Memory
T61 Long-Term Memory
T62 Model for Sensory/Short-Term/Long-Term Memory
T63 Schemas and Memory Distortions
T64 Examples of Top-Down Processing
T65 Examples of Gestalt Principles

In the Instructor's Resource Manual

Learning Activities and Related Research

7.1 **Background:** Sperling's Early Experiments
7.2 **Reflection/Journal Writing:** Elaborative Rehearsal: The Role of Meaning in Memory
7.3 **Teaching Tip:** Semantic Memory
7.4 **Reflection/Journal Writing:** Episodic Memory
7.5 **Background:** Reconstructive Elaborations
7.6 **Background:** Encoding and Retrieving Memory
7.7 **Field Experience:** Memory and Curriculum
7.8 **Background:** Teaching Memory Skills

Discussion Questions

Additional Resources for Teaching This Chapter

Recommended Films, Videotapes, and Audiocassettes

Guide to CNN Videotape

Handout Masters

7.0 Lecture Outline: Cognitive Views of Learning
7.1 Quiz on *Particularly Cats* Passage
7.2 KeyWord Mnemonic
7.3 Concept Map: Memory

In Other Supplements

Test Bank Items 7.1–7.127
   Answer Feedback

CNN Videotape Segment 7:
Learning Creatively   2:32 min

CHAPTER

8

Concept Learning, Problem Solving, Creativity, and Thinking

Content Changes in the Sixth Edition

- New section, "The Importance of Thinking and Understanding"
- New information on heuristics
- New information on expert knowledge
- Expanded coverage of expert knowledge in children
- New section, "Becoming an Expert Problem Solver: The ACT* Theory"
- New section, "The Language of Thinking"
- New section, "Thinking as a 'State of Mind' "
- New section, "Developing Thinking in Every Class"
- New Figure (8.3—"Representing a Problem")
- New Figure (8.6—"A Multicausal Analysis of Factors Affecting Rice Growth")
- Focus Questions for each major heading

Main Headings in Chapter 8

- The Importance of Thinking and Understanding
- Learning and Thinking about Concepts
- Problem Solving
- Effective Problem Solving: What Do the Experts Do?
- Creativity and Creative Problem Solving
- Teaching and Learning about Thinking
- Teaching for Transfer
- Cognitive Models of Teaching

Chapter Objectives

After studying chapter 8, the student should be able to do the following:

1. Explain the value of concepts, and integrate the two views of concept learning.
2. List the components of a concept that should be included in any lesson designed to teach that concept.
3. Define "problem solving," and describe the steps involved in the IDEAL process.
4. Give examples of heuristics and algorithms in various domains.

5. Name the factors that interfere with and the factors that factilitate problem solving.
6. Differentiate declarative and procedural knowledge, and describe their relationship to expert problem solving.
7. Explain how experts use pattern recognition to represent and to solve problems.
8. Show how Torrance assessed creativity as originality, fluency, and flexibility.
9. Define positive and negative transfer, and general and specific transfer. Give the principles involved in teaching for positive transfer.
10. Examine the work of Jerome Bruner by discussing his basic assumptions, his view of the learning process, and classroom implications and applications of his ideas.
11. State Ausubel's views about the learning process.
12. List the characteristics of expository methods of teaching.
13. Contrast the discovery and expository methods of teaching.

CHAPTER 8 AT A GLANCE

Acetate Transparencies

T66 A Propositional Network
T67 Example of Knowledge Arranged as a Hierarchy
T68 Example of the Use of Images to Aid Recall
T69 Schema for the Word *Bison*
T70 Illustrations Help Students to Understand Complex Concepts
T71 An Eighth Grader's Concept Map
T72 Problem Solving Using Algorithms and Heuristics
T73 Problem Solving
T74 Response Set and Insight—Problems
T74A Response Set and Insight—Solutions
T75 Problem Solving Process
T76 Events of Learning
T77 Influences on the Outcomes of Learning

In the Instructor's Resource Manual

Learning Activities and Related Research

8.1 **Teaching Tip:** Learning a Concept—Weetags Experiment
8.2 **Example:** Concept Attainment Lesson
8.3 **Cooperative Learning:** Teaching a Concept Effectively
8.4 **Background:** Students' Ideas in the Science Classroom
8.5 **Background:** Using Representation to Solve Problems
8.6 **Teaching Tip:** Functional Fixedness
8.7 **Critical Thinking:** Critical Thinking Strategies and Fallacies for Problem Solving
8.8 **Example:** Solving Arithmetic Problems
8.9 **Reflection/Journal Writing:** Using Critical Thinking

8.10 **Field Experience:** Dimensions of Critical Thinking
8.11 **Application:** Remodeling Lesson Plans to Incorporate Critical Thinking
8.12 **Field Experience:** Critical Thinking in the Classroom
8.13 **Example:** Discovery Learning in Action
8.14 **Background:** Cooperative Learning: Role-Playing an Expository Lesson
8.15 **Example:** Helping Novices Become Experts

Discussion Questions

Additional Resources for Teaching This Chapter

Recommended Films, Videotapes, and Audiocassettes

Guide to CNN Videotape

Handout Masters

8.0 Lecture Outline: Concept Learning, Problem Solving, Creativity, and Thinking
8.1 Weetags
8.2 Kinds of Relations: Encoding by Inference
8.3 Strategy List: 35 Dimensions of Critical Thought
8.4 Teacher Problem Solving: A Case Study
8.5 An Example of Expository Teaching
8.6 Concept Map: Problem Solving

In Other Supplements

Test Bank Items 8.1–8.112
   Answer Feedback

CNN *Videotape* Segment 8: Discovery Learning   8:00 min.

Motivation: Issues and Explanations

Content Changes in the Sixth Edition

- New opening classroom example
- New information on locus of causality
- New section, "Motivation to Learn in School"
- Expanded discussion of Ego-Involved Learners
- Revised Table (9.2—"Weiner's Theory of Causal Attribution")
- New section, "Feedback and Goal Acceptance"
- New research on Achievement
- New section, "The Need for Self-Determination"
- New section, "The Need for Relatedness"
- New section, "Beliefs about Self-Efficacy"
- New Figure (9.1—"Building a Concept of Motivation to Learn: Source of Motivation")
- New Figure (9.2—"Building a Concept of Motivation to Learn: Kinds of Goals and Type of Involvement")
- New Figure (9.4—"Building a Concept of Motivation to Learn: Need to Achieve vs. Fear of Failure")
- New Figure (9.5—"Building a Concept of Motivation to Learn: Likely Attributions")
- New Figure (9.6—"Building a Concept of Motivation to Learn: Beliefs about Ability")
- New Table (9.2—"Weiner's Theory of Causal Attributions")
- Focus Questions after each major heading

Main Headings in Chapter 9

- What Is Motivation?
- Students' Self-Esteem
- Goals and Motivation
- Needs and Motivation
- Attributions, Beliefs, and Motivation
- Anxiety in the Classroom

Chapter Objectives

After studying chapter 9, the student should be able to do the following:

1. Give examples of intrinsic and extrinsic motivation.
2. Define the concept of motivation from the behavioral, humanistic, cognitive, and social learning points of view.
3. Explain the concept of student motivation to learn.
4. Set motivating goals for self and students.
5. List Maslow's seven levels of needs and give a classroom example of each.
6. Explain how to encourage the need for achievement in your class.
7. Explain the relationship between self-determination and motivation.
8. Discuss the possible motivational effects of success and failure and how these effects relate to beliefs about ability.
9. Describe the characteristics of mastery-oriented, failure-avoiding, and failure-accepting students.
10. Develop a plan for helping an anxious student improve.

CHAPTER 9 AT A GLANCE

Acetate Transparencies

T78 The Components of Motivation
T79 Arousal and Quality of Performance
T80 Maslow's Hierarchy of Needs
T81 Social Facilitation: A Drive Theory
Approach
T82 Self-Esteem and Attributions for Successes
and Failures
T83 Expectancy Theory and Motivation
T84 Ambiguity and Risk in Decision Making
T85 Some Factors Affecting Individual
Motivation
T86 Example of a Task Analysis
T87 Theories of Motivation

In the Instructor's Resource Manual

Learning Activities and Related Research

9.1 Multicultural Awareness: Motivating
Adolescents from Minority Cultures
9.2 Reflection/Journal Writing: Guidance from
the Past
9.3 Application: Types of Motivation
9.4 Example: Self-Esteem Building: The Class
Quilt
9.5 Teaching Tip: Level of Aspiration
9.6 Teaching Tip: Maslow's Hierarchy
9.7 Field Experience: Comparing High and Low
Achievers
9.8 Background: Origins and Pawns
9.9 Teaching Tip: Internal-External Locus of
Control

9.10 Critical Thinking: Attribution of Motive
9.11 Application: Motivating the Discouraged
Learner
9.12 Readings: Preventing Dropouts
9.13 Teaching Tip: Encouraging Motivation
9.14 Background: Anxiety and Test Performance

Discussion Questions

**Additional Resources for Teaching
This Chapter**

**Recommended Films, Videotapes,
and Audiocassettes**

Guide to CNN Videotape

Handout Masters

9.0 Lecture Outline: Motivation: Issues and
Explanations
9.1 Locus of Control Test
9.2 Training Students to be Origins
9.3 Achievement Motivation: Observation Chart
9.4 Encouraging Motivation
9.5 Maslow's Hierarchy and Motivation
9.6 Concept Map: Attribution and Motivation

In Other Supplements

Test Bank Items 9.1–9.104
   Answer Feedback

CNN Videotape Segment 9:
Encouraging Self-Esteem   4:07 min.

Motivation, Teaching, and Learning

Content Changes in the Sixth Edition

- New section, "An Ultimate Goal of Teaching: Lifelong Learning"
- New section on Self-Regulated Learning
- New material on authentic tasks added to "Task Value" section
- New section, "Supporting Autonomy and Recognizing Accomplishment in the Classroom"
- New section on Time and Motivation
- New Table (10.1—"The TARGETT Model for Supporting Student Motivation to Learn")
- New Table (10.2—"Five Teaching Behaviors Found in Autonomy-Supportive Classrooms")
- Focus Questions after each major heading

Main Headings in Chapter 10

- The Ultimate Goal of Teaching: Lifelong Learning
- Tasks for Learning
- Supporting Autonomy and Recognizing Accomplishment in the Classroom
- Grouping: Cooperation and Competition
- Evaluation and Time
- Teacher Expectations
- Strategies to Encourage Motivation and Thoughtful Learning

Chapter Objectives

After studying chapter 10, the student should be able to do the following:

1. List some characteristics of a self-regulated learner, and describe how teachers can promote self-regulated learning in the classroom.
2. Explain how the ambiguity and risk of the learning task affect motivation and what can happen when students try to reduce risk and ambiguity.
3. Discuss how the value of a task affects motivation to learn.
4. Contrast the effects of cooperative, competitive, and individualistic goal structures on students' self-esteem and interpersonal relations.
5. Demonstrate how to set up three different models of cooperative learning in a classroom, and match each model with a subject area in which it can be most effective.

6. Explain how teaching methods and grouping arrangements can influence motivation.
7. Describe ways in which teachers, through their interaction patterns, communicate positive and negative expectations of students.
8. Devise a strategy for teaching a subject to an uninterested student.

CHAPTER 10 AT A GLANCE

Acetate Transparencies

T88 Theoretical Achievement Distributions during Traditional Instruction and Mastery Learning
T89 Computing Improvement Points

In the Instructor's Resource Manual

Learning Activities and Related Research

10.1 Cooperative Learning: Cooperative Learning Strategies for Elementary Reading
10.2 Application: Rewards for Cooperative Learning Groups
10.3 Background: Structures of the Cooperative Classroom
10.4 Background: Motivating High School Students to Achieve in Math
10.5 Multicultural Awareness: Bias against Science?
10.6 Background: Academic Counseling: Reflections on the Middle Grades

Discussion Questions

Additional Resources for Teaching This Chapter

Recommended Films, Videotapes, and Audiocassettes

Guide to CNN Videotape

Handout Masters

10.0 Lecture Outline: Motivation, Teaching, and Learning
10.1 Communicating Expectations
10.2 Observing Teacher Expectations
10.3 Cooperative Learning Structures
10.4 Concept Map: Motivational Strategies

In Other Supplements

Test Bank Items 10.1–10.85 Answer Feedback

CNN Videotape Segment 10: Teacher Expectations 7:47 min.

INSTRUCTOR'S SECTION

11

Creating Learning Environments

Content Changes in the Sixth Edition

- New section, "Spaces for Learning"
- New Figure (11.3—"Some Home-Base Formations")
- New Figure (11.4—"Some Special Formations")
- Focus Questions after each major heading

Main Headings in Chapter 11

- The Need for Organization
- Creating a Positive Learning Environment
- Maintaining a Good Environment for Learning
- Special Programs for Classroom Management
- The Need for Communication
- Spaces for Learning

Chapter Objectives

After studying chapter 11, the student should be able to do the following:

1. Describe the special managerial challenges of classrooms and relate these characteristics to the needs of students of different ages.
2. Explain how the age of the students can influence the management goals of the teacher.
3. Characterize classroom management that maximizes academic learning time.
4. Give examples of how the home environment can affect a student's ability to interact in the participation structures of a typical classroom.
5. Create a list of rules and procedures for an elementary and a secondary class.
6. List several categories of consequences that might be imposed for classroom rule infringement.
7. Develop a plan for organizing the first week of class.
8. Explain Kounin's suggestions for preventing management problems.
9. Describe how a teacher might respond to a student who seldom completes work.

10. Compare several types of group consequence behavioral management systems.
11. Give examples of classroom situations in which a token reinforcement system might be needed.
12. Suggest two different approaches for dealing with a conflict between a teacher and a student or between two students.
13. Give examples of various room arrangements that work well for both whole-class instruction and cooperative learning.

CHAPTER 11 AT A GLANCE

Acetate Transparencies

T90   Time Available for Academic Learning
T91   A Student Contract Appropriate for Primary Grades
T92   Group Contingency Program

In the Instructor's Resource Manual

Learning Activities and Related Research

11.1   **Background:** Increasing On-Task Time
11.2   **Field Experience:** Time on Task
11.3   **Background:** Fostering Student Self-Management
11.4   **Reflection/Journal Writing:** The Effective Classroom Manager
11.5   **Teaching Tip:** Classroom Management
11.6   **Teaching Tip:** Encouraging Responsibility
11.7   **Cooperative Learning:** Using Glasser's Principles
11.8   **Inquiry:** Using Behavior Modification in Classroom Discipline
11.9   **Example:** A Group Contingency Program to Improve Reading
11.10 **Application:** Who Owns the Problem?
11.11 **Teaching Tip:** Empathy Training
11.12 **Cooperative Learning:** I-Messages
11.13 **Cooperative Learning:** Confrontation

11.14 **Reflection/Journal Writing:** Self-Analysis
11.15 **Background:** Student Mediators

Discussion Questions

Additional Resources for Teaching This Chapter

Recommended Films, Videotapes, and Audiocassettes

Guide to CNN Videotape

Handout Masters

11.0   Lecture Outline: Creating Learning Environments
11.1   Classroom Management Observation Sheet
11.2   Who Owns the Problem?
11.3A and 11.3B   How Do You Handle Conflict?
11.4A and 11.4B   Assertiveness Scale
11.5   Contingency Contracts
11.6   Concept Map: Planning the First Day of Class

In Other Supplements

Test Bank Items 11.1–11.107
    Answer Feedback

CNN Videotape Segment 11:
Assertive Discipline   5:43 min.

CHAPTER

12

Teachers and Teaching

Content Changes in the Sixth Edition

- New section, "Objectives for Learning"
- New section, "Lecturing and Explaining"
- New section, "Characteristics of Effective Teachers"
- New section, "Putting It All Together: Models of Direct Instruction"
- New section, "Recitation and Questioning"
- New section, "Seatwork and Homework"
- Focus Questions after each major heading

Main Headings in Chapter 12

- The First Step: Planning
- Objectives for Learning
- How to Teach: Searching for the Keys to Success
- Characteristics for Effective Teachers
- Teaching Methods: Direct Instruction
- Criticisms of Direct Instruction

Chapter Objectives

After studying chapter 12, the student should be able to do the following:

1. Describe the role of planning in teaching.
2. Define "instructional objectives" and list the benefits of communicating objectives to students.
3. Compare and contrast behavioral and cognitive objectives. Give an example of each.
4. Identify the three components of a behavioral objective and write several examples in different academic areas.
5. Integrate Mager's and Gronlund's methods for writing objectives into a useful approach.
6. Evaluate two criticisms of the use of instructional objectives.
7. Contrast objectives in the cognitive, affective, and psychomotor domains in their definitions, uses, and assessment.
8. Outline the taxonomies in the cognitive, affective, and psychomotor domains. Be able to write an objective at each level in each domain.

9. Name the characteristics of effective teachers and explain the process through which each characteristic affects student learning.

10. Give examples of ways in which teachers must transform information as they create a curriculum of study.

11. Distinguish between lessons that are taught with clarity and those that are not.

12. Describe the processes involved in these teaching formats: recitation and questioning, lecturing and explaining, seatwork.

13. Describe various methods by which teacher effectiveness has been defined and measured.

14. State the goal and characteristics of direct instruction, and explain when direct instruction is appropriate.

15. Describe a program based on the principles of direct instruction. Evaluate the effectiveness of this program.

16. Compare the characteristics of instruction that are effective with high-ability students with those that are effective for low-ability groups.

CHAPTER 12 AT A GLANCE

Acetate Transparencies

T93   The Interplay of Different Kinds of Educational Objectives
T94   Mager's Three-Part Objectives
T95   Behavior-Content Matrix
T96   A Selective List of Verbs for Writing Cognitive Objectives
T97   Poorly Written Objectives
T98   Wait-Times Associated with Questioning
T99   Elementary Classroom Seating Arrangement
T100 Secondary Classroom Seating Arrangement
T101 Initial Kindergarten Room Arrangement
T102 Improved Kindergarten Room Arrangement
T103 Seven Steps of Delivering a Lesson
T104 Aptitude Treatment Interactions
T105 The General Inductive Model
T106 The Concept Attainment Model
T107 Effective Training
T108 Planning with a Topic Map

In the Instructor's Resource Manual

Learning Activities and Related Research

12.1 Teaching Tip: Effective Teaching
12.2 Reflection/Journal Writing: Assigned Competence
12.3 Multicultural Awareness: Effective Teaching with Different Students
12.4 Multicultural Awareness: Teaching Limited-English-Proficiency Students
12.5 Teaching Tip: An Interactive Teaching Presentation

12.6 Cooperative Learning: Different Teaching Approaches
12.7 Reflection/Journal Writing: Learning Educational Psychology
12.8 Observation/Field Experience: What Makes Lessons Effective?
12.9 Cooperative Learning: Selecting Instructional Strategies for Different Students

Discussion Questions

Additional Resources for Teaching This Chapter

Recommended Films, Videotapes, and Audiocassettes

Guide to CNN Videotape

Handout Masters

12.0   Lecture Outline: Teachers and Teaching
12.1A and 12.1B   Principles of Effective Teaching
12.2   Group Presentations Assignment on Teaching Approaches
12.3   An Example of Direct Instruction
12.4   Analysis of Teacher's Explanation
12.5   Objectives in the Cognitive Domain
12.6   Concept Map: Learning Objectives

In Other Supplements

Test Bank Items 12.1–12.123
   Answer Feedback

CNN Videotape Segment 12:
Students at Risk   9:05 min.

Rediscovering the Student in Teaching

Content Changes in the Sixth Edition

- NEW CHAPTER

Main Headings in Chapter 13

- Perspectives on Student-Centered Teaching
- Student-Centered Teaching Methods
- Constructivist Teaching for Different Ages
- Integrations: Beyond Models to Outstanding Teaching

Chapter Objectives

After studying chapter 13, the student should be able to do the following:

1. Contrast constructivist views of learning with direct instruction views.
2. Describe methods for studying the links between classroom teaching and student learning.
3. Summarize the American Psychological Association's twelve learner-centered psychological principles.
4. Describe characteristics shared by many constructivist approaches to teaching.
5. Describe situations in which each of the following formats would be most appropriate: individualized instruction, group discussion, inquiry, reciprocal teaching, and humanistic education.
6. Evaluate computer packages and microworld computer-based environments for use with your classes.
7. Explain how student-centered approaches can be incorporated into teaching.

INSTRUCTOR'S SECTION

CHAPTER 13 AT A GLANCE

Acetate Transparencies

T109 Five Standards of Authentic Instruction

In the Instructor's Resource Manual

Learning Activities and Related Research

13.1 Background: Reconstructing Children's Understanding of Science

13.2 Critical Thinking: Direct versus Indirect Instruction

13.3 Background: Children's Understanding of Science

13.4 Teaching Tip: Constructing Text in a Reading Class

13.5 Research: Meeting the Needs of Low Achievers

13.6 Background: Models for Teaching beyond the Basics: Simulations

13.7 Demonstration: Teaching Methods and Classroom Management: A Comparison

13.8 Critical Thinking: Direct versus Indirect Instruction

Discussion Questions

Additional Resources for Teaching This Chapter

Recommended Films, Videotapes, and Audiocassettes

Guide to CNN Videotape

Handout Masters

13.0 Lecture Outline: Rediscovering the Student in Teaching

13.1 Selecting Instructional Strategies for Students

13.2 A Story about Assigning Competence

13.3 Monitoring and Controlling Strategies for Self-Management

13.4 Reciprocal Teaching: Segment 1

13.5 Reciprocal Teaching: Segment 2

13.6 Inquiry Curriculum Design for Multicultural Education

13.7 Concept Map: Self-Regulated Learning

In Other Supplements

Test Bank **Items 13.1–13.77**
    Answer Feedback

CNN *Videotape* Segment 13:
Authentic Learning   12:00 min.

Standardized Testing

Content Changes in the Sixth Edition

- Focus Questions after each major heading

Main Headings in Chapter 14

- Measurement and Evaluation
- What Do Test Scores Mean?
- Types of Standardized Tests
- Issues in Standardized Testing
- New Directions in Standardized Testing

Chapter Objectives

After reading chapter 14, the student should be able to:

1. Differentiate measurement and evaluation, and describe the relationship between them.
2. Define norm-referenced testing and criterion-referenced testing. Give uses and limitations of each type of test.
3. Define the following terms: standardized test, norming sample, frequency distribution, central tendency, mean, median, mode, standard deviation, and normal distribution.
4. Be able to interpret percentile rank scores, grade-equivalent scores, and three types of standard scores. Give the advantages or limitations of each type of score.
5. Explain the concepts of reliability and validity, including definitions, importance, types, and related concepts.
6. Identify three kinds of standardized tests and the purpose of each kind of test.
7. Discuss the uses and misuses of testing, and name some areas where decisions are made on the basis of test scores.
8. Describe the purpose of readiness tests and of minimum competency and teacher assessment tests.
9. State the sources of test bias, and identify attempts that have been made to ensure the fair use of tests.
10. Describe ways to prepare students to take tests.
11. Discuss the advantages of assessing learning potential through process assessment.
12. Define authentic assessment, and give examples of authentic assessment approaches.

INSTRUCTOR'S SECTION

CHAPTER 14 AT A GLANCE

Acetate Transparencies

T110 Norm-Referenced versus Criterion-Referenced Tests

T111 Frequency of Scores Forming a Normal Curve

T112 Describing Measurement Data: A Histogram

T113 Normal Curve: Scores on a Standardized Test

T114 Example of Grading on a Curve

T115 Two Tests with the Same Mean and Different Standard Deviations

T116 Percentile Ranking on a Normal Distribution

T117 Stanines and Percentiles

T118 Four Types of Standard Scores

T119 Relationship between Various Types of Scores

T120 Halo Effects: Their Basic Nature

T121 Table of Specification for a Chemistry Unit

T122 Example of a Daily Report Card

In the Instructor's Resource Manual

Learning Activities and Related Research

14.1 **Application:** Central Tendency

14.2 **Application:** Using the Complete Standard Deviation Formula

14.3 **Application:** Types of Tests and the Interpretation of Test Scores

14.4 **Background:** Problems with Grade-Equivalent Scores

14.5 **Field Experience:** A Local School's Report

14.6 **Application:** Test Score Interpretation

14.7 **Background:** The Tyranny of Testing

14.8 **Issues:** Legal Issues in Testing

14.9 **Cooperative Learning:** Readiness Tests

14.10 **Background:** Teachers, Testing, and Time

14.11 **Critical Thinking:** Minimum Competency Testing

14.12 **Reflection/Journal Writing:** How Should Teachers Be Graded?

14.13 **Issues:** Accountability as a Reform Strategy

Discussion Questions

Additional Resources for Teaching This Chapter

Recommended Films, Videotapes, and Audiocassettes

Guide to CNN Videotape

Handout Masters

14.0 Lecture Outline: Standardized Testing

14.1 Types of Tests and the Interpretation of Test Scores

14.2 Calculating a Standard Deviation

14.3A and 14.3B Central Tendency and Standard Deviation: Exercises and Answers

14.4 Relationship of Test Scores to the Normal Curve

14.5 Concept Map: Standardized Test Scores

In Other Supplements

Test Bank Items 14.1–14.114
Answer Feedback

CNN *Videotape* Segment 14:
To Test or Not to Test 6:33 min.

Classroom Assessment and Grading

Content Changes in the Sixth Edition

- New section, "Evaluating Objective Test Items"
- New section, "Grades and Motivation"
- New section, "Evaluating Portfolios and Performances"
- New Figure (15.4—"A Sample Hands-on Score Form for Assessing Student Performance in a Laboratory Experiment")
- New Table (15.2—"Calculating the Difficulty and Discrimination Indices for Test Items")
- Focus Questions after each major heading

Main Headings in Chapter 15

- Formative and Summative Assessment
- Getting the Most from Traditional Assessment Approaches
- Innovations in Assessment
- Effects of Grades and Grading on Students
- Grading and Reporting: Nuts and Bolts
- Beyond Grading: Communication

Chapter Objectives

After completing chapter 15, the student should be able to:

1. Create multiple-choice and essay test items for a specific subject area.
2. Make a plan for testing students on a unit of work.
3. Evaluate tests that accompany textbooks and teacher's manuals.
4. Describe authentic assessment approaches, including portfolios, performances, and exhibitions.
5. Discuss the potential positive and negative effects of grades on students.
6. Give examples of criterion-referenced and norm-referenced grading systems.
7. Assign grades to a hypothetical group of students and defend decisions in class debate.
8. Role-play a conference with parents who do not understand the classroom grading system or their child's grades.

CHAPTER 15 AT A GLANCE

Acetate Transparencies

T123 Analyze Essay Questions
T124 Comparing Objective and Essay Tests
T125 Assign and Justify Grades
T126 A Sample Checklist for Assessing Student Performance in a Laboratory Experiment
T127 Linking Criterion-Referenced Criteria to Grades
T128 Example of a Performance Assessment Activity

In the Instructor's Resource Manual

Learning Activities and Related Research

15.1 **Critical Thinking:** Evaluating Test Items
15.2 **Cooperative Learning:** Writing Multiple-Choice Items
15.3 **Background:** Scoring Essay Tests
15.4 **Background:** Teaching to the Authentic Test
15.5 **Cooperative Learning:** Portfolio Content
15.6 **Field Experience:** Grading Students
15.7 **Reflection/Journal Writing:** Should Teachers Grade Everything?
15.8 **Application:** Dealing with a Student Who Refuses to Work
15.9 **Background:** Classroom Standard Setting and Grading Practices
15.10 **Application:** Norm-Referenced Grading
15.11 **Application:** Determining Grades
15.12 **Critical Thinking:** Evaluating Decisions
15.13 **Application:** Contracting

Discussion Questions

Additional Resources for Teaching This Chapter

Recommended Films, Videotapes, and Audiocassettes

Guide to CNN Videotape

Handout Masters

15.0 Lecture Outline: Classroom Assessment and Grading
15.1 Beliefs about Grades
15.2 Grading Systems
15.3 Checklist for Evaluating Test Items
15.4 Case Study: A Student Who Refuses to Work
15.5 Analyze Multiple Choice Questions
15.6 Different Kinds of Test Questions
15.7 Characteristics of Authentic Tests
15.8 Concept Map: Alternatives for Assessment

In Other Supplements

Test Bank Items 15.1–15.109
    Answer Feedback

CNN Videotape Segment 15:
To Test or Not to Test, Part II   4:12 min.

Notes

Notes

Notes

Educational Psychology

Educational Psychology

SIXTH EDITION

Anita E. Woolfolk
The Ohio State University

Allyn and Bacon

Boston ■ London ■ Toronto ■ Sydney ■ Tokyo ■ Singapore

Vice President, Education: Nancy Forsyth
Developmental Editor: Alicia Reilly
Series Editorial Assistant: Christine Nelson
Production Administrator: Susan McIntyre
Editorial Production Service: Kathy Smith
Photo Research: Susan Duane
Cover Administrator: Linda Dickinson
Composition Buyer: Linda Cox
Manufacturing Buyer: Megan Cochran
Marketing Manager: Ellen Mann

Library of Congress Cataloging-in-Publication Data

Woolfolk, Anita.
    Educational psychology / Anita E. Woolfolk. — 6th ed.
        p.   cm.
    Includes bibliographical references (p.) and indexes.
    ISBN 0-205-15542-1
    1. Educational psychology.   I. Title.
LB1051.W74   1995
370.15—dc20   94-28857
                                                          CIP

This textbook is printed on
recycled, acid-free paper.

Printed in the United States of America
10 9 8 7 6 5 4 3 2 1   99 98 97 96 95 94

Text Credits: pp. 3–4 F. Ruopp and M. Driscoll, reprinted with permission from *Harvard Education Letter*, January–February 1990 (vol. VI, no. 1, p. 5). Copyright President and Fellows of Harvard College. All rights reserved. p. 135 Worries about overactive kids, *Time* Magazine, January 16, 1989, p. 65. Copyright 1989 Time Inc. Reprinted by permission. p. 159 Reprinted with permission from Debra Viadero (November 28, 1990) Battle over multicultural education rises in intensity. *Education Week*, 10 (13), pp. 1, 11, 13. p. 452 From Charles Anderson, The role of education in the academic disciplines in teacher education, in A. Woolfolk (Ed.), *Research Bases for the Graduate Preparation of Teachers*. Copyright © 1989 by Allyn and Bacon. Reprinted by permission. pp. 479–481 Adapted from *Learner-centered psychological principles: Guidelines for school redesign and reform* by the Presidential Task Force on Psychology in Education of the American Psychological Association, 1993, Washington, DC: American Psychological Association. Copyright © 1993 by the American Psychological Association. Adapted with permission. This excerpt presents *draft guidelines*, which have not been adopted as official APA policy. pp. 481–482 Reprinted by permission from A. R. Baroody and H. P. Ginsburg (1990). Children's learning: A cognitive view. In R. Davis, C. Maher, and N. Noddings (Eds.), *Constructivist views on the teaching and learning of mathematics* (pp. 51–64). Monograph of the National Council of Teachers of Mathematics, Reston, VA. pp. 492–493 A. S. Palinscar and A. L. Brown (1984). Reciprocal teaching of comprehension-fostering and comprehension-monitoring activities. *Cognition and Instruction*, 1 (2), pp. 13–14. Reprinted by permission of the publisher and authors. p. 519 From John W. Best and James V. Kahn, *Research in Education*, 7/e. Copyright © 1993 by Allyn and Bacon. Reprinted by permission.

Photo credits are listed at the bottom of page 648 which constitutes a extension of the copyright page.

For Wayne,
who taught me to laugh and love again.

Contents

3 *Personal, Social, and Emotional Development*   64

Part Two
Individual Variations

5   *The Impact of Culture
and Community*   *152*

Part Three

Learning: Theory and Practice

6 *Behavioral Views of Learning*   194

Part Four

Motivation and Management

9 Motivation: Issues and Explanations 328

10 Motivation, Teaching, and Learning 364

11 *Creating Learning Environments* 400

Part Five

Teaching

13 *Rediscovering the
Student in Teaching* 476

Student Preface

M any of you reading this book will be enrolled in an educational psychology course as part of your professional preparation for teaching, counseling, speech therapy, or psychology. Others of you, while not planning to become teachers, are reading this book because you are interested in what educational psychology has to say about teaching and learning in a variety of settings. The material in this text should be of interest to everyone who is concerned about education and learning, from the nursery school volunteer to the instructor in a community program for disabled adults. No background in psychology or education is necessary to understand this material. It is as free of jargon and technical language as possible and many people have worked to make this edition clear, relevant, and interesting.

Since the first edition of *Educational Psychology* appeared, there have been many exciting developments in the field. This edition incorporates new insights and current trends while retaining the best features of the previous work. The sixth edition continues to emphasize the educational implications and applications of research on child development, cognitive science, learning, and teaching. Theory and practice are not separated but are considered together; the text shows how information and ideas drawn from research in educational psychology can be applied to solve the everyday problems of teaching. To explore the connections between knowledge and practice, there are many examples, lesson segments, case studies, guidelines, and practical tips from experienced teachers. Throughout the text you will be challenged to think about the value and use of the ideas in each chapter and you will see principles of educational psychology in action. Professors and students who used the first five editions found these features very helpful. But what about the new developments?

Recently, the study of teaching has taken a very logical turn to focus on the person being taught—the student—and the way that individual makes sense of the world. In this revision, there is a new chapter on *student-centered approaches to teaching*. In this chapter we will explore what is known about how to encourage and support students' learning as we consider teaching and learning from emerging constructivist perspectives.

Over 200 new citations have been added to this edition to bring prospective teachers the most current information. Topics include the following:

- assisted learning and scaffolding,
- instructional conversations,

- the brain cortex,
- changes in laws about individuals with disabilities,
- collaborative consultation in serving students with special needs,
- the development of prejudice,
- multicultural education,
- effective teaching for students placed at risk,
- gender-role identity and gender schemas,
- connectionist models of memory,
- the ACT* model of developing expertise and problem-solving skills,
- studies of children's expert knowledge,
- expert classroom managers,
- constructivist approaches to teaching,
- cooperative learning,
- self-efficacy,
- autonomy and motivation,
- self-determination,
- problem-based learning,
- motivation to learn,
- authentic assessment,
- portfolios, and
- judging test items.

The Plan of the Book.   The introductory chapter begins with you, the prospective teacher, and the questions you may be asking yourself about a teaching career. What is good teaching and what does it take to become an excellent teacher? How can educational psychology help you to become such a teacher? Part One, "Human Development" focuses on the students. How do they develop mentally, physically, emotionally, and socially, and how do all these aspects fit together? Part Two, "Individual Variations," addresses questions such as: Where do individual differences come from, and what do they mean for teachers? How can teachers adapt instruction for students with special needs? What does it mean to create a culturally compatible classroom, one that makes learning accessible to all students? Part Three, "Learning: Theory and Practice," looks at learning from two major perspectives, the behavioral and the cognitive, with an emphasis on the cognitive learning theories. Learning theories have important implications for instruction at every level. Cognitive research is particularly vital right now and promises to be a wellspring of ideas for teaching in the immediate future. Part Four, "Motivation and Management," discusses the ever present, linked issues of motivating and managing today's students. The information in these chapters is based on the most recent research in real classrooms. Part Five, "Teaching," includes chapters on both teacher-centered and student-centered approaches to teaching. Part Six, "Assessment," looks at many types of testing and grading, providing a sound basis for determining how well students have learned.

In addition to the 15 chapters, an Appendix, "Research in Educational Psychology," discusses basic vocabulary, concepts, and methods of psychological research. The appendix takes you through the processes of planning and evaluating a study. You will probably find the Appendix worthwhile reading, regardless of whether your instructor incorporates the appendix into your regular class work.

Aids to Understanding. At the beginning of each chapter you will find an *Outline* of the key topics with page numbers for quick reference. An *Overview* provides a chapter "orientation" along with a list of *Learning Objectives* (also useful for review later). Then I ask you, *"What Do You Think?"* about a subject related to the chapter. Before you read each chapter, take a moment to reflect on the questions raised.

Within the chapter, headings point out themes, questions, and problems as they arise, so you can look up information easily. These can also serve as a quick review of important points. When a new term or concept is introduced, it appears in boldface type along with a brief margin definition. These *Key Terms* are also listed alphabetically at the end of each chapter with page references and in the *Index of Key Terms* at the back of the text. This index gives the page in the text where the key term is discussed so you can study and understand the term in its larger context. After every major section of the chapter, a new feature of this edition asks you to *Focus on Learning* by checking your understanding of the material. Can you answer these questions? If not, you might review the material. Throughout the book, graphs, tables, photos, and cartoons have been chosen to clarify and extend the text material—and to add to your enjoyment.

Each chapter ends with a *Summary* of the key ideas in each main heading. With the information from the chapter as a base, you are ready to solve the problems posed in the *"What Would You Do?"* application exercises at the end of each chapter. These questions treat both elementary and secondary classrooms and include a cooperative learning activity.

Other Text Features. As in the previous editions, every chapter in the sixth edition includes *Guidelines* and the *Teachers' Casebook*. And because educational psychology is developing so rapidly today, I have added several new *Point/Counterpoints* on such issues as supported inclusion, values in the schools, "paying" kids to learn, and alternatives to direct teaching.

Guidelines. An important reason for studying educational psychology is to gain skills in solving classroom problems. Often texts give pages of theory and research findings but little assistance in translating theory into practice. This text is different. Included in each chapter are several sets of *Guidelines*. These are teaching tips and practical suggestions based on the theory and research discussed in the chapter. Each suggestion is clarified by two or three specific examples. Although the *Guidelines* cannot cover every possible situation, they do provide a needed bridge between knowledge and practice and should help you transfer the text's information to new situations.

Teachers' Casebook. This highly acclaimed and popular feature from the first five editions is back in revised form. At the end of each chapter, master teachers from all over the country, including many Teacher of the Year award winners, offer their own solutions to many of the diverse problems you are likely to encounter in the classroom at every grade level. Their ideas truly show educational psychology at work in a range of everyday situations. The *Teachers' Casebook* brings to life the topics and principles discussed in each chapter. This edition emphasizes real rather than hypothetical cases and how expert teachers handle them.

Point/Counterpoint. There is a section in every chapter called *Point/ Counterpoint,* a debate that examines two contrasting perspectives on an important question or controversy related to research or practice in educational psychology. Many of the topics considered in these *Point/Counterpoints* have "made the news" recently and are central to the discussions of educational reformers.

Student Supplements. A *Study Guide* designed to help you master the material in the text is also available. The *Study Guide* includes concept maps, case study applications, lists of key points, exercises with key terms and concepts, practice tests, and explanations of why answers are correct.

Student Responses. You are invited to respond to any aspect of this text. We welcome your feedback. You may wish to criticize the solutions in the *Teachers' Casebook,* for example, or suggest topics or materials you think should be added to future editions. We would also like to know what you think of the text features and student supplements. Please send letters to:

Woolfolk
EDUCATIONAL PSYCHOLOGY, 6/E
Allyn & Bacon
160 Gould Street
Needham Heights, MA 02194

ACKNOWLEDGMENTS

During the years I have worked on this book, from initial draft to this most recent revision, many people have supported the project. Without their help, this text simply could not have been written.

Many educators contributed to this project. Carol Weinstein wrote the section in chapter 11 on spaces for learning. Angela O'Donnell generously shared her insights about educational psychology with me and created the concept maps for the *Study Guide.* Steve Ross of Memphis State University and Kathryn Linden of Purdue University are responsible for the *Test Bank* and the answer feedback material that accompanies each item. The *Instructor's Resource Manual,* the *Study Guide,* and the Instructor's Section that accompanies the *Annotated Instructor's Edition* were written by Lynne Díaz-Rico and Ruth Sandlin, of the California State University, San Bernardino. They continue to bring creative thinking and exceptional dedication to the project. Their ideas have improved my teaching. The summaries of research for the *Instructor's Resource Manual* were written by Wayne K. Hoy II, now Vice President of Advanced Software Products. Chapters 9 and 10 on motivation were redesigned by Johnmarshall Reeve of the University of Wisconsin, Milwaukee. Hermine Marshall, San Francisco State University, Asghar Iran-Najad, University of Alabama, and

Kay Bull, Oklahoma State University, contributed ideas, information and insights to the cognitive and constructivist sections of the text.

My writing was guided by extensive and thoughtful reviews from the following individuals:

Joyce Alexander,
Indiana University

Kay Bull,
Oklahoma State University

Maureen Sherry Carr,
Oregon State University

Peggy Dettmer,
Kansas State University

Carlos Diaz,
Florida Atlantic University

Lynne Díaz-Rico,
*California State University
San Bernardino*

Miranda D'Amico,
McGill University

Roberta Dimord,
Delaware Valley College

Kathy Farber,
Bowling Green State University

Ricardo Garcia,
University of Idaho

Karl Haberlandt,
Trinity College

Daniel P. Hallahan,
University of Virginia

Sharon Lee Hiett,
University of Central Florida

Robert L. Hohn,
University of Kansas

Dianne Horgan,
The University of Memphis

Ali Iran-Nejad,
The University of Alabama

Sharon Lamb,
Bryn Mawr College

Kathryn Linden,
Purdue University

Hermine Marshall,
University of California, Berkeley

Marion Mason,
Bloomsburg University

Suzanne Morin,
Shippensburg University

Stephen A. Parker,
Chicago State University

Suzanne H. Pasch,
University of Wisconsin

Michael Piechowski,
Northland College

Johnmarshall Reeve,
University of Wisconsin

Leslie Rescorla,
Bryn Mawr College

Steven Richman,
Nassau Community College

Dianne Rivera,
Florida Atlantic University

Harry Robinson,
Muskegon Community College

Barak Rosenshine,
University of Illinois

Ruth Sandlin,
*California State University
San Bernardino*

Julie Turner,
Pennsylvania State University

Jerry Willis,
University of Houston

James Young,
Brigham Young University

As I made decisions about how to revise this edition, I benefited from the ideas of professors around the country who took the time to complete surveys and answer my questions. Thanks to: Jeanne Callihan, University of Texas, San Antonio; D. G. Underwood, Clemson University; Kathryn W. Linden, Purdue University; James M. Boland, Indiana University Northwest; David S. Bender, Pennsylvania State University, Berks; Keith W. Allred, Brigham Young University; Wensan Yan, Gonzaga University; George Vrhel, Sauk Valley College; Henri Groenheim, Towson State University; Dan G. Holt, Purdue University;

William L. Franzen, University of Missouri, St. Louis; Norma Y. Stevens, Belmont University; Richard H. Blake, Weber State University; Perry Castelli, Troy State University; John Wheeler, Southwest Baptist University; John Baer, Rider College; Melva M. Burke, Pfeiffer College; Sheila Drake, Kansas Wesleyan University; Jackson F. Lee, Jr., Francis Marion College; Joseph McCloskey, Gloucester County College; Linda Metzke, Lyndon State College; Arthur Hernandez, University of Texas, San Antonio; Robert R. Hayden, Siena College; Mary Ann Chapko, Indiana University Northwest; Tony Williams, Marshall University; Joe Bordeaux, Lindenwood College; Arthur Landry, Carthage College; Ron J. Sjoerdsma, Calvin College; Paula Hillman, University of Wisconsin, Waukesha; Brenna Beedle, Eastern Washington University; Ruth Anne Niles, Radford University; Gail C. Delicio, Clemson University; Daniel Fasko, Sr., Morehead State University; Mary R. Sudzina, University of Dayton; Stacey Neuharth-Pritchitt, Purdue University; Lynne Díaz-Rico, California State University, San Bernardino; Hagop S. Pambookian, Shawnee State University; Roberta Ralston Dimord, Delaware Valley College; Paul Berghoff, Pembroke State University; Marcia Salner, Sangamon State University.

Many classroom teachers across the country contributed their experience, creativity, and expertise to the *Teachers' Casebook*. I have thoroughly enjoyed my association with these master teachers and I am grateful for the perspective they brought to the book. Thanks to: Julie Addison (Roxborough Elementary School, Littleton, Colorado); Eileen D. Akers (Jackson-Via Elementary School, Charlottesville, Virginia); Kathy Andrews (Lane Center School for Exceptional Children, Houston, Texas); Laura Atkinson (Chapel Hill, North Carolina); Harriet Chipley (Lookout Mountain Elementary School, Lookout Mountain, Tennessee); Carolyn R. Cook (Ramona Elementary School, Ramona, California); Karen Beechy Creider (Central High School, Philadelphia, Pennsylvania); Kathryn Daniels (Fredericktown Elementary School, Fredericktown, Ohio); Rugth Ann Dearth (Fredericktown Junior High School, Fredericktown, Ohio); Jane Dusell (Medford Area Senior High School, Medford, Wisconsin); Stephen C. Ellwood IV (St. Francis Elementary School, St. Francis, Maine); Donald Falk (Fredericktown Intermediate School, Fredericktown, Ohio); Bruce Fisher (Fortuna Elementary School, Fortuna, California); Candice J. Gallagher (Fredericktown Intermediate School, Fredericktown, Ohio); Betty Garner (Pattonville I.D.E.A.L. Center, Maryland Heights, Missouri); Carol Gibbs (Happy Valley School, Rossville, Georgia); Nancy R. Gonzalez (Robert Frost School, Mount Prospect, Illinois); Mark Gray (Highland Middle School, Louisville, Kentucky); Joanne S. Groseclose (Marion Intermediate School, Marion, Virginia); Sarah Gustafsen (The Okeechobee Center, Okeechobee, Florida); K. Janice Hill (Dillingham School, Dillingham, Alabama); Bonnie Hettman (Lima Central Catholic High School, Lima, Ohio); Dori Hoffman-Latter (Walker Middle School, Charlottesville, Virginia); Malcolm Jarrell (Jackson-Via Elementary School, Charlottesville, Virginia); Don Knies (Brooklyn Friends School, Brooklyn, New York); Sharon Klotz (Kiel Middle School, Kiel, Wisconsin); James D. Kraft (Wausau West High School, Wausau, Wisconsin); Karen B. Kreider (Central High School, Philadelphia, Pennsylvania); Lawrence Leebens (Forest Hills Elementary School, Eden Prairie, Minnesota); Brenda M. Lloyd (St. Anne's-Belfield, Charlottesville, Virginia); Joan H. Lowe (Russell Elementary School, Hazelwood, Missouri); Phyllis N. Marshall (Hoech Middle School, St. Ann, Missouri); Louise Harrold Melucci (Greenwood School, Warwick, Rhode Island); Marcia E. Miller (Walker Elementary School, Charlottesville, Virginia); Kathy A. Minniear (LaVeta Bauer Elementary School, Dayton, Ohio); Deborah H. Platt (Eugene Field Elementary School, Mitchell, South Dakota); Ida Pofahl (Denison Elementary School, Denison, Iowa); Jan Reynolds (Fredericktown Intermediate School, Fredericktown, Ohio); R. Chris Rohde (Chippewa Falls Senior High School, Chippewa Falls, Wisconsin); Linda Stahl (Ponca City Senior High School, Ponca City, Oklahoma); Kay Toliver (East Harlem Tech Middle School, New York City, New York); Marie Vachon (St. Paul School, Ramsey, New Jersey); Darlene A. Walsh (Greenbush Elementary School, West Warwick, Rhode Island); Simone Wharton (New York, New York); Cynthia Newman Wisdom (Trace Crossings Elementary School, Hoover, Alabama).

In a project of this size so many people make essential contributions. Laurie Frankenthaler, Permissions Coordinator, worked diligently to obtain permissions for the material reproduced in this text and the supplements. Susan Duane guided the collection of photographs. The text designer, Debbie Schneck, and cover coordinator, Linda Knowles, made the look of this book my favorite yet. Kathy Smith, Production Coordinator, Susan McIntyre, Production Administrator, and Elaine Ober, Production Manager coordinated all aspects of the project, including the *Annotated Instructor's Edition*, with amazing skill and grace. Somehow they brought order to what could have been chaos. Now the book is in the able hands of Sandi Kirshner, Director of Marketing, Ellen Mann, Marketing Manager, Lou Kennedy, Director of Advertising, and their staff. I can't wait to see what they are planning for me now! What a talented and creative group of women—I am honored to work with them all.

On this edition, I was privileged to work with an outstanding editorial group. Bill Barke, President of Allyn and Bacon, brought his distinctive style and leadership to the project, making the effort a pleasure. Nancy Forsyth, the Editor in Chief for Education, brought her intelligence, creativity, sound judgment, and style to all our work. She will always have my deepest respect and enduring friendship. Christine Nelson, editorial assistant, kept everything running smoothly and kept my fax machine humming. On this edition I was fortunate to have the help of Alicia Reilly, an outstanding developmental editor with just the right combination of knowledge and organizational ability. She guided this revision in all its many aspects, always staying just ahead of whatever had to happen next—remarkable! The supplements package and the excellent pedagogical supports would not exist without her tireless efforts.

Finally, I want to thank my family and friends for their kindness and support during the long days and nights that I worked on this book. Again, to my daughter, Liz, thanks for your insights about teachers and students, shared over the years. You have been my greatest teacher—my continuing source of pride and humility. To my family, Anita Wieckert; Marion, Charlie, Bob, Lucas, Geoffrey, Eric, and Suzie Pratt; Claudia Casser; and Wayne C., Elsie, Wayne K., and Kelly Hoy—you are the greatest.

And finally, to Wayne Hoy, my friend, colleague, inspiration, passion, husband—the best is yet to be, thanks to you. Who would have thought life could be so good?

Anita Woolfolk Hoy

Teachers, Teaching, and Educational Psychology

I f you are like many students, you begin this course with a mixture of anticipation and wariness. Perhaps you are required to take educational psychology as part of a program in teacher education, speech therapy, nursing, or counseling. You may have chosen this class as an elective because you are interested in education or psychology. Whatever your reason for enrolling, you probably have questions about teaching, schools, students—or even about yourself—that you hope this course may answer. I have written the sixth edition of *Educational Psychology* with questions such as these in mind.

In this first chapter, we begin not with educational psychology but with education—more specifically, with the state of teaching today. Only when you are aware of the challenges teachers face can you appreciate the contributions of educational psychology. After a brief introduction to the world of the teacher, we turn to a discussion of educational psychology itself. We will consider what educational psychology is and why you should study it. How can principles identified by educational psychologists benefit teachers, therapists, parents, and others who are interested in teaching and learning? What exactly is the content of educational psychology, and where does this information come from? By the time you have finished this chapter, you will be in a much better position to answer these questions and many others such as:

- Would teaching be a good career for me?
- What do expert teachers know?
- What are the greatest concerns of beginning teachers?
- Why should I study educational psychology?
- What roles do theory and research play in this field?
- What specific kinds of problems will the study of educational psychology help me to solve?
- What is good teaching?

Take a minute to remember the names of the best teachers you ever had. What characteristics do you associate with these expert teachers? What was it about these teachers that made you remember them over the years? What effects did they have on you?

Describing teachers who made a difference in his life, Harvard professor Robert Coles (1990) said:

> I mention these teachers in my life because, in fact, they continue to be a great big part of it still. Their voices are in my head and are part of my voice, I am sure. Their thoughts and values inform what I consider and call my own thoughts and values. Their example—the things they did, the style of their teaching, the strategies they employed—continue to inform the way I work. . . .

> In a sense, then, all good teachers rescue us from the death of boredom, apathy, self-preoccupation, and self-satisfaction: the teacher as an intellectual and moral life saver who fortunately has come our way and, of course, the teacher as one who is rescued by rescuing others. (p. 59)

hat Is Good Teaching?

There are hundreds of answers to this question, including ideas based on your own experience. This question has been examined by educators, psychologists, philosophers, novelists, journalists, mathematicians, scientists, historians, policy makers, and parents, to name only a few groups. And good teaching is not confined to classrooms—it occurs in homes and hospitals, museums and sales meetings, therapists' offices and summer camps. In this book, we are primarily concerned with teaching in classrooms, but much of what you will learn applies to other settings as well.

Inside Five Classrooms

To begin our examination of good teaching, let's step inside the classrooms of several outstanding teachers. All the situations that follow are real. The first two teachers work with my student teachers in local elementary schools. I have chosen them because one of my colleagues at Rutgers, Carol Weinstein, has written about them in her book on classroom management (Weinstein & Mignano, 1993). The next three are secondary-school teachers who have been studied by other educational psychologists.

A Bilingual First Grade. There are 25 students in Viviana's class. Most have recently emigrated from the Dominican Republic; the rest come from Nicaragua, Mexico, Puerto Rico, and Honduras. Even though the children

Planning Tip: See the *Chapter-1-At-A-Glance Planning Guide* in the Instructor's Section at the front of this book.

Study Guide: The *Study Guide,* sold separately, contains exercises to help students determine if they have mastered each learning objective for this chapter.

Planning Tip: See the separate *Instructor's Resource Manual* for additional activities and resources for teaching this chapter, including Handout Masters. Also see the Allyn and Bacon *Transparencies in Educational Psychology.*

Planning Tip: See the *Test Bank* and *Study Guide* supplements as you plan for evaluation and measurement of student learning.

Planning Tip: For further information about audiovisual, multimedia, and computer-assisted resources for teaching this chapter, see the Video and Software Guide in the *Instructor's Resource Manual.*

Objective 1.1: Describe elements of good teaching.

Activity 1.1: If your class involves student discussion or cooperative group work, it is useful to do some ice-breaking activities during the first weeks of the course. See the Instructor's Section for a Getting Acquainted activity and the *Instructor's Resource Manual* for **Handout Master 1.1,** "Name Tags," and a Team Building activity.

speak little or no English when they begin school, by the time they leave in June, Viviana has helped them master the normal first-grade curriculum for their district. She accomplishes this by teaching in Spanish early in the year to aid understanding, then gradually introducing English as the students are ready. Viviana does not want her students segregated or labeled as disadvantaged. She encourages them to take pride in their Spanish-speaking heritage while using every available opportunity to support their developing English proficiency.

Viviana's expectations for her students are high, and she makes sure the students have the resources they need. She provides materials—pencils, scissors, colors—so no child lacks the means to learn. And she supplies constant encouragement. "Viviana's commitment to her students is evident in her first-grade bilingual classroom. With an energy level that is rare, she motivates, prods, instructs, models, praises, and captivates her students . . . The pace is brisk and Viviana clearly has a flair for the dramatic; she uses music, props, gestures, facial expressions, and shifts in voice tone to communicate the material" (Weinstein & Mignano, 1993).

Viviana's expectations for herself are high as well. She continually expands her knowledge of teaching through graduate work and participation in special training programs. To know more about her students each year, she spends hours in their homes. For Viviana, teaching is a not just a job; it is a way of life.

A Suburban Sixth Grade.   Ken teaches sixth grade in a suburban elementary school in central New Jersey. Ken emphasizes "process writing." His students complete first drafts, discuss them with others in the class, revise, edit, and "publish" their work. The students also keep daily journals and often use these to share personal concerns with Ken. They tell him of problems at home, fights, and fears; he always takes the time to respond in writing. The study of science is also placed in the context of the real world. The students use a National Geographic Society computer network to link with other schools in order to identify acid rain patterns around the world. For social studies, the class played two simulation games that focused on the first half of the 1800s. They "lived" as trappers collecting animal skins, and as pioneers heading west to search for gold.

Throughout the year Ken is very interested in the social and emotional development of his students—he wants them to learn about responsibility and fairness as well as science and social studies. This concern is evident in the way he develops his class rules at the beginning of the year. Rather than specifying dos and don'ts, Ken and his students devise a "Bill of Rights" for the class, describing the rights of the students and of the teacher. These rights cover most of the situations that might need a "rule."

An Inner-City Middle School.   Another excellent teacher is described in the *Harvard Education Letter.*

> Robert Moses, founder of the Algebra Project at the Martin Luther King School in Cambridge, Massachusetts, teaches students the concept of number and sign through a physical event: they go for a ride on a subway. Choosing one subway stop as a starting point, students relate inbound and outbound to positive and negative numbers. They translate their sub-

Activity 1.2 Reflection/Journal Writing: Characteristics of Your Best Teacher. See the *Instructor's Resource Manual* for an activity that asks your students to reflect on the qualities and characteristics of their "best" teachers.

Activity 1.3: To give students a feel for the many roles of a teacher, have them read one of the following:

1. In the separate *Instructor's Resource Manual* you will find "A Day in the Life of an Elementary School Teacher" and "A Day in the Life of a Secondary School Teacher." These **Handout Masters 1.2 and 1.3** vividly describe a typical day for two real teachers.

2. "About Teaching and Teachers: Two Teachers of Letters," by M. T. Metzger & C. Fox (*Harvard Educational Review*, November 1986), reprinted in the *Annual Editions: Educational Psychology 88/89* (Guilford, CT: Duskin, 1989) reveals the special joys and frustrations of secondary-school teaching.

After students have read one or more of these, ask them to analyze their potential strengths and weaknesses in filling the many roles of a teacher. In what areas will they need to improve?

Connections: Ken's process writing, student publishing, and journal writing are examples of a "whole language" approach, discussed in chapter 13. Ken's "Bill of Rights" is an example of an innovative approach to setting class rules, discussed in chapter 11.

Connections: Robert Moses's use of students' knowledge is a good example of the importance of prior knowledge in learning, discussed in chapter 7, and could be described as a constructivist approach to teaching, as discussed in chapters 7 and 13.

way ride into mathematical language by considering both the number of stops and their direction. By giving students such experiences before introducing the formal language of algebra, Moses . . . has made math more enjoyable and accessible. (Ruopp & Driscoll, 1990, p. 5)

Research: Borko, H., & Livingston, O. B. (1989). Cognition and improvisation: Differences in mathematics instruction by expert and novice teachers. *American Educational Research Journal, 26,* 473–498.

Connections: Ellen's flexible knowledge is a good example of the importance of teachers' thorough understanding of content, discussed in chapter 12.

Activity 1.4 Field Experience: Survey on Teaching Roles. See the *Instructor's Resource Manual* for an activity in which students use a form to interview teachers about the many roles of teachers today. This form is included as Handout Master 1.4 in the *Instructor's Resource Manual.*

Activity 1.5 Cooperative Learning: Advantages/Disadvantages of Teaching. See the *Instructor's Resource Manual* for an activity in which students work together to rank the advantages and disadvantages of teaching.

Background: Carter, K., Sabers, D., Cushing, K., Pinnegar, S., & Berliner, D. (1987). Processing and using information about students: A study of expert, novice, and postulant teachers. *Teaching and Teacher Education, 3,* 147–157.

Objective 1.2: Compare and contrast characteristics and methods of expert and novice teachers.

Two Advanced Math Classes.   Hilda Borko and Carol Livingston (1989) describe two expert secondary-school mathematics teachers. In one lesson for her advanced mathematics class, Ellen had her students identify any three problems about ellipses from their text. She asked if there were any questions or uncertainties about these problems. Ellen answered student questions, worked two of the problems, and then used the three problems to derive all the concepts and equations the students needed to understand the material. Ellen's knowledge of the subject and of her students was so thorough that she could create the explanations and derive the formulas on the spot, no matter which problems the students chose.

Another teacher, Randy, worked with his students' confusion to construct a review lesson about strategies for doing integrals. When one student said that a particular section in the book seemed "haphazard," Randy led the class through a process of organizing the material. He asked the class for general statements about useful strategies for doing integrals. He clarified their suggestions, elaborated on some, and helped students improve others. He asked the students to tie their ideas to passages in the text. Even though he accepted all reasonable suggestions, he listed only the key strategies on the board. By the end of the period, the students had transformed the disorganized material from the book into an ordered and useful outline to guide their learning. They also had a better idea about how to read and understand difficult material.

What do you see in these classrooms? The teachers are committed to their students. They must deal with a wide range of student abilities and challenges: different languages, different home lives, different needs. These teachers must understand their subjects and their students' thinking so well that they can spontaneously create new examples and explanations when students are confused. They must make the most abstract concepts, such as negative numbers, real and understandable for their particular students. And then there is the challenge of new technologies and techniques. The teachers must use them appropriately to accomplish important goals, not just to entertain the students. The whole time that these experts are navigating through the academic material, they also are taking care of the emotional needs of their students, propping up sagging self-esteem and encouraging responsibility. If we followed these individuals from the first day of class, we would see that they carefully plan and teach the basic procedures for living and learning in their classes. They can efficiently correct and collect homework, regroup students, give directions, distribute materials, collect lunch money, and deal with disruptions— do all of this while also making a mental note to check why one of their students is so tired.

Viviana, Ken, Robert, Ellen, and Randy are examples of expert teachers, the focus of much recent research in education and psychology. For another perspective on the question "What is good teaching?" let's examine this research on expertise in teaching.

Expert Teachers   Test Bank items 1.1–1.15, 1.56, 1.57, 1.67, 1.72, 1.73

What do **expert teachers** know that allows them to be so successful? How do they differ from beginners? Researchers are investigating how expert teachers think about their students, the subjects they teach, and the process of teaching itself.

Experts work from integrated sets of principles instead of dealing with each new event as a new problem. They look for patterns revealing similarities in situations that seem quite different at first glance. Experts focus more than beginners on analyzing a problem and mentally applying different principles to develop a solution. In one study of solutions to discipline problems, the expert teachers spent quite a bit of time framing each problem, forming questions, deciding what information was necessary, and considering alternatives (Swanson, O'Conner, & Cooney, 1990).

Expert teachers have a sense of what is typical in classrooms, of what to expect during certain activities or times of the day. Many of their teaching routines have become automatic—they don't even have to think about how to distribute materials, take roll, move students in and out of groups, or assign grades. This gives the teachers more mental and physical energy for being creative and focusing on their students' progress. For example, one study found that expert math teachers could go over the previous day's work with the class in two or three minutes, compared to 15 minutes for novices (Leinhardt, 1986).

We saw with Ellen and Randy that expert teachers can improvise explanations and create new examples on the spot. They can turn students' confusion into understanding by helping the students organize and expand upon what they know. Expert teachers are not bound by their plans but can follow the needs of the students (Borko & Livingston, 1989; Sabers, Cushing, & Berliner, 1991; Tochon & Munby, 1993).

So it seems that expert teachers, like expert dancers or gymnasts, have mastered a number of moves or routines that they can perform easily, almost without thinking. But they also know a great deal about their subject, so they can create new moves, improvise, and avoid trouble. And they are analytical. They can take a situation apart, diagnose the source of the problem, consider alternatives, and make decisions about what will work. Figure 1.1 on page 6 contrasts the problem solving of experts and beginners by presenting the "thoughts" of two teachers as they consider what to do about Robbie, who has just "fallen" out of his desk for the third time today. These thoughts are based on the findings of Swanson and associates (1990) and the experiences of my student teachers.

Expert teachers have more elaborate *systems of knowledge* for understanding problems in teaching. For example, when a beginning teacher is faced with students' wrong answers on math or history tests, all the wrong answers may seem about the same—wrong. The inexperienced teacher may have trouble connecting other facts or ideas with the students' wrong answers. But for an expert teacher, wrong answers are part of a rich system of knowledge that could include how to recognize several types of wrong answers, the misunderstanding or lack of information behind each kind of mistake, the best way to reteach and correct the misunderstanding, materials and activities that have

*T*eaching is one of the few professions in which an individual is expected to assume all the responsibilities of an experienced "pro" during the first week on the job. In this situation, a veteran teacher can be a real source of support and guidance.

Expert Teachers Experienced, effective teachers who have developed solutions for common classroom problems. Their knowledge of teaching process and content is extensive and well organized.

Novice Teachers Inexperienced teachers just beginning their career. They may be excellent teachers but have not yet developed a repertoire of solutions for common teaching problems or systems of well-organized knowledge about the many aspects of teaching.

FIGURE 1.1

EXPERT AND NOVICE TEACHERS THINK ABOUT A DISCIPLINE PROBLEM

Experts and novices think about classroom problems in different ways. For example, an expert goes through a series of problem-solving stages that allow the expert to apply extensive knowledge about students and teaching. Novices, on the other hand, often "leap" to the first solution that comes to mind.

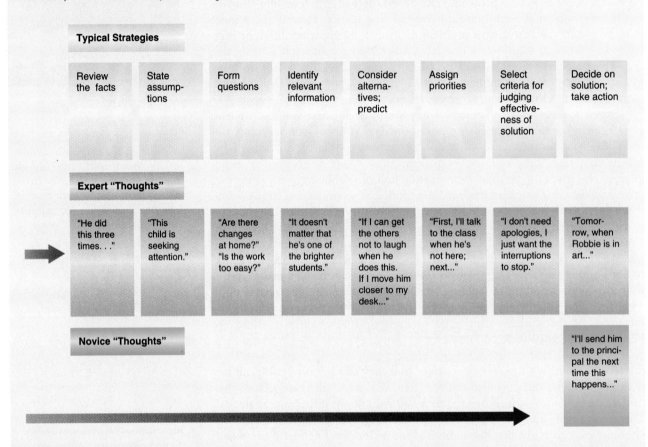

Source: H. Swanson, J. E. O'Conner, and J. B. Cooney (1990). An information processing analysis of expert and novice teachers' problem solving. *American Educational Research Journal, 27,* Appendix B. Copyright 1990 by the American Educational Research Association. Adapted by permission of the publisher.

worked in the past, and several ways to test whether the reteaching was successful (Floden & Klinzing, 1990; Leinhardt, 1988). Peterson and Comeaux (1989) argue that it is the quality of teachers' professional knowledge and their ability to be aware of their own thinking that make them expert. Let's look for a moment at the knowledge of expert teachers.

Expert Knowledge Test Bank items 1.54, 1.74

Lee Shulman (1987) has studied what teachers know, and he has identified seven areas of professional knowledge. Expert teachers know:

1. The academic subjects they teach.

2. General teaching strategies that apply in all subjects (such as the principles of classroom management, effective teaching, and evaluation that you will discover in this book).

3. The curriculum materials and programs appropriate for their subject and grade level.

4. Subject-specific knowledge for teaching: Special ways of teaching certain students and particular concepts, such as the best ways to explain negative numbers to lower-ability students.

5. The characteristics and cultural backgrounds of learners.

6. The settings in which students learn—pairs, small groups, teams, classes, schools, and the community.

7. The goals and purposes of teaching.

This is quite a list. Obviously, one course cannot give you all the information you need to teach. In fact, a whole program of courses won't make you an expert. That takes time and experience. But studying educational psychology can

Expert teachers not only know the content of the subjects they teach, they also know how to relate this content to the world outside the classroom and how to keep students involved in learning.

Application: Ask students to work in groups to create role plays that illustrate the thought processes of expert and novice teachers in response to common classroom situations. For example, a novice teacher might publicly reprimand a student who calls out answers, whereas an expert teacher might speak privately to the student who calls out.

Study Guide: Concept Map. See the *Study Guide* for the Concept Map of "Expert Teachers." This map also appears as **Handout Master 1.7.**

Objective 1.3: Describe Shulman's (1987) areas of professional knowledge.

Activity 1.6: Decision Making. See the *Instructor's Resource Manual* for an activity that emphasizes what is involved in the many decisions teachers must make.

Activity 1.7: Critical Thinking. One major goal of this first chapter is to make a case for the value of educational psychology. I describe the study of educational psychology as an examination of content and process, information and thinking. Students can examine research both to understand the findings (content) and to practice analytical, critical thinking (process). Students often are more comfortable with (and expect) content. They tend to want strategies and techniques. To make students think about both content and process, technique and reflective thinking, I sometimes conduct discussions or debates about teaching as art and science. See the separate *Instructor's Resource Manual* for Teaching: Art or Science—Technique or Reflection?

Objective 1.4: Contrast teaching as an art and as a science.

Casebook: See the Teachers' Casebook at the end of this chapter for one teacher's metaphor for teaching.

Whose Classroom Is It Anyway?

The Carnegie Forum on Education and the Economy report, *A Nation Prepared: Teachers for the 21st Century* (1986), introduced a new word to the vocabulary of educational reform—*restructuring*. The report argued that we must "restructure schools to provide a professional environment for teachers, freeing [teachers] to decide how to best meet the state and local goals for children" (p. 57). Is this recommendation becoming a reality? Is the structure of schools changing so teachers can use their expertise in deciding how to teach their students?

POINT **Teachers have a bigger say.**

The National Governors' Association, the National Education Association,

and the National Association of Secondary School Principals have issued reports supporting teacher participation in school decisions. The National Governors' Association (1989) states that restructuring should involve (1) modifying curriculum to support higher-order thinking and problem solving, creativity, and cooperation; (2) bringing together teachers, administrators, and parents at each school to make instructional decisions; (3) creating new staff roles to make better use of the teachers' expertise; and (4) holding schools accountable for students' achievement.

The April 1990 issue of *Educational Leadership* describes many elementary and secondary schools that have radically altered curriculum, decision-making, roles, and accountability systems. For example, the staff of

Central Park East Secondary School decided to limit the number of class periods for its students to allow more in-depth study:

> A typical week for students in grades 7–10, for example, includes several two-hour blocks of humanities and math-science, daily one-hour classes in Spanish, two to three hours of community service, and several advisory periods. During an extended lunch period and after school, students may participate in clubs, music, physical education, sports, and other activities. (O'Neil, 1990b, p. 7)

In 119 Dade County, Florida, schools, administrator/teacher/parent councils have been created to redesign the schools. Three of the innovations established by these councils are Saturday classes providing extra help, en-

Background: Jean Piaget (1973) had this to say about teaching: "The art of education is like the art of medicine: it is an art that cannot be practiced without special 'gifts,' but one that assumes exact and experimental knowledge relating to the human beings on which it is exercised" (*To Understand Is to Invent: The Future of Education*, p. 94).

Reflective Thoughtful and inventive. Reflective teachers think back over situations to analyze what they did and why and to consider how they might improve learning for their students.

add to your professional knowledge. In this book we will focus on general teaching strategies, the characteristics of students, and settings for learning. We will also touch on learning goals and subject-specific knowledge for teaching.

How do you grow from beginning teacher to expert? Can you learn to be an expert teacher, or are really great teachers just born? Is good teaching an art or a science? Answers to this last question provide another perspective on good teaching.

Teaching: Artistry, Technique, and a Lot of Work   Test Bank items 1.4, 1.55, 1.57, 1.67, 1.71–1.74

Because researchers have identified a number of effective teaching techniques, some educators argue that all teachers should learn these practices and be tested on them to earn or to keep their teaching certificates. Other educators believe that the mark of an excellent teacher is not the ability to apply techniques but the artistry of being **reflective**—thoughtful and inventive—about teaching (Schon, 1983). Educators who adopt this view tend to be more conrichment, and even ballet instruction; satellite schools in local businesses; and lead teachers who receive extra pay to support and guide their colleagues.

COUNTERPOINT Restructuring is not working.

In 1987 the Carnegie Foundation for the Advancement of Teaching surveyed teachers across the United States to see if they felt involved in decisions at their schools. Most teachers—about 79 percent—participated in choosing textbooks, and a good number (63 percent) felt they were involved in shaping the curriculum. But only 47 percent helped to set standards for students' behavior, only 43 percent participated in designing staff develop- ment programs, and a mere 20 percent had a say in school budgets.

Some researchers suggest that teachers must be so focused on their classrooms and students that they have little time or energy for participating in schoolwide decisions (Lortie, 1977). Other researchers suggest that teachers and administrators have a kind of agreement not to interfere in each other's "territory." In return for leaving school-level decisions to the administrators, teachers get to be autonomous in their classrooms (Corwin, 1981). Some critics fear that restructuring will require teachers to take on more responsibilities without giving them more time or resources to meet these new obligations (Conley, 1991).

Evidently, the problems persist. David Clark and Terry Astuto (1994) ask these questions about restructuring schools so that teachers are more involved in making decisions about their individual students:

Why do we focus on implementing site-based management systems for high schools while we retain the daily schedule of six to eight 50-minute class periods, which ensures that most high school teachers will never get to know about the lives of the 150 to 200 students whom they see each day? Does anyone believe that such an organizational structure provides the time for English teachers to tutor their students in writing . . . Or that it provides an opportunity for individualized instruction and counseling? (p. 514)

cerned with how teachers plan, solve problems, create instruction, and make decisions than they are with the specific techniques teachers apply. They believe teaching is a complicated, demanding activity that requires creative thinking and a commitment to lifelong learning (Borko, 1989; Peterson & Comeaux, 1989).

Most people agree that teachers must be both technically competent and inventive. They must be able to use a range of strategies, and they must also be able to invent new strategies. They must have some simple routines that work for managing classes, but they must also be willing and able to break from the routine when the situation calls for change. New problems arise all the time, and when the old solutions do not work, something else is needed.

With the growing understanding that teaching is a complex problem-solving activity has come a call to give teachers more freedom and responsibility. A number of educational reform movements seek to involve teachers in designing the curriculum and making the decisions for their own students, as you can see in the Point/Counterpoint section above.

You may be thinking that all this talk about expert teachers and expert knowledge, artistry, and technique is a bit idealistic and abstract. Right now, you may have other, more down-to-earth, concerns about becoming a teacher. You are not alone!

Connections: Teachers' knowledge of their own thinking is an example of metacognitive knowledge, discussed in chapter 7.

Objective 1.5: Describe how teaching requires a balance of reflection and technique.

Discussion: Have students read and discuss the article by Sparks-Langer, G. M., & Colton, A. S. B. (1991). Synthesis of research on teachers' reflective thinking. *Educational Leadership, 48*(6), 37–44. *Focus Questions:* What does it mean to be a reflective teacher? Why is reflection important in teaching?

Activity 1.8: Restructuring the Education of Teachers. See the *Instructor's Resource Manual* for a list of recommendations for educating teachers. Ask students to evaluate these recommendations.

Background: Restructuring Schools with Technology (1991, special section). *Phi Delta Kappan,* 73(1), 17–40.

Focus on . . .   Good Teaching

- What are some of the characteristics of expert teachers?
- What aspects of teachers' professional knowledge can you hope to develop by studying educational psychology?
- How are your concerns about teaching similar to or different from those reported in studies of beginning teachers?

Discussion: Have students read and discuss the article by Murphy, J., Evertson, C. M., & Radnofsky, M. L. (1991). Restructuring schools: Fourteen elementary and secondary teachers' perspectives on reform. *Elementary School Journal, 92,* 135–148. *Focus Question:* Are teachers becoming more involved in school decisions?

Objective 1.6: Identify the concerns of beginning teachers, and describe how these concerns change developmentally.

Teaching Tip: To gain a better sense of the problems and responsibilities of teaching, present the results of the latest "Gallup Poll of the Public's Attitude Toward the Public Schools," published each year in the September or October issue of *Phi Delta Kappan.* You might begin the class by taking a "poll" of your students on a few of the main Gallup questions, then compare their opinions to

Concerns of Beginning Teachers   Test Bank items 1.58, 1.66

Beginning teachers everywhere share many concerns. A review of studies conducted around the world found that beginning teachers regard maintaining classroom discipline, motivating students, accommodating differences among students, evaluating student work, and dealing with parents as the most serious challenges they face. Many teachers also experience what has been called "reality shock" when they take their first job and confront the "harsh and rude reality of everyday classroom life" (Veenman, 1984, p. 143). One source of shock may be that teachers really cannot ease into their responsibilities. On the first day of their first job, beginning teachers face the same tasks as teachers with years of experience. Student teaching, while a critical experience, does not really prepare prospective teachers for starting off a school year with a new class. And schools usually offer little chance for helpful contact between novice and experienced teachers, making mutual support and assistance difficult. If you have had any of these concerns, you shouldn't be troubled. It comes with the job of being a beginning teacher (Calderhead & Robson, 1991; Cooke & Pang, 1991; Veenman, 1984).

With experience, however, most teachers meet the challenges that seem difficult for beginners. They have more time to experiment with new methods or materials. Finally, as confidence grows, seasoned teachers can focus on the students' needs. Are my students learning? Are they developing positive attitudes? Is this the best way to teach the slower learners to write a persuasive essay? At this advanced stage, teachers judge their success by the successes of their students (Feiman-Nemser, 1983; Fuller 1969).

What about the Students?   Test Bank item 1.66

I have talked about good teachers because that is what many of you are planning to become. But all good teaching begins with an understanding of students and learning. As you will see throughout this text, today there is great interest in studying how people understand and apply knowledge. Just as educational psychologists have investigated how expertise develops in teaching, they have also explored how students come to be experts in particular subjects. Many of the chapters in this book are concerned with these issues.

I tell my class the first day of the semester that I hope they will "take educational psychology personally." By this I mean I want them to apply the ideas to their own lives as students. If you can become a more expert learner by applying the knowledge from this text about study strategies, motivation, active learning, and understanding, then you will be a better teacher as well. Years ago a wonderful principal told me that teachers are the *professional learners* and students are the *amateurs.* She encouraged the teachers in her school to be good guides and learning coaches so that their students would become expert learners too.

Of course, all experts were once beginners. How can educational psychology give you a basis for being an expert learner now and a good beginning teacher in the future?

The Role of Educational Psychology

Test Bank items 1.6, 1.7, 1.44, 1.68

We begin our consideration of the role of educational psychology by defining the term. For as long as educational psychology has existed—about 80 years—there have been debates about what it really is. Some people believe educational psychology is simply knowledge gained from psychology and applied to the activities of the classroom. Others believe it involves applying the methods of psychology to study classroom and school life (Clifford, 1984a; Grinder, 1981).

The view generally accepted today is that **educational psychology** is a distinct discipline with its own theories, research methods, problems, and techniques. "Educational psychology is distinct from other branches of psychology because it has the understanding and improvement of education as its primary goal" (Wittrock, 1992, p. 138). Educational psychologists "study what people think and do [I would add *feel*] as they teach and learn a particular curriculum in a particular environment where education and training are intended to take place" (Berliner, 1992, p. 145). Merle Wittrock sums it up well, saying that educational psychology focuses on "the psychological study of the everyday problems of education, from which one derives principles, models, theories, teaching procedures, and practical methods of instruction and evaluation, as well as research methods, statistical analyses, and measurement and assessment procedures appropriate for studying the thinking and affective processes of learners and the socially and culturally complex processes of schools." But are the findings of educational psychologists really that helpful for teachers? After all, most teaching is just common sense, isn't it? Let's take a few minutes to examine these questions.

Is It Just Common Sense?   Test Bank items 1.8–1.11, 1.62, 1.68

In many cases, the principles set forth by educational psychologists—after spending much thought, research, and money—sound pathetically obvious. People are tempted to say, and usually do say, "Everyone knows that!" Consider these examples:

Taking Turns.   What method should a teacher use in selecting students to participate in a primary-grade reading class?

Common Sense Answer.   Teachers should call on students randomly so that everyone will have to follow the lesson carefully. If a teacher were to use the same order every time, the students would know when their turn was coming up.

Gallup's reading of the national trends. This also allows you to discuss survey research as a method in educational psychology.

Handout: "Stress Test," presented in the *Instructor's Resource Manual* as **Handout Master 1.5**, assesses your students' vulnerability to stress. The test could serve as the basis for a discussion or an activity in which students determine how they will manage stress in their first year of teaching.

Activity 1.9 Field Experience: Expert Teacher Knowledge. See the *Instructor's Resource Manual* for questions students can use in interviewing practicing teachers.

Activity 1.10 Multicultural Awareness: Teacher Demographics versus Student Demographics. See the *Instructor's Resource Manual* for a discussion format to examine the shortage of minority-group teachers.

Background: For a slightly longer discussion of the value of technique versus reflective thinking in teacher preparation, see pages 109–111 of Hoy, W. K., and Woolfolk, A. E. (1989). Supervising student teachers. In A. Woolfolk (Ed.), *Research perspectives on the graduate preparation of teachers* (pp. 108–131). Boston: Allyn & Bacon.

Educational Psychology The discipline concerned with teaching and learning processes; applies the methods and theories of psychology and has its own as well.

Research: Evidence for the importance of technique and reflection in teaching can be found in a study of a teacher education program in the Netherlands that strongly emphasizes the development of reflective thinking: Korthagen, F. A. J. (1985). Reflective teaching and preservice teacher education in the Netherlands. *Journal of Teacher Education, 36*(5), 11–15. Over 50 percent of the program's graduates who responded to a survey said they had been insufficiently prepared for handling problems of motivation and management. Many of these graduates found that they had to abandon their attempts at analysis and inquiry in their early teaching years to develop ways to handle the day-to-day teaching problems. Beginning teachers need to master some basic teaching techniques and procedures in order to protect the capacity for reflection. Otherwise, they may spend all their time in the first years of teaching just learning to survive.

Objective 1.7: Define educational psychology and the areas of study that it includes.

Background: The Spring 1992 issue of *Educational Psychologist, 27,* (2), has a special section on "The Nature and Mission of Educational Psychology" with articles by Merle Wittrock, David Berliner, Robert Calfee, and Carol Goodenow.

Activity 1.11: Teaching Tip. To make the point that not all information in educational psychology is common sense, give the Test of Educational Psychology available in the separate *Instructor's Resource Manual.*

How should teachers select students to read out loud? Is oral reading an effective practice? Research provides some surprising perspectives on these questions.

Answer Based on Research.   Research by Ogden, Brophy, and Evertson (1977) indicates that the answer to this question is not so simple. In first-grade reading classes, for example, going around the circle in order and giving each child a chance to read led to better overall achievement than calling on students randomly. The critical factor in going around the circle may be that each child gets a chance to participate. Without some system for calling on everyone, many students can be overlooked or skipped. Research suggests there are better alternatives for teaching reading than going around the circle, but if teachers choose this alternative, they should make sure that everyone has the chance for practice and feedback (Tierney, Readence, & Dishner, 1990).

Classroom Management.   Students are engaged in an appropriate and educationally meaningful task, but still, some students are repeatedly out of their seats without permission, wandering around the room. What should the teacher do?

Common Sense Answer.   Each time they get up, the teacher should remind students to remain in their seats. These repeated reminders will help overactive students remember the rule. If the teacher does not remind them and lets them get away with breaking the rules, both the out-of-seat students and the rest of the class may decide the teacher is not really serious about the rule.

Answer Based on Research.   In a now-classic study, Madsen, Becker, Thomas, Koser, and Plager (1968) found that the more a teacher told students to sit down when they were out of their seats, the more often the students got out of their seats without permission. When the teacher ignored students who were out of their seats and praised students who were sitting down, the rate of out-of-seat behavior dropped greatly. When the teacher returned to the previous system of telling students to sit down, the rate of out-of-seat behavior increased once again. It seems that—at least under some conditions—the more a teacher says "Sit down!" the more the students stand up!

Skipping Grades. Should a school encourage exceptionally bright students to skip grades or to enter college early?

Common Sense Answer. No! Very intelligent students who are a year or two younger than their classmates are likely to be social misfits. They are neither physically nor emotionally ready for dealing with older students and would be miserable in the social situations that are so important in school, especially in the later grades.

Answer Based on Research. Maybe. According to Samuel Kirk and his colleagues (1993), "From early admissions to school to early admissions to college, research studies invariably report that children who have been accelerated have adjusted as well as or better than have children of similar ability who have not been accelerated" (p. 105). Whether acceleration is the best solution for a student depends on many specific individual characteristics, including the intelligence and maturity of the student, and on the other available options. For some students, moving quickly through the material and working in advanced courses with older students is a very good idea.

Lily Wong (1987) demonstrated that just seeing research results in writing can make them seem obvious. She selected 12 findings from research on teaching; one of them was the "taking turns" result noted above. She presented six of the findings in their correct form and six in *exactly the opposite form* to college students and to experienced teachers. Both the college students and teachers rated about half of the *wrong* findings as "obviously" correct. In a follow-up study, another group of subjects was shown the 12 findings and their opposites and was asked to pick which ones were correct. For 8 of the 12 findings, the subjects chose the wrong result more often than the right one.

You may have thought that educational psychologists spend their time discovering the obvious. The examples above point out the danger of this kind of thinking. When a principle is stated in simple terms, it can sound simplistic. A similar phenomenon takes place when we see a gifted dancer or athlete perform; the well-trained performer makes it look easy. But we see only the results of the training, not all the work that went into mastering the individual movements. And bear in mind that any research finding—or its opposite—may sound like common sense. The issue is not what *sounds* sensible, but what is demonstrated when the principle is put to the test (Gage, 1991).

Using Research to Understand and Improve Teaching

Conducting research to test possible answers is one of two major tasks of educational psychology. The other is combining the results of various studies into

Test Bank items 1.12–1.20, 1.23–1.43, 1.45–1.53, 1.59–1.61, 1.63–1.65, 1.69, 1.70, 1.75–1.77

Example: As an example of the teacher as model, motivator, and manager: An article in the *New York Times* (May 26, 1988, p. B1) described how Cornell University was bringing together some of the high school teachers of its top undergraduates in order to honor both the student and his or her former teacher. One of these undergraduates said of his high school math teacher, "She had so much enthusiasm in class, she made learning so interesting; we had fun learning calculus." According to the article, the teacher's techniques included such innovations as "classroom coupons" for excellent work, which gave students the privilege of leaving class early or being late to class without penalty. At the same time, the student spoke of his teacher's "absolute dedication and discipline in teaching mathematics. There was no doubt that you were in her class to learn."

Discussion: Have students read and discuss the article by Gage, N. L. (1991). The obviousness of social and educational research results. *Educational Researcher, 20*(1), 10–16. *Focus Questions:* What makes findings in educational research seem "obvious"? What is the danger in this kind of thinking?

Field Experiences: See the following activities in L. Benjamin & K. Lowman (Eds.). *Activities handbook for the teaching of psychology.* Washington, DC: American Psychological Association (phone: 202–833–7600):

Activity 1: Observation: A Standardized Experience

Activity 2: Accuracy of Observation

These activities have students make and then compare observations so as to understand better the difficulty and value of the process.

Objective 1.8: Compare descriptive and experimental research studies.

Activity 1.12: Experimental versus Correlational Research. See the *Instructor's Resource Manual* for an activity that asks students to discriminate between correlational and experimental research.

Descriptive Research Studies that collect detailed information about specific situations, often using observation, surveys, interviews, recordings, or a combination of these methods.

Ethnography A descriptive approach to research that focuses on life within a group and tries to understand the meaning of events to the people involved.

Participant Observation A method for conducting descriptive research in which the researcher becomes a participant in the situation in order to better understand life in that group.

Case Study Intensive study of one person or one situation.

Correlations Statistical descriptions of how closely two variables are related.

Positive Correlation A relationship between two variables in which the two increase or decrease together. Example: calorie intake and weight gain.

Negative Correlation A relationship between two variables in which a high value on one is associated with a low value on the other. Example: height and distance from top of head to the ceiling.

theories that attempt to present a unified view of such things as teaching, learning, and development.

The Research Guide at the end of this book provides an extensive discussion of research in educational psychology. The next few pages summarize many of the key ideas and terms that you will find in the Research Guide. Your instructor may ask you to read this Research Guide before continuing to the next chapters so you will have a better understanding of how to interpret the research results you encounter throughout this course.

Descriptive Research.   Educational psychologists design and conduct many different kinds of research studies in their attempts to understand teaching and learning. Some of these studies are "descriptive," that is, their purpose is simply to describe events in a particular class or several classes. Reports of **descriptive research** often include survey results, interview responses, samples of actual classroom dialogue, or records of the class activities.

One descriptive approach, classroom **ethnography,** is borrowed from anthropology. Ethnographic methods involve studying the naturally occurring events in the life of a group and trying to understand the meaning of these events to the people involved. For example, the descriptions of expert high school mathematics teachers in the opening pages of this chapter were taken from an ethnographic study by Hilda Borko and Carol Livingston (1989). The researchers made detailed observations in the teachers' classes and analyzed these observations, along with audio recordings and information from interviews with the teachers, in order to describe differences between novice and expert teachers.

In some descriptive research, researchers carefully analyze videotapes of classes to identify recurring patterns of teacher and student behaviors. In other studies, the researcher uses **participant observation** and works within the class or school to understand the actions from the perspectives of the teacher and the students. Researchers also may employ case studies. A **case study** investigates in depth how a teacher plans courses, for example, or how a student tries to learn specific material.

Correlations.   Often the results of descriptive studies include reports of correlations. We will take a minute to examine this concept, because you will encounter many correlations in the coming chapters. A **correlation** is a number that indicates both the strength and the direction of a relationship between two events or measurements. Correlations range from 1.00 to –1.00. The closer the correlation is to either 1.00 or –1.00, the stronger the relationship. For example, the correlation between height and weight is about .70 (a strong relationship); the correlation between height and number of languages spoken is about .00 (no relationship at all).

The sign of the correlation tells the direction of the relationship. A **positive correlation** indicates that the two factors increase or decrease together. As one gets larger, so does the other. Height and weight are positively correlated because greater height tends to be associated with greater weight. A **negative correlation** means that increases in one factor are related to decreases in the other. For example, the correlation between outside temperature and the weight of clothing worn is negative, since people tend to wear clothing of increasing weight as the temperature decreases.

It is important to note that correlations do not prove cause and effect (see Figure 1.2). Height and weight are correlated—taller people tend to weigh more than shorter people. But gaining weight obviously does not cause you to grow taller. Knowing a person's height simply allows you to make a general prediction about that person's weight. Educational psychologists identify correlations so they can make predictions about important events in the classroom.

Experimentation. A second type of research—**experimentation**—allows educational psychologists to go beyond predictions and actually study cause and effect. Instead of just observing and describing an existing situation, the investigators introduce changes and note the results. First, a number of comparable groups of subjects are created. In psychological research, the term **subjects** generally refers to the people being studied—such as teachers or eighth graders—not to subjects like math or science. One common way to make sure that groups of subjects are essentially the same is to assign each subject to a group using a random procedure. **Random** means each subject has an equal chance to be in any group.

In one or more of these groups, the experimenters change some aspect of the situation to see if this change or "treatment" has an expected effect. The results in each group are then compared. Usually statistical tests are conducted to see if the differences between the groups are significant. When differences are described as **statistically significant,** it means that they probably did not happen simply by chance. A number of the studies we will examine attempt to identify cause-and-effect relationships by asking questions such as this: If teachers ignore students who are out of their seats without permission and praise students who are working hard at their desks (cause), will students spend more time working at their desks (effect)?

Examples: Other examples of correlations:

Perfect positive (1.0) correlation: the radius of a circle and its circumference

Perfect negative (–1.0) correlation: the number of minutes of daylight and the number of minutes of dark each day

Less than perfect positive correlation: heights of husband and wife; the cost of a car and the cost of insuring it; mother's education and child's IQ score: .30 (Sattler, 1992); child's IQ score and school grades: .39 (Sattler, 1992)

Experimentation Research method in which variables are manipulated and the effects recorded.

Subjects People or animals studied.

Random Without any definite pattern; following no rule.

Statistically Significant Not likely to be a chance occurrence.

FIGURE 1.2

CORRELATIONS DO NOT SHOW CAUSATION
When research shows that broken homes and crime are correlated, it does not show causation. Poverty, a third variable, may be the cause of both crime and broken homes.

Faulty Assumption

More Likely Assumption

Less than perfect negative correlation: cost of a theater ticket and distance from the stage; teachers' beliefs about the effectiveness of education and their beliefs about controlling pupils: –.50; the more they believe in education the less they believe pupils have to be controlled (Woolfolk & Hoy, 1990)

Zero correlation: population of India and the winning percentage of the New York Yankees

Objective 1.9: Distinguish between principles and theories in educational psychology research.

Focus on . . .   **Educational Psychology**

- What is your definition of educational psychology?
- What would you say to someone who asserted that "teaching is just common sense"?
- What methods are used to study learning and teaching in educational psychology?

Application: Ask students to indicate whether the following studies are descriptive (D) or experimental (E).

(D) 1. Researchers observe teachers of classes that have high achievement in order to determine how these teachers are alike.

(E) 2. Teachers give three groups of impulsive children different types of training to determine which type of training is most effective in reducing impulsivity.

Principle Established relationship between factors.

Theory Integrated statement of principles that attempts to explain a phenomenon and make predictions.

In many cases, both descriptive and experimental research occur together. The study by Ogden, Brophy, and Evertson (1977) described at the beginning of this section is a good example. In order to answer questions about the relationship between how students are selected to read in a primary-grade class and their achievement in reading, these investigators first observed students and teachers in a number of classrooms and then measured the reading achievement of the students. They found that having students read in a predictable order was associated, or correlated, with gains in reading scores. With a simple correlation such as this, however, the researchers could not be sure that the strategy was actually causing the effect. In the second part of the study, Ogden and her colleagues asked several teachers to call on each student in turn. They then compared reading achievement in these groups with achievement in groups where teachers used other strategies. This second part of the research was thus an experimental study.

Theories for Teaching.   The major goal of educational psychology is understanding teaching and learning, and research is a primary tool. Reaching this goal is a slow process; there are very few landmark studies that answer a question once and for all. Human beings are too complicated. Instead, research in educational psychology examines limited aspects of a situation—perhaps a few variables at a time or life in one or two classrooms. If enough studies are completed in a certain area and findings repeatedly point to the same conclusions, we eventually arrive at a **principle**. This is the term for an established relationship between two or more factors—between a certain teaching strategy, for example, and student achievement.

Another tool for building a better understanding of the teaching and learning processes is **theory**. The common sense notion of theory (as in "Oh well, it was only a theory") is "a guess or hunch." But the scientific meaning of theory is quite different. "A theory in science is an interrelated set of concepts that is used to explain a body of data and to make predictions about the results of future experiments" (Stanovich, 1992, p. 21). Given a number of established principles, educational psychologists have developed explanations for the relationships among many variables and even whole systems of relationships. There are theories to explain how language develops, how differences in intelligence occur, and, as noted earlier, how people learn.

Few theories explain and predict perfectly. In this book, you will see many examples of educational psychologists taking different theoretical positions and disagreeing on the overall explanations of such issues as learning and motivation. Because no one theory offers all the answers, it makes sense to consider what each has to offer.

So why, you may ask, is it necessary to deal with theories? Why not just stick to principles? The answer is that both are useful. Principles of classroom management, for example, will give you help with specific problems. A good theory of classroom management, on the other hand, will give you a new way of thinking about discipline problems; it will give you tools for creating solutions to many different problems and for predicting what might work in new situations. A major goal of this book is to provide you with the best and the most useful theories for teaching—those that have solid evidence behind them. Although you may prefer some theories over others, consider them all as ways of understanding the challenges teachers face.

The Contents of This Book

Now that we have explored the role of theory and research, let us turn to a consideration of the topics studied by educational psychologists.

A Quick Tour of This Book

At the heart of educational psychology is a concern with learning wherever it occurs—in classrooms and corporations, in the military, and in medical internships, wherever people strive to become more knowledgeable and competent. No person can learn for another; students create their own knowledge and skills. The teacher's role is to orchestrate materials, tasks, environments, conversations, and explorations that encourage and support learning and the increasing independence of their students.

Parts One and Two of this text focus on the students. In Part One, we examine the ways in which students develop. Because children may differ from adolescents and adults in their thinking, language, and images about themselves, they may require different kinds of teaching. As a teacher, you will want to take into account the mental, physical, emotional, and social abilities and limitations of your students.

Part Two explores how children differ in their abilities, previous learning, learning styles, and in the ways that they have been prepared for schools by their cultural experiences. Classrooms today are becoming more and more diverse. Teachers are expected to work with students with learning disabilities and visual or hearing impairments, for example, and with both the retarded and the gifted. And most classrooms today are multicultural, with students who speak different languages and come from a variety of cultural backgrounds. Teachers must be able to recognize, respect, and adapt to these individual and group differences and to create classroom communities that allow students to belong and to thrive.

Having introduced the students, we will move to one of the most important topics in both educational psychology and the classroom: human learning. Part Three explores the two main approaches to the study of learning, the behavioral and the cognitive perspectives. We will also see how these approaches can be applied in a number of very practical ways, including strategies for classroom management and instruction in various subject areas. An understanding of how students learn is the basis for teachers' professional knowledge about both general and specific teaching strategies.

Having covered the dual foundations of teaching—the students and the processes of learning—we can concentrate in Parts Four, Five, and Six on actual practice.

(D) 3. Researchers administer IQ tests to a group of boys and girls to determine if there is a relationship between sex and verbal ability.

(E) 4. Teachers instruct two similar groups of math students by two different methods to determine which method leads to higher scores on a math achievement test.

Objective 1.10: Know the general organization of information in this textbook and how the information will be useful to teachers.

Discussion: Assign the article by Killion, J. P., & Todnem, G. R. (1991). A process for personal theory building. *Educational Leadership, 48*(6), 14–16. *Focus Question:* Why do teachers need a personal theory for teaching?

Discussion: The August 30, 1988, issue of *USA Today* had several stories about the attitudes of teachers based on a sample of 1,174 teachers randomly selected from the 10,000 delegates to the 1988 national conventions of the American Federation of Teachers and the National Education Association ("What Teachers Think," *USA Today,* August 30, 1988, Section D, p. 1). Some of the results:

The teachers averaged 44 years old and 19 years' teaching experience, and worked an average of 8 hours per day.

Of the teachers, 69 percent would go into teaching again; 29 percent would give their school a grade of A; 50 percent would give their school a grade of B. About 5 percent would give their school D or F. Most (71 percent) gave themselves a grade of A, 28 percent a grade of B, and 1 percent a C.

When asked what they dreaded most about their jobs, 15 percent said their bosses, 10 percent said their too-large classes, 5 to 6 percent named the paperwork, and 4 percent said discipline problems. The biggest problems in teaching: low pay and large classes. The greatest rewards: "Watching those mental lightbulbs go on."

You might discuss with your students the validity of these results. Are they representative of all teachers? Why or why not? Who are delegates to these professional meetings? Are they likely to be as satisfied with their careers as teachers in general? More or less satisfied? You might want to continue the discussion by noting the need to be "critical consumers" of the research results often reported in the press.

Casebook: See the Teachers' Casebook at the end of this chapter for a discussion of why several teachers chose their profession.

Transparency: Use acetate transparency **T 1**, "Components of Good Teaching." What are the goals of education, real and ideal? What does it mean to be an educated person? What makes a teacher effective? Describe the most effective teacher you ever had. How do you learn best? What do you hope to gain from this course? The students' answers provide the basis for a class discussion and an attempt at consensus. Throughout the course, you can relate information and ideas from the lectures back to these student beliefs about education, teaching, and learning.

Casebook: See the Teachers' Casebook at the end of this chapter for a discussion of what helps an experienced teacher to become more "expert."

Part Four examines theories of motivation and their applications to teaching. There is no learning without attention and engagement, so teachers and students must understand and incorporate the motivational factors that support active, engaged, independent learning. Because most learning and teaching happen in groups, we will examine how to organize and manage a classroom full of active learners. And because teachers deal with individuals as well as groups, we will spend some time discussing communication and interpersonal relationships.

In Part Five, we look at instruction from two perspectives: a teacher-focused, direct-instruction view that emphasizes the teacher's role in planning, providing, and monitoring instruction, and a student-centered view that emphasizes the students' active construction of understanding. Teachers owe it to their students to design powerful environments for learning, so the teachers must understand how different approaches can influence students' learning.

In Part Six, we consider how to evaluate what has been taught. Because to learn is to become more knowledgeable and competent, teachers must have at their disposal ways to assess knowledge and competence in order to guide students and give them useful information so they can guide themselves. We will look at standardized tests, teacher-made tests, grading systems, and various alternatives to the traditional systems of evaluation and grading.

How This Book Can Help You

In Table 1.1 you will find a list of sample questions drawn from different parts of this book. The questions do not begin to cover the many topics that will be included in each part, but they will give you a sense of the kind of information you will encounter.

The study of educational psychology involves both content and process. The content of facts, principles, and theories adds to the store of your professional knowledge for teaching. The process aspect of educational psychology helps you think critically about teaching so you can become a researcher on your own effectiveness.

Becoming an expert teacher takes time and experience, but you can start now by becoming a good beginner. You can develop a repertoire of effective principles and practices for your first years of teaching so that some activities quickly become automatic. You can also develop the habit of questioning and analyzing these accepted practices and your own teaching so you can solve new problems when they arise. You can learn to look behind the effective techniques identified in research to ask why: Why did this approach work with these students? What else might be as good or better? The answers to these questions and your ability to analyze the situations are much more important than the specific techniques themselves. As you ask and answer questions, you will be refining your personal theories of teaching.

My goal in writing this book is to help you become an excellent beginning teacher, one who can both apply and improve many techniques. Even more important, I hope this book will cause you to think about students and teaching in new ways, so you will have the foundation for becoming an expert as you gain experience.

TABLE 1.1 What Would You Like to Know? Educational Psychology Can Help	
Sample Questions	**Sources of Information**
■ What is good teaching? ■ Why study educational psychology? ■ How can a teacher use research and theory?	Educational Psychology and the Classroom Teacher
■ How might my students' thinking processes differ from my own? ■ What is the emotional and social world of my students like? ■ How can I help my students develop self-esteem? ■ What can I do when a student is terribly upset about his or her parents' divorce?	Part One: Human Development
■ What is intelligence and how can it be improved? ■ What if I am assigned a student who is mildly retarded? ■ How do I teach science to students who don't speak my language? ■ How can I help students from different cultures feel at home in my class?	Part Two: Individual Variations
■ What causes some students to develop fears about school? ■ Should I use punishment in my classes? ■ Why do students remember some things and forget others? ■ How can I study more effectively and help my students do the same? ■ How can I encourage students to be creative? ■ Will students use what I teach them?	Part Three: Learning: Theory and Practice
■ Can algebra ever be as interesting as sex education? ■ How can I help students take charge of their own learning? ■ How can I deal with a really defiant student? ■ What should I do when angry parents accuse me of treating their child unfairly?	Part Four: Motivation and Management
■ Where do I start in planning my first class? ■ Is lecture better than discussion or individualized instruction? ■ What makes a teacher effective? ■ How can I teach so students understand?	Part Five: Teaching
■ How can the results of standardized tests help me teach? ■ Are grades really necessary? ■ How should I assess my students?	Part Six: Assessment

Handout: See the *Instructor's Resource Manual* for **Handout Master 1.6,** a list of journals in education and educational psychology. It is helpful to provide this list to students if you assign research or term papers in your class.

SUMMARY

In this introductory chapter we have examined good teaching by looking in the classrooms of expert teachers and considering the research on what distinguishes experts from beginners. You also saw an overview of the field of educational psychology.

What Is Good Teaching?

It takes time and experience to become an expert teacher. For experts, accomplishing many classroom tasks has become automatic, so that routines are smooth. Less class time is wasted. Experts can apply well-practiced solutions or readily invent new ones. They have a rich store of well-organized knowledge about the many specific situations of teaching. This includes knowledge about the subjects they teach, their students, general teaching strategies, subject-specific ways of teaching, settings for learning, curriculum materials, and the goals of education.

Teaching is both an art and a science. Effective teaching requires an understanding of research findings on learning and instruction and knowledge of effective techniques and routines. Teaching also calls for the creativity, talent, and judgment of an artist.

Learning to teach is a gradual process. The concerns and problems of teachers change as they progress. During the beginning years, attention tends to be focused on survival. Maintaining discipline, motivating students, evaluating students' work, and dealing with parents are universal concerns for beginning teachers. The more experienced teacher can move on to concerns about professional growth and effectiveness with a wide range of students.

Becoming a good teacher means being a good learner. Much of the information in this text will help you become a more expert learner if you take the ideas personally and apply them to your own life.

The Role of Educational Psychology

The goals of educational psychology are to understand and to improve the teaching and learning processes. Educational psychologists develop knowledge and methods; they also use the knowledge and methods of psychology and other related disciplines to study learning and teaching in everyday situations.

Both descriptive studies and experimental research can provide valuable information for teachers. Correlations allow you to predict events that are likely to occur in the classroom; experimental studies can indicate cause-and-effect relationships and should help you implement useful changes.

Educational psychology involves content and process. The findings from research offer a number of possible answers to specific problems, and the theories offer perspectives for analyzing almost any situation that may arise. The process of analyzing research and theory will encourage you to think critically about teaching.

KEY TERMS

case study, p. 14
correlations, p. 14
descriptive research, p. 14
educational psychology, p. 11
ethnography, p. 14
experimentation, p. 15

expert teachers, p. 5
novice teachers, p. 5
negative correlation, p. 14
participant observation, p. 14
positive correlation, p. 14
principle, p. 16

random, p. 15
reflective, p. 8
statistically significant, p. 15
subjects, p. 15
theory, p. 16

WHAT WOULD YOU DO?

It is your second year as a teacher in Ben Franklin Middle School. The district has just received money from the state and a private foundation to give three awards in your school for "excellence in teaching." You have been assigned to a committee that will make recommendations to the principal about how to choose the recipients of these awards. You have a week before the first meeting. How would you prepare? Draft a position paper listing your ideas for the selection criteria. How would you back up your recommendations?

Cooperative Learning Activity

With four or five other members of your class who plan to teach the same grade level as you, develop a procedure and criteria for giving an "excellence in teaching" award. Present your group's plan to the class, and be prepared to explain why your system is appropriate.

TEACHERS' CASEBOOK

TO BECOME A VALUED PROFESSIONAL

Why Teaching?

Why did you choose teaching as a career? Would you choose it again?

I recommend the teaching profession to both my high school students and student teachers. First, teaching is never dull. Each year we meet an entirely new cast of characters, individuals who are unique and who represent both challenge and opportunity. Certainly at the secondary level, to observe the development from gawky adolescent in 9th grade to young adult at graduation is gratifying. To observe the concomitant development of the mind is even more rewarding. Yes, it is tiring, hectic, and often frustrating, but time flies. Second, teaching allows for continual refinement of our own techniques. Good teachers do not do things the same way each year and with each class. We are regularly provided with the opportunity for which researchers in the hard sciences must continually write grant proposals. We have the freedom to function professionally as teacher-researchers, exploring diverse ways to stimulate and discipline young minds. Third, teaching allows us to do what we ask of our students; that is, continue to learn. Much has been written concerning the deadly and debilitating boredom that accompanies jobs consisting primarily of repetitive tasks. Our profession not only encourages, it requires continuous self-education. Every history book I read is professional preparation. However, this reading also brings with it personal edification and enjoyment. We must be living models of the importance of lifelong learning, and that, indeed, is a professional perk. Finally, teaching can be hailed as one of the most gender liberating of the professions. The past decades have seen women make enormous gains in the battle to be accepted as men's equals, intellectually and professionally. Yes, teaching is demanding; it requires many hours beyond those of the school day. Yet its schedule does not force men and women to choose between a career and a family. While in the 1950s teaching was a trap to hold women back, in the 1990s it offers both men and women the liberating opportunity to both raise a family and be part of an intellectually stimulating and respected profession.

Karen Beechy Kreider, *Pennsylvania 1991 Teacher of the Year*
Central High School, Philadelphia, Pennsylvania

TO INFLUENCE AND GUIDE

The profile of a "typical" teacher frequently presents him or her as overworked, underpaid, frustrated, tired, and lacking recognition. All human beings, teachers included, need to feel valued, respected, fulfilled. As a human being, I sought a profession that would challenge and fulfill me at the same time. A summer as a counselor at a camp for handicapped boys convinced me that these youngsters had minds that needed healing as well as nurturing. That summer led me to conclude that two important components of health are attitude and knowledge. The knowledge that I had the opportunity to influence the intellectual, emotional, physical, mental, and psychological development and well-being of my students, as well as their attitudes and values, challenged me to expand my own horizons. Perhaps teaching is not financially rewarding; but would I still make it my career choice if I had to choose again? You bet—in a heartbeat! Why? Because I anticipate tomorrow knowing that today I gave my students my best—knowing that I made a difference today—knowing that despite the fatigue and the frustration, I'm valued, I'm respected, I'm fulfilled.

Laura Atkinson, *Special Education Teacher*
Chapel Hill, North Carolina

Becoming an Expert

Did you reach a point after you had been teaching for a while when you realized that you had learned to "think like a teacher"? What helped you become more expert in making decisions about teaching?

RELYING LESS ON COMMERCIAL TEXTS

My initial awareness that I had begun to "think like a teacher" occurred when I realized that textbooks and teacher's guides were not the panacea for classroom instruction. I discovered that the textbooks were guides or road maps, but not the vehicles for student learning. I began to seek additional sources of curriculum and to develop materials to increase motivation and to explore the interrelationships among subjects. Working collectively and cooperatively with colleagues enhanced my decision-making expertise concerning teaching. Additional in-service training was instrumental in my development as a professional educator.

Bruce D. Fisher, *California 1991 Teacher of the Year*
Fortuna Elementary School, Fortuna, California

CREATING CURRICULUM CONTENT

After several years of teaching straight from the textbooks, I began to realize that in many cases, my students were able to learn more information and retain it better when I trusted my own judgment about how and what to teach. I began to use textbook manuals as guides to the curriculum and textbooks as one resource. I learned to create units of study around the same topics, but I was able to bring content alive for my students, to involve them in the learning process, and to make learning more meaningful. It took several years for me to develop the self-confidence necessary to take control of the curriculum and learning process. However, that experience allowed me to use my gifts as a teacher fully and to regain the excitement of learning for myself and my students.

Sarah Gustafsen, *Florida 1991 Teacher of the Year*
The Okeechobee Center, Okeechobee, Florida

What do you feel are the qualities or capabilities of an outstanding teacher?

TOUCHING THE FUTURE

I believe that an outstanding teacher is someone who has great personal integrity and a compassionate spirit. Teaching is a heavy responsibility. A teacher has the power to influence how a child sees himself and his future, how a parent perceives his child, and how a class treats each member of the group. Few professionals deal with such raw social power. A teacher must constantly set a standard of kindness, honesty, and optimism. She must always remember that her words matter and that her voice carries far into the future.

Cynthia Newman Wisdom, *First-Grade Teacher*
Trace Crossings Elementary School, Hoover, Alabama

2

Cognitive Development and Language

*H*ow does the mind of the average 8-year-old work? What about the mind of the average 14-year-old? Can you explain geometry to second graders? Can you explain existentialism to seventh graders? The material in this chapter will help you answer these questions and many others about how young people think and how their thinking changes over time. These changes in thinking and understanding are called cognitive development.

In this chapter, we begin with a discussion of the general principles of human development and a brief look at the human brain. Then we will examine the ideas of two of the most influential cognitive developmental theorists, Jean Piaget and Lev Vygotsky. Piaget's ideas have implications for teachers about what their students can learn and when the students are ready to learn it. We will examine important criticisms of his ideas as well.

The work of Lev Vygotsky, a Russian psychologist, is becoming more and more influential. His theory highlights the important role teachers and parents play in the cognitive development of the child. Finally, we will explore language development and discuss the role of the school in developing and enriching language skills.

By the time you have completed this chapter, you should be able to:

- State three general principles of human development, and give examples of each.
- List Piaget's four stages of cognitive development.
- Explain how children's thinking differs at each stage of development.
- Summarize the implications of Piaget's theory for teaching students of different ages.
- Contrast Piaget's and Vygotsky's ideas about cognitive development.
- Give implications of Vygotsky's theory for teaching students of any age.
- Describe briefly the stages by which children learn language.
- Suggest ways a teacher can help children expand their language use and comprehension.

Think for a moment about how you would explain the concept of "symbol" to a 6-year-old and to a 14-year-old. Would you use words? Pictures? Specific examples? What kind? What do you know about how younger and older children differ in their thinking?

 A Definition of Development

Test Bank items 2.1–2.5, 2.75, 2.86, 2.99

Planning Tip: See the *Chapter-2-At-A-Glance Planning Guide* in the Instructor's Section at the front of this book.

Study Guide: The *Study Guide,* sold separately, contains exercises to help students determine if they have mastered each learning objective for this chapter.

Development Orderly, adaptive changes we go through from conception to death.

Physical Development Changes in body structure and function over time.

Personal Development Changes in personality that take place as one grows.

Social Development Changes over time in the ways we relate to others.

Cognitive Development Gradual, orderly changes by which mental processes become more complex and sophisticated.

Maturation Genetically programmed, naturally occurring changes over time.

The term **development** in its most general psychological sense refers to certain changes that occur in human beings (or animals) between conception and death. The term is not applied to all changes, but rather to those that appear in orderly ways and remain for a reasonably long period of time. A temporary change due to a brief illness, for example, is not considered to be a part of development. Psychologists also make a value judgment in determining which changes qualify as development. The changes, at least those that occur early in life, are generally assumed to be for the better and to result in behavior that is more adaptive, more organized, more effective, and more complex (Mussen, Conger, & Kagan, 1984).

Human development can be divided into a number of different aspects. **Physical development,** as you might guess, deals with changes in the body. **Personal development** is the term generally used for changes in an individual's personality. **Social development** refers to changes in the way an individual relates to others. And **cognitive development** refers to changes in thinking.

Many changes during development are simply matters of growth and maturation. **Maturation** refers to changes that occur naturally and spontaneously and that are, to a large extent, genetically programmed. Such changes emerge over time and are relatively unaffected by environment, except in cases of malnutrition or severe illness. Much of a person's physical development falls into this category. Other changes are brought about through learning, as individuals interact with their environment. Such changes make up a large part of a person's social development. But what about the development of thinking and personality? Most psychologists agree that in these areas, both maturation and interaction with the environment (or nature and nurture, as they are sometimes called) are important, but they disagree about the amount of emphasis to place on each.

Although there is disagreement about what is involved in development and about the way it takes place, there are a few general principles almost all theorists would support.

1. *People develop at different rates.* In your own classroom, you will have a whole range of examples of different developmental rates. Some students will be larger, better coordinated, or more mature in their thinking and social relationships. Others will be much slower to mature in these areas. Except in

rare cases of very rapid or very slow development, such differences are normal and to be expected in any large group of students.

2. *Development is relatively orderly.* People develop certain abilities before others. In infancy they sit before they walk, babble before they talk, and see the world through their own eyes before they can begin to imagine how others see it. In school, they will master addition before algebra, Bambi before Shakespeare, and so on. Theorists may disagree on exactly what comes before what, but they all seem to find a relatively logical progression.

3. *Development takes place gradually.* Very rarely do changes appear overnight. A student who cannot manipulate a pencil or answer a hypothetical question may well develop this ability, but the change is likely to take time.

The Brain and Cognitive Development

Test Bank items 2.6–2.9, 2.76, 2.89, 2.100

If you have taken an introductory psychology class, you have read about the brain and nervous system. You probably remember, for example, that there are several different areas of the brain and that certain areas are involved in particular functions. For example, the feathery-looking cerebellum seems to coordinate and orchestrate smooth, skilled movements—from the graceful gestures of the dancer to the everyday action of eating without stabbing yourself in the nose with a fork. The thalamus is involved in our ability to learn new information, particularly if it is verbal. The reticular formation plays a role in attention and arousal, blocking some messages and sending others on to higher brain centers for processing (Wood & Wood, 1993). Figure 2.1 on page 28 shows other functions related to other areas.

The large area all around the thalamus in Figure 2.1 is the cerebrum and its cortex. This is the part of the brain that allows the greatest human accomplishments. The outer 1/8-inch-thick covering of the cerebrum is the wrinkled-looking cerebral cortex. This crumpled sheet of neurons serves three major functions: receiving signals from sense organs such as visual or auditory signals, controlling voluntary movement, and forming associations. In humans, this area of the brain is much larger than in lower animals.

Even though areas of the cortex are somewhat specialized, they must work together. For example, many areas of the cortex are necessary in processing language. To answer a question, you must first hear it. This involves the primary auditory cortex. Movements controlled by the motor cortex are required to speak your response. Broca's area (near the area that controls the lips, jaw, and tongue) has a role in setting up a grammatically correct way of expressing an idea, and Wernicke's area (near the auditory cortex) is necessary for connecting meaning with particular words. A person with a functioning Broca's area but a damaged Wernicke's area will say meaningless things in a grammatically correct structure. Damage limited to Broca's area, on the other hand, is associated with short, ungrammatical sentences, but the words are appropriate (Anderson, 1990).

Another aspect of brain functioning that has implications for cognitive development is lateralization, or the specialization of the two hemispheres of the brain. We know that each half of the brain controls the opposite side of the body. Damage to the right side of the brain will affect movement of the left side of the body and vice versa. In addition, certain areas of the brain affect

FIGURE 2.1

THE BRAIN CORTEX

The cortex is the exterior covering of the brain's cerebral hemispheres. The cortex plays a special role in behavior because it is intimately involved with thought.

Area	Function
Frontal lobe	Involved with memory Concerned with movement Involved in speech and language production
Parietal lobe	Associated with activities involved in the sense of touch and body position
Temporal lobe	Involved with speech, hearing, and some visual information processing
Occipital lobe	Responsible for visual sense
Association cortex	Believed to play a role in complex behaviors that involve thinking and sensory processes

Source: From Lester A. Lefton, *Psychology,* 5/e. Copyright © 1994 by Allyn and Bacon. Reprinted by permission.

Application: To help students experience some of the ways children differ from adults in their thinking, have the students ask children of various ages the following questions:

What does it mean to be alive?

Can you name some things that are alive?

Is the moon alive?

Where do dreams come from?

particular behaviors. For most of us, the left hemisphere of the brain is the major factor in language processing, and the right hemisphere handles most of the spatial-visual information and emotions (nonverbal information). For some left-handed people, the relationship may be reversed, but for most left-handers there is less hemispheric specialization altogether (Berk, 1994).

Developmental psychologists are concerned about when lateralization occurs, because before specializations are established in particular areas of the brain, the brain is very adaptable, or *plastic.* If one area is damaged, other areas can take over functioning. So when very young children experience damage to part of their brain, other parts of the brain can handle the tasks usually accomplished by the damaged area—to a point. It appears that lateralization begins right after birth and proceeds for several years. Thus, the younger the child, the more he or she is able to recover from damage or deprivation.

Lateralization does not mean that one side or the other of the brain is in complete control, depending on the task. For people who have normal intact brains, both hemispheres are involved in all learning tasks, even if one side may be more or less involved at any given moment (Bjorklund, 1989). It is possible that researchers will trace certain learning problems to aspects of hemispheric specialization, but the evidence is not yet conclusive. In fact, some preliminary research indicates that the front-to-back functioning of the brain may be as important as left/right functioning in understanding learning disabilities (Jordan & Goldsmith-Phillips, 1994).

In the next decade we should see more and more research on the brain, development, learning, and teaching. Until recently, implications of brain research for teaching were not widely recognized, but we are moving into a time when this could change dramatically. For example, in 1992 there was a special issue of the *Educational Psychologist* on "Brain and Education." In it were articles describing research on variations in the development of different working brain systems that can affect learning to read and write and several models of learning and teaching based on brain research. A message of many of the authors of this volume is that the brain is a complex collection of systems working together to construct understanding, detect patterns, create rules, and make sense of experience. These systems change over the lifetime as the individual matures and learns.

The first theory of cognitive development we will consider was developed by a biologist turned psychologist, Jean Piaget.

Where do they go?

Which is farther, to go from the bottom of the hill all the way to the top or go from the top of the hill all the way to the bottom?

Can a person live in Chicago and in Illinois at the same time?

Will you be just as old as your big brother some day?

When is yesterday?

Where does the sun go at night?

Transparencies: Use acetate transparencies T 21, "Lateralization and Brain Functioning," and T 22, "Beware of Simplified Views of the Brain."

Focus on . . .   Development

- Distinguish between development and maturation.
- Summarize three principles of how development takes place.
- Give an example of the way different areas of the brain work together to produce language.

Piaget's Theory of Cognitive Development

During the past half-century, the Swiss psychologist Jean Piaget devised a model describing how humans go about making sense of their world by gathering and organizing information (Piaget, 1954, 1963, 1970). We will examine Piaget's ideas closely, because they provide an explanation of the development of thinking from infancy to adulthood.

According to Piaget (1954), certain ways of thinking that are quite simple for an adult are not so simple for a child. Sometimes all you need to do to teach a new concept is to give a student a few basic facts as background. At other times, however, all the background facts in the world are useless. The student simply is not ready to learn the concept. With some students, you can discuss the general causes of civil wars and then ask why they think the American Civil War broke out in 1861. But suppose the students respond with "When is 1861?" Obviously their concepts of time are different from your own. They may think, for example, that they will someday catch up to a sibling in age, or they may confuse the past and the future.

Jean Piaget was a Swiss psychologist whose insightful descriptions of children's thinking changed the way we understand cognitive development.

Influences on Development

As you can see, cognitive development is much more than the addition of new facts and ideas to an existing store of information. According to Piaget, our thinking processes change radically, though slowly, from birth to maturity. Why do these changes occur? Underlying Piaget's theory is the assumption that we constantly strive to make sense of the world. How do we do this? Piaget identified four factors—biological maturation, activity, social experiences, and equilibration—that interact to influence changes in thinking (Piaget, 1970). Let's briefly examine the first three factors. We'll return to a discussion of equilibration in the next section.

One of the most important influences on the way we make sense of the world is maturation, the unfolding of the biological changes that are genetically programmed in each human being at conception. Parents and teachers have little impact on this aspect of cognitive development, except to be sure that children get the nourishment and care they need to be healthy.

Activity is another influence. With physical maturation comes the increasing ability to act on the environment and learn from it. When a young child's coordination is reasonably developed, for example, the child may discover principles about balance by experimenting with a seesaw. So as we act on the environment—as we explore, test, observe, and eventually organize information—we are likely to alter our thinking processes at the same time.

As we develop, we are also interacting with the people around us. According to Piaget, our cognitive development is influenced by *social transmission,* or learning from others. Without social transmission, we would need to reinvent all the knowledge already offered by our culture. The amount people can learn from social transmission varies according to their stage of cognitive development.

Maturation, activity, and social transmission all work together to influence cognitive development. How do we respond to these influences?

Basic Tendencies in Thinking

As a result of his early research in biology, Piaget concluded that all species inherit two basic tendencies, or "invariant functions." The first of these tendencies is toward **organization**—the combining, arranging, recombining, and rearranging of behaviors and thoughts into coherent systems. The second tendency is toward **adaptation,** or adjusting to the environment.

Organization. Thus, according to Piaget, people are born with a tendency to organize their thinking processes into psychological structures. These psychological structures are our systems for understanding and interacting with the world. Simple structures are continually combined and coordinated to become more sophisticated and thus more effective. Very young infants, for example, can either look at an object or grasp it when it comes in contact with their hands. They cannot coordinate looking and grasping at the same time. As they develop, however, infants organize these two separate behavioral structures into a coordinated higher-level structure of looking at, reaching for, and grasping the object. They can, of course, still use each structure separately (Ginsburg & Opper, 1988).

Piaget gave a special name to these structures. In his theory, they are called schemes. **Schemes** are the basic building blocks of thinking. They are organized systems of actions or thought that allow us to mentally represent or "think about" the objects and events in our world. Schemes may be very small and specific, for example, the sucking-through-a-straw scheme or the recognizing-a-rose scheme. Or they may be larger and more general—the drinking scheme or the categorizing-plants scheme. As a person's thinking processes become more organized and new schemes develop, behavior also becomes more sophisticated and better suited to the environment.

Adaptation. In addition to the tendency to organize their psychological structures, people also inherit the tendency to adapt to their environment. Piaget believed that from the moment of birth, a person begins to look for ways to adapt more satisfactorily. Two basic processes are involved in adaptation: assimilation and accommodation.

Assimilation takes place when people use their existing schemes to make sense of events in their world. Assimilation involves trying to understand something new by fitting it into what we already know. At times, we may have to distort the new information to make it fit. For example, the first time many children see a skunk, they call it a "kitty." They try to match the new experience with an existing scheme for identifying animals.

Accommodation occurs when a person must change existing schemes to respond to a new situation. If data cannot be made to fit any existing schemes, then more appropriate structures must be developed. We adjust our thinking to fit the new information, instead of adjusting the information to fit our thinking. Children demonstrate accommodation when they add the scheme for recognizing skunks to their other systems for identifying animals.

People adapt to their increasingly complex environments by using existing schemes whenever these schemes work (assimilation) and by modifying and adding to their schemes when something new is needed (accommodation). In fact, both processes are required most of the time. Even using an established pattern like sucking through a straw may require some accommodation if the straw is of a different size or length than the type you are used to. If you have tried drinking juice from box packages, you know that you have to add a new skill to your sucking scheme—don't squeeze the box or you will shoot juice through the straw, straight up into the air and into your lap. Whenever new experiences are assimilated into an existing scheme, the scheme is enlarged and changed somewhat, so assimilation involves some accommodation.

There are also times when neither assimilation nor accommodation is used. If people encounter something that is too unfamiliar, they may ignore it. Experience is filtered to fit the kind of thinking a person is doing at a given time. For example, if you overhear a conversation in a foreign language, you probably will not try to make sense of the exchange unless you have some knowledge of the language.

Equilibration. According to Piaget, organizing, assimilating, and accommodating can be seen as a kind of complex balancing act. In his theory, the actual changes in thinking take place through the process of **equilibration**—the act of searching for a balance. Piaget assumed that people con-

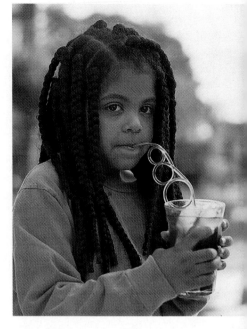

How are assimilation and accommodation involved in using this straw? Can the girl respond to this straw exactly as she does to a conventional one?

Critical Thinking: Class notes are often paraphrases of what the instructor actually said. Ask students to explain the roles of assimilation and accommodation in note taking.

Schemes Mental systems or categories of perception and experience.

Assimilation Fitting new information into existing schemes.

Accommodation Altering existing schemes or creating new ones in response to new information.

Equilibration Search for mental balance between cognitive schemes and information from the environment.

Activity 2.3: Reflection/Journal Writing. See the *Instructor's Resource Manual* for Cognitive Disequilibrium.

Background: For a good summary of Piaget's contributions to education, see Ginsburg, H. P. (1985). Piaget and education. In N. Entwistle (Ed.), *New directions in educational psychology. Vol. 1: Learning and teaching* (pp. 45–60). Philadelphia: Farmer Press, Taylor & Francis.

Activity 2.4: Cooperative Learning. See the *Instructor's Resource Manual* for Assessing Cognitive Development: Piagetian Tasks, an activity that asks students to develop Piagetian tasks and administer them to one another.

Objective 2.5: Name each of Piaget's four stages of cognitive development, and give one major accomplishment of children during each stage.

Activity 2.5: Cooperative Learning. See the separate *Instructor's Resource Manual* for Children's Understanding of Humor. This activity includes **Handout Master 2.2,** which relates children's sense of humor to Piagetian stages of development.

Disequilibrium In Piaget's theory, the "out-of-balance" state that occurs when a person realizes that his or her current ways of thinking are not working to solve a problem or understand a situation.

Sensorimotor Involving the senses and motor activity.

Object Permanence The understanding that objects have a separate, permanent existence.

Goal-Directed Actions Deliberate actions toward a goal.

tinually test the adequacy of their thinking processes in order to achieve that balance.

Briefly, the process of equilibration works like this: If we apply a particular scheme to an event or situation and the scheme works, then equilibrium exists. If the scheme does not produce a satisfying result, then **disequilibrium** exists, and we become uncomfortable. This motivates us to keep searching for a solution through assimilation and accommodation, and thus our thinking changes and moves ahead. In order to maintain a balance between our schemes for understanding the world and the data the world provides, we continually assimilate new information using existing schemes, and we accommodate our thinking whenever unsuccessful attempts to assimilate produce disequilibrium.

Test Bank items 2.21–2.42, 2.44–2.46, 2.78, 2.79, 2.88, 2.90, 2.91, 2.101, 2.102, 2.105–2.107

Four Stages of Cognitive Development

Now we turn to the actual differences that Piaget hypothesized for children as they grow. Piaget's four stages of cognitive development are called sensorimotor, preoperational, concrete operational, and formal operational. Piaget believed that all people pass through the same four stages in exactly the same order. These stages are generally associated with specific ages, as shown in Table 2.1. When you see ages linked to stages, remember that these are only general guidelines, not labels for all children of a certain age. Piaget was interested in the kinds of thinking abilities people are able to use, not in labeling. Often, people can use one level of thinking to solve one kind of problem and a different level to solve another. Piaget noted that individuals may go through long periods of transition between stages and that a person may show characteristics of one stage in one situation but characteristics of a higher or lower stage in other situations. So knowing a student's age is never a guarantee that you know how the child will think in every situation (Ginsburg & Opper, 1988).

Infancy: The Sensorimotor Stage. The earliest period is called the **sensorimotor stage,** because the child's thinking involves seeing, hearing, moving, touching, tasting, and so on. During this period, the infant develops **object permanence,** the understanding that objects in the environment exist whether the baby perceives them or not. As most parents discover, before infants develop object permanence, it is relatively easy to take something away from them. The trick is to distract them and remove the object while they are not looking— "out of sight, out of mind." The older infant who searches for the ball that has rolled out of sight is indicating an understanding that the objects still exist even though they can't be seen.

A second major accomplishment in the sensorimotor period is the beginning of logical, **goal-directed actions.** Think of the familiar container toy for babies. It is usually plastic, has a lid, and contains several colorful items that can be dumped out and replaced. A 6-month-old baby is likely to become frustrated trying to get to the toys inside. An older child who has mastered the basics of the sensorimotor stage will probably be able to deal with the toy in an orderly fashion. Through trial and error the child will slowly build a "con-

TABLE 2.1 Piaget's Stages of Cognitive Development

Stage	Approximate Age	Characteristics
Sensorimotor	0–2 years	Begins to make use of imitation, memory, and thought. Begins to recognize that objects do not cease to exist when they are hidden. Moves from reflex actions to goal-directed activity.
Preoperational	2–7 years	Gradually develops use of language and ability to think in symbolic form. Able to think operations through logically in one direction. Has difficulties seeing another person's point of view.
Concrete operational	7–11 years	Able to solve concrete (hands-on) problems in logical fashion. Understands laws of conservation and is able to classify and seriate. Understands reversibility.
Formal operational	11–adult	Able to solve abstract problems in logical fashion. Becomes more scientific in thinking. Develops concerns about social issues, identity.

Source: Piaget's Theory of Cognitive and Affective Development 4/e by Barry J. Wadsworth. Copyright © 1971, 1979, 1984, 1989 by Longman Publishing Group. Adapted with permission.

tainer toy" scheme: (1) get the lid off; (2) turn the container upside down; (3) shake if the items jam; (4) watch the items fall on the floor. Separate lower-level schemes have been organized into a higher-level scheme.

The child is soon able to reverse this action by refilling the container. Learning to reverse actions is a basic accomplishment of the sensorimotor stage. As we will soon see, however, learning to reverse thinking—that is, learning to imagine the reverse of a sequence of actions—takes much longer.

Early Childhood to the Early Elementary Years: The Preoperational Stage. By the end of the sensorimotor stage, the child can use many action schemes. As long as these schemes remain tied to physical actions, however, they are of no use in recalling the past, keeping track of information, or planning. For this, children need what Piaget called **operations,** or actions that are carried out and reversed mentally rather than physically. The stage after sensorimotor is called **preoperational,** because the child has not yet mastered these mental operations but is moving toward mastery.

According to Piaget, the first step from action to thinking is the internalization of action, performing an action mentally rather than physically. The first type of thinking that is separate from action involves making action schemes symbolic. The ability to form and use symbols—words, gestures, signs, images, and so on—is thus a major accomplishment of the preopera-

Transparency: Use acetate transparency T 5, "Piaget's Stages of Cognitive Development."

Handout Master 2.3: Piagetian Stages.

Operations Actions a person carries out by thinking them through instead of literally performing the actions.

Preoperational The stage before a child masters logical mental operations.

Guidelines

Teaching the Preoperational Child

Use concrete props and visual aids whenever possible.

Examples

1. When you discuss concepts such as "part," "whole," or "one-half," use shapes on a felt board or cardboard "pizzas" to demonstrate.
2. Let children add and subtract with sticks, rocks, or colored chips.

Make instructions relatively short, using actions as well as words.

Examples

1. When giving instructions about how to enter the room after recess and prepare for social studies, ask a student to demonstrate the procedure for the rest of the class by walking in quietly, going straight to his or her seat, and placing the text, paper, and a pencil on his or her desk.
2. Explain a game by acting out one of the parts.
3. Show students what their finished papers should look like. Use an overhead projector or display examples where students can see them easily.

Don't expect the students to be consistent in their ability to see the world from someone else's point of view.

Examples

1. Avoid social studies lessons about worlds too far removed from the child's experience.
2. Avoid long lectures on sharing. Be clear about rules for sharing or use of materials, but avoid long explanations of the rationales for the rules.

Be sensitive to the possibility that students may have different meanings for the same word or different words for the same meaning. Students may also expect everyone to understand words they have invented.

Examples

1. If a student protests, "I won't take a nap. I'll just rest!," be aware that a nap may mean something like "changing into pajamas and being in my bed at home."
2. Ask children to explain the meanings of their invented words.

Give children a great deal of hands-on practice with the skills that serve as building blocks for more complex skills like reading comprehension.

Examples

1. Provide cut-out letters to build words.
2. Supplement paper-and-pencil tasks in arithmetic with activities that require measuring and simple calculations—cooking, building a display area for class work, dividing a batch of popcorn equally.

Provide a wide range of experiences in order to build a foundation for concept learning and language.

Examples

1. Take field trips to zoos, gardens, theaters, and concerts; invite storytellers to the class.
2. Give students words to describe what they are doing, hearing, seeing, touching, tasting, and smelling.

Teaching Tip: Help students understand that teaching a child who is in the preoperational stage of cognitive development is a challenge. Ask: "Remembering the characteristics of the preoperational stage, how might you go about teaching a child in this stage to pop popcorn and give each person in the class a portion?"

Activity 2.6: Inquiry. See the separate *Instructor's Resource Manual* for Children's Conception of Death, a summary of the research on this topic. Children's ideas about death reflect many of the characteristics of preoperational thinking. **Handout Master 2.4,** provided with the summary, can guide class discussion.

Activity 2.7: Field Experience. See the *Instructor's Resource Manual* for Academic Versus Developmentally Appropriate Kindergartens, an activity that directs students' observations in kindergarten classes.

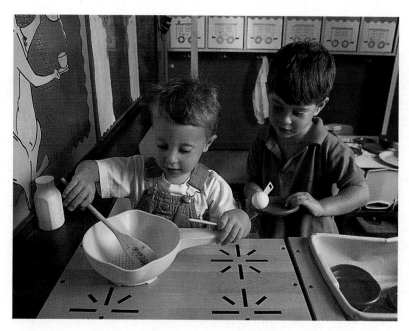

*P*retend games play an important role in children's cognitive development. Often, when children pretend, they use objects in a symbolic way to "stand for" other objects. A wooden table can become a stove or a tent, for example.

tional period and moves children closer to mastering the mental operations of the next stage. This ability to work with symbols, such as using the word "bicycle" or a picture of a bicycle to stand for a real bicycle that is not actually present, is called the **semiotic function.**

The child's earliest use of symbols is in pretending or miming. Children who are not yet able to talk will often use action symbols—pretending to drink from an empty cup or touching a comb to their hair, showing that they know what each object is for. This behavior also shows that their schemes are becoming more general and less tied to specific actions. The eating scheme, for example, may be used in playing house. During the preoperational stage, we also see the rapid development of that very important symbol system, language. Between the ages of 2 and 4, most children enlarge their vocabulary from about 200 to 2,000 words.

As the child moves through the preoperational stage, the developing ability to think about objects in symbolic form remains somewhat limited to thinking in one direction only, or using *one-way logic*. It is very difficult for the child to "think backwards," or imagine how to reverse the steps in a task.

Reversible thinking is involved in many tasks that are difficult for the preoperational child, such as the conservation of matter. **Conservation** is the principle that the amount or number of something remains the same even if the arrangement or appearance is changed, as long as nothing is added and nothing is taken away. You know that if you tear a piece of paper into several pieces, you will still have the same amount of paper. To prove this, you know that you can reverse the process by taping the pieces back together.

Application: As an example of young children's difficulties with reversibility and egocentric thinking, have students ask a child with only one sibling, "Do you have a brother (sister)?" The child should say, "Yes." Now ask, "Does your brother (sister) have a brother (sister)?" Young children have difficulty reversing the situation and putting themselves in their sibling's position, so they usually reply, "No." Now face the child and ask the child to point to your right hand. (For some children, you may have to say, "This is your right hand. Point to my right hand." Most young children assume your right hand is on the same side as theirs, even when they are facing you.

Semiotic Function The ability to use symbols—language, pictures, signs, gestures, etc.—to represent actions or objects mentally.

Reversible Thinking Thinking backward, from the end to the beginning.

Conservation Principle that some characteristics of an object remain the same despite changes in appearance.

Decentering Focusing on more than one aspect at a time.

Egocentric Assuming that others experience the world the way you do.

Collective Monologue Form of speech in which children in a group talk but do not really interact or communicate.

Concrete Operations Mental tasks tied to concrete objects and situations.

Identity Principle that a person or object remains the same over time.

A classic example of difficulty with conservation is found in the preoperational child's response to the following Piagetian task. Leah, a 5-year-old, is shown two identical glasses, both short and wide in shape. Both have exactly the same amount of colored water in them. The experimenter asks Leah if each glass has the same amount of water, and she answers, "Yes." The experimenter then pours the water from one of the glasses into a tall, narrow glass and asks Leah again if each glass has the same amount of water. Now she is likely to insist that there is more water in the tall, narrow glass, because the water level is higher. Notice, by the way, that Leah shows a basic understanding of identity (it's the same water) but not an understanding that the *amounts* are identical (Ginsburg & Opper, 1988).

Piaget's explanation for Leah's answer is that she is focusing, or centering, attention on the dimension of height. She has difficulty considering more than one aspect of the situation at a time, or **decentering.** The preoperational child cannot understand that increased diameter compensates for decreased height, since this would require taking into account two dimensions at once. Thus, children at the preoperational stage have trouble freeing themselves from their own perceptions of how the world appears. What looks like more must be more, even if logic says otherwise.

This brings us to another important characteristic of the preoperational stage. Preoperational children, according to Piaget, are very **egocentric;** they tend to see the world and the experiences of others from their own viewpoint. Egocentric, as Piaget intended it, does not mean selfish; it simply means children often assume that everyone else shares their feelings, reactions, and perspectives. For example, if a little boy at this stage is afraid of dogs, he may assume that all children share this fear. Very young children center on their own perceptions and on the way the situation appears to them. This is one reason it is difficult for these children to understand that your right hand is not on the same side as theirs when you are facing them.

Egocentrism is also evident in the child's language. You may have seen young children happily talking about what they are doing even though no one is listening. This can happen when the child is alone or, even more often, in a group of children—each child talks enthusiastically, without any real interaction or conversation. Piaget called this the **collective monologue.**

Recent research has shown that young children are not totally egocentric in every situation, however. Children as young as age 4 change the way they talk to 2-year-olds by speaking in simpler sentences, and even before age 2 children show toys to adults by turning the front of the toy to face the other person. So young children do seem quite able to take the needs and different perspectives of others into account, at least in certain situations (Gelman, 1979; Gelman & Ebeling, 1989).

Later Elementary to the Middle School Years: The Concrete-Operational Stage. Piaget coined the term **concrete operations** to describe this stage of "hands-on" thinking. The basic characteristics of the stage are the recognition of the logical stability of the physical world, the realization that elements can be changed or transformed and still conserve many of their original characteristics, and the understanding that these changes can be reversed.

Figure 2.2 shows examples of the different tasks given to children to assess conservation and the approximate age ranges when most children can

FIGURE 2.2

SOME PIAGETIAN CONSERVATION TASKS

Other tasks involve the conservation of number, length, weight, and volume. These tasks are all achieved over the concrete-operational period.

Liquid	6–7 yrs.	Is there the same amount of water in each glass?	Now is there the same amount of water in each glass, or does one have more?
Mass	6–7 yrs.	Is there the same amount of clay in each ball?	Now does each piece have the same amount of clay, or does one have more?
Area	8–10 yrs.	Does each of these two cows have the same amount of grass to eat?	Now does each cow have the same amount of grass to eat, or does one cow have more?

Source: From Laura E. Berk, *Child Development*, 2/e, p. 227. Copyright © 1991 by Allyn and Bacon. Reprinted by permission.

solve these problems. According to Piaget, a student's ability to solve conservation problems depends on an understanding of three basic aspects of reasoning: identity, compensation, and reversibility. With a complete mastery of **identity,** the student knows that if nothing is added or taken away, the material remains the same. With an understanding of **compensation,** the student knows that an apparent change in one direction can be compensated for by a change in another direction. That is, if the liquid rises higher in the glass, the glass must be narrower. And with an understanding of **reversibility,** the student can mentally cancel out the change that has been made. Note especially that a grasp of reversibility means the student at this stage has mastered two-way thinking.

Another important operation mastered at this stage is **classification.** Classification depends on a student's abilities to focus on a single characteristic of objects in a set and group the objects according to that characteristic. Given

Compensation The principle that changes in one dimension can be offset by changes in another.

Reversibility A characteristic of Piagetian logical operations—the ability to think through a series of steps, then mentally reverse the steps and return to the starting point; also called reversible thinking.

Classification Grouping objects into categories.

12 objects of assorted colors and shapes, the concrete-operational student can invariably pick out the ones that are round.

More advanced classification at this stage involves recognizing that one class fits into another. A city can be in a particular state or province and also in a particular country. As children apply this advanced classification to locations, they often become fascinated with "complete" addresses such as Lee Jary, 5116 Forest Hill Drive, Richmond Hill, Ontario, Canada, North America, Northern Hemisphere, Earth, Solar System, Milky Way, Universe.

Classification is also related to reversibility. The ability to reverse a process mentally now allows the concrete-operational student to see that there is more than one way to classify a group of objects. The student understands, for example, that buttons can be classified by color, then reclassified by size or by the number of holes.

Seriation is the process of making an orderly arrangement from large to small or vice versa. This understanding of sequential relationships permits a student to construct a logical series in which A < B < C (A is less than B is less than C) and so on. Unlike the preoperational child, the concrete-operational child can grasp the notion that B can be larger than A but smaller than C.

With the abilities to handle operations like conservation, classification, and seriation, the student at the concrete-operational stage has finally developed a complete and very logical system of thinking. This system of thinking, however, is still tied to physical reality. The logic is based on concrete situations that can be organized, classified, or manipulated. Thus, children at this stage can imagine several different arrangements for the furniture in their rooms before they act. They do not have to solve the problem strictly through trial and error by actually making the arrangements. But the concrete-operational child is not yet able to reason about hypothetical, abstract problems that involve the coordination of many factors at once. This kind of coordination is part of Piaget's next and final stage of cognitive development.

In any grade you teach, a knowledge of concrete-operational thinking will be helpful. In the early grades, the students are moving toward this logical system of thought. In the middle grades, it is in full flower, ready to be applied and extended by your teaching. In the high school years, it is often used by students whose thinking may not have fully developed to the next stage—the stage of formal operations.

Guidelines

Teaching the Concrete-Operational Child

Continue to use concrete props and visual aids, especially when dealing with sophisticated material.
Examples
1. Use time lines in history and three-dimensional models in science.
2. Use diagrams to illustrate hierarchical relationships like branches of government and the agencies under each branch.

Continue to give students a chance to manipulate and test objects.
Examples
1. Set up simple scientific experiments like the following involving the relationship between fire and oxygen. What happens to a flame when you blow on it from a distance? (If you don't blow it out, the flame gets larger briefly,

since it has more oxygen to burn.) What happens when you cover the flame with a jar?

2. Have students make candles by dipping wicks in wax, weave cloth on a simple loom, bake bread, set type by hand, or do other craft work that illustrates the daily occupations of people in the colonial period.

Make sure presentations and readings are brief and well organized.

Examples

1. Assign stories or books with short, logical chapters, moving to longer reading assignments only when students are ready.
2. Break up a presentation with a chance to practice the first steps before introducing the next.

Use familiar examples to explain more complex ideas.

Examples

1. Compare students' lives with those of characters in a story. After reading *Island of the Blue Dolphins* (the true story of a girl who grew up alone on a deserted island), ask "Have you ever had to stay alone for a long time? How did you feel?"
2. Teach the concept of area by having students measure two rooms in the school that are different sizes.

Give opportunities to classify and group objects and ideas on increasingly complex levels.

Examples

1. Give students separate sentences on slips of paper to be grouped into paragraphs.
2. Compare the systems of the human body to other kinds of systems: the brain to a computer, the heart to a pump. Break down stories into components, from the broad to the specific: author; story; characters, plot, theme; place, time; dialogue, description, actions.

Present problems that require logical, analytical thinking.

Examples

1. Use mind twisters, brain teasers, Master Mind, and riddles.
2. Discuss open-ended questions that stimulate thinking: "Are the brain and the mind the same thing?" "How should the city deal with stray animals?" "What is the largest number?"

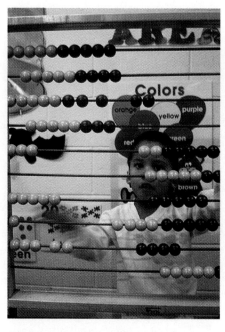

Being able to manipulate concrete objects helps children understand abstract relationships such as the connection between symbols and quantity.

Application: Point out that by the time children reach the concrete-operational stage of cognitive development, they have some operations and strategies that they are able to employ. Ask students, considering these new skills, how they might go about teaching a child in this stage (a) a history lesson about the American Revolution, and (b) the importance of the five food groups of nutrition.

Seriation Arranging objects in sequential order according to one aspect, such as size, weight, or volume.

Formal Operations Mental tasks involving abstract thinking and coordination of a number of variables.

Junior and Senior High: Formal Operations.   Some students remain at the concrete-operational stage throughout their school years, even throughout life. However, new experiences, usually those that take place in school, eventually present most students with problems that they cannot solve using concrete operations. What happens when a number of variables interact, as in a laboratory experiment? Then a mental system for controlling sets of variables and working through a set of possibilities is needed. These are the abilities Piaget called **formal operations.**

At the level of formal operations, all the earlier operations and abilities continue in force; that is, formal thinking is reversible, internal, and organized in a system of interdependent elements. The focus of thinking shifts, however, from what *is* to what *might be*. Situations do not have to be experienced to be imagined. Ask a young child how life would be different if people did not sleep,

Casebook: See the Teachers' Casebook for ideas about teaching abstract concepts to concrete thinkers.

Application: Have your class discuss how they would apply their knowledge in the following instance: You have been assigned to teach tenth-grade science. Your students are just beginning to use formal operations. What strategies will you keep in mind when forming your lesson plans?

Teaching Tip: Have your students discuss the differences (and similarities) between egocentrism in young children and egocentrism in adolescents. In young children, egocentrism tends not to be selfishness but rather an inability to see another person's point of view. An egocentric adolescent may understand that others have a different point of view but have difficulty accepting that another person's view has any value.

Hypothetico-Deductive Reasoning A formal-operations problem-solving strategy in which an individual begins by identifying all the factors that might affect a problem and then deduces and systematically evaluates specific solutions.

and the child might say, "People have to sleep!" In contrast, the adolescent who has mastered formal operations can consider contrary-to-fact questions. In answering, the adolescent demonstrates the hallmark of formal operations—**hypothetico-deductive reasoning.** The formal thinker can consider a hypothetical situation (people do not sleep) and reason deductively (from the general assumption to specific implications, such as longer workdays, more money spent on lighting, or new entertainment industries). Formal operations also include inductive reasoning, or using specific observations to identify general principles. For example, the economist observes many specific changes in the stock market and attempts to identify general principles about economic cycles. Formal-operational thinkers can form hypotheses, set up mental experiments to test them, and isolate or control variables in order to complete a valid test of the hypotheses.

The ability to consider abstract possibilities is critical for much of mathematics and science. After elementary school, most math is concerned with hypothetical situations, assumptions, and givens: "Let $x = 10$," or "Assume $x^2 + y^2 = z^2$," or "Given two sides and an adjacent angle . . . " Young children cannot reason based on symbols and abstractions, but this kind of reasoning is expected in the later grades (Bjorklund, 1989). Work in social studies and literature requires abstract thinking, too: "What did Wilson mean when he called World War I the 'war to end all wars'?" "What are some metaphors for hope and despair in Shakespeare's sonnets?" "What symbols of old age does T. S. Eliot use in *The Waste Land*?" "How do animals symbolize human character traits in Aesop's fables?"

The organized, scientific thinking of formal operations requires that students systematically generate different possibilities for a given situation. The following experiment can help you identify students who apply formal operations. The purpose is to test whether a person can determine, in an organized way, the number of different possibilities that exists within a reasonably limited framework. Ask your students: "How many different outfits can be made with the following clothes: (1) three tops—polo shirt, dress shirt, T-shirt; (2) three pairs of pants—jeans, shorts, slacks; and (3) three jackets—bomber, blazer, jeans jacket?" A student capable of formal operations would begin by laying out the possibilities systematically: first each jacket with the polo shirt and jeans, then each jacket with the polo shirt and shorts, then each jacket with the polo shirt and slacks; then on to the jackets with the dress shirt and jeans, then with the dress shirt and shorts, and so forth. A student at the concrete-operational stage, however, would be much less systematic; he or she might start with favorite clothes and continue in the order of preference. It would not be unusual for a student operating at the concrete level to mention only three outfits, using each garment only once. The underlying system of combinations is not yet available.

The ability to think hypothetically, consider alternatives, identify all possible combinations, and analyze one's own thinking has some interesting consequences for adolescents. Since they can think about worlds that do not exist, they often become interested in science fiction. Because they can reason from general principles to specific actions, they often are critical of people whose actions seem to contradict their principles. Adolescents can deduce the set of "best" possibilities and imagine ideal worlds (or ideal parents and teachers, for that matter). This explains why many students at this age develop interests in utopias, political causes, and social issues. They want to design better worlds, and their thinking allows them to do so. Adolescents can also imagine many possible futures for themselves and may try to decide which is best. Feelings about any of these ideals may be strong.

Another characteristic of this stage is **adolescent egocentrism.** Unlike egocentric young children, adolescents do not deny that other people may have different perceptions and beliefs; the adolescents just become very focused on their own ideas. They analyze their own beliefs and attitudes. They reflect on others' thinking as well but often assume that everyone else is as interested as they are in their thoughts, feelings, and behavior. This can lead to what Elkind (1981) calls the sense of an *imaginary audience*—the feeling that everyone is watching. Thus, adolescents believe that others are analyzing them: "Everyone noticed that I wore this shirt twice this week." "The whole class thought my answer was dumb!" "Everybody is going to love my new CD." You can see that social blunders or imperfections in appearance can be devastating if "everybody is watching." Luckily, this feeling of being "on stage" seems to peak in early adolescence by age 14 or 15.

Do We All Reach the Fourth Stage? As we have just seen, most psychologists agree that there is a level of thinking more sophisticated than concrete operations. But the question of how universal formal-operational thinking actually is, even among adults, is a matter of debate. According to Neimark (1975), the first three stages of Piaget's theory are forced on most people by physical realities. Objects really are permanent. The amount of water doesn't change when it is poured into another glass. Formal operations, however, are not so closely tied to the physical environment. They may be the product of experience and of practice in solving hypothetical problems and using formal scientific reasoning. These abilities tend to be valued and taught in literate cultures, particularly in colleges and universities.

Piaget himself (1974) suggested that most adults may be able to use formal-operational thought in only a few areas, areas where they have the greatest experience or interest. So do not expect every student in your junior high or high school class to be able to think hypothetically about all the problems you present. It is important to keep this in mind, since many of the tasks normally presented to high school and even junior high students require a good deal of formal thinking, especially in science and mathematics. Students who have not learned to go beyond the information presented to them are likely to fall by the wayside in these courses. Sometimes students find shortcuts for dealing with problems that are beyond their grasp; they may memorize formulas or lists of steps. These systems may be helpful for passing tests, but real understanding will take place only if students are able to go beyond this superficial use of memorization—only, in other words, if they learn to use formal-operational thinking.

Teaching Tip: David Elkind (1978) describes two dimensions of egocentric thinking characteristic of adolescents. Personal fable is a deep-rooted belief in one's personal uniqueness—"No one else in the world can possibly understand how I feel." The concept of the imaginary audience refers to the belief that everyone else in the world is preoccupied with the personal appearance and behavior of that adolescent. Adult support and understanding can help adolescents gradually eliminate this type of thinking. (Understanding the young adolescent. *Adolescence, 13*, 127–134).

Focus on . . . **Piaget's Theory**

- What is a scheme?
- Distinguish between assimilation and accommodation.
- As children move from sensorimotor to formal-operational thinking, what are the major changes?
- What are the characteristics of concrete-operational thinking?

Example: De Lisi and Staudt (1980) found support for this idea. In their experiment, college students from three different majors (physics, political science, and English) were asked to solve several types of problems. Almost all the students were able to use formal operations when the problems were similar to ones they encountered in their own majors. When given unfamiliar types of problems, however, only about half the students attempted to apply formal thinking in finding solutions.

Adolescent Egocentrism Assumption that everyone else shares one's thoughts, feelings, and concerns.

Guidelines

**Helping Students
to Use Formal
Operations**

Continue to use concrete-operational teaching strategies and materials.

Examples
  1. Use visual aids such as charts and illustrations as well as somewhat more sophisticated graphs and diagrams.
  2. Compare the experiences of characters in stories to students' experiences.

Give students the opportunity to explore many hypothetical questions.

Examples
  1. Have students write position papers, then exchange these papers with the opposing side and have debates about topical social issues—the environment, the economy, national health insurance.
  2. Ask students to write about their personal vision of a utopia; write a description of a universe that has no sex differences; write a description of Earth after humans are extinct.

Give students opportunities to solve problems and reason scientifically.

Examples
  1. Set up group discussions in which students design experiments to answer questions.
  2. Ask students to justify two different positions on animal rights, with logical arguments for each position.

Whenever possible, teach broad concepts, not just facts, using materials and ideas relevant to the students' lives.

Examples
  1. When discussing the Civil War, consider other issues that have divided the United States since then.
  2. Use lyrics from popular songs to teach poetic devices, to reflect on social problems, and to stimulate discussion on the place of popular music in our culture.

Implications of Piaget's Theory for Teachers

Piaget has taught us that we can learn a great deal about how children think by listening carefully, by paying close attention to their ways of solving problems. If we understand children's thinking, we will be better able to match teaching methods to children's abilities.

Objective 2.6: Describe the implications for teachers of Piaget's theory stating the importance of understanding students' thinking and matching teaching strategies to abilities.

Understanding Students' Thinking

Test Bank items 2.43, 2.101, 2.105, 2.106, 2.109

The students in any class will vary greatly both in their level of cognitive development and in their academic knowledge. As a teacher, how can you determine whether students are having trouble because they lack the necessary thinking abilities or because they simply have not learned the basic facts? To do this, Case (1985b) suggests you observe your students carefully as they try to solve the problems you have presented. What kind of logic do they use? Do they focus on only one aspect of the situation? Are they fooled by appearances? Do they suggest solutions systematically or by guessing and forgetting what they have already tried? Ask your students how they tried to solve the problem. Listen to their strategies. What kind of thinking is behind repeated mistakes or problems? The students are the best sources of information about their own thinking abilities (Confrey, 1990a).

Application: To help students understand children's thinking at different stages, instruct them to ask children between the ages of 5 and 18, "What are you afraid of? What do you fear?" Then compare answers and see what conclusions can be drawn.

Matching Strategies to Abilities   Test Bank items 2.101, 2.105, 2.108

An important implication of Piaget's theory for teaching is what Hunt years ago (1961) called "the problem of the match." Students must be neither bored by work that is too simple nor left behind by teaching they cannot understand. According to Hunt, disequilibrium must be kept "just right" to encourage growth. Setting up situations that lead to errors can help create an appropriate level of disequilibrium. When students experience some conflict between what they think should happen (a piece of wood should sink because it is big) and what actually happens (it floats!), they may rethink their understanding, and new knowledge may develop.

It is worth pointing out, too, that many materials and lessons can be understood at several levels and can be "just right" for a range of cognitive abilities. Classics such as *Alice in Wonderland,* myths, and fairy tales can be enjoyed at both concrete and symbolic levels. It is also possible for students to be introduced to a topic together, then work individually on follow-up activities matched to their level. Tom Good and Jere Brophy (1991) describe activity cards for three or four ability levels. These cards provide different readings and assignments, but all are directed toward the overall class objectives. One of the cards should be a good "match" for each student.

Piaget's fundamental insight was that individuals construct their own understanding; learning is a constructive process. At every level of cognitive development, you will also want to see that students are actively engaged in the learning process. They must be able to incorporate the information you present into their own schemes. To do this, they must act on the information in some way. Schooling must give the students a chance to experience the world. This active experience, even at the earliest school levels, should not be limited to the physical manipulation of objects. It should also include mental manipulation of ideas that arise out of class projects or experiments (Ginsburg & Opper, 1988). For example, after a social studies lesson on different jobs, a primary-grade teacher might show the students a picture of a woman and ask, "What could this person be?" After answers like "teacher," "doctor," "secretary," "lawyer," "saleswoman," and so on, the teacher could suggest, "How about a daughter?" Answers like "sister," "mother," "aunt," and "granddaughter" may follow. This should help the children switch dimensions in their classification and center on another aspect of the situation. Next, the teacher might suggest "American," "jogger," or "blonde." With older children, hierarchical classification might be involved: it is a picture of a woman, who is a

Application: Ask students: "Suppose you are teaching the concept clouds to a third-grade class and to a tenth-grade class. How would your presentations and expectations differ? Why would they differ?" (Explain in terms of organizational changes and the development of more complex schemes.)

Background: For a useful discussion of the "problem of the match," see Donaldson, M. (1985). The mismatch between school and children's minds. In N. Entwistle (Ed.), *New directions in educational psychology. Vol. 1: Learning and teaching* (pp. 61–70). Philadelphia: Farmer Press, Taylor & Francis.

Application: Ask your students, "Suppose you were teaching the concept of prejudice to a third-grade class and to a twelfth-grade class. How and why would your presentations and expectations differ?"

Application: Ask students, at what stage of cognitive development would it be appropriate to teach the following concepts: city, sharing, mammal, superstition, honesty?

Activity 2.9: Cooperative Learning. See the *Instructor's Resource Manual* for Piagetian Theory: What Does It Mean to Teachers?—an activity that asks students to work in groups to identify teaching implications of Piaget's theory.

Activity 2.10: See the separate *Instructor's Resource Manual* for Speeding Up Cognitive Development: Pro and Con, a summary of the arguments for and against accelerating cognitive development. Piaget called this "the American Question." An argument against acceleration appears in David Elkind's article, "Formal Education and Early Childhood Education: An Essential Difference," in the May 1986 issue of *Phi Delta Kappan*.

Objective 2.7: Explain three criticisms or limitations of Piaget's theory.

human being; a human being is a primate, which is a mammal, which is an animal, which is a life form.

Another important part of cognitive development is the ability to apply the principles learned in one situation to new situations. Teachers should constantly ask students to apply recently learned principles in different situations. For example, the student who has learned how to form plurals by dropping the *y* and adding *-ies* should be asked to form plurals not only of words like *party* and *pony* (where the rule fits) but of words like *donkey* (where the rule does not work). If the principle applies, the student will gain practice in using it. If the principle does not fit, disequilibrium will occur, and new thinking abilities may develop.

All students need to interact with teachers and peers in order to test their thinking, to be challenged, to receive feedback, and to watch how others work out problems. Disequilibrium is often set in motion quite naturally when the teacher or another student suggests a new way of thinking about something. As a general rule, students should act, manipulate, observe, and then talk and/or write (to the teacher and each other) about what they have experienced. Concrete experiences provide the raw materials for thinking. Communicating with others makes students use, test, and sometimes change their thinking abilities. Discussions about the implications of Piaget's theory often center on the question of whether cognitive development can be accelerated, as you can see in the Point/Counterpoint.

Some Limitations of Piaget's Theory

Test Bank items 2.47, 2.48, 2.106, 2.107

Piaget's influence on developmental psychology and education has been enormous, even though recent research has not supported all his ideas. Although most psychologists agree with Piaget's insightful descriptions of how children think, many disagree with his explanations of why thinking develops as it does.

The Trouble with Stages. Some psychologists have questioned the existence of four separate stages of thinking, even though they agree that children do go through the changes that Piaget described (Gelman & Baillargeon, 1983). One problem with the stage model is the lack of consistency in children's thinking. Psychologists reason that if there are separate stages, and if the child's thinking at each stage is based on a particular set of operations, then once the child has mastered the operations, he or she should be somewhat consistent in solving all problems requiring those operations. In other words, once you can conserve, you ought to know that the number of blocks does not change when they are rearranged (conservation of number) and that the weight of a ball of clay does not change when you flatten it (conservation of weight). But it doesn't happen this way. Children can conserve *number* a year or two before they can conserve *weight*. Piagetian theorists have tried to deal with these inconsistencies, but not all psychologists are convinced by their explanations (Siegler, 1991).

Some psychologists have pointed to research on the brain to support Piaget's stage model. Epstein observed changes in rates of growth in brain weight and skull size and changes in the electrical activity of the brain between infancy and adolescence. These growth spurts occur at about the same time as transi-

Can Cognitive Development Be Accelerated?

Ever since Piaget described his stages of cognitive development, some people have asked if progress through the stages could be accelerated. More recently, the question has focused on whether we should accelerate learning for preschoolers and young children at risk of academic failure. Can learning be accelerated, and if so, is this a good idea?

POINT Every child deserves a head start.

Some of the strongest arguments in favor of "speeding up" cognitive development are based on the results of cross-cultural studies of children (studies that compare children growing up in different cultures). These results suggest that certain cognitive abilities are indeed influenced by the environment and education. Children of pottery-making families in one area of Mexico, for example, learn conservation of substance earlier than their peers in families who do not make pottery (Ashton, 1978). Furthermore, children in non-Western cultures appear to acquire conservation operations later than children in Western cultures. It seems likely that factors in the environment contribute to the rate of cognitive development.

But even if cognitive development can be accelerated, is this a good idea? Two of the most vocal (and heavily criticized) advocates of early academic training are Siegfried and Therese Engelmann (1981). In their book, *Give Your Child a Superior Mind*, they suggest that children who learn academic skills as preschoolers will be smarter throughout their school years, are less likely to fail, and are more likely to enjoy school. They contend:

> Children respond to the environment. Their capacity to learn and what they learn depends on what the environment teaches. . . . Instead of relying on the traditional environment that is rich in learning opportunities for the child, we can take the environment a step further and mold it into a purposeful instrument that teaches and that guarantees your child will have a superior mind. (p. 10)

COUNTERPOINT Acceleration is ineffective and may be harmful.

The position of Piagetian psychologists who attempt to apply his theory to education is that development should not be speeded up. This traditional view has been well summarized by Wadsworth:

> The function of the teacher is not to accelerate the development of the child or speed up the rate of movement from stage to stage. The function of the teacher is to insure that development within each stage is thoroughly integrated and complete. (1978, p. 117)

According to Piaget, cognitive development is based on the self-selected actions and thoughts of the student, not on the teacher's action. If you do try to teach a student something the student is not ready to learn, he or she may learn to give the "correct" answer. But this will not really affect the way the student thinks about this problem. Therefore, why spend a long time teaching something at one stage when students will learn it by themselves much more rapidly and thoroughly at another stage?

Today the pressure is on parents and preschool teachers to create "superkids," 3-year-olds who read, write, and speak a second language. David Elkind (1991) asserts that pushing children can be harmful. Elkind believes that preschool children who are given formal instruction in academic subjects often show signs of stress such as headaches. These children may become dependent on adults for guidance. Early focus on "right" and "wrong" answers can lead to competition and loss of self-esteem. Elkind asserts:

> The miseducation of young children, so prevalent in the United States today, ignores well-founded and non-controversial differences between early education and formal education. As educators, our first task is to reassert this difference and insist on its importance. (p. 31)

tions between the stages described by Piaget (Epstein, 1978, 1980). Evidence from animal studies indicates that infant rhesus monkeys show dramatic increases in synaptic (nerve) connections throughout the brain cortex at the same time that they master the kinds of sensorimotor problems described by Piaget (Berk, 1994). This may be true in human infants as well. Transition to the higher cognitive states in humans has also been related to changes in the brain, such as production of additional synaptic connections.

Activity 2.11: Inquiry. See the separate *Instructor's Resource Manual* for Simplifying Instructions, a summary of research suggesting that Piaget underestimated the cognitive abilities of young children.

Underestimating Children's Abilities.

It now appears that Piaget underestimated the cognitive abilities of children, particularly younger ones. The problems he gave young children may have been too difficult and the directions too confusing. His subjects may have understood more than they could show on these problems. For example, work by Gelman and her colleagues (Gelman, Meck, & Merkin, 1986; Miller & Gelman, 1983) shows that preschool children know much more about the concept of number than Piaget thought, even if they sometimes make mistakes or get confused. As long as preschoolers work with only three or four objects at a time, they can tell that the number remains the same, even if the objects are spread far apart or clumped close together. Recent studies of infants show us that they too are much more competent than Piaget thought. Instead of having to learn that objects are permanent, they may just have to learn how to look for them. In other words, we may be born with a greater store of cognitive tools than Piaget suggested. Some basic understandings, like the permanence of objects or the sense of number, may be part of our evolutionary equipment, ready for use in our cognitive development.

Piaget's theory does not explain how even young children can perform at an advanced level in certain areas, areas where they have highly developed knowledge and expertise. An expert 9-year-old chess player may think abstractly about chess moves, while a novice 20-year-old player may have to resort to more concrete strategies to plan and remember moves (Siegler, 1991). As John Flavell (1985) noted, "the expert [child] looks very, very smart—very 'cognitively mature'—when functioning in her area of expertise" (p. 83).

Multicultural Awareness: Ask students if they think Piaget's theory applies to the development of children in other cultures. What observations or information do students have to support their hypotheses?

Background: See Rogoff, B., & Morelli, G. (1989). Perspectives on children's development from cultural psychology. *American Psychologist, 44*, 343–348.

Cognitive Development and Culture.

A final criticism of Piaget's theory is that it overlooks the important effects of the child's cultural and social group. Children in Western cultures may master scientific thinking and formal operations because this is the kind of thinking required in Western schools. Even basic concrete operations such as classification may not be so basic to people of other cultures. For example, when African subjects from among the Kpelle people were asked to sort 20 objects, they created groups that made sense to them—a hoe with a potato, a knife with an orange. The experimenter could not get the Kpelle to change their categories; they said this is how a wise man would do it. Finally the experimenter asked in desperation, "Well, how would a fool do it?" The subjects promptly created the four neat classification piles the experimenter had expected—food, tools, and so on (Rogoff & Morelli, 1989).

There is an increasingly influential view of cognitive development that offers an alternative perspective to that of Piaget. Proposed years ago by Lev Vygotsky and recently rediscovered, this theory ties cognitive development to culture.

Focus on . . .   **Implications of Piaget's Theory**

- How can teachers get a sense of the kind of thinking (preoperational, concrete, or formal) their students use to solve problems?
- What is the "problem of the match"?
- What is active learning? Why is Piaget's theory of cognitive development consistent with active learning?

Background: Moll, L. (1990). *Vygotsky and education: Instructional implications and applications of sociohistorical psychology.* New York: Cambridge University Press.

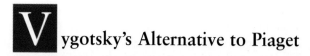ygotsky's Alternative to Piaget

Test Bank items 2.52, 2.106

Psychologists today recognize that the child's culture shapes cognitive development by determining what and how the child will learn about the world. For example, young Zinacanteco Indian girls of southern Mexico learn complicated ways of weaving cloth. In Brazil, without going to school, children who sell candy on the streets learn sophisticated mathematics in order to buy from wholesalers, sell, barter, and make a profit. Cultures that prize cooperation and sharing teach these skills early, whereas cultures that encourage competition nurture these abilities in their children (Bakerman et al., 1990; Childs & Greenfield, 1982; Saxe, 1988). The stages observed by Piaget are not necessarily "natural" for all children. These stages reflect to some extent the expectations and activities of the children's culture (Laboratory of Comparative Human Cognition, 1983).

Lev Vygotsky's theories challenge many of Piaget's ideas and highlight the importance of social interaction and support in cognitive development.

A major spokesperson for this cultural view was a Russian psychologist who died more than 50 years ago. Lev Semenovich Vygotsky was only 38 when he died, but his ideas about language, culture, and cognitive development were very mature. Recent translations of his work show that he provided an alternative to many of Piaget's ideas.

Whereas Piaget described the child as a little scientist, constructing an understanding of the world largely alone, Vygotsky (1978, 1986) suggested that cognitive development depends much more on the people in the child's world. Children's knowledge, ideas, attitudes, and values develop through interactions with others. Vygotsky also believed that culture and language play very important roles in cognitive development.

The Role of Language and Private Speech

Test Bank items 2.50, 2.51, 2.81, 2.92, 2.94, 2.108

In Vygotsky's mind, language is critical for cognitive development. Language provides a means for expressing ideas and asking questions, and it provides the categories and concepts for thinking. When we consider a problem, we generally think in words and partial sentences. Vygotsky placed much more emphasis than Piaget on the role of language in cognitive development. In fact, Vygotsky believed that language in the form of **private speech** (talking to yourself) guides cognitive development.

Vygotsky's and Piaget's Views Compared. If you have spent much time around young children, you know that they often talk to themselves as they play. We saw earlier that Piaget called children's self-directed talk "egocentric speech." He assumed that this egocentric speech is another indication that young children can't see the world through the eyes of others. They talk about what matters to them, without taking into account the needs or interests of their listeners. As they mature, and especially as they have disagreements with peers, Piaget believed, children develop socialized speech. They learn to listen and exchange ideas.

Vygotsky had very different ideas about young children's private speech. Rather than being a sign of cognitive immaturity, Vygotsky suggested that

Private Speech Children's self-talk, which guides their thinking and action. Eventually these verbalizations are internalized as silent inner speech.

these mutterings play an important role in cognitive development. The children are communicating—they are communicating with themselves to guide their behavior and thinking. In any preschool room you might hear 4- or 5-year-olds saying, "No, it won't fit. Try it here. Turn. Turn. Maybe this one . . . " while they do a puzzle. As these children mature, their self-directed speech goes underground, changing from spoken to whispered speech and then to silent lip movements. Finally, the children just "think" the guiding words. The use of private speech peaks at around 5 to 7 years of age and has generally disappeared by 9 years of age. Brighter children seem to make this transition earlier (Bee, 1992).

Vygotsky identified this transition from audible private speech to silent inner speech as a fundamental process in cognitive development. Through this process the child is using language to accomplish important cognitive activities such as directing attention, solving problems, planning, forming concepts, and gaining self-control. Research supports Vygotsky's ideas (Bivens & Berk, 1990; Kohlberg, Yaeger, & Hjertholm, 1969). Children tend to use more private speech when they are confused, having difficulties, or making mistakes. Inner speech not only helps us solve problems but also allows us to regulate our behavior. Have you ever thought to yourself something like, "Let's see, the first step is . . . " or "Where did I use my glasses last . . . ?" or "If I work to the end of this page, then I can . . . "? You were using inner speech to remind, cue, encourage, or guide yourself. In a really tough situation, you might even find that you return to muttering out loud. Table 2.2 contrasts Piaget's and Vygotsky's theories of private speech.

TABLE 2.2 Differences between Piaget's and Vygotsky's Theories of Egocentric or Private Speech

	Piaget	Vygotsky
Developmental Significance	Represents an inability to take the perspective of another and engage in reciprocal communication	Represents externalized thought; its function is to communicate with the self for the purpose of self-guidance and self-direction
Course of Development	Declines with age	Increases at younger ages and then gradually loses its audible quality to become internal verbal thought
Relationship to Social Speech	Negative; least socially and cognitively mature children use more egocentric speech	Positive; private speech develops out of social interaction with others
Relationship to Environmental Contexts	—	Increases with task difficulty. Private speech serves a helpful self-guiding function in situations where more cognitive effort is needed to reach a solution

Source: L. E. Berk and R. A. Garvin (1984). Development of private speech among low-income Appalachian children. *Developmental Psychology, 20,* p. 272. Copyright 1984 by the American Psychological Association. Adapted by permission.

Self-Talk and Learning. Because private speech helps students to regulate their thinking, it makes sense to allow, even encourage, students to use private speech in school. Insisting on total silence when young students are working on difficult problems may make the work even harder for them. You may notice when muttering increases—this could be a sign that students need help. One approach, called **cognitive self-instruction,** teaches students to use self-talk to guide learning. For example, students learn to give themselves reminders to go slowly and carefully. They "talk themselves through" tasks, saying such things as "Okay, what is it I have to do? . . . Copy the picture with the different lines. I have to go slowly and carefully. Okay, draw the line down, down, good; then to the right, that's it; now . . . " (Meichenbaum, 1977, p. 32).

Assisted Learning   Test Bank items 2.53, 2.54, 2.82, 2.93, 2.103, 2.108

Language plays another important role in development. Vygotsky believed that cognitive development occurs through the child's conversations and interactions with more capable members of the culture, adults or more able peers. These people serve as guides and teachers, providing the information and support necessary for the child to grow intellectually. The adult listens carefully to the child and provides just the right help to advance the child's understanding. Thus, the child is not alone in the world "discovering" the cognitive operations of conservation or classification. This discovery is assisted by family members, teachers, and peers. Most of this guidance is communicated through language, at least in Western cultures. In some cultures, observing a skilled performance, not talking about it, guides the child's learning (Rogoff, 1990).

Jerome Bruner called this adult assistance **scaffolding** (Wood, Bruner, & Ross, 1976). The term aptly suggests that children use this help for support while they build a firm understanding that will eventually allow them to solve the problems on their own. **Assisted learning,** or assisted discovery in the classroom, involves giving information, prompts, reminders, encouragement at the right time and in the right amounts, then gradually allowing the students to do more and more on their own. Cognitive self-instruction is an example of assisted learning. Reciprocal teaching (chapter 7) is another example. Teachers can assist learning by demonstrating skills, walking students through the steps of a complicated problem, doing part of the problem (for example, in algebra, the students set up the equation and the teacher does the calculations or vice versa), or giving detailed feedback and allowing revisions (Rosenshine & Meister, 1992).

For Vygotsky, social interaction and assistance were more than methods of teaching, they were the origin of higher mental processes such as problem solving. He assumed that "the notion of mental function can properly be applied to group as well as individual forms of activity" (Wertsch, 1991, p. 27). For example, Vygotsky believed that groups could "remember." Consider this example:

> A six-year-old has lost a toy and asks her father for help. The father asks her where she last saw the toy; the child says "I can't remember." He asks a series of questions—did you have it in your room? Outside? Next door? To each question, the child answers, "no." When he says "in the car?",

Cognitive Self-Instruction Approach in which students "talk themselves through" a learning task.

Scaffolding Support for learning and problem solving. The support could be clues, reminders, encouragement, breaking the problem down into steps, providing an example, or anything else that allows the student to grow in independence as a learner.

Assisted Learning Providing strategic help in the initial stages of learning, gradually diminishing as students gain independence.

Sometimes the best teachers are other students who have just understood a particular concept. These "teachers" may be operating in the zone of proximal development for their fellow students.

Background: For a concise summary of the role of adult mediators in children's learning, see Feuerstein, R., & Hoffman, M. B. (1985, summer). The importance of mediated learning for the child. *Human Intelligence International Newsletter, 6*(2), 1–2.

Activity 2.12: Critical Thinking. See the *Instructor's Resource Manual* for Comparison of Piaget and Vygotsky, an activity that asks the students to compare these two psychologists using eight guiding questions.

Objective 2.8: Discuss Vygotsky's theory of cognitive development, including his concept of a "zone of proximal development."

Zone of Proximal Development Phase at which a child can master a task if given appropriate help and support.

she says "I think so" and goes to retrieve the toy. (Tharp & Gallimore, 1988, p. 14)

Who remembered? The answer is really neither the father nor the daughter, but the two together. The remembering and problem solving was in the interaction, but the child may have internalized strategies to use next time something is lost. At some point, the child will be able to function independently to solve this kind of problem. Vygotsky believed that all higher mental functions have their origins in social interactions. Like the strategy for finding the toy, these higher functions appear first between a child and a "teacher" before they exist within the individual child (Kozulin, 1990).

How can you know what kind of help to give and when to give it? One answer has to do with the student's zone of proximal development.

The Zone of Proximal Development

Test Bank items 2.49, 2.54, 2.55, 2.93, 2.103, 2.108

According to Vygotsky, at any given point in development there are certain problems that a child is on the verge of being able to solve. The child just needs some structure, clues, reminders, help with remembering details or steps, encouragement to keep trying, and so on. Some problems, of course, are beyond the child's capabilities, even if every step is explained clearly. The **zone of proximal development** is the area where the child cannot solve a problem alone, but can be successful under adult guidance or in collaboration with a more advanced peer (Wertsch, 1991). This is the area where instruction can succeed, because this is the area where real learning is possible.

We can see how Vygotsky's beliefs about the role of private speech in cognitive development fit with the notion of the zone of proximal development. Often, an adult helps a child to solve a problem or accomplish a task using verbal prompts and structuring. This scaffolding may be gradually reduced as the child takes over the guidance, perhaps first by giving the prompts as private speech and finally as inner speech. Let's move forward to a future day in the life of the girl in the example above who had lost her toy and *listen to* her thoughts when she realizes that a schoolbook is missing. They might sound something like this:

> "Where's my math book? Used it in class. Thought I put it in my bookbag after class. Dropped my bag on the bus. That dope Larry kicked my stuff, so maybe . . . "

The girl can now systematically search for ideas about the lost book without help from anyone else.

An implication of Vygotsky's zone of proximal development is that students should be put in situations where they have to reach to understand, but where support from other students or from the teacher is also available. Sometimes the best teacher is another student who has just figured out the problem, because this student is probably operating in the learner's zone of proximal development. Vygotsky's theory suggests that teachers need to do more than just arrange the environment so that students can discover on their own. The students should be guided by explanations, demonstrations, and work with other students—opportunities for cooperative learning. Having a student work with someone who is just a bit better at the activity would also be a good idea. In addition, students should be encouraged to use language to organize their thinking, to talk about what they are trying to accomplish.

Instructional Conversations   Test Bank items 2.56, 2.83, 2.108

One implication of Vygotsky's theory of cognitive development is that important learning and understanding require interaction and conversation. Students need to grapple with problems in their zone of proximal development, and they need the scaffolding provided by interaction with a teacher or other students. Instructional conversations provide these opportunities. **Instructional conversations** are *instructional* because they are designed to promote learning, but they are *conversations,* not lectures or traditional discussions. One national study sponsored by the U.S. Department of Education reported that:

> Direct observations reveal that teachers do most of the talking in classrooms. . . . In over half the interactions that teachers have with students, students do not produce any language. . . . When students do respond, typically they provide only simple information recall statements. This pattern of teacher/student interaction not only limits a student's opportunity to create and manipulate language, but also limits the student's ability to engage in more complex learning. (Ramirez, Yuen, & Ramey, 1991, p. 8)

Instructional conversations are an alternative to this dominance of teacher talk. The teacher's goal is to keep everyone engaged in a substantive discussion. The teacher is a guide, helping students construct their own understandings. Table 2.3 on page 52 summarizes the elements of productive instructional conversations.

Research supports Vygotsky's beliefs about the importance of language in cognitive development. Language both reflects and influences students' mental development. In the next section, we examine how language develops and what teachers can do to encourage this development.

Background: For more information on instructional conversations, including examples of class transcripts and instruments to assess instructional conversations, contact: Dissemination Center, National Center for Research on Cultural Diversity and Second Language Learning, Center for Applied Linguistics, 1118 22nd Street NW, Washington, DC 20037.

Focus on . . .   Vygotsky

- What are the differences between Piaget's and Vygotsky's perspectives on private speech and its role in development?
- What is assisted learning, and what role does scaffolding play in learning?
- Describe the characteristics of a good instructional conversation.

The Development of Language

All children in every culture master the complicated system of their native language, unless severe deprivation or physical problems interfere. This knowledge is remarkable. As you might expect, there are different theories about how people master the complex process of communication.

How Do We Learn Language?   Test Bank items 2.57, 2.83, 2.108

One early view of language development assumed that children learn language just as they learn anything else, by repeating those behaviors that lead to some kind of positive result. The child makes a sound, the parent smiles and replies.

Objective 2.9: Trace the development of language through the beginning of the school years, using the following terms: holophrases, overextension, telegraphic speech, and overregulation.

Instructional Conversation Situation in which students learn through interactions with teachers and/or other students.

TABLE 2.3   Elements of the Instructional Conversation

Good instructional conversations must have elements of both instruction and conversation.

Instructional

1. *Thematic focus.* Teacher selects a theme on which to focus the discussion and has a general plan for how the theme will unfold, including how to "chunk" the text to permit optimal exploration of the theme.
2. *Activation and use of background knowledge.* Teacher either "hooks into" or provides students with pertinent background knowledge necessary for understanding a text, weaving the information into the discussion.
3. *Direct teaching.* When necessary, teacher provides direct teaching of a skill or concept.
4. *Promotion of more complex language and expression.* Teacher elicits more extended student contributions by using a variety of elicitation techniques: invitations to expand, questions, restatements, and pauses.
5. *Promotion of bases for statements or positions.* Teacher promotes students' use of text, pictures, and reasoning to support an argument or position, by gently probing: "What makes you think that?" or "Show us where it says ____."

Conversational

6. *Fewer "known-answer" questions.* Much of the discussion centers on questions for which there might be more than one correct answer.
7. *Responsiveness to student contributions.* While having an initial plan and maintaining the focus and coherence of the discussion, teacher is also responsive to students' statements and the opportunities they provide.
8. *Connected discourse.* The discussion is characterized by multiple, interactive, connected turns; succeeding utterances build on and extend previous ones.
9. *Challenging, but non-threatening, atmosphere.* Teacher creates a challenging atmosphere that is balanced by a positive affective climate. Teacher is more collaborator than evaluator and students are challenged to negotiate and construct the meaning of the text.
10. *General participation, including self-selected turns.* Teacher does not hold exclusive right to determine who talks; students are encouraged to volunteer or otherwise influence the selection of speaking turns.

Source: Claude Goldenberg (1991). *Instructional Conversations and Their Classroom Application* (p. 7). Santa Cruz, CA and Washington, DC: National Center for Research on Cultural Diversity and Second Language Learning. Reprinted by permission.

Background: Rice, M. L. (1989). Children's language acquisition. *American Psychologist, 44,* 149–156 provides a synthesis of research on this topic.

The child says, "Mmm," in the presence of milk, and the parent says, "Yes, milk, milk," and gives the child a drink. The child learns to say milk because it leads to a happy parent and a drink of milk. Children add new words by imitating the sounds they hear and improve their use of language when they are corrected by the adults around them. This explanation of language learning is based on the behavioral perspective described in chapter 6.

Such a theory is appealing, but research has shown that many of a child's earliest utterances are not imitations but original creations. And they are unlikely to be rewarded, because they are "incorrect," even though they make sense to the people involved. Examples are such phrases as "paper find," "car mosquito," "tooth-guy" (dentist), or "all gone kitty" (Moshman, Glover, & Bruning, 1987). In addition, researchers studying interactions between young children and their parents have discovered that parents rarely correct pronunciation and grammar during the early stages of language development. They are much more likely to respond to the content of a child's remarks (Brown & Hanlon, 1970; Demetras & Post, 1985). In fact, if parents spent all their time correcting a child's language and never "heard" what the child was trying to say, the child might give up trying to master a system as complicated as language.

Adults caring for children seem continually to adapt their language to stay just ahead of the child. Before children begin talking, adults may direct long, complicated sentences to them, but as soon as a child utters identifiable words, adults simplify their language. As the child progresses, adults tend to change their language to stay just a bit more advanced than the child's current level of development, thus encouraging new understanding (Bohannon & Warren-Leubecker, 1989). It seems that in order to stretch the child's language development, adults give the kind of support, or scaffolding, that Vygotsky has recommended. Adults, by staying slightly more advanced in their language, may also create disequilibrium and encourage development as a result.

But even this rich learning environment cannot explain how children learn so much language so quickly and correctly. Think of all the sounds that could be combined in different orders and linked with many different meanings. Why don't children create wild languages or make crazy associations between a sound and a meaning? Why, for example, when their parents say, "Look, a rabbit," do children learn to connect the word *rabbit* with the whole animal, not with the animal's ears, or movements, or size, or fur? Some psychologists explain this amazing accomplishment by assuming that humans are born with a special capacity for processing, understanding, and creating language (Chomsky, 1965, 1986; Eimas, 1985; Maratsos, 1989). Humans may have built-in biases, rules, and constraints about language that restrict the number of possibilities considered. For example, young children seem to have a constraint specifying that a new label refers to a whole object, not just a part. Another built-in bias leads children to assume that the label refers to a class of similar objects. So the child learning about the rabbit is equipped naturally to assume that *rabbit* refers to the whole animal (not just its ears) and that other similar-looking animals are also rabbits. These built-in constraints simplify language learning (Markman, 1990). Also, humans may share a universal grammar, a set of specifications and rules that limit the range of language created. In other words, only certain possibilities are considered as the child figures out the puzzle of language (Chomsky, 1980).

It is likely that many factors—biological and experiential—play a role in language development. The important point is that children develop language as they develop other cognitive abilities by actively trying to make sense of what they hear and by looking for patterns and making up rules to put together the jigsaw puzzle of language. In this process, built-in biases and rules may limit the the search and guide the pattern recognition. Reward and correction play a role in helping children learn correct language use, but the child's thinking and creativity in putting together the parts of this complicated system

Elementary-school-age children may understand complex language structure when they hear others use it, but they do not necessarily use it in their own conversations.

are very important (Rosser, 1994). In the process a child makes some very logical "mistakes," as you will see.

Test Bank items
2.58–2.67, 2.84,
2.95, 2.97, 2.104

Stages in the Process of Language Acquisition

Before they learn to speak, children communicate through crying, smiling, and body movements. By the end of the first year, more or less, most children have spoken their first word. They have entered what psychologists call the one-word stage.

First Words. After the first word, for the next three or four months, children add slowly to their vocabulary until they have about ten words. After this, words are added rapidly. By about 20 months, the vocabulary includes approximately 50 words (Nelson, 1981).

Even at this early stage, language is more complex than it might appear. One word can be used to communicate a variety of sophisticated ideas. For example, my daughter's first word was *ite* (translated: light). Said loudly while reaching toward the light switch on the wall, "ITE!" meant "I want to flip the switch on and off (and on and off, and on and off)." When someone else flipped the switch while she was playing on the floor, Elizabeth might remark "Ite," meaning "You turned on the light." When single words are used in this way, they are called **holophrases**, because they express whole phrases or complex ideas.

A second, related characteristic of this period is **overextension**. Children may use one word to cover a range of concepts. For example, on a trip to the zoo, the 13-month-old son of a friend pointed excitedly at every animal, including peacocks and elephants, saying "Dug, dug" (translated: dog, dog). This was the only word he had that came close to being adequate. He wisely rejected his other possibilities: "bye-bye," "more," "Mama," and "Dada." He used the language tools available to him to make sense of his world and to communicate. Children sometimes show **underextension** as well; they use words too specifically. For example, Siegler (1991) tells about the child who used the word "bottle" only for her baby bottle and not for soda bottles or water bottles.

First Sentences. At about 18 months, many children enter the two-word stage. They begin to string words together in two-word sentences like "Daddy book," "Play car," "Allgone milk," and "More light." This is **telegraphic speech** (R. Brown, 1973). The nonessential details are left out, and the words that carry the most meaning are included, as in a telegram. Even though sentences are short, semantics can be complex. Children can express possession ("Daddy book"), recurrence ("More light"), action on an object ("Play car"), and even disappearance or nonexistence ("Allgone milk").

For about one year, children continue to focus on the essential words even as they lengthen their sentences. At a certain point that varies from child to child, new features are added. Children begin to elaborate their simple language by adding plurals, endings for verbs such as *-ed* and *-ing*, and small words like *and, but,* and *in*. In the process of figuring out the rules governing these aspects of language, children make some very interesting mistakes.

Holophrases Single words that express complex ideas.

Overextension Using one word to cover a range of concepts.

Underextension Being too specific in using a word, limiting the word's meaning to a narrow range of possible examples.

Telegraphic Speech Children's speech using only essential words, as in a telegram.

Learning Grammar.   For a brief time, children may use irregular forms of particular words properly, as if they are saying what they have heard. Then, as they begin to learn rules, they **overregularize** words by applying the rules to everything. Children who once said, "Our car is broken" begin to insist, "Our car is broked." Parents often wonder why their child seems to be "regressing." Actually, these "mistakes" show how logical and rational children can be as they try to assimilate new words into existing schemes. Because most languages have many irregular words, accommodation is necessary in mastering language.

Another aspect of overregularizing language involves the order of words in a sentence. Since the usual order in English is subject–verb–object, preschoolers just mastering the rules of language have trouble with sentences in any different order. For example, if they hear a statement in the passive voice, like "The truck was bumped by the car," they usually think the truck did the bumping to the car (Berger, 1986). So in talking with young children, it is generally better to use direct language.

Learning Vocabulary.   During the preschool years, children learn new words very rapidly, doubling their vocabulary about every six months between ages 2 and 4, from about 200 to 2,000 words. During this time they may enjoy making up words. Because their thinking is egocentric, they may assume you know exactly what these words mean. They also tend to center on one meaning for a word.

Preschool children like to play with language. They enjoy sounds and silliness. The young son of a friend of mine wanted to name his new baby sister "Brontosaurus" because he "just liked to say it!" Think of all the language games, rhymes, taunts, chants, secret languages (pig Latin, Obish), and rituals that filled your early days. In my time it was "Sticks and stones may break my bones, but words will never hurt me," and the ever-popular "School's out, school's out . . . ."

Language Development in the School Years

By about age 5 or 6, most children have mastered the basics of their native language. As noted earlier, the language of these children can still be quite egocentric. Preschoolers may have special meanings for words. They may talk to themselves as they work, first clearly, then in a whisper, and finally silently. What remains for the school-age child to accomplish?

Pronunciation.   The majority of first graders have mastered most of the sounds of their native language, but a few may remain unconquered. As you can see from Figure 2.3 on page 56, the *j, v, th,* and *zh* sounds are the last to develop. About 10 percent of 8-year-olds still have some trouble with *s, z, v, th,* and *zh* (Rathus, 1988). Young children may understand and be able to use many words but prefer to use the words they can pronounce easily.

Intonation or word emphasis may also cause problems for young children. If the meaning of a sentence is ambiguous and intonation makes the difference, then children as old as 8 or 9 may misunderstand. Moshman, Glover, and Bruning (1987) give this example. Consider the sentence, "George gave the

"WHEN I SAY 'RUNNED,' YOU KNOW I MEAN 'RAN.' LET'S NOT QUIBBLE."

© 1994 *by Sidney Harris*

Test Bank items 2.68–2.72, 2.98, 2.104

Transparency: Use acetate transparency **T 12**, "Vocabulary Changes in Childhood."

Overregularize Apply a learned rule to all situations, including inappropriate ones.

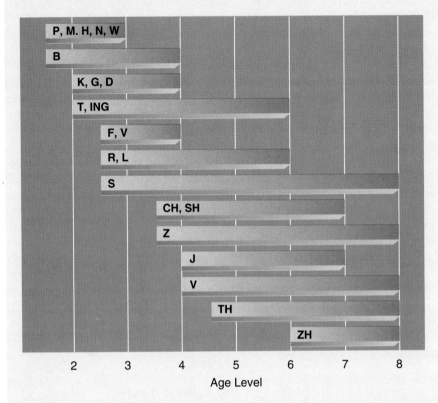

FIGURE 2.3

ACQUISITION OF THE SOUNDS OF SPEECH
The solid bar for each sound of speech begins at the age by which 50 percent of children pronounce it properly. The bar ends at the age by which 90 percent of children are pronouncing the sound correctly.

Source: Figure from *Understanding Child Development* by Spencer A. Rathus and Peter Favaro, copyright © 1988 by Holt, Rinehart and Winston, Inc., reproduced by permission of the publisher.

book to David, and he gave one to Bill." If you emphasize the *he*, then the meaning is "George gave the book to David, and David gave another book to Bill." With a different intonation, emphasizing the *and*, for example, the meaning is changed to "George gave the book to David, and George also gave one to Bill." Don't expect early elementary-school students to pick up subtle meanings in intonation.

Syntax. Children master the basics of word orders, or **syntax**, in their native language early. But the more complicated forms, such as the passive voice, take longer to master. By early elementary school, many children can understand the meaning of passive sentences, yet they do not use such construc-

Syntax The order of words in phrases or sentences.

tions in their normal conversations. Other accomplishments during elementary school include first understanding and then using complex grammatical structures such as extra clauses, qualifiers, and conjunctions.

Vocabulary and Meaning.   Between the ages of 2 and 6, the average child learns between six and ten words a day. This means the average 6-year-old has a vocabulary of 8,000 to 14,000 words. From ages 9 to 11, about 5,000 new words are added to this repertoire. It seems that the time before puberty, especially the preschool years, is a sensitive period for language growth. Research has shown that we can learn much about language after puberty, but that very positive or very negative conditions during the sensitive period before puberty can greatly help or hinder language development (Berger, 1986; Johnson & Newport, 1989).

In the early elementary years, some children may have trouble with abstract words such as *justice* or *economy*. They may also take statements literally and thus misunderstand sarcasm or metaphor. Many children are in their preadolescent years before they are able to distinguish being kidded from being taunted or before they know that a sarcastic remark is not meant to be taken literally (Gardner, 1982b).

Pragmatics.   **Pragmatics** involves the appropriate use of language to communicate. Children show an understanding of pragmatics when they talk in simpler sentences to younger children or command their pets to "Come here!" in louder, deeper voices (Rice, 1984). But there is much more to successful communicating. For instance, children must learn the rules of turn-taking in conversation. The conversations of young children tend to follow the rules of turn-taking, even if the children don't seem to listen to each other, as illustrated in Figure 2.4 on page 58. What seem to adults to be disjointed, unrelated remarks do not bother young children at all. They are paying attention to their own remarks, not the other children's, and they probably assume that everyone else is doing the same.

When children begin to have arguments, you can tell that they are listening to each other. In later elementary school, children's conversations start to sound like conversations. Contributions are usually on the same topic. By adolescence, students become interested in analyzing the feelings and views of others. They want to understand the perspective of the other speakers. You will hear "How did you feel when she did that?" or "Why aren't you sitting with Jonah? Did you have a fight?" (Dorval & Eckerman, 1984).

Teaching and Language   Test Bank items 2.73, 2.74

Around the age of 5, students begin to develop **metalinguistic awareness**. This means their understanding about language and how it works becomes explicit. They have knowledge about language itself. They are ready to study and extend the rules that have been implicit—understood but not consciously expressed. This process continues throughout life, as we all become better able to manipulate and comprehend language. Teachers can develop the language abilities and knowledge of their students in a variety of ways.

Teachers can enrich students' language environment by focusing not just on correct or incorrect usage, but on the idea expressed. Probe and extend stu-

Casebook: See the Teachers' Casebook for ideas about encouraging language development.

Objective 2.10: Describe strategies that teachers can use to help students develop language abilities and knowledge.

Research: Chall, J. S., & Snow, C. E. (1988). School influences on the reading development of low-income children. *Harvard Education Letter,* 4(1), 1–4. This article talks about classroom factors that make a difference in helping low-income students learn to read. Vocabulary development is an important aspect of successful programs. To develop vocabulary, good programs:

1. Stress vocabulary during content-area instruction as well as during reading, using many materials such as encyclopedias, maps, magazines, comics, and trade books.

2. Place less emphasis on looking up words in the dictionary.

3. Have reading materials at all levels so even the best readers are challenged.

4. Use field trips and other activities to expose students to new vocabulary in context, so students can build background knowledge for understanding the words and any future reading based on the experiences.

Background: See the special issue on Reading and Writing in *Educational Leadership,* 47(6), 1990.

Pragmatics Area of language involving the effects of contexts on meaning.

Metalinguistic Awareness Understanding about one's own use of language.

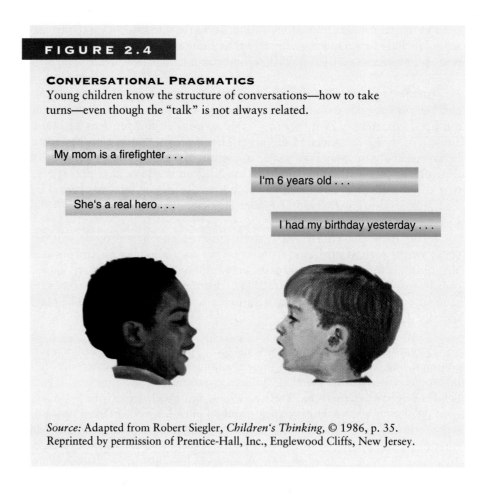

FIGURE 2.4

CONVERSATIONAL PRAGMATICS
Young children know the structure of conversations—how to take turns—even though the "talk" is not always related.

My mom is a firefighter . . .

I'm 6 years old . . .

She's a real hero . . .

I had my birthday yesterday . . .

Source: Adapted from Robert Siegler, *Children's Thinking,* © 1986, p. 35. Reprinted by permission of Prentice-Hall, Inc., Englewood Cliffs, New Jersey.

dents' ideas. For example, if a student says, "I writed my name on my picture," the teacher could respond, "You wrote your name above the rocket. Where is your astronaut going?" In this way, the teacher maintains the student's interest and at the same time introduces a different grammatical construction that the student can observe and perhaps adopt (Rice, 1989).

Cazden (1988) suggests that word meanings are most easily learned through interactions and conversations with an adult in which the adult introduces new words. For example, when a student complains, "He does that on purpose, just to make me mad!" the teacher might respond, "So you think he is intentionally tripping by your desk just to irritate you? What's your evidence for that conclusion?" Instructional conversations, described earlier, provide other examples.

Focus on . . . **Language Development**

- How are humans predisposed to develop language? What role does learning play?
- What do children's mistakes in using irregular verbs (i.e., "broked" for broken or "goed" for went) tell about the way they learn language?
- How can teachers extend and enrich students' language development?

Reading aloud is also a potent form of language stimulation. Reading to students often leads to conversations about the pictures or ideas in the books. The importance of one-to-one interaction with an adult in developing language abilities has been stressed by many psychologists (Rice, 1989). This is in keeping with Vygotsky's theory of cognitive development.

Throughout this text you will read about other ways that teachers can encourage language development. For example, we will discuss bilingual education in chapter 5, reciprocal teaching in chapter 7, the language of thinking in chapter 8, and whole language teaching in chapter 13.

SUMMARY

A Definition of Development

Theorists differ greatly in their approach to the study of development, but all tend to agree that people develop at different rates, that development is an orderly process, and that development takes place gradually. The brain begins to lateralize soon after birth and thus to specialize certain functions in certain areas. The younger the child, the more plastic the brain and the more easily the child's brain can adapt to damage. Even though certain functions are associated with certain parts of the brain, the various parts and working systems of the brain work together to learn and perform complex human activities and to construct understanding.

Piaget's Theory of Cognitive Development

Piaget's theory of cognitive development is based on the assumption that people try to make sense of the world and actively create their knowledge through direct experience with objects, people, and ideas. Maturation, activity, social transmission, and the need for equilibrium all influence the way thinking processes and knowledge develop. In response to these influences, according to Piaget's theory, thinking processes and knowledge develop through adaptation (including the complementary processes of assimilation and accommodation) and changes in the organization of thought (the development of schemes).

Piaget believed that young people pass through four stages as they develop: sensorimotor, preoperational, concrete-operational, and formal-operational. In the sensorimotor stage, infants explore the world through their senses and motor activity, and work toward mastering object permanence and performing goal-directed activities. In the preoperational stage, symbolic thinking and logical operations begin. Children in the stage of concrete operations can think logically about tangible situations and can demonstrate conservation, reversibility, classification, and seriation. The ability to perform hypothetico-deductive reasoning, coordinate a set of variables, and imagine other worlds marks the stage of formal operations.

Implications of Piaget's Theory for Teachers

Teachers can use Piaget's theory of cognitive development to understand students' thinking, to match instructional strategies to students' abilities, and to directly foster students' cognitive development. Piaget's theory has been criticized because children and adults often think in ways that are inconsistent with the notion of invariant stages. It also appears that Piaget underestimated children's cognitive abilities. Piaget's work is also criticized for overlooking cultural factors in child development. Critics often point to the work of Vygotsky as an example of a theory of cognitive development that does include the important role of culture.

Vygotsky's Alternative to Piaget

Vygotsky's view is that cognitive development hinges on social interaction and the development of language. As an example, Vygotsky describes the role of children's self-directed talk in guiding and monitoring thinking and problem solving. Vygotsky proposed the concept of a zone of proximal development, in which children in challenging situations can develop their own thinking abilities through timely, appropriate guidance and support from teachers or peers, called scaffolding. Assisted learning is the process of providing appropriate scaffolding within the student's zone of proximal development. Instructional conversations are one example of assisted learning.

The Development of Language

Closely linked to cognitive development are the development of language and metalinguistic awareness. Children try to understand and apply language rules. Chomsky and others suggest that some of these rules are inborn in humans. Using their capacity for language, children try to solve the puzzle of the language they hear, moving from holophrasic to telegraphic speech through overextension, underextension, and overregularization to a basic understanding of pronunciation, vocabulary, grammar and syntax, semantics, and pragmatics by around age 5 or 6.

Teachers have a significant role in helping children develop language ability and knowledge about language. Teachers can focus on effective communication, meaning, comprehension, and respect for language in the classroom.

KEY TERMS

accommodation, p. 31
adaptation, p. 30
adolescent egocentrism, p. 41
assimilation, p. 31
assisted learning, p. 49
classification, p. 37
cognitive development, p. 26
cognitive self-instruction, p. 49
collective monologue, p. 36
compensation, p. 37
concrete operations, p. 36
conservation, p. 35
decentering, p. 36
development, p. 26
disequilibrium, p. 32
egocentric, p. 36
equilibration, p. 31

formal operations, p. 39
goal-directed actions, p. 32
holophrases, p. 54
hypothetico-deductive reasoning, p. 40
identity, p. 36
instructional conversation, p. 51
maturation, p. 26
metalinguistic awareness, p. 57
object permanence, p. 32
operations, p. 33
organization, p. 30
overextension, p. 54
overregularize, p. 55
personal development, p. 26
physical development, p. 26

pragmatics, p. 57
preoperational, p. 33
private speech, p. 47
reversibility, p. 37
reversible thinking, p. 35
scaffolding, p. 49
schemes, p. 31
semiotic function, p. 35
sensorimotor, p. 32
seriation, p. 39
social development, p. 26
syntax, p. 56
telegraphic speech, p. 54
underextension, p. 54
zone of proximal development, p. 50

WHAT WOULD YOU DO?

Preschool and Kindergarten

A group of vocal parents wants you to introduce workbooks to teach basic arithmetic in your class for 4- and 5-year-olds. They seem to think that "play" with blocks, water, sand, clay, and so on is "wasted time." How would you respond?

Elementary and Middle School

The district curriculum guide calls for a unit on poetry, including lessons on symbolism in poems. You are concerned that many of your students may not be ready to understand this abstract concept. How would you approach this unit? What would you do to "listen" to your students' thinking so you could match your teaching to their level of thinking? How would you give them concrete experience with symbolism?

Two very concerned parents want to have a conference with you about their son's "language problems." He is in first grade and has some trouble with pronunciation. How would you prepare for the conference?

Junior High and High School

The students in your class persist in memorizing definitions for many of the important abstract concepts in your class. They insist, "That's what you have to do to make a good grade in this class." Even though they can repeat the definitions precisely, they seem to have no conception of what the terms mean; they can't recognize examples of the concept in problems or give their own examples. It is almost as if they don't believe there is any real hope of understanding the ideas. Pick one important, difficult concept in your field, and design a lesson to teach it to students who believe only in memorization.

It seems as if every fourth word from the mouths of your students is *like* or *you know.* Also, their understanding of the material in your class is limited, because they don't know the meaning of many words that you assumed high school students would certainly understand, such as *former* and *latter.* What would you do to encourage language development along with teaching your subject?

Cooperative Learning Activity

Working with four or five other members of your educational psychology class, solve either the "poetry" or the "memorization" problem described above. Then pair up with another group and take turns teaching the lessons you designed.

TEACHERS' CASEBOOK

Encouraging Language Development

One of your students seldom speaks and communicates only in short, incomplete sentences or monosyllables. The student is a middle child in a large family, and you suspect there is little conversation or reading at home. How would you encourage language development for this student?

FOSTER SELF-EXPRESSION

In a situation like this you as a teacher need to provide an outlet for the child to express him- or herself. This can be done by first using written communication, such as daily journals. The student writes down thoughts or events, and the teacher responds, also in writing. After you learn more about the student (likes, dislikes, interests), you can engage him or her in brief conversations and build from that. From there, you can go on to sharing books orally and so forth. School may be the most stable and comfortable environment for some students, and we as teachers need to utilize that situation.

Candice J. Gallagher, *Fourth-Grade Teacher*
Fredericktown Intermediate School, Fredericktown, Ohio

Teaching Abstract Concepts

How would you teach the abstract concept of "justice" to students who think very concretely?

ROLE PLAYS

Justice is such an abstract idea that many students have a difficult time in grasping the concept. One of the best ways to demonstrate the idea of justice in a democratic society is to role play.

I would have the students take the roles of court personnel: judge, jury, defense, prosecutor. The defense would then present the story of *The Three Little Pigs*. The defendant would be the Wolf, and the prosecuting witness would be the Third Little Pig.

The prosecution would bring in exhibits: straw, sticks, and so forth. The Third Little Pig could tell his side of the story. The defense could take another approach. The Wolf could tell his side of the story as told in the book *The True Story of the Three Little Pigs* by Jon Scieszka. When the prosecution and defense had finished, the verdict would be left up to the jury and the sentencing up to the judge.

The method of role playing, using a basic story, allows the students to think and interact with an abstract concept. The concept of justice is transformed into a concrete element. The idea of role playing could also be used in illustrating what justice looks like in different cultures.

Julie A. Addison, *Sixth-Grade Teacher*
Roxborough Elementary School, Littleton, Colorado

MOCK COURTROOMS

I would role play "injustice" for the students by arbitrarily dividing the class into two groups and giving one group a special privilege such as fifteen minutes of game time while I asked the other group to complete a boring task like copying all the "a" words in the dictionary. After fifteen minutes I would bring the students back together to discuss how they felt and contrast the injustice they had experienced with the concept of justice. I might set up a mock courtroom and put a familiar character like Goldilocks on trial or read excerpts from books like *Tom Sawyer, Charlotte's Web, The Three Little Pigs,* and *A Cricket in Times Square* and have the class record if they believe a character experienced justice or injustice.

Joanne S. Groseclose, *Virginia 1991 Teacher of the Year*
Marion Intermediate School, Marion, Virginia

I would relate the concept of justice to their world in a sense of fairness with things that happen to them and to their peers. I would even at times lead the students to make decisions as a group when certain events are related to this concept. Even young children, who are at a very concrete stage of development, are able to recognize the fairness of events in their world and are able to come to decisions that represent fairness or justice. The problem with students this age is that everything is black or white; there is no gray for them, therefore they cannot see that certain circumstances may dictate a certain response. However, there are times when discussion can help them to see the unusualness or specialness of what is happening, and they can be led to alter a decision to meet the situation. As students reach fifth grade, they are more able to assess situations individually and understand the concept of justice in its full flavor.

Brenda M. Lloyd, *Third- and Fourth-Grade Teacher*
St. Anne's-Belfield, Charlottesville, Virginia

Experiencing Others' Points of View

In childhood and adolescence, children tend to be egocentric and have difficulty seeing the world from another person's point of view. When you notice students experiencing this difficulty, what do you do?

The first day of school I want the students to realize that each of them is unique and essential to the class. The interdependence and value of everyone's resources enhance all that we do. I glue a large poster onto a piece of tag board, then cut it into thirty odd-shaped puzzle pieces (enough for each student to have one with a few extra pieces left over). The pieces have plenty of notches and grooves for secure assembly. The pieces are in a brown paper bag.

At the beginning of the class, I explain how glad I am that each of them is a part of the class, and how everybody had something unique and special to offer to the group. I emphasize that I have as much to learn from them as they do from me. As I talk, I walk around and personally hand each of the students a brightly colored piece of the puzzle. I then pair the students with the person next to them. Student one is directed to talk for one minute without stopping about his piece while student two listens without saying a word. At the end of one minute, student two has to tell student one what he said. (They are always taken off guard and realize that they have not really heard too much.) The exercise is repeated with student two talking for one minute while student one listens and later repeats what was said.

The students realize that no other piece is like theirs, but they still have no idea what the big picture for the puzzle is. We gather around one table, or on the floor, and I share a few words on how important each piece is to the whole picture. They then have to figure out how to put the picture together. I add the extra pieces, and explain how I need the students' pieces just as much as they need mine.

Some very interesting interactions take place, depending on the grade level and the chemistry of the group; but they always manage to get the picture together and experience considerable satisfaction in finding out what the poster is. We then glue it together and hang it in the room for the rest of the year as a reminder that "we are all in this together."

Betty Garner, *Elementary Art Teacher*
Pattonville I.D.E.A.L. Center, Maryland Heights, Missouri

Personal, Social, and Emotional Development

A s we all know from experience, schooling involves more than cognitive development. In this chapter we examine emotional, social, and moral development.

We begin with the work of Erik Erikson, whose comprehensive theory provides a framework for studying personal and social development. Next, we explore ideas about how we come to understand ourselves and others. What is the meaning of the self-concept, and how is it shaped? How do our views of others change as we grow? What factors determine our views about morality? What can teachers do to foster such personal qualities as honesty, cooperation, empathy, and self-esteem? We then consider the two major influences on children's personal and social development: families and schools. Families today have gone through many transitions, and these changes affect the roles of teachers.

With an understanding of these aspects of personal and social development, we can consider a pressing question: "What is a developmentally appropriate education for students?" Several issues are important in the early years—physical development, reactions to preschool experience, and the child's changing relationships with friends. As the child enters adolescence, other issues become important—physical and sexual maturing and health risks such as drugs and AIDS.

By the time you have completed this chapter, you should be able to:

- Describe Erikson's stages of psychosocial development and list several of his theory's implications for teaching.
- Suggest how teachers can foster self-esteem in their students.
- Describe Kohlberg's stages of moral reasoning and give an example of each.
- Evaluate alternatives to Kohlberg's theory.
- Explain the factors that encourage cheating and aggression in classrooms and discuss possible responses to each.
- Take a stand on affective and moral education.
- Describe the child's changing view of friendship.
- List the problems of early and late maturers.
- Suggest ways to help adolescents make responsible decisions about sex and drugs.

Planning Tip: See the *Chapter-3-At-A-Glance Planning Guide* in the Instructor's Section at the front of this book.

Study Guide: The *Study Guide,* sold separately, contains exercises to help students determine if they have mastered each learning objective for this chapter.

Planning Tip: See the separate *Instructor's Resource Manual* for additional activities and resources for teaching this chapter, including Handout Masters. Also see the Allyn and Bacon *Transparencies in Educational Psychology.*

Planning Tip: See the *Test Bank* and *Study Guide* supplements as you plan for evaluation and measurement of student learning.

WHAT DO YOU THINK?

Remember a teacher who helped to shape your sense of who you are—your abilities, aspirations, or values. What did the teacher do or say that influenced you? How old were you at the time, and how did you feel about the teacher? Is this teacher a model for your own work with students? Why or why not? Do you know someone whose career choice was affected by a teacher or a coach? What role did the teacher or coach play?

Erik Erikson proposed a theory of psychosocial development that describes tasks to be accomplished at different stages of life.

Psychosocial Describing the relation of the individual's emotional needs to the social environment.

Developmental Crisis A specific conflict whose resolution prepares the way for the next stage.

The Work of Erikson

Test Bank items 3.1–3.6, 3.73, 3.84, 3.104

Like Piaget, Erik Erikson did not start out as a psychologist. In fact, Erikson never graduated from high school. He spent his early adult years studying art and traveling around Europe. A meeting with Sigmund Freud in Vienna led to an invitation from Freud to study psychoanalysis. Erikson then emigrated to America to practice his profession and to escape the threat of Hitler.

In his influential *Childhood and Society* (1963), Erikson offered a basic framework for understanding the needs of young people in relation to the society in which they grow, learn, and later make their contributions. His later books, *Identity, Youth, and Crisis* (1968) and *Identity and the Life Cycle* (1980), expanded on his ideas. Although Erikson's approach is not the only explanation of personal and social development, I have chosen it to organize our discussion because Erikson emphasizes the emergence of the self, the search for identity, and the individual's relationships with others throughout life.

After studying child-rearing practices in several cultures, Erikson concluded that all humans have the same basic needs and that each society must provide in some way for those needs. Emotional changes and their relation to the social environment follow similar patterns in every society. This emphasis on the relationship of culture and the individual led Erikson to propose a **psychosocial** theory of development.

Like Piaget, Erikson saw development as a passage through a series of stages, each with its particular goals, concerns, accomplishments, and dangers. The stages are interdependent: accomplishments at later stages depend on how conflicts are resolved in the earlier years. At each stage, Erikson suggests, the individual faces a **developmental crisis**. Each crisis involves a conflict between a positive alternative and a potentially unhealthy alternative. The way in which the individual resolves each crisis will have a lasting effect on that person's self-image and view of society. An unhealthy resolution of problems in the early stages can have potential negative repercussions throughout life, although sometimes damage can be repaired at later stages. We will look briefly at all eight stages in Erikson's theory—or, as he calls them, the "eight ages of man." Table 3.1 presents the stages in summary form.

TABLE 3.1 Erikson's Eight Stages of Psychosocial Development

Stages	Approximate Age	Important Event	Description
1. Basic trust versus basic mistrust	Birth to 12–18 months	Feeding	The infant must form a first loving, trusting relationship with the caregiver or develop a sense of mistrust
2. Autonomy versus shame/doubt	18 months to 3 years	Toilet training	The child's energies are directed toward the development of physical skills, including walking, grasping, controlling the sphincter. The child learns control but may develop shame and doubt if not handled well.
3. Initiative versus guilt	3 to 6 years	Independence	The child continues to become more assertive and to take more initiative but may be too forceful, which can lead to guilt feelings.
4. Industry versus inferiority	6 to 12 years	School	The child must deal with demands to learn new skills or risk a sense of inferiority, failure, and incompetence.
5. Identity versus role confusion	Adolescence	Peer relationships	The teenager must achieve identity in occupation, gender roles, politics, and religion.
6. Intimacy versus isolation	Young adulthood	Love relationships	The young adult must develop intimate relationships or suffer feelings of isolation.
7. Generativity versus stagnation	Middle adulthood	Parenting	Each adult must find some way to satisfy and support the next generation.
8. Ego integrity versus despair	Late adulthood	Reflection on and acceptance of one's life	The culmination is a sense of acceptance of oneself as one is and a sense of fulfillment.

Source: From Lester A. Lefton, *Psychology,* 5/e. Copyright © 1994 by Allyn and Bacon. Reprinted by permission.

The Preschool Years: Trust, Autonomy, and Initiative

Erikson identifies *trust versus mistrust* as the basic conflict of infancy. In the first months of life, babies begin to find out whether they can depend on the world around them. According to Erikson, the infant will develop a sense of trust if its needs for food and care are met with comforting regularity. Closeness and responsiveness on the part of the parents at this time contribute greatly to this sense of trust (Bretherton & Waters, 1985; Isabella & Belsky, 1991). In this first year, infants are in Piaget's sensorimotor stage and are just beginning to learn that they are separate from the world around them. This realization is part of what makes trust so important: infants must trust the aspects of their world that are beyond their control (Bretherton & Waters, 1985).

Erikson's second stage, **autonomy** *versus shame and doubt,* marks the beginning of self-control and self-confidence. Young children are capable of doing more and more on their own. They must begin to assume important responsibilities for self-care like feeding, toileting, and dressing.

Test Bank items 3.5, 3.7–3.11, 3.74, 3.85, 3.96

Planning Tip: For further information about audiovisual, multimedia, and computer-assisted resources for teaching this chapter, see the Video and Software Guide in the *Instructor's Resource Manual.*

Objective 3.1: State the general characteristics of Erikson's theory of psychosocial development.

Transparency: Use acetate transparency T 16, "Comparing Erikson's and Piaget's Stages."

Autonomy Independence.

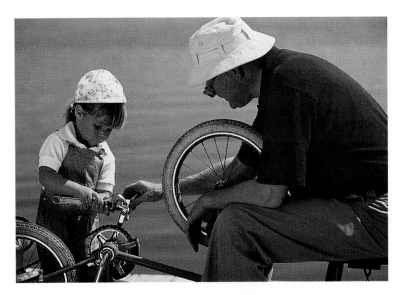

It would certainly be faster for this grandfather to fix the bike himself, but by letting his granddaughter join in, he nurtures her sense of initiative.

Transparency: Use acetate transparency **T 15,** "Erikson's Stages of Psychosocial Development."

Handout: See the *Instructor's Resource Manual* for **Handout Master 3.1,** "Conditions That Encourage Positive Resolutions of Erikson's Developmental Crises."

Objective 3.2: Name Erikson's eight developmental crises and environmental conditions that encourage positive resolution of the crises.

Study Guide: Concept Map. See the *Study Guide* for the Concept Map "Erikson's Theory of Psychosocial Development." This concept map also appears in the *Instructor's Resource Manual* as **Handout Master 3.7.**

Planning Tip: See the *Test Bank* and *Study Guide* supplements as you plan for evaluation and measurement of student learning.

Teaching Tip: The eight conditions that foster positive resolutions of Erikson's developmental crises are listed on **Handout Master 3.2** in the *Instructor's Resource Manual.*

Initiative Willingness to begin new activities and explore new directions.

Industry Eagerness to engage in productive work.

During this period parents must tread a fine line; they must be protective—but not overprotective. If parents do not maintain a reassuring, confident attitude and do not reinforce the child's efforts to master basic motor and cognitive skills, children may begin to feel shame; they may learn to doubt their abilities to manage the world on their own terms. Erikson believes that children who experience too much doubt at this stage will lack confidence in their own powers throughout life.

For Erikson, "initiative adds to autonomy the quality of undertaking, planning, and attacking a task for the sake of being active and on the move" (Erikson, 1963, p. 255). But with **initiative** comes the realization that some activities are forbidden. At times, children may feel torn between what they want to do and what they should (or should not) do. The challenge of this period is to maintain a zest for activity and at the same time understand that not every impulse can be acted on.

Again, adults must tread a fine line, this time in providing supervision without interference. If children are not allowed to do things on their own, a sense of guilt may develop; they may come to believe that what they want to do is always "wrong."

Elementary and Middle School Years: Industry versus Inferiority

Test Bank items 3.12–3.14, 3.16, 3.86, 3.96

In the early school years, students are developing what Erikson calls a sense of **industry.** They are beginning to see the relationship between perseverance and the pleasure of a job completed. The crisis at this stage is *industry versus inferiority.* For children in modern societies, the school and the neighborhood offer a new set of challenges that must be balanced with those at home. Interaction

Encourage children to make and to act on choices.

Examples

1. Have a free-choice time when children can select an activity or game.
2. As much as possible, avoid interrupting children who are very involved in what they are doing.
3. When children suggest an activity, try to follow their suggestions or incorporate their ideas into ongoing activities.
4. Offer positive choices: instead of saying, "You can't have the cookies now," ask, "Would you like the cookies after lunch or after naptime?"

Make sure that each child has a chance to experience success.

Examples

1. When introducing a new game or skill, teach it in small steps.
2. Avoid competitive games when the range of abilities in the class is great.

Encourage make-believe with a wide variety of roles.

Examples

1. Have costumes and props that go along with stories the children enjoy. Encourage the children to act out the stories or make up new adventures for favorite characters.
2. Monitor the children's play to be sure no one monopolizes playing "teacher," "Mommy," "Daddy," or other heroes.

Be tolerant of accidents and mistakes, especially when children are attempting to do something on their own.

Examples

1. Use cups and pitchers that make it easy to pour and hard to spill.
2. Recognize the attempt, even if the product is unsatisfactory.

with peers becomes increasingly important as well. The child's ability to move between these worlds and to cope with academics, group activities, and friends will lead to a growing sense of competence. Difficulty with these challenges can result in feelings of inferiority.

Adolescence: The Search for Identity

Test Bank items 3.15, 3.17–3.21, 3.75, 3.87, 3.88, 3.96

The central issue for adolescents is the development of an **identity** that will provide a firm basis for adulthood. The individual has of course been developing a sense of self since infancy. But adolescence marks the first time that a conscious effort is made to answer the now-pressing question, "Who am I?" The conflict defining this stage is *identity versus role confusion.*

Exactly what do we mean by identity, and what does the crisis of this adolescent stage involve? Identity refers to the organization of the individual's drives, abilities, beliefs, and history into a consistent image of self. It involves deliberate choices and decisions, particularly about vocation, sexual orienta-

Research: Mary Ainsworth (1979) has studied the differences between babies who are "securely attached" to their mothers and those who are "anxiously attached." Babies in the first group have mothers who are more responsive to their needs. As they grow older, they become more competent and sympathetic with peers and explore their environment with greater enthusiasm and persistence than the anxiously attached babies (Campos, Barrett, Lamb, Goldsmith, & Sternberg, 1983). By the preschool years, children who were securely attached as infants are rated by their teachers as more self-reliant and less dependent.

Sources: Ainsworth, M. D. S. (1979). Infant-mother attachment. *American Psychologist, 34,* 932–937; Campos, J. J., Barrett, K. C., Lamb, M. E., Goldsmith, H. H., & Sternberg, C. (1983). Socioemotional development. In P. Mussen (Ed.), *Handbook of child development (Vol. 2).* New York: Wiley.

Identity The complex answer to the question, "Who am I?"

Guidelines

Encouraging Industry

Make sure that students have opportunities to set and work toward realistic goals.

Examples

1. Begin with short assignments, then move on to longer ones. Monitor student progress by setting up progress checkpoints.
2. Teach students to set reasonable goals. Write down goals and have students keep a journal of progress toward goals.

Give students a chance to show their independence and responsibility.

Examples

1. Tolerate honest mistakes.
2. Delegate to students tasks like watering class plants, collecting and distributing materials, monitoring the computer lab, grading homework, keeping records of forms returned, and so on.

Provide support to students who seem discouraged.

Examples

1. Use individual charts and contracts that show student progress.
2. Keep samples of earlier work so students can see their improvements.
3. Have awards for most improved, most helpful, most hardworking.

Critical Thinking: Ask students to relate this information to concepts they learned in chapter 2. For example, what aspects of formal-operational thought are helpful (or perhaps necessary) in achieving identity formation? Can you think of people who seem to have established their identity but who do not seem to have achieved the formal-operational stage? Is identity formation necessarily a conscious process?

Identity Achievement Strong sense of commitment to life choices after free consideration of alternatives.

Identity Foreclosure Acceptance of parental life choices without consideration of options.

Identity Diffusion Uncenteredness; confusion about who one is and what one wants.

Moratorium Identity crisis; suspension of choices because of struggle.

tion, and a "philosophy of life" (Marcia, 1987; Waterman, 1985). If adolescents fail to integrate all these aspects and choices, or if they feel unable to choose at all, role confusion threatens.

Identity Statuses. Elaborating on Erikson's work, James Marcia and his colleagues have suggested that there are four alternatives for adolescents as they confront themselves and their choices (Marcia, 1980; Schiedel & Marcia, 1985). The first is **identity achievement.** This means that after considering the realistic options, the individual has made choices and is pursuing them. It appears that few students achieve this status by the end of high school. Most are not firm in their choices for several more years; students who attend college may take a bit longer to decide (Archer, 1982). **Identity foreclosure** describes the situation of adolescents who do not experiment with different identities or consider a range of options, but simply commit themselves to the goals, values, and lifestyles of others, usually their parents. **Identity diffusion,** on the other hand, occurs when individuals reach no conclusions about who they are or what they want to do with their lives; they have no firm direction. Adolescents experiencing identity diffusion may have struggled unsuccessfully to make choices, or they may have avoided thinking seriously about the issues at all.

Finally, adolescents in the midst of struggling with choices are experiencing what Erikson called a **moratorium.** Erikson used the term *moratorium* to describe a delay in the adolescent's commitment to personal and occupational choices. This delay is very common, and probably healthy, for modern adolescents. Marcia expands the meaning of moratorium to include the adolescent's active efforts to deal with the crisis of shaping an identity. Erikson

The search for identity during adolescence often involves experimenting with, or "trying on," various alternatives.

believed that adolescents in complex societies experience this *identity crisis,* or temporary period of moratorium and confusion. Today, the period is no longer referred to as a crisis because, for most people, the experience is a gradual exploration rather than a traumatic upheaval (Baumeister, 1990). Table 3.2 gives examples of the four alternatives in the adolescent's search for identity.

TABLE 3.2   Marcia's Identity Statuses

James Marcia suggested four possible statuses for adolescent identity. Here are examples of responses he received from adolescents in each status to questions like, "How willing would you be to give up your current plans for your career if something better came along?"

Identity achievement: "It's hard to imagine anything really better for me. I guess I might consider it, but I've thought about my decision for a long time—it's the right one for me."

Identity foreclosure: "I wouldn't want to change my plans. My family and I have been working toward this ever since I can remember. Actually, I can't even imagine doing anything else; I just wouldn't feel comfortable."

Identity diffusion: "I don't really have any plans, so there must be something better than the last couple of things I've been turning over in my mind. I don't really know what might work for me, anyway, or what I'd be able to do . . . ."

Moratorium: "Certainly, I might be willing to change. But I've been focusing on this one idea for a while, looking at it from all kinds of angles. It's driving me crazy, but I'm almost to the point where I can say it looks like the best idea for me. But I couldn't say I'm sure yet."

Source: Based on ideas found in J. E. Marcia (1980), Identity formation in adolescence. In J. Adelson (Ed.), *Handbook of Adolescent Psychology.* New York: Wiley.

Teaching Tip: Have your students debate the following viewpoints:

a. In order to establish their identity, adolescents need to separate themselves from their parents so they can discover who they are, other than being their parents' children. If parents are very strict and controlling, children have to give so much energy to establishing the separation that they don't have the time and effort to give to defining their own identity. For this reason, parents and teachers of adolescents would be more helpful if they were lenient with teenagers.

b. Adolescents are similar to large 2-year-olds in that they are egocentric and exhibit out-of-bounds behavior. They derive a sense of security from knowing that there are limits they must observe. They are in a transition stage with no clear-cut standards of behavior, since they are neither child nor adult. For this reason, parents and teachers of adolescents should be strict and impose rules to help a teenager make the transition more easily and safely.

Both identity achievement and moratorium are considered healthy alternatives. The natural tendency of adolescents to "try on" identities, experiment with life-styles, and commit to causes is an important part of establishing a firm identity. But adolescents who can't get past either the identity diffusion or foreclosure stage have difficulties adjusting. For example, identity-diffused adolescents and young adults often give up, trust their lives to fate, or go along with the crowd, so they are more likely to abuse drugs (Archer & Waterman, 1990). Foreclosed adolescents tend to be rigid, intolerant, dogmatic, and defensive (Frank, Pirsch, & Wright, 1990).

Ethnic Pride and Identity. For all students, pride in family and community is part of the foundation for a stable identity. Because ethnic-minority students are members of both a majority culture and a subculture, it is sometimes difficult for them to establish a clear identity. Values, learning styles, and communication patterns of the students' subculture may be inconsistent with the expectations of the school and the larger society. If the students' first language is not English, the problem may be even greater, especially if the school places little value on the students' language and culture. Special efforts to encourage **ethnic pride** are especially important so these students do not get the message that differences are deficits. For example, differences in skin color, hair length, dress, dialect, or accent are just that—differences, not inferior or superior qualities (Spencer & Markstrom-Adams, 1990).

Research indicates that members of minority groups who have achieved an identity by exploring and adopting values from both their ethnic heritage and the dominant culture have a stronger sense of self-esteem, feel more competent, and have more positive relations with others (Phinney & Alipuria, 1990). Each of us has an ethnic heritage. When majority adolescents are knowledgeable and secure about their own heritage, they are also more respectful of the heritage of others. So exploring the ethnic roots of all students should foster both self-esteem and acceptance of others (Rotherham-Borus, 1994).

Focus on... **The Work of Erikson**

- Why is Erikson's theory considered a psychosocial perspective?
- Describe the capabilities of a preschool child who has successfully emerged from Erikson's first three stages of personal-social development.
- How might an adolescent experiencing identity foreclosure answer the question, "Why did you choose that major?"

Ethnic Pride A positive self-concept about one's racial or ethnic heritage.

Generativity Sense of concern for future generations.

Integrity Sense of self-acceptance and fulfillment.

Beyond the School Years   Test Bank items 3.22–3.24

The crises of Erikson's stages of adulthood all involve the quality of human relations. The first of these stages is *intimacy versus isolation*. Intimacy in this sense refers to a willingness to relate to another person on a deep level, to have a relationship based on more than mutual need. Someone who has not achieved a sufficiently strong sense of identity tends to fear being overwhelmed or swallowed up by another person and may retreat into isolation.

The conflict at the next stage is *generativity versus stagnation*. **Generativity** extends the ability to care for another person and involves caring and guidance for the next generation and for future generations. While generativity frequently refers to having and nurturing children, it has a broader meaning. Productivity and creativity are essential features.

The last of Erikson's stages is *integrity versus despair*, coming to terms with death. Achieving **integrity** means consolidating one's sense of self and

Give students many models for career choices and other adult roles.

Examples
1. Point out models from literature and history. Have a calendar with the birthdays of eminent women, minority leaders, or people who made a little-known contribution to the subject you are teaching. Briefly discuss the person's accomplishments on his or her birthday.
2. Invite guest speakers to describe how and why they chose their professions. Make sure all kinds of work and workers are represented.

Help students find resources for working out personal problems.

Examples
1. Encourage them to talk to school counselors.
2. Discuss potential outside services.

Be tolerant of teenage fads as long as they don't offend others or interfere with learning.

Examples
1. Discuss the fads of earlier eras (neon hair, powdered wigs).
2. Don't impose strict dress or hair codes.

Give students realistic feedback about themselves.

Examples
1. When students misbehave or perform poorly, make sure they understand the consequences of their behavior—the effects on themselves and others.
2. Give students model answers or show them other students' completed projects so they can compare their work to good examples.
3. Since students are "trying on" roles, keep the roles separate from the person. You can criticize behavior without criticizing the student.

fully accepting its unique and now unalterable history. Those unable to attain a feeling of fulfillment and completeness sink into despair.

Understanding Ourselves and Others

With Erikson's theory of psychosocial development as a framework, we can now examine several aspects of personal and social development that are issues throughout childhood and adolescence.

What is self-concept? How do we come to understand ourselves and other people? How do we develop a sense of right and wrong—and do these beliefs affect our behavior? You will see that developments in these areas follow patterns similar to those noted in chapter 2 for cognitive development. Children's understandings of themselves are concrete at first, and then become more abstract. Early views of self and friends are based on immediate behaviors and

Discussion: What do your students think Erikson's reply would be to the following questions?

a. Do you recommend following a rigid feeding schedule for infants?
b. Isn't it possible to spoil an infant by picking it up whenever it cries?
c. Should you help a child do things before the child reaches the point of frustration?
d. What advice would you give a parent who tends to be overprotective and consistently curtails a child's exploration?
e. If a child is attempting to do something, isn't it helpful to show the child the right way or a better way to do it?
f. Isn't it possible that a child will become conceited if he or she is consistently praised for accomplishments?
g. Do you think adolescents should be treated as adults before the law? Do you think it's fair to have more lenient punishments for juveniles than for adults? (Introduce the idea of psychosocial moratorium.)

Objective 3.3: List the factors that influence the development of self-concept and specific ways in which teachers can encourage positive self-esteem.

appearances. Children assume that others share their feelings and perceptions. Their thinking about themselves and others is simple, segmented, and rule-bound, not flexible and integrated into organized systems. In time, children are able to think abstractly about internal processes—beliefs, intentions, values, motivations. With these developments, knowledge of self, others, and situations can incorporate more abstract qualities (Berk, 1994).

Self-Concept and Self-Esteem

Test Bank items 3.25–3.31, 3.76, 3.96, 3.98, 3.106, 3.108, 3.109

The term **self-concept** is part of our everyday conversation. We talk about people who have a "low" self-concept or individuals whose self-concept is not "strong," as if self-concept were fluid levels in a car or a muscle to be developed. In psychology, the term generally refers to "the composite of ideas, feelings, and attitudes people have about themselves" (Hilgard, Atkinson, & Atkinson, 1979, p. 605). We could also consider the self-concept to be our attempt to explain ourselves to ourselves, to build a scheme (in Piaget's terms) that organizes our impressions, feelings, and attitudes about ourselves. But this model or scheme is not permanent, unified, or unchanging. Our self-perceptions vary from situation to situation and from one phase of our lives to another.

Self-esteem is our evaluation of our own self-concept. If people have positive self-concepts—if they "like what they see" in themselves—we say that they have high self-esteem. The terms are often used interchangeably, even though they have distinct meanings.

How Self-Concept Develops. Young children see themselves in terms of their physical appearance, name, actions, and abilities, but do not have a sense of their enduring characteristics or "personality." As they mature, children move from concrete, fragmented views of themselves to more abstract, organized, and objective views that include psychological characteristics. In answer to the question, "Who are you?" a 7-year-old might say, "I am a girl. I have long, brown hair. My favorite color is blue, and my favorite food is nachos." A 9- or a 10-year-old might answer the same question by listing traits such as, "I'm funny and lazy, but I'm smart in arithmetic. I'm silly sometimes." Older children's self-descriptions include interpersonal and social characteristics such as friendly, shy, a good team member, a Girl Scout. As they enter adolescence, children begin to think of themselves in terms of abstract values and attitudes. As Erikson and Marcia noted, decisions about religion, philosophy of life, sexual beliefs, and career choices become part of the self-concept during high school and college, when identity issues are being resolved.

There is another change as students mature. From about fourth grade on, self-esteem tends to increase, at least for boys. One exception is just after transition to a new school, especially the transition to high school. Until students adjust to the new demands of schedules and workload, they may experience a decrease in self-esteem.

A recent study, however, found that women and men do not show the change in self-esteem during adolescence. Girls, aged 8 and 9, reported feeling confident, assertive, and authoritative about themselves. But they emerged from adolescence with a poor self-image, constrained views of their future and

Self-Concept Our perceptions about ourselves.

Self-Esteem The value each of us places on our own characteristics, abilities, and behaviors.

their place in society, and much less confidence about themselves and their abilities (American Association of University Women, 1991). Other studies indicate that for most ethnic groups (except African-American) males are more confident about their abilities in school, particularly in math and science (Grossman & Grossman, 1994).

The developing self-concept of the child is influenced by parents and other family members in the early years and by friends, schoolmates, and teachers as the child grows. Before about age 7, children tend to see themselves in global terms—if they have a positive self-concept, they assume that they are good in all areas of performance (Harter, 1990). But as they mature, children's views of themselves become more differentiated; that is, multiple concepts of the self come into play. For example, an 11-year-old girl may see herself simultaneously as a loyal friend, an alienated family member, a strong math student, an uncoordinated athlete, and so on. As part of this differentiation, separate concepts of self as student (academic self-concepts) and self beyond school (nonacademic self-concepts) emerge (Byrne & Shavelson, 1986; Marsh, 1990; Shavelson, Hubner, & Stanton, 1976). One view of the structure of self-concept is shown in Figure 3.1.

Research: American Association of University Women (1991). *Shortchanging girls, shortchanging America.* Washington, DC: AAUW. This report of a nationwide poll to assess the self-esteem, educational experiences, interest in math and science, and career aspirations of boys and girls ages 9 to 15 is available from the American Association of University Women Sales Office, P.O. Box 251, Annapolis Junction, MD 20701-0251 (phone 800-225-9998).

Handout Master 3.5. "Self-Esteem Index," in the *Instructor's Resource Manual* graphically represents the results of this poll. See also Prose, F. (1990). Confident at 11, confused at 16. *The New York Times Magazine.*

FIGURE 3.1

STRUCTURE OF SELF-CONCEPT
Students have many separate but sometimes related concepts of themselves. The overall sense of self appears to be divided into at least three separate, but slightly related, self-concepts—English, mathematics, and nonacademic.

Source: H. W. Marsh and R. J. Shavelson (1985). Self-concept: Its multifaceted, hierarchical structure. *Educational Psychologist, 20,* p. 114. Adapted by permission of the publisher and authors.

Transparency: Use acetate transparency T 17, "The Structure of Self-Concept." This diagram shows the interrelationships among academic and nonacademic aspects of self-concept.

As you can see, the person's general view of self is made up of other, more specific concepts, including the nonacademic self-concept, self-concept in English, and self-concept in mathematics. These self-concepts at the second level are themselves made up of more specific, separate conceptions of the self, such as conceptions about physical ability, appearance, relations with peers, and relations with family (particularly parents), based on many experiences and events such as how well we do in sports; how we regard our body, skin, or hair; our friendships; our artistic abilities; our contributions to community groups, and so on.

The self-concept evolves through constant self-evaluation in different situations (Shavelson & Bolus, 1982). Children and adolescents are continually asking themselves, in effect, "How am I doing?" They compare their performance with their own standards and with the performances of peers. They also gauge the verbal and nonverbal reactions of significant people—parents, best friends, leaders, teachers. The context of school makes a difference too. Students who are strong in math in an average school feel better about their math skills than students of equal ability in high-achieving schools. Marsh (1990) calls this the "Big-Fish-Little-Pond Effect." The way individuals explain their successes or failures also is important. We must attribute our successes to our own actions, not to luck or to special assistance, in order to build self-esteem.

Background: See Canfield, J. (1990). Improving students' self-concepts. *Educational Leadership, 48*(1), 48–50.

Self-Concept and School Life. For teachers, there are at least two questions to ask about self-concept: (1) How does self-concept affect a student's behavior in school? (2) How does life in school affect a student's self-concept?

In answer to the first question, it appears that students with higher self-esteem are somewhat more likely to be successful in school (Marsh, 1990), although the strength of the relationship varies greatly, depending on the characteristics of the students and the research methods used (Hansford & Hattie, 1982; Marsh & Holmes, 1990). In addition, higher self-esteem is related to more favorable attitudes toward school, more positive behavior in the classroom, and greater popularity with other students (Cauley & Tyler, 1989; Metcalfe, 1981; Reynolds, 1980). Of course, as we discussed in chapter 1, knowing that two variables are related (correlated) does not tell us that one is causing the other. It may be that high achievement and popularity lead to positive self-concept, or vice versa. In fact, it probably works both ways (Marsh, 1987; Shavelson & Bolus, 1982).

This leads us to the second question of how school affects self-concept. Good and Weinstein (1986) make this observation:

> School is a place where children develop or fail to develop a variety of competencies that come to define self and ability, where friendships with peers are nurtured, and where the role of the community member is played out, all during a highly formative period of development. Thus the building of self-esteem, interpersonal competence, social problem solving, and leadership becomes important in its own right and as a critical underpinning of success in academic learning. (p. 1095)

Is school really so important? A recent study that followed 322 sixth-grade students for two years would say yes. Hoge, Smit, and Hanson (1990) found that students' satisfaction with the school, their sense that classes were interesting and that teachers cared, and teacher feedback and evaluations influ-

TABLE 3.3	Suggestions for Encouraging Self-Esteem

1. Value and accept all pupils, for their attempts as well as their accomplishments.

2. Create a climate that is physically and psychologically safe for students.

3. Become aware of your own personal biases (everyone has some biases) and expectations.

4. Make sure that your procedures for teaching and grouping students are really necessary, not just a convenient way of handling problem students or avoiding contact with some students.

5. Make standards of evaluation clear; help students learn to evaluate their own accomplishments.

6. Model appropriate methods of self-criticism, perseverance, and self-reward.

7. Avoid destructive comparisons and competition; encourage students to compete with their own prior levels of achievement.

8. Accept a student even when you must reject a particular behavior or outcome. Students should feel confident, for example, that failing a test or being reprimanded in class does not make them "bad" people.

9. Remember that positive self-concept grows from success in operating in the world *and* from being valued by important people in the environment.

10. Encourage students to take responsibility for their reactions to events; show them that they have choices in how to respond.

11. Set up support groups or "study buddies" in school and teach students how to encourage each other.

12. Help students set clear goals and objectives; brainstorm about resources they have for reaching their goals.

13. Highlight the value of different ethnic groups—their cultures and accomplishments.

Sources: Information from J. Canfield (1990), Improving students' self-esteem, *Educational Leadership, 48*(1) pp. 48–50; M. M. Kash & G. Borich (1978), *Teacher behavior and student self-concept* (Menlo Park, CA: Addison-Wesley); H. H. Marshall (1989), The development of self-concept, *Young Children, 44*(5) pp. 44–51.

enced students' self-esteem. Teacher feedback and grades in particular subjects affected self-concepts in those subjects. In physical education, teachers' opinions were especially powerful in shaping students' conceptions of their athletic abilities. Interestingly, special programs like "Student of the Month" or admission to advanced math classes had little effect on self-esteem. (Relate this to the "Big-Fish-Little-Pond Effect.")

So teachers can make a difference in how students feel about their abilities in particular subjects. Given this responsibility, what can teachers do? The recommendations in Table 3.3 are a beginning.

The Self and Others   Test Bank items 3.32, 3.33, 3.89, 3.98

As we seek our own identity and form images of ourselves in various academic and social situations, we are also seeking and forming ways to understand the "significant others" around us. Children learn to see themselves as separate and to see others as separate people as well, with their own identities. How do we learn to interpret what others are thinking and feeling?

Intention.   Around the age of 2, children have a sense of intention, at least of their own intentions. They will announce, "I'm gonna get a puppy" or "I wanna peanut butter sandwich." They can say firmly, "I didn't drop it on purpose!" By 2-1/2 or 3 years old, children extend the understanding of intention to others. Older preschoolers who get along well with their peers are

Research: Hartup, W. W. (1989). Social relationships and their developmental significance. *American Psychologist, 44*, 120–126.

Multicultural Awareness: American Guidance Service (Publishers' Building, Circle Pines, MN 55014–1796, phone 800-328-2560. In Minnesota, 800-247-5053) publishes DUSO-Revised: Developing Understanding of Self and Others. In this program for elementary students are story books, audio cassettes, puppets, activities, and a teacher's guide. Topics covered include appreciation of individual differences, social skills, making choices, recognizing the consequences of actions, communication, and awareness of feelings. This program was the focus of controversy in Pennsylvania when parents protested the teaching of values in schools.

able to separate intentional from unintentional actions and react accordingly. For example, they will not get angry when another child accidentally knocks over their block tower. But aggressive children have more trouble assessing intention. They are likely to attack anyone who topples their tower, even accidentally (Berk, 1994; Dodge & Somberg, 1987). As children mature, they are more able to assess and consider the intentions of others.

Taking the Perspective of Others.   Very young children don't understand that other people have different feelings and experiences. But this **perspective-taking ability** develops over time until it is quite sophisticated in adults. Robert Selman has developed a five-stage model to describe the development of perspective-taking. Consider this situation:

> Holly is an 8-year-old girl who likes to climb trees. She is the best tree climber in the neighborhood. One day while climbing a tree she falls off the bottom branch but does not hurt herself. Her father sees her fall. He is upset and asks her to promise not to climb trees anymore. Holly promises.
>
> Later that day, Holly and her friends meet Sean. Sean's kitten is caught up in a tree and cannot get down. Something has to be done right away or the kitten may fall. Holly is the only one who climbs trees well enough to reach the kitten and get it down, but she remembers her promise to her father. (Selman & Byrne, 1974, p. 805)

If children of different ages are presented with this problem and asked such questions as, "If Holly climbs the tree, should she be punished?" "Will her father understand if she climbs the tree?" "Will Sean understand why Holly has trouble deciding what to do?" the children will give answers like those in Table 3.4. As children mature, they take more information into account. They realize that different people can react differently to the same situation. They develop the ability to analyze the perspectives of several people involved in a situation from the viewpoint of an objective bystander, and they can even imagine how different cultural or social values would influence the perceptions of the bystander (Berk, 1993).

Focus on . . .   **Understanding Ourselves and Others**

- Distinguish between self-concept and self-esteem.
- How does self-concept change as children develop?
- Describe the changes in perspective-taking that occur as students mature.

Objective 3.4: Describe Kohlberg's stages of moral reasoning, and give an example of each.

Perspective-Taking Ability Understanding that others have different feelings and experiences.

Moral Realism Stage of development wherein children see rules as absolute.

Moral Development   Test Bank items 3.34–3.36, 3.104

If you have spent time with young children, you know that there is a period when you can say, "Eating in the living room is not allowed!" and get away with it. For young children, rules simply exist. Piaget (1965) called this the state of **moral realism**. At this stage, the child of 5 or 6 believes that rules about conduct or rules about how to play a game are absolute and can't be changed. If a rule is broken, the child believes that the punishment should be determined by how much damage is done, not by the intention of the child or by other cir-

TABLE 3.4 Selman's Five Stages of Perspective-Taking

Children's responses to Holly's dilemma show developmental changes in perspective-taking—the ability to imagine what other people are thinking and feeling.

Stage	Age	Description	Typical Response to the "Holly" Dilemma
Undifferentiated perspective-taking	3–6	Children recognize that the self and others can have different thoughts and feelings, but they frequently confuse the two.	The child predicts that Holly will save the kitten because she does not want it to get hurt and believes that Holly's father will feel just as she does about her climbing the tree: "Happy, he likes kittens."
Social-informational perspective-taking	5–9	Children understand that different perspectives may result because people have access to different information.	When asked how Holly's father will react when he finds out that she climbed the tree, the child responds, "If he didn't know anything about the kitten, he would be angry. But if Holly shows him the kitten, he might change his mind."
Self-reflective perspective-taking	7–12	Children can "step in another person's shoes" and view their own thoughts, feelings, and behavior from the other person's perspective. They also recognize that others can do the same.	When asked whether Holly thinks she will be punished, the child says, "No. Holly knows that her father will understand why she climbed the tree." This response assumes that Holly's point of view is influenced by her father being able to "step in her shoes" and understand why she saved the kitten.
Third-party perspective-taking	10–15	Children can step outside a two-person situation and imagine how the self and other are viewed from the point of view of a third, impartial party.	When asked whether Holly should be punished, the child says, "No, because Holly thought it was important to save the kitten. But she also knows that her father told her not to climb the tree. So she'd only think she shouldn't be punished if she could get her father to understand why she had to climb the tree." This response steps outside the immediate situation to view both Holly's and her father's perspectives simultaneously.
Societal perspective-taking	14–Adult	Individuals understand that third-party perspective-taking can be influenced by one or more systems of larger societal values.	When asked if Holly should be punished, the individual responds, "No. The value of humane treatment of animals justifies Holly's action. Her father's appreciation of this value will lead him not to punish her."

Source: From Laura E. Berk, *Infants, Children, and Adolescents,* p. 467. Copyright © 1993 by Allyn and Bacon. Reprinted by permission.

cumstances. So accidentally breaking three cups is worse than intentionally breaking one, and in the child's eyes, the punishment for the three-cup offense should be greater.

As children interact with others, develop perspective-taking abilities, and see that different people have different rules, there is a gradual shift to a **morality of cooperation.** Children come to understand that people make rules and

Morality of Cooperation Stage of development wherein children realize that people make rules and people can change them.

people can change them. When rules are broken, both the damage done and the intention of the offender are taken into account. These developmental changes and others are reflected in Kohlberg's theory of moral development, based in part on Piaget's ideas.

POINT ■ COUNTERPOINT   Should Schools Teach Values?

For years, educators, parents, religious leaders, and politicians have debated whether the schools are responsible for moral education. Should the schools teach students about morality, or is this the sole responsibility of families and the community? Should values be transmitted to students by direct teaching, modeling, and exhortation, or should students be taught to make judgments and decisions, and clarify their own values?

POINT Moral education belongs in the schools.

According to Edward Wynne (1986):

> The transmission of moral values has been the dominant educational concern of most cultures throughout history. Most educational systems have been simultaneously concerned with the transmission of cognitive knowledge—skills, information, and techniques of intellectual analysis—but these admittedly important educational aims have rarely been given priority over moral education. The current policies in American education that give secondary priority to transmitting morality represent a sharp fracture with the great tradition. (p. 4)

Wynne goes on to argue that all societies must socialize young people to work for the good of the society and not to act on purely selfish instincts. Children must be taught not just to mouth abstract moral principles, but to conduct themselves morally in the everyday spaces of their lives. No one segment of society has the sole responsibility for this teaching. In fact, all the people and institutions of a society—the family, the schools, religious institutions, community organizations, the media—must model and teach moral values. In the 1990s, as we are dismayed by rising crime, rampant drug use, violence, racial hatred, and the disintegration of the family, we cannot leave moral education to any one group: all institutions, including the schools, must assume this responsibility.

COUNTERPOINT The schools should not teach morality or values.

There are two very different arguments against the direct teaching of morals and values in schools. The first argument is that moral education is the sole responsibility of the family. If schools teach values, whose values will they teach? Which culture or religion, if any, should be the guide? What if the school's teachings contradict the values of a child's family? Of course, we might all agree on the values of honesty, equality, and justice, but what do these values mean when applied to issues such as school prayer, abortion, divorce, safe sex, gun control, or capital punishment? If the school has no position on these issues, it has no moral authority. It seems to communicate that "anything goes." But if the school takes a position, how can it help but offend some students and their families?

The second argument often made against moral education in the schools is that schools should not teach values directly but should instead "help students *clarify their own values,* learn higher levels of *moral reasoning,* and learn the skills of *value analysis*" (Kirschenbaum, 1992, p. 771). In a pluralistic society there is no consensus about the "best" values. In addition, the moral dilemmas of the future cannot be anticipated today. So it is better for students to learn *how to reason* about moral issues than *what to think.*

Howard Kirschenbaum (1992) suggests that schools take a comprehensive approach to moral education by both teaching moral values and helping students learn to reason about morality.

> Young people deserve to be exposed to the inculcation of values by adults who care: family members, teachers, and the community. They deserve to see models of adults with a joy for living. And they deserve to have opportunities that encourage them to learn the skills of guiding their own lives. (p. 775)

Test Bank items
3.37–3.44, 3.78,
3.79, 3.90, 3.96, 3.99

Kohlberg's Stages of Moral Development

Lawrence Kohlberg (1963, 1975, 1981) has proposed a detailed sequence of stages of **moral reasoning,** or judgments about right and wrong, and has led the field in studying their evolution. He has divided moral development into three levels: (1) preconventional, where judgment is based solely on a person's own needs and perceptions; (2) conventional, where the expectations of society and law are taken into account; and (3) postconventional, where judgments are based on abstract, more personal principles that are not necessarily defined by society's laws. Each of these three levels is then subdivided into stages, as shown in Table 3.5.

Kohlberg has evaluated the moral reasoning of both children and adults by presenting them with **moral dilemmas,** or hypothetical situations in which

Background: With the death of Lawrence Kohlberg in 1987, American psychology reflected back on his work and how it shaped the field, particularly in the study of morality. The publication *Counseling and Values* (April 1988) was dedicated to his work. It contains numerous articles by researchers influenced by Kohlberg. It also includes a short biography.

TABLE 3.5   Kohlberg's Stage Theory of Moral Reasoning

Level 1. Preconventional Moral Reasoning

Judgment is based on personal needs and others' rules.

Stage 1   Punishment-Obedience Orientation
Rules are obeyed to avoid punishment. A good or bad action is determined by its physical consequences.

Stage 2   Personal Reward Orientation
Personal needs determine right and wrong. Favors are returned along the lines of "You scratch my back, I'll scratch yours."

Level 2. Conventional Moral Reasoning

Judgment is based on others' approval, family expectations, traditional values, the laws of society, and loyalty to country.

Stage 3   Good Boy–Nice Girl Orientation
Good means "nice." It is determined by what pleases, aids, and is approved by others.

Stage 4   Law and Order Orientation
Laws are absolute. Authority must be respected and the social order maintained.

Level 3. Postconventional Moral Reasoning

Stage 5   Social Contract Orientation
Good is determined by socially agreed-upon standards of individual rights. This is a morality similar to that of the U.S. Constitution.

Stage 6* Universal Ethical Principle Orientation
Good and right are matters of individual conscience and involve abstract concepts of justice, human dignity, and equality.

---

*In later work Kohlberg questioned whether Stage 6 exists separately from Stage 5.

Source: Adapted by permission of the *Journal of Philosophy* from L. Kohlberg (1975). The cognitive-developmental approach to moral education. *Phi Delta Kappan, 56,* p. 671.

Moral Reasoning   The thinking processes involved in judgments about questions of right and wrong.

Moral Dilemmas   Situations in which no choice is clearly and indisputably right.

Research: For a concise discussion of the recent research on moral development, see Nucci, L. (1987). Synthesis of research on moral development. *Educational Leadership, 44*(5), 86–92. This article is reprinted in the *Annual editions: Educational psychology 88/89* (Guilford, CT: Duskin). Highlights of the article: Nucci's article is a nice contrast to Kohlberg's analysis of moral development. Nucci suggests that even young children can distinguish between conventions and moral issues. Conventions are rules and expectations that vary from one group to the next, such as dating practices, "politeness" norms, or rules about talking in study hall. Moral issues have to do with such actions as physically or psychologically hurting others, stealing, lying—any activity that would be "wrong" even if there were no rule or law forbidding it. One goal of moral education should be to help children differentiate between the norms and conventions of their culture and universal moral concerns for justice, fairness, and human welfare. To help children understand these distinctions, Nucci suggests: (1) Moral education should focus on issues of justice and human welfare. (2) These concerns should be integrated into the curriculum, not taught as separate programs. (3) Moral discussion promotes moral development when students are at slightly different levels of moral development, are allowed to disagree about solutions to moral dilemmas, and really listen to each other, trying to understand, expand on, or refute each other's opinions. (4) Cooperative goal structures encourage moral development. (5) Firm, fair, flexible classroom management practices contribute to moral development.

Objective 3.5: Describe alternatives to Kohlberg's theory of moral development.

people must make difficult decisions. Subjects are asked what the person caught in the dilemma should do, and why. In these situations there is no obvious answer; no action will provide a complete solution.

One of the most commonly used moral dilemmas can be summarized as follows: A man's wife is dying. There is one drug that could save her, but it is very expensive, and the druggist who invented it will not sell it at a price low enough for the man to buy it. Finally, the man becomes desperate and considers stealing the drug for his wife. What should he do, and why?

At level 1 (preconventional), the child's answer might be, "It is wrong to steal because you might get caught." This answer reflects the child's basic egocentrism. The reasoning might be: "What would happen to me if I stole something? I might get caught and punished."

At level 2 (the conventional level), the subject is able to look beyond the immediate personal consequences and consider the views, and especially the approval, of others. Laws, religious or civil, are very important and are regarded as absolute and unalterable. One answer stressing adherence to rules is, "It is wrong to steal because it is against the law." Another answer, placing high value on loyalty to family and loved ones but still respecting the law, is, "It's right to steal because the man means well—he's trying to help his wife. But he will still have to pay the druggist when he can or accept the penalty for breaking the law."

At level 3 (the postconventional level), an answer might be, "It is not wrong to steal because human life must be preserved. The worth of a human life is greater than the worth of property." This response considers the underlying values that might be involved in the decision. Abstract concepts are no longer rigid, and, as the name of this level implies, principles can be separated from conventional values. A person reasoning on this level understands that what is considered right by the majority may not be considered right by an individual in a particular situation. Rational, personal choice is stressed.

Moral reasoning is related to both cognitive and emotional development. As we have seen, abstract thinking becomes increasingly important in the higher stages of moral development, as children move from decisions based on absolute rules to decisions based on principles such as justice and mercy. The ability to see another's perspective and to imagine alternative bases for laws and rules also enters into judgments at the higher stages.

Alternatives to Kohlberg's Theory   Test Bank item 3.82

Kohlberg's stage theory has been criticized, first, because the stages do not seem in reality to be separate, sequenced, and consistent. People often give reasons for moral choices that reflect several different stages simultaneously. Or a person's choices in one instance may fit one stage and in a different situation may reflect another stage. When asked to reason about helping someone else versus meeting their own needs, both children and adolescents reason at higher levels than when they are asked to reason about breaking the law or risking punishment (Eisenberg et al., 1987; Sobesky, 1983).

Social Conventions versus Moral Issues.   Another criticism is that Kohlberg's theory does not differentiate between social conventions and true moral issues until the higher stages of moral reasoning. Social conventions are the social rules and expectations of a particular group or society—for example, "It is rude to eat with your hands." Such behavior would not be inappropriate if there were no social convention prohibiting it. True moral issues, on the other hand, involve the rights of individuals, the general welfare of the group, or the avoidance of harm. "Stealing" would be wrong, even if there were no "rule" against it. Children as young as 3 can distinguish between social conventions and moral issues. They know, for example, that being noisy in school would be fine if there were no rule requiring quiet but that it would not be right to hit another child, even if there were no rule against it. So even very young children can reason based on moral principles that are not tied to social conventions and rules (Nucci, 1987; Smetana & Braeges, 1990; Turiel, 1983).

Cultural Differences in Moral Reasoning.   Another criticism of Kohlberg's stage theory is that stages 5 and 6 in moral reasoning are biased in favor of Western, male values that emphasize individualism. In cultures that are more family centered or group oriented, the highest moral value might involve putting the opinions of the group before decisions based on individual conscience. There has been much disagreement over the "highest" moral stage. Kohlberg himself has questioned the applicability of stage 6. Few people other than trained philosophers reason naturally or easily at this level. Kohlberg (1984) suggested that for all practical purposes, stages 5 and 6 might be combined.

The Morality of Caring.   One of the most hotly debated criticisms of Kohlberg's theory is that the stages are biased in favor of males and do not represent the way moral reasoning develops in women. Because the stage theory was based on a longitudinal study of men only, it is very possible that the moral reasoning of women and the stages of women's development are not adequately represented (Gilligan, 1982; Gilligan & Attanucci, 1988). Carol Gilligan (1982) has proposed a different sequence of moral development, an "ethic of care." Gilligan suggests that individuals move from a focus on self-interests to moral reasoning based on commitment to specific individuals and relationships, and then to the highest level of morality based on the principles of responsibility and care for all people.

The highest stage in Kohlberg's theory of moral development involves decisions based on universal principles of justice and fairness. Reasoning based on caring for others and maintaining relationships is scored at a lower level. Many of Kohlberg's early studies of moral reasoning found that most men progressed to stages 4 and 5 by adulthood, while most women "stayed" at stage 3. This makes it appear as if women are moral midgets. But recent studies find few significant differences between men and women, or boys and girls, in their level of moral reasoning as measured by Kohlberg's procedures (Thoma, 1986).

In order to study moral reasoning as it actually happens in real life, and to get an idea about the basis for decisions, Walker and his colleagues (Walker, 1989; Lawrence, Walker, de Vries, & Trevarthan, 1987) asked children, adolescents, and adults to describe a personal moral problem and to analyze a traditional moral dilemma. For both types of problems, males and females revealed both a morality of caring and a concern with justice. Andrew Garrod

Activity 3.1: Multicultural Awareness. See the *Instructor's Resource Manual* for Culture and Morality, an activity that explores cultural differences in moral reasoning. **Handout Master 3.4** in the *Instructor's Resource Manual* provides a form for self-assessment on moral issues evaluated by Hindu and American children in a 1987 study.

Transparency: Use acetate transparency **T 16**, "Stages of Moral Reasoning." This chart compares the theories of L. Kohlberg and C. Gilligan.

Background: Harvard Graduate School of Education (1990, July/August). Girls at 11: An interview with Carol Gilligan. *Harvard Education Newsletter, 6*(4), 5–7.

Activity 3.2: Background. See the *Instructors' Resource Manual* for a summary of Caring Kids: The Role of the School, an article by A. Kohn in the March 1991 issue of *Phi Delta Kappan.*

and his colleagues (1990) used fables to study the moral reasoning of first, third, and fifth graders and found that both boys and girls tended to adopt a care orientation. With the exception of a few fifth-grade boys who suggested solutions involving violence or tricks, there were no differences between first- and third-grade boys and girls. So justice and caring seem to be important bases for moral reasoning for both men and women. Gilligan's criticisms and ideas have broadened the view of what constitutes morality.

Empathy.   **Empathy** is the ability to feel an emotion as it is experienced by another person—to put yourself in another's shoes. Both adults and children respond emotionally to signs of distress in others. But the emotional reaction of a young child is not based on an understanding of how another feels, since the child cannot yet see the other's emotions as separate. Very young children may respond to seeing another child hurt as if they had been hurt themselves. A little later, children begin to be aware that others' feelings are separate but assume that those feelings must be the same as their own. For example, a young boy might give his "blankie" to a friend who is crying, assuming that the friend would want exactly the same comfort he himself usually wants in a time of trouble. Children eventually become more and more able to imagine how other people would feel in a given situation. As they develop perspective-taking skills, their sense of empathy develops as well.

Empathy plays an important part in our ability to understand and get along with one another (Chapman, Zahn-Waxler, Cooperman, & Iannotti,

Empathy Ability to feel emotion as experienced by others.

The ability to empathize with others and respect their views can be learned more readily by working toward common goals than by listening to a lecture from the teacher on the importance of respect. Here these "study buddies" check each other's work.

1987). Children who are empathetic are more compassionate and more likely to help others (Eisenberg & Miller, 1987; Eisenberg et al., 1987). Teachers can encourage the development of empathy by allowing students to work together and discuss emotional reactions to various experiences. When disputes arise in the later elementary and the secondary grades, teachers can resist the temptation to quote rules or act as a judge; instead, they can help the students see one another's point of view.

Moral Behavior   Test Bank items 3.45–3.48, 3.96

As people move toward higher stages of moral reasoning, they also evidence more sharing, helping, and defending of victims of injustice. This relationship between moral reasoning and moral behavior is not very strong, however (Berk, 1993). Many other factors besides reasoning affect behavior. Two important influences on moral behavior are internalization and modeling.

Most theories of moral behavior assume that young children's moral behavior is first controlled by others through direct instruction, supervision, rewards and punishments, and correction. But in time, children **internalize** the moral rules and principles of the authority figures who have guided them; that is, children adopt the external standards as their own. If children are given reasons when they are corrected or instructed about their actions, then they are more likely to internalize moral principles. They can then behave morally even when "no one is watching." Reasons that highlight the effects of actions on others, stated in language the child can understand, are helpful (Berk, 1994; Hoffman, 1988).

A second important influence on the development of moral behavior is modeling. Children who have been consistently exposed to caring, generous adult models will tend to be more concerned for the rights and feelings of others (Lipscomb, MacAllister, & Bregman, 1985). Let's consider several moral issues that arise in classrooms.

Cheating.   Early research indicates that cheating seems to have more to do with the particular situation than with the general honesty or dishonesty of the individual (R. Burton, 1963). A student who cheats in math class is probably more likely to cheat in other classes, but may never consider lying to a friend or taking candy from the store. Most students will cheat if the pressure to perform well is great and the chances of being caught are slim. When asked why students cheat, the 1,100 high school subjects in a study by Schab (1980) listed three reasons: being too lazy to study, fear of failure, and parental pressure for good grades. These students were very pessimistic about the incidence of cheating. Both boys and girls in the survey believed that over 97 percent of their peers had cheated at one time or another. However, this estimate may have been high; figures depend partly on how cheating is defined.

The implications for teachers are straightforward. To prevent cheating, try to avoid putting students in high-pressure situations. Make sure they are well prepared for tests, projects, and assignments so they can do reasonably well without cheating. Make extra help available for those who need it. Be clear about your policies in regard to cheating, and enforce them consistently. Help students resist temptation by monitoring carefully during testing.

Discussion: Moral action does not necessarily follow directly from moral judgment. But is it necessary for moral judgment to precede moral action? That is, can a person behave in a moral way even if he or she cannot make a cognitive statement about how one "should" behave?

Background: Lickona, T. (1988). Four strategies for fostering character development in children. *Phi Delta Kappan, 70,* 419–423.

Objective 3.6: Explain the factors that encourage cheating and aggression in classrooms, and discuss possible responses to each.

Multicultural Awareness: In a classroom discussion about stealing, the teacher finds that many students express the opinion that it is all right to steal if you don't get caught. How should a teacher respond? Would the race, culture, gender, or socioeconomic status of the student influence the teacher's response?

Activity 3.3: Background. See the *Instructor's Resource Manual* for a summary of Cheating and Plagiarism, an article in the September 1987 issue of the *Harvard Education Letter.*

Activity 3.4: Application. See the *Instructor's Resource Manual* for Moral Dilemma, an activity that asks your students to respond to a common moral issue—cheating.

Connections: To lessen the emphasis on tests in grading, teachers can use authentic assessment techniques, discussed in chapter 15.

Internalize Process whereby children adopt external standards as their own.

Guidelines

Dealing with Aggression and Encouraging Cooperation

Casebook: See the Teachers' Casebook at the end of this chapter for tips on handling student aggression.

Activity 3.5: Cooperative Learning. See the *Instructor's Resource Manual* for Issues of Socialization, a group activity that considers the problem of gang violence.

"SCOTT, YOU'VE BEEN WATCHING TOO MUCH TV."

(© *Stan Fine*—Phi Delta Kappan)

Aggression Bold, direct action that is intended to hurt someone else or take property; unprovoked attack.

Present yourself as a nonaggressive model.

Examples
1. Do not use threats of aggression to win obedience.
2. When problems arise, model nonviolent conflict-resolution strategies.

Ensure that your classroom has enough space and appropriate materials for every student.

Examples
1. Prevent overcrowding.
2. Make sure prized toys or resources are plentiful.
3. Remove or confiscate materials that encourage personal aggression, such as toy guns.

Make sure students do not profit from aggressive behaviors.

Examples
1. Comfort the victim of aggression and ignore the aggressor.
2. Use reasonable punishment, especially with older students.

Teach directly about positive social behaviors.

Examples
1. Incorporate lessons on social ethics/morality through reading selections and discussions.
2. Discuss the effects of antisocial actions such as stealing, bullying, and spreading rumors.

Provide opportunities for learning tolerance and cooperation.

Examples
1. Emphasize the similarities among people rather than the differences.
2. Set up group projects that encourage cooperation.

Aggression. **Aggression** is not to be confused with assertiveness, which means affirming or maintaining a legitimate right. Helen Bee (1981) gives this example of the difference between the two types of behavior: "A child who says, 'That's my toy!' is showing assertiveness. If he bashes his playmate over the head to reclaim it, he has shown aggression" (p. 350).

Modeling plays an important role in the expression of aggression (Bandura, Ross, & Ross, 1963). Children who grow up in homes filled with harsh punishment and family violence are more likely to use aggression to solve their own problems (Emery, 1989; Holden & Ritchie, 1991).

One very real source of aggressive models is found in almost every home in America—television. Most children spend more time watching television than they do in any other activity except sleep (Timmer, Eccles, & O'Brien, 1988). You can reduce the negative effects of TV violence by stressing three points with your students: most people do not behave in the aggressive ways shown on television; the violent acts on TV are not real, but are created by special effects and stunts; and there are better ways to resolve conflicts, and these are the ways most real people use to solve their problems (Huessmann, Eron, Klein, Brice, & Fischer, 1983).

Many popular films and video games are also filled with graphic depictions of violence, sometimes performed by the "hero." Students growing up in the inner cities see street gangs and drug deals. Newspapers, magazines, and the radio are filled with stories of murders, rapes, and robberies. In some preschools the children don't play "Mommy" and "Daddy"; they pretend to sell "nickel bags" of heroin to their playmates. This description appeared in the *Washington Post* (June 2, 1988):

> As children huddle, drug games begin. From one child's pocket comes chalk, crushed to resemble cocaine, inside plastic sandwich bags smuggled from home. Soon another child passes cash—thick knots of Monopoly money, or notebook paper, wrapped with rubber bands and dubbed "bankroll."

Socialization: The Home and the School

Socialization is the process by which the mature members of a society, such as parents and teachers, shape the behaviors of children, enabling them to fully participate in and contribute to the society. In this section we will consider two of the most important influences on the development and socialization of children—the family and the school.

American Families Today

Test Bank items 3.49–58, 3.60, 3.80, 3.81, 3.91, 3.100, 3.103–3.107

The most appropriate expectation to have about your students' families is no expectation at all. The idea of two parents, 2.2 children, Dad with the only job, and Mom in the kitchen is no longer the norm. In fact, this pattern held true for only 7 percent of American families in the mid-1980s, down from 60 percent in the 1950s (Hodgkinson, 1985).

More students today will have only one or no sibling, or they may be part of **blended families,** with stepbrothers or stepsisters who move in and out of their lives. Some of your students may live with an aunt, with grandparents, with one parent, in foster or adoptive homes, or with an older brother or sister. So the best advice is to drop the phrases "your parents" and "your mother and father" and to speak of "your family" when talking to students.

Many middle-class couples are waiting longer to have children and are providing more material advantages. Children in these homes may have more "things," but they may also have less time with their parents. Of course, not all students are middle-class. About one-quarter of all children under 18 live with one parent, usually their mother, and almost half of these families have incomes below the poverty level (U.S. Bureau of the Census, 1990). Your students are likely to be alone or unsupervised much of the day. The growing

Transparency: Use acetate transparency **T 23,** "The Effects of Media Violence: Underlying Processes."

Background: For an interesting discussion of aggressive children in school, see Bullies and their victims (1987, November). *Harvard Education Letter, 3*(6), 1–3.

Background: See Noll, J. W. (1991). *Taking sides: Clashing views on controversial educational issues* (pp. 44–63) for Lawrence Kohlberg's and Edward Wynne's positions on "Should Values Be Developed Rather than Transmitted?" Professor Wynne feels that the schools, largely under the influence of Kohlberg's work, have abandoned important educational traditions.

Background: Involving parents (1991, special section). *Phi Delta Kappan, 72*(5), 344–388.

Socialization The ways in which members of a society encourage positive development for the immature individuals of the group.

Blended Families Parents, children, and stepchildren merged into families through remarriages.

© *1989 M. Twohy*—Phi Delta Kappan.

number of these *latchkey children* has prompted many schools to offer before- and after-school programs.

Growing Up Too Fast.   Joan Isenberg (1991) summarizes the situation confronting children in this way:

Today's youth live in a fast-paced, changing world characterized by social pressures that push them to grow up too fast. They are pressured to adapt to changing family patterns, to achieve academically at early ages, and to participate and compete in sports and specialized skills. Moreover, they are pressured to cope with adult information in the media before they have mastered the problems of childhood. Such pressure places increased responsibility and stress on children while simultaneously redefining the essence of childhood itself. (p. 38)

David Elkind (1986) talks about the "hurried child," and other psychologists note the "adultification" of children's television and literature. An article in *Newsweek* (1991) on "The End of Innocence" began with this story:

A 16-year-old Houston girl was babysitting for two boys, 6 and 9 years old. The kids were glued to the George Michael "I Want Your Sex" video on MTV. Singing along, the boys came to the words "sex with you alone." The younger one looked a little puzzled. "What's that thing when it isn't alone, when lots of people do it?" he asked. "A borney?" "No," his older brother shot back contemptuously. "You're so dumb. It's an orgy." (p. 62)

Student teachers in my classes are amazed at the seeming sophistication of their young students. Every night on the news, these children hear about drugs, sex, AIDS, and other "adult" subjects. But don't assume that because your students know the vocabulary, they really understand these subjects or are emotionally ready to deal with them.

Children of Divorce.   Many of your students, ready or not, have to deal with one adult issue—divorce. The divorce rate in the United States is the highest in the world, almost double that of the second-ranked nation, Sweden. By the year 2000, only about 30 percent of the students in the United States will live with both of their biological parents throughout their teen years (Nielsen, 1993).

As many of us know from experiences in our own families, separation and divorce are stressful events for all participants, even under the best circumstances. The actual separation of the parents may have been preceded by years of conflict in the home or may come as a shock to all, including friends and children. During the divorce itself, conflict may increase as property and custody rights are being decided.

After the divorce, more changes may disrupt the children's lives. The parent who has custody (today, as in the past, usually the mother) may have to move to a less-expensive home, find new sources of income, go to work for the first time, or work longer hours. For the child, this can mean leaving behind important friendships in the old neighborhood or school, just when support is needed the most. It may mean having just one parent, who has less time than ever to be with the children.

The economic hardships of divorce seem particularly great for women who take over as heads of their households. Only one in 19 two-parent families lives

Guidelines

Take note of any sudden changes in behavior that might indicate problems at home.

Examples

1. Be alert to physical symptoms like repeated headaches or stomach pains, rapid weight gain or loss, fatigue or excess energy.
2. Be aware of signs of emotional distress, like moodiness, temper tantrums, difficulty in paying attention or concentrating.
3. Let parents know about the students' signs of stress.

Talk individually to students about their attitude or behavior changes. This gives you a chance to find out about unusual stress such as divorce.

Examples

1. Be a good listener. Students may have no other adult willing to hear their concerns.
2. Let students know you are available to talk, and let the student set the agenda.

Watch your language to make sure you avoid stereotypes about "happy" (two-parent) homes.

Examples

1. Simply say "your families" instead of "your mothers and fathers" when addressing the class.
2. Avoid statements such as "We need volunteers for room mother" or "Your father can help you."

Help students maintain self-esteem.

Examples

1. Recognize a job well done.
2. Make sure the student understands the assignment and can handle the workload. This is not the time to pile on new and very difficult work.
3. The student may be angry at his or her parents, but may direct the anger at teachers. Don't take the student's anger personally.

Find out what resources are available at your school.

Examples

1. Talk to the school psychologist, guidance counselor, social worker, or principal about students who seem to need outside help.
2. Consider establishing a discussion group, led by a trained adult, for students going through a divorce.

Be sensitive to both parents' rights to information.

Examples

1. When parents have joint custody, both are entitled to receive information and attend parent-teacher conferences.
2. The noncustodial parent may still be concerned about the child's school progress. Check with your principal about state laws regarding the noncustodial parent's rights.

Background: Disappearance of childhood. What about the endless hours spent in front of the television? Are we simply robbing our children of time to play by letting them be entertained? Marie Winn has written a thought-provoking book on this subject: *The Plug-In Drug* (New York: Viking, 1985). See also *Children Without Childhood* (New York: Pantheon, 1983). In Isenberger, J., & Quisenberry, N. L. (1988, February). Play: A necessity for all children. *Childhood Education*, 138–144, the Association for Childhood Education International (ACEI) defends children's right to play: "ACEI recognizes the need for children of all ages to play and affirms the essential role of play in children's healthy development. ACEI believes that as today's children move into the 21st century and continue to experience pressure to succeed in all areas of life, the necessity for play becomes even more critical."

Casebook: See the Teachers' Casebook for ideas about helping students when parents are getting divorced.

Transparency: Use acetate transparency **T 18**, "Projected Number of Students Not Living with Both Parents through the Year 2020."

Background: For a concise discussion of the effects of divorce on children and suggestions for ways that teachers can help their students cope with divorce, see Clarke-Stewart, K. A. (1989). Single-parent families: How bad for the children. *NEA Today,* 7(6), 60–64.

A few highlights:

1. Teachers need to be informed about what to expect. Children, especially boys, are likely to act up and act out, to be distracted or withdrawn. This may go on for a long time after the actual divorce.

2. Teachers can do only so much. Children need time and support to understand and cope with the changes in their lives.

3. Teachers may need to educate the other students in the class about the effects of divorce so that these students will be more tolerant and supportive of peers who are in crisis. Sometimes a child needs a fresh start in a new group that did not witness the child's acting out during the divorce.

4. Looking toward the future, students need preparation for the difficulties and challenges of family life so they will make decisions about marriage very carefully. Girls especially need to prepare for careers that will allow them to be self-sufficient, because women after a divorce tend to experience a dramatic drop (as much as 75 percent) in their standard of living, making it difficult for them to care for themselves and their children.

Background: Peterson, M. P. (1993). Physical and sexual abuse among school children: Prevalence and prevention. *Educational Psychology Review, 5,* 63–86. Bear, T., Schenk, S., & Buckner, L. (1993). Supporting victims of child abuse. *Educational Leadership, 50*(4), 44.

below the poverty level, but almost one in two female single-parent families is in this category (Hetherington, 1989; Moshman, Glover, & Bruning, 1987). Money shortages lead to fewer toys and trips, and less recreation in general. Children may also be asked to accept their parents' new lovers or even new stepparents. In some divorces there are few conflicts, ample resources, and the continuing support of friends and extended family. But divorce is never easy for anyone.

The first two years after the divorce seem to be the most difficult period for both boys and girls. During this time, children may have problems in school, lose or gain an unusual amount of weight, develop difficulties sleeping, and so on. They may blame themselves for the breakup of their family or hold unrealistic hopes for a reconciliation (Hetherington, 1989; Pfeffer, 1981). Long-term adjustment is also affected. Boys tend to show a higher rate of behavioral and interpersonal problems at home and in school than girls in general or boys from intact families. Girls may have trouble in their dealings with males. They may become more sexually active or have difficulties trusting males (Wallerstein & Blakeslee, 1989). But living with one fairly content, if harried, parent may be better than living in a conflict-filled situation with two unhappy parents (Nielsen, 1993).

Judith Wallerstein (1991) suggests that all children of divorce must face several tasks. They must separate real changes brought by the divorce from fantasy fears of abandonment or losing their parents. They must separate themselves from their parents' pain and get on with their own lives. Parents often make this very difficult by inflicting their own anger and loneliness on their children. Students experiencing divorce must deal with the very real loss of their family unit and usually lose the company of one parent as well. Ultimately, students have to accept that the divorce is permanent, that their family system is forever changed. Yet they must still be willing to take a chance on loving in this uncertain world of relationships.

Child Abuse. Accurate information about the number of abused children in the United States is difficult to find; estimates range from 1.5 to 2.2 million children per year (National Organization for Victims' Assistance, 1989; Peterson, 1993; Straus, Gelles, & Steinmetz, 1980). However, most experts agree that an enormous number of cases go unreported. About half of all abusive parents could change their destructive behavior patterns if they received help. Without assistance, probably only about 5 percent of abusing parents improve (Starr, 1979). Of course, parents are not the only people who abuse children. Siblings, other relatives, and even teachers have been responsible for the physical and sexual abuse of children.

As a teacher, you must alert your principal, school psychologist, or school social worker if you suspect abuse. In all 50 states of the United States, in the District of Columbia and the U.S. territories, the law requires certain professionals, often including teachers, to report suspected cases of child abuse. The legal definition of abuse has been broadened in many states to include neglect and failure to provide proper care and supervision. Most laws also protect teachers who report suspected neglect in good faith (Beezer, 1985). Be sure to understand the laws in your state or province on this important issue *and* your own moral responsibility. Approximately 2,000 children die of abuse or neglect each year in the United States, in many cases because no one would "get involved." Table 3.6 lists possible indicators of abuse.

TABLE 3.6   Indicators of Child Abuse

The following are some of the signs of abuse. Not every child with these signs is abused, but these indicators should be investigated.

	Physical Indicators	Behavioral Indicators	
Physical Abuse	■ unexplained bruises (in various stages of healing) welts, human bite marks, bald spots ■ unexplained burns, especially cigarette burns or immersion-burns (glove-like) ■ unexplained fractures, lacerations, or abrasions	■ self-destructive ■ withdrawn and aggressive—behavioral extremes ■ uncomfortable with physical contact ■ arrives at school early or stays late, as if afraid	■ chronic runaway (adolescents) ■ complains of soreness or moves uncomfortably ■ wears clothing inappropriate to weather, to cover body
Physical Neglect	■ abandonment ■ unattended medical needs ■ consistent lack of supervision ■ consistent hunger, inappropriate dress, poor hygiene ■ lice, distended stomach, emaciation	■ regularly displays fatigue or listlessness, falls asleep in class ■ steals food, begs from classmates ■ reports that no caretaker is at home	■ frequently absent or tardy ■ self-destructive ■ school dropout (adolescents)
Sexual Abuse	■ torn, stained, or bloodied underclothing ■ pain or itching in genital area ■ difficulty walking or sitting ■ bruises or bleeding in external genitalia ■ venereal disease ■ frequent urinary or yeast infections	■ withdrawn, chronic depression ■ excessive seductiveness ■ role reversal, overly concerned for siblings ■ poor self-esteem, self-devaluation, lack of confidence ■ peer problems, lack of involvement ■ massive weight change	■ suicide attempts (especially adolescents) ■ hysteria, lack of emotional control ■ sudden school difficulties ■ inappropriate sex play or premature understanding of sex ■ threatened by physical contact, closeness ■ promiscuity

Source: T. Bear, S. Schenk, and L. Buckner (1993). "Supporting victims of child abuse." *Educational Leadership, 50*(4), p. 44. Reprinted with permission of the Association for Supervision and Curriculum Development. Copyright 1993 by ASCD. All rights reserved.

New Roles for Teachers   Test Bank items 3.59, 3.60, 3.95, 3.100

When we consider the high rates of divorce and child abuse, we see that teachers today are dealing with issues that once stayed outside the walls of the school. The first and most important task of the teacher is to educate, but student learning suffers when there are problems with personal and social development. What do teachers think about their responsibilities for **affective education**—for encouraging personal and social growth in school?

Teachers are sometimes the best source of help for students facing emotional or interpersonal problems. When students have chaotic and unpredictable home lives, they need warm, firm structure in school. They need

Background: Hetherington, E. M. (1989). Coping with family transitions: Winners, losers, and survivors. *Child Development, 60,* 1–14.

Affective Education   Education focusing on emotional growth.

Guidelines

Affective Education Programs

Background: Nielsen, L. (1993). Students from divorced and blended families. *Educational Psychology Review, 5,* 177–199.

Background: In recent years there has been growing interest among educators in affective and moral education. See the December 1985/January 1986 issue of *Educational Leadership 43*(4) and the May 1988 issue of *Educational Leadership 45*(8). These two issues are devoted almost entirely to the question of the school's role in moral education and the development of character. There are articles about moral development and the teaching of values, affective education, global education, leadership, Christian schools, ethics, censorship, prejudice, parents and values, and related topics. In the February 1988 issue of *Phi Delta Kappan 69*(6) is a section on moral development and character education. In the June, 1992 issue of *Phi Delta Kappan 73*(10) is an article by Howard Kirschenbaum entitled, "A comprehensive mode for values education and moral education."

Objective 3.7: Take a stand on affective and moral education.

Help students examine the kinds of dilemmas they are currently facing or will face in the near future.

Examples

1. In elementary school, discuss sibling rivalries, teasing, stealing, prejudice, treatment of new students in the class, behavior toward handicapped classmates.
2. In high school, discuss cheating, letting friends drive when they are intoxicated, conforming to be more popular, protecting a friend who has broken a rule.

Help students see the perspectives of others.

Examples

1. Ask a student to describe his or her understanding of the views of another, then have the other person confirm or correct the perception.
2. Have students exchange roles and try to "become" the other person in a discussion.

Help students make connections between expressed values and actions.

Examples

1. Follow a discussion of "What should be done?" with "How would you act? What would be your first step? What problems might arise?"
2. Help students see inconsistencies between their values and their own actions. Ask them to identify inconsistencies, first in others, then in themselves.

Safeguard the privacy of all participants.

Examples

1. Remind students that in a discussion they can "pass" and not answer questions.
2. Intervene if peer pressure is forcing a student to say more than he or she wants to.
3. Don't reinforce a pattern of telling "secrets."

Make sure students are really listening to each other.

Examples

1. Keep groups small.
2. Be a good listener yourself.
3. Recognize students who pay careful attention to each other.

Make sure that as much as possible your class reflects concern for moral issues and values.

Examples

1. Make clear distinctions between rules based on administrative convenience (keeping the room orderly) and rules based on moral issues.
2. Enforce standards uniformly. Be careful about showing favoritism.

Source: Adapted with permission from J. W. Eiseman (1981), What criteria should public school moral education programs meet? *The Review of Education, 7,* pp. 226–227.

teachers who set clear limits, are consistent, enforce rules firmly but not punitively, respect students, and show genuine concern. As a teacher, you can be available to talk about personal problems without requiring that your students do so. One of my student teachers gave a boy in her class a journal entitled "Very Hard Thoughts" so that he could write about his parents' divorce. Sometimes he talked to her about the journal entries, but at other times he just recorded his feelings. The student teacher was very careful to respect the boy's privacy about his writings.

Focus on . . .   Socialization

- What are some examples of the ways that children are pressured to grow up quickly?
- What challenges face children whose parents are divorced?
- How would you recognize a child who is being abused?

The Preschool Years

In the next few pages we examine three important issues: physical development during the preschool years, the effects of day care on children, and the need for developmentally appropriate preschools.

Physical Development   Test Bank item 3.61

Preschool children are very active. Their **gross-motor skills,** which involve control of the large muscles, improve greatly over the years from ages 2 to 5, as you can see in Table 3.7. Between ages 2 and about 4 or 5, preschoolers' muscles grow stronger, their balance improves, and their center of gravity moves lower, so they are able to run, jump, climb, and hop. Most of these movements develop naturally if the child has normal physical abilities and the opportunity to play. Children with physical problems, however, may need special training to develop these skills. For young children, physical activity can be an end in itself. It is fun just to improve. But preschoolers may literally run till they drop. They need periods of rest scheduled after physical exertion.

Fine-motor skills such as tying shoes or fastening buttons, which require the coordination of small movements, also improve greatly during the preschool

Application: Ask students how they might integrate affective goals into the following topics:

1. Slavery as a cause of the Civil War.
2. Community helpers such as police officers, firefighters, nurses.
3. Columbus's voyage to America.
4. Proper nutrition: the basic food groups.
5. A democratic versus a dictatorial form of government.

TABLE 3.7 Motor Skills Improve throughout the Preschool Years		
Approximate Age	**Gross-Motor Skills**	**Fine-Motor Skills**
Birth to 3 years	sits and crawls; walks; begins to run	picks up, grasps, stacks, and releases objects
3 to 4.5 years	walks up and down stairs; jumps with both feet; throws ball	holds crayon; uses utensils; buttons; copies shapes
4.5 to 6 years	skips; rides two-wheel bicycle; catches ball; plays sports	uses pencil; makes representational drawings; cuts with scissors; prints letters

Gross-Motor Skills Voluntary body movements that involve the large muscles.

Fine-Motor Skills Voluntary body movements that involve the small muscles.

Teaching Tip: There are a number of social skills training packages available to help students develop prosocial behaviors. Research Press (Box 3177, Dept. K, Champaign, IL 61821, phone 217–352–3273) offers training packages for teachers. Many are based on the social learning and behavioral learning principles described in this text. The following are a few examples of the materials available:

McGinnis, E., & Goldstein, A. P. *Skillstreaming the elementary school child: A guide for teaching prosocial skills.*

Goldstein, A. P., Sprafkin, R. P., Gershaw, N. J., & Klein, P. *Skillstreaming the adolescent: A structured learning approach to teaching prosocial skills.*

Background: For a discussion of affective education, see Preaching, practicing, and prodding: What works in character education (1987, January). *Harvard Education Letter, 3*(1), 1–3.

Background: For interesting discussions of the effects of day care and preschool, see Effects of infant day care: A note of caution (1986, November). *Harvard Education Letter, 2*(6), 6–7, and Preschool: It does make a difference (1985, June). *Harvard Education Letter, 1*(3), 1–3.

Research: Kagan, J., Kearsley, R., & Zelazo, P. (1980). *Infancy.* Cambridge, MA: Harvard University Press, showed no major or minor differences between infants aged 3 to 6 months who were served in day care and those who stayed home. In some situations, the day-care experience proved to be somewhat better. Fallow, D. (1985). *A Mother's Work.* Boston: Houghton Mifflin, argued that Kagan's findings are not conclusive. Her writing argues that there is no effective substitute for the mother.

years, as shown in Table 3.7. Children need to work with large paintbrushes, fat pencils and crayons, large pieces of drawing paper, and soft clay or playdough to accommodate their developing skills. During this time, children will begin to show a preference for their right or left hand. Most students, about 85 percent during this time, will prefer their right hand, but those who prefer their left should not be forced to change. This means that there must be a good supply of left-handed scissors for preschool classes.

The Impact of Day Care   Test Bank items 3.62, 3.92, 3.101

With increases in two-career families and single-parent households, more and more children are spending part of their daily lives in group settings outside the family. What are the effects of day-care arrangements on the millions of children involved?

During the 1960s and 1970s, research on the effects of preschool experiences generally focused on compensatory programs, programs for children from low-income families, like Operation Head Start. Results indicated that benefits did not last, but recent findings are more optimistic. For example, studies of 12 experimental preschool programs for economically disadvantaged children compared program participants to children of similar age and background who did not attend special preschools (Berrueta-Clement, Schweinhart, Barnett, Epstein, & Weikart, 1984; Haskins, 1989; Smith, 1991). Children who attended the preschool programs had to repeat fewer grades, were assigned less often to special education classes, were classified less often as mentally retarded, were arrested less frequently, had fewer illegitimate children, graduated from high school and went on to advanced schooling more often, depended less on welfare, and worked more.

So good preschool programs can benefit children from low-income families. But what about other children? Here, the answer is not clear. In the first two years, children benefit from frequent one-to-one interactions with adults.

*D*evelopmentally appropriate toys should fit a range of ages. A 2-year-old can use blocks to improve motor development, while a 4-year-old can use the same blocks to develop counting and cooperation.

It is possible that very young children in day-care situations do not get enough of this kind of intensive interaction (Belsky & Braungart, 1991). After age 3 or 4, however, the stimulation of other children, teachers, and new environments may become important. At least it seems clear that day care for older children does not harm intellectual development and that it may help (Harvard University, 1985).

Good day-care and preschool programs have generally positive effects on social development as well. Children in these programs are more assertive, self-confident, socially mature, and outgoing. But children who attend preschool programs tend to interact more with their peers in negative as well as in positive ways. Some results indicate that these children may be more aggressive. Apparently, most children in preschools will not learn to solve conflicts peacefully unless special efforts are made to teach them how. The effect of this aggression in later years has not yet been determined (Clarke-Stewart, 1989).

Findings about the potential positive effects of preschool have led some educators to favor more formal academic schooling for young children. Is this a good idea? Some psychologists answer with a loud *"no!"*

Developmentally Appropriate Preschools

Test Bank items
3.63–3.64, 3.82,
3.101, 3.103–3.107

David Elkind (1989, 1991) has been a vocal critic of formal education for preschool children. He suggests that before 1960 there were few preschools as we know them today. But changing family styles and pressure on education to improve sinking test scores led to an emphasis on teaching children more, sooner. Middle-class working parents paid for preschool experiences that promised to make up for time lost with Mom and Dad. Elkind (1989) believes that ". . . teaching young children in a didactic way, as if they were miniature second or third graders, can have lasting negative effects on their academic careers and their successful adaptation to the larger society" (p. 47).

These negative effects include stress reactions such as headaches, stomach aches, and behavior problems. In addition, children who are given too much teacher direction at a time when they need to follow their own direction may develop a sense of guilt rather than initiative (in Erikson's terms), diminished self-confidence, and decreased motivation for academic learning later in life. They may learn to wait to be told what to learn and how to learn it. Furthermore, after a few years of elementary school, they will be no farther ahead than children who spent their preschool years playing instead of "studying."

What is a **developmentally appropriate education** for preschoolers, an education that fits their physical, social, emotional, and cognitive needs? Many suggestions echo the ideas we examined in the Guidelines in chapter 2 for teaching preoperational children and in this chapter for encouraging initiative. Because young children are so variable in their development at this time, Elkind suggests grouping several ages together so that slower 5-year-olds can play and interact with more advanced 4-year-olds, and so on. If children must be grouped by age, then activities and materials must take into account the wide range of development. Materials should be nongraded, that is, appropriate for a range of ages. You have seen these before: blocks, water, sand, dolls, pretend props, a range of books, animals, cars, and

Discussion: This issue of day care lends itself easily to debate. Ask students: At what point should a mother return to work? Before the child enters school? Do you think we will ultimately see problems with children who have been "raised" in day care?

Background: Elkind, D. (1991). Formal education and early childhood education: An essential difference. In K. M. Cauley, F. Linder, & J. H. McMillan (Eds.), *Annual Editions: Educational Psychology 1991/92* (pp. 26–31). Guilford, CT: Duskin.

Research: See the research synthesis by R. Haskins (1989), "Beyond metaphor: The efficacy of early childhood education," originally published in the *American Psychologist, 44,* 274–282.

Objective 3.8: Describe developmentally appropriate education for students of different ages.

Focus on . . .   **the Preschool Years**

- What are the effects of good-quality day preschool programs?
- In general, who benefits the most from preschool?
- Describe a developmentally appropriate preschool.

Developmentally Appropriate Education   Educational programs and activities designed to meet the cognitive, emotional, social, and physical needs of students.

Background: See David Elkind (1989). Developmentally appropriate practice: Philosophical and practical implications. *Phi Delta Kappan*, 71, 2 (October), 113–117. Dr. Elkind contrasts the psychometric philosophy with the developmental philosophy, arguing in favor of the latter. He states that if we would teach with a developmental approach we would create "students who want to know, not students who know what we want."

Casebook: See the Teachers' Casebook at the end of this chapter for one teacher's view on helping emotionally immature students with their social development.

Application: According to Erikson, why should a teacher be concerned with social isolates in his or her classroom? How can a teacher help a student become more socially integrated into the class?

Objective 3.9: Describe the child's changing view of friendship.

As children grow into adolescence, qualities such as loyalty and shared philosophies come into play. At every stage of development, girls are more likely than boys to have one "best" friend.

playdough. A 2-year-old can stack three blocks and improve motor development. A 4-year-old can use the same blocks with a friend to develop some basic idea about counting and cooperating. The teacher is a matchmaker between child and materials, understanding what children are ready to learn and providing situations that support that learning (Bredekemp, 1986).

The Elementary-School Years

As children move out of their families and into school, new challenges greet them. This can be a happy time for many children. They are growing physically, becoming more and more skillful. They are learning to read, write, solve problems, and understand their world. They are developing good friends. But failures in these areas can be devastating. The child who continually fails in school or who is rejected by other children can be a very unhappy person.

Physical Development   Test Bank items 3.65, 3.102

During the elementary-school years, physical development is fairly steady for most children. They become taller, leaner, and stronger, so they are better able to master sports and games. There is tremendous variation, however. A particular child can be much larger or smaller than average and still be perfectly healthy. Since children at this age are very aware of physical differences but are not the most tactful people, you may hear comments like "You're too little to be in fifth grade. What's wrong with you?" or "How come you're so fat?"

Throughout elementary school, many of the girls are likely to be as large as or larger than the boys in their classes. Between the ages of 11 and 14, girls are, on the average, taller and heavier than boys of the same age (Tanner, 1970). The size discrepancy can give the girls an advantage in physical activities, though some girls may feel conflict over this and, as a result, downplay their physical abilities.

Friendships in Childhood   Test Bank items 3.66, 3.67, 3.97

Psychologists have found that as children mature, the meaning of friendship changes for them (Damon, 1977; Selman, 1981; Youniss, 1980). Damon has described three levels of friendship. At the first level, friends are the other children a child plays with often. But friendships can begin and end quickly, based on acts of kindness or "meanness." There is little sense that friends have stable characteristics, so moment-to-moment actions define the friendship (Berndt & Perry, 1986). Teachers working with young children should be aware that these rapidly changing allegiances are a normal part of development. Note, too, that a child's view of friends at this level may be related to the level of cognitive development: young children have difficulty seeing beyond the immediate situation.

Friendships at the next level are defined by a willingness to help when help is needed. Friends are playmates and companions. Children begin to base their choices for friends on concrete but stable personal qualities in another child, such as, "She always shares her lunch with me." This level of friendship may be linked to concrete operational cognitive abilities and the development of empathy and perspective-taking.

At the highest level, as children move into adolescence, friends are seen as people who share common interests and values, faithfully keep one's most private revelations a secret, and provide psychological support when necessary. The personal qualities of a friend—loyalty, similar philosophy of life—are more abstract and less tied to behaviors (Furman & Bierman, 1984). The cognitive abilities required to understand abstract concepts and to base judgments upon them may come into play here. Friendship is now a long-term proposition and usually cannot be destroyed by one or even several incidents. At this stage, friendships can be very intense, especially for girls. At every stage, girls are more likely than boys to have one "best" friend and are more reluctant than boys to admit new members to a tight group of friends (Berndts & Perry, 1990).

At every level, friendships play a very significant role in healthy personal and social development. There is strong evidence that adults who had close friends as children have higher self-esteem and are more capable of maintaining intimate relationships than adults who spent lonely childhoods. Adults who were rejected as children tend to have more problems, such as dropping out of school or committing crimes (Hartup, 1989; Kupersmidt, Coie, & Dodge, 1990). Teachers sometimes forget just how central friendships are to their students' lives. When a student is having a problem with a friend, when there has been a falling-out or an argument, when one child is not invited to a sleep-over, when rumors are started and pacts are made to ostracize someone, the results can be devastating to the children involved. Even when students begin to mature and know intellectually that rifts will soon be healed, they may still be emotionally crushed by temporary trouble in the friendship.

A teacher should also be aware of how each student gets along with the group. Are there outcasts? Do some students play the bully role? Careful adult intervention can often correct such problems, especially at the middle elementary-school level.

Issues Affecting Adolescents

As students enter adolescence, they undergo dramatic changes. Differences in rates of physical and sexual development have important repercussions for personal/social development. In addition, adolescents today face risks that were much less prevalent a few generations ago—pregnancy, depression, drugs, and AIDS. We will turn our attention first to the effects of individual differences in the rate of physical and sexual development.

Early and Late Maturers   Test Bank items 3.68–3.70, 3.93, 3.94, 3.102

Puberty marks the beginning of sexual maturity. It is not a single event, but a series of changes involving almost every part of the body. The outcome of the changes is the ability to reproduce. The sex differences in physical development

Activity 3.6: Field Experience. See the *Instructor's Resource Manual* for Estimating Social Relations, an activity in which your students create a sociogram. An example of a sociogram is presented in **Handout Master 3.3** in the *Instructor's Resource Manual*. The students collect data to create two sociograms, one based on children's most desired work partners and the other on choices for their least desired partner. In your discussion of the results of this data collection, note particularly the problems of rejected, unpopular children.

Focus on . . .   The Elementary Years
- How do students develop physically during the elementary years?
- How does the meaning of friendship change as students mature?

Activity 3.7: Field Experience. See the *Instructor's Resource Manual* for Interviewing Children about Friendship, an activity that provides your students with interview questions for children of different ages about the meaning of friendship.

Activity 3.8: Application. See the *Instructor's Resource Manual* for a summary of Unpopular Children, an article in the January/February 1989 issue of the *Harvard Education Letter*.

Objective 3.10: List the problems of early and late maturers.

Puberty The period in early adolescence when individuals begin to reach physical and sexual maturity.

Teaching Tip: Using the teacher expectations and self-fulfilling prophecy phenomenon (described in chapter 9), explain how an early-maturing boy is likely to be academically advanced and a leader among his classmates.

Research: See Livson, N., & Peskin, H. (1980). Perspectives on adolescence from longitudinal research. *Handbook of Adolescent Psychology.* Summarizes research on early and late maturation. The early-maturing male seems to be readily accepted by adults. What is his position with his adolescent peers? The early-maturing female is looked at with contempt; she almost seems to pose a threat to adolescents and adults alike. What can teachers do to help students who are not fitting in?

Background: For information about other problems facing children and adolescents, see the March 1988 issue of *Educational Leadership*, *45*(6), which includes a special section on "Helping Youngsters Cope with Life." There are articles on drug abuse, suicide, sex education, and decision making.

Background: In the June 1987 issue of *Phi Delta Kappan*, *68*(10), are two articles on teenage pregnancy: Kenney, A. M. (1987). Teen pregnancy: An issue for the schools, pp. 728–736; and Buie, J. (1987). Teen pregnancy: It's time for the schools to tackle the problem, pp. 737–739.

Research: Brooks-Gunn, J., & Furstenberg, F. F., Jr. (1989). Adolescent sexual behavior. *American Psychologist, 44,* 2249–2257.

Background: Sexuality Education (1991, special section). *Educational Leadership, 49*(1), 51–68.

we saw during the later elementary years become even more pronounced at the beginning of puberty. Generally, girls begin puberty about two years ahead of boys and reach their final height by age 16; most boys continue growing until about age 18. For the typical girl, the adolescent growth spurt begins with breast development between the ages of 10 and 11 and continues for about three years. While this is the average time frame for girls, the actual range is from 9 to 16 years. Eighty percent of American girls have their first menstrual period between the ages of 11-1/2 and 14-1/2. For the typical boy, the growth spurt begins between the ages of 12 and 13.

The physical changes of adolescence have significant effects on the individual's identity. Psychologists have been particularly interested in the academic, social, and emotional differences they have found between adolescents who mature early and those who mature later.

First, there seems to be an academic advantage in early maturation. Students who are physically mature tend to score higher on tests of mental ability than less mature students of the same age (Fein, 1978). Second, early maturation seems to have certain special advantages for boys. The early maturers' taller, broader-shouldered body type fits the cultural stereotype for the male ideal. Early-maturing boys are more likely to enjoy high social status; they tend to be popular and to be leaders. On the other hand, boys who mature late have an especially difficult time. Since girls mature well ahead of boys, even late-maturing girls have developed by the time the late-maturing boy finally has his chance. The last to leave childhood, he may have been surrounded by mature peers for years. These late-maturing boys tend to be less popular, more talkative, and hungrier for attention (Kaplan, 1984). However, some studies show that in adulthood, males who matured early are less flexible and less creative in their thinking, whereas males who matured later tend to be more creative, tolerant, and perceptive. Perhaps the trials and anxieties of maturing late teach some boys to be better problem solvers (Brooks-Gunn, 1988; Seifert & Hoffnung, 1991).

For girls, these effects are reversed. Maturing way ahead of classmates can be a definite disadvantage. Being larger than everyone else in the class is not a valued characteristic for girls in our culture, particularly because our cultural ideal of female beauty is a girlish, long-legged, "Barbie doll" (Simmons & Blythe, 1987). A girl who begins to mature early probably will be the first in her peer group to start the changes of puberty. This can be very upsetting to some girls, especially if they have not been prepared for the changes or if friends tease them. Later-maturing girls seem to have fewer problems, but they may worry that something is wrong with them. All students can benefit from knowing that the "normal" range in rates of maturation is great and that there are advantages for both early and late maturers.

Adolescents at Risk   Test Bank items 3.71, 3.72, 3.73

It has always been difficult to navigate the adolescent years, but today the waters seem more dangerous than ever. Many challenges confront junior and senior high school students today. We will touch on only a few.

Teenage Sexuality and Pregnancy. Today, about 80 percent of American men and 75 percent of American women have had sexual intercourse by

Guidelines
_____

Do not call unnecessary attention to physical differences among students.

Examples

1. Avoid seating arrangements that are obviously based on height, but try to seat smaller students so they can see and participate in class activities.
2. Avoid games that call attention to differences in height, size, or strength.
3. Don't use or allow students to use nicknames based on physical traits.

Help students obtain factual information on differences in physical development.

Examples

1. Set up science projects on sex differences in growth rates.
2. Have readings and discussions that focus on differences between early and late maturers. Make sure that you present the positives and the negatives of each.
3. Find out the school policy on sex education and on informal guidance for students. Some schools, for example, encourage teachers to talk to girls who are upset about their first menstrual period, while other schools expect teachers to send the girls to talk to the school nurse.
4. Give the student models in literature or in their community of high-achieving individuals who do not fit the ideal physical stereotypes.

Accept that concerns about appearance and the opposite sex will occupy much time and energy for adolescents.

Examples

1. Allow students a few moments at the end of class to socialize.
2. Deal with some of these issues in curriculum-related materials.

_____

age 19 (Guttmacher Institute, 1991). *Newsweek* (1991) reported that 50 percent of 15-year-old girls have had intercourse. The emotional impact of these early sexual experiences may have repercussions in the school, both for the students involved and for fellow students who hear about the experiences. One consequence of this early sexual activity is unexpected and unwanted pregnancy. Each year, more than 1 million teenage girls become pregnant—30,000 of them are younger than 15 years old (DeRidder, 1993; Scarr, Weinberg, & Levine, 1986).

A remarkable number of American adolescents have little information, or indeed the wrong information, about birth control. For example, about one-half of the adolescent girls who become pregnant do so in their first six months of sexual activity; often, they haven't decided yet what to do about birth control, partly because they don't expect anything to happen so quickly. It can! In fact, many teenage girls don't know when in their menstrual cycle they can become pregnant. Some adults fear that giving adolescents accurate information about sex will encourage them to experiment. Research indicates that this is not a danger. The main effect of providing the facts appears to be fewer unwanted pregnancies (Brooks-Gunn & Furstenberg, 1989; DeRidder, 1993).

Background: For more information about teenage pregnancy, see The family crisis and what we can do about it: An interview with Marian Wright Edelman (1987, May). *Harvard Education Letter, 3*(3), 4–6.

Objective 3.11: Suggest ways to help adolescents make responsible decisions about sex and drugs.

Background: DeRidder, L. M. (1993). Teenage pregnancy: Etiology and educational interventions. *Educational Psychology Review, 5,* 87–107.

Research: Newcomb, M. D., & Bentler, P. M. (1989). Substance use and abuse among children and teenagers. *American Psychologist, 44,* 242–248.

Background: The December 1988 issue of *Phi Delta Kappan* had a special section on adolescent suicide. One of the articles is "Adolescent suicide: An open letter to counselors" by Jane Wolfle, the mother of a 16-year-old boy who killed himself.

Background: Range, L. M. (1993). Suicide prevention: Guidelines for schools. *Educational Psychology Review, 5,* 135–154.

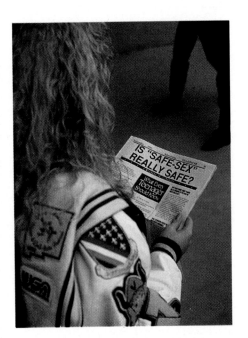

This girl is getting the facts about sexually transmitted diseases, but will she act on this information? One problem with teenagers is that they feel somewhat "invulnerable" and assume that nothing bad will happen to them, only to someone else.

Focus on . . . **Issues Affecting Adolescents**

- Describe the worlds of the late-maturing adolescent boy and girl.
- Why has there been an increase in teenage pregnancy?
- What are some of the danger signs that an adolescent might attempt suicide?

Bulimia Eating disorder characterized by overeating, then getting rid of the food by self-induced vomiting or laxatives.

Anorexia Nervosa Eating disorder characterized by very limited food intake.

Eating Disorders. Adolescents going through the changes of puberty are very concerned about their bodies. This has always been true, but today, the emphasis on fitness and appearance makes adolescents even more likely to worry about how their bodies "measure up." For some, the concern becomes excessive. One consequence is eating disorders such as **bulimia** (binge eating) and **anorexia nervosa** (self-starvation), both of which are much more common in females than in males. Bulimics often binge, eating an entire gallon of ice cream or a whole cake. Then, to avoid gaining weight, they force themselves to vomit, or they use strong laxatives, to purge themselves of the extra calories. Bulimics tend to maintain a normal weight, but their digestive systems can be permanently damaged. Anorexia is an even more dangerous disorder, for anorexics refuse to eat or eat practically nothing. In the process they may lose 20 to 25 percent of their body weight, and some (about 5 percent) literally starve themselves to death. Anorexic students may appear pale, with brittle fingernails, and fine, dark hairs developing all over their bodies. The are easily chilled because they have so little fat to insulate their bodies. These eating disorders often begin in adolescence and require professional help (Harris, 1991).

Drug Abuse. Modern society makes growing up a very confusing process. Notice the messages from films and billboards. "Beautiful," popular people drink alcohol and smoke cigarettes with little concern for their health. We have over-the-counter drugs for almost every common ailment. Coffee wakes us up, and a pill helps us sleep. And then we tell students to "Just say no!" to drugs.

For many reasons, not just because of these contradictory messages, drug use has become a problem for students. Accurate statistics are hard to find, but estimates from the National Center for Education Statistics indicate that 92 percent of high school seniors report some experience with alcohol—66 percent using it in the past month. About 20 percent of seniors are daily smokers, and 30 percent have tried at least one illegal drug.

What can be done about drug use among our students? First, we should distinguish between experimentation and abuse. Many students try something at a party but do not become regular users. The best way to help students who have trouble saying no appears to be through peer programs that teach how to say no assertively. The successful programs also teach general social skills and build self-esteem (Newcomb & Bentler, 1989). Also, the older students are when they experiment with drugs, the more likely they are to make responsible choices, so helping younger students say no is a clear benefit.

AIDS. A growing health risk for everyone, but especially for adolescents, is the spread of AIDS (acquired immune deficiency syndrome). As of 1992, only about 3 percent of all AIDS cases are individuals under the age of 21, and many of these are young children. But the frightening fact is that this percentage is growing rapidly, especially among adolescents. In most cases, adolescents contract AIDS through intimate sexual contact or intravenous drug use. For the virus to be transmitted, people have to exchange bodily fluids without the fluids coming into contact with the air first. Obviously, this can happen a number of ways, but contact has to be more than casual. Many students do not understand that the AIDS virus is unable to survive in air or water, so AIDS cannot be transmitted by casual day-to-day touching, hugging, or sharing food—or even by being spit on (Seifert & Hoffnung, 1991). The Task Force on Pediatric AIDS of the American Psychological Association (1989) recommends education about AIDS for students, beginning in the early years and continuing through high school. In this area, education can be life-saving and does not appear to encourage experimentation.

Suicide. For young people ages 15 to 24, the suicide rate has tripled in the past 30 years. Figure 3.2 shows a steady climb in the number of suicides among all males and among white females.

Suicide often comes as a response to life problems—problems that parents and teachers sometimes dismiss. There are a number of warning signs that trouble is brewing. Watch for changes in eating or sleeping habits, weight, grades, disposition, activity level, or interest in friends. Students at risk sometimes suddenly give away prized possessions such as stereos, CDs, clothing, or pets. They may seem depressed or hyperactive. It is especially dangerous if the student not only talks about suicide, but also has a plan for acting. If you suspect that there is a problem, talk to the student directly. One feeling shared by many people who attempt suicide is that no one really takes them seriously. "A question about suicide does not provoke suicide. Indeed, teens (and adults) often experience relief when someone finally cares enough to ask" (Range, 1993, p. 145). Be realistic, not poetic, about suicide. Ask about specifics, and take the student seriously. Table 3.8 lists common myths and facts about suicide.

INCREASING SUICIDE RATES AMONG ADOLESCENTS

From 1960 through 1987 the number of suicides per 100,000 adolescents has steadily increased for all groups except nonwhite females. The increase for white males has been the greatest.

Source: U.S. Department of Health and Human Services, as reported in *Newsweek Special Issue, Education: A Consumer's Handbook* (Fall–Winter 1990-91), p. 15.

TABLE 3.8 Myths and Facts about Suicide

Myth: People who talk about suicide don't kill themselves.
Fact: Eight out of ten people who commit suicide tell someone that they're thinking about hurting themselves before they actually do it.

Myth: Only certain types of people commit suicide.
Fact: All types of people commit suicide—male and female, young and old, rich and poor, country people and city people. It happens in every racial, ethnic, and religious group.

Myth: When a person talks about suicide, you should change the subject to get his or her mind off it.
Fact: You should take them seriously. Listen carefully to what they are saying. Give them a chance to express their feelings. Let them know you are concerned. And help them get help.

Myth: Most people who kill themselves really want to die.
Fact: Most people who kill themelves are confused about whether they want to die. Suicide is often intended as a cry for help.

Source: From R. Bell (1980), *Changing bodies, changing lives: A book for teens on sex and relationships.* New York: Random House, p. 142.

This has been a brief, selective look at the needs of children. As we saw earlier, educators and psychologists are concerned about providing a developmentally appropriate education for preschool students. All students, whatever their age, require an education that fits their physical, cognitive, personal, and social levels of development.

SUMMARY

The Work of Erikson

According to Erik Erikson's theory of emotional development, people go through eight life stages between infancy and old age, each of which involves a central crisis. Adequate resolution of each crisis leads to greater personal and social competence and a stronger foundation for solving future crises. In the first two stages, an infant must develop a sense of trust over mistrust and a sense of autonomy over shame and doubt. In early childhood, the focus of the third stage is on developing initiative and avoiding feelings of guilt. In the child's elementary-school years, the fourth stage involves achieving a sense of industry and avoiding feelings of inferiority.

In Erikson's fifth stage, identity versus role confusion, adolescents consciously attempt to solidify their identity. According to James Marcia, these efforts may lead to identity achievement, foreclosure, diffusion, or moratorium. Pride in family, community, and ethnicity is an important part of a strong and stable identity. Erikson's three stages of adulthood involve struggles to achieve intimacy, generativity, and integrity.

Understanding Ourselves and Others

Our self-concept and self-esteem—our definition and evaluation of ourselves—become increasingly complex, differentiated, and abstract as we mature. Self-concept evolves through constant self-evaluation, social interaction, and experiences in and out of school. Teachers can have a profound effect on students' self-concept and self-esteem.

An understanding of intentions develops as children mature, but aggressive students often have trouble understanding the intentions of others. Social-perspective-taking also changes as we mature. Young children believe that everyone has the same thoughts and feelings they do. Later, they learn that others have separate identities and therefore separate feelings and perspectives on events.

Moral Development

Lawrence Kohlberg's theory of moral development includes three levels: (1) a preconventional level, where judgments are based on self-interest; (2) a conventional level, where judgments are based on traditional family values and social expectations; and (3) a postconventional level, where judgments are based on more abstract and personal ethical principles. Critics suggest that Kohlberg's view does not account for possible sex differences in moral reasoning or differences between moral reasoning and moral behavior. Moral behavior is influenced by the internalization of rules (made easier if children are given reasons for rules) and by modeling. Cheating and aggression are two common behavior problems in the schools that involve moral issues.

Socialization: The Home and the School

Changes in family structures, childhood stress, divorce, and child abuse profoundly affect development. Teachers must report suspected cases of child abuse. In light of social challenges, teachers are faced with new roles, including supporting the affective development of their students.

The Preschool Years

The preschool years see the rapid development of children's gross- and fine-motor skills. Quality day-care and preschool programs generally have positive effects on emotional, intellectual, and social growth, as well as on the development of motor skills. Developmentally appropriate education does not hurry children's progress but responds to unfolding needs.

The Elementary-School Years

Physical development continues throughout the elementary-school years, with girls often ahead of boys in size. Friendships progress from play relationships based on immediate situations, through companionship based on a growing understanding of stable personal qualities, to close and psychologically supportive relationships that can be long-lasting, and which are tied to abstract values. Individuals who had close friends as children tend to be happier, more productive adults.

Issues Affecting Adolescents

With adolescence comes puberty and emotional struggles to cope with all the related changes. Females mature about two years ahead of males. Early maturation is generally beneficial for males, though it is not without its disadvantages. Early maturation is not generally beneficial for girls. Adolescents face many risks today, including pregnancy, eating disorders, drug abuse, AIDS, and suicide.

At all stages of development, teachers must address students' needs for education that is appropriate to their physical, cognitive, personal, and social levels of development.

KEY TERMS

affective education, p. 91
aggression, p. 86
anorexia nervosa, p. 100
autonomy, p. 67
blended families, p. 87
bulimia, p. 100
developmental crisis, p. 66
developmentally appropriate
 education, p. 95
empathy, p. 84
ethnic pride, p. 72

fine-motor skills, p. 93
generativity, p. 72
gross-motor skills, p. 93
identity, p. 69
identity achievement, p. 70
identity diffusion, p. 70
identity foreclosure, p. 70
industry, p. 68
initiative, p. 68
integrity, p. 72
internalize, p. 85

moral dilemmas, p. 81
moral realism, p. 78
moral reasoning, p. 81
morality of cooperation, p. 79
moratorium, p. 70
perspective-taking ability, p. 78
psychosocial theory, p. 66
puberty, p. 97
self-concept, p. 74
self-esteem, p. 74
socialization, p. 87

WHAT WOULD YOU DO?

Preschool
Two students in your 4-year-old group will soon have new babies in their families. As the time draws nearer, the students become more and more disruptive. What would you do?

Elementary and Middle School
One of the girls in your class is desperate for friends but can't keep them. She gives special gifts, tries to be helpful, but always seems to be the one exploited or hurt. How would you help this student form some genuine relationships?

You notice a fairly dramatic change in one of your students. This boy seems very tired and anxious, and he is not doing his homework. How would you approach this problem?

Junior High and High School
Several of your junior high school students are afraid to go to gym class because a gang of students has been extorting money and personal possessions. What steps would you take to end this situation?

You hear from one of your students that a group of seniors has a small "business" selling college applications essays. What would you do?

Cooperative Learning Activity
With four or five other members of your class, select a moral issue and develop a plan for integrating discussion of that issue into a lesson for the age level you will teach. How would you assess the effectiveness of your lesson?

Handling Aggression

You have heard from several parents that a student in your class is threatening their children and extorting money, articles of clothing, and other possessions. The student's parents seem unable to exercise control. How would you deal with this student's aggression?

FACING THE CONSEQUENCES

When threatening situations interrupt a student's environment, teachers and administrators need to be involved, and all strategies should be utilized. If a rapport exists between the teacher and the extortionist, a discussion outlining logical consequences is the first intervention. The consequences must be unpleasant, requiring an inventory analysis of the student by the teacher to learn what consequences are most uncomfortable for the student. If extortion is the case and is proven, the student must compensate the victim by returning the goods or items taken. Suspension in or out of school may be in order. There should be good documentation of the evidence and a contingency plan for future incidents. Proving that the incident occurred is difficult. Students who extort will lie, so witnesses are valuable. Questioned well and in the proper setting, other students are willing collaborators in the search for truth.

Marc Gray, *Science Teacher*
Highland Middle School, Louisville, Kentucky

DIRECT INTERVENTION

Dealing with a child's aggression toward his/her classmates is a particularly difficult situation, especially because the aggressive behavior usually occurs out of the teacher's sight. This requires the teacher to rely on so-called hearsay evidence, making it difficult to confront the child directly with irrefutable proof of the behavior. Thus, I would take a number of steps to circumvent extortion and other negative behaviors. First, I would try to exercise more direct supervision over the child during recess or other more unstructured activities, when the child is more likely to be practicing extortion. If necessary, I would enlist the assistance of other teachers. I would also discuss the matter with the entire class, without specifically naming the guilty student. Developmental guidance activities focused on building positive peer relationships, creating a sense of honesty and trust in the group, and respecting other people's property would be good for all the students, not just the offender. Other instructional concepts, such as developing self-esteem and learning decision-making skills, would also assist the students in resisting the aggressive behavior of the student offender.

Jane C. Dusell, *English Teacher*
Medford Area Senior High School, Medford, Wisconsin

Helping Students Cope

Is stress a problem for your students?

STRESSED-OUT STUDENTS

I believe stress is a big problem for young children. Children reflect their environment. Families are under tremendous time stress. When both parents work, time is very limited. Getting out the door in the morning is hectic and reconvening in the evening is worse. Everyone is tired and hungry. Dinner must be made, clothes washed, homework done. Every day is rushed, and there is little time for quiet, relaxed conversations. Children must also take on complex responsibilities early in life. This was very poignantly illustrated for me when I watched one of my first graders laying out four envelopes on his desk. It was early September and he could not read yet. Each carefully labeled envelope contained money. One was for lunch, one was for a field trip, one was for daycare, and one was for his book order. I listened as he studied the envelopes and talked to himself. "Don't lose your money, Chad. It is important to take care of money. You have to be responsible. One is for the daycare. One is for lunchroom. One is for the field trip. One is for your books. I don't know which envelopes to give to Mrs. Wisdom. There are so many envelopes. There is so much money. I have to take care of the money." Looking at the envelopes and struggling to read them, Chad began to cry quietly. I have no doubt that he was stressed and overwhelmed.

I help children handle stress in many ways. I try to structure our classroom so that it is predictable and easy to live in. I make an effort to be calm no matter what the circumstances. When the children make mistakes, I am kind and never ridicule them. They know they can come to me for help in straightening out problems. Smiling and taking pleasure in their growth is important, too. When I know that a child is especially stressed, I make some time to talk and listen privately. Most importantly, I help them learn the skills they need to manage their lives: reading, math, organizational skills, and how to get along with others.

Cynthia Newman Wisdom, *First-Grade Teacher*
Trace Crossings Elementary School, Hoover, Alabama

The parents of one of your students are going through a nasty divorce. The student is often upset, distracted, tired, or withdrawn and is not doing well in schoolwork or homework. The parents seem too concerned with their own problems to notice the effects they are having on their child. Can you do anything to help?

SUPPORT GROUPS

Our guidance department runs a series of specialized support groups to help students deal with intense, immediate problems such as this. These support groups have provided effective help in the past, so I would contact them to work with the student. If a school does not have such an ad hoc student support group system, but could have, I would encourage its implementation.

James D. Kraft, *Social Studies Teacher*
Wausau West High School, Wausau, Wisconsin

CHILD ADVOCACY

Children need to feel and believe that their teachers care about their welfare. Children who are experiencing the heartbreak of divorce may need their teachers to become advocates for them.

A teacher who recognizes behaviors that are the result of family strain and tensions should attempt to meet with the parents of the student. Parents who are embroiled in a divorce may be completely unaware of the impact on their children. A conference explaining the effects that the family pressures are having on the student may be enough to make the parents more sensitive to the child.

Parents who are still unresponsive after attempts by the teacher may be experiencing too many of their own problems to be able to react to a child's problems. When this is the case, the teacher must realize that a friendly word, smile, and an offer to help with tutoring will show the student that the teacher is there for support and guidance. Sometimes we can do little more than stand by our students and let them know we care. They understand we sometimes can't make certain situations better, but they can be strengthened by our support.

Darlene A. Walsh, *Rhode Island 1991 Teacher of the Year*
Greenbush Elementary School, West Warwick, Rhode Island

4

Learning Abilities and Learning Problems

*S*o far we have talked little about individuals. We have discussed principles of development that apply to everyone—stages, processes, conflicts, and tasks. Our development as human beings is similar in many ways—but not in every way. Even among members of the same family, there are marked contrasts in appearance, interests, abilities, and temperament.

We will begin our discussion of individual differences in learning with a look at the names and labels that have been applied to some students. Then we turn to an extended examination of intellectual abilities, which vary so greatly from individual to individual and have proved so difficult to define and measure. How can teachers work with such a wide range of abilities? Is ability grouping a good answer? What are the special needs of the gifted and the retarded? How do individual cognitive styles and learning preferences affect learning?

Next we explore the kinds of learning problems students may have. As we discuss each problem area, we will consider how a teacher might recognize problems, seek help from school and community resources, and plan instruction based on individuals' needs. Recent changes in federal legislation mean that you probably will have at least one exceptional student in your class, whatever grade you teach. We will discuss the laws and how to cope with their effects.

By the time you have completed this chapter, you should be able to:

- Discuss the potential problems in categorizing and labeling students.
- Begin to develop a personal concept of intelligence to aid you in your teaching.
- Discuss how you might recognize and teach students who are mildly retarded or who are gifted.
- Adapt lessons to make them appropriate for students with varying learning styles.
- List indicators of hearing, vision, language, and behavior problems, as well as indicators of specific learning disabilities.
- Adapt teaching methods to meet the needs of exceptional students.
- Discuss the implications of the Individuals with Disabilities Act for your teaching.

Have you ever had the experience of being the only one in a group who had trouble doing something? The first time you tried to skate, throw a football, play tennis, or bowl, perhaps you were the only one who didn't know how. How would you feel if every day in school you faced the same kind of difficulty, while everyone else seemed to find the work easier than you? What kind of support and teaching would you need to keep trying?

Language and Labeling

Planning Tip: See the *Chapter-4-At-A-Glance Planning Guide* in the Instructor's Section at the front of this book.

Study Guide: The *Study Guide*, sold separately, contains exercises to help students determine if they have mastered each learning objective for this chapter.

Planning Tip: See the separate *Instructor's Resource Manual* for additional activities and resources for teaching this chapter, including Handout Masters. Also see the Allyn and Bacon *Transparencies in Educational Psychology.*

Planning Tip: See the *Test Bank* and *Study Guide* supplements as you plan for evaluation and measurement of student learning.

Exceptional Students Students who have abilities or problems so significant that the students require special education or other services to reach their potential.

Every child is a distinctive collection of talents, abilities, and limitations. In that sense we all are "exceptional." But some students are called exceptional because they have learning abilities or problems and require special education or other services to reach their potential. **Exceptional students** may have mental retardation, learning disabilities, communication disorders, emotional or behavioral disorders, physical disabilities, autism, traumatic brain injury, impaired hearing, impaired vision, or special abilities and talents. Even though we will use these terms throughout the chapter, a caution is in order: labeling students is a controversial issue.

No child is born "mildly retarded," "gifted," or "learning disabled" in the same way that a child is born female or with blood type O. The decision that an individual has mental retardation is a judgment based on the way the individual performs certain tasks. For many years, the purpose of labels was to determine eligibility for special services in the school or community. The medical model was the guiding perspective; the assumption of the medical model is that each condition has a particular treatment that is usually effective.

Unfortunately, few specific "treatments" automatically follow from a "diagnosis" of mental retardation. Many different teaching strategies and materials are appropriate for students who have been labeled retarded. Critics of labeling claim the categories have no educational relevance, because a label does not tell the teacher which methods or materials to use with individual students. Further, the labels can become self-fulfilling prophecies. Everyone—teachers, parents, classmates, and even the students themselves—may see a label as a permanent problem, a stigma that cannot be changed. Finally, labels are mistaken for explanations, as in, "Chris gets into fights because he has a behavior disorder." "How do you know he has a behavior disorder?" "Because he gets into fights."

On the other hand, some educators argue that for younger students, at least, being labeled as special helps protect the child. For example, if classmates know a student is retarded, they will be more willing to accept his or her behaviors. And when a child is classified, parents and teachers have some guidelines in seeking information on particular problems. Of course, labels still open doors to some special programs or financial assistance.

Labels probably both stigmatize and help students (Brantlinger & Guskin, 1987; Heward & Orlansky, 1992). But until we are able to make diagnoses with greater accuracy, we should be very cautious about describing a whole human being with one or two words.

This caution also applies to many of the common descriptions heard in schools every day. Today some people object to labels such as "the mentally retarded" or "at-risk student," because describing a complex person with one or two words implies that the condition labeled is the most important aspect of the person. Actually the individual has many abilities, and to focus on the disability is to misrepresent the individual. An alternative is to speak of "students with mental retardation" or "students placed at risk." Here the emphasis is on the students first, not on the special challenges they face.

In the next section we consider a concept that has provided the basis for many labels—intelligence.

Individual Differences in Intelligence

Test Bank item 4.123

Because the concept of intelligence is so important in education, so controversial, and so often misunderstood, we will spend quite a few pages discussing it. Let us begin with a basic question.

What Does Intelligence Mean?

Test Bank items 4.3–4.11, 4.88, 4.89, 4.100, 4.116

The idea that people vary in what we call intelligence has been with us for a long time. Plato discussed similar variations over 2,000 years ago. Most early theories about the basic nature of intelligence involved one or more of the following three themes: (1) the capacity to learn; (2) the total knowledge a person has acquired; and (3) the ability to adapt successfully to new situations and to the environment in general.

In this century, there has been considerable controversy over the meaning of intelligence. In 1921, 14 psychologists offered 14 different views about the nature of intelligence in a symposium on the subject, reported in the *Journal of Educational Psychology* (Neisser, 1979). Sternberg and Detterman repeated this process in 1986, asking 24 experts for their definitions of intelligence. Again, opinion was divided. One point of disagreement in 1921 (and still today) is whether intelligence is a single ability or many separate abilities.

Intelligence: One Ability or Many? Some theorists believe intelligence is a basic ability that affects performance on all cognitively oriented tasks. An "intelligent" person will do well in computing mathematical problems, analyzing poetry, taking history essay examinations, and solving riddles. Evidence for this position comes from correlational evaluations of intelligence tests. In study after study, moderate to high positive correlations are found among all

Planning Tip: For further information about audiovisual, multimedia, and computer-assisted resources for teaching this chapter, see the Video and Software Guide in the *Instructor's Resource Manual.*

Handout: See **Handout Master 4.1** in the *Instructor's Resource Manual,* "Myths and Facts about Special Education."

Objective 4.1: Discuss the potential problems in categorizing and labeling students.

Objective 4.2: Begin to develop a personal concept of intelligence to aid in teaching.

Research: Lohman, D. L. (1989). Human intelligence: An introduction to advances in theory and research. *Review of Educational Research, 59,* 333–374. See also the *Instructor's Resource Manual* for Definitions of Intelligence, a summary of 11 classic and more recent definitions of intelligence.

Examples: Here are a few current ideas about the meaning of intelligence:

goal-directed adaptive behavior

ability to solve novel problems

ability to acquire and think with new conceptual systems

problem-solving ability

planning and other metacognitive skills

memory access speed

what people think intelligence is

what IQ tests measure

the ability to learn from bad teaching

Faces of Intellect In Guilford's theory, the three basic categories of thinking—operations, contents, and products.

the different tests that are designed to measure separate intellectual abilities (Lohman, 1989; McNemar, 1964). What could explain these results?

Charles Spearman (1927) suggested there is one factor or mental attribute, which he called *g* or *general intelligence,* that is used to perform any mental test, but that each test also requires some specific abilities in addition to *g.* For example, performance on a test of memory for numbers probably involves both *g* and some specific ability for immediate recall of what is heard. Spearman assumed that individuals vary in both general intelligence and specific abilities, and that together these factors determine performance on mental tasks.

Critics of Spearman's position insisted that there are several "primary mental abilities," not just one. Thurstone (1938) listed verbal comprehension, memory, reasoning, ability to visualize spatial relationships, numerical ability, word fluency, and perceptual speed as the major mental abilities underlying intellectual tasks. But tests of these "separate" factors showed that ability in one area was correlated with ability in the others.

Multiple Intelligences. J. P. Guilford (1988) and Howard Gardner (1983) are the most prominent modern proponents of the concept of multiple cognitive abilities. Guilford suggests that there are three basic categories, or **faces of intellect:** *mental operations,* or the processes of thinking; *contents,* or what we think about; and *products,* or the end results of our thinking (see Figure 4.1). In this model, mental operations are divided into six subcategories: cognition (recognizing old information and discovering new), convergent thinking (where there is only one answer or solution), divergent thinking (used when many answers may be appropriate), evaluation (decisions about how good, accurate, or suitable something is), memory recording (immediate memory), and memory retention (memory over several days). The contents on which people operate are divided into five subcategories: visual content, auditory content, word meanings, symbols, and behaviors. The different products that may result are units, classes, relations, systems, transformations, and implications.

According to this view, carrying out a cognitive task is essentially performing a mental operation on some specific content to achieve a product. For example, listing the next number in the sequence 3, 6, 12, 24, . . . requires a *convergent operation* (there is only one right answer) with *symbolic content* (numbers) to achieve a *relationship product* (each number is double the one before). Painting an abstract conception of a still life requires a *divergent-thinking operation* (many possible "answers") about *visual content* to create a *transformational product* (the actual objects are transformed into the artist's view). There are 180 combinations of operations, contents, and products— $6 \times 5 \times 6$.

Guilford's model of intelligence broadens our view of the nature of intelligence by adding such factors as social judgment (the evaluation of others' behavior) and creativity (divergent thinking). On the other hand, even though human mental abilities are complex, Guilford's model may be too complex to serve as a guide for predicting behavior in real situations or for planning instruction. In addition, when people are tested on these different abilities, the abilities prove to be related. The problem of explaining the positive correlations among all these supposed separate mental abilities remains unsolved.

Howard Gardner (1983, 1993c) has proposed a theory of **multiple intelligences.** According to Gardner there are at least seven separate kinds of intelligences: linguistic (verbal), musical, spatial, logical-mathematical, bodily-kinesthetic, understanding of others (interpersonal), and understanding of self (intrapersonal) (see Figure 4.2 on page 113). Gardner has based his notion of separate abilities in part on evidence that brain damage (from a stroke, for example) often interferes with functioning in one area, such as language, but does not affect functioning in other areas. Gardner has also noted that individuals often excel in one of these seven areas but have no remarkable abilities in the other six.

Intelligence as a Process.   As you can see, the theories of Spearman, Thurstone, Guilford, and Gardner tend to describe how individuals differ in the *content* of intelligence—the different abilities underlying intelligent behavior. Recent work in cognitive psychology has emphasized instead the thinking *processes* that may be common to all people. How do humans gather and use information to solve problems and behave intelligently? New views of intelligence are growing out of this work.

Background: Gardner, H., & Hatch, T. (1989). Multiple intelligences go to school. *Educational Researcher, 18*(8), 4–10.

Transparency: Use acetate transparency **T 25,** "Sternberg's Triarchic Theory of Intelligence."

FIGURE 4.1

GUILFORD'S MODEL OF THE STRUCTURE OF INTELLECT
Each of Guilford's three dimensions of intellectual abilities and activities—operation, content, and product—has many attributes. Through various combinations, these dimensions and their attributes produce 180 separate factors.

Multiple Intelligences In Gardner's theory of intelligence, a person's seven separate abilities: logical-mathematical, verbal, musical, spatial, bodily-kinesthetic, interpersonal, intrapersonal.

*H*oward Gardner's model of multiple intelligences broadened our view of intelligent behavior to include such factors as creativity and the ability to coordinate body movements.

Triarchic Theory of Intelligence A three-part description of the mental abilities (thinking processes, coping with new experiences, and adapting to context) that lead to more or less intelligent behavior.

Components In an information-processing view, basic problem-solving processes underlying intelligence.

Insight The ability to deal effectively with novel situations.

Robert Sternberg's (1985, 1990) **triarchic theory of intelligence** is an example of a cognitive process approach to understanding intelligence. As you might guess from the name, this theory has three parts.

The first describes the mental processes of the individual that lead to more or less intelligent behavior. These processes are defined in terms of **components**. A component is "an elementary information process that operates upon internal representations of objects or symbols" (Sternberg, 1985, p. 97). Components are classified by the functions they serve and by how general they are. There are at least three different functions served. The first function—higher-order planning, strategy selection, and monitoring—is performed by *metacomponents*. Examples of metacomponents are identifying the problem, allocating attention, and monitoring how well a strategy is working. A second function served by components—executing the strategies selected—is handled by *performance components*. One performance component allows us to perceive and store new information. The third function—gaining new knowledge—is performed by *knowledge-acquisition components*, such as separating relevant from irrelevant information as you try to understand a new concept (Sternberg, 1985).

Some components are specific; that is, they are necessary for only one kind of task, such as solving analogies. Other components are very general and may be necessary in almost every cognitive task. For example, metacomponents are always operating to select strategies and keep track of progress. This may help to explain the persistent correlations among all types of mental tests. People who are effective in selecting good problem-solving strategies, monitoring progress, and moving to a new approach when the first one fails are more likely to be successful on all types of tests. Metacomponents may be the modern-day version of Spearman's *g*.

FIGURE 4.2

SEVEN INTELLIGENCES
Howard Gardner's theory of multiple intelligences suggests that there are seven different categories of human abilities. An individual might have strengths or weaknesses in one or several areas. The figure gives explanations of each capacity and examples of occupations that draw upon that ability.

Intelligence	End States	Core Components
Logical-mathematical	Scientist Mathematician	Sensitivity to, and capacity to discern, logical or numerical patterns; ability to handle long chains of reasoning.
Linguistic	Poet Journalist	Sensitivity to the sounds, rhythms, and meanings of words; sensitivity to the different functions of language.
Musical	Composer Violinist	Abilities to produce and appreciate rhythm, pitch, and timbre; appreciation of the forms of musical expressiveness.
Spatial	Navigator Sculptor	Capacities to perceive the visual-spatial world accurately and to perform transformations on one's initial perceptions.
Bodily-kinesthetic	Dancer Athlete	Abilities to control one's body movements and to handle objects skillfully.
Interpersonal	Therapist Salesman	Capacities to discern and respond appropriately to the moods, temperaments, motivations, and desires of other people.
Intrapersonal	Person with detailed, accurate self-knowledge	Access to one's own feelings and the ability to discriminate among them and draw upon them to guide behavior; knowledge of one's own strengths, weaknesses, desires, and intelligence.

Source: H. Gardner and T. Hatch (1989). Multiple intelligences go to school. *Educational Researcher, 18* (8), p. 6. Copyright 1989 by the American Educational Research Association. Reprinted by permission of the publisher and the authors.

The second part of Sternberg's triarchic theory involves coping with new experiences. Intelligent behavior is marked by two characteristics: (1) **insight,** or the ability to deal effectively with novel situations, and (2) the ability to become efficient and automatic in thinking and problem solving. So intelligence involves creative thinking in solving new problems and **automaticity**—quickly turning new solutions into routine processes that can be applied without much cognitive effort.

Automaticity The result of learning to perform a behavior or thinking process so thoroughly that the performance is automatic and does not require effort.

FIGURE 4.3

STERNBERG'S TRIARCHIC THEORY OF INTELLIGENCE

Sternberg's triarchic theory suggests that intelligent behavior is the product of applying thinking strategies, handling new problems creatively and quickly, and adapting to contexts by selecting and reshaping our environment.

Contextual Intelligence	Experiential Intelligence	Componential Intelligence
Ability to adapt to a changing environment and to shape one's world to optimize opportunities. Contextual intelligence deals with an individual's ability to prepare for problem solving in specific situations. For example, some students take their telephones off the hook or put a "do not disturb" sign on the door while studying, because they know they will be distracted by calls and visitors.	Ability to formulate new ideas and combine unrelated facts. A test of experiential intelligence assesses a person's ability to deal with novel tasks in an automatic manner. Examples include learning to remember all the words containing the letter *t* in a particular paragraph and diagnosing a problem with an automobile engine.	Ability to think abstractly, process information, and determine what needs to be done. Tasks that can be used to measure the elements of componential intelligence are analogies, vocabulary, and syllogisms.

Teaching Tip: Describe the various subtests of the WISC-III. Ask students what kinds of abilities and thinking are tested by each subscale. What does it take to do well on each test? Describe how Wechsler developed the tests and how the tests predict school achievement. A good reference for this information is Sattler, J. (1992). *Assessment of children* (3rd ed. rev.). San Diego: Jerome Sattler Publisher.

Transparency: Use acetate transparency T 27, "Distribution of Intelligence Test Scores."

Transparency: Use acetate transparency T 28, "Illustration of Items Used in Intelligence Testing."

The third part of Sternberg's theory highlights the importance of choosing an environment in which a person can succeed and adapting to that environment or reshaping it if necessary. Here, culture is a major factor in defining successful choice, adaptation, and shaping. What works in one cultural group will not work in another. For example, abilities that make a person successful in a rural farm community may be useless in the inner city or at a country club in the suburbs. People who are successful often seek situations in which their abilities will be valuable, then work hard to capitalize on those abilities and compensate for any weaknesses. Thus, intelligence in this third sense involves practical matters such as career choice or social skills. Figure 4.3 summarizes the elements of Sternberg's triarchic theory of intelligence and shows how they may relate mental abilities to one another and to the thinking processes underlying these abilities.

How Is Intelligence Measured?

Test Bank items 4.12–4.19, 4.90, 4.91, 4.101, 4.116, 4.124

Because cognitive process approaches like Sternberg's are relatively new, they have not produced any widely used tests of intelligence. The tests of intelligence used in schools are based almost entirely on the definition of intelligence as content—specific and general abilities. Even though psychologists do not agree about what intelligence is, they do agree that intelligence, as measured by these standard tests, is related to learning in school. Why is this so? It has to do in part with the way intelligence tests were first developed.

Binet's Dilemma. In 1904, Alfred Binet was confronted with the following problem by the minister of public instruction in Paris: How can students who will need special teaching and extra help be identified early in their school careers, before they fail in regular classes? At the time, many of these students, who are now called mentally retarded, were likely to spend several years in regular classes, falling farther and farther behind, when they might have been in classes designed to meet their needs. Binet's task was to devise some way to identify these students. Binet was also a political activist, very concerned with the rights of children. He believed that having an objective measure of learning ability could protect students from poor families who might be forced to leave school because they were the victims of discrimination and assumed to be slow learners.

Binet and his collaborator Theophile Simon wanted to measure not merely school achievement, but the intellectual skills students needed to do well in school. They searched first for test items that could discriminate between students who were doing well and students of the same age who were doing poorly. They tested students in regular schools and students of the same age in institutions for the retarded and then compared the results. After trying many different tests and eliminating items that did not discriminate between successful and unsuccessful students, Binet and Simon finally identified 58 tests, several for each age group from 3 to 13. Binet's tests allowed the examiner to determine a **mental age** for a child. A child who succeeded on the items passed by most 6-year-olds, for example, was considered to have a mental age of 6, whether the child was actually 5, 6, or 7 years old. Some sample items from Binet's test are shown in Table 4.1.

The concept of **intelligence quotient,** or **IQ,** was added after Binet's test was brought to the United States and revised at Stanford University to give us the Stanford-Binet test. An IQ score was computed by comparing the mental-age score to the person's actual chronological age. The formula was

$$\text{intelligence quotient} = \frac{\text{mental age}}{\text{}} \times 100$$

The early Stanford-Binet has been revised four times, most recently in 1986 (Thorndike, Hagen, & Sattler, 1986). The practice of computing a mental age proved problematic. As children grow older, the range and variability of mental ages increase. For this reason, IQ scores calculated on the basis of

Alfred Binet developed a systematic procedure for assessing learning aptitudes. His goal was to understand intelligence and use this knowledge to help children.

Objective 4.3: Trace the development of IQ tests, and interpret the meaning of an IQ test score.

Connections: The deviation IQ score takes into account variations in performance at different ages by calculating individual deviation from the age-group average. This idea is discussed more fully in chapter 14.

Mental Age In intelligence testing, a score based on average abilities for that age group.

Intelligence Quotient (IQ) Score comparing mental and chronological ages.

TABLE 4.1 Intelligence Test Items at Three Different Age Levels of Binet's Test, 1911 Version

Year 3	Year 7	Year 15
1. Point to eyes, nose, and mouth	1. Show right hand and left ear	1. Repeat 7 digits
2. Repeat 2 digits	2. Describe a picture	2. Find 3 rhymes for a given word in 1 minute
3. Identify objects in a picture	3. Carry out 3 commands given simultaneously	3. Repeat a sentence of 26 syllables
4. Repeat a sentence of 6 syllables	4. Count the value of 6 coins	4. Interpret a set of given facts

Source: J. Darley, S. Glucksberg, and R. Kinchla (1988), *Psychology,* 5th ed., © 1991, p. 298. Reprinted by permission of Prentice-Hall, Englewood Cliffs, New Jersey.

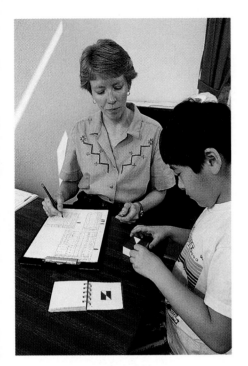

This boy is trying to arrange the red and white blocks so that they match the pattern in the booklet. His performance is timed. This subtest of the Wechsler Intelligence Scale for Children assesses spatial ability.

Activity 4.2: Application. See the *Instructor's Resource Manual* for Taking an Intelligence Test, an activity that gives your students experience in taking an actual intelligence test.

Activity 4.3: Critical Thinking. See the *Instructor's Resource Manual* for Interview on IQ Testing, an activity that asks your students to prepare questions for an interview with a school psychologist.

Deviation IQ   Score based on statistical comparison of individual's performance with the average performance of others in that age group.

mental age do not have the same meaning at every age. To cope with this problem, the concept of **deviation IQ** was introduced. The deviation IQ score is a number that tells exactly how much above or below the average a person scored on the test, compared to others in the same age group.

Group versus Individual IQ Tests.   The Stanford-Binet is an *individual intelligence test.* It has to be administered to one student at a time by a trained psychologist and takes about two hours. Psychologists also have developed *group tests* that can be given to whole classes or schools. A group test is much less likely to yield an accurate picture of any one person's abilities. When students take tests in a group, they may do poorly because they do not understand the instructions, because their pencils break, because they are distracted by other students, or because they do not shine on paper-and-pencil tests. But on an individual test, most of the questions are asked orally and do not require reading or writing. A student usually pays closer attention and is more motivated to do well when working directly with an adult. *As a teacher, you should be very wary of IQ scores based on group tests.*

What Does an IQ Score Mean?   Test Bank items 4.20–4.24

Most intelligence tests are designed so that they have certain statistical characteristics. Like college entrance examinations, intelligence tests have a standard average score. For IQ tests the average score is 100. Fifty percent of the people from the general population who take the tests will score 100 or above, and 50 percent will score below 100. About 68 percent of the general population will earn IQ scores between 85 and 115. Only about 16 percent of the population will receive scores below 85, and only 16 percent will score above 115. Note, however, that these figures hold true for white, native-born Americans whose first language is Standard English. Whether IQ tests should even be used with ethnic minority-group students is hotly debated.

Intelligence and Achievement.   People often wonder what IQ scores mean in terms of future achievement. Intelligence test scores predict achievement in schools quite well, at least for large groups. For example, the correlation is about .65 between school achievement and scores on a popular individual intelligence test, the revised Wechsler Intelligence Scale for Children (WISC-III) (Sattler, 1992). This isn't surprising because the tests were designed to predict school achievement. Remember, Binet threw out test items that did not discriminate between good and poor students.

But do people who score high on IQ tests achieve more in life? Here the answer is less clear. There is evidence that *g*, or general intelligence, correlates with "real-world academic, social, and occupational accomplishments" (Ceci, 1991), but there is great debate about the size and meaning of these correlations (*Current Directions in Psychological Science,* Special Section: Controversies, February 1993). People with higher intelligence-test scores tend to complete more years of school and to have higher-status jobs. However, when the number of years of education is held constant, IQ scores and school achievement are not highly correlated with income and success in later life. Even if predictions hold for large groups, they often are wrong for individu-

Guidelines

Check to see if the score is based on an individual or a group test. Be wary of group test scores.

Examples

1. Individual tests include the Wechsler Scales (WPPSI, WISC-III, WAIS-R), the Stanford-Binet, the McCarthy Scales of Children's Abilities, the Woodcock-Johnson Psycho-Educational Battery, and the Kaufman Assessment Battery for Children.
2. Group tests include the Lorge-Thorndike Intelligence Tests, the Analysis of Learning Potential, the Kuhlman-Anderson Intelligence Tests, the Otis-Lennon Mental Abilities Tests, and the School and College Ability Tests (SCAT).

Remember that IQ tests are only estimates of general aptitude for learning.

Examples

1. Ignore small differences in scores among students.
2. Bear in mind that even an individual student's scores may change over time for many reasons, including measurement error.
3. Be aware that a total score is usually an average of scores on several kinds of questions. A score in the middle or average range may mean that the student performed at the average on every kind of question or that the student did quite well in some areas (for example, on verbal tasks) and rather poorly in other areas (for example, on quantitative tasks).

Remember that IQ scores reflect a student's past experiences and learning.

Examples

1. Consider these scores as predictors of school abilities, not measures of innate intellectual abilities.
2. If a student is doing well in your class, do not change your opinion or lower your expectations just because one score seems low.
3. Be wary of IQ scores for minority students and for students whose first language was not English. Even scores on "culture-free" tests are lower for disadvantaged students.

---

als. If you complete college, your chances of doing well in your career, in comparison to your classmates, cannot be predicted accurately from your scores on IQ tests (McClelland, 1973, 1993). Within a given type of job, success does not seem to be related to measured intelligence. Other factors like motivation, social skills, and luck may make the difference (Sternberg & Wagner, 1993).

Intelligence: Heredity or Environment? Nowhere, perhaps, has the nature-versus-nurture debate raged so hard as in the area of **intelligence**. The main topic of controversy is whether intelligence should be seen as a potential, limited by our genetic makeup, that once fulfilled cannot be exceeded. Or does intelligence simply refer to an individual's current level of intellectual functioning, as fed and influenced by experience and education? In fact, it is almost

Transparency: Use acetate transparency **T 25**, "Sternberg's Triarchic Theory of Intelligence."

Teaching Tip: For a concise discussion of the history of intelligence testing and the major theories of intelligence, see chapter 3 of Sattler, J. (1992). *Assessment of children* (3rd ed. rev.). San Diego: Jerome Sattler Publisher.

Transparency: Use acetate transparency **T 26**, "The Modern Stanford-Binet Intelligence Scale."

Intelligence Ability or abilities to acquire and use knowledge for solving problems and adapting to the world.

impossible to separate intelligence "in the genes" from intelligence "due to experience." Today, most psychologists believe that differences in intelligence are due to both heredity and environment, probably in about equal proportions. "Genes do not fix behavior. Rather they establish a range of possible reactions to the range of possible experiences that the environment can provide" (Weinberg, 1989, p. 101).

So what can we conclude about intellectual abilities? Abilities as measured by standard IQ tests seem to be strongly influenced by heredity, but what people do with these abilities, their level of achievement, seems very much influenced by environment. And environmental influences can range from the health of a child's mother during pregnancy to the quality of teaching a child receives. As a teacher, it is especially important for you to realize that cognitive skills, like any other skills, are always improvable. *Intelligence is a current state of affairs,* affected by past experiences and open to future changes—probably within limits, but limits that are not yet fully understood. Even if intelligence is a limited potential, the potential is still quite large, and that potential is a challenge to all teachers.

Focus on . . . **Intelligence**

- Explain your personal definition of intelligence.
- Give an original example of each of Gardner's seven intelligences.
- What roles do new experiences play in Sternberg's theory of intelligence?
- What do IQ scores predict?

---

bility Differences and Teaching   Test Bank item 4.123

In this section we consider how you might handle differences in academic ability in your classes. First we examine a commonly used approach—ability grouping. Is this a solution to the challenge of ability differences? If so, when and for whom? Then we turn our attention to students who represent the extremes in ability, the retarded and the gifted. Both groups need teachers who understand their particular needs.

Research: Slavin, R. E. (1990). Achievement effects of ability grouping in secondary schools: A best-evidence synthesis. *Review of Educational Research, 60,* 471–500.

Objective 4.4: Identify the methods, common practices, and implications of ability grouping.

Background: For a concise discussion of ability grouping and tracking, see Oakes, J. (1988). Tracking: Can schools take a different route. *NEA Today, 6*(6), 41–47.

Ability Grouping   Test Bank items 4.25–4.29, 4.102, 4.117, 4.125

The expressed goal of ability grouping is to make teaching more appropriate for students. As we will see, this does not always happen.

Between-class ability grouping involves forming whole classes based on ability. It is a common practice in secondary schools and can be found in many elementary schools as well. Most high schools have "college prep" courses and "general" courses or, for example, high-, middle-, and low-ability classes in a particular subject. Although this seems on the surface to be an efficient way to teach, research has consistently shown that segregation by ability may benefit high-ability students slightly but causes problems for low-ability students (Good & Marshall, 1984; Slavin, 1987, 1990a).

There are several problems with between-class grouping. Low-ability classes seem to receive lower-quality instruction in general. Teachers tend to focus on lower-level objectives and routine procedures. There are more management problems. Teacher enthusiasm and enjoyment are less in the low-

Between-Class Ability Grouping System of grouping in which students are assigned to classes based on their measured ability or their achievements.

ability classes. These differences in instruction and the teachers' negative attitudes may mean that low expectations are communicated to the students. Student self-esteem suffers almost as soon as the assignment to "dummy" English or math is made. Attendance may drop along with self-esteem. The lower tracks often have a disproportionate number of minority-group and economically disadvantaged students, so ability grouping, in effect, becomes resegregation in school. Possibilities for friendships become limited to students in the same ability range. Assignments to classes are often made on the basis of group IQ tests instead of tests in the subject area itself. Yet group IQ tests are not good guides for what someone is ready to learn in a particular subject area (Corno & Snow, 1986; Good & Brophy, 1984; Kulik & Kulik, 1982; Slavin, 1987, 1990a; Slavin & Karweit, 1985).

There are two exceptions to the general finding that between-class ability grouping leads to lower achievement. The first is found in honors or gifted classes, where high-ability students tend to perform better than comparable students in regular classes. The second exception is the **nongraded elementary school** and the related **Joplin Plan.** In these arrangements, students are grouped by ability in particular subjects, regardless of their age or grade. A reading class might therefore have students from several grades, all working on the same level on reading. This cross-grade grouping seems to be effective for students of all abilities as long as the grouping allows teachers to give more direct instruction to the groups. When cross-age grouping is used to implement individualized instruction, the effects are much less positive (Gutierrez & Slavin, 1992).

A second method, **within-class ability grouping,** clustering students by ability within the same class, is another story. Many elementary-school classes are grouped for reading, and some are grouped for math. The results are generally positive for students at all ability levels if the following conditions are met (Good & Brophy, 1991; Slavin, 1987).

1. The groups should be formed and reformed on the basis of students' *current performance* in the subject being taught. This means students are grouped on the basis of current reading level for reading instruction and on the basis of current math achievement for math instruction. This also means frequent changes in group placement when students' achievement changes.

2. The teacher should discourage comparisons between groups and encourage students to develop a whole-class spirit. Group by ability for one or, at the most, two subjects. Make sure there are many lessons and projects that mix members from the groups. Experiment with learning strategies in which cooperation is stressed (described in chapter 10).

3. The number of groups should be kept small (two or three at most) so that the teacher can provide as much direct teaching as possible. When we discuss effective teaching in chapter 12, you will see that leaving students alone for too long leads to less learning.

4. Make sure teachers, methods, and pace are adjusted to fit the needs of the group. Putting similar-ability students together will not be effective unless the teaching is appropriate for the students' level of understanding.

There are alternatives to within-class grouping that appear more effective for some subjects. For example, DeWayne Mason and Tom Good (1993) found

Research: Another review of the research on ability grouping is: Organizing Classes by Ability (1987, July). *Harvard Education Letter, 3*(4), 1–4. Highlights:

Heterogeneous groups make sense in the elementary schools.

At the secondary level, it is worth trying less tracking than schools now have.

Teachers and counselors need to work harder at getting students to understand the consequences of their course choices.

The results of homogeneous grouping in secondary schools do not justify its strong support among teachers. (p. 2)

Background: For a discussion of the effects of ability grouping in reading, see First grade reading: Who learns and who doesn't (1987, January). *Harvard Education Letter, 3*(1), 4–6.

Research: For a comprehensive review of research on the effects of between- and within-class ability grouping on the achievement of elementary-school students, see Slavin, R. E. (1987). Ability grouping and student achievement in elementary schools: A best-evidence synthesis. *Review of Educational Research, 57,* 293–336.

Nongraded Elementary School/ The Joplin Plan Arrangement wherein students are grouped by ability in particular subjects, regardless of their ages or grades.

Within-Class Ability Grouping System of grouping in which students in a class are divided into two or three groups based on ability in an attempt to accommodate student differences.

Teaching Tip: Note that the Joplin Plan avoids some of the problems of ability grouping. In every group there are high-, middle-, and low-ability students (for example, high-ability second graders with middle-ability third graders and low-ability fourth graders).

Research: For an examination of how tracking has persisted nationally in the middle grades, see Braddock, J. H. (1990). Tracking the middle grades: National patterns of grouping for instruction. *Phi Delta Kappan, 71*, 445–452.

Casebook: See the Teachers' Casebook for practicing teachers' views on ability groupings.

Objective 4.5: Discuss how one might recognize and teach students who are either mildly retarded or gifted.

Background: Westling, D. L. (1989). Leadership for education of the mentally handicapped. *Educational Leadership, 46*(6), 19–23.

Transparency: Use acetate transparency T 31, "Defining Mental Retardation."

Handout: See Handout Master 4.2 in the *Instructor's Resource Manual*, "Myths and Facts about the Mentally Retarded."

Mental Retardation Significantly below-average intellectual and adaptive social behavior, evident before age 18.

Down Syndrome Retardation caused by presence of an extra chromosome.

that supplementing whole-class instruction in math with remediation and enrichment for students when they needed it worked better than dividing the class into two ability groups and teaching these groups separately.

What should teachers do when they face more extreme differences in student ability? We turn to this question next.

Mental Retardation   Test Bank items 4.30–4.37, 4.92, 4.103, 4.104

Before the 1970s, mental retardation was often defined simply as a score below a particular cutoff point on an intelligence test. Since one school district might use a cutoff of, say, 75, and another a cutoff of 67, a student could be labeled mentally retarded in one district but not in another. Using an IQ score alone is *never* an appropriate way to classify a student. Almost every definition of mental retardation includes the idea that mentally retarded individuals *cannot adapt adequately* to their environment.

Definition and Prevalence. According to the American Association on Mental Deficiency (AAMD Ad Hoc Committee on Terminology and Classification, 1992, p. 5), **mental retardation** refers to:

> substantial limitations in present intellectual functioning. It is characterized by significantly subaverage intellectual functioning existing concurrently with related limitations in two or more of the following applicable adaptive skill areas: communication, self-care, home living, social skills, community use, self-direction, health and safety, functional academics, leisure, and work. Mental retardation manifests before age 18.

Intellectual function is usually measured by IQ tests with a cutoff score of 70 to 75 as one indicator of retardation. But remember, an IQ score below the 70 to 75 range is *not* enough to diagnose a child as having mental retardation. There must also be problems with adaptive behavior, day-to-day independent living and social functioning. This caution is especially important when interpreting the scores of students from different cultures. Defining retardation based on test scores alone can create what some critics call "6-hour retardates"—students who are seen as retarded only for the part of the day they attend school.

Only about 1 to 1.5 percent of the population fit the AAMD's definition of retarded in both intellectual functioning and adaptive behavior (Hallahan & Kauffman, 1994). Of this group, most—about 75 percent—are mildly retarded, and only 5 percent are severely or profoundly affected. Table 4.2 describes typical behaviors for mildly, moderately, severely, and profoundly retarded people at preschool- and school-age levels.

Causes of Retardation. At least 75 percent of the time we don't know what causes mental retardation. Organic (physical) causes of retardation have been identified for only about 10 to 25 percent of the individuals involved. One organic cause is **Down syndrome,** a condition caused by the presence of an extra chromosome (though the extra chromosome does not appear to be inherited). Children with Down syndrome range in intelligence from very severely retarded to almost normal.

TABLE 4.2 Developmental Characteristics of Individuals with Mental Retardation

Degree of Retardation and IQ Range	Preschool Years (0–5)	School Years (6–20)
Mild 50–55 to approx. 70	Capable of developing social and communication skills Minimal sensorimotor retardation Retardation may not be obvious at this age	By late teens, can attain about sixth-grade academic level Social conformity and acceptance with guidance "Educable"
Moderate 35–50 to 50–55	Can talk or communicate Poor social awareness Fair motor development Moderate supervision necessary Training in self-help useful	Progress beyond second-grade academic level unlikely Training in social and occupational skills beneficial Can learn to get around alone in familiar places
Severe 20–25 to 35–40	Minimal speech; few or no communication skills Poor motor development Self-help training generally unprofitable	Can talk or learn to communicate Systematic training in basic hygiene and other self-care habits beneficial
Profound Below 20–25	Minimal sensorimotor functioning capacities Nursing care required	Some motor development Limited self-help training may be useful

Sources: Samuel Kirk and James Gallagher, *Educating Exceptional Children,* Third Edition, p. 142. Copyright © 1979 by Houghton Mifflin Company. Used with permission. Originally from the President's Committee on Mental Retardation, 1975. Also H. G. Grossman (Ed.) (1983), *Classification in Mental Retardation,* p. 13. Adapted by permission of the American Association on Mental Deficiency.

Other causes of mental retardation include maternal infections such as rubella (German measles), syphilis, or herpes simplex during pregnancy; blood-type incompatibility between the mother and the unborn baby; maternal alcohol or drug use during pregnancy; premature birth; lead poisoning in young children; or the inherited diseases phenylketonuria (PKU) or Tay-Sachs (Hardman, Drew, Egan, & Wolf, 1993).

Teaching Learners with Retardation.   As a regular teacher, you may not have contact with severely or moderately retarded children unless your school is participating in a full inclusion program for exceptional students (described later in this chapter), but you probably will work with mildly retarded children. In the early grades, these students may simply learn more slowly than their peers. By the third or fourth grade, they will probably have fallen far behind.

Learning goals for mildly retarded students between the ages of 9 and 13 include basic reading, writing, arithmetic, learning about the local environment, social behavior, and personal interests. In junior and senior high school, the emphasis is on vocational and domestic skills; literacy for living (using the

Teaching Tip: You may want to discuss the fact that most measures of adaptive behavior—such as the Vineland Adaptive Behavior Scale or the Woodcock-Johnson Scales of Independent Behavior—are nationally norm-referenced and do not have separate norms for separate cultural groups.

Activity 4.4: Teaching Tip. Teaching Retarded Students— see the *Instructor's Resource Manual.*

Research: Depending on one's conception of intelligence, the strategies used to treat the problems of children with low intelligence may vary. See Wagner, R. K., & Sternberg, R. J. (1984). Alternative conceptions of intelligence and their implications for education. *Review of Educational Research, 54,* 179–223.

telephone book; reading signs, labels, and newspaper ads; completing a job application); job-related behaviors like courtesy and punctuality; health self-care; and citizenship skills. Today there is a growing emphasis on **transition programming**—preparing the retarded student to live and work in the community. As you will see later in the chapter, the law requires that schools design an IEP, or individualized educational program, for every disabled child. An ITP, or individualized transition plan, may be part of the retarded student's IEP (Hallahan & Kauffman, 1994).

The Guidelines list suggestions for teaching students with below-average general intelligence.

Guidelines

Teaching Students with Mental Retardation

1. Determine readiness: however little a child may know, he or she is ready to learn a next step.
2. State and present objectives simply.
3. Base specific learning objectives on an analysis of the child's learning strengths and weaknesses.
4. Present material in small, logical steps. Practice extensively before going on to the next step.
5. Work on practical skills and concepts based on the demands of adult life.
6. Do not skip steps. Students with average intelligence can form conceptual bridges from one step to the next, but retarded children need every step and bridge made explicit. Make connections for the student. Do not expect him or her to "see" the connections.
7. Be prepared to present the same idea in many different ways.
8. Go back to a simpler level if you see the student is not following.
9. Be especially careful to motivate the student and maintain attention.
10. Find materials that do not insult the student. A junior high boy may need the low vocabulary of "See Spot run" but will be insulted by the age of the characters and the content of the story.
11. Focus on a few target behaviors or skills so you and the student have a chance to experience success. Everyone needs positive reinforcement.
12. Be aware that retarded students must overlearn, repeat, and practice more than children of average intelligence. They must be taught how to study, and they must frequently review and practice their newly acquired skills in different settings.
13. Pay close attention to social relations. Simply including retarded students in a regular class will not guarantee that they will be accepted or that they will make and keep friends.

Research: MacMillan, D. L., Keogh, B. K., & Jones, R. L. (1986). Special education research on mildly handicapped learners. In M. Wittrock (Ed.), *Handbook of research on teaching* (3rd ed., pp. 686–726). New York: Macmillan.

Transition Programming Gradual preparation of exceptional students to move from high school into further education or training, employment, or community involvement.

Gifted and Talented   Test Bank items 4.38–4.44, 4.105, 4.118

There is another group of students with special educational needs that is often overlooked by the schools: the gifted and talented. In the past, providing an enriched education for extremely bright or talented students was seen as undemocratic and elitist. Now there is a growing recognition that **gifted students** are being poorly served by most public schools. A recent national survey found that more than one-half of all gifted students do not achieve in school at a level equal to their ability (Tomlinson-Keasey, 1990).

Who Are the Gifted?   There is no agreement about what constitutes a gifted student. Individuals can have many different gifts. Remember that Gardner (1983) identified seven separate kinds of "intelligences," and Guilford (1988) claims there are 180. J. S. Renzulli (1982) suggests that we should distinguish between academic giftedness and "creative/productive" giftedness. The academically gifted learn lessons very easily and quickly and generally score well on tests of intelligence. These indicators do not, however, necessarily predict success in later life. The creatively gifted tend to excel in situations that require the application of information to solve problems in new and effective ways. These characteristics are more likely to be associated with success in adulthood.

Using these ideas, Renzulli and Reis (1991) have defined giftedness as a combination of three basic characteristics: above-average general ability, a high level of creativity, and a high level of task commitment or motivation to achieve in certain areas. Truly gifted children are not the students who simply learn quickly with little effort. The work of gifted students is original, extremely advanced for their age, and potentially of lasting importance.

What do we know about these remarkable individuals, whom former U.S. Commissioner of Education Sidney P. Marland has called "our most neglected students"? A classic study of the characteristics of the gifted was started decades ago by Lewis Terman and colleagues (1925, 1947, 1959). This huge project is following the lives of 1,528 gifted males and females and will continue until the year 2010. The subjects all have IQ scores in the top 1 percent of the population (140 or above on the Stanford-Binet individual test of intelligence). They were identified on the basis of teacher recommendations and IQ tests, so they probably fall into Renzulli's academically gifted category.

Terman and colleagues found that these gifted children were larger, stronger, and healthier than the norm. They often walked sooner and were more athletic. They were more emotionally stable than their peers and became better-adjusted adults than the average. They had lower rates of delinquency, emotional difficulties, divorces, drug problems, and so on. Of course, the teachers in Terman's study who made the nominations may have selected students who were better adjusted initially.

What Problems Do the Gifted Face?   In spite of Terman's findings, it would be incorrect to say that every gifted student is superior in adjustment and emotional health. Many problems confront a gifted child, including boredom and frustration in school as well as isolation (sometimes even ridicule) from peers because of seemingly unbridgeable differences in interests and concerns. For example, schoolmates may be consumed with a passion for baseball or worried about failing math, while the gifted child is fascinated with Mozart, focused on a social problem, or totally absorbed in computers, drama, or geology. Gifted children may also find it difficult to accept their own emotions, since the mismatch between mind and emotion can be great. They may be im-

Current definitions of giftedness include the characteristics of above-average ability, creativity, and motivation to achieve.

Research: Torrance, E. P. (1986). Teaching creative and gifted learners. In M. Wittrock (Ed.), *Handbook of research on teaching* (3rd ed., pp. 630–647). New York: Macmillan.

Handout: See the *Instructor's Resource Manual* for **Handout Master 4.3,** which outlines the indicators of giftedness.

Gifted Student A very bright, creative, and talented student.

Research: Feldhusen, J. F. (1989, March). Synthesis of research on gifted youth. *Educational Leadership, 46*(6), 6–12.

Highlights: Voluminous research on gifted and talented students provides several guidelines:

Identification. Schools are often ineffective in identifying gifted students, especially children from poverty and minority backgrounds, very young children, and under-achievers. Multiple data sources should be used to identify giftedness.

Acceleration. Acceleration motivates gifted students by challenging them to realize their potential, and acceleration does not damage social-emotional adjustment.

Grouping. Grouping gifted and talented youth for all or part of the school day or week serves as a motivator. Mutual reinforcement of enthusiasm for academic interests prevails.

To provide for the gifted, we must upgrade instruction to fit their abilities, achievement levels, and interests. The only suitable enrichment is instruction on special topics at a high level and a fast pace.

Activity 4.5: Teaching Tip. See the *Instructor's Resource Manual* for Thoughts about Being Gifted, the observations of elementary students describing the unhappy side of being gifted.

Research: Maker, C. J. (1987). Gifted and talented. In V. Richardson-Koehler (Ed.), *Educator's handbook: A research perspective* (pp. 420–456). White Plains, NY: Longman. See the *Instructor's Resource Manual* for Handout Master 4.3, which summarizes the indicators of giftedness taken from Maker's chapter.

TABLE 4.3   The Eight Great Gripes of Gifted Students

Being gifted is not all positive. Here are the eight biggest complaints of gifted students.

1. No one explains what being gifted is all about—it's kept a big secret.
2. The stuff we do in school is too easy and it's boring.
3. Parents, teachers, and friends expect us to be perfect, to "do our best" all the time.
4. Kids often tease us about being smart.
5. Friends who really understand us are few and far between.
6. We feel too different and wish people would accept us for what we are.
7. We feel overwhelmed by the number of things we can do in life.
8. We worry a lot about world problems and feel helpless to do anything about them.

Source: J. Galbraith (1985). The eight great gripes of gifted kids: Responding to special needs, *Roeper Review, 8,* p. 15. Reprinted with permission of *Roeper Review,* Bloomfield Hills, MI.

---

patient with friends, parents, and even teachers who do not share their interests or abilities. Table 4.3 lists the most frequent complaints of gifted students.

A recent follow-up of Terman subjects 60 years later reached some surprising conclusions about the relationship between popularity as a student and intellectual accomplishment as an adult. Terman's subjects who were popular and outgoing as children were less likely to maintain serious intellectual interests as adults. The authors of the study speculate that gifted students who became more accomplished as adults may have preferred adult company as children, or may have been comfortable being alone. It is possible that an active social life diverts interest away from intellectual pursuits (Tomlinson-Keasey & Little, 1990). Each path has its benefits and its liabilities for the individual.

Recognizing Students' Special Abilities.   It may seem to you that identifying a gifted child would be simple. This is not always the case. Many parents provide early educational experiences for their children. A preschool or primary student coming to your class may read above grade level, play an instrument quite well, or whiz through every assignment. But even very advanced reading in the early grades does not guarantee that students will still be outstanding readers years later (Mills & Jackson, 1990). How do you separate gifted students from hardworking or parentally pressured students? In junior high and high school, some very able students deliberately earn lower grades, making their abilities even harder to recognize.

Teachers are successful only about 10 to 50 percent of the time in picking out the gifted children in their classes (Fox, 1981). These seven questions, taken from an early study of gifted students, are still good guides today (Walton, 1961):

■ Who learns easily and rapidly?

■ Who uses a lot of common sense and practical knowledge?

- Who retains easily what he or she has heard?
- Who knows about many things that the other children don't?
- Who uses a large number of words easily and accurately?
- Who recognizes relations and comprehends meanings?
- Who is alert and keenly observant and responds quickly?

Based on Renzulli and Reis's (1991) definition of giftedness, we might add:

- Who is persistent and highly motivated on some tasks?
- Who is creative, often has unusual ideas, or makes interesting connections?

Giftedness and Formal Testing. The best single predictor of academic giftedness is still the individual IQ test. Many schools identify the academically gifted as those who score in the top 3 percent for their ethnic or cultural group (an IQ of about 130 for white, native-born Americans). But an individual intelligence test is costly and time-consuming—and far from perfect.

Group achievement and intelligence tests tend to underestimate the IQs of very bright children. Group tests may be appropriate for screening, but they are not appropriate for making placement decisions. Many psychologists recommend a case study approach to identifying gifted students. This means gathering many kinds of information, test scores, grades, examples of work, projects and portfolios, letters or ratings from teachers, self-ratings, and so on (Renzulli & Reis, 1991; Sisk, 1988). Especially for recognizing artistic talent, experts in the field can be called in to judge the merits of a child's creations. Science projects, exhibitions, performances, auditions, and interviews are all possibilities. Creativity tests may identify some children not picked up by other measures, particularly minority students who may be at a disadvantage on the other types of tests (Maker, 1987).

Teaching Gifted Students. There are at least two issues in making educational plans for gifted students. One is how students should be grouped and paced; the other is what teaching methods are most effective.

Educators disagree about grouping and pacing. Some educators believe that gifted students should be *accelerated*—moved quickly through the grades or through particular subjects. Other educators prefer *enrichment*—giving the students additional, more sophisticated, and more thought-provoking work, but keeping them with their age-mates in school. Actually, both may be appropriate (Torrance, 1986).

Many people object to acceleration, but most careful studies indicate that truly gifted students who begin primary, elementary, junior high, high school, college, or even graduate school early do as well as, and usually better than, nongifted students who are progressing at the normal pace. Social and emotional adjustment does not appear to be impaired. Gifted students tend to prefer the company of older playmates and may be miserably bored if kept with children of their own age. Skipping grades may not be the best solution for a particular student, but it does not deserve the bad name it has received (Jones & Southern, 1991; Kulik & Kulik, 1984; Richardson & Benbow, 1990). An alternative to skipping grades is to accelerate students in one or two particu-

Research: Schneider, B. H., Clegg, M., Byrne, B. M., Ledingham, J. E., & Crombie, G. (1989). Social relations of gifted children as a function of age and school program. *Journal of Educational Psychology, 81,* 48–56.

Abstract: This study examined social and personal concomitants of exceptional academic capability. Students in grades 5, 8, and 10 participated in the study. At each grade level there were students in classes for the gifted (self-contained gifted), gifted students in regular classes (integrated gifted), and classmates of the integrated gifted (matched and random controls). The integrated gifted children at all three grade levels had higher scores for academic self-concept than the other groups; there were no differences in social or physical self-concept. Only in grade 5 were the integrated gifted rated by their classmates as higher than controls in social competence.

Background: Richardson, T. M., & Benbow, C. P. (1990). Long-term effects of acceleration on the social-emotional adjustment of mathematically precocious youths. *Journal of Educational Psychology, 82,* 464–470.

Background: Grouping and the Gifted (1991, special section). *Educational Leadership, 48*(6), 60–74.

Transparency: Use acetate transparency T 30, "Example of Instrumental Enrichment."

Handout: Handout Master 4.10 is a table taken from Garger, S., & Guild, P. (1984). Learning styles: The crucial differences. *Curriculum Review, 23,* 9–12. The table lists differences between field-dependent and field-independent cognitive styles for students and teachers.

Transparency: Use acetate transparency T 29, "A Test of Cognitive Style."

Focus on...   Ability Differences

- If you have a wide range of academic abilities in your class, what are your options in grouping students for learning?
- How would you teach the concept of "safety" to a moderately retarded student?
- You have two students in your class who are way ahead of the others in their understanding. How would you help these two learn?

Teaching Tip: When students fail a grade or a course, they are often "recycled" through the same material on the assumption that repetition will produce learning. Use the concept of cognitive style to argue against this practice.

Background: Reflective children are less likely to fail an early grade (Messer, 1970). The causes of the early development of reflectivity or impulsivity as cognitive styles is not known, but genetic factors may play a role (Sigel & Brodzindky, 1977).

Objective 4.6: Critically analyze the concepts of cognitive-style and learning-style preference, describing any implications for teachers.

Cognitive Styles Different ways of perceiving and organizing information.

lar subjects but keep them with peers for most classes (Reynolds & Birch, 1988). For students who are extremely advanced intellectually (for example, those scoring 160 or higher on an individual intelligence test), the only practical solution may be to accelerate their education (Gross, 1992).

Teaching methods for gifted students should encourage abstract thinking (formal-operational thought), creativity, and independence, not just the learning of greater quantities of facts. In working with gifted and talented students, a teacher must be imaginative, flexible, and unthreatened by the capabilities of these students. The teacher must ask, What does this child need most? What is she or he ready to learn? Who can help me to help? Answers might come from faculty members at nearby colleges, retired professionals, books, museums, or older students. Strategies might be as simple as letting the child do math with the next grade. Increasingly, more flexible programs are being devised for gifted students: summer institutes; courses at nearby colleges; classes with local artists, musicians, or dancers; independent research projects; selected classes in high school for younger students; honors classes; and special-interest clubs. All are options for offering gifted students appropriate learning experiences (Mitchell, 1984).

We have spent quite a bit of time considering differences in cognitive ability. However, there are many more differences among students that have implications for teachers. We turn to these next.

 ognitive and Learning Styles   **Test Bank** items 4.45–4.49, 4.93, 4.119

In this section we examine individual differences that have very little to do with intelligence but can influence students' learning in school. These differences have been called *cognitive styles* or *learning styles*. Be aware that you may hear these terms used interchangeably. In general, educators prefer the term *learning styles,* and include many kinds of differences in this broad category. Psychologists tend to prefer the term *cognitive styles,* and to limit their discussion to differences in the ways people process information (Bjorklund, 1989).

Cognitive Styles

The notion of **cognitive styles** is fairly new. It grew out of research on how people perceive and organize information from the world around them. Results from these studies suggest that individuals differ in how they approach a task, but these variations do not reflect levels of intelligence or patterns of special abilities. Instead, they have to do with "preferred ways that different individuals have for processing and organizing information and for responding to environmental stimuli" (Shuell, 1981a, p. 46). For example, certain individuals respond very quickly in most situations. Others are more reflective and slower to respond, even though both types of people may be equally knowledgeable about the task at hand.

Field Dependence and Field Independence.   In the early 1940s, Herman Witkin became intrigued by the observation that certain airline pilots would fly into a bank of clouds and fly out upside down, without realizing that they had changed position. His interest led to a great deal of research on how people separate one factor from the total visual field. Based on his research, Witkin identified the cognitive styles of field dependence and field independence (Witkin, Moore, & Goodenough, 1977). People who are **field dependent** tend to perceive a pattern as a whole, not separating one element from the total visual field. Field-dependent individuals have difficulty focusing on one aspect of a situation, picking out details, or analyzing a pattern into different parts. They tend to work well in groups, have a good memory for social information, and prefer subjects such as literature and history.

Field-independent people, on the other hand, are more likely to perceive separate parts of a total pattern and are able to analyze a pattern according to its components. They are not as attuned to social relationships as field-dependent people, but they do well in math and science where their analytical abilities pay off.

Although you will not necessarily be able to determine all the variations in your students' cognitive styles, you should be aware that students approach problems in different ways. Some may need help learning to pick out important features and to ignore irrelevant details. They may seem lost in less-structured situations and need clear, step-by-step instructions. Other students may be great at organizing but less sensitive to the feelings of others and not as effective in social situations.

Impulsive and Reflective Cognitive Styles.   Another aspect of cognitive style is impulsivity versus reflectiveness. An **impulsive** student works very quickly but makes many mistakes. The more **reflective** student, on the other hand, works slowly and makes fewer errors. As with field dependence/independence, impulsive and reflective cognitive styles are not highly related to intelligence within the normal range. However, as children grow older, they generally become more reflective, and for school-age children, being more reflective does seem to improve performance on school tasks such as reading (Kogan, 1983; Smith & Caplan, 1988).

Students can learn to be more reflective, however, if they are taught specific strategies. One that has proved successful in many situations is **self-instruction,** described in chapter 2. This approach capitalizes on the beneficial use of private speech described by Vygotsky (Meichenbaum, 1986). Another possibility is learning scanning strategies. For example, students taking multiple-choice tests might be encouraged to cross off each alternative as they consider it, so that no possibilities will be ignored. They might work in pairs and talk about why each possibility is right or wrong. In math classes, impulsive children need to be given specific strategies for checking their work. Just slowing down is not enough. These students must be taught effective strategies for solving the problem at hand by considering each reasonable alternative.

Objective 4.7: Adapt lessons to make them appropriate for students with varying learning styles.

Research: For an analysis of the validity and usefulness of cognitive style measures, see Tiedemann, J. (1989). Measures of cognitive styles: A critical review. *Educational Psychologist, 24,* 261–275.

Abstract: Analysis demonstrates the limitations of evidence in support of cognitive styles. The measures of cognitive styles do not sufficiently match the criteria on the conceptual level; consistent convergent and discriminant validity is lacking. Most style measures are best interpreted as ability tests. Sufficient empirical evidence of any cognitive-style dimension in the sense of a bipolar, value-differentiated preference construct cutting across domains is lacking.

Background: Learning styles and the brain (1990, special issue). *Educational Leadership, 48*(2).

Field Dependence Cognitive style in which patterns are perceived as wholes.

Field Independence Cognitive style in which separate parts of a pattern are perceived and analyzed.

Impulsive Characterized by cognitive style of responding quickly but often inaccurately.

Reflective Characterized by cognitive style of responding slowly, carefully, and accurately.

Self-Instruction Talking oneself through the steps of a task.

Examples: *The Learning Style Inventory* by Renzulli and Smith (1978) asks students to indicate preferences for different types of instruction, such as lecture, discussion, projects, games, and so on. *The Learning Style Inventory* by Dunn, Dunn, and Price (1984) measures preferences for 23 elements of the instructional program, including the immediate environment (temperature, noise level, etc.); emotional involvement (motivational strategies, structure, etc.); social support (working alone or with others, etc.); physical characteristics (time of day, visual versus auditory materials, etc.); and psychological inclinations (impulsive or reflective, global or analytic, etc.). The *Learning Style Profile* (Keefe & Monk, 1986) is a 126-item test based on a broad definition of learning style that includes cognitive, affective, and physiological differences.

Teaching Tip: You might want to discuss a very controversial source of differences in learning and cognitive styles, **hemispheric specialization**, or a person's preference for right-brain versus left-brain processing. According to some educators, many students have problems learning because they tend to process information using the right hemisphere of their brain, whereas the tasks of school require mostly left-hemisphere processing. Is this true? Two basic assumptions underlying these ideas are that different abilities are completely controlled by one side of the brain or the other and that individuals favor one hemisphere

Learning-Style Preferences Preferred ways of studying and learning, such as using pictures instead of text, working with other people versus alone, learning in structured or in unstructured situations, and so on.

I have also encountered several bright students who seem too reflective. They turn 30 minutes of homework into an all-night project. They need help in learning to work steadily through a project.

Learning-Style Preferences   Test Bank item 4.50

Since the late 1970s a great deal has been written about differences in students' learning-style preferences (Dunn, 1987; Dunn & Dunn, 1978, 1987; Gregorc, 1982; Keefe, 1982). Workshops and in-service training sessions around the country focus on this topic. Learning preferences are usually called learning styles in these workshops, but I believe preferences is a more accurate label. **Learning-style preferences** are individual preferences for particular learning environments. They could be preferences for where, when, with whom, or with what lighting, food, or music you like to study. Think for a minute about how you learn best. I like to study and write during large blocks of time, late at night. I usually make some kind of commitment or deadline every week so that I have to work under pressure in long stretches to finish the work before that deadline. Then I take a day off. When I plan or think, I have to see my thinking in writing. I have a colleague who draws diagrams of relationships when she listens to a speaker or plans a paper. You may be similar or very different, even though we all work effectively.

There are a number of instruments for assessing students' learning preferences—for example, *The Learning Style Inventory* (Renzulli & Smith, 1978), *The Learning Style Inventory* (Dunn, Dunn, & Price, 1984), and the *Learning Style Profile* (Keefe & Monk, 1986). Tests of learning style have been criticized for lacking evidence of reliability and validity. This led Snider (1990) to conclude, "People are different, and it is good practice to recognize and accom-

People have different preferences for how and where they like to learn. Students who are very distracted by noise may work better in a quiet space, even if that place is on the floor in the hall.

modate individual differences. It is also good practice to present information in a variety of ways through more than one modality, but it is not wise to categorize learners and prescribe methods solely on the basis of tests with questionable technical qualities. . . . The idea of learning styles is appealing, but a critical examination of this approach should cause educators to be skeptical" (p. 53).

It may be too much to expect the teacher to provide every student with his or her preferred setting and support for learning. But the teacher can make options available. Having quiet, private corners as well as large tables for working; comfortable cushions as well as straight chairs; brightly lighted desks along with darker areas; headphones for listening to music as well as earplugs; structured as well as open-ended assignments; information available from films and tapes as well as in books—all these options will allow students to work and learn in their preferred mode at least some of the time.

Will making these alterations lead to greater learning? Here the answer is not clear. Results of some research indicate that students learn more when they study in their preferred setting and manner (Dunn, Beaudry, & Klavas, 1989; Dunn & Dunn, 1987). There is some evidence that very bright students need less structure and prefer quiet, solitary learning (Torrance, 1986). But before you try to accommodate all your students' learning styles, remember that students, especially younger ones, may not be the best judges of how they should learn. Preference for a particular style may not always guarantee that using the style will be effective. Sometimes students, particularly poorer students, prefer what is easy and comfortable; real learning can be hard and uncomfortable. Sometimes students prefer to learn in a certain way because they have no alternatives; it is the only way they know how to approach the task. These students may benefit from developing new—and perhaps more effective—ways to learn (Weinstein & McCombs, in press).

Focus on . . . **Cognitive Styles**

- Distinguish between cognitive style and learning preference.
- Are you more field dependent or field independent? How do you know?
- What are the advantages and disadvantages of matching teaching to individual learning styles?

over the other in processing information. In other words, they are "right-brained" or "left-brained." There is little evidence for either of these assumptions. For people who have normal intact brains, both hemispheres are involved in all learning tasks, even if one side may be more or less involved at any given moment (Bjorklund, 1989). Poets write in words but paint images and patterns with their verse. Sculptors often plan analytically, think logically, and perform calculations as they sculpt (Caine & Caine, 1991). It is possible that researchers will trace certain learning problems to aspects of hemispheric specialization, but the evidence is not yet conclusive. In fact, some preliminary research indicates that the front-to-back functioning of the brain may be as important as left/right functioning in understanding learning disabilities (Jordan & Goldsmith-Phillips, 1994).

Students with Learning Challenges

Thus far we have focused mostly on teachers' responses to the varying abilities and styles of students. For the rest of the chapter we will consider several kinds of problems or disabilities that can interfere with learning. Before we continue, though, let's analyze the difference between a disability and a handicap. A **disability** is just what the word implies—an inability to do something specific such as see or walk. A **handicap** is a disadvantage in certain situations. Some disabilities lead to handicaps. For example, being blind (a visual disability) is a handicap if you are doing work that requires sight. But this disability is not a handicap when you are doing work that requires other skills, such as composing music, finding your way around in complete darkness, or talking on the telephone. Not all disabilities are handicaps in every situation. And not all handicaps are due to disabilities; they may be caused by lack of

Disability The inability to do something specific such as walk or hear.

Handicap A disadvantage in a particular situation, sometimes caused by a disability.

experience or training. It is important that we do not *create* handicaps for people by the way we react to their disabilities.

Students with Physical Challenges

Test Bank items 4.51–4.60, 4.94, 4.95, 4.106

Some students must have special **orthopedic devices** such as braces, special shoes, crutches, or wheelchairs to participate in a normal school program. Accidents, disease, or birth defects can lead to conditions that require these devices. If the school has the necessary architectural features, such as ramps, elevators, and accessible rest rooms, and if teachers allow for the physical limitations of students, little needs to be done to alter the usual educational program.

Seizure Disorders (Epilepsy).   A seizure is "an abnormal discharge of electrical energy in certain brain cells" (Hallahan & Kauffman, 1994, p. 393). The effects of the seizure depend on where the discharge of energy starts in the brain and how far it spreads. People with **epilepsy** have seizures, but not all seizures are the result of epilepsy; temporary conditions such as high fevers or infections can also trigger seizures.

There are two major types of epilepsy you may encounter in the classroom. A **partial seizure** involves only a small part of the brain, whereas a **generalized seizure** includes much more of the brain.

Most generalized seizures (once called *grand mal*) are accompanied by uncontrolled jerking movements that ordinarily last two to five minutes, followed by a deep sleep or coma. Upon regaining consciousness the student may be very weary, confused, and in need of extra sleep. Most seizures are controlled by medication. If it occurs in class, a seizure accompanied by convulsions requires action by the teacher. The major danger to a student having such a seizure is getting hurt by striking a hard surface during the violent jerking. But do not try to restrain the child's movements—you can't stop the seizure once it starts. Lower the child gently to the floor, away from furniture or walls. Move hard objects away. Turn the child's head gently to the side and loosen any tight clothing. Never put anything in the student's mouth. Find out from the student's parents how the seizure is usually dealt with. If one seizure follows another and the student does not regain consciousness in between or if the seizure goes on more than 10 minutes, get medical help right away (Hallahan & Kauffman, 1994).

During a seizure the student may perspire heavily, foam at the mouth, seem to stop breathing briefly, or lose bladder or bowel control. As a teacher, your calm and sympathetic response is very important. If you seem fearful or disgusted, the other students will learn to respond in similar ways. Some students may believe that epilepsy is contagious; this and any other mistaken notions should be corrected.

Not all seizures are dramatic. Sometimes the student just loses contact briefly. The student may stare, fail to respond to questions, drop objects, and miss what has been happening for 1 to 30 seconds. These were once called *petit mal*, but they are now referred to as *absence seizures* and can easily go undetected. If a child in your class appears to daydream frequently, does not seem to know what is going on at times, or cannot remember what has just happened when you ask, you should consult the school psychologist or nurse. The

---

Objective 4.8: List indicators of hearing, vision, language, and behavior problems as well as indicators of specific learning disabilities.

Objective 4.9: Adapt teaching methods to the needs of exceptional students.

Background: Smith, S. L. (1989, April). The masks students wear. *Instructor*, 27+.

Orthopedic Devices Devices such as braces and wheelchairs that aid people with physical disabilities.

Epilepsy Disorder marked by seizures and caused by abnormal electrical discharges in the brain.

Partial Seizure A seizure beginning in a localized area and involving only a small part of the brain.

Generalized Seizure A seizure involving a large portion of the brain.

major problem for students with absence seizures is that they miss the continuity of the class interaction. If their seizures are frequent, they will find the lessons confusing. As a teacher, you should question these students to be sure they are understanding and following the lesson. Be prepared to repeat yourself periodically.

Cerebral Palsy. Damage to the brain before or during birth or during infancy can cause a child to have difficulty moving and coordinating his or her body. The problem may be very mild, so the child simply appears a bit clumsy, or so severe that voluntary movement is practically impossible. The most common form of **cerebral palsy** is characterized by **spasticity** (overly tight or tense muscles). The damage to the brain may be such that only movement is affected. Children with this form of cerebral palsy may wear a brace or use a wheelchair and need no special educational program. But many children with cerebral palsy have secondary handicaps (Kirk, Gallagher, & Anastasiow, 1993). In the classroom, these secondary handicaps are the greatest concern—and these are generally what the regular teacher can help with most. For example, many children with cerebral palsy also have hearing impairments, speech problems, or mild mental retardation. The strategies described in this chapter should prove helpful in such situations.

Hearing Impairment. Students with severe hearing or vision losses, especially younger students who have not yet learned how to function in regular classrooms, spend most of their school time in special classes. But students with mild impairments and students with more severe problems who have had special training are frequently placed in regular classrooms for most or all of their instruction.

Hearing losses may be caused by genetic factors: maternal infections (such as rubella) during pregnancy, complications during birth, or early childhood diseases, such as mumps or measles. Many children today are protected from hearing loss by vaccinations against such infections.

Signs of hearing problems are turning one ear toward the speaker, favoring one ear in conversation, or misunderstanding conversation when the speaker's face cannot be seen. Other indications include not following directions, seeming distracted or confused at times, frequently asking people to repeat what they have said, mispronouncing new words or names, and being reluctant to participate in class discussions. Take note particularly of students who have frequent earaches, sinus infections, or allergies.

In the past, educators have debated whether oral or manual approaches are better for children with hearing impairments. Oral approaches involve **speech reading** (also called lip reading) and training students to use whatever limited hearing they may have. Manual approaches include **sign language** and **finger spelling**. Research indicates that children who learn some manual method of communicating perform better in academic subjects and are more socially mature than students who are exposed only to oral methods. Today, the trend is to combine both approaches (Hallahan & Kauffman, 1994).

Vision Impairment. Mild vision problems can be overcome with corrective lenses. Only about 1 in 1,000 children in this country have visual im-

Teaching Tip: You might point out that students with AIDS can have many of the problems discussed in this chapter: mental retardation, attention-deficit disorder, seizures, neurological impairments similar to cerebral palsy, behavior disorders, and so on. Most states have policies that emphasize the education of children with AIDS in the regular classroom.

Handout: See the *Instructor's Resource Manual* for **Handout Master 4.4,** "Guidelines for Teaching the Hearing-Impaired Student."

Cerebral Palsy Condition involving a range of motor or coordination difficulties due to brain damage.

Spasticity Overly tight or tense muscles, characteristic of some forms of cerebral palsy.

Speech Reading Using visual cues to understand language.

Sign Language Communication system of hand movements that symbolize words and concepts.

Finger Spelling Communication system that "spells out" each letter with a hand position.

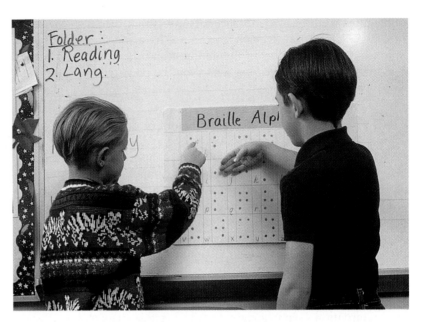

All students can benefit from learning about alternative ways of communicating, such as Braille and signing. Such understanding encourages mutual respect between students with disabilities and their classmates and gives all students a broader appreciation of the variety of human abilities.

Handout: See Handout Master 4.5 in the *Instructor's Resource Manual,* "Myths and Facts about Vision Impairment."

pairments so serious that special educational services are needed. Most of this group needing special services is classified as having **low vision.** This means they can read with the aid of a magnifying glass or large-print books. A small group of students, about 1 in every 2,500, are **educationally blind.** These students must use hearing and touch as the predominant learning channels (Kirk, Gallagher, & Anastasiow, 1993).

Special materials and equipment that help visually impaired students to function in regular classrooms include large-print typewriters; variable-speed tape recorders (allowing teachers to make time-compressed tape recordings, which speed up the rate of speech without changing the voice pitch); special calculators; the abacus; three-dimensional maps, charts, and models; and special measuring devices. For students with visual problems, the quality of the print is often more important than the size, so watch out for hard-to-read handouts and ditto sheets. The Instructional Materials Reference Center of the American Printing House for the Blind (1839 Frankfort Avenue, Louisville, KY 40206) has catalogs of instructional materials for visually impaired students.

Students who have difficulty seeing often hold books either very close to or very far from their eyes. They may squint, rub their eyes frequently, or complain that their eyes burn or itch. The eyes may actually be swollen, red, or encrusted. Students with vision problems may misread material on the chalkboard, describe their vision as being blurred, be very sensitive to light, or hold their heads at an odd angle (De Mott, 1982). Any of these signs should be reported to a qualified school professional.

Low Vision Vision limited to close objects.

Educationally Blind   Needing Braille materials in order to learn.

Communication Disorders

Test Bank items 4.61–4.64, 4.96, 4.107, 4.108, 4.120

Language is a complex learned behavior. Language disorders may arise from many sources, since so many different aspects of the individual are involved in learning language. A child with a hearing impairment will not learn to speak normally. A child who hears inadequate language at home will learn inadequate language. Children who are not listened to, or whose perception of the world is distorted by emotional problems, will reflect these problems in their language development. Since speaking involves movements, any impairment of the motor functions involved with speech can cause language disorders. And because language development and thinking are so interwoven, any problems in cognitive functioning can affect ability to use language.

Speech Impairments. Students who cannot produce sounds effectively for speaking are considered to have a **speech impairment**. About 5 percent of school-age children have some form of speech impairment. Articulation problems and stuttering are the two most common problems.

Articulation disorders include substituting one sound for another (*thunthine* for *sunshine*), distorting a sound (*shoup* for *soup*), adding a sound (*ideer* for *idea*), or omitting sounds (*po-y* for *pony*) (Cartwright, Cartwright, & Ward, 1981). But keep in mind that most children are 6 to 8 years old before they can successfully pronounce all English sounds in normal conversation. The sounds of the consonants *l, r, y, s,* and *z* and the consonant blends *sh, ch, zh,* and *th* are the last to be mastered.

Stuttering generally appears between the ages of 3 and 4. It is not yet clear what causes stuttering, but it can cause embarrassment and anxiety for the sufferer. In about 50 percent of cases, stuttering disappears during early adolescence (Wiig, 1982). If stuttering continues more than a year or so, the child should be referred to a speech therapist. Early intervention is critical (Onslow, 1992).

Voicing problems, a third type of speech impairment, include speaking with an inappropriate pitch, quality, or loudness or in a monotone (Wiig, 1982). A student with any of these problems should be referred to a speech therapist. Recognizing the problem is the first step. Be alert for students whose pronunciation, loudness, voice quality, speech fluency, expressive range, or rate is very different from that of their peers. Pay attention also to students who seldom speak. Are they simply shy, or do they have difficulties with language?

Oral Language Disorders. There are four kinds of language disorders, summarized in Figure 4.4 on page 134. Language differences are not necessarily language disorders. Students with language disorders are those who are markedly deficient compared with other students of their own age and cultural group. Students who seldom speak, who use few words or very short sentences, or who rely only on gestures to communicate should be referred to a qualified school professional for observation or testing.

Emotional/Behavioral Disorders

Test Bank items 4.65–4.67, 4.97

Students with emotional and behavioral disorders can be among the most difficult to teach in a regular class. Behavior becomes a problem when it deviates

Speech Impairment Inability to produce sounds effectively for speaking.

Articulation Disorders Any of a variety of pronunciation difficulties, such as the substitution, distortion, or omission of sounds.

Stuttering Repetitions, prolongations, and hesitations that block flow of speech.

Voicing Problems Inappropriate pitch, quality, loudness, or intonation.

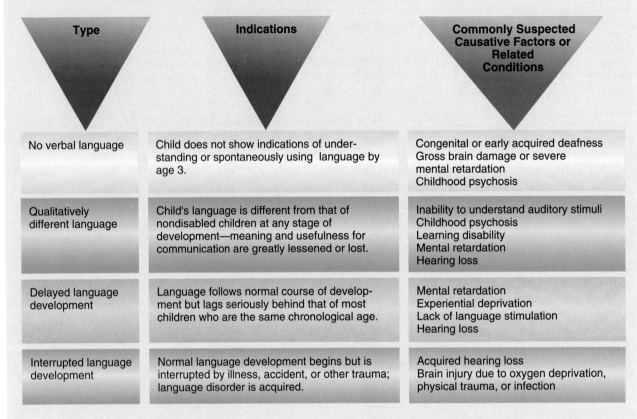

FIGURE 4.4

TYPES OF LANGUAGE DISORDERS

There are four kinds of language disorders, stemming from different causes.

Type	Indications	Commonly Suspected Causative Factors or Related Conditions
No verbal language	Child does not show indications of understanding or spontaneously using language by age 3.	Congenital or early acquired deafness Gross brain damage or severe mental retardation Childhood psychosis
Qualitatively different language	Child's language is different from that of nondisabled children at any stage of development—meaning and usefulness for communication are greatly lessened or lost.	Inability to understand auditory stimuli Childhood psychosis Learning disability Mental retardation Hearing loss
Delayed language development	Language follows normal course of development but lags seriously behind that of most children who are the same chronological age.	Mental retardation Experiential deprivation Lack of language stimulation Hearing loss
Interrupted language development	Normal language development begins but is interrupted by illness, accident, or other trauma; language disorder is acquired.	Acquired hearing loss Brain injury due to oxygen deprivation, physical trauma, or infection

Source: Rita C. Naremore, "Language Disorders in Children, in *Introduction to Communication Disorders,* T.J. Hixon, L.P. Shriberg, and J. H. Saxman (eds.), © 1980, pp. 154 – 161. Adapted by permission of Prentice-Hall, Englewood Cliffs, New Jersey.

so greatly from appropriate behaviors for the child's age group that it significantly interferes with the child's own growth and development and/or the lives of others. Clearly, deviation implies a difference from some standard, and standards of behavior differ from one situation, age group, culture, and historical period to another. Thus, what passes for team spirit in the football bleachers might be seen as disturbed behavior in a bank or restaurant. In addition, the deviation must be more than a temporary response to stressful events; it must be consistent across time and different situations.

Quay and Peterson (1987) describe six dimensions of emotional/behavioral disorders. Children who have *conduct disorders* are aggressive, destructive, disobedient, uncooperative, distractible, disruptive, and persistent. They have been corrected and punished for the same misbehavior countless times.

Many of these children are disliked by the adults and even the other children in their lives. The most successful strategies for helping these children are the behavior management approaches described in chapter 6. These students need very clear rules and consequences, consistently enforced. The future is not promising for students who never learn to control their behavior and who also fail academically. Waiting for the students to "outgrow" their problems is seldom effective (O'Leary & Wilson, 1987).

Children who are extremely anxious, withdrawn, shy, depressed, and hypersensitive, who cry easily and have little confidence, are said to have an *anxiety-withdrawal disorder*. These children have few social skills and consequently very few friends. The most successful approaches with them appear to involve the direct teaching of social skills (Gresham, 1981).

The third category is *attentional problems immaturity*. Characteristics include a short attention span, frequent daydreaming, little initiative, messiness, and poor coordination. If an immature student is not too far behind others in the class, she or he may respond to the behavior management strategies described in chapter 6. But if these approaches fail or if the problem is severe, you should consult the school psychologist, guidance counselor, or another mental health professional. Related to this dimension is the category of *motor excess*. These students are restless and tense; they seem unable to sit still or stop talking.

The fifth category of behavior disorders is *socialized aggression*. Students in this group are often members of gangs. They may steal or vandalize because their peer culture expects it.

Finally, some students exhibit *psychotic behavior*. You are not likely to work with many of these students. Their behavior may be bizarre, and they may express very farfetched ideas. These six categories are very general. If you are concerned about the behavior of one of your students, it is best to consult the school psychologist or guidance counselor.

Hyperactivity and Attention Disorders

Test Bank items 4.68–4.72, 4.109, 4.110, 4.21, 4.126–4.128

You have probably heard and may even have used the term **hyperactivity**. The notion is a modern one; there were no hyperactive children 30 to 40 years ago. Today, if anything, the term is applied too often and too widely. Hyperactivity is not one particular condition; it is "a set of behaviors—such as excessive restlessness and short attention span—that are quantitatively and qualitatively different from those of children of the same sex, mental age, and SES [socioeconomic status]" (O'Leary, 1980, p. 195).

Today most psychologists agree that the main problem for children labeled hyperactive is directing and maintaining attention, not simply controlling their restlessness and physical activity. The American Psychiatric Association has established a diagnostic category called **attention deficit-hyperactive disorder** to identify children with this problem.

Hyperactive children are not only more physically active and inattentive than other children; they also have difficulty responding appropriately and working steadily toward goals (even their own goals), and they may not be able to control their behavior on command, even for a brief period. The problem behaviors are generally evident in all situations and with every teacher. It

Teaching Tip: An article in *Time* (January 16, 1989) addressed "Worries about overactive kids: Are too many youngsters being misdiagnosed and medicated?" (p. 65). A few facts from the article:

Up to 750,000 American children take drugs to control attention deficit hyperactive disorder (ADHD). The number was expected to reach 1 million in the early 1990s.

Results of a study indicated that 40 percent of the children brought to the University of Chicago ADHD clinic did not suffer from hyperactivity. The article ended with these words:

Doctors emphasize that drugs should be a last, not a first, resort. Minor interventions, such as moving a child to the front row in class or allowing him more time to complete tasks, can lead to improvement. Rewards—extra television or a favorite snack—can help reinforce good behavior. And psychological therapy can bolster a child's flagging self-esteem and address social problems, like a lack of friends, that contribute to his distress. Only when these remedies fail should parents try medication on their overly active youngsters.

Casebook: See the Teachers' Casebook at the end of this chapter for one expert's ideas about how to help a student with symptoms of attention disorder.

Hyperactivity Behavior disorder marked by atypical, excessive restlessness and inattentiveness.

Attention Deficit–Hyperactive Disorder Current term for disruptive behavior disorders marked by overactivity, excessive difficulty sustaining attention, or impulsiveness.

Transparency: Use acetate transparency T 36, "LD is Fastest Growing Category."

Connections: In chapter 5 is a discussion of cognitive behavior modification and self-instruction, and in chapter 7 you will find ideas for teaching learning strategies. These skills are particularly helpful for learning-disabled students.

Research: Chapman, J. W. (1989). Learning disabled children's self-concepts. *Review of Educational Research, 58,* 347–371.

From the abstract: Studies of learning-disabled (LD) children's self-concepts show that LD students have lower self-concepts than nonhandicapped students. Greater decrements occur for academic self-concept than for general self-concept. Significant variations in results were found as a function of the group LD students were compared with, and the instruments used (the Piers-Harris scale or the Student's Perception of Ability Scale). For most LD children, decrements in self-concept occur by grade 3 and remain fairly stable through high school. Mainstreamed settings did not lead to higher self-concepts than segregated settings. But unplaced LD students clearly had lower self-concepts than LD students who were receiving remedial assistance.

Specific Learning Disability Problem with acquisition and use of language; may show up as difficulty with reading, writing, reasoning, or math.

is difficult to know how many children should be classified as hyperactive. The most common estimate is 5 percent of the elementary-school population (O'Leary, 1980). More boys than girls are identified as hyperactive. Adolescents are rarely classified in this category (Haring & McCormick, 1986).

There is great disagreement about the cause or causes of attention disorders and hyperactivity. The list includes subtle damage to the brain, slower than normal neurological development, chemical imbalances in the body, genetic factors, food allergies, lead poisoning, maternal drinking or smoking during pregnancy, and inappropriate learning (O'Leary & Wilson, 1987). The underlying problem may not be the same for each child.

As a teacher or parent, you are more concerned with cures than causes. Unfortunately, there are no completely effective approaches. Many children, about 750,000 in fact, receive stimulant medication, usually Dexedrine or Ritalin. These stimulants in particular dosages tend to have paradoxical effects on these children: short-term effects include possible improvements in social behaviors such as cooperation, attention, and compliance. Research suggests that about 70 percent of hyperactive children are more manageable when on medication. But for many there are negative side effects such as increased heart rate and blood pressure, interference with growth rate, insomnia, weight loss, nausea (Pelham & Murphy, 1986; Walden & Thompson, 1981). In addition, little is known about the long-term effects of drug therapy. There also is no evidence that the drugs lead to improvement in academic learning or peer relationships, two areas where hyperactive children have great problems. Since students appear to improve dramatically in their behavior, parents and teachers, relieved to see change, may assume the problem has been cured. It hasn't. The students still need special help in learning.

The methods that have proved most successful in helping students with attention deficits are based on the behavioral principles described in chapter 6. One promising approach combines instruction in learning and memory strategies with motivational training. The goal is to give students the "skill and will" (Paris, 1988) to improve their achievement. Students learn how and when to apply learning strategies and study skills. They are also encouraged to be persistent and to see themselves as "in control" (Reid & Borkowski, 1987). These methods should be thoroughly tested with the student before drugs are used. Even if students in your class are on medication, it is critical that they also learn the academic and social skills they will need to survive. Again, this will not happen by itself, even if behavior improves with medication (Kneedler, 1984).

Specific Learning Disabilities Test Bank items 4.73–4.76, 4.111

How do you explain what is wrong with a student who is not mentally retarded, emotionally disturbed, or educationally deprived; who has normal vision, hearing, and language capabilities; and who still cannot learn to read, write, or compute? One explanation is that the student has a **specific learning disability.** This is a relatively new and controversial category of exceptional students. There is no fully agreed upon definition. In fact, Cartwright, Cartwright, and Ward (1989) list 38 different definitions. The definition included in federal legislation is:

"Specific learning disability" means a disorder in one or more of the basic psychological processes involved in understanding or using language, spoken or written, which may manifest itself in an imperfect ability to listen, think, speak, read, write, spell, or to do mathematical calculations. The term includes such conditions as perceptual handicaps, brain injury, minimal brain dysfunction, dyslexia, and developmental aphasia. (*Federal Register,* August 23, 1977)

The definition goes on to say that these disorders of listening, thinking, and so on are not due primarily to other conditions, such as mental retardation, emotional disturbance, or educational disadvantages.

This definition reflects an older, medical orientation to learning disabilities and assumes that the disability results from disorders in psychological processing, a position that many psychologists question today. An alternative definition is proposed by a group of parents and professionals, the National Joint Committee on Learning Disabilities (1989):

Learning disabilities is a general term that refers to a heterogeneous group of disorders manifest by significant difficulties in the acquisition and use of listening, speaking, reading, writing, reasoning, or mathematical abilities. These disorders are intrinsic to the individual, presumed to be due to central nervous system dysfunction, and may occur across the life span. (p. 1)

This definition eliminates references to psychological processes, avoids the use of older terms such as *brain injury* or *minimal brain dysfunction,* and indicates that learning disabilities may pose a lifelong challenge. Most definitions agree that learning-disabled students are at least average in intelligence, but have significant academic problems and perform significantly below what would be expected.

There is no agreement about the causes of learning disabilities. Explanations include mild or slight physical damage to the brain; oxygen deprivation before, during, or after birth; chemical imbalances in the body due to allergies to foods or additives; poor early nutrition; genetic factors; immaturity of the central nervous system; underdeveloped perceptual motor skills; poor teaching; lack of motivation; and inadequate structure in the educational program (Mercer, 1992). You can see that some explanations refer to factors within the child and others refer to environmental factors.

Some educators and psychologists believe the learning disability label is overused and abused. Almost one-half of all students receiving some kind of special education services in the public schools are diagnosed as learning disabled. This is by far the largest category of disabled student. Some researchers have suggested that many of the students called learning disabled are really slow learners in average schools, average learners in high-achieving schools, students with second-language problems, or class "troublemakers" or that they may simply be behind in their work because they are absent frequently or have to change schools often (Gartner & Lipsky, 1987).

Students with Learning Disabilities.   As with any of the groups of disabled students described thus far, students with learning disabilities are not all alike. The most common characteristics are specific difficulties in one or more

Teaching Tip: Dolgins, J., Myers, M., Flynn, P. A., & Moore, J. (1984, February). How do we help the learning disabled? *Instructor,* 29–36.

Allow assignments to be typed, taped, or dictated.

Have material to be copied or directions for an assignment on the child's desk rather than on the board.

Increase the time allowed or decrease the amount of writing.

Omit handwriting as a criterion for evaluating reports.

Construct tests that require minimal writing, such as multiple-choice, matching.

Tape selections that a child cannot read but can comprehend.

Provide opportunities for group projects, peer tutoring, contracts, and/or learning centers.

Write summaries of reading assignments.

Decrease the number of spelling words required at one time.

To increase exposure, use spelling words that are also required in reading or science.

Avoid spelling as a criterion for evaluating assignments.

Require fewer math problems for an assignment.

Allow the use of calculators or other manipulative aids.

Provide concrete examples.

Encourage estimation skills.

Teaching Tip: You might discuss the issue of the social construction of learning disabilities, the observation that learning disabilities are defined, in part, by difficulties with particular activities valued by the culture.

Connections: The concept of learned helplessness will be discussed again in chapter 5 as one explanation for the lower achievement of children of poverty and again in chapter 9 as a factor influencing motivation.

Handout: See the *Instructor's Resource Manual* for **Handout Master 4.6,** "Indicators of Learning Problems," which asks students to match symptoms of learning problems with types of problems.

Background: See Noll, J. W. (1991). *Taking sides: Clashing views on controversial educational issues* (5th ed.). Guilford, CT: Duskin, for "Is Mainstreaming Beneficial to All?" (pp. 256–273). Dean Corrigan defends mainstreaming and W. N. Bender raises criticisms.

Transparency: Use acetate transparency T 35, "Models of Special Education Services."

Focus on . . . | **Learning Challenges**

- Distinguish between a disability and a handicap.
- How can schools accommodate the needs of physically disabled students?
- What are some signs of hearing impairment?
- What are the advantages and disadvantages of drug therapy for attention deficit disorders?
- Describe some teaching strategies that have been successful for learning-disabled students.

Learned Helplessness The expectation, based on previous experiences with a lack of control, that all one's efforts will lead to failure.

academic areas; poor coordination; problems paying attention; hyperactivity and impulsivity; problems organizing and interpreting visual and auditory information; disorders of thinking, memory, speech, and hearing; and sharp emotional ups and downs (Hallahan & Kauffman, 1994). As you can see, many students with other disabilities (such as attention deficit disorder) and many normal students may have some of the same characteristics. To complicate the situation even more, not all students with learning disabilities will have these problems, and few will have all of the problems.

Most students with learning disabilities have difficulties reading. These difficulties appear to be due to problems with relating sounds to letters that make up words, making spelling hard as well (Stanovich, 1991). Math, both computation and problem solving, is the second most common problem for learning-disabled students. The writing of some learning-disabled students is virtually unreadable, and their spoken language can be halting and disorganized. Many researchers trace some of these problems to the students' inability to use effective learning strategies like those we will discuss in chapter 7. Learning-disabled students often lack effective ways to approach academic tasks. They don't know how to focus on the relevant information, get organized, apply learning strategies and study skills, change strategies when one isn't working, or evaluate their learning. They tend to be passive learners, in part because they don't know *how* to learn. Working independently is especially trying, so homework and seatwork are often left incomplete (Hallahan & Kauffman, 1994).

Early diagnosis is important so that learning-disabled students do not become terribly frustrated and discouraged. The students themselves do not understand why they are having such trouble, and they may become victims of **learned helplessness.** This condition was first identified in learning experiments with animals. The animals were put in situations where they received punishment (electric shocks) that they could not control. Later, when the situation was changed and they could have escaped the shocks or turned them off, the animals didn't even bother trying (Seligman, 1975). They had learned to be helpless victims. Learning-disabled students may also come to believe that they cannot control or improve their own learning. This is a powerful belief. The students never exert the effort to discover that they can make a difference in their own learning, so they remain passive and helpless.

Learning-disabled students may also try to compensate for their problems and develop bad learning habits in the process, or they may begin avoiding certain subjects out of fear of not being able to handle the work. To prevent these things from happening, the teacher should refer the students to the appropriate professionals in the school.

Teaching Students with Learning Disabilities. There is also controversy over how best to help these students. Many programs have been developed to "train" the underlying learning processes. In general, attempts to train perceptual processes directly have not been very successful in improving academic performance (Reid, Hresko, & Swanson, 1991). A more promising ap-

"YOUR FEELINGS OF INSECURITY SEEM TO HAVE STARTED WHEN MARY LOU GURNBLATT SAID, 'MAYBE I DON'T HAVE A LEARNING DISABILITY—MAYBE YOU HAVE A TEACHING DISABILITY.'"

(© 1975 Tony Saltzman)

proach seems to be to emphasize study skills and methods for processing information in a given subject like reading or math. Many of the principles of cognitive learning from chapters 7 and 8 can be applied to help all students improve their attention, memory, and problem-solving abilities (Sawyer, Graham, & Harris, 1992). *The Kansas Learning Strategies Curriculum* is one example of this approach (Deshler & Schumaker, 1986). No set of teaching techniques will be effective for every learning-disabled child. You should work with the special education teachers in your school to design appropriate instruction for individual students. Table 4.4 on page 140 summarizes problem areas and the most effective teaching approaches for learning-disabled students across the life span.

Mainstreaming

We have been discussing in detail the many special problems of exceptional students because, no matter what grade or subject you teach, you will encounter these students in your classroom. The movement to educate exceptional students in regular classrooms sometimes is called **mainstreaming,** because the exceptional students are educated in the mainstream of American education.

Changes in the Law

Test Bank items 4.77–4.80, 4.98, 4.99, 4.111–4.113, 4.122

In 1975 a law was passed that began revolutionary changes in the education of disabled children. The Education for All Handicapped Children Act (Public Law 94-142) required states to provide "a free, appropriate public education for every child between the ages of 3 and 21 (unless state law does not provide free public education to children 3 to 5 or 18 to 21 years of age) regardless of how, or how seriously, he may be handicapped." In 1986, PL

Mainstreaming Teaching disabled children in regular classes for part or all of their school day.

TABLE 4.4   Learning Disabilities across the Life Span

Learning disabilities are not limited to the school years. This table lists the problems that may occur during different phases of life and the treatments that have the strongest support from research or from expert teachers in the field.

	Preschool	Grades K–1
Problem Areas	Delay in developmental milestones (e.g., walking) Receptive language Expressive language Visual perception Auditory perception Short attention span Hyperactivity	Academic readiness skills (e.g., alphabet knowledge, quantitative concepts, directional concepts, etc.) Receptive language Expressive language Visual perception Auditory perception Gross and fine motor Attention Hyperactivity Social skills
Treatments with Most Research and/or Expert Support	Direct instruction in language skills Behavioral management Parent training	Direct instruction in academic and language areas Behavioral management Parent training

Source: Reprinted with permission of Macmillan College Publishing Company from *Students with learning disabilities,* 4/e, by Cecil D. Mercer, p. 50. Copyright © 1992 by Macmillan College Publishing Company, Inc.

Regular Education Initiative An educational movement that advocates giving regular education teachers, not special education teachers, responsibility for teaching mildly (and sometimes moderately) handicapped students.

Individuals with Disabilities Education Act (IDEA) Amendment to PL 94-142.

Americans with Disabilities Act (ADA) Legislation prohibiting discrimination against persons with disabilities in employment, transportation, public access, local government, and telecommunications.

99-457 extended the requirement for a free, appropriate education to all handicapped children ages 3 to 5, even in states that do not have public schooling for children this age. Also in the mid-1980s, some special educators and educational policymakers suggested that regular and special education should be merged so that regular teachers would have to take even more responsibility for the education of exceptional students. This movement is called the **regular education initiative.**

In 1990, PL 94-142 was amended by the **Individuals with Disabilities Education Act (IDEA)**. This legislation replaced the word "handicapped" with "disabled," and expanded the services for disabled students. Also in 1990, the **Americans with Disabilities Act (ADA)** extended civil rights protection in employment, transportation, public accommodations, state and local government, and telecommunications to people with disabilities (an issue considered in the movie, *Philadelphia*, about an AIDS victim who loses his job).

Let's examine the requirements in these laws. There are three major points of interest to teachers: the concept of "least restrictive placement"; the indi-

Grades 2–6	Grades 7–12	Adult
Reading skills	Reading skills	Reading skills
Arithmetic skills	Arithmetic skills	Arithmetic skills
Written expression	Written expression	Written expression
Verbal expression	Verbal expression	Verbal expression
Receptive language	Listening skills	Listening skills
Attention span	Study skills (meta-	Study skills
Hyperactivity	cognition)	Social-emotional
Social-emotional	Social-emotional-delinquency	
Direct instruction in academic areas	Direct instruction in academic areas	Direct instruction in academic areas
Behavioral management	Tutoring in subject areas	Tutoring in subject (college) or job area
Self-control training	Direct instruction in learning strategies (study skills)	Compensatory instruction (i.e., using aids such as tape recorder, calculator, computer, dictionary)
Parent training	Self-control training	
	Curriculum alternatives	

vidualized education program (IEP); and the protection of the rights of disabled students and their parents.

Least Restrictive Placement. The laws require states to develop procedures for educating each child in the **least restrictive placement**. This means a setting that is as normal and as much in the mainstream of education as possible. Some disabled students may spend most of the day in a special class, but attend one or two regular classes in physical education and art. In most schools severely disabled students are not integrated into regular classes; but in some districts there is a movement toward **full inclusion**—integrating all students, even those with severe disabilities, into regular classes. Advocates of full inclusion believe that disabled students can benefit from involvement with their nondisabled peers and should be educated with them in their regular home-district school, even if doing so calls for special aids, services, and training or consultation for the regular teaching staff (Stainback & Stainback, 1992). As you can see in the Point/Counterpoint on pages 142–143, full inclusion is a hotly debated issue.

Connections: The IEP is discussed later in this chapter, and an example IEP is included as Handout Masters 4.8A and 4.8B in the *Instructor's Resource Manual*.

Transparency: Use acetate transparency **T 37**, "Flowchart for Individualized Program Process."

Study Guide: Concept Map. See the *Study Guide* for the Concept Map "Adapting Instruction for Learner Differences." This map also appears as **Handout Master 4.9** in the *Instructor's Resource Manual*.

Background: One group that advocates total inclusion of disabled students in regular classrooms is Schools Are For Everyone (SAFE), 360 South Third Street, Suite 101, Columbus, OH 43215.

Activity 4.9: Critical Thinking. See the *Instructor's Resource Manual* for Mainstreaming, an activity asking students to determine how they would adapt teaching for students with specific challenges.

Transparency: Use acetate transparency **T 32**, "Percentage of Children Served by Special Education."

Least Restrictive Placement Placement of each child in as normal an educational setting as possible.

Full Inclusion The integration of all students, including those with severe disabilities, into regular classes.

Is Full Inclusion a Reasonable Approach to Teaching Exceptional Students?

In his booklet entitled *Inclusion: Issues of educating students with disabilities in regular educational settings,* Michael Hardman (1994) summarizes the arguments for and against full inclusion.

POINT Full inclusion makes sense.

Supporters of full inclusion, such as Marsha Forest, believe that:

All children need to learn with and from other children. . . . All children need to belong and feel wanted. . . . All children need to have fun and enjoy noise and laughter in their lives. . . . All children need to take risks and fall and cry and get hurt. . . . All children need to be in real families and real schools and real neighborhoods. (p. 403).

These opportunities are limited in special class placements. No matter how good the teaching, disabled students will never learn to cope with the world outside their special classroom if they are not allowed to live in that world. Furthermore, many researchers believe that special education has failed. For example, only 56 percent of students in special education earn a high school diploma and only 21 percent of these graduates go on to pursue any kind of post-secondary education. Segregation away from the mainstream, in special classes, robs disabled students of the opportunity to learn to participate fully in society, robs nondisabled students of the opportunity to develop understanding and acceptance of the disabled, and increases the likelihood that disabled individuals will be stigmatized.

COUNTERPOINT Full inclusion will not work.

Just because a disabled student is physically present in a class does not mean that student feels a sense of belonging. Disabled students can be just as socially isolated and alone in a regular class as they would be in a "special" class across the hall or across the state. Children can be cruel, and they may not necessarily provide opportunities for their disabled peers to "have fun and enjoy noise and laughter in their

Trends toward supported inclusion of students with disabilities may encourage teachers to develop more specialized skills such as knowledge of signing.

Individual Education Program. The drafters of the laws recognized that each student is unique and may need a specially tailored program to make progress. The **individualized education program,** or **IEP,** is written by a team that includes the student's teacher or teachers, a qualified school psychologist or special education supervisor, the parent(s) or guardian(s), and (when possible) the student. The program must be updated each year and must state in writing:

1. The student's present level of achievement.
2. Goals for the year and short-term measurable instructional objectives leading to those goals.
3. A list of specific services to be provided to the student and details of when those services will be initiated.
4. A description of how fully the student will participate in the regular school program.
5. A schedule telling how the student's progress toward the objectives will be evaluated and approximately how long the services described in the plan will be needed.
6. Beginning at age 16, a statement of needed transitional services to move the student toward further education or work in adult life.

The Rights of Students and Parents. Several stipulations in these laws protect the rights of parents and students. Schools must have procedures for lives." Furthermore, many researchers believe that special education has been quite successful. Seventy-seven percent of parents of students with disabilities are satisfied with the education programs of their children (Harris, 1989). In fact, parents of children with disabilities are more satisfied with the public schools than are parents of school-age children in general (Robert Wood Johnson, 1988). And special classes cannot be held responsible for low graduation and high drop-out rates among special education students. Ninety-two percent of all students with disabilities spend at least some of their time in regular classes already. Shouldn't these classes be held responsible too?

Finally, can we really expect regular teachers who are already overburdened with responsibilities for low-achieving students, students coping with family crises, and students who speak little or no English to also handle the wide range of disabilities that could confront them? Regular educators are unprepared, unsupported, and unable to handle all these challenges at once. The idea that extra support and consultation will be provided is good in theory, but will it actually come to pass in practice? Albert Shanker, President of the American Federation of Teachers (AFT), speaking to members of his union during an AFT conference, *Inclusion: Where We Stand,* said the following:

I do believe very large numbers of students now separated into special education could be included and integrated into regular classes and it would be beneficial. . . . [But] We must put the brakes on the helter-skelter, even tumultuous rush toward full inclusion so that everyone involved—parents, school boards, legislators, Congress, and even the Clinton administration—can develop a policy based on what is best for all children in our public schools . . . Full inclusion is becoming more widely practiced based on budgetary and social motivation and not on what most Americans think classrooms ought to be about, which is education. (Inclusive Education Programs, 1994, p. 1+)

maintaining the confidentiality of school records. Testing practices must not discriminate against students from different cultural backgrounds. Parents have the right to see all records relating to the testing, placement, and teaching of their child. If they wish, parents may obtain an independent evaluation of their child. Parents may bring an advocate or representative to the meeting at which the IEP is developed. Students whose parents are unavailable must be assigned a surrogate parent to participate in the planning. Parents must receive written notice (in their native language) before any evaluation or change in placement is made. Finally, parents have the right to challenge the program developed for their child, and are protected by due process of law.

Today, about 9 to 10 percent of the schoolchildren in the United States participate in special education programs. Many are in regular classes for at least part of the day.

Effective Teaching in Mainstreamed Classrooms

Test Bank items 4.81–4.86, 4.115

When you think about working with disabled students, what are your concerns? Do you have enough training? Will you get the support you need from school administrators or specialists? Will working with the disabled students take time away from your other responsibilities? These are common questions, and sometimes concerns are justified. But effective teaching for mainstreamed students is not a unique set of skills. It is a combination of good teaching prac-

Multicultural Awareness: Ask students to consider and discuss the following findings in *The Condition of Education 1991,* prepared by the U.S. Department of Education:

The percentage of children living in poverty is two to three times greater for minorities than whites.

Minority-group students are overrepresented in special education classes.

Individualized Education Program (IEP) Annually revised program for an exceptional student, detailing present achievement level, goals, and strategies, drawn up by teachers, parents, specialists, and (if possible) student.

Background: Gartner, A., & Lipsky, D. K. (1987). Beyond special education: Toward a quality system for all students. *Harvard Educational Review, 57,* 367–395.

Background: Scruggs, T. E., & Mastropieri, M. A. (1992). Effective mainstreaming for mildly handicapped students. *Elementary School Journal 92,* 389–409.

Activity 4.10: Background. See the *Instructor's Resource Manual* for Effects of Handicapped Students Tutoring Regular Students. This is a summary of Top, B. L., & Osguthrope, R. T. (1987). Reverse-role tutoring: The effects of handicapped students tutoring regular class students. *The Elementary School Journal, 87,* 413–424.

Casebook: See the Teachers' Casebook for suggestions about how to deal with mainstreaming concerns, such as moving a student from a special to a regular classroom.

Research: Ferguson, D. L., Ferguson, P. M., & Bogdan, R. C. (1987). If mainstreaming is the answer, what is the question? In V. Richardson-Koehler (Ed.), *Educator's handbook: A research perspective* (pp. 394–419). White Plains, NY: Longman.

Background: Margolis, H., & Schwartz, E. (1989, January). Facilitating mainstreaming through cooperative learning. *The High School Journal,* 83–88.

Resource Room Classroom with special materials and a specially trained teacher.

Cooperative Teaching Collaboration between regular and special education teachers.

tices and sensitivity to all your students. Disabled students need to *learn the academic material,* and they need to be *full participants in the day-to-day life of the classroom.*

To accomplish the first goal of academic learning, Larrivee (1985) concluded that effective teachers of mainstreamed students do the following:

1. Use time efficiently by having smooth management routines, avoiding discipline problems, and planning carefully.
2. Ask questions at the right level of difficulty.
3. Give supportive, positive feedback to students, helping them figure out the right answer if they are wrong but on the right track.

To accomplish the second goal of integrating disabled students into the day-to-day life of the classroom, Ferguson, Ferguson, and Bogdan (1987) give the following guidelines:

1. Mix students with disabilities into groups with nondisabled students. Avoid resegregating the disabled students into separate groups.
2. Instead of sending students out for special services like speech therapy, remedial reading, or individualized instruction, try to integrate the special help into the class setting, perhaps during a time when the other students are working independently too.
3. Make sure your language and behavior with disabled students is a good model for everyone.
4. Teach about differences among people as part of the curriculum. Let students become familiar with aids for the disabled, such as hearing aids, sign language, communication boards, and so on.
5. Have students work together in cooperative groups or on special projects such as role plays, biographical interviews, or lab assignments.
6. Try to keep the schedules and activity patterns of disabled and nondisabled students similar.

Resource Rooms, Collaborative Consultation, and Cooperative Teaching. Many schools provide additional help for classroom teachers working with disabled students. A **resource room** is a classroom with special materials and equipment and a specially trained teacher. Students may come to the resource room each day for several minutes or several hours and receive instruction individually or in small groups. The rest of the day the students are in regular classes.

The resource room can also be used as a crisis center. Individual students may spend an hour, a day, or a week there during a crisis, when their regular teacher is unable to give them the necessary attention and guidance. Besides working with students directly, a resource teacher may also work with them indirectly by giving the regular teacher ideas, materials, or actual demonstrations of teaching techniques.

Increasingly, special and regular educators are working together, collaborating to assume equal responsibility for the education of disabled students. The collaboration may work through consultation, planning, and problem solving about how to teach specific students or the special education teacher might work directly alongside the regular teacher in a class made up of students with and without disabilities. The latter is called **cooperative teaching.**

The teachers assume different roles, depending on the age of the students and their needs. For example, in a secondary class the regular teacher might be responsible for academic content, while the special instructor teaches study skills and learning strategies. In another classroom the regular teacher might deal with core content, while the special teacher provides remediation, enrichment, or reteaching when necessary. The two teachers might also try team teaching, where each is responsible for different parts of the lesson.

In using cooperative teaching, it is important that regular and disabled students aren't resegregated in the class, with the regular teacher always working with the "regular" students and the special teacher always working with the mainstreamed students. I observed one class in which the mainstreamed students worked only with the special education teacher but often looked longingly over their shoulders at the activities of their classmates working with the regular teacher. Rather than integrating the disabled students into the class, this cooperative teaching arrangement accentuated their separateness.

Making a Referral. If you wanted to refer a student for evaluation, how would you begin? Table 4.5 guides you through the referral process.

Activity 4.11: Background. See the *Instructor's Resource Manual* for The Needs of Special Needs Children, a list of 16 suggestions for working with special needs children.

TABLE 4.5 Making a Referral

1. Contact the student's parents. It is very important that you discuss the student's problems with the parents *before* you refer.
2. Before making a referral, check *all* the student's school records. Has the student ever:

- had a psychological evaluation?
- qualified for special services?
- been included in other special programs (e.g., for disadvantaged children; speech or language therapy)?
- scored far below average on standardized tests?
- been retained?

Do the records indicate:

- good progress in some areas, poor progress in others?
- any physical or medical problem?
- that the student is taking medication?

3. Talk to the student's other teachers and professional support personnel about your concern for the student. Have other teachers also had difficulty with the student? Have they found ways of dealing successfully with the student? Document the strategies that you have used in your class to meet

the student's educational needs. Your documentation will be useful as evidence that will be helpful to or required by the committee of professionals who will evaluate the student. Demonstrate your concern by keeping written records. Your notes should include items such as:

- exactly what you are concerned about
- why you are concerned about it
- dates, places, and times you have observed the problem
- precisely what you have done to try to resolve the problem
- who, if anyone, helped you devise the plans or strategies you have used
- evidence that the strategies have been successful or unsuccessful

Remember that you should refer a student only if you can make a convincing case that the student may have a handicapping condition and probably cannot be served appropriately without special education. Referral for special education begins a time-consuming, costly, and stressful process that is potentially damaging to the student and has many legal ramifications.

Source: P. L. Pullen and J. M. Kaufmann (1987). *What should I know about special education? Answers for classroom teachers* (Austin, Texas: Pro-Ed, 1987). Reprinted by permission.

Research: Rich, H. L., & Ross, S. M. (1989). Students' time on learning tasks in special education. *Exceptional Children, 55,* 508–515.

Brief abstract: This study measured, through naturalistic observation procedures, the use of time among handicapped students in four special education alternatives: regular class, resource room, special class, and special school. Findings revealed that the least restrictive alternatives, particularly the resource room, made more in-class learning time available.

Research: Woodword, J., Carnine, D., & Gersten, R. (1988). Teaching problem solving through computer simulations. *American Educational Research Journal, 25,* 72–80.

Brief abstract: This study investigated the effectiveness of a computer simulation in enhancing student learning in a unit of health. Test results indicated significant differences on basic facts and concepts that were reinforced by the simulation. The most significant differences were in problem-solving skills. That is, the combination of structured teaching and computer simulation was effective in teaching not only factual knowledge but higher cognitive skills.

Focus on . . . **Mainstreaming**

■ Describe the main legal requirements in the Individuals with Disabilities Act.
■ What is your position on full inclusion?
■ What should you do before referring a child for evaluation by special education professionals?

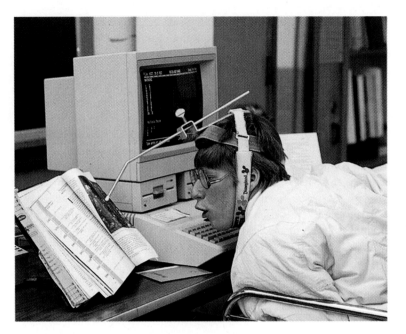

Computers and other technology can support learning for disabled students so that disabilities are less handicapping.

Computers and Exceptional Students   Test Bank item 4.87

Computers have improved the education of exceptional children in countless ways. Given the record keeping and program planning needed to meet federal regulations, teachers can use computers to manage instruction. For students who require small steps and many repetitions to learn a new concept, computers are the perfect patient tutors, repeating steps and lessons as many times as necessary. A well-designed computer instructional program is engaging and interactive—two important qualities for students with problems paying attention or with a history of failure that has eroded motivation. For example, a math or spelling program might use images, sounds, and gamelike features to maintain the attention of a student with an attention-deficit disorder. Interactive videodisc programs are being developed to help hearing people use sign language. Many programs do not involve sound, so hearing-impaired students can get the full benefit from the lessons. Students who have trouble reading can use programs that will "speak" a word for them if they touch the unknown word with a light pen or the cursor. With this immediate access to help, the students are much more likely to get the reading practice they need to prevent falling further and further behind. And for the learning-disabled student whose writing can't be read, word processors produce perfect penmanship so the ideas can finally get on paper. Once the ideas are on paper, the student can reorganize and improve the writing without the agony of rewriting by hand (Hallahan & Kauffman, 1994; Hardman, Drew, Egan, & Wolf, 1993; Reynolds & Birch, 1988).

For gifted students, computers can be a connection with databases and computers in universities, museums, and research labs. Computer networks allow students to work on projects and share information with others across the country. It is also possible to have gifted students write programs for students and teachers. Quite a few principals around the country rely on their students to make the technology in the school work. These are just a few examples of what technology can do. Check with the resource teachers in your district to find out what is available in your school.

Background: Salomon, G., Perkins, D. N., & Globerson, T. (1991). Partners in cognition: Extending human intelligence with intelligent technologies. *Educational Researcher, 20*(3), 2–9.

SUMMARY

Language and Labels

Exceptional learners have learning abilities or problems that require special education. In the past, education for children with learning problems or physical disabilities followed a medical disease model and often meant segregating children in separate classes or programs.

Labels and diagnostic classifications of exceptional students can easily become both stigmas and self-fulfilling prophecies, but can also open doors to special programs and help teachers develop appropriate instructional strategies.

Individual Differences in Intelligence

Psychologists disagree on what intelligence is—a collection of discrete abilities; a general mental ability to learn new information and cope with the world; abilities for problem solving; or an array of multiple intelligences that include, for example, social judgment and creativity. The models of Spearman, Guilford, and Gardner describe the content of intelligence, while Sternberg's triarchic theory views intelligence as a process.

IQ, as it is measured today through individually administered tests such as the Stanford-Binet and the Wechsler Scales, is closely related to success in school, but not necessarily to success in life. In the past, IQ compared mental age with chronological age, but today these tests compare the individual's performance with average scores for the same age group. IQ scores must be interpreted with caution, because many factors other than intelligence influence scores. Both heredity and environment play a role in intelligence, which is never fixed but is continually open to change.

Ability Differences and Teaching

Academic ability groupings can have both disadvantages and advantages for students and teachers. For low-ability students, however, between-class ability grouping generally has a negative effect on achievement, social adjustment, and self-esteem. Cross-age grouping by subject can be an effective way to deal with ability differences in a school. Within-class ability grouping, if handled sensitively and flexibly, can have positive effects, but alternatives such as cooperative learning are also possible.

Mentally retarded students have significantly below-average intellectual skills and difficulty adapting adequately to social norms. Transition programming prepares retarded students to live and work in the community. Gifted students—those who are exceptionally bright, creative, or talented—also may have social adjustment problems and are often unable to fulfill their potential in public schools. Acceleration, enrichment, or out-of-school programs can help meet the needs of exceptionally able students.

Cognitive and Learning Styles

Individuals have characteristic differences in personality, in the way they organize and process information, and in the conditions in which they learn best. Field dependence versus field independence and impulsive versus reflective cognitive styles are examples of these differences. While cognitive styles and learning preferences are not related to intelligence or effort, they do affect school performance. Applied with caution, learning style inventories can be used to modify instructional strategies and the classroom environment to take advantage of individual differences that help students learn.

Students with Learning Challenges

A disability and a handicap are not the same, and teachers must avoid imposing handicaps on disabled learners. Physically challenged students may rely on orthopedic devices, may have health problems such as epilepsy or cerebral palsy, or may be hearing or vision impaired to varying degrees. Communication disorders include speech impairments (articulation disorders, stuttering, and voicing problems) and oral language disorders. Behavioral and emotional problems include conduct disorders, anxiety-withdrawal, attentional problems/immaturity, motor excess, socialized aggression, and psychotic behavior. In some cases, attention deficit-hyperactive disorders can be helped by medication. All programs must include help for academic problems.

Specific learning disabilities often involve physical, behavioral, and emotional challenges. Learning-disabled students may become victims of learned helplessness when they come to believe that they cannot control or improve their own learning and therefore cannot succeed. A focus on learning strategies often helps students with learning disabilities.

Mainstreaming

Public Law 94-142 (1975) requires that each exceptional learner or special-needs student be educated in the least restrictive environment according to an individualized education program. The law also protects the rights of special needs students and their parents. Public Law 99-457 extends the mainstreaming law to preschool-age children, and IDEA, the Individuals with Disabilities Act, extends services to include transition programming for exceptional learners 16 years old and older. The regular education initiative calls for regular classroom teachers to receive training in teaching exceptional learners. Well-developed instructional strategies and technologies exist for helping exceptional students to learn.

KEY TERMS

Americans with Disabilities Act (ADA), p. 140
articulation disorders, p. 133
attention deficit-hyperactive disorder, p. 135
automaticity, p. 113
between-class ability grouping, p. 118
cerebral palsy, p. 131
cognitive styles, p. 126
components, p. 112
cooperative teaching, p. 144
deviation IQ, p. 116
disability, p. 129
Down syndrome, p. 120
educationally blind, p. 132
epilepsy, p. 130
exceptional students, p. 108
faces of intellect, p. 110
field dependence, p. 127
field independence, p. 127

finger spelling, p. 131
full inclusion, p. 141
generalized seizure, p. 130
gifted student, p. 123
handicap, p. 129
hyperactivity, p. 135
impulsive, p. 127
Individuals with Disabilities Act (IDEA), p. 140
individualized education program (IEP), p. 142
insight, p. 112
intelligence, p. 117
intelligence quotient (IQ), p. 115
Joplin Plan, p. 119
learned helplessness, p. 138
learning-style preferences, p. 128
least restrictive placement, p. 141
low vision, p. 132
mainstreaming, p. 139

mental age, p. 115
mental retardation, p. 120
multiple intelligences, p. 111
nongraded elementary school, p. 119
orthopedic devices, p. 130
partial seizure, p. 130
reflective, p. 127
regular education initiative, p. 140
resource room, p. 144
self-instruction, p. 127
sign language, p. 131
spasticity, p. 131
specific learning disability, p. 136
speech impairment, p. 133
speech reading, p. 131
stuttering, p. 133
transition programming, p. 122
triarchic theory of intelligence, p. 112
voicing problems, p. 133
within-class ability grouping, p. 119

WHAT WOULD YOU DO?

Preschool and Kindergarten

A little girl in your kindergarten class seldom speaks. When she does, she usually says only a word or two. She seems to understand when others talk, but almost never responds verbally. How would you approach this situation?

Elementary and Middle School

The school psychologist tells you that one of your students is going to start taking medication designed to "calm him down." What would you want to know? How would you respond?

The principal tells you that she is assigning two more students to your class because you are "new, and have more training in mainstreaming than the older teachers." One student is mildly retarded and has problems making friends. The other is blind. How would you prepare your class and modify your teaching for these students?

Junior High and High School

A student in your fifth-period class is failing. When you look at your grade book, you see that it is the written work that is giving the student trouble. Multiple-choice test scores and class participation are fine. How would you identify the source of the problem?

Your school has just received the results of the fall testing, including scores for all your students on a group test of intelligence. What would you do with the results?

How would you adapt your teaching to accommodate a hearing-impaired student in your biology lab class?

Cooperative Learning Activity

Assume the faculty at your school has decided to reconsider how students are assigned to classes. The traditional way in the school has been between-class ability grouping, because your school serves a very wide range of students. Work with four or five members of your educational psychology class to design a system, then present your recommendations to the entire class. Be prepared to justify your recommendations and explain how you would implement them.

Managing Disruptive Students

You have a student in your class who seems unable to sit still, responds impulsively, and continually interrupts other students, How would you deal with these symptoms of "attention-deficit disorder" in your classroom?

The first thing you should analyze is the reason for the interruptions. If it is to receive your attention, moving the child closer to you may help. If the reason is to be a "class clown" and perform for the others, moving the child to the back of the room may help the situation. In the back of the room the rest of the class can't see the child and will usually ignore the antics. If the child is interrupting out of habit or impulse, a behavior management program might help.

For the program to be most effective, parental involvement is desirable. If the parent or parents will support your efforts and those of the child, changing behavior is quicker and easier. But even if the teacher has no parental support, the program can still be effective. The teacher makes a grid showing the different activities of the day or time period. If the behavior is favorable, a token or sticker can be given to the child. If the behavior is not satisfactory, no reward is given. When a preset limit is reached, a reward is given, such as a reward letter, a small trinket, time at the computer or listening center, or extra time at the media center. The reward should be something that the child will strive to reach. The teacher must be sure that the child will succeed right away, or discouragement will dissolve the program. After the child has achieved success for a while, the limits and restrictions can be increased before an award is earned. Eventually the program can be tapered off entirely.

Many teachers are reluctant to use this system because they feel it shows favoritism to one student. However, the other students know that the behavior being addressed is not allowed, and they want everyone to follow the rules. The class will be supportive and encouraging to the child.

Ida Pofahl, *Second-Grade Teacher*
Denison Elementary School, Denison, Iowa

Mainstreaming Concerns

A new student has just been assigned to your class from a special education class. You don't believe the student is ready for full-time participation in your class, but the administration disagrees. What would you do?

First I would discuss the child with the administration to find out their reason for wanting the child in the regular classroom. I would also voice my concerns. Then I would suggest placing the child in the classroom for partial days for about three weeks. During this time I would keep notes on the child's adjustment. It would be helpful to videotape the child on several occasions. I would also request the administration to make several observations. Thus if the child were not ready for full-time participation in the classroom, the administration should realize this from the documentation presented.

Kathryn Daniels, *Second-Grade Teacher*
Fredericktown Elementary School, Fredericktown, Ohio

Ability Groupings

Do you use ability groupings in your classes? If so, why and for what subjects? Which type of ability grouping do you use? If not, why not?

The "cluster model" for grouping of gifted/talented (G/T) students has been successfully incorporated with the "inclusive model" for special services students.

Within this framework, identified G/T students are clustered together in home-rooms. This allows these students to interact throughout the day with three to four others that share common strengths and needs. Clustering four to five students together in a homeroom also ensures that enrichment activities will be provided to this "visible" group. The classroom teacher can group by interest, by learning style, or by another heterogeneous grouping pattern. The "inclusive model" allows special service teachers to come into the classroom and adapt or provide alternative teaching strategies on the spot. This allows learning-disabled and other special service students the opportunity to work with their peers as often as possible.

There are times when grouping ability is still necessary for exceptional learners determined on a case by case analysis. There will be times when special service students will need to be put in a resource setting for individual or small-group instruction. Time, space, and availability of resources and money dictate this as well as the need of the child. Educators tend to overreact to current trends, and I believe this is the case with the area of ability grouping for exceptional learners. We, as educators, need to be flexible and creative when determining the most appropriate grouping for each activity or lesson. Ability grouping should be included as a possible form of alternative grouping strategies.

Lawrence Leebens, *Curriculum Resource Coordinator*
Forest Hills Elementary School, Eden Prairie, Minnesota

IT DEPENDS ON THE SUBJECT

Ability grouping is a strategy that can be helpful in certain subject areas and a hindrance in others. Where skills mastery is essential prior to learning the next skill, such as in reading and math, it is better to have a homogeneous class. In those classes the students will be working on the same level and the teacher can spend as long as the group needs on that skill. In classes such as science and social studies, where the emphasis is more on oral discussion and student participation, I think that the low-achieving students gain a great deal from what they hear their peers say.

Dori Hoffman-Latter, *Special Education Teacher*
Walker Middle School, Charlottesville, Virginia

Working with Parents

Have you had to inform a child's parents of his or her learning disability?

ENLISTING SUPPORT

Yes. This is a situation that requires great tact. The teacher must keep in mind a number of things as she talks with parents. First and foremost she must remember that the only thing we really know about children is that they are bundles of potential. We must not be fooled into thinking that any kind of test or even our professional judgment enables us to really know what a child is capable of or what he will do in the future. Responsible teachers do not use the term learning disability to put a child in a pigeon hole. Second, the teacher must remember that this will be unpleasant news to the parent and that the parent is very likely to be upset. The teacher must be prepared to do a great deal of listening. She must guide the parent into learning more about the nature of the problem, accepting whatever help the school system offers, and becoming an informed advocate for their child. She must also help the parent become aware of self-fulfilling prophecies. The parent must be a cheerleader for his child and continue to hold high hopes for the future. In this situation the teacher must support the parent as well as the child.

Cynthia Newman Wisdom, *First-Grade Teacher*
Trace Crossings Elementary School, Hoover, Alabama

5

The Impact of Culture and Community

*T*he face of American classrooms is changing. In this chapter we examine the many cultures that form the fabric of our society. We begin by tracing the schools' responses to different ethnic and cultural groups and consider the concept of multicultural education. With a broad conception of culture as a basis, we then examine three important dimensions of every student's identity: social class, ethnicity, and gender. For each dimension, we will explore the experiences of the various groups in the schools, possible differences in achievement and learning styles, and explanations for the lower achievement of some groups. Then we turn to a consideration of language and bilingual education. The last section of the chapter presents three general principles for teaching every student.

By the time you have completed this chapter you should be able to:

- Compare the old notion of the melting pot with current views about multicultural education.
- Define *culture* and list the various groups that make up your own cultural identity.
- Explain why the school achievement of low-income students often falls below that of middle- and upper-income students.
- Give examples of conflicts and compatibilities between home and school cultures.
- Describe the school's role in the development of gender differences.
- Summarize the arguments for and against bilingual education.
- Incorporate multicultural concepts into your teaching.

Melting Pot A metaphor for the absorption and assimilation of immigrants into the mainstream of society so that ethnic differences vanish.

Today's Multicultural Classrooms

Who are the students in American classrooms today? Here are a few statistics:

- 1 in 5 Americans under the age of 18 lives in poverty. For children under age 3, the number is 1 in 3.
- Nearly 50 percent of all African-American children are poor.
- 1 in 3 children lives with a single parent, usually a working mother.
- 12 percent of all students are in bilingual classes.
- 15 percent of the children entering school in 1986 were immigrants who spoke little or no English; 10 percent had poorly educated or illiterate parents.
- 3 in 10 students probably will not finish high school; many of these will be members of minority groups (3 in 10 African Americans, 4 in 10 Hispanics, 4 in 10 Native Americans, 1 in 10 whites).
- By the year 2010, 38 percent of all students will be members of minority groups. (Grant & Sleeter, 1989; *Teacher Magazine*, April 1991)

How should the schools respond to these challenges? First, we consider the approaches of earlier times, when educators assumed all students—rich and poor, minority or majority group, male or female—should adapt to the expectations of traditional schools.

Old Views: The Students Must Adapt

Since the beginning of the twentieth century, a flow of immigrants has entered the United Kingdom, western Europe, Canada, Australia, the United States, and many other developed countries. As these new immigrants arrived, in most areas they were expected to assimilate—that is, to enter the cultural **melting pot** and become like those who had arrived earlier. For years, the goal of American schools was to be the fire under the melting pot. Immigrant children who spoke different languages and had different religious and cultural heritages were expected to come to the schools, master standard English, and learn to become mainstream Americans.

In the 1960s and 1970s, some educators suggested that minority-group and poor students had problems in school because they had not fully assimilated into mainstream American life; they had not adopted the "right" values and skills. The students were described as "culturally disadvantaged" or "culturally handicapped." The assumption of this **cultural deficit model** was that the students' home culture was inferior because it had not prepared them to fit into the schools. Today most people reject the idea of cultural deficits. They believe that no culture is deficient, but rather that there may be incompatibilities between the student's home culture and the cultural expectations of the school.

What are the expectations of schools? Many reformers have noted that American schools typically reflect the white, Anglo-Saxon, Protestant, middle-class, male-dominated values that have characterized mainstream America. Schedules are tight and planned months in advance (I just got my daughter's college vacation and exam schedule for the next four years!). Students are expected to be on time and to do one activity at a time. The future is paramount. Students are told to do well so they will get good grades, graduate from high school, get into college, and then (finally) find a good job. Competition is encouraged, and the phrase "Do your own work!" is repeated daily. Unless it is part of the teacher's lesson plan, "cooperation" is seen as cheating. Words, ideas, and knowledge are more important than feelings. Individuals are to work hard and achieve; they are responsible for their own destinies. Generally, the teacher talks more than the students, and students are expected to respect the teacher's authority. Teachers ask and initiate; students answer and react—one at a time. Spontaneous student talk, or several students talking at once, is discouraged. Working fast and being neat are valued (Banks, 1994; Bennett, 1995; Boykin, 1986).

But these values and expectations are not shared by all people. As you will see later in this chapter, some groups teach people to put the good of the group ahead of the needs of the individual. Cooperation is valued, not individualism and competition. People are taught to rely on family and friends (Harrison, Wilson, Pine, & Buriel, 1990) particularly when resources are scarce. There is a growing recognition that schools have a responsibility to adapt to some extent to the values and skills of students instead of expecting every student to adapt to all the traditional expectations of the school.

New Views: Multicultural Education

Test Bank items 5.4–5.6, 5.50, 5.73

Multicultural education, according to James Banks (1991, 1994), is an idea, an educational reform movement, and a process.

The *idea* of multicultural education is that all students—male, female, disabled, rich, poor, from different racial and ethnic groups, or speaking different languages—*all students* should have a full and equal opportunity to learn in school and to be respected. To make this statement more than just a slogan, teachers must understand the barriers some students face in attaining an education. Why is it that girls and boys achieve equally in science and math during the early grades, but that beyond elementary school the girls' performance drops off? By the time they reach college, even in the top schools, women often have less to say in class and doubt their abilities more than men (Sadker, Sad-

Background: Multicultural Education (1992, special issue). *Educational Leadership, 49*(4).

Background: See Noll, J. W. (1993). *Taking sides: Clashing views on controversial educational issues* (7th ed.). Guilford, CT: Duskin (pp. 228–251), for Molefi Asante and Arthur Schlesinger, Jr. debating "Do Black Students Need an Afrocentric Curriculum?"

Cultural Deficit Model A model that explains the school achievement problems of ethnic minority students by assuming that their culture is inadequate and does not prepare them to succeed in school.

Multicultural Education Education that teaches the value of cultural diversity.

Should Multicultural Education Emphasize Similarities or Differences?

"In principle, virtually all of the experts who have studied, advocated, and criticized the various forms of multicultural education now taking shape in the United States agree on one point: Such education should provide students with a fuller, more balanced truth about their own history and culture than they have had up to now" (Viadero, 1990, p. 14). The question is how. Should education emphasize the similarities or the differences among people?

POINT **Emphasize what is common among all students (traditional approaches).**

Richard Rodriguez (1987), a well-known contemporary writer and editor, made a case for emphasizing what is common to all citizens in his criticism of a report by the Study Commission on Global Education:

Few words issue from the commission's 52-page report with more frequency or less precision than does the word, "diversity." The dilemma of our national diversity becomes, with a little choke on logic, the solution: American educators "must understand diversity." "Appreciate diversity." "Deal constructively with diversity." Pay "greater attention to . . . diversity . . . around the world and within the United States. . . . "

Diversity is a liquid noun. Diversity admits everything, stands for nothing. . . .

I do not agree that the primary purpose of early education is to teach diversity. I believe something closer to the reverse—that education's primary purpose, its distinguishing obligation, is to foster commonality. It is in the classroom that the child comes to learn a public identity. The child learns the skills of numbers and words crucial to public survival, and learns to put on a public self, apart from family or ethnic community.

I submit that America is not a tale for sentimentalists. I read writings of 18th-century white men who powdered their wigs and kept slaves, because they were the men who shaped the country that shapes my life. I am brown and of Mexican ancestry, one generation into this country. I claim Thomas Jefferson as a cultural forefather.

COUNTERPOINT **Emphasize diversity (ethnocentric approaches).**

In response to Rodriguez's position, Alba Rosenman (1987) believes:

Education that values cultural diversity does not say that "diversity admits everything and stands for nothing," as Mr. Rodriguez puts it, but rather that a culture is not wrong because it is different. Knowledge of other societies and customs gives students choices that may be more meaningful to them than those offered in our society. It is possible that there are other and better ways to live than those we have grown to know and love. We might yet learn something from that imprecise mass called American "diversity." . . . A multicultural curriculum tries, while valuing differences, to teach a fair curriculum to students with diverse backgrounds. There is no threat to society here, simply a relevant education.

Rosenman agrees with Rodriguez that "the primary purpose of an early education should not be to 'teach diversity.' Its primary purposes are to teach students that in school they will learn how to survive in our society and to solidify their feelings of worth."

James Banks (1993) suggests that the notion that multicultural education will divide the nation "assumes that the nation is already united. While we are one nation politically, sociologically our nation is deeply divided along lines of race, gender, and class" (p. 23).

Objective 5.2: Define *culture* and list the various groups that make up a person's cultural identity.

ker, & Klein, 1991). A similar pattern occurs for African-American, Hispanic-American, and Native-American students. The longer they stay in school, the more their achievement lags behind that of white students (Banks, 1991).

As an *educational reform movement,* multicultural education seeks to change the effects described above. Exactly how to do this is the topic of heated debate. Some reformers urge schools to focus on improving human relations so that students will learn to respect all people. Other educators press for in-depth studies of various racial and ethnic groups as part of the curriculum. But critics believe this is not enough. They want to infuse the entire curriculum with material written by and about minority group members. Still another approach to multicultural education is to transform the entire educational system so that students learn to be politically effective in reshaping society (Grant & Sleeter, 1989).

An examination of the alternative approaches to multicultural education is beyond the scope of an educational psychology text, but be aware that there is no general agreement about the "best" approach, as you can see in the Point/Counterpoint section.

As a *process,* multicultural education is ongoing. Schools cannot just institute a program or hire a consultant to "solve" the problem. Teachers have to reach out to all children every day—and keep trying. James Banks (1994) suggests that multicultural education has five dimensions, as shown in Figure 5.1 on page 158. Many people are familiar only with the dimension of *content integration,* using examples and content from a variety of cultures when teaching a subject. Because they believe that multicultural education is simply a change in curriculum, many people assume that it is irrelevant for subjects such as science and mathematics. But if you consider the other four dimensions—helping students understand how knowledge is influenced by beliefs, reducing prejudice, creating social structures in schools that support learning and development for all students, and using teaching methods that reach all students—then we see that this view of multicultural education is relevant to all subjects and all students.

Multicultural education rejects the idea of the melting pot. According to the multicultural ideal, America should be transformed into a society that values diversity (Casanova, 1987; Grant & Sleeter, 1989). Let's take a closer look at the differences that make up the mosaic of cultural diversity.

American Cultural Diversity

In this text we take a broad interpretation of culture and multicultural education, so we will examine social class, race, ethnicity, and gender as aspects of diversity. We begin with a look at the meaning of culture. Many people associate this concept with the "cultural events" section of the newspaper—art galleries, museums, Shakespeare, classical music, and so on. Culture has a much broader meaning; it embraces the whole way of life of a group of people.

Culture and Group Membership.   There are many definitions of **culture.** Most include the knowledge, rules, traditions, attitudes, and values that guide behavior in a particular group of people (Betancourt & Lopez, 1993). The group creates a culture—a program for living—and communicates the culture to members. Thus people are members of groups, they are not members of cultures. Groups can be defined along regional, ethnic, religious, racial, gender, social class, or other lines. Each of us is a member of many groups (see Figure 5.2 on page 159), so we all are influenced by many different cultures. Sometimes the influences are incompatible or even contradictory. For example, if you are a feminist but also a Roman Catholic, you may have trouble reconciling the two different cultures' beliefs about the ordination of women as

Activity 5.1: Cooperative Learning. See the *Instructor's Resource Manual* for Clarifying the Goals of a Multicultural Curriculum, an activity in which your students work individually and then in groups to rank five goals of multicultural education. **Handout Master 5.1** in the *Instructor's Resource Manual* supports this activity.

Activity 5.2: Field Experience. See the *Instructor's Resource Manual* for Observing Diversity in the Classroom, a field experience activity that focuses students' attention on diversity in classrooms.

Culture The knowledge, values, attitudes, and traditions that guide the behavior of a group of people and allow them to solve the problems of living in their environment.

FIGURE 5.1

THE DIMENSION OF MULTICULTURAL EDUCATION

Multicultural education is more than a change in the curriculum. To make education appropriate for all students, we must consider other dimensions as well. The way the athletics and counseling programs are structured, the teaching methods used, lessons about prejudice, perspectives on knowledge—these and many more elements contribute to true multicultural education.

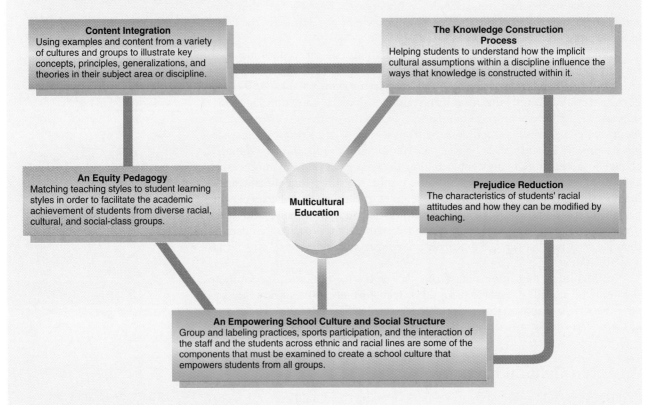

Source: J. A. Banks (1994). *Multiethnic education: Theory and practice,* 3/e, p. 5. Boston: Allyn and Bacon. Adapted with permission of the author and the publisher.

Transparency: Use acetate transparency T 38, "The Dimensions of Multicultural Education."

Activity 5.3: Reflection/Journal Writing. See the *Instructor's Resource Manual* for Cultural Identity, a journal-writing activity that encourages students to evaluate their own ethnic backgrounds and identities.

priests. Your personal belief on the issue will be based, in part, on how strongly you identify with each group (Banks, 1994).

There are many different cultures, of course, in every modern country. In the United States, students growing up in a small rural town in the Deep South are part of a cultural group that is very different from that of students in a large urban center or students in a West Coast suburb. In Canada, students living in the suburbs of Toronto certainly differ in a number of ways from students growing up in a Montreal high-rise apartment or on a farm in Quebec. Within those small towns in the Deep South or Quebec, the child of a gas station attendant grows up in a different culture from the child of the town doctor or dentist. Individuals of African, Asian, Hispanic, Native-American, or

FIGURE 5.2

INDIVIDUALS BELONG TO MANY DIFFERENT GROUPS

Each of us is a member of many different groups, and each group brings a different set of influences. The memberships shown here are not the only ones, but they are the major memberships for most people. Think of all the circles as overlapping.

Source: J. A Banks (1994). *Multiethnic education: Theory and practice,* 3/e, p. 89. Boston: Allyn and Bacon. Adapted with the permission of the author and the publisher.

European descent have distinctive histories and traditions. The experiences of males and females are different in most ethnic and economic groups. Everyone living within a particular country shares many common experiences and values, especially because of the influence of the mass media. But other aspects of their lives are shaped by differing cultural backgrounds.

Cautions in Interpreting Cultural Differences.   Before we examine the bases for cultural differences, two cautions are necessary. First, we will consider social class, ethnicity, and gender separately, because much of the available research focuses on only one of these variables. Of course, real children are not just African American, or middle class, or female; they are complex beings and members of many groups.

The second caution comes from James Banks (1993), who has written several books on multicultural education:

> Although membership in a gender, racial, ethnic, social-class, or religious group can provide us with important clues about an individual's behavior, it cannot enable us to predict behavior. . . . *Membership in a particular group does not determine behavior but makes certain types of behavior more probable.* (pp. 13–14)

Transparency: Use acetate transparency T 39, "Individuals Belong to Many Different Groups."

Background: The following paragraphs are quoted with permission from *Education Week* for Debra Viadero (1990), "Battle over multicultural education rises in intensity," *Education Week, 10* (13), November 28, pp. 1, 11, 13:

> While the ethnic-studies approach is meant to embrace a number of ethnic groups, it is talked about most often in relation to Afrocentric curricula. In their most commonly envisioned form, Afrocentric programs are embodied in the model used in the Portland public schools since 1989. School officials commissioned scholars to write "baseline essays" on the contributions of African and American blacks in six fields of study: art, language, mathematics, science, social studies, and music. Teachers are now expected to "infuse" that information throughout their teaching. Similar essays will be developed over the next few years on Hispanics, American Indians, Asians, and Pacific Islanders.

> "We're recognizing that most education programs use a European lens to view the world," says Carolyn M. Leonard, coordinator of the Portland district's program. "We're saying, 'I'm using another lens to view the world and my way of looking at it is different than yours.' "

Focus on ...   **Multicultural Classrooms**

- What group memberships particularly influence your identity?
- Explain multicultural education as an idea, an educational reform movement, and a process.

Keep this in mind as you read about characteristics of economically disadvantaged students or Asian Americans or males. The information we will examine reflects tendencies and probabilities. It does not tell you about a specific person. Remember that you will be teaching individual students. Each child is a unique product of many influences, a member of a variety of groups. For example, if a minority-group student in your class consistently arrives late, you should not assume that the student's behavior reflects a cultural difference in beliefs about punctuality. It may be that the student has a job before school or must walk a long distance, or even that he or she hates school.

Social Class Differences   Test Bank item 5.74

Activity 5.4: Field Experience. See the *Instructor's Resource Manual* for Experiencing Social Class Differences, an activity that gives your students a firsthand experience in stores or restaurants in neighborhoods of different socioeconomic levels.

The term used by sociologists for variations in wealth, power, and prestige is **socioeconomic status,** or **SES.** In modern societies, levels of wealth, power, and prestige are not always consistent. Some people—for instance, university professors—are members of professions that are reasonably prestigious but provide little wealth or power. Other people have political power though they are not wealthy. No single variable, not even income, is an effective measure of SES. In spite of these inconsistencies, most researchers identify four general levels of SES: upper, middle, working, and lower. The main characteristics of these four levels are summarized in Table 5.1.

Social class is a powerful dimension of cultural differences, often overpowering other differences such as ethnicity or gender. For example, upper-class Anglo-Europeans, African Americans, and Hispanic Americans typically find that they have more in common with each other than they have with lower-class individuals from their own ethnic groups.

Who Are the Poor?   Test Bank items 5.9–5.11, 5.52, 5.61

Background: Reed, S., & Sautter, R. C. (1990). Children of poverty: The status of 12 million Americans. *Phi Delta Kappan, 71*(10), K1–K12.

Transparency: Use acetate transparency T. 40, "Projected Number of Students in Poverty."

Socioeconomic Status (SES) Relative standing in the society based on income, power, background, and prestige.

Over one in five Americans under the age of 18 lives in poverty, defined in 1990 as an income below $13,359 for a family of four living in an urban area (Macionis, 1994). By 2020 this number will be *one in four.* But these percentages don't tell the whole story. As you can see in Figure 5.3 on page 162, the absolute number of poor children will increase substantially. By 2020, schools will have to teach 5.4 million more poor students than they taught in 1984. The United States has the highest rate of poverty for children of all developed nations, as much as three times higher than most other industrialized countries. And these children are not concentrated in the inner cities. Twice as many poor children live outside as within large urban areas (Reed & Sautter, 1990).

The majority of these poor children, about 65 percent, are white, because the total number of poor white families is greater than any other ethnic group. But even though the total number of poor African-American and Hispanic-American children is smaller than the number of poor white children, the per-

TABLE 5.1 Selected Characteristics of Different Social Classes

	Upper Class	Middle Class	Working Class	Lower Class
Income	$100,000+	$40,000–$100,00 (1/3) $25,000–$39,999 (2/3)	$12,000–$40,000	Below $12,000
Occupation	Corporate, professional, family money	White-collar, skilled blue-collar	Blue-collar	Minimum-wage unskilled labor
Education	Prestigious colleges and professional schools	High school, college, or professional school	High school	High school or less
Home ownership	At least one home	Usually own home	About half own a home	No
Health coverage	Full	Usually	Limited	No
Access to community resources	All	Many	Some	Few
Neighborhoods	Exclusive or comfortable	Comfortable	Modest	Deteriorating
Ability to send children to college	Easily	Depends on income and number of children	Seldom	No
Political power	National, state, or local	State or local	Limited	No

Source: Information from J. J. Macionis (1994), *Sociology,* 4th ed. (Englewood Cliffs, NJ: Prentice-Hall), pp. 270–274.

centages are higher. About 36 percent of all Hispanic-American children and 44 percent of all African-American children live in poverty. Compare this to an overall poverty rate of 20 percent for all children in the United States (Macionis, 1994).

SES and Achievement

Test Bank items 5.12–5.19, 5.53, 5.62–5.64, 5.74

There are many relationships between SES and school performance. For example, it is well documented that high-SES students of all ethnic groups show higher average levels of achievement on test scores, receive better grades, and stay in school longer than low-SES students (Alwin & Thornton, 1984; Goleman, 1988; White, 1982). When SES is measured solely in terms of parents' education, income, or occupation, the relationship between SES and achievement is weaker. But when SES is measured in terms that include family atmosphere variables such as parents' attitudes toward education, their aspirations for their children, or the intellectual activities of the family, then

Teaching Tip: Ask students to write down their perceptions of their family's social class, income last year, total wealth, and highest level of education attained (mother and father). Stress the importance of honesty and confidentiality. Reports must be anonymous and private. Collect the papers and tally some of the results. Do students use income, wealth, and education in similar ways to define social class? Most Americans consider themselves "middle class," even if sociologists would disagree.

Discussion: Assign Knapp, M., Turnbull, B. J., & Shields, P. M. (1990). New directions for educating children of poverty. *Educational Leadership, 48*(1), 4–9. *Focus Question:* Ask your students to contrast traditional approaches for teaching students at risk of failing with the newer recommendations of Knapp and Turnbull. Why should the new approaches be more effective?

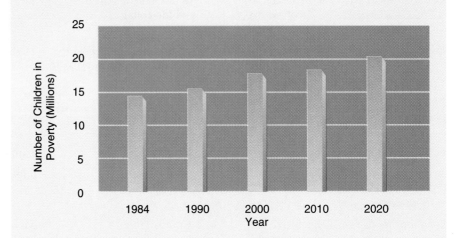

FIGURE 5.3

PROJECTED NUMBER OF CHILDREN IN POVERTY

The number of children who live in poverty in the United States grows each year and is projected to reach 20 million by the year 2020.

Source: A. M. Pallas, G. Natriello, and E. L. McDill (June–July 1989). The changing nature of the disadvantaged population: Current dimensions and future trends. *Educational Researcher, 18,* p. 19. Copyright 1989 by the American Educational Research Association. Reprinted by permission of the publisher.

Objective 5.3: Explain why the school achievement of low-income students often falls below that of middle- and upper-income students.

Background: Teaching the Children of Poverty (1991, special section). *Phi Delta Kappan, 73*(4), 282–310.

Connections: The concepts of teacher expectation effects and self-fulfilling prophecies are very important in a consideration of cultural differences in the classroom. These concepts are discussed fully in chapter 10.

the correlation is stronger (Laosa, 1984; Peng & Lee, 1992; White, 1982). This is an encouraging result. It indicates that lack of income may not be as important for school achievement as the actual attitudes and behaviors of the child's family life.

What are the effects of low socioeconomic status that might explain the lower school achievement of these low-SES students? Many factors maintain a cycle of poverty. Poor health care for mother and child, limited resources, family stress, interruptions in schooling, discrimination, and other factors lead to school failures, low-paying jobs—and another generation born in poverty. Garcia (1991), while cautioning that research on this question is meager, lists five other possible explanations. Let's take a closer look at each of them.

Low Expectations—Low Self-Esteem. Because low-SES students may wear old clothes, speak ungrammatically, or be less familiar with books and school activities, teachers and other students may assume that these students are not bright. The teacher may avoid calling on them to protect them from the embarrassment of giving wrong answers or because they make the teachers uncomfortable. The children come to believe that they aren't very good at schoolwork. The following true story shows how powerful this effect on self-esteem can be. Terrence Quinn, principal of an elementary school in New York, spends his mornings serving coffee and doughnuts in a welfare hotel six blocks from his school, trying to convince parents to send their children to school.

> Last spring, Jacqueline, a sixth-grader who had lived at the hotel, was selected as the school's valedictorian. One month before the official announcement, she entered Quinn's office and asked to speak to him in private.
>
> "Can someone on welfare actually be the valedictorian?" she asked.
>
> Quinn reassured Jacqueline, a youngster who has overcome many obstacles. . . . Why should a child such as Jacqueline feel so humiliated and ashamed of her predicament? (Reed & Sautter, 1990, p. K2)

Learned Helplessness.   Low-SES children may be the victims of learned helplessness, described in the previous chapter. That is, low-SES students (or any students who fail continually) may come to believe that doing well in school is hopeless. Many of their friends and relatives never finished school, so it seems normal to quit. In fact, about one-fourth of children from poor families drop out of school (Bennett, 1990). Without a high school diploma, these students find few rewards awaiting them in the work world. Many available jobs barely pay a living wage. If the head of a family of three works full-time at the minimum wage, the family's income will still be $2,500 below the poverty line (Reed & Sautter, 1990). Low-SES children, particularly those who also encounter racial discrimination, "become convinced that it is difficult if not impossible for them to advance in the mainstream by doing well in school" (Goleman, 1988).

Resistance Cultures.   Some researchers have suggested that low-SES students may become part of a **resistance culture.** To members of this culture, making it in school means selling out and trying to act "middle-class." In order to maintain their identity and their status within the group, low-SES students must reject the behaviors that would make them successful in school—studying, cooperating with teachers, even coming to class (Bennett, 1995; Ogbu, 1987). John Ogbu linked identification in a resistance culture to poor Hispanic-American, Native-American, and African-American groups, but similar reactions have been noted for poor white students both in the United States and in England (Willis, 1977).

Tracking.   Another explanation for the lower achievement of many low-SES students is that these students experience a different academic socialization, that is, they are actually taught differently. If they are tracked into "low-ability" or "general" classes, they may be taught to memorize and be passive. Their classes may be low-level and teacher-dominated. Middle-class students are more likely to be encouraged to think and create in their classes (Anyon, 1980). When low-SES students receive an inferior education, their academic skills are inferior and their life chances are limited. In an interview with Marge Scherer, Jonathan Kozol described the cruel predictive side of tracking:

> [T]racking is so utterly predictive. The little girl who gets shoved into the low reading group in 2nd grade is very likely to be the child who is urged

Connections: The concept of learned helplessness was discussed in chapter 4 as one explanation for the lower achievement of learning-disabled students and will be discussed again in chapter 9 as a factor influencing motivation.

Background: For a discussion of possible clashes between the culture of the school and the culture of the black adolescent, see " 'The burden of 'acting white' " (1987, November). *Harvard Education Letter, 3*(6), 6.

Connections: Related information on the effects of ability grouping and tracking appears in chapter 4.

Resistance Culture Group values and beliefs about refusing to adopt the behaviors and attitudes of the majority culture.

to take cosmetology instead of algebra in the 8th grade, and most likely to be in vocational courses, not college courses, in the 10th grade, if she hasn't dropped out by then. (Scherer, 1993, p. 8)

Childrearing Styles.   The oldest explanation for the academic problems of low-SES children is that their home environment does not give them the head start in school provided by middle- and upper-class homes. Adjustment to school may be more difficult for these children, since schools tend to value and expect the behaviors more often taught in middle-class homes. Let's take a closer look at this last explanation.

Studies have shown that middle-class mothers talk more; give more verbal guidance; help their children understand the causes of events, make plans, and anticipate consequences; direct their children's attention to the relevant details of a problem; and, rather than impose solutions, encourage children to solve problems themselves (Hess & Shipman, 1965; L. Hoffman, 1984; Willerman, 1979). By assisting their children in these ways, mothers are actually following Vygotsky's advice to provide intellectual support, or scaffolding, in the children's zone of proximal development, as we discussed in chapter 2. Contrast these two interactions as a mother works with a child on a puzzle:

> "What shape is that piece? Can you find a spot that is straight like the piece? Yes, that's straight, but look at the color. Does the color match? No? Look again for a straight, red piece. Yes—try that one. Good for you! You finished the corner."

> "No, that piece goes here!"

You can see how the first approach is more likely to encourage learning concepts (straight, shape, color, corner, match) and problem solving. Hess and McDevitt (1984) studied mothers and children over an eight-year period and

Research: For a description and evaluation of a program for at-risk children that avoids the use of a "pull out" orientation by using regrouping and tutoring, see Slavin, R. E., Madden, N. A., Karweit, N. L., Livermon, B. J., & Dolan, L. (1990). Success for all: First-year outcomes of a comprehensive plan for reforming urban education. *American Educational Research Journal, 27,* 255–278.

*W*hen families stress the value of reading, studying, and learning, their children are usually at an advantage in school.

found evidence that this "teaching as opposed to telling" style, often used by middle-class mothers, is related to higher achievement test scores for children ages 4 through 12. These differences in parental interaction styles may account for some of the differences among children from various SES groups.

You should be wary, however, of prejudging families based on their socioeconomic status. Many low-income families provide a rich learning environment for their children. When parents of any SES level support and encourage their children—by reading to them, providing books and educational toys, taking the children to the library, making time and space for learning—the children tend to become better, more enthusiastic readers (Morrow, 1983; Peng & Lee, 1992; Shields, Gordon, & Dupree, 1983). Remember, White (1982) found that the actual behaviors of the parents were more predictive of their children's school achievement than income level or parents' occupation.

Focus on . . . **Social Class Differences**

- Define SES.
- Why might children from lower SES backgrounds have greater difficulties in schools?

Ethnic and Racial Differences

Test Bank items 5.20, 5.54, 5.65

Ethnicity is used to refer to "groups that are characterized in terms of a common nationality, culture, or language" (Betancourt & Lopez, 1993, p. 631). This shared sense of identity may be based on geography, religion, race, or language. We all have some ethnic heritage, whether our background is Italian, Jewish, Ukrainian, Hmong, Vietnamese, Chinese, Japanese, Korean, Navajo, Hawaiian, Puerto Rican, Cuban, Eskimo, German, African, or Irish—to name only a few. **Race,** on the other hand, is defined as "a category composed of men and women who share biologically transmitted traits that are defined as socially significant" such as skin color or hair texture (Macionis, 1991, p. 308). Depending on the traits you measure and the theory you follow, there are between 3 and 300 races. In effect, race is a label people apply to themselves and to others based on appearances. There are no biologically pure races (Betancourt & Lopez, 1993).

Sociologists sometimes use the term **minority group** to label a group of people that receives unequal or discriminatory treatment. Strictly speaking, however, the term refers to a numerical minority compared to the total population. Referring to particular racial or ethnic groups as "minorities" is technically incorrect in some situations, because in certain places the "minority" group is actually the majority, for example, African Americans in Chicago or Mississippi. The practice of referring to people as "minorities" because of their racial or ethnic heritage has been criticized for this reason.

The Changing Demographics

Test Bank items 5.21, 5.60, 5.66

Between 1981 and 1990, the number of immigrants entering the United States was the largest ever. Results of the 1990 census, shown in Table 5.2 on page 166, reveal that the number of ethnic Americans has increased substantially.

Background: Dealing with Diversity (1989, special section). *Educational Leadership,* 46(6), 2–58.

Transparency: Use acetate transparency T 41, "Projections of the Number of Children in the U.S. by Ethnic Group."

Ethnicity A cultural heritage shared by a group of people.

Race A group of people who share common biological traits that are seen as self-defining by the people of the group.

Minority Group A group of people who have been socially disadvantaged—not always a minority in actual numbers.

Activity 5.5: Cooperative Learning. See the *Instructor's Resource Manual* for Cultural Differences: Possible Sources of Conflict, an activity that asks your students to role play positive and negative interactions between teachers and students with contradictory culture-based expectations. **Handout Master 5.2** in the *Instructor's Resource Manual* lists sources of conflict to stimulate students' thinking as they develop role plays.

Activity 5.6: Critical Thinking. See the *Instructor's Resource Manual* for Historical Perspectives and Cultural Consciousness, an activity that asks your students to work in groups to analyze the experiences of several ethnic groups. **Handout Master 5.3,** "Multicultural Societies: A Definition Guide," is provided to support this activity.

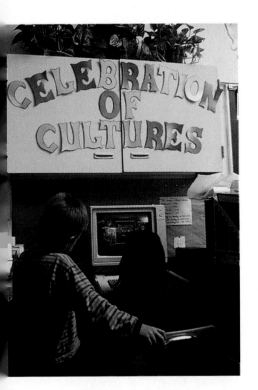

Changing demographics make it inaccurate to refer to ethnic groups as "minorities."

TABLE 5.2 Results of the 1990 Census for Selected Ethnic Groups		
Group	**Total Number**	**Increase Since 1980**
African American	30.0 million	13.2%
Asian	7.3 million	107.8%
Native American	2.0 million	37.9%
Hispanic	22.4 million	53.0%
Other	9.8 million	

Source: U.S. Bureau of the Census, 1990.

By the year 2020, almost half of the population of the country will be from African-American, Asian, Latino, or other ethnic groups.

What do these numbers mean for teaching? First, let's consider the ways that different ethnic cultures influence their members.

Cultural Differences   Test Bank items 5.22, 5.23

Ricardo Garcia (1991) compares culture to an iceberg. One-third of the iceberg is visible; the rest is hidden and unknown. The visible signs of culture, such as costumes and marriage traditions, represent only a small portion of the differences among cultures. Many of the differences are "below the surface." They are implicit, unstated, even unconscious biases and beliefs. Each cultural group teaches its members certain "lessons" about living (Casanova, 1987; Kagan, 1983; Maehr, 1974).

Cultures differ in rules for conducting interpersonal relationships, for example. In some groups listeners give a slight affirmative nod of the head and perhaps an occasional "uh huh" to indicate they are paying attention and understand what the speaker is saying. But members of other cultures listen without giving acknowledgment, or with eyes downcast, as a sign of respect. In some cultures high-status individuals initiate conversations and ask the questions, and low-status individuals only respond. In other cultures, the pattern is reversed.

Cultural influences are widespread and pervasive. Some psychologists even suggest that culture defines intelligence. For example, physical grace is essential in Balinese social life, so the ability to master physical movements is a mark of intelligence in that culture. Manipulating words and numbers is important in Western societies, so in these cultures such skills are indicators of intelligence (Gardner, 1983).

Cultural Conflicts.   The above are just a few areas where cultures may teach different lessons about living. The differences may be very obvious, such as holiday customs, or they may be very subtle, such as how to get your turn in conversations. The more subtle and unconscious the difference, the more difficult it is to change or even recognize (Casanova, 1987). Cultural conflicts are usually about below-the-surface differences, because when subtle cultural differences meet, misunderstandings are common. Thus, the members of a different culture may be misperceived as rude, slow, or disrespectful.

For example, Erickson and Shultz (1982) studied school counselors working with students from the same and from different cultures. The researchers found that the culturally different students did not nod and say "uh huh" as they listened to the counselors. Not having received this expected feedback, the counselors assumed that the culturally different students had not understood, and so the counselors repeated their remarks in simpler form. Again no nod, so the counselors simplified and repeated once more. When the students were interviewed afterwards, many said that the counselors had made them feel stupid. In fact, the counselors had decided that these students were not very bright. Neither participant realized that a subtle cultural difference in how to listen was probably to blame for the impressions. In contrast, when students and counselors shared the same background, discussions proceeded smoothly, without the cycles of simplifying and repeating. The students knew the counselors' tacit rules for listening (or at least appearing to listen), because both counselor and student had learned from the same teacher—their common culture.

Cultural Compatibility.   Not all cultural differences lead to clashes, however. In the Vietnamese culture, for example, children learn to value self-improvement and accept the directions of legitimate authorities like parents, employers, or teachers. These values fit the demands of American schools, so Vietnamese children often do well.

A study comparing mothers in the People's Republic of China, Chinese-American mothers, and Caucasian-American mothers found dramatic differences in beliefs about motivation and the value of education (Hess, Chih-Mei, & McDevitt, 1987). For example, the mothers from the Republic of China attributed school failure to lack of effort more often than the Caucasian-American mothers. The Chinese-American mothers were in the middle, attributing failure to lack of effort more often than the Caucasian-American mothers but less often than the Republic of China mothers.

This does not mean that all Vietnamese- or Chinese-American children are perfectly equipped for the American school, however. Children may perform well on tests and assignments but feel uncomfortable in social situations, where subtle rules for interacting are not second nature to them (Casanova, 1987; Yee, 1992). Later in this chapter, we will explore ways to make classrooms compatible with the home cultures of students. First, however, we need to see some of the effects of cultural conflicts and discrimination on student achievement.

Ethnic and Racial Differences in School Achievement
Test Bank items 5.24–5.25

A major concern in schools is that some ethnic groups consistently achieve below the average for all students. Table 5.3 on page 168 gives examples. This pattern of results tends to hold for all standardized achievement tests, but the gaps have been narrowing over the past two to three decades.

Casebook: See the Teachers' Casebook at the end of this chapter for teachers' suggestions about how to deal with cultural differences in the classroom.

Background: For a concise discussion of cultural styles and the possible clashes of styles in classrooms, see Hilliard, A. G., III (1989). Teachers and cultural styles in a pluralistic society. *NEA Today,* 7(6), 65–69. Hilliard notes: " . . . the misunderstanding of behavioral styles leads teachers to mistake achievement in academic areas such as creative expression . . . Many teachers from Eurocentric cultures have a linear storytelling style. Many African-American children, on the other hand, exhibit a spiraling storytelling style with many departures from an initial point, but a return to make a story whole. Many teachers of these children are unable to follow the children's coherent stories. Some teachers even believe that the children's stories have no coherence at all. Some lose patience with the children and indicate that they are doing badly." (p. 69)

Objective 5.4: Give examples of conflicts and compatibilities between home and school cultures.

Background: See *Educational Psychology Review,* March 1992, for two articles on multicultural education: Garcia, E. E. (1992). "Hispanic" children: Theoretical, empirical, and related policy issues, pp. 69–94; Yee, A. H. (1992). Asians as stereotypes and students: Misperceptions that persist, pp. 95–132.

TABLE 5.3	National Assessment of Educational Progress, by Subject and by Ethnic Group*		
Reading, 1987–88	**9-year-olds**	**13-year-olds**	**17-year-olds**
National average	211.8	257.5	290.1
White	217.7	261.3	294.7
Black	188.5	242.9	274.4
Hispanic	193.7	240.1	270.8
Writing, 1988	**4th graders**	**8th graders**	**11th graders**
National average	173.3	208.2	220.7
White	180.0	213.1	225.3
Black	150.7	190.1	206.9
Hispanic	162.2	197.2	202.0
Mathematics, 1985–86	**9-year-olds**	**13-year-olds**	**17-year-olds**
National average	222.0	269.0	302.0
White	227.0	274.0	308.0
Black	202.0	249.0	279.0
Hispanic	205.0	254.0	283.0

*National Assessment of Educational Progress scales in reading, writing, and mathematics range from 0 to 500.

Source: National Center for Education Statistics, *Digest of education statistics, 1990* (Washington, DC: National Center for Education Statistics, U.S. Department of Education, 1991), pp. 113, 116, 118, 120, 121.

Background: In the Chinese tradition, achievement is seen as dependent more on concentration, effort, and persistence than on talent. Centuries ago, Xu Gan, a revered Chinese scholar, said, "Will is the teacher of study and talent is the follower of study. If a person has no talent, [achievement] is possible. But if a person has no will, it is not worth talking about study" (Hess, Chih-Mei, & McDevitt, 1987, p. 180).

Activity 5.7: Teaching Tip. See the *Instructor's Resource Manual* for Cultural Differences, a summary of one teacher's cautions about overreacting to cultural differences.

Connections: Strategies for motivating minority-group students are discussed in chapter 10.

Activity 5.8: Application. See the *Instructor's Resource Manual* for Racial Attitudes, an activity asking students to assess their own racial attitudes and the impact of teachers' racial attitudes on students.

Although there are consistent differences among ethnic groups on tests of cognitive abilities, most researchers agree that these differences are mainly the legacy of discrimination, the product of cultural mismatches, or a result of growing up in a low-SES environment. Because many minority-group students are also economically disadvantaged, it is important to separate the effects of these two sets of influences on school achievement. When we compare students from different ethnic and racial groups who are all at the same SES level, then their achievement differences diminish (Gleitman, 1991; Scarr & Carter-Saltzman, 1982).

The Legacy of Discrimination

Test Bank items 5.26–5.30, 5.55, 5.67

When we considered explanations for why low-SES students have trouble in school, we listed the low expectations and biases of teachers and fellow students. This has been the experience of many ethnic minority students as well. Imagine that the child described below is your own. What would you do?

Almost forty years ago, in the city of Topeka, Kansas, a minister walked hand in hand with his seven-year-old daughter to an elementary school four blocks from their home. Linda Brown wanted to enroll in the second grade, but the school refused to admit her. Instead, public school officials required her to attend another school two miles away. This meant that she had to walk six blocks to a bus stop, where she sometimes waited half an hour for the bus. In bad weather, Linda Brown would be soaking wet by the time the bus came; one day she became so cold at the bus stop that she walked back home. Why, she asked her parents, could she not attend the school only four blocks away? (Macionis, 1991, p. 307)

Her parents' answer to this question, with the help of other concerned families, was to file a suit challenging the school policy. You know the outcome of *Brown v. the Board of Education of Topeka.* "Separate but equal" schools for black children were declared inherently unequal. Even though segregation in schools became illegal in 1954, about two-thirds of all African-American students still attend schools where members of minority groups make up at least 50 percent of the student body. For about one-third of all black students, this figure is over 90 percent (Schofield, 1991). This is because segregation in housing and neighborhoods persists and because not every district has fully complied with Supreme Court decisions on desegregation (Calmore, 1986).

Years of research on the effects of desegregation have mostly shown that legally mandated integration is not a quick solution to the detrimental effects of centuries of racial inequality. Too often, minority-group students are resegregated in low-ability tracks even in integrated schools. Simply putting people in the same building does not mean that they will come to respect each other or even that they will experience the same quality of education (Schofield, 1991).

What is the legacy of unequal treatment and discrimination? Part of the testimony during the *Brown v. Board of Education* case in the 1950s was that when black children in a study were asked to pick the more attractive or smarter doll, they usually chose a white doll and rejected a black one. This test was repeated in 1990 with the same results (Pine & Hilliard, 1990).

Continuing Prejudice. The word *prejudice* is closely related to the word *prejudge.* **Prejudice** is a rigid and irrational generalization—a prejudgment—about an entire category of people (Macionis, 1994). Prejudice may be positive or negative, that is, you can have positive as well as negative irrational beliefs about a group, but the word usually refers to negative attitudes. Prejudice may target people in particular racial, ethnic, religious, political, geographic, or language groups or may be directed towards the sex or sexual orientation of the individual. Racial prejudice is pervasive. A 1991 survey by the National Opinion Research Center found that even though racial attitudes had improved somewhat since 1970, most of the groups surveyed felt at least some prejudice against all the other groups. For example, 78 percent of non-Hispanic Americans (whites, blacks, and Asian Americans) agreed with the statement that Hispanic Americans prefer to live off welfare, and 55 percent believed that Hispanic Americans are less intelligent.

The results were virtually the same when whites were asked their opinions of African Americans. The United States is a racist society, and this racism is not confined to one group. Tom Smith, a survey director for the National Opinion Research Center, noted that education is one of the strongest influences counteracting prejudice. If schools emphasize acceptance and teach

Nine-year-old Linda Brown, the plaintiff in Brown v. the Board of Education of Topeka.

Background: Pine, G. J., & Hilliard, A. G., III (1990). Rx for racism: Imperatives for America's schools. *Phi Delta Kappan, 71,* 593–600.

Activity 5.9: Critical Thinking. See the *Instructor's Resource Manual* for Racism, an activity that asks your students to work in groups to decide if racist reading material should be censored.

Background: The May 1988 issue of *The Elementary School Journal* (Vol. 88, No. 5) is entirely devoted to articles about minority students in the schools.

Transparency: Use acetate transparency T 42, "Prejudice and the Processing of Social Information."

Prejudice Prejudgment, or irrational generalization about an entire category of people.

Children do not instinctively dislike or mistrust people; they learn such attitudes from the words and actions of family and friends.

about the history and contributions of all ethnic groups, then attitudes may change (Armstrong, 1991).

The Development of Prejudice.   There are many theories about how and why prejudice develops. Early explanations tended to emphasize a single factor such as an instinctive mistrust of people who are physically or culturally different, economic competition among different groups, or a traumatic experience with a member of the "other" group (Rose, 1962). But these simple explanations proved inaccurate or incomplete. Children do not instinctively dislike and mistrust certain groups. They learn these attitudes from the words and actions of family and friends. And people can be prejudiced against certain groups even when there is no economic competition or when they have never actually met a member of the group.

Current explanations of prejudice combine personal and social factors. Extreme prejudice may develop as part of an **authoritarian personality**—a person who rigidly conforms to conventional values and believes that society is naturally competitive, with the "better" people rightly reaping the rewards (Macionis, 1994). But prejudice is more than a personality trait—it is also a set of cultural values. Children learn about valued traits and characteristics from their families, friends, teachers, and the world around them. For years, most of the models presented in books, films, television, and advertising were middle- and upper-class European Americans. People of different ethnic and racial backgrounds were seldom the "heroes" (Gerbner, Gross, Signorelli, & Morgan, 1986). This is changing.

Prejudice is difficult to combat because it can be part of our thinking processes. You saw in chapter 2 that children develop *schemas*—organized bodies of knowledge—about objects, events, and actions. We have schemas that organize our knowledge about drinking from a straw, people we know, the meaning of words, and so on. We can also form schemas about groups of people. If I were to ask you to list the traits most characteristic of college freshman, politicians, African Americans, Asian Americans, athletes, Buddhists, lesbians, or members of the National Rifle Association, you probably could generate a list. That list would show that you have a **stereotype**—a schema—that organizes what you know about the group (Wyler, 1988).

As with any schema, we use our stereotype to make sense of the world. You will see in chapter 7 that having a schema allows you to process information more quickly and efficiently, but it also allows you to distort information to make it fit your schema better. This is the danger in racial and ethnic stereotypes. We notice information that confirms or agrees with our stereotype—our schema—and miss or dismiss information that does not fit. For example, if a juror has a negative stereotype of Asian Americans and is listening to evidence in the trial of an Asian American, the juror may interpret the evidence more negatively. The juror may actually forget testimony in favor of the defendant but remember more damaging testimony. Information that fits the stereotype is even processed more quickly (Anderson, Klatzky, & Murray, 1990; Baron, 1992).

Continuing Discrimination.   Prejudice is an attitude, feelings and beliefs (usually negative), about an entire category of people. **Discrimination** is behavior, treating particular categories of people unequally. Clearly, ethnic

---

Authoritarian Personality Rigidly conforming to belief that society is naturally competitive, with "better" people reaping its rewards.

Stereotype Schema that organizes knowledge or perceptions about a category.

Discrimination Treating particular categories of people unequally.

Americans face prejudice and discrimination in subtle or blatant ways every day. One of the most discouraging findings I encountered while writing this chapter is that only 4 percent of the scientists, engineers, and mathematicians in the United States are either African American or Hispanic American—whereas more than 20 percent of the total population is from one of these groups. Even though their attitudes toward science and math are more favorable than the attitudes of white students, black and Hispanic students begin to lose out in science and math as early as elementary school. They are chosen less often for gifted classes and acceleration or enrichment programs. They are more likely to be tracked into "basic skills" classes. As they progress through junior high, high school, and college, their paths take them farther and farther out of the pipeline that produces our scientists. If they do persist and become scientists or engineers, they, along with women, will still be paid less than whites for the same work (National Science Foundation, 1988; Oakes, 1990).

Casebook: See the Teachers' Casebook for teachers' suggestions about how to deal with ethnic-group cliques in the classroom.

Focus on . . .   **Ethnic and Racial Differences**

- Explain how prejudice might develop.
- What is meant by ethnic pride?
- Distinguish between prejudice and discrimination.

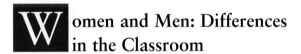

Women and Men: Differences in the Classroom

While I was proofreading this very page for the last edition, riding cross-country on a train, the conductor stopped beside my seat. He said, "I'm sorry, dear, for interrupting your homework, but do you have a ticket?" I had to smile at his (I'm sure unintended) sexism. I doubt that he made the same comment to the man across the aisle writing on his legal pad. Like racial discrimination, messages of sexism can be subtle. In this section we will examine how men and women are socialized and the role of teachers in providing an equitable education for both sexes.

Background: Grossman, H., & Grossman, S. H. *Gender issues in education.* Boston: Allyn & Bacon.

Background: For a lively debate on the terminology of gender and sex, see the March 1993 issue of *Psychological Science.*

Background: Lytton, H., & Romney, D. M. (1991). Parents' sex-related differential socialization of boys and girls: A meta-analysis. *Psychological Bulletin, 109,* 267–296.

Gender-Role Identity   Test Bank items 5.3–5.33, 5.56, 5.75

The word *gender* usually refers to judgments about masculinity and femininity, judgments that are influenced by culture and context. In contrast, *sex* refers to biological differences (Deaux, 1993). **Gender-role identity** is the image each of us has of ourselves as masculine or feminine in characteristics—a part of our self-concept. People with a "feminine" identity would rate themselves high on characteristics usually associated with females, such as "sensitive" or "warm," and low on characteristics traditionally associated with males, such as "forceful" and "competitive." Most people see themselves in gender-typed terms, as high on *either* masculine or feminine characteristics. Some children and adults, however, are more **androgynous**—they rate themselves high on *both* masculine and feminine traits. They can be assertive or sensitive, depending on the situation. Having either a masculine or an androgynous identity is associated with higher self-esteem than having a feminine identity, possibly because feminine characteristics are not as valued (Bem, 1974; Boldizar, 1991).

Gender-Role Identity Beliefs about characteristics and behaviors associated with one sex as opposed to the other.

Androgynous Having some typically male and some typically female characteristics apparent in one individual.

FIGURE 5.4

GENDER SCHEMA THEORY

According to *gender schema theory*, children and adolescents use gender as an organizing theme to classify and understand their perceptions about the world.

Society's beliefs about the traits of females and males

Gender Schema

Influences processing of social information

Influences self-esteem (only behavior or attitudes consistent with gender schema are acceptable)

Teaching Tip: To help students become more sensitive to subtle encouragement of sex differences, discuss TV commercials as a source of influence on the development of sex roles.

Casebook: See the Teachers' Casebook for teachers' suggestions about how to broaden students' conceptions of male and female social roles.

Gender Schemas Organized networks of knowledge about what it means to be male or female.

How do gender-role identities develop? All of us may learn very early what it means to be male or female because of the actions of our parents in the first years of our lives. Both parents play more roughly and vigorously with sons than they do with daughters. Parents tend to touch male infants more at first; later, they keep male toddlers at a greater distance than females. Parents also seem to spend more time interacting with sons, trying to get the babies to smile (Jacklin, DiPietro, & Maccoby, 1984). Parents are more likely to react positively to assertive behavior on the part of their sons and emotional sensitivity in their daughters (Fagot & Hagan, 1991; Lytton & Romney, 1991). When white middle-class parents are asked about what they value in their children, they list achievement, competitiveness, and emotional control for their sons and warmth and "ladylike" behavior for their daughters (Block, 1983; McGuire, 1988).

Through their interactions with family, peers, teachers, and the environment in general, children begin to form **gender schemas,** or organized networks of knowledge about what it means to be male or female (see Figure 5.4). These schemas help the children make sense of the world and guide their behavior. So a young girl whose schema for "girls" includes "girls play with dolls and not with trucks" or "girls can't be scientists" will pay attention to, remember, and interact more with dolls than trucks, and she may avoid science activities (Martin & Little, 1990).

*T*hrough their experiences, children begin to form gender schemas about what it means to be male or female.

Gender-Role Stereotyping in the Preschool Years. Different treatment of the sexes and gender-role stereotyping continue in early childhood. Boys are encouraged to be more physically active; girls are encouraged to be affectionate and tender. Researchers have found that boys are given more freedom to roam the neighborhood, and they are not protected for as long a time as girls from potentially dangerous activities like playing with sharp scissors or crossing the street alone. Parents quickly come to the aid of their daughters, but are more likely to insist that their sons handle problems themselves (Block, 1983; Fagot, Hagan, Leinbach, & Kronsberg, 1985). Thus, independence and initiative seem to be encouraged more in boys than in girls.

For an eye-opening experience, visit a large toy store. Recently, in buying a birthday gift for my 2-year-old nephew, I could choose between two sets of sandbox toys. The boys' set featured drills and hammers; the girls got muffin pans and dishes. Had my nephew been a niece, I could have chosen the box of lavender and pink plastic construction blocks!

Many of my student teachers are surprised when they hear young children talk about gender roles. Even in this era of great progress toward equal opportunity of the sexes, a preschool girl is more likely to tell you she wants to become a secretary than to say she wants to be an engineer. After she had given a lecture on the dangers of sex stereotyping in schools, a colleague of mine brought her young daughter to her college class. The students asked the little girl, "What do you want to be when you grow up?" The child immediately replied, "A doctor," and her professor/mother beamed with pride. Then the girl whispered to the students in the front row, "I really want to be a nurse, but my Mommy won't let me." Actually, this is a common reaction for young children. Preschoolers tend to have more stereotyped notions of sex roles than

Objective 5.5: Describe the school's role in the development of gender differences.

older children, and all ages seem to have more rigid and traditional ideas about male occupations than about what females do (Martin, 1989).

Gender Bias in the Curriculum.   During the elementary-school years, children continue to learn about what it means to be male or female. Unfortunately, schools often foster these **gender biases** in a number of ways. Most of the textbooks produced for the early grades before 1970 portrayed both males and females in sexually stereotyped roles. Materials for the later grades often omitted women altogether from illustrations and text. In a study of 2,760 stories in 134 books from 16 publishers, a group called *Women on Words and Images* (1975) found the total number of stories dealing with males or male animals to be four times greater than the number of stories dealing with females or female animals. They also found that females tended to be shown in the home, behaving passively and expressing fear or incompetence. Males were usually more dominant and adventurous; they often rescued the females.

In recent years textbook publishers have recognized these problems to some extent and established guidelines to prevent them. It still makes sense to check your teaching materials for such stereotypes, however. When Purcell and Stewart (1990) used the same design as *Women on Words and Images* to analyze 62 elementary readers, they found that the numbers of male and female characters were about equal. Girls were shown in a wide range of activities, but were still portrayed as more helpless than boys. And don't assume that books for older children are free of sexual stereotypes. Despite new publishers' guidelines, problems have not disappeared entirely (Powell, Garcia, & Denton, 1985).

Discussion: Assign Purcell, P., & Stewart, L. (1990). Dick and Jane in 1989. *Sex Roles, 22,* 177–185. This study replicates analyses of textbooks and children's books conducted in the 1970s. *Focus Question:* What evidence of sexism, if any, remains in texts today?

Gender Biases Different views of males and females, often favoring one gender over the other.

The teacher's own attitude toward sex differences may be influential as well. One reason there have been more children's books and stories with male characters is the belief held by many teachers that boys like to read stories about boys and girls don't mind reading stories about boys—so why not assign stories about boys? It will help the boys be motivated to read, and it won't hurt the girls. Publishers seem to agree with this logic. When Scott O'Dell was looking for a publisher for his *Island of the Blue Dolphins,* he was told by several editors that he needed to make a small change—turn this story of a girl's courageous fight for survival into a story about a boy. O'Dell refused, and the book went on to win a Newbery Award for children's literature (Sadker, Sadker, & Klein, 1991).

The truth about reading preferences is not so simple. It appears that boys do like to read about male characters, but girls appear to prefer female characters. Both sexes find stories about nontraditional females to be at least as interesting as stories about traditional male characters (Sadker, Sadker, & Klein, 1991).

Sex Discrimination in Classrooms.   There has been quite a bit of research on teachers' treatment of male and female students. One of the best documented findings of the past 20 years is that teachers interact more with boys than with girls. This is true from preschool to college. Teachers ask more questions of males, give males more feedback (praise, criticism, and correction), and give more specific and valuable comments to boys. As girls move through the grades, they have less and less to say. By the time students reach college, men are twice as likely to initiate comments as women (Bailey, 1993; Sadker & Sadker, 1985, 1986b; Serbin & O'Leary, 1975; Wingate, 1986). The effect of these differences is that from preschool through college girls, on the average, receive 1,800 fewer hours of attention and instruction than boys (Sadker, Sadker, & Klein, 1991). Of course, these differences are not evenly distributed. Some boys, generally high-achieving white students, receive more than their share. Minority-group boys, like girls, tend to receive much less attention from the teacher. The imbalances of teacher attention given to boys and girls are particularly dramatic in science classes. In one study, boys were questioned on the subject matter 80 percent more often than girls (Baker, 1986). Boys also dominate the use of equipment in science labs, often dismantling the apparatus before the girls in the class have a chance to perform the experiments (Rennie & Parker, 1987).

Stereotypes are perpetuated in many ways, some obvious, some subtle. Guidance counselors, parents, and teachers often do not protest at all when a bright girl says she doesn't want to take any more math or science courses, but when a boy of the same ability wants to forget about math or science, they will object. In these subtle ways, students' stereotyped expectations for themselves can be reinforced (Sadker & Sadker, 1985).

Sex Differences in Mental Abilities

Test Bank items 5.34–5.38, 5.68, 5.69

From infancy through the preschool years, most studies find few differences between boys and girls in overall mental and motor development or in specific abilities. During the school years and beyond, psychologists find no differences in general intelligence on the standard measures—but these tests have been de-

Activity 5.10: Field Experience. See the *Instructor's Resource Manual* for Gender Equity, a field-experience activity that focuses students' attention on a teacher's interactions with boys and with girls.

Research: Linn, M. C., & Hyde, J. S. (1989). Gender, mathematics, and science. *Educational Researcher, 18,* 17–27.

Background: See Girls' math achievement: What we know and don't know (1986, January). *Harvard Education Letter, 3*(4), 1–4.

Teaching Tip: Emphasize to students that, in contrast to the Maccoby and Jacklin (1974) findings of almost two decades ago, recent findings are showing decreasing achievement differences between males and females, even in mathematics. Recent articles on this subject include Linn, M. C., & Hyde, J. S. (1989). Gender, mathematics, and science. *Educational Researcher, 118,* 17–28. Also Marsh, H. W. (1989). Sex differences in the development of verbal and mathematics constructs: The high school and beyond study. *American Educational Research Journal, 26,* 191–225. Differences persist between academically gifted males and females in mathematics reasoning. See Mills, C. J., Ablard, K. E., & Stumpf, H. (1993). Gender differences in academically talented young students' mathematical reasoning: Patterns across age and subskills. *Journal of Educational Psychology, 85,* 340–346.

signed and standardized to minimize sex differences. The overall IQ scores of males and females are not significantly different on the average; however, scores on several subtests show sex differences.

Studies conducted before 1974 showed that males performed significantly better than females on tests of spatial ability. Since 1974 the differences have virtually disappeared, except on tests that require mental rotation of a figure in space. Here males are faster, though not more accurate. This quickness in mental rotation of objects has been related to male participation in athletics (Linn & Hyde, 1989; Newcombe & Baenninger, 1990). Males' extensive experiences with video and arcade games may play a role as well.

Sex and Mathematics. In studies conducted before 1974, males outperformed females in mathematics. Again, in studies conducted over the past 20 years, the differences are disappearing, though males still maintain an edge overall compared to females (Linn & Hyde, 1989; Mills, Ablard, & Stumpf, 1993). There is a caution, however. In most studies of sex differences, race and socioeconomic status are not taken into account. When racial groups are studied separately, African-American females outperform African-American males in high school mathematics; there is little or no difference in the performance of Asian-American girls and boys in math or science (Grossman & Grossman, 1994; Yee, 1992).

It is important to realize that when differences are found between the average scores of boys and girls on tests of spatial and mathematical ability, the differences are rather small (Linn & Hyde, 1989). Some researchers have found that girls are better than boys on some kinds of problems—for example, on computational problems and logical, abstract problems—while boys do better than girls on other kinds of problems—for example, story problems and spatial relations problems (Hyde, Fennema, & Lamon, 1990; Mills, Ablard, & Stumpf, 1993).

The difference in mathematics performance between males and females is more pronounced among academically talented students. On the SAT quantitative tests, the highest scores still go to males (but again, these differences were not examined by race). For example, for the 1988–1989 administrations of the SAT math section, 89 percent of the students who earned a score of 750 or higher were males (National Center for Education Statistics, 1990). There is some evidence that male superiority on this test is related to their ability to work quickly and to estimate answers (Linn & Hyde, 1989; Mills, Ablard, & Stumpf, 1993). Why this may be so is not fully understood.

One controversial question is whether boys are better in mathematics because they take more math courses than girls. There appear to be few or no differences between boys and girls in math achievement at the beginning of high school (although differences show up earlier for academically gifted students), but during high school girls take fewer math courses (Pallas & Alexander, 1983). As soon as mathematics courses become optional, many girls avoid them, as you can see in Table 5.4. There is mounting evidence that the differences between boys and girls in math achievement decrease substantially or disappear altogether when the actual number of previous math courses taken by each student is considered (Fennema & Sherman, 1977; Oakes, 1990; Pallas & Alexander, 1983). But other researchers have reported that high-ability boys are superior to high-ability girls in mathematics reasoning, even when

TABLE 5.4   Who Finishes What Courses?

A government survey revealed the following data on the percentages of males and females who enrolled in and then completed high school courses in several areas.

Courses	Percent Males Completing	Percent Females Completing
Algebra	81.6	76.8
Trigonometry or geometry	60.1	50.3
Chemistry or physics	54.2	42.3
English, 3 years or more	92.8	94.1
Foreign language, 2 years or more	39.1	48.1

Source: National Center for Education Statistics, *Digest of Education Statistics, 1990* (Washington, DC: National Center for Education Statistics, U.S. Department of Education, 1991), p. 130.

participation in previous math courses is taken into account (Benbow & Minor, 1986; Benbow & Stanley, 1980, 1983a & b; Kolata, 1980).

When Oakes (1990) analyzed the reasons why only 15 percent of the scientists, engineers, and mathematicians in the United States are women, she concluded that academically qualified girls choose not to take advanced science and math courses in high school. Thus, they don't develop their abilities in this area. In the process, they limit their college and career choices because colleges require applicants to possess some proficiency in mathematics and many jobs also demand abilities in this area.

Transparency: Use acetate transparency T 44, "Gender Schema Theory."

The historical disparity between male and female performance in math and technical subjects has diminished over the past couple of decades, but teachers still must monitor classroom practices. Why are there so many boys and so few girls working with computers in this classroom?

Guidelines

Avoiding Sexism in Teaching

Check to see if textbooks and other materials you are using present an honest view of the options open to both males and females.

Examples

1. Are both males and females portrayed in traditional and nontraditional roles at work, at leisure, and at home?
2. Discuss your analyses with students, and ask them to help you find sex role biases in other materials—magazine advertising, TV programs, news reporting, for example.

Watch for any unintended biases in your own classroom practices.

Examples

1. Do you group students by sex for certain activities? Is the grouping appropriate?
2. Do you call on one sex or the other for certain answers—boys for math and girls for poetry, for example?

Look for ways in which your school may be limiting the options open to male or female students.

Examples

1. What advice is given by guidance counselors to students in course and career decisions?
2. Is there a good sports program for both girls and boys?

Use gender-free language as much as possible.

Examples

1. Do you speak of "law-enforcement officer" and "mail carrier" instead of "policeman" and "mailman"?
2. Do you name a committee "head" instead of a "chairman"?

Research: Are females socialized to select or not select scientific careers? See Ware, N. C., & Lee, V. E. (1988). Sex differences in choice of college student majors. *American Educational Research Journal, 25,* 593–614.

Brief abstract: The process of choosing a scientific major was examined in a nationally representative sample of male and female college students of above-average ability. Women who were attending a four-year college, who reported having been influenced by high school teachers and guidance counselors in making plans for college, and who placed a high priority upon aspects of their future family and personal lives were less likely to major in science than their female peers. High socioeconomic status, positive assessments of their high schools, and attending a four-year college predicted science majoring for men.

Another controversial question is whether teachers are responsible, in part, for the lower participation of girls in math and science studies. There is some evidence that teachers treat girls and boys differently in mathematics classes. For example, some elementary-school teachers spend more academic time with boys in math and with girls in reading. In one study, high school geometry teachers directed most of their questions to boys, even though the girls asked questions and volunteered answers more often. Several researchers have found that some teachers tend to accept wrong answers from girls, saying, in effect, "Well, at least you tried." But when boys give the wrong answer, the teachers are more likely to say, "Try harder! You can figure this out." These messages, repeated time and again, can convince girls that they just aren't cut out for mathematics (Harvard University, 1986). If you are like a few of the student teachers I have supervised who "really hate math," please don't pass this attitude on to your students. You may have been the victim of sex discrimination yourself.

Eliminating Gender Bias.   We don't know what the situation would be like if all students, boys and girls, received appropriate instruction and encouragement in math. For example, Patricia Casserly of the Educational Testing Service studied 20 high schools where no sex differences in mathematics performance were found. Even though the schools were not alike in all ways, they shared several common features. The teachers had strong backgrounds in mathematics, engineering, or science, not just in general education. They were enthusiastic about mathematics. The brightest students, male and female, were grouped together for instruction in math, and there was heavy emphasis on reasoning in the classes (Kolata, 1980). The activities used to teach math may make a difference as well. Elementary-age girls may do better in math if they learn in cooperative as opposed to competitive activities. Certainly it makes sense to balance both cooperative and competitive approaches so that students who learn better each way have equal opportunities (Fennema & Peterson, 1988). The Guidelines on the facing page provide additional ideas for how to avoid sexism in your teaching.

Focus on . . .   **Girls and Boys in the Classroom**

- Distinguish between sex and gender.
- What are gender schemas and how do they develop?
- How do males and females differ in mathematical abilities?
- How can teachers promote gender equity in classrooms?

anguage Differences in the Classroom

Test Bank items 5.39–5.40

In the classroom, quite a bit happens through language. Communication is at the heart of teaching, but as we have seen in this chapter, culture affects communication. In this section, we will examine two kinds of language differences—dialect differences and bilingualism.

Dialects

A **dialect** is a language variation spoken by a particular ethnic, social, or regional group. The rules for a language define how words should be pronounced, how meaning should be expressed, and the ways the basic parts of speech should be put together to form sentences. Dialects appear to differ in their rules in these areas, but it is important to remember that these differences are not errors. Each dialect within a language is just as logical, complex, and rule-governed as the standard form of the language (often called **standard speech**).

An example of this is the use of the double negative. In Standard English the redundancy of the double negative is not allowed. But in many dialects, like "black English," just as in many other languages (for instance, Russian, French, Spanish, and Hungarian), the double negative is required by the grammatical rules. To say "I don't want anything" in Spanish, you must literally say, "I don't want nothing," or "No quiero nada." Haitian dialects differ from "black English" because French is the primary language, and some Hispanic-English dialects reflect the influence of Spanish and Creole language variations.

Transparency: Use acetate transparency T 42, "Could You Pass This Test?"

Dialect   Rule-governed variation of a language spoken by a particular group.

Standard Speech   The most generally accepted and used form of a given language.

Guidelines

Teaching Dialect-Dominant Students

1. Become familiar with features of the students' dialect. This will allow you to understand students better and to distinguish a reading miscue (a noncomprehension feature) from a comprehension error. Students should not be interrupted during the oral reading process. Correction of comprehension features is best done after the reading segment.
2. Allow students to listen to a passage or story first. This can be done in two ways: (a) finish the story and then ask comprehension questions, or (b) interrupt the story at key comprehension segments and ask students to predict the outcome.
3. Use predictable stories, which can be familiar episodes in literature, music, or history. They can be original works or experiential readers.
4. Use visual aids to enhance comprehension. Visual images, whether pictures or words, will aid word recognition and comprehension.
5. Use "cloze procedure" deletions to focus on vocabulary and meaning. Cloze procedures are selected deletions of words from a passage in order to focus on a specific text feature. *Examples:* (a) The little red hen found an ear of corn. The little red _____ said, "Who will dry the ear of _____?" (vocabulary focus) (b) Today I feel like a (*noun*). (grammar focus) (c) There was a (*pain*) in the pit of his stomach. (semantic focus)
6. Allow students to retell the story or passage in various speech styles. Have students select different people to whom they would like to retell the story (family member, principal, friend), and assist them in selecting synonyms most appropriate to each audience. This allows both teacher and student to become language authorities.
7. Integrate reading, speaking, and writing skills whenever possible.
8. Use the microcomputer (if available) as a time-on-task exercise. The microcomputer can effectively assist in teaching the reading techniques of skimming (general idea), scanning (focused reference), reading for comprehension (mastery of total message), and critical reading (inference and evaluation).

Source: From Christine I. Bennett, *Comprehensive Multicultural Education, Theory and Practice, 2/e,* pp. 234–235. Copyright © 1990 by Allyn and Bacon. Reprinted by permission.

Research: Hakuta, K., & Garcia, E. E. (1989). Bilingualism and education. *American Psychologist, 44,* 374–379.

Background: Harvard Graduate School of Education (1991, November/December). Kids who speak Spanish: Schools that help them learn. *Harvard Education Newsletter, 7*(6), 1–4. *Focus Question:* What are the characteristics of schools that help Spanish-speaking students learn?

Background: Romero, M., Mercado, C., & Vazquez-Faria, J. A. (1987). Students of limited English proficiency. In V. Richardson-Koehler (Ed.), *Educator's handbook: A research perspective* (pp. 348–369). White Plains, NY: Longman; When Children Speak Little English: How Effective Is Bilingual Education? (1987, November). *Harvard Education Letter, 2*(6), 1–4; Watson, D. L., Northcutt, L., & Rydell, L. (1989, February). Teaching bilingual students successfully. *Educational Leadership, 46*(5), 59–61.

Dialects and Language Skills. Another area in which nonstandard dialects differ from Standard English is pronunciation, which can lead to spelling problems. In "black English" and in Southern dialects, for instance, there is less attention paid to pronouncing the ends of words than in Standard English. A lack of attention to final consonants, such as *s,* can lead to failure to indicate possession, third-person singular verbs, and plurals in the standard way. So *John's book* might be *John book,* and words such as *thinks, wasps,* and *lists* may be difficult to pronounce. When endings are not pronounced, there are more *homonyms* (words that sound alike but have different meanings) in the student's language than the unknowing teacher may expect; *spent* and *spend* might sound alike, for example. Even without the confusions caused by dialect differences, there are many homonyms in English. Usually, special attention is given to words such as these when they come up in the spelling lesson. If the teacher is aware of the special homonyms in student dialects, direct teaching of these spelling differences is also possible.

Dialects and Teaching. Now we turn to a very important issue. While the various dialects of a language may be equally logical, complex, and rule-governed, should teachers make learning easier for children by teaching in the dialect of the majority of students? To do this would show respect for the children's language, but the children would be robbed of the opportunity to learn the standard speech of the dominant culture. Being able to communicate effectively in standard speech allows adults to take advantage of many social and occupational opportunities.

The best teaching approach seems to be to focus on understanding the children and to accept their dialect as a valid and correct language system, but to teach as an alternative the standard form of English (or whatever the dominant language is in your country). Learning the standard speech is easy for most children whose original language is a dialect, as long as they have good models.

What does all this mean for teachers? How can they cope with linguistic diversity in the classroom? First, they can be sensitive to their own possible negative stereotypes about children who speak a different dialect. Taylor (1983) found that teachers who held negative attitudes toward "black English" gave lower ratings for reading comprehension to students using that dialect, even when the accuracy of the students' performance was the same as that of Standard English speakers. Second, teachers can ensure comprehension by repeating instructions using different words and by asking students to paraphrase instructions or give examples.

Bilingualism   Test Bank items 5.41–5.43, 5.57, 5.70, 5.76, 5.78–5.80

Bilingualism is a topic that sparks heated debates and touches many emotions. One reason is the changing demographics discussed earlier in this chapter. In the United States in the late 1980s, 2.5 million school-age children were not native-English-speaking. This number is expected to double by the year 2000. In some states almost one-fourth of all students speak a first language other than English—usually Spanish. Two terms that you will see associated with bilingualism are **English as a second language (ESL),** describing classes for students whose primary language is not English, and **limited English proficiency (LEP),** referring to students whose English skills are limited.

What Does Bilingualism Mean? There are disagreements about the meaning of *bilingualism*. Some definitions focus exclusively on a language-based meaning: bilingual people, or bilinguals, speak two languages. But this limited definition minimizes the significant problems that bilingual students face. Consider the words of these two students:

> A ninth-grade boy, who recently arrived in California from Mexico: "There is so much discrimination and hate. Even from other kids from Mexico who have been here longer. They don't treat us like brothers. They hate even more. It makes them feel more like natives. They want to be American. They don't want to speak Spanish to us, they already know English and how to act. If they are with us, other people will treat them more like wetbacks, so they try to avoid us." (Olsen, 1988, p. 36)

> A tenth-grade Chinese-American girl who had been in America for several years: "I don't know who I am. Am I the good Chinese daughter? Am I

Discussion: Is the increasing cultural plurality of the United States making the learning of foreign languages (namely, Spanish) more important in U.S. schools than was the case in the past?

Research: Commins, N. L., & Miramontes, O. B. (1989). Received and actual linguistic components: A descriptive study of four low-achieving Hispanic bilingual students. *American Educational Research Journal, 26,* 427–443.

Brief abstract: This ethnographic study investigated four Hispanic bilingual students perceived to have limited language abilities. The study provided data on the students' language use and abilities in a variety of settings. The data indicated that the organization of instruction limited the students' abilities to demonstrate their full range of competence in their two languages and that teachers interpreted their lack of English structural proficiency and lack of vocabulary in Spanish as a lack of conceptual ability. Observed over a variety of contexts, however, students showed the ability to use language as a vehicle for effective self-expression both socially and cognitively.

Objective 5.6: Summarize the arguments for and against bilingual education.

Bilingualism Speaking two languages fluently.

English as a Second Language (ESL) Designation for programs and classes to teach English to students who are not native speakers of English.

Limited English Proficiency (LEP) Descriptive term for students who have limited mastery of English.

Background: See Noll, J. W. (1993). Taking sides: Clashing views on controversial educational issues (7th ed.). Guilford, CT: Duskin (pp. 252–273), for "Should Bilingual Education be Abandoned?" Donaldo Macedo defends bilingual education, while Diane Ravitch questions the research on bilingual education.

Transparency: Use acetate transparency **T 43**, "Two Approaches to Balanced Bilingual Instruction."

Research: Filmore, L. W., & Valadez, C. (1986). Teaching bilingual learners. In M. Wittrock (Ed.), *Handbook of research on teaching* (3rd ed., pp. 648–685). New York: Macmillan.

Activity 5.11: Application. See the *Instructor's Resource Manual* for Immigrant Student Project, a summary of recommendations for teaching immigrant students.

Activity 5.12: Multicultural Awareness. See the *Instructor's Resource Manual* for Promoting the Success of Language-Minority Students, a summary of the features of secondary schools that promote motivation and achievement for language-minority students.

Second-Language Acquisition The process of learning a second language, very similar to the process of first-language learning.

Monolinguals Individuals who speak only one language.

an American teenager? I always feel I am letting my parents down when I am with my friends because I act so American, but I also feel that I will never really be an American. I never feel really comfortable with myself anymore." (Olsen, 1988, p. 30)

The experiences of these two students show that there is more to being bilingual than just speaking two languages. You must also be able to move back and forth between two cultures while still maintaining a sense of your own identity (Hakuta & Garcia, 1989). Being bilingual and bicultural means mastering the knowledge necessary to communicate in two cultures as well as dealing with potential discrimination. As a teacher, you will have to help your students learn all these skills.

Becoming Bilingual. Early research on bilingualism concluded that speaking two languages was so taxing on the mental development of the child that cognitive abilities suffered. Thus, the child should learn English as quickly as possible. Better designed studies today show that the opposite is true. Higher degrees of bilingualism are correlated with increased cognitive abilities in such areas as concept formation, creativity, knowledge of the workings of language, and cognitive flexibility. These findings seem to hold as long as there is no stigma attached to being bilingual and as long as students are not expected to abandon their first language to learn English (Dias, 1983; Galambos & Goldin-Meadow, 1990; Garcia, 1992; Hakuta & Garcia, 1989).

Psychologists studying **second-language acquisition** now believe that people learn a second language in much the same way as they learned the first—by making sense of the language puzzle, building schemas, and understanding meaning. Learning the second language does not interfere with understanding in the first language. In fact, the more proficient the speaker is in the first language, the faster she or he will master a second language (Cummins, 1984). If children learn two languages simultaneously as toddlers, there is a period between ages 2 and 3 when they progress more slowly because they have not yet figured out that they are learning two different languages. They may mix up the grammar of the two. But researchers believe that by age 4, if they have enough exposure to both languages, they get things straight and speak as well as native **monolinguals** (Reich, 1986).

Proficiency in a second language has two separate aspects: face-to-face communication (known as "contextualized language skills") and academic uses of language like reading and doing grammar exercises ("decontextualized language skills") (Snow, 1987). It takes students about two years in a good-quality program to be able to communicate face-to-face in a second language, but mastering decontextualized, academic language skills in the new language takes five to seven years. So students who seem in conversation to "know" a second language may still have great difficulty with complex schoolwork in that language (Ovando, 1989).

Bilingual Education. Virtually everyone agrees that all citizens should learn the official language of their country. But when and how should instruction in that language begin? Is it better to teach non–English-speaking and limited-English-proficiency students to read first in their native language or to begin reading instruction in English? Do these children need some oral lessons in English before reading instruction can be effective? Should other subjects, such as mathematics and social studies, be taught in the primary (home) language until the children are fluent in English? On these questions there are two basic positions, which have given rise to two contrasting teaching approaches.

Proponents of the first approach believe that English ought to be introduced as early as possible; they argue that valuable learning time is lost if students are taught in their native language. Most bilingual programs today follow this line of thinking. Critics, however, raise three important issues. First, children who are forced to try to learn math or science in an unfamiliar language are bound to have trouble. Think of how you would have done with math if you had been forced to learn fractions or algebra in a second language that you had studied for only a semester. Some psychologists believe students taught by this approach may become **semilingual,** inadequate speakers of both languages. Second, students may get the message that their home languages (and therefore, their families and cultures) are second class. You saw the seeds of these feelings in the stories of the two students at the beginning of this section.

Third, ironically, by the time students have mastered academic English and let their home language deteriorate, they reach secondary school and are encouraged to learn a second language. Had both the home language and English been developed all along, they would already be fluent in two languages without having to take French I or Introductory Spanish. Kenji Hakuta (1986) expresses this hope:

> Perhaps the rosiest future for bilingual education in the United States can be attained by dissolving the paradoxical attitude of admiration and pride for school-attained bilingualism on the one hand and scorn and shame for home-brewed immigrant bilingualism on the other. The goals of the educational system could be seen as the development of all students as functional bilinguals, including monolingual English speakers. (p. 229)

The second approach to teaching advocates using the child's native language for some subject teaching while simultaneously developing English proficiency. Supporters of this approach believe that children have a right to be proficient speakers of their native language and to become fully competent speakers of the dominant language of their country. One new approach to reaching this goal is to create classes that mix students who are learning a second language with students who are native speakers. The goal is for both groups to become fluent in both languages (Snow, 1986). My daughter spent a summer in such a program in Quebec and has been ahead in every French class ever since. For truly effective bilingual education, we will need many bilingual teachers. If you have a competence in another language, you might want to develop it fully for your teaching.

We have dealt with a wide range of differences in this chapter. How can teachers provide an appropriate education for all their students? One response is to make the classroom compatible with the students' cultural heritage. Such a classroom is described as being culturally compatible.

Teachers in today's bilingual classrooms must help their students learn skills to communicate in more than one culture.

Focus on . . .   Language Differences

- How should teachers deal with different dialects in the classroom?
- How does being bilingual affect learning?
- What are the advantages and disadvantages of the different approaches to bilingual education?

Semilingual Not proficient in any language; speaking one or more languages inadequately.

Culturally Compatible Classrooms
Classrooms in which procedures, rules, grouping strategies, attitudes, and teaching methods do not cause conflicts with the students' culturally influenced ways of learning and interacting.

Creating Culturally Compatible Classrooms

The goal of creating **culturally compatible classrooms** is to eliminate racism, sexism, and ethnic prejudice while providing equal educational opportunities for all students. Roland Tharp (1989) states that "two decades of data on cultural issues in classroom interactions and school outcomes have accumulated. When schools are changed, children's experiences and achievement also change" (p. 349). Tharp outlines several dimensions of classrooms that can be tailored to fit the needs of students. Three dimensions are social organization, learning style, and sociolinguistics.

Social Organization   Test Bank items 5.48, 5.81, 5.82

Tharp states that "a central task of educational design is to make the organization of teaching, learning, and performance compatible with the social structures in which students are most productive, engaged, and likely to learn" (p. 350). Social structure or social organization in this context means the ways people interact to accomplish a particular goal. For example, the social organization of Hawaiian society depends heavily on collaboration and cooperation. Children play together in groups of friends and siblings, with older children often caring for the younger ones. When cooperative work groups of four or five boys and girls were established in Hawaiian classrooms, student learning and participation improved. The teacher worked intensively with one group while the children in the remaining groups helped each other. But when the same structure was tried in a Navajo classroom, students would not work together. These students are socialized to be more solitary and not to play with the opposite sex. By setting up same-sex working groups of only two or three Navajo students, teachers encouraged them to help each other.

Learning Styles   Test Bank items 5.44–5.46, 5.58, 5.71, 5.77

Some psychologists have found ethnic-group differences in students' cognitive styles. You may remember from the previous chapter that cognitive styles are the ways that individuals typically process information. The following are a few examples.

Hispanic Americans. Results of some research suggest that Mexican Americans tend to be field dependent, preferring holistic, concrete, social approaches to learning. Because being field independent is related to achievement in mathematics, the tendency to be field dependent may interfere with performance in mathematics if it is taught in the usual abstract, analytical way (Buenning & Tollefson, 1987). Other researchers have suggested that Hispanic-American students are more oriented toward family and group loyalty and less individualistic. This may mean that Hispanic-American students prefer cooperative activities and dislike being made to compete with fellow students (Garcia, 1992; Vasquez, 1990).

African Americans. Bennett (1990) summarizes research that suggests the learning styles of African Americans may be inconsistent with teaching approaches in most schools. Some of the characteristics of this learning style are a visual/global rather than a verbal/analytic approach; a preference for reasoning by inference rather than formal logic; a focus on people and relationships; a preference for energetic involvement in several activities simultaneously rather than routine, step-by-step learning; and a greater dependence on nonverbal communication. To capitalize on these learning styles, Hale-Benson (1986) recommends the following strategies with young African-American children:

Use appropriate nonverbal cues, gestures, and eye contact

Allow equal "talking time" for teacher and students

Emphasize small-group learning and hands-on contact with the teacher

Use a variety of learning activities that include movement, games, poetry, and music.

Native Americans.   Native Americans also appear to have a more global, visual style of learning. For example, Navajo students prefer hearing a story all the way through to the end before discussing parts of the story. Teachers who stop to ask questions seem odd to these students and interrupt the learning process (Tharp, 1989). Also, these students sometimes show strong preferences for learning privately, through trial and error, rather than having their mistakes made public (Vasquez, 1990).

Asian Americans.   There has been little research on the learning styles of Asian Americans, perhaps because they are seen as "successful minorities." As we discussed earlier, many of the values and attitudes taught by some Asian cultures, such as respect for teachers, hard work, and persistent effort, can support academic achievement. One recent study among refugee students found that they tended to be field dependent and global in their approach to problem solving. They tended to be more passive and learned best in cooperative settings with good support from peers and the teacher. Of course, strong support may be helpful for any group trying to cope with a new and very different culture.

> There are dangers when teachers stereotype Asian Americans as hardworking and passive. This practice tends to reinforce conformity and stifle creativity. Asian and Pacific American students, therefore, frequently do not develop the ability to assert and express themselves verbally and are channeled in disproportionate numbers into the technical/scientific fields. As a result, many Asian and Pacific American students undergo traumatic family/school discontinuities, suffer from low self-esteem, are overly conforming, and have their academic and social development narrowly circumscribed. (Suzuki, 1983, p. 9)

Suzuki's cautions are echoed by many critics of the research on ethnic differences in learning styles (Yee, 1992).

Criticisms of Learning-Styles Research.   In considering this research on learning styles, you should keep two points in mind. First, the validity of some of the learning-styles research has been strongly questioned, as we saw in the previous chapter. Second, there is a heated debate today about whether identifying ethnic-group differences in learning styles and preferences is a dangerous, racist, sexist exercise. In our society we are quick to move from the notion of "difference" to the idea of "deficit." I have included the information about learning-style differences because I believe that, used sensibly, this information can help you better understand your students.

*O*ne goal of creating culturally compatible classrooms is to encourage mutual acceptance and respect among students from all backgrounds.

Background: McCarty, T. L., Wallace, S., & Lynch, R. H. (1989, February). Inquiry-based curriculum development in a Navajo school. *Educational Leadership, 46*(5), 66–71.

Discussion: Assign O'Neil, J. (1990). Link between style, culture proves divisive. *Educational Leadership, 48*(2), 8. *Focus Question:* Why do some educators argue against linking learning styles to cultural differences?

Background: See Cultural differences in the classroom (1988, March). *Harvard Education Letter, 2*(2), 1–4. This article describes the KEEP program and Shirley Heath's project in the Piedmont Carolinas and offers four conclusions:

1. Interaction is the key to learning, and language is the key to interaction. "When teachers in both projects became aware of specific communication and interaction skills children were developing in their homes, they adapted classroom practice to build on these skills. In addition, teachers specifically demonstrated respect for the language of their students" (p. 3).

2. Academic standards and teacher expectations for students should not be lowered. Standard English skills were still emphasized in both projects but without devaluing the children's own dialect.

3. Schools can work with local colleges, parents, and other community members to learn more about students' home cultures.

4. By attending to students' cultures teachers can expand and improve their teaching skills. The new ways of teaching developed in the two projects proved helpful for all the students in the classes, not just those from different cultures.

Sociolinguistics The study of the formal and informal rules for how, when, about what, to whom, and how long to speak in conversations within cultural groups.

Participation Structures The formal and informal rules for how to take part in a given activity.

It is dangerous and incorrect, however, to assume that every individual in a group shares the same learning style. Also, information about the "typical" learning styles of a given ethnic group can become just one more basis for stereotyping, as mentioned above (Gordon, 1991; O'Neil, 1990a). The best advice for teachers is to be sensitive to individual differences in all your students and to make available alternative paths to learning. Never prejudge how a student will learn best on the basis of assumptions about the student's ethnicity or race. Get to know the individual.

Sociolinguistics   Test Bank items 5.47, 5.48, 5.59, 5.81, 5.82

Sociolinguistics is the study of "the courtesies and conventions of conversation across cultures" (Tharp, 1989, p. 351). A knowledge of sociolinguistics will help you understand why communication sometimes breaks down in classrooms. The classroom is a special setting for communicating; it has its own set of rules for when, how, to whom, about what subject, and in what manner to use language. Sometimes the sociolinguistic skills of students do not fit the expectations of teachers.

Participation Structures.   In order to be successful, students must know the communication rules; that is, they must understand the pragmatics of the classroom—when, where, and how to communicate. (See chapter 2 for a discussion of pragmatics.) This is not such an easy task. As class activities change, rules change. Sometimes you have to raise your hand (during the teacher's presentation), but sometimes you don't (during storytime on the rug). Sometimes it is good to ask a question (during discussion), but other times it isn't so good (when the teacher is scolding you). The differing activity rules are called **participation structures**. These structures define appropriate participation for each class activity. Most classrooms have many different participation structures.

To be competent communicators in the classroom, students sometimes have to read very subtle, nonverbal cues telling them which participation structures are currently in effect. For example, in one classroom, when the teacher stood in a particular area of the room, put her hands on her hips, and leaned forward at the waist, the children in the class were signaled to "stop and freeze," look at the teacher, and anticipate an announcement (Shultz & Florio, 1979).

Sources of Misunderstandings.   Some children are simply better than others at reading the classroom situation because the participation structures of the school match the structures they have learned at home. The communication rules for most school situations are similar to those in middle-class homes, so children from these homes often appear to be more competent communicators. They know the unwritten rules. Students from different cultural backgrounds may have learned participation structures that conflict with the behaviors expected in school. For example, one study found that the home conversation style of Hawaiian children is to chime in with contributions to a story. In school, however, this overlapping style is seen as "interrupting." When the teachers in one school learned about these differences and made their reading groups more like their students' home conversation groups, the young Hawaiian children in their classes improved in reading (Au, 1980; Tharp, 1989).

The source of misunderstanding can be a subtle sociolinguistic difference, such as how long the teacher waits to react to a student's response. White and Tharp (1988) found that when Navajo students in one class paused in giving a response, their Anglo teacher seemed to think that they were finished speaking. As a result, the teacher often unintentionally interrupted students. In another study, researchers found that Pueblo Indian students participated twice as much in classes where teachers waited longer to react. Waiting longer also helps girls to participate more freely in math and science classes (Grossman & Grossman, 1994).

So it seems that even students who speak the same language as their teachers may still have trouble communicating, and thus learning school subjects, if their knowledge of pragmatics does not fit the school situation. What can teachers do? Especially in the early grades, you should make communication rules for activities clear and explicit. Do not assume students know what to do. Use cues to signal students when changes occur. Explain and demonstrate appropriate behavior. I have seen teachers show young children how to "talk in your inside voice" or "whisper so you won't disturb others." One teacher said and then demonstrated, "If you have to interrupt me while I'm working with other children, stand quietly beside me until I can help you." Be consistent in responding to students. If students are supposed to raise their hands, don't call on those who break the rules.

Bringing It All Together: Teaching Every Student

Test Bank items 5.81, 5.82

The goal of this chapter is to give you a sense of the diversity in today's and tomorrow's schools and to help you meet the challenges of teaching in a multicultural classroom. How will you understand and build on all the cultures of your students? How will you deal with many different languages? Here are three general teaching principles to guide you in finding answers to these questions.

Objective 5.7: Incorporate multicultural concepts into teaching.

Know Your Students. Nothing you read in a chapter on cultural differences will teach you enough to understand the lives of all your students. If you can take other courses in college or read about other cultures, I encourage you to do it. But reading and studying are not enough. You should get to know your students' families and communities. Try to spend time with students and parents on projects outside school. Ask parents to help in class or to speak to your students about their jobs, their hobbies, or the history and heritage of their ethnic group. In the elementary grades, don't wait until a student is in trouble to have the first meeting with a family member. Watch and listen to the ways that your students interact in large and small groups. Have students write to you, and write back to them. Eat lunch with one or two students. Spend some nonteaching time with them.

Respect Your Students. From knowledge ought to come respect for your students' learning strengths—for the struggles they face and the obstacles they overcome. For a child, genuine acceptance is a necessary condition for developing self-esteem. Self-esteem and pride are important accomplishments of the school years. Sometimes the self-image and occupational aspirations of minority children actually decline in their early years in public school, probably because of the emphasis on majority culture values, accomplishments, and history. By presenting the accomplishments of particular members of an ethnic group or by bringing that group's culture into the classroom (in the form of, say, literature, art, or music), teachers can help students maintain a sense of pride in their cultural group. This integration of culture must be more than the "tokenism" of sampling ethnic foods or wearing costumes. Students should learn about the socially and intellectually important contributions of the various groups.

Tiedt and Tiedt (1990) have provided a great many useful suggestions for multicultural teaching. Here are just a few:

Ask students to draw a picture or bring in a photograph of themselves. Have each student list all her or his group memberships on a page with this picture. For example, Sue Wong is a female, a daughter, a Chinese American, a Methodist, a Camp Fire Girl . . . Display the pages around the room or bind them into a book.

Study in depth one cultural group such as Cherokees, Puerto Ricans, Chicanos, Haitians, or Vietnamese Americans.

Create a learning center based on a particular culture. Use maps, postcards, books, encyclopedias, recordings of the native language, posters, flags, biographies, art.

Have students draw maps, calculate distances, convert money, act out historical events or important holiday traditions, write their own "encyclopedia" articles or travelogues, or write for more information to the appropriate public or private agencies within that country.

Introduce lessons based on a multicultural calendar. Tiedt and Tiedt provide a calendar for each school month showing the important holidays of various cultures and the contributions of these groups to American society.

Teach Your Students. The most important thing you can do for your students is teach them to read, write, speak, compute, think, and create. Too often, goals for low-SES or minority-group students have focused exclusively on basic skills. Students are taught words and sounds, but the meaning of the story is supposed to come later. Knapp, Turnbull, and Shields (1990) make these suggestions:

Focus on meaning and understanding from beginning to end—for example, by orienting instruction toward comprehending reading passages, communicating important ideas in written text, or understanding the concepts underlying number facts.

Balance routine skill learning with novel and complex tasks from the earliest stages of learning.

Provide context for skill learning that establishes clear reasons for needing to learn the skills.

Influence attitudes and beliefs about the academic content areas as well as skills and knowledge.

Eliminate unnecessary redundancy in the curriculum (e.g., repeating instruction in the same mathematics skills year after year). (p. 5)

Handout: Use Handout Master 5.4 in the *Instructor's Resource Manual*, "Goals of a Multicultural Approach to Teaching," a diagram that summarizes multicultural approaches to teaching.

Activity 5.14: Discussion. See the *Instructor's Resource Manual* for Teaching to the Distinctive Traits of Minority Students, describing James Vasquez's three-step model for adapting instruction. This model is also presented in **Handout Master 5.5.**

And finally, teach students directly about how to be students. In the early grades this could mean directly teaching the courtesies and conventions of the classroom: how to get a turn to speak, how and when to interrupt the teacher, how to whisper, how to get help in a small group, how to give an explanation that is helpful. In the later grades it may mean teaching the study skills that fit your subject. You can ask students to learn "how we do it in school" without violating principle number two above—respect your students. Ways of asking questions around the kitchen table at home may be different from ways of asking questions in school, but students can learn both ways, without deciding that either way is superior. The Guidelines give more ideas.

Guidelines

Creating Culturally Compatible Classrooms

Experiment with different grouping arrangements to encourage social harmony and cooperation.

Examples

1. Try "study buddies" and pairs.
2. Organize heterogeneous groups of four or five.
3. Establish larger teams for older students.

Provide a range of ways to learn material to accommodate a range of learning styles.

Examples

1. Give students verbal materials at different reading levels.
2. Offer visual materials—charts, diagrams, models.
3. Provide tapes for listening and viewing.
4. Set up activities and projects.

Teach classroom procedures directly, even ways of doing things that you thought everyone would know.

Examples

1. Tell students how to get the teacher's attention.
2. Explain when and how to interrupt the teacher if students need help.
3. Show which materials students can take and which require permission.
4. Demonstrate acceptable ways to disagree with or challenge another student.

Learn the meaning of different behaviors for your students.

Examples

1. Ask students how they feel when you correct or praise them. What gives them this message?
2. Talk to family and community members and other teachers to discover the meaning of expressions, gestures, or other responses that are unfamiliar to you.

Emphasize meaning in teaching.

Examples

1. Make sure students understand what they read.
2. Try storytelling and other modes that don't require written materials.
3. Use examples that relate abstract concepts to everyday experiences; for instance, relate negative numbers to being overdrawn in your checkbook.

Continued

Get to know the customs, traditions, and values of your students.

Examples

1. Use holidays as a chance to discuss the origins and meaning of traditions.
2. Analyze different traditions for common themes.
3. Attend community fairs and festivals.

Help students detect racist and sexist messages.

Examples

1. Analyze curriculum materials for biases.
2. Make students "bias detectives," reporting comments from the media.
3. Discuss the ways that students communicate biased messages about each other and what should be done when this happens.
4. Discuss expressions of prejudice such as anti-Semitism.

SUMMARY

Today's Multicultural Classrooms

Statistics point to increasing cultural diversity in American society. Old views—that minority-group members and immigrants should lose their cultural distinctiveness in the American "melting pot" or be regarded as culturally deficient—are being replaced by new emphases on multicultural education, equal educational opportunity, and the celebration of cultural diversity.

Everyone is a member of many cultural groups, defined in terms of geographic region, nationality, ethnicity, race, gender, social class, and religion. Membership in a particular group does not determine behavior or values but makes certain values and kinds of behavior more likely. Wide variations exist within each group.

Social Class Differences

Socioeconomic status (SES) is determined by several factors—not just income—and often overpowers other cultural differences. Disproportionate numbers of low-SES families are African American and Hispanic American.

Socioeconomic status and academic achievement are closely related. Low-SES students may suffer from teachers' lowered expectations of them, low self-esteem, learned helplessness, participation in resistance cultures, school tracking, and understimulating childrearing styles.

Ethnic and Racial Differences

Ethnicity (culturally transmitted behavior) and race (biologically transmitted physical traits) are socially significant categories people use to describe themselves and others. Minority groups (either numerically or historically unempowered) are rapidly increasing in population.

Conflicts between groups can arise from differences in culture-based beliefs, values, and expectations. Differences among ethnic groups in cognitive and academic abilities are largely the legacy of racial segregation and continuing prejudice and discrimination.

Women and Men: Differences in the Classroom

Educational equity for females and males is also an issue. Research shows that gender-role stereotyping begins in the preschool years and continues through gender bias in the school curriculum and sex discrimination in the classroom. Teachers often unintentionally perpetuate these problems.

Some measures on IQ and SAT tests have shown small sex-linked differences, especially in spatial abilities and mathematics. Research on the causes of these differences has been inconclusive, except to indicate that academic socialization and teachers' treatment of male and female students in mathematics classes do play a role. Teachers can use many strategies for reducing gender bias.

Language Differences in the Classroom

Language differences among students include dialects, bilingualism, and culture-based communication styles. Dialects are not inferior languages and should be respected, but Standard English should be taught for academic contexts.

Bilingual students speak a first language other than English, learn English as a second language, may have some degree of limitation in English proficiency, and also must often struggle with social adjustment problems relating to biculturalism. While there is much debate over the best way to help bilingual students master English, studies show it is best if they are not forced to abandon their first language. The more proficient students are in their first language, the faster they will master the second. Mastering academic language skills in any new language takes five to seven years.

Creating Culturally Compatible Classrooms

Culturally compatible classrooms are free of racism, sexism, and ethnic prejudice and provide equal educational opportunities for all students. Dimensions of classroom life that can be modified to that end are social organization, learning-style formats, and participation structures. Teachers, however, must avoid stereotypes of culture-based learning styles and must not assume that every individual in a group shares the same style.

Communication may break down in classrooms because of differences in sociolinguistic styles and skills. Teachers can directly teach appropriate participation structures and be sensitive to culture-based communication rules. To help create compatible multicultural classrooms, teachers must know and respect all their students, have high expectations of them, and teach them what they need to know to succeed.

KEY TERMS

androgynous, p. 171
authoritarian personality, p. 170
bilingualism, p. 181
cultural deficit model, p. 155
culturally compatible classrooms, p. 184
culture, p. 157
dialect, p. 179
discrimination, p. 170
English as a second language (ESL), p. 181

ethnicity, p. 165
gender biases, p. 174
gender-role identity, p. 171
gender schemas, p. 172
limited English proficiency (LEP), p. 181
melting pot, p. 154
minority group, p. 165
monolinguals, p. 182
multicultural education, p. 155

participation structures, p. 186
prejudice, p. 169
race, p. 165
resistance culture, p. 163
second-language acquisition, p. 182
semilingual, p. 183
socioeconomic status (SES), p. 160
sociolinguistics, p. 186
standard speech, p. 179
stereotype, p. 170

WHAT WOULD YOU DO?

Preschool
You overhear children arguing in the block area. Two boys are saying to a girl, "You can't play here. These toys are for boys and you're a girl. Girls can't build space stations!" What would you do?

Elementary and Middle School
Several of your students are from a public housing project in the district and clearly have fewer advantages than the other students in your class. You are concerned that the "project" students never seem to work or play with the others in the class. What would you do?

Every year the number of non-English-speaking students in your class increases. This year there are four different language groups represented—and you know only about five words in each language. The school's resources are very limited. Pick one topic and tell how you would teach it to accommodate the limited English proficiency of your students.

Junior High and High School
One day you notice that the males are doing most of the talking in your classes, particularly the advanced classes.

Just out of curiosity, you start to note each day how many girls and boys make contributions and ask questions. You are really surprised to see that your first impression was correct. What would you do to encourage more participation on the part of your female students?

For some reason, this year there have been several racial incidents in your school. Each incident seems a bit nastier and more dangerous than the one before. What would you do in your classes to improve the situation?

Cooperative Learning Activity
Your school has received a $30,000 grant from a private foundation to "improve cross-cultural communications in the school."

Suggestions for accomplishing this include assessing the learning styles of all the students, hiring a consultant, buying new curriculum materials, sending teachers to multicultural workshops, and hiring more teachers' aides. With four or five other members of your educational psychology class, prepare a set of recommendations for spending the money so that the greatest benefit is achieved.

Teacher-Student Differences

Suppose you have a student in your class who is different from you racially, culturally, and temperamentally and who has a different background and values from your own. You notice that you tend to avoid this student and that other students follow your example. How could you establish a relationship and reverse the trend toward estrangement and isolation?

AWARENESS FIRST

Students who are different racially, culturally, and with a different background are often intimidating to a teacher. Particularly in this age of "political correctness," teachers often revert to the technique of least resistance—we tend to avoid any confrontation between values by ignoring the student. *Noticing* that one tends to avoid a relationship with such a student is clearly the first, and perhaps most important, step. A second step is deliberately to engage that student on a one-to-one basis. Using the content of the class is a "values neutral" method of doing so. A debate with a student of any race or ethnic background on the subject of Rome's downfall or the steps to a geometry proof will reveal the commonality of human logic as greater than the differences in background. I have often found that once such a dialogue is established, the relationship can proceed to a less formal one, which invariably reveals that young adults of all backgrounds have common fears and aspirations. Finally, enough trust is established that we can venture into areas in which variation in cultural values may, in fact, lead to a different interpretation of data or conflicting conclusions. By this time, however, the differences can be accepted or even debated within an accepting relationship.

Karen B. Kreider, *Pennsylvania 1991 Teacher of the Year*
Central High School, Philadelphia, Pennsylvania

EXTRA EFFORT PAYOFF

In teaching a child with a different cultural background, value system, or temperament, a teacher must first acknowledge the student's right to be respected and treated with consideration in the classroom. The teacher must also recognize his or her responsibility as a role model for the other students. Students will learn to accept individual differences only if the teacher demonstrates compassion and understanding toward all students.

When I feel tension between myself and a student, it is usually due to a lack of mutual understanding. If I am confused by a child's behavior or attitude, I attempt to learn more about the student and the student's background. I may examine the child's school records to obtain further information. I will visit with the child and get to know him or her personally. Conversely, I also want the student to acquire a better, personal understanding of me.

Often, I can better understand a student if I meet the student's family and, perhaps, visit the home. In the secure and sterile environment of the school, it is easy to ignore the poverty and broken homes that many students must endure. Furthermore, I may talk to other persons with similar cultural backgrounds or read about the student's culture in order to gain more insight.

Kathy Andrews, *Special Education Teacher*
Lane Center School for Exceptional Children, Houston, Texas

Gender Schemas

Do you feel the social and emotional needs of boys and girls are different or that they should be handled differently?

ENCOURAGE SELF-ESTEEM

Although I feel that boys and girls are more alike than different, I do feel that they have some special needs. I was deeply concerned to discover that most of the little girls in my first grade classroom felt that they were overweight and needed to diet. The feeling that they were overweight had no basis in reality. My little girls are much more concerned about appearance and tend to judge themselves by their appearance. Since I realized this, I have made a special effort to address the issue every year. We spend a great deal of time talking about the outside of a person, the inside of a person, and the things that really matter. I find that these conversations go better if only girls are present. The girls are more willing to open up and discuss their concerns. I also address these issues in whole group discussions. I believe that these kinds of conversations with adult women help to arm the girls for the assaults on their self-esteem that come with adolescence. Our culture puts tremendous pressure on girls to be thin, pretty, and sexy. Girls often feel that they can never live up to the standard.

Cynthia Newman Wisdom, *First-Grade Teacher*
Trace Crossings Elementary School, Hoover, Alabama

Improving Classroom Social Relations

In your class are students from four main cultural groups, speaking a first language other than English. The groups are becoming cliquish and disrespectful of one another. What would you do to improve social relations in your class?

**TEACH HONOR
AND RESPECT**

I believe that in any class it's important to teach honor and respect for individual differences, whether they be cultural, physically limiting, or academic. Beyond modeling respect for each student or cultural group, I would want to teach the entire class about the gifts of each of the cultures and the gift of diversity. I would create units to study each culture represented, making the learning fun and exciting. I would introduce students to foods, beliefs, music, literature, language, and ways of life from each one. Throughout, I would initiate discussions focusing on how rich and full our world and our lives are because of the diversity that is found in every part of life—cultures, animals, plant life, even snowflakes—and how boring our lives would be without that diversity.

Sarah Gustafson, *Florida 1991 Teacher of the Year*
The Okeechobee Center, Okeechobee, Florida

**FOSTER COOPERATIVE
LEARNING**

Educators must create learning environments that enhance the self-worth and mutual respect of each and every child. It is imperative to teach and to demonstrate valuing of different cultures and ideologies. Students working together in teams of cooperative learning models learn to rely upon the collective input and combined skills of their partners for a common goal or purpose. Role playing of hypothetical conflicts, situations, and dilemmas allows students to examine their own values and beliefs. Switching roles provides personal insight on feelings from a different perspective and point of view. Classroom climate can be enhanced by celebrations of multicultural days and events. Develop activities that are rich in cultural tradition and ethnicity. Invite community participation and provide cultural role models for each group.

Bruce D. Fisher, *California 1991 Teacher of the Year*
Fortuna Elementary School, Fortuna, California

Behavioral Views of Learning

*I*f you were asked to give 10 to 20 different examples of learning, what would your response be? You might begin by listing academic subjects or certain activities you had set about mastering at some point in your life. You might also list different emotional reactions or insights you have had. But unless you've already had a few courses in psychology, it is likely that the examples you chose would cover only a few of the aspects included in the psychological definition of learning. We will spend the next three chapters looking at learning and its applications.

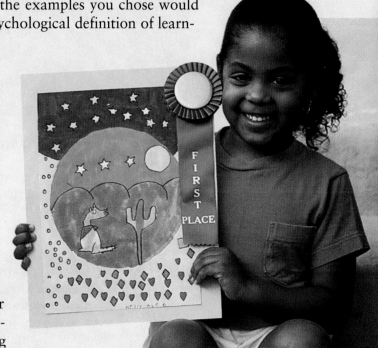

We begin this chapter with a general definition of learning that takes into account the opposing views of different theoretical groups. We will then highlight one of these groups, the behavioral theorists in this chapter and the other major group, the cognitive theorists, in chapters 7 and 8.

Our discussion in this chapter will focus on four behavioral learning processes: contiguity, classical conditioning, operant conditioning, and observational learning, with the greatest emphasis on the last two processes. After examining the implications of applied behavior analysis for teaching, we look at three recent directions in behavioral approaches to learning—social learning theory, self-management, and cognitive behavior modification.

By the time you have completed this chapter, you should be able to:

- Define learning.
- Compare contiguity, classical conditioning, and operant conditioning, and give examples of each.
- Give examples of four different kinds of consequences that may follow any behavior and the effect each is likely to have on future behavior.
- Select a common academic or behavior problem and design an intervention based on applied behavior analysis.
- Describe situations in which a teacher may wish to use modeling.
- Compare self-management and cognitive behavior modification.
- Discuss potential dangers and ethical issues involved in the use of any behavior change technique.

Are you one of those people whose blood pressure goes up when it is taken in the doctor's office? Have you ever worn something new and received so many compliments that you found yourself wearing that outfit often? What happens when you tell a joke and no one laughs?

Are you more or less likely to tell the joke in the future? If you see someone severely reprimanded for reading a newspaper in class, are you more or less likely to read the paper in that class? What explains these behaviors?

Understanding Learning

Planning Tip: See the Chapter-6-At-A-Glance Planning Guide in the Instructor's Section at the front of this book.

Study Guide: The *Study Guide,* sold separately, contains exercises to help students determine if they have mastered each learning objective for this chapter.

Planning Tip: See the separate *Instructor's Resource Manual* for additional activities and resources for teaching this chapter, including Handout Masters. Also see the *Allyn & Bacon Transparencies in Educational Psychology.*

Planning Tip: See the *Test Bank* and *Study Guide* supplements as you plan for evaluation and measurement of student learning.

Planning Tip: For further information about audiovisual, multimedia, and computer-assisted resources for teaching this chapter, see the Video and Software Guide in the *Instructor's Resource Manual.*

Learning Process through which experience causes permanent change in knowledge or behavior.

When we hear the word "learning," most of us think of studying and school. We think about subjects or skills we intend to master, such as algebra, Spanish, chemistry, or karate. But learning is not limited to school. We learn every day of our lives. Babies learn to kick their legs to make the mobile above their cribs move, teenagers learn the lyrics to all their favorite songs, middle-aged people like me learn to change their diet and exercise patterns, and every few years we all learn to find a new style of dress attractive when the old styles (the styles we once loved) go out of fashion. This last example shows that learning is not always intentional. We don't try to like new styles and dislike old; it just seems to happen that way. We don't intend to become nervous when we see the dentist fill a syringe with Novocain or when we step onto a stage, yet many of us do. So what is this powerful phenomenon called learning?

Learning: A Definition

Test Bank items 6.1, 6.3, 6.4, 6.86, 6.97, 6.110

In the broadest sense, **learning** occurs when experience causes a relatively permanent change in an individual's knowledge or behavior. The change may be deliberate or unintentional, for better or for worse. To qualify as learning, this change must be brought about by experience—by the interaction of a person with his or her environment. Changes due simply to maturation, such as growing taller or turning gray, do not qualify as learning. Temporary changes due to illness, fatigue, or hunger are also excluded from a general definition of learning. A person who has gone without food for two days does not learn to be hungry, and a person who is ill does not learn to run more slowly. Of course, learning plays a part in how we respond to hunger or illness.

Our definition specifies that the changes resulting from learning are in the individual's knowledge or behavior. While most psychologists would agree with this statement, some tend to emphasize the change in knowledge, others the change in behavior. Cognitive psychologists, who focus on changes in knowledge, believe learning is an internal mental activity that cannot be observed directly. As you will see in the next chapter, cognitive psychologists studying learning are interested in unobservable mental activities such as thinking, remembering, creating, and solving problems (Schwartz & Reisberg, 1991).

The psychologists discussed in this chapter, on the other hand, favor **behavioral learning theories.** The behavioral view generally assumes that the outcome of learning is change in behavior and emphasizes the effects of external events on the individual. Some early behaviorists like J. B. Watson took the radical position that since thinking, intentions, and other internal mental events could not be seen or studied rigorously and scientifically, these "mentalisms," as he called them, should not even be included in an explanation of learning. Before we look in depth at behavioral explanations of learning, let's step into an actual classroom and note the possible results of learning.

Learning Is Not Always What It Seems

Elizabeth was beginning her first day of solo teaching. After weeks of working with her cooperating teacher in an eighth-grade social studies class, she was ready to take over. As she moved from behind the desk to the front of the room, she saw another adult approach the classroom door. It was Mr. Ross, her supervisor from college. Elizabeth's neck and facial muscles suddenly became very tense and her hands trembled.

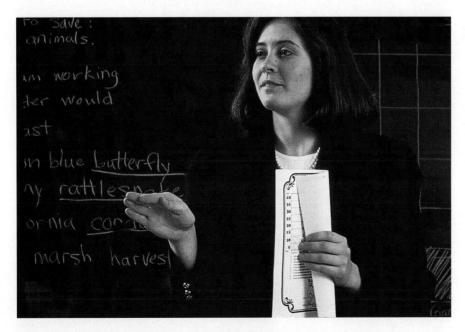

How will you feel about being evaluated when you student teach? Are there any experiences in your "learning history" that have made you anxious about speaking in public or taking tests? How could you use behavioral principles of learning to explain the development of these anxieties?

Behavioral Learning Theories Explanations of learning that focus on external events as the cause of changes in observable behaviors.

Example: Elizabeth's sweaty palms may be an example of a classically conditioned reaction to being evaluated. The fact that the students associate "slavery" with "Civil War" and "Lincoln" is an example of contiguity learning. Elizabeth provides a model for her students, indicating that laughing is appropriate in this situation.

Example: The students' laughter serves as a reinforcer for the silly remarks.

Example: Elizabeth attempts to use punishment.

"I've stopped by to observe your teaching," Mr. Ross said. "This will be my first of six visits. I tried to reach you last night to tell you."

Her worst fear was confirmed: he was going to observe her on her first solo day. She tried to hide her reaction, but her hands trembled as she gathered the notes for the lesson. Elizabeth had planned a slightly unorthodox introduction. She now found herself wishing she had chosen something a bit less risky; but after a few seconds of reflection, she decided to stick to her original plan.

"Let's start today with a kind of game. I will say some words, then I want you to tell me the first words you can think of. Don't bother to raise your hands. Just say the words out loud, and I will write them on the board. Don't all speak at once, though. Wait until someone else has finished to say your word. Okay, here is the first word: Slavery."

"Civil War." "Lincoln." "Freedom." "Emancipation Proclamation." The answers came very quickly, and Elizabeth was relieved to see that the students understood the game.

"All right, very good," she said. "Now try another one: South."

"South Carolina." "South Dakota." "South Street Seaport," "No, the Confederacy, you dummy." "*Gone with the Wind*." "Clark Gable." With this last answer, a ripple of laughter moved across the room.

"Clark Gable!" Elizabeth sighed dreamily. "*Gone with the Wind* was on television last month." Then she laughed too. Soon all the students were laughing. "Okay, settle down," Elizabeth said. "Here is another word: North."

"Bluebellies." The students continued to laugh. "Yellowbellies." "Bellydancers." More laughter and a few appropriate gestures.

"Just a minute," Elizabeth pleaded. "These ideas are getting a little off base!"

"Off base? Baseball," shouted the boy who had first mentioned Clark Gable. He stood up and started throwing balls of paper to a friend in the back of the room, simulating the style of Roger Clemens.

"The Atlanta Braves." "No, the Mets." "Shea Stadium." "Hot dogs." "Popcorn." "Home videos." "*Gone with the Wind*." "Clark Gable." The responses now came too fast for Elizabeth to stop them. For some reason, the Clark Gable line got an even bigger laugh the second time around, and Elizabeth suddenly realized she had lost the class.

"Okay, since you know so much about the Civil War, close your books and take out a pen," Elizabeth said, obviously angry. She passed out the worksheet that she had planned as a cooperative, open-book project. "You have 20 minutes to finish this test!"

"You didn't tell us we were having a test!" "This isn't fair!" "We haven't even covered this stuff yet!" "I didn't do anything wrong!" There were moans and disgusted looks, even from the most mellow students. "I'm reporting you to the principal; it's a violation of students' rights!"

This last comment hit hard. The class had just finished discussing human rights as preparation for this unit on the Civil War. As she listened to the protests, Elizabeth felt terrible. How was she going to grade these "tests"? The first section of the worksheet involved facts about events during the Civil War, and the second section asked students to create a news-style program interviewing ordinary people touched by the war.

"All right, all right, it won't be a test. But you do have to complete this worksheet for a grade. I was going to let you work together, but your behavior this morning tells me that you are not ready for group work. If you can complete the first section of the sheet working quietly and seriously, you may work together on the second section." Elizabeth knew that her students would like to work together on writing the script for the news interview program.

It appears, on the surface at least, that very little learning of any sort was taking place in Elizabeth's classroom. In fact, Elizabeth had some good ideas; but she also made some mistakes in her application of learning principles. We will return throughout the chapter to analyze this episode. To get us started, four events can be singled out, each possibly related to a different learning process.

First, Elizabeth's hands trembled when her college supervisor entered the room. Second, the students were able to associate the words *Carolina* and *Dakota* with the word *South*. Third, one student continued to disrupt the class with inappropriate responses. And fourth, after Elizabeth had laughed at a student comment, the class joined in her laughter. The four learning processes represented are classical conditioning, contiguity, operant conditioning, and observational learning. In the following pages we will examine these four kinds of learning, starting with contiguity.

Test Bank items 6.2, 6.3, 6.5–6.14, 6.17, 6.18, 6.87, 6.88, 6.98–6.100, 6.111, 6.120, 6.123

Early Explanations of Learning: Contiguity and Classical Conditioning

One of the earliest explanations of learning came from Aristotle (384–322 B.C.). He said that we remember things together (1) when they are similar, (2) when they contrast, and (3) when they are *contiguous*. This last principle is the most important, because it is included in all explanations of *learning by association*. The principle of **contiguity** states that whenever two or more sensations occur together often enough, they will become associated. Later, when only one of these sensations (a **stimulus**) occurs, the other will be remembered too (a **response**) (Rachlin, 1991).

Contiguity plays a role in some school learning. Doing spelling drills, practicing multiplication tables, and reciting states and capitals are examples of attempts to form associations. Some results of contiguous learning were evident in Elizabeth's class. When she said "South," students associated the words "Carolina" and "Dakota." They had heard these words together many times. Other learning processes may be involved as well when students learn these phrases, but contiguity plays a part. Contiguity also plays a major role in another learning process best known as classical conditioning.

Pavlov's Dilemma and Discovery: Classical Conditioning

Classical conditioning focuses on the learning of *involuntary* emotional or physiological responses such as fear, increased heart beat, salivation, or sweat-

Example: The Premack principle—use a higher-frequency (more-desired) activity to reinforce a lower-frequency behavior.

Transparency: Acetate transparency T 52 presents "Six Examples of Learning" as an in-class test of students' understanding of kinds of learning.

Transparency: Use acetate transparency T 47 "Three Stages of Classical Conditioning."

Teaching Tip: To demonstrate classical conditioning, have the students sit in pairs facing one another so they can look at each other's eyes. Explain that you are going to blow a whistle, then immediately turn off the light in the classroom. (The darkness will cause the pupils of the eyes to dilate.) After repeating this sequence several times, you will blow the whistle but will not turn off the light. They should watch their partner's eyes to see if the pupils become larger in response to just the whistle. This works best if the room gets quite dark without the lights. Some students are more responsive or "conditionable" than others.

Objective 6.3: Define the terms "stimulus" and "response," and give several examples of each.

Objective 6.4: Explain the process of contiguity learning.

Contiguity Association of two events because of repeated pairing.

Stimulus Event that activates behavior.

Response Observable reaction to a stimulus.

Classical Conditioning Association of automatic responses with new stimuli.

Neutral Stimulus Stimulus not connected to a response.

Unconditioned Stimulus (US) Stimulus that automatically produces an emotional or physiological response.

Unconditioned Response (UR) Naturally occurring emotional or physiological response.

Conditioned Stimulus (CS) Stimulus that evokes an emotional or physiological response after conditioning.

Conditioned Response (CS) Learned response to a previously neutral stimulus.

Generalization Responding in the same way to similar stimuli.

Discrimination Responding differently to similar, but not identical stimuli.

Extinction Gradual disappearance of a learned response.

ing—sometimes called *respondents* because they are automatic responses to stimuli. Through the process of classical conditioning, humans and animals can be trained to react involuntarily to a stimulus that previously had no effect—or a very different effect—on them. The stimulus comes to *elicit,* or bring forth, the response automatically.

Classical conditioning was discovered by Ivan Pavlov, a Russian physiologist, in the 1920s. In his laboratory, Pavlov was plagued by a series of setbacks. He was trying to answer questions about the digestive system of dogs, including how long it took a dog to secrete digestive juices after it had been fed. But the intervals of time kept changing. At first, the dogs salivated in the expected manner while they were being fed. Then the dogs began to salivate as soon as they saw the food. Finally, they salivated as soon as they saw the scientist enter the room. The white coats of the experimenters, the sound of their footsteps, all *elicited* salivation. Pavlov decided to make a detour from his original experiments and examine these unexpected interferences in his work.

In one of his first experiments, Pavlov began by sounding a tuning fork and recording a dog's response. As expected, there was no salivation. At this point, the sound of the tuning fork was a **neutral stimulus** because it brought forth no salivation. Then Pavlov fed the dog. The response was salivation. The food was an **unconditioned stimulus** because no prior training or "conditioning" was needed to establish the natural connection between food and salivation. The salivation was an **unconditioned response,** again because it occurred automatically—no conditioning required.

Using these three elements—the food, the salivation, and the tuning fork—Pavlov demonstrated that a dog could be conditioned to salivate after hearing the tuning fork. He did this by contiguous pairing of the sound with food. At the beginning of the experiment, he sounded the fork and then quickly fed the dog. After Pavlov repeated this several times, the dog began to salivate after hearing the sound but before receiving the food. Now the sound had become a **conditioned stimulus** that could bring forth salivation by itself. The response of salivating after the tone was now a **conditioned response.** Figure 6.1 is a schematic diagram of what happened in Pavlov's laboratory.

Generalization, Discrimination, and Extinction

Pavlov's work also identified three other processes in classical conditioning: *generalization, discrimination,* and *extinction.* After the dogs learned to salivate in response to hearing one particular sound, they would also salivate after hearing other similar tones, those that were slightly higher or lower. This process is called **generalization** because the conditioned response of salivating generalized or occurred in the presence of similar stimuli. Pavlov could also teach his dogs **discrimination**—to respond to one tone but not to others that are similar—by making sure that food always followed only one tone, not any others. **Extinction** occurs when a conditioned stimulus (a particular tone) is presented repeatedly but is not followed by the unconditioned stimulus (food).

FIGURE 6.1

PAVLOV'S EXPERIMENT
In a classical conditioning experiment, an animal comes to respond to a stimulus that once prompted no response. The process is as follows: before conditioning, the unconditioned stimulus (meat, in this case) prompts an unconditioned response (salivation), but the neutral stimulus (a bell tone) prompts no response. During conditioning the neutral stimulus (bell tone) is presented, immediately followed by the unconditioned stimulus (meat). After several such pairings, the neutral stimulus (bell tone) becomes a conditioned stimulus, and prompts the conditioned response (salivation) by itself.

The conditioned response (salivating) gradually fades away and finally is "extinguished"—it disappears altogether.

Pavlov's findings and those of other researchers who have studied classical conditioning have implications for teachers. It is possible that many of our emotional reactions to various situations are learned in part through classical conditioning. For example, Elizabeth's trembling hands when she saw her college supervisor might be traced to previous unpleasant experiences. Perhaps she had been embarrassed during past evaluations of her performance, and now just being observed elicits a pounding heart and sweaty palms. Remember that emotions and attitudes as well as facts and ideas are learned in classrooms. This emotional learning can sometimes interfere with academic learning. By the same token, procedures based on classical conditioning can be used to help people learn more adaptive emotional responses, as the Guidelines on page 202 suggest.

Focus on . . . **Classical Conditioning**

- How does a neutral stimulus become a conditioned stimulus?
- Discriminate between generalization and discrimination.
- After several painful visits to the dentist, you feel your heart rate increase when you sit down in the dentist's chair to have your teeth cleaned. Analyze this situation in terms of classical conditioning.

Guidelines

Using Principles of Classical Conditioning

Associate positive, pleasant events with learning tasks.

Examples

1. Emphasize group competition and cooperation over individual competition. Many students have negative emotional responses to individual competition that may generalize to other learning.
2. Make division drills fun by having students decide how to divide refreshments equally, then letting them eat the results.
3. Make voluntary reading appealing by creating a comfortable reading corner with pillows, colorful displays of books, and reading props such as puppets (see Morrow & Weinstein, 1986, for more ideas).

Help students to risk anxiety-producing situations voluntarily and successfully.

Examples

1. Assign a shy student the responsibility of teaching two other students how to distribute materials for map study.
2. Devise small steps toward a larger goal. For example, give ungraded practice tests daily, and then weekly, to students who tend to "freeze" in test situations.
3. If a student is afraid of speaking in front of the class, let the student read a report to a small group while seated, then read it while standing, then give the report from notes instead of reading it verbatim. Next, move in stages toward having the student give a report to the whole class.

Help students recognize differences and similarities among situations so they can discriminate and generalize appropriately.

Examples

1. Explain that it is appropriate to avoid strangers who offer gifts or rides but safe to accept favors from adults when parents are present.
2. Assure students who are anxious about taking college entrance exams that this test is like all the other achievement tests they have taken.

Objective 6.5: Draw a diagram of classical conditioning learning, explaining how a child can become afraid of school. Include the concepts of generalization and discrimination in this explanation.

Objective 6.6: Use the classical conditioning diagram to suggest how to prevent and extinguish a child's fear of animals.

Discussion: How can contiguity learning explain the development of superstitions? Can superstitions be better explained by classical or operant conditioning than by contiguity?

Respondents Responses (generally automatic or involuntary) elicited by specific stimuli.

Operants Voluntary (and generally goal-directed) behaviors emitted by a person or an animal.

Operant Conditioning Learning in which voluntary behavior is strengthened or weakened by consequences or antecedents.

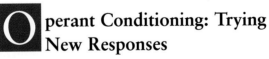

Operant Conditioning: Trying New Responses

Test Bank items 6.3, 6.16

So far we have concentrated on the automatic conditioning of involuntary responses such as salivation and fear. These involuntary actions are often called **respondents.** Clearly, not all human learning is so automatic and unintentional. Most behaviors are not elicited by stimuli, they are *emitted* or voluntarily enacted. People actively "operate" on their environment to produce different kinds of consequences. These deliberate actions are called **operants.** The learning process involved in operant behavior is called **operant conditioning** because we learn to behave in certain ways as we operate on the environment.

The Work of Skinner   Test Bank item 6.15

The person generally thought to be responsible for developing operant conditioning is B. F. Skinner (1953). Skinner began with the belief that the principles of classical conditioning account for only a small portion of learned behaviors. Many human behaviors are operants, not respondents. Classical conditioning describes only how existing behaviors might be paired with new stimuli; it does not explain how new operant behaviors are acquired.

Behavior, like response or action, is simply a word for what a person does in a particular situation. Conceptually, we may think of a behavior as sandwiched between two sets of environmental influences: those that precede it (its **antecedents**) and those that follow it (its **consequences**) (Skinner, 1950). This relationship can be shown very simply as antecedent–behavior–consequence, or A–B–C. As behavior is ongoing, a given consequence becomes an antecedent for the next ABC sequence. Research in operant conditioning shows that operant behavior can be altered by changes in the antecedents, the consequences, or both. Early work focused on consequences.

To study the effects of consequences on behavior under carefully controlled conditions, Skinner designed a special cagelike apparatus. The subjects of Skinner's studies were usually rats or pigeons placed in the cages, which soon came to be called **Skinner boxes.** A typical Skinner box is a small enclosure containing only a food tray and a lever or bar (for rats) or a disk (for pigeons). The lever or disk is connected to a food hopper. Modifications of this basic box include lights close to the lever or disk and electrified floors used to give mild shocks to the animals. In one experiment, a hungry pigeon is placed in the box and proceeds to explore it. Since pigeons tend to peck, the animal will eventually get around to pecking the disk. At that point a small food pellet will drop into the food tray. The hungry bird eats the pellet, moves around the box, and soon pecks the disk again. There is more food, and before long the pigeon is pecking and eating continuously. The next time the pigeon is placed in the box, it will go directly to the disk and begin pecking.

Using this approach, Skinner studied many questions about the effects of consequences on behavior. For example, how is the rate of pecking affected if the pigeons do not get food every time they peck? How long will the pigeons continue to peck if no food follows at all? What happens if food appears only when the pigeon pecks the red key but not when it pecks the green key?

Types of Consequences   Test Bank items 6.19–6.22, 6.25–6.29, 6.31, 6.89, 6.101, 6.121

According to the behavioral view, consequences determine to a great extent whether a person will repeat the behavior that led to the consequences. The type and timing of consequences can strengthen or weaken behaviors. We will look first at consequences that strengthen behavior.

Reinforcement.   While **reinforcement** is commonly understood to mean "reward," this term has a particular meaning in psychology. A **reinforcer** is any consequence that strengthens the behavior it follows. So, by definition, *reinforced behaviors increase in frequency or duration.* Whenever you see a behavior persisting or increasing over time, you can assume the consequences of

Skinner's work on operant conditioning changed the way we think about consequences and learning.

Objective 6.7: Define the following terms: operant, behavior, antecedents, consequences, and cueing.

Objective 6.8: State the basic principle of operant conditioning.

Antecedents   Events that precede an action.

Consequences   Events that follow an action.

Skinner Box   Experimental chamber designed to isolate stimulus-response connections.

Reinforcement   Use of consequences to strengthen behavior.

Reinforcer   Any event that follows a behavior and increases the chances that the behavior will occur again.

Examples: These examples of operant conditioning are taken from Morris, C. G. (1988). *Psychology: An introduction* (6th ed.). Englewood Cliffs, NJ: Prentice-Hall, pp. 1–27:

Operant conditioning has been applied to the treatment of the mentally ill, convicted criminals, and people suffering from various kinds of phobias. Recently, operant conditioning has been applied to weight reduction programs. . . . Unlike many of the fad diets that have become so much a part of our weight-conscious society, behavior modification methods seem to be more successful in that they reinforce the more appropriate eating behaviors that will lead to permanent weight loss.

Teaching Tip: For a class project that demonstrates some of the principles of operant conditioning, see Chrisler, J. C. (1988). Conditioning the instructor's behavior: A class project in psychology of learning. *Teaching of Psychology, 15,* 135–137.

Background: In some of his last writings, Skinner analyzed his own life in terms of his operant view of learning [Skinner, B. F. (1987). *Upon further reflection.* Englewood Cliffs, NJ: Prentice-Hall]. He noted that the older scholar doesn't need frequent reinforcement if he has been reinforced through the years on a schedule that encourages persistence.

Objective 6.9: Identify the four forms consequences can take and the effect of each on the behavior that it follows. Give an example of each.

Positive Reinforcement Strengthening behavior by presenting a desired stimulus after the behavior.

Negative Reinforcement Strengthening behavior by removing an aversive stimulus.

Aversive Irritating or unpleasant.

---

that behavior are reinforcers for the individual involved. The reinforcement process can be diagrammed as follows:

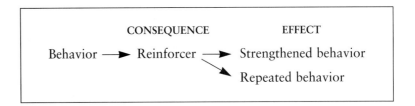

We can be fairly certain that food will be a reinforcer for a hungry animal, but what about people? It is not clear why an event acts as a reinforcer for an individual, but there are many theories about why reinforcement works. For example, some psychologists suggest that reinforcers satisfy needs, while other psychologists believe that reinforcers reduce tension or stimulate a part of the brain (Rachlin, 1991). Whether the consequences of any action are reinforcing probably depends on the individual's perception of the event and the meaning it holds for her or him. For example, students who repeatedly get themselves sent to the principal's office for misbehaving may be indicating that something about this consequence is reinforcing for them, even if it doesn't seem desirable to you.

Reinforcers are those consequences that strengthen the associated behavior (Skinner, 1953, 1989). There are two types of reinforcement. The first, called **positive reinforcement,** occurs when the behavior produces a new stimulus. Examples include a peck on the red key producing food for a pigeon, wearing a new outfit producing many compliments, or falling out of your chair producing cheers and laughter from classmates.

Notice that positive reinforcement can occur even when the behavior being reinforced (falling out of a chair) is not "positive" from the teacher's point of view. In fact, positive reinforcement of inappropriate behaviors occurs unintentionally in many classrooms. Teachers help maintain problem behaviors by inadvertently reinforcing them. For example, Elizabeth may have unintentionally reinforced problem behavior in her class by laughing the first time the boy answered, "Clark Gable." The problem behavior may have persisted for other reasons, but the consequence of Elizabeth's laughter could have played a role.

When the consequence that strengthens a behavior is the *appearance* (addition) of a new stimulus, the situation is defined as positive reinforcement. In contrast, when the consequence that strengthens a behavior is the *disappearance* (subtraction) of a stimulus, the process is called **negative reinforcement.** If a particular action leads to stopping, avoiding, or escaping an **aversive** situation, the action is likely to be repeated in a similar situation. A common example is the car seatbelt buzzer. As soon as you attach your seatbelt, the irritating buzzer stops. You are likely to repeat this action in the future (reinforcement) because the behavior made an aversive stimulus disappear (negative). Consider students who continually "get sick" right before a test and are sent to the nurse's office. The behavior allows the students to escape aversive situations—tests—so getting "sick" is being maintained, in part, through negative reinforcement. It is negative because the stimulus (the test) disappears; it is reinforcement because the behavior that caused the stimulus to disappear (getting "sick") increases or repeats. It is also possible that classical conditioning plays a role. The students may have been conditioned to experience unpleasant physiological reactions to tests.

The "negative" in negative reinforcement does not imply that the behavior being reinforced is necessarily negative. The meaning is closer to that of "negative" numbers—something is subtracted. Associate positive and negative reinforcement with adding or subtracting something following a behavior.

Punishment. Negative reinforcement is often confused with punishment. The process of reinforcement (positive or negative) always involves strengthening behavior. **Punishment,** on the other hand, involves *decreasing or suppressing behavior.* A behavior followed by a "punisher" is less likely to be repeated in similar situations in the future. Again, it is the effect that defines a consequence as punishment, and different people have different perceptions of what is punishing. One student may find suspension from school punishing, while another student wouldn't mind at all. The process of punishment is diagrammed as follows:

```
              CONSEQUENCE          EFFECT
Behavior ──▶ Punisher ──▶ Weakened behavior
                        ↘
                          Decreased frequency of behavior
```

Like reinforcement, punishment may take one of two forms. The first type has been called Type I punishment, but this name isn't very informative, so I use the term **presentation punishment.** It occurs when the appearance of a stimulus following the behavior suppresses or decreases the behavior. When teachers assign demerits, extra work, running laps, and so on, they are using presentation punishment. The other type of punishment (Type II punishment) I call **removal punishment** because it involves removing a stimulus. When teachers or parents take away privileges after a young person has behaved inappropriately, they are applying removal punishment. With both types, the effect is to decrease the behavior that led to the punishment. Figure 6.2 on page 206 summarizes the processes of reinforcement and punishment we have just discussed.

Reinforcement Schedules

Test Bank items 6.23, 6.24, 6.30, 6.32–6.36, 6.90, 6.102, 6.112, 6.123

When people are learning a new behavior, they will learn it faster if they are reinforced for every correct response. This is a **continuous reinforcement schedule.** Then, when the new behavior has been mastered, they will maintain it best if they are reinforced intermittently rather than every time. An **intermittent reinforcement schedule** helps students to maintain skills without expecting constant reinforcement.

There are two basic types of intermittent reinforcement schedules. One—called an **interval schedule**—is based on the amount of time that passes between reinforcers. The other—a **ratio schedule**—is based on the number of responses learners give between reinforcers. Interval and ratio schedules may be either *fixed* (predictable) or *variable* (unpredictable). Table 6.1 on page 207 summarizes the five possible reinforcement schedules (the continuous schedule and the four kinds of intermittent schedules).

Punishment Process that weakens or suppresses behavior.

Presentation Punishment Decreasing the chances that a behavior will occur again by presenting an aversive stimulus following the behavior; also called Type I punishment.

Removal Punishment Decreasing the chances that a behavior will occur again by removing a pleasant stimulus following the behavior; also called Type II punishment.

Continuous Reinforcement Schedule Presenting a reinforcer after every appropriate response.

Intermittent Reinforcement Schedule Presenting a reinforcer after some but not all responses.

Interval Schedule Length of time between reinforcers.

Ratio Schedule Number of responses between reinforcers.

Teaching Tip: Negative reinforcement is often confused with punishment. To clarify the distinction, see Robert Tauber [Overcoming misunderstanding about the concept of negative reinforcement. *Teaching of Psychology, 15* (October 1988), 152–153]. Tauber has a brief negative reinforcement quiz with questions such as, "What is another word for negative reinforcement?" and "What is the effect of negative reinforcement on behavior?" When the results are in and students see that they are having problems, you can try one of Tauber's six remedies. Both the quiz and the reprint of the article detailing the six remedies are available from Robert Tauber, Division of Humanities and Social Sciences, Behrend College, Erie, PA 16563.

Objective 6.10: Define continuous and intermittent reinforcement. State the purpose for which each should be used.

Transparency: Use acetate transparency T 48 "Kinds of Reinforcement and Punishment."

Reflection/Journal Writing: To help students become aware of the prevalence of reinforcement in daily life, ask them to keep a log, noting every time they give or receive reinforcement. Remind them to look for positive and negative reinforcement and also to record the kind of schedule operating. Another possibility is to note reinforcement and schedules in a field placement classroom or even in college classes. Ask your students what examples of reinforcement are present in your class.

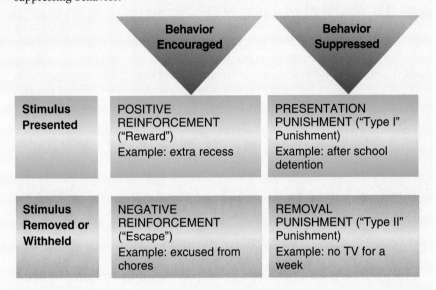

FIGURE 6.2

KINDS OF REINFORCEMENT AND PUNISHMENT
Negative reinforcement and punishment are often confused. It may help you to remember that negative reinforcement is always associated with increases in behavior, and punishment always involves decreasing or suppressing behavior.

Summarizing the Effects of Reinforcement Schedules

Speed of performance depends on control. If reinforcement is based on the number of responses you give, then you have more control over the reinforcement: the faster you accumulate the correct number of responses, the faster the reinforcement will come. Therefore, people work faster on ratio than on interval schedules. A teacher who says, "As soon as you complete these ten problems correctly, you may go to the student lounge," can expect higher rates of performance than a teacher who says, "Work on these ten problems for the next 20 minutes. Then I will check your papers and those with ten correct may go to the lounge."

Persistence in performance depends on predictability. Continuous reinforcement and both kinds of fixed reinforcement (ratio and interval) are quite predictable. We come to expect reinforcement at certain points and are generally quick to give up when the reinforcement does not meet our expectations. To encourage persistence of response, variable schedules are most appropriate. In fact, if the schedule is gradually changed until it becomes very "lean"— meaning that reinforcement occurs only after many responses or a long time interval—then people can learn to work for extended periods without any reinforcement at all. Just watch gamblers playing slot machines to see how powerful a lean reinforcement schedule can be.

Schedule	Definition	Example	Response Pattern	Reaction When Reinforcement Stops
Continuous	Reinforcement after every response	Turning on the television	Rapid learning of response	Very little persistence; rapid disappearance of response
Fixed-interval	Reinforcement after a set period of time	Weekly quiz	Response rate increases as time for reinforcement approaches, then drops after reinforcement	Little persistence; rapid drop in response rate when time for reinforcement passes and no reinforcer appears
Variable-interval	Reinforcement after varying lengths of time	Pop quizzes	Slow, steady rate of responding; very little pause after reinforcement	Greater persistence; slow decline in response rate
Fixed-ratio	Reinforcement after a set number of responses	Piece work Bake sale	Rapid response rate; pause after reinforcement	Little persistence; rapid drop in response rate when expected number of responses are given and no reinforcer appears
Variable-ratio	Reinforcement after a varying number of responses	Slot machines	Very high response rate; little pause after reinforcement	Greatest persistence; response rate stays high and gradually drops off

TABLE 6.1   Reinforcement Schedules

Reinforcement schedules influence how persistently we will respond when reinforcement is withheld. What happens when reinforcement is completely withdrawn?

Extinction.   In classical conditioning, we saw that the conditioned response was extinguished (disappeared) when the conditioned stimulus appeared but the unconditioned stimulus did not follow (tone, but no food). In operant conditioning, a person or an animal will not persist in a certain behavior if the usual reinforcer is withheld. The behavior will eventually be extinguished (stop). For example, if you go for a week without selling even one magazine door-to-door, you may give up. Removal of reinforcement altogether leads to extinction. The process may take a while, however, as you know if you have tried to extinguish a child's tantrums by withholding your attention. Often the child wins—you give up ignoring and instead of extinction, intermittent reinforcement occurs. This, of course, may encourage even more persistent tantrums in the future.

Focus on...   **Consequences**

- What defines a consequence as a reinforcer? As a punisher?
- How are negative reinforcement and punishment different?
- How can you encourage persistence in a behavior?

Examples: *Positive reinforcement:* Praise for good grades, bonus points on tests, a class pizza party when everyone makes above 85 on the weekly spelling test. *Negative reinforcement:* Removing a stone from your shoe; calling on a child who is madly waving his hand and shouting, "I know, I know!"(you are negatively reinforced because the noise stops); wearing a certain pair of shoes on trips to avoid aching feet; saying "I'm really sorry" to your spouse to avoid his or her anger. *Presentation punishment:* Running extra laps; reprimands; bad grades; corporal punishment. *Removal punishment:* Fines; being grounded; missing recess; not being allowed to go on the field trip; getting fired.

Objective 6.11: Contrast the effects of the four schedules of reinforcement.

Transparency: Acetate transparency T 49 provides a table for schedules of intermittent reinforcement.

Activity 6.2: See the *Instructor's Resource Manual* for Schedules of Reinforcement, an activity that involves dispensing tokens on different reinforcement schedules.

Teaching Tip: It sometimes helps students to understand reinforcement schedules if they see a graph of the responses under different schedules.

Discussion: When a teacher decides to begin ignoring a behavior that he or she wants to extinguish, there is frequently an increase in the behavior for a short time before it decreases. How do your students explain this phenomenon?

Stimulus Control Capacity for the presence or absence of antecedents to cause behaviors.

Cueing Providing a stimulus that "sets up" a desired behavior.

*P*eople "learn" to be persistent in losing their money to slot machines by being reinforced intermittently.

Antecedents and Behavior Change

Test Bank items 6.37, 6.38, 6.117

In operant conditioning, antecedents—the events preceding behaviors—provide information about which behaviors will lead to positive consequences and which to negative. Skinner's pigeons learned to peck for food when a light was on, but not to bother when the light was off, because no food followed pecking when the light was off. In other words, they learned to use the antecedent light as a cue to discriminate the likely consequence of pecking. The pigeons' pecking was under **stimulus control,** controlled by the discriminative stimulus of the light. You can see that this idea is related to discrimination in classical conditioning, but here we are talking about voluntary behaviors like pecking, not reflexes like salivating.

We all learn to discriminate—to read situations. When should you ask to borrow your roommate's car, after a major disagreement or after you both have had a great time at a party? The antecedent cue of a school principal standing in the hall helps students discriminate the probable consequences of running or attempting to break into a locker. We often respond to such antecedent cues without fully realizing that they are influencing our behavior. But teachers can use cues deliberately in the classroom.

Cueing. By definition, **cueing** is the act of providing an antecedent stimulus just before a particular behavior is to take place. Cueing is particularly useful in setting the stage for behaviors that must occur at a specific time but are easily forgotten. In working with young people, teachers often find themselves correcting behaviors after the fact. For example, they may ask students, "When are you going to start remembering to . . . ?" Such reminders often lead to irritation. The mistake is already made, and the young person is left with only two choices, to promise to try harder or to say, "Why don't you leave me alone?" Neither response is very satisfying. Presenting a nonjudgmental cue can help prevent these negative confrontations. When a student performs the appropriate behavior after a cue, the teacher can reinforce the student's accomplishment instead of punishing the student's failure.

Prompting.   Sometimes students need help in learning to respond to a cue in an appropriate way so the cue becomes a discriminative stimulus. One approach is to provide an additional cue, called a **prompt,** following the first cue. There are two principles for using a cue and a prompt to teach a new behavior (Becker, Engelmann, & Thomas, 1975). First, make sure the environmental stimulus that you want to become a cue occurs immediately before the prompt you are using, so students will learn to respond to the cue and not rely only on the prompt. Second, fade the prompt as soon as possible so students do not become dependent on it.

An example of cueing and prompting is providing students with a checklist or reminder sheet. Figure 6.3 is a checklist for the steps in peer tutoring. Working in pairs is the cue; the checklist is the prompt. As students learn the procedures, the teacher may stop using the checklist, but may remind the stu-

Prompt A reminder that follows a cue to make sure the person reacts to the cue.

FIGURE 6.3

WRITTEN PROMPTS: A PEER-TUTORING CHECKLIST
By using this checklist, students are reminded how to be effective tutors. As they become more proficient, the checklist may be less necessary.

Remember to…   ____ 1. Have the lesson ready.   ____ 2. Talk clearly.   ____ 3. Be friendly.   ____ 4. Tell the student when he is right.

____ 5. Correct mistakes. STOP! Give the right answer. Have the student do it.   ____ 6. Praise good work!   ____ 7. Make the lesson fun.   ____ 8. Do not give TOO MUCH help.   ____ 9. Fill out the daily sheet.   ____ 10. Can you add a suggestion?

Source: Figure from *Achieving educational excellence: Behavior analysis for school personnel,* p. 89. Copyright © 1994 by Beth Sulzer-Azaroff and G. Roy Mayer (San Marcos, CA: Western Image, P.O. Box 427). Reprinted by permission of the authors.

Teaching Tip: Introduce the idea of "stimulus control," or coming to respond somewhat automatically to the antecedents in a situation. I use the example of finding myself (more than once) about to turn into my old office parking lot, even after my department had been moved to a new building across town. The old cues kept me heading automatically to the old office. Another example is the supposedly true story of a getaway car driver in a bank robbery who sped through town, only to be caught by the police when she dutifully stopped at a red light. The stimulus of the red light had come to have automatic control.

Examples: Here are a few other examples of antecedents serving as cues about what behaviors will be rewarded in a particular situation:

Antecedent: Teacher giving lecture—taking notes will be rewarded, reading the newspaper will not.

Antecedent: Substitute teacher—rule breaking may not be punished in this situation.

Antecedent: Desks in a circle—discussion will be rewarded.

Applied Behavior Analysis The application of behavioral learning principles to understand and change behavior.

Behavior Modification Systematic application of antecedents and consequences to change behavior.

dents of the steps. When no written or oral prompts are necessary, the students have learned to respond appropriately to the environmental cue of working in pairs—they have learned how to behave in tutoring situations. But the teacher should continue to monitor the process, recognize good work, and correct mistakes. Before a tutoring session, the teacher might ask students to close their eyes and "see" the checklist, focusing on each step. As students work, the teacher could listen to their interactions and continue to coach students as they improve their tutoring skills.

Applied Behavior Analysis

Test Bank items 6.41, 6.113, 6.126

Applied behavior analysis is the application of behavioral learning principles to change behavior. The method is sometimes called **behavior modification,** but this term has negative connotations for many people and is often misunderstood (Alberto & Troutman, 1990; Kaplan, 1991).

Ideally, applied behavior analysis requires clear specification of the behavior to be changed, careful measurement of the behavior, analysis of the antecedents and reinforcers that might be maintaining inappropriate or undesirable behavior, interventions based on behavioral principles to change the behavior, and careful measurement of changes. In research on applied behavior analysis, an ABAB design is common. That is, researchers take a baseline measurement of the behavior (A), then apply the intervention (B), then stop the intervention to see if the behavior goes back to the baseline level (A), and then reintroduce the intervention (B).

In classrooms, teachers usually cannot follow all the ABAB steps, but they can do the following:

1. Clearly specify the behavior to be changed and note the current level. For example, if a student is "careless," does this mean 2, 3, 4, or more computation errors for every 10 problems?

2. Plan a specific intervention using antecedents, consequences, or both. For example, offer the student one extra minute of computer time for every problem completed with no errors.

3. Keep track of the results, and modify the plan if necessary.

Let's consider some specific methods for accomplishing step 2—the *intervention.*

Test Bank items 6.39, 6.40, 6.42–6.58, 6.83, 6.84, 6.92, 6.93, 6.103, 6.104, 6.113, 6.115–6.117, 6.122, 6.126

Methods for Encouraging Behaviors

As we discussed earlier, to encourage behavior is to reinforce it. There are several specific ways to use positive and negative reinforcement to encourage existing behaviors or teach new ones. These include praise, the Premack principle, shaping, and positive practice.

Reinforcing with Teacher Attention. Based on early work such as that of Madsen, Becker, and Thomas (1968) demonstrating that teachers can improve student behavior by ignoring rule-breakers and praising students who are following the rules, many psychologists advised teachers to "accentuate the positive"—liberally praise students for good behavior while ignoring mistakes and misbehavior. This *praise-and-ignore approach* can be helpful, but we should not expect it to solve all classroom management problems. Several studies have shown that disruptive behaviors persist when teachers use positive consequences (mostly praise) as their only classroom management strategy (Pfiffner, Rosen, & O'Leary, 1985; Rosen, O'Leary, Joyce, Conway, & Pfiffner, 1984).

The praise-and-ignore approach should be considered a method for dealing with minor misbehaviors or an option to accompany other strategies. There is a second consideration in using praise. The positive results found in research occur when teachers carefully and systematically praise their students. Unfortunately, praise is not always given appropriately and effectively. Merely "handing out compliments" will not improve behavior. To be effective, praise must (1) be contingent on the behavior to be reinforced, (2) specify clearly the behavior being reinforced, and (3) be believable (O'Leary & O'Leary, 1977). In other words, the praise should be sincere recognition of a well-defined behavior so students understand what they did to warrant the recognition. Teachers who have not received special training often violate these conditions (Brophy, 1981). Ideas for using praise effectively, based on Brophy's extensive review of the subject, are presented in the Guidelines on page 212.

Some psychologists have suggested that teachers' use of praise tends to focus students on learning to win approval rather than on learning for its own sake. Perhaps the best advice is to be aware of the potential dangers of the overuse or misuse of praise and to navigate accordingly.

Selecting Reinforcers: The Premack Principle. In most classrooms, there are many readily available reinforcers other than teacher attention, such as the chance to talk to other students or feed the class animals. But teachers tend to offer these opportunities in a rather haphazard way. Just as with praise, by making privileges and rewards directly contingent on learning and positive behavior, the teacher may greatly increase both learning and desired behavior.

A helpful guide for choosing the most effective reinforcers is the Premack principle, named for David Premack (1965). According to the **Premack principle,** a high-frequency behavior (a preferred activity) can be an effective reinforcer for a low-frequency behavior (a less-preferred activity). This is sometimes referred to as "Grandma's rule": first do what I want you to do, then you may do what you want to do. Elizabeth used this principle in her class when she told them they could work together on their Civil War news program after they quietly completed the first section of the worksheet on their own.

If students didn't have to study, what would they do? The answers to this question may suggest many possible reinforcers. For most students, talking, moving around the room, sitting near a friend, being exempt from assignments or tests, reading magazines, or playing games are preferred activities. The best way to determine appropriate reinforcers for your students may be to watch

"HEY, WAIT A MINUTE! YOU'RE CLEANING ERASERS AS A PUNISHMENT? I'M CLEANING ERASERS AS A REWARD!"

(© 1991 Tony Saltzman)

Premack Principle Principle stating that a more-preferred activity can serve as reinforcer for a less-preferred activity.

Guidelines

Using Praise Appropriately

Be clear and systematic in giving praise.

Examples

1. Make sure praise is tied directly to appropriate behavior.
2. Make sure the student understands the specific action or accomplishment that is being praised. Say, "You returned this poster on time and in good condition," not, "You were very responsible."

Recognize genuine accomplishments.

Examples

1. Reward the attainment of specified goals, not just participation.
2. Do not reward uninvolved students just for being quiet and not disrupting the class.
3. Tie praise to students' improving competence or to the value of their accomplishment. Say, "I noticed that you double-checked all your problems. Your score reflects your careful work."

Set standards for praise based on individual abilities and limitations.

Examples

1. Praise progress or accomplishment in relation to the individual student's past efforts.
2. Focus the student's attention on his or her own progress, not on comparisons with others.

Attribute the student's success to effort and ability so the student will gain confidence that success is possible again.

Examples

1. Don't imply that the success may be based on luck, extra help, or easy material.
2. Ask students to describe the problems they encountered and how they solved them.

Make praise really reinforcing.

Examples

1. Don't attempt to influence the rest of the class by singling out some students for praise. This tactic often backfires, since students know what's really going on. In addition, you risk embarrassing the student you have chosen to praise.
2. Don't give undeserved praise to students simply to balance failures. It is seldom consoling and calls attention to the student's inability to earn genuine recognition.

Objective 6.13: Give two ways of selecting effective reinforcers and illustrate how they would be used according to the Premack principle.

Casebook: See the Teachers' Casebook at the end of this chapter for practicing teachers' ideas about how to catch students being good.

Research: An interesting study of the Premack principle is described in Hall, J. F. (1989). *Learning and memory* (2nd ed.). Englewood Cliffs, NJ: Prentice-Hall, p. 132.

what they do in their free time. If you find yourself saying to a student, "Stop doing that and pay attention!" or "Please put that away until the end of class!" you have probably found a perfect reinforcer for the student.

For the Premack principle to be effective, the low-frequency (less preferred) behavior must happen first. In the following dialogue, notice how the teacher loses a perfect opportunity to use the Premack principle:

Students: Oh, no! Do we have to diagram sentences again today? The other classes got to discuss the film we saw in the auditorium this morning.

Teacher: But the other classes finished the lesson on sentences yesterday. We're almost finished too. If we don't finish the lesson, I'm afraid you'll forget the rules we reviewed yesterday.

Students: Why don't we finish the sentences at the end of the period and talk about the film now?

Teacher: Okay, if you promise to complete the sentences later.

Discussing the film could have served as a reinforcer for completing the lesson. As it is, the class may well spend the entire period discussing the film. Just as the discussion becomes fascinating, the teacher will have to end it and insist that the class return to diagramming sentences.

Some teachers use questionnaires like the one in Table 6.2 to identify effective reinforcers for their students. Remember, what works for one student may not be right for another. And students can get "too much of a good thing"—reinforcers can lose their potency if they are overused.

Shaping. What happens when students continually fail to gain reinforcement because they simply cannot perform a skill in the first place? Consider these examples:

A fourth-grade student looks at the results of the latest mathematics test. "No credit on almost half of the problems again because I made one dumb mistake in each problem. I hate math!"

A 10th-grade student tries each day to find some excuse for avoiding the softball game in gym class. The student cannot catch a ball and now refuses to try.

In both situations the students are receiving no reinforcement for their work because the end product of their efforts is not good enough. A safe prediction is that the students will soon learn to dislike the class, the subject, and

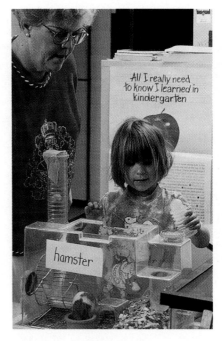

This student looks a bit tentative about reaching into the hamster's cage. If you are sure students are not in danger, encourage them to take small steps to approach the things they fear.

TABLE 6.2	What Do You Like? Reinforcement Ideas from Students

Name _____ Grade _____ Date_____

Please answer all the questions as completely as you can.

1. The school subjects I like best are:
2. Three things I like most to do in school are:
3. If I had 30 minutes' free time at school each day to do what I really liked, it would be:
4. My two favorite snacks are:
5. At recess I like most to (three things):
6. If I had $1 to spend on anything, I would buy:
7. Three jobs I would enjoy in the class are:
8. The two people I most like to work with in school are:
9. At home I really enjoy (three things):

Source: G. Blackham and A. Silberman (1979). *Modification of child and adolescent behavior* (3rd ed.). Belmont, CA: Wadsworth, pp. 281–283. © 1979 by Wadsworth Publishing Co., Inc. Reprinted by permission of the publisher.

Activity 6.3: Field Experience. See the *Instructor's Resource Manual* for What Is Rewarding? This field-experience activity asks your students to survey public school students about what is rewarding to them. Questions to use in surveying are provided in the text (Table 6.2) and in **Handout Master 6.1** in the separate *Instructor' Resource Manual*.

Activity 6.4: Multicultural Awareness. See the *Instructor's Resource Manual* for Reinforcer Preferences, an activity that asks your students to survey public school pupils from different cultural groups about their preferences for reinforcers. **Handout Master 6.1** is provided to help students conduct the survey.

Guidelines

Using Positive Reinforcement

Make sure you recognize positive behavior in ways that students value.
Examples
1. When presenting class rules, set up positive consequences for following rules as well as negative consequences for breaking rules.
2. Recognize honest admissions of mistakes by giving a second chance: "Because you admitted that you copied your paper from a book, I'm giving you a chance to rewrite it."
3. Offer desired rewards for academic efforts, such as extra recess time, exemptions from homework or tests, extra credit on major projects.

When students are tackling new material or trying new skills, give plenty of reinforcement.
Examples
1. Find and comment on something right in every student's first life drawing.
2. Reinforce students for encouraging each other. "French pronunciation is difficult and awkward at first. Let's help each other by eliminating all giggles when someone is brave enough to attempt a new word."

After new behaviors are established, give reinforcement on an unpredictable schedule to encourage persistence.
Examples
1. Offer surprise rewards for good participation in class.
2. Start classes with a short, written extra-credit question. Students don't have to answer, but a good answer will add points to their total for the semester.
3. Make sure the good students get compliments for their work from time to time. Don't take them for granted.

Use cueing to help establish new behaviors.
Examples
1. Put up humorous signs in the classroom to remind students of rules.
2. At the beginning of the year, as students enter class, call their attention to a list on the board of the materials they should have with them when they come to class.

Make sure all students, even those who often cause problems, receive some praise, privileges, or other rewards when they do something well.
Examples
1. Review your class list occasionally to make sure all students are receiving some reinforcement.
2. Set standards for reinforcement so that all students will have a chance to be rewarded.

Establish a variety of reinforcers.
Examples
1. Let students suggest their own reinforcers or choose from a "menu" of reinforcers with "weekly specials."
2. Talk to other teachers or parents about ideas for reinforcers.

Use the Premack principle to identify effective reinforcers.
Examples
1. Watch what students do with their free time.
2. Notice which students like to work together. The chance to work with friends is often a good reinforcer.

Connections: Token reinforcement programs, group consequences, and contracts are discussed in chapter 11.

Objective 6.14: Describe three methods for developing new behaviors in students.

Activity 6.5: See the *Instructor's Resource Manual* for The Case of Bobby Richard, an activity that asks your students to apply behavior principles to help a disorganized student.

Example: As an example of specifying subskills, elicit a list of subskills required to divide a three-digit number. See Jenson, W. R., Sloane, H. N., & Young, K. R. (1988). *Applied behavior analysis in education: A structured teaching approach*. Englewood Cliffs, NJ: Prentice-Hall, p. 288.

perhaps the teacher and school in general. One way to prevent this problem is the strategy of **shaping**, also called **successive approximations.** Shaping involves reinforcing progress instead of waiting for perfection.

In order to use shaping, the teacher must break down the final complex behavior the student is expected to master into a number of small steps. One approach identifying the small steps is **task analysis**, originally developed by R. B. Miller (1962) to help the armed services train personnel. Miller's system begins with a definition of the final performance requirement, what the trainee (or student) must be able to do at the end of the program or unit. Then the steps that will lead to the final goal are specified. The procedure simply breaks skills and processes down into subskills and subprocesses.

In the classroom, the teacher begins by asking, "What will the students have to do before they can reach the final goal I have in mind?" The answer to this question may help identify several underlying skills. Let's say five skills are identified. The teacher then asks, "What must the students be able to do to succeed at each of these five skills?" The answer this time should produce a number of subskills for each of the basic skills. This working backward should give a full picture of all the abilities a student must have to accomplish the objective successfully.

Consider the example of task analysis in Figure 6.4 on page 216, in which students must write a position paper based on library research. If the teacher assigned the position paper without analyzing the task in this way, what could happen? Some of the students might not know how to use the card catalog. They might search through one or two encyclopedias, then write a summary of the issues based only on the encyclopedia articles. Another group of students might know how to use the card catalog, tables of contents, and indexes, but have difficulty reaching conclusions. They might hand in lengthy papers listing summaries of different ideas. Another group of students might be able to draw conclusions, but their written presentations might be so confusing and grammatically incorrect that the teacher could not understand what they were trying to say. Each of the groups would have failed in fulfilling the assignment, but for different reasons.

A task analysis gives a picture of the logical sequence of steps leading toward the final goal. An awareness of this sequence can help teachers make sure that students have the necessary skills before they move to the next step. In addition, when students have difficulty, the teacher can pinpoint problem areas.

Krumboltz and Krumboltz (1972) have described the following four methods of shaping:

1. **Reinforce each subskill.** For example, as shown in Figure 6.4, a research paper can be broken down into organizing, using indexes and tables of contents, summarizing information from several sources, drawing conclusions, writing footnotes, and so on.

2. **Reinforce improvements in accuracy.** A French teacher, for example, might first reinforce a vague approximation of the correct pronunciation of "monsieur," then continue to raise standards gradually until pronunciation is close to that of a native.

3. **Reinforce longer and longer periods of performance.** Students often can perform in a desirable fashion, but only for a few minutes at a time. As you learned in the section on reinforcement schedules, students can be encouraged to persist at a task if they are reinforced at longer and longer intervals.

Transparency: Acetate transparency **T 86** presents a "Task Analysis for Making a Pizza" in the form of a flow chart.

Background: McDaniel, T. R. (1989). Practicing positive reinforcement: Ten behavior management techniques. In Annual editions: *Educational Psychology 88/89* (pp. 91–94). Guilford, CT: Duskin.

In this article you will find descriptions and examples of the following ten strategies:

1. Teach specific directions
2. Look for good behavior
3. Praise effectively
4. Model good behavior
5. Use nonverbal reinforcement
6. Establish token economies
7. Use "Premacking"
8. Teach kids to reinforce one another
9. Teach kids to reinforce themselves
10. Vary positive reinforcement

Teaching Tip: This example makes task analysis seem very linear and straightforward. A slightly more complex task analysis in diagram form appears in **Handout Master 12.3** in the *Instructor's Resource Manual.*

Shaping Reinforcing each small step of progress toward a desired goal or behavior.

Successive Approximations Small components that make up a complex behavior.

Task Analysis System for breaking down a task hierarchically into basic skills and subskills.

FIGURE 6.4

Task Analysis for a Library Assignment

This incomplete task analysis reveals some of the specific knowledge and skills required to write a position paper based on library research. Many of the skills are interrelated, but all are necessary.

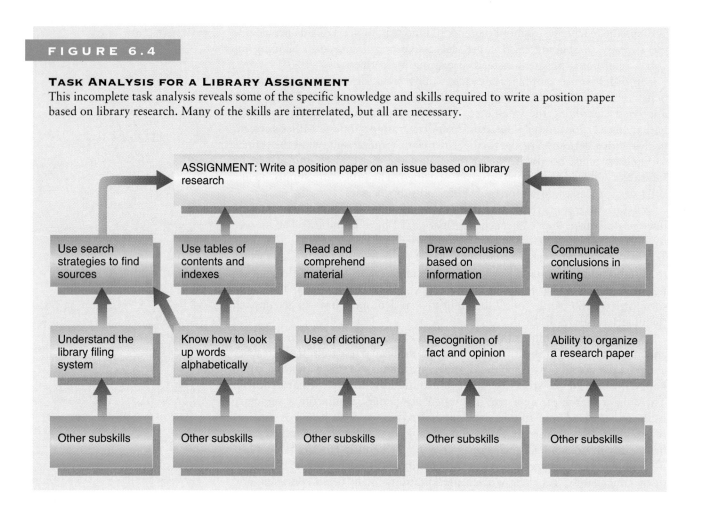

4. **Reinforce longer and longer periods of participation.** Students are sometimes reluctant to participate because they have been embarrassed in the past. In this case a teacher could begin by reinforcing, in a matter-of-fact way, even the smallest contributions of a student who seldom participates in class.

Many behaviors can be improved through shaping, especially skills that involve persistence, endurance, increased accuracy, greater speed, or extensive practice to master. Because shaping is a time-consuming process, however, it should not be used if success can be attained through simpler methods like cueing.

Positive Practice. A strategy for helping students replace one behavior with another is **positive practice**. This approach is especially appropriate for dealing with academic errors. When students make a mistake, they must correct it as soon as possible and practice the correct response (Gibbs & Luyben, 1985; Kazdin, 1984). The same principle can be applied when students break

Activity 6.6: See the *Instructor's Resource Manual* for Positive Practice, an example of applying overcorrection.

Positive Practice Practicing correct responses immediately after errors.

classroom rules. Instead of being punished, the student might be required to practice the correct alternative action.

Coping with Undesirable Behavior

Test Bank items 6.59–6.70, 6.91, 6.105, 6.126

No matter how successful you are at accentuating the positive, there are times when you must cope with undesirable behavior, either because other methods do not seem sufficient or because the behavior itself is dangerous or calls for direct action. For this purpose, negative reinforcement, satiation, reprimands, and punishment all offer possible solutions.

Negative Reinforcement. Recall the basic principle of negative reinforcement: if an action stops or avoids something unpleasant, then the action is likely to occur again in similar situations. Negative reinforcement was operating in Elizabeth's classroom. When she gave in to the moans and complaints of her class and canceled the test, her behavior was being negatively reinforced. She escaped the unpleasant student comments by changing her assignment.

Negative reinforcement may also be used to enhance learning. To do this, you place students in mildly unpleasant situations so they can "escape" when their behavior improves. Consider these examples:

Teacher to a third-grade class: "When the supplies are put back in the cabinet and each of you is sitting quietly, we will go outside. Until then, we will miss our recess."

High school teacher to a student who seldom finishes in-class assignments: "As soon as you complete the assignment, you may join the class in the auditorium. But until you finish, you must work in the study hall."

You may wonder why these examples are not considered punishment. Surely staying in during recess or not accompanying the class to a special program is punishing. But the focus in each case is on strengthening specific behaviors (putting away supplies or finishing in-class assignments). The teacher strengthens (reinforces) the behaviors by removing something aversive *as soon as the desired behaviors occur.* Since the consequence involves removing or "subtracting" a stimulus, the reinforcement is negative.

Negative reinforcement also gives students a chance to exercise control. Missing recess and staying behind in study hall are unpleasant situations, but in each case the students retain control. As soon as they perform the appropriate behavior, the unpleasant situation ends. In contrast, punishment occurs after the fact, and a student cannot so easily control or terminate it.

Krumboltz and Krumboltz (1972) offer several rules for negative reinforcement: Describe the desired change in a positive way. Don't bluff. Make sure you can enforce your unpleasant situation. Follow through despite complaints. Insist on action, not promises. If the unpleasant situation terminates when students promise to be better next time, you have reinforced making promises, not making changes.

Satiation. Another way to stop problem behavior is to insist that students continue the behavior until they are tired of doing it. This procedure,

"OF COURSE YOU DON'T HAVE TO GO TO SCHOOL, DEAR. WOULD YOU GET SOME LIVER OUT OF THE FREEZER TO DEFROST FOR OUR LUNCH?"

(© Martha Campbell)

Objective 6.15: Identify three methods for dealing with undesirable behaviors, and give a classroom example of each.

Transparency: Use acetate transparency T 54 to help students clarify the different viewpoints on learning.

Activity 6.7: Cooperative Learning. See the *Instructor's Resource Manual* for Behavior Problem Scenarios, an activity that asks your students to work in groups to design behavioral interventions for specific classroom problems. Handout Masters 6.2 and 6.3 are provided in the Teachers' Resource Manual to guide planning.

Example: *Negative Reinforcement:*
A 10th-grade teacher tells her class that those students who turn in sloppy, careless work will have to use their free-choice time to redo it.
A first-grade teacher tells an angry boy that he must sit by the tree until he feels able to rejoin the kickball game without arguing.

Teaching Tip: Divide the class into groups of four or five. Give them 2 minutes of silence in which to recall an instance of punishment they have experienced at some time during their lives. Then ask them to tell you the feeling they had when they were being punished. List the feelings on the board. (Negative feelings, such as embarrassment, resentment, hurt, anger, etc., will account for 90 percent of the responses.)

Ask: Does the punishment work?

What are some other negative effects of punishment? List these on the board.

If punishment is ineffective and also produces negative side effects, why do so many teachers rely on it so much?

Activity 6.8: Cooperative Learning. See the *Instructor's Resource Manual* for Reinforcement versus Punishment, an activity in which students work in groups to describe how and when they would use different behavioral principles in teaching.

Activity 6.9: Field Experience. See the *Instructor's Resource Manual* for Interview, a short list of guiding questions for interviewing teachers on reinforcement and punishment.

Example: *Satiation:* A sixth-grade teacher discovered one of his students making paper airplanes during an independent work time. He gave that student a stack of paper and told her to continue making airplanes until

Satiation Requiring a person to repeat a problem behavior past the point of interest or motivation.

Reprimands Criticisms for misbehavior; rebukes.

Response Cost Punishment by loss of reinforcers.

called **satiation**, should be applied with care. Forcing students to continue some behaviors may be physically or emotionally harmful or even dangerous.

An example of an appropriate use of satiation is related by Krumboltz and Krumboltz (1972). In the middle of a ninth-grade algebra class, the teacher suddenly noticed four students making all sorts of unusual motions. In response to persistent teacher questioning, the students finally admitted they were bouncing imaginary balls. The teacher pretended to greet this idea with enthusiasm and suggested the whole class do it. At first, there was a great deal of laughing and joking. After a minute this stopped, and one student even quit. The teacher, however, insisted that all the students continue. After 5 minutes and a number of exhausted sighs, the teacher allowed the students to stop. No one bounced an imaginary ball in that class again.

Teachers also may allow students to continue some action until they stop by themselves, if the behavior is not interfering with the rest of the class. A teacher can do this by simply ignoring the behavior. Remember that responding to an ignorable behavior may actually reinforce it.

In using satiation, a teacher must take care not to give in before the students do. It is also important that the repeated behavior be the one you are trying to end. If the algebra teacher above had insisted that the students write, "I will never bounce imaginary balls in class again" 500 times, the students would have become satiated with writing rather than with bouncing balls.

Reprimands. In an issue of the *Junction Journal,* my daughter's elementary-school newspaper, I read the following lines in a story called "Why I Like School," written by a fourth grader: "I also like my teacher. She helps me understand and learn. She is nice to everyone. . . . I like it when she gets mad at somebody, but she doesn't yell at them in front of the class, but speaks to them privately."

A study by Dan O'Leary and his associates examined the effectiveness of soft, private **reprimands** versus loud, public reprimands in decreasing disruptive behavior (O'Leary, Kaufman, Kass, & Drabman, 1970). Reprimanding a problem student quietly so that only the student can hear seems to be much more effective. When the teacher in the study spoke to offenders loudly enough for the entire class to hear, the disruptions increased or continued at a constant level. Some students enjoy public recognition for misbehavior. Perhaps public condemnation encourages a student to save face by having the last word. At any rate, the extra time and effort required to use private reprimands seems to be a good investment in making lasting improvements. If reprimands are not used too often, and if the classroom is generally a positive, warm environment, then students usually respond quickly (Van Houten & Doleys, 1983).

Response Cost. The concept of **response cost** is familiar to anyone who has ever paid a fine. For certain infractions of the rules, people must lose some reinforcer (money, time, privileges, pleasures). In a class, the concept of response cost may be applied in a number of ways. The first time a student breaks a class rule, the teacher gives a warning. The second time, the teacher makes a mark beside the student's name in the grade book. The student loses 2 minutes of recess for each mark accumulated. For older students, a certain number of marks might mean losing the privilege of working in a group or going on a class trip.

Try to structure the situation so you can use negative reinforcement rather than punishment.

Examples

1. Allow students to escape unpleasant situations (completing additional workbook assignments, weekly tests of math facts) when they reach a level of competence.
2. Insist on actions, not promises. Don't let students convince you to change terms of the agreement.

Be consistent in your application of punishment.

Examples

1. Avoid inadvertently reinforcing the behavior you are trying to punish. Keep confrontations private, so that students don't become heroes for standing up to the teacher in a public showdown.
2. Let students know in advance the consequences of breaking the rules by posting major class rules for younger students or outlining rules and consequences in a course syllabus for older students.
3. Tell students they will receive only one warning before punishment is given. Give the warning in a calm way, then follow through.
4. Make punishment as unavoidable and immediate as is reasonably possible.

Focus on the students' actions, not on the students' personal qualities.

Examples

1. Reprimand in a calm but firm voice.
2. Avoid vindictive or sarcastic words or tones of voice. You might hear your own angry words later when students imitate your sarcasm.
3. Stress the need to end the problem behavior instead of expressing any dislike you might feel for the student.

Adapt the punishment to the infraction.

Examples

1. Ignore minor misbehaviors that do not disrupt the class, or stop these misbehaviors with a disapproving glance or a move toward the student.
2. Don't use homework as a punishment for misbehaviors like talking in class.
3. When a student misbehaves to gain peer acceptance, removal from the group of friends can be effective, since this is really time out from a reinforcing situation.
4. If the problem behaviors continue, analyze the situation and try a new approach. Your punishment may not be very punishing, or you may be inadvertently reinforcing the misbehavior.

the stack of paper was gone. The student thought it was great fun for the first 10 minutes, but then she got weary and wanted to stop. After this experience, this student made better use of her independent work times.

Example: *Soft reprimands:* During reading in Miss McCormick's first-grade class, she noticed that Kenny wasn't concentrating on his book. She was working with a group at the time and could have called out, "Kenny, you'd better get back to work. You're not concentrating," but she decided this would embarrass him as well as disturb the concentration of others. Instead, Miss McCormick walked over to him, asked him a couple of questions about the story, and asked him to let her know how the story ended. She achieved her goal without causing embarrassment, and she provided Kenny with an impetus and motive to concentrate on his story again.

Time Out Technically, the removal of all reinforcement. In practice, isolation of a student from the rest of the class for a brief time.

Social Isolation Removal of a disruptive student for 5 to 10 minutes.

Social Isolation. One of the most controversial behavioral methods for decreasing undesirable behavior is the strategy of **social isolation**, often called **time out** from reinforcement. The process involves removing a highly disruptive student from the classroom for 5 to 10 minutes. The student is placed in an empty, uninteresting room alone. It seems likely that the factor that actually decreases behavior is the punishment of brief isolation from other people (O'Leary & O'Leary, 1976). A trip to the principal's office or confinement to a chair in the corner of the regular classroom does not have the same effect as sitting alone in an empty room.

Some Cautions.   Punishment in and of itself does not lead to any positive behavior. Thus, whenever you consider the use of punishment, you should make it part of a two-pronged attack. The first goal is to carry out the punishment and suppress the undesirable behavior. The second goal is to make clear what the student should be doing instead and to provide reinforcement for those desirable actions. Thus, while the problem behaviors are being suppressed, positive alternative responses are being strengthened.

Versions of social isolation are sometimes used as methods for decreasing undesirable behavior.

Social Cognitive Theory Theory that emphasizes learning through observation of others.

Reciprocal Determinism An explanation of behavior that emphasizes the mutual effects of the individual and the environment on each other.

Social Learning Theory   Test Bank items 6.74, 6.94, 6.126

In recent years, most behavioral psychologists have found that operant conditioning offers too limited an explanation of learning. Many have expanded their view of learning to include the study of cognitive processes that cannot be directly observed, such as expectations, thoughts, and beliefs. A prime example of this expanded view is Albert Bandura's (1986) **social cognitive theory.** Bandura believes that the traditional behavioral views of learning, while accurate, are incomplete. They give only a partial explanation of learning and overlook important aspects of the situation, particularly the important social influences on learning.

Bandura distinguishes between the *acquisition of knowledge* (learning) and the *observable performance based on that knowledge* (behavior). In other words, Bandura suggests that we all may know more than we show. Students may have learned how to simplify fractions, but perform badly on a test because they are anxious or ill or have misread the problem. While learning may have occurred, it may not be demonstrated until the situation is right. In social cognitive theory, therefore, both internal and external factors are important. Environmental events, personal factors (such as thinking and motivation), and behavior are seen as interacting, each influencing the others in the process of learning. Bandura calls this interaction of forces **reciprocal determinism.**

One factor overlooked by traditional behavioral theories is the powerful effect that modeling and imitation can have on learning. People and animals can learn merely by observing another person or animal learn, and this fact challenges the behaviorist idea that cognitive factors are unnecessary in an explanation of learning. If people can learn by watching, they must be focusing their attention, constructing images, remembering, analyzing, and making decisions that affect learning.

Learning by Observing Others

Test Bank items 6.71, 6.72, 6.76, 6.124

When Elizabeth laughed at the "Clark Gable" comment in class, she communicated that laughing was appropriate in this situation. Soon all the students were laughing along with her, and she did not try to stop them until it was too late. They were learning through modeling or observation, even though this was not the type of learning Elizabeth had intended. Elizabeth, through her behavior, provided a model for her students to imitate.

There are two main modes of **observational learning.** First, observational learning can take place through **vicarious reinforcement.** This happens when we see others being rewarded or punished for particular actions and then modify our behavior as if we had received the consequences ourselves. For example, if you compliment two students on the attractive illustrations in their lab reports, several other students who observe your compliments may turn in illustrated lab reports next time. This demonstrates vicarious reinforcement. Punishment can also be vicarious: you may slow down on a stretch of highway after seeing several people get speeding tickets there. Through modeling we learn not only how to perform a behavior but also what will happen to us in specific situations if we do perform it.

In the second kind of observational learning, the observer imitates the behavior of a model even though the model receives no reinforcement or punishment while the observer is watching. Often the model is demonstrating something the observer wants to learn and expects to be reinforced for mastering; for example, the proper way to position hands while playing a piano or the correct way to assemble laboratory equipment. But imitation can also occur when the observer simply wants to become more like an admired or high-status model. Models need not be real people. We may also use fictional characters or stereotypical images as models and try to behave as we imagine the model would (Hill, 1990).

Observation can be a very efficient learning process. The first time children hold hairbrushes, cups, tennis rackets, or steering wheels, they usually brush, drink, swing, or steer as well as they can, given their current muscle development and coordination. Let's take a closer look at how observational learning occurs.

Elements of Observational Learning

Test Bank items 6.73, 6.75, 6.106, 6.107, 6.114, 6.124

Bandura (1986) notes that there are four important elements to be considered in observational learning. They are *paying attention, retaining information or impressions, producing behaviors,* and *being motivated* to repeat the behaviors.

Attention.   In order to learn through observation, we have to pay attention. We typically pay attention to people who are attractive, popular, competent, or admired (Sulzer-Azaroff & Mayer, 1986). For younger children this could mean parents, older brothers or sisters, or teachers. For older students it may mean popular peers, rock stars, or TV idols.

In teaching, you will have to ensure students' attention to the critical features of the lesson by making clear presentations and highlighting important

Casebook: See the Teachers' Casebook for practicing teachers' ideas about how to handle inappropriate behavior in the classroom.

Objective 6.16: Identify negative side effects of punishment and explain how punishment can be used appropriately.

Teaching Tip: A good topic for class discussion is whether corporal punishment should be used in schools. Three possible formats: whole-class discussion, in which students can express whatever views they want; class debate, in which students are assigned a certain position to take; and small-group discussion, in which the issue is discussed in groups of four to seven students, each group reporting to the class as a whole.

Discussion: What are some forms of punishment used in the public schools? In the long run, does the punishment decrease or extinguish the behavior for which it is given? Ask students to give some examples of punishment (according to the teacher's view) being experienced by the student as reinforcement.

Examples: Other examples of learning through the observation of others include: learning how to kiss by watching TV and movies; avoiding air travel after witnessing a plane wreck; cheating on a test after seeing someone else cheat without getting caught.

Observational Learning Learning by observation and imitation of others.

Vicarious Reinforcement Increasing the chances that we will repeat a behavior by observing another person being reinforced for that behavior.

Transparency: Use acetate transparency T 53 as an example of how advertisers use classical conditioning.

Transparency: Use acetate transparency T 51, "Key Factors in Observational Learning."

Connections: Sense of self-efficacy is discussed more fully in chapter 9, as is the related concept of teacher efficacy.

Example: *Modeling:*

In Mrs. B's second-grade classroom, the use of vicarious reinforcement brings many positive results: improved concentration, neater work habits, responsible behavior, interest, and enthusiasm for extra projects.

As the children were working on a social studies project, Mrs. B. noticed that at a table with four children, two were concentrating and two were fooling around. Her comments to the two children who were working helped the other two children to focus their attention back onto their tasks. "Why, Christine and Robert, you're doing such a fine job on your map. I can tell you're concentrating and putting your best effort into it." When she noticed that the other two had gone back to work, she commented, "I'm happy to see that you're both working so well. You do such a nice job when you concentrate." All four children worked responsibly throughout the rest of the period. Similar procedures are used to help achieve neat work habits and responsible behavior.

Objective 6.17: Define observational learning. Include its five effects in the definition.

Self-Efficacy A person's sense of being able to deal effectively with a particular task.

points. In demonstrating a skill (for example, threading a sewing machine or operating a lathe), you may need to have students look over your shoulder as you work. Seeing your hands from the same perspective as they see their own directs their attention to the right features of the situation and makes observational learning easier.

Retention.   In order to imitate the behavior of a model, you have to remember it. This involves mentally representing the model's actions in some way, probably as verbal steps ("Hwa-Rang, the eighth form in Tae Kwan Do karate, is a palm-heel block, then a middle riding stance punch, then . . ."), or as visual images, or both. Retention can be improved by mental rehearsal (imagining imitating the behavior) or by actual practice. In the retention phase of observational learning, practice helps us remember the elements of the desired behavior, such as the sequence of steps.

Production.   Once we "know" how a behavior should look and remember the elements or steps, we still may not perform it smoothly. Sometimes we need a great deal of practice, feedback, and coaching about subtle points before we can reproduce the behavior of the model. In the production phase, practice makes the behaviors smoother and more expert. A sense of **self-efficacy,** the belief that we are capable of performing the behavior, is important at this phase and influences our motivation to perform.

Motivation and Reinforcement.   As mentioned earlier, social cognitive theory distinguishes between acquisition and performance. We may acquire a new skill or behavior through observation, but we may not perform that behavior until there is some motivation or incentive to do so. Reinforcement can play several roles in observational learning. If we anticipate being reinforced for imitating the actions of a model, we may be more motivated to pay attention, remember, and reproduce the behaviors. In addition, reinforcement is important in maintaining learning. A person who tries a new behavior is unlikely to persist without reinforcement (Barton, 1981; Ollendick, Dailey, & Shapiro, 1983). For example, if an unpopular student adopted the dress of the "in" group but was greeted with teasing and ridicule, it is unlikely that the imitation would continue.

Bandura identifies three forms of reinforcement that can encourage observational learning. First, of course, the observer may reproduce the behaviors of the model and receive direct reinforcement, as when a gymnast successfully executes a front flip/round-off combination and the coach/model says, "Excellent!" But the reinforcement need not be direct—it may be vicarious reinforcement as well. As mentioned earlier, the observer may simply see others reinforced for a particular behavior and then increase his or her production of that behavior. Most TV ads hope for this kind of effect. People in commercials become deliriously happy when they drive a particular car or drink a specific juice, and the viewer is supposed to do the same; the viewer's behavior is reinforced vicariously by the actors' obvious pleasure. The final form of reinforcement is self-reinforcement, or controlling your own reinforcers. This sort of reinforcement is important for both students and teachers. We want our students to improve not because it leads to external rewards but because the students value and enjoy their growing competence. And as a teacher, sometimes self-reinforcement is all that keeps you going.

Observational Learning in Teaching

Test Bank items 6.76–6.79, 6.95, 6.124

There are five possible outcomes of observational learning: teaching new behaviors and attitudes, encouraging existing behaviors, changing inhibitions, directing attention, and arousing emotions. Let's look at each of these as they occur in classrooms.

Teaching New Behaviors.   **Modeling** has long been used, of course, to teach dance, sports, and crafts, as well as skills in subjects such as home economics, chemistry, and shop. Modeling can also be applied deliberately in the classroom to teach mental skills and to broaden horizons—to teach new ways of thinking. Teachers serve as models for a vast range of behaviors, from pronouncing vocabulary words, to reacting to the seizure of an epileptic student, to being enthusiastic about learning. For example, a teacher might model sound critical thinking skills by thinking "out loud" about a student's question. Or a high school teacher concerned about girls who seem to have stereotyped ideas about careers might invite women with nontraditional jobs to speak to the class.

Modeling, when applied deliberately, can be an effective and efficient means of teaching new behavior (Bandura, 1986; Schunk, 1987). Studies indicate that modeling can be most effective when the teacher makes use of all the elements of observational learning described in the previous section, especially reinforcement and practice.

Models who are the same age as the students may be particularly effective. For example, Schunk and Hanson (1985) compared two methods for teaching subtraction to second graders who had difficulties learning this skill. One group of students observed other second graders learning the procedures, then participated in an instructional program on subtraction. Another group of students watched a teacher's demonstration, then participated in the same instructional program. Of the two groups, the students who observed peer models learning not only scored higher on tests of subtraction after instruction, but also gained more confidence in their own ability to learn. For students who doubt their own abilities, a good model is a low-achieving student who keeps trying and finally masters the material (Schunk, 1987).

Encouraging Already-Learned Behaviors.   All of us have had the experience of looking for cues from other people when we find ourselves in unfamiliar situations. Observing the behavior of others tells us which of our already-learned behaviors to use: the proper fork for eating the salad, when to leave a gathering, what kind of language is appropriate, and so on. Adopting the dress and grooming styles of TV idols is another example of this kind of effect.

Strengthening or Weakening Inhibitions.   If class members witness one student breaking a class rule and getting away with it, they may learn that undesirable consequences do not always follow rule-breaking. The class may

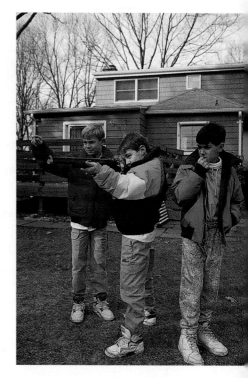

Models of aggressive or violent behavior are readily available to children who watch television or go to the movies.

Activity 6.10: Background. For a complete review of the research on peer modeling, see Schunk, D. H. (1987). Peer models and children's behavioral change. *Review of Educational Research, 57,* 149–174. The abstract for the article appears in the *Instructor's Resource Manual.*

Modeling   Changes in behavior, thinking, or emotions that occur through observing another person —a model.

Application: Students tend to "test limits," especially with new teachers. Why is it important for a teacher to deal decisively with such a situation? (Use the concepts of observational learning and the ripple effect.)

Focus on . . .   **Social Learning Theory**

- What is vicarious reinforcement?
- Describe the four elements of observational learning.
- What are the possible outcomes of obervational learning? Give an example of each outcome from your own experience.

Research: Zimmerman, B. J. (1990). Self-regulated learning and academic achievement: An overview. *Educational Psychologist, 21,* 3–18. Zimmerman's article introduces a special issue of *Educational Psychologist* on self-regulated learning.

Activity 6.11: Background. See the *Instructor's Resource Manual* for Self-Management, a summary of research conducted by B. H. Manning on cognitive behavior modification.

Connections: Point out that concern with self-management is not restricted to any one group or theory. Psychologists who study Vygotsky's ideas about cognitive development (chapter 2) are involved, as are cognitive psychologists interested in learning strategies (chapters 7 and 8) and motivational psychologists pointing to self-regulation as a critical factor in motivation (chapters 9 and 10).

Ripple Effect "Contagious" spreading of behaviors through imitation.

Self-Management Use of behavioral learning principles to change your own behavior.

be less inhibited in the future about breaking this rule. If the rule-breaker is a well-liked, high-status class leader, the effect of the modeling may be even more pronounced. One psychologist has called this phenomenon the **ripple effect** (Kounin, 1970). The ripple effect can work for the teacher's benefit. When the teacher deals effectively with a rule-breaker, especially a class leader, the idea of breaking this rule may be inhibited for the other students viewing the interaction. This does not mean that teachers must reprimand each student who breaks a rule, but once a teacher has called for a particular action, following through is an important part of capitalizing on the ripple effect.

Directing Attention.   By observing others, we not only learn about actions, we also notice the objects involved in the actions. For example, in a preschool class, when one child plays enthusiastically with a toy that has been ignored for days, many other children may want to have the toy, even if they play with it in different ways or simply carry it around. This happens, in part, because the children's attention has been drawn to that particular toy.

Arousing Emotion.   Finally, through observational learning people may develop emotional reactions to situations they themselves have never experienced, such as flying or driving. A child who watches a friend fall from a swing and break an arm may become fearful of swings. Students may be anxious when they are assigned to a certain teacher because they've heard frightening stories about how "mean" that teacher is. Note that hearing and reading about a situation are also forms of observation. The Guidelines will give you some ideas about using observational learning in the classroom.

Self-Regulation and Cognitive Behavior Modification

Test Bank items 6.80, 6.82, 6.108, 6.119, 6.125–6.127

The most recent application of behavioral views of learning emphasizes **self-management**—helping students gain control of their own learning. As you will see throughout this book, the role of students in their own learning is a major concern of psychologists and educators today. This concern is not restricted to any one group or theory. Different areas of research and theory all converge on one important idea, that responsibility and the ability to learn rest within the student. No one can learn for someone else (Manning, 1991; Zimmerman, 1990; Zimmerman & Schunk, 1989).

One reason that behavioral psychologists became interested in self-management is that students taught with classic behavioral methods seldom generalized their learning to new situations. For example, in my dissertation research I found that inattentive students could learn to pay excellent attention to lessons when they were systematically reinforced in a small group. But when they returned to the regular classroom, they did not take their new skill back with them (Woolfolk & Woolfolk, 1974). Many behavioral psychologists de-

Guidelines

Using Observational Learning

Model behaviors and attitudes you want your students to learn.

Examples

1. Show enthusiasm for the subject you teach.
2. Be willing to demonstrate both the mental and the physical tasks you expect the students to perform. I once saw a teacher sit down in the sandbox while her 4-year-old students watched her demonstrate the difference between "playing with sand" and "throwing sand."
3. When reading to students, model good problem solving. Stop and say, "Now let me see if I remember what happened so far," or "That was a hard sentence. I'm going to read it again."

Use peers as models.

Examples

1. In group work, pair students who do well with those who are having difficulties.
2. Ask students to demonstrate the difference between "whispering" and "silence—no talking."

Make sure students see that positive behaviors lead to reinforcement for others.

Examples

1. Point out the connections between positive behavior and positive consequences in stories.
2. Be fair in giving reinforcement. The same rules for rewards should apply to the problem students as to the good students.

Enlist the help of class leaders in modeling behaviors for the entire class.

Examples

1. Ask a well-liked student to be friendly to an isolated, fearful student.
2. Let high-status students lead an activity when you need class cooperation or when students are likely to be reluctant at first. Popular students can model dialogues in foreign-language classes or be the first to tackle dissection procedures in biology.

cided that generalization would be encouraged if students became partners in the behavior change procedures. About this same time, Donald Meichenbaum (1977) was having success teaching impulsive students to "talk themselves through" tasks, so there was evidence that students could benefit from what Meichenbaum termed "cognitive behavior modification" (Manning, 1991).

Self-Management

If one goal of education is to produce people capable of educating themselves, then students must learn to manage their own lives, set their own goals, and provide their own reinforcement. In adult life, rewards are sometimes vague

Objective 6.19: State the value and the procedures in a self-management program.

Application: Self-management can be used to encourage social behavior. This self-recording form is taken from Jenson, W. R., Sloane, H. N., & Young, K. R. (1988). *Applied behavior analysis in education: A structured teaching approach.* Englewood Cliffs, NJ: Prentice-Hall, p. 272.

SOCIAL SKILLS PRACTICE CARD

Name _____

Date _____

Things to remember:

Use your new skill.

Take this card with you and mark it when you use the social skill.

Social Skill: _____

Where?	How many times?				
	1	2	3	4	5
1. In class					
2. On the playground					
3. At lunch					
4. At home					
5. Other					

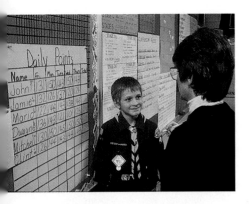

Students may benefit from participating in the evaluation, or self-recording, of their own performance.

and goals often take a long time to reach. Think how many small steps are required to complete an education and find your first job. Life is filled with tasks that call for this sort of self-management (Kanfer & Gaelick, 1986).

Students may be involved in any or all of the steps in implementing a basic behavior change program. They may help set goals, observe their own work, keep records of it, and evaluate their own performance. Finally, they can select and deliver reinforcement. Such involvement can help students learn to perform all the steps on their own in the future (Kaplan, 1991).

Goal Setting.   It appears that the goal-setting phase is very important in self-management. In fact, some research suggests that setting specific goals and making them public may be the critical elements of self-management programs. For example, S. C. Hayes and his colleagues identified college students who had serious problems with studying and taught them how to set specific study goals. Students who set goals and announced them to the experimenters performed significantly better on tests covering the material they were studying than students who set goals privately and never revealed them to anyone (Hayes, Rosenfarb, Wulfert, Munt, Korn, & Zettle, 1985).

Higher standards tend to lead to higher performance (McLaughlin & Gnagey, 1981). Unfortunately, student-set goals have a tendency to become lower and lower. Teachers can help students maintain high standards by monitoring the goals set and reinforcing high standards. In one study, a teacher helped first-grade students raise the number of math problems they set for themselves to work on each day by praising them whenever they increased their objective by 10 percent. The students maintained their new, higher work standards, and the improvements even generalized to other subjects (Price & O'Leary, 1974).

Recording and Evaluating Progress.   Students may also participate in the recording and evaluation phases of a behavior change program. Some examples of behaviors that are appropriate for self-recording are the number of assignments completed, time spent practicing a skill, number of books read, and number of times out of seat without permission. Tasks that must be accomplished without teacher supervision, like homework or private study, are also good candidates for self-monitoring. Students keep a chart, diary, or checklist recording the frequency or duration of the behaviors in question.

A progress record card can help older students break down assignments into small steps, determine the best sequence for completing the steps, and keep track of daily progress by setting goals for each day. The record card itself serves as a prompt that can be faded out (Jenson, Sloane, & Young, 1988). Because cheating on records is a potential problem, especially when students are rewarded for improvements, intermittent checking by the teacher plus bonus points for accurate recording may be helpful (Hundert & Bucher, 1978).

Self-evaluation is somewhat more difficult than simple self-recording because it involves making a judgment about quality. Very few studies have been conducted in this area, but it appears that students can learn to evaluate their behavior with reasonable accuracy (Rhode, Morgan, & Young, 1983). One key seems to be periodically checking students' self-evaluations and giving reinforcement for accurate judgments. Older students may learn accurate self-evaluation more readily than younger students. Again, bonus points can be awarded when the teachers' and students' evaluations match (Kaplan, 1991).

A study conducted by Mark Morgan (1985) combined goal setting, self-recording, and self-evaluation. Morgan taught self-monitoring strategies to all the education students in the required educational psychology course at his college. The students who set specific short-term objectives for each study unit and monitored their progress toward the objectives outperformed the students who simply monitored study time, even though the students who monitored their time actually spent more hours studying!

Self-Reinforcement.   The last step in self-management is **self-reinforcement**. There is some disagreement, however, as to whether this step is actually necessary. Some psychologists believe that setting goals and monitoring progress alone are sufficient and that self-reinforcement adds nothing to the effects (Hayes et al., 1985). Others believe that rewarding yourself for a job well done can lead to higher levels of performance than simply setting goals and keeping track of progress (Bandura, 1986). If you are willing to be tough and really deny yourself something you want until your goals are reached, then perhaps the promise of the reward can provide extra incentive for work. With that in mind, you may want to think of some way to reinforce yourself when you finish reading this chapter. A similar approach helped me write the chapter in the first place.

Teaching Tip: Show students examples of recording forms for self-monitoring, such as those available in E. Workman's *Teaching Behavioral Self-Control to Students* (1982).

Discussion: There is one student in your class who is never prepared to do his work. He doesn't have a pencil, has misplaced his book, left his homework at home, doesn't understand the assignment, forgot to buy notebook paper, and so on. The result of all this is that he seldom hands in his homework assignments. How would you approach this problem? Develop several alternative strategies, such as reward and punishment, shaping, or self-management.

Guidelines

Instituting Self-Management Programs

Introduce the system in a positive way.

Examples

1. Emphasize the system in a positive way.
2. Consider starting the program just with volunteers.
3. Describe how you use self-management programs yourself.

Help students learn to set appropriate goals.

Examples

1. Monitor goals frequently at first, and praise reasonably high standards.
2. Make goals public by having students tell you or members of their work group what they want to accomplish.

Provide a way for students to record and evaluate their progress.

Examples

1. Divide the work into easily measured steps.
2. Provide models of good work where judgments are more difficult, such as in creative writing.
3. Give students a record form or checklist to keep track of progress.

Check the accuracy of student records from time to time, and encourage students to develop forms of self-reinforcement.

Examples

1. Have many checkups when students are first learning, fewer later.
2. Have students check one another's records.
3. Where appropriate, test the skills that students are supposed to be developing and reward students whose self-evaluations match their test performances.
4. Have students brainstorm ideas for rewarding themselves for jobs well done.

Self-Reinforcement   Providing yourself with positive consequences, contingent on accomplishing a particular behavior.

Sometimes, teaching students self-management can solve a problem for teachers and provide fringe benefits as well. For example, the coaches of a competitive swim team with members aged 9 to 16 were having difficulty persuading swimmers to maintain high work rates. Then the coaches drew up four charts indicating the training program to be followed by each member and posted the charts near the pool. The swimmers were given the responsibility of recording their numbers of laps and completion of each training unit. Because the recording was public, swimmers could see their own progress and that of others, give and receive congratulations, and keep accurate track of the work units completed. Work output increased by 27 percent. The coaches also liked the system because swimmers could begin to work immediately without waiting for instructions (McKenzie & Rushall, 1974).

Cognitive Behavior Modification

Test Bank items 6.81, 6.96, 6.109, 6.119, 6.125, 6.127, 6.128

Objective 6.18: Describe the processes of self-regulation and cognitive behavior modification.

Discussion: Assign Harris, K. R. (1990). Developing self-regulated learners: The role of private speech and self-instruction. *Educational Psychologist, 21,* 35–50. *Focus Question:* Ask your students to summarize the ways that private speech can help guide children's learning.

Self-management generally means getting students involved in the basic steps of a behavior change program. **Cognitive behavior modification** adds an emphasis on thinking and self-talk to the package. For this reason, many psychologists consider cognitive behavior modification more a cognitive than a behavioral approach. I present it here because it serves as a bridge to the coming chapters on cognitive learning.

As noted in chapter 2, there is a stage in cognitive development when young children seem to guide themselves through a task using private speech. They talk to themselves, often repeating the words of a parent or teacher. In cognitive behavior modification, students are taught directly how to use **self-instruction.** Meichenbaum (1977) outlined the steps:

1. An adult model performs a task while talking to self out loud (cognitive modeling).

2. The child performs the same task under the direction of the model's instructions (overt, external guidance).

3. The child performs the task while instructing self aloud (overt, self-guidance).

4. The child whispers the instructions to self as he/she goes through the task (faded, overt self-guidance).

5. The child performs the task while guiding his/her performance via private speech (covert self-instruction). (p. 32)

Cognitive Behavior Modification Procedures based on both behavioral and cognitive learning principles for changing your own behavior by using self-talk and self-instruction.

Self-Instruction Talking oneself through the steps of a task.

Actually, cognitive behavior modification as it is practiced by Meichenbaum and others has many more components than just teaching students to use covert self-instruction. Meichenbaum's methods also include dialogue and interaction between teacher and student, modeling, guided discovery, motivational strategies, feedback, careful matching of the task with the student's developmental level, and other principles of good teaching. The student is even involved in designing the program (Harris, 1990; Harris & Pressley, in press). Given all this, it is no surprise that students do seem to generalize to new learning situations the skills developed with cognitive behavior modification (Harris, Graham, & Pressley, in press).

Should Students Be Rewarded for Learning?

For years educators and psychologists have debated whether students should be rewarded for school work and academic accomplishments. As a recent example, Paul Chance and Alfie Kohn exchanged opinions in several issues of *Phi Delta Kappan:* Kohn, A. (1991, March). "Caring kids: The role of the schools"; Chance, P. (1991, June). "Backtalk: A gross injustice"; Chance, P. (1992, November). "The rewards of learning"; Kohn, A. (1993, June). "Rewards versus learning: A response to Paul Chance"; Chance, P. (1993, June). "Sticking up for rewards."

POINT **Students are punished by rewards.**

Alfie Kohn (1993) argues that "Applied behaviorism, which amounts to saying, 'do this and you'll get that,' is essentially a technique for controlling people. In the classroom it is a way of doing things *to* children rather than working *with* them" (p. 784). Kohn goes on to contend that rewards are ineffective because when the praise and prizes stop, the behaviors stop too. "Rewards (like punishments) can get people to do what we want: buckle up, share a toy, read a book. . . . But they rarely produce effects that survive the rewards themselves. . . . They do not create an enduring *commitment* to a set of values or to learning;

they merely, and temporarily, change what we do" (p. 784).

The problem with rewards does not stop here. According to Kohn, rewarding students for learning actually makes them less interested in the material:

All of this means that getting children to think about learning as a way to receive a sticker, a gold star, or a grade—or even worse, to get money or a toy *for* a grade, which amounts to an extrinsic motivator for an extrinsic motivator—is likely to turn learning from an end into a means. Learning becomes something that must be gotten through in order to receive the reward. Take the depressingly pervasive program by which children receive certificates for pizzas when they have read a certain number of books. John Nicholls of the University of Illinois comments, only half in jest, that the likely consequence of this program is 'a lot of fat kids who don't like to read.' (p. 785)

COUNTERPOINT **Learning should be rewarding.**

According to Paul Chance (1993):

Behavioral psychologists in particular emphasize that we learn by *acting on* our environment. As B. F. Skinner put it: "[People] act on the world, and change it, and are changed in turn by the consequences of their actions." Skinner, unlike Kohn, understood that people learn best in a responsive envi-

ronment. Teachers who praise or otherwise reward student performance provide such an environment. . . . If it is immoral to let students know they have answered questions correctly, to pat students on the back for a good effort, to show joy at a student's understanding of a concept, or to recognize the achievement of a goal by providing a gold star or a certificate—if this is immoral, then count me a sinner (p. 788).

Even psychologists such as Edward Deci and Mark Lepper who suggest that rewards might undermine intrinsic motivation agree that rewards can also be used positively. When rewards provide students with information about their growing mastery of a subject or when the rewards show appreciation for a job well done, then the rewards bolster confidence and make the task more interesting to the students. Nothing succeeds like success. If students master reading or mathematics with the support of rewards, they are able to read or solve problems in ways they could not before. They will not forget what they have learned when the praise stops. Would they have learned without the rewards? Some would, but some might not. Would you continue working for a company that didn't pay you? Would the freelance writer Alfie Kohn, for that matter, lose interest in writing because he gets paid fees and royalties?

Poor readers have been taught a set of self-instructions to guide reading. They learn to ask themselves questions about the content as they go along, outline each passage in their heads, relate the ideas in the reading to other information, and so on (Bornstein, 1985; Dush, Hirt, & Schroeder, 1983; Meichenbaum, 1977). One important aspect of the self-instructional approach is to give students something concrete to do that focuses their attention. This

Activity 6.12: Background. Extrinsic versus Intrinsic Rewards. See the *Instructor's Resource Manual* for a demonstration of intrinsic reward as education's future.

task must fit the goals of the particular situation. Asking questions as you read, for example, not only helps maintain attention but also helps you understand what you are reading. Some other system, like imagining painful punishment every time your mind wanders, might keep you focused on the words in the book, but it probably would not improve comprehension. Of course, students must also be capable of the tasks they are instructing themselves to do. Self-instructional support for reading will do little good if the passage is too difficult for the student (Harris, 1990).

roblems and Issues

The preceding sections provide an overview of several strategies for changing classroom behavior. However, you should be aware that these strategies are tools that may be used responsibly or irresponsibly. What, then, are some issues you should keep in mind?

Ethical Issues   Test Bank items 6.85, 6.118

Objective 6.20: Discuss the ethical issues involved in a behavior change program.

Objective 6.21: Name two potential drawbacks to the use of behavioral methods and explain how they can be counteracted in the classroom.

Discussion: Assign Canter, L. (1989). Assertive discipline—More than names on the board and marbles in a jar. *Phi Delta Kappan*, 71(1) 41–56. *Focus Question:* Ask your students to evaluate Canter's claims for his approach. What are the similarities between the criticisms of behavioral approaches to learning and the criticisms of "assertive discipline?"

Background: See Noll, J. W. (1991). *Taking sides: Clashing views on controversial educational issues* (5th ed.). Guilford, CT: Duskin (pp. 82–97), for "Do External Controls Provide the Best Learning Stimulus?"

The ethical questions related to the use of the strategies described in this chapter are similar to those raised by any process that seeks to influence people. What are the goals? How do these goals fit in with those of the school as a whole? Might students be rewarded for the "wrong" thing, though it seems "right" at first? By what criteria should strategies be chosen? What effect will a strategy have on the individuals involved? Is too much control being given to the teacher, or to a majority?

Goals.   The strategies described in this chapter could be applied exclusively to teach students to sit still, raise their hands before speaking, and remain silent at all other times (Winett & Winkler, 1972). This certainly would be an unethical use of the techniques. It is true that a teacher may need to establish some organization and order, but stopping with improvements in conduct will not ensure academic learning. On the other hand, in some situations, reinforcing academic skills may lead to improvements in conduct. Whenever possible, emphasis should be placed on academic learning. Academic improvements generalize to other situations more successfully than do changes in classroom conduct.

Strategies.   As noted earlier, punishment can have negative side effects: it can serve as a model for aggressive responses, and it can encourage negative emotional reactions. Punishment is unnecessary and even unethical when positive approaches, which have fewer potential dangers, might work as well. A set of guidelines originally prepared to select programs for retarded students

Guidelines

1. Use behavioral methods in appropriate contexts to reinforce positive academic and social learning behaviors, not merely to enforce rules of conduct.
2. Encourage student awareness of and cooperation in behavioral change programs. So far as possible, make sure changes in behavior occur for reasons students themselves understand and accept.
3. Know your students. Fit behavioral strategies to the special needs of each one, carefully considering all possible consequences. This includes carefully selecting reinforcers and fitting rewards to the individual. Consult with parents and school professionals to ensure that a reinforcement program is appropriate for, and will not harm, the student. At the same time, consider the needs of other students and of the whole group when implementing reinforcement programs that target particular individuals.
4. Use reinforcement selectively and only when needed. Try the simplest, most positive, least restrictive, and least intrusive procedures first. Leave as much responsibility for learning as possible in the hands of students.
5. Encourage reliance on intrinsic rewards and incentives first and whenever possible. Make sure extrinsic rewards are understood as symbols of task mastery and not as ends in themselves. Phase out reward systems as student motivation and success improve.

Making Ethical Use of Behavioral Methods

offers a logical progression of strategies that may be applied in any classroom setting (American Psychological Association, 1976). When simpler, less-restrictive procedures fail, then more complicated procedures should be tried. Table 6.3 shows a general hierarchy based on these guidelines.

A second consideration in the selection of a strategy is the impact of the strategy on the individual student. For example, some teachers arrange for students to be rewarded at home with a gift or activities based on good work in school. But if a student has a history of being severely punished at home for bad reports from school, a home-based reinforcement program might be very harmful to that student. Reports of unsatisfactory progress at school could lead to increased abuse at home.

Activity 6.13: Background. See the *Instructor's Resource Manual* for Extrinsic Rewards Are Education's Past, Not Its Future, a summary of several recent *Educational Leadership* articles debating the use of external rewards.

Teaching Tip: You might note that many critics agree behavior modification works, but not for the reasons stated by behaviorists. These critics say that consequences provide information, not strengthening of associations.

Background: For a debate on the value of using rewards in teaching, see Chance, P. (1992). The rewards of learning. *Phi Delta Kappan, 73;* Kohn, A. (1993). Rewards versus learning: A response to Paul Chance. *Phi Delta Kappan, 74,* 783–787; and Chance, P. (1993). Sticking up for rewards. *Phi Delta Kappan, 74,* 787–790.

TABLE 6.3 Choosing Strategies for Classroom Management

First try:	Praising positive behaviors and ignoring undesirable behaviors.
If that doesn't work, try:	Praise-and-ignore techniques with prompting and cueing, soft reprimands, modeling, or shaping.
If that doesn't work, try:	Praise-and-ignore techniques with negative reinforcement, satiation, response cost, or social isolation.

Criticisms of Behavioral Methods   Test Bank items 6.85, 6.118

Properly used, the strategies in this chapter can be effective tools to help students learn academically and grow in self-sufficiency. Effective tools, however, do not automatically produce excellent work. The indiscriminate use of even the best tools can lead to difficulties. Critics of behavioral methods point to two basic problems that may arise.

Some psychologists fear that rewarding students for all learning will cause the students to lose interest in learning for its own sake (Deci, 1975; Deci & Ryan, 1985; Kohn, 1993; Lepper & Greene, 1978). Studies have suggested that using reward programs with students who are already interested in the subject matter may, in fact, cause students to be less interested in the subject when the reward program ends as you can see in the Point/Counterpoint on page 229.

Just as you must take into account the effects of a reward system on the individual, you must also consider the impact on other students. Using a reward program or giving one student increased attention may have a detrimental effect on the other students in the classroom. Is it possible that other students will learn to be "bad" in order to be included in the reward program? Most of the evidence on this question suggests that reward programs do not have any adverse effects on students who are not participating in the program if the teacher believes in the program and explains the reasons for using it to the nonparticipating students (Christy, 1975). If the conduct of some students does seem to deteriorate when their peers are involved in special programs, many of the same procedures discussed in this chapter should help them return to previous levels of appropriate behavior (Chance, 1992, 1993).

Focus on ...   **Criticisms of Behavioral Approaches**

- Is it ever appropriate to reward students for learning? Why or why not?
- What are the main criticisms of behavioral approaches?

SUMMARY

Understanding Learning

Although theorists disagree about the definition of learning, most would agree that learning occurs when experience causes a change in a person's knowledge or behavior. Behavioral theorists emphasize the role of environmental stimuli in learning and focus on behavior—observable responses. Behavioral learning processes include contiguity learning, classical conditioning, operant conditioning, and observational learning.

Early View of Learning: Contiguity and Classical Conditioning

In contiguity learning, two events that repeatedly occur together become associated in the learner's mind. Later, the presence of one event causes the learner to remember the other.

In classical conditioning, discovered by Pavlov, a previously neutral stimulus is repeatedly paired with a stimulus that evokes an emotional or physiological response. Later, the previously neutral stimulus alone evokes the response—that is, the conditioned stimulus brings forth a conditioned response. Conditioned responses are subject to the processes of generalization, discrimination, and extinction.

Operant Conditioning: Trying New Responses

In operant conditioning, a theory of learning developed by B. F. Skinner, people learn through the effects of their deliberate responses. Operant conditioning is most applicable to classroom learning. For an individual, the effects of consequences following an action may serve as reinforcement or punishment. Positive and negative reinforcement strengthens a response, while punishment decreases or suppresses the behavior. In addition, the scheduling of reinforcement influences the rate and persistence of responses. Ratio schedules encourage higher rates of response, and variable schedules encourage persistence of responses. In addition to controlling consequences of behavior, teachers can also control the antecedents of behavior through cueing and prompting.

Applied Behavior Analysis

Applied behavior analysis provides teachers with methods for encouraging positive behaviors and coping with undesirable ones. Teachers can reinforce positive, appropriate student behavior through attention, recognition, praise, and the judicious use of reinforcers. The Premack principle, that a more-preferred activity can be used as a reinforcer for a less-preferred one, can help teachers choose effective reinforcers for individuals as well as groups. Teachers can use shaping and positive practice to help students develop new responses. Negative reinforcement, satiation, and forms of punishment—such as reprimands, response cost, and social isolation—can also help change behavior but must be used with caution.

Social Learning Theory

Social learning theorists such as Bandura emphasize the role of observation in learning and in nonobservable cognitive processes, such as thinking and knowing. Observational learning occurs through vicarious conditioning and imitation of high-status models and involves paying attention, retaining information or impressions, producing behaviors, and repeating behaviors through reinforcement or motivation. Teachers can use observational learning to teach new behaviors (providing peer models, for example), encourage already-learned behaviors, strengthen or weaken inhibitions, focus attention, or arouse emotions.

Self-Regulation and Cognitive Behavior Modification

Cognitive psychologists have influenced behavioral views, pointing, for example, to the importance of self-regulation in learning. Students can apply behavior analysis on their own to manage their own behavior. Teachers can encourage the development of self-management skills by allowing students to participate in setting goals, keeping track of progress, evaluating accomplishments, and selecting and giving their own reinforcements. Teachers can also use cognitive behavior modification, a behavior change program described by Meichenbaum in which students are directly taught how to use self-instruction.

Problems and Issues

The misuse or abuse of behavioral learning methods is unethical. Critics of behavioral methods also point out the danger that reinforcement could decrease interest in learning by overemphasizing rewards and could have a negative impact on other students. Guidelines do exist, however, for helping teachers use behavioral learning principles appropriately and ethically.

KEY TERMS

antecedents, p. 203
applied behavior analysis, p. 210
aversive, p. 204
behavioral learning theories, p. 197
behavior modification, p. 210
classical conditioning, p. 199
cognitive behavior modification,
    p. 228
conditioned response, p. 200
conditioned stimulus, p. 200
consequences, p. 203
contiguity, p. 199
continuous reinforcement schedule,
    p. 205
cueing, p. 208
discrimination, p. 200
extinction, p. 200
generalization, p. 200
intermittent reinforcement schedule,
    p. 205
interval schedule, p. 205

learning, p. 196
modeling, p. 223
negative reinforcement, p. 204
neutral stimulus, p. 200
observational learning, p. 221
operant conditioning, p. 202
operants, p. 202
positive practice, p. 216
positive reinforcement, p. 204
Premack principle, p. 211
presentation punishment,
    p. 205
prompt, p. 209
punishment, p. 205
ratio schedule, p. 205
reciprocal determinism, p. 220
reinforcement, p. 203
reinforcer, p. 203
removal punishment, p. 205
reprimands, p. 218
respondents, p. 202

response, p. 199
response cost, p. 218
ripple effect, p. 224
satiation, p. 218
self-efficacy, p. 222
self-instruction, p. 228
self-management, p. 224
self-reinforcement, p. 227
shaping, p. 215
Skinner box, p. 203
social cognitive theory, p. 220
social isolation, p. 219
stimulus, p. 199
stimulus control, p. 208
successive approximations, p. 215
task analysis, p. 215
time out, p. 219
unconditioned response, p. 200
unconditioned stimulus, p. 200
vicarious reinforcement, p. 221

WHAT WOULD YOU DO?

Preschool and Kindergarten

A student in your class is terrified of the class's pet guinea pigs. The child won't get close to the cages and wants you to "give them away." How would you help the child overcome this fear?

Elementary and Middle School

You were hired in January to take over the class of a teacher who moved away. The class is a nightmare! Evidently the teacher had no control over the students. They get up and walk around while you are reading to the class, interrupt you when you are working with a group, and seldom finish their classwork or homework. How would you approach the situation?

You want your students to improve their time management and self-management abilities so they will be prepared for the increased demands of high school next year. What would you do?

Junior High and High School

You have been assigned an emotionally disturbed student. She seemed fine at first, but now you notice that when she encounters difficult work, she often interrupts or teases other students. How would you work with this student and the class to improve the situation?

It takes you 10 minutes to get your class to settle down after the bell rings. Analyze this situation. What could be maintaining this problem? What would you do?

Cooperative Learning Activity

Work with two or three other members of your educational psychology class to develop a plan using applied behavior analysis to tackle one of the following problems:

> Three students who "hang out" together in your class repeatedly say insulting and disrespectful things to you, often in front of the entire class.

> Your class has gotten into the habit of ignoring due dates.

> One of the students in your class continues to attack other students verbally and physically.

Dealing with Inappropriate Behavior

The boys in your class perennially imitate the latest action heroes. Years ago it was
StarWars heroes wielding "the force"; then it was karate-chopping Ninja Turtles.
What do you do about this kind of behavior during class?

**RULES FOR IN-SCHOOL
PLAY**

Knowing that the average child spends 20 hours or better each week in front of a
television set compounds this problem. When we're having behavior problems, I
take some time and talk to the students about what is appropriate and inappropriate behavior for school. We talk about what is after-school play and in-school
play. From this basis, I lay down some ground rules of what will happen if they
choose to use inappropriate school behavior (lose a set amount of recess time or
special time), and then I always follow through with it.

Candice J. Gallagher, *Fourth-Grade Teacher*
Fredericktown Intermediate School, Fredericktown, Ohio

Behavior Management Programs

Have you ever used a systematic reward and/or punishment program with your
students, such as marbles in a jar for good behavior, demerits for rule violations,
or some other system? Why did you establish the program, and how did it work?

GRAB-BAG POINTS

I have used a point system to motivate students to stay on task and to do their best.
Before beginning the reward program, I surveyed the students to discover the type
of items they found rewarding. When a student accumulated 20 points, he or she
could choose from a grab bag filled with items such as free homework passes, pencils, markers, Hot Wheels, jewelry, stickers, books, game time cards, opportunity
to be the teacher for an instructional period cards, bookmarks, and even one class
pizza party certificate. The element of surprise created by the grab bags proved to
be the most motivating. I found the system to be very effective, but some expense
of time and money was involved for the teacher.

Joanne S. Groseclose, *Virginia 1991 Teacher of the Year*
Marion Intermediate School, Marion, Virginia

SIGNATURE CARDS

Systematic rewards for positive and negative behaviors work only if the students
have a say in the process.

I have used a system called Signature Cards. The Signature Card, a note card,
is placed either on an individual's desk or at a group table. When the individual or
group is not behaving according to set standards (set by the class), the student(s)
get my signature on the card. Each signature, or lack thereof, has positive and negative consequences. The type of consequence is a difficult problem. If the students
do not "buy in," the most elaborate system is useless. Recently, I tried a consensus-

building activity using a "fishbowl" to arrive at class consequences. The process is as follows:

1. Each student generates a list of positive and negative consequences for their appropriate actions. They are limited to six.
2. Each student then gets a partner and together they compromise on a list of six consequences, using each of their lists as a starting place.
3. Each pair joins another pair; this group of four then compromises on a set of six consequences.
4. Each group of four picks a spokesperson to support and defend the group's ideas.
5. All the spokespersons make a small circle in the middle of the room, while the other members make a large circle encompassing them.
6. The inner circle discusses and decides, by consensus, on six consequences for the class. The outer circle is to listen carefully.
7. If anyone in the room has a question or concern they call a time out. As in a football game, when one team calls a time out, the other teams consult also.
8. The teacher's role is to facilitate and record.
9. At the end of the process, six consequences for inappropriate behavior are generated by a consensus model and the students have "bought in" to the system.

Julie A. Addison, *Sixth-Grade Teacher*
Roxborough Elementary School, Littleton, Colorado

Catch the Child Being Good

According to one of the principles of operant conditioning, if you want to increase a child's desirable behavior, positively reinforce that behavior when it occurs. Teachers are told, "Catch the child being good." In the course of a busy school day, however, it is often difficult, especially for beginning teachers, to act on this advice and to feel natural and comfortable about it. How did you get yourself into the habit of noticing desirable behaviors?

REWARDS FOR PERSEVERANCE

As a first-year teacher, I quickly realized that I could "catch more flies with honey than vinegar." When I accentuated attention on the appropriate behavior displayed by students, discipline problems were substantially reduced and a healthy classroom environment was established. By constantly giving my attention to minor infractions, I was encouraging misbehavior and defiance of the school rules! I discovered that most of the same students who misbehaved for negative attention just as readily behaved for positive reinforcement.

Praise must be sincere to be effective. Children quickly recognize insincerity. They do not trust authority figures who are less than honest. In addition, descriptive praise is the most productive. A teacher should reinforce specific behavior. "Johnny, I like the way you blended the paints to make such an interesting blue sky," is a more descriptive and personal form of praise than "Johnny, that's a pretty picture."

Kathy Andrews, *Special Education Teacher*
Lane Center for Exceptional Children, Houston, Texas

Cognitive Views
of Learning

I n this chapter we turn from behavioral theories of learning to the cognitive perspective. This means a shift from "viewing the learners and their behaviors as products of incoming environmental stimuli" to seeing the learners as "sources of plans, intentions, goals, ideas, memories, and emotions actively used to attend to, select, and construct meaning from stimuli and knowledge from experience" (Wittrock, 1982, pp. 1–2). We will begin with a discussion of the general cognitive approach to learning and memory and the importance of knowledge in learning. To understand memory, we will consider a widely accepted cognitive model, information processing, which suggests that information moves through three different storage systems. We will briefly consider two alternatives to the three-store model of memory: depth of processing and connectionist views. Next we will explore metacognition, a field of study that may provide insights into individual and developmental differences in learning. Then we turn to ideas about how teachers can help their students become more knowledgeable, particularly about the process of learning itself. Finally, we consider a recent challenge to the information processing view, constructivism. By the time you have completed this chapter, you should be able to:

- Discuss the role of knowledge in learning.
- Describe three models of human information processing—the three-store model, levels of processing, and connectionism.
- Give examples of the roles of perception and attention in learning.
- Define declarative, procedural, and conditional knowledge.
- Explain how schemas and scripts influence learning and remembering.
- Explain why we remember some things and forget others.
- Discuss individual differences in short- and long-term memory.
- Describe the stages in the development of cognitive skills.
- Use memory strategies and study skills derived from cognitive theory to prepare for the test you may have to take on this chapter.
- Develop a plan for teaching learning strategies and study skills to your students.
- Contrast information processing and constructivist perspectives on learning.

Cognitive View of Learning A general approach that views learning as an active mental process of acquiring, remembering, and using knowledge.

WHAT DO YOU THINK?

What makes a lesson easy to learn and remember? Think about the classes you are taking this semester. What information that you studied in the last two or three days do you expect to remember next week? Next year? What is different about the information you expect to remember as opposed to the information you probably will forget? What is different about the way you learned the information you expect to remember?

Elements of the Cognitive Perspective

The cognitive perspective is both the oldest and the youngest member of the psychological community. It is old because discussions of the nature of knowledge, the value of reason, and the contents of the mind date back at least to the ancient Greek philosophers (Hernshaw, 1987). Then, from the late 1800s, cognitive studies fell from favor and behaviorism thrived. But research during World War II on the development of complex human skills, the computer revolution, and breakthroughs in understanding language development all stimulated a resurgence in cognitive research. Evidence accumulated indicating that people do more than simply respond to reinforcement and punishment. For example, we plan our responses, use systems to help us remember, and organize the material we are learning in our own unique ways (Miller, Galanter, & Pribram, 1960; Shuell, 1986). With the growing realization that learning is an active mental process, educational psychologists became interested in how people think, learn concepts, and solve problems (e.g., Ausubel, 1963; Bruner, Goodnow, & Austin, 1956).

Interest in concept learning and problem solving soon gave way, however, to interest in how knowledge is represented in the mind and particularly how it is remembered. Remembering and forgetting became major topics for investigation in cognitive psychology, and the information processing model of memory dominated research.

Today, there are other models of memory besides information processing. In addition, many cognitive theorists have a renewed interest in learning, thinking, and problem solving. The **cognitive view of learning** can best be described as a generally agreed-upon philosophical orientation. This means that cognitive theorists share basic notions about learning and memory. Cognitive theorists believe, for example, that learning is the result of our attempts to make sense of the world. To do this, we use all the mental tools at our disposal. The ways we think about situations, along with our knowledge, expectations, feelings, and interactions with others, influence how and what we learn.

Comparing Cognitive and Behavioral Views

Test Bank items 7.1, 7.4, 7.90, 7.91, 7.109

The cognitive and behavioral views differ in their assumptions about what is learned. In the cognitive view, knowledge is learned, and changes in knowledge make changes in behavior possible. In the behavioral view, the new behaviors themselves are learned (Shuell, 1986). Both behavioral and cognitive theorists believe reinforcement is important in learning but for different reasons. The strict behaviorist maintains that reinforcement strengthens responses; cognitive theorists see reinforcement as a source of feedback about what is likely to happen if behaviors are repeated.

The cognitive view sees people as active learners who initiate experiences, seek out information to solve problems, and reorganize what they already know to achieve new insights. Instead of being passively influenced by environmental events, people actively choose, practice, pay attention, ignore, and make many other decisions as they pursue goals. Older cognitive views emphasized the *acquisition* of knowledge, but newer approaches stress its *construction* (Mayer, 1992).

Differences between behavioral and cognitive views are also apparent in the methods each group has used to study learning. Much of the work on behavioral learning principles has been with animals in controlled laboratory settings. The goal is to identify a few general laws of learning that apply to all higher organisms (including humans, regardless of age, intelligence, or other individual differences).

Cognitive psychologists, on the other hand, study a wide range of learning situations. Because of their focus on individual and developmental differences in cognition, they have not sought general laws of learning. This is one of the reasons that there is no single cognitive model or theory of learning representative of the entire field.

The Importance of Knowledge in Learning

Test Bank items 7.5, 7.109

Knowledge is the outcome of learning. When we learn a name, the history of cognitive psychology, the rules of tennis, or when to ask a friend for a favor, we know something new. Knowledge is more than the end product of previous learning; it also guides new learning. The cognitive approach suggests that one of the most important elements in the learning process is what the individual brings to the learning situation. What we already know determines to a great extent what we will learn, remember, and forget (Peeck, van den Bosch, & Kreupeling, 1982; Resnick, 1981; Shuell, 1986).

A study by Recht and Leslie (1988) shows the importance of knowledge in understanding and remembering new information. These psychologists identified junior high school students who were either very good or very poor readers. They tested the students on their knowledge of baseball and found that knowledge of baseball was not related to reading ability. So the researchers were able to identify four groups of students: *good readers/high baseball knowledge, good readers/low baseball knowledge, poor readers/high baseball knowledge, and poor readers/low baseball knowledge.* Then all the subjects read a passage describing a baseball game and were tested in a number of ways to see if they understood and remembered what they had read.

Objective 7.2: Contrast behavioral views of the learning process with those of cognitivists.

Teaching Tip: Read a few of these proverbs about memory taken from Klatzky, R. L. (1984). *Memory and awareness: An information processing perspective.* New York: Freeman, p. 122.

On Learning
Learning teacheth more in one year than experience in twenty. (Roger Ascham)

What we have to learn to do, we learn by doing. (Aristotle)

On Memory
The true art of memory is the art of attention. (Samuel Johnson)

A man's memory may almost become the art of continually varying and misrepresenting his past, according to his interests in the present. (George Santayana)

On Forgetting
The mind is slow in unlearning what it has been long in learning. (Seneca)

Soon learnt, soon forgotten. (Proverb)

Out of sight, out of mind. (Proverb)

An injury is much sooner forgotten than an insult. (Lord Chesterfield)

On Aging
I am too old to learn. (Shakespeare, *King Lear*)

No one is so old that he cannot still learn something. (German proverb)

An old dog will learn no new tricks. (Thomas D'Urfey)

Source for proverbs: Christy, R. (1887). *Proverbs, Maxims, and Phrases of All Ages.* New York: G. P. Putnam's Sons.

Source for quotations: Evans, B. (1968). *Dictionary of Quotations.* New York: Delacorte.

Focus on . . .   **The Cognitive Perspective**

■ Contrast cognitive and behavioral views of learning in terms of what is learned and the role of reinforcement.
■ How does knowledge affect learning?

Background: "What people learn is virtually never a direct replica of what they have read or been told or even what they have been drilled on. We know that to understand something is to interpret it and, further, that our interpretation is based partly on what we've been told or have read but also on what we already know and on general reasoning and logical abilities." Resnick, L. (1989). *Educational Leadership, 46*(4), 15.

Study Guide: Concept Map. See chapter 7 of the *Study Guide* for the Concept Map "Memory." This concept map is also presented as Handout Master 7.3 in the *Instructor's Resource Manual.*

Information Processing Human mind's activity of taking in, storing, and using information.

General Knowledge Information that is useful in many different kinds of tasks; information that applies to many situations.

Domain-Specific Knowledge Information that is useful in a particular situation or that applies only to one specific topic.

Declarative Knowledge Verbal information; facts; "knowing that" something is the case.

The results demonstrated the power of knowledge. Poor readers who knew baseball remembered more than good readers with little baseball knowledge and almost as much as good readers who knew baseball. Poor readers who knew little about baseball remembered the least of what they had read. So a good basis of knowledge can be more important than good learning strategies in understanding and remembering.

As a framework for examining learning and memory, we will use a well-researched model, information processing.

The Information Processing Model of Memory

There are a number of theories of memory, but the most common are the **information processing** explanations, including the newer neural-network or connectionist approaches (Martindale, 1991). Information processing models often include distinctions about different kinds of knowledge.

Kinds of Knowledge   Test Bank items 7.6, 7.7, 7.77, 7.92

Some knowledge is general—it applies to many different situations. For example, **general knowledge** about how to read or spell or use a word processor is useful in and out of school. **Domain-specific knowledge,** on the other hand, pertains to a particular task or subject. For example, knowing that the shortstop plays between second and third base is specific to the domain of baseball. Of course, there is no absolute line between general and domain-specific knowledge. When you were first learning to read, you may have studied specific facts about the sounds of letters. At that time, knowledge about letter sounds was specific to the domain of reading. But now you can use both knowledge about sounds and the ability to read in more general ways (Alexander, 1992; Schunk, 1991a).

Another way of categorizing knowledge is as declarative, procedural, or conditional (Paris, Lipson, & Wixson, 1983). **Declarative knowledge** is "knowing that" something is the case. The commonsense use of the term *knowledge* usually refers to declarative knowledge—facts, beliefs, theories, opinions; poems or passages or song lyrics; rules, names, and so on. Robert Gagne (1985) calls this category *verbal information.* The range of declarative knowledge is tremendous. You can know very specific facts (the atomic weight of gold is 196.967), or generalities (leaves of some trees change color in autumn), or personal preferences (I don't like lima beans), or personal events (What happened at my brother's wedding), or rules (to divide fractions, invert the divisor and multiply). Small units of declarative knowledge can be organized into larger units; for example, principles of reinforcement and punishment can be organized in your thinking into a theory of behavioral learning (Gagne, Yekovich, & Yekovich, 1993).

TABLE 7.1   Kinds of Knowledge

	General Knowledge	Domain-Specific Knowledge
Declarative	Hours the library is open Rules of grammar	The definition of "hypotenuse" The lines of the poem "The Raven"
Procedural	How to use your word processor How to drive	How to solve an oxidation-reduction equation How to throw a pot on a potter's wheel
Conditional	When to give up and try another approach When to skim and when to read carefully	When to use the formula for calculating volume When to rush the net in tennis

Procedural knowledge is "knowing how" to do something such as divide fractions or clean a carburetor. Notice that repeating the rule "to divide fractions, invert the divisor and multiply" shows *declarative* knowledge—the student can state the rule. But to show *procedural* knowledge, the student must act. When faced with a fraction to divide, the student must divide correctly. Robert Gagne (1985) calls this kind of knowledge *intellectual skills*. Students demonstrate procedural knowledge when they translate a passage into Spanish or correctly categorize a geometric shape or diagram a sentence.

Conditional knowledge is "knowing when and why" to apply your declarative and procedural knowledge. Robert Gagne (1985) calls this kind of knowledge *cognitive strategies*. Given many kinds of math problems, it takes conditional knowledge to know when to apply one procedure and when to apply another to solve each. It takes conditional knowledge to know when to read every word in a text and when to skim. For many students, conditional knowledge is a stumbling block. They have the facts and can do the procedures, but they don't seem to apply what they know at the appropriate time.

Table 7.1 shows that we can combine our two systems for describing knowledge. Declarative, procedural, and conditional knowledge can be either general or domain-specific.

Information Processing: Three Memory Stores

Test Bank item 7.19

Information processing views of memory rely on the computer as a model. Like the computer, the human mind takes in information, performs operations on it to change its form and content, stores the information, retrieves it when needed, and generates responses to it. Thus, processing involves gathering and representing information, or *encoding;* holding information, or *storage;* and getting at the information when needed, or *retrieval.* The whole system is guided by *control processes* that determine how and when information will flow through the system.

For some cognitive psychologists, the computer model is only a metaphor for human mental activity. But other cognitive scientists, particularly those studying artificial intelligence, try to design and program computers to "think" and solve problems like human beings (Schunk, 1991a). Some theorists suggest that the operation of the brain resembles a large number of very slow com-

Objective 7.4: Diagram the sequence of information processing from sensory input to long-term memory.

Procedural Knowledge Knowledge that is demonstrated when we perform a task; "knowing how."

Conditional Knowledge "Knowing when and why" to use declarative and procedural knowledge.

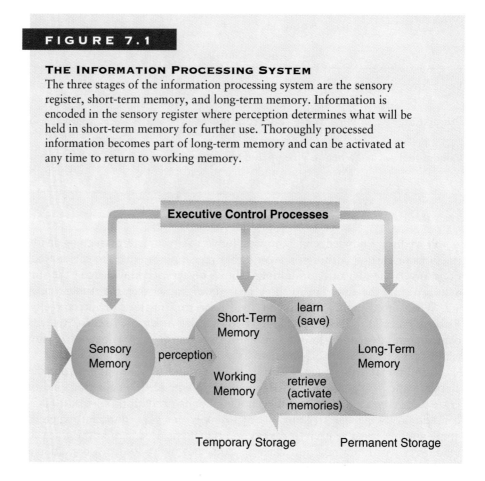

FIGURE 7.1

THE INFORMATION PROCESSING SYSTEM
The three stages of the information processing system are the sensory register, short-term memory, and long-term memory. Information is encoded in the sensory register where perception determines what will be held in short-term memory for further use. Thoroughly processed information becomes part of long-term memory and can be activated at any time to return to working memory.

Executive Control Processes

Sensory Memory

perception

Short-Term Memory

Working Memory

learn (save)

retrieve (activate memories)

Long-Term Memory

Temporary Storage   Permanent Storage

Transparency: Acetate transparency T 55, "The Information Processing System," presents the classic model of information processing.

Teaching Tip: Much of the sensory input we receive is not registered. Demonstrate this by asking the class what color shoes you have on (or whatever). They won't be able to answer even though that environmental input was available to them before you asked the question. It is only when we focus our attention on a fact that it is noticed and registered.

Receptors Parts of the human body that receive sensory information.

Sensory Register System of receptors holding sensory information very briefly.

puters, all operating in parallel (at the same time), with each computer dedicated to a different, specific task (Martindale, 1991).

Information processing theorists approach learning primarily through a study of memory. Figure 7.1 is a schematic representation of a typical information processing model of memory, derived from the ideas of several theorists (Atkinson & Shiffrin, 1968; R. Gagne, 1985). Other models have been suggested, but all of the models, despite their variations, resemble flow charts. In order to understand this model, let's examine each element.

Sensory Memory

Test Bank items 7.8–7.12, 7.18, 7.20, 7.21, 7.28, 7.78, 7.79, 7.94, 7.95, 7.112, 7.118

Stimuli from the environment (sights, sounds, smells, etc.) constantly bombard our receptors. **Receptors** are the body's mechanisms for seeing, hearing, tasting, smelling, and feeling. The sensory memory, also called the **sensory register** or *sensory information store*, holds all these sensations—very briefly.

Capacity, Duration, and Contents of Sensory Memory. The *capacity* of sensory memory is very large, more information than we can possibly handle at once. But this vast amount of sensory information is fragile in *duration*.

It lasts between one and three seconds. You can experience this brief holding of sensory information in your own sensory register. Wave a pencil (or your finger) back and forth before your eyes while you stare straight ahead. See the shadowy image that trails behind the object? The sensory input remains very briefly after the stimulus has left. You can see a trace of the pencil after the actual stimulus has been removed (Lindsay & Norman, 1977). The *content* of sensory memory resembles the sensations from the original stimulus. Visual sensations are coded briefly by the sensory register as images, almost like photographs. Auditory sensations are coded as sound patterns. It may be that the other senses also have their own codes. Thus, for a second or so, a wealth of data from sensory experience remains intact. In these moments, we have a chance to select and organize information for further processing. Perception and attention are critical at this stage.

Perception.   The meaning we attach to the raw information received through our senses is called **perception**. This meaning is constructed based on both objective reality and our existing knowledge. For example, consider these marks: β. If asked what the letter is, you would say "B." If asked what the number is, you would say "13." The actual marks remain the same; the perception of them—their meaning—changes in keeping with your expectation to recognize a number or a letter. To a child without appropriate knowledge to perceive either a number or a letter, the marks would probably be meaningless (Smith, 1975).

There are two explanations in information processing theory for how we recognize patterns and give meaning to sensory events. The first is called *feature analysis*, or **bottom-up processing** because the stimulus must be analyzed into features or components and assembled into a meaningful pattern "from the bottom up." For example, a capital letter A consists of two relatively straight lines joined at a 45-degree angle (/\) and a horizontal line (—) through the middle. Whenever we see these features, or anything close enough, including **A**, *A*, A, *A*, A, and *A*, we recognize an A (Anderson, 1990). This explains how we are able to read words written in other people's handwriting.

If all perception relied on feature analysis, learning would be very slow. Luckily, humans are capable of another type of perception, based on knowledge and expectation often called **top-down processing**. To recognize patterns rapidly, in addition to noting features, we use what we already know about the situation—what we know about words or pictures or the way the world generally operates. For example, you would not have seen the marks above as the letter B if you had no knowledge of the Roman alphabet. So what you know also affects what you are able to perceive. If you catch only a fleeting glimpse of a medium-sized, four-legged animal being led down a city street on a leash, you are likely to perceive a dog, based on what you know about dogs (their size and number of legs) and cities (the kinds of animals on leashes in cities). Of course you may be wrong, but not very often.

The Role of Attention.   If every variation in color, movement, sound, smell, temperature, and so on had to be perceived, life would be impossible. By paying attention to certain stimuli and ignoring others, we select from all the possibilities what we will process. But **attention** is a very limited resource. We can pay attention to only one demanding task at at time (Anderson, 1990).

Activity 7.1: See the separate *Instructor's Resource Manual* for Sperling's Early Experiments, a summary of Sperling's studies of visual perception.

Objective 7.6: Compare top-down and bottom-up perceptual processing.

Transparency: Use acetate transparency **T 64** for an example of top-down processing.

Objective 7.7: Describe the role of attention in learning and identify the implications for teaching.

Perception Interpretation of sensory information.

Bottom-Up Processing Perceiving based on noticing separate defining features and assembling them into a recognizable pattern.

Top-Down Processing Perceiving based on the context and the patterns you expect to occur in that situation.

Attention Focus on a stimulus.

TABLE 7.2   Suggestions for Focusing Attention

1. Tell students the purpose of the lesson. Indicate how learning the material will be useful or important to them.
2. Ask students why they think learning the material will be important.
3. Arouse curiosity with questions such as "What would happen if . . . ?"
4. Create shock by staging an unexpected event such as a loud argument just before a lesson on communication.
5. Alter the physical environment by changing the arrangement of the room or moving to a different setting.
6. Shift sensory channels by giving a lesson that requires students to touch, smell, or taste.
7. Use movements, gestures, and voice inflection—walk around the room, point, speak softly and then more emphatically.
8. Avoid distracting behaviors such as tapping a pencil.

Source: E. Emmer and G. Millett (1970). *Improving teaching through experimentation: A laboratory approach.* Adapted by permission of Allyn and Bacon.

Transparency: Acetate transparency T 59, "Memory and Meaning," presents the well-known picture of a black-and-white-spotted dog in a black-and-white-spotted setting.

The first step in learning is paying attention; students cannot process something they do not recognize or perceive.

Automaticity The ability to perform thoroughly learned tasks without much mental effort.

Short-Term Memory Working memory, holding a limited amount of information briefly.

For example, there was a time when I was learning to drive when I couldn't listen to the radio and drive at the same time. After some practice, I could listen, but I had to turn the radio off when traffic was heavy. After years of practice, I can plan a class or talk on the phone as I drive. This is because many processes that initially require attention and concentration become automatic with practice. Actually, **automaticity** probably is a matter of degree—we are not completely automatic but rather more or less automatic in our performances depending on how much practice we have had (Anderson, 1990).

Attention and Teaching.   The first step in learning is paying attention. Students cannot process something that they do not recognize or perceive. Many factors in the classroom influence student attention. Eye-catching or startling displays or actions can draw attention at the beginning of a lesson. A teacher might begin a science lesson on air pressure by blowing up a balloon until it pops. Bright colors, underlining, highlighting of written or spoken words, surprise events, and changes in voice level, lighting, or pacing can all be used to gain attention. Table 7.2 offers additional ideas for capturing students' attention.

Short-Term Memory

Test Bank items 7.13–7.16, 7.23, 7.29, 7.80, 7.81, 7.93, 7.96, 7.110, 7.118

Once transformed into patterns of images or sounds (or perhaps other types of sensory codes), the information in sensory memory can enter the **short-term memory** system.

Capacity, Duration, and Contents of Short-Term Memory.   Short-term memory *capacity* is limited by the number of "bits" of information that can be held at one time. In experimental situations based on the information processing model, it appears that the capacity is only about five to nine separate new items at once (Miller, 1956). This limitation holds true to some degree in everyday life. It is quite common to remember a new phone number after looking it up, as you walk across the room to make the call. But what if you have two phone calls to make in succession? Two new phone numbers (14 digits) probably cannot be stored simultaneously.

Remember—put in your short-term memory—that we are discussing the recall of *new* information. In daily life we certainly can hold more than five to nine bits of information at once. While you are dialing that seven-digit phone number you just looked up, you are bound to have other things "on your mind"—in your memory—such as how to use a telephone, whom you are calling, and why. You don't have to pay attention to these things; they are not new knowledge. Some of the processes, such as dialing the phone, have become automatic. However, because of the short-term memory's limitations, if you were in a foreign country and were attempting to use an unfamiliar telephone system, you might very well have trouble remembering the phone number because you were trying to figure out the phone system at the same time.

The *duration* of information in short-term memory, as in sensory memory, is short, about 20 to 30 seconds at the most. It may seem to you that a memory system with a 20-second time limit is not very useful. But without this system, you would have already forgotten what you read in the first part of this sentence before you came to these last few words. This would clearly make understanding sentences difficult.

Short-term memory is sometimes known as **working memory** because its *content* is activated information—what you are thinking about at the moment. This activated information may be knowledge from long-term memory that you are currently thinking about or something new you have just encountered (Anderson, 1990). For this reason, some psychologists consider the working memory to be synonymous with "consciousness." The information in short-term memory may be in the form of images that resemble the perceptions in sensory memory, or the information may be structured more abstractly, based on meaning.

Retaining Information in Short-Term Memory.   Because information in short-term memory is fragile and easily lost, it must be kept activated to be retained. Activation is high as long as you are focusing on information, but activation decays or fades quickly when attention shifts away (Anderson, 1990). When activation fades, forgetting follows, as shown in Figure 7.2 on page 248. To keep information activated in short-term memory for longer than 20 seconds, most people rehearse the information mentally.

There are two types of rehearsal (Craik & Lockhart, 1972). **Maintenance rehearsal** involves repeating the information in your mind. As long as you repeat the information, it can be maintained in short-term memory indefinitely. Maintenance rehearsal is useful for retaining something you plan to use and then forget, like a phone number.

Elaborative rehearsal involves associating the information you are trying to remember with something you already know, with information from long-term memory. For example, if you meet someone at a party whose name is the same as your brother's, you don't have to repeat the name to keep it in memory, you just have to make the association. This kind of rehearsal not only retains information in working memory but helps move information from short-term to long-term memory. Rehearsal is thus an "executive control process" that affects the flow of information through the information processing system.

Working Memory The information that you are focusing on at a given moment.

Maintenance Rehearsal Keeping information in working memory by repeating it to yourself.

Elaborative Rehearsal Keeping information in working memory by associating it with something else you already know.

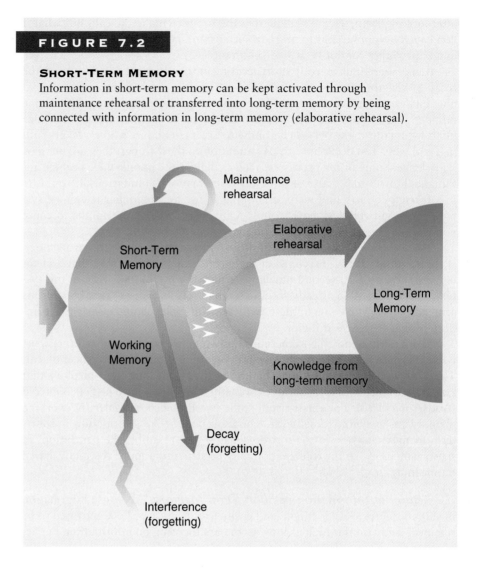

FIGURE 7.2

SHORT-TERM MEMORY
Information in short-term memory can be kept activated through maintenance rehearsal or transferred into long-term memory by being connected with information in long-term memory (elaborative rehearsal).

Maintenance rehearsal

Short-Term Memory

Elaborative rehearsal

Long-Term Memory

Working Memory

Knowledge from long-term memory

Decay (forgetting)

Interference (forgetting)

Teaching Tip: To illustrate the advantages of chunking information, ask the class to try to remember the following letters by writing them down after you read them consecutively:

A P D I B O H G T

Then repeat the exercise with the following list of identical letters:

D O G B A T H I P

Ask students to compare their two performances. From an information processing standpoint, why is the second list easier to recall? How many "bits" are really involved in each list?

Transparency: Acetate transparencies T 56 and T 57, "The Information Processing Model," are overlays showing the relationships between short-term memory and long-term memory and the processes of forgetting.

Chunking Grouping individual bits of data into meaningful larger units.

The limited capacity of short-term memory can also be somewhat circumvented by the control process of **chunking.** Because the number of bits of information, not the size of each bit, is the limitation for short-term memory, you can retain more information if you can group individual bits of information. For example, if you have to remember the six digits 3, 5, 4, 8, 7, and 0, it is easier to put them together into three chunks of two digits each (35, 48, 70) or two chunks of three digits each (354, 870). With these changes, there are only two or three bits of information rather than six to hold at one time. Chunking helps you remember a telephone number or a social security number.

Forgetting. Information may be lost from short-term memory through interference or decay. Interference is fairly straightforward: remembering new information interferes with or gets in the way of remembering old information. The new thought replaces the old one. As new thoughts accumulate, old information is lost from short-term memory. Information is also lost from short-term memory by time **decay.** If you don't continue to pay attention to information, the activation level decays (weakens) and finally drops so low that the information cannot be reactivated—it disappears altogether.

Forgetting is very useful. Without forgetting, people would quickly overload their short-term memories and learning would cease. Also, it would be a problem if you remembered permanently every sentence you ever read. Finding a particular bit of information in all that sea of knowledge would be impossible. It is helpful to have a system that provides temporary storage.

Long-Term Memory

Short-term memory holds the information that is currently activated, such as a telephone number you have just found and are about to dial. **Long-term memory** holds the information that is well learned, such as all the other telephone numbers you know. Well-learned information is said to be high in **memory strength** or *durability* (Anderson, 1990).

Capacity and Duration of Long-Term Memory.   There are a number of differences between short-term and long-term memory, as you can see in Table 7.3. Information enters short-term memory very quickly. To move information into long-term storage requires more time and a bit of effort. Whereas the capacity of short-term memory is limited, the capacity of long-term memory appears to be, for all practical purposes, unlimited. In addition, once information is securely stored in long-term memory, it can remain there permanently. Theoretically, we should be able to remember as much as we want for as long as we want. Of course, the problem is to find the right information when it is needed. Our access to information in short-term memory is immediate because information in short-term memory is what we are thinking about at that very moment. But access to information in long-term memory requires time and effort.

Transparency: Acetate transparency T 58, "Three Types of Memory."

Objective 7.9: Contrast the short-term and long-term memory systems.

Transparencies: Use transparencies T 60, "Short-Term Memory," T 61, "Long-Term Memory," and T 62, "A Model," for an overview of memory structure.

Decay The weakening and fading of memories with the passage of time.

Long-Term Memory Permanent store of knowledge.

Memory Strength The durability of a memory; if information is well learned, it is more durable.

Test Bank items 7.17, 7.22, 7.24–7.27, 7.30–7.34, 7.36–7.41, 7.82, 7.83, 7.97–7.102, 7.111, 7.118, 7.119–7.122

TABLE 7.3   Short-Term and Long-Term Memory

Type of Memory	Input	Capacity	Duration	Contents	Retrieval
Short-term	Very fast	Limited	Very brief: 20–30 sec.	Words, images, ideas, sentences	Immediate
Long-term	Relatively slow	Practically unlimited	Practically unlimited	Propositional networks, schemata, productions, episodes, perhaps images	Depends on representation and organization

Source: Adapted by permission of the author from F. Smith (1975), *Comprehension and learning: A conceptual framework for teachers,* published by Holt, Rinehart and Winston.

Research: Clark, J. M., & Paivio, A. (1991). Dual coding theory and education. *Educational Psychology Review, 3,* 149–210. This is a current statement of the dual coding theory.

Discussion: Why would drawing pictures of events or objects facilitate learning?

Activity 7.3: Teaching Tip. See the separate *Instructor's Resource Manual* for Semantic Memory, an activity demonstrating that the meaning and not the surface structure of information is stored in long-term memory. This activity includes **Handout Master 7.1,** a quiz in which students test their recall and explain their errors in terms of what they have learned about semantic memory.

Transparency: Acetate transparency T 59, "A Propositional Network," graphically illustrates the network of components in a propositional statement.

Objective 7.8: Explain how various types of information and knowledge may be stored in memory. Use the concepts of propositional networks, images, and schemas in the explanation.

Semantic Memory Memory for meaning.

Propositional Network Set of interconnected concepts and relationships in which long-term knowledge is held.

Images Representations based on the physical attributes—the appearance—of information.

Contents of Long-Term Memory. Allan Paivio (1971, 1986; Clark & Paivio, 1991) suggests that information is stored in long-term memory as either visual images, or verbal units, or both. Psychologists who agree with this point of view believe that information coded both visually and verbally is easiest to remember. (This may be one reason why explaining an idea with words and representing it visually in a figure, as we do in textbooks, has proved helpful to students.) Paivio's ideas have some support, but critics contend that the capacity of the brain is not large enough to store all the images we can imagine. They suggest that many images are actually stored as verbal codes and then translated into visual information when an image is needed (Schunk, 1991). Most cognitive psychologists distinguish three categories of long-term memory: semantic, episodic, and procedural.

Semantic memory is memory for meaning. These memories are stored as *propositions, images,* and *schemas.* Because these are very important concepts for teaching, we will spend some extra time on them.

Propositions and Propositional Networks. A *proposition* is the smallest unit of information that can be judged true or false. The statement, "Ida borrowed the antique tablecloth," has two propositions:

1. Ida borrowed the tablecloth.
2. The tablecloth is an antique.

A **propositional network** is interconnected bits of information. Different cognitive psychologists have slightly different methods for diagramming propositional networks. Figure 7.3 is a common way of representing the relationships in the sentence "Ida (the *agent*) borrowed the antique tablecloth (the *object*)." Since the verb is in the past tense, the *time* of action is in the past. The same propositional network would apply to these sentences: "The antique tablecloth was borrowed by Ida," or "Ida borrowed the tablecloth, which was an antique." The meaning is the same, and it is this *meaning* that is stored in memory as a set of relationships.

It is possible that most information is stored and represented in propositional networks. When we want to recall a bit of information, we may translate its meaning (as represented in the propositional network) into familiar phrases and sentences, or mental pictures. Also, because of the network, recall of one bit of information can trigger or *activate* recall of another. We are not aware of these networks, for they are not part of our conscious memory (Anderson, 1990). In much the same way, we are not aware of underlying grammatical structure when we form a sentence in our own language; we don't have to diagram a sentence in order to say it.

Images. Images are representations based on *perceptions*—on the structure or appearance of the information (Anderson, 1990). **Images** mirror what they represent—they preserve the physical attributes and spatial structure of information. For example, when asked how many window panes are in their living room, most people call up an image of the windows "in their mind's eye" and count the panes—the more panes, the longer it takes to respond. If the information were represented in a proposition such as "my living room has seven window panes," then everyone would take about the same time to answer, whether the number was one or 24 (Mendell, 1971). Images are useful in mak-

FIGURE 7.3

A PROPOSITIONAL NETWORK

The sentence "Ida borrowed the antique tablecloth" has two propositions:
(1) Ida borrowed the tablecloth [in the past] and (2) The tablecloth is an
antique.

Source: Developed from material in J. Anderson (1985), *Cognitive psychology
and its implications* (2nd ed.). San Francisco: W. H. Freeman; and D. Gentner
(1975), Evidence for the psychological reality of semantic components: The
verbs of possession. In D. Norman and D. Rumelhart (Eds.), *Explorations in
Cognition.* San Francisco: W. H. Freeman.

ing many practical decisions such as how a sofa might look in your living room
or how to line up a golf shot. Images may also be helpful in abstract reasoning. Physicists, such as Faraday and Einstein, report creating images to reason
about complex new problems (Gagne, Yekovich, & Yekovich, 1993).

   Schemas.   As Ellen Gagne and her colleagues have noted, propositions
and images are fine for representing single ideas and relationships. But often our
knowledge about a topic combines images and propositions. "In order to deal
with the fact that much of our knowledge seems integrated, psychologists have
developed the idea of a schema" (Gagne, Yekovich, & Yekovich, 1993, p. 81).
Schemas (sometimes called *schemata*) are abstract data structures that organize vast amounts of information. A **schema** (the singular form) is a pattern or
guide for understanding an event, a concept, or a skill. Figure 7.4 on page 252
is a partial representation of a schema for knowledge about an "antique."
   The "antique" schema is an example of a *natural category schema.* This
kind of schema represents objects in nature such as "minerals" or "birds" or
culturally created categories such as "antiques." The schema tells you what
features are typical of a category, what to expect. The schema is like a proto-

Schemata (singular, **Schema**) Basic structures for organizing information; concepts.

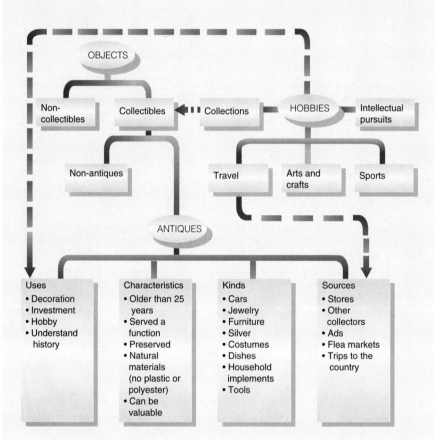

FIGURE 7.4

A Schema for "Antique"
The concept of "antique" falls under the general category of "collectible object." It is related to other concepts, such as "hobby" and "traveling to flea markets," depending on the individual's experience with antiques.

OBJECTS

Non-collectibles Collectibles ← Collections HOBBIES → Intellectual pursuits

Non-antiques Travel Arts and crafts Sports

ANTIQUES

Uses
• Decoration
• Investment
• Hobby
• Understand history

Characteristics
• Older than 25 years
• Served a function
• Preserved
• Natural materials (no plastic or polyester)
• Can be valuable

Kinds
• Cars
• Jewelry
• Furniture
• Silver
• Costumes
• Dishes
• Household implements
• Tools

Sources
• Stores
• Other collectors
• Ads
• Flea markets
• Trips to the country

Transparency: Use acetate transparency T 69 for an example of a schema diagram for the word "bison."

Multicultural Awareness: Ask students to discuss how schemas about differences among individuals, groups, and social contexts can determine how new information about people and situations is interpreted.

Activity 7.4: Reflection/Journal Writing. See the separate *Instructor's Resource Manual* for Episodic Memory, a journal-writing activity that encourages students to recall two memories from two different times in their lives. Using these two memories, students reflect on episodic memory and the factors that influence it.

Story Grammar Typical structure or organization for a category of stories.

Script Schema or expected plan for the sequence of steps in a common event such as buying groceries or ordering take-out pizza.

Episodic Memory Long-term memory for information tied to a particular time and place, especially memory of the events in a person's life.

---

type or pattern, specifying the "standard" relationships in an object or situation. The pattern has "slots" that are filled with specific information as we apply the schema in a particular situation. And schemas are individual. For example, my schema of an antique is less richly developed than the schema of an antique collector. You encountered the very similar concept of scheme in the discussion of Piaget's theory of cognitive development in chapter 2.

When you hear the sentence, "Ida borrowed the antique tablecloth," you know even more about it than the propositions in Figure 7.3. This is because you have schemas about borrowing, tablecloths, antiques, and maybe even Ida herself. You know without being told, for example, that the lender does not have the tablecloth now, because it is in Ida's possession, and that Ida has an obligation to return the tablecloth to the lender (Gentner, 1975). None of this information is explicitly stated, but it is part of our schema for understanding the meaning of "borrow." Other schemas allow you to infer that the cloth is not plastic (if it is a real antique) and that Ida has probably invited guests for a meal. Your schema about Ida may even allow you to predict how promptly the cloth will be returned and in what condition.

Another type of schema, a **story grammar** (sometimes called a schema for text or **story structure**) helps students to understand and remember stories (Gagne, Yekovich, & Yekovich, 1993; Rumelhart & Ortony, 1977). A story grammar could be something like this: murder discovered, search for clues, murderer's fatal mistake identified, trap set to trick suspect into confessing, murderer takes bait . . . mystery solved! In other words, a story grammar is a typical general structure that could fit many specific stories. To comprehend a story, we select a schema that seems appropriate. Then we use this framework to decide which details are important, what information to seek, and what to remember. It is as though the schema is a theory about what should occur in the story. The schema guides us in "interrogating" the text, filling in the specific information we expect to find so that the story makes sense. If we activate our "murder mystery schema" we may be alert for clues or a murderer's fatal mistake (Resnick, 1981). Without the appropriate schema, trying to understand a story, textbook, or classroom lesson is a very slow, difficult process, something like finding your way through a new town without a map.

A schema representing the typical sequence of events in an everyday situation is called a **script** or an *event schema*. Children as young as 3 have basic scripts for the familiar events in their lives (Nelson, 1986). A kindergartner's script for "lunch" might be something like the one in Figure 7.5.

Storing knowledge of the world in schemas and scripts has advantages and disadvantages. A schema can be applied in many contexts, depending on what part of the schema is relevant. You can use what you know about antiques, for example, to plan trips, decide if a particular article is worth the price asked, or enjoy a museum display. Having a well-developed schema about Ida lets you recognize her (even as her appearance changes), remember many of her characteristics, and make predictions about her behavior. But it also allows you to be wrong. You may have incorporated incorrect or biased information into your schema of Ida. For example, if Ida is a member of an ethnic group different from yours and if you believe that group is dishonest, you may assume that Ida will keep the tablecloth. In this way, racial and ethnic stereotypes can function as schemas for misunderstanding individuals and for racial discrimination.

Episodic Memory.   Memory for information tied to a particular place and time, especially information about the events of your own life, is called **episodic memory**. Episodic memory keeps track of the order of things, so it is also a good place to store jokes, gossip, or plots from films. Martindale (1991) distinguishes between semantic and episodic memory as follows:

> Semantic memory contains the basic elements of knowledge, and episodic memory is made up from these elements. Semantic memory is like a dictionary containing the meanings of all of the words and images you know. Episodic memory is like a novel or movie that puts these concepts together in particular ways. (p. 181)

FIGURE 7.5

"LUNCHTIME" SCRIPT
This script is typical of ones generated by children 5 or 6 years of age. Younger children give scripts that are less detailed and that contain fewer main acts.

First you play outside for a while.

When the teacher calls your name, you go in.

You get your lunchbox and sit down.

Then you eat.

Then you throw away your trash.

You get ready for your nap.

Source: From Laura E. Berk, *Child Development,* 2/e, p. 282. Copyright © 1991 by Allyn and Bacon. Reprinted by permission.

Procedural learning may go slowly at first, but once this boy masters the skills of riding a bike, he'll remember them automatically for a long time.

Objective 7.10: Give examples of how information may be processed to enhance long-term storage.

Procedural Memory Long-term memory for how to do things.

Productions The contents of procedural memory; rules about what actions to take, given certain conditions.

Elaboration Adding and extending meaning by connecting new information to existing knowledge.

Organization Ordered and logical network of relations.

Context The physical or emotional backdrop associated with an event.

Procedural Memory. Memory for how to do things is called **procedural memory.** It may take a while to learn a procedure—such as how to ski, serve a tennis ball, or factor an equation—but once learned, this knowledge tends to be remembered for a long time. Procedural memories are represented as *condition-action rules,* sometimes called productions. **Productions** specify what to do under certain conditions: if A occurs, then do B. A production might be something like, "If you want to ski faster, lean back slightly," or "If your goal is to increase student attention, and a student has been paying attention a bit longer than usual, then praise the student." People can't necessarily state all their condition-action rules, but they act on them nevertheless. The more practiced the procedure, the more automatic the action (Anderson, 1990).

Storing Information in Long-Term Memory. Just what is done to "save" information permanently—to create procedural, semantic, or episodic memories? How can we make the most effective use of our practically unlimited capacity to learn and remember? The way you learn information in the first place—the way you process it at the outset—seems to affect its recall later. One important requirement is that you integrate new material with information already stored in long-term memory as you construct an understanding. Here *elaboration, organization,* and *context* play a role.

Elaboration is the addition of meaning to new information through its connection with already existing knowledge. In other words, we apply our schemas and draw on already existing knowledge to build an understanding of new information and perhaps to change our existing knowledge in the process. We often elaborate automatically. For example, a paragraph about an historic figure in the seventeenth century tends to activate our existing knowledge about that period; we use the old knowledge to understand the new.

Material that is elaborated when first learned will be easier to recall later. First, as we saw earlier, elaboration is a form of rehearsal. It keeps the information activated in working memory long enough to have a chance for permanent storage in long-term memory. Second, elaboration builds extra links to existing knowledge. The more one bit of information or knowledge is associated with other bits, the more routes there are to follow to get to the original bit. To put it another way, you have several "handles," or retrieval cues, by which you can recognize or "pick up" the information you might be seeking (Schunk, 1991a). Psychologists have also found that the more precise and sensible the elaborations, the easier recall will be (Bransford, Stein, Vye, Franks, Auble, Mezynski, & Perfetto, 1982; Stein, Littlefield, Bransford, & Persampieri, 1984).

Organization is a second element of processing that improves learning. Material that is well organized is easier to learn and to remember than bits and pieces of information, especially if the information is complex or extensive. Placing a concept in a structure will help you learn and remember either general definitions or specific examples. The structure serves as a guide back to the information when you need it. For example, Table 7.1 on page 243 organizes information about types of knowledge; Table 7.3 on page 249 gives an organized view of the capacity, duration, contents, and retrieval of information from short- and long-term memory; and Figure 7.2 on page 248 organizes my (limited) knowledge about antiques.

Context is a third element of processing that influences learning. Aspects of physical and emotional context—places, rooms, how we are feeling on a particular day, who is with us—are learned along with other information. Later, if you try to remember the information, it will be easier if the current context is similar to the original one. This has been demonstrated in the laboratory. Students who learned material in one type of room performed better on tests taken in a similar room than they did on tests taken in a very different-looking room (Smith, Glenberg, & Bjork, 1978). So studying for a test under "testlike" conditions may result in improved performance. Of course, you can't always go back to the same or to a similar place in order to recall something. But you can picture the setting, the time of day, and your companions, and you may eventually reach the information you seek.

Retrieving Information from Long-Term Memory. When we need to use information from long-term memory, we search for it. Sometimes the search is conscious, as when you see a friend approaching and search for her name. At other times locating and using information from long-term memory is automatic, as when you dial a telephone or solve a math problem without having to search for each step. Think of long-term memory as a huge shelf full of tools and supplies ready to be brought to the workbench of working memory to accomplish a task. The shelf (long-term memory) stores an incredible amount, but it may be hard to find quickly what you are looking for. The workbench (working memory) is small, but anything on it is immediately available. Because it is small, however, supplies (bits of information) sometimes are lost when the workbench overflows (E. Gagne, 1985).

The size of the memory network is huge, but only one small area is activated at any one time. Only the information we are currently thinking about is in working memory. Information is retrieved in this network through the **spread of activation.** When a particular proposition or image is active—when we are thinking about it—other closely associated knowledge can be activated as well, and activation can spread through the network (Anderson, 1993; Gagne, Yekovich, & Yekovich, 1993). Thus, as I focus on the propositions, "I'd like to go for a drive to see the fall leaves today," related ideas such as, "I should rake leaves," and "The car needs an oil change," come to mind. As activation spreads from the "car trip" to the "oil change," the original thought, or active memory, disappears from working memory because of the limited space. So **retrieval** from long-term memory is partly through the spreading of activation from one bit of knowledge to related ideas in the network. We often use this spreading in reverse to retrace our steps in a conversation, as in, "Before we got onto the topic of where to get the oil changed, what were we talking about? Oh yes, seeing the leaves."

In long-term memory the information is still available, even when it is not activated, even when you are not thinking about it at the moment. If spreading activation does not "find" the information we seek, then we might still come up with the answer through **reconstruction,** a problem-solving process that makes use of logic, cues, and other knowledge to *construct* a reasonable answer by filling in any missing parts.

Sometimes reconstructed recollections are incorrect. For example, in 1932, F. C. Bartlett conducted a series of famous studies on remembering stories. He read a complex, unfamiliar Native-American tale to students at England's Cambridge University and after various lengths of time, asked the students to recall the story. Students' recalled stories were generally shorter than the original and were translated into the concepts and language of the Cambridge stu-

Critical Thinking: Ask students to suggest analogies for the relationship between the effective coding or mediation of information before it enters long-term memory and the successful retrieval of that information. (You might suggest the analogy of a library, in which storage is no problem, but retrieval depends on the manner in which material was stored.)

Activity 7.5: Background. See the *Instructor's Resource Manual* for Reconstructive Elaborations, a summary of Scruggs, T. E., & Mastropieri, M. A. (1991). Reconstructive elaborations: A model for content area learning. *American Educational Research Journal.*

Research: Garner, R. (1990). When children and adults do not use learning strategies: Toward a theory of settings. *Review of Educational Research, 60,* 517–530.

Spread of Activation Retrieval of pieces of information based on their relatedness to one another. Remembering one bit of information activates (stimulates) recall of associated information.

Retrieval Process of searching for and finding information in long-term memory.

Reconstruction Recreating information by using memories, expectations, logic, and existing knowledge.

256 CHAPTER 7 Cognitive Views of Learning

Example: Reconstruction also occurs when retrieved information is only partially correct—"The book is blue with white letters" when the book is actually green with white letters. Information may have been encoded incorrectly to begin with, or not elaborated enough to make it to long-term memory.

Activity 7.6: See the separate *Instructor's Resource Manual* for Encoding and Retrieving from Memory, two activities demonstrating the difference between recall and recognition memory and the role of meaning in memory.

Background: For the original Indian myth used in Bartlett's study and an example of how one subject recalled the story, see Bartlett, F. (1932). *Remembering.* Cambridge: Cambridge University Press. British college students tended to systematically forget, distort, and revise details of a North American Indian myth in ways that made the recalled story less unusual to them.

Teaching Tip: Point out that not all reconstructed memories are distorted and that reconstruction strategies can be remarkably successful. To demonstrate, ask students to experiment with the following retrieval challenge (Lindsay & Normal, 1977, p. 372): "What were you doing on Monday afternoon in the third week of September two years ago?"

Objective 7.11: Name three possible reasons for "forgetting" information.

dent culture. The story told of a seal hunt, for instance, but many students remembered a "fishing trip," an activity closer to their experiences. Instead of remembering the exact words of the story, the students remembered the meaning, but the meaning they remembered was altered slightly to fit their cultural expectations and stereotypes—in other words, their schemas.

Forgetting and Long-Term Memory. Information lost from short-term memory truly disappears. No amount of effort will bring it back. But information stored in long-term memory may be available, given the right cues. Some researchers believe that nothing is ever lost from long-term memory; but recent research casts doubts on this assertion (Schwartz & Reisberg, 1991). (The learning and retrieving processes of long-term memory are diagrammed in Figure 7.6.)

Freud suggested that we sometimes intentionally forget or "repress" certain information or experiences we do not really want to remember. But this

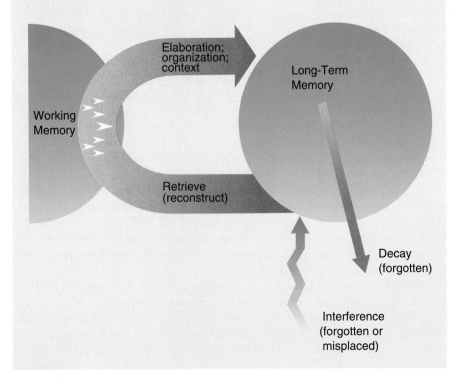

FIGURE 7.6

LONG-TERM MEMORY
We activate information from long-term memory to help us understand new information in short-term memory. With mental work and processing (elaboration, organization, context) the new information can be stored permanently in long-term memory. Forgetting is caused by interference and time decay.

Elaboration; organization; context

Working Memory

Long-Term Memory

Retrieve (reconstruct)

Decay (forgotten)

Interference (forgotten or misplaced)

does not explain why some painful experiences are remembered vividly, while others that are pleasant or neutral are forgotten. What else causes problems in long-term memory?

Information appears to be lost from long-term memory through time decay and interference. For example, memory for Spanish-English vocabulary decreases for about three years after a person's last course in Spanish, then stays level for about 25 years, then drops again for the next 25 years. One explanation for this decline is that neural connections, like muscles, grow weak without use. After 25 years, it may be that the memories are still somewhere in the brain but are too weak to be reactivated (Anderson, 1990).

The idea that **interference** causes forgetting in long-term as well as in short-term memory seems to be supported by evidence from research. Newer memories may interfere with or obscure older memories, and older memories may interfere with memory for new material. It seems that interference occurs when the same schema or script is used on several different occasions and elements of the different situations get confused (Schunk, 1991b).

The Guidelines below give applications of information processing for teaching.

Guidelines

Using Information Processing Ideas in the Classroom

Make sure you have the students' attention.

Examples

1. Develop a signal that tells students to stop what they are doing and focus on you. Some teachers move to a particular spot in the room, flick the lights, or play a chord on the class piano.
2. Move around the room, use gestures, avoid speaking in a monotone.
3. Begin a lesson by asking a question that stimulates interest in the topic.
4. Regain the attention of individual students by walking closer to them, using their names, or asking them a question.

Help students separate essential from nonessential details and focus on the most important information.

Examples

1. Summarize instructional objectives to indicate what students should be learning. Relate the material you are presenting to the objectives as you teach: "Now I'm going to explain exactly how you can find the information you need to meet Objective One on the board—determining the tone of the story."
2. When you make an important point, pause, repeat, ask a student to paraphrase, note the information on the board in colored chalk, or tell students to highlight the point in their notes or readings.

Help students make connections between new information and what they already know.

Examples

1. Review prerequisites to help students bring to mind the information they will need to understand new material: "Who can tell us the definition of a quadri-

Continued

Interference   The process that occurs when remembering certain information is hampered by the presence of other information.

lateral? Now, what is a rhombus? Is a square a quadrilateral? Is a square a rhombus? What did we say yesterday about how you can tell? Today we are going to look at some other quadrilaterals."
2. Use an outline or diagram to show how new information fits with the framework you have been developing. For example, "Now that you know the duties of the FBI, where would you expect to find it in this diagram of the branches of the U.S. government?
3. Give an assignment that specifically calls for the use of new information along with information already learned.

Provide for repetition and review of information.
Examples
1. Begin the class with a quick review of the homework assignment.
2. Give frequent, short tests.
3. Build practice and repetition into games, or have students work with partners to quiz each other.

Present material in a clear, organized way.
Examples
1. Make the purpose of the lesson very clear.
2. Give students a brief outline to follow. Put the same outline on an overhead so you can keep yourself on track. When students ask questions or make comments, relate these to the appropriate section of the outline.
3. Use summaries in the middle and at the end of the lesson.

Focus on meaning, not memorization.
Examples
1. In teaching new words, help students associate the new word to a related word they already understand: "*Enmity* is from the same base as *enemy....*"
2. In teaching about remainders, have students group 12 objects into sets of 2, 3, 4, 5, 6, and 7. Ask them to count the "leftovers" in each case.

Another View of Information Processing: Levels of Processing

Test Bank items 7.35, 7.36, 7.84

Objective 7.12: Integrate the stages of information processing theory with the levels of processing theory.

Levels of Processing Theory Theory that recall of information is based on how deeply it is processed.

Not all cognitive psychologists believe that human memory can be completely explained by the three-store (sensory, short-term, long-term memory) model. Craik and Lockhart (1972) first proposed their **levels of processing theory** as an alternative to three-store models. They suggested that what determines how long information is remembered is not *where* it is stored but *how completely* the information is analyzed and connected with other information. The more completely information is processed, the better our chances of remembering it. For example, according to the levels of processing theory, if I ask you to sort pictures of dogs based on the color of their coats, you might not remember many of the pictures later. But if I ask you to rate each dog on how likely it is to chase you as you jog, you probably would remember more of the pictures. To rate the dogs you must pay attention to details in the pictures, relate features of the dogs to characteristics associated with danger, and so on. This rating procedure requires "deeper" processing and more focus on the *meaning* of the features in the photos.

Craik (1979) suggested that the three-store model and the levels of processing view are not entirely incompatible. There may be different structural components or memory stages similar to the sensory, short-term, and long-term distinctions, as well as different strategies or levels of processing that "move" information from one stage to the next (Reed, 1992). Even though researchers have turned away from a levels of processing approach, Schwartz and Reisberg (1991) argue that "there is an important and correct insight at the heart of the levels view: Finding meaningful connections between what you know and what you learn is very important. Conversely, thinking about what you learn in superficial ways tends not to promote learning" (p. 285).

Connectionism: Another Alternative to the Three-Store Model

Test Bank items 7.42, 7.43, 7.103

Some of the most recent explanations of how memory works are **connectionist models** that assume all knowledge is stored in patterns of connections among basic processing units in a vast network of the brain. The processing of information is assumed to be distributed across this network. So connectionist models use the brain's physical network of neurons as a metaphor for memory networks. Some connectionist models, such as **Parallel Distributed Processing (PDP)**, stay at the metaphorical level and try to describe memory in a way that is consistent with human behavior. Brain-based theories, on the other hand, focus directly on how the nervous system might operate and not on the network-like physical appearance of the nervous system (Iran-Nejad, Marsh, & Clements, 1992; Driscoll, 1994).

In connectionist models, the building blocks of memory are *subsymbolic*, that is, they are more basic than *symbolic* units that have meaning such as propositions or schemas. The subsymbolic units in connectionist models are simple processing devices that interact with one another through connections that are differentially "weighted." Knowledge (proposition and schemas) is represented as patterns of activation in this network. In order to get some idea how a connectionist network might operate, Bereiter (1991) gave the analogy shown in Figure 7.7 on page 260.

In Figure 7.7, every time a particular pattern of frisbees is created by clamping different frisbees to the walls, a particular bit of knowledge is activated. Learning is the tuning and adjustment of different weights (rubber band length and width) among the (frisbee) connections. Exactly how this happens at the level of neurons is not so important. What is important is that many ad-

---

Teaching Tip: To demonstrate levels of processing effects, construct a list of 20 common nouns. Prepare two sets of written instructions, one that asks students to try to count the length of each word as it is read, and another that asks them to rate the personal desirability of the thing named on a 1–5 scale. Distribute the lists to the class so that half receives each version. Read the nouns, and after a 5-minute interval, ask students to recall as many as they can. Read the nouns again and ask the students to determine the number they correctly recalled. Discuss the results and the reasons why one set of instructions (the ratings) is likely to promote better recall than the other instructions.

> *Focus on . . .*   **Information Processing**
>
> - Compare declarative, procedural, and conditional knowledge.
> - Give two explanations for perception.
> - How is information retained in working memory?
> - How is information represented in long-term memory?
> - A child from a large city has trouble understanding and remembering a story about endangered species in a national park. Explain this situation using information processing theory.

Connectionist Models Views of knowledge as being stored in patterns of connections among basic processing units in the brain.

Parallel Distributed Processing Connectionist model that uses the brain's physical network of neurons as a metaphor for memory networks.

FIGURE 7.7

A FRISBEE AND RUBBER-BAND MODEL OF A CONNECTIONIST NETWORK

To understand how a connectionist network of elements might work, consider this rough physical analogy. Imagine there is a bare room, with a clamp on each wall. In the middle of the room is a pile of frisbees attached to one another by rubber bands of different lengths and thicknesses. If you pick any four frisbees and clamp one to each wall, the mass of connected frisbees will vibrate for a while, but finally form a pattern. If you changed the length and thickness of the bands, a different pattern would emerge. Knowledge in a connectionist model of memory is assumed to be *in the connections* – different weights (band length and thickness) create different output patterns. For example, one pattern of activation might suggest the output of the letter A.

- Clamped units
- Activated units
- Hidden units
- Unactivated units
- High connection weights
- Low connection weights

Source: C. Bereiter (1991). Implications of connectionism for thinking about rules. *Educational Researcher, 20* (3), p. 12. Copyright 1991 by the American Educational Research Association. Reprinted by permission of the publisher.

justments can take place simultaneously because the processing is assumed to be parallel, like many computers working at the same time.

Connectionist models have certain advantages. They can account for more than recall of information, and they can explain the slowly developing, incremental, ever-changing nature of human learning. As connection weights are constantly adjusted, learning occurs. When an output doesn't match a goal, the weights can be adjusted, so PDP models provide "for the first time a convenient way of incorporating goals into the dynamics of information processing systems" (Estes, 1988, p. 207). However, connectionist models may not be developed enough to be useful for teachers except to remind us that learning involves the continued building, elaboration, and adjustment of knowledge (Driscoll, 1994; Iran-Nejad, Marsh, & Clements, 1992; Seidenberg, 1993).

Metacognition, Self-Regulation, and Individual Differences

Test Bank items 7.44–7.47, 7.85, 7.113

One question that intrigues many cognitive psychologists is why some people learn and remember more than others. For those who hold an information processing view, part of the answer lies in the executive control processes shown in Figure 7.1. **Executive control processes** guide the flow of information through the information processing system.

We have already discussed a number of control processes, including selective attention, maintenance rehearsal, elaborative rehearsal, organization, and elaboration. These executive control processes are sometimes called *metacognitive skills*. **Metacognition** literally means knowledge about cognition. Donald Meichenbaum and his colleagues describe metacognition as people's "awareness of their own cognitive machinery and how the machinery works" (Meichenbaum, Burland, Gruson, & Cameron, 1985, p. 5). Because people differ in their metacognitive knowledge and skills, they differ in how well and how quickly they learn.

Some of the differences in metacognitive abilities are due to development. As children grow older they are more able to exercise executive control and use strategies. For example, they are more able to determine if they have understood instructions (Markman, 1977, 1979) or if they have studied enough

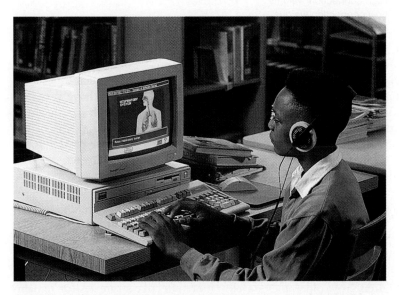

Using computer "menus" is analogous to the use of metacognitive skills in information processing. In both cases, the individual decides what procedure is needed next, selects procedures from several choices, monitors the effect of making the choice, and returns to the menu if the results are unsatisfactory or if a new procedure is needed.

Multicultural Awareness: See Carrell, P. L., Pharis, B. G., & Liberto, J. C (1989). Metacognitive strategy training for ESL reading. *TESOL Quarterly,* 23, 647–678; and Reyes, M. L., & Molnar, L. A. (1991). Instructional strategies for second-language learners in content areas. *Journal of Reading,* 35 (2, October), 96–103.

Background: Flavell (1985) described four aspects of attention in developing children:

1. *Controlled:* Develop longer attention spans and ability to focus on important details, ignoring minor ones.

2. *Tailored to task:* Older children focus attention on most difficult material being learned (Berk 1994).

3. *Directive:* They develop a feel for cues (teachers' voice, gestures) telling then when/how to direct their attention.

4. *Self-monitoring:* They learn to decide if they are using the right strategy, and to change if it's not working.

Executive Control Processes Processes such as selective attention, rehearsal, elaboration, and organization that influence encoding, storage, and retrieval of information in memory.

Metacognition Knowledge about our own thinking processes.

Cognitive Monitoring Monitoring of our thinking and learning strategies.

to remember a set of items (Flavell, Friedrichs, & Hoyt, 1970). Older children automatically use more efficient techniques than younger children for memorizing information (Flavell, 1985; Pressley, 1982). Metacognitive abilities begin to develop around ages 5 to 7 and improve throughout school. Most children go through a transitional period when they can apply a particular strategy if reminded, but will not apply it on their own (Garner, 1990).

Not all differences in metacognitive abilities have to do with age or maturation. There is great variability even among students of the same developmental level. Some individual differences in metacognitive abilities are probably caused by biological differences or by variations in learning experiences. Students can vary greatly in their ability to attend selectively to information in their environment. In fact, many students diagnosed as learning disabled actually have attention disorders (Hallahan & Kauffman, 1994), particularly with long tasks (Pelham, 1981). Attention is also influenced by the individual and cultural differences we examined in chapters 4 and 5, such as learning abilities and preferences, cognitive styles, and cultural background. Students who are field dependent, for example, have difficulty perceiving elements in a pattern and tend to focus on the whole.

Metacognition involves at least two separate components: declarative and procedural knowledge of the skills, strategies, and resources needed to perform a task—knowing *what* to do and *how* to do it; and conditional knowledge to ensure the completion of the task—knowing *when* to do it. The use of these regulatory or metacognitive abilities is known as **cognitive monitoring** (Flavell, 1985). Let's examine some of the individual differences in metacognitive abilities that affect short-term memory and long-term memory.

Individual Differences and Working Memory

As you might expect, there are both developmental and individual differences in short-term memory. Research indicates that young children have very limited working memories, but their memory span improves with age. It is not clear whether these differences are due to changes in memory *capacity* or improvements in *strategy* use. Case (1985a & b) suggests that the total amount of "space" available for processing information is the same at each age, but young children must use quite a bit of this space to remember how to execute basic operations, like reaching for a toy, finding the right word for an object, or counting. Using a new operation takes up quite a bit of the child's working memory. Once an operation is mastered, however, there is more working memory available for short-term storage of new information. Biology may play a role too. As the brain and neurological system of the child mature, processing may become more efficient so that more working-memory space is available.

As children grow older, they develop more effective strategies for remembering information. Most children spontaneously discover rehearsal around age 5 or 6. Siegler (1991) describes a 9-year-old boy who witnessed a robbery, then mentally repeated the license number of the getaway car until he could give the number to the police. Younger children can be taught to rehearse, and will use the strategy effectively as long as they are reminded. But they will not apply the strategy spontaneously. Children are 10 to 11 years old before they have adultlike working memories.

According to Case (1985a & b), young children often use reasonable, but incorrect, strategies for solving problems because of their limited memories. They try to simplify the task by ignoring important information or skipping steps to reach a correct solution. This puts less strain on memory. For example, when comparing quantities, young children may consider only the height of the water in a glass, not the diameter of the glass, because this approach demands less of their memory. According to Case, this explains young children's inability to solve the classic Piagetian conservation problem.

There are several developmental differences in how students use organization, elaboration, and knowledge to process information in working memory. Around age 6, most children discover the value of using *organizational strategies* and by 9 or 10 they use these strategies spontaneously. So, given the following words to learn:

> couch, orange, rat, lamp, pear, sheep, banana, rug, pineapple, horse, table, dog

an older child or an adult might organize the words into three short lists of furniture, fruit, and animals. Younger children can be taught to use organization to improve memory, but they probably won't apply the strategy unless they are reminded. Children also become more able to use elaboration as they mature, but this strategy is developed late in childhood. Creating images or stories to remember ideas is more likely for older elementary-school students and adolescents (Siegler, 1991).

Besides developmental differences, there are other individual variations in short-term memory. Some people seem to have more efficient short-term memories than others (Dempster, 1981), and differences in working memory may be associated with giftedness in math and verbal areas. For example, subjects in one research study were asked to remember lists of numbers, the locations of marks on a page, letters, and words (Dark & Benbow, 1991). Subjects who excelled in mathematics remembered numbers and locations significantly better than subjects talented in verbal areas. The verbally talented subjects, on the other hand, had better memories for words. Based on these results, Dark and Benbow believe that basic differences in information processing abilities play a role in the development of mathematical and verbal talent.

Because working memory is limited, students, particularly younger and less able students, often try to simplify new information by ignoring some elements. This can lead to errors. Case (1985b) suggests the following procedures for dealing with young children or with any students whose working-memory capacity is limited. First, observe the students who are failing at a particular task and determine if they are trying to oversimplify the task. Second, find some way to point out what they are ignoring and why their oversimplified approach won't work. Then demonstrate a better strategy. Finally, have the students practice the new approach. Throughout this process, try to minimize the amount of information the students have to remember by reducing the number of items involved, using familiar terms, emphasizing what is really important, keeping the steps small, and giving lots of practice so that each step becomes as automatic as possible.

Casebook: See the Teachers' Casebook for practicing teachers' ideas about how to help students retain and retrieve information.

Cooperative Learning: To demonstrate several principles of memory, see the following activities in Benjamin, L. T., & Lowman, K. D. (Eds.) (1981). *Activities handbook for the teaching of psychology.* Washington, DC: American Psychological Association.

Wertheimer. Activity 32. *Memory and forgetting.* After being placed in one of four groups, students are asked to memorize a list of words, both meaningful and nonsense, with one emphasized word. Then each group is asked to recall the words at different times. The forgetting curve, meaningfulness, repetition, emphasis, and serial position effect are all memory principles that are exemplified by this exercise.

Kasschau, R. A. Activity 33. *Reconstructive nature of memory.* Students are presented with a series of figures to remember. Before being asked to recall the figures, they are given varying lists of words designed to interfere with the memory of the figures. This exercise demonstrates how a memory is reconstructed and does not just reappear.

What's Wrong with Memorizing?

For years students have relied on memorization to learn vocabulary, procedures, steps, names, and facts. Is this a bad idea?

POINT Rote memorization creates inert knowledge.

Years ago William James (1912) described the limitations of rote learning by telling a story about what can happen when students memorize but do not understand:

A friend of mine, visiting a school, was asked to examine a young class in geography. Glancing at the book, she said: Suppose you should dig a hole in the ground, hundreds of feet deep, how should you find it at the

bottom—warmer or colder than on top?" None of the class replying, the teacher said: "I'm sure they know, but I think you don't ask the question quite rightly. Let me try." So, taking the book, she asked: "In what condition is the interior of the globe?" And received the immediate answer from half the class at once. "The interior of the globe is in a condition of igneous fusion." (p. 150)

The students had memorized the answer, but they had no idea what it meant. Perhaps they didn't understand the meaning of "interior," "globe," or "igneous fusion." At any rate, the knowledge was useful to them only when they were answering test questions, and only then when the questions were phrased exactly as they had

been memorized. Students often resort to memorizing the exact words of definitions when they have no hope for actually understanding the terms or when teachers count off for definitions that are not exact.

Most recently, Howard Gardner has been a vocal critic of rote memorization and a champion of "teaching for understanding." In an interview in *Phi Delta Kappan* (Siegel & Shaughnessy, 1994), Gardner says:

My biggest concern about American education is that even our better students in our better schools are just going through the motions of education. In *The Unschooled Mind*, I review ample evidence that suggests an absence of understanding—the inability of students to take knowledge,

Individual Differences and Long-Term Memory

The major individual difference that affects long-term memory is knowledge. When students have more *domain-specific declarative* and *procedural knowledge,* they are better at learning and remembering material in that domain. Think what it is like for you to read a very technical textbook in an area you know little about. Every line is difficult. You have to stop and look up words or turn back to read about concepts you don't understand. It is hard to remember what you are reading because you are trying to understand and remember at the same time. But with a good basis of knowledge, learning and remembering become easier; the more you know, the easier it is to know more. This is true in part because having knowledge improves strategy use.

Now that we have examined the information processing explanation of how knowledge is represented in memory, how memory might work, and the ways that individual students differ, let's turn to the really important question: What does this tell us about how teachers can help students learn and remember better? How can teachers support the development of knowledge?

Focus on . . .   **Metacognition**

■ Give some examples of your own metacognitive abilities.
■ How can using better metacognitive strategies improve memory?

skills, and other apparent attainments and apply them successfully in new situations. In the absence of such flexibility and adaptability, the education that the students receive is worth little. (pp. 563–564)

COUNTERPOINT Rote memorization can be effective.

Memorization may not be such a bad way to learn new information that has little inherent meaning, such as foreign language vocabulary. Alvin Wang, Margaret Thomas, and Judith Ouellette (1992) compared learning Tagalog (the national language of the Philippines) using either rote memorization or the keyword approach. The

keyword method is a way of creating connections and meaning for associating new words with existing words and images. In their study, even though the keyword method led to faster and better learning initially, long-term forgetting was *greater* for students who had used the keyword method than for students who had learned by rote memorization.

There are times when students must memorize and we do them a disservice if we don't teach them how. Every discipline has its own terms, names, facts, and rules. As adults, we want to work with physicians who have memorized the correct names for the bones and organs of the body or the drugs needed to combat particular infections. Of course, they can look up some informa-

tion or research certain conditions, but they have to know where to start. We want to work with accountants who give us accurate information about the new tax codes, information they probably had to memorize because it changes from year to year in ways that are not necessarily rational or meaningful. We want to deal with computer sales people who have memorized their stock and know exactly which printers will work with our computer. Just because something was learned through memorization does not mean it is inert knowledge. The real question, as Gardner points out above, is whether you can *use* the information flexibly and effectively to solve new problems.

Becoming Knowledgeable: Some Basic Principles

Test Bank items 7.49, 7.51, 7.123

We have discussed the development of conditional knowledge in our consideration of the metacognitive strategies that guide and monitor learning. Next we explore the development of declarative and procedural knowledge. In real-life, this learning is intertwined. Understanding a concept such as "antique" involves *declarative knowledge* about characteristics and images and *procedural knowledge* about how to apply rules to categorize specific antiques. We will discuss the development of declarative and procedural knowledge separately, but keep in mind that real learning is holistic and interrelated.

Development of Declarative Knowledge

Test Bank items 7.53–7.67, 7.86, 7.87, 7.104, 7.105–7.107, 7.115, 7.123–7.125

Within the information processing perspective, to learn declarative knowledge is really to integrate new ideas with existing knowledge and construct an understanding. For example, a teacher says:

"In vitro experiments show vitamin C increases the formation of white blood cells."

Students may ignore the phrase "in vitro" because they have no existing schemas for making sense of it. But through *spreading of activation* the con-

Activity 7.7: Field Experience. See the separate *Instructor's Resource Manual* for Memory and Curriculum, an interview guide for gathering teachers' ideas about how they help their students remember what is taught.

Background: The December 1988/January 1989 issue of *Educational Leadership* (Vol. 46, No. 4) has 10 articles on teaching implications of research on cognitive learning. There are articles on teaching students to summarize, use learning strategies, reading instruction, and reciprocal teaching.

Activity 7.8: Background. See the separate *Instructor's Resource Manual* for Teaching Memory Skills, a summary of Moely, B. E., et al. (1986). How do teachers teach memory skills? *Educational Psychologist, 21,* 55–71. The summary describes the 12 strategies teachers use most often to help their students learn memory skills.

Background: Darley, J. M., Glucksberg, S., & Kinchla, R. A. (1989). *Psychology* (4th ed., p. 226). Englewood Cliffs, NJ: Prentice-Hall. The authors give this example of the effects of massed versus distributed practice: Researchers gave a Spanish vocabulary test to people who had studied the vocabulary eight years earlier. The earlier studying was done during two practice sessions separated by either 720, 48, 24, or zero hours. (i.e., 720 hours was 30 days; zero hours indicated immediately consecutive sessions.) Even after eight years, recall was significantly better the greater the distribution of practice.

Background: Smith, S. M. (1985). A method for teaching name mnemonics. *Teaching of Psychology, 12*, 156–158. A classroom demonstration teaches students how to construct and use name mnemonics. In small groups students create keyword mnemonics for each other's names. The name mnemonics are then presented to the whole class.

Background: Hall, J. W. (1991). More on the utility of the keyword method. *Journal of Educational Psychology, 83*, 171–172. Hall questions the effectiveness of the keyword method.

Rote Memorization Remembering information by repetition without necessarily understanding the meaning of the information.

Part Learning Breaking a list of rote items into shorter lists.

Serial-Position Effect The tendency to remember the beginning and the end but not the middle of a list.

Distributed Practice Practice in brief periods with rest intervals.

Massed Practice Practice for a single extended period.

Mnemonics Techniques for remembering; also, the art of memory.

cepts of "white blood cells" and "vitamin C" cue the retrieval of prior knowledge such as "vitamin C fights colds," "viruses cause colds," and "white blood cells destroy viruses." Using this prior knowledge about colds, viruses, and vitamin C, along with the new information that vitamin C increases white blood cells, the students may infer that "vitamin C fights colds *because* it increases the formation of the white blood cells." This information was neither in their long-term memories nor in the teacher's statement, but it was constructed by the students as they elaborated and organized their understanding of vitamin C. The resulting elaborated, reorganized network of knowledge includes the students' interpretations of the new information from the teacher in addition to their constructions and inferences (Gagne, Yekovich, & Yekovich, 1993). Let's examine factors that support the construction of declarative knowledge.

As you have seen, people learn best when they have a good base of knowledge in the area they are studying. With many well-elaborated schemas and scripts to guide them, new material makes more sense, and there are many possible networks for connecting new information with old. But students don't always have a good base of knowledge. In the early phases of learning, students of any age must grope around the landscape a bit, searching for landmarks and direction. Even experts in an area must use some learning strategies when they encounter unfamiliar material or new problems (Alexander, 1992; Garner, 1990; Perkins & Salomon, 1989; Shuell, 1990).

First we will discuss **rote memorization** strategies, which help students remember information that, while it has little inherent meaning, may provide the basic building blocks for other learning—the populations of the 10 largest cities in the world, for example. Next we will examine *mnemonic strategies*, which build in meaning by connecting what is to be learned with established words or images. Then we explore approaches that build on *meaning*.

Rote Memorization. Very few things need to be learned by rote. The greatest challenge teachers face is to help students think and understand, not just memorize. Unfortunately, many students see memorizing and learning as the same thing (Iran-Nejad, 1990). There are times when we have to memorize something word-for-word, such as lines in a song, poem, or play.

If you must memorize, how would you do it? If you have tried to memorize a list of items that are all similar to one another, you may have found that you tended to remember items at the beginning and at the end of the list but forgot those in the middle. This is called the **serial-position effect. Part learning,** breaking the list into smaller segments, can help prevent this effect, because breaking a list into several shorter lists means there will be fewer middle items to forget.

Another strategy for memorizing a long selection or list is the use of **distributed practice.** A student who studies Hamlet's soliloquy intermittently throughout the weekend will probably do much better than a student who tries to memorize the entire speech on Sunday night. Studying for an extended period, rather than for briefer periods with rest time in between, is called **massed practice.** Distributed practice is more effective than massed practice because long study sessions lead to fatigue, and motivation lags.

Mnemonics. **Mnemonics** are systematic procedures for improving one's memory. These techniques have been demonstrated to be effective for students of all ages, from preschool to college (Levin, 1985; McCormick & Levin, 1987). Many of these mnemonic strategies use imagery.

The **loci method** derives its name from the plural of the Latin word *locus,* meaning "place." To use loci, you must first imagine a very familiar place, such as your own house or apartment, and pick out particular locations. Every time you have a list to remember, the same locations serve as "pegs" to "hang" memories. Simply place each item from your list in one of these locations. For instance, let's say you want to remember to buy milk, bread, butter, and cereal at the store. Imagine a giant bottle of milk blocking the entry hall, a lazy loaf of bread sleeping on the living room couch, a stick of butter melting all over the dining room table, and dry cereal covering the kitchen floor. When you want to remember the items, all you have to do is take an imaginary walk through your house. Other **peg-type mnemonics** use a standard list of words (one is bun, two is shoe . . .) as pegs.

If you need to remember information for long periods of time, an acronym may be the answer. An **acronym** is a form of abbreviation—a word formed from the first letter of each word in a phrase. Examples include NAFTA (North American Free Trade Agreement), scuba (self-contained underwater breathing apparatus), and laser (light amplification by stimulated emission of radiation). Another method forms phrases or sentences out of the first letter of each word or item in a list, for example, Every Good Boy Does Fine to remember the lines on the G clef—E, G, B, D, F. Since the words must make sense as a sentence, this approach also has some characteristics of **chain mnemonics**, methods that connect the first item to be memorized with the second, the second item with the third, and so on. In one type of chain method, each item on a list is linked to the next through some visual association or story. Another chain-method approach is to incorporate all the items to be memorized into a jingle with rhymes, like "i before e except after c," or "Thirty days hath September."

The mnemonic system that has been most extensively applied in teaching is the **keyword method.** The approach has two stages. To remember a foreign word, for example, you first choose an English word, preferably a concrete noun, that sounds like the foreign word or a part of it. Next, you associate the meaning of the foreign word with the English word through an image or sentence. For example, the Spanish word *carta* (meaning "letter") sounds like the English word "cart." Cart becomes the keyword: you imagine a shopping cart filled with letters on its way to the post office, or you make up a sentence such as "The cart full of letters tipped over" (Pressley, Levin, & Delaney, 1982). Figure 7.8 on page 268 offers another example of this method, this time used to learn English vocabulary.

One problem, however, is that the keyword method does not work well if it is difficult to identify a keyword for a particular item. Many words and ideas that students need to remember do not lend themselves to associations with keywords (Hall, 1991; Pressley, 1991). Also, vocabulary learned with keywords may be more easily forgotten than vocabulary learned in other ways, especially if students are given keywords and images instead of being asked to supply the words and images. When the teacher provides the memory links, these associations may not fit the students' existing knowledge and may be forgotten or confused later, so remembering suffers (Wang, Thomas, & Ouelette, 1992). Younger students have some difficulty forming their own images. For them, memory aids that rely on auditory cues—rhymes like "i before e except after c," and "Thirty days hath September" seem to work better.

"HOW MANY TIMES MUST I TELL YOU—IT'S 'CAT' BEFORE 'TEMPLE' EXCEPT AFTER 'SLAVE.'"

(By permission of Bo Brown. from Phi Delta Kappan*)*

Transparency: Acetate transparency T 68, for an example of the use of images to aid recall.

Objective 7.15: Define "mnemonics" and explain four mnemonic strategies for helping students to remember information. Give examples of each.

Handout: For an illustration of the use of keyword mnemonics, see **Handout Master 7.2.** As an application activity, you might ask your students to create similar cartoons for other vocabulary items that express abstractions.

Loci Method Technique of associating items with specific places.

Peg-Type Mnemonics Systems of associating items with cue words.

Acronym Technique for remembering names, phrases, or steps by using the first letter of each word to form a new, memorable word.

Chain Mnemonics Memory strategies that associate one element in a series with the next element.

Keyword Method System of associating new words or concepts with similar-sounding cue words.

Source: J. R. Levin, C. B. McCormick, G. E. Miller, J. K. Berry, and M. Pressley (1982). Mnemonic versus nonmnemonic vocabulary—learning strategies for children. *American Educational Research Journal, 19,* pp.121–136. Copyright 1982 by the American Educational Research Association. Reprinted by permission of the publisher and authors.

Until a student has some knowledge to guide learning, it may help to use some rote memorization and mnemonic approaches to build vocabulary and facts. Not all educators agree, as is noted in the Point/Counterpoint. As knowledge grows, other learning strategies become more helpful.

Making It Meaningful. Perhaps the best single method for helping students learn is to make each lesson as meaningful as possible. Meaningful lessons are presented in vocabulary that makes sense to the students. New terms are clarified through associations with more familiar words and ideas. Meaningful lessons are also well organized, with clear connections between the different elements of the lesson. Finally, meaningful lessons make natural use of old information to help students understand new information through examples or analogies.

The importance of meaningful lessons is emphasized in an example presented by Smith (1975). Consider the three lines below:

1. KBVODUWGPJMSQTXNOGMCTRSO

2. READ JUMP WHEAT POOR BUT SEEK

3. KNIGHTS RODE HORSES INTO WAR

Meaningful lessons are presented in vocabulary that makes sense to the student. New terms are clarified through associations with more familiar words and ideas.

Begin by covering all but the first line. Look at it for a second, close the book, and write down all the letters you remember. Then repeat this procedure with the second and third lines. Each line has the same number of letters, but the chances are great that you remembered all the letters in the third line, a good number of letters in the second line, and very few in the first line.

The first line makes no sense. There is no way to organize it in a brief glance. The second line is more meaningful. You do not have to see each letter because you bring prior knowledge of spelling rules and vocabulary to the task. The third line is the most meaningful. Just a glance and you can probably remember all of it because you bring to this task prior knowledge not only of spelling and vocabulary but also of rules about syntax and probably some historical information about knights (they didn't ride in tanks). This sentence is meaningful because you have existing schemas for assimilating it. It is relatively easy to associate the words and meaning with other information already in long-term memory.

The challenge for teachers is to make lessons less like learning the first line and more like learning the third line. Although this may seem obvious, think about the times when you yourself have read a sentence in a text, or heard an explanation from a professor that might just as well have been KBVO-DUWGPJMSQTXNOGMCTRSO. In chapter 8 we will examine a variety of ways that teachers can support meaningful learning and understanding.

Becoming an Expert: Development of Procedural Knowledge

Test Bank items 7.50, 7.52, 7.68, 7.89, 7.117

Experts in a particular field have a wealth of domain-specific knowledge, that is knowledge that applies specifically to their area or domain. They not only

Teaching Tip: Have students identify the encoding process or memory strategy used in each of the following examples:

a. In order to help children remember the symbol for the number eight, the teacher makes a snowman out of the figure 8 while telling a story about the snowman with eight buttons who lives for eight days.

b. To remember that Bismarck is the capital of North Dakota, a student imagines N.D. on a biscuit.

c. To help students remember how to spell "separate," the teacher says, "There is a rat in separate."

d. A student lists the products of Alabama so that the first letters spell CAPS—for cotton, apples, paper products, and soybeans.

e. Columbus sailed the ocean blue in fourteen hundred and ninety-two.

f. To remember a grocery list, Mrs. Tarent imagines cheese on her TV, limes on the sofa, milk on the table, beans in the wicker basket, and tomatoes on the stove.

g. The teacher uses a time line to show the major events before, during, and after the Vietnam War.

h. Students are asked to compare their present home chores with chores they might have if they lived during Civil War times.

have *declarative knowledge* (facts and verbal information), they also have at their command considerable *procedural knowledge,* an understanding of how to perform various cognitive activities. And they know when and why to apply their understandings; that is, they have *conditional knowledge,* so they can manipulate their declarative and procedural knowledge to solve problems.

Another characteristic distinguishes experts from novices in an area. Much of the expert's declarative knowledge has become "proceduralized," that is, incorporated into routines that can be applied automatically without making many demands on working memory. Skills that are applied without conscious thought are called **automated basic skills.** An example is shifting gears in a standard transmission car. At first you had to think about every step, but as you became more expert (if you did), the procedure became automatic. But not all procedures (sometimes called *cognitive skills*) can be automatic, even for experts in a particular domain. For example, no matter how expert you are in driving, you still have to consciously watch the traffic around you. This kind of conscious procedure is called a *domain-specific strategy.* Automated basic skills and domain-specific strategies are learned in different ways (Gagne, Yekovich, & Yekovich, 1993).

Automated Basic Skills. Most psychologists identify three stages in the development of an automated skill: *cognitive, associative,* and *autonomous* (Anderson, 1990; Fitts & Posner, 1967). At the **cognitive stage,** when we are first learning, we rely on declarative knowledge and general problem-solving strategies to accomplish our goal. For example, to learn to assemble a gas grill, we might try to follow steps in the instruction manual, putting a check beside each step as we complete it to keep track of progress. At this stage we have to "think about" every step and perhaps refer back to the pictures of parts to see what a "1/4 inch metal bolt with lock nut" looks like. The load on working memory is heavy. There can be quite a bit of trial-and-error learning at this stage when, for example, the bolt we chose doesn't fit.

At the **associative stage,** individual steps of a procedure are combined, or "chunked" into larger units. We reach for the right bolt and put it into the right hole, tightening it just enough. One step smoothly cues the next. With practice, the associative stage moves to the **autonomous stage,** where the whole procedure can be accomplished without much attention. So if you assemble enough gas grills, you can have a lively conversation as you do, paying little attention to the grill assembly task. This movement from the cognitive to the associative to the autonomous stage holds for the development basic cognitive skills in any area, but science, medicine, chess, and mathematics have been most heavily researched.

What helps students pass through these three stages? In other words, what can teachers do to help their students become more expert? In general, it appears that two factors are critical: prerequisite knowledge and practice with feedback. First, if students don't have the essential prior knowledge (schemas, skills, etc.), the load on working memory will be too great. In order to compose a poem in a foreign language, for example, you must know some of the vocabulary and grammar of that language, and you must have some understanding of poetry forms. To learn the vocabulary, grammar, and forms as you also try to compose the poem would be too much. Second, practice with feedback allows you to form associations, recognize cues automatically, and combine small steps into larger condition-action rules or *productions.* Even from

---

Casebook: See the Teachers' Casebook at the end of this chapter for practicing teachers' ideas about how to make lessons meaningful and relevant to students.

Automated Basic Skills Skills that are applied without conscious thought.

Cognitive Stage The initial learning of an automated skill when we rely on general problem-solving approaches to make sense of steps or procedures.

Associative Stage Individual steps of a procedure are combined or "chunked" into larger units.

Autonomous Stage Final stage in the learning of automated skills. The procedure is fine-tuned and becomes "automatic."

the earliest stage, this practice should include a simplified version of the whole process in a real context, *not* isolated practice on subskills disconnected from the situations where the skills might be applied. Practice in real contexts helps students learn not only *how* to do a skill but also *why* and *when* (Collins, Brown, & Newman, 1989; Gagne, Yekovich, & Yekovich, 1993).

Domain-Specific Strategies. As we saw earlier, some procedural knowledge, such as monitoring the traffic while you drive, is not automatic because conditions are constantly changing. Once you decide to change lanes, the maneuver may be fairly automatic, but the decision to change lanes was conscious, based on the traffic conditions around you. **Domain-specific strategies** are these consciously applied skills of organizing thoughts and actions to reach a goal. To support this kind of learning, teachers need to provide opportunities for practice in many different situations—practice reading with newspapers, package labels, magazines, books, letters, operating manuals, and so on. In the next chapter, when we discuss problem solving, you will learn other ways to help students develop domain-specific strategies.

Some procedures apply across many domains, as you saw in Table 7.1. In school the most important general procedural knowledge concerns how to study and how to learn. Let's look at these cognitive skills next.

Becoming an Expert Student: Learning Strategies and Study Skills

Test Bank items 7.68, 7.69–7.72, 7.88, 7.116, 7.126

Research on learning reveals one undeniable fact: Students must be cognitively engaged in order to learn. They must be thoughtful. The emphasis today is on helping students develop effective learning strategies and tactics.

Learning Strategies and Tactics. **Learning strategies** are ideas for accomplishing learning goals, a kind of overall plan of attack. **Learning tactics** are the specific techniques that make up the plan (Derry, 1989). Your *strategy* for learning the material in this chapter might include the *tactics* of using mnemonics to remember key terms, first skimming the chapter to identify the organization, and then writing sample answers to possible essay questions. Your use of strategies and tactics reflects your metacognitive knowledge.

Fortunately, teaching these procedural skills has become a high priority in education, and several important principles have been identified.

1. Students must be exposed to a number of *different strategies,* not only general learning strategies but very specific tactics, such as the mapping strategies described later in this chapter.

2. *Teach conditional knowledge* about when, where, and why to use various strategies (Pressley, 1986). Although this may seem obvious, teachers often neglect this step, either because they do not realize its significance or because they assume students will make inferences on their own. A strategy is more likely to be maintained and employed if students know when, where, and why to use it.

3. Students may know when and how to use a strategy, but unless they also *develop the desire to employ these skills,* general learning ability will not improve. Several learning strategy programs (Borkowski, Johnston, & Reid, 1986; Dansereau, 1985) include a motivational training component. In chapters 9 and 10 we look more closely at this important issue of motivation.

Background: Pintrich, P. R., McKeachie, W. J., & Lin, Y. Teaching a course in learning to learn. *Teaching of Psychology, 14,* 81–86. This article describes a college course in personal use of learning strategies based on cognitive learning principles.

Background: Pressley, M. (1986). The relevance of the good strategy user model to the teaching of mathematics. *Educational Psychologist, 21,* 139–161. Teachers are advised (a) to teach strategies; (b) to teach knowledge about when, where, and how to use strategies; (c) to teach general knowledge about factors that promote strategy functioning; (d) to teach relevant nonstrategic knowledge; and (e) to have students practice good strategy use.

Discussion: Assign Pressley, M., & Harris, K. (1990). What we really know about strategy instruction. *Educational Leadership, 48*(1), 31–34. Focus Questions: Is it helpful to teach learning strategies directly? When? With whom?

Objective 7.16: Identify four principles of learning strategy instruction for students.

Background: Derry, S. J. (1989). Putting learning strategies to work. *Educational Leadership, 47*(5), 4–10. Focus Questions: For what kinds of students and learning goals would these learning strategies work best? Why?

Domain-Specific Strategies Consciously applied skills to reach goals in a particular subject or problem area.

Learning Strategies General plans for approaching learning tasks.

Learning Tactics Specific techniques for learning, such as using mnemonics or outlining a passage.

Background: Thomas, J. W., &
Rohwer, W. D. (1986). Academic
studying: The role of learning
strategies. *Educational Psychologist, 21*, 19–41.

Brief abstract: The phenomena
of studying in academic domains
are characterized and analyzed
with special reference to the role
of learning strategies. An autonomous learning model of
studying is presented; its major
components are study outcomes,
study activities, course characteristics (including the nature of criterion performance), and student
characteristics. The article suggests four determinants of the
effectiveness of studying: specificity, generativity, executive monitoring, and personal efficacy.

4. *Direct instruction in schematic knowledge* is often an important component of strategy training. In order to identify main ideas—a critical skill for a number of learning strategies—you must have an appropriate schema for making sense of the material. Table 7.4 summarizes of several learning tactics for learning declarative (verbal) and procedural information (Derry, 1989).

Study Skills. Do you underline or highlight key phrases in textbooks? Are my words turning yellow or pink at this very moment? What about outlining or taking notes? Underlining and note taking are probably two of the most commonly used strategies among college students. Yet few students have ever received any direct instruction in the best ways to underline and take notes. So it is not surprising that many students use ineffective strategies.

One common problem is that students underline or highlight too much. It is far better to be selective. In studies that limit how much students can underline—for example, only one sentence per paragraph—learning has improved (Snowman, 1984). In addition to being selective, you also should actively transform the information into your own words as you underline or take notes. Don't rely on the words of the book or lecturer. Note connections between what you are hearing or reading and other things you already know.

TABLE 7.4   Examples of Learning Tactics

	Examples	Use When?
Tactics for Learning Verbal Information	1. Attention Focusing ■ Making outlines, underlining ■ Looking for headings and topic sentences	With easy, structured materials; for good readers For poorer readers; with more difficult materials
	2. Schema Building ■ Story grammars ■ Theory schemas ■ Networking and mapping	With poor text structure, goal is to encourage active comprehension
	3. Idea Elaboration ■ Self-questioning ■ Imagery ■ PQ4R	To understand and remember specific ideas
Tactics for Learning Procedural Information	1. Pattern Learning ■ Hypothesizing ■ Identifying reasons for actions	To learn attributes of concepts To match procedures to situations
	2. Self-instruction ■ Comparing own performance to expert model	To tune, improve complex skills
	3. Practice ■ Part practice ■ Whole practice	When few specific aspects of a performance need attention To maintain and improve skill

Source: Based on S. Derry (1989), Putting learning strategies to work, *Educational Leadership*, January, pp. 5–6.

Draw diagrams to illustrate relationships. Finally, look for organizational patterns in the material and use them to guide your underlining or note taking (Irwin, 1991; Kiewra, 1988).

Effective use of underlining and note taking depends on an understanding of the organization of the text. Some study strategies have been developed to help students with this key element. Armbruster and Anderson (1981) taught students specific techniques for diagramming relationships among ideas presented in a text. "Mapping" these relationships by noting causal connections, comparison/contrast connections, and examples improved recall. Davidson (1982) suggested that students compare one another's "maps" and discuss the differences. As you can see, the map in Figure 7.9 uses a main idea/detail structure to organize information about the Puritans. There are usually many different ways to map the ideas in a passage.

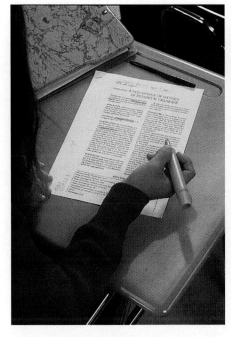

FIGURE 7.9

MAPPING A SOCIAL STUDIES CHAPTER
This student has mapped information related to the concept of "Puritan values" by relating ideas about history, literature, work, and education.

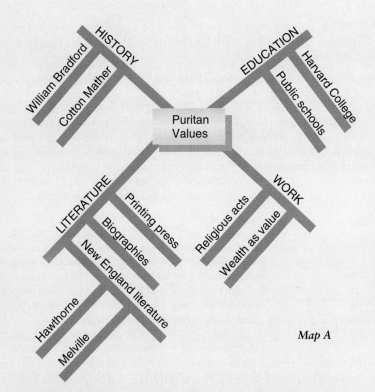

Map A

Source: From Judith Westphal Irwin, *Teaching Reading Comprehension Processes,* p. 55. Copyright © 1986 by Allyn and Bacon. Reprinted by permission.

One common problem students have in studying is underlining or highlighting too much. Studies that limit how much students are allowed to highlight correlate this strategy with higher learning.

Research: Paris, S. G., Lipson, M. Y., & Wixson, K. K. (1983). Becoming a strategic reader. *Contemporary Educational Psychology, 8,* 293–316.

Connections: Remind students that the guidelines for study skills apply to everyone who wishes to become an expert learner and involve the metacognitive abilities and executive control processes discussed earlier in this chapter.

Research: Belmont, J. M. (1989). Cognitive strategies and strategic learning. *American Psychologist, 44,* 142–148. Recent developmental studies have focused on children's learning strategies and on the socio-instructional dynamics that foster strategic learning. Vygotsky's concept of the zone of proximal development has been central to this research effort, both in the context of traditional cognitive strategies research and in terms of its practical applications.

Background: Weinstein, C., Ridley, D. S., Dahl, T., & Weber, E. S. (1988/1989). Helping students develop strategies for effective learning. *Educational Leadership, 46*(4), 17–19.

The authors give many examples of elaboration strategies.

What is the main idea of this story?

If this principle were not true, what would that imply?

What does this remind me of?

How could I use this information in the project I am working on?

How could I represent this in a diagram?

How do I feel about the author's opinion?

How could I put this in my own words?

What might be an example of this?

If I were going to interview the author, what would I ask her?

How does this apply to my life?

Objective 7.18: Show how the PQ4R reading technique can assist a student in reading a chapter of this textbook.

Focus on . . . **Developing Knowledge**

- How would you use the keyword method to teach the exports of foreign countries?
- Describe some procedures for developing procedural knowledge.
- How would you use study skills to study this chapter?

PQ4R A method for studying text that involves six steps: Preview, Question, Read, Reflect, Recite, Review.

PQ4R. There have been many suggestions for understanding and remembering what you read. One of the most enduring systems is the SQ3R (Survey, Question, Read, Recite, Review) approach developed by F. P. Robinson (1961). You may have been exposed to this study strategy at some point during your academic career. A more recent variation is called **PQ4R** (Thomas & Robinson, 1972). In this system the extra R is for reflection, and the P stands for preview; so the acronym means Preview, Question, Read, Reflect, Recite, and Review. To use PQ4R to study this chapter, you would:

1. *Preview.* Introduce yourself to the chapter you are about to read by surveying the major topics and sections. Read the overview, the objectives, the section headings and subheadings, the summary, and perhaps the initial sentences of the major sections. All of these procedures will help activate schemas so you can interpret and remember the text that follows. Previewing also allows you to formulate your own general purpose for reading each section, whether it is to identify the main idea or to note the general biases of the author.

2. *Question.* For each major section, write questions that are related to your reading purposes. One way is to turn the headings and subheadings into questions. For example, in this chapter you might ask: "Why is knowledge important in learning?"

3. *Read.* At last! The questions you have formulated can be answered through reading. Pay attention to the main ideas, supporting details, and other data in keeping with your purposes. You may have to adjust your reading speed to suit the difficulty of the material and your purpose in reading.

4. *Reflect.* While you are reading, try to think of examples or create images of the material. Elaborate and try to make connections between what you are reading and what you already know.

5. *Recite.* After reading each section, sit back and think about your initial purposes and questions. Can you answer the questions without looking at the book? In doing this, you give your mind a second chance to connect what you have read with what you already know. If your mind is blank after reading the section, it may have been too difficult to read comfortably, or you may have been daydreaming. Reciting helps you to monitor your understanding and tells you when to reread before moving on to the next section. Reciting should take place after each headed section, but you may need to do it more often when you are reading difficult material.

6. *Review.* Effective review incorporates new material more thoroughly into your long-term memory. As study progresses, review should be cumulative, including the sections and chapters you read previously. Rereading is one form of review, but trying to answer key questions without referring to the book is the best way. Wrong answers can direct you to areas that need more study, especially before an exam.

Anderson (1990) suggests several reasons for PQ4R's effectiveness. First, following the steps makes students more aware of the organization of a given chapter. How often have you skipped reading headings entirely and thus missed major clues to the way the information was organized? Next, these steps require students to study the chapter in sections instead of trying to learn all the information at once. This makes use of distributed practice. Creating and answering questions about the material forces students to process the information more deeply and with greater elaboration (Doctorow, Wittrock, & Marks, 1978; Hamilton, 1985).

As you may have guessed, the PQ4R method is most appropriate for older children. Very little is known about teaching study skills to students before fifth grade. The effective application of study skills probably requires metacognitive development beyond the range of most very young children. And of course, young children are still focusing much of their attention on learning the basics of word recognition.

Constructivism: Challenging Symbolic Processing Models

Test Bank items 7.73–7.75, 7.127

The information processing perspectives presented in this chapter share several features, even if they differ in their views of memory. All of these approaches see the human mind as a physical symbol-processing system that converts sensory input into symbol structures (e.g., propositions, images, schemas) then processes those symbol structures so knowledge can be held in memory and retrieved, thus modifying the symbol structures in light of new learning. Symbolic processing research has focused on knowledge representation and memory, and recently on the learning of school subjects such as reading, writing, science, and mathematics.

Information processing theorists believe that we actively *construct* knowledge based on what we already know and the new information we encounter, so these approaches are "constructivist," at least in a narrow sense. But, as you will soon see, many researchers and educators believe that these symbolic processing approaches do not take the idea of knowledge construction far enough (Derry, 1992).

Even though symbolic processing models dominated cognitive research for many years, other views of learning were developing as well. Today, there is a strong challenge to cognitive views of learning—the **constructivist perspective.** This perspective is grounded in the research of Piaget, Vygotsky, the Gestalt psychologists, Bartlett, and Bruner as well as the educational philosophy of John Dewey, to mention just a few intellectual roots. As with information processing views, there is no one constructivist theory of learning. For example, there are constructivist approaches in science and mathematics education, in educational psychology and anthropology, and in computer-based education. Some constructivist views emphasize the *shared, social construction of knowledge;* others see social forces as less important (Cognition and Technology Group at Vanderbilt, 1991; Driscoll, 1994; Iran-Nejad, 1990; Perkins, 1991; Spiro, Feltovich, Jacobson, & Coulson, 1991; Tobin, 1990; von Glaserfeld, 1990; Wittrock, 1992).

One of the beginnings of constructivist approaches can be traced to studies of perception conducted early in this century in Germany (and later in the United States) by psychologists called Gestalt theorists. **Gestalt,** which means something like pattern or configuration in German, refers to people's tendency to organize sensory information into patterns or relationships. Instead of perceiving bits and pieces of unrelated information, "the human brain transforms

Connections: Direct instruction in learning strategies is especially important for students with learning disabilities, as described in chapter 4.

Casebook: See the Teachers' Casebook for practicing teachers' ideas about how to help students monitor their reading comprehension so they know when they have not understood what they have read.

Background: Marshall, H. H. (Ed.) (1992). *Redefining student learning: Roots of educational change.* Norwood, NJ: Ablex.

Transparency: Acetate transparency T 65, "Gestalt Principles of Organization," provides a visual self-test for students that illustrates Gestalt principles.

Examples: For an example of a test of figure-ground perception, refer to Subtest II of the Frostig Developmental Test of Visual Perception. Also discuss "Hidden Pictures" (a picture in which objects are concealed and the child has to find them) as an example of practice in improving figure-ground perception. ("Hidden Pictures" can be found in *Highlights* magazine and in other children's magazines.)

Constructivist Perspective View that emphasizes the active role of the learner in building understanding and making sense of information.

Gestalt German for pattern or whole; Gestalt theorists hold that people organize their perceptions into coherent wholes.

FIGURE 7.10

EXAMPLES OF GESTALT PRINCIPLES

Gestalt principles of perception explain how we "see" patterns in the world around us.

a. Figure-ground
What do you see?
Faces or a vase?
Make one figure—the
other ground.

b. Proximity
You see these lines as
3 groups because of
the proximity of lines.

c. Similarity
You see these lines as
an alternating pattern because
of the similarity in height
of lines.

**d. Proximity
outweighing similarity**
You see these lines as
proximal groups instead
similar heights.

e. Common direction
You perceive a continuous
line going up and down.

f. Simplicity
You perceive two whole shapes
instead of five separate shapes.

g. Closure
You perceive a circle
instead of dotted curved lines.

Source: Reprinted with the permission of Macmillan College Publishing Company from *Learning Theories: An Educational Perspective* by Dale H. Schunk, p. 131. Copyright © 1991 by Macmillan College Publishing Company Inc.

objective reality into mental events organized as meaningful wholes" (Schunk, 1991, p. 129). Figure 7.10 presents a few Gestalt principles.

F. C. Bartlett (1932) was another early constructivist theorist. His studies of the constructive nature of remembering (described earlier) highlighted the fact that remembering is more than recall. As we remember, we often create meaning based on what we know and expect.

Knowledge: Accuracy versus Usefulness

Test Bank items 7.75, 7.108

A fundamental difference between symbolic processing and constructivist perspectives is that symbolic theorists assume the world is knowable; there is an objective reality "out there," and an individual can form a relatively complete understanding of it. This understanding may be more or less accurate. Our knowledge constructions may be filled with misconceptions about how the world operates. For example, young children sometimes construct a subtraction procedure that says, "subtract the smaller number from the larger number, no matter which number in a problem is on top."

Many of the more radical **cognitive constructivist perspectives,** on the other hand, do not assume that the world is knowable. They suggest that all knowledge is constructed and based upon not only prior knowledge, but also the cultural and social context. They point out that what is true in one time and place—such as the "fact" before Columbus's time that the earth was flat—becomes false in another time and place. Constructivists are not concerned with accurate, "true" representations of the world, but only with *useful* constructions.

> Radical constructivists hold that we live in a relativistic world that can only be understood from individually unique perspectives, which are constructed through experimental activity in the social/physical world. No individual's viewpoint thus constructed should be viewed as inherently distorted or less correct than another's, although it is certainly true that one individual perspective can be more useful than another. (Derry, 1992, p. 415)

Particular ideas may be useful within a specific **community of practice,** such as fifteenth century navigation, but useless outside that community. What counts as new knowledge is determined in part by how well the new idea fits with current accepted practice. Over time, the current practice may be questioned and even overthrown, but until such major shifts occur, current practice will shape what is considered useful.

Learning: Individual versus Social   Test Bank items 7.76, 7.127

A second difference between information processing and many of the current constructivist perspectives is that information processing theorists tend to focus on the individual information processor as he or she tries to make sense of the world. Thus cognitive psychologists study individual and developmental differences, but may ignore the social situation in which learning occurs. In contrast, **social constructivist approaches** affirm Vygotsky's notion that learning is inherently social and embedded in a particular cultural setting. Learning in the real world is not like studying in school. It is more like an apprenticeship where novices, with the support of an expert guide and model, take on more and more responsibility until they are able to function independently. For the social constructivist, this explains learning in factories, around the dinner table, in high school halls, in street gangs, in the business office, and on the playground. Because learning takes place in a social situation, the norms of the group and the identity of the individual in the group must be considered (Derry, 1992).

Much of the work within the constructivist perspective has focused on teaching. In chapters 8 and 13 we consider many of these implications for teaching. As a summary of the different perspectives on learning, Table 7.5 on page 278 presents the behavioral, information processing, cognitive constructivist, and social constructivist assumptions about learning.

Cognitive Constructivist Perspective   The view of learning emphasizing that learners create or construct their own knowledge through acting on and interacting with the world. The role of other people may be important but is not considered essential.

Community of Practice   Social situation or context in which ideas are judged useful or true.

Social Constructivist Approaches   Views that consider the social context in which learning occurs and emphasizes the importance of social interaction and negotiation in learning.

TABLE 7.5 Four Views of Learning

	Transmissive		Constructivist-Derived	
	Behavioral	**Information/Symbolic Processing**	**Cognitive**	**Social**
Knowledge	Fixed body of knowledge to acquire	Fixed body of knowledge to acquire	Changing body of knowledge, individually constructed in social world	Socially constructed knowledge
	Stimulated from outside	Stimulated from outside Prior knowledge influences how information is processed	Built on what learner brings	Built on what participants contribute, construct together
Learning	Acquisition of facts, skills, concepts	Acquisition of facts, skills, concepts, and strategies	Active construction, restructuring prior knowledge	Collaborative construction of socially defined knowledge and values
	Occurs through drill, guided practice	Occurs through the effective application of strategies	Occurs through multiple opportunities and diverse processes to connect to what is already known	Occurs through socially constructed opportunities
Teaching	Transmission Presentation (Telling)	Transmission Guide students toward more "accurate" and complete knowledge	Challenge, guide thinking toward more complete understanding	Co-construct knowledge with students
Role of Teacher	Primary source of knowledge	A source of knowledge (along with materials)	A source of knowledge (along with student, materials, environment)	A source of knowledge (along with others, materials, social artifacts, environment)
	Manager, supervisor	Teach and model effective strategies	Facilitator, guide	Facilitator, guide Co-participant
	Correct wrong answers	Correct misconceptions	Listen for student's current conceptions, ideas, thinking	Co-construct different interpretation of knowledge; listen to socially constructed conceptions
Role of Peers	Not usually considered	Not necessary but can influence information processing	Not necessary but can stimulate thinking, raise questions	Ordinary part of process of knowledge construction
Role of Student	Passive reception of information	Active processor of information	Active construction (within mind)	Active co-construction with others and self
	Worker	Strategy user	Generator, constructor	Co-generator, co-constructor
	Active listener, direction-follower	Organizer and reorganizer of information Rememberer	Active thinker, explainer, interpreter, questioner	Active thinker, explainer, interpreter, questioner Active social participator

There are variations within each of these views of learning that differ in emphasis. There is also an overlap in constructivist views.

Source: H. H. Marshall (1992, April). *Reconceptualizing learning for restructured schools.* Paper presented at the Annual Meeting of the American Educational Research Association, April, 1992. Adapted by permission of the author.

SUMMARY

Elements of the Cognitive Perspective

Cognitive learning theorists focus on the human mind's active attempts to make sense of the world. The ways we think about situations—along with our beliefs, expectations, and feelings—influence what and how we learn. Cognitivists view knowledge as the outcome of learning and the power of knowledge as the driving element in learning.

The Information Processing Model of Memory

Knowledge can be general or domain specific and can be classified as declarative, procedural, and conditional. Different kinds of knowledge require different teaching approaches.

One widely used cognitive model of the structure and processes of learning is the information processing model, based on the analogy between the mind and the computer. This model includes three storage systems: the sensory register, short-term memory, and long-term memory. Information processing involves encoding, retention, retrieval, and other processes. The sensory register takes in sensory stimuli and briefly holds the information. Attention and perception—the meaning and importance we attach to data received through our senses—affect the contents of the sensory register. Perception is based on bottom-up processing (recognizing familiar elements) and top-down processing (using previous knowledge to fill in incomplete patterns).

Short-term memory, or working memory, holds five to nine bits of information at a time for 20 to 30 seconds. The duration of short-term memory can be extended through maintenance rehearsal, elaboration rehearsal, and chunking. Forgetting in short-term memory results from both interference and time decay.

Long-term memory seems to hold an unlimited amount of information permanently. Information may be coded only verbally or both verbally and visually as part of our semantic, episodic, or procedural memory. In long-term memory, bits of information may be stored and interrelated in terms of propositional networks and schemas (such as story grammars and scripts)—data structures that allow us to represent large amounts of complex information, make inferences, and understand new information.

Information is retrieved from long-term memory through the spread of activation, as one memory activates other related information. Remembering is a reconstruction process leading to accurate, partly accurate, or inaccurate recall. Accurate retrieval depends on the extent to which information is elaborated, organized, and embedded in a context. As in short-term memory, forgetting in long-term memory occurs through interference and decay.

A view of memory that does not depend on the information processing model is the levels of processing theory, in which recall of information is determined by how completely it is processed. Recent connectionist models explain memory in terms of simple processing devices connected in a massive network, like many computers working simultaneously.

Metacognition, Self-Regulation, and Individual Differences

Metacognition—knowledge about thinking—and monitoring are powerful executive controls in the information processing system. Metacognition involves an awareness of what thinking strategies to use and when, how, and why to apply them. There are both developmental and individual differences in metacognitive abilities. As children grow older they are more able to monitor and direct their attention and learning strategies. Teachers can teach metacognitive skills to help students become strategic learners.

Becoming Knowledgeable: Some Basic Principles

Declarative knowledge develops as we integrate new information with our existing understanding. The least effective way to accomplish this is rote memorization, which can best be improved by part learning and distributed practice. Mnemonics as memorization aids include peg-type approaches such as the loci method; acronyms; chain mnemonics; and the keyword method. The best way to learn and remember is to understand. Making the information to be remembered meaningful is important and often is the greatest challenge for teachers.

Teachers also need to help students develop procedural knowledge by teaching learning strategies (plans) and learning tactics (techniques), including study skills. Examples of study skills that aid both memory and comprehension are underlining, note taking, concept mapping, and PQ4R.

Constructivism: Challenging Symbolic Processing Models

Today there is a strong challenge to the information processing perspective—constructivism. Grounded in the work of the Gestalt psychologists, Piaget, Vygotsky, Bruner, Bartlett, and Dewey, this general orientation emphasizes the individual's active construction of meaning. The focus is on meaning-making and knowledge construction, not memory for information. Many constructivist perspectives also consider the social context a major factor in determining what people come to know about themselves and the world.

KEY TERMS

acronym, p. 267
associative state, p. 270
attention, p. 245
automated basic skills, p. 270
autonomous stage, p. 270
automaticity, p. 246
bottom-up processing, p. 245
chain mnemonics, p. 267
chunking, p. 248
cognitive constructivist perspective, p. 277
cognitive monitoring, p. 262
cognitive stage, p. 270
cognitive view of learning, p. 240
community of practice, p. 277
conditional knowledge, p. 243
connectionist models, p. 259
constructivist perspective, p. 275
context, p. 254
decay, p. 249
declarative knowledge, p. 242
distributed practice, p. 266
domain-specific knowledge, p. 242

domain-specific strategies, p. 271
elaboration, p. 254
elaborative rehearsal, p. 247
episodic memory, p. 253
executive control processes, p. 261
general knowledge, p. 242
Gestalt, p. 275
images, p. 250
information processing, p. 242
interference, p. 257
keyword method, p. 267
learning strategies, p. 271
learning tactics, p. 271
levels of processing theory, p. 258
loci method, p. 267
long-term memory, p. 249
maintenance rehearsal, p. 247
massed practice, p. 266
memory strength, p. 249
metacognition, p. 261
mnemonics, p. 266
organization, p. 254
parallel distributed processing (PDP), p. 259

part learning, p. 266
peg-type mnemonics, p. 267
perception, p. 245
PQ4R, p. 274
procedural knowledge, p. 243
procedural memory, p. 254
productions, p. 254
propositional network, p. 250
receptors, p. 244
reconstruction, p. 255
retrieval, p. 255
rote memorization, p. 266
schemata; schema, p. 251
script, p. 253
semantic memory, p. 250
sensory register, p. 244
serial-position effect, p. 266
short-term memory, p. 246
social constructivist approaches, p. 277
spread of activation, p. 255
story grammar, p. 253
top-down processing, p. 245
working memory, p. 247

WHAT WOULD YOU DO?

Preschool and Kindergarten

The first-grade teachers believe that the kindergarten teachers could do a better job of preparing their students to "pay attention" in class. As a kindergarten teacher, what would you do? How would you justify your plans to the first-grade teachers?

Elementary and Middle School

The principal and curriculum coordinator in your school have decided that study skills will be a high priority this year. How would you approach teaching study skills to your third-grade class? To your sixth-grade class?

Several students in your class are recent immigrants and have limited knowledge of the kinds of experiences described in your basal reader series (county fairs, zoos, trips to the beach, shopping malls, etc.). The students speak and read English, but still have difficulty understanding and remembering what they read. What would you do?

Junior High and High School

You have reached a very complicated chapter in your text—one that is difficult for students every year. How would you make the highly abstract concepts (such as sovereignty and jurisprudence) understandable for your students?

The students in your classes seem to equate understanding with memorizing. They prepare for each unit test by memorizing the exact words of the textbook definitions. How would you help them understand that comprehension is the goal?

Cooperative Learning Activity

You just learned that next week the school must begin emergency construction right outside your classroom window. With four or five other members of your class, develop a plan for the week of the construction that will keep your students' attention on the lessons and away from the forklift.

TEACHERS' CASEBOOK

Making It Meaningful

Research shows that we remember best the information that is most meaningful to us: information that makes sense in terms of what we already know and that is clear, organized, and personally relevant. What strategies do you use in your classes to make lessons meaningful and relevant to students?

CURRICULUM INTEGRATION

Integrating the elementary curriculum helps students see that all learning is inter-related. I teach using a hands-on, investigative approach to learning. Instead of teaching math and language separately, lessons often incorporate these two sub-jects. We keep math journals with daily entries. Using the newspaper is an excel-lent way to incorporate all subjects. We use many manipulatives, and I encourage students to use manipulatives at home as well as at school.

Integration takes a lot of teacher preparation. You need to know where you're going with the idea and how you'll end the idea, and you must acquire the needed materials. It's well worth the effort, as my students think learning is fun.

Kathy A. Minniear, *Third-Grade Teacher*
LaVeta Bauer Elementary School, Dayton, Ohio

PERSONALIZED KNOWLEDGE

Kahlil Gibran once wrote, "For thought is a bird of flight that in a cage of words may indeed unfold its wings, but cannot fly." My students say the same thing when they say, "I know what I want to say, but can't put it into words." Students must constantly be encouraged to "put it into words" in both their writing and their class discussions. To accomplish this, we constantly work on a process I call the "personalization of knowledge." It involves (1) defining concepts in one's own words without destroying the meaning, (2) providing one's own examples, (3) cross-referencing items with other experiences and situations, and (4) review-ing repeatedly from varied perspectives. (I have found that one of the best ways to review is to have students convert key phrases into topic sentences, then support them with evidence.)

To make the personalization of knowledge process effective, students must know about it and consciously and consistently practice it. In addition, knowledge must be seen as cumulative. If you are not using ideas from the beginning of the year in new and varied ways at the end of the year, you are doing something wrong.

James D. Kraft, *Social Studies Teacher*
Wausau West High School, Wausau, Wisconsin

STUDENT PROJECTS

Obviously the best way to make something meaningful is to apply it to one's own set of circumstances. One of my favorite classroom projects comes after the lesson on operant conditioning. Each student designs his or her own behavior modifica-tion project, establishing a baseline, determines reinforcers and contingencies, and starts to work on the selected behavior. After three weeks of modification, the stu-dents outline their projects and discuss the outcomes. I find that each student winds up displaying a thorough understanding of the material.

Linda Stahl, *Psychology Teacher*
Ponca City Senior High School, Ponca City, Oklahoma

Helping Them Remember What You Teach

How do you help students with those basic skills, retaining and retrieving information? Do you have special techniques for preventing boredom in the unavoidable rote memorization tasks? What about teaching vocabulary, facts, or concepts?

MAKE IT FUN

One method I have found helpful in memorizing and retaining information is to have a catchy sentence. For example, to help my students memorize the names of the planets, I give them the following sentence: My Very Efficient Mother, Jean, Serves Unusually Nice Pies.

For my poetry lessons, I read one line at a time leaving out one word. The children fill it in. Next we follow the same procedure leaving out two or more words. I have found this technique very successful and enjoyable for all.

Marie Vachon, *Eighth-Grade Teacher*
St. Paul School, Ramsey, New Jersey

ACTIVE AND CREATIVE PARTICIPATION

There are a variety of methods I have found helpful. Here are some examples.

- Role playing: "If you were a medieval laborer after the Black Death had reduced the population by 40 percent, would your labor be worth more or less than previously?"

- Reading aloud from literature: "Here, you look like a good Falstaff. Read these outrageous lines with a yawn every 10 seconds."

- Blackboard: Tactile use of pen on paper to copy. Arrangement of ideas in space on blackboard.

- "Everybody Participates": "John here has this view on these poems. Who agrees? Who disagrees? Looks like the vote is 10 to 5. Who would like to speak for the majority? Who would like to refute?"

Don Knies, *Head and English Teacher*
Brooklyn Friends School, Brooklyn, New York

Reading Comprehension

Many students do not seem to realize they have not fully understood what they have read. How do you help them learn to monitor their own reading comprehension and get the most out of their reading?

BRING THE TEXTS TO LIFE

There are several ways to deepen students' reading and self-monitoring abilities—and to develop a greater appreciation of reading in the process. Students can pick out the three main points of a text or themes of a story and do three drawings to illustrate each. They can make up their own tests based on the text to give to one another. Sometimes checklists of who, what, where, and when are useful for younger students to refer to as they read. Older students often enjoy reversals—let them pick out three minor details or characters and rewrite the text using these as the main points or characters. Set up a talk show around several texts: some students play the authors and are interviewed by student-hosts about their work. Or have a trial based on a novel or play, with the main action as the crime and each character interrogated about his role. Students not taking active roles can be journalists covering the trial.

Simone Wharton, *English Teacher*
New York, New York

8

Concept Learning, Problem Solving, Creativity, and Thinking

I n the previous chapter we focused on the development of knowledge— how people make sense of and remember information and ideas. In this chapter we will focus on understanding and thinking. Specifically, we will examine instructional approaches that have evolved from the cognitive orientation. We will be concerned with the implications of cognitive theories for the day-to-day practice of teaching, particularly for the development of students' thinking and understanding.

Since the cognitive perspective is a philosophical orientation and not a unified theoretical model, teaching methods derived from it are varied. In this chapter, we will first examine four important areas in which cognitive theorists have made suggestions for learning and teaching: concept learning, problem solving, creativity, and thinking. Next, we will explore the question of how to encourage the transfer of learning from one situation to another to make learning more useful. In the final section, we will discuss the instructional theories of two cognitive psychologists—Jerome Bruner's discovery learning and David Ausubel's expository teaching.

By the time you have completed this chapter, you should be able to:

- Design a lesson for teaching a key concept in your subject area.
- Describe the steps in solving complex problems and explain the role of problem representation.
- List three ways you might encourage creativity in your students.
- Discuss the implications of cognitive theories for teaching critical thinking.
- List three ways a teacher might encourage positive transfer of learning.
- Develop lessons using Bruner's and Ausubel's approaches.

List three skills you learned in junior high or high school that you use regularly. These could be procedures, learning strategies, or just useful information. Why do you remember and apply this knowledge? How was it taught?

Planning Tip: See the "Chapter-8-At-A-Glance Planning Guide" in the "Instructor's Section" at the front of this book.

Study Guide: *The Study Guide,* sold separately, contains exercises to help students determine if they have mastered each learning objective for this chapter.

Planning Tip: See the separate *Instructor's Resource Manual* for additional activities and resources for teaching this chapter, including Handout Masters. Also see the Allyn and Bacon *Transparencies in Educational Psychology.*

Planning Tip: See the *Test Bank* and *Study Guide* supplements as you plan for evaluation and measurement of student learning.

Planning Tip: For further information about audiovisual, multimedia, and computer-assisted resources for teaching this chapter, see the "Video and Software Guide" in the *Instructor's Resource Manual.*

Background: Gardner, H. (1991). *The unschooled mind: How children think and how schools should teach.* New York: Basic Books. Gardner, H. (1993). *Educating the unschooled mind: A science and public policy seminar.* Washington, DC: American Educational Research Association. Brandt, R. (1993). On teaching for understanding: A Conversation with Howard Gardner. *Educational Leadership, 50*(7), 4–7.

Concept A general category of ideas, objects, people, or experiences whose members share certain properties.

The Importance of Thinking and Understanding

Understanding is more than memorizing. It is more than retelling in your own words. Howard Gardner(1993b) defines understanding as:

> the capacity to take knowledge, skills, and concepts and apply them appropriately in new situations. If someone only parrots back what he or she has been taught, we do not know whether the individual understands. If that person applies the knowledge promiscuously, regardless of whether it is appropriate, then I would not say he or she understands either. . . . But if that person knows where to apply and where not to apply, and can do it to new situations, he or she understands. (p. 2)

Is thinking different from understanding? We could say that good thinking leads to understanding—so thinking is the process that produces the outcome of understanding. What is good thinking? Some psychologists believe that thinking is the effective use of general strategies, like the learning strategies and tactics described in the previous chapter. Other psychologists associate thinking with problem solving and creativity. Still others talk about critical thinking skills such as evaluating evidence or making judgments.

A simple, practical definition is *good thinking is thinking that achieves its goal* (Baron, 1985). Different goals require different kinds of thinking. In deciding which car to buy, critical thinking and the evaluation of advertisers' claims may be necessary. When faced with a flat tire and no jack, creative problem solving is required to reach your goal (Perkins, Jay, & Tishman, 1993). In the following sections we will explore what is known about different aspects of thinking: problem solving, creativity, and critical thinking, and how teachers can support these paths to understanding. We begin with a discussion of the building blocks of thinking—concepts.

Learning and Teaching about Concepts

Most of what we know about the world involves concepts and relations among concepts (Schwartz & Reisberg, 1991). But what exactly is a concept? A **concept** is a category used to group similar events, ideas, objects, or people. When we talk about a particular concept like *student,* we refer to a category of people who are similar to one another—they all study a subject. The people may be old or young, in school or not; they may be studying baseball or Bach, but they can all be categorized as students. Concepts are abstractions. They do not exist in the real world. Only individual examples of concepts exist.

Concepts help us organize vast amounts of information into manageable units. For instance, there are about 7.5 million distinguishable differences in colors. By categorizing these colors into some dozen or so groups, we manage to deal with this diversity quite well (Bruner, 1973). Without the ability to form concepts, we would find life a confusing series of unrelated experiences. There would be no way of grouping things together, no symbols or shorthand for talking and thinking about similar objects and events. Nothing would be like anything else, and communication would be impossible (Reed, 1992).

Views of Concept Learning

Test Bank items 8.2–8.10, 8.71, 8.72, 8.84, 8.85, 8.98

Traditionally, psychologists have assumed that members of a category share a set of **defining attributes,** or distinctive features. Students all study; books all contain pages of printed, drawn, or photographed materials that are bound together in some way. The defining attributes theory of concepts suggests that we recognize specific examples by noting key features.

Since about 1970, however, these long-popular views about the nature of concepts and category systems have been challenged (Benjafield, 1992). While some concepts, such as equilateral triangle, have clear-cut defining attributes, most concepts do not. Take the concept of *party.* What are the defining attributes? You might have difficulty listing these attributes, but you probably recognize a party when you see (or hear) one. What about the concept of *bird?* Your first thought might be that birds are animals that fly. But is an ostrich a bird? What about a penguin?

Prototypes and Exemplars. According to critics of the traditional view of concept learning, we have in our minds a prototype of a party and a bird—an image that captures the essence of each concept. A **prototype** is the best representative of its category. For instance, the best representative of the "birds" category for many Americans might be a robin (Rosch, 1973). Other members of the category may be very similar to the prototype (sparrow) or similar in some ways but different in others (chicken, ostrich). At the boundaries of a category, it may be difficult to determine if a particular instance really belongs. For example, is a telephone a piece of "furniture"? Is an elevator a "vehicle"? Is an olive a "fruit"? Whether something fits into a category is a matter of degree. Thus, categories have fuzzy boundaries and **graded membership** (Schwartz & Reisberg, 1991). Some events, objects, or ideas are simply better examples of a concept than others.

Another explanation of concept learning suggests that we identify members of a category by referring to exemplars. **Exemplars** are our actual memories of specific birds, parties, furniture, and so on that we use to compare with an item in question to see if that item belongs in the same category as our exemplar. For example, if you see a strange steel-and-stone bench in a public park, you may compare it to the chair in your living room to decide if the uncomfortable-looking creation is still a chair or if it has crossed a fuzzy boundary into "sculpture."

"CITY CHILDREN HAVE TROUBLE WITH THE CONCEPT OF HARVEST."

(© Martha Campbell)

Background: Quote: "The greatest enemy of understanding is coverage. As long as you are determined to cover everything, you actually ensure that most kids are not going to understand." Howard Gardner in Brandt, R. (1993). On teaching for understanding: A Conversation with Howard Gardner. *Educational Leadership, 50*(7), p. 7.

Background: Perkins, D., Jay, E., & Tishman, S. (1993). New Conceptions of thinking: From ontology to education. *Educational Psychologist, 28,* 67–85.

Objective 8.1: Explain the value of concepts and integrate the two views of concept learning.

Defining Attributes Distinctive features shared by members of a category.

Prototype Best representative of a category.

Graded Membership The extent to which something belongs to a category.

Exemplar A specific example of a given category that is used to classify an item.

Focus on . . . **Learning and Teaching about Concepts**

- Distinguish between thinking and understanding.
- What are the defining attributes of the concept of "cup"? What attributes are irrelevant?
- What does it mean for a category to have graded membership?
- Distinguish between prototypes and exemplars.

Prototypes probably are built from experiences with many exemplars. This happens naturally because episodic memories of particular events tend to blur together over time, creating an average or typical chair prototype from all the chair exemplars you have experienced (Schwartz & Reisberg, 1991).

Concepts and Schemas. In addition to prototypes and exemplars, there is a third element involved when we recognize a concept—our schematic knowledge related to the concept. How do we know that counterfeit money is not "real" money, even though it perfectly fits our "money" prototype and exemplars? We know because of its history. It was printed by the "wrong" people. So our understanding of the concept of money is connected with concepts of crime, forgery, the federal treasury, and many others.

In order to understand a concept, it often helps to use visual representations— diagrams, models, drawings, and so on—to "see" the concept more clearly. Here, the teacher has created a visual reminder of the ways students might be "polite."

Strategies for Teaching Concepts

Test Bank items 8.11–8.15, 8.73, 8.86, 8.98

Most of the current approaches to teaching concepts still rely heavily on the traditional analysis of defining attributes. Interest is growing, however, in the prototypes view of concept learning, partly because children first learn many concepts in the real world from best examples or prototypes, pointed out by adults (Tennyson, 1981). The teaching of concepts can combine both distinctive features and prototypes.

Lesson Components. Whatever strategy you use for teaching concepts, you will need to have four components in any lesson: the name of the concept, a definition, relevant and irrelevant attributes, and examples and nonexamples (Joyce & Weil, 1992). In addition, visual aids such as pictures, diagrams, or maps can improve learning of many concepts (Anderson & Smith, 1987).

The name of the concept is important for communicating, but it is somewhat arbitrary. Simply learning a label does not mean the person understands the concept, although the label is necessary for the understanding.

A definition makes the nature of the concept clear. A good definition has two elements: a reference to any more *general category* that the new concept falls under, and a statement of the new concept's *defining attributes* (Klausmeier, 1976). For example, an equilateral triangle is defined as a plane, simple, closed figure (general category), with three equal sides and three equal angles (defining attributes). This kind of definition helps place the concept in a schema of related knowledge.

The identification of relevant and irrelevant attributes is another aspect of teaching concepts. The ability to fly, as we've seen, is not a relevant attribute for classifying animals as birds. Even though many birds fly, some birds do not (ostrich, penguin), and some nonbirds do (bats, flying squirrels). The ability to fly would have to be included in a discussion of the bird concept, but students should understand that flying does not define an animal as a bird.

Examples are essential in teaching concepts. More examples are needed in teaching complicated concepts and in working with younger or less-able students. Both examples and nonexamples (sometimes called *positive* and *negative instances*) are necessary to make the boundaries of the category clear. So a discussion of why a bat (nonexample) is not a bird will help students define the boundaries of the bird concept.

In teaching some concepts "a picture is worth a thousand words"—or at least a few hundred. Seeing and handling specific examples, or pictures of examples, helps young children learn concepts. For students of all ages, the complex concepts in history, science, and mathematics can often be illustrated in diagrams or graphs. For example, Anderson and Smith (1983) found that when the students they taught just read about the concept, only 20 percent could understand the role of reflected light in our ability to see objects. But when the students worked with diagrams such as the one in Figure 8.1, almost 80 percent understood the concept.

FIGURE 8.1

UNDERSTANDING COMPLEX CONCEPTS

Words alone may not be enough. Illustration can help students grasp a difficult concept.

Q. When sunlight strikes the tree it helps the girl to see the tree. How does it do this?

Q. When sunlight strikes the tree it helps the girl to see the tree. How does it do this?

A. Some of the light bounces (is reflected) off the tree and goes to the girl's eyes.

Source: The Educator's Handbook: A Research Perspective, edited by Virginia Richardson-Koehler. Copyright © 1987 by Longman Publishing Group. Reprinted with permission.

Discussion: According to Piaget, a person cannot think in abstract terms until the stage of formal operations is reached. How then can a child learn abstract concepts such as "yesterday" and "happy"?

Discussion: Can abstract concepts be taught through the use of prototypes?

Activity 8.1: Teaching Tip. See the separate *Instructor's Resource Manual* for "Learning a Concept: Weetags Experiment," a class activity that gives students experience learning a novel concept. **Handout Master 8.1** presents examples and nonexamples of the "weetag" concept.

Objective 8.2: List the components of a concept that should be included in any lesson designed to teach the concept.

Research: Tennyson, R. D., & Cocchiarella, M. M. (1986). An empirically based instructional design theory for teaching concepts. *Review of Educational Research, 56,* 40–71.

Brief abstract: An instructional design theory views concept learning as a two-phase process: (a) formation of conceptual knowledge, and (b) development of procedural knowledge. Two fundamental components of the proposed theoretical model are content structure variables and instructional design variables. A rational combination of these components provides the means for the selection of one of four basic instructional design strategies. The theoretical model is described with reference to instructional methods and cognitive processes.

Transparency: Acetate transparency T 70, "Illustrations Help Students to Understand Complex Concepts," shows how concrete visual representations of abstract concepts aid in understanding.

Application: How can a teacher determine if a student has learned a concept?

Research: Novak, J. D., & Musonda, D. (1991). A twelve-year longitudinal study of science concept learning. *American Educational Research Journal, 28,* 117–154.

Cooperative Learning: To help students learn to teach a concept effectively, have them work in pairs or small teams to prepare and give a brief lesson on one concept. Have the students alternate as they role-play presenters, subjects, and observers. Discuss with students how they would evaluate subjects' attainment of the concept.

Activity 8.2: Example. See the *Instructor's Resource Manual* for "Concept Attainment Lesson," an example of an eighth-grade social studies lesson.

Activity 8.3: Cooperative Learning. See the *Instructor's Resource Manual* for "Teaching a Concept Effectively," a group activity.

Activity 8.4: Background. See the *Instructor's Resource Manual* for "Students' Ideas in the Science Classroom," a summary of an article from the January 1988 issue of the *Harvard Education Letter.*

Undergeneralization Exclusion of some true members from a category; limiting a concept.

Overgeneralization Inclusion of nonmembers in a category; overextending a concept.

Concept Mapping Student's diagram of his or her understanding of a concept.

Problem Any situation in which you are trying to reach some goal and must find a means to do so.

Problem Solving Creating new solutions for problems.

Lesson Structure.   Start your concept lesson with prototypes, or best examples, to help the students establish the category. For instance, if you were teaching the concept of *liquid,* you might start with examples such as water or juice. Then move to more difficult, less obvious examples such as cake batter, shampoo, or honey. These examples show the wide range of possibilities the category includes and the variety of irrelevant attributes within a category. This information helps students avoid focusing on an irrelevant attribute as a defining feature. The cake batter example tells students that liquids can be thick and opaque as well as thin and clear. The shampoo example indicates that liquids do not have to be edible. Including liquids that are thick and thin, clear and opaque, edible and inedible, will prevent **undergeneralization,** or the exclusion of some substances from their rightful place in the category *liquid.*

Nonexamples should be very close to the concept, but miss by one or just a few critical attributes. For instance, sand is not an example of liquid, even though it shares one of the characteristics of liquids. You can pour it. Including nonexamples will prevent **overgeneralization,** or the inclusion of substances that are not liquids.

Once students have a good sense of a concept, they should use it. This might mean doing exercises, solving problems, writing, reading, explaining, or any other activity that requires them to apply their new understanding. This will connect the concept into the students' web of related schematic knowledge. One new approach that you may see in some texts and workbooks is **concept mapping** (Novak & Musonda, 1991). Students "diagram" their understanding of the concept, as Amy has in Figure 8.2. Amy's map shows a reasonable understanding of the concept of *molecule,* but also indicates that Amy holds one misconception. She thinks that there is no space between the molecules in solids.

Problem Solving

"Educational programs," Robert Gagne has written, "have the important ultimate purpose of teaching students to solve problems—mathematical and physical problems, health problems, social problems, and problems of personal adjustment" (1977, p. 177). A **problem** has an initial state—the current situation, a goal—the desired outcome, and a path for reaching the goal. Problem solvers often have to set and reach subgoals as they move toward the final solution (Schunk, 1991a). **Problem solving** is usually defined as formulating new answers, going beyond the simple application of previously learned rules to create a solution. Problem solving is what happens when routine or automatic responses do not fit the current situation. Some psychologists suggest that most human learning involves problem solving (Anderson, 1993).

Problem Solving: General or Domain-Specific?

Test Bank items 8.16, 8.17, 8.87, 8.99

There is an interesting debate about problem solving. Some psychologists believe that effective problem-solving strategies are specific to the problem area. That is, the problem-solving strategies in mathematics are unique to math, the

FIGURE 8.2

AMY'S MOLECULE

Amy, an eighth grader, has drawn a map to represent her understanding of the concept of "molecule." Her concept includes one misconception—that there is no space between molecules in solids.

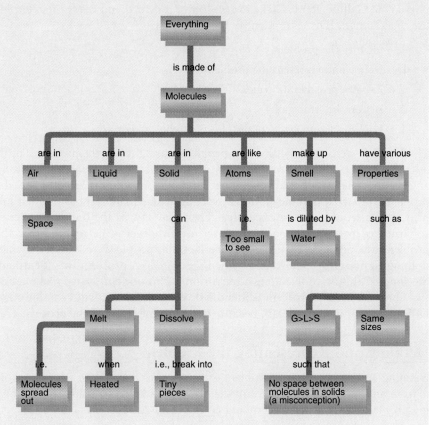

Source: J.D. Novak and D. Musonda (1991). A twelve-year longitudinal study of science concept learning. *American Educational Resource Journal, 28,* p.137. Copyright 1991 by the American Educational Research Association. Reprinted by permission of the publisher.

Transparency: Acetate transparency **T 71,** "An Eighth Grader's Concept Map," illustrates a student's mapping of the concept of molecule. The diagram also shows how misconceptions can become incorporated into concept maps.

Study Guide: Concept Map. See the *Study Guide* for the Concept Map "Problem Solving," also available as **Handout Master 8.6.**

Discussion: Assign Perkins, D. N., & Salomon, G. (1989). Are cognitive skills context-bound? *Educational Researcher, 18,* 16–25. *Focus Questions:* Ask your students to describe how the role of general and specific problem-solving skill changes with the learning situation. What is the evidence for the assertion that cognitive skills are specific to situations and content domains?

strategies in art are unique to art, and so on. Becoming an expert problem solver in an area requires that you master the strategies of the area. The other side of the debate claims that there are some general problem-solving strategies that can be useful in many areas.

There is evidence for both sides of the argument. In fact, it appears that people move between general and specific approaches, depending on the situation and their level of expertise. Early on, when we know little about a problem area or domain, we may rely on general learning and problem-solving strategies to make sense of the situation. As we gain more domain-specific knowledge (particularly procedural knowledge about how to do things in the domain), we need the general strategies less and less. But if we encounter a problem outside our current knowledge, we may return to relying on general strategies to attack the problem (Alexander, 1992; Perkins & Salomon, 1989; Shuell, 1990).

Think of a general problem-solving strategy as a beginning point, a broad outline. Such strategies usually have five stages (Derry, 1991; Derry & Murphy, 1986; Gallini, 1991; Gick, 1986). John Bransford and Barry Stein (1984) use the acronym IDEAL to identify the five steps:

I Identify the problem.

D Define and represent the problem.

E Explore possible strategies.

A Act on the strategies.

L Look back and evaluate the effects of your activities.

Teaching Tip: You might want to note that, although interest in problem solving is great today, many of the early ideas of John Dewey are consistent with the recent emphasis on teaching students to be effective problem solvers.

The first step, identifying that a problem exists, begins the process. This is not always straightforward. There is a story describing tenants who were angry about the slow elevators in their building. Consultants hired to "fix the problem" reported that the elevators were no worse than average and that improvements would be very expensive. Then one day, as the building supervisor watched people waiting impatiently for an elevator, he realized that the problem was not slow elevators but the fact that people were bored; they had nothing to do while they waited. When the boredom problem was identified, the simple solution of installing a mirror on each floor eliminated complaints.

Once a solvable problem is identified, what next? We will examine steps D, E, A, and L in some detail, because these are the heart of the process.

Objective 8.3: Define "problem solving," and describe the steps involved in the *Ideal* process.

Research: Cummins, D. D. (1991). Children's interpretation of arithmetic word problems. *Cognition and Instruction, 8,* 261–289. Stern, E. (1993). What makes certain arithmetic word problems involving the comparison of sets so difficult for children? *Journal of Educational Psychology, 85,* 7–23.

Defining and Representing the Problem

Test Bank items 8.18–8.22, 8.74, 8.88, 8.99

Defining and representing a problem often requires finding the relevant information and ignoring the irrelevant details. For example, consider the following problem adapted from Sternberg & Davidson (1982):

> If you have black socks and white socks in your drawer, mixed in the ratio of four to five, how many socks will you have to take out to make sure of having a pair the same color?

What information is relevant to solving this problem? Did you realize that the information about the four-to-five ratio of black socks to white socks is irrelevant? As long as you have only two different colors of socks in the drawer, you will have to remove only three socks before two of them have to match.

In addition to identifying the relevant information in a problem, you must develop an accurate representation of the situation involved. This may require knowledge that is specific to the problem area. Let's assume we are dealing with story problems, problems that are stated orally or written out, like the socks problem above. To represent these problems successfully, you must (1) understand the *words* and *sentences,* and (2) activate the right *schema* to understand the whole problem (Mayer, 1983a & b, 1992).

Understanding the Words.   The first task in representing a story problem is **linguistic comprehension**, understanding the meaning of each sentence. Take, for example, the following sentence from an algebra story problem:

> The riverboat's rate in still water is 12 miles per hour more than the rate of the river current.

This is a *relational proposition*. It describes the relationship between two rates, that of the riverboat and that of the current. Here is another sentence from a story problem:

> The cost of the candy is $2.75 per pound.

This is an *assignment proposition*. It simply assigns a value to something, in this case the cost of one unit of candy.

Research shows that relational propositions are harder to understand and remember than assignment propositions. In one study, when students had to recall relational and assignment propositions like those above, the error rate for recalling relational propositions was about three times higher than the error rate for assignment propositions. (Mayer, 1982). If you misunderstand the meaning of individual statements in a problem, you will have a hard time representing the whole problem correctly.

The main stumbling block in representing many word problems is the students' understanding of *part-whole relations* (Cummins, 1991). Students have trouble figuring out what is part of what, as evident in this dialogue between a teacher and a first grader:

Teacher: Pete has three apples; Ann also has some apples; Pete and Ann have nine apples altogether; how many apples does Ann have?

Student: Nine.

Teacher: Why?

Student: Because you just said so.

Teacher: Can you retell the story?

Student: Pete had three apples; Ann also had some apples; Ann had nine apples; Pete also has nine apples. (adapted from De Corte & Verschaffel, 1985, p. 19)

The student interprets "altogether" (the whole) as "each" (the parts).

Understanding the Whole Problem.   The second task in representing a problem is to assemble all the sentences into an accurate understanding or *translation* of the total problem. Even if you understand every sentence, you may still misunderstand the problem as a whole. Consider this example:

> Two train stations are 50 miles apart. At 2 P.M. one Saturday afternoon two trains start toward each other, one from each station. Just as the trains pull out of the stations, a bird springs into the air in front of the first train and flies ahead to the front of the second train. When the bird reaches the second train it turns back and flies toward the first train. The bird continues to do this until the trains meet. If both trains travel at the rate of 25 miles per hour and the bird flies at 100 miles per hour, how many miles will the bird have flown before the trains meet? (Posner, 1973)

Activity 8.5: Background. See the *Instructor's Resource Manual* for "Using Representation to Solve Problems," a summary of Fuscon, K. C., & Willis, G. B. (1988). Teaching children to use schematic drawings to solve addition and subtraction problems. *Journal of Educational Psychology, 80*, 192–201.

Example: Piaget identified children's difficulties with part-whole relations years ago when he asked questions like, "There are six daisies and two daffodils; are there more daisies or flowers?" Young children usually answer, "Daisies!"

Linguistic Comprehension Understanding of the meaning of sentences.

Teaching Tip: Guidelines for encouraging problem solving in children:

1. Provide problems, not just solutions.

2. Encourage viewing problems from different angles.

3. Make sure students have necessary background information.

4. Make sure students understand the problem.
   - Make accurate and useful representation
   - Math: ensure linguistic comprehension, use problem schemas
   - Understand through associations and analogies

5. Help students tackle the problem systematically.
   - Verbalize
   - Describe and compare
   - Practice with worked-out examples
   - Watch for "bugs" in math

Your interpretation of the problem is called a translation because you translate the problem into a schema that you understand. If you translate this as a *distance* problem ("I have to figure out how far the bird travels before it meets the oncoming train and turns around, then how far it travels before it has to turn again, and finally add up all the trips back and forth . . . "), then you have a very difficult problem on your hands. But there is a better way to structure the problem. You can represent it as a question of *time* and focus on the time the bird is in the air. If you know how long the bird is in the air, then you can easily determine the distance it will cover, since you know exactly how fast it flies. The solution could be stated like this:

Since the stations are 50 miles apart and the trains are moving toward each other at the same speed, the trains will meet in the middle, 25 miles from each station. Because they are traveling 25 mph, it will take the trains one hour to reach the meeting point. In the one hour it takes the trains to meet, the bird will cover 100 miles because it is flying at 100 miles per hour. Easy!

Research shows that students can be too quick to decide what a problem is asking. The subjects in one study made their decisions about how to categorize standard algebra problems after reading only the first few sentences of a problem (Hinsley, Hayes, & Simon, 1977). Once a problem is categorized—"Aha, it's a distance problem!"—a particular schema is activated. The schema directs attention to relevant information and sets up expectations for what the right answer should look like (Hayes, Waterman, & Robinson, 1977; Robinson & Hayes, 1978).

When students do not have the necessary schemas to represent problems, they often rely on surface features of the situation and represent the problem incorrectly—like the student who wrote "15 + 24 = 39" as the answer to the question, "Joan has 15 bonus points and Louise has 24. How many more does Louise have?" This student saw two numbers and the word "more," so he applied the *add to get more* procedure. When students use the wrong schema, they overlook critical information, use irrelevant information, and may even misread or misremember critical information so that it fits the schema. Errors in representing the problem and difficulties in solving it are the results. But when students use the proper schema for representing a problem, they are less likely to be confused by irrelevant information or tricky wording, like *more* in a problem that really requires *subtraction* (Resnick, 1981). Figure 8.3 gives examples of different ways students might represent a simple mathematics problem.

Translation and Schema Training. How can students improve translation and schema selection? To answer this question, we often have to move from general to area-specific problem-solving strategies. In mathematics, for example, it appears that students benefit from seeing many different kinds of example problems worked out correctly for them. The common practice of showing students a few examples, then having students work many problems on their own, is less effective. Especially when problems are unfamiliar or difficult, worked-out examples are helpful (Cooper & Sweller, 1987). The most effective examples seem to be those that do not require students to integrate several sources of information, such as a diagram and a set of statements about the problem. This kind of attention splitting may put too much strain on the

---

FIGURE 8.3

FOUR DIFFERENT WAYS TO REPRESENT A PROBLEM

A teacher asks, "How many wildlife stamps will Jane need to fill her book if there are three empty pages and each page holds 30 stamps?" The teacher gives the students supplies such as squared paper, number lines, and place-value frames and encourages them to think of as many ways as possible to solve the problem. Here are four different solutions, based on four different but correct representations:

Source: From J. E. Schwartz and C. A. Riedesel, (1994). *Essentials of Classroom Teaching: Elementary Mathematics,* pp. 123–124. Copyright © 1994 by Allyn and Bacon. Reprinted by permission of the publisher.

---

working memory. When students are learning, worked examples should deal with one source of information (Ward & Sweller, 1990). Ask students to compare examples. What is the same about each solution? What is different? Why? The same procedures may be effective in areas other than mathematics.

How else might students develop the schemas they will need to represent problems in a particular subject area? Mayer (1983b) has recommended giving students practice in the following:

1. Recognizing and categorizing a variety of problem types.

2. Representing problems—either concretely in pictures, symbols, or graphs, or in words.

3. Selecting relevant and irrelevant information in problems.

The Results of Problem Representation. There are two main outcomes of the problem representation stage of problem solving, as shown in Figure 8.4 on page 296. If your representation of the problem suggests an immediate solution, your task is done. In the language of the cognitive scientist, you have activated the right schema and the solution is apparent because it is part of the

Discussion: Assign Solving the arithmetic problem. *Harvard Education Letter,* pp. 5–6 (1987, July). A summary of this article appears in the Instructor's Section (IS-61). Focus Question: Ask your students to consider how they might use their pupils' intuitive notions of numbers to teach a basic concept in arithmetic.

FIGURE 8.4

DIAGRAM OF THE PROBLEM-SOLVING PROCESS

There are two paths to a solution. In the first, the correct schema for solving the problem is activated and the solution is apparent. But if no schema is available, searching and testing may become the path to a solution.

Source: M. L. Gick (1986). Problem-solving strategies. *Educational Psychologist, 21,* p. 101. Adapted by permission of the publisher and author.

Transparency: Acetate transparency T 75, "Diagram of the Problem-Solving Process," shows this process in a flow chart.

Objective 8.4: Give examples of heuristics and algorithms in various domains.

Schema-Driven Problem Solving Recognizing a problem as a "disguised" version of an old problem for which one already has a solution.

Algorithm Step-by-step procedure for solving a problem; prescription for solutions.

---

schema. In one sense, you haven't really solved a new problem, you have simply recognized the new problem as a "disguised" version of an old problem that you already know how to solve. This has been called **schema-driven problem solving,** a kind of matching between the situation and your store of systems for dealing with different problems (Gick, 1986). In terms of Figure 8.4, you have taken the *schema-activated route* and have proceeded directly to a solution. But what if you have no existing way of solving the problem or if your activated schema fails? Time to search for a solution!

Exploring Possible Solution Strategies

Test Bank items 8.23–8.29, 8.75, 8.89, 8.90, 8.99, 8.104–8.108

If you do not have existing schemas that suggest an immediate solution, then you must take the *search-based route* indicated in Figure 8.4. Obviously, this path is not as efficient as activating the right schema, but sometimes it is the only way. In conducting your search for a solution, you have available two general kinds of procedures, algorithmic and heuristic.

Algorithms. An **algorithm** is a step-by-step prescription for achieving a goal. It usually is domain-specific; that is, tied to a particular subject area. In solving a problem, if you choose an appropriate algorithm and implement it properly, a right answer is guaranteed. Unfortunately, students often apply algorithms haphazardly. They try first this, then that. They may even happen upon the right answer, but not understand how they found it.

In math classes you probably experienced some success applying algorithms. As long as you were careful in your computations, you were able to solve even such complicated problems as

$$.17\left[43\left(90+\frac{15}{78}\right)\right]-\left[\frac{5}{9}\left(\frac{12356}{2}\right)\right].$$

Later, if you were given geometry proofs to verify or equations to differentiate, you soon discovered that there were no algorithms guaranteeing a solution. At that point, if you did not learn some heuristics, you probably bailed out of math classes as soon as possible.

Heuristics.   A **heuristic** is a general strategy that might lead to the right answer. Since many of life's problems are fuzzy, with ill-defined problem statements and no apparent algorithms, the discovery or development of effective heuristics is important. Let's examine a few.

In **means-ends analysis,** the problem is divided into a number of intermediate or subgoals and then a means of solving each is figured out. For example, writing a 20-page term paper can loom as an insurmountable problem for some students. They would be better off breaking this task into several intermediate goals, such as selecting a topic, locating sources of information, reading and organizing the information, making an outline, and so on. As they attack a particular intermediate goal, they may find that other goals arise. For example, locating information may require that they find someone to refresh their memory about using the library computer search system. Keep in mind that psychologists have yet to discover an effective heuristic for students who are just starting their term paper the night before it is due.

A second aspect of means-ends analysis is *distance reduction,* or pursuing a path that moves directly toward the final goal. People tend to look for the biggest difference between the current state of affairs and the goal and then search for a strategy that reduces the difference. We resist taking detours or making moves that are indirect as we search for the quickest way to reach the goal. So when you realize that reaching the goal of completing a term paper may require a detour of relearning the library computer search system, you may resist at first because you are not moving directly and quickly toward the final goal (Anderson, 1993).

Some problems lend themselves to a **working-backward strategy,** in which you begin at the goal and move back to the unsolved initial problem. Working backward is sometimes an effective heuristic for solving geometry proofs. It can also be a good way to set intermediate deadlines ("Let's see, if I have to submit this chapter in three weeks, then it has to be in the mail by the 28th, so I should have a first draft by the 11th . . . ").

Another useful heuristic is **analogical thinking** (Copi, 1961), which limits your search for solutions to situations that have something in common with the one you currently face. When submarines were first designed, for example, engineers had to figure out how battleships could determine the presence and location of vessels hidden in the depths of the sea. Studying how bats solve an analogous problem of navigating in the dark led to the invention of sonar.

Analogical reasoning can lead to faulty problem solving too. When they are first learning to use a word processor, some people use the analogy of the typewriter and fail to take advantage of the features of a computer. It seems that

Transparency: Acetate transparency T 72, "Problem Solving Using Algorithms and Heuristics," is a flow chart representing the solving of a problem with the goal of writing a good term paper.

Research: Vosniadou, S., & Schommer, M. (1988). Explanatory analogies can help children acquire information from expository text. *Journal of Educational Psychology, 80,* 524–536. This article describes the results of an experiment in which analogies were used to help young children learn new information from science texts. For example, "an infection is like a war," "a stomach is like a blender," etc. Results showed that children in the analogy condition communicated more information than those in the control condition. Implication: Analogies can facilitate learning.

Heuristic General strategy used in attempting to solve problems.

Means-Ends Analysis Heuristic in which goal is divided into subgoals.

Working-Backward Strategy Heuristic in which one starts with the goal and moves backward to solve the problem.

Analogical Thinking Heuristic in which one limits the search for solutions to situations that are similar to the one at hand.

Background: The following five heuristics that might help students solve college math problems are from Schoenfeld, A. H. (1979). Explicit heuristic training as a variable in problem solving performance. *Journal for Research in Mathematics Education, 10,* 173–187.

1. Draw a diagram, if possible.

2. If the problem has an "N" that takes on integer values, try substituting numbers such as 1, then 2, then 3, then 4 for the "N," and look for a pattern in the results.

3. If you are trying to prove a statement, for example, "If X is true, then Y is true," try proving the contrapositive, "If X is false, then Y is false," or try assuming the statement you want to prove is false and look for a contradiction.

4. Try solving a similar problem with fewer variables.

5. Try to set up subgoals.

Example: A student was given the problem, find the value of *x* and *y* that solves both equations:

$$8x + 4y = 28$$
$$4x + 2y = 10$$

The student quickly responded *x* = 2, *y* = 3, correctly addressing the first problem, but neglecting to check the solution on the second.

Connections: In chapter 15 we will again encounter the idea of correcting buggy algorithms, and will note what teachers can do to give helpful feedback.

Objective 8.5: Name the factors that interfere with and the factors that facilitate problem solving.

Verbalization Putting your problem-solving plan and its logic into words.

---

people need knowledge both in the problem domain and the analogy domain in order to use an analogy effectively (Gagne, Yekovich, & Yekovich, 1993).

Putting your problem-solving plan into words and giving reasons for selecting it can lead to successful problem solving (Cooper & Sweller, 1987). You may have discovered the effectiveness of this **verbalization** process accidentally, when a solution popped into your head as you were explaining a problem to someone else. Gagne and Smith (1962) found that when ninth- and tenth-grade students were instructed to state a reason for each step they were taking, they were much more successful in solving the problem than students who did not state reasons.

Acting on the Strategies and Looking Back

Test Bank items 8.99, 8.107

After representing the problem and selecting the approach, the next step is to execute the plan. If the plan primarily involves the use of algorithms, it is important to keep in mind that systematic "bugs," or erroneous algorithms, may have developed in the procedures. Brown and Burton (1979) developed computer programs that located bugs created by students in solving subtraction problems. Their research indicated that children's algorithms contain many more bugs than teachers realize. One buggy algorithm they found, for example, was the consistent subtraction of the smaller from the larger number, regardless of which one was on top. Once teachers discover a bug, they can give specific tips for reworking problems. This corrective feedback is much more helpful than merely advising the child to try again and be more careful.

After you choose a solution strategy and implement it, evaluate the results by checking for evidence that confirms or contradicts your solution. Many people tend to stop working before reaching the best solution and simply accept an answer that works in some cases.

In mathematical problems, evaluating the answer might mean applying a checking routine, such as adding to check the result of a subtraction problem or, in a long addition problem, adding the column from bottom to top instead of top to bottom. Another possibility is estimating the answer. For example, if the computation was 11 x 21, the answer should be around 200, since 10 x 20 is 200. A student who reaches an answer of 2,311 or 23 or 562 should quickly realize these cannot be correct. Estimating an answer is particularly important when students rely on calculators, since they cannot go back and spot an error in the figures.

Factors That Hinder Problem Solving

Test Bank items 8.30, 8.31, 8.76, 8.99, 8.104, 8.105

Consider the following situation:

> You enter a room. There are two ropes suspended from the ceiling. You are asked by the experimenter to tie the two ends of the ropes together and assured that the task is possible. On a nearby table are a few tools, including a hammer and pliers. You grab the end of one of the ropes and walk toward the other rope. You immediately realize that you cannot possibly reach the end of the other rope. You try to extend your reach using the pliers but still cannot grasp the other rope. What can you do? (Maier, 1933)

Functional Fixedness. This problem can be solved by using an object in an unconventional way. If you tie the hammer or the pliers to the end of one

FIGURE 8.5

OVERCOMING FUNCTIONAL FIXEDNESS
In the two-string problem, the subject must set one string in motion in order to tie both strings together.

rope and start swinging it like a pendulum, you will be able to catch it while you are standing across the room holding the other rope, as shown in Figure 8.5. You can use the weight of the tool to make the rope come to you instead of trying to stretch the rope. People often fail to solve this problem, because they seldom consider unconventional uses for materials that have a specific function. This difficulty is called **functional fixedness** (Duncker, 1945). Problem solving requires seeing things in new ways. In your everyday life, you may often exhibit functional fixedness. Suppose a screw on a dresser-drawer handle is loose. Will you spend 10 minutes searching for a screwdriver? Or will you think to use another object not necessarily designed for this function, like a knife or a dime?

Response set can be another block to effective problem solving. Consider the following:

In each of the four matchstick arrangements below, move only one stick to change the equation so that it represents a true equality such as V = V.

$$\lor = \lor || \qquad \lor | = \times | \qquad \times || = \lor || \qquad \lor | = ||$$

You probably figured out how to solve the first example quite quickly. You simply move one matchstick from the right side over to the left to make $\lor | = \lor |$. Examples two and three can also be solved without too much difficulty by moving one stick to change the $\lor$ to an $\times$ or vice versa. But the

Activity 8.6: Teaching Tip. See the *Instructor's Resource Manual* for "Functional Fixedness," an activity that demonstrates the power of functional fixedness to interfere with problem solving.

Teaching Tip: To demonstrate response set, see Activity 42 in Benjamin, L. T., & Lowman, K. D. (Eds.) (1981). *Activities handbook for the teaching of psychology.* Washington, DC: American Psychological Association.

Functional Fixedness Inability to use objects or tools in a new way.

Response Set Rigidity; tendency to respond in the most familiar way.

Focus on . . .   Problem Solving

- What are the steps in the general problem-solving process?
- Why is the representation stage of problem solving so important?
- Describe factors that can interfere with problem solving.

Teaching Tip: In the transparency set there are two problems for your students:

Display transparency T 69, which shows six boxes and a "random" cluster of trees. One object is to move any three toothpicks (lines) to change the arrangement of boxes to five squares. You may even want your students to work with actual toothpicks. When you reveal the solution, note that the original arrangement was a misleading cue; you assume the squares must be adjoining. This is an example of response set.

The other object, an example of insight, presents this problem: How can 10 trees be planted in 5 rows so that there are 4 trees in each row? Allow students to contemplate the solution for a minute or so. Then overlay transparency T 70, which shows the solutions. From Sternberg, R., & Davidson, J. (1982, June). The mind of the puzzler. *Psychology Today*, pp. 37–44.

Insight Sudden realization of a solution.

fourth example (taken from Raudsepp & Haugh, 1977) probably has you stumped. To solve this problem you must change your response set or switch schemas, because what has worked for the first three problems will not work this time. The answer here lies in changing from Roman numerals to Arabic numbers and using the concept of square root. By overcoming response set, you can move one matchstick from the right to the left to form the symbol for square root; the solution reads $\sqrt{1} = 1$, which is simply the symbolic way of saying that the square root of 1 equals 1.

The Importance of Flexibility. Functional fixedness and response set point to the importance of flexibility in understanding problems. If you get started with an inaccurate or inefficient representation of the true problem, it will be difficult—or at least very time-consuming—to reach a solution (Wessells, 1982). Sometimes it is helpful to "play" with the problem. Ask yourself: "What do I know? What do I need to know to answer this question? Can I look at this problem in other ways?" Try to think conditionally rather than rigidly and divergently rather than convergently. Ask, "What could this be?" instead of "What is it?" (Benjafield, 1992).

If you open your mind to multiple possibilities, you may have what the Gestalt psychologists called an insight. **Insight** is the sudden reorganization or reconceptualization of a problem that clarifies the problem and suggests a feasible solution. The supervisor described earlier, who suddenly realized that the problem in his building was not slow elevators but impatient, bored tenants, had an insight that allowed him to reach the solution of installing mirrors by the elevators.

Effective Problem Solving: What Do the Experts Do?

Test Bank items 8.36, 8.100

Most psychologists agree that effective problem solving is based on an ample store of knowledge about the problem area. In order to solve the matchstick problem, for example, you had to understand Roman and Arabic numbers as well as the concept of square root. You also had to know that the square root of 1 is 1. Experts in any given field have a good supply of knowledge, facts, concepts, and procedures. This rich store of knowledge is *elaborated* and *organized* so that it is easy to retrieve from long-term memory when needed. And the knowledge is high in *strength*—it is well practiced (Anderson, 1993).

Experts not only have a wealth of declarative knowledge—facts and verbal information; they also have at their command considerable procedural knowledge—an understanding of how to perform various cognitive activities. And they know when and why to apply their understandings; they have conditional knowledge so they can readily manipulate their declarative and procedural knowledge to solve problems. Let's examine how this expertise develops.

Becoming an Expert Problem Solver: The ACT* Theory

Test Bank items 8.33, 8.77, 8.100

John Anderson (1993) has developed the ACT* theory to explain how we become proficient problem solvers. In the early stages of solving a problem in a new area, when there appear to be no ready-made paths to follow, the novice problem solver often searches for an analogy to use as a guide. What worked before in a similar situation? This first stage is called the *interpretive stage* because the problem solver recalls specific examples and interprets them, checking for similarities to the current problem. This may or may not require drawing on long-term memory. For example, sometimes students use worked-out problems in a mathematics or physics text to guide their search for a solution, even though they never memorize these problems. The knowledge called upon at this point is *declarative*—knowing that something is the case. The problem solvers may rely on words to "talk their way through" the application of the analogy to solve the new problem.

As the problem solver becomes more practiced and proficient in an area, the knowledge that guides problem solving changes from declarative to *procedural*—from knowing *that* to knowing *how*. As declarative knowledge is compiled into productions or *condition-action rules,* the problem solver moves from the interpretive stage to the *procedural stage* where he or she can identify and apply solutions quickly—in situation Y, do X. The more practice and experience an individual has in a problem area, the more accessible and immediate are solutions to problems in that area. At the procedural stage our expert mathematics or physics problem solvers no longer search the text for similar problems to guide them. Instead they (almost automatically) apply the right rules to solve the problem at hand.

Connections: See chapter 7 for a discussion of declarative, procedural, and conditional knowledge.

Objective 8.6: Differentiate declarative and procedural knowledge and describe their relationship to expert problem solving.

Expert Knowledge

Test Bank items 8.32, 8.35, 8.100

The modern study of expertise began with investigations of chess masters (Simon & Chase, 1973). Results indicated that masters can quickly recognize about 50,000 different arrangements of chess pieces. They can look at one of these patterns for a few seconds and remember where every piece on the board was placed. It is as though they have a "vocabulary" of 50,000 patterns. Michelene Chi (1978) demonstrated that third- through eighty-grade chess experts had a similar ability to remember chess piece arrangement. For all the masters, patterns of pieces are like words. If you were shown any word from your vocabulary store for just a few seconds, you would be able to remember every letter in the word in the right order (assuming you could spell the word).

But a series of letters arranged randomly is hard to remember, as you saw in chapter 7. An analogous situation holds for chess masters. When chess pieces are placed on a board randomly, masters are no better than average players at remembering the positions of the pieces. The master's memory is for patterns that make sense or could occur in a game.

A similar phenomenon occurs in other fields. There may be an intuition about how to solve a problem based on recognizing patterns and knowing the "right moves" for those patterns. Experts in physics, for example, organize their knowledge around central principles, whereas beginners organize their smaller amounts of physics knowledge around the specific details stated in the

Objective 8.7: Explain how experts use pattern recognition to represent and to solve problems.

Research: Joshua, S., & Dupin, J. J. (1988). Taking into account student conceptions in instructional strategy: An example in physics. *Cognition and Instruction, 5,* 193–222.

Brief abstract: Several studies have emphasized the predominant influence of students' conceptions in the learning process in physics. But, more often than not, these conceptions are somehow considered in a negative way, as "errors." This article describes taking students' conceptions as an active basis for scientific reasoning in real class situations with groups approximately 12 and 14 years old.

The subject matter taught was basic electricity. The article

Focus on . . . Expert Problem Solving

- Explain the ACT* theory of developing expertise in problem solving.
- What are the differences between expert and novice knowledge in a given area?
- How do misconceptions interfere with learning?
- What are some common misconceptions about being an expert?

---

shows how preinstruction conceptions were actually used (or not used) by the students to explain the electricity phenomena, and how these conceptions subsequently changed, increasing in internal consistency, without moving closer to scientific conceptions. Analogical explanation helped overcome this situation.

Teaching Tip: You might ask students to brainstorm about intuitive models in other fields besides science and mathematics. What are some common misconceptions about cultural differences, history, government, or educational psychology? See chapter 4 of the *Instructor's Resource Manual* for common misconceptions about disabled students.

problems. The experts can find the patterns needed to solve a particular problem very quickly. So they literally don't have to think as hard (Glaser, 1981).

In addition to representing a problem very quickly, experts know what to do next. They have a large store of productions or condition-action schemas about what action to take in various situations. So the steps of understanding the problem and choosing a solution happen simultaneously and fairly automatically (Norman, 1982). Of course, this means that they must have many, many schemas available. A large part of becoming an expert is simply acquiring a great store of knowledge about a particular field. To do this, you must encounter many different kinds of problems in that field, see problems solved by others, and practice solving many yourself.

Experts can use their knowledge to organize information for easier learning and retrieval. Compared to fourth graders with little knowledge of soccer, fourth-graders who were soccer experts learned and remembered far more new soccer terms, even though the abilities of the two groups to learn and remember nonsoccer terms was the same. The soccer experts organized and clustered the soccer terms to aid in recall (Schneider & Bjorklund, 1992). Even very young children who are experts on a topic can use strategies to organize their knowledge. One 4-year old who had learned the names and characteristics of over 40 kinds of dinosaurs organized the information in logical categories much like an adult (Chi & Koeske, 1983). To get an example of this use of dinosaur category knowledge, I called my nephews, Lucas and Geoffrey (4 and 3 years old), who promptly ran down the list of large and small plant- and meat-eating dinosaurs, from the well-known stegosaurus (large, plant eater) to the less familiar ceolophysis (small, meat eater).

Chi, Glaser, and Farr (1988) summarize the superior capabilities of experts. Experts (1) perceive large, meaningful patterns in given information, (2) perform tasks quickly and with few errors, (3) deal with problems at a deeper level, (4) have superior short- and long-term memories, and (5) take a great deal of time to analyze a given problem.

When the area of problem solving is fairly well defined, such as chess or physics or computer programming, then these skills of expert problem solvers hold fairly consistently. But when the problem-solving area is less well-defined and has fewer clear underlying principles, such as problem solving in economics or psychology, then the differences between experts and novices are not as clear-cut (Alexander, 1992).

Novice Knowledge   Test Bank item 8.34

Studies of the differences between experts and novices in particular areas have revealed some surprising things about how novices understand and misunderstand a subject. Physics again provides many examples. Most beginners approach physics with a great deal of misinformation, partly because many of their intuitive ideas about the physical world are wrong. Most elementary-school children believe that light helps us see by brightening the area around objects. They do not realize that we see an object because the light is reflected by the object to our eyes. This concept does not fit with the everyday experience of turning on a light and "brightening" the dark area. Researchers from the Elementary Science Project at Michigan State University found that even after completing a unit on light in which materials explicitly stated the idea of reflected light and vision, most fifth-grade students—about 78 percent—continued to cling to their intuitive notions. But when new materials were designed that directly confronted the students' misconceptions, only about 20 percent of the students failed to understand (Eaton, Anderson, & Smith, 1984).

It seems quite important for science teachers to understand their students' intuitive models of basic concepts. If the students' intuitive model includes misconceptions and inaccuracies, then the students are likely to develop inadequate or misleading representations of a problem. In order to learn new information and solve problems, students must sometimes "unlearn" common sense ideas (Joshua & Dupin, 1987).

Guidelines

Problem Solving

Ask students if they are sure they understand the problem.
Examples
1. Can they separate relevant from irrelevant information?
2. Are they aware of the assumptions they are making?
3. Encourage them to visualize the problem by diagramming or drawing it.
4. Ask them to explain the problem to someone else. What would a good solution look like?

Encourage attempts to see the problem from different angles.
Examples
1. Suggest several different possibilities yourself and then ask students to offer some.
2. Give students practice in taking and defending different points of view on an issue.

Help students develop systematic ways of considering alternatives.
Examples
1. Think out loud as you solve problems.
2. Ask, "What would happen if . . . ?"
3. Keep a list of suggestions.

Teach heuristics.
Examples
1. Ask students to explain the steps they take as they solve problems.
2. Use analogies to solve the problem of limited parking in the downtown area. How are other "storage" problems solved?
3. Use working backward to plan a party.

Let students do the thinking; don't just hand them solutions.
Examples
1. Offer individual problems as well as group problems, so that each student has the chance to practice.
2. Give partial credit if students have good reasons for "wrong" solutions to problems.
3. If students are stuck, resist the temptation to give too many clues. Let them think about the problem overnight.

Research: Resnick, L. B. (1989). Developing mathematical knowledge. *American Psychologist, 44,* 162–169.

Brief abstract: Research has given rise to new ideas about the nature of children's number-knowledge development. This article shows how infants' and preschoolers' implicit protoquantitative reasoning schemas combine with early counting knowledge to produce mathematical concepts of number. It also discusses elementary school children's informal and invented arithmetic, as well as implications for mathematics education.

Research: Delclos, V. R., & Harrington, C. (1991). Effects of strategy monitoring and proactive instruction on children's problem-solving performance. *Journal of Educational Psychology, 83,* 35–42.

Casebook: See the "Teachers' Casebook" for practicing teachers' suggestions on how to help students become effective problem solvers.

Transparency: Acetate transparency T 73, "Problem Solving," provides two common types of problems your students can solve.

Handout: See **Handout Master 8.4** in the *Instructor's Resource Manual* for "Teacher Problem Solving: A Case Study." This case study describes a calculus teacher who struggles to help her advanced math students think creatively and solve problems when they care only about doing well on their tests.

Background: Gardner, H. (1993). *Creating minds: An anatomy of creativity seen through the lives of Freud, Einstein, Picasso, Stravinsky, Elliot, Graham, and Gandhi.* New York: Basic Books.

Connections: See chapter 4 for a figure portraying Sternberg's three aspects of intelligence.

Creativity Imaginative, original thinking or problem solving.

Restructuring Conceiving of a problem in a new or different way.

Incubation Unconscious work toward a solution while one is away from the problem.

Helping Novices Become Experts　Test Bank items 8.37, 8.91

When people have little knowledge in a particular area, they usually have difficulties solving problems. They often reach an impasse in the early stages of problem solving, particularly at the problem-representation stage. Three factors seem to improve problem solving in a particular area (Delclos & Harrington, 1991).

1. Present the needed facts as well as several examples of how to use the facts in solving the problem at hand.

2. Let students practice using the facts in actual problem-solving situations.

3. Provide some way for students to monitor their use of problem-solving strategies as they work.

Creativity and Creative Problem Solving

To some psychologists, **creativity** is a personal quality or trait. We often talk about creative people. Other psychologists suggest that creativity is not a personality trait but a skill or process that produces a "creative" product, such as a painting, invention, computer program, or solution to a personal problem. Howard Gardner (1993a) defines the creative individual as "a person who regularly solves problems, fashions products, or defines new questions in a domain in a way that is initially considered novel but that ultimately becomes accepted in a particular cultural setting" (p. 35). This conception suggests that there is no such thing as "all-purpose creativity;" people are creative *in a particular area.* But to be creative, the "invention" must be intended. An accidental spilling of paint that produces a novel design is not creative unless the artist recognizes the potential of the "accident" or uses the spilling technique intentionally to create new works (Weisberg, 1993). Although we frequently associate the arts with creativity, any subject can be approached in a creative manner.

Creativity and Cognition　Test Bank items 8.43, 8.47

Robert Sternberg (1985) suggests that creativity comes from using the *knowledge-acquisition components* (one of the three aspects of intelligence described in chapter 4) in an insightful way. Having a rich store of knowledge in an area is the basis for creativity, but something more is needed. For many problems, that "something more" is the ability to break set—**restructuring** the problem to see things in a new way, which leads to a sudden insight. Often this happens when a person has struggled with a problem or project, then sets it aside for a while.

　Some psychologists have attributed these sudden solutions to the process of **incubation,** a kind of unconscious working through the problem while you are away from it. But it is more likely that leaving the problem for a time in-

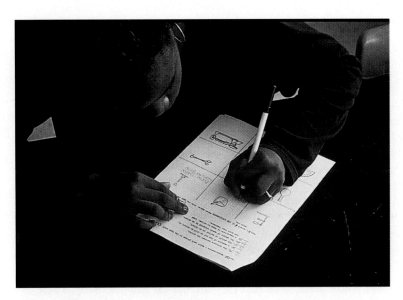

Paper and pencil tests of creativity are difficult to construct and difficult to evaluate as indicators of real-life creativity.

terrupts rigid ways of thinking, such as functional fixedness and response set, so you can restructure it (Gleitman, 1991).

Howard Gardner's (1982a) description of Charles Darwin's creativity downplays sudden, dramatic insight but still highlights the role of knowledge restructuring.

> Darwin experienced no sudden epiphany of inspiration, no wholly novel thoughts or theories. Instead, Darwin marshalled endless lists of thoughts, images, questions, dreams, sketches, comments, arguments, and notes to himself, all of which he continually organized and reorganized. . . . Pivotal insights were anticipated in earlier scribbles, and occasionally discovered twice. (p. 353)

So it seems that creativity requires extensive knowledge, flexibility, and the continual reorganizing of ideas. Darwin's work also shows that motivation and persistence play important roles in creative problem solving.

Assessing Creativity   Test Bank items 8.38–8.40, 8.42, 8.44, 8.47, 8.78

Psychologists and educators confront all the usual research problems when they attempt to study creativity. "How shall we define creativity?" becomes "How shall we measure creativity?" Several answers have been proposed. One answer has been to equate creativity with divergent thinking. As we saw when we discussed Guilford's faces of intellect, **divergent thinking** is the ability to propose many different ideas or answers. **Convergent thinking** is the more common ability to identify only one answer.

Paper-and-Pencil Tests of Creativity. E. P. Torrance has developed two types of creativity tests, verbal and graphic (Torrance, 1972; Torrance &

Teaching Tip: Point out that creativity is not the same as intelligence. It appears that at least average intelligence is required to be creative. Beyond this, IQ and creativity are not related.

Teaching Tip: Two class activities related to creativity are in Benjamin, L. T., & Lowman, K. D. (Eds.) (1981). *Activities handbook for the teaching of psychology*, Washington, DC: American Psychological Association.

LaVoie, A. L. Activity 46. Creativity. The instructor asks small groups of students to devise significant new improvements for everyday objects using unrelated stimulus words. This lets students experience creativity through analogical thinking without the need to suspend reality.

Walls, R. E. Activity 82. A general model for developing classroom creativity exercises. This general model develops a creativity exercise that allows students to identify and experience a drawing process resulting in richer and more artistic drawings.

Connections: See chapter 4 for a discussion of Guilford's faces of intellect and the role played by divergent thinking in this model.

Objective 8.8: Show how Torrance assessed creativity as originality, fluency, and flexibility.

Divergent Thinking Coming up with many possible solutions.

Convergent Thinking Narrowing possibilities to the single answer.

Teaching Tip: To give students a sense of how creativity has been measured, administer this divergent thinking test based on the work of J. P. Guilford:

Ask the class to respond in writing to the following questions:

1. List all the things you can think of that are solid and flexible.

2. Write as many four-word sentences as possible using the same initial letters, without repeating any words. Use these letters:

   W   c   e   n

3. List all the uses you can think of for a paper clip.

After they have finished, tell the class that these questions were designed to measure creativity. Discuss what abilities were required to do well on the test. (Originality, fluency, and flexibility factors, as well as intellectual ability, should be included in the discussion.) Do you think these types of questions are good measures of creativity?

Hall, 1980). In the verbal test, you might be instructed to think up as many uses as possible for a tin can or asked how a particular toy might be changed to make it more fun to play with. On the graphic test, you might be given 30 pairs of parallel vertical lines and asked to create 30 different drawings, each drawing including one pair of lines (Sattler, 1992).

Responses to all these tasks are scored for *originality, fluency,* and *flexibility,* three aspects of divergent thinking. *Originality* is usually determined statistically. To be original, a response must be given by fewer than 5 or 10 people out of every 100 who take the test. *Fluency* is the number of different responses. *Flexibility* is generally measured by the number of different categories of responses. For instance, if you listed 100 uses for a tin can but each use was as some type of container, your fluency score might be high, but your flexibility score would be quite low. Of the three measures, fluency—the number of responses—is the best predictor of divergent thinking (Bjorklund, 1989).

Do measures of divergent thinking really assess creativity? David Bjorklund (1989) says,

> The answer would seem to be that they do, but far from perfectly. There are individual differences in divergent thinking among children. There is only moderate stability of patterns of divergent thinking over childhood, and divergent thinking is marginally related to some aspects of real-life creative activity. Creativity is an elusive concept and one not easily measured by paper-and-pencil tests. (p. 279)

Teachers' Judgments of Creativity. If test scores are not reliable indicators of creativity, what about teachers' opinions? Teachers are not always the best judges of creativity. In fact, Torrance (1972) reports data from a 12-year follow-up study indicating no relationship between teachers' judgments of their students' creative abilities and the actual creativity these students revealed in their adult lives. Some psychologists suggest that the best way to identify creative students is through their achievements. Jerome Sattler (1992) recommends the rating scale in Table 8.1 to identify creative students. As you can see, many of the traits of creative individuals can make them a challenge in the classroom.

Creativity in the Classroom   Test Bank items 8.41, 8.45, 8.79

Even though creative students may be difficult to identify (and sometimes difficult to handle), creativity is worth fostering. Certainly the many social, environmental, and economic problems facing our society will require creative solutions. How can teachers promote creative thinking?

Perhaps the most important step teachers can take to encourage creativity is to make sure students know that their creativity will be appreciated. "Individuals who ultimately make creative breakthroughs tend from their earliest days to be explorers, innovators, and tinkers. . . . Often this adventurousness is interpreted as insubordination, though more fortunate tinkerers receive from teachers or peers some form of encouragement for their experimentation" (Gardner, 1993a, pp. 32–33). All too often, in the crush of day-to-day classroom life, teachers stifle creative ideas without realizing what they are doing. Teachers are in an excellent position to encourage or discourage creativity through their acceptance or rejection of the unusual and imaginative.

TABLE 8.1   Rating Scale

Rating Scale: 1 Not present   4 Moderately present
           2 Minimally present   5 Strongly present
           3 Somewhat present

Trait	Rating (circle one number)	Trait	Rating (circle one number)
1. Ability to concentrate	1 2 3 4 5	19. Internal locus of control and evaluation	1 2 3 4 5
2. Ability to defer judgment	1 2 3 4 5	20. Inventiveness	1 2 3 4 5
3. Above-average IQ	1 2 3 4 5	21. Lack of tolerance for boredom	1 2 3 4 5
4. Adaptability	1 2 3 4 5	22. Need for supportive climate	1 2 3 4 5
5. Aesthetic appreciation	1 2 3 4 5	23. Nonconformism	1 2 3 4 5
6. Attraction to the complex and mysterious	1 2 3 4 5	24. Openness to experience	1 2 3 4 5
7. Curiosity	1 2 3 4 5	25. Playfulness	1 2 3 4 5
8. Delight in beauty of theory	1 2 3 4 5	26. Willingness to take risks	1 2 3 4 5
9. Delight in invention for its own sake	1 2 3 4 5	27. Self-confidence	1 2 3 4 5
10. Desire to share products and ideas	1 2 3 4 5	28. Sense of identity as originator	1 2 3 4 5
11. Eagerness to resolve disorder	1 2 3 4 5	29. Sense of mission	1 2 3 4 5
12. Extensive knowledge background	1 2 3 4 5	30. Sensitivity	1 2 3 4 5
13. Flexibility	1 2 3 4 5	31. Ability to see that solutions generate new problems	1 2 3 4 5
14. Good memory, attention to detail	1 2 3 4 5	32. Spontaneity	1 2 3 4 5
15. High energy level, enthusiasm	1 2 3 4 5	33. Commitment to task	1 2 3 4 5
16. Humor (perhaps bizarre)	1 2 3 4 5	34. Tolerance for ambiguity and conflict	1 2 3 4 5
17. Imagination, insight	1 2 3 4 5	35. Willingness to face social ostracism	1 2 3 4 5
18. Independence	1 2 3 4 5	36. Willingness to daydream and fantasize	1 2 3 4 5

Some of the possible characteristics of creative students are listed on this form.

Source: J. Sattler (1988). *Assessment of children* (3rd. ed.) p. 682. San Diego: Jerome M. Sattler Publisher. Reprinted by permission.

The Brainstorming Strategy.   In addition to encouraging creativity through everyday interactions with students, teachers can try **brainstorming.** The basic tenet of brainstorming is to separate the process of creating ideas from the process of evaluating them because evaluation often inhibits creativity and problem solving (Osborn, 1963). In discussions such as the following, for example, the attempt to have creative ideas about solving a problem often turns into a debate about the merits of one idea:

> We have to decide on a senior project.
> How about cleaning up the river by the park?
> No, that won't work. Someone's bound to get hurt.
> Not necessarily. Five years ago the senior class did it and everything went fine.
> Yes, but . . .

Many participants in such discussions become bored and tune out.

Brainstorming   Generating ideas without stopping to evaluate them.

Research: Clements, D. H. (1991). Enhancement of creativity in computer environments. *American Educational Research Journal, 28,* 173–188.

The goal of brainstorming is to generate as many ideas as possible, no matter how impractical they seem at first. Evaluation, discussion, and criticism are postponed until all possible suggestions have been made. In this way, one idea inspires others; people do not withhold potentially creative solutions out of fear of criticism. After all the ideas are expressed, they can be evaluated, modified, or combined to produce a creative solution.

Individuals as well as groups may benefit from brainstorming. In writing this book, for example, I have sometimes found it helpful to list all the different topics that could be covered in a chapter, then leave the list and return to it later to evaluate the ideas.

Take Your Time—and Play! Years ago, Sigmund Freud (1959) linked creativity and play: "Might we not say that every child at play behaves like a creative writer, in that he creates a world of his own, or, rather, rearranges the things of his world in a new way which pleases him? . . . The creative writer does the same as the child at play. He creates a world of phantasy which he takes very seriously—that is, which he invests with large amounts of emotion . . ." (p. 143–144). There is some evidence that preschool children who spend more time in fantasy and pretend play are more creative. In fact, playing before taking a creativity test resulted in higher scores on the test for the young students in one study (Bjorklund, 1989). Teachers can encourage students of all ages to be more reflective—to take time for ideas to grow, develop, and be restructured. Recent evidence suggests that working in Logo computer environments can enhance both visual and verbal creativity in young children (Clements, 1991). The Guidelines on the facing page, adapted from Frederiksen (1984) and Sattler (1992), describe other possibilities for encouraging creativity.

Focus on . . . Creativity

- Think of a time that you solved a problem in a creative way. What helped you see a different approach?
- What can teachers do to support creativity?

Activity 8.7: Critical Thinking. See the *Instructor's Resource Manual* for "Critical Thinking Strategies and Fallacies for Learning," a description of five commonly held fallacies about how to learn and solve problems.

Activity 8.8: Example. See the *Instructor's Resource Manual* for "Solving Arithmetic Problems."

Examples: The following description of the Odyssey program is abridged from the *Human Intelligence International Newsletter* (1985, winter). Odyssey: A curriculum for thinking, p. 9:

Odyssey, which can be introduced between grades 4 and 8, includes six books:

Foundations of Reasoning, the introductory book. It teaches the basic concepts that are developed in other Odyssey books: processes for gathering, organizing, and interpreting information in systematic and critical ways.

Teaching and Learning about Thinking

Even if we are successful in teaching reading and the other basics, can we be sure that our students will be able to analyze and evaluate what they read? Will they be able to go beyond the information given to apply their knowledge, make judgments, and generate new ideas? In other words, will they be able to think (Prawat, 1991)? Many educational psychologists believe that good thinking can and should be developed in school. But clearly, teaching thinking entails much more than the standard classroom practices of completing worksheets, answering "thought" questions at the end of the chapter, and participating in teacher-led discussions. What else is needed?

One approach has been to focus on the development of *thinking skills,* either through stand-alone programs that teach skills directly, or through indirect methods that embed development of thinking in the regular curriculum.

Encouraging Creativity

Accept and encourage divergent thinking.

Examples
1. During class discussion, ask: "Can anyone suggest a different way of looking at this question?"
2. Reinforce attempts at unusual solutions to problems, even if the final product is not perfect.

Tolerate dissent.

Examples
1. Ask students to support dissenting opinions.
2. Make sure nonconforming students receive an equal share of classroom privileges and rewards.

Encourage students to trust their own judgment.

Examples
1. When students ask questions you think they can answer, rephrase or clarify the questions and direct them back to the students.
2. Give ungraded assignments from time to time.

Emphasize that everyone is capable of creativity in some form.

Examples
1. Avoid describing the feats of great artists or inventors as if they were superhuman accomplishments.
2. Recognize creative efforts in each student's work. Have a separate grade for originality on some assignments.

Be a stimulus for creative thinking.

Examples
1. Use a class brainstorming session whenever possible.
2. Model creative problem solving by suggesting unusual solutions for class problems.
3. Encourage students to delay judging a particular suggestion for solving a problem until all the possibilities have been considered.

Understanding Language. This book helps students extend their analytical skills to vocabulary, sentences, and paragraphs.

Verbal Reasoning. Students learn how to recognize, analyze, produce, and evaluate assertions and arguments.

Problem Solving. Teaches students graphic representation and simulation of problem statements, use of trial and error, and ways to think through the implications of a solution.

Decision Making. How to gather and sort information along the dimensions of relevance, consistency, and credibility.

Inventive Thinking. Designs as descriptions, comparisons, and experimentation; ways to evaluate, improve, and invent designs.

For information contact Don Robb, Charles Bridge Publisher, 85 Main Street, Watertown, MA 02172, 617–926–0329.

Stand-Alone Programs for Developing Thinking

Test Bank item 8.46

There are many different programs that teach thinking skills directly. A resource book for educators (Costa, 1985) lists over 15 different programs, including *de Bono's CoRT* system; *Odyssey: A Curriculum for Thinking*; *Winocur's Project Impact*; *Lipman's Philosophy for Children*; and *Meeker's SOI*. In these programs students learn skills such as comparing, ordering, classifying, and making inferences. The advantage of these **stand-alone thinking skills programs** is that students do not need extensive subject matter knowl-

Stand-Alone Thinking Skills Programs Programs that teach thinking skills directly without need for extensive subject matter knowledge.

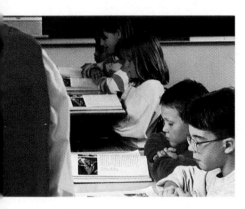

These students seem engrossed in the reading, but what sense are they making of what they read? What are they understanding about the text?

Background: Perkins, D., Jay, E., & Tishman, S. (1993). New conceptions of thinking: From ontology to education. *Educational Psychologist, 28,* 67–85; see also Tishman, S., Perkins, D., and Jay, E. (1995). *The thinking classroom: Learning and teaching in a culture of thinking.* Boston: Allyn and Bacon.

Background: Adams, M. J. (1989). Thinking skills curricula. *Educational Psychologist, 24,* 25–27. This article addresses the explosion of interest in the teaching of thinking. What content or processes should a thinking skills curriculum include? How should it be organized? In what ways would such a curriculum differ in force or effect from thoughtful delivery of conventional school topics? This article concludes that the direct teaching of thinking offers an important complement to conventional school regimen for all students, and is invaluable for those with scholastic difficulties.

edge to master the skills. Students who have had trouble with the traditional curriculum may achieve success—and perhaps an enhanced sense of self-esteem—through these programs. The disadvantage is that the general skills often are not used outside the program unless teachers make a concerted effort to show students how to apply the skills in specific subjects. As you will see shortly when we discuss transfer, encouraging students to apply knowledge and skills to new situations is a challenge for all teachers (Prawat, 1991).

Developing Thinking in Every Class

Test Bank items 8.47–8.50, 8.92

Another way to develop students' thinking is encourage analysis, problem solving, and reasoning through the regular lessons of the curriculum. David Perkins and his colleagues (Perkins, Jay, & Tishman, 1993) propose that teachers do this by creating a *culture of thinking* in their classrooms. This means that there is a spirit of inquisitiveness and critical thinking, a respect for reasoning and creativity, and an expectation that students will learn and understand. In such a classroom, education is seen as *enculturation,* a broad and complex process of acquiring knowledge and understanding. We all learned language by being a member of a particular cultural group. We also learned rules of interaction, norms of appropriate behavior, and many other complicated rules and procedures through living in a culture that supports certain knowledge and values. Just as our home culture taught us lessons about the use of language, the culture of a classroom can teach lessons about thinking by giving us *models* of good thinking; providing *direct instruction* in thinking processes; and encouraging *practice* of those thinking processes through *interactions* with others.

Let's consider how this might happen in a classroom described by Perkins, Jay, and Tishman (1993).

Suppose an eighth-grade teacher wants his students to learn how to construct explanations that involve *multiple causes.* The class is studying the agriculture of eastern Asia, specifically the important rice crops. The teacher introduces a lesson by *modeling* good thinking about multiple causes:

> Have you noticed that the roses in the park bloomed early this year? I'm asking myself why. What factors caused these early blooms? I recall it was a warm winter. That was probably an important factor. But certainly there are other factors involved—probably some hidden ones—and I know it is important to search for them. In fact, now that I have stopped to think, I remember that we had very heavy rains in March. This may be a factor too . . . (Perkins, Jay, & Tishman, 1993, p. 80)

After providing this model, the teacher points out other effects that have multiple causes such as winning a football game or staying healthy. Next, the teacher gives straightforward, *direct instruction* about how to analyze causes, such as considering how causal factors may work together or separately. He teaches the students to draw diagrams that depict multiple causes. Then he gives the students *practice* in analyzing multiple causes by asking them to diagram the causes involved in rice growth and how the causes work together or separately to produce rice. The teacher stimulates their thinking by suggesting that the students cast a wide net—consider many factors such as weather, soil, insects, and farming practices. One student's diagram is presented in Figure 8.6.

FIGURE 8.6

A MULTICAUSAL ANALYSIS OF FACTORS AFFECTING RICE GROWTH

Students are taught how to use the *and/or* convention to diagram causes that work together (*and*) or separately (*or*) to produce an effect, in this case, the growth of rice.

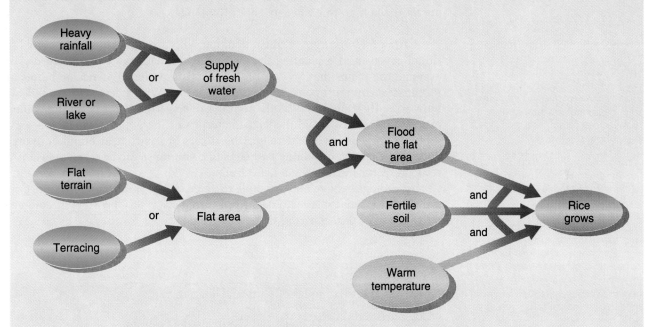

Source: A. Collins and W. Ferguson (1993). Epistemic forms and epistemic games: Structures and strategies to guide inquiry. *Educational Psychologist, 28,* p. 35. Adapted by permission of the publisher and authors.

When the students finish their diagrams, the teacher asks them to discuss their analysis with a partner. He guides the *interaction* with questions such as "How did you identify causes?" "Was it hard to figure out if causes worked together or alone?" "What questions can you invent about this multifactor causal analysis game?" "Can you envision other situations where you could use this kind of causal analysis?"

In this lesson, the four factors of modeling, direct instruction, practice, and interaction help students become expert members of the thinking community.

The Language of Thinking.   How many words can you find in the above lesson that describe aspects of thinking? A quick look finds "search," "asking why," "hidden factors," "analyze," "identify," "figure out," "envision," "effects," "contributing causes," and "invent." My computer's thesaurus just found over 100 more words when I highlighted "thinking." "The language of thinking consists of natural language terms that refer to mental processes and mental products. Words like think—*believe, guess, conjecture, hypothesis,*

Teaching Tip: Ask your students to list all the different words related to thinking that they hear during one of their college classes. They might contrast the "thinking language" in a class that seems to challenge them to think with a class that focuses on skills and facts.

Activity 8.9: Reflection/Journal Writing. See the *Instructor's Resource Manual* for "Using Critical Thinking," a journal-writing activity that encourages students to consider how, when, and why they have engaged in critical thinking in the last week.

Activity 8.10: Field Experience. See the *Instructor's Resource Manual* for "Dimensions of Critical Thinking."

Activity 8.11: Application. See the *Instructor's Resource Manual* for "Remodeling Lessons to Incorporate Critical Thinking," an example of how a didactic lesson on the nervous system can be remodeled to incorporate critical thinking.

Background: *Educational Leadership* (1988, April), *Vol. 45*, No. 7, has a special section called "Teaching Thinking Throughout the Curriculum."

Critical Thinking Evaluating conclusions by logically and systematically examining the problem, the evidence, and the solution.

evidence, suspect, doubt, and *theorize*—form a vocabulary used to describe thinking" (Perkins, Jay, & Tishman, 1993). The classroom should be filled with a clear, precise, and rich vocabulary of thinking. Rather than saying, "What do you think about Jamie's answer?" the teacher might ask questions that expand thinking such as, "What evidence can you give to refute or support Jamie's answer?" "What assumptions is Jamie making?" "What are some alternative explanations?" Students surrounded by a rich language of thinking are more likely to think deeply about thinking.

Critical Thinking. Critical thinking skills are useful in almost every life situation—even in evaluating the media ads that constantly bombard us. To evaluate the claim that 99 out of 100 dentists prefer a particular brand of toothpaste, you must consider such questions as: Which dentists were polled? How were they chosen? Was the toothpaste company involved in the polling process? If so, how could this bias the results of the poll? Or when you see a group of gorgeous people extolling the virtues of a particular brand of orange juice as they frolic in skimpy bathing suits, you must decide if sex appeal is a relevant factor in choosing a fruit drink.

Psychologists have not been able to agree on the skills that constitute critical thinking, but Table 8.2, taken from Kneedler (1985), provides a representative list of critical thinking skills.

TABLE 8.2 Examples of Critical Thinking Skills

Defining and Clarifying the Problem

1. Identify central issues or problems.
2. Compare similarities and differences.
3. Determine which information is relevant.
4. Formulate appropriate questions.

Judging Information Related to the Problem

5. Distinguish among fact, opinion, and reasoned judgment.
6. Check consistency.
7. Identify unstated assumptions.
8. Recognize stereotypes and clichés.
9. Recognize bias, emotional factors, propaganda, and semantic slanting.
10. Recognize different value systems and ideologies.

Solving Problems/Drawing Conclusions

11. Recognize the adequacy of data.
12. Predict probable consequences.

Source: P. Kneedler (1985). California assesses critical thinking. In A. Costa (Ed.), *Developing minds: A resource book for teaching thinking*, p. 277. Alexandria, VA: Association for Supervision and Curriculum Development. Reprinted with permission of the Association for Supervision and Curriculum Development and the author. Copyright 1985 by ASCD. All rights reserved.

No matter what approach you use to develop critical thinking, it is important to follow up with additional practice. One lesson is not enough. For example, if your class examined a particular historical document to determine if it reflected bias or propaganda, you should follow up by analyzing other written historical documents, contemporary advertisements, or news stories. Until thinking skills become overlearned and relatively automatic, they are not likely to be transferred to new situations. Instead, students will use these skills only to complete the lesson in social studies, not to evaluate the claims made by friends, politicians, toy manufacturers, or diet plans. What else is needed to apply good thinking?

Thinking as a "State of Mind."   If people have a rich language for thinking and can be critical thinkers, they need one more quality to use their abilities—*mindfulness.* "Mindfulness is a state of mind that results from drawing novel distinctions, examining information from new perspectives, and being sensitive to context. It is an open, creative, probabilistic state of mind in which the individual might be led to finding differences among things thought to be similar and similarities among things thought to be different" (Langer, 1993, p. 44). The classroom culture should support the development of mindfulness by encouraging students to take intellectual risks, explore, inquire, seek challenges, and invest effort. Otherwise students will learn the language and skills of thinking, but seldom apply them outside the lessons of school. The challenge of transferring knowledge and understanding beyond the school house door has a long history of research in educational psychology.

Activity 8.12: Field Experience. See the *Instructor's Resource Manual* for "Critical Thinking in the Classroom," a field-experience activity that asks your students to observe a lesson and note how to incorporate dimensions of critical/creative thinking. **Handout Master 8.3** is provided to guide the students' observation and planning.

Focus on . . .   Thinking

- What is meant by a culture of thinking in the classroom?
- How is critical thinking required in your everyday life?
- How can a teacher encourage or discourage "mindfulness"?

Research: Greeno, J. G. (1989). A perspective on thinking. *American Psychologist, 44,* 134–141.

Abbreviated abstract: Research on general thinking abilities—productive, higher-order, critical, and creative thinking—has progressed slowly compared with the rapid progress in the study of cognitive structures and procedures. Three framing assumptions for the study of thinking are proposed, involving situated cognition, personal and social epistemologies, and conceptual competence; topics in the psychology of thinking are discussed in relation to the assumptions.

One of the challenges of teaching is helping students develop the ability to use their knowledge in a variety of situations.

Objective 8.9: Define positive and negative transfer, general and specific transfer. Give the principles involved in teaching for positive transfer.

Teaching Tip: To demonstrate negative transfer, see Activity 30 in Benjamin, L. T., & Lowman, K. D. (Eds.) (1981). *Activities handbook for the teaching of psychology.* Washington, DC: American Psychological Association.

Discussion: Ask students what transfer in learning the sound "o" could be expected from learning to read the following words:

First group: does oh Spot good dog (negative transfer)
Second group: hot stop clock pop Tom (positive transfer)

Which group of words is more likely to be found in a first-grade basal reading program?

Application: What principles do you anticipate teaching that could be expected to have general transfer?

Teaching for Transfer

Think back for a moment to a class in one of your high school subjects you did not go on to study in college. Imagine the teacher, the room, the textbook. If you can do all of this, you are using your information processing strategies for search and retrieval very well. Now remember what you actually studied in class. If it was a science class, what were some of the formulas you learned? How about chemical reactions? Oxidation reduction? If you are like most of us, you may remember that you learned these things, but you will not be quite sure exactly what you learned. Were those hours wasted? These questions are about the transfer of learning.

Defining Transfer   Test Bank items 8.51, 8.56–8.80, 8.93, 8.101

Whenever something previously learned influences current learning, **transfer** has occurred. If students learn a mathematical principle in first period and use it to solve a physics problem in fifth period, then positive transfer has taken place. Even more rewarding for teachers is when a math principle learned in October is applied to a physics problem in March.

However, the effect of past learning on present learning is not always positive. *Functional fixedness* and *response set* are examples of negative transfer because they involve the attempt to apply familiar but *inappropriate* strategies to a new situation.

Specific transfer occurs when a rule, fact, or skill learned in one situation is applied in another, very similar situation; for example, applying rules of punctuation to write a job application letter or using knowledge of the alphabet to find a word in the dictionary. *General transfer* involves applying to new problems the principles and attitudes learned in other, often dissimilar situations. Thus, general transfer might mean using problem-solving heuristics to solve issues in your personal life—for example, applying working backward to decide when to call for an appointment to have a dentist check a sore tooth in time to get any necessary treatment done before you leave for spring break.

A Contemporary View of Transfer. Gavriel Salomon and David Perkins (1989) describe two kinds of transfer, termed low-road and high-road transfer. **Low-road transfer** "involves the spontaneous, automatic transfer of highly practiced skills, with little need for reflective thinking" (p. 118). For example, you probably have little trouble driving a friend's car, even though it is different from your car, because you have practiced the skill of driving until it is automatic. You might have trouble, of course, if your friend's car has a standard transmission and you haven't driven a stick shift in years, because you lack recent practice with this kind of car. The key to low-road transfer is practicing a skill often, in a variety of situations, until your performance becomes automatic. So if you worked one summer for a temporary secretarial service and were sent to many different offices to work on all kinds of typewriters and word processors, by the end of the summer you probably would be able to handle most machines easily. Your practice with many machines would let you transfer your skill automatically to a new situation.

Transfer Influence of previously learned material on new material.

Low-Road Transfer Spontaneous and automatic transfer of highly practiced skills.

TABLE 8.3   Kinds of Transfer

	Low-Road Transfer	High-Road Transfer
Definition	Automatic transfer of highly practiced skill	Conscious application of abstract knowledge to a new situation
Key Conditions	Extensive practice Variety of settings and conditions Overlearning to automaticity	Mindful focus on abstracting a principle, main idea, procedure that can be used in many situations.
Examples	Driving many different cars Finding your gate in an airport	Applying PQ4R in reading texts Applying procedures from math in designing a page layout for the school newspaper

---

High-road transfer, on the other hand, involves consciously applying abstract knowledge learned in one situation to a different situation. This can happen in one of two ways. You may learn a principle or a strategy, intending to use it in the future. For example, if you plan to apply what you learn in anatomy class this semester to work in a life-drawing course you will take next semester, you may search for principles about human proportions, muscle definition, and so on. This is called *forward-reaching transfer,* because you are looking forward to applying the knowledge gained. *Backward-reaching transfer* occurs when you are faced with a problem and look back on what you have learned in other situations to help you in this new one. Analogical thinking is an example of this kind of transfer. You search for other, related situations that might provide clues to the current problem. The key to high-road transfer is *mindful abstraction,* or the deliberate identification of a principle, main idea, strategy, or procedure that is not tied to one specific problem or situation but could apply to many. Such an abstraction becomes part of your metacognitive knowledge, available to guide future learning and problem solving. Table 8.3 summarizes the types of transfer.

Test Bank items 8.57–8.64, 8.67, 8.81, 8.82, 8.94, 8.101, 8.103, 8.110–8.112

Teaching for Positive Transfer

Years of research and experience show that teachers cannot expect students to automatically transfer what they learn to new problems. We have seen repeatedly in this book that students will master new knowledge, problem-solving procedures, and learning strategies, but not use them unless prompted or guided. This is because learning is situated, that is, it is learned in particular situations. We learn solutions to particular problems, not general all-purpose solutions that can fit any problem. Because knowledge is learned as a tool to solve particular problems, we may not realize that the knowledge is relevant when we encounter a problem that seems different, at least on the surface. We tend to use knowledge only in situations where it is obviously appropriate (Driscoll, 1994; Singley & Anderson, 1989). How can you make sure your students will use what they learn, even when situations change?

Research: Winkles, J. (1986). Achievement, understanding, and transfer in a learning hierarchy. *American Educational Research Journal, 23,* 275–288.

Brief abstract: A set of skills is defined in the trigonometry of the right triangle, and a learning hierarchy is identified, including examples of lateral and vertical transfer. Two instructional treatments identified as "achievement only" and "achievement with understanding" are used in ordinary math classes with 90 eighth-grade students and 87 ninth-grade students. The "achievement with understanding" treatment is better for the development of lateral transfer for the more mathematically able students. A small amount of additional instruction on vertical-transfer items produces much better performance under both treatments.

Discussion: Ask students why they think information that is overlearned is resistant to forgetting. Do we overlearn all information that is practiced and rehearsed?

High-Road Transfer Application of abstract knowledge learned in one situation to a different situation.

"I DON'T GET IT! THEY MAKE US LEARN READING, WRITING AND ARITHMETIC TO PREPARE US FOR A WORLD OF VIDEOTAPES, COMPUTER TERMINALS AND CALCULATORS!"

(Harley Schwadron—Phi Delta Kappan*)*

Background: Salomon, G., & Perkins, D. N. (1989). Rocky roads to transfer: Rethinking mechanisms of a neglected phenomenon. *Educational Psychology, 25,* 113–142.

Casebook: See the "Teachers' Casebook" for ideas about how to encourage transfer of learning outside the classroom.

Focus on . . . **Transfer**

- Distinguish between specific and general transfer.
- How do low-road and high-road transfer relate to the ACT* theory of the development of expertise?
- Why is it important to ask students to apply new knowledge to both well-defined and ill-defined problems?

Overlearning Practicing a task past the point of mastery to combat forgetting and improve transfer.

What Is Worth Learning? First you must answer the question "What is worth learning?" The learning of basic skills like reading, writing, computing, and speaking will definitely transfer to other situations, because these skills are necessary for later work both in and out of school—writing job applications, reading novels, paying bills, locating and evaluating health care services, among others. All later learning depends on positive transfer of these basics to new situations.

Teachers must also be aware of what the future is likely to hold for their students, both as a group and as individuals. What will society require of them as adults? What will their careers require of them? As a child growing up in Texas in the 1950s and 1960s, I studied nothing about computers, even though my father was a computer systems analyst; yet now I spend hours at this word processor. Computer programming and word processing were not part of my high school curriculum, but learning to use a slide rule *was* taught. Now calculators and computers have made this skill obsolete. Undoubtedly changes as extreme and unpredictable as these await the students you will teach. For this reason, the general transfer of principles, attitudes, critical thinking ability, and problem-solving strategies will be just as important to these students as the specific transfer of basic skills.

How Can Teachers Help? To have something to transfer, students must first learn and understand.

Students will be more likely to transfer information to new situations if they have been actively involved in the learning process. They must be encouraged to form abstractions that they will apply later. For example, Salomon and Perkins (1989) give this advice for teaching history:

[The] history teacher can introduce direct discussion of contemporary events. To provoke forward-reaching transfer, the teacher can select an episode in history and encourage students to seek contemporary analogs. To provoke backward-reaching transfer, the teacher can choose a current phenomenon . . . and urge students to reach into their historical repertoires for analogies and disanalogies. (p. 136)

Newly mastered concepts, principles, and strategies must be practiced in a wide variety of situations. Positive transfer is encouraged when skills are practiced under authentic conditions, similar to those that will exist when the skills are needed later. Students can learn about multiplication by figuring how many ways they can make $1.67 cents using only dimes and pennies. They can learn historical research methods by researching their own family. Some of these applications should involve complex, unstructured problems, since many of the problems to be faced in later life, in school and out, will not come to students complete with instructions.

Greater transfer can also be ensured by **overlearning,** practicing a skill past the point of mastery. Many of the basic facts students learn in elementary school, such as the multiplication tables, are traditionally overlearned. Overlearning helps students retrieve the information quickly and automatically when it is needed.

Cognitive Models of Teaching

Many instructional models are consistent with cognitive theories of learning. We will consider Jerome Bruner's discovery learning and David Ausubel's expository teaching.

Discovery Learning

Jerome Bruner's early research on thinking (Bruner, Goodnow, & Austin, 1956) stirred his interest in educational approaches that encourage the development of thinking. Bruner's work emphasized the importance of understanding the structure of a subject being studied, the need for active learning as the basis for true understanding, and the value of inductive reasoning in learning.

Structure and Discovery. **Subject structure** refers to the fundamental ideas, relationships, or patterns of the field—the essential information. Because structure does not include specific facts or details about the subject, the essential structure of an idea can be represented simply as a diagram, set of principles, or formula. According to Bruner, learning will be more meaningful, useful, and memorable for students if they focus on understanding the structure of the subject being studied. For example, if you learned the concepts *figure, plane, simple, closed, quadrilateral, isosceles, scalene, equilateral,* and *right,* you would be on your way to understanding one aspect of geometry. But how do these terms relate to one another? If you can place the terms into a coding system such as the one in Figure 8.7 on page 318, you will have a better understanding of the basic structure of this part of geometry.

A **coding system** is a hierarchy of related concepts. At the top of the coding system is the most general concept, in this case *plane, simple, closed figure.* More specific concepts are arranged under the general concept.

In order to grasp the structure of information, Bruner believes, students must be active—they must identify key principles for themselves rather than simply accepting teachers' explanations. He believes that teachers should provide problem situations stimulating students to question, explore, and experiment. This process has been called discovery learning. In **discovery learning,** the teacher presents examples and the students work with the examples until they discover the interrelationships—the subject's structure. Thus, Bruner believes that classroom learning should take place through **inductive reasoning,** that is, by using specific examples to formulate a general principle. For instance, if students are presented with enough examples of triangles and nontriangles, they will eventually discover what the basic properties of any triangle must be. Encouraging inductive thinking in this way is sometimes called the **eg-rule method,** from the Latin e.g., meaning "for example."

Discovery in Action. An inductive approach requires **intuitive thinking** on the part of students. Bruner suggests that teachers can nurture this intuitive thinking by encouraging students to make guesses based on incomplete evidence and then to confirm or disprove the guesses systematically (Bruner, 1960). After learning about ocean currents and the shipping industry, for example, students might be shown old maps of three harbors and asked to guess which one became a major port. Then students could check their guesses through systematic re-

Jerome Bruner's writings about education have influenced teaching for several decades.

Subject Structure According to Bruner, the fundamental framework of ideas.

Coding System A hierarchy of ideas or concepts.

Discovery Learning Bruner's approach, in which students work on their own to discover basic principles.

Inductive Reasoning Formulating general principles based on knowledge of examples and details.

Eg-Rule Method Teaching or learning by moving from specific examples to general rules.

Intuitive Thinking Making imaginative leaps to correct perceptions or workable solutions.

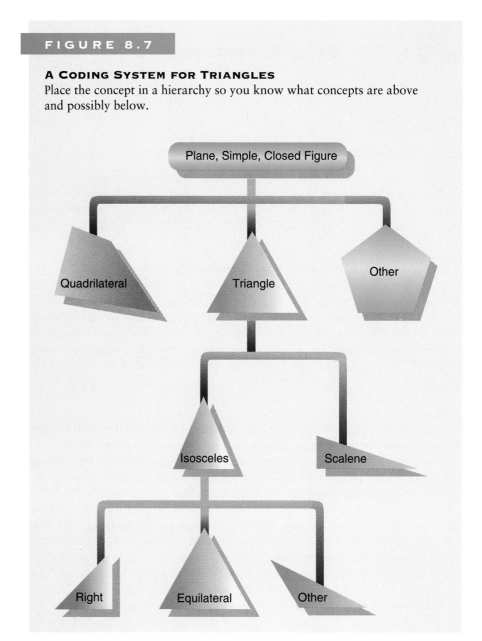

FIGURE 8.7

A CODING SYSTEM FOR TRIANGLES
Place the concept in a hierarchy so you know what concepts are above and possibly below.

Background: Wilcox, R. T. (1987). Rediscover discovery learning. *The Clearing House,* 53–56. Focus Question: Ask your students to describe ways to incorporate discovery learning into their teaching.

Teaching Tip: To demonstrate the eg-rule method of concept teaching, see Activity 44 in Benjamin, L. T., & Lowman, K. D. (Eds.) (1981). *Activities handbook for the teaching of psychology.* Washington, DC: American Psychological Association.

Activity 8.13: Example. See the *Instructor's Resource Manual* for "Discovery Learning in Action," an example comparing an inductive approach to teaching a botany lesson with a more traditional approach.

Casebook: See the "Teachers' Casebook" for ideas about how to conduct discovery lessons so that everyone, not just the brightest or quickest, makes discoveries.

Guided Discovery An adaptation of discovery learning, in which the teacher provides some direction.

search. Unfortunately, educational practices often discourage intuitive thinking by punishing wrong guesses and rewarding safe but uncreative answers.

Notice that in Bruner's discovery learning, a teacher organizes the class so that the students learn through their own active involvement. A distinction is usually made between discovery learning, in which the students work on their own to a very great extent, and **guided discovery,** in which the teacher provides some direction. Unguided discovery is appropriate for preschool children, but in a typical elementary or secondary classroom, unguided activities usually prove unmanageable and unproductive. For these situations, guided discovery is preferable. Students are presented with intriguing questions, baffling situa-

An important principle of discovery learning is that students learn best when they play an active role in problem situations, discovering the key factors for themselves, rather than simply accepting teachers' explanations.

tions, or interesting problems: Why does the flame go out when we cover it with a jar? Why does this pencil seem to bend when you put it in water? What is the rule for grouping these words together? Instead of explaining how to solve the problem, the teacher provides the appropriate materials and encourages students to make observations, form hypotheses, and test solutions. Feedback must be given at the optimal moment, when students can either use it to revise their approach or take it as encouragement to continue in the direction they've chosen. The Guidelines on page 320 should help you apply Bruner's suggestions to various classroom situations.

Discovery learning appears to have many advantages, but even Bruner believes that it is not appropriate in every situation. The Point/Counterpoint section on page 321 examines the pros and cons of this approach.

Reception Learning

Test Bank items 8.83, 8.95–8.97, 8.102, 8.109–8.112

David Ausubel's (1963, 1977) view of learning offers an interesting contrast to that of Bruner. According to Ausubel, people acquire knowledge primarily through reception rather than through discovery. Concepts, principles, and ideas are presented and understood, not discovered. As you saw in the previous chapter, the more organized and focused the presentation, the more thoroughly the person will learn.

Ausubel stresses what is known as **meaningful verbal learning**—verbal information, ideas, and relationships among ideas, taken together. Rote memorization is not considered meaningful learning, since material learned by rote is not connected with existing knowledge. Unfortunately, despite the ineffectiveness of rote learning, many lessons seem to rely on little else (Ausubel, 1977). Ausubel has proposed his **expository teaching** model to encourage

---

Teaching Tip: See Eggen, P. D., & Kauchak, D. P. (1988). *Strategies for teachers: Teaching content and thinking skills* (2nd ed.). Englewood Cliffs, NJ: Prentice-Hall, pp. 265–269 for an exercise that requires students to analyze a deductive or rule-eg lesson. There are questions and answers provided to aid in the analysis.

Example: The following advance organizer is taken from Joyce, B., & Weil, M. (1988). *Models of teaching* (3rd ed.). Englewood Cliffs, NJ: Prentice-Hall, pp. 70–71.

A guide, beginning a tour of an art museum with a group of high school students, says, "I want to give you an idea that will help you understand the paintings and sculpture we are about to see. The idea is simply that art, although it is a personal expression, reflects in many ways the culture and times in which it was produced. This may seem obvious to you at first when you look at the difference between Oriental and Western art. However, it is also true that, within each culture, as the culture changes, so the art will change—and that is why we can speak of periods of art. The changes are often reflected in the artists' techniques, subject matter, colors, and style. Major changes are often reflected in the forms of art that are produced." In the tour that follows, as the students look at paintings and sculpture, the guide points out to them the differences.

Objective 8.11: State Ausubel's views about the learning process.

Meaningful Verbal Learning Focused and organized relationships among ideas and verbal information.

Expository Teaching Ausubel's method—teachers present material in complete, organized form, moving from broadest to more specific concepts.

Guidelines

**Applying Bruner's
Ideas in the
Classroom**

Present both examples and nonexamples of the concepts you are teaching.

Examples

1. In teaching about mammals, include people, kangaroos, whales, cats, dolphins, and camels as examples, and chickens, fish, alligators, frogs, and penguins as nonexamples.
2. Ask students for additional examples and nonexamples.

Help students see connections among concepts.

Examples

1. Ask questions such as these: What else could you call this apple? (Fruit.) What do we do with fruit? (Eat.) What do we call things we eat? (Food.)
2. Use diagrams, outlines, and summaries to point out connections.

Pose a question and let students try to find the answer.

Examples

1. How could the human hand be improved?
2. What is the relation between the area of one tile and the area of the whole floor?

Encourage students to make intuitive guesses.

Examples

1. Instead of giving a word's definition, say, "Let's guess what it might mean by looking at the words around it."
2. Give students a map of ancient Greece and ask where they think the major cities were.
3. Don't comment after the first few guesses. Wait for several ideas before giving the answer.
4. Use guiding questions to focus students when their discovery has led them too far astray.

Deductive Reasoning Drawing conclusions by applying rules or principles; logically moving from a general rule or principle to a specific solution.

Rule-Eg Method Teaching or learning by moving from general principles to specific examples.

Advance Organizer Statement of inclusive concepts to introduce and sum up material that follows.

meaningful rather than rote reception learning. (Here, exposition means *explanation,* or the setting forth of facts and ideas.) In this approach, teachers present materials in a carefully organized, sequenced, and somewhat finished form, and students thus receive the most usable material in the most efficient way. Ausubel does agree with Bruner that people learn by organizing new information into hierarchies or coding systems. Ausubel calls the general concept at the top of the system the *subsumer,* because all other concepts are subsumed under it, as in Figure 8.6. However, Ausubel believes that learning should progress, not inductively as Bruner recommends, but deductively: from the general to the specific, or from the rule or principle to examples. The **deductive reasoning** approach is sometimes called the **rule-eg method.**

Advance Organizers. Optimal learning generally occurs when there is a potential fit between the student's schemas and the material to be learned. To make this fit more likely, a lesson following Ausubel's strategy always begins with an **advance organizer.** This is an introductory statement of a relationship

Is Discovery Learning Effective?

Most psychologists and educators agree that students must make sense of information in order to learn and remember it. Simply memorizing lists and facts leads to superficial understanding and rapid forgetting. When students struggle with perplexing problems, test possible solutions, and finally discover for themselves the fundamental structure of a key concept, they are more likely to understand and remember the information. But critics of discovery learning raise some important questions. Is discovery learning an effective method?

POINT Discovery learning matches cognitive development.

Educators favoring discovery learning note that this approach is consistent with the ways that people learn and develop. For example, Jerome Bruner (1966, 1971) identified three stages of cognitive growth, similar to the stages identified by Piaget. Bruner believes that children move from an *enactive* stage to an *iconic* stage and finally to a *symbolic* stage. In the enactive stage (similar to Piaget's sensorimotor stage), the child represents and understands the world through actions—to understand something is to manipulate it, taste it, throw it, break it and so on. At the iconic stage, the child represents the world in images—appearances dominate. This stage corresponds to Piaget's preoperational thinking, in which the

higher the water level, the more water there must be in the glass, because that's what appears to be true. At the final level, the child is able to use abstract ideas, symbols, language, and logic to understand and represent the world. Actions and images can still be used in thinking, but they do not dominate.

Discovery learning allows students to move through these three stages as they encounter new information. First the students manipulate and act on materials; then they form images as they note specific features and make observations; and finally they abstract general ideas and principles from these experiences and observations. Because they have experienced each stage of representation, Bruner believes, the students will have a better understanding of the topic. When students are motivated and really participate in the discovery project, discovery learning leads to superior learning (Strike, 1975).

COUNTERPOINT Discovery learning is impractical.

In theory, discovery learning seems ideal, but in practice there are problems. To be successful, discovery projects often require special materials and extensive preparations. And these preparations can't guarantee success. For example, a discovery lesson on the effects of light on plants takes many hours and often falls flat because the plants grown in darkness and those

grown in light don't always behave as they should— many factors other than light affect growth (Anderson & Smith, 1987).

In order to benefit from a discovery situation, students must have basic knowledge about the problem and must know how to apply problem-solving strategies. Without this knowledge and skill, they will flounder and grow frustrated. Instead of learning from the materials, they may simply play with them. The brightest students may make some discoveries, while the others lose interest or just wait passively for someone else to complete the project. Instead of benefiting from a teacher's organized explanation, these "nondiscovering" students may get an inadequate explanation from a fellow student who can't quite communicate his or her discoveries. Everyone may grow frustrated as the teacher seems to withhold the solutions and explanations needed.

Critics believe that discovery learning is so inefficient and so difficult to organize successfully that other methods are preferable. This seems especially true for lower-ability students. Discovery methods may make too many demands on these students, because they lack the background knowledge and problem-solving skills needed to benefit. Some research has shown that discovery methods are ineffective and even detrimental for lower-ability students (Corno & Snow, 1986; Slavin, Karweit, & Madden, 1989).

or a high-level concept broad enough to encompass all the information that will follow.

The function of advance organizers is to provide scaffolding or support for the new information. You can also see the advance organizer as a kind of conceptual bridge between new material and students' current knowledge (Faw & Waller, 1976). Textbooks often contain advance organizers—the chapter

Connections: See chapter 2 for a discussion of Vygotsky and scaffolding.

When presenting material that is unfamiliar or complex, advance organizers seem to help; concrete models seem to work especially well.

Objective 8.12: List the characteristics of expository teaching and give an example of its application.

Activity 8.14: Cooperative Learning. See the *Instructor's Resource Manual* for "Role Playing an Expository Lesson," an activity that asks students to role play an expository lesson and analyze the elements. **Handout Master 8.5,** "An Example of Expository Teaching," is provided for this activity.

Objective 8.13: Contrast the discovery and expository methods of teaching.

overviews in this book are examples. The organizers can serve three purposes: they direct your attention to what is important in the coming material; they highlight relationships among ideas that will be presented; and they remind you of relevant information you already have. In teaching a lesson on the caste system in India, for example, the organizer might deal with the concepts of social classes and social stratification in societies (Joyce & Weil, 1986).

In general, advance organizers fall into one of two categories, *comparative* and *expository* (Mayer, 1979, 1984). Each fulfills an important function. Comparative organizers *activate* (bring into working memory) already existing schemas. They remind you of what you already know, but may not realize is relevant. A comparative advance organizer for a history lesson on revolutions might be a statement that contrasts military uprisings with the physical and social changes involved in the Industrial Revolution; you could also compare the common aspects of the French, English, Mexican, Russian, Iranian, and American revolutions (Salomon & Perkins, 1989).

In contrast, *expository organizers* provide *new* knowledge that students will need to understand the upcoming information. An expository organizer is thus a statement of a subsumer, a definition of a general concept. In an English class, you might begin a large thematic unit on rites of passage in literature with a very broad statement of the theme and why it has been so central in literature—something like, "A central character coming of age must learn to know himself or herself, often makes some kind of journey of self-discovery, and must decide what in the society is to be accepted, what rejected . . . "

The general conclusion of research on advance organizers is that they do help students learn, especially when the material is quite unfamiliar, complex, or difficult (Corkill, 1992; Mayer, 1984; Shuell, 1981b). Of course, the effects of advance organizers depend on how good they are and how students actually use them. First, to be effective, the organizer must be processed and understood by the students. This was demonstrated dramatically in a study by Dinnel and Glover (1985). They found that instructing students to paraphrase an advance organizer—which, of course, requires them to understand its meaning—increased the effectiveness of the organizer. Second, the organizer must really be an organizer: It must indicate relations among the basic concepts and terms that will be used. In other words, a true organizer isn't just a statement of historical or background information. No amount of student processing can make a bad organizer more effective. Concrete models, diagrams, or analogies seem to be especially good organizers (Mayer 1983a, 1984).

Steps in an Expository Lesson. After presenting an advance organizer, the next step in a lesson using Ausubel's approach is to present content in terms of basic similarities and differences, using specific examples. To learn any new material, students must see not only the similarities between the material presented and what they already know; they must also see the differences so that interference—the confusion of old and new material—can be avoided.

It is often helpful in an expository lesson to ask students to supply similarities and differences themselves. In a grammar lesson, you might ask, "What are the differences between the way commas and semicolons are used?" Or suppose in teaching the coming-of-age theme in literature, you choose *The Diary of Anne Frank* and *The Adventures of Huckleberry Finn* as the basic material for the unit. As the students read the first book, you might ask them to compare the central character's growth, state of mind, and position in soci-

Guidelines

Use advance organizers.

Examples

1. English: Shakespeare used the social ideas of his time as a framework for his plays—*Julius Caesar, Hamlet,* and *Macbeth* dealt with concepts of natural order, a nation as the human body, etc.
2. Social studies: Geography dictates economy in preindustrialized regions or nations.
3. History: Important concepts during the Renaissance were symmetry, admiration of the classical world, the centrality of the human mind.

Use a number of examples.

Examples

1. In mathematics class, ask students to point out all the examples of right angles that they can find in the room.
2. In teaching about islands and peninsulas, use maps, slides, models, postcards.

Focus on both similarities and differences.

Examples

1. In a history class, ask students to list the ways in which the North and South were alike and different before the Civil War.
2. In a biology class, ask students how they would transform spiders into insects or an amphibian into a reptile.

Applying Ausubel's Ideas in the Classroom

---

ety with characters from other novels, plays, and films. When the class moves on to the second book, you can start by asking students to compare Anne Frank's inner journey with Huck Finn's trip down the Mississippi. As comparisons are made, whether within a single class lesson or during an entire unit, it is useful to underscore the goal of the lesson and occasionally to repeat the advance organizer (with amendments and elaborations).

Along with the comparisons, specific examples must come into play. You can see that the best way to point out similarities and differences is with examples. There must be specific examples of comma and semicolon usage; the specific elements of Huck Finn's and Anne Frank's dilemmas must be clear. Finally, when all the material has been presented, ask students to discuss how the examples can be used to expand on the original advance organizer.

Making the Most of Expository Teaching. As with any teaching approach, expository teaching works better in some situations than in others. First, this approach is most appropriate when you want to teach about the relationships among several concepts. Students must have some knowledge of the actual concepts first. What if students in a history class had never heard of the French Revolution or the Industrial Revolution? How could they compare these specific events to get a better understanding of elements that characterize different kinds of revolutions? They might

Application: Ask students to outline one lesson plan using the expository teaching approach and another using the discovery learning approach for teaching the concept of "civil disobedience." Which approach is the most efficient? Which do students think would be most effective?

Focus on . . . **Cognitive Models of Teaching**

- When is discovery learning appropriate?
- What are the steps in expository teaching?
- When are advance organizers helpful?
- Can you combine discovery and expository approaches? Give an example.

Discussion: What characteristics of cognitive development would support the statement that expository teaching is more appropriate for the secondary than the elementary level?

resort to memorizing definitions and lists, such as "the five characteristics of a revolution are . . ." Even in a lesson on what poetry is, students who don't have a basic understanding of the concept of literature—why people write and why they read—will be at a loss.

Another consideration with expository teaching is the age of the students. This approach requires students to manipulate ideas mentally, even if the ideas are simple and based on physical realities such as rocks and minerals. This means that expository teaching is more developmentally appropriate for students at or above later elementary school, that is, around the fifth or sixth grade (Luiten, Ames, & Ackerson, 1980). The Guidelines on page 323 should help you follow the main steps in expository teaching.

SUMMARY

This chapter has covered quite a bit of territory, partly because the cognitive perspective has so many implications for instruction. Although they are varied, you can see that most of the cognitive ideas for teaching concepts, problem-solving skills, and thinking emphasize the role of the student's prior knowledge in learning and the need for active, mindful learning.

The Importance of Thinking and Understanding

The ultimate goal of teaching is student understanding. Students demonstrate understanding when they can use knowledge appropriately in new situations. Thinking, in the form of problem solving, creativity, or critical analysis, is the avenue to understanding.

Learning and Teaching about Concepts

Concepts are categories used to group similar events, ideas, people, or objects. We probably learn concepts from prototypes or exemplars of the category, understand in terms of our schematic knowledge, and then refine concepts through our additional experience of relevant and irrelevant features. Lessons about concepts include four basic components: concept name, definition, attributes, and examples.

Problem Solving

Problem solving is both general and domain-specific. The five stages of problem solving are identifying the problem, understanding the problem through representation, exploring possible solutions, selecting a strategy or executing a plan, and evaluating the results. A critical element in solving problems in school is representing the problem accurately, showing understanding of both the whole problem and its discrete elements. Translation and schema training may improve this ability.

Effective Problem Solving: What Do the Experts Do?

The application of algorithms and heuristics—such as means-ends analysis, analogical thinking, working backward, and verbalization—may help students solve problems. Factors that hinder problem solving include functional fixedness or rigidity (response set). These disallow the flexibility needed to represent problems accurately and to have insight into solutions. Expert problem solvers have a rich store of declarative, procedural, and conditional knowledge. They organize this knowledge around general principles or patterns that apply to large classes of problems.

Creativity and Creative Problem Solving

Creativity is a process that involves independently restructuring problems to see things in new, imaginative ways. Creativity is difficult to measure, but tests of divergent thinking can assess originality, fluency, and flexibility. Teachers can encourage creativity by providing opportunities for play, using brainstorming techniques, and accepting divergent ideas.

Teaching and Learning about Thinking

Two approaches to teaching thinking skills are to use stand-alone programs or to embed programs in the regular curriculum. In every class, teachers can use a rich language of thinking, develop critical thinking skills, model good thinking, and encourage the practice of specific skills.

Teaching for Transfer

The transfer of learning from one situation to another may be positive or negative, general or specific. Transfer involving spontaneity and automaticity in familiar situations has been called low-road transfer. High-road transfer involves reflection and conscious application of abstract knowledge to new situations. Teachers can promote thinking and learning skills by teaching for mastery, and for the positive, general transfer of knowledge.

Cognitive Models of Teaching

According to Jerome Bruner's discovery model of teaching, students learn best when they themselves discover the structure of a subject through inductive reasoning (the eg-rule method) and intuitive thinking. In guided discovery, the teachers ask leading questions and give directive feedback. According to David Ausubel's reception model, learning should be primarily deductive (the rule-eg method) and based on meaningful verbal learning. In expository teaching, teachers present material that is fully organized and sequenced from the general (subsumers and advance organizers) to the specific.

KEY TERMS

advance organizer, p. 320
algorithm, p. 296
analogical thinking, p. 297
brainstorming, p. 307
coding system, p. 317
concept, p. 286
concept mapping, p. 290
convergent thinking, p. 305
creativity, p. 304
critical thinking, p. 312
deductive reasoning, p. 320
defining attributes, p. 287
discovery learning, p. 317
divergent thinking, p. 305
exemplar, p. 287
expository teaching, p. 319

functional fixedness, p. 299
graded membership, p. 287
guided discovery, p. 318
heuristic, p. 297
high-road transfer, p. 315
incubation, p. 304
inductive reasoning, p. 317
insight, p. 300
intuitive thinking, p. 317
linguistic comprehension, p. 293
low-road transfer, p. 314
meaningful verbal learning, p. 319
means-ends analysis, p. 297
overgeneralization, p. 290
overlearning, p. 316

problem, p. 290
problem solving, p. 290
prototype, p. 287
response set, p. 299
restructuring, p. 304
rule-eg method, p. 320
schema-driven problem solving, p. 296
stand-alone thinking skills programs, p. 309
subject structure, p. 317
transfer, p. 314
undergeneralization, p. 290
verbalization, p. 298
working-backward strategy, p. 297

WHAT WOULD YOU DO?

Preschool and Kindergarten
Several students in your class still have trouble discriminating between simple shapes. What would you do to help them understand?

Elementary and Middle School
Students in your class are having a really hard time with the concepts of heat and energy. What would you do?

Your students' first attempt at writing an essay comparing two short poems is a disaster. They write a few lines giving superficial descriptions of each poem and then tell which one they liked best. There is no critical thinking or analysis. Where would you go from here?

Junior High and High School
Students in your math class can solve problems for homework, but get confused on tests that cover several chapters. They don't seem to know when to apply one procedure and when to apply another. How would you help them?

You decide to give an essay test that requires creativity and critical thinking. Your students perform very badly and protest loudly that the test is "unfair." They want to use the definitions and facts they have so carefully memorized. What would you do?

Cooperative Learning Activity
With four or five other members of your class, design a lesson or series of lessons that teach important content and thinking skills at the same time. How would you introduce the lessons, and how would you evaluate students' learning?

Effective Problem Solving

How do you help students in your class to become effective problem solvers, particularly when they are dealing with the complex, often ambiguous, problems of daily life?

Students become effective problem solvers by developing the mental structures needed to gather, organize, and evaluate information. I encourage students to (1) "notice" details and suspend judgment until all relevant information is gathered; (2) use reflective thinking to find patterns and relationships with previous knowledge and experience; (3) create meaning within a personal context; and (4) organize information for output according to accepted conventions of language and expression. I ask questions that cannot be answered with yes/no or one-word responses. Students must explain why and how they arrived at an answer so that they see a need for logical justification rather than guesses about what the teacher wants to hear. I challenge students to use comparative thinking and explain how the material is alike or different from other contexts and contents. When students are invited to do hypothetical ("what if") thinking, they utilize their creative capabilities to come up with unexpected solutions and then use reflective thinking to manipulate the variables mentally and evaluate the possible outcomes.

When students are dealing with complex personal problems, I encourage them to write down what they perceive the problems to be or draw how they feel about the situation. Once the students have given "form" to their problems, they are more able to talk about cause/effect relationships, alternative solutions, and why they feel the way the do. My role is to empower the students through the systematic collection and analysis of data so that they can solve their own problems.

Betty Garner, *Art Teacher*
Pattonville I.D.E.A.L. Center, Maryland Heights, Missouri

In order for students to learn to solve problems, they must be allowed to make decisions and to learn the consequences of inappropriate choices. Start with simple choices such as listing two assignments and letting them choose the one they want to do first. Then increase the choices and let them choose which ones to do and which ones to ignore. Gradually give them the power to make other decisions that affect the whole class. Plan a class walk, and let the children decide what they should be seeing and the route they should take. Have them draw out a map and show the most direct or the most enlightening way. The class should vote for the preferred route, and that route should be the one taken.

Another method would be to make up simulation exercises in which different decisions will affect the outcome. Discussing the pros and cons of the decisions will give the students useful insights on managing their choices. Empowering the students with decision making is going to give them the confidence to make complex decisions in the future.

Ida Pofahl, *Second-Grade Teacher*
Denison Elementary School, Denison, Iowa

Aiding Transfer

What kinds of in-class activities have you found aid students' transfer of learning? How do you make connections between lessons and the "real life" beyond the school walls?

BRING OUTSIDE WORLD INSIDE

I feel students transfer learning best if they actually get involved in their work. In math, we have a week of following the stock market. We keep a chart in the room to see if we make money. We also write checks and balance a family budget for a month. In spelling, we play games like the Great American Giveaway, which reinforces learning so students can retain and transfer it. If students spell three unit words correctly, they can choose one of two doors. Behind each door is a picture from a magazine of something the children enjoy or want—for example, Oreo-cookie ice cream. The child who opens that door wins an imaginary month's supply of the ice cream.

Sharon Klotz, *Sixth-Grade Teacher*
Kiel Middle School, Kiel, Wisconsin

USE NEIGHBORHOOD RESOURCES

To make learning more applicable to life outside the classroom, I have days when students bring in calculators for math. I also try to utilize the resource people of the neighborhood—artists or nurses, for example—who speak to the class about relevant topics. For each of the seven social studies units, we have a guest speaker who has lived or traveled in the area being studied. I think children want to feel connected to the outside world. They appreciate knowing that classroom lessons are not restricted to teachers and students, that the broader community also uses the same knowledge.

Louise Harrold Melucci, *Fourth-Grade Teacher*
Greenwood School, Warwick, Rhode Island

Discovery Learning

Describe a "discovery learning" lesson that really seemed to work well with your students. Why do you think it was so successful?

HANDS-ON EXPERIENCES

In second grade we do a unit on magnets. At the beginning of the unit, the children (in small groups) go to five various centers to make their own discoveries. At each center is a card that tells the children to do various things with the magnet. For example, they try to pull a paper fish (with a paper clip underneath) through water with a magnet. Then they write down their discovery. In this instance they find that magnets do work through water. The children work together to make their discoveries. This is much more effective and enjoyable than a lecture on magnets.

Kathryn Daniels, *Second-Grade Teacher*
Fredericktown Elementary School, Fredericktown, Ohio

CHANNELING ENERGY

It's difficult to restrain children who are overflowing with energy and ideas. They can take over a classroom if you let them. What can teachers do? We can talk to the whole class about respecting the rights of all and giving everyone an opportunity to respond. Perhaps we can allow the advanced children to lead the discussions, at least in part, after we have modeled this behavior. Another thing to do is encourage all the children to come up with many different ideas, avoid acknowledging any correct response, and have each child back up his or her answers. We can also have children draw pictures or write out their discoveries before verbalizing them. Some discovery activities have no right or wrong answers, and these can be used to encourage all children to respond without feeling threatened.

Carolyn R. Cook, *Kindergarten Teacher*
Ramona Elementary School, Ramona, California

Motivation: Issues and Explanations

"Why don't the students pay attention?" "Kids today don't seem to care about school." "The trouble is these kids have no motivation!" If you have spent much time in schools, you have heard these laments before. Is lack of motivation really at the heart of school failure? Or are students motivated, but not necessarily to do what their teachers want? Whatever the answers, most educators agree that motivating students toward appropriate goals is one of the critical tasks of teaching.

We begin with the question "What is motivation?" and examine many of the answers that have been proposed. This leads to a discussion of intrinsic and extrinsic motivation and four general theories of motivation: behavioral, humanistic, cognitive, and social learning.

The remainder of the chapter examines more closely several personal factors that frequently appear in discussions of motivation: goals, needs for self-actualization and for achievement, beliefs about the causes of success and failure in school, notions about ability and self-worth, and anxiety. In chapter 10 we will complete the picture with an examination of the external factors that can affect motivation.

By the time you have completed this chapter, you should be able to:

- Give examples of intrinsic and extrinsic motivation.
- Define the concept of motivation from the behavioral, humanistic, cognitive, and social learning points of view.
- Explain the concept of student motivation to learn.
- Set motivating goals for yourself and your students.
- List Maslow's seven levels of needs and give a classroom example of each.
- Explain how to encourage the need for achievement in your class.
- Explain the relationship between self-determination and motivation.
- Discuss the possible motivational effects of success and failure and how these effects relate to beliefs about ability.
- Describe the characteristics of mastery-oriented, failure-avoiding, and failure-accepting students.
- Develop a plan for helping an anxious student improve.

Why are you reading this chapter? Why did you start reading it instead of doing something else? How deeply involved are you? How long will you continue reading and why will you stop? These are the basic questions about motivation: Why start? Are you involved? Why stop? Did you open the book because you are curious about motivation and interested in the topic? Or is there a test in your near future? How do you feel about the activity? Does reading this chapter feel like play and entertainment or more like work and obligation? Do you feel guilty or relieved when you stop reading? Do you expect to understand what you read, or do you anticipate a struggle? Do you need this course to earn a teaching certificate or to graduate? Maybe you believe that you have a good chance to do well in this class, and that belief keeps you working. Perhaps it is some combination of these reasons. What motivates you to study motivation?

Planning Tip: See the Chapter-9-At-A-Glance Planning Guide in the Instructor's Section at the front of this book.

Study Guide: The *Study Guide,* sold separately, contains exercises to help students determine if they have mastered each learning objective for this chapter.

Planning Tip: See the separate *Instructors' Resource Manual* for additional activities and resources for teaching this chapter, including Handout Masters. Also see the *Allyn and Bacon Transparencies in Educational Psychology.*

Planning Tip: See the *Test Bank* and *Study Guide* supplements as you plan for evaluation and measurement of student learning.

Planning Tip: For further information about audiovisual, multimedia, and computer-assisted resources for teaching this chapter, see the Video and Software Guide in the *Instructors' Resource Manual.*

hat Is Motivation?   Test Bank items 9.1, 9.3

Motivation is usually defined as an internal state that arouses, directs, and maintains behavior. Psychologists studying motivation have focused on three basic questions (Pintrich, Marx, & Boyle, 1993). First, what causes a person to initiate some action? For example, why do some students start their homework as soon as they can, while others wait until the last minute or never start at all? Second, what is the level of involvement in the chosen activity? Once the book bag is opened, is the student absorbed and focused or just going through the motions? And third, what causes a person to persist or to give up? Will a student read the entire Shakespeare assignment or just a few pages? Why?

Answering these questions about real students in classrooms is a challenge. As you will see in this chapter and the next, there are many factors that influence motivation. To get a sense of the complexity, let's step into a middle school general science classroom and survey the motivational problems that might confront you as the teacher. The students are taken from Stipek (1993).

The assignment: "In your lab notebook, describe the procedures for tomorrow's chemistry experiment. Indicate all the materials you will need and how you will set up the apparatus." As soon as you finish your instructions, the hands go up. "Do we have to write in paragraphs or can we outline?" "Do we have to draw the apparatus or just describe it?" "Can we work together?" Some students begin right away, while others wait for answers to these questions. A few students seem to be in another world.

Hopeless Henry won't even start the assignment—as usual. He just keeps saying, "I don't understand," or "This is too hard." When you try to help him, he answers your questions correctly, but then says he "guessed" and he "doesn't really know." Henry causes no management problems because he spends most of his time starring into space, but he is falling farther and farther behind.

Safe Sally checks with you about every step—she wants to be perfect. You once gave her bonus points for doing an excellent color drawing of the apparatus and now she produces a work of art for lab every time. But Sally never takes any chances. She does well in science, but plans to take only the required science courses so she won't risk getting a B. If it isn't required or on the test, Sally isn't interested.

Satisfied Sam, on the other hand, *is* interested in this project. In fact, he knows more than you do about it. Evidently he has set up a lab in his garage and spends hours reading about chemistry and performing experiments. But his overall grade in your class is between B– and C+ because when you were studying biology, Sam couldn't have cared less. He was satisfied with the C he could get on tests without even trying. Homework didn't interest him. His only participation was to make jokes about the illustrations in the text. Judging by his standardized test scores, Sam could do much better.

Defensive Diana doesn't have her lab manual—again. You tell her that she may share with another student. Then Diana pretends to be working, but she spends most of her time making fun of the assignment or trying to get answers from other students when your back is turned. She wants everyone to know that she "isn't really trying." That way, if her grades are low she has an excuse. She is afraid to try because if she makes an effort and fails, she fears that everyone will know she is "dumb."

Anxious Amy is a good student in most subjects, but she freezes on science tests. She seems fine in group projects and doing her homework, but "forgets" everything she knows when she has to answer questions in class or take a test. Her parents are scientists and expect her to become one too, but her prospects for this future look dim.

Example: Hopeless Henry is an example of a student experiencing *learned helplessness*, discussed later in the chapter.

Example: Safe Sally is an example of a student who is motivated by *extrinsic* factors, sets *performance goals*, fears *failure*, and views *ability as fixed*. She is also a (successful) *failure-avoiding student.* All these concepts will be discussed later in the chapter.

Example: Satisfied Sam is an example of a student motivated by *intrinsic* factors. He set *learning goals* in his areas of interest, but just wants to perform "OK" in other areas. These concepts are discussed later in the chapter.

Example: Defensive Diana is an example of a student who is motivated by *extrinsic* factors, sets *performance goals, fears failure,* and views *ability as fixed.* She is also a *failure-avoiding student.* Because she avoids work, she may soon become a *failure-accepting student.* All of these concepts will be discussed later in the chapter.

Example: Anxious Amy is an example of a student experiencing debilitating *anxiety,* discussed later in the chapter.

Each student presents a different motivational problem, yet you have to teach the entire class. In the next few pages we will look more closely at the meaning of motivation so we can better understand these students.

Intrinsic and Extrinsic Motivation

Test Bank items 9.34, 9.66, 9.79

We all know how it feels to be motivated, to move energetically toward a goal. We also know what it is like to work hard, even if we are not fascinated by the task. What energizes and directs our behavior? Answers include descriptions of drives, needs, incentives, fears, goals, social pressure, self-confidence, interests, curiosity, attributions for success and failure, beliefs, values, expectations, and more. Some psychologists have explained **motivation** in terms of personal *traits* or individual characteristics. Certain people, so the theory goes, have a strong need to achieve, a fear of tests, or an enduring interest in art, so they behave accordingly. They work hard to achieve, avoid tests, or spend hours in art galleries. Other psychologists see motivation more as a *state,* a

Motivation An internal state that arouses, directs, and maintains behavior.

"WHAT DO I GET FOR JUST NEATNESS?"

(© Glenn Bernhardt)

Activity 9.1: Multicultural Awareness. See the *Instructors' Resource Manual* for Motivating Adolescents from Minority Cultures. This extended discussion covers factors that influence the motivation of minority-group students and characteristics of minority-group learners that place them at risk.

Transparency: Acetate transparency T 77, "Influences on the Outcomes of Learning," represents simply the internal and external conditions that affect learning.

Objective 9.1: Give examples of intrinsic and extrinsic motivation.

Activity 9.2: Reflection/Journal Writing. See the separate *Instructors' Resource Manual* for Guidance from the Past, an activity that asks your students to imagine what advice two of their best teachers would give about how to encourage intrinsic motivation.

Intrinsic Motivation   Motivation associated with activities that are their own reward.

Extrinsic Motivation   Motivation created by external factors like rewards and punishments.

Locus of Causality   The location—internal or external—of the cause of behavior.

temporary situation. If, for example, you are reading this paragraph because you have a test tomorrow, you are motivated (at least for now) by the situation. Of course, the motivation we experience at any given time usually is a combination of trait and state. You may be studying because you value learning *and* because your professor often gives pop quizzes.

As you can see, some explanations of motivation rely on internal, personal factors such as needs, interests, curiosity, and enjoyment. Other explanations point to external, environmental factors—rewards, social pressure, punishment, and so on. Motivation that stems from factors such as interest or curiosity is called intrinsic motivation. **Intrinsic motivation** is the natural tendency to pursue personal interests and exercise capabilities and in doing so, seek out and conquer challenges (Deci & Ryan, 1985). When we are intrinsically motivated, we do not need incentives or punishments to make us work, because *the activity itself is rewarding*. We enjoy the task or the sense of accomplishment that it brings. Satisfied Sam studies chemistry outside school simply because he loves the activity; no one makes him do it. In contrast, when we do something in order to earn a grade or reward, avoid punishment, please the teacher, or for some other reason that has very little to do with the task itself, we experience **extrinsic motivation.** We are not really interested in the activity for its own sake; we care only about what it will gain us. Safe Sally works for the grade; she has little interest in the subject itself.

It is impossible to tell just by looking if a behavior is intrinsically or extrinsically motivated. The essential difference between the two types of motivation is the student's reason for acting, that is, whether the **locus of causality** for the action (the location of the cause) is internal or external—inside or outside the person. Students who read or practice their backstroke or paint may be reading, stroking, or painting because they freely chose the activity based on personal interests (*internal* locus of causality/intrinsic motivation), or because someone or something else outside is influencing them (*external* locus of causality/extrinsic motivation).

Is your motivation for reading this page intrinsic or extrinsic? Is your locus of causality internal or external? As you try to answer this question, you probably realize that the dichotomy between intrinsic and extrinsic motivation is too simple—too all-or-nothing. Our activities fall along a continuum from fully *self-determined* (internal locus of causality/intrinsic motivation) to fully *determined by others* (external locus of causality/extrinsic motivation). For example, students may freely choose to work hard on activities that they don't find particularly enjoyable, because they know the activities are important in reaching a valued goal—like spending hours studying anatomy in order to become a physician. Is this intrinsic or extrinsic motivation? Actually it is in between—the person is freely choosing to respond to outside causes such as medical school requirements. The person has *internalized an external cause.*

In school, both intrinsic and extrinsic motivation are important. Many activities are, or could be, interesting to students. Teaching can create intrinsic motivation by stimulating the students' curiosity and making them feel more competent as they learn. But you know this won't work all the time. Did you find long division or grammar inherently interesting? Was your curiosity piqued by the states and their capitals? If teachers count on intrinsic motivation to energize all their students all of the time, they will be disappointed. There are situations when incentives and external supports are necessary. Teachers must encourage and nurture intrinsic motivation while making sure that the level of extrinsic motivation is right (Brophy, 1988). To do this, they need to know about the factors that influence motivation.

Four General Approaches to Motivation

Test Bank items 9.7–9.20, 9.67, 9.68, 9.80–9.82, 9.93

Motivation is a vast and complicated subject with many, many theories. Some theories were developed through work with animals in laboratories. Others are based on research with humans in situations that used games or puzzles. Some theories grow out of the work done in clinical or industrial psychology. Our examination of the field will be selective, otherwise we would never finish the topic.

Behavioral Approaches to Motivation.   Behaviorists explain motivation with concepts such as "reward" and "incentive." A **reward** is an attractive object or event supplied as a consequence of a particular behavior. For example, Safe Sally was rewarded with bonus points when she drew an excellent apparatus diagram. An **incentive** is an object or event that encourages or discourages behavior. The promise of an A+ was an incentive to Sally. Actually receiving the grade was a reward. Thus, according to the behavioral view, an understanding of student motivation begins with a careful analysis of the incentives and rewards present in the classroom.

If we are consistently reinforced for certain behaviors, we may develop habits or tendencies to act in certain ways. For example, if a student is repeatedly rewarded with affection, money, praise, or privileges for earning letters in baseball but receives little recognition for studying, the student will probably work longer and harder on perfecting her fastball than on understanding geometry. Providing grades, stars, and so on for learning—or demerits for misbehavior—is an attempt to motivate students by extrinsic means of incentives, rewards, and punishments. Of course, in any individual case, many other factors will affect how a person behaves.

Humanistic Approaches to Motivation.   The **humanistic view** is sometimes referred to as "third-force" psychology, because it developed in the 1940s as a reaction against the two forces then dominant, behaviorism and Freudian psychoanalysis. Proponents of humanistic psychology such as Abraham Maslow and Carl Rogers felt that neither behavioral nor Freudian psychology adequately explained why people act as they do.

Humanistic interpretations of motivation emphasize such intrinsic sources of motivation as a person's needs for "self-actualization" (Maslow, 1970, 1968), the inborn "actualizing tendency" (Rogers & Freiberg, 1994), or the need for "self-determination" (Deci, Vallerand, Pelletier, & Ryan, 1991). What these theories have in common is the belief that people are continually motivated by the inborn need to fulfill their potential. So from the humanistic perspective, to motivate students means to encourage their inner resources—their sense of competence, self-esteem, autonomy, and self-actualization. One current reflection of the humanistic perspective is the "self-esteem movement," a controversial approach to meeting students' needs for dignity and self-esteem. The Point/Counterpoint section on page 334 explores this issue.

When we examine the role of *needs* in motivation, we will see two examples of the humanistic approach to motivation, Maslow's theory of the hierarchy of needs and Deci's self-determination theory.

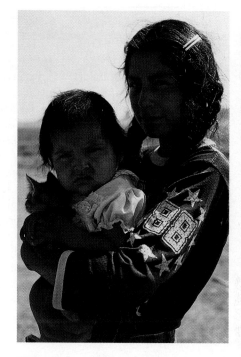

Respect for ethnic heritage, one's own and that of others, supports the development of self-esteem.

Objective 9.2: Define the concept of motivation from the behavioral, humanistic, cognitive, and social learning points of view.

Activity 9.4: Example. See the separate *Instructors' Resource Manual* for Self-Esteem Building: The Class Quilt. This activity asks your students to design individual "squares" of a quilt to reflect significant personal attributes, then assemble the individual elements into a class "quilt."

Reward   An attractive object or event supplied as a consequence of a behavior.

Incentive   An object or event that encourages or discourages behavior.

Humanistic View   Approach to motivation that emphasizes personal freedom, choice, self-determination, and striving for personal growth.

POINT ■ COUNTERPOINT

What Should Schools Do to Encourage Students' Self-Esteem?

James Beane (1991) begins his article "Sorting Out the Self-Esteem Controversy" with this statement: "In the '90s, the question is not whether schools should enhance students' self-esteem, but how they propose to do so" (p. 25). The attempts to improve students' self-esteem have taken three main forms: personal development activities such as sensitivity training; self-esteem programs where the curriculum focuses directly on improving self-esteem; and structural changes in schools that place greater emphasis on cooperation, student participation, community involvement, and ethnic pride.

POINT **The self-esteem movement has problems.**

Attempts to encourage self-esteem directly through sensitivity training or self-esteem courses have not proven very successful. As Beane notes, "Saying 'I like myself and others' in front of a group is not the same as actually feeling that way, especially if I am only doing it because I am supposed to. Being nice has a place in enhancing self-esteem, but it is not enough" (p. 26). Many of the self-esteem courses are commercial packages—costly for schools but without solid evidence that they make a difference for students (Crisci, 1986; Leming, 1981).

Sensitivity training and self-esteem courses share a common conceptual problem. They assume that we encourage self-esteem by changing the individual's beliefs, making the young person work harder against the odds. But what if the student's environment is truly unsafe, debilitating, and unsupportive? Some people have overcome tremendous problems, but to expect everyone to do so "ignores the fact that having positive self-esteem is almost impossible for many young people, given the deplorable conditions under which they are forced to live by the inequities in our society" (Beane, 1991, p. 27).

Because many attempts to encourage self-esteem have been superficial, commercial, and filled with "pop psychology," the self-esteem movement has become an easy target for critics in magazine articles such as "Education: Doing Bad and Feeling Good" (*Time*, February 5, 1990) and "The Trouble with Self-Esteem" (*U.S. News and World Report*, April 2, 1990).

COUNTERPOINT **The self-esteem movement has promise.**

Beyond the "feel-good psychology" of some aspects of the self-esteem movement is a basic truth: "Self-esteem is a central feature of human dignity and thus an inalienable human entitle-

ment. As such, schools and other agencies have a moral obligation to help build it and avoid debilitating it" (Beane, 1991, p. 28). If we view self-esteem accurately as a product of our thinking and our actions—our values, ideas, and beliefs as well as our interactions with others—then we see a significant role for the school. Practices that allow authentic participation, cooperation, problem solving, and accomplishment should replace policies that damage self-esteem, such as tracking and competitive grading.

Beane suggests four principles to guide educators:

First, being nice is surely a part of this effort, but it is not enough. Second, there is a place for some direct instruction regarding affective matters, but this is not enough either. Self-esteem and affect are not simply another school subject to be placed in set-aside time slots. Third, the negative affect of "get tough" policies is not a promising route to self-esteem and efficacy. This simply blames young people for problems that are largely not of their own making. Fourth, since self-perceptions are powerfully informed by culture, comparing self-esteem across cultures without clarifying cultural differences is distracting and unproductive. (pp. 29–30)

Cognitive Approaches to Motivation.   In many ways, cognitive theories of motivation also developed as a reaction to the behavioral views. Cognitive theorists believe that behavior is determined by our thinking, not simply by whether we have been rewarded or punished for the behavior in the past (Schunk, 1991a; Stipek, 1993). Behavior is initiated and regulated by plans (Miller, Galanter, & Pribram, 1960), goals (Locke & Latham, 1990), schemas (Ortony, Clore, & Collins, 1988), expectations (Vroom, 1964), and attributions (Weiner, 1992). One of the central assumptions in cognitive approaches is that people respond not to external events or physical conditions like hunger, but rather to their interpretations of these events. You may have had the experience of being so involved in a project that you missed a meal, not realizing you were hungry until you noticed the time. Food deprivation did not automatically motivate you to seek food.

In cognitive theories, people are seen as active and curious, searching for information to solve personally relevant problems. People work hard because they enjoy the work and because they want to understand. Thus, cognitive theorists emphasize intrinsic motivation. We will see examples of cognitive theories of motivation when we examine Bernard Weiner's attribution theory and Martin Covington's self-worth theory.

Social Learning Approaches to Motivation. Social learning theories of motivation are integrations of behavioral and cognitive approaches: They take into account both the behaviorists' concern with the effects or outcomes of behavior and the cognitivists' interest in the impact of individual beliefs and expectations. Many influential social learning explanations of motivation can be characterized as **expectancy × value theories**. This means that motivation is seen as the product of two main forces, the individual's expectation of reaching a goal and the value of that goal to him or her. In other words, the important questions are, "If I try hard, can I succeed?" and "If I succeed, will the outcome be valuable or rewarding to me?" Motivation is a product of these two forces, because if either factor is zero, there is no motivation to work toward the goal. For example, if I believe I have a good chance of making the basketball team (high expectation), and if making the team is very important to me (high value), then my motivation should be strong. But if either factor is zero (I believe I haven't a prayer of making the team, or I couldn't care less about playing basketball), then my motivation will be zero, too. Bandura's social cognitive theory, discussed later in this chapter, is an example of an expectancy × value approach to motivation.

The behavioral, humanistic, cognitive, and social learning approaches to motivation are summarized in Table 9.1. These theories differ in their answers to the question "What is motivation?" but each contributes in its own way toward a comprehensive understanding of human motivation.

Discussion: Based on expectancy theory, ask students to predict the level of motivation in each of the following:

a. Perceived probability of success under minimum effort is high; incentive value is high.

b. Perceived probability of success under maximum effort is high; incentive value is moderate.

c. Perceived probability of success under maximum effort is low; incentive value is moderate.

Transparency: Acetate transparency T 77, "The Relationships of Reciprocal Determinism," shows interrelationships among environmental, personal, and behavioral variables as causes in learning.

Transparency: Acetate transparency T 81, "The Drive Theory of Social Facilitation," schematically presents social conditions that may improve or impair performance.

Objective 9.3: Define motivation to learn.

Expectancy × Value Theories Explanations of motivation that emphasize individuals' expectations for success combined with their valuing of the goal.

TABLE 9.1 Four Views of Motivation

Behaviorists emphasize the importance of environmental events, particularly positive and negative consequences, in energizing behavior. Cognitivists point to the role of thoughts and beliefs. Humanists stress the power of needs for growth and autonomy. Social learning theories look to both the power of consequences and the role of thoughts and expectations in motivating action.

	Behavioral	Humanistic	Cognitive	Social Learning
Source of Motivation	Extrinsic reinforcement	Intrinsic reinforcement	Intrinsic reinforcement	Extrinsic and intrinsic reinforcement
Important Influences	Reinforcers, rewards, incentives, and punishers	Need for self-esteem, self-fulfillment, and self-determination	Beliefs, attributions for success and failure, expectations	Value of goals, expectation of reaching goals
Key Theorists	Skinner	Maslow Deci	Weiner Covington	Bandura

Motivation to Learn in School   Test Bank items 9.2, 9.5, 9.6, 9.78

Teachers are concerned about developing a particular kind of motivation in their students—the motivation to learn. Jere Brophy (1988) describes **student motivation to learn** as " . . . a student tendency to find academic activities meaningful and worthwhile and to try to derive the intended academic benefits from them. Motivation to learn can be construed as both a general trait and a situation-specific state" (pp. 205–206).

Many elements make up the motivation to learn. These include planning, concentration on the goal, metacognitive awareness of what you intend to learn and how you intend to learn it, the active search for new information, clear perceptions of feedback, pride and satisfaction in achievement, and no anxiety or fear of failure (Johnson & Johnson, 1985). Motivation to learn thus involves more than wanting or intending to learn. It includes the quality of the student's mental efforts. For example, reading the text 10 times may indicate persistence, but motivation to learn implies more thoughtful, active study strategies, like summarizing, elaborating the basic ideas, outlining in your own words, drawing graphs of the key relationships, and so on (Brophy, 1988).

Focus on . . .   Motivation

- It is sometimes suggested that one way of improving education would be to pay students for successful school achievement. What would be the likely effects of doing this?
- Why would a student be motivated to study for a test according to a behavioral viewpoint? A cognitive viewpoint? A humanistic viewpoint?
- How might teachers' attempts to help students "find the fun in learning" undermine the long-term development of the trait of motivation to learn?

It would be wonderful if all our students came to us filled with the motivation to learn, but they don't. And even if they did, work in school might still seem boring or unimportant to some students. As teachers, we have three major goals. The first is to get students productively involved with the work of the class; in other words, to create a *state* of motivation to learn. The second and longer-term goal is to develop in our students the *trait* of being motivated to learn so they will be able " . . . to educate themselves throughout their lifetime" (Bandura, 1993, p. 136). And finally, we want our students to be cognitively engaged—to think deeply about what they study. In other words, we want them to be *thoughtful* (Blumenfeld, Puro, & Mergendoller, 1992).

In the next pages we will examine the role of goals, needs, and beliefs in supporting motivation to learn. In fact, we will use the concept of motivation to learn to develop a chart summarizing the many factors that influence motivation. Figure 9.1 is the first entry in the chart.

oals and Motivation

A **goal** is what an individual is striving to accomplish (Locke & Latham, 1990). When students strive to read a chapter, earn an A on a report, or make a 4.0 GPA, they are involved in *goal-directed behavior*. In pursuing goals, students are generally aware of some current condition (I haven't even opened my book), some ideal condition (I have read and understood every page), and the

FIGURE 9.1

BUILDING A CONCEPT OF MOTIVATION TO LEARN: SOURCE OF MOTIVATION

Motivation to learn is a complex collection of beliefs and behaviors. Motivation to learn is encouraged when the sources of motivation are intrinsic.

	Optimum Characteristics of Motivation to Learn	Characteristics That Diminish Motivation to Learn
Source of Motivation	INTRINSIC: Personal factors such as needs, interests, curiosity, enjoyment	EXTRINSIC: Environmental factors such as rewards, social pressure, punishment

discrepancy between the current and ideal situations. Goals motivate people to act in order to reduce the discrepancy between "where they are" and "where they want to be." Goal setting is usually effective for me. In addition to the routine tasks, like eating lunch that will happen without much attention, I often set goals for each day. For example, today I intend to finish this chapter, run, paint the front door, and send a birthday gift to my daughter (who is melting on the August pavement in summer school at the University of Texas). Having decided to do these things, I will feel uncomfortable if I don't complete the list.

According to Locke and Latham (1990), there are four main reasons why goal setting improves performance. First, goals direct our attention to the task at hand. (Every time my mind wanders from this chapter, my goal of finishing helps direct my attention back to the writing.) Second, goals mobilize effort. (The harder the goal, to a point, the greater the effort.) Third, goals increase persistence. (When we have a clear goal we are less likely to be distracted or to give up until we reach the goal.) Finally, goals promote the development of new strategies when old strategies fall short. For example, if your goal is making an A and you don't reach that goal on your first quiz, you might drop the strategy of reading the text over and over and try a new study approach for the next quiz, such as explaining the key points to a friend.

Types of Goals

Test Bank items 9.21–9.24, 9.54, 9.69, 9.83, 9.102–9.104

The types of goals we set influence the amount of motivation we have to reach them. Goals that are specific, moderately difficult, and likely to be reached in the near future tend to enhance motivation and persistence (Schunk, 1991a & b). Specific goals provide clear standards for judging performance. If perfor-

Background: Lepper, M. R. (1988). Motivational considerations in the study of instruction. *Cognition and Instruction, 5,* 289–309.

The hours of practice required to master a musical instrument surely involves a large measure of intrinsic motivation, but extrinsic motivation, in the form of praise and rewards, may be helpful, especially in the early stages of learning.

Objective 9.4: Set motivating goals for yourself and students.

Discussion: Assign Clifford, M. M. (1990). Students need challenge, not easy success. *Educational Leadership* 48(1), 22–26. *Focus Questions:* Ask your students to evaluate Clifford's claim that students need some experience with failure. For whom is this experience most needed?

Background: Ames, C. (1992). Classrooms: Goals, structures, and student motivation. *Journal of Educational Psychology, 84,* 261–271. A good statement integrating many concepts about goals and providing a frame for the next chapter in this text. The following article expands on Ames's ideas: Blumenfeld, P. C. (1992). Classroom learning and motivation: Clarifying and expending goal theory. *Journal of Educational Psychology, 84,* 272–281.

mance falls short, we keep going. For example, I have decided to "finish this chapter" instead of deciding to "work on the book." Since it is clear when I am finished (the chapter is in the mail), I know when I have met the goal. Anything short of having the chapter in the mail means "keep working." Moderate difficulty provides a challenge, but not an unreasonable one. I can finish this chapter if I stay with it. Finally, goals that can be reached fairly soon are not likely to be pushed aside by more immediate concerns. Groups like Alcoholics Anonymous show they are aware of the motivating value of short-term goals when they encourage their members to stop drinking "one day at a time."

In classrooms there are two main categories of goals—learning and performance. The point of a **learning goal** is to improve, to learn, no matter how many mistakes you make or how awkward you appear. Students who set learning goals tend to seek challenges and persist when they encounter difficulties. Nicholls and Miller (1984) call these students **task-involved learners** because they are concerned with mastering the task and are not worried about how their performance "measures up" compared to others in the class. We often say that these people "get lost in their work."

The second kind of goal is a performance goal. Students with **performance goals** are focused on how they are judged by others. They want to look smart and avoid seeming incompetent. The evaluation of their performance, not what they learn or how hard they try, is what matters. Nicholls and Miller (1984) refer to these students as **ego-involved learners** because they are preoccupied with themselves. Because their goal is to perform and not to learn, ego-involved learners try to look smarter than others in the class. If this seems impossible, they may adopt defensive, failure-avoiding strategies like Defensive Diana described earlier—they pretend not to care, make a show of "not really trying," or they may simply give up (Jagacinski & Nicholls, 1987; Schunk, 1991a). Deborah Stipek lists these behaviors as indicative of a student who is ego-involved with classwork.

- Uses short cuts to complete tasks (tries to finish without doing the work it would take to really learn the material)
- Cheats/copies classmates' papers
- Seeks attention for good performance
- Only works hard on graded assignments
- Is upset by and hides papers with low grades
- Compares grades with classmates
- Chooses tasks that are most likely to result in positive evaluations
- Is uncomfortable with assignments that have unclear evaluation criteria

Learning Goal A personal intention to improve abilities and understand, no matter how performance suffers.

Task-Involved Learners Students who focus on mastering the task or solving the problem.

Performance Goal A personal intention to seem competent or perform well in the eyes of others.

Ego-Involved Learners Students who focus on how well they are performing and how they are judged by others.

Brophy's description of motivation to learn is consistent with the distinction between learning goals and performance goals and task- versus ego-involved students. Motivation to learn means working toward learning, not performance, goals and staying focused on the task at hand. The point is to understand and improve, not just to perform well. (Ames, 1992; Dweck, 1986). As we will see later in this chapter, students' beliefs about ability and effort affect the kinds of goals they set. Figure 9.2 shows how goals and type of involvement fit the concept of motivation to learn.

FIGURE 9.2

BUILDING A CONCEPT OF MOTIVATION TO LEARN: SOURCES, GOALS, AND INVOLVEMENT
Motivation to learn is encouraged when the sources of motivation are intrinsic, the goals are personally challenging, and the individual is focused on the task.

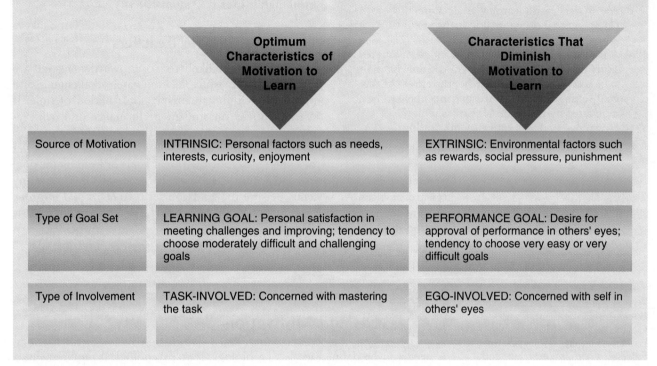

	Optimum Characteristics of Motivation to Learn	Characteristics That Diminish Motivation to Learn
Source of Motivation	INTRINSIC: Personal factors such as needs, interests, curiosity, enjoyment	EXTRINSIC: Environmental factors such as rewards, social pressure, punishment
Type of Goal Set	LEARNING GOAL: Personal satisfaction in meeting challenges and improving; tendency to choose moderately difficult and challenging goals	PERFORMANCE GOAL: Desire for approval of performance in others' eyes; tendency to choose very easy or very difficult goals
Type of Involvement	TASK-INVOLVED: Concerned with mastering the task	EGO-INVOLVED: Concerned with self in others' eyes

Feedback and Goal Acceptance   Test Bank items 9.25, 9.104

Besides having specific, challenging, attainable learning goals and focusing on the task, there are two additional factors that make goal-setting in the classroom effective. The first is *feedback*. In order to be motivated by a discrepancy between "where you are" and "where you want to be," you must have an accurate sense of where you are and how far you have to go. When feedback tells a student that current efforts have fallen short of the goal, the student can exert more effort or even try another strategy. When feedback tells the student that the goal is reached or exceeded, the student should feel satisfied and competent—competent enough perhaps to set a higher goal for the future. There is evidence that feedback emphasizing progress is the most effective. In one study, feedback to adults emphasized either that they had accomplished 75 percent of the standards set or that they had fallen short of the standards by 25 percent. When the feedback highlighted accomplishment, the subjects' self-confidence, analytic thinking, and performance were all enhanced (Bandura, 1993).

Research: Butler, R. (1987). Task-involving and ego-involving properties of evaluation: Effects of different feedback conditions on motivational perceptions, interest, and performance, *Journal of Educational Psychology, 79,* 474–482. Does the impact of information about performance on subsequent intrinsic motivation depend significantly on the degree to which this information promotes a task-involved or an ego-involved motivational orientation? Butler's findings support the conceptualization of feedback conditions as task-involving (comments), ego-involving (grades and praise), or neither (no feedback).

The second factor affecting motivation to pursue a goal is *goal acceptance.* When students accept the goals set by their teachers or establish their own goals, then the power of goal setting to motivate learning can be tapped. But if students reject goals set by others or refuse to set their own goals, then motivation will suffer. Generally, students are more willing to adopt the goals of others if the goals seem realistic, reasonably difficult, and meaningful (Erez & Zidon, 1984).

Goals: Lessons for Teachers

Test Bank items 9.25, 9.104

Students are more likely to work toward goals that are clear, specific, reasonable, moderately challenging, and attainable within a relatively short period of time. If teachers focus on student performance and achievement, they may undermine their students' ability to learn and become task-involved. Students may not yet be expert at setting their own goals or keeping the goal in mind, so encouragement and accurate feedback are necessary. If you use any reward or incentive systems, be sure the goal you set is to *learn and improve* in some area, not just to perform well or look smart. And be sure the goal is not too difficult.

Needs and Motivation

A need can be defined as " . . . a biological or psychological requirement; a state of deprivation that motivates a person to take action toward a goal" (Darley, Glucksberg, & Kinchla, 1991, p. 743). Our needs are seldom satisfied completely and perfectly; improvement is always possible. People are thus motivated by the tensions the needs create to move toward goals that could satisfy the needs. Let's look at one very influential *humanistic* theory of motivation that deals with this central concept.

Maslow's Hierarchy

Test Bank items 9.26–9.33, 9.70, 9.71, 9.80, 9.84, 9.94

Abraham Maslow has had a great impact on psychology in general and on the psychology of motivation in particular. Maslow (1970) suggested that humans have a **hierarchy of needs** ranging from lower-level needs for survival and safety to higher-level needs for intellectual achievement and finally self-actualization. **Self-actualization** is Maslow's term for self-fulfillment, the realization of personal potential. Figure 9.3 is a diagram of Maslow's model.

Maslow (1968) called the four lower-level needs—survival, safety, belonging, and self-esteem—**deficiency needs.** When these needs are satisfied, the motivation for fulfilling them decreases. He labeled the three higher-level needs—intellectual achievement, aesthetic appreciation, and self-actualization—**being needs.** When they are met, a person's motivation does not cease; in-

Background: Graham, S., & Golan, S. (1991). Motivational influences on cognition: Task involvement, ego involvement, and depth of information processing. *Journal of Educational Psychology, 83,* 187–194.

Hierarchy of Needs   Maslow's model of seven levels of human needs, from basic physiological requirements to the need for self-actualization.

Self-Actualization   Fulfilling one's potential.

Deficiency Needs   Maslow's four lower-level needs, which must be satisfied first.

Being Needs   Maslow's three higher-level needs, sometimes called growth needs.

FIGURE 9.3

MASLOW'S HIERARCHY OF NEEDS

The four lower-level needs in Maslow's hierarchy are called deficiency needs because when they are met, the motivation to satisfy them decreases. But when the being needs are met, motivation to seek further fulfilment of these needs increases.

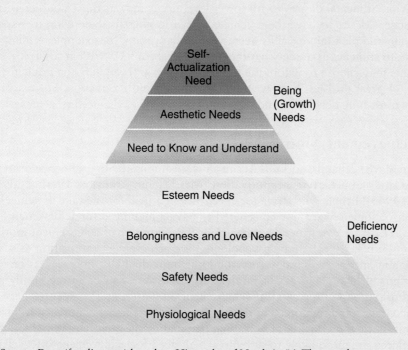

Source: Data (for diagram) based on Hierarchy of Needs in "A Theory of Human Motivation" in *Motivation and Personality,* 2d ed., by Abraham Maslow. Copyright © 1970 by Abraham H. Maslow. Reprinted by permission of Harper & Row, Publishers, Inc.

stead, it increases to seek further fulfillment. For example, the more successful you are in your efforts to know and understand, the harder you are likely to strive for even greater knowledge and understanding. Unlike the deficiency needs, these being needs can never be completely filled. The motivation to achieve them is endlessly renewed.

Maslow's theory has been criticized for the very obvious reason that people do not always appear to behave as the theory would predict. Most of us move back and forth among different types of needs and may even be motivated by many different needs at the same time. Some people deny themselves safety or friendship in order to achieve knowledge, understanding, or greater self-esteem.

Teaching Tip: Write the needs from Maslow's hierarchy in random order on the board. Ask students to pretend they are shipwrecked on a desert island. Their task is to order the needs based on the sequence in which they would be motivated to satisfy them. Compare their hierarchies with Maslow's.

Activity 9.5: Teaching Tip. See the separate *Instructors' Resource Manual* for Level of Aspiration, a class activity that demonstrates the effects of group standards and previous performance on level of aspiration.

Objective 9.5: List Maslow's seven levels of needs and give a classroom example of each.

Activity 9.6: Teaching Tip. See the separate *Instructors' Resource Manual* for Maslow's Hierarchy, an activity that asks your students to examine their own motivation in terms of Maslow's hierarchy of needs. **Handout Master 9.5** supports this activity.

Transparency: Acetate transparency T 80, "Maslow's Hierarchy of Needs," presents this famous model from humanistic psychology.

It's difficult to be motivated to learn when you are hungry. In many schools, students' basic needs for physiological safety are met through breakfast programs.

Application: Ask students to give a rationale, based on Maslow's hierarchy, for teacher support of a school breakfast program.

Objective 9.6: Explain how to encourage the need for achievement in the classroom.

Achievement Motivation Desire to excel; impetus to strive for excellence and success.

Resultant Motivation Whichever is the stronger tendency—the need to achieve or the need to avoid failure.

Criticisms aside, Maslow's theory does give us a way of looking at the whole person, whose physical, emotional, and intellectual needs are all interrelated. This has important implications for education. Students who come to school hungry, sick, or hurt are unlikely to be motivated to seek knowledge and understanding. A child whose feelings of safety and sense of belonging are threatened by divorce may have little interest in learning to divide fractions. If the classroom is a fearful, unpredictable place and students seldom know where they stand, they are likely to be more concerned with security and less with learning. Maslow's hierarchy can provide other insights into students' behavior. Students' desires to fill lower-level needs may at times conflict with a teacher's desire to have them achieve higher-level goals. Belonging to a social group and maintaining self-esteem within that group, for example, are important to students. If doing what the teacher says conflicts with group rules, students may choose to ignore the teacher's wishes or even defy the teacher.

A great deal has been written about needs and motivation. For teaching, the most fully developed and relevant work involves the need to achieve.

Achievement Motivation   Test Bank items 9.34–9.37, 9.72

David McClelland and John Atkinson were among the first to concentrate on the study of **achievement motivation** (McClelland, Atkinson, Clark, & Lowell, 1953). People who strive for excellence in a field for the sake of achieving, not for some reward, are considered to have a high need for achievement.

There are two general explanations for the source of achievement motivation (Stipek, 1993). Some psychologists see achievement motivation as a stable and unconscious trait—something the individual has more or less of. The origins of high achievement motivation are assumed to be in the family and cultural group of the child. If achievement, initiative, and competitiveness are encouraged and reinforced in the home, and if parents let children solve problems on their own without becoming irritated by the children's initial failures, children are more likely to develop a high need for achievement (McClelland & Pilon, 1983). Children who see that their actions can have an impact on their environment and who are taught how to recognize a good performance are more likely to grow up with the desire to excel (Lefton, 1994; Schunk, 1991a).

Other theorists see achievement motivation as a set of conscious beliefs and values shaped mainly by recent experiences with success and failure and by factors in the immediate situation such as the difficulty of the task or the incentives available. Thus you might have high achievement motivation in your educational psychology class because you are doing well and you value the material, but low achievement motivation in a required government class because you have had trouble with that subject in the past and the assignments seem unnecessarily long and difficult (Stipek, 1993).

Atkinson (1964) added a new consideration to the theory of achievement need when he noted that all people have a need to avoid failure as well as a need to achieve. If our need to achieve in a particular situation is greater than the need to avoid failure, the overall tendency, or **resultant motivation,** will be to take the risk and try to achieve. On the other hand, if the need to avoid failure is greater, the risk will be threatening rather than challenging, and the resultant motivation will be to avoid the situation. An extended example should help clarify Atkinson's views.

A coach wants the school team to try a new routine at the gymnastic meet coming up in two months. The routine involves several new, difficult movements. If the movements are executed well, the team is certain to win the meet. If the team tries but fails, it is sure to lose.

Jennifer is one of the best gymnasts on the team and could probably master the movements with ease. But she insists on perfecting the old routine instead of learning a new one. She is immobilized by her fear of embarrassing herself in front of so many people. For Jennifer, the fear of failure is greater than the need for achievement in this particular situation.

Another member of the team, Kelly, is very eager to try the new routine. While she and Jennifer are similar in ability, Kelly is less afraid of embarrassment and is willing to work at mastering the new movements. She is generally the last to leave every practice session and seems to look forward to new challenges. Kelly's need for achievement overcomes any fear of failure.

If students' motivation to achieve is greater than their motivation to avoid failure, a moderate amount of failure can often enhance their desire to pursue a problem. They are determined to achieve, so they try again. If Kelly, for example, were to fall off the balance beam, she would be likely to try even harder to master the balance beam movements. On the other hand, success gained too easily can actually decrease motivation for those with high achievement needs. Kelly probably realizes this. Just relying on the old routine is not particularly motivating for her.

In contrast, students motivated by the need to avoid failure are usually discouraged by failure and encouraged by success. Jennifer, for example, might quit the team if she were embarrassed publicly by her mistakes. If the old routine won the meet, however, she probably would experience unqualified pleasure as well as relief. Figure 9.4 on page 344 integrates achievement motivation into the idea of motivation to learn.

The Need for Self-Determination

Self-determination is the need to experience choice in what we do and how we do it. It is the desire to have our own wishes, rather than external rewards or pressures, determine our actions (Deci & Ryan, 1985; Deci, Vallerand, Pelletier, & Ryan, 1991). According to deCharms (1976, 1983), people strive to be *causal agents*—to be the main locus of causation for their behavior. Because people strive to be in charge of their own behavior, they constantly struggle against pressure from external controls such as the rules, schedules, deadlines, orders, and limits imposed by others. Sometimes even help is rejected so that the individual can remain in command.

To capture the difference between self- and other-determination, deCharms used the metaphor of people as "origins" and "pawns." As origins, people perceive themselves as the origin or source of their intention to act in a certain way. As pawns, people see themselves as powerless participants in a game controlled by others. When people feel like pawns, play becomes work, leisure feels like obligation, and intrinsic motivation becomes extrinsic motivation (Lepper & Greene, 1978). For example, you may have had the experience of deciding to wash the car or clean your room, only to have your motivation dampened by a parent who insists that you tackle the chore. Your chance to be an origin

Test Bank items 9.38, 9.39, 9.85

Activity 9.7: Field Experience. See the separate *Instructors' Resource Manual* for Comparing High and Low Achievers, a field-experience activity that guides your students' observations of the class behavior of high- and low-achieving students. An observation chart is provided in **Handout Master 9.3** in the *Instructors' Resource Manual.*

Teaching Tip: Describe the Thematic Apperception Test. To evaluate an individual's need to achieve, David McClelland used the Thematic Apperception Test, often called the TAT (Murray, 1938), although other methods are now available. In the TAT, people are shown ambiguous pictures and asked to tell or write stories about them. The stories are scored on the basis of the themes or needs implied. A major assumption behind such a test is that people project their own fantasies, thoughts, and needs into the characters and situations in their stories. For this reason, tests such as the TAT are called projective tests. Here is an example of a story that was scored high on n-Ach (need to achieve):

The boy is trying to reconcile the philosophies of Descartes and Thomas Aquinas—at the tender age of 18. He has read several books on philosophy and feels the weight of the world on his shoulders.

Looking at the same picture, another individual wrote a story that received a low n-Ach score:

Ed is thinking of leaving home for a while in the hope that this might shock his parents into getting along.

Activity 9.8: Background. See the separate *Instructors' Resource Manual* for Origins and Pawns, a brief summary of deCharms's program for encouraging student self-motivation. **Handout Master 9.2** provides your students with guidelines for training their students to be "origins."

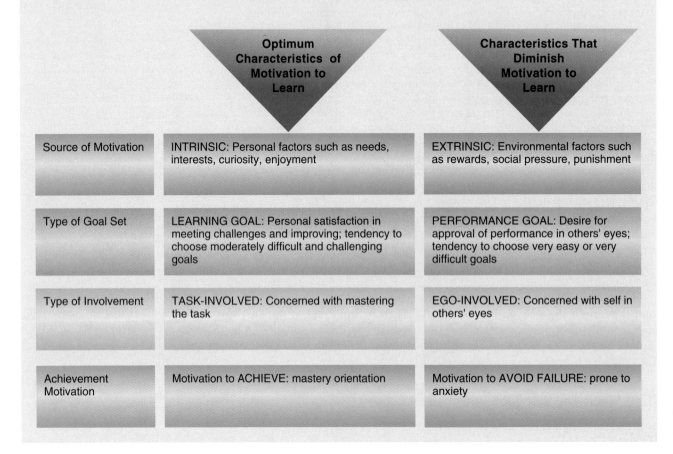

FIGURE 9.4

BUILDING A CONCEPT OF MOTIVATION TO LEARN: NEED TO ACHIEVE VERSUS FEAR OF FAILURE

Motivation to learn is encouraged when the sources of motivation are intrinsic, the goals are personally challenging, and the individual is focused on the task and has a mastery orientation.

	Optimum Characteristics of Motivation to Learn	Characteristics That Diminish Motivation to Learn
Source of Motivation	INTRINSIC: Personal factors such as needs, interests, curiosity, enjoyment	EXTRINSIC: Environmental factors such as rewards, social pressure, punishment
Type of Goal Set	LEARNING GOAL: Personal satisfaction in meeting challenges and improving; tendency to choose moderately difficult and challenging goals	PERFORMANCE GOAL: Desire for approval of performance in others' eyes; tendency to choose very easy or very difficult goals
Type of Involvement	TASK-INVOLVED: Concerned with mastering the task	EGO-INVOLVED: Concerned with self in others' eyes
Achievement Motivation	Motivation to ACHIEVE: mastery orientation	Motivation to AVOID FAILURE: prone to anxiety

seems spoiled by outside attempts at control. You don't want to wash the car anymore because your sense of self-determination is taken away.

DeCharms was struck by his observation that students are too little governed by their own intrinsic motivation and too powerless over external controls and demands. As origins students are active and responsible, but as pawns they are passive, and they take little responsibility for school work. DeCharms developed programs to help teachers support student self-determination. The programs emphasized setting realistic goals, personal planning of activities to reach the goals, personal responsibility for actions, and feelings of self-confidence. Results of some studies show that when students feel more like origins and less like pawns, they have higher self-esteem, feel more competent and in charge of their learning, score higher on standardized tests, and are absent less (deCharms, 1976; Ryan & Grolnick, 1986).

The Need for Relatedness   Test Bank item 9.73

Relatedness is the need to establish close emotional bonds and attachments with others and reflects the desire to be emotionally connected to the important people in our lives (Ryan, 1991). When children are denied the interpersonal involvement they seek from adults—when adults, for example, are unresponsive to their needs—the children lose intrinsic motivation. But when teachers and parents are responsive and demonstrate that they care about the children's interests and well-being, the children show high intrinsic motivation (Grolnick, Ryan, & Deci, 1991).

Relatedness has two components, involvement and autonomy support. Involvement is the degree to which teachers and parents are interested in and knowledgeable about, and devote time to their childrens' activities and experiences. Autonomy support is the degree to which teachers and parents encourage children to make their own choices rather than applying pressure to control the children's behavior. When teachers and parents show high involvement and autonomy support, children show greater competence, academic achievement, and responsibility, as well as less aggression (Grolnick & Ryan, 1989; Grolnick, Ryan, & Deci, 1991).

Needs and Motivation: Lessons for Teachers   Test Bank item 9.94

All people need to feel safe, secure, accepted, competent, effective, connected, and in charge of their own behavior. Some people may have developed a par-

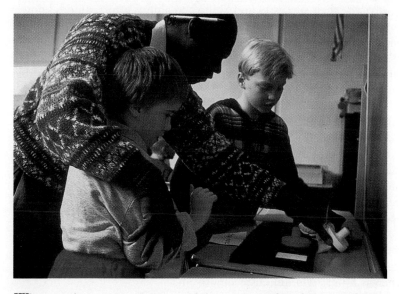

When teachers are responsive and demonstrate that they care about children's interests and well-being, the children show high intrinsic motivation.

ticularly strong need to achieve. Most people are more motivated when they are involved with tasks that give them a sense of achievement and a chance to form positive relationships with others. No one enjoys failure, and for some people it is crushing. Students, like adults, are unlikely to stick with tasks or respond well to teachers who make them feel insecure or incompetent and cause them to fail. They are less likely to take responsibility for learning if they feel like pawns rather than origins in the classroom or if they believe that the teacher doesn't really care about them.

 # ttributions, Beliefs, and Motivation

Thus far, we have talked about goals and needs, but there is another factor that must be considered in explaining motivation. Success will not encourage motivation if you believe it was "just lucky" and probably won't happen again. Failure is not threatening unless you believe that it implies something is "wrong" with you. In other words, our *beliefs and attributions* about what is happening and why—about why we succeed and why we fail—affect motivation.

Attribution Theory

Test Bank items 9.40–9.51, 9.54, 9.74, 9.75, 9.86, 9.87, 9.88, 9.95

Cognitive explanations of motivation, called **attribution theories**, begin with the assumption that we all ask "Why?" in our attempts to understand our successes and failures. Students may ask themselves, Why did I flunk my midterm? What's wrong with my essay? Why did I do so well this grading period? Students may *attribute* their successes and failures to ability, effort, mood, knowledge, luck, help, interest, clarity of instructions, the interference of others, unfair policies, and so on. Attribution theories of motivation describe how the individual's explanations, justifications, and excuses influence motivation.

Bernard Weiner is one of the main educational psychologists responsible for relating attribution theory to school learning (Weiner, 1979, 1990, 1992; Weiner & Graham, 1989). According to Weiner, most of the causes to which students attribute their successes or failures can be characterized in terms of three dimensions: *locus* (location of the cause internal or external to the person), *stability* (whether the cause stays the same or can change), and *responsibility* (whether the person can control the cause). Table 9.2 shows how a student might explain failing a test using the eight possible combinations of these dimensions as causes.

Weiner (1984, 1992) believes that these three dimensions have important implications for motivation. The *internal/external locus*, for example, seems to be closely related to feelings of self-esteem (Weiner, 1980). If success or failure is attributed to internal factors, success will lead to pride and increased motivation, whereas failure will diminish self-esteem.

The *stability* dimension seems to be closely related to expectations about the future. If, for example, students attribute their success (or failure) to stable factors such as the difficulty of the subject, they will expect to succeed (or

Attribution Theories Descriptions of how individuals' explanations, justifications, and excuses influence their motivation and behavior.

TABLE 9.2   Weiner's Theory of Causal Attribution

There are many explanations students can give for why they fail a test. Below are eight reasons representing the eight combinations of locus, stability, and responsibility in Weiner's model of attributions.

Dimension Classification	Reason for Failure
Internal-stable-uncontrollable	Low aptitude
Internal-stable-controllable	Never studies
Internal-unstable-uncontrollable	Sick the day of the exam
Internal-unstable-controllable	Did not study for this particular test
External-stable-uncontrollable	School has hard requirements
External-stable-controllable	Instructor is biased
External-unstable-uncontrollable	Bad luck
External-unstable-controllable	Friends failed to help

Source: B. Weiner (1992). *Human motivation: Metaphors, theories and research*, p. 253. Newbury Park, CA: Sage Publications, Inc. Adapted by permission.

fail) in that subject in the future. But if they attribute the outcome to unstable factors such as mood or luck, they will expect (or hope for) changes in the future when confronted with similar tasks. The *responsibility* dimension is related to emotions such as anger, pity, gratitude, or shame. If we fail at something that we believe is controllable, we may feel shame or guilt; if we succeed, we may feel proud. Failing at an uncontrollable task may lead to anger toward the person or institution in control, while succeeding leads to feeling lucky or grateful.

Weiner's locus and responsibility dimensions are closely related to Deci's concept of *locus of causality* and deCharm's origin/pawn distinction, discussed earlier. J. B. Rotter's (1954) idea of **locus of control** also captures the distinction between self-determination and control by others. Rotter suggested that locus of control is a relatively stable trait. For example, some people have an internal locus of control and believe they are responsible for their own fate. They like to work in situations where skill and effort can lead to success. Other people tend to have an external locus of control, generally believing that people and forces outside themselves control their lives. These individuals prefer to work in situations where luck determines the outcome (Lefcourt, 1966). Locus of control can be influenced by the behavior of others. Continuing discrimination against women, people of color, and individuals with special needs can affect these individuals' perceptions of their own ability to control their lives (Beane, 1991). If people feel that they are not in control of their own lives their self-esteem is likely to be diminished.

Whatever the label, most theorists agree that a sense of choice, control, and self-determination is critical if people are to feel intrinsically motivated. When people come to believe that the events and outcomes in their lives are mostly uncontrollable, they have developed **learned helplessness** (Seligman, 1975). To understand the power of learned helplessness, consider this experiment (Hiroto

Research: Graham, S. (1991). A review of attribution theory in achievement contexts. *Educational Psychology Review, 3*, 5–39. This article reviews several major principles of attribution theory as they relate to achievement strivings, including the antecedents to particular self-ascriptions, the emotional consequences of causal attributions for success and failure, help seeking and help giving, peer acceptance and rejection, achievement evaluation, and attributional process in African American populations.

Transparency: Use acetate transparency **T 82**, "Attributions for Successes and Failures."

Study Guide: Concept Map. See the *Study Guide* for the Concept Map "Attributions and Motivation," which is also presented in **Handout Master 9.6.**

Activity 9.9: Teaching Tip. See the separate *Instructors' Resource Manual* for Internal-External Locus of Control, a class activity that asks students to analyze their answers to a locus of control test. This activity is supported by **Handout Master 9.1,** located in the *Instructors' Resource Manual.*

Casebook: For ideas about how to help students attribute their successes and failures to their own efforts, see the *Teachers' Casebook.*

Casebook: See the *Teachers' Casebook* for practicing teachers' ideas about how to help a student who completely lacks self-confidence.

Locus of Control "Where" people locate responsibility for success and failures—inside or outside themselves.

Learned Helplessness The expectation, based on previous experiences with a lack of control, that all one's efforts will lead to failure.

& Seligman, 1975). Subjects receive either solvable or unsolvable puzzles. In the next phase of the experiment, all subjects are given a series of solvable puzzles. The subjects who struggled with unsolvable problems in the first phase of the experiment usually solve significantly fewer puzzles in the second phase. They have learned that they cannot control the outcome, so why should they even try?

Learned helplessness appears to cause three types of deficits: motivational, cognitive, and affective. Students who feel hopeless will be unmotivated and reluctant to attempt work. Like Helpless Henry described earlier, they expect to fail so why even try—thus motivation suffers. Because they are pessimistic about learning, these students miss opportunities to practice and improve skills and abilities, so they develop cognitive deficits. Finally, they often suffer from affective problems such as depression, anxiety, and listlessness (Alloy & Seligman, 1979). Once established, it is very difficult to reverse the effects of learned helplessness. As we saw in chapters 4 and 5, learned helplessness is a particular danger for students with learning disabilities and students who are the victims of discrimination.

Attributions and Student Motivation. Most students try to explain their failures to themselves. When usually successful students fail, they often make *internal, controllable* attributions: they misunderstood the directions, lacked the necessary knowledge, or simply did not study hard enough, for example. When students see themselves as capable and attribute failure to lack of effort or insufficient knowledge—controllable causes—they usually focus on strategies for succeeding next time. This is an adaptive, mastery-oriented response, one that often leads to achievement, pride, a greater feeling of control, and a sense of self-determination (Ames, 1992).

The greatest motivational problems arise when students attribute failures to stable, uncontrollable causes. Such students may seem resigned to failure, depressed, helpless—what we generally call "unmotivated" (Weiner, Russell, & Lerman, 1978). These students respond to failure by focusing even more on their own inadequacy; their attitudes toward schoolwork may deteriorate even further (Ames, 1992). Apathy is a logical reaction to failure if students believe the causes are stable, unlikely to change, and beyond their control. In addition, students who view their failures in this light are less likely to seek help—they believe nothing and no one can help (Ames & Lau, 1982). Figure 9.5 adds the role of attributions to motivation to learn.

Cues about Causes. How do students determine the causes of their successes and failures? Sandra Graham (1991) gives some surprising answers. There is evidence that when teachers respond to students' mistakes with pity, praise for a "good try," or unsolicited help, the students are more likely to attribute their failure to an uncontrollable cause—usually lack of ability. For example, Graham and Barker (1990) asked subjects of various ages to rate the effort and ability of two boys on a videotape. On the tape was a teacher circulating around the class while students worked. The teacher stopped to look at the two boys' papers, did not comment to the first boy, but said to the second, "Let me give you a hint. Don't forget to carry your tens." The second boy had not asked for help and did not appear to be stumped by the problem. All the age groups watching the tapes, even the youngest, perceived the helped boy as lower in ability than the boy who did not get help. It is as if the subjects

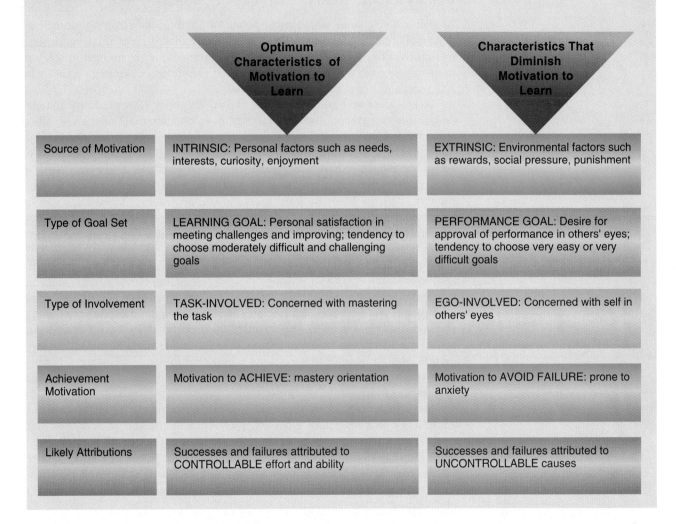

FIGURE 9.5

BUILDING A CONCEPT OF MOTIVATION TO LEARN: LIKELY ATTRIBUTIONS
Motivation to learn is encouraged when the sources of motivation are intrinsic, the goals are personally challenging, and the individual is focused on the task, has a mastery orientation, and attributes successes and failures to controllable causes.

	Optimum Characteristics of Motivation to Learn	Characteristics That Diminish Motivation to Learn
Source of Motivation	INTRINSIC: Personal factors such as needs, interests, curiosity, enjoyment	EXTRINSIC: Environmental factors such as rewards, social pressure, punishment
Type of Goal Set	LEARNING GOAL: Personal satisfaction in meeting challenges and improving; tendency to choose moderately difficult and challenging goals	PERFORMANCE GOAL: Desire for approval of performance in others' eyes; tendency to choose very easy or very difficult goals
Type of Involvement	TASK-INVOLVED: Concerned with mastering the task	EGO-INVOLVED: Concerned with self in others' eyes
Achievement Motivation	Motivation to ACHIEVE: mastery orientation	Motivation to AVOID FAILURE: prone to anxiety
Likely Attributions	Successes and failures attributed to CONTROLLABLE effort and ability	Successes and failures attributed to UNCONTROLLABLE causes

read the teacher's behavior as saying, "You poor child, you just don't have the ability to do this hard work, so I will help."

Does this mean that teachers should be critical and withhold help? Of course not! But it is a reminder that "praise as a consolation prize" for failing (Brophy, 1985) or oversolicitous help can give unintended messages. Graham (1991) suggests that many minority-group students could be the victims of well-meaning pity from teachers. Seeing the very real problems that the students face, teachers may "ease up" on requirements so the students will "experience success" and "feel good about themselves." But a subtle communication may accompany the pity, praise, and extra help: "You don't have the ability to do this,

Activity 9.10: Critical Thinking. See the separate *Instructors' Resource Manual* for Attribution of Motive, a class activity that gives experience analyzing external and internal attributions of motivation.

Transparency: Use acetate transparency T 85, "Some Factors Affecting Individual Motivation."

Objective 9.7: Discuss the possible motivational effects of success and failure and how these effects relate to beliefs about ability.

Research: Blumenfeld, P. C., Pintrich, P. R., & Hamilton, V. L. (1986). Children's concepts of ability, effort, and conduct. *American Educational Research Journal, 23,* 95–104.

Brief abstract: Children's self-perceptions of ability may reflect assessments of their effort and good conduct as well as academic performance. In a study of 158 second and sixth graders, ability was generally linked to effort and effort to conduct, but not ability to conduct, in either ratings or judgment criteria. Children generally used absolute standards in judging ability and did so almost exclusively in judging effort and conduct. The results suggest that children's judgments of ability, effort, and conduct are interrelated but distinguishable.

Teaching Tip: McAndrew, F. T. (1985). A classroom demonstration of the primacy effect in the attribution of ability. *Teaching of Psychology, 12,* 209–211. Students participate in a simple experiment designed to provide firsthand experience with the "primacy effect" (people's judgment of others is influenced more by early information than by later information). The demonstration can serve as a jumping-off point for a discussion on teacher expectations, attribution theory, and experimental design.

so I will overlook your failure." Graham says, "The . . . pertinent question for blacks is whether their own history of academic failure makes them more likely to be the targets of sympathetic feedback from teachers and thus the recipients of low-ability cues" (1991, p. 28). This kind of sympathetic feedback, even if well-intended, can be a subtle form of racial discrimination.

Beliefs about Ability   Test Bank items 9.52–9.54, 9.76, 9.89, 9.90, 9.96

As you can see, some of the most powerful attributions affecting motivation in school are beliefs about *ability*. By examining these beliefs and how they affect motivation, we will understand why some people set inappropriate, unmotivating goals; why some students adopt self-defeating strategies; and why some students seem to give up altogether.

Adults use two basic concepts of ability. An **entity view of ability** assumes that ability is a *stable, uncontrollable* trait—a characteristic of the individual that cannot be changed. According to this view, some people have more ability than others, but the amount each person has is set. An **incremental view of ability,** on the other hand, suggests that ability is *unstable* and *controllable*— ". . . an ever-expanding repertoire of skills and knowledge" (Dweck & Bempechat, 1983, p. 144). By hard work, study, or practice, knowledge can be increased and thus ability can be improved. Table 9.3 shows how these two conceptions of ability would fit into Weiner's model of causal attribution (Table 9.2).

Young children tend to hold an exclusively incremental view of ability (Nicholls & Miller, 1984). Through the early elementary grades, most students believe that effort is the same as intelligence. Smart people try hard and trying hard makes you smart. If you fail, you aren't smart and you didn't try hard; if you succeed, you must be a smart, hard worker (Stipek, 1993). Children are age 11 or 12 before they can differentiate among effort, ability, and performance. About this time, they come to believe that someone who succeeds without working at all must be *really* smart. This is when beliefs about ability begin to influence motivation.

Students who hold an entity view of intelligence tend to set performance goals. They seek situations where they can look smart and protect their self-esteem. Like Jennifer on the gymnastics team or Safe Sally, they keep doing what they can do well without expending too much effort or risking failure, since either one—working hard *or* failing—indicates (to them) low ability. And to work hard but still fail would be a devastating blow to their sense of competence.

Entity View of Ability Belief that ability is a fixed characteristic that cannot be changed.

Incremental View of Ability Belief that ability is a set of skills that can be changed.

TABLE 9.3   A Revised View of the Internal Attribution Model with Two Kinds of Ability

| | Internal Attribution | |
	Stable	Unstable
Controllable	Never studies	Did not study for this particular test *Incremental ability*
Uncontrollable	*Entity ability*	Sick day of exam

Another strategy is to make a point of not trying at all, like Defensive Diana described earlier. If you don't try and fail, no one can accuse you of being dumb. Just before a test a student might say, "I didn't study at all!" or "All I want to do is pass." Then, any grade above passing is a success. Procrastination is another self-protective strategy. Low grades do not imply low ability if the student can claim, "I did okay considering I didn't start the term paper until last night." Some evidence suggests that blaming anxiety for poor test performance can also be a self-protective strategy (Covington & Omelich, 1987). Of course, even though these strategies may help students avoid the negative implications of failure, very little learning is going on.

Incremental theorists, in contrast, tend to set learning goals and seek situations in which they can improve their skills, since improvement means getting smarter. Failure is not devastating; it simply indicates more work is needed. Ability is not threatened. Incremental theorists tend to set moderately difficult goals, the kind we have seen are the most motivating. Figure 9.6 on page 352 merges beliefs about ability into the concept of motivation to learn.

Beliefs about Self-Efficacy   Test Bank items 9.55, 9.56, 9.91

Bandura (1986, 1993) suggests that one source of motivation is thoughts and predictions about possible outcomes of behavior. "Will I succeed or fail? Will I be liked or laughed at?" We imagine future consequences based on past experiences and our observations of others. These predictions are also affected by our sense of **self-efficacy**. This concept, an important aspect of Bandura's theory, refers to our beliefs about our personal competence *in a given area*. Clearly, our expectations for succeeding or failing at a particular task will be influenced by our sense of self-efficacy in that area.

Sense of self-efficacy also affects motivation through goal setting, influencing the goals we will attempt to reach and our persistence. If we have a high

Sense of self-efficacy is an important component of motivation. For many young women, a diminished sense of efficacy in math and science has undermined their motivation and achievement. All students should be encouraged to tackle courses that provide challenges and build a sense of efficacy.

Research: Ames, C., & Archer, J. (1987). Mothers' beliefs about the role of ability and effort in school learning. *Journal of Educational Psychology, 79,* 409–423.

The researchers studied the achievement goals of mothers in relation to their interpretation of school success, preferences for certain types of school feedback, task choices, causal attributions, and valuing of certain personal characteristics in their children. Over 500 mothers of children in kindergarten through fifth grade were surveyed. The findings showed that mothers who emphasized mastery (as opposed to performance-based achievement goals) had different beliefs about how learning occurs, how it is fostered, how it is evidenced, and how it should be evaluated. These findings suggest mothers with different achievement goals may encourage their children to pursue different types of achievement activities, may evaluate children on different aspects of their behavior, and may communicate different types of expectations to children. The findings also suggest that a performance-goal priority may have especially negative consequences for children who have doubts about their ability or who do not compare favorably with others.

Background: Bandura, A. (1993). Perceived self-efficacy in cognitive development and functioning. *Educational Psychologist, 28,* 117–114.

Self-Efficacy Beliefs about personal competence in a particular situation.

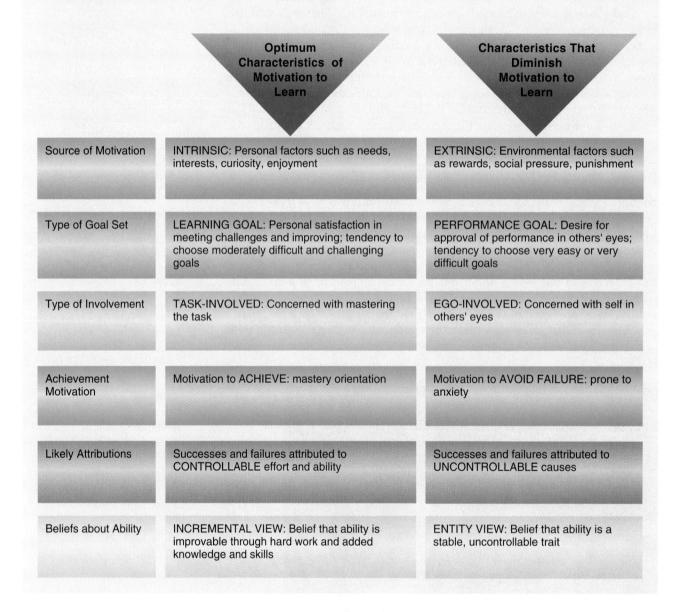

FIGURE 9.6

BUILDING A CONCEPT OF MOTIVATION TO LEARN: BELIEFS ABOUT ABILITY
Motivation to learn is encouraged when the sources of motivation are intrinsic, the goals are personally challenging, and the individual is focused on the task, has a mastery orientation, attributes successes and failures to controllable causes, and believes ability can be improved.

	Optimum Characteristics of Motivation to Learn	Characteristics That Diminish Motivation to Learn
Source of Motivation	INTRINSIC: Personal factors such as needs, interests, curiosity, enjoyment	EXTRINSIC: Environmental factors such as rewards, social pressure, punishment
Type of Goal Set	LEARNING GOAL: Personal satisfaction in meeting challenges and improving; tendency to choose moderately difficult and challenging goals	PERFORMANCE GOAL: Desire for approval of performance in others' eyes; tendency to choose very easy or very difficult goals
Type of Involvement	TASK-INVOLVED: Concerned with mastering the task	EGO-INVOLVED: Concerned with self in others' eyes
Achievement Motivation	Motivation to ACHIEVE: mastery orientation	Motivation to AVOID FAILURE: prone to anxiety
Likely Attributions	Successes and failures attributed to CONTROLLABLE effort and ability	Successes and failures attributed to UNCONTROLLABLE causes
Beliefs about Ability	INCREMENTAL VIEW: Belief that ability is improvable through hard work and added knowledge and skills	ENTITY VIEW: Belief that ability is a stable, uncontrollable trait

Research: Norwich, B. (1987). Self-efficacy and mathematics achievement: A study of their relation. *Journal of Educational Psychology, 79,* 384–387.

sense of efficacy in a given area, we will set high goals and persist when we encounter difficulties. If our sense of efficacy is low, however, we may avoid a task altogether or give up easily when problems arise (Bandura, 1993; Zimmerman, Bandura, & Martinez-Pons, 1992).

FIGURE 9.7

THE ATTRIBUTIONAL APPROACH TO EXPLAINING ACHIEVEMENT MOTIVATION

There are many factors influencing achievement motivation. Experiencing success or failure and receiving feedback from adults that highlights either effort or ability affects children's attributions to mastery or helplessness. Attributions shape academic self-esteem, and self-esteem influences expectancies for future success and sense of efficacy for future related tasks. Expectations and sense of efficacy together affect achievement motivation. The cycle begins again as motivation influences whether a child succeeds or fails.

Source: From Laura E. Berk, *Child Development*, 2/e, p. 443. Copyright © 1991 by Allyn and Bacon. Adapted with permission.

Self-efficacy also seems to be related to attributions. People with a strong sense of self-efficacy for a given task ("I'm good at math") attribute their failures to lack of effort ("I should have double-checked my work"). But people with a low sense of efficacy ("I'm terrible at math") tend to attribute their failures to lack of ability ("I'm just dumb"). You can see that if a student held an entity view of ability (it cannot be changed) and a low sense of self-efficacy, motivation would be destroyed when failures were attributed to lack of (unchangeable) ability ("I just can't do this and I'll never be able to learn") (Bandura, 1993; Schunk, 1991b). The cycle of attributions, expectations, self-efficacy, motivation, and outcomes is depicted in Figure 9.7.

Much of my own recent research has focused on a particular kind of self-efficacy—sense of efficacy in teaching (Hoy & Woolfolk, 1990, 1993; Woolfolk & Hoy, 1990; Woolfolk, Rosoff, & Hoy, 1990). **Teaching efficacy,** a teacher's belief that he or she can reach even difficult students to help them learn, appears to be one of the few personal characteristics of teachers that is correlated with student achievement (Ashton & Webb, 1986). Self-efficacy theory predicts that teachers with a high sense of efficacy work harder and persist longer even when students are difficult to teach, in part because these teachers believe in themselves and in their students.

This study investigated the relationship between self-efficacy and mathematics achievement when other factors such as self-concept of math ability, prior task achievement, and prior self-efficacy were taken into account. Results of four trials with 72 children, aged 9 to 10 years, indicated small or no predictive relation between self-efficacy and task performance, depending on task familiarity, when these other factors were included in the analysis. These results illustrate the complexity of self-efficacy, its sources, and its consequences.

Teaching Efficacy A teacher's belief that he or she can reach even the most difficult students and help them learn.

Background: For ideas about what can be done to prevent discouraged students from dropping out of school, see Sagor, R. (1989). Teetering on the edge of failure. *Annual editions: Educational psychology 89/90*. Guilford, CT: Duskin, pp. 140–144.

Activity 9.11: Application. See the separate *Instructors' Resource Manual* for Motivating the Discouraged Learner, an activity that asks your students to apply different theoretical perspectives to motivate a discouraged learner.

Objective 9.8: Describe the characteristics of mastery-oriented, failure-avoiding, and failure-accepting students.

Connections: How can the ideas presented in chapter 6 about using praise appropriately be applied to help failure-avoiding students recognize their own accomplishments?

Mastery-Oriented Students Students who focus on learning goals because they value achievement and see ability as improvable.

We have found that prospective teachers tend to increase in their personal sense of efficacy as a consequence of completing student teaching. Teachers' sense of personal efficacy is higher in schools where the other teachers and administrators have high expectations for students and where teachers receive help from their principals in solving instructional and management problems (Hoy & Woolfolk, 1993). Another important conclusion from our research is that efficacy grows from real success with students, not just from the moral support or cheerleading of professors and colleagues. Any experience or training that helps you succeed in the day-to-day tasks of teaching will give you a foundation for developing a sense of efficacy in your career.

Attributions, Achievement Motivation, and Self-Worth

Test Bank items 9.57, 9.58, 9.77, 9.99

What are the connections between our need for achievement, attributions for success and failure, beliefs about ability, self-efficacy, and self-worth? Covington and his colleagues suggest that these factors come together in three kinds of motivational sets: *mastery-oriented, failure-avoiding*, and *failure-accepting*, as shown in Table 9.4 (Covington, 1984; Covington & Omelich, 1984, 1987).

Mastery-oriented students tend to value achievement and see ability as improvable, so they focus on learning goals in order to increase their skills and abilities. They are not fearful of failure, since failing does not threaten their sense of competence and self-worth. This allows them to set moderately difficult goals, take risks, and cope with failure constructively. They generally attribute success to their own effort, and so they assume responsibility for learning and have a strong sense of self-efficacy. They perform best in competitive situations, learn fast, have more self-confidence and energy, are more aroused, welcome concrete feedback (it does not threaten them), and are eager to learn "the rules of the game" so that they can succeed. All of these factors make for persistent, successful learning (Alderman, 1985; McClelland, 1985; Morris, 1991).

TABLE 9.4   Mastery-Oriented, Failure-Avoiding, and Failure-Accepting Students

	Need for Achievement	Goals Set	Attributions	View of Ability	Strategies
Mastery-oriented	High need for achievement; low fear of failure	Learning goals: moderately difficult and challenging	Effort, use of right strategy, sufficient knowledge is cause of success	Incremental; improvable	Adaptive strategies: e.g., try another way, seek help, practice/study more
Failure-avoiding	High fear of failure	Performance goals; very hard or very easy	Lack of ability is cause of failure	Entity; set	Self-defeating strategies: e.g., make a feeble effort, pretend not to care
Failure-accepting	Expectation of failure; depression	Performance goals or no goals	Lack of ability is cause of failure	Entity; set	Learned helplessness; likely to give up

Failure-avoiding students tend to hold an entity view of ability, so they set performance goals. They lack a strong sense of their own competence and self-worth separate from their performance. In other words, they feel only as smart as their last test grade, so they never develop a solid sense of self-efficacy. In order to feel competent, they must protect themselves (and their self-images) from failure. If they have been generally successful, they may avoid failure simply by taking few risks and "sticking with what they know." If, on the other hand, they have experienced some successes but also a good bit of failure, they may adopt the strategies we discussed earlier—procrastination, feeble efforts, setting very low or ridiculously high goals, or claiming not to care. Both Safe Sally and Defensive Diana are failure-avoiding students.

Unfortunately, as we have seen, failure-avoiding strategies are self-defeating, generally leading to the very failure the students were trying to avoid. If failures continue and excuses wear thin, the students may finally decide that they are incompetent. This is what they feared in the first place, but they come to accept it. Their sense of self-worth and self-efficacy deteriorate. They give up and thus become **failure-accepting students**. They are convinced that their problems are due to low ability, and they can no longer protect themselves from this conclusion. As we saw earlier, those students who attribute failure to low ability and believe ability is set are likely to become depressed, apathetic, and helpless. Like Hopeless Henry, they have little hope for change.

Teachers may be able to prevent some failure-avoiding students from becoming failure-accepting by helping them to find new and more realistic goals. Also, some students may need support in aspiring to higher levels in the face of sexual or ethnic stereotypes about what they "should" want or what they "should not" be able to do well. This kind of support could make all the difference. Instead of pitying or excusing these students, teachers can teach them how to learn and hold them accountable.

Background: See Noll, J. W. (1991). *Taking sides: Clashing views on controversial educational issues*, (5th ed.). Guilford, CT: Duskin, for "Can Schools Prevent Urban Dropouts?" pp. 162–173. Larry Cuban describes what schools can do to prevent dropouts, while Paul Wooding argues that the changes must take place beyond the school.

Focus on... Attributions, Beliefs, and Motivation

- If a person has a strong sense of self-efficacy, what kind of goals would he or she set? Why?
- Explain how beliefs about the nature of ability might be associated with students' self-protective, self-defeating behaviors such as procrastination or not trying.
- Describe the development of learned helplessness. What kinds of goals would a student set if the student felt helpless?
- Why are students more likely to learn if they attribute successes and failures to controllable causes? How does the attribution to controllable causes relate to the need for self-determination?

Attributions and Beliefs: Lessons for Teachers

Test Bank items 9.59, 9.60

At the heart of attribution theory is the notion of individual perception. If students believe they lack the ability to deal with higher mathematics, they will probably act on this belief even if their actual abilities are well above average. These students are likely to have little motivation to tackle trigonometry or calculus, since they expect to do poorly in these areas. If students believe that failing means they are stupid, they are likely to adopt many self-protective, but also self-defeating, strategies.

Just telling students to "try harder" is not particularly effective. Students need real evidence that effort will pay off, that setting a higher goal will not lead to failure, that they can improve, and that abilities can be changed. The Guidelines on page 356 provide ideas for encouraging self-worth.

Failure-Avoiding Students Students who avoid failure by sticking to what they know, by not taking risks, or by claiming not to care about their performance.

Failure-Accepting Students Students who believe their failures are due to low ability and there is little they can do about it.

Guidelines

**Encouraging
Students'
Self-Worth**

Emphasize students' progress in a particular area.

Examples

1. Return to earlier material in reviews and show how "easy" it is now.
2. Encourage students to redo and improve projects when they have learned more.
3. Keep examples of particularly good work in portfolios.

Make specific suggestions for improvement, and revise grades when improvements are made.

Examples

1. Return work with comments noting what the students did right, what they did wrong, and why they might have made the mistakes.
2. Experiment with peer editing.
3. Show students how their revised, higher grade reflects greater competence and raises their class average.

Stress connections between past efforts and past accomplishments.

Examples

1. Have individual goal-setting and goal-review conferences with students, in which you ask students to reflect on how they solved difficult problems.
2. Confront self-defeating, failure-avoiding strategies directly.

Set learning goals for your students, and model a mastery orientation for them.

Examples

1. Recognize progress and improvement.
2. Share examples of how you have developed your abilities in a given area.
3. Read stories about students who overcame physical, mental, or economic challenges.
4. Don't excuse failure because a student has problems outside school. Help the student succeed inside school.

Activity 9.12: Background. Ask students to read the article "Some third graders are passing because I work with them" (1987, July). *Harvard Education Letter, 3(2),* 2. A summary of this article, Preventing Dropouts, appears in the separate *Instructors' Resource Manual. Focus Questions:* Why does tutoring younger students increase the school motivation of potential dropouts? Why does tutoring younger students increase the motivation of the tutor as well as the tutee?

Activity 9.13: See the separate *Instructors' Resource Manual* for Encouraging Motivation. **Handout Master 9.4** presents four cases and asks students to apply their knowledge of motivation to solve the problem presented in the case.

Anxiety General uneasiness, a feeling of tension.

Anxiety in the Classroom   Test Bank item 9.98

Students who are worried that they will not be able to complete a task satisfactorily often end up with a feeling of **anxiety**, or " . . . an experience of general uneasiness, a sense of foreboding, a feeling of tension" (Hansen, 1977, p. 91). The effects of anxiety on school achievement are clear. "From the time of the earliest work on this problem, starting with the pioneering work of Yerkes and Dodson (1908), to the present day, researchers have consistently reported a negative correlation between virtually every aspect of school achievement and a wide range of anxiety measures" (Covington & Omelich, 1987, p. 393). Anxiety can be both a cause and an effect of school failure—

students do poorly because they are anxious, and their poor performance increases their anxiety.

What Causes Anxiety in School?   Test Bank items 9.61, 9.92

In the classroom, the conditions surrounding a test can influence the performance of highly anxious individuals. For example, Hill and Eaton (1977) found that very anxious fifth and sixth graders worked as quickly and accurately as their less-anxious classmates when there was no time limit for solving arithmetic problems. With a time limit, however, the very anxious students made three times as many errors as their classmates, spent about twice as much time on each problem, and cheated twice as often as the less-anxious group. Williams (1976) found that very anxious students outperformed all other groups when they did not have to put their names on test papers, which seemed to remove some of the personal cost of failing. Whenever there are pressures to perform, severe consequences for failure, and competitive comparisons among students, anxiety may be encouraged (Wigfield & Eccles, 1989).

Sigmund Tobias (1985) suggests a model to explain how anxiety interferes with learning and test performance at three points in the learning and performance cycle. When students are learning new material, they must pay attention to it. Highly anxious students evidently divide their attention between the new material and their preoccupation with how nervous they are feeling. Instead of concentrating on a lecture or on what they are reading, they keep noticing the tight feelings in their chest, thinking, "I'm so tense, I'll never understand this stuff!" Much of their attention is taken up with negative thoughts about performing poorly, being criticized, and feeling embarrassed. From the beginning, anxious students may miss much of the information they are supposed to learn because their thoughts are focused on their own worries (Hill & Wigfield, 1984; Paulman & Kennelly, 1984).

But the problems do not end here. Even if they are paying attention, many anxious students have trouble learning material that is somewhat disorganized and difficult—material that requires them to rely on their memory. Unfortunately, much material in school could be described this way. Anxious students may be more easily distracted by irrelevant or incidental aspects of the task at hand. They seem to have trouble focusing on the significant details (Hill & Wigfield, 1984). In addition, many highly anxious students have poor study habits. Simply learning to be more relaxed will not automatically improve these students' performance; their learning strategies and study skills must be improved as well (Naveh-Benjamin, 1991).

Finally, anxious students often know more than they can demonstrate on a test. They may lack critical test-taking skills, or they may have learned the materials but "freeze and forget" on tests. So anxiety can interfere at one or all three points—attention, learning, and testing (Naveh-Benjamin, McKeachie, & Lin, 1987).

Helping Anxious Students   Test Bank items 9.64, 9.99

Teachers should help highly anxious students to set realistic goals, since these individuals often have difficulty making wise choices. They tend to select either extremely difficult or extremely easy tasks. In the first case, they are likely to

Research: Hunsley, J. (1987). Cognitive processes in mathematics anxiety and test anxiety: The role of appraisals, inner dialogue, and attributions. *Journal of Educational Psychology, 79,* 388–392. Ninety-six undergraduates in a psychology statistics course completed test and math anxiety measures early in the course. Before and after each of their five midterm examinations, students also completed questionnaires that assessed their anxiety, appraisals, internal dialogue, and performance attributions. The results: both math and test anxiety accounted for variance in preexam appraisals, negative internal dialogue, postexam appraisals, pre- and postexam anxiety, and several types of performance attributions. Only test anxiety, however, accounted for variance in actual examination performances.

Research: Meece, J. L., Wigfield, A., & Eccles, J. (1990). Predictors of math anxiety and its influence on young adolescents' course enrollment intentions and performance in mathematics. *Journal of Educational Psychology, 92,* 6–70. This study found that math anxiety was most directly related to students' math ability perceptions, performance expectancies, and value perceptions. Students' performance expectancies predicted subsequent math grades, whereas their value perception predicted course enrollment intentions.

Objective 9.9: Develop a plan for helping an anxious student improve.

fail, which will increase their sense of hopelessness and anxiety about school. In the second case, they will probably succeed on the easy tasks, but they will miss the sense of satisfaction that could encourage greater effort, ease their fears about schoolwork, and nurture a sense of self-efficacy. Anxious students may need a good deal of guidance in choosing both short- and long-term goals. They may also need help working at a moderate pace, especially when taking tests. Often, these students either work too quickly and make many careless errors or work too slowly and are never able to finish the task. If possible, consider eliminating time limits on important tests. Since anxiety appears to interfere with both attention and retention (Wittrock, 1978), highly anxious students (at least those of average or high ability) benefit most from instruction that is very structured and allows for repetition of parts of the lesson that are missed or forgotten (Seiber, O'Neil, & Tobias, 1977; Wigfield & Eccles, 1989).

Anxiety: Lessons for Teachers

Test Bank items 9.62, 9.63, 9.65, 9.100, 9.101

You need to work at keeping the level of **arousal** right for the task at hand. If students are going to sleep, energize them by introducing variety, piquing their curiosity, surprising them, or giving them a brief chance to be physically active. If arousal is too great, follow the Guidelines for dealing with anxiety.

Focus on... Anxiety in the Classroom

- Name some sources of anxiety in typical classroom situations.
- How does anxiety interfere with learning?

Research: Naveh-Benjamin, M. (1991). A comparison of training programs intended for different types of test-anxious students: Further support for an information-processing model. *Journal of Educational Psychology, 83,* 134–139. This study investigates the distinction between two types of test-anxious students. The first type consists of students with good study habits who have difficulties mostly in retrieval for a test. The second type consists of students with poor study habits who have problems in all stages of processing.

Guidelines

Dealing with Anxiety

Arousal Physical and psychological reactions causing a person to be alert, attentive, wide awake.

Use competition carefully.

Examples
1. Monitor activities to make sure no students are being put under undue pressure.
2. During competitive games, make sure all students involved have a reasonable chance of succeeding.
3. Experiment with cooperative learning activities.

Avoid situations in which highly anxious students will have to perform in front of large groups.

Examples
1. Ask anxious students questions that can be answered with a simple yes or no, or some other brief reply.
2. Give anxious students practice in speaking before smaller groups.

Make sure all instructions are clear.

Examples
1. Write test instructions on the board or on the test itself instead of giving them orally.
2. Check with students to make sure they understand. Ask several students how they would do the first question or an exercise or the sample question on a test. Correct any misconceptions.

3. If you are using a new format or starting a new type of task, give students examples or models to show how it is done.

Avoid unnecessary time pressures.

Examples
1. Give occasional take-home tests.
2. Make sure all students can complete classroom tests within the period given.

Remove some of the pressures from major tests and exams.

Examples
1. Teach test-taking skills; give practice tests; provide study guides.
2. Avoid basing most of a report-card grade on one test.
3. Make extra-credit work available to add points to course grades.
4. Use different types of items in testing, since some students have difficulty with certain types.

Develop alternatives to written tests.

Examples
1. Try oral, open-book, or group tests.
2. Have students do projects, organize portfolios of their work, make oral presentations, or create a finished product.

Research: Silverman, W. K., & Kearney, C. A. (1991). The nature and treatment of childhood anxiety. *Educational Psychology Review, 3,* 335–362. This article reviews several issues pertinent to childhood anxiety and related disorders: the reliability and validity of existing classification systems; the diversity and shortcomings of behavioral assessment techniques; the nature and efficacy of intervention strategies; and the need to interface taxonomic, assessment, and treatment methods.

Background: Wigfield, A., & Eccles, J. (1989). Test anxiety in elementary and secondary school students. *Educational Psychologist, 24,* 159–183.

Activity 9.14: Background. See the separate *Instructors' Resource Manual* for Anxiety and Performance, a summary of Covington, M., & Omelich, C. L. (1987). "I knew it cold before the exam": A test of the anxiety-blockage hypothesis. *Journal of Educational Psychology, 79,* 393–400.

SUMMARY

What Is Motivation?

The study of motivation is essentially a study of how and why people initiate actions directed toward specific goals, how intensively they are involved in the activity, and how persistent they are in their attempts to reach these goals. Explanations of motivation include both personal and environmental factors as well as intrinsic and extrinsic sources of motivation.

Behaviorists tend to emphasize extrinsic motivation caused by incentives, rewards, and punishment. Humanistic views stress the intrinsic motivation created by the need for personal growth and fulfillment. Cognitive psychologists stress a person's active search for meaning, understanding, and competence, and the power of the individual's beliefs and interpretations. Social learning views suggest that motivation to reach a goal is the product of our expectations for success and the value of the goal to us. If either is zero, our motivation is zero also. This general approach is called the expectancy × value theory of motivation.

Teachers are interested in a particular kind of motivation—student motivation to learn. Student motivation to learn is both a trait and a state. It involves taking academic work seriously, trying to get the most from it, and applying appropriate learning strategies in the process.

Goals and Motivation

Many theories of motivation feature a prominent role for goals. Goals increase motivation if they are specific, moderately difficult, and able to be reached in the near future. An important distinction is between performance goals (the intention to appear smart or capable in the eyes of others) and learning goals (the intention to gain knowledge and master skills). Students who are motivated to learn set learning rather than performance goals and are task-involved rather than ego-involved. In order for goal-setting to be effective in the classroom, students need accurate feedback about their progress toward goals and they must accept the goals rather than reject them.

Needs and Motivation

Needs are also an important component of many theories of motivation. Maslow has suggested that people are motivated by a hierarchy of needs, beginning with basic physiological requirements and moving up to the need for self-fulfillment. Lower-level needs must by met before higher-level needs can influence motivation. The need for achievement has been viewed as a personal characteristic nurtured by early experiences in the family and as a reaction to recent experiences with success or failure. The need to achieve is balanced by the need to avoid failure. Together these are strong motivating forces. Several theorists emphasize the role of choice and self-determination in motivation and the need for positive relations with others.

Attributions, Beliefs, and Motivation

The attribution theory of motivation suggests that the explanations people give for behavior, particularly their own successes and failures, have strong influences on future plans and performance. One of the important features of an attribution is whether it is internal and within a person's control or external and beyond control. Teachers may cue attributions by the way they respond to students' work. Surprisingly, praise, sympathy, and unsolicited help can communicate to students that they lack the ability to do the work.

When people believe that ability is fixed, they tend to set performance goals and strive to protect themselves from failure. When they believe ability is improvable, however, they tend to set learning goals and handle failure constructively. A low sense of self-worth seems to be linked with the failure-avoiding and failure-accepting strategies intended to protect the individual from the consequences of failure. These strategies may seem to help in the short term, but are damaging to motivation and self-esteem in the long run.

Bandura suggests that sense of self-efficacy, the belief that you will be effective in a given situation, is a powerful influence on motivation. If an individual has a strong sense of self-efficacy, he or she tends to set more challenging goals and to persist even when obstacles are encountered.

Anxiety in the Classroom

Severe anxiety is an example of arousal that is too high for optimal learning. Anxiety can be the cause or the result of poor performance; it can interfere with attention to, learning of, and retrieval of information. Many anxious students need help in developing effective test-taking and study skills.

KEY TERMS

achievement motivation, p. 342
anxiety, p. 356
arousal, p. 358
attribution theories, p. 346
being needs, p. 340
deficiency needs, p. 340
ego-involved learners, p. 338
entity view of ability, p. 350
expectancy × value theories, p. 335
extrinsic motivation, p. 332
failure-accepting students, p. 355

failure-avoiding students, p. 355
goal, p. 336
hierarchy of needs, p. 340
humanistic view, p. 333
incentive, p. 333
incremental view of ability, p. 350
intrinsic motivation, p. 332
learned helplessness, p. 347
learning goal, p. 338
locus of causality, p. 332
locus of control, p. 347

mastery-oriented students, p. 354
motivation, p. 331
performance goal, p. 338
reward, p. 333
resultant motivation, p. 342
self-actualization, p. 340
self-efficacy, p. 351
student motivation to learn, p. 336
task-involved learners, p. 338
teaching efficacy, p. 353

WHAT WOULD YOU DO?

Preschool and Kindergarten

How would you create an environment that communicates the value of learning to young children without becoming too directive or academic in your teaching? How could you help students build a foundation for self-efficacy in school?

Elementary and Middle School

Your district has no money for new math materials, and the only resources are the workbooks. How would you arouse student curiosity and interest about the material in the workbooks?

Several of your students seem to have given up in science. They almost expect to fail. This is especially troubling because a number of the students are girls who believe that "girls are no good in science." What would you do?

Junior High and High School

You are the faculty advisor for the student newspaper. Your students have grand ideas for stories and features, but they seem to run out of steam and never quite finish. The production of the paper is always last-minute and rush, rush. How would you help the students stay motivated and work steadily?

As the time to take the PSAT nears, a few of your students are becoming so anxious that you wonder if they will make it through the test. What can you do to help them?

Cooperative Learning Activity

With four or five other members of your class, identify ways you can respond to student mistakes without communicating to students that their mistakes are due to low ability. You also want to avoid being unrealistic about what they can do or implying that the material is "easy."

TEACH SELF-ESTEEM

Building Confidence

How do you encourage your students' self-esteem?

I believe that self-esteem has become a buzz word with little meaning. I am appalled at some of the packaged programs that are sold to teach self-esteem at the elementary level. These packages usually contain a unit entitled "All About Me" or "I Like Myself." I have come to believe that real self-esteem is far more complex than just appreciating yourself or gathering information about yourself. Real self-esteem is a deep matter that involves a child's sense of his or her growing capabilities. Real self-esteem grows as a child forms a relationship with teachers and classmates and is fostered by a carefully constructed classroom environment. I have one ironclad rule in my classroom. All actions taken and words spoken must be both true and kind. With this as our base we can build a supportive environment for all the learners. A secondary necessary element is the recognition that we are all at school for a common purpose: learning and growing. We are in the class together to encourage and support one another. I strongly send the message that each member is important.

Cynthia Wisdom, *First-Grade Teacher*
Trace Crossings Elementary School, Hoover, Alabama

CROSS-AGE TUTORING

A student who lacks confidence in his/her ability sometimes needs more than verbal praise for a "job well done." I have found that by actively involving this student in the subject matter, in this case math, I can help the student develop confidence in a meaningful way. I begin by having the student tutor a younger student who is having difficulty. This gives the tutor a feeling of importance because he/she is responsible for helping another learn. As the tutor develops confidence, I change the tutoring situation to an older student and gradually move up until the student has the confidence to tutor someone in his/her own class. Nothing makes students feel more important than helping others.

For subject areas that do not readily lend themselves to a tutor/tutee situation, a student can build confidence by being actively involved in a project that is significant to him/her. Special projects that are pertinent to the student allow the use of learned skills in meaningful ways and can change negative attitudes into positive ones.

Malcolm Jarrell, *Remedial Mathematics and Reading Teacher*
Jackson-Via Elementary School, Charlottesville, Virginia

Motivating Learners

Students are better motivated in school when they attribute their successes and failures to personally controllable causes, such as their own efforts. Suppose you have a student who gives up easily and tends to blame poor performance on assignments, on you, or on presumed lack of ability. What can you do to help this student?

PERSONAL GOALS

Goal setting is an important source of personal motivation. My students and I write personal goals at the beginning of each ranking period. We discuss the whole-person model of a balanced life. Specifically, we write two goals in each of four main categories: mental, social, emotional (feelings), and physical. The students write their individual goals on an index card and place the card in a private place (usually in their desk). The goals are personal, and no one is required to discuss their goals. Each morning while I'm taking attendance and completing the school lunch form, the students silently read their goals. At the end of each quarter, we evaluate our progress. Those students who wish to discuss their goals openly do so at this time. We applaud each other's progress and write new goals (or continue past goals) for the next ranking period. As the goals become internalized, motivation naturally develops.

> Stephen C. Ellwood IV, *Maine 1991 Teacher of the Year*
> *St. Francis Elementary School, St. Francis, Maine*

Teaching for Relevance

Your students complain that the lessons you are teaching are not relevant to their lives. How do you motivate them to learn, understand, and relate to your lessons?

USE STUDENTS' REALITIES

Perhaps it is not so much that I must "motivate them to learn, understand, and relate to my lessons" as it is incumbent upon me to make my lessons relevant to the students. Learning has to take place within their universe and in their words. If I cannot figure out why something is relevant to my students, perhaps it isn't. In that case, I need to change what I am teaching. This is not as simple as it sounds. I am in no way suggesting that students have to "like" everything they study or that learning has to be dressed up in a "rap mode" in order to entice students in the way that popular entertainment does. Rather, I am promoting the idea that students' learning must be in student words and concepts, must involve student evaluation and require student judgments. Intellectually important ideas will demand this kind of involvement; tasks requiring rote memorization will not.

> Karen B. Kreider, *Pennsylvania 1991 Teacher of the Year*
> *Central High School, Philadelphia, Pennsylvania*

TAP STUDENTS' SENSE OF OWNERSHIP

At the beginning of the school year I photograph my students individually with black and white film. Once the pictures are developed, I cut each youngster's face out and glue it on paper which I've ruled into one-inch boxes. Each child's picture is on this one paper, which I then photocopy. I usually make 30 to 40 copies of my original picture paper. The next task is to cut out each child's set of pictures of himself/herself and put these 30 to 40 pictures into an envelope with the youngster's name on it. These pictures are used for many different activities and give the children a sense of ownership in lessons.

At Halloween children come to school in costumes. They stand on an enormous floor graph to explain if their costume is pretty, scary, funny, or an occupation. Once their "real graph" is discussed, children return to their desks to draw their costume on a four-inch square. Their photograph is pasted to this costume drawing, and their drawings are taped to a graph on the wall. Once again discussion ensues, and each child is asked to make a comment about the graph. One comment might be, "There are three more funny costumes than pretty ones." These comments are written on strips of paper, and the picture of the youngster who made the comment is glued to the strip of paper. These strips may be placed in strategic spots around the graph. Children are motivated by this kind of activity and certainly find it relevant.

> Darlene A. Walsh, *Rhode Island 1991 Teacher of the Year*
> *Greenbush Elementary School, West Warwick, Rhode Island*

10

Motivation, Teaching, and Learning

I n the previous chapter we saw that motivation is an extremely complex concept. Many factors seem to affect the goals we choose and our energy and persistence in working toward them. We saw that goals, needs, beliefs, attributions, expectations, and anxiety can all affect motivation.

How do we put all this information together in teaching? How do we create environments, situations, and relationships that encourage motivation? These are the questions we will consider in the next several pages. First we focus on the overall goal in motivating students—the development of self-regulated learners. Then we examine how motivation is influenced by the academic work of the class, the value of the work, and the setting in which the work must be done. Having considered the task and the setting, we turn to a very important influence on student motivation—the teacher. Finally, we discuss a number of strategies for developing motivation as a constant state in your classroom and as a permanent trait in your students.

By the time you have completed this chapter, you should be able to:

- List some characteristics of a self-regulated learner, and describe how teachers can promote self-regulated learning in the classroom.
- Explain how the ambiguity and risk of the learning task affect motivation and what can happen when students try to reduce risk and ambiguity.
- Discuss how the value of a task affects motivation to learn.
- Describe the characteristics of classrooms that support students' autonomy.
- Explain how evaluation procedures and grouping arrangements can influence motivation.
- Design a unit using cooperative learning.
- Describe potential effects on students of teachers' positive and negative expectations.
- Devise a strategy for teaching your subject to an uninterested student.

Planning Tip: See the *Chapter-10-At-A-Glance Planning Guide* in the Instructor's Section at the front of this book.

Study Guide: The *Study Guide*, sold separately, contains exercises to help students determine if they have mastered each learning objective for this chapter.

Planning Tip: See the separate *Instructors' Resource Manual* for additional activities and resources for teaching this chapter, including Handout Masters. Also see the *Allyn and Bacon Transparencies in Educational Psychology*.

Planning Tip: See the *Test Bank* and *Study Guide* supplements as you plan for evaluation and measurement of student learning.

Planning Tip: For further information about audiovisual, multimedia, and computer-assisted resources for teaching this chapter, see the *Video and Software Guide* in the separate *Instructors' Resource Manual*.

Objective 10.1: List some characteristics of a self-regulated learner, and describe how teachers can promote self-regulated learning in the classroom.

Research: Zimmerman, B. J. (1990). Self-regulated learning and academic achievement: An overview. *Educational Psychologist, 21*, 3–18. Zimmerman's article introduces a special issue of the *Educational Psychologist* on self-regulated learning.

Study Guide: Concept Map. See the *Study Guide* for the Concept Map "Self-Regulated Learning." This Concept Map also appears as **Handout Master 13.8**.

Self-Regulated Learners Students whose academic learning abilities and self-discipline make learning easier so motivation is maintained.

WHAT DO YOU THINK?

When you are facing a difficult task, what do you do? How do you handle distractions? Can other people encourage you to be persistent and resist the temptation to quit? How do they do it? Are there activities that you have no trouble doing—that you have to "make yourself quit?" What are they? Are you more motivated when you are a member of a team and others are counting on you or when you are on your own? Think about these issues and then list 10 characteristics of people, tasks, or situations that motivate you the most.

An Ultimate Goal of Teaching: Lifelong Learning

Today, people change jobs an average of seven times before they retire. Many of these are career changes requiring new knowledge and skills (Weinstein, 1994). Students entering the workforce in the next 10 to 20 years probably will experience the same need for continuous learning. Thus, one goal of teaching should be to free students from the need for teachers so the students can continue to learn independently throughout their lives.

Self-Regulated Learning

Test Bank items 10.1, 10.2, 10.44, 10.45, 10.57

To continue learning independently throughout life, you must be a self-regulated learner. **Self-regulated learners** have a combination of academic learning skills and self-control that makes learning easier, so they are more motivated to learn; in other words, they have the *skill* and the *will* to learn (McCombs & Marzano, 1990; Weinstein & McCombs, in press). The concept of self-regulated learning integrates much of what is known about effective learning and motivation. Three factors influence skill and will: knowledge, motivation, and self-discipline or volition.

Knowledge. To be self-regulated learners, students need *knowledge* about themselves, the subject, the task, strategies for learning, and the contexts in which they will apply their learning. "Expert" students know about *themselves* and how they learn best. For example, they know their preferred learning styles, what is easy and what is hard for them, how to cope with the hard parts, what their interests and talents are, and how to use their strengths. These experts also know quite a bit about the *subject* being studied—and the more they know, the easier it is to learn more. They probably understand that different *learning tasks* require different approaches on their part. A simple memory task, for example, might require a mnemonic strategy, while a complex comprehension task might be approached by means of concept maps of the key ideas.

These expert students not only know what each task requires, they can also apply the *strategy* needed. They can skim or read carefully. They can use mnemonics or reorganize the material. In short, they have mastered a large repertoire of learning strategies and tactics.

Finally, expert learners think about the *contexts* where they will apply their knowledge—when and where they will use their learning—so they can set motivating goals and connect present work to future accomplishments (Wang & Palincsar, 1989; Weinstein, 1994).

Motivation. Self-regulated learners are *motivated to learn.* They find many tasks in school interesting because they value learning, not just performing well in the eyes of others. But even if they are not intrinsically motivated by a particular task, they are serious about getting the intended benefit from it. They know *why* they are studying, so their actions and choices are self-determined and not controlled by others. However, knowledge and motivation are not always enough. Self-regulated learners need volition or self-discipline. "Where motivation denotes commitment, volition denotes follow-through" (Corno, 1992, p. 72).

Volition. It is Halloween night. I have been writing almost all day. I want to keep writing because the deadline for this chapter is very near. I have knowledge and motivation, but to keep going I need a good dose of volition. **Volition** is an old-fashioned word for willpower. Self-regulated learners know how to protect themselves from distractions—where to study, for example, so they are not interrupted. They know how to cope when they feel anxious, drowsy or lazy (Corno, 1992). And they know what to do when tempted to stop working and watch *60 Minutes*—the temptation I'm facing now—that, and a large bowl of Halloween candy.

Creating Environments for Self-Regulated Learning. Lyn Corno (1992) describes four cases, each revealing a different aspect of the environment that encourages student volition and responsibility for learning. In the first case, a fourth-grade student who never joined in the classwork was allowed to pursue an interest in drawing without the pressure of being evaluated. This freedom to draw without evaluation proved to be the magnet that drew the student into classwork and encouraged him stick with assignments. "Investing heavily in students' own interests at the start of the school year may pay off later in the students' willingness to invest in *teachers'* interests" (Corno, 1992, p. 76). We will look more closely at the power of evaluative climate and at tapping students' interests later in this chapter.

The second case describes a teacher who used revisions to help students take responsibility for being clear in their writing. Rather than just grade written work, the teacher returned early efforts with suggestions for revisions. Then the teacher moved from providing feedback herself about revised work to having other students guide the revising process. In the third case, Corno highlights the value of peers as learning partners. When students study together, they often ask questions and make suggestions about each others' work. These prompts can cause students to be more reflective and thoughtful about the task at hand.

Connections: Self-regulated learning brings together insights about cognitive skill-metacognition, expert learning, and strategies (chapter 7)—with the information about affective will or motivation (chapter 9). Volition can be seen as the mindful, cognitive side of motivation, knowing how to make yourself do what must be done to learn.

Handout: Handout Master 13.7 provides a flow chart showing "Monitoring and Controlling Strategies for Self-Management."

Research: Lepper, M. R. (1988). Motivational considerations in the study of instruction. *Cognition and Instruction, 5,* 289–309.

Volition Willpower; self-discipline.

The final case describes students in a urban school learning to program in LOGO. The teachers gradually moved from participant modeling—demonstrating what to do—to providing only feedback as the students took over responsibility for the programming. As much as possible the students were expected to handle difficulties on their own. This gradual shift from teacher direction to student independence is a characteristic of many approaches that strengthen volition.

Obviously, not all of your students will be self-regulated learners. In fact, some psychologists suggest that you think of this capacity as an individual difference characteristic. Some students are much better at it than others. How can you help more students become self-regulated learners? We discussed the development of *knowledge,* particularly knowledge of learning strategies and tactics (the *skill* to learn) in earlier chapters, so in this chapter we will focus on *will*—motivation and volition. What can teachers do to encourage and support motivation to learn? To organize our discussion, we will use the TARGETT model.

Focus on . . .   Self-Regulated Learning

- Distinguish between motivation and volition.
- How does knowledge play a role in self-regulated learning?
- What are the TARGETT areas?

Research: Butler, R. (1987). Task-involving and ego-involving properties of evaluation: Effects of different feedback conditions on motivational perceptions, interest, and performance. *Journal of Educational Psychology, 79,* 474–482.

Does the impact of information about performance on subsequent intrinsic motivation depend significantly on the degree to which this information promotes a task-involved or an ego-involved motivational orientation? Two hundred fifth- and sixth-grade students were given interesting divergent thinking tasks in each of three sessions. Individual comments, numerical grades, standardized praise, or no feedback were received after Sessions 1 and 2. At Session 3 (post-test), interest, performance, and attributions of effort, outcome, and the impact of evaluation to task involved causes were highest after receipt of comments. Ego-involved attributions were highest after receipt of grades and praise. These findings support the conceptualization of feedback conditions as task involving (comments), ego involving (grades and praise), or neither (no feedback).

On TARGETT for Self-Regulated Learning

Test Bank items 10.3, 10.46, 10.58

Carol Ames (1990, 1992) has identified six areas where teachers make decisions that can influence student motivation to learn: the nature of the *task* that students are asked to do, the *autonomy* students are allowed in working, how students are *recognized* for their accomplishments, *grouping* practices, *evaluation* procedures, and the scheduling of *time* in the classroom. Epstein (1989) coined the acronym TARGET to organize these areas of possible teacher influence. We will add *teacher expectations* to the model, so ours will be a TARGETT for motivation to learn. Table 10.1 summarizes the model. In the following pages we will examine each of these areas more closely.

Tasks for Learning

To understand how an **academic task** can affect students' motivation, we need to analyze the task. Tasks can be interesting or boring for students. Tasks have a particular subject content and also involve certain cognitive operations such as *memorize, infer, classify, apply,* and so on. As students work on a task they are learning content and practicing operations. Tasks also vary in terms of how clear-cut or ambiguous they are and how much risk is involved in doing them (Doyle, 1983). Finally, tasks have a certain value to students, determined in part by how authentic and meaningful the tasks are for them.

Academic Tasks The work the student must accomplish, including the content covered and the mental operations required.

Tapping Interests and Arousing Curiosity

Test Bank item 10.71

It seems logical that learning experiences should be related to the interests of the students. However, this is not always an easy or even a desirable strategy; there are times when students must master basic skills that hold no intrinsic interest for them. Nevertheless, if a teacher knows what students' interests are,

TABLE 10.1	The TARGETT Model for Supporting Student Motivation to Learn		

Teachers make decisions in many areas that can influence motivation to learn. The TARGETT acronym highlights task, autonomy, recognition, grouping, evaluation, time, and teacher expectations.

TARGETT Area	Focus	Objectives	Examples of Possible Strategies
Task	How learning tasks are structured—what the student is asked to do	Enhance intrinsic attractiveness of learning tasks Make learning meaningful	Encourage instruction that relates to students' backgrounds and experience Avoid payment (monetary or other) for attendance, grades, or achievement Foster goal setting and self-regulation
Autonomy/Responsibility	Student participation in learning/school decisions	Provide optimal freedom for students to make choices and take responsibility	Give alternatives in making assignments Ask for student comments on school life—and take them seriously Encourage students to take initiatives and evaluate their own learning Establish leadership opportunities for *all* students
Recognition	The nature and use of recognition and reward in the school setting	Provide opportunities for *all* students to be recognized for learning Recognize *progress* in goal attainment Recognize challenge seeking and innovation	Foster "personal best" awards Reduce emphasis on "honor rolls" Recognize and publicize a wide range of school-related activities of students
Grouping	The organization of school learning and experiences	Build an environment of acceptance and appreciation of all students Broaden the range of social interaction, particularly of at-risk students Enhance social skills development	Provide opportunities for cooperative learning, problem solving, and decision making Encourage multiple group membership to increase range of peer interaction Eliminate ability-grouped classes
Evaluation	The nature and use of evaluation and assessment procedures	Grading and reporting processes Practices associated with use of standardized tests Definition of goals and standards	Reduce emphasis on social comparisons of achievement Give students opportunities to improve their performance (e.g., study skills, classes) Establish grading/reporting practices that portray student progress in learning Encourage student participation in the evaluation process
Time	The scheduling of the school day	Allow the learning task and student needs to dictate scheduling Provide opportunities for extended and significant student involvement in learning tasks	Allow students to *progress at their own rate* whenever possible Encourage flexibility in the scheduling of learning experiences Give teachers greater control over time usage through, for example, block scheduling
Teacher Expectations	Beliefs and predictions about students' abilities	Hold appropriate but high expectations for all students Communicate that you expect growth	Give all students the chance to revise and improve their work Monitor who gets which opportunities Make sure materials show diversity in achievement

Source: M. L. Maehr and E. M. Andermann (1993). Reinventing schools for early adolescents: Emphasizing task goals. *The Elementary School Journal*, 93, pp. 604–605. Published by The University of Chicago Press. Adapted by permission.

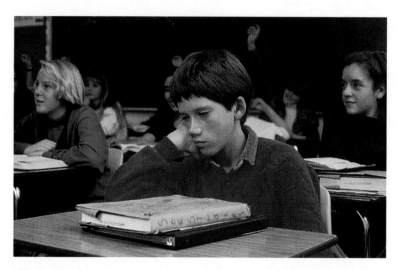

*W*hile it is important to try to tap students' interest and curiosity, there are times when students must master basic skills that hold no intrinsic interest for them.

Research: Graham, S., & Golan, S. (1991). Motivational influences on cognition: Task involvement, ego involvement, and depth of information processing. *Journal of Educational Psychology, 83,* 187–194.

Background: The January 1988 issue of the *Elementary School Journal* is devoted to the topic of "Schoolwork and Academic Tasks."

Objective 10.2: Explain how the ambiguity and risk of the learning task affect motivation and what can happen when students try to reduce risk and ambiguity.

these can be part of many teaching strategies. For example, one music teacher encouraged an interest in Bach by helping students see how certain popular music used a similar style.

For younger students, the chance to manipulate and explore objects relevant to what is being studied may be the most effective way to keep curiosity stimulated. For older students, well-constructed questions, logical puzzles, and paradoxes can have the same effect. Example: ranchers in an area killed the wolves on their land. The following spring they noticed that the deer population was much smaller. How could this be, since wolves hunt the deer and fewer wolves should mean more deer? In searching for a solution, students learn about ecology and the balance of nature: without wolves to eliminate the weaker and sicker deer, the deer population expanded so much that the winter food supply could not sustain the deer herds. Many deer died of starvation.

Task Operations: Risk and Ambiguity

Test Bank items 10.4–10.9, 10.47, 10.48, 10.59, 10.71

Doyle (1983) has suggested that there are four general categories of academic tasks, defined by the operations required: *memory, routine procedure, comprehension,* and *opinion,* as shown in Figure 10.1. The kind of operation in a task determines how ambiguous and risky the task is, and this, in turn, affects student motivation, as you will see.

Some tasks involve less *risk* than others, because failure is unlikely. For example, opinion tasks are very low-risk tasks—there are no right or wrong answers. Simple memory or procedural tasks also involve few risks, because getting the right answer is easy: you just follow the steps. But the stakes can be very high with longer and more complex memory or procedural tasks. Reciting 100 lines from Shakespeare is risky, especially if you are graded on how well you do, because there is a great deal to memorize.

Another characteristic of tasks is level of *ambiguity*—how straightforward the expected answer is. Opinion and understanding tasks are ambiguous: it is hard to predict the right answer (if there is one) or how to find it. The "right" answer may involve the teacher's opinion. Memory and procedural tasks, on the other hand, are straightforward and unambiguous. If you are reciting a soliloquy from *Hamlet,* the "right" answer is clear, even though the task is difficult. Figure 10.1 summarizes how tasks can be categorized by risk and ambiguity.

What does this have to do with motivation? Most students want to *lower the risk* and *decrease the ambiguity* involved in schoolwork, because their grades are at stake. This is especially true for highly anxious students or those who are trying to avoid failure. Many times teachers plan a complicated *comprehension* task that is both ambiguous and risky. They want their students to think and solve problems. But the students want more guidance. They may ask for models, rules, minimums, or formulas: "How many references do you

Transparency: In acetate transparency T 84, the variables in "Riskiness in Decision Making" is presented in a diagram.

FIGURE 10.1

AMBIGUITY AND RISK ASSOCIATED WITH ACADEMIC TASKS IN CLASSROOMS
Academic tasks can be characterized by their levels of risk and ambiguity. Because students often find high-ambiguity/high-risk tasks very threatening, they need extra support and fewer pressures when completing them.

Comprehension tasks
require students to go a step beyond—to transform information, choose the best among many approaches, combine several ideas to solve a new problem, or write a passage in a particular style.

Opinion tasks
ask students to state a preference, such as which character in a story is the bravest.

Memory tasks
require students to recognize or reproduce information they have encountered before, as in matching states and capitals or reciting lines from a play.

Routine or procedural tasks
involve using a set of steps to solve a problem. If students apply the procedure correctly, they will get the right answer: if they use the formula πr^2 for example, they will find the area of a circle.

Source: W. Doyle (1983). Academic work. *Review of Educational Research, 53,* p. 183. Copyright 1983 by the American Educational Research Association. Adapted by permission of the publisher.

want?" "How many pages?" "Will we have to know dates and names?" "Give us a model to follow." In other words, students *negotiate the task*. These negotiations can lead to management problems. If the students are very confused, they may become restless, turn to other students for help, get discouraged, or lose interest in the task.

Under this kind of pressure, the teacher often responds by stating the three main points that should be addressed, giving a minimum number of references or a page limit, and providing books that would be helpful. This transforms the *comprehension* task into a *procedural* one. Risk and ambiguity are reduced and motivation may seem to increase, at least temporarily. But the task itself is not as interesting. Doing well on the procedural task is not as rewarding, because achievement does not lead to a sense of increased competence. So the results of the "task negotiation" may be a temporary *state* of motivation, but it is motivation to perform, to get the grade, not motivation to learn. And little has been done to foster the long-term development of the *trait* of motivation to learn. Furthermore, since students learn the operations that they practice, these students have learned how to do a procedure—and how to negotiate with teachers (Doyle, 1983). But they probably have not improved the problem-solving or critical-thinking skills that the teacher had intended to develop.

Obviously, some balance is needed. Tasks that are clear-cut and low-risk may encourage immediate motivation but undermine the development of long-term motivation and persistence in the face of frustration. Teachers must make wise choices, then stick with them even when students try to negotiate changes. Instructions should be clear, but not too restricting. The penalties for taking a risk or making a mistake should not be too great. Finally, tasks must have some value to students. Let's take a closer look now at the value of classroom tasks.

Task Value   Test Bank items 10.10–10.14, 10.49, 10.60, 10.61

As you recall from the previous chapter, many theories suggest that the strength of our motivation in a particular situation is determined by our *expectation* that we can succeed and the *value* of that success to us. We can think of a task as having three kinds of value to the students (Eccles & Wigfield, 1985). **Attainment value** is the importance of doing well on the task. This aspect of value is closely tied to the needs of the individual (for example, the need to be competent, well-liked, etc.) and the meaning of success to that person. For instance, if someone has a strong need to appear smart and believes that a high grade on a test shows you are smart, then the test has high attainment value for that person. A second kind of value is **intrinsic or interest value.** This is simply the enjoyment one gets from the activity itself. Some people like the experience of learning. Others enjoy the feeling of hard physical effort or of solving puzzles. Finally, tasks have **utility value;** that is, they help us achieve a short-term or long-term goal.

You see from our discussion of task value that it is very difficult to separate personal and environmental influences on motivation. The two influences interact constantly. The task we ask students to accomplish is an aspect of the environment; it is external to the student. But the value of accomplishing the task is bound up with the internal needs, beliefs, and goals of the individual.

Recently there has been a great deal written about the use of authentic tasks in teaching. An **authentic task** is one that has some connection to the real-

---

Objective 10.3: Discuss how the value of a task affects motivation to learn.

Background: See the special issue on "authentic learning" in the April, 1993 issue of *Educational Leadership.*

Attainment Value The importance of doing well on a task; how success on the task meets personal needs.

Intrinsic or Interest Value The enjoyment a person gets from a task.

Utility Value The contribution of a task to meeting one's goals.

Authentic Task Tasks that have some connection to real-life problems the students will face outside the classroom.

life problems and situations that students will face outside the classroom, now and in the future. If you ask students to do busywork, to memorize definitions they will never use, to learn the material only because it is on the test, or to repeat work they already understand, then there can be little motivation to learn. But if the tasks are authentic, students are more likely to see the genuine utility value of the work and are also more likely to find the tasks meaningful and interesting.

Problem-based learning is one example of the use of authentic tasks in teaching. According to William Stepien and Shelagh Gallagher (1993), "problem-based learning turns instruction topsy-turvy. Students meet an ill-structured problem before they receive any instruction. In place of covering the curriculum, learners probe deeply into issues searching for connections, grappling with complexity, and using knowledge to fashion solutions" (p. 26). Teachers act as coaches and tutors, asking questions, modeling thinking, helping students organize and monitor their own problem solving.

An example problem presented to one group of seventh and eighth graders in Illinois is, "What should be done about a nuclear waste dump site in our area?" The students soon learn that this real problem is not a simple one. Scientists disagree about the dangers. Environmental activists demand that the materials be removed, even if this bankrupts the company involved—one that employs many local residents. Some members of the state assembly want the material taken out of state, even though no place in the country is licensed to receive the toxic materials. The company believes the safest solution is to leave the materials buried. The students must research the situation, interview parties involved, and develop recommendations to be presented to state experts and community groups. "In problem-based learning students assume the roles of scientists, historians, doctors, or others who have a real stake in the proposed problem. Motivation soars because students realize it's their problem" (Stepien & Gallagher, 1993, p. 26).

Background: Maehr, M. L., & Anderman, E. M. (1993). Reinventing schools for early adolescents: Emphasizing task goals. *The Elementary School Journal, 93,* 593–610.

Focus on . . . **Tasks for Learning**

- What does it mean for students to "negotiate a task?"
- What makes a task risky?
- Name some ways other than problem-based learning to make learning tasks more authentic.

Supporting Autonomy and Recognizing Accomplishment in the Classroom

Test Bank items 10.72, 10.85

The second area in the TARGETT model involves how much choice and autonomy students are allowed. We saw in the previous chapter that the need for self-determination—the need to be an *origin* not a *pawn*—is an important factor in motivation. There is no intrinsic motivation without self-determination.

Advantages of Autonomy in the Classroom

Test Bank item 10.15

Classroom environments that support student autonomy are associated with greater student interest, sense of competence, self-esteem, creativity, conceptual learning, and preference for challenge. These relationships appear to hold from first grade through graduate school (Ryan & Grolnick, 1986; Williams, Wiener, Markakis, Reeve, & Deci, 1993). In autonomy-oriented classrooms,

Problem-based Learning Methods that provide students with realistic problems that don't necessarily have "right" answers.

Calvin and Hobbes   by Bill Watterson

*CALVIN AND HOBBES © 1991 Watterson. Dist. by Universal Press Syndicate.
Reprinted with permission. All rights reserved.*

students are more likely to believe that the work is important, even if it is not "fun." Thus they tend to internalize educational goals and take them as their own. For example, the problem-based project described above might encourage autonomy and self-determination as the students made choices about how best to solve the problem of toxic-waste dumps.

Controlling environments tend to improve performance only on rote recall tasks. When students are pressured to perform, they often seek the quickest, easiest solution. One discomforting finding, however, is that both students and parents seem to prefer more controlling teachers, even though the students learn more when their teachers support autonomy (Flink, Boggiano, & Barrett, 1990). Popular images of good teaching favor teachers who use extrinsic incentives and pressure students to perform.

Assuming you are willing to risk going against popular images, how can you support student autonomy? One answer is to focus on *information,* not *control,* in your interactions with students.

Information and Control   Test Bank item 10.16

Many things happen to students throughout the school day. They are praised or criticized, reminded of deadlines, assigned grades, given choices, lectured on rules, and on and on. **Cognitive evaluation theory** (Deci & Ryan, 1985; Deci, Vallerand, Pelletier, & Ryan, 1991) explains how these events can influence the students' intrinsic motivation by affecting their sense of self-determination and competence. According to this theory, all events have two aspects, controlling and informational. If an event is highly controlling, that is, if it pressures students to act or feel a certain way, then students will experience less control and their *intrinsic motivation* will be diminished. If, on the other hand, the event provides information that increases the students' sense of competence and efficacy, then intrinsic motivation will increase. Of course, if the information provided makes students feel less competent, it is likely that motivation will decrease.

For example, a teacher might praise a student by saying, "Good for you! You got an A because you finally followed my instructions correctly." This is a highly controlling statement, giving the credit to the teacher thus undermining the student's sense of self-determination and intrinsic motivation. The

Cognitive Evaluation Theory Suggests that events affect motivation through the individual's perception of the events as controlling behavior or providing information.

teacher could praise the same work by saying, "Good for you! Your understanding of the author's use of metaphors has improved tremendously. You earned an A." This statement provides information about the student's growing competence and should increase intrinsic motivation. But if the information is negative, as in "You still have not grasped the concept of metaphor and your grade shows it," then motivation is likely to diminish.

Autonomy Supporting Class Climates   Test Bank item 10.72

What can teachers do to support student autonomy? An obvious first step is to limit their controlling messages to their students and make sure the information they provide highlights students' growing competence. Unfortunately, when teachers are under pressure and "controlled" by the school administration, they are likely to treat students the same way. In one study, teachers told to "make sure" their students performed well in solving problems were more critical and gave students more hints and less time for independent work than teachers who were told that their job was to "help" the students learn how to solve the problems themselves. And the students of the pressured teachers actually performed worse (Boggiano, Flink, Shields, Seelbach, & Barrett, in press). Table 10.2 on page 376 lists five essential elements that support student autonomy.

Recognizing Accomplishment   Test Bank item 10.72

The third TARGETT area is *recognition*. How should students' accomplishments be acknowledged and rewarded? In chapter 6 we discussed the importance of authentic praise that focuses on progress, growing competence, and independence. We have also seen that giving students rewards for activities that they already enjoy can undermine intrinsic motivation. Students should be recognized for improving on their own personal best, for tackling difficult tasks, for persistence, and for creativity—not just for performing better than others. The next section explains one way to use personal progress as a basis for recognition in classrooms.

Focus on... **Supporting Autonomy and Recognizing Accomplishment**

- Name three characteristics of a classroom environment that supports students' autonomy.
- How can recognition undermine motivation and a sense of self-efficacy?
- Why would providing rationales for class rules help students feel more autonomous?

Grouping: Cooperation and Competition

You may remember a teacher who made you want to work hard—someone who made a subject come alive. Or you may remember how many hours you spent practicing as a member of a team, orchestra, choir, or theater troupe. If you do, then you know the motivational power of relationships with other people. David Johnson and Roger Johnson (1985) describe the power this way:

> Motivation to learn is inherently interpersonal. It is through interaction with other people that students learn to value learning for its own sake, enjoy the process of learning, and take pride in their acquisition of knowledge and development of skill. Of the interpersonal relationships available in the classroom, peers may be the most influential on motivation to learn. (p. 250)

TABLE 10.2 Five Teaching Behaviors Found in Autonomy-Supportive Classrooms

1. *Teacher acknowledges the students' points-of-view.*
The teacher strives to understand and appreciate the students' points-of-view in the classroom. The teacher puts the proverbial shoe on the other foot in order to adopt the frame-of-reference the students have as they engage each educational task. The teacher constantly tries to identify the needs and feelings of the students.

2. *Teacher encourages students' choice and self-initiative.*
The teacher creates opportunities for students to take greater initiative in whether to participate in educational tasks, when to do them, and how to solve the problems that arise. The teacher provides students with choices, and the teacher resists telling students to behave and feel a particular way.

3. *Teacher communicates rationale for any behavioral limit or constraint he or she places on students.*
When the teacher places behavioral constraints on students (e.g., "no talking," "keep the table clean"), he or she explains the importance and necessity of the constraints. The teacher explains why the constraint is imposed by clearly spelling out what the good reason for the "no talking" or "keeping the table clean" constraints are.

4. *Teacher acknowledges that negative emotion from students is a valid reaction to teacher-imposed limits, restraints, or tasks.*
The teacher anticipates that students will sometimes (even most of the time) experience negative emotion when behavioral constraints are placed upon them (e.g., feel frustrated by having to wait their turn) and when they are asked to do some educational tasks (e.g., feel confused while reading a difficult book). The teacher communicates that it is "Okay" to feel that way, and that the teacher will continue to accept and respect the student during any experience or expression of negative emotions.

5. *Teacher relies on noncontrolling, positive feedback.*
When students perform poorly or behave in a problematic way, the teacher treats the poor performance or behavioral problem as a problem to be solved rather than as a target for criticism. The teacher resists using critically negative feedback (e.g., "your handwriting is sloppy") and resists using controlling, pressuring, and coercive language (e.g., avoids saying students "should," "must," "ought to," or "have to" do such-and-such).

Background: Ames, C. (1992). Classrooms: Goals, structures, and student motivation. *Journal of Educational Psychology, 84,* 261–271.

Students in the classroom function as part of a large group. Johnson and Johnson (1994) have given considerable attention to this in their work on motivation. They have found that motivation can be greatly influenced by the ways we relate to the other people who are also involved in accomplishing a particular goal. Johnson and Johnson have labeled this interpersonal factor the **goal structure** of the task. There are three such structures: cooperative, competitive, and individualistic, as shown in Figure 10.2.

Cooperative Learning

Test Bank items 10.18–10.31, 10.50–10.53, 10.62–10.65, 10.73, 10.74, 10.77–10.81

Goal Structure The way students relate to others who are also working toward a particular goal.

Several studies have shown that when the task involves complex learning and problem-solving skills, cooperation leads to higher achievement than competition, especially for low-ability students (Johnson & Johnson, 1985; Slavin 1995). In one study, achievement for all students was increased when the group was rewarded based on the average learning of the group members (Slavin, 1983).

FIGURE 10.2

DIFFERENT GOAL STRUCTURES

Each goal structure is associated with a different relationship between the individual and the group. This relationship influences motivation to reach the goal.

Cooperative
Students believe their goal is attainable if and only if other students will also reach the goal.

Competitive
Students believe they will reach their goal if and only if other students do *not* reach the goal.

Individuaiistic
Students believe their own attempt to reach a goal is not related to other students' attempts to reach goals.

Source: D. Johnson and R. Johnson (1975). *Learning together and alone: Cooperation, competition, and individualization.* Adapted by permission of Allyn and Bacon.

In addition, **cooperative learning** seems to result in improved ability to see the world from another person's point of view, better relations among different ethnic groups in schools and classrooms, increased self-esteem, and greater acceptance of handicapped and low-achieving students (Slavin, 1995). Students learn to negotiate and to be more tolerant of others. The interaction with peers that students enjoy so much becomes a part of the learning process. The result? The need for belonging described by Maslow is more likely to be met.

Many activities can be approached cooperatively. For example, students can work together in conducting local surveys. How do people feel about the plan to build a new mall that will bring more shopping and more traffic? Would the community support or oppose the building of a nuclear power plant?

Background: Cooperative learning (1986, September). Harvard Education Letter, *Vol. 2,* No. 5, pp. 4–6. This article describes STAD and the approach of Roger and David Johnson. One advantage of cooperative learning, as noted by Nel Noddings of Stanford University, is that "children solve problems at a more thoughtful, deliberate pace than they do when working as a class. Without any teacher to approve or reject a proposed solution, they debate strategies for some time." Noting how often children in groups call out, "Wait, wait!" Noddings wonders how many would like to slow down the pace of full-class instruction so they could feel that they really understood.

Cooperative Learning Arrangement in which students work in mixed-ability groups and are rewarded on the basis of the success of the group.

Objective 10.4: Contrast the effects of cooperative, competitive, and individualistic goal structures on students' self-esteem and interpersonal relations.

Research: Slavin, R. R. (1991). Synthesis of research on cooperative learning. *Educational Leadership, 48*(5), 71–82. *Focus Question:* When is cooperative learning most effective, and with which students?

Background: Cooperative Learning (1990, special section). *Educational Leadership, 47,*(4), 4–67, and Cooperative Learning (1991, special section). *Educational Leadership, 48,* 71–95.

Activity 10.1: Cooperative Learning. See the separate *Instructors' Resource Manual* for Cooperative Learning Strategies for Elementary Reading, a summary of three techniques for using cooperative learning.

Activity 10.2: Background. See the separate *Instructors' Resource Manual* for Rewards for Cooperative Learning Groups, a discussion of rewards that could be incorporated into a cooperative goal structure.

Connections: Remind students that the need for belonging is the third level of Maslow's hierarchy, discussed in chapter 9. The need to maintain relationships is strong. I was reminded of this when my daughter was reprimanded by her fourth-grade teacher for passing notes during class. Liz's explanation was that there had been a fight during lunch, " . . . and we had to work it out!"

Objective 10.5: Demonstrate how to set up three different models of cooperative learning in a classroom, and match each model with a subject area in which it can be most effective.

Students working in pairs or teams can support each other's learning. Motivation is greater since immediate help from team members is available when a student has problems.

But cooperative learning is not limited to specific or elaborate activities like these. Many of the most ordinary assignments can be enhanced by cooperation. If students must learn 10 new definitions in a biology class, why not let students divide up the terms and definitions and teach one another? Be sure, however, that everyone in the group can handle the task. Sometimes a cooperative effort ends with one or two students doing the work of the entire group. Work groups should be monitored to make sure that each person is contributing and that hostilities, if they develop, are resolved in a positive way.

Setting Up Cooperative Groups. In setting up learning groups, it often makes sense to balance the number of boys and girls. Some research indicates that when there are just a few girls in a group, they tend to be left out of the discussions unless they are the most able or assertive members. By contrast, when there are only one or two boys in the group, they tend to dominate and be "interviewed" by the girls unless these boys are less able than the girls or very shy. In general, for very shy and introverted students, individual learning may be a better approach (Webb, 1980, 1985). Whatever the case, teachers must monitor groups to make sure everyone is contributing and learning.

Even if the group as a whole is successful in reaching the goal, there is still no guarantee that every student has benefited equally. In practice, the effects of learning in a group vary, depending on what actually happens in the group and who is in it. If only a few people take responsibility for the work, these people will learn, but the nonparticipating members probably will not. Students who ask questions, get answers, and attempt explanations are more likely to learn than students whose questions go unasked or unanswered. In fact, there is evidence that the more a student provides elaborated, thoughtful explanations to other students in a group, the more the *explainer* learns. Giving good explanations appears to be even more important for learning than receiving explanations (Webb, 1989). In order to explain, you have to organize the information, put it into your own words, think of examples and analogies (which connect the information to things you already know), and test your understanding by answering questions. These are excellent learning strategies (King, 1990).

STAD. Robert Slavin and his associates have developed a system for overcoming the disadvantages of the cooperative goal structure while maintaining its advantages. The system is called **Student Teams–Achievement Divisions,** or **STAD** (Slavin, 1995). Each team has about five members with a mix of abilities, ethnic backgrounds, and sexes. The teacher calculates an **individual learning expectation (ILE)** score, or base score, for each team member. This score represents the student's average level of performance. Details about how to determine the base scores are given in Table 10.3.

Students work in their teams to study and prepare for twice-weekly quizzes, but they take the quizzes individually, just as in a regular class. Based on test performance, each team member can earn from one to three points for the group. Table 10.3 shows how points are awarded by comparing each student's current test score to his or her base (ILE) score (Slavin, 1995). As you can see from the table, every student has an equal chance to contribute the maximum number of points to the team total. Thus, every student, not just the most able or motivated, has reason to work hard. This system avoids the problem of students' unequal contributions to a group project. Every week the group earning the greatest number of points is declared the winner. Team accomplishments should be recognized in a class newsletter or a bulletin board display.

Activity 10.3: Background. See the separate *Instructors' Resource Manual* for Structures of the Cooperative Classroom, a summary of Kagan, S. (1989/90). The structural approach to cognitive learning. *Educational Leadership, 47*(4), 12–15. Handout Master 10.4 is an overview of several cooperative learning structures as a basis for class discussion.

Transparency: Acetate transparency T 89, "Computing Improvement Points," explains a system of evaluation that enhances student motivation to achieve.

Casebook: For the ideas of practicing teachers about how to get students to participate effectively in cooperative learning, see the Teachers' Casebook at the end of this chapter.

TABLE 10.3 Using Individual Learning Expectations

The idea behind individual learning expectations, or ILEs, is that students ought to be judged in relation to their own abilities and not compared to others. The focus is on improvement, not on comparisons among students.

To calculate an ILE score, the teacher simply averages the student's grades or test scores from previous work. These scores are usually on a 100-point scale. Letter grades can be converted to points based on the school's system—for example, A = 90 points, B = 80 points, and so on. The student's average score is her or his initial base score. The ILE score becomes the standard for judging each student's work.

If the teacher is using the STAD system of cooperative learning, then students earn points for their group based on the following system:

Test Score	Points Earned for Group
A perfect score	3
10 or more points above ILE score	3
5 to 9 points above ILE score	2
4 points below to 4 points above ILE score	1
5 or more points below ILE score	0

Student Teams–Achievement Divisions (STAD) Cooperative learning with heterogeneous groups and elements of competition and reward.

Individual Learning Expectation (ILE) Constantly recomputed average score in a subject.

Example: In cooperative learning programs such as STAD or Teams-Games-Tournaments, student groups compete. Within each group, members help each other to learn the required material and prepare for assessment.

Research: Chambers, B., & Abrami, P. C. (1991). The relationship between student learning outcomes and achievement, causal attributions, and effect. *Journal of Educational Psychology, 83,* 140–146.

Research: King, A. (1990). Enhancing peer interaction and learning in the classroom through reciprocal questioning. *American Educational Research Journal, 27,* 664–687.

Focus on . . .   Cooperative Learning

- What are the advantages and disadvantages of all-male and all-female cooperative groups?
- How is an ILE score calculated?
- What are the three characteristics of cooperative learning?

Teams-Games-Tournaments (TGT) Learning arrangement in which team members prepare cooperatively, then meet comparable individuals of competing teams in a tournament game to win points for their team.

Cooperative Integrated Reading and Composition (CIRC) Cooperative learning technique in which pairs of students from each reading group work together on reading and writing projects, then teams are rewarded on the basis of their work.

Reciprocal Questioning Approach where groups of two or three students ask and answer each other's questions after a lesson or presentation.

Every few weeks the teams can be changed so that students have a chance to work with many different class members. Every two weeks or so the teacher must recompute each student's ILE score by averaging the old base score with grades on the recent tests. With this system, improvement pays off for all students. Those with less ability can still earn the maximum for their team by scoring 10 or more points above their own base score. Those with greater ability are still challenged because they must score well above their own average or make a perfect score to contribute the maximum to the group total.

TGT. **Teams-Games-Tournaments** or **TGT** is similar to STAD. After the teacher's presentation, students move into their heterogeneous groups to help each other answer problems or questions about the material. Instead of taking written tests, however, each student meets once a week at a "tournament table" with two other students of comparable ability from the other teams. The three students at each tournament table compete, answering questions similar to the problems practiced in their study teams. The winner at each table earns 6 points for his or her team. Each week the participants at the tournament tables are adjusted—the winners are "bumped" up to a higher-ability table to keep the competition fair. This way, every student has the chance to contribute equally to the team's total score (Slavin, 1990).

Some recent research on TGT raises a caution. Bette Chambers and Philip Abrami (1991) found that members of successful teams did learn more than members of unsuccessful teams, but also they were happier about the outcome and rated their ability higher than members of losing teams. For low-achieving students who tend to be anxious, failure-accepting, or helpless, being on a losing team could make matters worse. Chambers and Abrami suggest experimenting with cooperation both within and between teams. For example, the whole class might earn recognition if each team reaches a specified level of learning.

CIRC. A recent addition to the list of cooperative learning techniques is **Cooperative Integrated Reading and Composition (CIRC).** This system supports the traditional approach of using ability-based reading groups. Students are assigned to teams made up of pairs from each reading group in the class. While the teacher works with one reading group, the teams work in their pairs using many of the methods of reciprocal teaching described in chapter 13—reading aloud, making predictions, asking questions, summarizing, and writing about the stories they are reading. Teams help each other prepare for tests, write and edit work, and often "publish" team books. Teams are rewarded based on the average performance of all their members on all the reading and writing assignments. Thus, there is equal opportunity for success, group support for learning, and individual accountability for final performance. These three elements are characteristic of many cooperative learning strategies (Slavin, 1995).

Reciprocal Questioning. Another cooperative approach can be used with a wide range of ages and subjects. **Reciprocal questioning** requires no special materials or testing procedures. After a lesson or presentation by the teacher, students work in pairs or triads to ask and answer questions about the material. The teacher provides question stems like the following taken from King (1990):

How would you use . . . to . . . ?

What is a new example of . . . ?

Explain why . . . ?

How are . . . and . . . similar?

What do you think would happen if . . . ?

What are the strengths and weaknesses of . . . ?

Students are taught how to develop specific questions on the material using these generic question stems. The students create questions, then take turns asking and answering. This process has proven more effective than traditional discussion groups because it seems to encourage deeper thinking about the material.

 valuation and Time

The last two TARGETT areas identified by Ames (1990) are *evaluation* and *time*. Students must take tests, answer questions in class, and complete assignments, and they must perform within certain time limits. Doyle (1983) suggests that students look upon most classroom work as "an exchange of performance for grades" (p. 181). Grading here refers to more than marks on a report card. It includes both the formal and informal evaluations of teachers.

Evaluation   Test Bank items 10.10–10.32

The greater the emphasis on competitive evaluation and grading, the more students will focus on performance goals rather than learning goals and the more they will be ego-involved as opposed to task-involved.

Of course, not all students are caught up in an exchange of performance for grades. Low-achieving students who have little hope of either "making the grade" or mastering the task may simply want to finish. One study of first graders found that low-achieving students made up answers, filled in the page with patterns, or copied from other students, just to get through their seatwork. As one student said when she finished a word/definition matching exercise, "I don't know what it means, but I did it" (Anderson, Brubaker, Alleman-Brooks, & Duffy, 1985, p. 132). On closer examination, the researchers found that the work was much too hard for these students, so they connected words at random.

How can teachers prevent students from simply focusing on the grade or doing the work "just to get finished"? The most obvious answer is to de-emphasize grades and emphasize learning in the class. Students need to understand the value of the work. Instead of saying, "You will need to know this for the test," tell students how the information will be useful in solving problems they want to solve. Suggest that the lesson will answer some interesting questions. Communicate that understanding is more important than finishing.

Activity 10.4: Background. See the separate *Instructors' Resource Manual* for Motivating High School Students to Achieve in Math, a summary of Escalante, J., & Dirmann, J. (1990). The Jamie Escalante math program. *Journal of Negro Education, 59*(3), 407–423. Because this summary is good background reading for the CNN segment on Escalante and Garfield High School, a condensed version of it is presented in CNN Video Master 10 in the *Video and Software Guide.*

Activity 10.5: Multicultural Awareness. See the separate *Instructors' Resource Manual* for Bias Against Science.

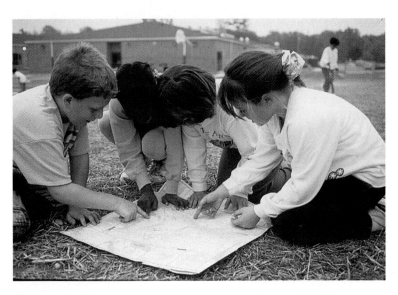

One approach to encouraging motivation is to engage students in "authentic" tasks—activities that have practical value such as reading a map.

Unfortunately, many teachers do not follow this advice. Brophy (1988) reports that when he and several colleagues spent about 100 hours observing how six teachers introduced their lessons, they found that most introductions were routine, apologetic, or unenthusiastic. The introductions described procedures, made threats, emphasized finishing, or promised tests on the material. A few examples are:

"You don't expect me to give you baby work to do every day, do you?"

"My talkers are going to get a third page to do during lunch."

"If you are done by 10 o'clock, you can go outside." (Brophy, 1988, p. 204)

During 100 hours, only nine introductions included statements that described the value of the work or suggested that it would be interesting, and these often were brief. One example is, "Answer the comprehension questions with complete sentences. All these stories are very interesting. You'll enjoy them" (Brophy, 1988, p. 203).

While many teachers are similar to the six Brophy studied, there are exceptions. Hermine Marshall (1987) described a few elementary-school teachers who seem to establish a *learning orientation* in their classrooms. They stress understanding instead of performing, being graded, or finishing work. Later in the chapter we will examine strategies for establishing such an orientation in your class.

Connections: Chapter 11 discusses how to make more time for learning by decreasing disruptions, smoothing transitions, and avoiding discipline problems.

Time

How does the use of time affect student motivation? Most experienced teachers know that there is too much work and not enough time in the school day.

Students seldom have the opportunity to stick with an activity. Even if they become engrossed in a project, students must stop and turn their attention to another subject when the bell rings or the schedule demands. Furthermore, students must progress as a group. If particular individuals can move faster or if they need more time, they may still have to follow the pace of the whole group. So scheduling often interferes with motivation by making students move faster or slower than would be appropriate or by interrupting their involvement. It is difficult to develop persistence and a sense of efficacy in the face of difficulties when students are not allowed to stick with an activity.

We have examined the TARGET influences on student motivation to learn, *task, autonomy, recognition, grouping, evaluation,* and *time.* Before we summarize strategies to encourage motivation let's add the last T—teacher expectations.

Teacher Expectations

Over 25 years ago, a study by Robert Rosenthal and Lenore Jacobson (1968) captured the attention of the national media in a way that few studies by psychologists have since. Articles in newspapers across the country reported the seemingly remarkable effects of "Pygmalion in the classroom," a term taken from the title of the book about the experiment. The study also caused great controversy within the professional community. Debate about the meaning of the results prompted much research (Braun, 1976; Brophy, 1982; Cooper & Good, 1983; Good, 1988; Mendels & Flanders, 1973; Rosenthal, 1987).

What did Rosenthal and Jacobson say that caused such a stir? They chose several students at random in a number of elementary-school classrooms, then told the teachers that these students probably would make significant intellectual gains during the year. The students did indeed make larger gains than normal that year. The researchers presented data suggesting the existence of a self-fulfilling prophecy in the classroom. A **self-fulfilling prophecy** is a groundless expectation that comes true simply because it has been expected. In the classroom this means that a teacher's beliefs about students' abilities or behaviors bring about the very behaviors the teacher expects. The Point/Counterpoint section on page 384 examines the debate over the existence of a self-fulfilling prophecy or **Pygmalion effect.**

Research: Tal, Z., & Babad, E. (1990). The teachers' pet phenomenon: Rate of occurrence, correlates, and psychological costs. *Journal of Educational Psychology, 82,* 637–645.

Two Kinds of Expectation Effects

Test Bank items 10.33–10.36, 10.38, 10.54, 10.55, 10.66, 10.67, 10.75, 10.82

Actually, two kinds of expectation effects can occur in classrooms. The first is the self-fulfilling prophecy described above. In this situation the teacher's beliefs about the student's abilities have no basis in fact, but student behavior comes to match the initially inaccurate expectation. The second kind of expectation effect occurs when teachers are fairly accurate in their initial reading of students' abilities and respond to students appropriately. So far, so good. There is nothing wrong with forming and acting on accurate estimates of student ability. Indeed, many teachers do this almost automatically. The problems

Self-Fulfilling Prophecy A groundless expectation that is confirmed because it has been expected.

Pygmalion Effect Exceptional progress by a student as a result of high teacher expectations for that student; named for mythological king, Pygmalion, who made a statue, then caused it to be brought to life.

Can Teachers' Expectations Affect Students' Learning?

The answer to this question is more complicated than it might seem. There are two ways to investigate the question. One is to give teachers unfounded expectations about their students and note if these baseless expectations have any effects. The other approach is to identify the naturally occurring expectations of teachers and study the effects of these expectations. The answer to the question of whether teacher expectations can affect student learning depends in part on which approach is taken to study the question.

POINT Teachers' expectations have less effect than we think.

The original Rosenthal and Jacobson experiment used the first approach—giving teachers groundless expectations and noting the effects. The study was heavily criticized for the experimental and statistical methods used (Elashoff & Snow, 1971; Weinberg, 1989). A careful analysis of the results revealed that even though first-through sixth-grade students participated in the study, the self-fulfilling prophecy effects were confined mostly to those in grades one and two. When other researchers tried to replicate the study, they did not find evidence of a self-fulfilling prophecy effect, even for children in these lower grades (Claiborn, 1969; Wilkins & Glock, 1973). Critics argued that even if higher expectations do lead to greater learning in the early grades, this does not prove that lower expectations will lead to decreased learning. Besides, the critics pointed out, giving teachers false expectations is an unnatural situation. Several studies found that when teachers did not believe the information they were given, no expectation effects occurred. After reviewing the research on teacher expectations, Raudenbush (1984) concluded that these expectations have only a small effect on student IQ scores (the outcome measure used by Rosenthal and Jacobson) and only in the early years of a new school setting—in the first years of elementary school and then again in the first years of junior high school.

COUNTERPOINT Teachers' expectations can have powerful effects.

When researchers study the naturally occurring expectations of teachers, they find that teachers do indeed form beliefs about students' capabilities. Many of these beliefs are accurate assessments based on the best available data and are corrected as new information is collected (Good & Brophy, 1991). Even so, some teachers do favor certain students (Rosenthal, 1987). For example, in a study of over 400 classrooms in the southwest United States, the Civil Rights Commission (1973) found that Hispanic-American students consistently received less praise and encouragement and fewer positive teacher responses and questions than Anglo-American students. In classes where teachers treat high-achieving students differently from lower-achieving students, the teachers' evaluation of students' ability appears to affect the students' achievement in the class. "Even though measures of student ability or prior achievement available at the beginning of a school year are highly accurate predictors of the students' achievement at the end of the year, adding measures of teacher expectations will produce significant increases in the level of accuracy of the prediction that can be achieved" (Good & Brophy, 1991, p. 135). In other words, teachers' evaluations of students' ability may cause the students to achieve more or less than they would have otherwise. Just how powerful the expectation effect is depends on how differently a teacher treats high- versus low-expectation students.

Sustaining Expectation Effect Student performance maintained at a certain level because teachers don't recognize improvements.

arise when students show some improvement but teachers do not alter their expectations to take account of the improvement. This is called a **sustaining expectation effect,** because the teacher's unchanging expectation sustains the student's achievement at the expected level. The chance to raise expectations, provide more appropriate teaching, and thus encourage greater student achievement is lost. In practice, sustaining effects are more common than self-fulfilling prophecy effects (Cooper & Good, 1983).

Teacher expectations may affect students in the following manner. Teachers begin by forming expectations about how individual students will behave or how well each will do in the class. The teachers then treat each student according to these expectations. If they expect a student to do well, that student may be given more encouragement or more time to answer a question. Students given more time and more encouragement answer correctly more often. If this pattern is repeated daily for months, the students given more time and encouragement will do better academically and score better on achievement tests. Over time, the students' behavior moves closer and closer to the kind of performance originally expected by the teachers (Good & Brophy, 1984; Jussim, 1986). The same cycle of expectation, teacher behavior, and student response can occur with groups within a class or with whole classes.

A student's achievement, motivation, aspiration level, and self-concept may all be affected by a teacher's expectations. Of course, students differ. Some are more sensitive than others to the teacher's opinions. In general, students who are young, dependent, and conforming, or who really like the teacher are most likely to have their self-esteem affected by the teacher's views (Brophy, 1982).

Sources of Expectations Test Bank items 10.75, 10.82, 10.83

Braun (1976) has developed a model based on research findings to explain the origins of teacher expectations and the ways in which these expectations are communicated to students and then perpetuated by student behavior. Figure 10.3 on page 386 shows the basic elements of this model.

Braun lists 10 possible sources of teacher expectations. Intelligence test scores are an obvious source, especially if teachers do not interpret the scores appropriately. Sex also influences teachers; most teachers expect more behavior problems from boys than from girls. The notes from previous teachers and the medical or psychological reports found in cumulative folders (permanent record files) are another obvious source of expectations. Knowledge of ethnic background also seems to have an influence, as does knowledge of older brothers and sisters. The influence of students' physical characteristics is shown in several studies, indicating that teachers hold higher expectations for attractive students. Previous achievement, socioeconomic class, and the actual behaviors of the student are also often used as sources of information.

Teacher Behavior and Student Reaction

Test Bank items 10.37, 10.39, 10.68, 10.75, 10.84, 10.85

In Figure 10.3, you see five areas in which teacher behavior toward students varies. The first and last of these, grouping and different activities, involve instructional strategies.

Instructional Strategies. As we have seen, different grouping processes may well have a marked effect on students. And some teachers leave little to the imagination; they make their expectations all too clear. For example, Alloway (1984) recorded comments like these directed to low-achieving groups:

"I'll be over to help you slow ones in a minute."

"The blue group will find this hard."

In these remarks the teacher not only tells the students that they lack ability, the teacher also communicates that finishing the work, not understanding, is the goal.

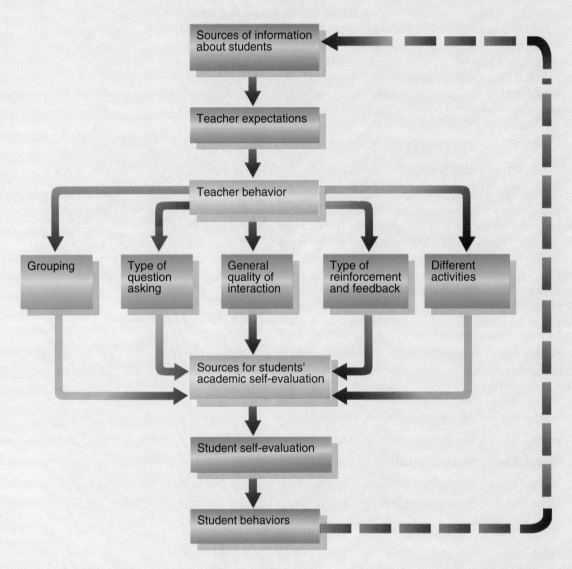

Source: C. Braun (1976). Teacher expectations: Sociopsychological dynamics. *Review of Educational Research, 46,* pp.185–213. Copyright © 1976 American Educational Research Association. Adapted by permission of the publisher.

Once teachers assign students to ability groups, they usually assign different learning activities. To the extent that teachers choose activities that challenge students and increase achievement, these differences are probably necessary. Activities become inappropriate, however, when students who are ready for more challenging work are not given the opportunity to try it because teachers believe they cannot handle it. This is an example of a sustaining expectation effect.

Other problems occur when teachers make accurate predictions about students' abilities but at the outset select inappropriate teaching methods. For example, a teacher may be correct in predicting that one group of students will have great difficulty with a particular lesson and another group will learn the new material easily. The teacher may decide against spending much time with either group, since one group "can't benefit from help" and the other "doesn't need help." But in this way both groups are robbed of the chance to do their best (Brophy, 1982).

Teacher-Student Interactions.

However the class is grouped and whatever the assignments, the quantity and the quality of student-teacher interactions are likely to affect the students. Students who are expected to achieve tend to be asked more and harder questions, to be given more chances and a longer time to respond, and to be interrupted less often than students who are expected to do poorly (Allington, 1980; Good & Brophy, 1984; Rosenthal, 1973). Teachers also give these high-expectation students cues and prompts, communicating their belief that the students can answer the question (Rosenthal, 1973). Teachers tend to be more encouraging in general toward those students for whom they have high expectations. They smile at these students more often and show greater warmth through such nonverbal responses as leaning toward the students and nodding their heads as the students speak (Woolfolk & Brooks, 1983, 1985). In contrast, with students for whom expectations are low, teachers ask easier questions, allow less time for answering, and are much less likely to give prompts.

It appears that feedback and reinforcement are also somewhat dependent on teacher expectations. Good and Brophy (1984) have noted that teachers demand better performance from high-achieving students, are less likely to accept a poor answer from them, and praise them more for good answers. Teachers are more likely, on the one hand, to accept or even reinforce inadequate answers from low-achieving students or, on the other, to criticize these students for wrong answers. Even more disturbing, low-achieving students receive less praise than high-achieving students for similar correct answers. On tests when an answer is "almost right," the teacher is more likely to give the benefit of the doubt (and thus the better grade) to high-achieving students (Finn, 1972).

This inconsistent feedback can be very confusing for low-ability students. Imagine how hard it would be to learn if your wrong answers were sometimes praised, sometimes ignored, and sometimes criticized, and your right answers received little recognition (Good 1983a & b).

The Effects of Teacher Behavior on Students.

Teacher behaviors can communicate to students how they are viewed by a very significant person, their teacher. Think about students' attributions. If youngsters see the inevitable mistakes that accompany learning as a consequence of their own lack of ability, they are likely to lower their level of aspiration. Decreased motivation follows lowered expectations. The student and the teacher set lower standards, persistence is discouraged, and poorer performance results. Students start saying "I don't know" or nothing at all rather than risk failure again.

Objective 10.7: Describe ways in which teachers, through their interaction patterns, communicate positive and negative expectations of students.

Transparency: In acetate transparency T 83, the relationships in "Expectancy Theory and Motivation" are presented in the form of a graph.

| |
Here the teacher's attributions enter the picture: the teacher accepts the poor performance and attributes it to lack of ability. The lower expectation for the student thus seems to be confirmed, and as the dotted line in Figure 10.3 shows, the cycle continues.

Even when student performance does not fit expectations, the teacher may rationalize and attribute the performance to external causes beyond the student's control. For example, a teacher may assume that the low-ability student who did well on a test must have cheated and that the high-ability student who failed must have been upset that day. In both cases, behavior that seems out of character is dismissed. It may take many instances of supposedly uncharacteristic behavior to change the teacher's beliefs about a particular student's abilities. Thus, expectations often remain in the face of contradictory evidence (Brophy, 1982).

You may be promising yourself that you will never communicate low expectations to your students, especially now that you know about the dangers involved. Of course, not all teachers form inappropriate expectations or act on their expectations in unconstructive ways (Babad, Inbar, & Rosenthal, 1982). But avoiding the problem may be more difficult than it seems. In general, low-expectation students also tend to be the most disruptive students. (Of course, low expectations can reinforce their desire to disrupt or misbehave.) Teachers may call on these students less, wait a shorter time for their answers, and give them less praise for right answers, partly to avoid the wrong, careless, or silly answers that can cause disruptions, delays, and digressions (Cooper, 1979). The challenge is to deal with these very real threats to classroom management without communicating low expectations to some students or fostering their own low expectations of themselves. The Guidelines may help you avoid some of these problems.

Focus on...   **Teacher Expectations**

- What are some sources of teacher expectations?
- What are the two kinds of expectation effects and how do they happen?
- What are the different avenues for communicating teacher expectations?
- How can teacher expectations set up a cycle of expectation and confirmation?

Guidelines

Avoiding the Negative Effects of Teacher Expectations

Use information about students from tests, cumulative folders, and other teachers very carefully.
Examples
1. Some teachers avoid reading cumulative folders at the beginning of the year.
2. Be critical and objective about the reports you hear from other teachers.

Be flexible in your use of grouping strategies.
Examples
1. Review work of students in different groups often and experiment with new groupings.
2. Use different groups for different subjects.
3. Use mixed-ability groups in cooperative exercises.

Make sure all the students are challenged.
Examples
1. Don't say, "This is easy, I know you can do it."

2. Offer a wide range of problems, and encourage all students to try a few of the harder ones for extra credit. Try to find something positive about these attempts.

Be especially careful about how you respond to low-achieving students during class discussions.

Examples

1. Give them prompts, cues, and time to answer.
2. Give ample praise for good answers.
3. Call on low achievers as often as high achievers.

Use materials that show a wide range of ethnic groups.

Examples

1. Check readers and library books. Is there ethnic diversity?
2. If few materials are available, ask students to research and create their own, based on community or family sources.

Make sure that your teaching does not reflect racial, ethnic, or sexual stereotypes or prejudice.

Examples

1. Use a checking system to be sure you call on and include all students.
2. Monitor the content of the tasks you assign. Do boys get the "hard" math problems to work at the board? Do you avoid having students with limited English give oral presentations?

Be fair in evaluation and disciplinary procedures.

Examples

1. Make sure equal offenses receive equal punishment. Find out from students in an anonymous questionnaire whether you seem to be favoring certain individuals.
2. Try to grade student work without knowing the identity of the student. Ask another teacher to give you a "second opinion" from time to time.

Communicate to all students that you believe they can learn—and mean it.

Examples

1. Return papers that do not meet standards with specific suggestions for improvements.
2. If students do not have the answers immediately, wait, probe, and then help them think through an answer.

Involve all students in learning tasks and in privileges.

Examples

1. Use some system to make sure you give each student practice in reading, speaking, and answering questions.
2. Keep track of who gets to do what job. Are some students always on the list while others seldom make it?

Monitor your nonverbal behavior.

Examples

1. Do you lean away or stand farther away from some students? Do some students get smiles when they approach your desk while others get only frowns?
2. Does your tone of voice vary with different students?
3. Do you avoid touching some students in your class?

Strategies to Encourage Motivation and Thoughtful Learning

The influences on students' motivation to learn in a particular situation can be summarized in three basic questions: Can I succeed at this task? Do I want to succeed? What do I need to do to succeed? (Eccles & Wigfield, 1985). As reflected in these questions, we want students to have confidence in their ability so they will approach learning with energy and enthusiasm. We want them to see the value of the tasks involved and work to learn, not just try to get the grade or get finished. We want students to believe that success will come when they apply good learning strategies instead of believing that their only option is to use self-defeating, failure-avoiding, face-saving strategies. When things get difficult, we want students to try to solve the problem and stay focused on the task, not get so worried about failure that they "freeze."

Necessary Conditions in Classrooms

Until four basic conditions are met, no motivational strategies will succeed. Once these requirements are in place, there are numerous strategies to help students gain confidence, value learning, and stay involved with the task (Brophy, 1988; Lepper, 1988).

First, the classroom must be relatively organized and free from constant interruptions and disruptions. (Chapter 11 will give you the information you need to make sure this requirement is met.) Second, the teacher must be a patient, supportive person who never punishes, criticizes, or embarrasses students for mistakes. Everyone in the class should see mistakes as opportunities for learning (Clifford, 1990, 1991). Third, the work must be challenging but reasonable. If work is too easy or too difficult, students will have little motivation to learn. They will focus on finishing, not on learning. Finally, the learning tasks must be authentic (Brophy 1983; Brophy & Kher, 1986; Stipek, 1993).

Table 10.4 summarizes the basic requirements and strategies for encouraging student motivation to learn, all of which are discussed at length in the next few pages.

Can I Do It? Building Confidence and Positive Expectations

Test Bank items 10.40, 10.41, 10.69, 10.85

Let's assume these conditions are met in your classroom. What's next? One of the most important factors in building expectations for success is past success. No amount of encouragement or "cheerleading" will substitute for real accomplishment. To ensure genuine progress:

1. *Begin work at the students' level and move in small steps.* The pace should be brisk, but not so fast that students have to move to the next step before they understand the previous one. This may require assigning different tasks to different students. One possibility is to have very easy and very difficult questions on every test and assignment, so all students are sure to pass some questions

TABLE 10.4 Strategies to Encourage Motivation to Learn	
Fulfill basic requirements ■ Provide an organized class environment ■ Be a supportive teacher ■ Assign challenging work, but not too difficult ■ Make tasks worthwhile **Build confidence and positive expectations** ■ Begin work at the students' level ■ Make learning goals clear, specific, and attainable ■ Stress self-comparison, not competition ■ Communicate that academic ability is improvable ■ Model good problem solving **Show the value of learning** ■ Connect the learning task to the needs of the students ■ Tie class activities to the students' interests	■ Arouse curiosity ■ Make the learning task fun ■ Make use of novelty and familiarity ■ Explain connections between present learning and later life ■ Provide incentives and rewards, if needed **Help students stay focused on the task** ■ Give students frequent opportunities to respond ■ Provide opportunities for students to create a finished product ■ Avoid heavy emphasis on grading ■ Reduce task risk without oversimplifying the task ■ Model motivation to learn ■ Teach learning tactics

This table refers to the entire Strategies to Encourage Motivation and Thoughtful Learning section of the text.

and fail others. This provides both success and challenge for everyone. When grades are required, make sure all the students in class have a chance to make at least a C if they work hard.

2. *Make sure learning goals are clear, specific, and possible to reach in the near future.* When long-term projects are planned, break the work into subgoals and help students feel a sense of progress toward the long-term goal. For example, a big research paper could be broken down into identifying a topic and a few basic references, doing an outline, taking notes, finding additional references and learning the form for a bibliography, writing an introduction, doing a first draft, and finally writing the polished paper. If possible, give students a range of goals at different levels of difficulty and let them choose.

3. *Stress self-comparison, not comparison with others.* Help students see the progress they are making by showing them how to use self-management strategies like those described in chapter 6. Give specific feedback and corrections. Tell students what they are doing right as well as what is wrong and *why* it is wrong. Periodically, give students a question or problem that was once hard for them but now seems easy. Point out how much they have improved. Show the connections between their efforts and their accomplishments.

4. *Communicate to students that academic ability is improvable* and specific to the task at hand. In other words, the fact that a student has trouble in algebra doesn't necessarily mean that geometry will be difficult or that he or she is a bad English student. Even when a task is hard, students can improve if they stick with it. Don't undermine your efforts to stress improvement by displaying only the 100 percent papers on the bulletin board.

5. *Model good problem solving,* especially when you yourself have to try several approaches to get a solution. Students need to see that learning is not smooth and error-free, even for the teacher.

Do I Want to Do It? Seeing the Value of Learning

Test Bank items 10.56, 10.85

Teachers can use intrinsic and extrinsic motivation strategies to help students see the value of the learning task. In this process the age of the student must be taken into consideration. For younger children, intrinsic or *interest value* is a greater determinant of motivation than attainment or utility value. Because younger students have a more immediate, concrete focus, they have trouble seeing the value of an activity that is linked to distant goals such as getting a good job—or even preparing for the next grade. Older students, on the other hand, have the cognitive ability to think more abstractly and connect what they are learning now with goals and future possibilities, so *utility value* becomes important to these students (Eccles & Wigfield, 1985).

Attainment and Intrinsic Value. To establish *attainment value,* we must connect the learning task with the needs of the students. First, it must be possible for students to meet their needs for safety, belonging, and achievement in our classes. The classroom should not be a frightening or lonely place. Second, we must be sure that sexual or ethnic stereotypes do not interfere with motivation. For example, if students subscribe to rigid notions of masculinity and femininity, we must make it clear that both women and men can be high achievers in all subjects and that no subjects are the territory of only one sex. It is not "unfeminine" to be strong in mathematics, science, shop, or sports. It is not "unmasculine" to be good in literature, art, music, or French.

There are many strategies for encouraging *intrinsic* (interest) motivation. Several of the following are taken from Brophy (1988).

1. *Tie class activities to student interests* in sports, music, current events, pets, common problems or conflicts with family and friends, fads, television and cinema personalities, or other significant features of their lives (Schiefele, 1991). But be sure you know what you are talking about. For example, if you use a verse from a REM song to make a point, you had better have some knowledge of the music and the group members. When possible, give students choices of research paper or reading topics so they can follow their own interests.

2. *Arouse curiosity.* Point out puzzling discrepancies between students' beliefs and the facts. For example, Stipek (1993) describes a teacher who asked her fifth-grade class if there were "people" on some of the other planets. When the students said yes, the teacher asked if people needed oxygen to breathe. Since the students had just learned this fact, they responded yes to this question also. Then the teacher told them that there is no oxygen in the atmosphere of the other planets. This surprising discrepancy between what the children knew about oxygen and what they believed about life on other planets led to a rousing discussion of the atmospheres of other planets, the kinds of beings that could survive in these atmospheres, and so on. A straight lecture on the atmosphere of the planets might have put the students to sleep, but this discussion led to real interest in the subject.

3. *Make the learning task fun.* Many lessons can be taught through simulations or games. For example, when my daughter was in the eighth grade, all the students in her grade spent three days playing a game her teachers had designed

Learning to read and write is more interesting when students are personally invested in the task. Here, students are encouraged to write their own books and submit work in the "Authors' Basket."

called ULTRA. Students were divided into groups and formed their own "countries." Each country had to choose a name, symbol, national flower, and bird. They wrote and sang a national anthem and elected government officials. The teachers allocated different resources to the countries. To get all the materials needed for the completion of assigned projects, the countries had to establish trade with one another. There was a monetary system and a stock market. Students had to work with their fellow citizens to complete cooperative learning assignments. Some countries "cheated" in their trades with other nations, and this allowed debate about international relations, trust, and war. Liz says she had fun—but she also learned how to work in a group without the teacher's supervision and gained a deeper understanding of world economics and international conflicts.

4. *Make use of novelty and familiarity.* Don't overuse a few teaching approaches or motivational strategies. We all need some variety. Varying the goal structures of tasks (cooperative, competitive, individualistic) can help, as can using different teaching media. When the material being covered in class is abstract or unfamiliar to students, try to connect it to something they know and understand. For example, talk about the size of a large area, such as the Acropolis in Athens, in terms of football fields. Brophy (1988) describes one teacher who read a brief passage from *Spartacus* to personalize the unit on slavery in the ancient world.

Instrumental Value. Sometimes it is difficult to encourage intrinsic motivation, and so teachers must rely on the utility or "instrumental" value of tasks. That is, it is important to learn many skills because they will be needed in more advanced classes or because they are necessary for life outside school.

1. When these connections are not obvious, you should *explain the connections to your students.* Jeanette Abi-Nader (1991) describes one project, the PLAN program, that makes these connections come alive for Hispanic high school students. The three major strategies used in the program to focus students' attention on their future are: (1) working with mentors and models—often PLAN graduates—who give advice about how to choose courses, budget time, take notes, and deal with cultural differences in college; (2) storytelling about the achievements of former students—sometimes the college term papers of former students are posted on PLAN bulletin boards; and (3) filling the classroom with future-oriented talk such as "When you go to college, you will encounter these situations . . . " or, "You're at a parents' meeting—you want a good education for your children—and you are the ones who must speak up; that's why it is important to learn public speaking skills" (p. 548).

2. In some situations teachers need to *provide incentives and rewards for learning.* Chapter 6 details the use of extrinsic reinforcement through the application of positive and negative consequences, self-management systems, and other behavioral approaches, so we need not spend time on those topics here. Remember, though, that giving rewards when students are already interested in the activity may undermine intrinsic motivation. As Stipek (1993) has noted, if teachers began testing and grading students on their memory of the television programs they watched the previous evening, even television viewing would lose some of its intrinsic appeal.

3. Use *ill-structured problems and authentic tasks* in teaching. Connect problems in school to real problems outside.

Research: Nolen, S. B. (1988). Reasons for studying: Motivational orientations and study strategies. *Cognition and Instruction, 5,* 269–288.

Brief Abstract: This study of eighth graders explored the relationship among (a) individual differences in three motivational or goal orientations and (b) valuing and use of study strategies. Task orientation was positively correlated with both valuing and use of strategies requiring deep processing of information. Ego orientation was positively related to valuing and use of surface-level strategies only. Work avoidance was negatively related to valuing and use of both kinds of strategies. Analysis indicated that task orientation, more than perceived ability or knowledge of the value of deep-processing strategies, predicts the spontaneous use of these strategies. The prediction held over four to six weeks, suggesting the importance of individual differences in motivational orientation.

In the same issue are two commentaries on this study:

Lepper, M.R. (1988). Motivational considerations in the study of instruction. *Cognition and Instruction, 5,* 289–310.

Brown, A.L. (1988). Motivation to learn and understand: Taking charge of one's own learning. *Cognition and Instruction, 5,* 311–322.

Background: Abi-Nader, J. (1991). Creating a vision of the future: Strategies for motivating minority students. *Phi Delta Kappan, 72,* 546–549. Focus Questions: Why do minority-group students sometimes find schooling unmotivating? What can be done?

Computer/Software: Note the positive effects of computers on motivation as described in:

Kulik, J. A. (1983). Synthesis of research on computer-based instruction. *Educational Leadership, 41*(1), 19–21.

Kulik, J. A., Bangert, R. L., & Williams, G. W. (1983). Effects of computer-based teaching on secondary school students. *Journal of Educational Psychology, 75*(1), 19–26.

Kulik, J. A., & Kulik, C. L. C. (1987a, spring). *Computer-based instruction: What 200 evaluations say.* Paper presented at the Annual Convention of the Association for Educational Communications and Technology. (ERIC Document No. 285521.)

Kulik, J. A., & Kulik, C. L. C. (1987b). Review of recent research literature on computer-based instruction. *Contemporary Educational Psychology, 12*(3), 222–230.

Activity 10.6: Background. See the separate *Instructors' Resource Manual* for Academic Counseling: Reflections on the Middle Grades, a summary of Fenwick, J. J. (1986). The middle school years. San Diego, CA: Fenwick Associates.

Research: Brophy, J. (1987, October). Synthesis of research on strategies for motivating students to learn. *Educational Leadership, 44*, 40–48. This article is also reprinted in the *Annual editions: Educational psychology 89/90*, Guilford, CT: Duskin.

Discussion: Assign Newby, T. J. (1991). Classroom motivation: Strategies of first-year teachers. *Journal of Educational Psychology, 83*, 195–200. *Focus Question:* Ask your students to list examples of the four basic motivational strategies used by beginning teachers.

What Do I Need to Do to Succeed? Staying Focused on the Task

When students encounter difficulties, as they must if they are working at a challenging level, they need to keep their attention on the task. If the focus shifts to worries about performance, fear of failure, or concern with looking smart, then motivation to learn is lost. Here are some ideas for keeping the focus on learning.

1. *Give students frequent opportunities to respond* through questions and answers, short assignments, or demonstrations of skills. Make sure you check the students' answers so you can correct problems quickly. You don't want students to practice errors too long. Computer learning programs give students the immediate feedback they need to correct errors before they become habits.

2. When possible, *have students create a finished product*. They will be more persistent and focused on the task when the end is in sight. We all have experienced the power of the need for closure. For example, I often begin a house-painting project thinking I will work for just an hour and then find myself still painting hours later because I want to see the finished product.

3. *Avoid heavy emphasis on grades and competition*. You will force students to be ego-involved rather than task-involved. Anxious students are especially hard hit by highly competitive evaluation.

4. *Reduce task risk without oversimplifying the task*. When tasks are risky (failure is likely and the consequences of failing are grave), student motivation suffers. For difficult, complex, or ambiguous tasks, provide students with plenty of time, support, resources, help, and the chance to revise or improve work.

5. *Model motivation to learn for your students*. Talk about your interest in the subject and how you deal with difficult learning problems.

6. *Teach the particular learning tactics* that students will need to master the material being studied. Show students how to learn and remember so they won't be forced to fall back on self-defeating strategies or rote memory.

Table 10.4 (refer back to page 391) summarizes these ideas for helping students to have confidence in their abilities, value learning, and stay focused on the right task.

How Do Beginning Teachers Motivate Students?

Test Bank items 10.42, 10.43, 10.70, 10.76

Timothy Newby (1991) trained classroom observers to record the motivational strategies of 30 first-year elementary-school teachers over a 16-week period. He found that the teachers used about 10 different strategies per hour—half were rewards and punishments. Figure 10.4 gives examples of the four types of strategies used by these beginning teachers. As you can see, commenting on the relevance of the lessons and building student confidence each accounted for about 7 percent of strategies, focusing student attention made up 27 percent, and rewards and punishments accounted for 58 percent.

Another interesting finding is that commenting on relevance was positively correlated with students being on task, while using rewards/punishments was

FIGURE 10.4

MOTIVATIONAL STRATEGIES OF BEGINNING TEACHERS

First-year teachers tend to rely on reward and punishment strategies to motivate students, even though these are not necessarily the most effective approaches.

Reward/Punishment Strategies
Teacher gives verbal reinforcement (praise), provides tangible rewards (extra points), or takes away a privilege (time at recess).

Attention-Focusing Strategies
Teacher waits until all is quiet.
Student work groups switch to new locations and tasks at the sound of a bell.
Students work on story problem for the first 5 minutes of class.

58%   27%   8%   7%

Confidence-Building Strategies
Teacher explains that it is okay to make mistakes. Teacher states explicit instructions with pertinent examples (listing the critical steps to the assignment on the board, then reviewing each step with the class).

Relevance Strategies
Teacher uses familiar experiences to introduce a subject (playing in the snow for a lesson on how animals prepare for winter). Teacher has a guest relate an experience (parent describes his or her job).

Source: T. J. Newby (1991). Classroom motivation: Strategies of first-year teachers. *Journal of Educational Psychology, 83,* pp. 195–200. Copyright 1991 by the American Psychological Association. Adapted by permission.

negatively correlated. So beginning teachers tended to use less effective strategies more often. It may be that these new teachers turned to extrinsic reinforcement (rewards and punishments) only when it became difficult to keep the students interested in their work.

SUMMARY

The Ultimate Goal: Lifelong Learning

One important goal of teaching is to prepare students for lifelong learning. To reach this goal, students must be self-regulated learners, that is, they must have a combination of the knowledge, motivation to learn, and volition that provides the skill and will to learn independently and effectively. Knowledge includes an understanding of self, subject, task, learning strategy, and contexts for application. Motivation to learn provides the commitment, and volition is the follow-through that combats distraction and protects persistence.

Teachers make many decisions that influence student motivation to learn. The TARGETT acronym highlights decisions about tasks, autonomy, recognition, grouping, evaluation, time, and teacher expectations.

Tasks for Learning

The tasks that teachers set affect motivation. When students encounter tasks that are related to their interests, stimulate their curiosity, or are connected to real-life situations, the students are more likely to be motivated to learn. Tasks that are difficult and require critical thinking are risky and ambiguous. Students often seek to lower the risk and ambiguity in tasks through negotiation with the teacher.

Tasks can have attainment, intrinsic, or utility value for students. Attainment value is the importance to the student of succeeding. Intrinsic value is the enjoyment the student gets from the task. Utility value is determined by how much the task contributes to reaching short-term or long-term goals.

Supporting Autonomy and Recognizing Accomplishment

In order to experience intrinsic motivation, students must have a sense of self-determination about their activities in school. When students experience autonomy, they are more interested in their work, have a greater sense of self-esteem, and learn more. Whether students experience self-determination depends in part on whether the teacher's communications with students provide information or seek to control them. In addition, teachers must acknowledge the students' perspective, offer choices, provide rationales for limits, and treat poor performance as a problem to be solved rather than a target for criticism.

Recognition and reward in the classroom will support motivation to learn if the recognition is for personal progress rather than competitive victories. Praise and rewards should focus on students' growing competence.

Grouping: Cooperation and Competition

Cooperative learning arrangements can encourage motivation and increase learning, especially for low-achieving students. There are a number of approaches, including STAD, TGT, CIRC, and reciprocal questioning. Many cooperative learning strategies are designed to allow each student equal access to success, social support for learning, and individual accountability for final performance.

Evaluation and Timing

The evaluative climate of the class—that is, the relative emphasis on competition and grading—influences motivation. The more competitive the grading, the more students set performance goals and focus on "looking competent"; that is, the more they are ego-involved. When the focus is on performing rather than learning students often see the goal of classroom tasks as simply finishing, especially if the work is difficult.

In order to foster motivation to learn and support volition, teachers should be flexible in their use of time in the classroom. Students who are forced to move faster or slower than they should or who are interrupted as they become involved in a project are not likely to develop the willpower for learning.

Teacher Expectations

Several studies have pointed to the important role teachers' expectations play in motivating students. Some teachers tend to treat students differently, depending on their own views of how well the students are likely to do. Students may behave accordingly, fulfilling teachers' predictions or staying at an expected level of achievement.

Strategies to Encourage Motivation to Learn

Strategies to encourage motivation to learn should help students feel confidence in their abilities to improve, value the tasks of learning, and stay involved in the process without being threatened by fear of failure.

KEY TERMS

Preschool and Kindergarten

What would you do to help your students develop persistence without discouraging their spontaneity and enthusiasm?

Elementary and Middle School

You are talking to the parents of one of your lower-achieving students. You really like the student, but he seems not to apply himself to the work. Suddenly the boy's mother says, "We think our son is doing badly in your class because you don't like him. You just seem to expect him to fail!" What would you do?

There are students from four different ethnic groups in your class. Each group seems to stick together, never making friends with students from the other groups. How would you structure the class to help the students feel more comfortable together?

Junior High and High School

You want to prepare your senior classes for the kind of independent work they will face in college, so you assign a research project. As soon as you make the assignment, the questions begin: "How many sources?" "How many pages?" "What exactly do you mean by 'support your conclusions with evidence'?" "What kind of evidence?" How do you make the assignment clear without turning it into a "spoon feeding"?

How could you use cooperative learning strategies with ninth-grade students?

Cooperative Learning Activity

With four or five other members of your educational psychology class, develop a self-monitoring procedure for identifying the expectations that you communicate to your students.

Making Cooperative Learning Work

You have decided to use small-group cooperative learning in your classroom, but your students do not seem to be able to help each other well. They rely on you for everything. What would you do to help them benefit more from cooperative learning?

Students are often asked to work in small groups without learning the skills necessary to be successful in those situations. Before my students work in groups, they are given a summary of their role. This summary includes:

1. "*Needs to . . .* "—This area defines the role, the responsibilities that need to be carried out by the student.
2. "*Sounds like . . .* "—This section gives examples of words or phrases that should be used by the student serving in this role.
3. "*Looks like . . .* "—This part includes reminders of important gestures, including eye contact, leaning forward to show interest, and other ways to show other group members that you are interested and involved.

Group evaluation is based on how well individual members are able to implement all three areas in their role. The role description provides key words for students who are more reluctant to be involved and reinforces all group members for ensuring that everyone is involved.

The last technique that has worked successfully in my classroom is called "The Fishbowl Technique." A small group is placed in the middle of the classroom. They are given an activity that includes role descriptions. The other members of the class are divided into three or four groups and are given a specific group skill to evaluate. They closely watch the small group, looking for an example of the designated skill. They might be looking for "specific examples when someone encouraged another member to speak" or "specific examples of statements that moved the group closer to a solution."

Lawrence Leebens, *Curriculum Resource Coordinator*
Forest Hills Elementary School, Eden Prairie, Minnesota

Focusing on Learning

What strategies have you found successful in helping your students to focus on learning rather than on the grade they will receive?

Learning is a lifelong process. My school is a community school for lifelong learners. The entire concept of the school centers around learning, not grades.

Within my classroom, I am very open with the students about my deficiencies, but I tell them that I am still learning and achieving. I model by using a dictionary to compensate for my poor spelling and I ask a proofreader to help me in my writing. I have even gone as far as joining beginning band. I attempted to play the flute and failed miserably. The students saw that I was discouraged, but they also saw me try again. I am now trying my hand at the electric piano.

Julie A. Addison, *Sixth-Grade Teacher*
Roxborough Elementary School, Littleton, Colorado

We talk a lot in my classroom about the responsibility for learning being with the students. I stress that making mistakes is the way we learn, and that a low grade may be the chance for a great learning experience. We then have the opportunity to go over the material again and really concentrate on what we're learning. We discuss the importance of everyone doing their best, and that we're all individuals. Therefore, what's "best" for one person may not be "best" for another. One person's best job may earn an A while another person's best may earn a C.

Building self-esteem is one of the greatest ways to encourage students to concentrate on learning for learning's sake instead of worrying about the grade they get. Another strategy I use is cooperative learning and other group or partner work. When children are working together, they tend to enjoy themselves more and be less concerned about a letter grade.

Deborah H. Platt, *Third-Grade Teacher*
Eugene Field Elementary School, Mitchell, South Dakota

NON-GRADED PRACTICE

I set up a series of units in which the students select a required number of activities to complete. No grades are given, but completion of each unit is required before a student receives an "expert" award. Topics are chosen by the students and have included sign language, Australia, whales, Mexico, bats, and Greenland. Activities have included cooperative learning activities, independent and paired reading, construction of picture books, guest lecturers, movies, crafts, map skills, brainstorming, writing summaries, and cooking experiences. I find the students to be highly motivated, and we all have fun.

Joanne S. Groseclose, *Virginia 1991 Teacher of the Year*
Marion Intermediate School, Marion, Virginia

HIGH EXPECTATIONS

One of my strategies for helping my students concentrate on learning rather than on the grade they will receive is to hold very high expectations of each pupil. I tell students that they all can be successful and that their success is based on a step-by-step process in which skills are developed. I focus on each pupil's effort in various ways, such as writing comments on papers pointing out specific areas where their diligence was reflected to make them aware that it was the hard work channeled into their studies that has been shown, not luck. This is an integral part of the process to de-emphasize grades and call attention to learning so that students persevere even though they may not be as successful in getting the grade desired.

Phyllis N. Marshall, *Seventh-Grade Teacher*
Hoech Middle School, St. Ann, Missouri

Controlling Teacher Bias

It is natural and inevitable for teachers to form impressions of their students. How do you control your biases toward favorite students and toward students for whom you have little regard or low expectations?

FOCUS ON GOOD QUALITIES

Every child is special, regardless of faults. All parents trust teachers with their children's self-esteem. As an educator, part of my job is to find a good quality in each student in my class and focus on that quality. As a teacher, I also need to ignore the forewarnings from previous teachers and form my own opinions. Too often children are labeled as "good" or "bad." Many times a student reacts to different teachers in very different ways. I have had "warnings" about students in the past only to find that we get along just fine, respect each other, and there isn't a behavior problem.

Candice J. Gallagher, *Fourth-Grade Teacher*
Fredericktown Intermediate School, Fredericktown, Ohio

11

Creating Learning Environments

*T*his chapter examines the ways that teachers create social and physical environments for learning. We will look at classroom management—one of the main concerns of teachers, particularly beginning teachers, as well as of administrators and parents.

The very nature of classes, teaching, and students makes good management a critical ingredient of success; we will look at why this is true. Next, we will turn to the goals of classroom management. Successful managers create more time for learning, involve more students, and help students to become self-managing.

A positive learning environment must be established and maintained throughout the year. One of the best ways to do this is to try to prevent problems from occurring at all. But when problems arise—as they always do—an appropriate response is important. What will you do when students challenge you openly in class, when one student asks your advice on a difficult personal problem, or when another withdraws from all participation? We will examine the ways that teachers can communicate effectively with their students in these and many other situations.

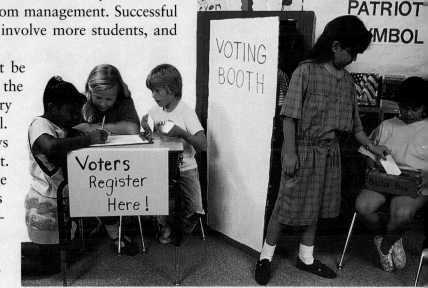

By the time you have completed this chapter, you should be able to:

- Describe the special managerial demands of classrooms and relate these demands to students of different ages.
- Create a list of rules and procedures for a class.
- Develop a plan for organizing your first week of teaching.
- Explain Kounin's suggestions for preventing management problems.
- Describe how you might respond to a student who seldom completes work.
- Describe how and when you might use group consequences, token economies, and contingency contracts to enhance classroom management.
- Suggest two different approaches for dealing with a conflict between teacher and student, or between two students.
- Arrange the physical environment of your classroom to fit your learning goals and teaching methods.

When you imagine facing 25 or 30 students on the first day of class, what are your concerns? List the management problems that you find most difficult. What are your strengths in dealing with classroom management problems?

The Need for Organization   Test Bank item 11.2

In 1993, *Phi Delta Kappa* published the 25th annual Gallup Poll of the public's attitude toward public schools. For 16 of the first 17 years of the poll, "lack of discipline" was named as the number one problem facing the schools. From 1986 to 1991, "use of drugs" took over first place on the list of problems, but "lack of discipline" was not far behind as the number two concern. In the 1992 poll, "drug use" and "lack of discipline" were virtually tied for first place, and in 1993, these two concerns were tied for second place, with lack of proper financial support taking over as the number one problem facing the schools (Elam, Rose, & Gallup, 1993). Clearly, the public sees discipline as an important challenge for teachers. In order to understand the role of management in teaching, let's take a closer look at the classroom itself.

The Ecology of Classrooms   Test Bank items 11.2–11.8, 11.93

The word *ecology* is usually associated with nature. But classrooms are ecological systems, too. The environment of the classroom and the inhabitants of that environment—students and teachers—are constantly interacting. Each aspect of the system affects all others. The characteristics of classrooms, the tasks of teaching, and the needs of students all influence classroom management.

Characteristics of Classrooms. Classes are particular kinds of environments. They have "distinctive properties affecting participants regardless of how students are organized for learning or what educational philosophy the teacher espouses" (Doyle, 1986, p. 394). Let's look at six of the features described by Doyle.

Classrooms are *multidimensional.* They are crowded with people, tasks, and time pressures. Many individuals, all with differing goals, preferences, and abilities, must share resources, accomplish various tasks, use and reuse materials without losing them, move in and out of the room, keep track of what is happening, and so on. In addition, actions can have multiple effects. Calling on low-ability students may encourage their participation and thinking but may slow the discussion and lead to management problems if the students cannot answer.

So much is happening at once in a typical classroom that teachers, especially beginning teachers, may feel distracted or overwhelmed.

There is *simultaneity.* Everything happens at once. A teacher explaining a concept must also notice if students are following the explanation, decide whether two whispering youngsters should be ignored or stopped, determine if there is enough time to start the next topic, and decide who should answer the question that Jill just asked.

The next characteristic, *immediacy,* refers to the fast pace of classroom life. Teachers have literally hundreds of exchanges with students during a single day.

In this rapid-fire existence, events are *unpredictable.* Even when plans are carefully made, the overhead projector is in place, and the handouts are ready, the lesson can still be interrupted by a burned-out bulb in the projector, a child who suddenly becomes ill, or a loud, angry discussion right outside the classroom window.

Because classrooms are *public,* the way the teacher handles these unexpected intrusions is seen and judged by all. Students are always noticing if the teacher is being "fair." Is there favoritism? What happens when a rule is broken?

Finally, classrooms have *histories.* The meaning of a particular teacher's or student's actions depends in part on what has happened before. The 15th time a student arrives late requires a different response from the teacher than the first late arrival. In addition, the history of the first few weeks of school affects life in the class all year.

The Basic Task: Gain Their Cooperation.

No productive activity can take place in a group without the cooperation of all members. This obviously applies to classrooms. Even if some students don't participate, they must allow others to do so. (You have probably seen one or two students bring an entire class to a halt.) So the basic management task for teachers is to achieve order

Background: Evertson, C. (1987). Managing classrooms: A framework for teachers. In D. Berliner & B. Rosenshine (Eds.), *Talks to teachers* (pp. 54–74). New York: Random House. Emmer, E. (1987). Classroom management and discipline. In V. Richardson-Koehler (Ed.), *Educator's Handbook: A research perspective* (pp. 233–258). White Plains, NY: Longman.

Computer/Software: Many computer programs exist to help teachers manage their own activities inside and outside the classroom. Typical activities include on-line standard forms, IEPs, student home and school data bases, student reports, letters to parents, archiving and locating information, electronic mail, financial planning, and scheduling. complete classroom management systems and computer-managed instruction (CMI) are also available. For more information see:

Geisert, P., & Futrell, M. (1990). *Teachers, computers, and curriculum.* Boston: Allyn & Bacon.

by gaining and maintaining student cooperation in class activities (Doyle, 1986). Given the multidimensional, simultaneous, immediate, unpredictable, public, and historical nature of classrooms, this is quite a challenge.

Gaining student cooperation means much more than dealing effectively with misbehavior. It means planning activities, having materials ready, making appropriate behavioral and academic demands on students, giving clear signals to students, accomplishing transitions smoothly, foreseeing problems and stopping them before they start, selecting and sequencing activities so that order and flow are maintained—and much more. Also, different activities require different managerial skills. For example, a new or complicated activity may be a greater threat to classroom management than a familiar or simple activity.

Age-Related Needs. Other necessary considerations are the age-related needs of students. Obviously, gaining the cooperation of kindergarteners is not the same task as gaining the cooperation of high school seniors. Jere Brophy and Carolyn Evertson (1978) have identified four general stages of classroom management, defined by age-related needs. Let's look briefly at each.

During kindergarten and the first few years of elementary school, children are learning how to go to school. They are being socialized into a new role. Direct teaching of classroom rules and procedures is important during this stage. Little learning will take place until the children master these basics.

Children in the middle elementary years are usually familiar with the student role, even if they are not always perfect examples of it. Many school and classroom routines have become relatively automatic. Specific new rules and procedures for a particular activity may have to be taught directly, however. And you may hear the familiar refrain, "My teacher last year didn't do it that way!" Still, at this stage you will spend more time monitoring and maintaining the management system than teaching it directly.

One of the challenges of managing students in the elementary grades is to deal effectively with defiant or aggressive behavior and achieve a positive outcome.

Toward the end of elementary school and the beginning of high school, friendships and status within peer groups take on tremendous importance. Pleasing the teacher may be replaced by pleasing peers. Some students begin to test and defy authority. The management challenges at this stage are to deal productively with these disruptions and to motivate students who are becoming less concerned with teachers' opinions and more interested in their social lives.

By the end of high school, the focus of most students returns to academics. By this time, unfortunately, many of the students with overwhelming behavioral problems have dropped out. Classroom management at this stage involves managing the curriculum, fitting academic material to students' interests and abilities, and helping students become more self-managing in their learning. The first few classes each semester may be devoted to teaching particular procedures for using materials and equipment, or for keeping track of and submitting assignments. But most students know what is expected.

The Goals of Classroom Management

Test Bank items 11.9–11.13, 11.67–11.69, 11.79–11.81

The aim of **classroom management** is to maintain a positive, productive learning environment. But order for its own sake is an empty goal. As we discussed in chapter 6, it is unethical to use class management techniques just to keep students docile and quiet. What, then, is the point of working so hard to manage classrooms? There are at least three reasons why management is important.

More Time for Learning. As a child, I once used a stopwatch to time the commercials during a TV quiz show. I was amazed to find that half of the program was devoted to commercials. Actually, very little quizzing took place. If you used a similar approach in classrooms, timing all the different activities throughout the day, you might be surprised by how little actual teaching takes place. Many minutes each day are lost through interruptions, disruptions, late starts, and rough transitions. Sometimes the causes are unavoidable, as with fire drills, but often they could be prevented (Karweit, 1989; Karweit & Slavin, 1981).

Obviously, students will learn only the material they have a chance to learn. Almost every study examining time and opportunity to learn has found a significant relationship between amount of content covered and student learning (Berliner, 1988). In fact, the correlations between content covered and student learning are usually larger than the correlations between specific teacher behaviors and student learning (Rosenshine, 1979). So one important goal of classroom management is to expand the sheer number of minutes available for learning. This is sometimes called **allocated time.**

But simply making more time for learning will not automatically lead to achievement. To be valuable, time must be used effectively. As you saw in the chapters on cognitive learning, the way students process information is a central factor in what they learn and remember. Basically, students will learn what they practice and think about (Doyle, 1983). Time spent actively involved in specific learning tasks is often called **engaged time,** or sometimes **time on task.**

Again, however, just being engaged doesn't guarantee learning. Students may be engaged, but struggling with such difficult material that they learn very little. When students are working with a high rate of success—really learning and understanding—we call the time spent **academic learning time.** A second

Objective 11.2: Explain how the age of the students can influence the management goals of a teacher.

Connections: Chapter 3 included a discussion of the power of the adolescent's peer group to influence beliefs and behavior.

Objective 11.3: Characterize the features of classroom management that increase academic learning time.

Research: Walberg, H. (1988, March). Synthesis of research on time and learning. *Educational Leadership,* 76–80+. This article is reprinted in *Annual editions: Educational psychology 89* (pp. 120–127). Guilford, CT: Duskin.

Film/Video: The videotape series, "Effective Teaching for Higher Achievement," available from the Association for Supervision and Curriculum Development, 125 N. West Street, Alexandria, VA 22314 (phone 703-549-9110), has a useful segment on the concept of academic learning time.

Classroom Management Techniques used to maintain a healthy learning environment, relatively free of behavior problems.

Allocated Time Time set aside for learning.

Engaged Time Time spent actively learning.

Time on Task Time spent actively engaged in the learning task at hand.

Academic Learning Time Time when students are actually succeeding at the learning task.

Activity 11.1: Background. See the *Instructor's Resource Manual* for Increasing On-Task Time, excerpts from an article by an elementary-school principal that appeared in *Educational Leadership* (1988, March).

Research: See Berliner, D. (1983). Developing concepts of classroom environments: Some light on the T in studies of ATI. *Educational Psychologist, 18,* 1–13.

Activity 11.2: Field Experience. See the *Instructor's Resource Manual* for Time-on Task, a field activity designed to heighten your students' awareness of the challenge of time management in the classroom.

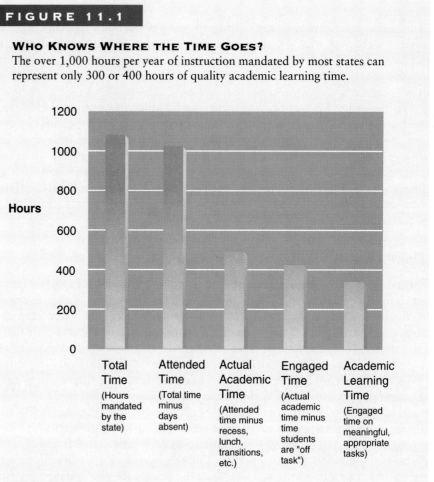

FIGURE 11.1

WHO KNOWS WHERE THE TIME GOES?
The over 1,000 hours per year of instruction mandated by most states can represent only 300 or 400 hours of quality academic learning time.

Hours

- **Total Time** (Hours mandated by the state)
- **Attended Time** (Total time minus days absent)
- **Actual Academic Time** (Attended time minus recess, lunch, transitions, etc.)
- **Engaged Time** (Actual academic time minus time students are "off task")
- **Academic Learning Time** (Engaged time on meaningful, appropriate tasks)

Source: C. Weinstein and A. Mignano (1993). *Elementary classroom management: Lessons from research and practice.* Copyright © 1993 by McGraw-Hill. Adapted with permission of McGraw-Hill.

goal of class management is to increase academic learning time by keeping students actively engaged in worthwhile, appropriate learning activities. Figure 11.1 shows how the 1,000+ hours of time mandated for school in most states can become only about 333 hours of quality academic learning time for a typical student.

Access to Learning. Each classroom activity has its own rules for participation. Sometimes these rules are clearly stated by the teacher, but often they are implicit and unstated. Teacher and students may not even be aware that they are following different rules for different activities (Berliner, 1983). And the differences are sometimes quite subtle. For example, in a reading group students may have to raise their hands to make a comment, but in a show-and-tell circle in the same class they may simply have to catch the teacher's eye.

As we saw in chapter 5, the rules defining who can talk; what they can talk about; and when, to whom, and how long they can talk are often called **participation structures**. In order to participate successfully in a given activity, students must understand the participation structure. Some students, however, seem to come to school less able to participate than others. The participation structures they learn at home in interactions with siblings, parents, and other adults do not match the participation structures of school activities (Tharp, 1989). But teachers are not necessarily aware of this conflict. Instead, the teachers see that a child doesn't quite fit in, always seems to say the wrong thing at the wrong time, or is very reluctant to participate, and they are not sure why.

What can we conclude? In order to involve all your students, you must make sure that everyone knows how to participate in each specific activity. The key is awareness. What are your rules and expectations? Are they understandable, given your students' cultural backgrounds and home experiences? What unspoken rules or values may be operating? Are you clear and consistent in signaling your students about how to participate? To reach the second goal of good classroom management—giving all students access to learning—you must make sure everyone knows how to participate in class activities.

Management for Self-Management.   The third goal of any management system is to help students become better able to manage themselves. Encouraging **self-management** requires extra time, but teaching students how to

Encouraging self-management is well worth the extra effort required, both for the smooth running of the class, and as a valuable skill for individual students.

Objective 11.4: Give examples of ways that the home environment can affect a student's ability to interact in the participation structures of a typical classroom.

Focus on . . .   **Classroom Organization**

- Why do classrooms need managers?
- What are the goals of good classroom management?
- Explain academic-learning time.

Multicultural Awareness: You might discuss with your students any cultural differences in the verbal and nonverbal ways that students show respect, pay attention, bid for a turn in conversation, and so on. How can cultural differences in interaction styles and expectations make classroom management more challenging?

Transparency: Acetate transparency **T 90**, "Who Knows Where the Time Goes?", is a bar graph showing factors that affect the number of hours typically available for academic learning.

Background: Brophy, J. (1985, fall). Classroom management as instruction: Socializing self-guidance in students. *Theory into Practice*, 233–240.

Activity 11.3: Background. See the *Instructor's Resource Manual* for Fostering Student Self-Management, a summary of the report of the Phi Delta Kappa Commission on Discipline.

Participation Structures Rules defining how to participate in different activities.

Self-Management Management of your own behavior and acceptance of responsibility for your own actions.

take responsibility is an investment well worth the effort. When elementary and secondary teachers have very effective class management systems but neglect to set student self-management as a goal, their students often find that they have trouble working independently after they graduate from these "well-managed" classes.

Connections: You might want to remind students that motivation and classroom management are closely related. The motivational strategies described in chapters 9 and 10 are good first steps in effective class management.

Connections: In chapter 12 students will learn about the importance of careful planning and clear objectives. Good planning is an important aspect of classroom management.

Background: Orderly classrooms and corridors: Why some schools have them and others don't (1987, September). *Harvard Education Letter*, Vol. 3, No. 5, pp. 1–5.

Activity 11.4: Reflection/Journal Writing. See the *Instructor's Resource Manual* for The Effective Classroom Manager, a journal-writing activity that encourages students to analyze the approach of the most effective classroom manager they have observed in their field experiences.

Activity 11.5: Teaching Tip. See the *Instructor's Resource Manual* for Classroom Management.

Background: Three excellent and very practical discussions of classroom management are: Evertson, C. M., Emmer, E. T., Clements, B. S., & Worsham, M. E. (1994). *Classroom management for elementary teachers* (3rd ed.). Boston: Allyn & Bacon; Emmer, E. T., Evertson, C. M., Clements, B. S. & Worsham, M. E. (1994). *Classroom management for secondary teachers* (3rd ed.). Boston: Allyn & Bacon; and Weinstein, C. S., & Mignano, A. J. Jr. (1993). *Elementary classroom management: Lessons from research and practice.* New York: McGraw-Hill.

reating a Positive Learning Environment

In making plans for your class, much of what you have already learned in this book should prove helpful. You know, for example, that problems are prevented when individual variations, such as those discussed in chapters 2, 3, 4, and 5, are taken into account in instructional planning. Sometimes students become disruptive because the work assigned is too difficult. Students who are bored by lessons well below their ability levels may be interested in finding more exciting activities to fill their time.

In one sense, teachers prevent discipline problems whenever they make an effort to motivate students. A student involved in mastering course objectives is usually not involved in a clash with the teacher or other students at the same time. All plans for motivating students are steps toward preventing problems.

Some Research Results   Test Bank items 11.96, 11.101

What else can teachers do to be good managers? For several years, educational psychologists at the University of Texas at Austin studied classroom management quite thoroughly (Emmer, Evertson, & Anderson, 1980; Emmer, Evertson, Clements, & Worsham, 1994; Evertson, 1988; Evertson, Emmer, Clements, & Worsham, 1994). Their general approach was to study a large number of classrooms, making frequent observations the first weeks of school and less-frequent visits later in the year. After several months there were dramatic differences among the classes. Some had very few management problems, while others had many. The most and least effective teachers were identified on the basis of the quality of classroom management and student achievement later in the year.

Next, the researchers looked at their observation records of the first weeks of class to see how the effective teachers got started. Other comparisons were made between the teachers who ultimately had well-behaved, high-achieving classes and those whose classes were fraught with problems. On the basis of these comparisons, management principles were developed. The researchers then taught these principles to a new group of teachers; the results were quite positive. Teachers who applied the principles had fewer problems; their students spent more time working and less time disrupting; and achievement was higher. The findings of these studies formed the basis for two books on classroom management (Emmer et al., 1994; Evertson et al., 1994). Many of the ideas in the following pages are from these books.

Rules and Procedures Required

Test Bank items 11.14–11.24, 11.82, 11.83, 11.96, 11.101, 11.102

At the elementary-school level, teachers must lead 20 to 30 students of varying abilities through many different activities each day. Without efficient rules and procedures, a great deal of time is wasted answering the same question over and over. "My pencil broke. How can I do my math?" "I'm finished with my story. What should I do now?" "Steven hit me!" "I left my homework in my locker. May I get it?"

At the secondary-school level, teachers must deal daily with over 100 students who use dozens of materials and often change rooms for each class. Secondary-school students are also more likely to challenge teachers' authority. The effective managers studied by Emmer, Evertson, and their colleagues had planned procedures and rules for coping with these situations.

Procedures.   How will materials and assignments be distributed and collected? Under what conditions can students leave the room? How do students respond to the bell at the beginning and end of a period? How will grades be determined? What are the special routines for handling equipment and supplies in science, art, or vocational classes? **Procedures** describe how activities are accomplished in classrooms, but they are seldom written down; they are simply the ways of getting things done in class. Carol Weinstein and Andy Mignano (1993) suggest that teachers establish procedures to cover the following areas:

1. *Administrative routines,* such as taking attendance.

2. *Student movement,* such as entering and leaving the room or going to the bathroom.

Research: For the description of a study that tested the Emmer/Evertson management principles along with other approaches, such as reinforcement strategies with adolescents in several schools, see Gottfredson, D. C., Gottfredson, G. D., & Hybl, L. G. (1993). Managing adolescent behavior: A multiyear, multischool study. *American Educational Research Journal, 30,* 179–217. Generally, the application of these principles improved behavior.

Discussion: What are the differences between procedures and rules? What rewards and penalties are appropriate for the grade levels your students will teach?

Objective 11.5: Create a list of rules and procedures for an elementary and a secondary class.

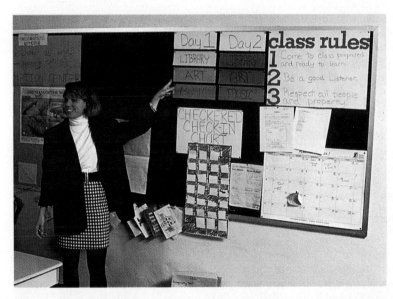

This teacher is preventing problems by posting the class rules and the daily schedule.

Procedures   Prescribed steps for an activity.

---

3. *Housekeeping,* such as watering plants or storing personal items.

4. *Routines for accomplishing lessons,* such as how to collect assignments or return homework.

5. *Interactions between teacher and student,* such as how to get the teacher's attention when help is needed.

6. *Talk among students,* such as giving help or socializing.

You might use these six areas as a framework for planning your class procedures and routines. The Guidelines should help you as you plan.

Guidelines

Establishing Class Procedures

Determine procedures for student upkeep of desks, classroom equipment, and other facilities.

Examples.
1. Some teachers set aside a cleanup time each day or once a week in self-contained classes.
2. You might demonstrate and have students practice how to push chairs under the desk, take and return materials stored on shelves, sharpen pencils, use the sink or water fountain, assemble lab equipment, and so on.
3. In some classes a rotating monitor is in charge of equipment or materials.

Decide how students will be expected to enter and leave the room.

Examples
1. How will students know what they should do as soon as they enter the room? Some teachers have a standard assignment ("Have your homework out and be checking it over").
2. Under what conditions can students leave the room? When do they need permission?
3. If students are late, how do they gain admission to the room?
4. Many teachers require students to be in their seats and quiet before they can leave at the end of class. The teacher, not the bell, dismisses class.

Establish a signal and teach it to your students.

Examples
1. In the classroom, some teachers flick the lights, sound a chord on a piano or recorder, move to the podium and stare silently at the class, use a phrase like "Eyes, please," take out their grade books, or move to the front of the class.
2. In the halls, a raised hand, one clap, or some other signal may mean "Stop."
3. On the playground, a raised hand or whistle may mean "Line up."

Set procedures for student participation in class.

Examples
1. Will you have students raise their hands for permission to speak or simply require that they wait until the speaker has finished?
2. How will you signal that you want everyone to respond at once? Some teachers raise a cupped hand to their ear. Others preface the question with "Everyone . . . "
3. Make sure you are clear about differences in procedures for different activities: reading group, learning center, discussion, teacher presentation, seatwork, film, peer learning group, library, and so forth.

4. How many students at a time can be at the pencil sharpener, teacher's desk, learning center, sink, bookshelves, reading corner, or bathroom?

Determine how you will communicate, collect, and return assignments.

Examples
1. Some teachers reserve a particular corner of the board for listing assignments. Others write assignments in colored chalk. For younger students it may be better to prepare assignment sheets or folders, color-coding them for math workbook, reading packet, and science kit.
2. Some teachers collect assignments in a box or bin; others have a student collect work while they introduce the next activity.

Rules. **Rules** specify expected and forbidden actions in the class. They are the do's and don'ts of classroom life. Unlike procedures, rules are often written down and posted. In establishing rules, you should consider what kind of atmosphere you want to create. What student behaviors will help you teach effectively? What limits do the students need to guide their behavior? The rules you set should be consistent with school rules, and also in keeping with principles of learning. For example, we know from the research on small-group learning that students benefit when they explain work to peers. They learn as they teach. A rule that forbids students to help each other may be inconsistent with good learning principles. Or a rule that says, "No erasures when writing" may make students focus more on preventing mistakes than on communicating clearly in their writing (Weinstein & Mignano, 1993).

Having a few general rules that cover many specifics is better than listing all the do's and don'ts. If specific actions are forbidden, such as chewing gum in class or smoking in the bathrooms, then a rule should make this clear.

Rules for Elementary School. Evertson and her colleagues (1994) give five examples of general rules for elementary-school classes:

1. *Be polite and helpful.* This applies to behavior toward adults (including substitute teachers) and children. Examples of polite behavior include waiting your turn, saying "please" and "thank you," and not fighting or calling names.
2. *Respect other people's property.* This might include picking up litter; returning library books; not marking on walls, desks, or buses; and getting permission before using other people's things.
3. *Listen quietly while others are speaking.* This applies to the teacher and other students, in large-class lessons or small-group discussions.
4. *Do not hit, shove, or hurt others.* Make sure you give clear explanations of what you mean by "hurt." Does this apply to hurt feelings as well as hurt bodies?
5. *Obey all school rules.* This reminds students that all school rules apply in your classroom. Then students cannot claim, for example, that they thought it was okay to chew gum or listen to a radio in your class, even though these are against school rules, "because you never made a rule against it for us."

Whatever the rule, students need to be taught the behaviors that the rule includes and excludes. Examples, practice, and discussion will be needed before learning is complete.

Casebook: See the Teachers' Casebook at the end of this chapter for practicing teachers' ideas about how and when to involve students in setting class rules.

Field Experience: An interesting field activity is for students to visit elementary-school classes and note the rules posted by different teachers at the same grade level. Have your students identify rules that are common to all or most classes, as well as those that are unusual.

Rules Statements specifying expected and forbidden behaviors; dos and don'ts.

As you've seen, different activities often require different rules. This can be confusing for elementary students until they have thoroughly learned all the rules. To prevent confusion, you might consider making signs that list the rules for each activity. Then, before the activity, you can post the appropriate sign as a reminder. This provides clear and consistent cues about participation structures so all students, not just the "well-behaved," know what is expected. Of course, these rules must be explained and discussed before the signs can have their full effect.

Rules for Secondary School.   Emmer and colleagues (1994) suggest six examples of rules for secondary students:

1. *Bring all needed materials to class.* The teacher must specify the type of pen, pencil, paper, notebook, texts, and so on.

2. *Be in your seat and ready to work when the bell rings.* Many teachers combine this rule with a standard beginning procedure for the class, such as a warm-up exercise on the board or a requirement that students have paper with a proper heading ready when the bell rings.

3. *Respect and be polite to everyone.* This covers fighting, verbal abuse, and general troublemaking.

4. *Respect other people's property.* This means property belonging to the school, the teacher, or other students.

5. *Listen and stay seated while someone else is speaking.* This applies when the teacher or other students are talking.

6. *Obey all school rules.* As with the elementary class rules, this covers many behaviors and situations, so you do not have to repeat every school rule for your class. It also reminds the students that you will be monitoring them inside and outside your class. Make sure you know all the school rules. Some secondary students are very adept at convincing teachers that their misbehavior "really isn't against the rules."

Consequences.   As soon as you decide on your rules and procedures, you must consider what you will do when a student breaks a rule or does not follow a procedure. It is too late to make this decision after the rule has been broken. For many infractions, the logical consequence is having to go back and "do it right." Students who run in the hall may have to return to where they started and walk properly. Incomplete papers can be redone. Materials left out should be put back. Sometimes consequences are more complicated. In their case studies of four expert elementary-school teachers, Weinstein and Mignano (1993) found that the teachers' negative consequences fell into seven categories, as shown in Table 11.1.

Connections: See the description of Ken's teaching approach in chapter 1.

In the first chapter I described Ken, an expert teacher who worked with his students to establish a students' and teacher's "Bill of Rights" instead of defining rules. These "rights" cover most situations that might require a "rule" and help the students move toward the goal of becoming self-managing. The rights for one recent year's class are listed in Table 11.2 on page 414. The main point here is that decisions about penalties (and rewards) must be made early on, so students know before they break a rule or use the wrong procedure what this will mean for them. I encourage my student teachers to get a copy of the school rules and their cooperating teacher's rules, then plan their own.

TABLE 11.1   Seven Categories of Penalties for Students

1. *Expressions of disappointment* If students like and respect their teacher, then a serious, sorrowful expression of disappointment may cause students to stop and think about their behavior.

2. *Loss of privileges* Students can lose free time. If they have not completed homework, for example, they can be required to do it during a free period or recess.

3. *Exclusion from the group* Students who distract their peers or fail to cooperate can be separated from the group until they are ready to cooperate. Some teachers give a student a pass for 10 to 15 minutes. The student must go to another class or study hall where the other students and teachers ignore the offending student for that time.

4. *Written reflections on the problem* Students can write in journals, write essays about what they did and how it affected others, or write letters of apology—if this is appropriate. Another possibility is to ask students to describe objectively what they did; then the teacher and the student can sign and date this statement. These records are available if parents or administrators need evidence of the students' behavior.

5. *Detentions* Detentions can be very brief meetings after school, during a free period, or at lunch. The main purpose is to talk about what has happened. (In high school, detentions are often used as punishments; suspensions and expulsions are available as more extreme measures.)

6. *Visits to the principal's office* Expert teachers tend to use this penalty rarely, but they do use it when the situation warrants. Some schools require students to be sent to the office for certain offenses, such as fighting. If you tell a student to go to the office and the student refuses, you might call the office saying the student has been sent. Then the student has the choice of either going to the office or facing the principal's penalty for "disappearing" on the way.

7. *Contact with parents* If problems become a repeated pattern, most teachers contact the student's family. This is done to seek support for helping the student, not to blame the parents or punish the student.

Source: C. Weinstein and A. Mignano (1983). *Elementary classroom management: Lessons from research and practice.* Copyright © 1993 by McGraw-Hill. Adapted with permission of McGraw-Hill.

Getting Started: The First Weeks of Class

Test Bank items 11.25–11.27, 11.84, 11.94, 11.97, 11.105

Having a plan and knowing how you will respond to problems is a first step toward having a well-managed class—which brings us to another very important question. What do effective teachers really do during those first critical days and weeks? One study carefully analyzed the first weeks' activities of effective and ineffective elementary teachers, and found striking differences (Emmer, Evertson, & Anderson, 1980).

Effective Managers for Elementary Students. In the effective teachers' classrooms, the very first day was well organized. Name tags were ready. There was something interesting for each child to do right away. Materials were set up. The teachers had planned carefully to avoid any last-minute tasks that might take them away from their students. These teachers dealt with the children's pressing concerns first. "Where do I put my things? How do I pronounce my teacher's name? How do I get the teacher's attention? Can I whisper to my neighbor? Where is the bathroom?" The effective teachers had a workable, easily understood set of rules and taught the students the most important rules right away. They taught the rules like any other subject, with lots of explanation, examples, and practice.

Objective 11.6: List several categories of penalties for breaking classroom rules, and give examples of each category appropriate for the grade levels to be taught.

Objective 11.7: Develop a plan for organizing the first week of the class.

Study Guide: Concept Map. See the *Study Guide* for the Concept Map "Planning the First Day of Class." This Concept Map also appears as **Handout Master 11.6** in the *Instructors' Resource Manual.*

TABLE 11.2 A Bill of Rights for Students and Teachers

Students' Bill of Rights

Students in this class have the following rights:

To whisper when the teacher isn't talking or asking for silence.
To celebrate authorship or other work at least once a month.
To exercise outside on days there is no physical education class.
To have 2-minute breaks.
To have healthy snacks during snack time.
To participate in choosing a table.
To have privacy. No one may touch anyone else's possessions without permission.
To be comfortable.
To chew gum without blowing bubbles or making a mess.
To make choices about the day's schedule.
To have free work time.
To work with partners.
To talk to the class without anyone else talking.
To work without being disturbed.

Teacher's Bill of Rights

The teacher has the following rights:

To talk without anyone else talking, or moving about, or disturbing the class.
To work without being disturbed.
To have everyone's attention while giving directions.
To punish someone who is not cooperating.
To send someone out of the group, or room, or to the office.

Source: C. Weinstein and A. Mignano (1993). *Elementary classroom management: Lessons from research and practice.* Copyright © 1993 by McGraw-Hill. Adapted with permission of McGraw-Hill.

Throughout the first weeks, the effective managers continued to spend quite a bit of time teaching rules and procedures. Some used guided practice to teach procedures; others used rewards to shape behavior. Most taught students to respond to a bell or some other signal to gain their attention. These teachers worked with the class as a whole on enjoyable academic activities. They did not rush to get students into small groups or to get them started in readers. This whole-class work gave the teachers a better opportunity to continue monitoring all students' learning of the rules and procedures. Misbehavior was stopped quickly and firmly, but not harshly.

In the poorly managed classrooms, the first weeks were quite different. Rules were not workable; they were either too vague or very complicated. For example, one teacher made a rule that students should "be in the right place at the right time." Students were not told what this meant, so their behavior could not be guided by the rule. Neither positive nor negative behaviors had clear, consistent consequences. After students broke a rule, ineffective managers might give a vague criticism, such as "Some of my children are too noisy," or issue a warning, but not follow through with the threatened consequence.

In the poorly managed classes, procedures for accomplishing routine tasks varied from day to day and were never taught or practiced. Instead of dealing with these obvious needs, ineffective managers spent time on procedures that could have waited. For example, one teacher had the class practice for a fire drill the first day, but left unexplained other procedures that would be needed every day. Students wandered aimlessly and had to ask each other what they should be doing. Often the students talked to one another because they had nothing productive to do. Ineffective teachers frequently left the room. Many became absorbed in paperwork or in helping just one student. They had not made plans for how to deal with late-arriving students or interruptions. One ineffective manager tried to teach students to respond to a bell as a signal for attention, but later let the students ignore it. All in all, the first weeks in these classrooms were disorganized and filled with surprises for teachers and students alike.

Effective Managers for Secondary Students. What about getting started in a secondary-school class? It appears that many of the differences between effective and ineffective elementary-school teachers hold at the secondary level as well. Again, effective managers focus on establishing rules, procedures, and expectations on the first day of class. These standards for academic work and class behavior are clearly communicated to students and consistently enforced during the first weeks of class. Student behavior is closely monitored, and infractions of the rules are dealt with quickly. In classes with lower-ability students, work cycles are shorter; students are not required to spend long, unbroken periods on one type of activity. Instead, during each period they are moved smoothly through several different tasks. In general, effective teachers carefully follow each student's progress, so students cannot avoid work without facing consequences (Emmer & Evertson, 1982).

> **Focus on . . . Creating a Positive Learning Environment**
> - Distinguish between rules and procedures.
> - What basic rules would you use for your students and how would you teach them?
> - Contrast the first school week of effective and ineffective classroom managers.

With all this close monitoring and consistent enforcement of the rules, you may wonder if effective secondary teachers have to be grim and humorless. Not necessarily. The effective managers in one study also smiled and joked more with their students (Moskowitz & Hayman, 1976). As any experienced teacher can tell you, there is much more to smile about when the class is cooperative and well behaved.

Maintaining a Good Environment for Learning

A good start is just that—a beginning. Effective teachers build on this beginning. They maintain their management system by preventing problems and keeping students engaged in productive learning activities. We have discussed several ways to keep students engaged. In the chapters on motivation, for example, we noted such approaches as stimulating curiosity, relating lessons to student interests, encouraging cooperative learning, establishing learning goals instead of performance goals, and having positive expectations. What else can teachers do?

Encouraging Engagement   Test Bank items 11.28, 11.29

The format of a lesson affects student involvement. In general, as teacher supervision increases, students' engaged time also increases (Emmer & Evertson, 1981). A recent study, for example, found that elementary students working directly with a teacher were on task 97 percent of the time, while students working on their own were on task only 57 percent of the time (Frick, 1990). This does not mean that teachers should eliminate independent work for students. It simply means that this type of activity usually requires careful monitoring.

When the task provides continuous cues for the student about what to do next, involvement will be greater. Activities with clear steps are likely to be more absorbing, since one step leads naturally to the next. When students have all the materials they need to complete a task, they tend to stay involved (Kounin & Doyle, 1975). If their curiosity is piqued, students will be motivated to continue seeking an answer. And as you now know, students will be more engaged if they are involved in authentic tasks—activities that have connections to real life.

Of course, teachers can't supervise every student all the time or rely on curiosity. Something else must keep students working and completing assignments on their own. In their study of elementary and secondary teachers, Evertson, Emmer, and their colleagues found that effective class managers at both levels had well-planned systems for encouraging students to manage their own work (Evertson et al., 1994, Emmer et al., 1994). The Guidelines on page 417 are based on their findings.

Prevention Is the Best Medicine   Test Bank items 11.30–11.34, 11.70, 11.71, 11.85–11.87, 11.95

What else can you do to maintain your management system? The ideal way to manage problems, of course, is to prevent them in the first place. In a classic study, Jacob Kounin (1970) examined classroom management by comparing effective teachers, whose classes were relatively free of problems, with ineffective teachers, whose classes were continually plagued by chaos and disruption. Observing both groups in action, Kounin found that they were not very different in the way they handled discipline once problems arose. The difference was that the successful managers were much better at preventing problems. Kounin concluded that effective classroom managers were especially skilled in four areas: *"withitness," overlapping activities, group focusing, and movement management* (Doyle, 1977). More recent research confirms the importance of these factors (Emmer & Evertson, 1981; Evertson, 1988).

Withitness.   **Withitness** means communicating to students that you are aware of everything that is happening in the classroom, that you aren't missing anything. "With-it" teachers seem to have eyes in the back of their heads. They avoid becoming absorbed or interacting with only a few students, since

---

Objective 11.8: Explain Kounin's suggestions for preventing management problems.

Activity 11.6: See the *Instructor's Resource Manual* for Encouraging Responsibility, a summary of William Glasser's eight steps for implementing effective classroom management.

Activity 11.7: Cooperative Learning. See the *Instructor's Resource Manual* for Using Glasser's Principles, a group activity that asks your students to identify two typical behavioral and learning problems of middle-school-age students, and then apply William Glasser's principles of effective classroom management to solve the problems.

Withitness According to Kounin, awareness of everything happening in a classroom.

Make basic work requirements clear.

Examples

1. Specify and post the routine work requirements for headings, paper size, pen or pencil use, and neatness.
2. Establish and explain rules about late or incomplete work and absences. If a pattern of incomplete work begins to develop, deal with it early; speak with parents if necessary.
3. Make due dates reasonable, and stick to them unless the student has a very good excuse for lateness.

Communicate the specifics of assignments.

Examples

1. With younger students, have a routine procedure for giving assignments, such as writing them on the board in the same place each day. With older students, assignments may be dictated, posted, or given in a syllabus.
2. Remind students of coming assignments.
3. With complicated assignments, give students a sheet describing what to do, what resources are available, due dates, and so on. Older students should also be told your grading criteria.
4. Demonstrate how to do the assignment, do the first few questions together, or provide a sample worksheet.

Monitor work in progress.

Examples

1. When you make an assignment in class, make sure each student gets started correctly. If you check only students who raise their hands for help, you will miss those who think they know what to do but don't really understand, those who are too shy to ask for help, and those who don't plan to do the work at all.
2. Check progress periodically. In discussions, make sure everyone has a chance to respond.

Give frequent academic feedback.

Examples

1. Elementary students should get papers back the day after they are handed in.
2. Good work can be displayed in class and graded papers sent home to parents each week.
3. Students of all ages can keep records of grades, projects completed, and extra credits earned.
4. For older students break up long-term assignments into several phases, giving feedback at each point.

this encourages the rest of the class to wander. They are always scanning the room, making eye contact with individual students, so the students know they are being monitored (Brooks, 1985).

These teachers prevent minor disruptions from becoming major. They also know who instigated the problem, and they make sure the right people are dealt with. In other words, they do not make what Kounin called timing errors (waiting too long before intervening) or target errors (blaming the wrong student and letting the real perpetrators escape responsibility for their behavior).

If two problems occur at the same time, effective managers deal with the more serious one first. For example, a teacher who tells two students to stop whispering but ignores even a brief shoving match at the pencil sharpener communicates to students a lack of awareness. Students begin to believe they can get away with almost anything if they are clever (Charles, 1989).

Overlapping and Group Focus. **Overlapping** means keeping track of and supervising several activities at the same time. Success in this area also requires constant monitoring of the class. In many ways, a teacher must continually manage what Dunkin and Biddle (1974) called a three-ring circus. For example, a teacher may have to check the work of an individual and at the same time keep a small group working by saying, "Right, go on" (Charles, 1985).

Maintaining a **group focus** means keeping as many students as possible involved in appropriate class activities and avoiding narrowing in on just one or two students. All students should have something to do during a lesson. For example, the teacher might ask everyone to write the answer to a question, then call on individuals to respond while the other students compare their answers. Choral responses might be required while the teacher moves around the room to make sure everyone is participating (Charles, 1985). Some teachers have their students use small blackboards or colored cards for responding in groups. This lets the teacher check for understanding as well. For example, during a grammar lesson the teacher might say, "Everyone who thinks the answer is *have run,* hold up the red side of your card. If you think the answer is *has run,* hold up the green side" (Hunter, 1982). This is one way teachers can ensure that all students are involved and check that they all understand the material.

Movement Management. **Movement management** means keeping lessons and the group moving with smooth transitions, variety, and at an appropriate (and flexible) pace. The effective teacher avoids abrupt transitions, such as announcing a new activity before gaining the students' attention or starting a new activity in the middle of something else. In these situations, one-third of the class will be doing the new activity, many will be on the old lesson, several will be asking other students what to do, some will be taking the opportunity to have a little fun, and most will be confused.

Another transition problem Kounin noted is the *slowdown,* or taking too much time to start a new activity. Sometimes teachers give too many directions. Problems also arise when teachers have students work one at a time while the rest of the class waits and watches. Charles (1985, p. 26) gives this example:

> During a science lesson the teacher began, "Row 1 may get up and get their beakers. Row 2 may get theirs. Now Row 3. Now, Row 1 may line up to put some bicarbonate of soda in their beakers. Row 2 may follow them," and so forth. When each row had obtained their bicarbonate of soda the teacher had them go row by row to add water. This left the remainder of the class sitting at their desks with no direction, doing nothing or else beginning to find something with which to entertain themselves.
>
> . . . After every student had the necessary substances in their beakers the teacher proceeded: "Okay Roy, now pour in the vinegar while we watch.

Overlapping Supervising several activities at once.

Group Focus The ability to keep as many students as possible involved in activities.

Movement Management Ability to keep lessons and groups moving smoothly.

Good. Now Susie, it's your turn. Patti, you're next." The teacher had individuals doing the activity when it would have made more sense to have the class do it together.

A teacher who successfully demonstrates withitness, overlapping activities, group focus, and movement management tends to have a class filled with actively engaged students who do not escape his or her all-seeing eye. This need not be a grim classroom. It is more likely a busy place where students are actively learning and gaining a sense of self-worth rather than misbehaving in order to get attention and achieve status.

Dealing with Discipline Problems   Test Bank items 11.35, 11.36

Being an effective manager does not mean publicly correcting every minor infraction of the rules. This kind of public attention may actually reinforce the misbehavior, as we saw in chapter 6. Teachers who frequently correct students do not necessarily have the best behaved classes (Irving & Martin, 1982). The key is to know what is happening and what is important so you can prevent problems. Emmer and colleagues (1994) suggest four simple ways to stop misbehavior quickly:

1. *Make eye contact* with, or move closer to, the offender. Other nonverbal signals, such as pointing to the work students are supposed to be doing, might be helpful. Make sure the student actually stops the inappropriate behavior and gets back to work. If you do not, students will learn to ignore your signals.

2. If they are not performing a class procedure correctly, *remind the students* of the procedure and have them follow it correctly.

3. In a calm, unhostile way, *ask the student to state the correct rule or procedure* and then to follow it.

4. Tell the student in a clear, assertive, and unhostile way to *stop the misbehavior.* (Later in the chapter we will discuss assertive messages to students in more detail.)

If you must impose penalties, the Guidelines on page 420, taken from Weinstein and Mignano (1993), give ideas about how to do it. The examples are taken from the actual words of the four expert teachers described in their book.

Special Problems with Secondary Students   Test Bank items 11.37–11.39

Many secondary students never complete their work. Besides encouraging student responsibility, what else can teachers do to deal with this frustrating problem? Since students at this age have many assignments and teachers have many students, both teacher and students may lose track of what has and hasn't been completed. The teacher must keep accurate records so everyone will be sure what the students are actually doing, but the most important thing is to enforce the established consequences for incomplete work. Do not pass a student because you know he or she is "bright enough" to pass. Make it clear to these students that the choice is theirs: they can do the work and pass, or they can refuse to do the work and face the consequences.

There is also the problem of students who continually break the same rules, always forgetting materials, for example, or getting into fights. What should you do? Seat these students away from others who might be influenced

Discussion: Assign Petty, R. (1989). Managing disruptive students. *Educational Leadership, 46(6), 26–28. Focus Question:* Ask students to list the discipline problems that they find most troubling, then to develop possible responses to these problems based on Petty's ideas.

Objective 11.9: Describe how a teacher might respond to a student who seldom completes work.

Casebook: See the Teachers' Casebook for ideas about how to handle the problem of students who regularly hand in incomplete work or no work at all.

Activity 11.8: Background. See the *Instructor's Resource Manual* for Using Behavior Modification in Classroom Discipline, a summary of Siggers, W. (1980). Changing teacher correcting behavior: Using aversive and positive contingencies. *Educational Research Quarterly, 5,* 25–32.

Guidelines

Imposing Penalties

Delay the discussion of the situation until you and the students involved are calmer and more objective.

Examples

1. Say calmly to a student, "Sit there and think about what happened. I'll talk to you in a few minutes," or, "I don't like what I just saw. Talk to me during your free period today."
2. Say, "I'm really angry about what just happened. Everybody take out journals; we are going to write about this." After a few minutes of writing, the class can discuss the incident.

Impose penalties privately.

Examples

1. Make arrangements with students privately. Stand firm in enforcing arrangements.
2. Resist the temptation to "remind" students in public that they are not keeping their side of the bargain.
3. Move close to a student who must be disciplined and speak so that only the student can hear.

After imposing a penalty, reestablish a positive relationship with the student immediately.

Examples

1. Send the student on an errand or ask him or her for help.
2. Compliment the student's work or give a real or symbolic "pat on the back" when the student's behavior warrants. Look hard for such an opportunity.

Set up a graded list of penalties that will fit many occasions.

Example

1. For not turning in homework: (1) receive reminder; (2) receive warning; (3) hand homework in before close of school day; (4) stay after school to finish work; (5) participate in a teacher-student-parent conference to develop an action plan.

Research: For a description of an extensive research project examining how teachers cope with problem behaviors, see Brophy, J., & McCaslin, M. (1992). Teachers' reports of how they perceive and cope with problem students. *Elementary School Journal, 93,* 3–68.

Discussion: A child continually acts aggressively toward other children, pushing in line and hitting and kicking others during recess. Ask your students what they would do to set up a behavior modification program to eliminate this behavior.

Discussion: Try this scenario with your students: Almost every day in your sixth-grade class, Rod talks out of turn and loses the reward for his group. The other group members are giving Rod a difficult time, and the parents of two students have called you to complain that the group reward system is unfair. What would you do to resolve this problem?

by them. Try to catch them before they break the rules, but if rules are broken, be consistent in applying established consequences. Do not accept promises to do better next time. Teach the students how to monitor their own behavior; some of the self-management techniques described in chapter 6 should be helpful. Finally, remain friendly with the students. Try to catch them in a good moment so you can talk to them about something other than their rule-breaking.

The defiant, hostile student can pose serious problems. If there is an outbreak, try to get out of the situation as soon as possible; everyone loses in a public power struggle. One possibility is to give the student a chance to save face and cool down by saying, "It's your choice to cooperate or not. You can take a minute to think about it." If the student complies, the two of you can talk later about controlling the outbursts. If the student refuses to cooperate, you can tell him or her to wait in the hall until you get the class started on work, then step outside for a private talk. If the student refuses to leave, send another class member for the assistant principal. Again, follow through. If the student complies before help arrives, do not let him or her off the hook. If outbursts occur frequently, you might have a conference with the counselor, parents, or other teachers. If the problem is an unreconcilable clash of personalities, the student should be transferred to another teacher.

Violence or destruction of property is a difficult and potentially dangerous problem. The first step is to send for help and get the names of participants and witnesses. Then get rid of any crowd that may have gathered; an audience will only make things worse. Do not try to break up a fight without help. Make sure the school office is aware of the incident: usually the school has a policy for dealing with these situations.

> *Focus on . . .*   **Maintaining a Good Environment for Learning**
>
> - Explain the factors identified by Kounin that prevent management problems in the classroom.
> - Will you use penalties in your class when students violate rules? What kinds?

Special Programs for Classroom Management

In some situations you may want to consider using a much more formal classroom management system. Three possibilities, all based on behavioral principles, are group consequences, token programs, and contingency contracts.

Group Consequences

Test Bank items 11.10, 11.40–11.43, 11.72, 11.103

A teacher can base reinforcement for the class on the cumulative behavior of all members of the class, usually by adding each student's points to a class or a team total. The **good behavior game** is an example of this approach. A class is divided into two teams. Specific rules for good behavior are cooperatively developed. Each time a student breaks one of the rules, that student's team is given a mark. The team with the fewest marks at the end of the period receives a special reward or privilege (longer recess, first to lunch, and so on). If both teams earn fewer than a preestablished number of marks, both teams receive the reward. Most studies indicate that even though the game produces only small improvements in academic achievement, it can produce definite improvements in the behaviors listed in the good behavior rules.

You can also use **group consequences** without dividing the class into teams, that is, you can base reinforcement on the behavior of the whole class. Wilson and Hopkins (1973) conducted a study using group consequences to reduce noise levels. Radio music served effectively as the reinforcer for students in a home economics class. Whenever noise in the class was below a predetermined level, students could listen to the radio; when the noise exceeded the level, the radio was turned off. Given the success of this simple method, such a procedure might be considered in any class where music does not interfere with the task at hand.

Group consequences are recommended for situations in which students care about the approval of their peers. If the misbehavior of several students seems to be encouraged by the attention and laughter of other students, then

Objective 11.10: Compare several kinds of group consequence behavioral management systems, citing the advantages and disadvantages of each.

Activity 11.9: Background. In the *Instructor's Resource Manual* see A Group Contingency Program to Improve Reading, which provides an extended example of designing and implementing a group contingency program.

Transparency: Acetate transparency T 92 shows how students' talking-out and out-of-seat behavior in math and reading classes declined as a consequence of group contingency games.

Good Behavior Game Arrangement where a class is divided into teams and each team receives demerit points for breaking agreed-upon rules of good behavior.

Group Consequences Rewards or punishments given to a class as a whole for adhering to or violating rules of conduct.

Cooperative Learning: Divide the class into groups according to students' teaching level of interest (e.g., elementary, middle school, high school, adult). Ask each group to generate a list of the classroom rewards that appear to serve as the strongest motivators for the age level concerned. Have the groups present their lists; compare and discuss them.

Discussion: The teacher has divided the class into small groups to work on different aspects of a class assignment. In one group there is a child who is preventing the group from completing its task because of crazy antics and remarks. How would you set up a program that would encourage the group to take responsibility for getting the student to cooperate?

Objective 11.11: Give examples of classroom situations in which a token reinforcement system might be needed.

Research: For a study of the use of students to manage a token program, see Salend, S. J., Tintle, L., & Balber, H. (1988). Effects of a student-managed response cost system on the behavior of two mainstreamed students. *The Elementary School Journal, 89,* 89-97.

Discussion: Despite the obvious advantages of home-based token reinforcement programs, a problem in many cases is ensuring that parents will participate fully. What are some things that teachers can do to encourage parents' involvement?

Token Reinforcement System System in which tokens earned for academic work and positive classroom behavior can be exchanged for some desired reward.

group consequences could be helpful. Also, using positive group consequences can help build cooperation among students (Jenson, Sloane, & Young, 1988).

However, caution is needed in group approaches. The whole group should not suffer for the misbehavior or mistakes of one individual if the group has no real influence over that person. I saw an entire class break into cheers when the teacher announced that one boy was transferring to another school. The chant "No more points! No more points!" filled the room. The "points" referred to the teacher's system of giving one point to the whole class each time anyone broke a rule. Every point meant 5 minutes of recess lost. The boy who was transferring had been responsible for many losses. He was not very popular to begin with, and the point system, though quite effective in maintaining order, had led to rejection and even greater unpopularity.

Peer pressure in the form of support and encouragement, however, can be a positive influence. Teachers might show students how to give support and constructive feedback to classmates. If a few students seem to enjoy sabotaging the system, those students may need separate arrangements.

Token Reinforcement Programs   Test Bank items 11.44–11.46

Often it is difficult to provide positive consequences for all the students who deserve them. A **token reinforcement system** can help solve this problem by allowing all students to earn tokens for both academic work and positive classroom behavior. The tokens may be points, checks, holes punched in a card, chips, play money, or anything else that is easily identified as the student's property. Periodically the students exchange the tokens they have earned for some desired reward (Martin & Pear, 1992).

Depending on the age of the student, the rewards could be small toys, school supplies, free time, special class jobs, or other privileges. When a "token economy," as this kind of system is called, is first established, the tokens should be given out on a fairly continuous schedule, with chances to exchange the tokens for rewards often available. Once the system is working well, however, tokens should be distributed on an intermittent schedule and saved for longer periods of time before they are exchanged for rewards. In order to establish an intermittent schedule, the teacher might set a timer for various lengths of time, then give a token to every student who is working when the timer goes off. Of course, the students would not know when the next signal was coming, so they would have to work steadily. An alarm watch makes a good timer for this purpose.

Another variation is to allow students to earn tokens in the classroom and then exchange them for rewards at home. These plans are very successful when parents are willing to cooperate. Usually a note or report form is sent home daily or twice a week. The note indicates the number of points earned in the preceding time period. The points may be exchanged for minutes of television viewing, access to special toys, or private time with parents. Points can also be saved up for larger rewards such as trips. Do not use this procedure, however, if you suspect the child might be severely punished for poor reports.

Token reinforcement systems are complicated and time-consuming. Generally, they should be used in only three situations: to motivate students who are completely uninterested in their work and have not responded to other approaches; to encourage students who have consistently failed to make academic progress; and to deal with a class that is out of control. Some groups of

Before presenting the program to students, make sure you have all the details worked out.

Examples
1. Establish rules that clearly specify requirements, such as how many problems done correctly will earn a point.
2. Make sure your system is workable and not too complicated. You might discuss it with another teacher to identify possible sources of problems.

You may want to have different goals for different groups of students.

Examples
1. Focus on cooperative behaviors for students who are disruptive.
2. For high-achieving students, give tokens for enrichment work, peer tutoring, or special projects.
3. Match the token to the age of the student—colored chips for younger children, points for older students.

Offer a variety of rewards at different "prices."

Examples
1. Offer rewards that can be purchased for only two or three tokens, so that all students will be motivated to try.
2. Offer rewards that make more extensive efforts or saving up tokens worthwhile.

Gradually increase the requirements for each token.

Examples
1. Begin with one token for each correct answer, then give a token for every three correct answers, and so on.
2. Offer tokens for 5 minutes of attention to assignments, then eventually for a whole day of attentive work.

Gradually change from tangible rewards and privileges to time focused on enjoyable learning experiences.

Examples
1. With young students, start with candy or small toys, but move to assisting the teacher and free reading time.
2. With older students, start with such things as magazines and move toward free time to spend on special projects, the chance to tutor younger children, or the opportunity to work in the computer lab.

students seem to benefit more than others from token economies. Mentally retarded students, slow learners, children who have failed often, students with few academic skills, and students with behavior problems all seem to respond to the concrete, direct nature of token reinforcement.

Before you try a token system, you should be sure that your teaching methods and materials are right for the students. Sometimes class disruptions or lack of motivation indicate that teaching practices need to be changed. Maybe

Handout: Example of contingency contracts are provided in **Handout Master 11.5.**

Transparency: Acetate transparency T 91 presents a "Student Contract Appropriate for the Primary Grades."

the class rules are unclear or are enforced inconsistently. Maybe the teacher provides too little social reinforcement, praise, or warmth. Maybe the text is too easy or too hard. Maybe the pace is wrong. If these problems exist, a token system may improve the situation temporarily, but the students will still have trouble learning the academic material (Jenson, Sloane, & Young, 1988).

Contingency Contract Programs   Test Bank items 11.47, 11.73

In a **contingency contract** program, the teacher draws up an individual contract with each student, describing exactly what the student must do to earn a particular privilege or reward. In some programs, students participate in deciding on the behaviors to be reinforced and the rewards that can be gained. The negotiating process itself can be an educational experience, as students learn to set reasonable goals and abide by the terms of a contract.

An example of a contract for completing assignments that is appropriate for intermediate and upper-grade students is presented in Figure 11.2. This chart serves as a contract, assignment sheet, and progress record. Something like this might even help you keep track of your assignments and due dates in college.

The few pages devoted here to token reinforcement and contingency contracts can offer only an introduction to these programs. If you want to set up a large-scale reward program in your classroom, you should probably seek professional advice. Often the school psychologist, counselor, or principal can help. In addition, remember that, applied inappropriately, external rewards can undermine the students' motivation to learn (Deci, 1975; Lepper & Greene, 1978).

Focus on . . .   **Special Management Programs**

- What are the uses and limitations of group consequences?
- Describe a situation in which you might use a contingency contract.

Casebook: See the Teachers' Casebook for practicing teachers' ideas about classroom management for beginning teachers: how to strike a balance between friendship and respect.

The Need for Communication   Test Bank items 11.98, 11.105–11.107

Communication between teacher and students is essential when problems arise. Communication is more than "teacher talks—student listens." It is more than simply the words exchanged between individuals. We communicate in many ways. Our actions, movements, voice tone, facial expressions, and many other nonverbal behaviors send messages to our students. Many times the messages we intend to send are not the messages our students receive.

Message Sent—Message Received   Test Bank items 11.89, 11.98

Teacher: Carl, where is your homework?

Carl: I left it in my Dad's car this morning.

Teacher: Again? You will have to bring me a note tomorrow from your father saying that you actually did the homework. I won't grade it without the note.

Message Carl receives: You are lying. I can't trust you. I need proof you did the work.

Contingency Contract A contract between the teacher and an individual student specifying what the student must do to earn a particular privilege or reward.

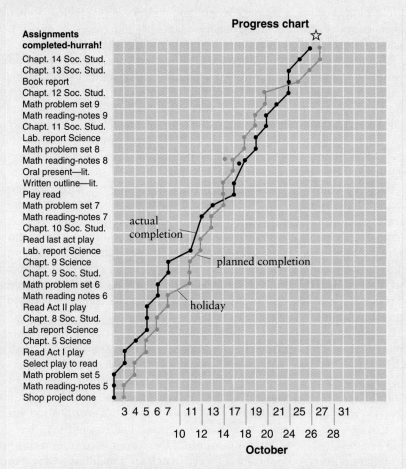

FIGURE 11.2

A CONTINGENCY CONTRACT FOR COMPLETING ASSIGNMENTS

This contract can serve as a visual reminder of due dates for projects and assignments. Whenever the "actual completion" line is above the "planned completion" line, work is on time and the contract is met.

Progress chart

Assignments completed-hurrah!

Chapt. 14 Soc. Stud.
Chapt. 13 Soc. Stud.
Book report
Chapt. 12 Soc. Stud.
Math problem set 9
Math reading-notes 9
Chapt. 11 Soc. Stud.
Lab. report Science
Math problem set 8
Math reading-notes 8
Oral present—lit.
Written outline—lit.
Play read
Math problem set 7
Math reading-notes 7
Chapt. 10 Soc. Stud.
Read last act play
Lab. report Science
Chapt. 9 Science
Chapt. 9 Soc. Stud.
Math problem set 6
Math reading notes 6
Read Act II play
Chapt. 8 Soc. Stud.
Lab report Science
Chapt. 5 Science
Read Act I play
Select play to read
Math problem set 5
Math reading-notes 5
Shop project done

actual completion

planned completion

holiday

3 4 5 6 7 11 13 17 19 21 25 27 31
10 12 14 18 20 24 26 28

October

The teacher and student agree on the due dates for each assignment, marking them in blue on the chart. Each time an assignment is turned in, the date of completion is marked in black on the chart. As long as the actual completion line is above planned completion line, the student earns free time or other contracted rewards.

Source: Figure from *Achieving educational excellence: Behavior analysis for improving instruction*, p. 277. Copyright © 1994 by Beth Sulzer-Azaroff and G. Roy Mayer (San Marcos, CA: Western Image, P.O. Box 427). Reprinted by permission of the authors.

Example: Token Reinforcement at work:

Michael, a second-grade student, was capable of producing neat and accurate work but generally preferred to rush, completing his work quickly and haphazardly. His teacher knew of Michael's great interest in dinosaurs and decided to use this to help him. She asked him to bring in a decorated CAN which would represent Careful And Neat work. For every carefully produced assignment, she would deposit a red bead into the CAN. After accumulating five beads, Michael would earn 15 minutes' free time at the dinosaur center or on a dinosaur project of his own. His teacher noticed a dramatic improvement in the quality of his work and made sure to praise him each time. Continuing to use praise as reinforcement, she slowly increased the number of tokens required to earn free time. After Michael's work habits had become consistently neat and thorough, the teacher phased out her system of token reinforcement, replacing it with verbal reinforcement alone.

"THEY'RE TESTING YOU."

(James Warren—Phi Delta Kappan)

Activity 11.10: See the *Instructors' Resource Manual* for Who Owns the Problem? a whole-class activity that allows your students to analyze typical classroom situations. **Handout Master 11.2** lists the situations and can be used as an independent or class activity.

Discussion: Ask your students what they believe to be a teacher's responsibility if he or she finds out that a pupil is involved in illegal acts such as selling drugs or stolen property.

Paraphrase Rule Policy whereby listeners must accurately summarize what a speaker has said before being allowed to respond.

Teacher: Sit at every other desk. Put all your things under your desk. Jane and Laurel, you are sitting too close together. One of you move!

Message Jane and Laurel receive: I expect you two to cheat on this test.

A new student comes to Ms. Lincoln's kindergarten. The child is messy and unwashed. Ms. Lincoln puts her hand lightly on the girl's shoulder and says, "I know you will like it here." Her muscles tense, and she leans away from the child.

Message student receives: I don't like you. I think you are bad.

In all interactions, a message is sent and a message is received. Sometimes teachers believe they are sending one message, but their voices, body positions, choices of words, and gestures may communicate a different message.

Students may hear the hidden message and respond to it. For example, a student may respond with hostility if she or he feels insulted by the teacher (or by another student) but may not be able to say exactly where the feeling of being insulted came from. Perhaps it was in the teacher's tone of voice, not the words actually spoken. In such cases, the teacher may feel attacked for no reason. "What did I say? All I said was . . ." The first principle of communication is that people respond to what they *think* was said or meant, not necessarily to the speaker's intended message.

There are many exercises for practicing sending and receiving messages accurately. Students in my classes have told me about one instructor who encourages accurate communication by using the **paraphrase rule.** Before any participant, including the teacher, is allowed to respond to any other participant in a class discussion, he or she must summarize what the previous speaker said. If the summary is wrong, indicating the speaker was misunderstood, the speaker must explain again. The respondent then tries again to paraphrase. The process continues until the speaker agrees that the listener has heard the intended message.

Paraphrasing is more than a classroom exercise. It can be the first step in communicating with students. Before teachers can deal appropriately with any student problem, they must know what the real problem is. A student who says, "This book is really dumb! Why did we have to read it?" may really be saying, "The book was too difficult for me. I couldn't read it, and I feel dumb." A teacher who responds to the "why" question with a justification for the choice of reading material has missed the point. The student may feel even worse as a result: "Now I'm not just dumb, I've also missed out on this thing the teacher thinks is so important. I'll never catch up. I might as well just quit!"

Diagnosis: Whose Problem Is It?

Test Bank items 11.48, 11.49, 11.51–11.53, 11.88, 11.98, 11.104

As a teacher, you may find many student behaviors unacceptable, unpleasant, or troubling. It is often difficult to stand back from these problems, take an objective look, and decide on an appropriate response. According to Thomas Gordon (1981), the key to good teacher-student relationships is determining why you are troubled by a particular behavior and whose problem it is. The teacher must begin by asking who "owns" the problem. The answer to this question is critical. If it is really the student's problem, the teacher must become a counselor and supporter, helping the student find his or her own solution. But if the teacher "owns" the problem, it is the teacher's responsibility to find a solution through problem solving with the student.

Diagnosing who owns the problem is not always straightforward. Let's look at three troubling situations to get some practice in this skill:

1. A student writes obscene words and draws sexually explicit illustrations in a school encyclopedia.
2. A student tells you that his mother and father had a bad fight and he hates his father.
3. A student quietly reads a newspaper in the back of the room.

Why are these behaviors troubling? If you cannot accept the student's behavior because it has a serious effect on you as a teacher—if you are blocked from reaching your goals by the student's action—then *you* own the problem. It is your responsibility to confront the student and seek a solution. A teacher-owned problem appears to be present in the first situation described above—the young pornographer—because teaching materials are damaged.

If you feel annoyed by the behavior because it is getting in the student's own way or because you are embarrassed for the child, but the behavior does not directly interfere with your teaching, then it is probably the student's problem. The test question is this: does this student's action tangibly affect you or prevent you from fulfilling your role as a teacher? The student who hates his father would not prevent you from teaching, even though you might wish the student felt differently. The problem is really the student's, and he must find his own solution. (In both the first and second situations, teachers may want to help students confront moral or emotional problems. Nevertheless, teachers must still clarify whose emotions and values are involved, how they are involved, and why.)

Situation 3 is more difficult to diagnose. I have had lengthy debates in my class about whose problem it is when a student reads a newspaper in class. One argument is that the teacher is not interfered with in any way, so it is the student's problem. Another argument is that teachers might find reading the paper distracting during a lecture, so it is their problem, and they must find a solution. In a gray area such as this, the answer probably depends on how the teacher actually experiences the student's behavior. Having decided who owns the problem, it is time to act.

Counseling: The Student's Problem

Test Bank items 11.50, 11.54, 11.55, 11.74, 11.75, 11.98

Let's pick up the situation in which the student found the reading assignment "dumb." How might a teacher handle this positively?

Student: This book is really dumb! Why did we have to read it?

Teacher: You're pretty upset. This seemed like a worthless assignment to you. [Teacher paraphrases the student's statement, trying to hear the emotions as well as the words.]

Student: Yeah! Well, I guess it was worthless. I mean, I don't know if it was. I couldn't exactly read it.

Teacher: It was just too hard to read, and that bothers you.

Student: Sure, I felt really dumb. I know I can write a good report, but not with a book this tough.

Teacher: I think I can give you some hints that will make the book easier to understand. Can you see me after school today?

Student: Okay.

Activity 11.11: See the *Instructor's Resource Manual* for Empathy Training, a class activity that gives students practice in active listening.

Objective 11.12: Suggest two different approaches for dealing with a conflict between teacher and student or between two students.

Empathetic Listening Hearing the intent and emotions behind what another says and reflecting them back by paraphrasing.

"I" Message Clear, nonaccusatory statement of how something is affecting you.

Here the teacher used **empathetic listening** to allow the student to find a solution. (As you can see, this approach relies heavily on paraphrasing.) By trying to hear the student and by avoiding the tendency to jump in too quickly with advice, solutions, criticisms, reprimands, or interrogations, the teacher keeps the communication lines open. Here are a few *unhelpful* responses the teacher might have made:

I chose the book because it is the best example of _____ in our library. You will need to have read it before your English II class next year. (The teacher justifies the choice; this prevents the student from admitting that this "important" assignment is too difficult.)

Did you really read it? I bet you didn't do the work, and now you want out of the assignment. (The teacher accuses; the student hears, "The teacher doesn't trust me!" and must defend herself or himself or accept the teacher's view.)

Your job is to read the book, not ask me why. I know what's best. (The teacher pulls rank, and the student hears, "You can't possibly decide what is good for you!" The student can rebel or passively accept the teacher's judgment.)

Empathetic, active listening can be a helpful response when students bring problems to you. You must reflect back to the student what you hear him or her saying. This reflection is more than a parroting of the student's words; it should capture the emotions, intent, and meaning behind them. Sokolove, Garrett, Sadker, and Sadker (1986, p. 241) have summarized the components of active listening:

1. Blocking out external stimuli.
2. Attending carefully to both the verbal and nonverbal messages.
3. Differentiating between the intellectual and the emotional content of the message.
4. Making inferences regarding the speaker's feelings.

When students realize they really have been heard and not evaluated negatively for what they have said or felt, they feel freer to trust the teacher and to talk more openly. Sometimes the true problem surfaces later in the conversation.

Confrontation and Assertive Discipline

Test Bank items 11.56–11.60, 11.76, 11.77, 11.90, 11.91, 11.99, 11.105– 11.107

Now let's assume a student is doing something that actively interferes with teaching. The teacher decides the student must stop. The problem is the teacher's. Confrontation, not counseling, is required.

"I" Messages. Gordon (1974) recommends sending an **"I" message** in order to intervene and change a student's behavior. Basically, this means telling a student in a straightforward, assertive, and nonjudgmental way what she or he is doing, how it affects you as a teacher, and how you feel about it. The student is then free to change voluntarily, and often does so. Here are two "I" messages:

When you leave your locker open, I sometimes bump into it and hurt myself.

When you all call out answers, I cannot concentrate on each answer, and I feel frustrated.

Assertive Discipline.   Lee and Marlene Canter (1992; Canter, 1989) suggest other approaches for dealing with a teacher-owned problem. They call their method **assertive discipline.** Teachers are assertive when they make their expectations clear and follow through with established consequences. Students then have a straightforward choice: they can follow the rules or accept the consequences. Many teachers are ineffective with students because they are either wishy-washy and passive or hostile and aggressive.

The *passive style* can take several forms. Instead of telling the student directly what to do, the teacher tells, or often asks, the student to *try* or to *think about* the appropriate action. The passive teacher might comment on the problem behavior without actually telling the child what to do differently: "Why are you doing that? Don't you know the rules?" or "Sam, are you disturbing the class?" Or teachers may clearly state what should happen, but never follow through with the established consequences, giving the students "one more chance" every time. Finally, teachers may ignore behavior that should receive a response or may wait too long before responding.

A *hostile response style* involves different mistakes. Teachers may make "you" statements that condemn the student without stating clearly what the student should be doing: "You should be ashamed of the way you're behaving!" or "You never listen!" or "You are acting like a baby!" Teachers may also threaten students angrily but follow through too seldom, perhaps because the threats are too vague—"You'll be very sorry you did that when I get through with you!"—or too severe. For example, a teacher tells a student in a physical education class that he will have to "sit on the bench for *three weeks.*" A few days later the team is short one member and the teacher lets the student play, never returning him to the bench to complete the three-week sentence. Often a teacher who has been passive becomes hostile and explodes when students persist in misbehaving.

In contrast with both the passive and hostile styles, an *assertive response* communicates to the students that you care too much about them and the process of learning to allow inappropriate behavior to persist. Assertive teachers clearly state what they expect. To be most effective, the teachers often look into a student's eyes when speaking, address the student by name, and perhaps touch the student's shoulder. The teacher's voice is calm, firm, and confident. They are not sidetracked by accusations such as "You just don't understand!" or "You don't like me!" Assertive teachers do not get into a debate about the fairness of the rules. They expect changes, not promises or apologies.

Even though many teachers and school administrators have given enthusiastic testimonies about the assertive discipline approach, some educators and psychologists question its effectiveness. The Point/Counterpoint section on page 430 further explores the issue.

Conflict and Negotiations.   If "I" messages or assertive responses fail and a student persists in misbehaving, teacher and student are in a conflict.

In giving an "I message" to a student, it is important to give an "eye message" as well. State your case calmly but directly, and focus on the student.

Activity 11.14: Reflection/Journal Writing. See the *Instructor's Resource Manual* for Self-Analysis. Using **Handout Masters 11.3A** and **11.3B** (on handling conflict) and **Handout Masters 11.4A** and **11.4B** (assertiveness scale), students evaluate their approaches to conflict resolution and their levels of assertiveness.

Activity 11.15: Background: See the *Instructor's Resource Manual* for Student Mediators, excerpts from Talking it out: Students mediate disputes (1989). *Harvard Education Letter, 5*(1), 4–5.

Assertive Discipline Clear, firm, unhostile response style.

POINT ■ COUNTERPOINT   Does Assertive Discipline Work?

L ee Canter, the developer of "assertive discipline," describes his observations of effective teachers:

> I found that, above all, the master teachers were assertive; that is they taught students how to behave. They established clear rules for the classroom, they communicated those rules to the students, and they taught students how to follow them. (1989, p. 58)

Is assertive discipline effective? There are strong opinions both against and in favor of the approach, as you will see. Researchers are skeptical, but some practitioners are committed to assertive discipline.

POINT   Research results do not support assertive discipline.

In an article entitled "What research really shows about Assertive Discipline," Gary Render, Je Neil Padilla, and H. Mark Krank (1989) note that very little unbiased information is available about the effectiveness of this approach. Even though reports claim that 500,000 people have been trained in assertive discipline, Render and his colleagues were able to find only 16 systematic studies of assertive discipline. Their analysis of these studies led them to conclude that:

> The claims made by Canter (1988) ... are simply not supported by the existing and available literature. We would agree that Assertive Discipline

could be helpful in severe cases where students are behaving inappropriately more than 96 percent of the time, as in the study by Mandlebaum et al. (1983). We would also argue that teachers such as the one in that study would benefit from any intervention. However, we can find no evidence that Assertive Discipline is an effective approach deserving schoolwide or districtwide adoption. (p. 72)

A second criticism of assertive discipline is that while it may stop misbehavior in the short run, the long-term effects on students are damaging. Richard Curwin and Allen Mendler (1988) remind teachers that classroom management systems not only manage behavior, they also teach students lessons about their own self-worth, their ability to act responsibly and solve problems, how much control they have over their own lives, and how to use that control. What lessons are taught by systems such as assertive discipline? "If Richard shapes up after the third mark on the chalkboard because the fourth means a call home to an abusive parent, did the program improve his self-control, or did it simply transfer the inner turmoil of a child caught in a dysfunctional family?" (Curwin & Mendler, 1988, p. 68). This concern is echoed by John Covaleskie (1992): "What helps children become moral is not knowledge of the rules, or even obedience to the rules, but discussions about the reasons for acting in certain ways (p. 56).

COUNTERPOINT   Practitioners know that assertive discipline works.

In response to the assertion by Render and his colleagues that research does not support assertive discipline, Sammie McCormack (1989) says, "The decision to implement a program should be based on many factors, in addition to research; from a practitioner's standpoint, Assertive Discipline works" (p. 77). McCormack reports the reactions of more than 8,700 teachers from four school districts and a confederation of schools in Oregon. In these schools, 78 to 99 percent of the teachers saw improvements in student behavior as a consequence of using assertive discipline. McCormack does not explain how these particular samples were selected or if teachers in other schools had different reactions.

In response to Curwin and Mendler's (1988) concerns that classroom management models such as assertive discipline may undermine students' self-worth and sense of responsibility, Lee Canter (1988) notes that several studies have found improvements in both teachers' and students' self-concepts after the introduction of assertive discipline. Further, Canter states that the basis of assertive discipline is giving students choices and that it is through making choices and accepting the consequences that students learn about responsibility.

Several pitfalls now loom. The two individuals become less able to perceive each other's behavior accurately. Research has shown that the angrier you get with another person, the more you see the other as the villain and yourself as an innocent victim. Since you feel the other person is in the wrong, and since he or she feels just as strongly that the conflict is all your fault, very little mutual trust is possible. A cooperative solution to the problem is almost impossible. In fact, by the time the discussion has gone on a few minutes, the original problem is lost in a sea of charges, countercharges, and self-defense (Johnson & Johnson, 1994).

There are three methods of resolving a conflict between teacher and student. One is for the teacher to impose a solution. This may be necessary during an emergency, as when a defiant student refuses to go to the hall to discuss a public outbreak, but it is not a good solution for most conflicts. The second method is for the teacher to give in to the student's demands. You might be convinced by a particularly compelling student argument, but again, this should be used sparingly. It is generally a bad idea to be talked out of a position. Problems arise when either the teacher or the student gives in completely. In each case, someone is the loser and has no impact on the final decision.

Gordon recommends a third approach, which he calls the "no-lose method." Here the needs of both the teacher and the students are taken into account in the solution. No one person is expected to give in completely, and all participants retain respect for themselves and each other. The no-lose method is a six-step, problem-solving strategy:

1. *Define the problem.* What exactly are the behaviors involved? What does each person want? (Use active listening to help students pinpoint the real problem.)

2. *Generate many possible solutions.* Brainstorm, but remember, don't allow any evaluations of ideas yet.

3. *Evaluate each solution.* Any participant may veto any idea. If no solutions are found to be acceptable, brainstorm again.

4. *Make a decision.* Choose one solution through consensus—no voting. In the end, everyone must be satisfied with the solution.

5. *Determine how to implement the solution.* What will be needed? Who will be responsible for each task? What is the timetable?

6. *Evaluate the success of the solution.* After trying the solution for a while, ask, "Are we satisfied with our decision? How well is it working? Should we make some changes?"

So far we have considered the social and procedural aspects of creating positive learning environments. There is another aspect of classroom management that often is overlooked—the space itself.

Teaching Tip: See Makovsky, V. P., Whittenmore, L. G., & Rogers, A. M. (1987). Activities handbook for the teaching of psychology (Vol. 2). Washington, DC: American Psychological Association, for two activities that allow students to assess their own assertiveness and evaluate the assertive behaviors of others. The first activity (Eison, J. Activity 80: Assessing student assertiveness, pp. 294–298) uses an instrument designed by the author as a stimulus for discussion. The second (Karten, S. J. Activity 81: Assertiveness: A simulation in social skills training, pp. 299–300) helps students better understand the meaning of assertive behavior and see how assertiveness training is conducted.

Focus on . . .   **Communication**

- What is meant by "empathetic listening"?
- Distinguish among assertive, passive, and hostile response styles.
- What are the steps in Gordon's problem-solving approach?

Spaces for Learning

To understand the impact of the physical environment on learning in classrooms, you should be familiar with two basic ways of organizing space: interest areas and personal territories. These two ways of organizing space are not mutually exclusive; many teachers use a design that combines the two. Individual students' desks are placed in the center, with interest areas in the back or around the periphery of the room. This allows the flexibility needed for both large- and small-group activities.

Objective 11.12: List the steps involved in designing a classroom arrangement organized by function.

Interest-Area Arrangements   Test Bank items 11.62–11.64, 11.100

The design of interest areas can influence the way the areas are used by students. For example, working with a classroom teacher, Carol Weinstein (1977) was able to make changes in interest areas that helped the teacher meet her objectives of having more girls involved in the science center and having all students experiment more with a variety of manipulative materials. In a second study, changes in a library corner led to more involvement in literature activities throughout the class (Morrow & Weinstein, 1986).

To plan your classroom space, first decide what activities the classroom should accommodate. For example, if you are in a self-contained elementary classroom, you might set up interest areas for reading, arts and crafts, science, and math. If you are teaching one particular subject on the junior or senior high level, you might divide your room into several areas, perhaps for audiovisual activities, small-group instruction, quiet study, and projects. Certain activities pose special spatial requirements. For example, art and science should be near the sink; science should also be near windows if you want to grow plants; small-group instruction should be near the blackboard.

Next, you are ready to draw several possible floor plans. Use graph paper if possible, and draw to scale. As you work, keep in mind these principles:

1. *Note the fixed features* that you must deal with—doors, windows, outlets. You don't want an audiovisual center in a corner without an electrical outlet!

2. *Have easy access to materials and a well-organized place to store them.* Materials must be easy to reach if you want students to use them. Shelves toward the center of the room seem to be more likely to attract attention than those placed in the corners. There should be enough shelves so that materials need not be stacked on top of one another.

3. *Provide students with clean, convenient surfaces on which to use equipment.* The closer these surfaces are to the materials, the better.

4. *Make sure work areas are private and quiet,* and segregate activities. Tables or work areas should not be placed in the middle of traffic lanes, and a person should not have to pass through one area to get to another. Noisy activities should be placed as far as possible from quiet ones. You can increase the feeling of quiet and privacy by placing partitions, such as bookcases or pegboards, between areas or within large areas.

5. *Arrange things so you can see your students and they can see all instructional presentations.* If you plan to put up partitions, make sure they are low enough for you to see over them comfortably. If possible, students should be able to see instruction without moving their chairs or desks.

6. *Avoid dead spaces and "racetracks."* Check to see that you have not placed all the interest areas around the outside of the room, leaving a large dead space in the middle. You also want to avoid placing a few items of furniture right in the middle of this large space, creating a "racetrack" around the furniture.

7. *Provide choices.* Different people have different spatial needs. Some people prefer closed, small spaces in which to work; others may find such places too confining.

8. *Provide flexibility.* At times you may wish to have students work alone, in small groups, or with many others. If you cannot arrange to have spaces for

Transparency: Acetate transparencies T 104 and T 105 present a "before-and-after" picture of an initial and an improved room arrangement for a kindergarten classroom.

all these possibilities at one time, try to ensure that your design is flexible enough so that it can be changed to meet the requirements of new activities.

9. *Give students a place to keep their personal belongings.* This is especially important if students don't have personal desks.

Once you have chosen your room design, try the new arrangement, evaluate it, and make any needed changes. The goal of these suggestions is to remove as much physical friction from the classroom system as possible, so that students can easily select and use materials. The only way to know whether you have reached this goal is to monitor the use of the environment, identify problems, and try again. Incidentally, enlist the aid of your students. They have to live in the room, too, and designing a classroom can be a very challenging educational experience.

Personal Territories

Test Bank items 11.61, 11.65, 11.66, 11.78, 11.92, 11.100

Can the physical setting influence teaching and learning in classrooms organized by territories? Firsthand experience in college tells me that the most interested students sit at the front, and those who yearn for an early escape station themselves as close to the door as possible. In early studies of elementary and secondary classes, Adams and Biddle (1970) found that verbal interaction between teacher and students was concentrated in the center front of the classroom and in a line directly up the center of the room. The data were so dramatic that Adams and Biddle coined the term **action zone** to refer to this area of the room. Later research modified this finding. Even though most rooms have an action zone where participation is greatest, this area is not always "front and center." In some classes it may be on one side, or near a particular learning center (Good, 1983a).

Front-seat location does seem to increase participation for students who are predisposed to speak in class, whereas a seat in the back will make it more difficult to participate and easier to sit back and daydream (Woolfolk & Brooks, 1983). To "spread the action around," Weinstein and Mignano (1993) suggest that teachers move around the room when possible, establish eye contact with students seated far away, and direct comments to students seated at a distance.

Many teachers vary the seating in their classrooms so the same students are not always consigned to the back of the room. Another reason to change seating is to make the arrangement more appropriate for particular objectives and activities. But because too much rearranging can be a waste of time and an invitation to chaos, Musgrave (1975) distinguishes between home-base formations, semipermanent arrangements that are suitable for a wide number of teaching and learning situations, and "special formations," which give needed variety and are suited to a particular lesson.

Figure 11.3 on page 434 shows several **home-base formations** other than rows and columns. Horizontal rows share many of the advantages of row and column arrangements. Both are useful for independent seatwork, presentations, and recitations; they encourage students to focus on the teacher; and they simplify housekeeping. Horizontal rows permit students to work more easily in pairs. This formation is also best for demonstrations, since students are closer to the teacher. However, it is a poor arrangement for large-group interaction.

Objective 11.13: Give examples and appropriate uses of different types of home-base and special formations in classroom arrangements.

Transparency: Acetate transparencies T 99 and T 100, respectively, show seating arrangements in an elementary and in a secondary classroom.

Action Zone Area of a classroom where the greatest amount of interaction takes place.

Home-Base Formations Arrangements for students' desks that allow flexibility in activities.

FIGURE 11.3

SOME HOME-BASE FORMATIONS
These home-base formations work well for whole-class instruction and also allow for some cooperative work.

Horizontal rows

Clusters of four

Circle

Source: G. R. Musgrave, I*ndividualized instruction: Teaching strategies focusing on the learner,* pp. 49, 52, 54. Copyright © 1975. Adapted with permission of Allyn and Bacon.

Connections: You might highlight for your students the connections among the various elements discussed in this chapter and chapter 12: clear objectives, appropriate teaching methods, the physical arrangement of the room, and ease of classroom management.

Objective 11.14: State some general principles a teacher should consider when planning a classroom arrangement.

Clusters of four or circle arrangements are best for student interaction. Circles are especially useful for discussions but still allow for independent seatwork. Clusters permit students to talk, help one another, share materials, and work on group tasks. Both arrangements, however, are poor for whole-group presentations and may make class management more difficult.

Figure 11.4 shows several special formations. The debate arrangement and interest stations are probably familiar. The stack formation, where students sit close together near the focus of attention (the back row may even be standing), should be used only for short periods of time, because it is not comfortable and can lead to discipline problems. On the other hand, the stack can create a feeling of group cohesion and is helpful when the teacher wants students to watch a demonstration, brainstorm on a class problem, or see a small visual aid.

FIGURE 11.4

SOME SPECIAL FORMATIONS

These special seating plans are appropriate when certain activities, such as a debate or demonstration, require room rearrangements.

Source: G. R. Musgrave, *Individualized instruction: Teaching strategies focusing on the learner,* pp. 48, 63, 65. Copyright © 1975. Adapted with permission of Allyn and Bacon.

Although the physical environment can help or hinder the realization of a teacher's goals, it is not all-powerful. Arranging desks in a circle will not guarantee increased participation in a discussion. A cozy reading area will not solve reading problems. Nevertheless, it is important to consider the classroom space as you plan because space can play an important role in creating an optimal learning environment.

Focus on . . . Spaces for Learning

- Distinguish between personal territories and interest-area spatial arrangements.
- What is meant by an "action zone"?
- How can the physical arrangement of the room promote learning?

SUMMARY

The Need for Organization

Classrooms are by nature multidimensional, full of simultaneous activities, fast-paced and immediate, unpredictable, public, and affected by the history of students' and teachers' actions. A manager must juggle all these elements every day.

Productive classroom activity requires students' cooperation. Maintaining cooperation is different for each different age group. Young students are learning how to "go to school" and need to learn the general procedures of school. Older students need to learn the specifics required for working in different subjects. Working with adolescents requires teachers to understand the power of the adolescent peer group.

The goals of effective classroom management are to make ample time for learning; improve the quality of time use by keeping students actively engaged; make sure participation structures are clear, straightforward, and consistently signaled; and encourage student self-management.

Creating Positive Learning Environments

The most effective teachers set rules and establish procedures for handling predictable problems. Procedures should cover administrative tasks, student movement, housekeeping, routines for running lessons, interactions between students and teachers, and interactions among students. Consequences should be established for following and breaking the rules and procedures so that the teacher and the students know what will happen.

Maintaining a Good Environment for Learning

For effective classroom management, it is essential to spend the first days of class teaching basic rules and procedures. Students should be occupied with organized, enjoyable activities and learn to function cooperatively in the group.

Quick, firm, clear, and consistent responses to infractions of the rules characterize effective teachers.

To create a positive environment and prevent problems, teachers must take individual differences into account, maintain student motivation, and reinforce positive behavior.

Successful problem preventers are skilled in four areas described by Kounin: "withitness," overlapping, group focusing, and movement management. When penalties have to be imposed, teachers should impose them calmly and privately.

Special Programs for Classroom Management

There are several special procedures that may be helpful in maintaining positive management, including group consequences, token economies, and contingency contracts. A teacher must use these programs with caution, emphasizing learning and not just "good" behavior.

The Need for Communication

Communication between teacher and student is essential when problems arise. All interactions between people, even silence or neglect, communicate some meaning.

Techniques such as paraphrasing, empathetic listening, determining whether the teacher or the student "owns" the problem, assertive discipline, avoidance of passive and hostile responses, and active problem solving with students help teachers open the lines of positive communication.

Spaces for Learning

There are two basic kinds of spatial organization, territorial (the traditional classroom arrangement) and functional (dividing space into interest or work areas). Flexibility is often the key. Access to materials, convenience, privacy when needed, ease of supervision, and a willingness to reevaluate plans are important considerations in the teacher's choice of physical arrangements.

KEY TERMS

academic learning time, p. 405
action zone, p. 433
allocated time, p. 405
assertive discipline, p. 429
classroom management, p. 405
contingency contract, p. 424
empathetic listening, p. 428
engaged time, p. 405

good behavior game, p. 421
group consequences, p. 421
group focus, p. 418
home-base formations, p. 433
"I" message, p. 428
movement management, p. 418
overlapping, p. 418
paraphrase rule, p. 426

participation structures, p. 407
procedures, p. 409
rules, p. 411
self-management, p. 407
time on task, p. 405
token reinforcement system, p. 422
withitness, p. 416

WHAT WOULD YOU DO?

Preschool and Kindergarten

Your class is larger than ever this year, and it is very difficult to get everyone dressed for play outside. How would you handle the situation?

Elementary and Middle School

It takes your class 15 minutes to settle down each morning and begin work. What would you do?

A few students in your class always seem to be out of step with the rest of the class. They call out when they shouldn't, interrupt others, and get up and walk around when they should be seated and working. What would you do?

Junior High and High School

You tell a student to put away a radio, and she says, "Try and make me!" What would you do?

One of your students who is bright and able has stopped doing homework. What would you do?

Cooperative Learning Activity

With four or five other members in your educational psychology class, plan the rules and procedures for a class you might teach.

Setting Classroom Rules

Do you involve students in setting classroom rules? Why or why not? How do you do it?

Beginning teachers and veteran teachers need to establish clear and reasonable classroom rules. One successful way to develop these rules is to have one or two brainstorming sessions with students at the beginning of the year. With kindergarten youngsters as well as high school seniors, students who are given an opportunity to set classroom standards will feel an ownership of the rules and be more apt to follow them. It is the teacher's task to enforce the rules with consistency.

The teacher who is judged fair by her/his students will receive their respect. Finally, the teacher who has established rules but also responds to students with a smile, a kind word, a helping hand, and genuine concern has achieved the right relationship with her/his students. Students want what we all want, to be cared about. Youngsters will react positively and respectfully to the teacher they believe genuinely cares about their welfare.

Darlene A. Walsh, *Rhode Island 1991 Teacher of the Year*
Greenbush Elementary School, West Warwick, Rhode Island

Can You Be Accepted and Respected?

Many beginning teachers want so much to be accepted by their students that any distinction between being friendly and being friends becomes blurred. Others go to the opposite extreme and interpret advice to be assertive as a warning that they must be grim disciplinarians. What advice would you give new teachers about establishing appropriate relationships with students?

Everyone wants to be received favorably and to be well liked. But students expect an authority figure to be in charge of the class. They need someone they can turn to if they have a problem, someone who can guide them through difficult times. Someone who acts and talks to them as a peer will have trouble being believed and respected as the person in charge. The students will feel they have as much authority and independence as the teacher. A teacher can certainly joke and have fun with students, but he or she needs to know where and when to draw the line—without any arguments—*before* the situation gets out of hand. Be firm, fair, caring, supportive, and understanding, and your students will not only like you, they will respect you.

Ida Pofahl, *Second-Grade Teacher*
Denison Elementary School, Denison, Iowa

There's no substitute for well-organized, enthusiastic teaching. If your students are interested and you are well prepared, behavior is easier to manage. Start with these assumptions: you like to teach; your students want to learn; you have something important to give them. Whatever your game plan for discipline, whether it be names posted, seating changed, extra assignments, removal from class, or after-school detainment, administer it consistently—this means consistency in your expectations and in what you will not tolerate. Carry out your plan with firmness, but without shouting. Do it fairly, without sarcasm or shaming. And from the beginning, try hard to create a climate of optimism and cheerfulness, expecting the very best effort from everyone.

Harriet Chipley, *Elementary Art Teacher*
Lookout Mountain Elementary School, Lookout Mountain, Tennessee

Strategies for Discipline Problems

A critical part of successful classroom management is having a strategy to deal with discipline problems. How do you deal with students who regularly hand in incomplete work or no work at all?

CONSISTENT CONSEQUENCES

The rules of the classroom must be clear and consistently enforced. At the beginning of the year, students discuss at length with me the rules and the consequences of violating them. I remind students of a rule when it is disobeyed and restate the consequences. In my classroom students are allowed to miss only one homework assignment. After that, they must stay after school in detention if their homework is incomplete. I consistently enforce this rule, with no exceptions or excuses. If students receive more than two detentions for incomplete work, I call their parent(s) and discuss the assignments for completeness. I also stress that completing their homework is part of their job and is necessary to pass fifth grade. Because of my consistency I have few problems with managing homework.

I was not as strict in enforcing these rules in my first year of teaching. Consequently, many students did not complete homework. I have also found that a homework chart, signed by me each afternoon and by a parent in the evening, is helpful to some chronic problem students.

Marcia E. Miller, *Fifth-Grade Teacher*
Walker Elementary School, Charlottesville, Virginia

TEACH RESPONSIBILITY

First of all, the teacher should assign work that can realistically be done in the allotted time and is appropriate to the child's independent working level.

To keep track of completed work, I have a Completed Work folder for each reading and math group. As each child finishes an assignment, he/she puts the work in the appropriate folder. Sometime during the day I quickly go through the folders and make a check next to the child's name and assignment on a checksheet that I have attached to the folder. A more responsible group of children will be able to use the checksheet appropriately.

I try to put some time in each day's schedule for "catching up." At this time I allow the students who haven't finished their work to complete it. I am available, if possible, to answer questions and give help. The other children have a special time when they can choose to go to the various centers in the room . . . library, art, listening, writing, and so on. Most of the children soon decide to make good use of their time during the assigned time period so that they can also enjoy some "free time" activities. I try to make this less of a punitive time period; I've chosen to make it much more positive, and it seems to work better. I also find that using older students and other volunteers to help during this time period make it much more profitable for all.

Eileen D. Akers, *First-Grade Teacher*
Jackson-Via Elementary School, Charlottesville, Virginia

Teachers and Teaching

eachers make many decisions affecting the lives of students. These decisions range from how to position desks to how long to spend in silent reading or reviewing homework each day. Even when students are working independently or in small, unsupervised groups, they are influenced by decisions the teacher has made about such things as materials, grouping, and timing. In this chapter we focus on the *teachers*—on their decisions, plans, knowledge, and actions.

We look first at how teachers plan, including some basic definitions of instructional objectives, their function in the classroom, different kinds of written objectives, and some criticisms of written objectives. Next, we consider how to use taxonomies of learning outcomes as a basis for planning.

What else do we know about teachers? Are there particular characteristics that distinguish effective from ineffective teachers? We will examine teacher knowledge, clarity, and enthusiasm. Next we turn to the teaching of basic skills. Research in recent years has identified a cluster of principles that can guide the teaching of basic, explicit information and procedures. We will examine teaching methods such as lecturing, questioning, recitation, and homework, and then look at three models of teacher-direct instruction that incorporate these methods.

By the time you have completed this chapter, you should be able to:

- Describe the functions and levels of teacher planning.
- Write objectives, applying Mager's or Gronlund's approach, for cognitive, affective, and psychomotor learning.
- Describe a number of characteristics that effective teachers seem to share.
- List steps that can ensure clarity in presentation.
- Give examples of lessons based on the principles of direct instruction, on the Hunter model, and on the Missouri Mathematics Program.
- Summarize the criticisms of direct instruction.
- Plan a unit in your subject for a low-ability class.
- Choose one lesson in your own area and explain how you would go about presenting it to the students you will be teaching.

In the first chapter of this book I asked you to list the characteristics of those teachers you found truly outstanding. Review (or redo) that list now. Can you add or delete any characteristics based on what you have learned so far? Consider what you now know about student learning and suggest why the teacher characteristics you listed might promote learning.

Planning Tip: See Chapter-12-At-A-Glance Planning Guide in the Instructor's Section at the front of this book.

Study Guide: The *Study Guide,* sold separately, contains exercises to help students determine if they have mastered each learning objective for this chapter.

Planning Tip: See the separate *Instructor's Resource Manual* for additional activities and resources for teaching this chapter, including Handout Masters. Also see the *Allyn and Bacon Transparencies in Educational Psychology.*

Planning Tip: See the *Test Bank* and *Study Guide* supplements as you plan for evaluation and measurement of student learning.

Planning Tip: For further information about audiovisual, multimedia, and computer-assisted resources for teaching this chapter, see the "Video and Software" section of the *Instructor's Resource Manual.*

Objective 12.1: Describe the role of planning in teaching.

Casebook: See the Teachers' Casebook for practicing teachers' views about the value of lesson planning.

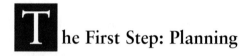

The First Step: Planning

Test Bank items 12.1, 12.2, 12.89

In the past few years educational researchers have become very interested in teachers' planning. They have interviewed teachers about how they plan, asked teachers to "think out loud" while planning or to keep journals describing their plans, and even studied teachers intensively for months at a time. What have they found?

First, planning is a very important step in teaching. In many ways, the plan determines what students will learn, because planning transforms the available time and curriculum materials into activities, assignments, and tasks for students. Class activities create the environment for learning. When a teacher decides to devote 7 hours to language arts and 15 minutes to science in a given week, the students in that class will learn more language than science. In fact, differences as dramatic as this do occur. Nancy Karweit (1989) reported that in one school the time allocated to mathematics ranged from 2 hours and 50 minutes a week in one class to 5 hours and 55 minutes a week in a class down the hall (Clark & Peterson, 1986; Clark & Yinger, 1988; Doyle, 1983).

Second, teachers engage in several levels of planning—by the year, term, unit, week, and day. All the levels must be coordinated. Accomplishing the year's plan requires breaking the work into terms, the terms into units, and the units into weeks and days. Planning done at the beginning of the year is particularly important, because many routines and patterns are established early. For experienced teachers, unit planning seems to be the most important level, followed by weekly and then daily planning (Clark & Peterson, 1986; Clark & Yinger, 1988).

Third, plans reduce—but do not eliminate—uncertainty in teaching. Even the best plans cannot (and should not) control everything that happens in class. There is some evidence that when teachers "overplan"—fill every minute and stick to the plan no matter what—their students do not learn as much as students whose teachers are flexible (Shavelson, 1987). Chris Clark (1983) suggests that beginning teachers should think of their plans as "flexible frameworks for action, as devices for getting started in the right direction, as something to depart from or elaborate on, rather than as rigid scripts" (p. 13).

Finally, there is no one model for effective planning. For experienced teachers, planning is a creative problem-solving process (Shavelson, 1987). Experienced teachers know how to accomplish many lessons and segments of lessons. They know what to expect and how to proceed, so they don't necessarily continue to follow the detailed lesson-planning models they learned during their teacher-preparation programs. But many experienced teachers think it was helpful to learn this detailed system as a foundation (Clark & Peterson, 1986). We will examine one approach to planning that focuses on determining objectives.

Research: Clark, C. M., & Yinger, R. J. (1987). Teacher planning. In D. Berliner & B. Rosenshine (Eds.), *Talks to teachers* (pp. 342–365). New York: Random House.

Objectives for Learning

Test Bank items 12.3–12.13, 12.77, 12.90–12.92, 12.116, 12.117, 12.119–12.121

The items listed in the overview at the beginning of this chapter are examples of learning objectives. Although there are many different approaches to writing objectives, each assumes that the first step in teaching is to decide what changes should take place in the learner—what is the goal of teaching. This leads us to a general definition of an **instructional objective**: it is a clear and unambiguous description of your educational intentions for your students.

Kinds of Objectives

At a very general, abstract level are the grand goals society may have for graduates of public schools, such as increased intellectual development and effective citizenship. But very general goals become meaningless as potential guidelines for instruction. On the other hand, objectives that are too specific may teach poor study habits by focusing the students' attention on specific facts and encouraging them to skip anything that is not mentioned in the objective (TenBrink, 1986).

Most psychologists and educators agree that we need something between grand generalities and specific item-by-item instructions for each student. But here the agreement ends. Objectives written by people with behavioral views focus on observable and measurable changes in the learner. **Behavioral objectives** use terms such as *list, define, add,* or *calculate*. Objectives written by cognitivists, on the other hand, emphasize internal changes. Their objectives are more likely to include words such as *understand, recognize, create,* or *apply*. Not surprisingly, **cognitive objectives** tend to be more general and less clearly measurable than behavioral objectives. They also tend to be less restricting. Let's look at one well-developed method of writing specific objectives.

Mager: Start with the Specific.   Robert Mager has developed a very influential system for writing instructional objectives. Mager's idea is that objectives ought to describe what students will be doing when demonstrating their achievement and how you will know they are doing it (Mager, 1975). Mager's objectives are generally regarded as behavioral.

According to Mager, a good objective has three parts. First, it describes the intended student behavior—what must the student do? Second, it lists the con-

Objective 12.2: Define "instructional objectives" and list the benefits of communicating objectives to students.

Objective 12.3: Compare and contrast behavioral and cognitive objectives. Give an example of each.

Background: Cuban, L. (1990). Four stories about national goals for American education. *Phi Delta Kappan, 72*(4), 264–314. *Focus Questions:* What should be the goals of American education? Should we have a national agenda that shapes our instructional objectives?

Instructional Objective Clear statement of what students are intended to learn through instruction.

Behavioral Objectives Instructional objectives stated in terms of observable behaviors.

Cognitive Objectives Instructional objectives stated in terms of higher-level thinking operations.

Research: Brown, D. S. (1988). Twelve middle-school teachers' planning. *Elementary School Journal*, 89, 69—88.

Meticulous case studies of 12 middle-school teachers' instructional yearly, unit, weekly, and daily planning showed that the teachers used a pattern of "nested" decision making in instructional planning, but (unlike elementary teachers) did not engage in term planning. Yinger's three-stage process model provides a better description of yearly, unit, and weekly planning than the "rational" model, because teachers focused on activities rather than on objectives. At the daily level, Leinhardt's agenda-formulation model provides a closer fit than the rational model. Teachers made planning decisions on the basis of what had worked for them in the past, the school schedule, the availability of instructional materials, and the interests and abilities of students.

Study Guide: Concept Map. See the *Study Guide* for the Concept Map "Learning Objectives." This map is also presented as **Handout Master 12.6** in the *Instructor's Resource Manual.*

Example: For examples of the need to operationalize instructional objectives, see Jenson, W. R., Sloane, H. N., & Young, K. R. (1988). *Applied behavior analysis in education: A structured teaching approach.* Englewood Cliffs, NJ: Prentice-Hall, p. 283.

Objective 12.4: Identify the three components of a behavioral objective and write several examples in different academic areas.

FIGURE 12.1

MAGER'S THREE-PART SYSTEM

Robert Mager believes that a good learning objective has three parts: the student behavior, the conditions under which the behavior will be performed, and the criteria for judging a performance.

Part	Central Question	Example
Student behavior	Do what?	Mark statements with an *F* for fact or an *O* for opinion
Conditions of performance	Under what conditions?	Given an article from a newspaper
Performance criteria	How well?	75% of the statements are correctly marked

Source: R. F. Mager, *Preparing instructional objectives*, 1975, by Fearon, Belmont, CA. Reprinted by permission of David S. Lake Publishers.

---

ditions under which the behavior will occur—how will this behavior be recognized or tested? Third, it gives the criteria for acceptable performance on the test. Figure 12.1 shows how the system works. This system, with its emphasis on final behavior, requires a very explicit statement. Mager contends that such an effort is worthwhile. He believes that often students can teach themselves if they are given well-stated objectives.

Gronlund: Start with the General. Norman Gronlund (1993) offers a different approach. He believes that an objective should be stated first in general terms (*understand, solve, appreciate,* etc.). Then the teacher should clarify by listing a few sample behaviors that would provide evidence that the student has attained the objective. Gronlund's system is often used for writing cognitive objectives.

Look at the example in Table 12.1, taken from Cangelosi (1990). The goal here really is problem solving. The teacher does not want the student to stop with discriminating, stating, computing, and so on. Instead, the teacher looks at performance on these sample tasks to decide if the student can solve real-life problems. The teacher could just as well have chosen six different tasks to indicate ability to solve problems.

Gronlund's emphasis on specific objectives as samples of more general student ability is important. A teacher could never list all the behaviors that might be involved in solving problems in the subject area, but stating an initial, general objective makes it clear that the ability to solve problems is the purpose.

TABLE 12.1   Gronlund's Combined Method for Creating Objectives

General Objective

For sixth-grade mathematics: Student can efficiently solve real-life problems that require finding sizes of surface areas.

Specific Examples

1. Discriminates between the surface area of a figure and other quantitative characteristics of that figure (e.g., height and volume).
2. States the formula for the area of a rectangle.
3. Given the dimensions of a rectangle, computes its area.
4. Given the dimensions of a right triangle, computes its area.
5. Given the dimensions of a right cylinder, computes its surface area.
6. When confronted with a real-life problem, determines whether computing the area of a surface will help solve that problem.

Source: Designing Tests for Evaluating Student Achievement by James S. Cangelosi, p. 6. Copyright © 1990 by Longman Publishing Group. Adapted with permission.

The most recent research on instructional objectives tends to favor approaches similar to Gronlund's. It seems reasonable to state a few central objectives in general terms and clarify them with samples of specific behaviors, as in Table 12.1 (Hamilton, 1985; Popham, 1993).

Are Objectives Useful?   Test Bank items 12.14, 12.15, 12.116, 12.120

Having objectives seems to improve achievement, but only under certain conditions. First, objectives can promote learning with loosely organized and less-structured activities such as lectures, films, and research projects. With very structured materials such as programmed instruction, objectives seem less important (Tobias & Duchastel, 1974). Second, if the importance of some information is not clear from the learning materials and activities themselves, instructional objectives will probably help focus students' attention and thus increase achievement (Duchastel, 1979). But when the task involves simply getting the gist of the passage or transferring the information to a new situation, objectives are not as effective. In these situations, it is better to use questions that focus on meaning, inserting the questions right before the passage to be read (Hamilton, 1985).

Criticisms of Objectives.   Not all educators believe writing objectives is valuable. According to some critics, because trivial, short-term goals are easier to specify than higher-level, more relevant goals, instructional objectives are likely to be trivial and irrelevant. Many critics feel that the use of instructional objectives has a potential effect of spoon-feeding students. If only low-level abilities are specified as outcomes, and if tests are merely a collection of instructional objectives turned into questions, spoon-feeding is indeed likely. The

Transparency: Acetate transparency T 94, "Mager's Three-Part Objectives," provides an in-class test on writing learning objectives properly according to Mager's model. The students write "yes" if all three parts are present in an objective; otherwise they identify the missing part or parts by letter, as follows: A = behavior; B = conditions of performance; C = performance criteria. Suggested answers: 1. C; 2. B; 3. Yes; 4. Yes; 5. C; 6. B; 7. Yes.

Transparency: Acetate transparency T 96 provides "A Selected List of Verbs for Writing Cognitive Objectives." Ask students to write objectives based on this list.

Objective 12.5: Integrate Mager's and Gronlund's methods for writing objectives into a useful approach.

Transparency: Acetate transparency T 97 provides five examples of "Poorly Written Objectives" for your students to analyze in class.

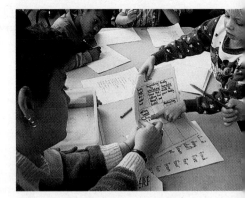

Objectives can help focus students' attention on what is important about learning materials, especially if it is not clear from the materials themselves.

Discussion: What is your students' reaction to this statement: Behavioral objectives often may be appropriate for training (an end in itself) but seldom are appropriate for education (which is concerned with understanding).

Objective 12.6: Evaluate two criticisms of the use of instructional objectives.

Casebook: See the Teachers' Casebook for thoughts on telling students a teacher's specific objectives and performance standards.

Cooperative Learning: Ask students: "Do you think behavioral objectives are really objectives in themselves, or are they a means to an end?" Have students work in two groups to develop arguments with examples for these two views. Students might present their arguments in the form of dialogues or role playing.

students' opportunities to question and explore may well be limited. In addition, having the same objectives for all students implies that everyone starts with the same background and is heading toward the same destination. This is seldom the case.

In Defense of Objectives.   Learning objectives do not have to be limiting. Consider this objective, prepared for a relatively high-level secondary course in history:

> In class, without access to notes, given three presidential elections between 1900 and 1944, write a 200-word essay describing how domestic policy might have changed if the defeated presidential candidate had been elected.

For the test the teacher selects the elections of 1900, 1912, and 1940. Since these particular years were not specified in the objective, students must know a number of facts. What president was chosen in each election year between 1900 and 1944? Who were their opponents? What was the domestic policy advocated by each candidate? What were key events during each president's term in office? Besides understanding these facts and concepts, the students would have to be able to make inferences, give evidence to support hypotheses, and think divergently (come up with many possible right answers). This is hardly spoon-feeding!

Even if a teacher never specifies objectives, students will become aware of them when the tests or assignments are graded. If, for example, the top grades go to students who are best at memorizing facts, the students will realize that the objective was to memorize facts. If, on the other hand, the objectives are supplied in advance—and especially if students have a role in designing objectives—both students and teacher will know what the criteria are. In thinking about objectives, both teachers and students must consider what is important, what is worth learning. The Guidelines should help you whether you decide to make thorough use of objectives or just to prepare them for certain assignments.

Guidelines

Developing Instructional Objectives

Avoid "word magic"—phrases that sound noble and important but say very little.
Examples
1. Keep the focus on specific changes that will take place in the students' knowledge of skills.
2. Ask students to explain the meaning of the objectives. If they can't give specific examples of what you mean, the objectives are not communicating your intentions to your students.

Suit the activities to the objectives.
Examples
1. If the goal is the memorization of vocabulary, give the students memory aids and practice exercises.
2. If the goal is the ability to develop well-thought-out positions, consider position papers, debates, projects, or mock trials.
3. If you want students to become better writers, give many opportunities for writing and rewriting.

Make sure your tests are related to your objectives.

Examples

1. Write objectives and rough drafts for tests at the same time.
2. Weight the tests according to the importance of the various objectives and the time spent on each.

Taxonomies

Test Bank items 12.16–12.38, 12.78, 12.79, 12.93, 12.94, 12.118

Several decades ago, as interest in defining educational objectives was increasing, a group of experts in educational evaluation led by Benjamin Bloom studied the idea of defining objectives systematically. They developed a **taxonomy,** or classification system, of educational objectives. Objectives were divided into three domains: cognitive, affective, and psychomotor. A handbook describing the objectives in each area was eventually published. In real life, of course, behaviors from these three domains occur simultaneously. While students are writing (psychomotor), they are also remembering or reasoning (cognitive), and they are likely to have some emotional response to the task as well (affective).

The Cognitive Domain.   Six basic objectives are listed in Bloom's taxonomy of the thinking or **cognitive domain** (Bloom, Engelhart, Frost, Hill, & Krathwohl, 1956):

1. *Knowledge:* Remembering or recognizing something without necessarily understanding, using, or changing it.

2. *Comprehension:* Understanding the material being communicated without necessarily relating it to anything else.

3. *Application:* Using a general concept to solve a particular problem.

4. *Analysis:* Breaking something down into its parts.

5. *Synthesis:* Creating something new by combining different ideas.

6. *Evaluation:* Judging the value of materials or methods as they might be applied in a particular situation.

It is common in education to consider these objectives as a hierarchy, each skill building on those below, but this is not entirely accurate (Seddon, 1978). Some subjects, such as mathematics, do not fit this structure very well (Pring, 1971). Still, you will hear many references to *lower-level* and *higher-level objectives,* with knowledge and comprehension considered lower level and the other categories considered higher level. As a rough way of thinking about objectives, this can be helpful.

Consider how Bloom's taxonomy might suggest objectives for a course. Figure 12.1 gave one example of a specific objective at the *analysis* level in a social studies class—distinguishing between fact and opinion in news stories. At the *synthesis* level, an objective for the class could be written this way:

> Given a list of three facts, write a two-paragraph news story taking a position on an issue and documenting the position with the facts.

Objective 12.7: Contrast objectives in the cognitive, affective, and psychomotor domains in their definitions, uses, and assessment.

Handout: Distribute Handout Master 12.5, a detailed analysis of "Objectives in the Cognitive Domain."

Background: See the *Instructor's Resource Manual* for Gagne's Outcomes of Learning, a description of Robert Gagne's five possible outcomes of learning.

Taxonomy Classification system.

Cognitive Domain In Bloom's taxonomy, memory and reasoning objectives.

Affective Domain Emotional objectives.

At the evaluation level, the objective might be written like this:

Given two articles that present contradictory views of a recent event, decide which article gives the fairer presentation and justify your choice.

The taxonomy of objectives can also be helpful in planning evaluation, since different types of test items are appropriate for objectives at the various levels. Gronlund (1993) suggests that knowledge objectives can best be measured by true-false, short-answer, matching, or multiple-choice tests. Such tests will also work with the comprehension, application, and analysis levels of the taxonomy. For measuring synthesis and evaluation objectives, however, essays, reports, projects, and portfolios are more appropriate. Essay tests will also work at the middle levels of the taxonomy.

The Affective Domain. The objectives in the taxonomy of the **affective domain,** or domain of emotional response, run from least committed to most committed (Krathwohl, Bloom, & Masia, 1956). At the lowest level, a student would simply pay attention to a certain idea. At the highest level, the student would adopt an idea or a value and act consistently with that idea. There are five basic objectives in the affective domain.

1. *Receiving:* Being aware of or attending to something in the environment. This is the I'll-listen-to-the-concert-but-I-won't-promise-to-like-it level.

2. *Responding:* Showing some new behavior as a result of experience. At this level a person might applaud after the concert or hum some of the music the next day.

3. *Valuing:* Showing some definite involvement or commitment. At this point a person might choose to go to a concert instead of a film.

4. *Organization:* Integrating a new value into one's general set of values, giving it some ranking among one's general priorities. This is the level at which a person would begin to make long-range commitments to concert attendance.

5. *Characterization by value:* Acting consistently with the new value. At this highest level, a person would be firmly committed to a love of music and demonstrate it openly and consistently.

Like the basic objectives in the cognitive domain, these five objectives are very general. To write specific learning objectives, you must state what students will actually be doing when they are receiving, responding, valuing, and so on. For example, an objective for a nutrition class at the valuing level (showing involvement or commitment) might be stated:

After completing the unit on food contents and labeling, at least 50 percent of the class will commit to the junk-food boycott project by giving up candy for a month.

How can the teacher in the nutrition example be sure that students have given up candy in support of a junk-food boycott? The best method may be to ask them to report anonymously on their candy consumption; if students have to sign their names to their responses, the process may counteract the desire to reach another affective goal, honesty. Also, if students are graded on their success in boycotting candy, this process might really encourage the students to give false reports. In most cases, it is best not to grade the assessment of affective goals.

The Psychomotor Domain.   Until recently, the **psychomotor domain,** or realm of physical ability objectives, has been mostly overlooked by teachers not directly involved with physical education. There are several taxonomies in this domain (e.g., Harrow, 1972; Simpson, 1972). These taxonomies generally move from basic perceptions and reflex actions to skilled, creative movements. James Cangelosi (1990) provides a useful way to think about objectives in the psychomotor domain as either voluntary muscle capabilities that require endurance, strength, flexibility, agility, or speed; or the ability to perform a specific skill.

Objectives in the psychomotor domain should be of interest to a wide range of educators, including those in fine arts, vocational-technical education, and special education. Many other subjects, such as chemistry, physics, and biology, also require specialized movements and well-developed hand and eye coordination. Using lab equipment, the "mouse" on a computer, or art materials means learning new physical skills. Here are two psychomotor objectives:

> Four minutes after completing a one-mile run in eight minutes or under, your heart rate will be below 120.

> Without referring to notes or diagrams, assemble the appropriate laboratory apparatus to distill _____.

Learning in the psychomotor area means developing a particular performance ability. How do you assess a student's performance? The obvious answer is to ask the student to demonstrate the skill and then observe the student's proficiency. In some cases, the performance of the skill results in a product, so assessment of the product can be substituted for observation of the actual performance. An art student learning to use the potter's wheel, for example, should be able to produce a pot that is symmetrical, stands by itself, and doesn't crack when fired.

*P*sychomotor objectives, from general abilities to specific skills, are of interest to a wide range of educators, not just those in physical education departments.

Objective 12.8: Outline the taxonomies in the cognitive, affective, and psychomotor domains. Be able to write an objective at each level in each domain.

Psychomotor Domain   Physical ability objectives.

> **TABLE 12.2   Checklist to Evaluate Student's Performance of a Two-Arm Press**

The student, stationed in front of a barbell with only a light weight that would offer little resistance, is directed to demonstrate one two-arm press.

Scoring key: (11 points possible) +1 for each blank checked on the following form:

_____ feet properly positioned under the bar throughout the entire lift

_____ proper grip and hand spread

_____ back straight throughout

_____ head facing forward throughout

_____ clean initiated with knees flexed

_____ clean initiated with elbows extended

_____ clean properly executed

_____ pauses with bar just above the chest

_____ executes press properly

_____ returns bar to position just above chest and pauses

_____ gently returns bar to floor, flexing knees on the way down

Source: Designing Tests for Evaluating Student Achievement by James S. Cangelosi, p. 125. Copyright © 1990 by Longman Publishing Group. Adapted with permission.

Focus on . . .   **Learning Objectives**

- What are the three parts of Robert Mager's learning objectives?
- How does Gronlund's approach to creating objectives differ from Mager's?
- Specify an objective in the cognitive, affective, and psychomotor domains for a subject you will teach.

When students are actually demonstrating skills or performing, you need a checklist or rating scale to help you focus on the important aspects of the skill being evaluated. A checklist usually gives the measurable dimensions of performance, along with a series of blank spaces for judgments. Table 12.2 provides an example. A rating scale generally follows the same plan but has a numerical scale to rate each aspect of performance.

Now that you have a fairly good plan for *what* you want to teach, the next question is, "*How* should I teach it?"

How to Teach: Searching for the Keys to Success

Discussion: Ask students: "What are some ways that teachers you have had made a difference to you?"

The search for the secret of effective teaching is not a new one. However, until recently it hasn't been very successful. In the 1960s and 1970s, several widely publicized studies concluded that teachers have very little impact on student learning (Coleman, Campbell, Wood, Weinfeld, & York, 1966; Jencks et al., 1972). Based on these reports, it seemed that factors such as social class and student ability were the main influences on learning. Many people wondered . . .

Do Teachers Make a Difference?   Test Bank item 12.39

A closer look at the Coleman and Jencks reports reveals many problems in the design of this research (Good, 1983a & b). The studies did not try to relate what actually happened in individual classrooms to the achievement of students, nor did they examine the effects of individual teachers within each school. Because the research was purely correlational, we have no basis for inferring any causal relationships. So the studies did not answer the basic question: Do individual teachers make a difference in the day-to-day learning of their students?

Partly in response to the Coleman and Jencks reports, many researchers set out to answer this question. Most directed their attention to learning objectives that are measured using standardized tests. Often the focus was basics skills. The next part of this chapter describes what we have learned from this explosion of research on teachers and teaching.

Methods for Studying Effective Teaching   Test Bank item 12.95

How would you go about identifying the keys to effective teaching? You might ask students, principals, college professors of education, or experienced teachers to list the characteristics of good teachers. Or you could do intensive case studies of a few classrooms over a long period. You might observe classrooms, rate different teachers on certain characteristics, and then see which characteristics were associated with teachers whose students either achieved the most or were the most motivated to learn. (To do this, of course, you would have to decide how to assess achievement and motivation.) You could identify teachers whose students, year after year, learned more than students working with other teachers; then you could watch the more successful teachers, and note what they do. You might also train teachers to apply several different strategies to teach the same lesson and then determine which strategy led to the greatest student learning. You could videotape teachers, then ask them to view the tapes and report what they were thinking about as they taught and what influenced their decisions while teaching. You might study transcripts of classroom dialogue to learn what helped students understand.

All these approaches and more have been used to investigate effective teaching. Often researchers conduct a series of studies by making careful observations and identifying relationships between teaching and learning. The researchers then use these relationships as the basis for developing teaching approaches and testing these approaches in experimental studies. Let's examine some of the specific knowledge about effective teaching gained from these projects.

 haracteristics of Effective Teachers

Some of the earliest research on effective teaching focused on the personal qualities of the teachers themselves. Researchers thought that the key to success in teaching must lie in the characteristics of teachers (Medley, 1979). Although this assumption proved incorrect—or at least incomplete—it did teach us some lessons about three teacher characteristics: knowledge, clarity, and warmth.

Research: For a complete summary of the research on teaching by two experts in the field, see Porter, A., & Brophy, J. (1988). Synthesis of research on good teaching: Insights from the work of the Institute for Research on Teaching. *Educational Leadership, 45*(8), 74–85. The article depicts effective teachers as semi-autonomous professionals who:

- are clear about their instructional goals

- are knowledgeable about their content and the strategies for teaching it

- communicate to their students what is expected of them and why

- make expert use of existing instructional materials

- are knowledgeable about their students, adapting instruction to their needs

- teach students metacognitive strategies

- address higher- as well as lower-level cognitive objectives

- offer regular appropriate feedback

- integrate their instruction with that in other subject areas; accept responsibility for student outcomes

- are thoughtful and reflective about their practice

Objective 12.9: Name the characteristics of effective teachers and explain the process through which each characteristic affects student learning.

Teachers' Knowledge

Test Bank items 12.40–12.43, 12.96, 12.98, 12.99, 12.119

Do teachers who know more about their subject have a more positive impact on their students? When we look at teachers' knowledge of facts and concepts, as measured by test scores and college grades, the relationship to student learning is unclear and may be indirect. Teachers who know more facts about their subject do not necessarily have students who learn more. But teachers who know more may make clearer presentations and recognize student difficulties more readily. They are ready for any student questions and do not have to be evasive or vague in their answers. So knowledge is necessary but not sufficient for effective teaching.

Knowing about Knowing.   What else is needed? Today researchers are studying other aspects of teachers' knowledge. One conclusion is that, in addition to knowing the important facts, concepts, and procedures in their academic discipline, teachers must know how to transform their knowledge into curriculum—into lessons, explanations, assignments, games, tests, questions, examples, demonstrations, and all the other activities of teaching (Wilson, Shulman, & Richert, 1987). Good teachers can make facts, procedures, and concepts understandable for students, but to do so, the teachers must know more about their subject than facts, procedures, and concepts. Charles Anderson (1989) suggests that they must also know the structure, function, and development of the material they teach. He gives three examples of beginning teachers who lack this knowledge:

1. Ann has been very successful in her teacher education program, making grades of 4.0 in every course before student teaching. Now Ann, a biology major, is student teaching in a middle school life science class. I visit her for the first time as her university supervisor.

   Today Ann is teaching about atoms, molecules, elements, and compounds, and she does not look like a 4.0 student. Her teaching is uninspired and didactic, her way of distinguishing molecules from compounds is not quite right, and some of her examples are fictitious (He^2, Zn^2).

   When I talk to Ann after the lesson she acknowledges her disappointment in her performance and talks about how difficult she finds it to come up with good examples. When she asks for help I ask a question back: How are you going to use these concepts [molecules, atoms, elements, etc.] later in the year? Ann says that she doesn't know; it's just something that you have to teach. Her mentor teacher, however, quickly names several topics where these concepts play an important role: photosynthesis, digestion, respiration, ecological matter cycling. As he does this he mentions examples of elements and compounds that the middle school students will need to be familiar with. (Anderson, 1989, p. 94)

2. A group of elementary student teachers is meeting to discuss mathematics teaching. The discussion is led by Deborah Ball, who challenges them to develop a word problem that can be solved with the expression, "1-3/4 divided by 1/2." Only one student suggests an appropriate example: "How many half cakes are in 1-3/4 cakes?" Most students suggest problems that go through a variety of contortions to arrive at 3-1/2, which they all know to be the correct answer. The following is typical: "I buy 1-3/4 pizzas that are split into four slices each and divide them equally with my friend. How many slices does each of us get?" (Note that this problem actually involves division by two rather than division by 1/2. The logic of the problem is: 1-3/4 = 7/4 divided by 2 = 3-1/2 fourths.) (Anderson, 1989, p. 95)

Background: Stoddart, T., Connell, M, Stofflett, R., & Peck, D. (1993). Reconstructing elementary teacher candidates' understanding of mathematics and science content. *Teaching and Teacher Education, 9,* 229–241.

Background: For a complete discussion of this teacher's content knowledge, see Anderson, C. W. (1989). The role of education in the academic disciplines in teacher education. In A. Woolfolk (Ed.), *Research perspectives on the graduate preparation of teachers* (pp. 88–107). Englewood Cliffs, NJ: Prentice-Hall.

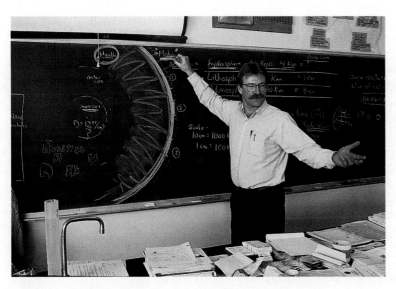

In addition to knowing the important facts, concepts, and procedures in their academic discipline, teachers must know how to transform their knowledge into effective examples, explanations, illustrations, and activities.

3. Several secondary biology majors are discussing their plans for teaching one-week units. Most of the unit plans share a common problem: They include far too much content for the time available. One student, for example, plans to cover the following topics in five-day units on fishes: evolution of fishes, classes of fishes (named in Latin) and their characteristics, adaptation of fishes to their environment, structure, and function of fish body systems (down to the level of parts of the brain). The methods course instructors immediately begin suggesting ways to reduce and simplify the content that she plans to teach. She demurs, "But it's all interconnected!" (Anderson, 1989, p. 96)

Problems Transforming Knowledge.   What is wrong here? Ann had trouble finding good examples and resorted to making up fictitious molecules because she did not know the *structure* of the material she was teaching. She did not understand the relationships among the different concepts, ideas, procedures, and areas of application in biology. Like most college students, she probably had studied and been tested on units of work in isolation without being encouraged to identify relationships across different courses in biology or even across different chapters in the same textbook. Consequently, she had trouble seeing relationships across units in her own class, from the unit on "molecules" to the unit on "digestion," for example. In the language of information processing, she did not have well-organized, richly elaborated, deeply processed knowledge.

The second example (develop a problem that can be solved with the expression "1-3/4 divided by 1/2") highlights another necessary kind of knowledge. Teachers must know the *function* of the information they teach. What is it used for? What problems will it solve? How will students encounter the need for that information in other classes or in everyday life? Too often we teach students a fact or procedure without teaching them how, why, or when or when not to use it.

Objective 12.10: Give examples of ways in which teachers must transform information as they create a curriculum of study.

Connections: Relate the teacher's need to understand the structure of information to the concept of schema and the organization of information in long-term memory discussed in chapter 7.

The problem in the final example, of teaching too much about fishes, could be solved if the teacher had a better understanding of *how knowledge develops* in individuals. How do students move from a simple to a highly developed understanding of a particular concept or idea? How can a teacher simplify complicated ideas without reducing them to definitions or steps to be memorized?

Educational psychology cannot give you the structure, function, or development of the subjects you will teach. Unfortunately, few of your college courses in specific subject areas will provide this kind of knowledge either. A recent study by Stoddart, Connell, Stofflett, and Peck, (1993) found that many prospective elementary teachers at a large university were seriously deficient in their understanding of mathematical and scientific content, even though most were in the top quartile of their college class. Just taking more advanced classes is not enough. I tell my students to construct these understandings for themselves and press their professors for explanations of the structure, function, and development of the material they are presenting. Teaching experience, especially tutoring slower students, can help as well.

Organization and Clarity

Test Bank items 12.44–12.46, 12.89, 12.97, 12.98, 12.100, 12.119

Students discussing a teacher are likely to say things like, "Oh, she can really explain," "He's so disorganized," or "Those two! They're impossible to follow!" When Barak Rosenshine and Norma Furst (1973) reviewed about fifty studies of teaching, they concluded that clarity was the most promising teacher behavior for future research on effective teaching. Recent studies confirm the importance of clarity. Teachers who provide clear presentations and explanations tend to have students who learn more and who rate their teachers more positively (Hines, Cruickshank, & Kennedy, 1982, 1985; Land, 1987).

What does it mean to be "clear"? Clear teachers are precise and specific, not vague. They avoid words and phrases that are ambiguous (somewhere, someplace); approximate or indeterminate (fairly, nearly, maybe, often, in general); or "bluffing" (as anyone can see, so to speak, you know). Teachers with more knowledge of the subject tend to be less vague in their explanations to the class. The less vague the teacher, the more the students learn (Land, 1987). Lack of knowledge may cause teachers to be vague—or to be anxious and nervous, which also causes them to be vague. Either way, students get lost.

Planning for Clarity. Recent research offers guidelines for greater clarity in teaching (Berliner, 1987; Evertson et al., 1994; Hines, Cruickshank, & Kennedy, 1982, 1985). When planning a lesson, try to anticipate the problems your students will have with the material. Turn to teachers' manuals and experienced teachers for help with this. You might also do the written parts of the lesson yourself to identify potential problems. Have definitions ready for new terms, and prepare several relevant examples for concepts. Think of analogies that will make ideas easier to understand. Organize the lesson in a logical sequence; include checkpoints that incorporate oral or written questions or problems to make sure the students are following the explanations.

Plan a clear introduction to the lesson. Tell students what they will be learning and how they could approach it. Often teachers are vague about both the "what" and the "how." For example, in a study by Duffy, Roehler, Meloth,

Discussion: Some teachers are very knowledgeable about their subject matter. In what ways is their knowledge likely to affect their teaching? Does teacher training in college allow students to become experts in their field?

Objective 12.11: Distinguish between lessons that are taught with clarity and those that are not.

Background: Cruickshank, D. R. (1985). Applying research on teacher clarity. *Educational Leadership*, 36(2), 44–48.

"AND THEN, OF COURSE, THERE'S THE POSSIBILITY OF BEING JUST THE SLIGHTEST BIT TOO ORGANIZED."

(Glen Dines—Phi Delta Kappan)

and Vavrus (1986), an ineffective reading teacher began her lesson on using context in reading by saying:

> Today we are going to learn about context. This skill will help you in your reading. (p. 206)

This is a vague and general statement of "what" the students will learn. An effective teacher in the same study began her lesson with an explicit, precise description:

> At the end of today's lesson, you will be able to use the other words in a sentence to figure out the meaning of an unknown word. The skill is one that you use when you come to a word that you don't know and you have to figure out what the word means. (p. 206)

Being precise about "how" to do the work is even harder. One study found that teachers seldom, if ever, explain the cognitive processes they want their students to practice in a seatwork activity. Bright students figure out the right process, but slower students often guess or give up. For example, an *ineffective* teacher might introduce a seatwork activity on words with prefixes by saying, "Here are some words with prefixes. Write the meaning of each in the blanks." An *effective* teacher, on the other hand, would demonstrate how to divide the words into a prefix and a root; how to determine the meaning of the root and the prefix; and how to put the two meanings together to make sense of the whole word (Berliner, 1987).

Clarity during the Lesson.   Make clear connections between facts or concepts by using **explanatory links** such as *because, if . . . then,* or *therefore.* For example, when a teacher says, "The Northern economy was based on manufacturing and the North had an advantage in the Civil War," students are given two facts, but no connection between them. If there is a relationship between the two ideas, it should be indicated with an explanatory link as in, "The North had an advantage in the Civil War *because* its economy was based on manufacturing." Explanatory links tie ideas together and make them easier to learn (Berliner, 1987). Explanatory links are also helpful in labeling visual material such as graphs, concept maps, or illustrations.

In general, stick with your plan and do not digress. Signal transitions from one major topic to another with phrases such as *"The next area . . . ," "Now we will turn to . . ,"* or *"The second step is . . ."* You might help students follow the lesson by outlining topics, or listing key points on the board or on an overhead projector. Continually monitor the group to see if everyone is following the lesson. Look for confident nods or puzzled stares. You should be able to tell if most students are keeping up.

Throughout the lesson, choose words that are familiar to the students. Define new terms and relate them to what the students already know. Be precise. Avoid vague words and ambiguous phrases: steer clear of "the somes": *something, someone, sometime, somehow;* "the not verys": *not very much, not very well, not very hard, not very often;* and other unspecific fillers, such as *most, not all, sort of, and so on, of course, as you know, I guess, in fact,* or *whatever,* and *more or less.* Use specific (and, if possible, colorful) names instead of *it, them,* and *thing.* Also, refrain from using pet phrases such as *you know, like,* and *Okay?* Another idea is to record a lesson on tape to check yourself for clarity.

Discussion: Would a person who tends to be disorganized be more suitable as an elementary or as a secondary school teacher? Or should he or she choose another profession?

Discussion: Ask students to name some strategies they have already learned that contribute to lesson organization and clarity of presentation.

Explanatory Links   Words and phrases such as "because" and "in order to" that specify the relationships between ideas.

Warmth and Enthusiasm   Test Bank items 12.47, 12.119

As you are well aware, some teachers are much more enthusiastic than others. Some studies have found that ratings of teachers' enthusiasm for their subject are correlated with student achievement gains (Rosenshine & Furst, 1973). Warmth, friendliness, and understanding seem to be the teacher traits most strongly related to student attitudes (Murray, 1983; Ryans, 1960; Soar & Soar, 1979). In other words, teachers who are warm and friendly tend to have students who like them and the class in general. But notice, these are correlational studies. The results do not tell us that teacher enthusiasm causes student learning or that warmth causes positive attitudes, only that the two variables tend to occur together. Teachers trained to demonstrate their enthusiasm have students who are more attentive and involved but not necessarily more successful on tests of content (Gillett & Gall, 1982).

The research we have looked at has identified teacher knowledge, clarity, organization, and enthusiasm as important characteristics of effective teachers. The Guidelines summarize the practical implications of this work for the classroom.

Focus on . . .   **Characteristics of Effective Teachers**

■ What methods have been used to study teaching?
■ What must a teacher know about a subject in order to transform subject knowledge into teaching activities and materials?
■ How can a teacher be clear during lesson presentations?

Guidelines

Teaching Effectively

Organize your lessons carefully.

Examples

1. Provide objectives that help students focus on the purpose of the lesson.
2. Begin lessons by writing a brief outline on the board, or work on an outline with the class as part of the lesson.
3. If possible, break the presentation into clear steps or stages.
4. Review periodically.

Strive for clear explanations.

Examples

1. Use concrete examples or analogies that relate to the students' own lives. Have several examples for particularly difficult points.
2. Give explanations at several levels so all students, not just the brightest, will understand.
3. Focus on one idea at a time and avoid digressions.

Communicate an enthusiasm for your subject and the day's lesson.

Examples

1. Tell students why the lesson is important. Have a better reason than "This will be on the test" or "You will need to know it next year." Emphasize the value of the learning itself.
2. Be sure to make eye contact with the students.
3. Vary your pace and volume in speaking. Use silence for emphasis.

Constantly broaden your knowledge in your area.

Examples
1. Read journals that report new research and suggest new ideas.
2. Go to workshops and conventions; take a course at a nearby college.

Teaching Methods: Direct Instruction

Let's assume you and your students have clear, valuable, and interesting objectives. You are prepared to be knowledgeable, clear, and enthusiastic. What next? You still need to decide what's happening on Monday. This section describes a variety of general teaching strategies or formats for turning objectives into action in the classroom. These strategies are not complete models of teaching, but rather building blocks that can be used to construct lessons and units. All the methods described in this chapter are more teacher-centered. In the next chapter we will examine learner-centered methods for teaching.

We begin with the strategy many people associate most directly with teaching: lecturing.

Lecturing and Explaining   Test Bank items 12.48–12.51, 12.122

Some studies have found that lecturing takes up one-sixth to one-fourth of all classroom time. High school teachers, of course, lecture more than teachers in the lower grades. You will probably learn about how to lecture in your methods classes. Many different approaches are available, and the one you choose will depend on your objectives and the subject you are teaching. You will certainly want to keep in mind the age of your students, because the younger your students, the briefer and simpler your explanations should be. You may also want to follow a basic three-part format suggested by Kindsvatter, Wilen, and Ishler (1988), shown in Table 12.3 on page 458.

Lecturing is appropriate for communicating a large amount of material to many students in a short period of time. The teacher can integrate information from many sources in less time than it would take for the students to integrate all the information themselves. Lecturing is a good method for introducing a new topic, giving background information, and motivating students to learn more on their own. Lecturing also helps students learn to listen accurately and critically and gives the teacher a chance to make on-the-spot changes to help students understand when they are confused (Gilstrap & Martin, 1975; Kindsvatter, Wilen, & Ishler, 1988). Lectures are therefore most appropriate for cognitive and affective objectives at the lower levels of the taxonomies described earlier: for knowledge, comprehension, application, receiving, responding, and valuing.

The lecture method also has some disadvantages. You may find that some students have trouble listening for more than a few minutes at a time and that they simply tune you out. Lecturing puts the students in a passive position. It does much of the cognitive work for the students and may prevent them from asking or thinking of questions. Also, students learn and comprehend at dif-

Background: For a concise discussion of recitation, discussion, and seatwork, see Doyle, W., & Carter, K. (1987). Choosing the means of instruction. In V. Richardson-Koehler (Ed.), *Educator's handbook: A research perspective* (pp. 188–206). White Plains, NY: Longman.

Handout: Use **Handout Master 12.4**, "Analysis of Teacher's Explanation," which shows the components of a good explanation through teacher-student dialogue.

"NOW THAT YOU'RE ALL PRESENT AND ACCOUNTED FOR, I'LL BEGIN TODAY'S LECTURE."

(Doug Redfern—Phi Delta Kappan)

Lecturing Organized explanation of a topic by a teacher.

TABLE 12.3   Three Phases in the Lecture Method

Entry: Preparation for Learning

A. State objectives and rationale.
B. Provide a context for the new material to be presented.
C. Focus attention on key concept, generalization, or principle that encompasses the lecture.

Presentation

A. Sequence content from simpler to complex understandings.
B. Enhance presentation with visual aids.
C. Stimulate attention with verbal and nonverbal behaviors.

Closure: Review of Learning

A. Integrate with students' knowledge and experiences.
B. Transition to next lesson or activity.

Source: Dynamics of effective teaching, 2/e by Richard Kindsvatter, William Wilen, and Margaret Ishler, p. 221. Copyright © 1988 and 1992 by Longman Publishing Group. Reprinted with permission.

Background: Duffy, G. G., Roehler, L. R., Meloth, M. S., & Varus, L. G. (1986). Conceptualizing instructional explanation. *Teaching and Teacher Education,* 2, 197–214.

Objective 12.12: Describe the processes involved in these teaching formats: recitation and questioning, lecturing and explaining, seatwork.

Discussion: Ask students: "If you are lecturing and becoming aware that you are losing the class's attention, what can you do?"

Casebook: See the Teachers' Casebook at the end of this chapter for practicing teachers' ideas about how to tell when an explanation "works" and what to do when it doesn't.

Background: Teacher questions: Why do you ask? (1987). *Harvard Education Letter, Vol. 3,* No. 3, p. 1. This article includes a discussion of asking higher-order questions, relates questioning to reciprocal teaching, and describes the advantages of allowing adequate time for students to answer.

Recitation Format of teacher questioning, student response, and teacher feedback.

ferent paces, whereas a lecture proceeds at the lecturer's own pace (Gilstrap & Martin, 1975). If your objectives include having students solve a problem; develop arguments; write essays, poems, or short stories; create paintings; or evaluate work, then you must go beyond lecturing to methods that require more active student involvement.

Recitation and Questioning

Test Bank items 12.52–12.59, 12.80, 12.81, 12.105

Recitation is a common approach to teaching that has been with us for many years (Stodolsky, 1988). Teachers pose questions, students answer. The teacher's questions generally follow some sort of plan to develop a framework for the subject matter involved. The students' answers are often followed by reactions from the teacher, such as statements of praise, correction, or requests for further information. The pattern from the teacher's point of view consists of *structure* (setting a framework), *solicitation* (asking questions), and *reaction* (praising, correcting, and expanding) (Clark et al., 1979). These steps are repeated over and over.

Let us consider the heart of recitation, the soliciting or *questioning* phase, by looking at the different kinds of questions, when to ask them, and how to respond to student answers. Of course, an important goal of teaching should be to encourage students to ask questions, but for now we will focus on teachers' questions, to make them as helpful as possible for students.

Kinds of Questions.   Some educators have estimated that high school teachers ask an average of 395 questions per day (Gall, 1970). What are these questions like? Many can be categorized in terms of Bloom's taxonomy of objectives in the cognitive domain. Figure 12.2 offers examples of questions at the different taxonomic levels.

FIGURE 12.2

CLASSROOM QUESTIONS FOR OBJECTIVES IN THE COGNITIVE DOMAIN

Questions can be posed that encourage thinking at every level of Bloom's taxonomy in the cognitive domain. Of course, the thinking required depends on what has gone before in the discussion.

Category	Type of Thinking Expected	Examples
Knowledge (recognition)	Recalling or recognizing information as learned	Define . . . . What is the capital of . . .? What did the text say about . . .?
Comprehension	Demonstrating understanding of the material; transforming, reorganizing, or interpreting	Explain in your own words . . . . Compare . . . . What is the main idea of . . .? Describe what you saw . . . .
Application	Using information to solve a problem with a single correct answer	Which principle is demonstrated in . . .? Calculate the area of . . . . Apply the rule of . . . to solve . . . .
Analysis	Critical thinking; identifying reasons and motives; making inferences based on specific data; analyzing conclusions to see if supported by evidence	What influenced the writings of . . .? Why was Washington, D.C. chosen . . .? Which of the following are facts and which are opinions? Based on your experiment, what is the chemical . . .?
Synthesis	Divergent, original thinking; original plan, proposal, design, or story	What's a good name for this . . .? How could we raise money for . . .? What would the United States be like if the South had won . . .?
Evaluation	Judging the merits of ideas, offering opinions, applying standards	Which U.S. senator is the most effective? Which painting do you believe to be better? Why? Why would you favor . . .?

Source: Adapted by permission from M. Sadker and D. Sadker (1986), Questioning skills. In J. Cooper (Ed.), *Classroom teaching skills: A handbook* (3rd ed.). Lexington, MA: D. C. Heath, pp. 143-160.

Teaching Tip: Beers, S. E. (1986). Questioning and peer collaboration as techniques for thinking and writing about personality. *Teaching of Psychology, 13*, 75–77, describes how an instructor encouraged analysis and evaluation of class content by having students ask questions as preparation for writing essays. Students wrote questions each week, classified them according to Bloom's taxonomy, and then twice during the term chose a question to develop into an essay.

Background: There is a journal devoted to questions, called *Questioning Exchange*, edited by J. T. Dillon, School of Education, University of California, Riverside, CA 92521.

Transparency: For a visual representation of the concept of "wait-time," see acetate transparency T 98, "Wait Times Associated with Questioning."

Another way to categorize questioning is in terms of **convergent questions** (only one right answer) or **divergent questions** (many possible answers). Questions about concrete facts are convergent: "Who ruled England in 1540?" "Who wrote the original *Peter Pan*?" Questions dealing with opinions or hypotheses are divergent: "In this story, which character is most like you and why?" "In 100 years, which of the past five presidents will be seen as the most successful?"

Quite a bit of space in education textbooks has been devoted to urging teachers to ask a greater number of higher-level (analysis, synthesis, and evaluation) and divergent questions. Is this really a better way of questioning? Research has provided several surprises.

Fitting the Questions to the Students. Early research found that lower-level (knowledge and comprehension) questions were positively correlated with learning in the primary grades when learning was measured with test questions at the knowledge and comprehension levels (Stallings & Kaskowitz, 1975; Soar, 1973). But Redfield and Rousseau (1981) examined 14 studies and concluded that higher-level questions can lead to achievement gains when teachers are trained to use this approach appropriately. It appears that both high- and low-level questions can be effective (Gall, 1984). Different patterns seem to be better for different students, however. The best pattern for younger students and for lower-ability students of all ages is simple questions that allow a high percentage of correct answers, ample encouragement, help when the student does not have the correct answer, and praise. For high-ability students, the successful pattern includes harder questions at both higher and lower levels and more critical feedback (Berliner, 1987; Good, 1988).

Whatever their age or ability, all students should have some experience with thought-provoking questions and, if necessary, help in learning how to answer them. As we saw in chapter 8, to master critical thinking and problem-solving skills, students must have a chance to practice the skills. They also need time to think about their answers. But research shows that teachers wait an average of only one second for students to answer (Rowe, 1974). Consider the following slice of classroom life (Sadker & Sadker, 1986a, p. 170):

Teacher: Who wrote the poem "Stopping by Woods on a Snowy Evening"? Tom?

Tom: Robert Frost.

Teacher: Good. What action takes place in the poem? Sally?

Sally: A man stops his sleigh to watch the woods get filled with snow.

Teacher: Yes. Emma, what thoughts go through the man's mind?

Emma: He thinks how beautiful the woods are . . . (She pauses for a second.)

Teacher: What else does he think about? Joe?

Joe: He thinks how he would like to stay and watch. (Pauses for a second.)

Teacher: Yes—and what else? Rita? (Waits half a second.) Come on, Rita, you can get the answer to this. (Waits half a second.) Well, why does he feel he can't stay there indefinitely and watch the woods and the snow?

Sarah: Well, I think it might be—(Pauses a second.)

Teacher: Think, Sarah. (Teacher waits for half a second.) All right then—Mike? (Waits again for half a second.) John? (Waits half a second.) What's the matter with everyone today? Didn't you do the reading?

Convergent Questions Questions that have a single correct answer.

Divergent Questions Questions that have no single correct answer.

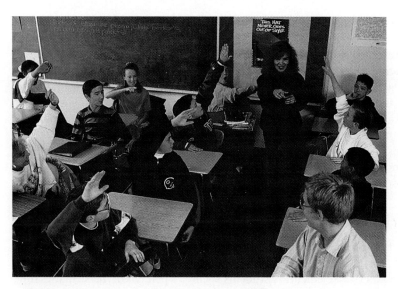

All students need experience answering thought-provoking questions to develop critical thinking and problem-solving skills.

Very little thoughtful responding can take place in this situation. When teachers learn to pose a question, then wait at least 3 to 5 seconds before calling on a student to answer, students tend to give longer answers; more students are likely to participate, ask questions, and volunteer appropriate answers; student comments involving analysis, synthesis, inference, and speculation tend to increase; and the students generally appear more confident in their answers (Berliner, 1987; Rowe, 1974; Sadker & Sadker, 1986a; Tobin, 1987). This seems like a simple improvement in teaching, but 5 seconds of silence is not that easy to handle. It takes practice. You might try asking students to jot down ideas or even discuss the question with another student. This makes the wait more comfortable and gives students a chance to think. Of course, if it is clear that students are lost or don't understand the question, waiting longer will not help. When your question is met with blank stares, rephrase the question or ask if anyone can explain the confusion.

A word about selecting students to answer questions. If you call only on volunteers, then you may get the wrong idea about how well students understand the material. Also, the same people volunteer over and over again. Many expert teachers have some systematic way of making sure that they call on everyone: They pull names from a jar or check names off a list as each student speaks (Weinstein & Mignano, 1993). Another possibility is to put each student's name on an index card, then shuffle the cards and go through the deck as you call on people. You can use the card to make notes about students' answers or extra help they may need.

Responding to Student Answers.   What do you do after the student answers? The most common response, occurring about 50 percent of the time in most classrooms, is simple acceptance—"OK" or "Uh-huh" (Sadker & Sadker, 1986a). But there are better reactions, depending on whether the student's

Research: Tobin, K. (1987). The role of wait time in higher cognitive level learning. *Review of Educational Research, 57,* 69–96.

This article reviews studies of wait time (the duration of pauses separating utterances during verbal interaction). When average wait time was greater than three seconds, higher cognitive achievement was obtained in elementary, middle, and high school science, as well as in middle-school mathematics. Wait time appears to facilitate higher-cognitive-level learning by providing teachers and students with additional time to think.

Research: Meyer, L. A. (1987). Strategies for correcting students' wrong answers. *Elementary School Journal, 87,* 227–241.

This article on teacher feedback to students' wrong responses describes the sustained feedback and paradigm that grew from work with direct instruction programs. Procedures and definitions are presented for classifying four categories of mistakes: lack of information, motor problems, confused information, and rule application. Five correction strategies—modeling, leading, testing, retesting, and mastery units—are described.

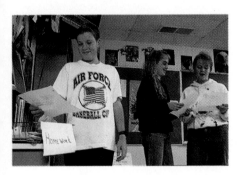

*T*o benefit from homework or seatwork students must stay involved and do the work. The work must be meaningful, not just busywork.

Background: Student questions in K–12 classrooms (1988). *Harvard Education Letter, Vol. 4,* No. 1, p. 7. This article concludes with the following statement: " . . . after the seventh grade low-achieving students may become less active participants than their more academically successful classmates . . . Over time, teachers may begin to expect that low achievers' questions will be inappropriate and avoid calling on them. Arrangements for grouping students by ability may prompt some teachers to adopt classroom management strategies that involve more seatwork and less spoken interaction for low achievers. Noting these possible patterns may help teachers become more aware of how their behavior shapes that of their students."

Research: Stigler, J. W., Lee, S., & Stevenson, H. W. (1987). Mathematics classrooms in Japan, Taiwan, and the United States. *Child Development, 58,* 1272–1285.

Discussion: Is homework a form of seatwork? What are the essential differences?

Casebook: See the Teachers' Casebook for expert teachers' ideas about how to make seatwork a valuable experience.

Seatwork Independent classroom work.

---

answer is correct, partially correct, or wrong. If the answer is quick, firm and correct, simply accept the answer or ask another question. If the answer is correct but hesitant, give the student feedback about *why* the answer is correct: "That's right, Chris, the Senate is part of the legislative branch of government because the Senate . . . " This allows you to explain the material again. If this student is unsure, others may be confused as well. If the answer is partially or completely wrong but the student has made an honest attempt, you should probe for more information, give clues, simplify the question, review the previous steps, or reteach the material. If the student's wrong answer is silly or careless, however, it is better simply to correct the answer and go on. (Good, 1988; Rosenshine & Stevens, 1986).

Seatwork and Homework

Test Bank items 12.60–12.62, 12.106, 12.108

There is little research on the effects of **seatwork,** or independent classroom-desk work, but it is clear that this technique is often overused. In fact, a study found that American elementary students spend 51 percent of mathematics time in school working alone, while Japanese students spend 26 percent and Taiwanese students spend only 9 percent (Stigler, Lee, & Stevenson, 1987). Some educators point to these differences as part of the explanation for Asian students' superiority in mathematics. Seatwork should follow up a lesson and give students supervised practice. It should not be the main mode of instruction.

In the 1980s several studies reported strong positive correlations between the amount of homework students were assigned and their grades (Keith, 1982). Many schools responded by requiring that more homework be assigned. But just assigning more homework is not necessarily a good idea. The seatwork and homework must be meaningful extensions of class lessons, not just busywork. Unfortunately, many workbook pages and "dittos" do little to support the learning of important objectives. Before you assign work, ask yourself, "Does doing this work help students learn anything that matters?" For example, consider this task, cited in the report of the Commission on Reading of the National Institute of Education (Anderson, Hiebert, Scott, & Wilkinson, 1985):

> Read each sentence. Decide which consonant letter is used the most. Underline it each time.

What's the point? This sort of activity communicates to students that reading isn't very important or useful.

Carol Weinstein and Andy Mignano (1993) describe several alternatives to workbooks and dittos, such as silent reading and reading aloud to a partner, "real" writing for an audience, letters, journals, transcribing conversations and punctuating them properly, making up problems, working on long-term projects and reports, brainteasers and puzzles, and computer activities. One of my favorites is a group story. Two students begin a story on the computer. Then two more add a paragraph. The story grows with each new pair's addition. The students are reading and writing, editing and improving.

To benefit from seatwork or homework, students must stay involved and do the work. The first step toward involvement is getting students started correctly by making sure they understand the assignment. It may help to do the first few questions as a class, to clear up any misconceptions. This is especially important for homework assignments, because students may have no one at home to consult if they have problems with the assignment. A second way to keep students involved is to hold them accountable for completing the work correctly, not just for filling in the page. This means the work should be checked, the errors corrected, and the results counted toward the class grade (Brophy & Good, 1986).

Seatwork particularly requires careful monitoring. As you saw in the previous chapter, effective teachers supervise students, keeping them actively involved in the materials so that the time spent on seatwork is not wasted. Being available to students doing seatwork is more effective than offering students help before they ask for it. To be available, you should move around the class and avoid spending too much time with one or two students. Short, frequent contacts are best (Brophy & Good, 1986; Rosenshine, 1977).

Sometimes you may be working with a small group while other students do seatwork. In these situations it is especially important for students to know what to do if they need help. One expert teacher described by Weinstein and Mignano (1993) taught students a rule, "Ask three, then me." Students have to consult three classmates before seeking help from the teacher. This teacher also spends time early in the year showing students *how* to help each other—how to ask questions and how to explain.

Students should see the connection between the seatwork or homework and the lesson. Tell them why they are doing the work. The objectives should be clear, all the materials that might be needed should be provided, and the work should be easy enough that students can succeed on their own. Success rates should be high—near 100 percent. When seatwork is too difficult, students often resort to guessing or copying just to finish (Anderson, 1985).

Putting It All Together: Models of Direct Instruction

The outcome of much of the research conducted during the 1970s and 1980s on effective teaching was to combine findings about teacher characteristics and teaching behaviors into models of effective teaching. In these models, the emphasis was on teaching basic skills.

The models described in this section fit a specific set of circumstances because they are based on a particular approach to research. The studies that provide the foundation for these models identified existing teaching practices that are effective in American classrooms. The research could not identify successful innovations because the focus was on traditional forms of teaching. Effectiveness was usually defined as average improvement in standardized test scores for a whole class or school. So the results hold for large groups, but not necessarily for every student in the group. Even when the average achievement of a group improves, the achievement of some individuals may decline.

Given these conditions, you can see that the models described below apply best to the teaching of **basic skills**—clearly structured knowledge and essential skills, such as science facts, mathematics computations, reading vocabulary, and grammar rules (Rosenshine & Stevens, 1986). These skills involve tasks that are relatively unambiguous; they can be taught step-by-step and tested by

Background: See Walberg, H. J. (1990). Productive teaching and instruction: Assessing the knowledge base. *Phi Delta Kappan, 72,* 470–478.

Objective 12.13: Describe various methods by which teacher effectiveness has been defined and measured.

Focus on... Teaching Methods
- What are three phases of a lecture?
- Give examples of convergent and divergent questions.
- Describe some alternatives to seatwork.

Background: For an excellent discussion of process-product research on teaching, including a complete analysis of several major studies, see Gage, N. L., & Needels, M. C. (1989). Process-product research on teaching: A review of criticisms. *The Elementary School Journal, 89,* 253–300.

Brief abstract: Four kinds of criticism of process-product research are reviewed and evaluated. Conceptual criticisms address the treatment of teachers' intentions, the context of teaching, the conception of causality, and theory. Methodological criticisms concern issues such as plausibility, the need for experiments, and the quality of outcome measures. Criticisms of productivity concern the yield in understanding, predictive power, and improvement of teaching. Interpretation-application criticisms relate to the use of meta-analysis and the conversion of findings into rules for teaching.

Test Bank items 12.63–12.69, 12.83–12.86, 12.101–12.104, 12.120, 12.121

Basic Skills Clearly structured knowledge that is needed for later learning and that can be taught step by step.

Objective 12.14: State the goal and characteristics of direct instruction, and explain when direct instruction is appropriate.

Discussion: If your students have observed in a primary grade, would they say that the teacher made use of direct instruction? Why or why not?

Activity 12.1: See the separate *Instructor's Resource Manual* for Effective Teaching, an activity that asks students to create examples of effective teaching principles. **Handout Masters 12.1 and 12.1a** list the principles derived from four studies of effective teaching.

Transparency: Acetate transparency **T 103** lists the "Seven Steps of Delivering a Lesson."

Transparency: Rosenshine's six teaching functions and nine factors that support complex learning are listed in acetate transparency **T 107**, "Effective Teaching."

standardized tests. The teaching approaches described below are not necessarily appropriate for objectives such as helping students to write creatively, solve complex problems, or mature emotionally.

Several psychologists have identified a teaching approach that is related to improved student learning. Barak Rosenshine calls this approach **direct instruction** (1979) or **explicit teaching** (1986). Tom Good (1983a) uses the term **active teaching** for a similar approach. Ausubel's expository teaching, described in chapter 8, is also an example of this approach. The goal of direct instruction is the mastery of basic skills as measured by the tests commonly given in schools. In Rosenshine's words:

> Direct instruction refers to academically focused, teacher-directed classrooms using sequenced and structured materials. It refers to teaching activities where goals are clear to students, time allocated for instruction is sufficient and continuous, coverage of content is extensive, the performance of students is monitored . . . and feedback to students is immediate and academically oriented. In direct instruction the teacher controls instructional goals, chooses materials appropriate for the student's ability, and paces the instructional episode. Interaction is . . . structured, but not authoritarian. Learning takes place in a convivial academic atmosphere. (1979, p. 38)

We will look at three elaborations on the basic model of direct instruction, Rosenshine's six teaching functions, Hunter's "mastery teaching," and the Good and Grouws's Missouri Mathematics Program.

Direct Instruction/Explicit Teaching Instruction for mastery of basic skills.

Active Teaching Teaching characterized by high levels of teacher explanation, demonstration, and interaction with students.

When students are involved in guided practice activities, the teacher should monitor and assist. Students need to know how to get the teacher's attention and what to do while they wait for the teacher to come to them. Some teachers encourage students to ask fellow classmates for help, or to go on to the rest of the seatwork.

Rosenshine's Six Teaching Functions.   Rosenshine and his colleagues (Rosenshine, 1988; Rosenshine & Stevens, 1986) have identified six teaching functions based on the research on effective instruction. These could serve as a checklist or framework for teaching basic skills.

1. *Review and check the previous day's work.* Reteach if students misunderstood or made errors.

2. *Present new material.* Make the purpose clear, teach in small steps, provide many examples and nonexamples.

3. *Provide guided practice.* Question students, give practice problems, and listen for misconceptions and misunderstandings. Reteach if necessary. Continue guided practice until students answer about 80 percent of the questions correctly.

4. *Give feedback and correctives* based on student answers. Reteach if necessary.

5. *Provide independent practice.* Let students apply the new learning on their own, either in seatwork, cooperative groups, or homework. The success rate during independent practice should be about 95 percent. This means that students must be well prepared for the work by the presentation and guided practice and that assignments must not be too difficult. The point is for the students to practice until the skills become overlearned and automatic—until the students are confident. Hold students accountable for the work they do—check it.

6. *Review weekly and monthly* to consolidate learning. Include some review items as homework. Test often, and reteach material missed on the tests.

These six functions are not steps to be followed in a particular order, but all of them are elements of effective instruction. For example, feedback, review, or reteaching should occur whenever necessary and should match the abilities of the students.

Hunter's Mastery Teaching Program.   Even before the research on basic skills became influential, Madeline Hunter had developed a system for designing lessons that had much in common with direct instruction. The most recent version of this system is the *Hunter Mastery Teaching Program* (Hunter, 1982, 1991). Like Rosenshine, Hunter emphasizes review, guided practice, checking for understanding, and independent practice, but she also includes ideas about how to get students ready to learn and how to present material effectively. Table 12.4 on page 466 is a summary of Hunter's approach.

Good and Grouws—The Missouri Mathematics Program.   Tom Good and Doug Grouws have spent years studying mathematics teachers who consistently improve the achievement of their students. On the basis of this research, Good and Grouws have developed a model for teaching elementary- and middle-school students. Again, the program emphasizes review, guided practice, checking for understanding, and independent practice.

Good and Grouws believe that the presentation or development portion of the math lesson is critical. The most successful teachers emphasize understanding and meaning in their presentations. They do not simply teach proce-

Background: Madeline Hunter's approaches have been remarkably popular over the years, but not without their critics. See the November 1986 issue of *Elementary School Journal* for five articles on a four-year Madeline Hunter follow-through project. There are findings of quantitative and qualitative analysis, commentaries by Andrew Porter and by Bob Slavin, and a response from Madeline Hunter. In general, the findings show some gains in the schools that used the Hunter program, but these gains were not maintained when consultation and support for the teachers were withdrawn in the final year of the program. The quantitative study is Stallings, J., & Krasavage, E. M. (1986). Program implementation and student achievement in a four-year Madeline Hunter Follow-Through Project. *Elementary School Journal, 87*, 117–138. This paper describes findings from a follow-through project in two Napa County, California, schools over a four-year period. The study explored relationships between program implementation and student engaged rate and achievement in reading and mathematics from 1982 to 1985.

TABLE 12.4   The Hunter Mastery Teaching Program: Selected Principles

Get students set to learn.

Make the best use of the prime time at the beginning of the lesson.

Give students a review question or two to consider while you call the roll, pass out papers, or do other "housekeeping" chores. Follow up—listen to their answers, and correct if necessary.

Create an *anticipatory set* to capture the students' attention. This might be an advance organizer, an intriguing question, or a brief exercise. For example, at the beginning of a lesson on categories of plants you could ask, "How is pumpkin pie similar to cherry pie but different from sweet potato pie?" Answer: Pumpkins and cherries are both fruits, unlike sweet potatoes.

Communicate the lesson objectives (unless withholding this information for a while is part of your overall plan.)

Provide information effectively.

Determine the basic information and organize it. Use this basic structure as scaffolding for the lesson.

Present information clearly and simply. Use familiar terms, examples, illustrations.

Model what you mean. If appropriate, demonstrate or use analogies—"If the basketball Ann is holding were the sun, how far away do you think I would have to hold this pea to represent Pluto . . . ?"

Check for understanding, and give guided practice.

Ask a question and have every student signal an answer—"Thumbs up if this statement is true, down if it's false."

Ask for a choral response: "Everyone, is this a dependent or an independent clause?"

Sample individual responses: "Everyone, think of an example of a closed system. Jon, what's your example?"

Allow for independent practice.

Get students started right by doing the first few few questions together.

Make independent practice brief. Monitor responses, giving feedback quickly.

dures and rules but strive to make students comprehend the material. Demonstrations, illustrations, concrete examples, diagrams, models, manipulatives, and clear explanations are important aspects of their presentations (Good & Grouws, 1979; Good, Grouws, & Ebmeier, 1983; Kutz, 1991; Mason & Good, 1993). A model for a math lesson is given in Table 12.5.

Adapting Models to Students' Abilities

In chapters 4 and 5 we explored several ways that students differ: intelligence, gender, cognitive style, socioeconomic status, race and ethnicity, and culture. In chapter 9 we discussed student differences in need for achievement,

---

TABLE 12.5   Missouri Mathematics Program: Key Instructional Elements

Opening (first 8 minutes except Mondays)

1. Briefly review the concepts and skills associated with the homework.
2. Collect and deal with homework assignments.
3. Ask students to do several mental computation exercises. ("Think: what's 4 × 4? Now, what's 40 × 4?")

Development (about 20 minutes)

1. Briefly focus on prerequisites—the skills and concepts that will be needed in the lesson.
2. Focus on meaning and on promoting student understanding by using explanations, demonstrations, and illustrations. Keep the pace lively.
3. Assess student comprehension frequently. Use both rapid short-answer questions (but give students enough time to respond) and single practice problems.
4. Repeat and elaborate on meaning as necessary. Use examples and analogies.

Seatwork (about 15 minutes)

1. Provide uninterrupted successful practice. Most students should get at least 80 percent of their items correct.

2. Maintain momentum—keep the ball rolling; get everyone involved, then sustain involvement.
3. Alert your students—let students know their work will be checked at the end of the period.
4. Require accountability—check the students' work.

Homework Assignment

1. Assign homework at the end of each math class except Fridays. The work should take about 15 minutes.
2. Include one or two review problems in homework assignments.

Special Reviews

1. Weekly review/maintenance: during the first 20 minutes each Monday. Focus on skills and concepts covered the previous week.
2. Monthly review/maintenance on every fourth Monday. Focus on skills and concepts covered since the last monthly review.

Source: T. Good, D. Grouws, and H. Ebmeier (1983), *Active mathematics teaching.* New York: Longman. Adapted by permission of the author.

---

locus of control, and anxiety. In analyzing effective teaching, we must ask whether one method of teaching can be equally effective with everyone. Even without turning to research for an answer, you might say no—and you would be right.

Aptitude-Treatment-Interactions.   The term **aptitude-treatment-interaction,** or **ATI,** refers to the ways individual differences—verbal ability, anxiety, cognitive style, or need to achieve—interact with particular teaching methods. We have seen the result: No single method is effective for everyone (Cronbach & Snow, 1977). You encountered a few examples of ATIs in chapter 9 when we discussed how approaches like programmed instruction and competitive grading could have very different effects on nonanxious and highly anxious students.

The interactions between student aptitudes and different teaching approaches can become complex and difficult to interpret. With the exception (discussed below) of student ability, most aptitudes interact differently with treatments, depending on the situation or study. There is one important general implication of the ATI research: *When students are having difficulty learning with one teaching approach, it makes sense to try something else.* Once more, flexibility is the key.

Transparency: This graph of "Aptitude-Treatment-Interactions" also appears as acetate transparency T 104.

Aptitude-Treatment-Interaction (ATI) Interaction of individual differences in learning with particular teaching methods.

Ability Differences and Prior Knowledge. There is one area of ATI research where findings have reasonably clear and consistent implications for teaching. This is the research that has focused on academic ability and prior knowledge. In ATI research the term *ability* refers not to a theoretical notion of potential but instead to having the necessary prior knowledge to understand new material (Cronbach & Snow, 1977; Good & Stipek, 1983).

If we look at ATI studies involving prior knowledge, we can identify some consistent findings. When students are quite knowledgeable about a particular subject, many methods can be successful. But when students have little prior knowledge, the method makes a difference. The less students know, the more they need instructional and emotional support, probably in the form of improved materials, help in focusing and sustaining attention, systematic feedback, and explicit teaching or direct instruction, recognition for gains, and encouragement (Rosenshine & Stevens, 1986; Sigmund Tobias, 1981, 1982). One goal of this extra instructional support is to reduce the information processing demands on the students (Corno, 1980; Snow, 1977). Appropriate materials and methods help the students organize the information, direct their attention to its critical features, and relieve some of the burden on their memories.

Lesson Formats for Low-Ability Classes. In most secondary-school subjects, teachers follow a lesson format that involves an opening, a presentation of the content of the lesson, student work on problems or questions based on the presentation, and a closing. In a low-ability class, however, this standard format can invite problems, because the students are expected to pay attention to one activity for long blocks of time. Teachers who are successful with low-ability classes tend to have more than one cycle of presentation and student seatwork in each period (Ebmeier & Ziomek, 1982). The teacher may make a short presentation, have the students work briefly, continue the lesson with more content development, then more student practice on the skill being developed, and perhaps give another presentation followed by student seatwork (Evertson, 1982). This pattern keeps the students attentive by giving small doses of both information and individual work. The different activities are short enough to be within the students' attention spans, and the teacher can make sure every student understands each step.

To give students a greater sense of responsibility for their own work, Emmer and colleagues (1994) have suggested short daily assignments. Students keep a record of grades on every assignment and of average grades for each week so they can see the results of their work (or lack of work). Class participation is part of the grading system, with daily or weekly grades awarded for appropriate contributions. In addition, students can be taught some of the learning and metacognitive strategies that more successful students tend to apply automatically. It is especially important to give low-achieving students techniques for monitoring their own learning and problem-solving processes so they can tell when they should use a particular strategy and if they are applying it correctly (Brown, Campione, & Day, 1981).

With all this emphasis on structure, the atmosphere of the class should remain as friendly and supportive as possible. Students who have failed repeat-

What Is the Best Way to Help Students at Risk of Failing

There are many ideas and models for teaching low-achieving students—students often referred to as "at risk" for failure. Some recommendations are based on direct instruction and basic skills teaching. Another approach bases its recommendations on cognitive theories of learning, and these recommendations question the value of direct instruction. What are the teaching strategies offered by each approach?

POINT **Adapt direct instruction for students' needs.**

Research on effective teachers of low achievers (Ebmeier & Ziomek, 1982; Emmer et al., 1989; Slavin, Karweit, & Madden, 1989) has identified these approaches as helpful:

Break instruction into small steps and provide short activities, chosen and sequenced by the teacher.

Cover material thoroughly and at a moderate pace. Give plenty of practice, immediate clear feedback, and specific praise.

Have students work as a whole class or in groups so the teacher can supervise. Avoid individualized, self-paced, or independent work.

Keep a level of difficulty that guarantees high rates of success.

Ask convergent questions—one correct answer.

Make sure to call on everyone and stay with a student until a question is answered.

Avoid interruptions, open-ended questions, and nonacademic conversations.

Emphasize short, frequent paper-and-pencil exercises, not games, arts, crafts, discovery learning activities, and interest centers. These are less helpful for learning.

COUNTERPOINT **Move beyond the basics.**

Educators and psychologists who hold a cognitive view of learning are critical of direct instruction. For example, Barbara Means and Michael Knapp (1991) decry the "basics" approach to teaching low achievers:

A recent summary of critiques of conventional approaches to teaching academic skills to at-risk students, offered by a group of national experts in reading, writing, and mathematics education, concluded that such approaches tend to:

underestimate what students are capable of doing;

postpone more challenging and interesting work for too long—in some cases, forever;

and deprive students of a meaningful or motivating context for learning or for employing the skills that are taught. (pp. 283–284)

What do critics of direct instruction offer in its place? The following are some principles recommended by Means and Knapp (1991):

Focus on complex, meaningful problems. Keep the level of tasks high enough that the purpose of the task is apparent and makes sense to students.

Embed basic skills instruction in the context of more global tasks such as class record keeping or letter writing.

Make connections with students' out-of-school experience and culture.

Model powerful thinking strategies for students; for example, think aloud as you try to figure out a difficult text passage.

Encourage multiple approaches to academic tasks. Have students describe how they reached their answers.

Provide scaffolding to enable students to accomplish complex tasks; for example, perform the calculations for students as they set up an algebra problem correctly.

Make dialogue the central medium for teaching and learning. Reciprocal teaching is one example. (See chapter 13.)

edly are more likely to need the kind of genuine, constant encouragement and nurturing that is effective with younger students (Good & Brophy, 1991). But you should know that not all educators agree with these findings. The Point/Counterpoint section above gives two perspectives on teaching strategies for these students.

Teaching High Achievers. The research on aptitude-treatment-interactions indicates that a wider range of methods and approaches can be effective with high achievers. During lecture-discussion sessions these students tend to learn more if the teacher keeps the pace of the class rapid and the tasks challenging, asks both factual questions and questions requiring higher-level thinking, sets high standards, and points out errors clearly (Brophy & Evertson, 1976). The more nurturing style of teaching seems less important in encouraging learning in high achievers, although this does not hold true for every individual. Presentations can be longer, and more material can be covered in one session. Guided practice sessions can be shorter. Less review and independent practice are necessary (Rosenshine, 1986).

Focus on ... Direct Instruction

■ Describe Rosenshine's six teaching functions.
■ How does Hunter's Mastery Teaching differ from Good and Grouws's Missouri Math Program?
■ What is an aptitude-treatment-interaction?

Connections: Recall the discussion about labeling in chapter 4. Some educators and educational psychologists prefer the expression "students placed at risk" instead of the more common "at-risk students." The reason given is that the label "at-risk students" implies that the "risk" is located in the child rather than in the child's environment.

Activity 12.4: Multicultural Awareness. See the *Instructor's Resource Manual* for Teaching Limited-English-Proficiency Students, a summary of the arguments against "sheltered content instruction."

Discussion: Assign Means, B., & Knapp, M. S. (1991). Cognitive approaches to teaching advanced skills to educationally disadvantaged students. *Phi Delta Kappan, 73,* 282–289. *Focus Questions:* Ask your students to contrast Means and Knapp's approach with traditional methods for teaching the disadvantaged. Will the cognitive approach be more effective? Why? How do Means and Knapp's suggestions differ from the methods that cognitive psychologists offer for nondisadvantaged students?

Cooperative Learning: Ask students to work in groups. Their task is to demonstrate an effective lesson presentation for high-ability students. Using the same content, alter the lesson presentation so it is appropriate for a low-ability class.

Criticisms of Direct Instruction

Critics say that direct instruction is limited to lower-level objectives, that it is based on traditional teaching methods that ignore innovative models, and that it discourages students' independent thinking. Some educational psychologists claim that the direct instruction model tells teachers to "do what works" without grounding the suggestions in a theory of student learning. Other critics disagree, saying that direct instruction is based on a theory of student learning—but it is the *wrong* theory. The learning theory underlying direct instruction, they believe, is a purely behavioral or transmission view. Teachers break material into small segments, present each segment clearly, and reinforce or correct, thus transmitting accurate understandings from teacher to student. The student is seen as an "empty vessel" waiting to be filled with knowledge (Anderson, 1989a; Berg & Clough, 1991; Davis, Maher, & Noddings, 1990). These images of teaching and learning are wrong, say the opponents of direct instruction:

> The key point for instructors to recognize, be they in grade schools or colleges, is that learners have minds—*minds of their own.* Learners are not empty vessels to be filled with content knowledge—they already possess knowledge and beliefs about the content to be learned. These preconceptions form a filter through which new information is processed and understood. (Stoddart, Connell, Stofflett, & Peck, 1993, p. 230)

These criticisms of direct instruction echo the criticisms of behavioral learning theories. As support for behavioral views of learning declined and cognitive perspectives became more influential, the study of teaching discovered a critical variable long overlooked—the student! In a talk to educators, Barak Rosenshine commented on changing thinking about teaching: "Before, we were asking students questions. Now we see we need to teach students how to ask questions. That's a watershed" (Association for Supervision and Curriculum Development, 1990, p. 5).

In response to these criticisms, many researchers expanded their conceptions of teaching. For example, Barak Rosenshine identified a set of factors that support complex learning.

Rosenshine's Factors That Support Complex Learning

Test Bank item 12.120

Earlier in this chapter we discussed Rosenshine's six teaching functions, his summary of effective teaching strategies for direct instruction in "explicit" basic skills. In 1990 he reviewed the research on teaching reading and language arts in first grade through college and identified nine factors that support student learning of "implicit" skills such as reading comprehension, creative writing, and complex problem solving. Table 12.6 summarizes these factors.

Being Sensible about Teaching

Test Bank item 12.122

Even though the research on direct instruction has been criticized, there are still lessons to be learned from it. Lecture, recitation, and seatwork have been overemphasized in many classrooms. Teaching must be more than telling, more even than clear and compelling telling. But there are times when an explanation or demonstration is helpful or when students need to practice basic skills. At these times, there is much a teacher can learn from the research on direct instruction about how to be effective. The critical question is, "What is the student doing while the teacher is talking?" In the next chapter we follow the research on teaching as it rediscovers the student. The emphasis shifts to student-centered approaches to teaching.

Application: Ask your students: "Do you think you will be able to remember which approaches are effective with students of different ages in different subjects? If not, how could you become aware of the different approaches and alternative teaching strategies so that you can choose the ones that you decide are most effective in a particular situation?"

Background: Brophy, J. E. (1992). Probing the subtleties of subject-matter teaching. *Educational Leadership, 49*(7), 4–8.

Teaching Tips: As you discuss different components of the teaching models described in this chapter, use examples of your lectures in this class as illustrations. Students enjoy hearing their professors talk about their own teaching. No one's teaching is perfect, so don't be afraid to point out negative examples.

Background: Rosenshine, B. & Meister, C. (1992). The use of scaffolds for teaching higher-level cognitive strategies. *Educational Leadership, 49*(7), 26–33.

TABLE 12.6 Factors That Support Complex Learning

- *Procedural facilitators.* These provide a "scaffold" to help students learn implicit skills. For example, students can be taught to use "signal words" such as who, what, where, when, why, and how to generate questions after reading a passage.
- *Modeling use of facilitators.* The teacher, in the above example, might model the generation of questions about the reading.
- *Thinking out loud.* This models the teacher's expert thought processes, showing students the revisions and choices the learner makes in using procedural facilitators to work on problems.
- *Anticipating difficult areas.* During the modeling and presentations phase of instruction, for example, the teacher anticipates and discusses potential student errors.
- *Proving prompt or cue cards.* Procedural facilitators were written on "prompt cards" that students kept for reference as they worked. As students practiced, the cards gradually became unnecessary.
- *Regulating the difficulty.* Tasks involving implicit skills were introduced by beginning with simpler problems, providing for student practice after each step, and gradually increasing the complexity of the task.
- *Providing half-done examples.* Giving students half-done examples of problems and having them work out the conclusions can be an effective way to teach students how to ultimately solve problems on their own.
- *Reciprocal teaching.* Having the teacher and students rotate the role of teacher. The teacher provides support to students as they learn to lead discussions and ask their own questions.
- *Providing checklists.* Students can be taught self-checking procedures to help them regulate the quality of their responses.

Source: Effective teaching redux, *ASCD Update, 32*(6), p. 5. Copyright © 1990 by Association for Supervision and Curriculum Development. All rights reserved. Reprinted with permission.

The First Step: Planning

Planning on several different levels is an important step in teaching. The plan determines how time and materials will be turned into activities for students. There is no single model of planning, but all plans should allow for flexibility.

Objectives for Learning

Instructional objectives state a teacher's intentions for what students will learn. Objectives help provide structure, let students know what they are studying for or working toward, and help guide the teacher in writing fair and balanced tests. Critics of instructional objectives have argued that objectives are time-consuming, tend to be irrelevant because trivial objectives are easier to create, and place too many restrictions on students' inclination to explore on their own. Two approaches to writing objectives are Mager's specific behavior objectives and Gronlund's combination of general and specific objectives. Many educators believe that Gronlund's approach is the most helpful.

Bloom and others have developed taxonomies categorizing basic objectives in the cognitive, affective, and psychomotor domains. A taxonomy encourages systematic thinking about relevant objectives and ways to evaluate them.

The Search for the Keys to Success

For years, researchers have tried to unravel the mystery of effective teaching. Studies conducted in the 1960s and early 1970s concluded that teachers don't make a difference, but this research did not study teaching in individual classrooms. Later research used a variety of methods including classroom observation, case studies, interviews, experimentation with different methods, and other approaches to study teaching in real classrooms.

Characteristics of Effective Teachers

Results of research on teacher characteristics indicate that thorough and expert knowledge of a subject, organization and clarity in presentation, and enthusiasm all play important parts in effective teaching. But no one way of teaching has been found to be right for each class, lesson, or day.

Teaching Methods: Direct Instruction

The teaching format for putting objectives into action should be suited to the objectives. Lecturing is efficient for communicating a large amount of new material to a large group, but may keep students too passive and ignore individual learning rates. The younger the student, the shorter the presentation should be. Recitation can involve various types of questions, and should fit students' abilities and motivation levels; teacher responses to answers should not be too hasty in most cases and should provide appropriate feedback.

Direct instruction seems most appropriate when teaching basic skills. A framework for direct instruction might involve reviewing yesterday's work, presenting new material, giving guided practice, giving feedback and corrections, providing independent practice, and reviewing weekly and monthly. Hunter's mastery teaching and the Missouri Mathematics Program are elaborations on direct instruction in the basics.

Teachers must deal with a wide range of student aptitudes for learning. Aptitude-treatment-interaction research has attempted to determine how particular methods affect students of different abilities. One clear implication is that teachers must be flexible, willing to try a new approach if one is not working well. Degree of prior knowledge can influence the effectiveness of teaching methods. Students with little prior knowledge need much more support and structure in learning.

Low-ability students need an emotionally supportive atmosphere and lessons broken up into small doses of presentation and seatwork, not too much of any one task at once. A wider range of methods and a faster pace are more appropriate for high achievers. Though there are no guarantees about effectiveness, it is clear that effective classrooms are pleasant, convivial, and fun.

Criticisms of Direct Instruction

Critics of direct instruction suggest that it is based on a misleading theory of student learning, one that sees students as passive recipients of knowledge from the teacher. Direct instruction focuses on teaching as it is and thus ignores innovations. In response to these criticisms, researchers studying teaching have expanded their conceptions of teaching to include the active role of students. Revised models of teaching such as Rosenshine's factors that support complex learning, are available. The shift of attention to the students doing the learning is consistent with an emphasis on student-centered teaching, discussed in the next chapter.

KEY TERMS

active teaching, p. 464
affective domain, p. 448
aptitude-treatment-interaction (ATI),
   p. 467
basic skills, p. 463
behavioral objectives, p. 443
cognitive domain, p. 447

cognitive objectives, p. 443
convergent questions, p. 460
direct instruction/explicit teaching,
   p. 464
divergent questions, p. 460
explanatory links, p. 455

instructional objective, p. 443
lecturing, p. 457
psychomotor domain, p. 449
recitation, p. 458
seatwork, p. 462
taxonomy, p. 447

WHAT WOULD YOU DO?

Preschool and Kindergarten

You have a very well supplied science corner in your class, but your students seldom visit it. When they do, they don't seem to take advantage of the learning possibilities available with the manipulatives. How would you help students benefit from the materials?

Elementary and Middle School

Your cooperating teacher wants a full lesson plan for each subject. What would you include in the plan to make it useful for you?

You are given a math workbook and text series and told that you must use these materials as the basis for your math teaching. What would you do to incorporate these materials into lessons that help students understand mathematical thinking and problem solving?

One of the teachers in your building is really disorganized and confusing. Your students have to go to this teacher for science and they hate it. The saddest part is that many of your students seem to have decided that science is impossibly difficult and they are just "too dumb" to learn it. What would you do?

Junior High and High School

You have been assigned a "developmental" class—25 students who are several years behind. How would you help them become better learners?

Identify three instructional objectives for a lesson in your subject to be used in a mixed-ability tenth-grade class. How would you make these learning objectives clear to your students?

Cooperative Learning Activity

With four or five other members of your educational psychology class, plan a unit. Include objectives, lesson formats, and room arrangements.

Making Explanations Work

*How do you know when an explanation "works"? What do you do if students
greet your well-planned presentation with blank stares?*

I know that an explanation "works" when my students are able to apply it to other
knowledge or work. Anytime I am greeted with blank stares, or for that matter,
even one blank stare, I try another angle. A great presentation is worthless if it
doesn't make sense to the audience. Frequently I will try a more involved, hands-
on approach or I will tie the new learning in to something they know well. I might,
for example, apply math concepts to batting records of famous baseball players, if
my students' interests were so directed.

Sarah Gustafson, *Florida 1991 Teacher of the Year*
The Okeechobee Center, Okeechobee, Florida

Blank stares indicate that I have not effectively presented material that will lead to
key student understanding. Students need to be *actively* involved in all areas of the
curriculum from introduction of a concept to the completion of a lesson. As a
teacher I must create activities that rely on my students' own experience base and
then constantly check for understanding in creative and engaging ways. I immediately recognize the success of an explanation when students "attack" the task at
hand, providing their own creative and divergent approaches to problem solving.
   If I'm still unsuccessful after modifying my approach, I will move on to something else. I will rethink the activity and consult other resources and colleagues before reteaching the lesson.

Bruce D. Fisher, *California 1991 Teacher of the Year*
Fortuna Elementary School, Fortuna, California

The Value of Lesson Plans

*A beginning teacher at your school tells you in confidence that he does not see the
value of writing the lesson plans as required by the school administration. What
would you say?*

I would first ask the teacher what he understood the purpose of the directive to be
and what he thought it entailed. If he thought writing lesson plans involved the detailed format used in teacher training classes, I would show him how to simplify the
process with a coding system or abbreviated statement of goals, materials needed,
and so forth. If he thought writing lesson plans meant recording the page numbers
of the textbook/manual/worksheet in the plan book, I'd tell him about some exciting, insightful ways of teaching. I would share how much more I enjoy teaching now
that I integrate learning, encourage the students to become their own teachers, use
textbooks as one of many resources, have the students create their own written application of what they have learned, and use alternative forms of assessment.
   Writing down plans and taking the time to evaluate them makes teachers reflective professionals. Writing the plans makes it possible for the teacher to document what has been done and demonstrate accountability, to protect the children
in case of teacher absence or extended emergency leave so that they can have continuity in their learning, to provide data for integrating previous information with

current lessons, and to have ready reference for parent conferences about material covered and the purpose of the material.

Betty Garner, *Art Teacher*
Pattonville I.D.E.A.L. Center, Maryland Heights, Missouri

Teaching Basic Skills

How do you incorporate basic skills into your teaching and homework assignments?

Plan reading and spelling instruction that is whole group with active participation of all students, followed by small group reading instruction time so that all children will have the opportunity to work at their own developmental levels. All of our homework assignments have a parental component, even if it is just the parent signing the homework sheet. I have had a great deal of success developing curriculum-specific homework assignments that students enjoy doing and parents thank me for. For example, we have been studying endangered species, focusing on the California Condor. Parents are always impressed by how much their children know. Students commonly show up with related newspaper clippings or a book that they have chosen together with their parents. I believe that parental involvement is the most important component in the success of these homework activities. It provides students with validation that they are successful second-grade students.

K. Janice Hill, *Second-Grade Teacher*
Dillingham School District, Dillingham, Alaska

Seatwork

A common criticism of seatwork is that it is busywork: students get bored, their attention wanders, and the time is wasted in the end. How can seatwork assignments be structured so that they are valid, positive learning experiences?

Seatwork can be a valid teaching tool if properly planned. The success of a seatwork assignment hinges on several variables that teachers must take into account—the who, what, where, when, how, and why of the students and the assignment: the personality ties of the students and the gestalt of the whole class; the background knowledge students bring to the subject and to the task; the physical environment and its conduciveness to the task; how fatigued, distracted, or stimulated students are at the particular time of day; the procedure and the essential materials and their accessibility; and the existing motivation for the task as well as the extra reinforcement necessary to encourage self-directed work.

In addition, teachers need a thorough knowledge of the subject matter, legitimate long-range goals, and specific, behaviorally stated short-range objectives. Seatwork then becomes one of the comprehensive, productive, daily assignments that are the culmination of this kind of extensive planning. As for the students, they must see a legitimate correlation between an assignment's purpose and its actual completion. There must be a predetermined criterion for success, and actual completion of the task must also be reinforced. Seatwork can and should be exciting and motivating.

Laura Atkinson, *Special Education Teacher*
Chapel Hill, North Carolina

HOMEWORK: INVOLVE THE PARENTS

A DIFFICULT BUT WORTHWHILE ENDEAVOR

13

Rediscovering the Student in Teaching

*T*he study of teaching has taken a very logical turn to focus on the person being taught—the student. In this chapter, we will explore what is known about how to encourage and support students' learning. This general approach is sometimes called student-centered teaching, but, of course, all teaching should ultimately be centered on the student.

First we consider different perspectives on student-centered teaching, including the research methods that help us understand how teaching and learning are linked. We compare two related perspectives that emphasize student-centered learning. Next we examine methods of planning and teaching that are consistent with a student-centered philosophy. Planning focuses on important ideas and themes, and on the thinking processes of the students. The methods are individualized learning, group discussion, inquiry, reciprocal teaching, humanistic education, and technology such as hypermedia. To explore larger, integrated student-centered approaches to teaching, we examine selected models that are appropriate for young children, elementary students, and adolescents.

By the time you have completed this chapter you should be able to:

- Describe methods for studying the links between classroom teaching and student learning.
- Summarize the American Psychological Association's 12 learner-centered psychological principles.
- Describe characteristics shared by many constructivist approaches to teaching.
- Describe situations in which each of the following formats would be most appropriate: individualized instruction, group discussion, inquiry, reciprocal teaching, and humanistic education.
- Evaluate computer packages and microworld computer-based environments for use with your classes.
- Incorporate student-centered approaches into your teaching.

Perspectives on Student-Centered Teaching

Test Bank item 13.65

As researchers studied effective teaching and the factors associated with learning, their findings pointed to the importance of students' cognitive engagement—their thinking. Results indicated that many different approaches and activities can be effective—if the activities create environments in which students think deeply. Rather than focus on what the *teacher* is doing, researchers turned their attention to what the *students* were doing. A good example of this student focus is in the work by a group of researchers from New Zealand.

The New Zealand Studies   Test Bank items 13.1, 13.2, 13.49, 13.66

Graham Nuthall and Adrienne Alton-Lee (1990, 1992, 1993) in New Zealand have conducted a series of studies focusing on how and what students learn. The researchers take a long-term view, trying to pinpoint what helps students construct accurate understandings and remember them a year later. The design of the studies includes careful development of *pretests* and *posttests* based on the actual material being taught in the class; *records* of everything that happens in class—and in-depth *case studies of selected students.*

Some Findings:

1. Students learn very different things from the same lesson. The class average test score "is more likely to misrepresent rather than reflect the learning of an individual student" (1990, p. 555).

2. Quantity of *academic learning time* (the amount of time students spend engaged with challenging but understandable tasks) is closely related to learning.

3. Watching demonstrations and looking at visual illustrations seem to be powerful influences on the students and promote learning that is remembered.

4. Students' prior knowledge in a subject area, including erroneous knowledge, is particularly important in shaping what they learn. For example, students' misconceptions make a significant difference in what they will learn and remember. Sometimes students in the study "learned" a concept temporarily, but remembered their initial misconception *as fact* a year later.

Conditions for Learning from Teaching. Nuthall and Alton-Lee (1990) are developing a theory of student learning based on these and other findings. They believe that three clusters of factors must come together for memorable learning to be strong and enduring.

1. The student must have *resources* to learn. These might include such personal, social, and technical resources as sufficient prior knowledge, support from home, materials and equipment, and relevant experiences.

2. The student must have many *opportunities* to learn. This means sufficient time spent with demonstrations, discussions, and projects; opportunities to clarify concepts; and challenges that will displace misconceptions.

3. The student must take *advantage of these resources and opportunities*. The student must pay attention, talk to the teachers and other students, and express an understanding of key concepts orally or in writing.

Nuthall and Alton-Lee (1993) have extended their theory by relating classroom events to the students' cognitive processes. As students are involved in activities about a topic, they store a representation of information about the topic in their working memories. These representations become connected and integrated with other related information in semantic memory—the propositions, images, schemas described in chapter 7. Any representations that do not get connected are lost, but if enough representations are integrated and connected, then the ideas become established in long-term memory. Sometimes information is misinterpreted. For example, on the test given right after the unit is taught and again months later, in answer to the question, "Why was William Caxton famous?" one student answered "He led the Peasants' Revolt." Looking back at the class transcripts, the researchers found that during a discussion of the Peasants' Revolt, the teacher described changes in society that brought about the collapse of the feudal system. One change was the printing press—invented by William Caxton. So the student had connected Caxton with the Peasants' Revolt and later "remembered" (or reconstructed) that Caxton *led* the revolt. This construction was strong and lasting.

We must provide resources and opportunities for learning, *and* we must help students benefit from resources and take advantage of learning opportunities. This means helping students become more effective, motivated learners. One perspective about how to support student learning comes from a task force of the American Psychological Association.

Learner-Centered Psychological Principles

Research: Nuthall, G., & Alton-Lee, A. (1990). Research on teaching and learning: Thirty years of change. *Elementary School Journal, 90,* 546–570; Nuthall, G., & Alton-Lee, A. (1993). Predicting learning from student experience of teaching: A theory of student knowledge in classrooms. *American Educational Research Journal, 30,* 799–840.

Background: Wang, M. C., Haertel, G. D., & Walberg, H. J. (1994). Synthesis of research: What helps students learn? *Educational Leadership, 51*(1), 74–79.

Casebook: For an example of one teacher's ideas about how to keep students actively engaged in learning, see the *Teachers' Casebook.*

Test Bank items 13.3, 13.4, 13.50, 13.67

In January of 1993, the Presidential Task Force on Psychology in Education of the American Psychological Association (APA) circulated the fourth draft of its *Learner-Centered Psychological Principles: Guidelines for School Redesign and Reform* (Presidential Task Force on Psychology in Education, 1993). The draft was met with both praise and criticism. In fact, discussions and debate continue even as I write this paragraph. The authors of the document plan to continue revisions, but this draft is a concise statement from advocates of student-centered learning and motivation. The principles are:

Principle 1: The nature of the learning process. Learning is a natural process of pursuing personally meaningful goals. It is active, volitional, and internally

Applications: Here are some ideas for ways to involve all students actively in a lesson. Ask them to:

1. Tell the answer to a neighbor.

2. Summarize the main idea in one or two sentences, writing the summary on a piece of paper and sharing this with a neighbor, or repeat the procedures to a neighbor.

3. Write the answer on a slate, then hold up the slate.

4. Raise their hand if they know the answer (thereby allowing the teacher to check the entire class).

5. Raise their hand if they agree with an answer someone else gave.

6. Raise different colored cards when the answer is a, b, or c.

Taken from Rosenshine, B. (1987). Explicit teaching. In D. Berliner & B. Rosenshine (Eds.), *Talks to teachers* (pp. 75–92). New York: Random House, p. 84.

motivated; it is a process of discovering and constructing meaning from information and experience, filtered through the learner's unique perceptions, thoughts, and feelings. Students are capable of assuming personal responsibility for their own learning if the educational situation takes into account their past learning, ties the new learning to personal goals, and actively involves the students in the learning process.

Principle 2: Goals of the learning process. The learner seeks to create meaningful, coherent representations of knowledge regardless of the quantity and quality of the data available. Students will make the best sense they can of learning activities, even poorly communicated facts, concepts, principles, or theories. Sometimes this can lead to misconceptions, but these misconceptions may be important steps on the road to deeper understanding.

Principle 3: The construction of knowledge. The learner links new information with existing and future-oriented knowledge in uniquely meaningful ways. Because each student has different experiences and because the mind works to link information meaningfully, each student will organize information in a way that is unique. Teachers can help students develop shared understandings about important knowledge and skills.

Principle 4: Higher-order thinking. Higher-order strategies for "thinking about thinking"—for overseeing and monitoring mental operations—facilitate creative and critical thinking and the development of expertise. These metacognitive abilities develop during middle childhood. To foster this self-awareness and sense of personal control, students need settings where their interests, values, and goals are respected and accommodated.

Principle 5: Motivational influences on learning. The depth and breath of information processed, and what and how much is learned and remembered, are influenced by (a) self-awareness and beliefs about personal control, competence, and ability; (b) clarity and saliency of personal values, interests, and goals; (c) personal expectations for success or failure; (d) affect, emotion, and general states of mind; and (e) the resulting motivation to learn. The inner world of beliefs, goals, and expectations can enhance or interfere with learning.

Principle 6: Intrinsic motivation to learn. Individuals are naturally curious and enjoy learning, but intense negative cognitions and emotions (e.g., feeling insecure, worrying about failure, being self-conscious or shy, and fearing corporal punishment, ridicule, or stigmatizing labels) thwart this enthusiasm. Teaching should support and nourish students' natural curiosity and intrinsic motivation rather than "driving" them to learn through fear of punishment.

Principle 7: Characteristics of motivation-enhancing learning tasks. Curiosity, creativity, and higher-order thinking are stimulated by relevant, authentic learning tasks of optimal difficulty and novelty for each student. Students need opportunities to make choices about learning in line with their personal interests. Students are more likely to be creative and think deeply about projects that are as complex as real-world situations.

Principle 8: Developmental constraints and opportunities. Individuals progress through stages of physical, intellectual, emotional, and social development that are a function of unique genetic and environmental factors. Students learn best when materials are developmentally appropriate.

Principle 9: Social and cultural diversity. Learning is facilitated by social interactions and communication with others in flexible, diverse (in age, culture, family background, etc.), and adaptive instructional settings. Learning situations that allow for and respect diversity encourage flexible thinking, social competence, and moral development.

Principle 10: Social acceptance, self-esteem, and learning. Learning and self-esteem are heightened when individuals are in respected and caring relationships with others who see their potential, appreciate their unique talents, and accept them as individuals. Self-esteem and learning are mutually reinforcing.

Principle 11: Individual differences in learning. Learners have different capabilities and preferences for learning modes and strategies. These differences are a function of environment (what is learned and communicated in different cultures or other social groups) and heredity (what occurs naturally as a function of the genes). Understanding and respecting cultural differences is fundamental to creating good learning environments for all students.

Principle 12: Cognitive filters. Personal beliefs, thoughts, and understandings resulting from prior learning and interpretations become the individual's basis for constructing reality and interpreting life experiences. Becoming aware of how personal beliefs and experiences influence each individual's construction of reality will lead to greater choice in what we believe, more control over our own lives, and a greater understanding of the perspectives of others.

Teaching based on these learner-centered principles would make sure that students are active in solving problems, practicing learning strategies, making choices, and discovering important ideas. Methods such as well-planned inquiry, debates, projects, and discussions (examined in an upcoming section) are consistent with these goals.

Constructivist Contributions

Test Bank items 13.5–13.8, 13.35, 13.36, 13.51, 13.52, 13.65, 13.71–13.74

Educators and psychologists who take a **constructivist approach** are among the strongest voices speaking in favor of student-centered teaching. These voices are not only from psychology but also from other arenas such as philosophy, science education, and educational technology. You saw in chapter 7 that constructivism is an orientation that emphasizes the students' construction of knowledge. "While there are several interpretations of what [constructivist] theory means, most agree that it involves a dramatic change in the focus of teaching, putting the students' own efforts to understand at the center of the educational enterprise" (Prawat, 1992, p. 357). Many of the ideas and approaches we already have considered—including discussions of Piaget and Vygotsky, the constructive nature of memory, problem solving, creativity, thinking, discovery learning, and attribution theories of motivation—are consistent with constructivist perspectives.

The Need for a Constructivist Approach. Some of the most compelling support for constructivist approaches to teaching comes from mathematics education. Critics of direct instruction believe that traditional mathematics instruction often teaches students an unintended lesson—that they "cannot understand mathematics," or worse, that mathematics doesn't have to make sense, you just have to memorize the formulas. Arthur Baroody and Herbert Ginsburg (1990, p. 62) give this example:

> Sherry, a junior high student, explained that her math class was learning how to convert measurements from one unit to another. The interviewer gave Sherry the following problem:

Background: John Cronin lists these four common misconceptions about authentic learning: **Misconception #1:** *If you can't take 'em to Spain, they might as well not learn Spanish at all.* The fact that living with native speakers is the best way to learn Spanish does not make using the language in classroom conversations a poor alternative. Look for the small and obvious ways to make learning more authentic—especially if you can't take 'em to Spain. **Misconception #2:** *If you don't have your chef's license, then you'll have to starve.* You don't need special training or materials to create authentic instruction. Good teachers have been doing it for years. **Misconception #3:** *If it isn't real fun, then it isn't real.* Important learning and valuable life skills are not always fun to learn or fun to use. Self-discipline is part of growing up authentically. **Misconception #4:** *If you want to learn to play the piano, you must start with mastering Chopin.* Not all learning has to be complicated; Some important life skills are simple. From Cronin, J. F. (1993). Four misconceptions about authentic learning. *Educational Leadership, 50*(7), 78–80.

Activity 13.1: Background. See the *Instructor's Resource Manual* for insights about Children's Understanding of Science.

Activity 13.2: Critical Thinking. See the *Instructor's Resource Manual* for Direct Versus Indirect Instruction, an activity that asks students which topics in a 5th-grade science curriculum they would teach with direct methods and which they would approach with indirect methods.

Objective 13.1: Contrast constructivist views of learning with a direct-instruction view.

Constructivist Approach View that emphasizes the active role of the learner in building understanding and making sense of information.

Connections: See chapter 6 for a discussion of the criticisms of behavioral teaching methods.

Example: Another example of how students solve mathematics problems by applying rules is taken from Merseth, K. K. (1993) How old is the shepherd? An essay about mathematics education. *Phi Delta Kappan, 74,* 548–554. Merseth cites findings from research showing that three out of four students will produce some numerical answer to the problem: *There are 125 sheep and 5 dogs in a flock. How old is the shepherd?* Here is how one child reached an answer. Notice that logic and reasoning play a role:

125 + 5 = 130 . . . this is too big, and

125 − 5 = 120 is still too big . . . while

125 ÷ 5 = 25. That works! I think the shepherd is 25 years old.

Complex Learning Environments Problems and learning situations which mimic the ill-structured nature of real life.

Social Negotiation Aspect of learning process that relies on collaboration with others and respect for different perspectives.

Multiple Representations of Content Considering problems using various analogies, examples, and metaphors.

To feed data into the computer, the measurements in your report have to be converted to one unit of measurement: feet. Your first measurement, however, is 3 feet 6 inches. What are you going to feed into the computer?

Sherry recognized immediately that the conversion algorithm taught in school applied . . . However, because she really did not understand the rationale behind the conversion algorithm, Sherry had difficulty in remembering the steps and how to execute them. After some time she came up with an improbable answer (it was less than 3 feet). Sherry knew she was in trouble and became flustered. At this point, the interviewer tried to help by asking her if there was any other way of solving the problem. Sherry responded sharply, "No!" She explained, "That's the way it has to be done." The interviewer tried to give Sherry a hint: "Look at the numbers in the problem, is there another way we can think about them that might help us figure out the problem more easily?" Sherry grew even more impatient, "This is the way I learned in school, so it has to be the way."

Sherry believed that there was only one way to solve a problem. Though Sherry knew that 6 inches was one-half a foot and that the fraction one-half was equivalent to the decimal expression .5, she did not use this knowledge to solve the problem informally and quickly ("3 feet 6 inches is 3 1/2 feet, or 3.5 feet"). Her beliefs prevented her from effectively using her existing mathematical knowledge to solve the problem.

Sherry had probably been taught to memorize the steps to convert one measurement to another. How would a constructivist approach teaching the same material? Even though there is no single constructivist theory, many constructivist approaches to teaching recommend complex, challenging learning environments; social negotiation and shared responsibility as a part of learning; multiple representations of content; understanding that knowledge is constructed; and student-centered instruction (Driscoll, 1994; Marshall, 1992).

Complex Learning Environments. Constructivists believe that students should not be given stripped down, simplified problems and basic skills drills, but instead should deal with complex situations and "fuzzy," ill-structured problems. The real world presents few simplified problems or step-by-step directions, so schools should be sure that *every* student has experience solving complex problems. Students may need support as they work on these complex problems, helping them find resources, keeping track of their progress, and so on. This is consistent with APA's Principle 7 above.

Social Negotiation. Many constructivists share Vygotsky's belief that higher mental processes develop through social interaction, so collaboration in learning is valued. The Language Development and Hypermedia Group (1992) suggests that a major goal of teaching is to develop students' abilities to establish and defend their own positions while respecting the positions of others. To accomplish this exchange, students must talk and listen to each other. This aspect of learning is not fully represented in the APA principles, though it is reflected in Principle 9, emphasizing respect for the perspectives of others.

Multiple Representations of Content. When students encounter only one model, one analogy, one way of understanding complex content, they

The real world seldom provides simplified problems or step-by-step directions, so schools should be sure that every student has experience solving complex problems.

often oversimplify as they try to apply that one approach to every situation. I saw this happen in my educational psychology class when six students were presenting an example of guided discovery learning. The students' presentation was a near copy of a guided discovery demonstration I had given earlier in the semester, but with some major misconceptions. Like Sherry above, who knew only one way to convert feet to inches, my students knew only one way to represent discovery learning. Resources for the class should have provided multiple representations of guided discovery using different analogies, examples, and metaphors. We'll do better this semester.

Richard Spiro and his colleagues (1991) suggest that "Revisiting the same material, at different times, in rearranged contexts, for different purposes, and from different conceptual perspectives is essential for attaining the goals of advanced knowledge acquisition" (p. 28). This idea is not entirely new. Years ago Jerome Bruner (1966) described the advantages of a *spiral curriculum*. This is a structure for teaching that introduces the fundamental structure of all subjects—the "big ideas"—early in the school years, then revisits the subjects in more and more complex forms over time.

> **Focus on . . .   Student-Centered Perspectives**
>
> - What three factors encourage durable learning, according to the findings of the New Zealand studies?
> - What are the dangers of direct instruction, according to the constructivist perspective?
> - What are four common elements in most constructivist views of teaching?

Understanding the Knowledge Construction Process.   Throughout this text you have encountered the concept of metacognition—knowledge of your own mental processes and how you learn. Constructivist approaches often go beyond helping students understand their own metacognitive processes to helping them be aware of their own role in constructing knowledge (Cunningham, 1992). The assumptions we make, our beliefs, and experiences shape what each of us comes to "know" about the world. Different assumptions and different experiences lead to different knowledge. Constructivists stress the importance of understanding the knowledge construction process so that students will be aware of the influences that shape their thinking; thus they will be able to choose, develop, and defend positions in a self-critical way while respecting the positions of others. This is consistent with APA Principles 1, 3, 9, and 12.

The last characteristic of constructivist teaching listed by Driscoll (1994) is student-centered instruction. Because student-centered teaching is the focus of this chapter, we will spend several pages discussing this topic.

Test Bank items 13.12, 13.13, 13.65, 13.73, 13.74

Student-Centered Teaching Methods

In this section we will examine examples of student-centered teaching practices and methods that are consistent with constructivist approaches. First we consider planning from a constructivist perspective. Next we explore constructivist teaching practices and student-centered teaching approaches.

Planning from a Constructivist Perspective

Test Bank items 13.9–13.11, 13.37, 13.53

In the teacher-centered approaches to planning discussed in the previous chapter, teachers begin by stating objectives for their students. Next, the teachers identify methods that are consistent with their objectives and design strategies to assess whether students have mastered the objectives. In other words, the teacher controls the "what" and "how" of learning. In constructivist approaches, planning is shared and negotiated. The teacher and students together make decisions about content, activities, and approaches. Students have the opportunity to pursue personally meaningful problems and projects.

All this does not mean that teachers have no goals. Rather than having specific student behaviors and skills as objectives, the teacher has overarching goals—"big ideas"—that guide planning. These goals are understandings or abilities that the teacher returns to again and again. For example, Vito Perrone (1994) has these goals for his secondary history students. He wants his student to be able to:

- use primary sources, formulate hypotheses, and engage in systematic study

- handle multiple points of view

- be close readers and active writers

- pose and solve problems

By the end of his class, Perrone believes his students " . . . should be able to develop a historical narrative and understand that history is created by the decisions people make or don't make" (p. 12).

The next step in the planning process is to create a learning environment that allows students to move toward these goals in ways that respect their individual interests and abilities. Perrone (1994) suggests identifying " . . . those

Research: White, B. Y. (1993). TinkerTools: Causal models, conceptual change, and science education. *Cognition and Instruction, 10,* 1–100.

Activity 13.3: Background. See the *Instructor's Resource Manual* for Reconstructing Children's Understanding of Science, a summary of Gega, P.C. (1994), Science in elementary education.

Activity 13.4: Teaching Tip. See the *Instructor's Resource Manual* for Constructing a Reading Class.

Background: Special issue on Authentic Learning: *Educational Leadership,* April 1993. There are 25 articles in this issue—everything from an interview with Howard Gardner to descriptions of Civil War reinactments.

ideas, themes, and issues that provide the depth and variety of perspective that help students develop significant understandings" (p. 12). For a secondary history course, a theme might be "democracy and revolution," "fairness," or "slavery." In math or music a theme might be "patterns"; in literature, "personal identity" might be the theme. Perrone suggests mapping the topic as a way of thinking about how the theme can generate learning and understanding. An example of a topic map, using the theme of "Immigrants in the United States," is shown in Figure 13.1.

FIGURE 13.1

PLANNING WITH A TOPIC MAP

With this map of the topic, "Immigrants to the United States," a secondary history teacher can identify those themes, issues, and ideas for study. Rather than "cover" the whole map, a few areas are examined in depth.

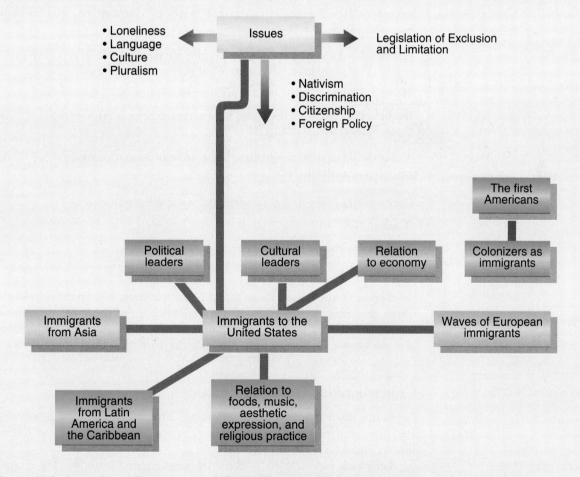

Source: V. Perrone (1994). "How to engage students in learning." *Educational Leadership, 51* (5), p. 13. Reprinted with permission of the Association for Supervision and Curriculum Development. Copyright 1990 by ASCD. All rights reserved.

With this topic map as a guide, teacher and students can work together to identify activities, materials, projects, and performances that will support the development of the students' understanding and abilities—the overarching goals of the class. The teacher spends less time planning specific presentations and assignments and more time gathering a variety of resources and facilitating students' learning. The focus is not so much on students' products as on the processes of learning and the thinking behind the products.

Assessment plans also differ within a constructivist classroom. Assessment is ongoing as teachers and students comment on each others efforts. *Authentic assessment* in the form of exhibitions, portfolios of work, and performances (described in chapters 14 and 15) substitutes for traditional testing. But perhaps most important, teacher and students share the authority to evaluate work. The students have a responsibility to assess their own and each others' thinking, explanations, and performances. The teacher gives up control of "correctness" in the classroom and instead asks students, "Does that explanation make sense?" "Can you improve it?" "Do you agree?" "Why?" The following excerpt shows how a third-grade teacher, Ms. Coleman, avoids correcting students during math class. The class has been considering one problem: $-10 + 10 = ?$ A student, Marta, has just tried to explain, using a number line, why $-10 + 10 = 0$:

Teacher: Marta says that negative ten plus ten equals zero, so you have to count ten numbers to the right. What do you think, Harold?

Harold: I think it's easy, but I don't understand how she explained it.

Teacher: OK. Does anybody else have a comment or a response to that? Tessa? (Peterson, 1992, p. 165)

As the discussion progresses, Ms. Coleman encourages students to talk directly to each other:

Teacher: You said you don't understand what she is trying to say?

Chang: No.

Teacher: Do you want to ask her?

Chang: What do you mean by counting to the right?

This dialogue reveals three things about planning in a constructivist classroom: the thinking processes of the students are the focus of attention; one topic is considered in depth rather than attempting to "cover" many topics; and assessment is ongoing and mutually shared by teacher and students.

Constructivist Teaching Practices   Test Bank items 13.11, 13.38

Given the above framework for planning, what practices might apply? Table 13.1 lists constructivist teaching practices suggested by Jacqueline Grennon Brooks and M. G. Brooks (1993).

Let's look more closely at some student-centered methods. The examples we will consider are individualized instruction, group discussion, inquiry, reciprocal teaching, humanistic education, and computers and hypermedia.

TABLE 13.1 Constructivist Teaching Practices

Many constructivist practices can be incorporated into any class.

1. Constructivist teachers encourage and accept student autonomy and initiative.
2. Constructivist teachers use raw data and primary sources, along with manipulative, interactive, and physical materials.
3. When framing tasks, constructivist teachers use cognitive terminology such as "classify," "analyze," "predict," and "create."
4. Constructivist teachers allow student responses to drive lessons, shift instructional strategies, and alter content.
5. Constructivist teachers inquire about students' understandings of concepts before sharing their own understandings of those concepts.
6. Constructivist teachers encourage students to engage in dialogue, both with the teacher and with one another.
7. Constructivist teachers encourage student inquiry by asking thoughtful, open-ended questions and encouraging students to ask questions of each other.
8. Constructivist teachers seek elaboration of students' initial responses.
9. Constructivist teachers engage students in experiences that might engender contradictions to their initial hypotheses and then encourage discussion.
10. Constructivist teachers allow wait-time after posing questions.
11. Constructivist teachers provide time for students to discover relationships and create metaphors.

Source: J. G. Brooks and M. G. Brooks (1993). "Becoming a Constructivist Teacher." *In Search of Understanding: The Case for Constructivist Classrooms.* excerpted from pp. 101–118. Reprinted with permission of the Association for Supervision and Curriculum Development. Copyright 1993 by ASCD. All rights reserved.

Individualized Instruction

Test Bank items 13.12–13.16, 13.39, 13.54

The defining characteristic of **individualized instruction** is that each student works with learning plans designed to fit his or her own needs, interests, and abilities. To accomplish this goal, individualized instruction takes many forms. Individualized instruction does not necessarily require independent or solitary work: Students may even work in small or large groups so long as the activities are designed to match the needs of the individuals involved. Let's consider how you would modify lessons to meet individual needs.

Modifying Lessons to Fit Individual Needs. Perhaps the simplest form of individualized instruction is to let students work at their own *pace* on the same assignment. The second variable in individualized instruction is choice of *learning objectives.* Instead of insisting that each student move through the same sequence of objectives, you can tailor the objectives to the needs, interests, and abilities of different students or different groups of students. For example, in Perrone's (1994) secondary history class, described above, some students might spend time in the library learning to use databases, while other students who already know how to access those resources might focus on their writing by reading and editing each other's drafts.

Individualized Instruction An approach tailored to individual students' needs, interests, abilities, and work pace.

A third variable in individualized instruction is the *learning activity* itself. Even if students have the same learning goals, they might use different means to achieve those goals. One student might rely on the textbook, while others might read library books or newspaper stories or use audiovisual resources. Students with reading problems, students who have impaired vision, or students who have difficulty remembering what they read might listen to tapes or play simulation games together. Individual projects, and library or field research are also possibilities. In your methods courses you may learn about other approaches, such as learning centers. Students can select different topics to study or research, based on their interests. For example, one group of students might use the topic map in Figure 13.1 on page 485 and decide to find out if immigrants came to the the United States from Mexico because they have family in that country. Other students with an interest in music might trace changes in popular music to influences from Latin America and the Caribbean. The teacher's overarching goals of working with primary sources, close reading and active writing, and so on, could be fostered with any topic the students selected.

A fourth variable has just been touched on—*reading level*. For example, most of the students in the history class may be able to research and write about the relation of the economy to immigration patterns, but some of them may need background reading material at the junior high level or even lower. It is not always possible to find such a wide range of reading materials. Information sources other than the printed word—tapes, films, photographs, cartoons, and so on—may have to be included.

The way in which students are required to *demonstrate their new learning* is the fifth variable that can be tailored to fit the needs of individual students. Students who have difficulty with written expression might first be given oral tests, or they might be asked to tape their answers to written tests. Some students might demonstrate learning by completing major papers or projects. For other students, frequent tests might be better. Students may also demonstrate some learning nonverbally, for instance by drawing pictures, graphing relationships, making a model, or assembling a collage.

Research on Individualized Instruction. In practice, the results of individualized instruction have not always matched the expectations. When used as the *only* form of instruction for elementary and secondary students, these approaches are not superior to traditional methods. But individualized methods do seem quite effective for college students (Bangert, Kulik, & Kulik, 1983). It is possible that completely individualized systems leave elementary and secondary students on their own too much. Only the most motivated and self-directed students can stay involved, and many students don't get the teaching and explanation they need. The teacher's time is absorbed with preparing and correcting individual assignments, leaving less time for demonstrating, presenting, explaining, discussing, and listening to students.

This doesn't mean that teachers should make every student work at the same pace, on the same objectives and activities, or at the same reading level as every other student. Many elements of individualized instruction can be incorporated into regular class lessons. For example, students can work at their own pace on assignments matched to their ability but study and practice together in cooperative, mixed-ability learning groups like those described in

Activity 13.5: Research. See the *Instructor's Resource Manual* for Meeting the Needs of Low Achievers.

Field Experience: Ask your students if the learning centers or learning packages they have observed in use in the classroom follow the purpose described in this text. If not, how are they different? Are learning centers or learning packages commonly found in classrooms? What provisions for individualized instruction are made if these are not present?

chapter 10. This variation of cooperative learning, called **team-assisted individualization,** has proved very effective in elementary-school mathematics classes (Slavin & Karweit, 1985).

Good teachers have been individualizing for years. Teachers individualize, for example, when they make sure that the books chosen for library assignments match the reading levels of the students. Individualized assignments can provide remediation and enrichment. At times it makes sense to send some children into a different grade for instruction in one subject. Two second-grade students, for example, joined my daughter's sixth-grade class for science.

Group Discussion   Test Bank items 13.17, 13.18, 13.69

Group discussion is in some ways similar to the recitation strategy described in the previous chapter, but should be more like the instructional conversations described in chapter 2 (Tharp & Gallimore, 1991; Wilen, 1991). A teacher may pose questions, listen to student answers, react, and probe for more information. But in a true group discussion, the teacher does not have a dominant role. Students ask questions, answer each other's questions, and respond to each other's answers. Remember how Ms. Coleman (above) encouraged students to speak directly to each other.

There are many advantages to group discussions. The students are directly involved and have the chance to participate. Group discussion helps students learn to express themselves clearly, to justify opinions, and to tolerate different views. Group discussion also gives students a chance to ask for clarification, examine their own thinking, follow personal interests, and assume responsibility by taking leadership roles in the group. Thus, group discussions help students evaluate ideas and synthesize personal viewpoints. Discussions are also useful when students are trying to understand difficult concepts that go against common sense. As we saw in chapter 8, many scientific concepts, like the role of

Class discussions enable students to explore lesson content from their own points of view and to develop valuable communication skills.

Team-Assisted Individualization Arrangement where students work at their own pace on individualized assignments, but practice together in cooperative, mixed-ability groups.

Group Discussions Conversations in which the teacher does not have the dominant role; students pose and answer their own questions.

light in vision or Newton's laws of motion, are difficult to grasp because they contradict commonsense notions. By thinking together, challenging each other, and suggesting and evaluating possible explanations, students are more likely to reach a genuine understanding.

Guidelines

Leading Class Discussions

Invite shy children to participate.

Examples

1. "What's your opinion, Joel? We need to hear from some other students."
2. Don't wait until there is a deadly silence to ask shy students to reply. Most people, even those who are confident, hate to break a silence.

Direct student comments and questions back to another student.

Examples

1. "That's an unusual idea, Steve. Kim, what do you think of Steve's idea?"
2. "That's an important question, John. Maura, do you have any thoughts about how you'd answer that?"
3. Encourage students to look at and talk to one another rather than wait for your opinion.

Make sure you understand what a student has said. If you are unsure, other students may be unsure as well.

Examples

1. Ask a second student to summarize what the first student said; then the first student can try again to explain if the summary is incorrect.
2. "Karen, I think you're saying. . . . Is that right, or have I misunderstood?"

Probe for more information.

Examples

1. "That's a strong statement. Do you have any evidence to back it up?"
2. "Tell us how you reached that conclusion. What steps did you go through?"

Bring the discussion back to the subject.

Examples

1. "Let's see, we were discussing . . . and Sarah made one suggestion. Does anyone have a different idea?"
2. "Before we continue, let me try to summarize what has happened thus far."

Give time for thought before asking for responses.

Example

"How would your life be different if television had never been invented? Jot down your ideas on paper, and we will share reactions in a minute." After a minute: "Jean, will you tell us what you wrote?"

When a student finishes speaking, look around the room to judge reactions.

Examples

1. If other students look puzzled, ask them to describe why they are confused.
2. If students are nodding assent, ask them to give an example of what was just said.

Of course, there are disadvantages. Class discussions are quite unpredictable and may easily digress into exchanges of ignorance. Some members of the group may have great difficulty in participating and may become anxious if forced to speak. In addition, you may have to do a good deal of preparation to ensure that participants have a background of knowledge on which to base the discussion. And large groups are often unwieldy. In many cases, a few students will dominate the discussion while the others daydream (Kindsvatter, Wilen, & Ishler, 1988).

Inquiry Methods   Test Bank items 13.19, 13.40, 13.55, 13.69

John Dewey described the basic **inquiry learning** format in 1910. There have been many adaptations of this strategy, but the form usually includes the following elements (Pasch, Sparks-Langer, Gardner, Starko, & Moody, 1991):

The teacher presents a puzzling event, question, or problem. The students:

- formulate hypotheses to explain the event or solve the problem
- collect data to test the hypotheses
- draw conclusions
- reflect on the original problem and on the thinking processes needed to solve it

At times, teachers present a problem and students ask yes/no questions to gather data and test hypotheses. This allows the teacher to monitor students' thinking and guide the process. Here is an example:

1. Teacher presents discrepant event (after clarifying ground rules). The teacher blows softly across the top of an 8-1/2" x 11" sheet of paper, and the paper rises. She tells students to figure out why it rises.

2. Students ask questions to gather more information and to isolate relevant variables. Teacher answers only "yes" or "no." Students ask if temperature is important (no). They ask if the paper is of a special kind (no). They ask if air pressure has anything to do with the paper rising (yes). Questions continue.

3. Students test causal relationships. In this case, they ask if the nature of the air on top causes the paper to rise (yes). They ask if the fast movement of the air results in less pressure on the top (yes). Then they test out the rule with other materials—for example, thin plastic.

4. Students form a generalization (principle): "If the air on the top moves faster than the air on the bottom of a surface, then the air pressure on top is lessened, and the object rises." Later lessons expand students' understanding of the principles and physical laws through further experiments.

5. The teacher leads students in a discussion of their thinking processes. What were the important variables? How did you put the causes and effects together? and so on (Pasch et al., 1991, pp. 188–189).

Inquiry teaching allows students to learn content and process at the same time (Kindsvatter, Wilen, & Ishler, 1988). In the example above, students learned about the effects of air pressure and how airplanes fly. In addition, they learned the inquiry process itself—how to solve problems, evaluate solutions, and think critically.

Discussion: Ask students to explain how they would deal with the following types of "problem individuals" while conducting a whole-group discussion:

a. A student who never participates

b. A student who monopolizes the discussion

c. Two students who begin arguing with one another during the discussion

Casebook: See the Teachers' Casebook at the end of this chapter for practicing teachers' ideas about how to conduct productive class discussions.

"WE DID THAT LAST YEAR—HOW COME WE HAVE TO DO IT AGAIN THIS YEAR?"

(© W. A. Vanselow—Phi Delta Kappan)

Inquiry Learning Approach in which the teacher presents a puzzling situation and students solve the problem by gathering data and testing their conclusions.

Connections: See chapter 8 for a discussion of discovery learning.

The inquiry approach has much in common with guided discovery learning and shares its advantages and disadvantages. Like discovery learning, inquiry methods require great preparation, organization, and monitoring to be sure everyone is engaged and challenged.

Reciprocal Teaching

Test Bank items 13.20, 13.21, 13.41, 13.56, 13.68

The goal of **reciprocal teaching** is to help students understand and think deeply about what they read (Palincsar, 1986; Palincsar & Brown, 1984). To accomplish this goal, students learn four strategies: *summarizing* the content of a passage, *asking a question* about the central point, *clarifying* the difficult parts of the material, and *predicting* what will come next. First the teacher introduces these strategies, perhaps focusing on one strategy each day. The teacher explains and models each strategy and encourages students to practice. Next the teacher and the students read a short passage silently. Then the teacher again provides a model by summarizing, questioning, clarifying, and predicting based on the reading. Everyone reads another passage, and the students gradually begin to assume the teacher's role. Often the students' first attempts are halting and incorrect. But the teacher gives clues, guidance, and encouragement (what Bruner might call "scaffolding") to help the students master these strategies. The goal is for students to learn to apply these strategies independently as they read so they can make sense of text.

An Example of Reciprocal Teaching.   Let's look at some examples of reciprocal teaching in action. The first example is an early lesson. Here the teacher is guiding a student as he tries to formulate a question about the central point in a passage on spiders (Harvard University, March 1986, p. 6):

Text: Spinner's mate is much smaller than she, and his body is dull brown. He spends most of his time sitting at one side of her web.

Charles: (No question)

Teacher: What's this paragraph about?

Charles: Spinner's mate. How do spinner's mate. . . .

Teacher: That's good. Keep going.

Charles: How do spinner's mate is smaller than. . . . How am I going to say that?

Teacher: Take your time with it. You want to ask a question about spinner's mate and what he does, beginning with the word "how."

Charles: How do they spend most of his time sitting?

Teacher: You're very close. The question would be, "How does spinner's mate spend most of his time?" Now, you ask it.

Charles: How does spinner's mate spend most of his time?

After a while, students are usually able to take more and more responsibility for the teaching. In the following example, Laura shows how much progress she has made after about 12 lessons (Harvard University, March 1986, p. 6):

Text: The second oldest form of salt production is mining. Unlike early methods that made the work extremely dangerous and difficult, today's methods use special machinery, and salt mining is easier and safer. The old expression "back to the salt mine" no longer applies.

Reciprocal Teaching A method, based on modeling, to teach reading comprehension strategies.

Laura: Name two words that often describe mining salt in the old days.

Kim: Back to the salt mines?

Laura: No. Angela?

Angela: Dangerous and difficult.

Laura: Correct. This paragraph is all about comparing the old mining of salt and today's mining of salt.

Teacher: Beautiful!

Laura: I have a prediction to make.

Teacher: Good.

Laura: I think it might tell when salt was first discovered . . . well, it might tell what salt is made of and how it's made.

Teacher: OK. Can we have another teacher?

Applying Reciprocal Teaching. Research on reciprocal teaching has shown some dramatic results. Although reciprocal teaching seems to work with almost any age student, most of the research has been done with younger adolescents who can read aloud fairly accurately, but who are far below average in reading comprehension. After 20 hours of practice with this approach, many students who were in the bottom quarter of their class moved up to the average level or above on tests of reading comprehension. Based on the results of several studies, Palincsar has identified three guidelines for effective reciprocal teaching (Harvard University, March 1986; Palincsar & Brown, 1984):

1. *Shift gradually.* The shift from teacher control to student responsibility must be gradual.

2. *Match demands to abilities.* The difficulty of the task and the responsibility must match the abilities of each student and grow as these abilities develop.

3. *Diagnose thinking.* Teachers should carefully observe the "teaching" of each student for clues about how the student is thinking and what kind of instruction the student needs.

Humanistic Education   Test Bank items 13.22, 13.23, 13.42, 13.57

Years ago a group of psychologists and educators such as Carl Rogers (1969; Rogers and Freiberg, 1994), Abraham Maslow (1970), and Art Combs (1984) called for student-centered teaching. They were not identified as constructivist at the time, though their **humanistic** philosophy and approach surely was consistent with constructivism. The basic principles of humanism include a belief that each person constructs his or her own reality. What a person perceives as real and important *is* reality for that individual and one person cannot fully know the reality of another.

Humanistic approaches to education stress the importance of feelings, open communication, and the value of every student. Humanistic education is a philosophy rather than a collection of strategies—an attitude of caring and respect for students. In their book, *Inviting School Success: A Self-Concept Approach to Teaching and Learning,* William Purkey and John Novak (1984) list many things that teachers can do to support self-esteem and make school an inviting place. A few of the ideas are listed in Table 13.2 on page 494.

Humanistic View An approach to motivation that emphasizes personal freedom, choice, self-determination, and striving for personal growth.

TABLE 13.2 Inviting School Success

Here is a sample from the list of practices recommended to invite success in school.

Elementary Teachers

1. *Give an apple on opening day.* Instead of an apple for the teacher, put an apple on each student's desk on the first day of school.
2. *Build a loft.* Create a snug place for reading or small meetings.
3. *Rotate the seating.* Make sure everyone has a chance to be in the favorite seats—near the teacher, close to class pets, etc.
4. *Dial-a-parent.* Each week, call one parent with honest and positive comments about his or her child.
5. *Use the Newspaper.* Watch for articles about students, their families, their interests, or course content. Share the articles with the class. Before a holiday, take out a classified ad to send a special greeting to your class.

Middle School

1. *Share decisions.* Whenever possible, get students involved in decisions about rules of conduct, activities, academic expectations, even textbook reviews.
2. *Start a trading library.* Set up a library in your classroom so students can share favorite books. Communicate that books are meant to be used and enjoyed, and the more people involved the better.
3. *Hold a fractions party.* Bring (or ask the class to bring) pies, cakes, and other goodies in various shapes. Ask students to recognize the difference between 3/4, 5/8, 1/2, and 1/3, and let them eat their answers.

4. *Build a poem.* Rather than having each student write a long poem (a daunting task for many students), ask everyone in the class to write a one-line poem about a particular topic (sunset is a good subject). A small group can assemble the lines into an outstanding class poem.
5. *Visit a graveyard.* Ask students to study the gravestones, imagine, then write about one of the people represented. What happened in this person's lifetime? What was life like in those days? Older students might even do some research in library files, old newspapers, etc.

High School

1. *Tap expertise.* Your school cafeteria worker may be a music buff, the school psychologist an amateur photographer. Have these people share their interests with your class.
2. *Invite participation.* When students are not joining in, divide into small discussion groups—first pairs, then fours, then eights, and so on.
3. *Arrange a Big-Pal program.* Organize tutoring programs for younger students.
4. *And now a word from our sponsor.* Divide the class into small groups and have each group write, design, and videotape a commercial for an academic concept to be shown to the entire class.
5. *Make and take.* Have students produce something—"invest" in the stock market and follow the outcome, design a better parking plan for the school, write letters to manufacturers to request donations for the class.

Source: W. W. Purkey and J. M. Novak (1984). *Inviting school success: A self-concept approach to teaching and learning,* 2nd ed., pp. 102–129. Copyright 1984 by Wadsworth Publishing Co. Adapted by permission.

Open Schools Schools in which students are grouped by activity rather than age.

One approach associated with humanistic education is **open schools.** Although there are many different approaches to open schools, most share certain characteristics. Students are grouped not by age or grade, but by project or activity. Instruction is individualized, with students working at learning stations or on individual or group projects. Objectives and activities are often negotiated with the teacher who acts more as a facilitator than an instructor. Sometimes the classes themselves are open, without walls, so that students can move freely from one area to another. Much of the learning is based on "hands-on," manipulative materials. Teachers use observation, work samples, performances, and discussions to guide teaching, not to determine grades (Giaconia & Hedges, 1982).

Research on open schools has generally demonstrated that these settings do encourage creativity, cooperation, self-esteem, and social adjustment, but academic learning is no greater than it is in traditional classrooms (Giaconia & Hedges, 1982; Rothenberg, 1989).

Computers, Videodiscs, and Beyond

Test Bank items 13.24, 13.25, 13.43–13.45, 13.58, 13.59, 13.69, 13.75

No discussion of student-centered teaching strategies would be complete without considering the role of computers in teaching and learning. In earlier times, I would have had a discussion of technology in teaching in the previous chapter because most computer-assisted instruction was little more than drill and practice, replacing the teacher in the center of teaching with a machine. But today, much more is possible. Technology allows students to explore different worlds, access resources all over the world, and confront complex problems. The uses of computers and other instructional technology are so broad and varied, we can only touch on a few key points here. Because this is such an important topic for today's teachers, I encourage you to learn all you can about it. Some of my student teachers have gotten teaching positions in difficult times partly because they knew how to use computers in their classroom.

Many of your students will have used computers for word processing, graphic design, or games since their preschool years. Other students will have had little experience with computers. Some schools will have computers in every classroom. Videodisc encyclopedias will make a tremendous amount of information available to students. Communications networks will connect your class with students around the country and with museums, research labs, or colleges. But in other schools, there will be a few old computers in a lab down the hall. Given this wide range in students' sophistication and in schools' resources, what can we say about using technology to teach? There are three main roles of computers in schools: as *learning environments* to help students learn content and problem-solving skills, as *tools* to help students and teachers with such tasks as word processing, computing, locating and managing information, doing graphics, or programming computers; and as what Roger Taylor (1980) called *tutees*. In this last role, the student teaches the computer what to do through programming using BASIC, LOGO, Pascal, or some other language. We will focus first on the computer as a learning environment.

Computers as Learning Environments.   Computer games encourage learning and problem solving through motivating activities that resemble video games. An elementary school in upstate New York was faced with an all too typical set of somewhat contradictory demands: improve students' knowledge of social studies and their ability to write and use reference skills, and get them computer literate while you're at it. Unfortunately, the school day was already filled and there were only 14 computers available. The school's computer coordinator put together a social studies unit built around the computer simulation program *Where in the World Is Carmen San Diego?* The unit begins with the whole class playing the game as it is presented on a large monitor, practicing the note-taking and other fact-finding skills that will be useful in successfully "capturing the criminal." After several days of guided instruction in

Background: Big kids teach little kids: What we know about cross-age tutoring (1987). *Harvard Education Letter, 3*(2), pp. 1–4.

Multicultural Awareness: Fresko and Chen (1989) examined the effects of tutor-tutee ethnic similarity, tutor expertise, and perceived goal attainment on the satisfaction of college student tutors of disadvantaged elementary-school children. Results showed that the major factor directly influencing satisfaction was the extent to which tutors felt they had achieved project goals. Ethnic similarity had only an indirect impact. Fresko, B., & Chen, M. (1989). Ethnic similarity, tutor expertise, and tutor satisfaction in cross-age tutoring. *American Educational Research Journal, 26*, 122–140.

Students in many classrooms today are familiar with computers as tools and as tutors.

Background: U.S. Congress, Office of Technology (1988, September). *Power on! New tools for teaching and learning.* OTA-SET-379. Washington, DC: U.S. Government Printing Office.

Background: Educational Technology (1990, special feature). *Phi Delta Kappan, 72*(2), 104–126; Selby, C. C. (1993). Technology: From myths to realities. *Phi Delta Kappan, 74*(9), 684–689.

Discussion: What are your students' thoughts, attitudes, fears, and so on about interacting with a computer? Ask students: Do you think computer programming should become a part of teacher education curriculum? Do you think you need to learn more about computers? There are many sources where students can learn more about computers and computer programming. Ask them to name several.

Discussion: Computer-based instruction provides four basic types of program: drill and practice, tutorial, simulation, and instructional games. Ask students to discuss how they might use each of these in their teaching.

Focus on . . .   **Student-Centered Methods**

- Describe planning from a constructivist perspective.
- What can teachers vary in order to individualize instruction?
- What is the main purpose of reciprocal teaching?
- In what ways are humanism and constructivism similar?

Computer Simulations Programs that require students to apply knowledge and skills to solve life-like problems.

Microworlds Simplified but complete computerized model of a real world working system.

---

using reference materials to unravel the clues that appear in the game, students pair off and, as a team, continue working with the program. The culminating activity for the student is the preparation of a report about the state he or she researched.

Computer simulations are simplified versions of situations that the student would encounter in real life. "In this simplified world, the student solves problems, learns procedures, comes to understand the characteristics of phenomena and how to control them, or learns what actions to take in different situations" (Alessi & Trollip, 1991, p. 119). One example is *SimCity,* which allows students to plan and build cities complete with transportation systems, law enforcement, and industrial, recreational, and residential development. Students must cope with problems as they build and plan—everything from mild discontent over traffic to major natural disasters. In the interactive videodisc world of *ScienceVision,* students can conduct experiments that would be too dangerous or costly to be accomplished in a typical middle-school laboratory (Tobin & Dawson, 1992). *Science 2000* is a multimedia, thematic science curriculum with a hypertext database that is tied into videodiscs. In one unit, for example, students study the ecosystem by participating in a simulated community that is concerned about the quality of water in a nearby lake. Working in cooperative groups, students play the roles of farmers, politicians, building developers, naturalists, and representatives from the Environmental Protection Agency. These groups use the database to research their positions and develop their cases. The unit involves more than science; social studies and language arts play a role as well as the groups debate and compromise (Coburn, 1993).

Microworlds are small but complete parts of real environments that encourage discovery through exploration (Papert, 1993). Working in the environments, students construct knowledge as they explore and experiment. For example, in LOGO, young children learn to program a computer by writing moves for a "turtle" (Papert, 1980). *TinkerTools,* a series of microworlds that incorporate simulations and game-like features, allows students as young as 11 or 12 to explore the world of Newtonian physics (White, 1993).

Computers and Learning. Are computers effective as learning environments? The answer in any given situation depends on the quality of the programs and how they are used, but in general, computer-assisted instruction appears to be moderately more effective than conventional methods (Niemiec & Walberg, 1987). Given all the possibilities for using instructional technology and the rapid pace of advances in the field, it would be foolhardy to specify exactly how students should use computers. However, some general ideas are listed in the Guidelines.

The notion that computers individualize instruction has been interpreted by many educators to mean that the computer should be used by one student at a time. As a result, computers have been underutilized as a means of providing small-group and large-group learning experiences. Research on cooperative or collaborative learning indicates that this approach may have numerous benefits for both cognitive and social development (Lieber & Semmel, 1988; Robinson, DePascale, & Deno, 1988; Slavin, 1984; Webb, 1982).

Using Computers and Other Technology

Take advantage of the capacity to individualize.

Because teachers are concerned about being fair and equitable, they often have all their students use the same software at the same time. Yet one of the most important benefits of computers is the variety of ways they can be used to encourage children to develop different skills at different times. For some, this can be accomplished through the use of drill-and-practice programs; for others, through learning a programming language or word processing.

Involve students in decisions about hardware and software for the class.

Have student teams review software and make recommendations to the administration. Take students on visits to other schools to see how technology is working for them.

Give students experience with technology as a tool.

Computer experience for students should be consistent with the ways computers are currently used in the adult world outside of school. Have students do research for projects on databases and using videodisc encyclopedias. Incorporate word processing, page layout, and spreadsheet applications in assignments.

Use computers as tools for your own work.

Focus on those aspects of computing that will enable you to do your job well by making work easier, more interesting, and more effective. Use electronic gradebooks, test generators, spreadsheets, databases, and word processors.

Constructivist Teaching for Different Ages

Test Bank item 13.70

The range of possibilities for student-centered teaching is tremendous. I can only begin to give you examples of the different ways that you can design learning environments that support the student's construction of knowledge. The following section is organized by the age of the students, but many ideas that work well for one age can be adapted for older or younger students.

Early Childhood/Elementary

Test Bank items 13.27–13.30, 13.46, 13.47, 13.61, 13.70

In the early years, teachers should help students develop abilities in many areas while retaining their curiosity and zest for learning. The goal of understanding, not just memorizing, has to be established early. We will consider how children come to understand numbers and how children's museums have provided inspiration for student-centered teaching approaches.

Constructing an Understanding of Numbers.   A constructivist approach to teaching about numbers creates an environment in which students can make sense of mathematics and use mathematics to make sense of the

Background: Upchurch, R. L., & Lochhead, J. (1987). Computers and higher-order thinking. In V. Richardson-Koehler (Ed.), *Educator's handbook: A research perspective* (139–164). White Plains, NY: Longman.

Computer/Software: Apart from drill and behaviorally supported software, computers can individualize only as well as the psychology of the learner is understood and can be reliably measured. See Psotka, J., Massey, L. D., & Mutter, S. A. (1988). *Intelligent tutoring systems: Lessons learned.* Hillsdale, NJ: LEA.

Background: Computer use and student achievement: More to learn (1988, March). *Harvard Education Letter*, 4(2), p. 7. The most important impact of computers on learning may occur when computers are used not only as an adjunct to instruction but also as a tool for inquiry.

Discussion: Assign Slavin, R. E. (1990). IBM's Writing to Read: Is it right for reading? *Phi Delta Kappan*, 72(3), 214–216. *Focus Question:* What does Slavin conclude about the value of Writing to Read?

Concrete materials (called "manipulatives") play an important role in mathematics learning.

Background: Contrasting views on the effectiveness of computers for improving thinking and problem solving are presented in the following two articles: Papert, S. (1987). Computer criticism vs. technocentric thinking. *Educational Researcher, 16,* 22–30 and Pea, R. D. (1987). The crime of software criticism: Reply to Professor Papert. *Educational Researcher, 16,* 30–34.

Casebook: See the Teachers' Casebook for practicing teachers' ideas about how to help students represent story problems in math so that finding a solution is easier.

world. To accomplish these goals, teaching begins with the student's current understanding. A major challenge for teachers is to capitalize on the student's natural ways of thinking about mathematics. Young children can create concrete, direct representations of problems and use counting to solve problems. To answer the question, "Melissa has three cookies—how many more does she need to have six altogether?" young children might use counters (sticks, fingers, pebbles, etc.) to represent three cookies, keep adding until there are six, then count how many were added (Peterson, Fennema, & Carpenter, 1989).

Teachers can capitalize on the natural use of counting strategies to see how many different ways students can solve a problem. The emphasis is on mathematical thinking, not on math "facts" or on learning the one best (teacher's) way to solve the problem. Here is an example of how one teacher encouraged mathematical thinking while doing the lunch count:

> During the first few minutes of the day, Ms. White asked how many children wanted hot lunches that day. Eighteen children raised their hands. Six children were going to eat cold lunches. Ms. White asked, "How many children are going to eat lunch here today?"
>
> By starting with 18 and counting on, several children got to the answer of 24. One child got out counters and counted out a set of 18 and another set of 6. He then counted all of them and said "24."
>
> Ms. White then asked, "How many more children are eating hot lunch than are eating cold lunch?"
>
> Several children counted back from 18 to 12. The child with the blocks matched 18 blocks with 6 blocks and counted the blocks left over.
>
> Ms. White asked the children who volunteered to tell the rest of the class how they got the answer. Ms. White continued asking for different solutions until no one could think of a new way to solve the problem. (Peterson, Fennema, & Carpenter, 1989, p. 45)

Children's Museums. Have you accompanied children to a museum designed just for them, like the "Exploratorium" in San Francisco? If you have, then you know the power of these places. Howard Gardner (1993b) describes what can happen:

> Kids who for weeks sit alienated, bored, dulled, and uninspired in science classrooms spend an afternoon or two in a children's museum. What happens? Those children are turned on; they try out things; and each child approaches these things in his or her own way at his or her own speed. Frank Oppenheimer, who developed the idea for the Exploratorium in San Francisco said, "Nobody flunks museum." (p. 11)

Classrooms cannot become museums, but we can learn from these institutions something about creating rich educational environments for children. Inspired in part by children's museums, Gardner and his colleagues have designed "Project Spectrum," an environment for assessing and developing the multiple intelligences of young children (Gardner, 1991, 1993b). The Spectrum assessment tasks that examine seven areas of cognitive abilities (intelligences) are described Table 13.3.

TABLE 13.3   Areas of Cognitive Ability Examined in Project Spectrum

One goal of Project Spectrum is to develop students' abilities in all seven areas of cognitive ability identified by Howard Gardner (described in chapter 4).

Numbers

Dinosaur Game: designed as a measure of a child's understanding of number concepts, counting skills, ability to adhere to rules, and use of strategy.

Bus Game: assesses a child's ability to create a useful notation system, perform mental calculations, and organize number information for one or more variables.

Science

Assembly Activity: designed to measure a child's mechanical ability. Successful completion of the activity depends on fine-motor skills and visual-spatial, observational, and problem-solving abilities.

Treasure Hunt Game: assesses a child's ability to make logical inferences. The child is asked to organize information to discover the rule governing the placement of various treasures.

Water Activity: used to assess a child's ability to generate hypotheses based on observations and to conduct simple experiments.

Discovery Area: includes year-round activities that elicit a child's observations, appreciation, and understanding of natural phenomena.

Music

Music Production Activity: designed to assess a child's ability to maintain accurate pitch and rhythm while singing and to recall a song's musical properties.

Music Perception Activity: assesses a child's ability to discriminate pitch. The activity consists of song recognition, error recognition, and pitch discrimination.

Language

Storyboard Activity: measures a range of language skills including complexity of vocabulary and sentence structure, use of connectors, use of descriptive language and dialogue, and ability to pursue a story line.

Reporting Activity: assesses a child's ability to describe an event with regard to the following criteria: ability to report content accurately, level of detail, sentence structure, and vocabulary.

Visual Arts

Art Portfolios: reviewed twice a year, and assessed on criteria that include use of lines and shapes, color, space, detail, and representation and design. Children also participate in three structured drawing activities. The drawings are assessed on criteria similar to those used in the portfolio assessment.

Movement

Creative Movement: the ongoing movement curriculum focuses on children's abilities in five areas of dance and creative movement: sensitivity to rhythm, expressiveness, body control, generation of movement ideas, and responsiveness to music.

Athletic Movement: an obstacle course focuses on the types of skills found in many different sports, such as coordination, timing, balance, and power.

Social

Classroom Model: assesses a child's ability to observe and analyze social events and experiences in the classroom.

Peer Interaction Checklist: a behavioral checklist is used to assess the behaviors in which children engage when interacting with peers. Different patterns of behavior yield distinctive social roles such as facilitator and leader.

Source: Table 6.1 Areas of Cognitive Ability from *Multiple intelligences: The theory in practice* by Howard Gardner pp. 91–92. Copyright © 1993 by Howard Gardner. Reprinted by permission of BasicBooks, a division of HarperCollins Publishers, Inc.

In Project Spectrum classrooms there are materials and activities designed to develop students' abilities in each of the seven areas. For example, there is a naturalist corner where students examine biological specimens, thus drawing on their powers of logic, language, and visual observation. Theme-related kits, such as "Day and Night" or "About Me," provide a variety of activities for home and school. These themes can be enhanced by trips to local museums. For example, students learning about day and night might visit a planetarium.

Background: See the February 1990 issue of *Educational Leadership* for several articles on integrating different approaches to teaching.

Activity 13.6: Background. See the *Instructor's Resource Manual* for Models for Teaching beyond the Basics: Simulations.

Casebook: See the Teachers' Casebook for a practicing teacher's ideas about how to help students learn to write. The teacher's response reflects a whole-language approach to writing.

Whole-Language Perspective A philosophical approach to teaching and learning that stresses learning through authentic, real-life tasks. Emphasizes using language to learn, integrating learning across skills and subjects, and respecting the language abilities of student and teacher.

Gardner describes two students whose lives may have been changed by their participation in a Spectrum environment. One 6-year-old boy from an abusive home was about to be retained in 1st grade. Donnie's teacher saw him as slow, almost unable to learn. But in Project Spectrum, Donnie was able to take apart and rebuild everything in the assembly corner. He was a mechanical marvel! When his classroom teacher saw videotapes of Donnie rebuilding food grinders and door knobs, she was overwhelmed. Her entire view of him changed, and she was able to find ways to reach him in class. Another boy, Gregory, was a first-grade teacher's dream student, learning to read and compute easily. But in Project Spectrum, Gregory would only try tasks that had right answers. He wouldn't take risks, and he made sure his answers were always what the teacher wanted. Knowing this, his teachers were able to help Gregory learn to deal with uncertainty and risk.

Middle Childhood

Test Bank items 13.27–13.30, 13.46, 13.47, 13.61, 13.70

In the middle years, students are extending their understanding in many areas, including language, numbers, the arts, science, and social studies. Whole-language teaching and apprenticeships might support this learning.

Whole Language. Most teachers agree that the first key to language development in school is to encourage students to use language by talking, listening, reading, and writing. Yetta and Kenneth Goodman (1990) make this argument:

> Language, written language included, is learned most easily in the context of use. When language is whole, relevant, and functional, learners have real purposes for using language, and through their language use, they develop control over the processes of language (p. 225).

Within this **whole-language perspective,** teaching and learning are seen as reciprocal and collaborative. The teacher becomes an astute observer of students, noticing what support or resources they need in order to learn. Teacher and students together make decisions about curriculum. When students write, they write for an audience; their goal is to communicate effectively. Writing is a relevant and meaningful activity. Vygotsky (1978) recognized the importance of authentic writing tasks: "[W]riting should be incorporated into a task that is necessary and relevant for life. Only then can we be certain that it will develop not as a matter of hand and finger habits but as a really new and complex form of speech" (p. 118). David Pearson (1989) makes a similar point: "[We] should ask students to read and write for real reasons (the kind real people in the real world have) rather than fake reasons we give them in school. School is too school-like" (p. 235).

The advocates of whole language insist that the curriculum should be integrated. There is no reason to work on spelling skills, then listening skills, then writing skills, and then social studies or science. All these abilities can be developed together if students work to solve authentic problems. For example, one teacher capitalized on current affairs to encourage student reading, writing, and social studies problem solving:

> Cathie's elementary class learned about the Alaskan oil spill. She brought a newspaper article to class that sequenced in logbook fashion the events

of the oil spill in Prince William Sound. To prepare her students to understand the article, she had her students participate in several background-building experiences. First, they used a world map, an encyclopedia, and library books to gather and share relevant information. Next, she simulated an oil spill by coating an object with oil. By then, the class was eager to read the article. (Espe et al., 1990, p. 45)

After they read and discussed the newspaper article, the teacher asked the class to imagine how the problem might have been prevented. Students had to explain and support their proposed solutions. The next week the students read another newspaper article about how people in their state were helping with the cleanup efforts in Alaska. The teacher asked if the students wanted to help, and they replied with an enthusiastic "Yes!" The students designed posters and made speeches requesting donations of clean towels to be used to clean the oil-soaked animals in Prince William Sound. The class sent four large bags of towels to Alaska to help in the cleanup. The teacher's and the students' reading, writing, research, and speaking were directed toward solving a real-life problem (Espe, Worner, & Hotkevich, 1990).

There are many approaches to whole-language learning, but most share an emphasis on authentic tasks and integrated curricula. The Contoocook Valley (CoVal) District in New Hampshire has adopted a whole-language approach with ten elements, listed in Table 13.4. Whatever your school's philosophy, you might adopt some of the ideas from the whole-language approach to encourage language and cognitive development in your students.

What is the status of whole-language approaches? You will hear opinions on both sides, as you can see in the Point/Counterpoint on page 502.

TABLE 13.4   Ten Elements of a Whole-Language Program

1. *Reading to children*—the teacher reads quality literature to children to encourage them to read.

2. *Shared book experience*—a cooperative language activity based on the bedtime story tradition; the teacher reads and rereads appealing rhymes, songs, poems, and stories.

3. *Sustained silent reading*—everyone, including the teacher, reads for an extended period of time.

4. *Guided reading*—the teacher assigns books to groups of eight to ten children for independent reading followed by reading conferences; books are selected to keep the children on the cutting edge of their reading ability.

5. *Individualized reading*—an organized alternative to guided reading; grows out of guided reading; careful monitoring of individual progress is done by both child and teacher.

6. *Language experience*—oral language is recorded by a scribe or on tape and made available to children in written format; firsthand or vicarious experience is translated into written language.

7. *Children's writing*—ConVal uses the writing process of rehearse, draft, revise, edit, publish, and receive responses.

8. *Modeled writing*—the teacher models writing process and behavior; children see and hear an "expert" writer in action.

9. *Opportunities for sharing*—a finished piece is presented to an audience; ConVal uses author's teas and published books as two methods.

10. *Content area reading and writing*—students see demonstrations of each type of text (by subject content) and learn about varying reading speed and looking for content clues.

Source: P. A. Robbins (1990). "Implementing whole language: Bridging children and books." *Educational Leadership*, 47(6) p. 53. Reprinted with permission of the Association for Supervision and Curriculum Development. Copyright © 1990 by ASCD. All rights reserved.

Whole Language versus Phonics in Learning to Read

For years, educators have debated whether students should be taught to read through code-based (phonics, skills) approaches that relate letters to sounds and sounds to words or through meaning-based (whole-language, literature-based, emergent literacy) approaches that *do not* dissect words and sentences into pieces, but instead focus on the meaning of the text (Goodman, 1986; Smith, 1992; Vellutino, 1992). Whole-language approaches have become very popular, but are they effective?

POINT Children learn best when language is kept whole.

Advocates of whole-language approaches believe that learning to read is a natural process, very much like mastering your native language. Reading is a kind of guessing game in which students sample words and make predictions and guesses about meaning based on the context of other words in the passage and on their prior knowledge. So words should not be presented out of context, and "sounding out" words and "breaking whole (natural) language into bite-size abstract little pieces" should be avoided (Goodman, 1986, p. 7). Rather, children should be emersed in a print-rich environment, surrounded by books worth reading and adults who read—to the children and for themselves.

Whole language, according to Frank Smith (1992), has nothing to do with methods, materials, or techniques. It is rather a philosophy:

The basis of the philosophy as respect—respect for language (which should be natural and "authentic," not contrived and fragmented) and respect for learners (who should be engaged in meaningful and productive activities, not pointless drills and memorization). The philosophy has attracted the enthusiastic support of scores of thousands of teachers. It is without a doubt the most vital movement in education today, and its political and social influence has been enormous. (p. 440)

COUNTERPOINT Skill in recognizing sounds and words supports reading.

Frank Vellutino (1992) says, "At the heart of the debate between code and meaning advocates is the question of

Apprenticeships.   Over the centuries, apprenticeships have proved to be an effective form of education. By working alongside a master and perhaps other apprentices, young people have learned many skills, trades, and crafts. Why are they so effective? Howard Gardner (1991) suggests that apprenticeships are rich in information because the master knows a great deal about the subject. Working with more knowledgeable guides provides models, demonstrations, and corrections, as well as a personal bond that is motivating. The performances required of the learner are real and important and grow more complex as the learner becomes more competent.

How can teaching provide **cognitive apprenticeships?** In the Key School, an inner-city public elementary school in Indianapolis, Indiana, students of different ages work side-by-side for part of every day on a "pod" designed to have many of the qualities of an apprenticeship. The pods might focus on a craft or a discipline. Examples include gardening, architecture, and "making money." Many levels of expertise are evident in the students of different ages, so students can move at a comfortable pace, but still have the model of a master available. Community volunteers, including many parents, visit to demonstrate a skill that is related to the pod topic.

The challenge with apprenticeships as well as all hands-on projects is to make them more than just "science fair" experiences in which parents do most of the learning. Teachers must understand the subject and the students very well to facilitate development.

Cognitive Apprenticeship A relationship in which a less experienced learner acquires knowledge and skills under the guidance of an expert.

whether fluency (automaticity) in identifying words out of context is a prerequisite for effective and efficient comprehension of what is read" (p. 437). Advocates of code-based approaches believe that being able to identify many words as you read does not depend on using context to guess meaning. In fact, it is almost the other way around—knowing words helps you make sense of context. Identifying words as you read is a highly automatic process. The more fluent and automatic you are in identifying words, the more effective you will be in getting meaning from context.

Many studies support the code-based position. For example, three different groups reported similar findings in the *Journal of Educational Psychology* (December, 1991). Summarizing the results of these investigations, Frank Vellutino states:

I think it is fair to say that the major theoretical assumptions on which whole-language approaches to instruction are based have simply not been verified in relevant research testing those assumptions. Aside from the fact that there are very sound reasons to reject the "natural" parallel between spoken and written language drawn by whole-language theorists, the research supports the following generalizations: (a) The most basic skill in learning to read is word identification; (b) an adequate degree of fluency in word identification is a basic prerequisite to successful reading comprehension; (c) word identification in skilled readers is a fast-acting, automatic, and in effect modular process that depends little on contextual information for execution; (d) even skilled readers can predict not more than one word out of four in sentence contexts, indicating that the predictive role of context must be extremely limited; (e) because of limited facility in word identification, beginning and poor readers are much more dependent on context than are more advanced readers; (p. 442)

Vellutino goes on to list two more generalizations, that alphabetic coding and awareness of letter sounds are essential skills for acquiring word identification, so some direct teaching of the alphabet and phonics is helpful in learning to read. The best approach probably makes sensible use of both phonics and whole language. After all, we want our students to be fluent *and* enthusiastic readers and writers.

High School and Beyond

Test Bank items 13.31, 13.48, 13.62, 13.70

As students move into high school, they are becoming more sophisticated in their understanding of subjects such as literature, mathematics, science, and history. Unfortunately, many students have also picked up some misinformation along the way. We will consider examples of student-centered approaches that might help high school students construct a more complete understanding of mathematics, learn ways of researching topics in the library, and confront and correct misconceptions in science.

Constructing Mathematics. Jere Confrey (1990b) analyzed an expert mathematics teacher in a class for high school girls who had difficulty with mathematics. Confrey identified five components in a model of this teacher's approach to teaching. These components are summarized in Table 13.5 on page 504.

Conducting Research. Judy Pitts (1992) describes two different "lessons" about doing library research. In the first, the library media specialist gives a clear, step-by-step presentation that describes how to use the *Readers' Guide*. After the presentation and a question-and-answer session, the media specialist passes out a worksheet with copies of *Readers' Guide* entries and questions about each selection. But the students never actually use the *Readers' Guide*. They do not confront the messy, ill-structured task of search-

Background: The May 1993 issue of *Educational Leadership* has over a dozen articles on the changing curriculum, including several on the ways that mathematics education has been changed by the National Council of Teachers of Mathematics (NCME) *Curriculum and Evaluation Standards for School Mathematics.*

Background: Peterson, P., Fennema, E., & Carpenter, T. (1989). Using knowledge of how students think about mathematics. *Educational Leadership, 46*(4), 42–46.

Research: Confrey, J. (1990). What constructivism implies for teaching. In R. Davis, C. Maher, & N. Noddings (Eds.), *Constructivist views on the teaching and learning of mathematics* (pp. 107–122). Monograph 4 of the National Council of Teachers of Mathematics, Reston, VA.

TABLE 13.5 A Constructivist Approach to Mathematics: Five Components

1. Promote students' autonomy and commitment to their answers

Examples:

- Question student answers, whether they are right or wrong.
- Insist that students at least try to solve a problem and be able to explain what they tried.

2. Develop students' reflective processes

Examples:

- Ask students to restate the problem in their own words.
- Question students to guide them to try different ways to resolve the problem.
- Ask students to explain what they are doing and why.
- Ask students what they mean by the terms they are using.

3. Construct a case history of each student

Examples:

- Note general tendencies in the way the student approaches problems.
- Note common misconceptions and strengths.

4. If the student is unable to solve a problem, intervene to negotiate a possible solution with the student

Examples:

- Based on the case study and your understanding of how the student is thinking about the problem, guide the student to think about a possible solution.
- Ask questions such as "Is there anything you did in the last one that will help you here?" or "Can you explain your diagram?"
- If the student is becoming frustrated, ask more direct, product-oriented questions.

5. When the problem is solved, review the solution

Examples:

- Encourage students to reflect on what they did and why.
- Note what students did well and build confidence.

Source: Adapted by permission from J. Confrey (1990). What constructivism implies for teaching. In R. Davis, C. Maher, and N. Noddings (Eds.), *Constructivist views on the teaching and learning of mathematics.* Monograph 4 of the National Council of Teachers of Mathematics, Reston, VA.

---

ing for information. Instead they complete a simplified task—one they will never encounter in a real library research project.

The second lesson is quite different. The geography teacher, Mr. Booth, works with the media specialist, Ms. Smythe. Students are in groups, with each member of the group responsible for mastering a particular resource and teaching other group members, if the need arises. Students use the actual resources—the *Readers' Guide, NewsBank,* reference sets, almanacs, and so on. Pitts (1992) describes this class:

> Next, Ms. Smythe reviews the assignment. "Each group is responsible for a different country. You are to decide what information to present and figure out how to make it interesting for your classmates. . . . By the end of the period, please explain your plans to either me or Mr. Booth."

> The students quickly began their work. The room was not quiet, but most discussions focused on the task at hand. One group decided to produce a travel poster and brochure. Group members spent nearly thirty minutes negotiating the types of information they wanted to include. "You can't include stuff about history in a travel brochure," one student insisted. "Yes you can, " another said. "You have to if you tell about historical monuments that tourists should visit." After several more exchanges

among group members, the first student changed his mind, agreeing to be responsible for the pertinent historical information.

Another group decided to write a skit and produce a videotape to present their findings while still another started planning a game about their country. . . . By the end of the period, most students were looking for information, and several mini-lessons with a student teaching another student had taken place. When the bell rang, nearly everyone looked surprised and then somewhat irritated at being interrupted. (pp. 16–17)

In the second class, students confront complex, real-life problems, not simplified worksheets. They learn by doing and by teaching others. The students must take positions and argue for them while being open to the ideas of others. They may encounter different representation of the same information—graphs, databases, maps, interviews, or encyclopedia articles—and have to integrate information from different sources. So this lesson exemplifies many of the characteristics of constructivist approaches. But the most important characteristic of the lesson is that students have a good chance of learning how to do library research.

Christopherian Encounters. We have seen a number of times that by high school many students have "learned" some unfortunate lessons in school. Like Sherry, described earlier in this chapter, they have learned that math is impossible to understand and you just have to apply the rules to get the answers. Or they may have developed some misconceptions about the world, such as the belief that the earth is warmer in the summer because it is closer to the sun. Howard Gardner (1991, 1993a) believes that these misconceptions and misunderstandings are prevalent in even the "best educated" students. He suggests that, in high school, "students must directly confront evidence that contradicts their intuitive theories" (1991, p. 227). Gardner calls this process **Christopherian encounters** after Christopher Columbus, whose voyages helped correct misconceptions about the shape of the world.

There are several Christopherian encounters that use the microworld format described earlier. Jeremy Roschelle (1991), working with James Greeno, created the "Envisioning Machine," a computer world with two windows. In the "object window," the student can simulate throwing a ball. A hand on the computer screen throws the ball and the ball travels just as it would in the real, observable world, except that the ball leaves a trace so the student can easily see the movement path. In the second window, the Newtonian world of constant acceleration and velocity is depicted (see Figure 13.2 on page 506). Students can see the path an object would follow, given any combination of initial velocity and acceleration chosen. Thus, the Envisioning Machine gives students a laboratory to experiment with "pure" Newtonian motion. The students might be asked to observe the movement of a ball in the observable-world window, and then select the correct initial velocity and acceleration to create the same path in the Newtonian window (Roschelle & Clancey, 1992). The Envisioning Machine confronts misconceptions by showing the students the actual path created by their selections in the Newtonian world.

Background: Gardner, H. (1991). *The unschooled mind: How children think and how schools should teach.* New York: Basic Books. Gardner, H. (1993). *Educating the unschooled mind: A science and public policy seminar.* Washington, DC: American Educational Research Association. Brandt, R. (1993). On teaching for understanding: A Conversation with Howard Gardner. *Educational Leadership, 50*(7), 4–7.

Transparency: "The General Inductive Model" of teaching is presented in acetate transparency T 108.

Transparency: "The Concept Attainment Model" of teaching is presented in acetate transparency T 109.

Focus on . . . **Constructivist Approaches for Different Ages**

- How might a 1st or 2nd grade teacher observe and develop student abilities in all seven "intelligences?"
- What is meant by an integrated curriculum? Give an example.
- What is meant by a "Christopherian encounter?" Give an example.

Christopherian Encounters Process by which students must confront evidence which contradicts their intuition or preconceptions.

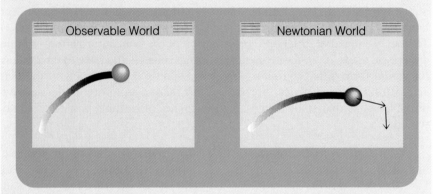

FIGURE 13.2

THE ENVISIONING MACHINE
This microworld allows students to simulate movement in a Newtonian World. Students can select different initial velocities and constant acceleration, then see how an object would move given these characteristics. Then the students can compare the actual movement of objects in the real world to different combinations of velocity and acceleration.

Observable World Newtonian World

Source: J. Roschelle and W. J. Clancey (1992). Learning as social and neural. *Educational Psychologist, 27,* 435–454. Adapted by permission of the publisher and authors.

Test Bank items 13.65, 13.69, 13.71–13.74

Integrations: Beyond Models to Outstanding Teaching

In this chapter and the previous one, we have examined two ways of studying teaching, one that centers on the teacher and another that focuses on the student. Of course, in practice teaching and learning cannot be separated—they are always connected. Let's take a minute to consider how both direct instructional and student-centered teaching could influence the ways students learn and remember.

Can Direct Instruction Encourage Understanding?

Test Bank items 13.32, 13.77

What aspects of direct instruction might explain its success? Linda Anderson (1989b) offers one clue. She suggests that lessons that help students perceive links among main ideas will help them construct accurate understandings. Well-organized presentations, clear explanations, the use of explanatory links, and reviews can all help students perceive connections among ideas. If done well, therefore, a direct instruction lesson could be a resource that students use to construct understanding. For example, reviews activate prior knowledge so the student is ready to understand. Brief, clear presentations and guided prac-

Activity 13.7: Demonstration. See the *Instructor's Resource Manual* for Teaching Methods and Classroom Management: A Comparison.

Discussion: Can different formats, such as lecture or seatwork, be used in the service of different models, such as direct instruction or constructivist approaches?

Background: If you want to discuss possible differences in effective teaching of mathematics for boys and girls, see Fennema, E., & Peterson, P. L. (1987). Effective teaching for girls and boys: The same or different? In D. Berliner & B. Rosenshine (Eds.), *Talks to teachers* (pp. 111–125). New York: Random House.

tice avoid overloading the students' information processing systems and taxing their memories. Numerous examples and explanations give many pathways and associations for building networks of concepts. Guided practice can also give the teacher a snapshot of the students' thinking and of their misconceptions, so these can be addressed directly as misconceptions rather than simply as "wrong answers."

What direct instruction cannot do is ensure that students understand. If badly done, it may encourage students to memorize and mimic but never to "own" the knowledge. To help students reach this goal, Eleanor Duckworth believes that teachers must pay very close attention to understanding their students' understandings (Meek, 1991). This process is the basis for cognitive/constructive models of teaching.

Matching Methods to Learning Goals

Test Bank items 13.34, 13.64, 13.65, 13.77

Penelope Peterson (1979) compared the more traditional teacher-centered direct instruction with more open, constructivist methods. She concluded that teacher-centered instruction leads to better performance on achievement tests; while the open, informal methods like discovery learning or inquiry approaches are associated with better performance on tests of creativity, abstract thinking, and problem solving. In addition, the open methods are better for improving attitudes toward school and for stimulating curiosity, cooperation among students, and lower absence rates (Walberg, 1990). According to these conclusions, when the goals of teaching involve problem solving, creativity, understanding, and mastering processes, many approaches besides direct instruction should be effective.

These guidelines are in keeping with Tom Good's conclusion that teaching should become less direct as students mature and when the goals involve affective development and problem solving or critical thinking (Good, 1983a). Of course, every subject, even college English or chemistry, can require some direct instruction. If you are teaching when to use "who" and "whom," or how to set up laboratory apparatus, direct instruction may be the best approach. Noddings (1990) reminds teachers that students may need some direct instruction in how to use various manipulative materials to get the possible benefits from them. Students working in cooperative groups may need guidance, modeling, and practice in how to ask questions and give explanations. And to solve difficult problems, students may need some direct instruction in possible problem-solving strategies. The message for teachers is to match instructional methods to learning goals.

Handout: For an extended example of the relationships between the inquiry method and the curriculum, see **Handout Master 13.6**, "Inquiry Curriculum Design for Multicultural Education."

Activity 13.8: Critical Thinking. See the *Instructor's Resource Manual* for Direct versus Indirect Instruction.

Background: Marshall, H. H. (Ed.) (1992). *Redefining student learning: Roots of educational change*. Norwood, NJ: Ablex.

SUMMARY

Perspectives on Student-Centered Teaching

Many researchers studying teaching today have turned their attention from a focus on teachers' behavior to an examination of student learning. Educators now see their main task to be helping their students become effective, motivated learners. The American Psychological Association is currently drafting a set of principles designed to define and promote student-centered learning practices. Teaching based on these principles would ensure that students are active in solving problems, practicing learning strategies, making choices, and discovering important ideas.

Educators and psychologists who take a constructivist approach are among the strongest voices speaking in favor of student-centered teaching. They emphasize the importance of students' construction of knowledge. Constructivist approaches to teaching recommend: complex, challenging learning environments; social negotiation and shared responsibility as part of learning; multiple representations of content; understanding that knowledge is constructed; and student-centered instruction.

Student-Centered Teaching Methods

In teacher-centered approaches, teachers select learning objectives and plan how to get students to meet those objectives. Teachers control the "what" and "how" of learning. In contrast, planning is shared and negotiated in student-centered, or constructivist, approaches. The teacher and students together make decisions about content, activities, and approaches. Students have the opportunity to pursue personally meaningful problems and projects. Rather than having specific student behaviors as objectives, the teacher has overarching goals or "big ideas" that guide planning. The focus is not so much on the products as on the processes of learning and thinking behind the products. Assessment of learning is ongoing and mutually shared by teacher and students. The point of assessment is to support learning, not to reward "getting the right answer."

Constructivist teaching practices include individualized instruction, group discussion, inquiry, reciprocal teaching, humanistic education, and computers and hypermedia. These methods make minimal use of rote memorization.

They strive instead to encourage in students an excitement about learning, a thrill in discovering how the world works.

Constructivist Teaching for Different Ages

When designing learning environments to support the construction of knowledge in young children, teachers should help them develop abilities while retaining their curiosity and zest for learning. The goal of understanding, not just memorizing, has to be established early.

In the middle years students are extending their understanding of many areas, including language, numbers, the arts, science, and social studies. Whole-language approaches, apprenticeships, and methods that emphasize authentic tasks, support such learning particularly well.

Teenagers are becoming more sophisticated in their understanding of subjects such as literature, mathematics, science, and history. Often, however, they have learned some misinformation along the way—like "math is impossible." Student-centered approaches can challenge misconceptions and help students learn how to deepen their understanding through inquiry and critical thinking.

Integrations

Many educators feel that the careful use of direct instruction methods—well-organized presentations, clear explanations, carefully delivered prompts, and guided discovery—can be a resource for students as they construct understanding. In all cases, teaching methods should match learning goals.

KEY TERMS

WHAT WOULD YOU DO?

Preschool and Kindergarten

One of your students is very fearful of taking risks or attempting any task that does not have a right answer. The child tries to tell other students "the right way" to do everything. How would you help the student tolerate uncertainty and become willing to try more open-ended, creative projects?

Elementary and Middle School

How would you help 3rd grade students understand negative numbers?

Your school district has adopted a whole-language, integrated curriculum approach. Students and teachers are generally pleased, but standardized test results indicate a drop in scores in some language areas, and several parents are complaining. As a teacher, what would you do about the parents' complaints?

Junior High and High School

Your school librarian wants to help all the history classes learn to use the print and database resources in the library. How would you take advantage of this opportunity?

The answers to the essay questions on your last exam are "right from the book." Develop an assignment that will help students move beyond the text to think more deeply about the questions.

Cooperative Learning

With a few other members of your class, identify a concept you will be teaching that is often misunderstood. Design a student-centered approach that will help students understand this difficult idea.

With four or five other members of your educational psychology class, brainstorm ways to "understand your students' understanding" in a particular content area. What would you do before, during, and after a class in this unit to make your students' knowledge and thinking processes visible to you and to them?

Learning Content

Describe your experience with the following learning approaches: whole-language, inquiry learning, and mathematics instruction.

WHOLE MATH APPROACH

I want to teach the whole child. I want them to start thinking and using some logical explanations for why things are the way they are and not just sitting back and waiting for the teacher to always communicate the idea. I like to use writing a lot because many of my kids are Spanish-dominant, and they come in with poor writing skills. So this is another way to get them to express themselves, other than in the English classes. They have to realize that writing and explanation are part of the mathematical process. I want them to find out that math can be a pleasurable experience. That's the whole idea. Math class shouldn't be something that they fear coming to. My greatest joy is just seeing my students enjoy math, coming to school, not shying away from it. It's an area where a lot of times minority kids feel they can't be successful. I want them to know they can be successful at it. I don't seek to embarrass my kids. If they get a wrong answer, then we've got to ask, 'How did you get that answer?' Then it becomes less intimidating if they're not correct.

Kay Toliver, *Math Teacher*
East Harlem Tech Middle School

Story Problems

Students often have difficulty with story problems in math because they are not representing the problems so they can "see" the appropriate solution strategies. What are some techniques you use to help students represent problems?

LET STUDENTS WORK TOGETHER

When we do story problems for homework I make it an in-class assignment and let the students work together. They are free to check any answers with me. On a test I use problems that they can identify with personally. They spend money at a street fair, baby-sit at different rates, work for so much an hour. I often let them use calculators. With story problems, I am more concerned about having students solve that problem than with the actual computation.

Donald Falk, *Math Teacher*
Fredericktown Intermediate School, Fredericktown, Ohio

A VARIETY OF STRATEGIES

I strongly urge students to sketch out some sort of model for each word problem. Brainstorming is an important problem-solving tool. I reward appropriate strategies even if the final answer is inaccurate. Also, we explore a variety of strategies that will effectively solve each problem. I often attack problem solving by employing cooperative learning. This model of teaching gives students exposure to each other's ideas and strategies.

Stephen C. Ellwood IV, *Maine 1991 Teacher of the Year*
St. Francis Elementary School, St. Francis, Maine

ROLE PLAYING

Role playing is an excellent way to help children visualize and understand the process of solving story problems. For instance, if a story problem involves two characters, I select two students for the roles. I set the scene by reading the story. To personalize it, each student plays himself and decides what lines he would say in that particular situation. (In the beginning, students may require some prompting.) Then I write the story on the chalkboard in equation form and explain it. A second story problem is presented, and new volunteers are selected for role playing. A volunteer is also selected to write the story on the board as an equation. The students soon learn to write their own story problems in this form. Should a student fail to understand the process, he can draw a picture or retell the story to me. Invariably the child will "see" the solution.

Nancy R. Gonzalez, *Bilingual First-Grade Teacher*
Robert Frost School, Mount Prospect, Illinois

Student Writing

Sometimes students get bogged down in the mechanics of writing . . . How do you encourage students to write creatively and imaginatively while also helping them learn correct grammar and vocabulary?

WRITE FOR A REASON

In order for students to write well, they must write for a reason. I have found that students are willing to write if they have something to say and believe that someone, either myself as their teacher or any other real audience, cares what they have to say. My students write to explain, to argue a point of view, to prove a hypothesis. My focus is on their message. Eventually their need to present a clear description or persuasive argument will lead to a concern with the clarity and logic of their message. First and foremost, my students are encouraged to write in order to discover and clarify their ideas. Editing is done only to strengthen the intelligibility of the ideas, and revisions are always acceptable. Students want to be heard. Clear writing, reflecting our shared symbolic conventions, allows them to be.

Karen B. Kreider, *Pennsylvania 1991 Teacher of the Year*
Central High School, Philadelphia, Pennsylvania

Strategies to Involve Students

We know that effective teaching relies in part on students' active involvement in lessons. What strategies do you use to keep students involved? How do you keep the rest of the class engaged when only a few are answering questions?

WINNING TECHNIQUES

Keeping all students involved is always a challenge. One way to meet the challenge is to make sure that all students believe they may be called on at any time. In my experience, secondary-school students should be selected to answer questions randomly. The question should be asked first, before anyone is called on. After the first student has responded, that answer can be used to generate a new question for others.

Another technique to help keep students focused on the task is to walk around the classroom while asking questions. Students tend to daydream less if the teacher is standing nearby. A third technique is to have students write individual responses to questions. After they've all had enough time to write their responses, an individual student can be called on. This way, all students think through the question and answer it, even if they don't respond orally.

Jane C. Dusell, *English Teacher*
Medford Senior High School, Medford, Wisconsin

14

Standardized Testing

W ould it surprise you to learn that published tests, such as the college entrance exams and IQ tests, are creations of the 20th century? In the 19th and early 20th centuries, college entrance was generally based on grades, essays, and interviews. From your own experience, you know that testing has come a long way since then. In fact, many educators and psychologists believe standardized testing has come too far. Some critics want to reshape testing as a way of reshaping the curriculum and reforming education. We will explore these new ideas.

In spite of the criticisms, schools still use many standardized tests, so teachers must be knowledgeable about testing. This chapter focuses on preparing for and interpreting standardized tests. Understanding how standardized test scores are determined, what they really mean, and how they can be used (or misused) provides you a framework for ensuring that the tests you give are appropriate.

First, we consider testing in general, including the various methods of interpreting test scores. Then we look at the different kinds of standardized tests used in schools. Finally, we examine the criticisms of testing and the alternatives being proposed. By the time you have completed this chapter, you should be able to do the following:

- Calculate mean, median, mode, and standard deviation.
- Define percentile ranks, standard deviations, *z* scores, *T* scores, and stanine scores.
- Explain how to improve reliability and validity in testing.
- Interpret the results of achievement, aptitude, and diagnostic tests in a realistic manner.
- Take a position on the testing issue and defend your position.
- Describe how to prepare students (and yourself) for taking standardized tests.
- Explain the strengths and weaknesses of alternative forms of assessment such as portfolios.

Evaluation Decision making about student performance and about appropriate teaching strategies.

Measurement An evaluation expressed in quantitative (number) terms.

Norm-Referenced Testing Testing in which scores are compared with the average performance of others.

WHAT DO YOU THINK?

How has standardized testing affected your life so far? What opportunities have opened or closed to you based on test scores? Was the process fair? Propose a better way to make these decisions.

Measurement and Evaluation

All teaching involves **evaluation**. At the heart of evaluation is judgment, making decisions based on values. In the process of evaluation, we compare information to criteria and then make judgments. Teachers must make all kinds of judgments. "Should we use a different text this year?" "Is the film appropriate for my students?" "Will Sarah do better if she repeats the first grade?" "Should Terry get a B– or a C+ on the project?"

Measurement is evaluation put in quantitative terms—the numeric description of an event or characteristic. Measurement tells how much, how often, or how well by providing scores, ranks, or ratings. Instead of saying, "Sarah doesn't seem to understand addition," a teacher might say, "Sarah answered only 2 of the 15 problems correctly in her addition homework." Measurement also allows a teacher to compare one student's performance on one particular task with a standard or with the performances of the other students.

Not all the evaluative decisions made by teachers involve measurement. Some decisions are based on information that is difficult to express numerically: student preferences, information from parents, previous experiences, even intuition. But measurement does play a large role in many classroom decisions, and properly done, it can provide unbiased data for evaluations.

The answers given on any type of test have no meaning by themselves; we must make some kind of comparison to interpret test results. There are two basic types of comparison: In the first, a test score is compared to the scores obtained by other people who have taken the same test. (This is called a norm-referenced comparison.) For instance, if you took a college entrance exam, the score you received told you (and the admissions offices of colleges) how your performance compared to the performances of many other people who had previously taken either the same test or one like it. The second type is criterion-referenced. Here, the comparison is to a fixed standard or minimum passing score. Most tests required for a driver's license are based on this kind of comparison.

Norm-Referenced Tests

In **norm-referenced testing**, the people who have taken the test provide the *norms* for determining the meaning of a given individual's score. You can think of a norm as being the typical level of performance for a particular group. By comparing the individual's raw score (the actual number correct) to the norm, we can determine if the score is above, below, or around the average for that group.

There are at least three types of **norm groups** (comparison groups) in education. One frequently used norm group is the class or school itself. When a teacher compares the score of one student in a 10th-grade American history class with the scores of all the other students in the class, the class itself is the norm group. If the teacher happens to have three American history classes, all of about the same ability, then the norm group for evaluating individual performance might be all three classes.

Norm groups may also be drawn from wider areas. Sometimes, for example, school districts develop achievement tests. When students take this kind of test, their scores are compared to the scores of all other students at their grade level throughout the district. Finally, some tests have national norm groups. When students take the college entrance exam, their scores are compared with the scores of students all over the country.

Norm-referenced tests cover a wide range of general objectives rather than assessing a limited number of specific objectives. Norm-referenced tests are especially useful in measuring the overall achievement of students who have come to understand complex material by different routes. Norm-referenced tests are also appropriate when only the top few candidates can be admitted to a program.

However, norm-referenced measurement has its limitations. The results of a norm-referenced test do not tell you whether students are ready to move on to more advanced material. For instance, knowing that a student is in the top 3 percent of the class on a test of algebraic concepts will not tell you if he or she is ready to move on to trigonometry; everyone in the class may have a limited understanding of the algebraic concepts.

Nor are norm-referenced tests particularly appropriate for measuring affective and psychomotor objectives. To measure individuals' psychomotor learning, you need a clear description of standards. (Even the best gymnast in school performs certain exercises better than others and needs specific guidance about how to improve.) In the affective area, attitudes and values are personal; comparisons among individuals are not really appropriate. For example, how could we measure an "average" level of political values or opinions? Finally, norm-referenced tests tend to encourage competition and comparison of scores. Some students compete to be the best. Others, realizing that being the best is impossible, may compete to be the worst. Either goal has its casualties.

Criterion-Referenced Tests

Test Bank items 14.3, 14.7, 14.8, 14.71, 14.84, 14.101

When test scores are compared, not to those of others, but to a given criterion or standard of performance, this is **criterion-referenced testing**. To decide who should be allowed to drive a car, it is important to determine just what standard of performance is appropriate for selecting safe drivers. It does not matter how your test results compare to the results of others. If your performance on the test was in the top 10 percent but you consistently ran through red lights, you would not be a good candidate for receiving a license, even though your score was high.

Objective 14.2: Define norm-referenced testing and criterion-referenced testing. Give uses and limitations of each type of test.

Background: For a brief overview of the types of tests, see Shepard, L. (1989). Norm-referenced versus criterion-referenced tests. In *Annual editions: Educational psychology 89/90* (pp. 198–203). Guilford, CT: Duskin.

Example: To get a teaching certificate in some states, you must pass a criterion-referenced test, that is, you must reach a certain standard of performance on a test such as the NTE (National Teachers' Examination).

Norm Group A group whose average score serves as a standard for evaluating any student's score on a test.

Criterion-Referenced Testing Testing in which scores are compared to a set performance standard.

Criterion-referenced tests measure the mastery of very specific objectives. The results of a criterion-referenced test should tell the teacher exactly what the students can and cannot do, at least under certain conditions. For example, a criterion-referenced test would be useful in measuring the ability to add three-digit numbers. A test could be designed with 20 different problems, and the standard for mastery could be set at 17 correct out of 20. (The standard is often somewhat arbitrary and may be based on such things as the teacher's experience.) If two students receive scores of 7 and 11, it does not matter that one student did better than the other since neither met the standard of 17. Both need more help with addition.

In teaching basic skills there are many instances where comparison to a preset standard is more important than comparison to the performance of others. It is not very comforting to know, as a parent, that your child is better in reading than most of the students in class if none of the students is able to read material suited for their grade level. Sometimes standards for meeting the criterion must be set at 100 percent correct. You would not like to have your appendix removed by a surgeon who left surgical instruments inside the body *only* 10 percent of the time.

But criterion-referenced tests are not appropriate for every situation. Many subjects cannot be broken down into a set of specific objectives. Moreover, although standards are important in criterion-referenced testing, they can often be arbitrary, as you have already seen. When deciding whether a student has mastered the addition of three-digit numbers comes down to the difference between 16 or 17 correct answers, it seems difficult to justify one particular standard over another. Finally, at times it is valuable to know how the students in your class compare to other students at their grade level both locally and nationally. Table 14.1 offers a comparison of norm-referenced and criterion-referenced tests. You can see that each type of test is well suited for certain situations, but each also has its limitations.

Focus on . . . **Measurement and Evaluation**

- What is the difference between measurement and evaluation?
- What examples of criterion-referenced and norm-referenced tests have you experienced in the past year?
- The doctor tells you that your cholesterol level is above average. What would you like to know about the norm group?
- Would you prefer a criterion-referenced or norm-referenced measure of your blood pressure? Why?

TABLE 14.1   Deciding on the Type of Test to Use

Norm-referenced tests may work best when you are

- Measuring general ability in certain areas, such as English, algebra, general science, or American history.
- Assessing the range of abilities in a large group.
- Selecting top candidates when only a few openings are available.

Criterion-referenced tests may work best when you are

- Measuring mastery of basic skills.
- Determining if students have prerequisites to start a new unit.
- Assessing affective and psychomotor objectives.
- Grouping students for instruction.

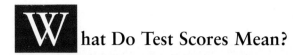hat Do Test Scores Mean?

On the average, more than 1 million standardized tests are given per school day in classes throughout this country (Lyman, 1986). Most of these are norm-referenced standardized tests. **Standardized tests** are those official-looking pamphlets and piles of forms purchased by school systems and administered to students. More specifically, the tests are called standardized because "the same directions are used for administering them in all classrooms and standard procedures are used for scoring and interpreting them" (Carey, 1994, p. 443). The tests are meant to be given under carefully controlled conditions so that students all over the country undergo the same experience. Standard methods of developing items, administering the test, scoring it, and reporting the scores are all implied by the term standardized test.

Basic Concepts

Test Bank items 14.11–14.18, 14.22, 14.23, 14.25, 14.72–14.74, 14.85–14.88, 14.102

In standardized testing the test items and instructions have been tried out to make sure they work and then rewritten and retested as necessary. The final version of the test is administered to a **norming sample,** a large sample of subjects as similar as possible to the students who will be taking the test in school systems throughout the country. This norming sample serves as a comparison group for all students who take the test.

The test publishers provide one or more ways of comparing each student's raw score (number of correct answers) with the norming sample. Let's look at some of the measurements on which comparisons and interpretations are based.

Frequency Distributions.   A **frequency distribution** is simply a listing of the number of people who obtain each score or fall into each range of scores on a test or other measurement procedure. For example, on a spelling test 19 students made these scores: 100, 95, 90, 85, 85, 85, 80, 75, 75, 75, 70, 65, 60, 60, 55, 50, 50, 45, 40. A graph, in this case a **histogram** (bar graph), of the spelling test scores is shown in Figure 14.1 on page 518, where one axis (the *x,* or horizontal, axis) indicates the possible scores and the other axis (the *y,* or vertical, axis) indicates the number of subjects who attained each score. As you can see, one student made a score of 100, three made 85, and so on.

Measurements of Central Tendency and Standard Deviation.   You have probably had a great deal of experience with means. A **mean** is simply the arithmetical average of a group of scores. To calculate the mean, you add the scores and divide the total by the number of scores in the distribution. For example, the total of the 19 spelling scores is 1,340, so the mean is 1,340/19, or 70.53. The mean offers one way of measuring **central tendency,** the score that is typical or representative of the whole distribution of scores.

Two other measures of central tendency are the median and the mode. The **median** is the middle score in the distribution, the point at which half the scores are larger and half are smaller. The median of the 19 scores is 75. Nine scores in the distribution are greater than or equal to 75, and nine are less. The

Objective 14.3: Define the following terms: standardized test, norming sample, frequency distribution, central tendency, mean, median, mode, standard deviation, and normal distribution.

Transparency: Acetate transparency **T 112** illustrates a histogram as a means of "Describing Measurement Data."

Activity 14.1: See the *Instructor's Resource Manual* for Central Tendency, a mini-case study of a teacher who is criticized by the superintendent for having the class with the lowest median score in the district on a standardized math test.

Discussion: At a PTA meeting parents were complaining because half of the students in the district scored below the district average on the achievement tests that were given. Is this a valid complaint?

Standardized Tests Tests given, usually nationwide, under uniform conditions and scored according to uniform procedures.

Norming Sample Large sample of students serving as a comparison group for scoring standardized tests.

Frequency Distribution Record showing how many scores fall into set groups.

Histogram Bar graph of a frequency distribution.

Mean Arithmetical average.

Central Tendency Typical score for a group of scores.

Median Middle score in a group of scores.

Mode Most frequently occurring score.

Bimodal Distribution Frequency distribution with two modes.

Standard Deviation Measure of how widely scores vary from the mean.

Variability Degree of difference or deviation from mean.

FIGURE 14.1

HISTOGRAM OF A FREQUENCY DISTRIBUTION
This bar graph or histogram shows the number of people who earned each score on a test. You can quickly see, for example, that three people earned a 75 and three people earned an 85.

mode is the score that occurs most often. The distribution in Figure 14.1 actually has two modes, 75 and 85, because each of these scores occurred three times. This makes it a **bimodal distribution.**

The measure of central tendency gives a score that is representative of the group of scores, but it does not tell you anything about how the scores are distributed. Two groups of scores may both have a mean of 50 but be alike in no other way. One group might contain the scores 50, 45, 55, 55, 45, 50, 50; the other group might contain the scores 100, 0, 50, 90, 10, 50, 50. In both cases the mean, median, and mode are all 50, but the distributions are quite different.

The **standard deviation** is a measure of how widely the scores vary from the mean. The larger the standard deviation, the more spread out the scores in the distribution. The smaller the standard deviation, the more the scores are clustered around the mean. For example, in the distribution 50, 45, 55, 55, 45, 50, 50, the standard deviation is much smaller than in the distribution 100, 0, 50, 90, 10, 50, 50. Another way of saying this is that distributions with very small standard deviations have less **variability** in the scores.

The standard deviation is relatively easy to calculate if you remember your high school math. It does take time, however. The process is similar to taking an average, but you use square roots. To calculate the standard deviation, you follow these steps:

1. Calculate the mean (written as $\bar{\chi}$) of the scores.

2. Subtract the mean from each of the scores. This is written as $(\chi - \bar{\chi})$.

3. Square each difference (multiply each difference by itself). This is written $(\chi - \overline{\chi})^2$.

4. Add all the squared differences. This is written $\Sigma\,(\chi - \overline{\chi})^2$.

5. Divide this total by the number of scores. This is written $\dfrac{\Sigma\,(\chi - \overline{\chi})^2}{N}$.

6. Find the square root. This is written $\sqrt{\dfrac{\Sigma(\chi - \overline{\chi})^2}{N}}$, which is the formula for calculating the standard deviation.

Knowing the mean and the standard deviation of a group of scores gives you a better picture of the meaning of an individual score. For example, suppose you received a score of 78 on a test. You would be very pleased with the score if the mean of the test were 70 and the standard deviation were 4. In this case, your score would be 2 standard deviations above the mean, a score well above average.

Consider the difference if the mean of the test had remained at 70 but the standard deviation had been 20. In the second case, your score of 78 would be less than 1 standard deviation from the mean. You would be much closer to the middle of the group, with a score above average, but not high. Knowing the standard deviation tells you much more than simply knowing the **range** of scores. No matter how the majority scored on the tests, one or two students may do very well or very poorly and thus make the range very large.

The Normal Distribution.   Standard deviations are very useful in understanding test results. They are especially helpful if the results of the tests form a **normal distribution.** You may have met the normal distribution before. It is the bell-shaped curve, the most famous frequency distribution because it describes many naturally occurring physical and social phenomena. Many scores fall in the middle, giving the curve its puffed appearance. You find fewer and fewer scores as you look out toward the end points, or *tails,* of the distribution.

The normal distribution has been thoroughly analyzed by statisticians. The mean of a normal distribution is also its midpoint. Half the scores are above the mean, and half are below it. In a normal distribution, the mean, median, and mode are all the same point.

Another convenient property of the normal distribution is that the percentage of scores falling within each area of the curve is known, as you can see in Figure 14.2 on page 520. A person scoring within 1 standard deviation of the mean obviously has a lot of company. Many scores pile up here. In fact, 68 percent of all scores are located in the area of ±1 standard deviation from the mean. About 16 percent of the scores are higher than 1 standard deviation above the mean. Of this higher group, only 2.5 percent are better than 2 standard deviations above the mean. Similarly, only about 16 percent of the scores are less than 1 standard deviation below the mean, and of that group only about 2.5 percent are worse than 2 standard deviations below. At 2 standard deviations from the mean in either direction, the scorer has left the pack.

The SAT college entrance exam is one example of a normal distribution. The mean of the SAT is 500 and the standard deviation is 100. If you know people who made scores of 700, you know they did very well. Only about 2.5 percent of the people who take the test do that well, because only 2.5 percent of the scores are better than 2 standard deviations above the mean in a normal distribution.

Transparency: Acetate transparency T 113 presents a graph showing how a frequency distribution forms a normal curve.

Transparency: "The Normal Distribution" is graphically illustrated in acetate transparency T 113.

Teaching Tip: You might note that the sum of all the deviations from the mean in a group of scores equals 0. For example, see the scores below, taken from Best, J. W., & Kahn, J. V. (1986). *Research in education* (5th ed.). Englewood Cliffs, NJ: Prentice-Hall, p. 216.

Reading		Arithmetic	
X	$(X - \overline{X})$	X	$(X - \overline{X})$
95	+20	76	+1
90	+15	78	+3
85	+10	77	+2
80	+5	71	−4
75	0	75	0
70	−5	79	+4
65	−10	73	−2
60	−15	72	−3
55	−20	74	−1
$\Sigma X = 675$	$\Sigma X = 0$	$\Sigma X = 675$	$\Sigma X = 0$
$N = 9$		$N = 9$	
$X = 75$		$X = 75$	

$$\Sigma(X - \overline{X}) = 0$$
$$\Sigma X = 0$$

In fact, we can give an alternative definition of the mean: the mean is that value in a distribution around which the sum of the deviation scores equals zero.

Range Distance between the highest and the lowest score in a group.

Normal Distribution The most commonly occurring distribution, in which scores are distributed evenly around mean.

FIGURE 14.2

THE NORMAL DISTRIBUTION

The normal distribution or bell-shaped curve has certain predictable characteristics. For example, 68 percent of the scores are clustered within 1 standard deviation below to 1 standard deviation above the mean.

Objective 14.4: Be able to interpret percentile rank scores, grade-equivalent scores, and three types of standard scores. Give the advantages or limitations of each type of score.

Activity 14.3: See the separate *Instructor's Resource Manual* for Types of Tests and the Interpretation of Test Scores, a test for your students that asks them to categorize particular commercial tests, match tests to appropriate situations, and apply measurement concepts. This activity is provided in **Handout Master 14.1.**

Transparency: Acetate transparency T 116 shows "Percentile Ranking on a Normal Distribution."

Percentile Rank Percentage of those in the norming sample who scored at or below an individual's score.

Types of Scores

Test Bank items 14.19–14.21, 14.24, 14.26–14.36, 14.38–14.40, 14.89–14.91, 14.103, 14.109–14.112

Now you have enough background for a discussion of the different kinds of scores you may encounter in reports of results from standardized tests.

Percentile Rank Scores. The concept of ranking is the basis for one very useful kind of score reported on standardized tests, a **percentile rank** score. In percentile ranking, each student's raw score is compared with the raw scores of the students in the norming sample. The percentile rank shows the percentage of students in the norming sample who scored at or below a particular raw score. If a student's score is the same as or better than three-quarters of the students in the norming sample, the student would score in the 75th percentile or have a percentile rank of 75. You can see that this does *not* mean that the student had a raw score of 75 correct answers or even that the student answered 75 percent of the questions correctly. Rather, the 75 refers to the percentage of people in the norming sample whose scores on the test were equal to or below this student's score. A percentile rank of 50 means that a student has scored as well as or better than 50 percent of the norming sample and has achieved an average score.

FIGURE 14.3

PERCENTILE RANKING ON A NORMAL DISTRIBUTION CURVE
One problem with percentile scores is that they have different meanings at
different places on the scale. For example, a difference of a few raw score
points near the mean might translate into a 10 point percentile difference,
while it would take 6 or 7 points to make a 10 point percentile difference
farther out on the scale.

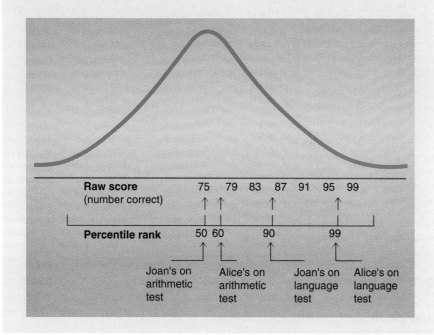

Figure 14.3 illustrates one caution in interpreting percentile scores. Differences in percentile ranks do not mean the same thing in terms of raw score
points in the middle of the scale as they do at the fringes. The graph shows
Joan's and Alice's percentile scores on the fictitious Test of Excellence in Language and Arithmetic. Both students are about average in arithmetic skills.
One equaled or surpassed 50 percent of the norming sample; the other, 60 percent. However, because their scores are in the middle of the distribution, this
difference in percentile ranks means a raw score difference of only a few
points. Their raw scores were actually 75 and 77. In the language test, the difference in percentile ranks seems to be about the same as the difference in arithmetic, since one ranked at the 90th percentile and the other at the 99th. But
the difference in their raw scores on the language test is much greater. It takes
a greater difference in raw score points to make a difference in percentile rank
at the extreme ends of the scale. On the language test the difference in raw
scores is about 10 points.

Grade-Equivalent Score Measure of grade level based on comparison with norming samples from each grade.

Standard Scores Scores based on the standard deviation.

z Score Standard score indicating the number of standard deviations above or below the mean.

T Score Standard score with a mean of 50 and a standard deviation of 10.

Grade-Equivalent Scores. Grade-equivalent scores are generally obtained from separate norming samples for each grade level. The average of the scores of all the 10th graders in the norming sample defines the 10th-grade equivalent score. Suppose the raw-score average of the 10th-grade norming sample is 38. Any student who attains a raw score of 38 on that test will be assigned a grade-equivalent score of 10th grade. Grade-equivalent scores are generally listed in numbers such as 8.3, 4.5, 7.6, 11.5, and so on. The whole number gives the grade. The decimals stand for tenths of a year, but they are usually interpreted as months.

Suppose a student with the grade-equivalent score of 10 is a 7th grader. Should this student be promoted immediately? Probably not. Different forms of tests are used at different grade levels, so the 7th grader may not have had to answer items that would be given to 10th graders. The high score may represent superior mastery of material at the 7th-grade level rather than a capacity for doing advanced work. Even though an average 10th grader could do as well as our 7th grader on this particular test, the 10th grader would certainly know much more than this test covered. Also, grade-equivalent score units do not mean the same thing at every grade level. For example, a 2nd grader reading at the 1st-grade level would have more trouble in school than an 11th grader who reads at the 10th-grade level.

Because grade-equivalent scores are misleading and so often misinterpreted, especially by parents, most educators and psychologists strongly believe they should not be used at all. There are several other forms of reporting available that are more appropriate.

Standard Scores. As you may remember, one problem with percentile ranks is the difficulty in making comparisons among ranks. A discrepancy of a certain number of raw-score points has a different meaning at different places on the scale. With standard scores, on the other hand, a difference of 10 points is the same everywhere on the scale.

Standard scores are based on the standard deviation. A very common standard score is called the **z score**. A z score tells how many standard deviations above or below the average a raw score is. In the example described earlier, in which you were fortunate enough to get a 78 on a test where the mean was 70 and the standard deviation was 4, your z score would be +2, or 2 standard deviations above the mean. If a person were to score 64 on this test, the score would be 1.5 standard deviation units *below* the mean, and the z score would be −1.5. A z score of 0 would be no standard deviations above the mean—in other words, right on the mean.

To calculate the z score for a given raw score, subtract the mean from the raw score and divide the difference by the standard deviation. The formula is:

$$z = \frac{X - \overline{X}}{SD}$$

Since it is often inconvenient to use negative numbers, other standard scores have been devised to eliminate this difficulty. The **T score** has a mean of 50 and uses a standard deviation of 10. Thus a T score of 50 indicates average performance.

If you multiply the z score by 10 (which eliminates the decimal) and add 50 (which gets rid of the negative number), you get the equivalent T score as the answer. The person whose z score was −1.5 would have a T score of 35.

First multiply by 10:

$$-1.5 \times 10 = -15$$

Then add 50:

$$-15 + 50 = 35$$

The scoring of the College Entrance Examination Board test is based on a similar procedure. The mean of the scores is set at 500, and a standard deviation of 100 is used.

Before we leave this section on types of scores, we should mention one other widely used method. **Stanine scores** (the name comes from "standard nine") are standard scores. There are only nine possible scores on the stanine scale, the whole numbers 1 through 9. The mean is 5, and the standard deviation is 2. Each unit from 2 to 8 is equal to half a standard deviation.

Stanine scores provide a method of considering a student's rank, since each of the nine scores includes a specific range of percentile scores in the normal distribution. For example, a stanine score of 1 is assigned to the bottom 4 percent of scores in a distribution. A stanine of 2 is assigned to the next 7 percent. Of course, some raw scores in this 7 percent range are better than others, but they all get a stanine score of 2.

Each stanine score represents a wide range of raw scores. This has the advantage of encouraging teachers and parents to view a student's score in more general terms instead of making fine distinctions based on a few points. Figure 14.4 on page 524 compares the four types of standard scores we have considered, showing how each would fall on a normal distribution curve.

Interpreting Test Scores

Test Bank items 14.37, 14.41–14.52, 14.75–14.77, 14.92–14.94, 14.105

One of the most common problems with the use of tests is misinterpretation of scores. This often happens because of the belief that numbers are precise measurements of a student's ability. No test provides a perfect picture of a person's abilities; a test is only one small sample of behavior. Two factors are important in developing good tests: reliability and validity. We must consider both when we interpret test scores.

Reliability. If you took a standardized test on Monday, then took the same test again a week later, and you received about the same score each time, you would have reason to believe the test was reliable. If 100 people took the test one day, then repeated it the following week, and the ranking of the individual scores was about the same for both tests, you would be even more certain the test was reliable. (Of course, this assumes that no one looks up answers or studies before the second test.) A reliable test gives a consistent and stable "reading" of a person's ability from one occasion to the next, assuming the person's ability remains the same. A reliable thermometer works in a similar manner, giving you a reading of 100°C each time you measure the temperature of boiling water. Measuring a test's **reliability** in this way, by giving the test on two different occasions, indicates *stability* or *test-retest reliability*. If a group of people takes two equivalent versions of a test and the scores on both tests are comparable, this indicates *alternate-form reliability*.

Reliability can also refer to the internal consistency or the precision of a test. This type of reliability, known as *split-half reliability*, is calculated by com-

Stanine Scores Whole-number scores from 1 to 9, each representing a wide range of raw scores.

Reliability Consistency of test results.

True Score Hypothetical average of all of an individual's scores if repeated testing under ideal conditions were possible.

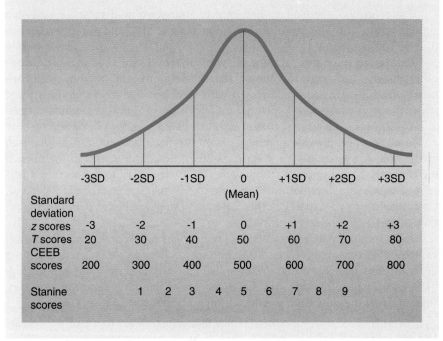

FIGURE 14.4

FOUR TYPES OF STANDARD SCORES ON A NORMAL DISTRIBUTION CURVE
Using this figure, you can translate one type of standard score into another.

paring performance on half of the test questions with performance on the other half. If, for example, someone did quite well on all the odd-numbered items and not at all well on the even-numbered items, we could assume that the items were not very consistent or precise in measuring what they were intended to measure. The most effective way to improve reliability is to add more items to a test. Generally speaking, longer tests are more reliable than shorter ones.

True Score. All tests are imperfect estimators of the qualities or skills they are trying to measure. There are errors in every testing situation. Sometimes the errors are in your favor, and you score higher than your ability might warrant. This can occur when you happen to review a key section just before the test or are unusually well rested and alert the day of a pop quiz. Sometimes the errors go against you. You don't feel well the day of the examination, have just gotten bad news from home, or focused on the wrong material in your review. But if you could be tested over and over again without becoming tired and without memorizing the answers, your good luck and bad luck would even out, and the average of the test scores would bring you close to a **true score.** In other words, we can think of a student's true score as the mean of all the scores the student would receive if the test were repeated many times.

In reality, however, students take a test only once. That means that the score each student receives is made up of the hypothetical true score plus some amount of error. How can error be reduced so that the actual score can be brought closer to a true score? As you might guess, this returns us to the question of reliability. The more reliable the test, the less error in the score actually obtained. On standardized tests, test developers take this into consideration and make estimations of how much the students' scores would probably vary if they were tested repeatedly. This estimation is called the **standard error of measurement.** It represents the *standard deviation* of the distribution of scores from our hypothetical repeated testings. Thus a reliable test can also be defined as a test with a small standard error of measurement. In their interpretation of tests, teachers must also take into consideration the margin for error.

Confidence Interval.   Teachers should never base an opinion of a student's ability or achievement on the exact score the student obtains. Many test companies now report scores using a **confidence interval,** or "standard error band," that encloses the student's actual score. This makes use of the standard error of measurement and allows a teacher to consider the range of scores that might include a student's true score.

Let us assume, for example, that two students in your class take a standardized achievement test in Spanish. The standard error of measurement for this test is 5. One student receives a score of 79; the other, a score of 85. At first glance, these scores seem quite different. But when you consider the standard error bands around the scores, not just the scores alone, you see that the bands overlap. The first student's true score might be anywhere between 74 and 84 (that is, the actual score of 79 plus and minus the standard error of 5). The second student's true score might be anywhere between 80 and 90. If these two students took the test again, they might even switch rankings. It is crucial to keep in mind the idea of standard error bands when selecting students for special programs. No child should be rejected simply because the obtained score missed the cutoff by one or two points. The student's true score might well be above the cutoff point.

Validity.   If a test is sufficiently reliable, the next question is whether it is valid, or more accurately, whether the judgments and decisions based on the test are valid. To have **validity,** the decisions and inferences based on the test must be supported by evidence. This means that validity is judged in relation to a particular use or purpose, that is, in relation to the actual decision being made and the evidence for that decision (Gronlund, 1993).

Traditionally, psychologists described three different kinds of validity: content, criterion, and construct. The move today is toward viewing validity as a single quality. Instead of different kinds of validity, there are different kinds of evidence to support a particular judgment. If the purpose of a test is to measure the skills covered in a particular course or unit, then we would hope to see test questions on all the important topics and not on extraneous topics. If this condition is met, we would have *content-related evidence of validity.* Have you ever taken a test that dealt only with a few ideas from one lecture or just a few pages of the textbook? Then decisions based on that test (like your grade) certainly lacked content-related evidence of validity.

Teaching Tip: Ask students the following questions taken from Popham, W. J. (1988). *Educational evaluation* (2nd ed.). Englewood Cliffs, NJ: Prentice-Hall, p. 127.

Indicate which of the following types of validity evidence is being gathered.

a. Subject-matter experts have been summoned to rate the consonance of a test's items with the objectives the test is supposed to measure.

b. A correlation is computed between a new test of student self-esteem and a previously validated and widely used test of student self-esteem.

c. Scores on a screening test (used to assign sophomores to standard or enriched English classes) are correlated with English competence of college juniors (as reflected by grades assigned at the close of junior-year English classes).

Answers: a. content b. construct c. criterion

Discussion: What makes any test or procedure a good predictor? Consider the relevance to the outcome, freedom from bias, reliability, convenience, cost.

Background: Moss, P. A. (1992). Shifting conceptions of validity in educational measurement: Implications for performance assessment. *Review of Educational Research, 62,* 229–258.

Standard Error of Measurement Hypothetical estimate of variation in scores if testing were repeated.

Confidence Interval Range of scores within which an individual's particular score is likely to fall.

Validity Degree to which a test measures what it is intended to measure.

Some tests are designed to predict outcomes. The SATs, for example, are intended to predict performance in college. If SAT scores correlate with academic performance in college as measured by, say, grade-point average in the first year, then we have *criterion-related evidence of validity* for the use of the SAT in admissions decisions. In other words, the test scores are fairly accurate predictors of the criterion—how well the student will do in college.

Most standardized tests are designed to measure some psychological characteristic or "construct" such as reasoning ability, reading comprehension, achievement motivation, intelligence, creativity, and so on. It is a bit more difficult to gather *construct-related evidence of validity,* yet this is a very important requirement, probably the most important. Construct-related evidence of validity is gathered over many years. It is indicated by a pattern of scores. For example, older children can answer more questions on intelligence tests than younger children. This fits with our construct of intelligence. If the average 5-year-old answered as many questions correctly on a test as the average 13-year-old, we would doubt that the test really measured intelligence. Construct-related evidence for validity can also be demonstrated when the results of a test correlate with the results of other well-established, valid measures of the same construct.

Today, many psychologists suggest that construct validity is the broadest category and that gathering content- and criterion-related evidence is another way of determining if the test measures the construct it was designed to measure. And new questions are being raised about validity. What are the consequences of using a particular assessment procedure for teaching and learning? Twenty years ago Sam Messick (1975) raised two important questions to consider in making any decisions about using a test: Is the test a good measure of the characteristic it is assumed to assess? Should the test be used for the proposed purpose? The first question is about construct validity; the second is about ethics and values (Moss, 1992).

A number of factors may interfere with the validity of tests given in classroom situations. One problem has already been mentioned—a poorly planned test with little or no relation to the important topics. Standardized achievement tests must be chosen so that the items on the test actually measure knowledge gained in the classes. This match is absent more often than we might assume: one group of teachers in St. Louis found that fewer than 10 percent of the items in their curriculum overlapped in both the textbooks and the standardized tests they were using (Fiske, 1988). Also, students must have the necessary skills to take the test. If students score low on a science test not because they lack knowledge about science, but because they have difficulty reading the questions, do not understand the directions, or do not have enough time to finish, then the test is not a valid measure of science achievement for those students.

A test must be reliable in order to be valid. For example, if, over a few months, an intelligence test yields different results each time it is given to the same child, then by definition it is not reliable. Certainly it couldn't be a valid measure of intelligence because intelligence is assumed to be fairly stable, at

---

Focus on . . .   **The Meaning of Test Scores**

- Which is the best measure of central tendency for indicating the typical performance in a group where only a few students did very well on the test?
- If 10 million people take the SAT, about how many should score between 400 and 600 on the verbal test? Remember, the mean is 500.
- A *z* score of 2.5 is the same as what *T* score?
- Which is better, a percentile score of 75 or a *T* score of 75? Which is easier to explain to a parent?
- Every time you check, your bathroom scale gives you the same weight, but you always weigh more at the doctor's office. Is your scale valid? Is it reliable?

Teaching Tip: If students have access to their own records, ask them to locate copies of standardized tests they have taken and to interpret the scores as if they were their own teacher.

Casebook: See the Teachers' Casebook for practicing teachers' ideas about how they would respond to students' cheating during standardized tests.

Guidelines

Make sure the test actually covers the content of the unit of study.

Examples

1. Compare test questions to course objectives. A behavior-content matrix might be useful here (see chapter 15).
2. Use local achievement tests and local norms when possible.
3. Check to see if the test is long enough to cover all important topics.
4. Are there any difficulties your students experience with the test, such as not enough time, level of reading, and so on? If so, discuss these problems with appropriate school personnel.

Make sure students know how to use all the test materials.

Examples

1. Several days before the testing, do a few practice questions with a similar format.
2. Demonstrate the use of the answer sheets, especially computer-scored answer sheets.
3. Check with new students, shy students, slower students, and students who have difficulty reading to make sure they understand the questions.
4. Make sure students know if and when guessing is appropriate.

Follow instructions for administering the test exactly.

Examples

1. Practice giving the test before you actually use it.
2. Follow the time limits exactly.

Make students as comfortable as possible during testing.

Examples

1. Do not create anxiety by making the test seem like the most important event of the year.
2. Help the class relax before beginning the test, perhaps by telling a joke or having everyone take a few deep breaths. Don't be tense yourself!
3. Make sure the room is quiet.
4. Discourage cheating by monitoring the room. Don't become absorbed in your own paper-work.

Remember that no test scores are perfect.

Examples

1. Interpret scores using bands instead of a single score.
2. Ignore small differences between scores.

least over a short period of time. However, reliability will not guarantee validity. If that intelligence test gave the same score every time for a particular child but didn't predict school achievement, speed of learning, or other characteristics associated with intelligence, then performance on the test would not be a true indicator of intelligence. The test would be reliable—but invalid. The Guidelines above should help you increase the reliability and validity of the standardized tests you give.

Discussion: A man aims his gun at the bull's-eye on a target and shoots five times. All five shots hit in the upper right-hand corner. Is the gun reliable? Is it valid? What are some possible sources of error?

"I HATE TAKING A TEST
WITHOUT AN ERASER."

(© Martha Campbell)

Objective 14.6: Identify three
kinds of standardized tests and
the purpose of each kind of test.

**Activity 14.5: Field Experience
Activity.** See the *Instructor's Resource
Manual* for A Local
School's Report, a guide for interviewing
a principal about standardized
testing and authentic
assessment.

Background: Koretz, D. (1989,
January). The new National Assessment:
What it can and cannot
do. *NEA Today* (Special issue: Issues
'89), 32–37.

Transparency: The relationship
between "Stanines and Percentiles"
is shown on acetate
transparency T 117.

Achievement Tests Standardized
tests measuring how much students
have learned in a given content
area.

Types of Standardized Tests   Test Bank item 14.106

Several kinds of standardized tests are used in schools today. If you have seen
the cumulative folders that include testing records for individual students over
several years, then you know the many ways students are tested in this country.
There are three broad categories of standardized tests: achievement, diagnostic,
and aptitude (including interest). As a teacher, you will probably
encounter achievement and aptitude tests most frequently.

Achievement Tests: What Has the Student Learned?

Test Bank items 14.53–14.54,
14.106

The most common standardized tests given to students are **achievement tests.**
These are meant to measure how much a student has learned in specific content
areas such as reading comprehension, language usage, computation, science,
social studies, mathematics, and logical reasoning.

Achievement tests can be designed to be administered either to a group or
individually. Group tests can be used for screening—to identify children who
might need further testing or as a basis for grouping students according to
achievement levels. Individual achievement tests are generally given to determine
a child's academic level more precisely, or to help diagnose learning problems.

Norm-referenced achievement tests that are commonly given to groups include
the California Achievement Test, the Metropolitan Achievement Test, the
Stanford Achievement Test, the Comprehensive Test of Basic Skills, the SRA
Achievement Series, and the Iowa Test of Basic Skills. Individually administered
norm-referenced tests include Part II of the Woodcock-Johnson Psycho-Educational
Battery: Tests of Achievement; the Wide-Range Achievement Test;
the Peabody Individual Achievement Test; and the Kaufman Assessment Battery
for Children. These tests vary in their reliability and validity.

Using Information from a Norm-Referenced Achievement Test. What
specific information can teachers expect from achievement test results? Test
publishers usually provide individual profiles for each student, showing scores
on each subtest. Figure 14.5 is an example of an individual profile for a fifth
grader, Ken Allen, on the California Achievement Test, Fifth Edition. Note that
the Individual Test Record reports the scores in many different ways. At the top
of the form, after the identifying information about Ken's grade and birthday,
is a list of the various tests—Reading Vocabulary, Reading Comprehension,
Total Reading (Vocabulary and Comprehension combined), Language Mechanics,
and so on. Beside each test are several different ways of reporting Ken's
score:

NS: Ken's National Stanine Score (his stanine score based on a national norming
sample comparison group).

NCE: Ken's Normal Curve Equivalent Score (a score used mostly for research
purposes to evaluate certain compensatory education programs).

SS: Ken's Scale Score. This describes growth in achievement that typically occurs
as a student progresses through the grades—the higher the grade the
higher the expected scale score.

FIGURE 14.5

AN INDIVIDUAL TEST RECORD

Test publishers provide several kinds of report forms for individual students and for entire classes. The form below gives both norm-referenced and criterion-referenced information about a fifth-grade boy.

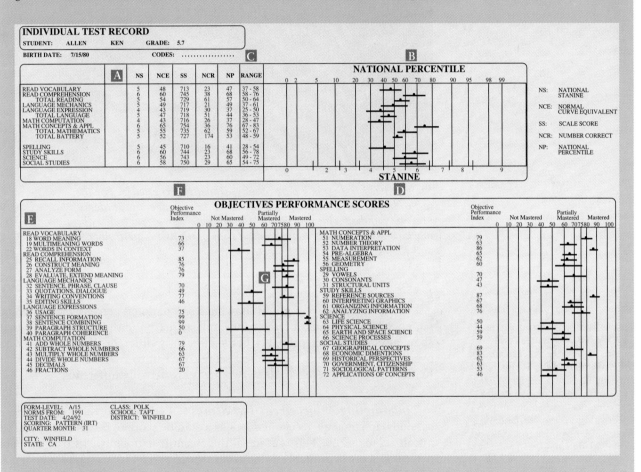

Source: Reproduced from the *California Achievement Test,* 5th edition, by permission of the publisher, CTB, a division of Macmillan/McGraw-Hill School Publishing Company. Copyright © 1992 CTB by Macmillan/McGraw-Hill School Publishing Company. All rights reserved.

NCR: Ken's actual number correct—his raw score.

NP: Ken's National Percentile Score, telling us where he stands in relation to students at his grade level across the country.

RANGE: The range of national percentile scores in which Ken's *true score* is likely to fall. You may remember from our discussion of true scores that this range, or confidence interval, is determined by adding and subtracting the standard error of the test from Ken's actual score. There is a 95 percent chance that Ken's true score is within this range.

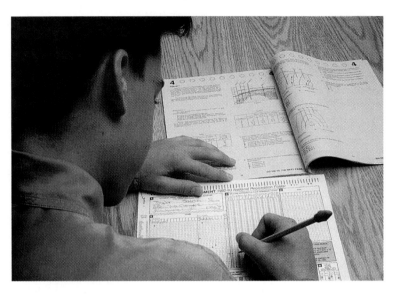

Standardized testing is a part of most students' experience. For the test to be a valid measure of the students' knowledge, the students must be familiar with procedures for taking a test—how to use the machine-scored sheets, what to do if they don't know an answer, and so on.

Discussion: Have students read At Odds: Performance Assessment (1991, special feature). *Phi Delta Kappan, 72*(9). This feature includes two articles: Cizek, G. J. Innovation or enervation: Performance assessment in perspective, pp. 695–699, and Wiggins, G. A response to Cizek, pp. 700–703. *Focus Questions:* Ask students to summarize the two positions on performance assessment expressed by the authors. Which position most closely represents your students' views? Why?

Casebook: See the Teachers' Casebook at the end of this chapter for practicing teachers' ideas about how to help ESL students who work slowly on standardized tests.

Casebook: See the Teachers' Casebook for a teacher's assessment of the advantages and disadvantages of standardized achievement tests.

Beside the scores is a graph showing Ken's national percentile and stanine scores, with the standard error bands indicated around the scores. Bands that show any overlap are probably not significantly different. When there is no overlap between bands for two test scores, we can be reasonably certain that Ken's achievement levels in these two areas are actually different.

Interpreting Achievement Test Scores. Let's look at Ken's scores more carefully. In language mechanics he has a stanine score of 5, which is equal to a scale score of 729. This is at the 57th percentile nationally. His true national percentile score is probably in the range from 50 to 64 (that is, plus and minus 1 standard error of measurement from the actual score of 57, so the standard error of the language mechanics test must be 7). By looking at the graph, we can see that Ken's language mechanics and language expression score bands overlap. His achievement in these areas is probably similar, even though there seems to be a difference when you look at the NP scores alone. Comparing language expression with reading comprehension, on the other hand, we see that the bands do not overlap. Ken is stronger in reading comprehension than in language expression.

The profile in Figure 14.5 tells us a number of things. First, we can see that all Ken's scores are within the average range compared to the national norming sample. Ken's highest score is in math concepts and applications. However, this score band overlaps several other score bands, so we cannot say for sure that this is his strongest area. Ken's strength in math concepts and applications raises his total math battery score to a percentile of 59, but his math computation score is significantly lower than his math concepts score (the bands do not overlap). With some work on math computations, Ken would probably improve his overall math performance. We can also see that Ken is weak in spelling. Improving his spelling might improve his vocabulary score and vice versa.

The scores we have just described are all norm-referenced. However, results from standardized tests like the one Ken took can also be interpreted in a criterion-referenced way. The bottom portion of Ken's Individual Test Record in Figure 14.5 breaks down the larger categories of the top section (reading vocabulary, reading comprehension, etc.) and shows criterion-referenced scores that indicate mastered, partially mastered, or not mastered for specific skills. These include reading vocabulary skills such as the use of word meanings and words in context and study skills such as using reference sources and interpreting graphics. The Objective Performance Index score is an estimate of the percentage of all possible items that Ken could be expected to answer correctly in each performance area. In other words, based on his performance on these test items, what percentage of all possible questions in this area (at his level) should he get right? Teachers can use these results to get an idea of Ken's strengths and weaknesses with these specific skills and thus determine his progress toward objectives in a given subject. Be aware, though, that some of these specific skill areas may be measured with only a few items each, and the fewer the items, the more potential problems there can be with reliability.

Diagnostic Tests: What Are the Student's Strengths and Weaknesses?

Test Bank items 14.55, 14.95, 14.106

If teachers want to identify specific learning problems, they may need to refer to results from the various diagnostic tests that have been developed. Most **diagnostic tests** are given to students individually by a highly trained professional. The goal is usually to identify the specific problems a student is having. Achievement tests, both standardized and teacher-made, identify weaknesses in academic content areas like mathematics, computation, or reading. Individually administered diagnostic tests identify weaknesses in learning processes. There are diagnostic tests to assess the ability to hear differences among sounds, remember spoken words or sentences, recall a sequence of symbols, separate figures from their background, express relationships, coordinate eye and hand movements, describe objects orally, blend sounds to form words, recognize details in a picture, coordinate movements, and many other abilities needed to learn, remember, and communicate learning.

Elementary-school teachers are more likely than secondary-school teachers to receive information from diagnostic tests. There are few such tests for older students. If you become a high school teacher, your students are more likely to be given aptitude tests.

Aptitude Tests: How Well Will the Student Do in the Future?
Test Bank items 14.56–14.58, 14.96, 14.100

Both achievement and aptitude tests measure developed abilities. Achievement tests may measure abilities developed over a short period of time, such as during a week-long unit on map reading, or over a longer period of time, such as

Background: Some diagnostic tests measure a student's ability in a variety of areas. These tests include the Detroit Test of Learning Aptitude and Part I of the Woodcock-Johnson Psycho-Educational Battery: Tests of Cognitive Ability.

Others, however, assess a student's ability in a more specific area. Tests of motor skills include the Bender Gestalt Test and the Purdue Perceptual Motor Survey. For assessing specific areas of perception, commonly used tests include the Wepman Auditory Discrimination Test, the Goldman-Fristoe-Woodcock Test of Auditory discrimination, the Frostig Developmental Test of Visual Perception, and the Motor-Free Visual Perception Test.

Diagnostic Tests Individually administered tests to identify special learning problems.

Background: Marzano, R. J., & Cost, A. L. (1988). Question: Do standardized tests measure general cognitive skills? Answer: No. *Educational Leadership*, 45(8), 66–73.

Activity 14.6: See the *Instructor's Resource Manual* for Test Score Interpretation. This activity requires your students to interpret the group intelligence test score of a third grader.

Transparency: "Normal Curve: Scores on a Standardized IQ Test" is presented in acetate transparency T 113.

Application: How should a teacher interpret an IQ score that is recorded in a student's cumulative folder? If there is a large discrepancy (in either direction) between the IQ score and the child's performance level in school, which would you be more concerned about? Which would you consider more valid? Why?

a semester. **Aptitude tests** are meant to measure abilities developed over many years and to predict how well a student will do in the future at learning unfamiliar material. The greatest difference between the two types of tests is that they are used for different purposes. Achievement tests measure final performance (and perhaps give grades), and aptitude tests predict how well people will do in particular programs like college or professional school (Anastasi, 1988).

Scholastic Aptitude. The purpose of a scholastic aptitude test, like the SAT (Scholastic Aptitude Test) or ACT (American College Testing Program), is to predict how well a student is likely to do in college. Colleges use such scores to help decide on acceptances and rejections. The SAT may have seemed like an achievement test to you, measuring what you had learned in high school. Although the test is designed to avoid drawing too heavily on specific high school curricula, the questions are very similar to achievement test questions.

Standardized aptitude tests—such as the SAT, the School and College Ability Tests (SCAT), and the Preliminary Scholastic Aptitude Test (PSAT) for younger students—seem to be reliable in predicting future achievement. Since standardized tests are less open to teacher bias, they may be even fairer predictors of future achievement than high school grades. Indeed, some psychologists believe grade inflation in high schools has made tests like the SAT even more important. Others believe that the SATs are not good predictors of success in college, particularly for women or members of cultural or ethnic minority groups. The controversy continues. As you will see later in this chapter, the name of the SAT is being changed to the Scholastic Assessment Test, but the purpose is still to predict scholastic performance.

IQ and Scholastic Aptitude. In chapter 4 we discussed one of the most influential aptitude tests of all, the IQ test. The IQ test as we know it could well be called a test of scholastic aptitude. Now that you understand the concept of standard deviation, you will be able to appreciate several statistical characteristics of the tests. For example, the IQ score is really a standard score with a mean of 100. The standard deviation is 15 for the Wechsler Scales; the Cognitive Abilities section of the Woodcock-Johnson Psycho-Educational Battery; and the Global Scale of the Kaufman Assessment Battery for Children. The standard deviation is 16 for the Stanford-Binet and the McCarthy Scales for Children. Thus about 68 percent of the general population would score between +1 and –1 standard deviations from the mean, or between about 85 and 115. Only about 2.5 percent of the general population would have a score higher than 2 standard deviations above the mean, that is, above 130 on the Wechsler Scales.

A difference of a few points between two students' IQ scores should not be viewed as important. Scores between 90 and 109 are within the average range. In fact, scores between 80 and 119 are considered within the range of low average to high average. To see the problems that may arise, consider the following conversation:

Focus on . . . **Standardized Tests**

- If you were Ken Allen's teacher (see Figure 14.5) how would you help him improve in reading? in math? in spelling?
- What is the purpose of achievement testing? of aptitude testing? How do you tell the difference in the two kinds of tests?
- Are the WISC III scores of 120 and 125 significantly different? Why or why not?
- If there are 100 million adults in a country, and every one takes a Wechsler Intelligence Test, about how many should have IQ test scores above 130?

Aptitude Tests Tests meant to predict future performance.

Parent: We came to speak with you today because we are shocked at our son's IQ score. We can't believe he has only a 99 IQ when his sister scored much higher on the same test. We know they are about the same. In fact, Sam has better marks than Lauren did in the fifth grade.

Teacher: What was Lauren's score?

Parent: Well, she did much better. She scored a 103!

Clearly, brother and sister have both scored within the average range. While the standard error of measurement on the WISC-III (Weschler Intelligence Scale for Children, third edition) varies slightly from one age to the next, the average standard error for the total score is 3.2. So the bands around Sam's and Lauren's IQ scores—about 96 to 102 and 100 to 106—are overlapping. Either child could have scored 100, 101, or 102. The scores are so close that on a second testing Sam might score slightly higher than Lauren.

Vocational Aptitude and Interest. In schools, the guidance counselor is generally the person most concerned with students' career decisions. It is the responsibility of people in the guidance office to know what aptitude test scores really mean and how to help each student make an appropriate decision. **Vocational aptitude tests** and **vocational interest tests** may provide useful information for educational planning, but, as with any tests, interpretation must be cautious.

If you teach in a junior high or high school, your school may administer vocational aptitude tests to the students. One test designed to measure aptitudes relevant to career decisions is the **Differential Aptitude Test (DAT)**. Students in grades 8 through 12 may take the test. Questions cover seven areas: (1) verbal reasoning, (2) numerical ability, (3) abstract reasoning, (4) clerical speed and accuracy, (5) mechanical reasoning, (6) space relations, and (7) spelling and language. The test results on the DAT are converted into percentiles, and a percentile band is reported for each subtest. After the tests have been scored, the guidance counselors in a school should be able to help students relate their DAT profile scores to career-planning decisions.

Many high schools also give vocational interest tests. Three examples are the Kuder Preference Record, the Strong-Campbell Interest Blank, and Part III of the Woodcock-Johnson Psycho-Educational Battery: Tests of Interest Level. In these tests students may be asked to indicate which of several activities (such as collecting books, collecting shells, or collecting postcards) they would like most and which they would like least. The pattern of the students' answers is then compared to the answer patterns of adults working in different occupations. Remember that the results on such a test indicate interests, not aptitude or talent. No career option should be permanently closed to an adolescent on the basis of an occupational interest test.

Issues in Standardized Testing

Test Bank items 14.59, 14.113, 14.114

Today, many important decisions about students, teachers, and schools are based in part on the results of standardized tests. Test scores may affect "admission" to first grade, high school graduation, access to special programs,

Vocational Aptitude Tests Tests designed to measure abilities needed in particular occupations.

Vocational Interest Tests Tests indicating possible areas of career interest.

Differential Aptitude Test (DAT) A vocational aptitude test that measures such abilities as mechanical reasoning, clerical speed and accuracy, and number ability.

Teaching Tip: Have students choose a partner to role-play a parent-teacher conference. Below are two examples of test results that the teacher should interpret to the parent. Each member of the dyad will take the role of the teacher or parent, then reverse the roles. The teacher should interpret the scores to the parent and make judgments or recommendations about the child's future educational experiences. The parent should feel free to ask questions concerning the interpretation and the recommendations.

Terry: 3rd grade, scores based on national norm.

 Math Computation: 6.0 (grade-equivalent score)

 Math Reasoning: 3.5 (grade-equivalent score)

 Reading Vocabulary: 85th percentile

 Reading Comprehension: 53rd percentile

 Group IQ score: 79 (test was given the day before Terry's birthday)

Bobbie: 10th grade, scores based on local norms

 Math Computation: 5 (stanine score)

 Math Reasoning: 4 (stanine score)

 Reading Vocabulary: 53 (*T* score)

 Reading Comprehension: 38 (*T* score)

 WISC-R: Verbal = 121

 Performance = 130

 Total Score = 125

High-Stakes Testing Standardized tests whose results have powerful influences when used by school administrators, other officials, or employers to make decisions.

Readiness Testing Testing procedures meant to determine if an individual is ready to proceed to the next level of education or training.

placement in special education classes, teacher certification and tenure, and school funding. Because the decisions affected by test scores are so critical, many educators call this process **high-stakes testing.** By 1991, 47 states had some form of statewide mandated testing for public school students (Ziomek & Maxey, 1993). Some groups are working to increase the role of testing—by establishing a national examination, for example—while others are working to cut back the use of standardized tests in schools (Madaus & Kellaghan, 1993).

In the next few pages we will consider two basic questions: What role should testing play in making decisions about people? Do some students have an unfair advantage in taking tests?

The Uses of Testing in American Society

Test Bank items 14.60–14.64, 14.78, 14.79, 14.97, 14.107, 14.113, 14.114

Tests are not simply procedures used in research. Every day, there are many decisions made about individuals that are based on the results of tests. Should Liz be issued a driver's license? How many and which students from the eighth grade would benefit from an accelerated program in science? Who belongs in a remedial class? Who will be admitted to college or professional school? Who will get a teaching certificate? In answering these questions, it is important to distinguish between the quality of the test itself and how the test is used. Even the best instruments can be, and have been, misused. In earlier years, for example, using otherwise valid and reliable individual intelligence tests, many students were inappropriately classified as mentally retarded. The problem was not with the tests, but with the fact that the test score was the only information used to classify students. Much more information must be considered before a student can be identified as retarded.

Behind all the statistics and terminology are issues related to values and ethics. Who will be tested? What are the consequences of choosing one test over another for a particular purpose with a given group? What is the effect of being tested on the students? How will the test scores of minority-group students be interpreted? What do we really mean by intelligence, competence, and scholastic aptitude? Do our views agree with those implied by the tests we use to measure these constructs? How will test results be integrated with other information about the individual to make judgments? Answering these questions requires choices based on values as well as accurate information about what tests can and cannot tell us.

Let's look at three uses: testing readiness, testing minimum competency, and testing teachers.

Readiness Testing. In 1988, Georgia became the first state to require that children pass a test before moving from kindergarten to first grade (Fiske, 1988; Linn, 1986). The test quickly became a symbol of the misuse of tests. Public outcry led to modifications of the policy and spurred many educators to reform the **readiness testing** process. In fact, the uproar over this group-administered, machine-scored, norm-referenced test for kindergarten children "probably did more to advance readiness assessment reform in this country than all other causes combined" (Engel, 1991, p. 41).

Critics of readiness tests (Engel, 1991; Meisels, 1989; Shepard & Smith, 1989) believe:

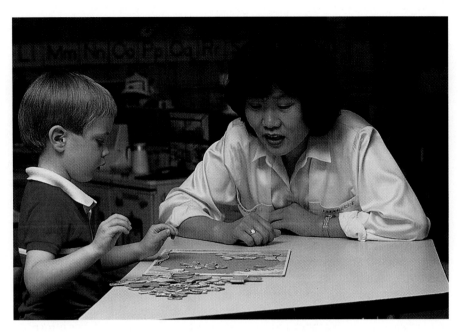

School "readiness" is a controversial construct. Individualized assessment is one response to criticisms of group-administered, machine-scored, norm-referenced tests for kindergarten placement.

Activity 14.7: Background. See the *Instructor's Resource Manual* for The Tyranny of Testing, a summary of Sternberg, R. J. (1989, March). The tyranny of testing. *Learning*, 60–63.

Background: Madaus, G. F., & Kellaghan, T. (1993). Testing as a mechanism of public policy: A brief history. *Measurement and Evaluation in Counseling and Development*, 26, 6–10.

Objective 14.7: Discuss the uses and misuses of testing, and name some areas where decisions are made on the basis of test scores.

Activity 14.8: Background. See the *Instructor's Resource Manual* for Legal Issues in Testing, a summary of several important court cases about testing.

Background: Testing: Is there a right answer? (1988, September/October). *Harvard Education Letter*, Vol. 4, No. 5, 1–4.

Objective 14.8: Describe the purpose of readiness tests, and of minimum competency and teacher assessment tests.

Activity 14.9: Cooperative Learning. See the *Instructor's Resource Manual* for Readiness Tests, a group activity that asks student teams to debate the value of first-grade readiness tests.

Research: Smith, M. L. (1991). Put to the test: The effects of external testing on teachers. *Educational Researcher*, 20(5), 8–11.

1. Group-administered paper-and-pencil tests are inappropriate for preschool children and thus should not be the basis for decisions about school entry.

2. Using readiness tests narrows the preschool curriculum, making it more academic and less developmentally appropriate.

3. The evidence shows that delaying entry into first grade or retaining students in kindergarten is not effective. Students who are retained do no better than similar students who are not held back.

In spite of these criticisms, today almost every state uses testing at the state or district level to determine if a child is "ready" for first grade or to place a child in a special "developmental kindergarten" (Kirst, 1991a). Several states, as well as a few test publishers, are trying to develop appropriate ways to determine readiness. Engel (1991) suggests that such procedures could be ongoing assessments about many different aspects of readiness—cognitive, social/emotional, physical, and so on. These assessments would be indirect, that is, they would be completed by adults rather than requiring the children to answer questions directly on paper. The observations would provide useful information for teaching; they would be conducted in a comfortable natural setting, often as part of the preschool program itself.

National Testing. *A Nation at Risk* (National Commission on Excellence in Education, 1983) reported that about 23 million American adults were functionally illiterate. About 13 percent of the teenagers in the United States (and up to 40 percent of minority youth) were not **functionally literate,** that is, they lacked a level of reading, writing, and communication skills necessary to

Functional Literacy A level of reading, writing, and communication ability that allows the individual to function independently in society.

Discussion: Assign Kirst, M. (1991a). Interview on assessment issues with Lorrie Shepard. *Educational Researcher, 20*(2), 21–23+. Kirst, M. (1991b). Interview on assessment issues with James Popham. *Educational Researcher, 20*(2), 24–27. *Focus Questions:* Ask students to summarize Shepard's and Popham's views on assessment. What kind of classroom assessment would each support?

Background: Worthen, B. R., & Spanel, V. (1991). Putting the standardized test debate in perspective. *Educational Leadership, 48*(5), 65–70.

Activity 14.10: Background. See the *Instructor's Resource Manual* for Teachers, Testing, and Time, a reprint of Pipho, C. (1991). Teachers, testing and time. *Phi Delta Kappan, 73*(3), 182–183.

Background: National Testing (1991, special section). *Phi Delta Kappan, 73*(3), 219–250.

Background: Special Issue: Mandatory testing: Issues in policy-driven assessment (1993, April). *Measurement and Evaluation in Counseling and Development, 26*(1).

Activity 14.11: Critical Thinking. See the *Instructor's Resource Manual* for Minimum Competency Testing, a set of questions to structure a debate or discussion about the value of a national competency examination.

Background: Bell, T. H. (1993). Reflections one decade after *A Nation at Risk. Phi Delta Kappan, 74*, 592–597.

Minimum Competency Testing
Standardized tests meant to determine if students meet minimum requirements to graduate or to proceed in school.

---

function independently in society. And in many studies comparing U.S. students with students from other industrialized nations, the American students have placed low in academic achievement (Educational Testing Service, 1992).

In response to these problems, many people believe that schools should rely on minimum competency testing. A **minimum competency test** is a standardized test meant to determine whether an individual meets the minimum standard for moving to the next level or graduating. Almost every state in the United States has some kind of high school competency testing program. Some people even suggest that a national examination would be helpful. "Escalating concern over low achievement, coupled with a growing belief that each pupil needs to be able to aim for a national standard of performance, has some policymakers, business leaders, and educators favoring a national exam (or set of exams) for all students" (O'Neil, 1991).

Will requiring minimum competency tests or a national exam improve education? Seventy-one percent of the people surveyed in the 1992 Gallup Poll of the public's attitude toward the public schools said they favored requiring the public schools in their community to use standardized national tests to measure the academic achievement of students (Elam, Rose, & Gallup, 1992). Those who support national testing believe that having the same test for all students will make teachers and students work harder and will focus efforts on content and skills that need improvement. Lauren Resnick, Director of the New Standards Project, notes that "The U. S. remains the only major nation in which no examination standard guides students as they work through school" (Association for Supervision and Curriculum Development, 1991).

However, many psychologists and teachers believe such tests are not a good idea. Their argument is that teachers would have less and less freedom in deciding what and how to teach. The tests would control the curriculum. In working to get everyone to the minimum level, a few slower students might monopolize the teacher's attention. Then teachers would have to ignore the faster students. New ways of organizing classes would be necessary to prevent holding everyone back. And finally, tests might discriminate against minority students. As educators and politicians have recognized these potential problems, the push for a national test has slowed in recent years, but the idea is still under discussion and the debate rages (Kirst, 1991a & b; O'Neil, 1993; Ziomek & Maxey, 1993). The Point/Counterpoint summarizes arguments for and against standardized testing.

Testing Teachers. Almost 90 percent of the people surveyed in the 1985 Gallup Poll believed that teachers should have to pass a basic competency test before being hired. When teachers answered the same question a year earlier, 63 percent agreed that testing was a good idea (Gallup, 1984). Edward Haertel (1991) notes that, like other standardized tests, "the teacher competency tests now in common use have been strenuously and justifiably criticized for their content, their format, and their impacts, as well as the virtual absence of criterion-related validity evidence supporting their use" (p. 3). In other words, high test scores do not predict good teaching.

New models of teacher assessment are in the planning and development stages. For example, the revision of the NTE is nearing completion as I am writing this page and will be available by the time you read these words. The revised NTE is a battery of tests called the *Praxis Series* and is given in three

To Test or Not to Test?

Student teachers are often astounded by the amount of time they must spend every spring preparing their students for "test week." Schools have been known to abandon innovations such as "whole language" and hands-on science teaching and to adopt drill-and-practice test-based programs in their place, just because test scores fell when these innovations were introduced. Yet there is talk of more, not less, testing and the development of a National Curriculum. Should standardized testing be continued?

POINT Testing should be stopped.

Critics of standardized testing state that these tests measure disjointed facts and skills that have no use or meaning in the real world. Often test questions do not match the curriculum of the schools, so the tests can't measure how well students have learned the curriculum. Even so, there is great pressure on teachers to produce high test scores. Teachers' jobs, principals' raises, and even the value of real estate in the school district are affected by the schools' test scores. So teachers find themselves "teaching to the test." Because tests are best at measuring lower-level objectives, facts, and basic skills, these facts and skills become the content of the curriculum. Too often, the results of tests are used to label

students as low achievers, and self-fulfilling prophecies are set into motion. Mary Lee Smith (1991) found the following effects of standardized testing on teachers:

When test scores are made public, teachers often feel embarrassed, angry, or ashamed. They sometimes change students' answers, excuse poor students from taking the test, drill students on the answers, or give unallowed "help" because the pressure for high scores is so great.

Teachers feel alienated from the test process, because when test scores are published, no one takes into account the fact that some of their students live in poverty or are just learning English.

Teachers are concerned that the tests take away valuable teaching time and make their students too anxious. Preparing for, giving, and recovering from the tests took an average of 100 hours of instructional time in the schools Smith studied.

COUNTERPOINT Tests can provide valuable information.

Defenders of standardized tests note that it is the responsibility of the school to select an appropriate test. Standardized tests are designed to sample what is typically taught, so the fit with any particular school's curriculum will not be perfect. Thus a standardized test

is only one source of information. To redesign the curriculum so that it matches the test or to make placement decisions based only on a test score is to overuse and misuse the test. No test is reliable and valid enough to serve as the only basis for making important decisions. But tests do provide useful information.

To make good use of test results, Blaine Worthen and Vicki Spandel (1991) suggest the following:

Don't test unless there is an important decision to make. Then choose a good test that will give useful information about the decision.

Never use the test as the only basis for the decision. Supplement with other information, including the teacher's judgment.

Assume every test score is imperfect. Take the score as an estimate.

Know what the test actually measures. Just because it is called a test of reading comprehension does not mean that a test measures everything about reading comprehension.

Know your students. A test of math achievement that uses word problems can be a test of reading comprehension for students whose English is limited.

Don't use test results to compare students or foster competition. Use the results to benefit students.

phases. Early in the prospective teacher's education program, *Praxis I: Academic Skills Assessment* tests basic skills such as reading, writing, and mathematics. A computer-based package is available to remediate any weak areas identified by the test. *Praxis II: Subject Assessments,* given at the end of the undergraduate program, tests subject matter knowledge and principles of teaching and learning. *Praxis III: Classroom Performance Assessments* is

Background: Ellwein, M. C., Glass, G. V., & Smith, M. L. (1988). Standards of competence: Propositions on the nature of testing reforms. *Educational Researcher, 17*(8), 4–9.

The authors address the determination of standards in teaching competency testing and examine the extent to which such procedures are affected by political and practical considerations. They also criticize the implementation of such testing and assert that competency tests and standards function more as symbolic and political gestures than as instrumental reforms. Five themes are discussed in support of this conclusion: the importance of the standard's image, the redundancy with preexisting standards, the loose coupling of test performance and decisions, the overemphasis on initial fail rates, and the striking contrast between early and late phases of competency testing reforms.

Background: See Noll, J. W. (1991). *Taking sides: Clashing views on controversial educational issues.* (5th ed.). Guilford, CT: Duskin, for "Are Current Educational Tests of Teacher Knowledge Fair?" pp. 344–360. Gregory Anrig, president of the Educational Testing Service, describes the value of the National Teacher Examination; Linda Darling-Hammond points out deficiencies in the test.

Activity 14.12: Journal Writing/Reflection. See the *Instructor's Resource Manual* for How Should Teachers Be Graded? This activity encourages students to consider how they would like to be assessed as teachers.

Activity 14.13: Background. See the *Instructor's Resource Manual* for Accountability: As a Reform Strategy, a summary of Lieberman, A. (1991). Accountability: As a reform strategy. *Phi Delta Kappan, 73*(3), 219–220.

based on the particular licensing requirements for each participating state. This assessment is conducted by trained local evaluators, mostly through classroom observations. Within each Praxis phase there are several modules to chose from. States can require any one—or a combination of two or all three—of the Praxis phases for certification (Dwyer & Villegas, 1993).

Like the alternatives to standardized tests we will examine shortly, the Praxis Series and other new teacher tests will make greater use of authentic performances and products. In *Praxis II,* teacher candidates might analyze case studies and suggest solutions to teaching problems. In *Praxis III,* teachers might complete a lesson-planning exercise and then be interviewed about what they planned and why. They might be asked to submit a portfolio containing an overview of a unit, details of two consecutive lessons, copies of student handouts, lists of the resources selected for background, a videotape of teaching samples showing large- and small-group lessons, and other examples of the teacher's actual work. Results of the assessment could be used to guide continuing professional development.

These procedures are not yet refined, but many look promising. Of course, every innovation has its shortcomings. Can these portfolios and performances be evaluated objectively? Will we see an explosion of businesses that specialize in helping teachers build a beautiful portfolio? Will the wealthier teachers and teacher candidates have the best portfolios and videos (Kirst, 1991b)?

Advantages in Taking Tests—Fair and Unfair

Test Bank items 14.65–14.68, 14.106

In this section we will consider three basic issues: Are standardized tests biased against minority students? Can students gain an advantage on admissions tests through coaching? Can they be taught test-taking skills?

Bias in Testing. As you saw in chapter 5, on most standardized measures of mental abilities the average performance of students of lower socioeconomic status and from minority groups is below that of middle-class white students, although the discrepancies are decreasing for some minority groups (Burton & Jones, 1982). Are tests such as the individual measures of intelligence or college admissions tests biased against minorities? This is a complex question.

Research on test bias shows that most standardized tests predict school achievement equally well across all groups of students. Items that might appear on the surface to be biased against minorities are not necessarily more difficult for minorities to answer correctly (Sattler, 1992). Even though standardized aptitude and achievement tests are not biased against minorities in predicting school performance, many people believe there are factors related to the specific content and procedures of such tests that put minority students at a disadvantage. Here are a few examples:

1. The language of the test and the tester is often different from the languages of the students.

2. The questions asked tend to center on experiences and facts more familiar to the dominant culture than to minority-group students.

3. Answers that support middle-class values are often rewarded with more points.

4. On individually administered intelligence tests, being very verbal and talking a lot is rewarded. This favors students who feel comfortable in that particular situation.

5. Minority-group children may not be oriented toward individual achievement and may not appreciate the value of doing well on tests.

Concern about cultural bias in testing has led some psychologists to try to develop **culture-fair** or **culture-free tests**. These efforts have not been very successful. On many of the so-called culture-fair tests, the performance of students from lower socioeconomic backgrounds and minority groups has been the same as or worse than their performance on the standard Wechsler and Binet Intelligence scales (Sattler, 1992).

Coaching and Test-Taking Skills. Courses to prepare students for college entrance exams are becoming more popular. As you probably know from experience, both commercial and public school coaching programs are available. It is difficult to evaluate the effects of these courses. In general, research has indicated that short high school training programs yield average gains of 10 points in SAT verbal scores and 15 points in SAT math scores, whereas longer commercial programs show gains of anywhere from 50 to as much as 200 points for some people (Owen, 1985). Kulik, Kulik, and Bangert (1984) analyzed the results of 40 different studies on aptitude and achievement test training and found that there were more substantial gains when students practiced on a parallel form of a test for brief periods. The design of the coaching program, therefore, may be the critical factor.

Two other types of training can make a difference in test scores. One is simple familiarity with the procedures of standardized tests. Students who have a lot of experience with standardized tests do better than those who do not. Some of this advantage may be due to greater self-confidence, less tendency to panic, familiarity with different kinds of questions (for example, analogies like house : garage : : ____ : car), and practice with the various answer sheets (Anastasi, 1988). Even brief orientations about how to take tests can help students who lack familiarity and confidence.

A second type of training that appears to be very promising is instruction in general cognitive skills such as solving problems, carefully analyzing questions, considering all alternatives, noticing details and deciding which are relevant, avoiding impulsive answers, and checking work. These are the kinds of metacognitive and study skills we have discussed before. Training in these skills is likely to generalize to many tasks (Anastasi, 1988). The Guidelines on page 540 give some ideas about how to be a more effective test-taker.

Test Bank items 14.108, 14.113, 14.114

ew Directions in Standardized Testing

Standardized tests continue to be controversial, as you saw in the Point/Counterpoint section on page 537. In response to dissatisfaction with traditional forms of assessment, new approaches have emerged to deal with some of the most common testing problems. However, each of these approaches has its

Objective 14.9: State the sources of test bias, and identify attempts that have been made to ensure the fair use of tests.

Cooperative Learning: After you have discussed the concept of intelligence and the question of cultural biases in testing, ask students to work in pairs or small groups to develop a culture-fair test. This could be done in class, but it is better as an assignment. The students' tests should be duplicated and distributed so that the class can evaluate them. Ask students what makes a test culture-fair. How could we go about developing such a test? How could we norm and standardize such a test?

Objective 14.10: Describe ways to prepare students to take tests.

Casebook: See the Teachers' Casebook for practicing teachers' accounts of how they prepare students for taking standardized tests.

Multicultural Awareness: According to data collected by U.S. Department of Education National Center for Education Statistics (*The Condition of Education* 1991, *Vol. 1*, p. 31), overall, college entrance examination scores have fallen modestly during the last few years. This finding is similar for both the SAT total score and the ACT composite score. Since 1976, however, average mathematics scores on the SAT increased for black and Mexican American students by 20 and 9 points, respectively. Black, Mexican American, American Indian, Asian American, and Puerto Rican students have all scored gains since 1976 on the SAT mathematics assessment. Black students scored the greatest gain, an increase of 31 points.

Culture-Fair/Culture-Free Test A test without cultural bias.

Guidelines

Taking a Test

Use the night before the test effectively.

Examples

1. Study the night before the exam, ending with a final look at a summary of the key points, concepts, and relationships.
2. Get a good night's sleep. If you know you generally have trouble sleeping the night before an exam, try getting extra sleep on several previous nights.

Set the situation so you can concentrate on the test.

Examples

1. Give yourself plenty of time to eat and get to the exam room.
2. Don't sit near a friend. It may make concentration difficult. If your friend leaves early, you may be tempted to do so too.

Make sure you know what the test is asking.

Examples

1. Read the directions carefully. If you are unsure, ask the instructor or proctor for clarification.
2. Read each question carefully to spot tricky words, such as *not, except, all of the following but one.*
3. On an essay test, read every question first, so you know the size of the job ahead of you and can make informed decisions about how much time to spend on each question.
4. On a multiple-choice test, read every alternative, even if an early one seems right.

Use time effectively.

Examples

1. Begin working right away and move as rapidly as possible while your energy is high.
2. Do the easy questions first.
3. Don't get stuck on one question. If you are stumped, mark the question so you can return to it easily later, and go on to questions you can answer more quickly.
4. If you are unsure about a question, answer it but mark it so you can go back if there is time.
5. On a multiple-choice test, if you know you will not have time to finish, fill in all the remaining questions with the same letter if there is no penalty for guessing.
6. If you are running out of time on an essay test, do not leave any questions blank. Briefly outline a few key points to show the instructor you "knew" the answer but needed more time.

Know when to guess on multiple-choice or true-false tests.

Examples

1. Always guess when only right answers are scored.
2. Always guess when you can eliminate some of the alternatives.
3. Don't guess if there is a penalty for guessing, unless you can confidently eliminate at least one alternative.

4. Are correct answers always longer? shorter? in the middle? more likely to be one letter? more often true than false?
5. Does the grammar give the right answer away or eliminate any alternatives?

Check your work.

Examples

1. Even if you can't stand to look at the test another minute, reread each question to make sure you answered the way you intended.
2. If you are using a machine-scored answer sheet, check occasionally to be sure the number of the questions you are answering corresponds to the number of the answer on the sheet.

On essay tests, answer as directly as possible.

Examples

1. Avoid flowery introductions. Answer the question in the first sentence and then elaborate.
2. Don't save your best ideas till last. Give them early in the answer.
3. Unless the instructor requires complete sentences, consider listing points, arguments, and so on by number in your answer. If will help you organize your thoughts and concentrate on the important aspects of the answer.

Learn from the testing experience.

Examples

1. Pay attention when the teacher reviews the answers. You can learn from your mistakes, and the same question may reappear in a later test.
2. Notice if you are having trouble with a particular kind of item; adjust your study approach next time to handle this type of item better.

own problems. We will examine proposed procedures for measuring learning potential, for making assessment more "authentic," and for improving the SAT.

Assessing Learning Potential   Test Bank item 14.81

One criticism of traditional forms of intelligence testing is that such tests are merely samples of performance at one particular point in time. These tests, critics say, fail to capture the child's potential for future learning. Reuven Feuerstein's **Learning Potential Assessment Device** attempts to look at the process of learning rather than its product (Feuerstein, 1979). The child is presented with various reasoning and memory tasks. When necessary, the examiner teaches the child how to solve the problems and then assesses how well the child has benefited from instruction. This approach reflects Vygotsky's ideas about the zone of proximal development—the range of functioning where a child cannot solve problems independently but can benefit from guidance. Results of the test have been difficult to interpret. Nevertheless, it offers a thought-provoking and radically different approach to intelligence testing.

Teaching Tip: In some school districts the accountability movement has resulted in teachers trying to "teach the test" so that their students will perform better. Therefore, mean test scores may gradually rise over the years as teachers' familiarity with the test increases.

Objective 14.11: Discuss the advantages of assessing learning potential through process assessment.

Objective 14.12: Define authentic assessment, and give examples of authentic assessment approaches.

Background: Wolf, D., Bixby, J., Glenn, J., III, & Gardner, H. (1991). To use their minds well: New forms of student assessment. *Review of Research in Education, 17,* 31–74.

Connections: Chapter 15 includes a discussion of alternatives for authentic assessment, including portfolios and exhibitions.

Learning Potential Assessment Device Innovative method for testing the student's ability to benefit from teaching, consistent with Vygotsky's theory of cognitive development.

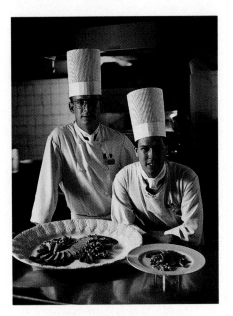

In many subjects, the most reasonable test is to demonstrate the ability to produce a finished product.

Background: Special Section on Authentic Assessment (1993, February). *Phi Delta Kappan, 74,* 444–479.

Background: For an interesting look at performance assessment, see the report of a conference, "What Works in Performance Assessment?" in the Spring 1993 issue of *Evaluation Comment,* from UCLA's Center for the Study of Evaluation and the National Center for Research on Evaluation, Standards, and Student Testing, Graduate School of Education, 405 Hilgard Ave., Los Angeles, CA 90024-1522.

Authentic Assessment Measurement of important abilities using procedures that simulate the application of these abilities to real-life problems.

Constructed-Response Format Assessment procedures that require the student to create an answer instead of selecting an answer from a set of choices.

Authentic Assessment   Test Bank items 14.69, 14.70, 14.81, 14.98

As the public and government demanded greater accountability in education in the 1980s and 1990s and as traditional standardized tests became the basis for high-stakes decisions, pressure to do well led many teachers and schools to "teach to the test." This tended to focus student learning on basic skills and facts. Even more troubling, say critics, the traditional tests assess skills that have no equivalent in the real world. Students are asked to solve problems or answer questions they will never encounter again; they are expected to do so alone, without relying on any tools or resources and while working under extreme time limits. Real life just isn't like this. Important problems take time to solve and often require using resources, consulting other people, and integrating basic skills with creativity and high-level thinking (Kirst, 1991a; Wolf, Bixby, Glenn, & Gardner, 1991).

In response to these criticisms, the **authentic assessment** movement was born. The goal was to create standardized tests that assess complex, important, real-life outcomes. The approach is also called *direct assessment, performance assessment,* or *alternative assessment.* These terms refer to procedures that are alternatives to traditional multiple-choice standardized tests because they directly assess student performance on "real-life" tasks (Worthen, 1993). Some states are developing procedures to conduct authentic assessments. For example, in 1990, Kentucky passed the Educational Reform Act. The act identifies six objectives for students, including such goals as applying knowledge from mathematics, the "hard" sciences, arts, humanities, and the social sciences to problems the students will encounter throughout their lives as they become self-sufficient individuals and responsible members of families, work groups, and communities.

According to Jack Foster (1991), the secretary of the Education and Humanities Cabinet for the governor of Kentucky, "The task now is to create prototypes of complex tasks that students can perform to demonstrate all these objectives in an interactive context. The tasks must have multiple objectives and require higher levels of thinking than is demanded by most paper-and-pencil tests" (p. 35). The state assessments will be tied to ongoing school and class assessments that guide instruction. The process will be criterion-referenced rather than norm-referenced, because students' performances will be compared to expected "benchmark" levels of attainment at grades 3, 5, 8, and 12. By 1995, Kentucky will have the first statewide assessment system that is totally performance based.

Many of the suggestions for improving standardized tests will require new forms of testing, more thoughtful and time-consuming scoring, and perhaps new ways of judging the quality of the tests themselves. Standardized tests of the future may be more like the writing sample you may have submitted for college entrance and less like the multiple-choice college entrance tests you also had to take. Newer tests will feature more **constructed-response formats**. This means that students will create responses (essays, problem solutions, graphs, diagrams, etc.), rather than simply selecting the (one and only) correct answer. This will allow tests to measure higher-level and divergent thinking.

In the excitement about authentic assessment, it is important to be sensible. Just being different from traditional standardized tests will not guarantee that the alternative tests are better. Many questions have to be answered. Assume, for example, that a new assessment requires students to complete a hands-on science project. If the student does well on one science project, does this mean the student "knows" science and would do well on other projects? One study found that students' performance on three different science tasks was quite variable: a student who did well on the absorbency experiment, for example, might have trouble with the electricity task. Thus it was hard to generalize about a student's knowledge in science based on just the three tasks. Many more tasks would be needed to get a good sense of science knowledge. But a performance assessment with many different tasks would be expensive and time-consuming (Shavelson, Gao, & Baxter, 1993). Also, if high-stakes decisions are based on performance on these tasks, will teachers begin to "teach to the assessment" by giving students practice in these science projects? And how will the projects be judged? Will different judges agree on the quality? When researchers examined the results of the 1992 Vermont Portfolio Assessment Program, they found that scorers assessing the same portfolio often gave very different ratings (Kotrez, Stecher, & Diebert, 1993). In other words, will judgments based on alternative assessments be reliable and valid? Will the assessment results generalize to tasks beyond those on the test itself? Will the new assessments have a positive effect on learning (Moss, 1992)?

> ### Focus on . . .   Issues in Testing
>
> - What does high-stakes testing mean? What are some decisions that should *not* be based on standardized test scores?
> - How would you judge the reliability and validity of a performance test in which a student was asked to show a knowledge of geometry by designing a tile floor using tiles of different shapes and sizes?
> - What are the possibilities for bias in alternative assessments?
> - What are the most effective ways to help students learn to take tests?

Many state legislatures are drafting laws that will require direct assessment of student performance to determine how well the schools, districts, and even the whole state is doing. These new, authentic, or alternative assessment procedures could be used to make the same high-stakes decisions as the traditional standardized tests and thus create some of the same problems (Worthen, 1993). Until more is known, it may be best to focus on authentic assessment at the classroom level, as we will discuss in the next chapter. Because this is a new area, it will take time to develop high quality alternative assessments for use by whole school districts or states.

Changes in the SAT   Test Bank items 14.71, 14.99, 14.100

Even the SAT is changing. For one thing, the title is changing from the Scholastic *Aptitude* Test to the Scholastic *Assessment* Test. The new SAT will have tests of verbal reasoning, mathematical reasoning, and subject matter. The verbal test will emphasize reading. The reading passages will be more engaging and more similar to the material that high school students have read in their classes. Each passage will be longer, and students will have to answer more questions about the passage. The verbal test will still have sentence-completion and analogy questions, but the antonym questions will be dropped. On the mathematical portion, students will generate their own answers (constructed-response format) for 20 percent of the questions. Hand-held calculators will be allowed, but not required. There will be a writing test consisting of two-thirds multiple-choice questions and one-third essay. The new SAT will be ready by March 1994. A new PSAT (Preliminary Scholastic Assessment Test)

Computer Software: An area of growing interest is computerized adaptive testing. For information on this area see:

Kingsbury, G. G. (1990). Adapting adaptive testing: Using the MicroCAT testing system in a local school district. Special issue: Computer Applications to Testing: Examples of Implementation in the Field. *Educational Measurement Issues and Practice, 9*(2), 3–6.

Rocklin, T. R., & O'Donnell, A. M. (1987). Self-adaptive testing: A performance improving variant of computerized adaptive testing. *Journal of Educational Psychology, 79*(3), 315–319.

Discussion: Scores on the ACTs and SATs correlate fairly highly with college grades, but is the practice of using these tests as a basis for college admission fair? Why or why not?

Background: Rosser, P. (1988, January). Girls, boys, and the SAT: Can we even the score? *NEA Today* (Special Issue: Issue '88), 48–53.

was introduced in fall 1993, so students who took the PSAT in fall 1993 will encounter the same format when they take their SATs later (J. Smith, 1991).

With a move to more authentic assessment, standardized tests and classroom tests can be better coordinated. This brings us to classroom testing and grading—the topics of the next chapter.

SUMMARY

Measurement and Evaluation

Evaluation of student learning can be based on measurements from norm-referenced tests in which a student's performance is compared to the average performance of others, or from criterion-referenced tests, in which scores are compared to a preestablished standard.

What Do Test Scores Mean?

Standardized tests are most often norm-referenced. They have been pilot-tested, revised, and then administered in final form to a norming sample, which becomes the comparison group for scoring. Important aspects of measurement in standardized testing are the frequency distribution, the central tendency, and the standard deviation. The mean (arithmetical average), median (middle score), and mode (most common score) are all measures of central tendency. The standard deviation reveals how scores spread out around the mean.

A normal distribution is a frequency distribution represented as a bell-shaped curve. Many scores cluster in the middle; the farther from the midpoint, the fewer the scores. Half the scores are above the mean; half are below.

There are several basic types of standardized test scores: percentile rankings, which indicate the percentage of others who scored at or below an individual's score; grade-equivalent scores, which indicate how closely a student's performance matches average scores for a given grade; and standard scores, which are based on the standard deviation. T and z scores are both common standard scores. A stanine score is a standard score that incorporates elements of percentile rankings.

Care must be taken in the interpretation of test results. Each test is only a sample of a student's performance on a given day. The score is only an estimate of a student's hypothetical true score. Some tests are more reliable than others, that is, they yield more stable and consistent estimates. The standard error of measurement takes into account the possibility for error and is one index of test reliability.

The most important consideration about a test is the validity of the decisions and judgments that are based on the test results. Some of these judgments are more valid than others because there is strong evidence for the interpreta-

tions and judgments made. Evidence of validity can be related to content, criterion, or construct. Construct-related evidence for validity is the broadest category and encompasses the other two categories of content and construct. Tests must be reliable to be valid, but reliability does not guarantee validity.

Types of Standardized Tests

Three kinds of standardized tests are used frequently in schools: achievement, diagnostic, and aptitude. Profiles from norm-referenced achievement tests can also be used in a criterion-referenced way to help a teacher assess a student's strengths and weaknesses in a particular subject. Diagnostic tests usually are given individually to elementary school students when learning problems are suspected. Aptitude tests are designed to predict how a student will perform in the future. For example, the Scholastic Assessment Test (SAT) predicts performance in the first year of college.

Issues in Standardized Testing

Controversy over standardized testing has focused on the role and interpretation of tests, the validity of readiness tests as a guide for decisions about young children, the fairness and usefulness of minimum competency testing, the testing of teachers, and the degree of bias against minority-group students inherent in tests.

The way test results are used is a major issue for teachers. Teachers should use results to improve instruction, not to stereotype students or justify lowered expectations. Performance on standardized tests can be improved if students gain experience with this type of testing and training in study skills and problem solving.

New Directions in Standardized Testing

Today there is great interest in authentic assessment—designing procedures that assess students' abilities to solve important real-life problems, think creatively, and act responsibly. Standardized tests of the future will be more varied and will use more constructed-response formats, requiring students to generate (rather than select) answers.

KEY TERMS

achievement tests, p. 528
aptitude tests, p. 532
authentic assessment, p. 542
bimodal distribution, p. 518
central tendency, p. 517
confidence interval, p. 525
constructed-response format, p. 542
criterion-referenced testing, p. 515
culture-fair/culture-free tests, p. 539
diagnostic tests, p. 531
differential aptitude test (DAT), p. 533
evaluation, p. 514
frequency distribution, p. 517
functional literacy, p. 535
grade-equivalent score, p. 522

high-stakes testing, p. 534
histogram, p. 517
Learning Potential Assessment Device, p. 541
mean, p. 517
measurement, p. 514
median, p. 517
minimum competency testing, p. 536
mode, p. 518
normal distribution, p. 519
norm group, p. 515
norming sample, p. 517
norm-referenced testing, p. 514
percentile rank, p. 520
range, p. 519

readiness testing, p. 534
reliability, p. 523
standard deviation, p. 518
standard error of measurement, p. 525
standardized tests, p. 517
standard scores, p. 522
stanine scores, p. 523
true score, p. 524
T score, p. 522
validity, p. 525
variability, p. 518
vocational aptitude tests, p. 533
vocational interest tests, p. 533
z score, p. 522

WHAT WOULD YOU DO?

Preschool and Kindergarten

Your district is considering establishing a first-grade readiness testing program. As the lead teacher for the kindergarten, you are asked to speak to the school board about the issue. What points would you make?

Elementary and Middle School

Your students seem very nervous about the spring testing. The local paper has carried stories about the school's "low" scores last year, and there is pressure on everyone to do better this time. How would you prepare your students?

The parents of one of your students are angry with you because their child was not selected for the special accelerated math group. Selection was based on both standardized test scores and class performance. How would you explain the school's decision?

Junior High and High School

The parents of one of your students want their child to receive credit for ninth-grade math without her having to take the course because she received a grade-equivalent score of 10.7 on her standardized math test in the spring of eighth grade. What would you say to the parents?

One of your students is very upset because the vocational interest test he took suggests that he "should be a forest ranger," but he wants to be a lawyer. What would you say to this student?

Cooperative Learning Activity

With four or five other members of your educational psychology class, analyze the test printout in Figure 14.5. If you were Ken's teacher, how would you use this information in teaching?

TEACHERS' CASEBOOK

Achievement Tests and ESL Students

Your district is giving standardized achievement tests. Two of your students have recently moved to the United States and are still having problems reading quickly. Although they are bright students, you know they will score low on the test because they must work slowly. What would you do?

SPECIAL TREATMENT

The first step I would take is to speak with the person administering the test and make him or her aware of the situation. In many instances, it would be possible to arrange for those two students to meet with a guidance counselor or other staff member and have that person orally read the test to the students. By doing this you would get a better idea of the students' actual abilities. This would also help to ensure that misplacement in a remedial program did not occur.

Candice J. Gallagher, *Fourth-Grade Teacher*
Fredericktown Intermediate School, Fredericktown, Ohio

EXTRA EFFORT NEEDED

I would give each student an *additional* answer sheet on which I would direct them to continue the test beyond the time limit. For example, had they completed 28 questions, I would tell them to begin on line 29 of the *second* answer sheet. The students would be given a specific amount of time, but under no condition would the additional time exceed the original allotted time. The teacher should copy the answers from the first answer sheet to the second. Both sheets should be submitted and corrected, and the ESL students will each have two scores.

Louise Harrold Melucci, *Fourth-Grade Teacher*
Greenwood School, Warwick, Rhode Island

GUIDE TO GENERAL ABILITY

Since the students are not discouraged enough to give up working on the test, they should be encouraged to finish what is possible. Achievement tests are used to measure general ability rather than just reading skills. Children should not be penalized for being slow readers. The results of most standardized tests have item analyses that the teacher can and should study for correct and incorrect answers. By analyzing the questions answered, the teacher can see the children's strengths and weaknesses. Though the composite scores may be lowered, there will still be enough information to be useful.

Ida Pofahl, *Second-Grade Teacher*
Denison Elementary School, Denison, Iowa

Coaching for Tests?

Do you do anything special to prepare students for standardized tests such as the College Boards? Why or why not?

PSYCHOLOGY OF THE GAME

Most of my students have experienced considerable success in their educational careers. They are accustomed to doing very well on their tests. I believe my most important role is to assure them that it is "okay" not to be able to answer all the questions on a standardized test. They do not fully understand that the test will purposely establish percentiles by asking some very difficult questions. I am convinced that many bright students become frustrated as they are taking the test and lose confidence in their ability and preparation. In many ways, I must become more of a coach than a teacher and must concentrate on the psychology of the "game."

R. Chris Rohde, *Chemistry Teacher*
Chippewa Falls Senior High School, Chippewa Falls, Wisconsin

Cheating

Several students tell you that three other students in your class were cheating during a statewide standardized test. What would you do?

MONITOR CLOSELY

The observers should be talked with separately. If they were very convincing, then I would tell the accused what had been observed. Depending on the situation and what was said, I might give the option to retake the test (if that was a possibility) in a closely monitored situation; or if the child admitted that cheating occurred, then the test results would need to note what had occurred. I would be careful not to accuse or throw out test results unless I was reasonably sure that cheating did occur.

Ruth Ann Dearth, *English and Reading Teacher*
Fredericktown Junior High School, Fredericktown, Ohio

SEEK THE TRUTH

My first step would be to talk to the students involved and to attempt to arrive at the truth. If I was sure that the accusation was correct, I would involve the parents and declare the test results to be invalid for those students. Then I would try to find out why those students felt the pressure to cheat.

Joanne S. Groseclose, *Virginia 1991 Teacher of the Year*
Marion Intermediate School, Marion, Virginia

Testing Advantages and Disadvantages

Achievement tests have become a way of life in schools. But the tests are an expense to the schools and a source of anxiety to the students (and teachers). What are the advantages and disadvantages of these tests? How can the results be used?

MEASURE INDIVIDUAL GROWTH

The advantages: (1) Achievements provide a basis of comparison for evaluating strengths and correcting weaknesses of students, classes, schools, and districts. (2) They provide support for teacher judgment. (3) They serve as tools for evaluating the worth of texts, instructional materials, and curriculum.

The disadvantages: (1) Tests do not always test what is taught. (2) Some administrators use tests to evaluate teachers and principals, pitting school against school and teacher against teacher. (3) Some teachers are pressured into teaching the tests, thereby invalidating the results. (4) Some students are not "test takers" and some are "superguessers," making results unreliable. (5) Test results are too often just filed and forgotten.

Joan H. Lowe, *Fifth-Grade Teacher*
Russell Elementary School, Hazelwood, Missouri

15

Classroom Assessment and Grading

W hen you think about elementary or secondary school, you probably have vivid memories of being tested and graded. In this chapter, we will look at both tests and grades, focusing not only on the effects these are likely to have on students, but also on practical means of developing more efficient methods for testing and grading.

We begin with a consideration of the many types of tests teachers prepare each year and some new approaches to assessment. Then we examine the effects grades are likely to have on students. Because there are so many grading systems, we also spend some time identifying the advantages and disadvantages of one system over another. Finally, we turn to the very important topic of communication with students and parents. How will you justify the grades you give?

By the time you have completed this chapter, you should be able to:

- Make a plan for testing students on a unit of work.
- Evaluate tests that accompany textbooks and teachers' manuals.
- Create multiple-choice and essay test items for your subject area.
- Describe authentic assessment approaches, including portfolios, performances, and exhibitions.
- Discuss the potential positive and negative effects of grades on students.
- Give examples of criterion-referenced and norm-referenced grading systems.
- Assign grades to a hypothetical group of students and defend your decisions in a class debate.
- Role-play a conference with parents who do not understand your grading system or their child's grades.

Think back on your report cards and grades over the years. Did you ever receive a grade that was lower than you expected? How did you feel about yourself, the teacher, the sub- ject, and school in general as a result of the lower grade? What could the teacher have done to help you understand and profit from the experience?

Test Bank items 15.1–15.9, 15.65–15.66, 15.78, 15.79, 15.95

Formative and Summative Assessment

As a teacher, you may or may not help in designing the grading system for your school or your class. Many school districts have a standard approach to grading. Still, you will have choices about how you use your district's grading system and how you assess your students' learning. Will you give tests? How many? What kinds? Will students do projects or keep portfolios of their work? How will homework influence grades? Will you grade on students' current academic performance or on their degree of improvement? How will you use the information from standardized student assessments?

There are two general uses or functions for assessment: formative and summative. **Formative assessment** occurs before or during instruction. It has two basic purposes: to guide the teacher in planning and to help students identify areas that need work. In other words, formative assessment helps *form* instruction. Often students are given a formative test prior to instruction, a **pretest** that helps the teacher determine what students already know. Sometimes a test is given during instruction to see what areas of weakness remain so teaching can be directed toward the problem areas. This is generally called a **diagnostic test** but should not be confused with the standardized diagnostic tests of more general learning abilities. A classroom diagnostic test identifies a student's areas of achievement and weakness in a particular subject. Older students are often able to apply the information from diagnostic tests to "reteach" themselves. For example, armed with the knowledge that you have difficulty interpreting standardized test reports like the one shown in Figure 14.5 in the preceding chapter, you could reread the section on this topic in chapter 14, read the interpretation section of a test manual, or ask another student or the instructor for an explanation.

Pretests and diagnostic tests are not graded. And since formative tests do not count toward the final grade, students who tend to be very anxious on "real" tests may find this low-pressure practice in test taking especially helpful.

A variation of formative measurement is ongoing measurement, often called **data-based instruction** or **curriculum-based assessment (CBA)**. This approach uses frequent "probes," brief tests of specific skills and knowledge drawn from the curriculum, to give a precise picture of a student's current per-

---

Planning Tip: See the *Chapter-15-At-A-Glance Planning Guide* in the *Instructor's Section* at the front of this book.

Study Guide: The *Study Guide*, sold separately, contains exercises to help students determine if they have mastered each learning objective for this chapter.

Planning Tip: See the separate *Instructor's Resource Manual* for additional activities and resources for teaching this chapter, including Handout Masters. Also see the *Allyn and Bacon Transparencies in Educational Psychology*.

Planning Tip: See the *Test Bank* and *Study Guide* supplements as you plan for evaluation and measurement of student learning.

Planning Tip: For further information about audiovisual, multimedia, and computer-assisted resources for teaching this chapter, see the Video and Software Guide Section in the *Instructor's Resource Manual*.

Formative Assessment Ungraded testing used before or during instruction to aid in planning and diagnosis.

Pretest Formative test for assessing students' knowledge, readiness, and abilities.

Diagnostic Test Formative test to determine students' areas of weakness.

Data-Based Instruction Assessment method using daily probes of specific-skill mastery.

Curriculum-Based Assessment (CBA) Evaluation method using frequent tests of specific skills and knowledge.

formance. Actually, CBA is not just one approach, but a whole family of approaches for linking teaching and assessment. CBA is "*any* set of measurement procedures that use direct observation and recording of a student's performance in the local curriculum as a basis for gathering information to make instructional decisions" (Deno, 1987, p. 41). This method has been used primarily with students who have learning problems, because it provides systematic assessment of both student performance and the teaching methods used. The assessment probes check to see if the difficulty level and the pace of instruction is right for the student. If a student shows inadequate progress on the assessment probes, the teacher should consider modifying or switching instructional strategies or pacing (Shapiro & Ager, 1992).

Summative assessment occurs at the end of instruction. Its purpose is to let the teacher and the students know the level of accomplishment attained. Summative assessment, therefore, provides a *summary* of accomplishment. The final exam is a classic example.

The distinction between formative and summative assessment is based on how the results are used. The same assessment procedure can be used for either purpose. If the goal is to obtain information about student learning for planning purposes, the assessment is formative. If the purpose is to determine final achievement (and help determine a course grade), the assessment is summative.

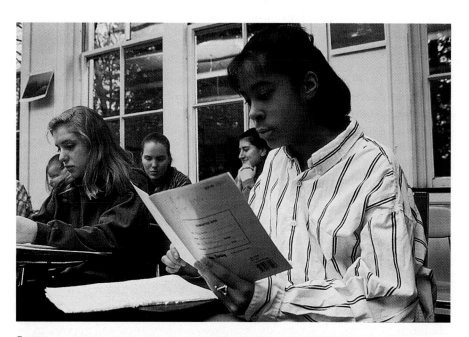

Is this assessment formative or summative? The answer depends on what is done with the results. If the teacher uses the outcome to shape future teaching and "form" instruction, then the assessment is formative. But if the results are used to determine how much the student has learned and to assign a grade or other final evaluation, then the assessment is summative because it provides a "summary" of the student's learning.

Background: Glaser, R. (1987). The integration of instruction and testing. In D. Berliner & B. Rosenshine (Eds.), *Talks to teachers* (pp. 329–341). New York: Random House.

Application: Ask students to give some specific ways in which formative evaluation can be implemented in the classroom.

Background: For a description of the different models of curriculum-based assessment and ideas for how it can be used with mainstreamed students, see Shapiro, E. S., & Ager, C. (1992). Assessment of special education students in regular education programs: Linking assessment to instruction. *The Elementary School Journal, 92,* 283–296.

Background: See Noll, J. W. (1991). *Taking sides: Clashing views on controversial educational issues* (5th ed.). Guilford, CT: Duskin, for "Is Measurement Driven Instruction Desirable?" pp. 224–241. W. James Popham argues in favor of linking teaching and testing; Gerald W. Bracey speaks against it.

Summative Assessment Testing that follows instruction and assesses achievement.

Objective 15.2: Make a plan for testing students on a unit of work.

Getting the Most from Traditional Assessment Approaches

When most people think of assessment, they usually think of testing. As you will see shortly, teachers today have many other options, but testing is still a significant activity in most classrooms. Let's consider your options for assessing students using the traditional testing approach. In this section we will examine how to plan effective tests, how to evaluate the tests that accompany standard curriculum materials, and how to write your own test questions.

Planning for Testing

Test Bank items 15.10–15.13, 15.86, 15.102

Both instruction and assessment are most effective when they are well organized and planned. Creating a behavior-content matrix can help teachers develop thoughtful learning objectives. The same process can be applied in planning classroom assessment. When you have a good plan, you are in a better position to judge the tests provided in teacher's manuals and texts and to write tests yourself.

Using a Behavior-Content Matrix.

Here is how you might use a behavior-content matrix to design a unit test. First you will need to decide how many items students can complete during the testing period, and then you must make sure that the items you write cover all the objectives you have set for the unit. More important objectives should have more items (Berliner, 1987).

An example of a plan that might be appropriate for a 40-question unit test in government is given in Figure 15.1. From the test plan, you can see that this teacher has decided the most important topic is *major political issues* and has accordingly allotted a total of 15 questions to it. The least important topic is *methods of inquiry.* Also, the teacher wants to emphasize students' abilities to make *generalizations* (14 questions) while giving considerable attention to *understanding concepts* and *locating information. Interpreting graphs* is the least important skill, but it is not to be overlooked.

By preparing such a plan, you can avoid a situation where you have written 15 great questions (out of 40), only to discover that all 15 ask students to deal with the same concept or topic. Making a test plan will also improve the validity of tests. You will be able to ask a reasonable number of questions that measure the skills you hoped to develop about each key topic.

When to Test?

Research: Dempster, F. (1991). Synthesis of research on reviews and tests. *Educational Leadership, 48*(7), 71–76. Focus Question: How can tests and reviews be used to encourage student learning?

Background: Dempster, F. N. (1993). Exposing our students to less should help them learn more. *Phi Delta Kappan, 74,* 432–437.

Frank Dempster (1991) examined the research on reviews and tests and reached these useful conclusions for teachers:

1. Frequent testing encourages the retention of information and appears to be more effective than a comparable amount of time spent reviewing and studying the material.

2. Tests are especially effective in promoting learning if you give students a test on the material soon after they learn it, then retest on the material later. The retestings should be spaced farther and farther apart.

3. The use of cumulative questions on tests is a key to effective learning. Cumulative questions ask students to apply information learned in previous units to solve a new problem.

FIGURE 15.1

TEST PLAN FOR A UNIT ON GOVERNMENT

In making a test plan, begin by deciding on the totals (the numbers in bold) and then allocate the number of questions to each particular type and skill combination.

Topics   Skills Tested

	Understanding Concepts	Making Generalizations	Locating Information	Interpreting Graphs	Total Questions
Social trends	4	4	1	1	**10**
National political events	2	3	3	2	**10**
Methods of inquiry	1	1	2	1	**5**
Major political issues	3	6	4	2	**15**
Total questions	**10**	**14**	**10**	**6**	**40**

Unfortunately, the curriculum in many schools is so full that there is little time for frequent tests and reviews. Dempster argues that students will learn more if we "teach them less," that is, if the curriculum includes fewer topics, but explores those topics in greater depth and allows more time for review, practice, testing, and feedback (Dempster, 1993).

Judging Textbook Tests.   Most elementary and secondary school texts today come complete with supplemental materials such as teaching manuals, handout masters, and ready-made tests. Using these tests can save time, but is this good teaching practice? The answer depends on your objectives for your students, the way you taught the material, and the quality of the tests provided (Airasian, 1994). If the textbook test matches your testing plan and the instruction you actually provided for your students, then it may be the right test to use. Table 15.1 on page 554 gives key points to consider in evaluating textbook tests.

Objective 15.3: Evaluate tests that accompany textbooks and teacher's manuals.

What if there are no tests available for the material you want to cover, or the tests provided in your teacher's manuals are not appropriate for your students? Then it's time for you to create your own tests. We will consider the two major kinds of tests—objective and essay.

Objective Testing

Test Bank items 15.14–15.17, 15.19, 15.25, 15.67, 15.68, 15.80–15.82, 15.96, 15.101, 15.105

Multiple-choice questions, matching exercises, true/false statements, and short-answer or fill-in items are all types of **objective testing**. The word "ob-

Objective Testing Multiple-choice, matching, true-false, short-answer, and fill-in tests; scoring answers does not require interpretation.

TABLE 15.1   Key Points to Consider in Judging Textbook Tests

The decision to use a textbook test must come *after* a teacher identifies the objectives that he or she taught and now wants to assess.

Textbook tests are designed for the typical classroom, but since few classrooms are typical, most teachers deviate somewhat from the text in order to accommodate their pupils' needs.

The more classroom instruction deviates from the textbook objectives and lesson plans, the less valid the textbook tests are likely to be.

The main consideration in judging the adequacy of a textbook test is the match between its test questions and what pupils were taught in their classes:

- Are questions similar to the teacher's objectives and instructional emphases?
- Do questions require pupils to perform the behaviors they were taught?
- Do questions cover all or most of the important objectives taught?
- Is the language level and terminology appropriate for pupils?
- Does the number of items for each objective provide a sufficient sample of pupil performance?

Source: P. Airasian (1994). *Classroom assessment* (2nd ed.), p. 154. Copyright © 1994 by McGraw-Hill. Adapted with permission of McGraw-Hill.

Handout: A diagram classifying "Different Kinds of Test Questions" is available in **Handout Master 15.6** in the *Instructor's Resource Manual.*

Activity 15.1: Critical Thinking. See the separate *Instructor's Resource Manual* for Evaluating Test Items. This activity asks your students to work in groups to analyze an achievement test, using as a criterion Gronlund's checklist for evaluating test items. The "Checklist for Evaluating Test Items" is provided in **Handout Master 15.3.**

jective" in relation to testing means "not open to many interpretations," or "not subjective." The scoring of these types of items is relatively straightforward compared to the scoring of essay questions because the answers are more clear-cut than essay answers.

Gronlund (1993) suggests that the guiding principle for deciding which item format is best is to "use the item types that provide the most direct measures of student performance specified by the intended learning outcome" (p. 28). In other words, if you want to see how well students can write a letter, have them write a letter, don't ask multiple-choice questions about letters. But if many different item formats will work equally well, then use multiple-choice questions because they are easier to score fairly and can cover many topics. Switch to other formats if writing good multiple-choice items for the material is not possible. For example, if related concepts need to be linked, such as terms and definitions, then a matching item is a better format than multiple-choice. If it is difficult to come up with several wrong answers for a multiple-choice item, try a true/false question instead. Alternatively, ask the student to supply a short answer that completes a statement (fill in the blank). Variety in objective testing can lower students' anxiety because the entire grade does not depend on one type of question that a particular student may find difficult. Here we look closely at the multiple-choice format, because it is the most versatile—and the most difficult to use well.

Using Multiple-Choice Tests.   People often assume that multiple-choice items are appropriate only for asking factual questions. But multiple-choice items can test higher-level objectives as well, although writing higher-level items is difficult. A multiple-choice item can assess more than recall and recognition if it requires the student to deal with new material by *applying* or *analyzing* the concept or principle being tested (Gronlund, 1993). For example, the following multiple-choice item is designed to assess students' ability to recognize unstated assumptions, one of the skills involved in analyzing an idea:

> An educational psychology professor states, "A *z* score of +1 on a test is equivalent to a percentile rank of approximately 84." Which of the following assumptions is the professor making?
>
> 1. The scores on the test range from 0 to 100.
> 2. The standard deviation of the test scores is equal to 3.4.
> 3. The distribution of scores on the test is normal. (correct answer)
> 4. The test is valid and reliable.

All test items require skillful construction, but good multiple-choice items are a real challenge.

Writing Multiple-Choice Questions.   Some students jokingly refer to multiple-choice tests as "multiple-guess" tests—a sign that these tests are often poorly designed. Your goal in writing test items is to design them so that they measure student achievement, not test-taking and guessing skills.

The **stem** of a multiple-choice item is the part that asks the question or poses the problem. The choices that follow are called *alternatives*. The wrong answers are called **distractors** because their purpose is to distract students who have only a partial understanding of the material. If there were no good distractors, students with only a vague understanding would have no difficulty in finding the right answer.

Stating the correct answer so that it is the only right answer, or clearly the best answer, is tricky. You probably have been on the student side of discussions about whether the correct answer was really correct or whether several of the answers might be correct. The teacher is just as unhappy as the students when half the class selects the same wrong answer. Often this means the item was poorly constructed. The Guidelines adapted from Gronlund (1993), should make writing multiple-choice and other objective test questions easier.

Activity 15.2: Cooperative Learning. See the separate *Instructor's Resource Manual* for Writing Multiple-Choice Items, an activity in which students work in groups to identify problems with multiple-choice items. Handout Master 15.5 presents the items.

Objective 15.1: Create multiple-choice and essay test items for the relevant subject area.

Stem The question part of a multiple-choice item.

Distractors Wrong answers offered as choices in a multiple-choice item.

Guidelines

Writing Objective Test Items

The stem should be clear and simple, and present only a single problem. Unessential details should be left out.

Poor
> There are several different kinds of standard or derived scores. An IQ score is especially useful because . . .

Better
> An advantage of an IQ score is . . .

The problem in the stem should be stated in positive terms. Negative language is confusing. If you must use words such as *not*, *no*, or *except*, underline them or type them in all capitals.

Poor
> Which of the following is not a standard score?

(continued)

Better

Which of the following is NOT a standard score?

Do not expect students to make extremely fine discrimination among answer choices.

Poor

The percentage of area in a normal curve falling between +1 and −1 standard deviations is about:

a. 66%.   **b.** 67%.   **c.** 68%.   **d.** 69%.

Better

The percentage of area in a normal curve falling between +1 and −1 standard deviations is about:

a. 14%   **b.** 34%.   (c.) 68%.   **d.** 95%.

As much wording as possible should be included in the stem so that phrases will not have to be repeated in each alternative.

Poor

A percentile score

a. indicates the percentage of items answered correctly.
b. indicates the percent of correct answers divided by the percent of wrong answers.
c. indicates the percent of people who scored at or above a given raw score.
d. indicates the percent of people who scored at or below a given raw score.

Better

A percentile score indicates the percentage of

a. items answered correctly.
b. correct answers divided by the percent of wrong answers.
c. people who scored at or above a given raw score.
(d.) people who scored at or below a given raw score.

Each alternative answer should fit the grammatical form of the stem, so that no answers are obviously wrong.

Poor

The Stanford-Binet test yields an

a. IQ score.   **c.** vocational preference.
b. reading level.   **d.** mechanical aptitude.

Better

The Stanford-Binet is a test of

(a.) intelligence.   **c.** vocational preference.
b. reading level.   **d.** mechanical aptitude.

Categorical words such as *always, all, only,* or *never* should be avoided unless they can appear consistently in all the alternatives. Most smart test takers know the categorical answers are usually wrong.

Poor

A student's true score on a standardized test is

a. never equal to the obtained score.
b. always very close to the obtained score.
c. always determined by the standard error of measurement.
d. usually within a band that extends from +1 to −1 standard errors of measurement on each side of the obtained score.

Better

Which one of the statements below would most often be correct about a student's true score on a standardized test?

a. It equals the obtained score.
b. It will be very close to the obtained score.
c. It is determined by the standard error of measurement.
d. It could be above or below the obtained score.

You should also avoid including two distractors that have the same meaning. If only one answer can be right and if two answers are the same, then these two must both be wrong. This narrows down the choices considerably.

Poor

The most frequently occurring score in a distribution is called the

a. mode.   **c.** arithmetical average.
b. median.   **d.** mean.

Better

The most frequently occurring score in a distribution is called the

a. mode.   **c.** standard deviation.
b. median.   **d.** mean.

Using the exact wording found in the textbook is another technique to avoid. Poor students may recognize the answers without knowing what they mean.

Avoid overuse of *all of the above* and *none of the above*. Such choices may be helpful to students who are simply guessing. In addition, using *all of the above* may trick a quick student who sees that the first alternative is correct and does not read on to discover that the others are correct, too.

Obvious patterns on a test also aid students who are guessing. The position of the correct answer should be varied, as should its length.

Evaluating Objective Test Items   Test Bank items 15.62–15.64

How will you evaluate the quality of the objective tests you give? One way is to conduct an item analysis to identify items that are performing well and those that should be changed or eliminated. There are many techniques for item analysis, but one simple approach is to calculate the difficulty and discrimination indices of the test. The difficulty index (p) of any item is simply the proportion or percentage of people who answered that item correctly. For norm-referenced tests, items with difficulty indices of around .50 are best. These items are most likely to identify individual differences in achievement levels. A simple way of calculating the difficulty index of an item when you have a large class is shown in Table 15.2 on page 558.

The discrimination index (d) tells you how well each test item discriminated between people who performed well overall on the test and those who did poorly. The assumption here is that good items are those that are answered correctly by students who do well on the entire test but are missed by the students who get low scores on the test. A test item that was passed more often by the low scorers than by the high scorers would be suspect. Table 15.2 on page 558 gives a simple way to estimate the discrimination index of an item.

TABLE 15.2   Calculating the Difficulty and Discrimination Indices for Test Items

To estimate the **Difficulty Index** (*p*) for each item:

- Rank the scores on the test from highest to lowest.
- Identify the people in the top one-third (the high-scoring group or HSG) and the people in the bottom one-third (the low-scoring group or LSG).
- For each item, count the number of people who answered correctly the HSG and the LSG combined and divide by the total in the two groups. The formula is:

$$\text{Difficulty Index of an item} = \frac{\text{number correct in HSG} + \text{number correct in LSG}}{\text{number in HSG} + \text{number in LSG}}$$

This calculation is a reasonable estimate of the proportion of students in the whole class who answered correctly. Ideally, most of the items on a norm-referenced test would have difficulty indices of .40 to .59, with only a few hard (.00 to .25) or easy (.75 to 1.00) items.

To estimate the **Discrimination Index** (*d*) for each item:

- Rank the scores on the test from highest to lowest.
- Identify the people in the top one-third of the scores (high-scoring group or HSG) and the people in the bottom one-third (low-scoring group or LSG).
- Subtract the percentage of students in the LSG who answered correctly from the percentage of students in the HSG who answered correctly. The formula is:

$$\text{Discrimination Index of an item} = \text{percent correct in HSG} - \text{percent correct in LSG}$$

The meaning of the discrimination index for any item is as follows:

$d = +.60$ to 1.00	*Very Strong* discriminator between high- and low-scoring students
$d = +.40$ to $.59$	*Strong* discriminator between high- and low-scoring students
$d = +.20$ to $.39$	*Moderate* discriminator between high- and low-scoring students (improve the item)
$d = -.19$ to $.19$	*Does Not* discriminate between high- and low-scoring students (improve or eliminate the item)
$d = -.20$ to -1.00	*Strong Negative* discriminator between high- and low-scoring students (check item for problems, miskeyed? two right answers? etc.)

Source: Adapted from Linden, K. (1992). *Cooperative learning and problem solving.* Prospect Heights, IL: Waveland Press, pp. 207–209.

Essay Testing

Test Bank items 15.18, 15.20–15.24, 15.26–15.28, 15.69, 15.84, 15.85, 15.97

The best way to measure some learning objectives is to require students to create answers on their own. An essay question is appropriate in these cases. The most difficult part of essay testing is judging the quality of the answers, but writing good, clear questions is not particularly easy, either. We will look at writing, administering, and grading essay tests, with most of the specific suggestions taken from Gronlund (1993). We will also consider factors that can bias the scoring of essay questions and ways you can overcome these problems.

Constructing Essay Tests.   Because answering takes time, true essay tests cover less material than objective tests. Thus, for efficiency, essay tests should generally be limited to the assessment of the more complex learning outcomes.

An essay question should give students a clear and precise task and should indicate the elements to be covered in the answer. Gronlund suggests the following as an example of an essay question that might appear in an educational psychology course to measure an objective at the *synthesis* level of Bloom's taxonomy in the cognitive domain:

> For a course that you are teaching or expect to teach, prepare a complete plan for assessing student achievement. Be sure to include the procedures

Transparency: An activity in which students "Analyze Essay Questions" and rewrite them as needed is presented in acetate transparency T 123.

Connections: See Chapter 12 for a discussion of Bloom's taxonomy of objectives in the cognitive domain.

you would follow, the instruments you would use, and the reasons for your choices.

This question requires students to apply information and values derived from course material to produce a complex new product.

Gronlund (1993) has offered a variety of specific suggestions for constructing and administering essay tests. First, students should be given ample time for answering. If more than one essay is being completed in the same class period, you may want to suggest time limits for each. Remember, however, that time pressure increases anxiety and may prevent accurate assessment of some students.

Whatever your approach, do not try to make up for the limited amount of material an essay test can cover by including a large number of essay questions. It would be better to plan on more frequent testing than to include more than two or three essay questions in a single class period. Combining an essay question with a number of objective items is one way to avoid the problem of limited sampling of course material.

Evaluating Essays: Dangers. In 1912, Starch and Elliot began a classic series of experiments that shocked educators into critical consideration of subjectivity in testing. These researchers wanted to find out the extent to which teachers were influenced by personal values, standards, and expectations in scoring essay tests. For their initial study, they sent copies of English examination papers written by two high school students to English teachers in 200 high schools. Each teacher was asked to score the papers according to his or her school's standards. A percentage scale was to be used, with 75 percent as a passing grade.

Discussion: One reason students prefer essay tests is that they can write down something, even if it doesn't answer the question, and receive at least partial credit for the question. Do your students think that granting partial credit is a common grading practice among teachers? Considering that essay questions sample only a limited amount of material, does the practice seem commendable or defensible?

Activity 15.3: Background. See the Instructor's Resource Manual for Scoring Essay Tests.

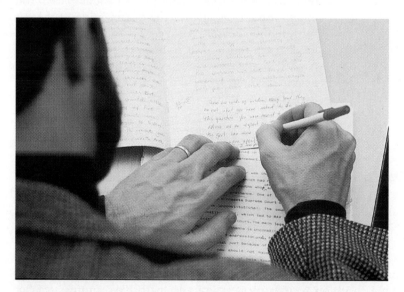

Often the best way to measure students' learning is to have them create their own answers in essay tests; however, grading essay tests is less straightforward than grading objective tests.

The results? Neatness, spelling, punctuation, and communicative effectiveness were all valued to different degrees by different teachers. The scores on one of the papers ranged from 64 to 98 percent, with a mean of 88.2. The average score for the other paper was 80.2, with a range between 50 and 97. The following year, Starch and Elliot (1913a & b) published similar findings in a study involving history and geometry papers. The most important result of these studies was the discovery that the problem of subjectivity in grading was not confined to any particular subject area. The main difficulties were the individual standards of the grader and the unreliability of scoring procedures.

Certain qualities of an essay may influence grades. For example, in a study of grading practices at 16 law schools, Linn, Klein, and Hart (1972) found that neatly written, verbose, jargon-filled essays with few grammatical and construction errors were given the best grades. Evidence indicates that teachers may reward quantity rather than quality in essays. In a series of studies described by Fiske (1981), many high school and college English teachers rated pairs of student essays that were identical in every way but linguistic style. One essay was quite verbose, with flowery language, complex sentences, and passive verbs. The other essay was written in the simple, straightforward language most teachers claim is the goal for students of writing. The teachers consistently rated the verbose essay higher.

Research: Vacc, N. N. (1989). Writing evaluation: Examining four teachers' holistic and analytic scores. *Elementary School Journal, 90,* 88–95.

Focus on . . .   **Traditional Assessment Approaches**

- What is the most important consideration in deciding whether to use a test that comes with the text for your class?
- Write three multiple-choice items for this chapter and then evaluate them using the Guidelines: Writing Objective Test Items.
- Would an objective test or an essay test be more appropriate under these circumstances:
  1. You wish to test the students' knowledge of the terminology used in lab experiments.
  2. The test must be given and graded in the two days before the end of the six-week grading period.
  3. You want to test the students' ability to present a logical argument.
  4. Your aim is to balance subjective judgments with a highly reliable measure.
  5. You are seeking to test student understanding of a few major principles.
  6. You want to test students' knowledge of foreign countries' major export goods.
  7. You have limited time to construct the test.
  8. You are interested in students' ability to differentiate between the major philosophies of democracy and socialism.

Evaluating Essays: Methods.   Gronlund (1993) offers several strategies for grading essays that avoid problems of subjectivity and inaccuracy. When possible, a good first step is to construct a model answer, then you can assign points to its various parts. You might also give points for the organization of the answer and the internal consistency. You can then assign grades such as 1 to 5 or A, B, C, D, and F, and sort the papers into piles by grade. As a final step, skim the papers in each pile to see if they are comparable in quality. These techniques will help ensure fairness and accuracy in grading.

When grading essay tests with several questions, it makes sense to grade all responses to one question before moving on to the next. This helps prevent the quality of a student's answer to one question from influencing your reaction to the student's other answers. After you finish reading and scoring the first question, shuffle the papers so that no students end up having all their questions graded first, last, or in the middle.

You may achieve greater objectivity if you ask students to put their names on the back of the paper, so that grading is anonymous. A final check on your fairness as a grader is to have another teacher who is equally familiar with your goals and subject matter grade your tests without knowing what grades you have assigned. This can give you valuable insights into areas of bias in your grading practices.

Educators concerned with the writing process have developed an approach to evaluating written work known as **holistic scoring.** The philosophy underlying the holistic approach is that a written passage is greater than the sum of its parts. When teachers focus on the specific parts of an essay, such as vocabulary, grammar, spelling, or inclusion of particular details, they may miss important qualities like the essential message and persuasiveness. Rather than assigning separate grades for style, grammar, and content, for example, the holistic approach would assess the essay as a whole and give just one grade (Vacc, 1989). To make sure holistic scores are reliable, White (1984) has recommended that teachers use one session to read essays, and at the outset choose sample essays for each grade level to serve as models, i.e., choose one essay as a model for an A, one for a B, and so on.

Now that we have examined both objective and essay testing, we can compare the two approaches. Table 15.3 presents a summary of the important characteristics of each.

Transparency: Acetate transparency **T 124** provides a chart "Comparing Objective and Essay Tests."

TABLE 15.3 Comparing Objective and Essay Tests

Objective tests include any tests that ask the student to select the answer from a set of choices (multiple choice, true/false, matching).

	Selection-Type Items	Essay Questions
Learning Outcomes Measured	Good for measuring outcomes at the knowledge, comprehension, and application levels of learning; inadequate for organizing and expressing ideas.	Inefficient for measuring knowledge outcomes; best for ability to organize, integrate, and express ideas.
Sampling of Content	The use of a large number of items results in broad coverage which makes representative sampling of content feasible.	The use of a small number of items limits coverage which makes representative sampling of content infeasible.
Preparation of Items	Preparation of good items is difficult and time consuming.	Preparation of good items is difficult but easier than selection-type items.
Scoring	Objective, simple, and highly reliable.	Subjective, difficult, and less reliable.
Factors Distorting Scores	Reading ability and guessing.	Writing ability and bluffing.
Probable Effect on Learning	Encourages students to remember, interpret, and use the ideas of others.	Encourages students to organize, integrate, and express their own ideas.

Source: From Norman E. Gronlund, *How to Make Achievement Tests and Assessments 5/e,* p. 83. Copyright © 1993 by Allyn & Bacon. Reprinted by permission.

Holistic Scoring Evaluation of a piece of written work as a whole, without separate grades for individual elements.

Innovations in Assessment

Study Guide: Concept Map. See the *Study Guide* for the Concept Map "Alternatives for Assessment." This Concept Map also appears as **Handout Master 15.8.**

Background: Cambourne, B., & Turbill, J. (1990). Assessment in whole-language classrooms: Theory into practice. *Elementary School Journal, 90,* 337–349.

Objective 15.4: Describe authentic assessment approaches, including portfolios and exhibitions.

Background 15.1: Wiggins, G. (1989). Teaching to the authentic test. *Educational Leadership, 46*(7), 41–47. This article is summarized in the *Instructor's Resource Manual. Focus Question:* Ask your students to describe what makes tests "authentic."

Activity 15.4: Background. See the *Instructor's Resource Manual* for Teaching to the Authentic Test.

We have been considering how to make traditional testing more effective; now let's look at a few new approaches to classroom assessment. One of the main criticisms of standardized tests—that they control the curriculum, emphasizing recall of facts instead of thinking and problem solving—is a major criticism of classroom tests as well. Few teachers would dispute these criticisms. Even if you follow the guidelines we have been discussing, traditional testing can be limiting. What can be done? Should innovations in classroom assessment make traditional testing obsolete? The Point/Counterpoint section addresses this question.

One solution that has been proposed to solve the testing dilemma is to apply the concept of authentic assessment to classroom testing.

Authentic Classroom Tests

Test Bank items 15.29, 15.70, 15.98, 15.103

Authentic tests ask students to apply skills and abilities as they would in real life. For example, they might use fractions to enlarge or reduce recipes. Grant Wiggins makes this argument:

> If tests determine what teachers actually teach and what students will study for—and they do—then the road to reform is a straight but steep one: test those capabilities and habits we think are essential, and test them in context. Make [tests] replicate, within reason, the challenges at the heart of each academic discipline. Let them be—authentic. (1989, p. 41)

Authentic Tests Assessment procedures that test skills and abilities as they would be applied in real-life situations.

Authentic assessment of reading skills would involve students actually reading as part of their performance.

To Test or Not to Test, Part II

We have seen the advantages and disadvantages of standardized tests, but what about classroom testing? Are traditional multiple-choice and essay tests useful in classroom assessment?

POINT **Traditional tests are a poor basis for classroom assessment.**

In his article "Standards, Not Standardization: Evoking Quality Student Work," Grant Wiggins (1991) makes a strong case for giving students standards of excellence against which they can judge their accomplishments. But these standards should not be higher scores on multiple-choice tests. When scores on traditional tests become the standard, the message to students is that only right answers matter and the thinking behind the answers is unimportant. Wiggins notes:

> We do not judge Xerox, the Boston Symphony, the Cincinnati Reds, or Dom Perignon vineyards on the basis of indirect, easy to test, and common indicators. Nor would the workers in those places likely produce quality if some generic, secure test served as the only measure of their success in meeting a standard. Demanding and getting quality, whether from students or adult workers, means framing standards in terms of the work that we undertake and value. And it means framing expectations about that work

which make quality a necessity, not an option. Consider:

> ■ the English teacher who instructs peer-editors to mark the place in a student paper where they lost interest in it or found it slapdash and to hand it back for revision at that point;

> ■ the professor who demands that all math homework be turned in with another student having signed off on it, where one earns the grade for one's work *and* the grade for the work that each person (willingly!) countersigned. (p. 22)

In a more recent article, Wiggins continues to argue for assessment that makes sense, that tests knowledge as it is applied in real-world situations. Understanding cannot be measured by tests that ask students to use skills and knowledge out of context. "In other words, we cannot be said to understand something unless we can employ our knowledge wisely, fluently, flexibly, and aptly in particular and diverse contexts" (Wiggins, 1993, p. 200).

COUNTERPOINT **Traditional tests can play an important role.**

Most psychologists and educators would agree with Wiggins that setting clear, high, authentic standards is important, but many also believe that traditional tests are useful in this process. Learning may be more than knowing the right answers, but right answers are

important. While schooling is about learning to think and solve problems, it is also about knowledge. Students must have something to think about—facts, ideas, concepts, principles, theories, explanations, arguments, images, opinions. Well-designed traditional tests can evaluate students' knowledge effectively and efficiently (Airasian, 1994; Kirst, 1991b).

Some educators believe that traditional testing should play an even greater role than it currently does. Educational policy analysts suggest that American students, compared to students in many other developed countries, lack essential knowledge because American schools emphasize process—critical thinking, self-esteem, problem solving—more than content. In order to teach more about content, teachers will need to determine how well their students are learning the content, and traditional testing provides useful information about content learning.

Tests are also valuable in motivating and guiding students' learning. There is research evidence that frequent testing encourages learning and retention (Nungester & Duchastel, 1982). In fact, students generally learn more in classes with more rather than fewer tests (Dempster, 1991).

Source: Grant Wiggins (1991). "Standards not standardization." *Educational Leadership, 48* (5), 18–25. Reprinted with permission of the Association for Supervision and Curriculum Development. Copyright © 1991 by ASCD. All rights reserved.

Wiggins goes on to say that if our instructional goals for students include the abilities to write, speak, listen, create, think critically, do research, solve problems, or apply knowledge, then our tests should ask students to write, speak, listen, create, think, solve, and apply. How can this happen?

Many educators suggest we look to the arts and sports for analogies to solve this problem. If we think of the "test" as being the recital, exhibition,

Connections: See chapter 14 for a discussion of authentic assessment and standardized tests.

Handout: "Characteristics of
Authentic Tests" are presented in
Handout Master 15.7 in the *Instructor's Resource Manual.* Students might use the information
on this handout to compare the
purposes of authentic and norm-
referenced tests.

Background: Herman, J. L.,
Aschbacher, P. R., & Winters, L.
(1992). *A practical guide to alternative assessment.* Alexandria,
VA: Association for Supervision
and Curriculum Development.

game, mock court trial, or other performance, then teaching to the test is just
fine. All coaches, artists, and musicians gladly "teach" to these "tests" because
performing well on these tests is the whole point of instruction. Authentic assessment asks students to perform. The performances may be thinking performances, physical performances, creative performances, or other forms.

It may seem odd to talk of thinking as a performance, but there are many
parallels. Serious thinking is risky, because real-life problems are not well defined. Often the outcomes of our thinking are public—our ideas are evaluated
by others. Like a dancer auditioning for a Broadway show, we must cope with
the consequences of being evaluated. Like a sculptor looking at a lump of clay,
a student facing a difficult problem must experiment, observe, redo, imagine and
test solutions, apply both basic skills and inventive techniques, make interpretations, decide how to communicate results to the intended audience, and often
accept criticism and improve the solution (Wolf, in press; Wolf, Bixby, Glenn, &
Gardner, 1991). Table 15.4 lists some characteristics of authentic tests.

TABLE 15.4 Characteristics of Authentic Tests

A. Structure and Logistics

1. Are more appropriately public; involve an audience, a panel, and so on.
2. Do not rely on unrealistic and arbitrary time constraints.
3. Offer known, not secret, questions or tasks.
4. Are more like portfolios or a *season* of games (not one-shot).
5. Require some collaboration with others.
6. Recur—and are *worth* practicing for, rehearsing, and retaking.
7. Make assessment and feedback to students so central that school schedules, structures, and policies are modified to support them.

B. Intellectual Design Features

1. Are "essential"—not needlessly intrusive, arbitrary, or contrived to "shake out" a grade.
2. Are "enabling"—constructed to point the student toward more sophisticated use of the skills or knowledge.
3. Are contextualized, complex intellectual challenges, not "atomized" tasks, corresponding to isolated "outcomes."
4. Involve the student's own research or use of knowledge, for which "content" is a means.
5. Assess student habits and repertoires, not mere recall or plug-in skills.
6. Are *representative* challenges—designed to emphasize *depth* more than breadth.

7. Are engaging and educational.
8. Involve somewhat ambiguous ("ill-structured") tasks or problems.

C. Grading and Scoring Standards

1. Involve criteria that assess essentials, not easily counted (but relatively unimportant) errors.
2. Are graded not on a "curve" but in reference to performance standards (criterion-referenced. not norm-referenced).
3. Involve demystified criteria of success that appear to *students* as inherent in successful activity.
4. Make self-assessment a part of the assessment.
5. Use a multifaceted scoring system instead of one aggregate grade.
6. Exhibit harmony with shared schoolwide aims—a *standard.*

D. Fairness and Equity

1. Ferret out and identify (perhaps hidden) strengths.
2. Strike a *constantly* examined balance between honoring achievement and native skill or fortunate prior training.
3. Minimize needless, unfair, and demoralizing comparisons.
4. Allow appropriate room for student learning styles, aptitudes, and interests.
5. Can be—should be—attempted by *all* students, with the test "scaffolded up," not "dumbed down," as necessary.

Performance in Context: Portfolios and Exhibitions

Test Bank items 15.30, 15.31, 15.71, 15.88

The concern with authentic assessment has led to the development of several new approaches based on the goal of *performance in context*. Instead of circling answers to "factual" questions on nonexistent situations, students are required to solve real problems. Facts are used in a context where they apply—for example, the student uses grammar facts to write a persuasive letter to a software company requesting donations for the class computer center. The following example of a test of performance is taken from the Connecticut Core of Common Learning:

> Many local supermarkets claim to have the lowest prices. But what does this really mean? Does it mean that every item in their store is priced lower, or just some of them? How can you really tell which supermarket will save you the most money? Your assignment is to design and carry out a study to answer this question. What items and prices will you compare and why? How will you justify the choice of your "sample"? How reliable is the sample, etc.? (Wolf, Bixby, Glenn, & Gardner, 1991, p. 61)

Students completing this "test" will use mathematical facts and procedures in the context of solving a real-life problem. In addition, they will have to think critically and write persuasively.

Portfolios and exhibitions are two new approaches to assessment that require performance in context. With these new approaches, it is difficult to tell where instruction stops and assessment starts because the two processes are interwoven.

Portfolios. According to Paulson, Paulson, and Meyer (1991), **portfolio** is:

> a purposeful collection of student work that exhibits the student's efforts, progress, and achievements in one or more areas. The collection must include student participation in selecting contents, the criteria for judging merit, and evidence of student self-reflection. (p. 60)

Portfolios often include work in progress, revisions, student self-analyses, and reflections on what the student has learned. For example, one student's self-reflection is presented in Figure 15.2 on page 566.

Written work or artistic pieces are common contents of portfolios, but students might also include graphs, diagrams, snapshots of displays, peer comments, audio- or videotapes, laboratory reports, computer programs—anything that demonstrates learning in the area being taught and assessed (Belanoff & Dickson, 1991; Camp, 1990; Wolf, Bixby, Glenn, & Gardner, 1991). The Vermont Mathematics Portfolio, for example, has (1) five to seven of the student's "best pieces," including at least one puzzle, one investigation, one application, and no more than two examples of group work; (2) a letter to the portfolio examiner; and (3) a collection of other pieces of mathematics work (Abruscato, 1993). The Guidelines give some ideas for using portfolios in your teaching.

Exhibitions. An **exhibition** is a performance test that has two additional features. First, it is public, so students preparing exhibitions must take the audience into account; communication and understanding are essential. Second, an exhibition often requires many hours of preparation, because it is

Discussion: Assign Paulson, F. L., Paulson, P. R., & Meyer, C. A. (1991). What makes a portfolio a portfolio? *Educational Leadership, 48*(5), 60–63. Focus Question: Ask your students to describe five entries that they might include in portfolios for their students.

Portfolio A collection of the student's work in an area, showing growth, self-reflection, and achievement.

Exhibition A performance test or demonstration of learning that is public and usually takes an extended time to prepare.

Activity 15.5: Cooperative Learning. See the separate *Instructor's Resource Manual* for Portfolio Content, a group activity that asks your students to determine how they would use portfolios in teaching.

Background: For a positive view of using portfolios as a statewide assessment process, see Ambruscato, J. (1993). Early results and tentative implications from the Vermont Portfolio Project. *Phi Delta Kappan, 74,* 474–477.

FIGURE 15.2

A STUDENT REFLECTS ON LEARNING: SELF-ANALYSIS OF WORK IN A PORTFOLIO
Not only has this student's writing improved, but the student has become a more self-aware and self-critical writer.

> Today I looked at all my stories in my writing folder I read some of my writing since September. I noticed that I've improved some stuff. Now I edit my stories, and revise Now I use periods, quotation mark. Sometimes my stories are longer I used to misspell my words and now I look in a dictionary or ask a friend and now I write exciting and scary stories and now I have very good endings. Now I use capitals I used to leave out words and write short simple stories.

Source: F. Leon Paulson, P. Paulson, and C. Meyers (1991). What makes a portfolio a portfolio? *Educational Leadership, 48* (5), p. 63. Reprinted with permission of the Association for Supervision and Curriculum Development. Copyright © 1991 by ASCD. All rights reserved.

Guidelines

Creating Portfolios

Students should be involved in selecting the pieces that will make up the portfolio.

Examples
1. During the unit or semester, ask each student to select work that fits certain criteria, such as "my most difficult problem," "my best work," "my most improved work," or "three approaches to. . . ."
2. For their final submissions, ask students to select pieces that best show how much they have learned.

A portfolio should include information that shows student self-reflection and self-criticism.

Examples
1. Ask students to include a rationale for their selections.
2. Have each student write a "guide" to his or her portfolio, explaining how strengths and weaknesses are reflected in the work included.

3. Include self- and peer critiques, indicating specifically what is good and what might be improved.
4. Model self-criticism of your own productions.

The portfolio should reflect the students' activities in learning.

Examples

1. Include a representative selection of projects, writings, drawings, etc.
2. Ask students to relate the goals of learning to the contents of their portfolios.

The portfolio can serve different functions at different times of the year.

Examples

1. Early in the year, it might hold unfinished work or "problem pieces."
2. At the end of the year, it should contain only what the student is willing to make public.

Portfolios should show growth.

Examples

1. Ask students to make a "history" of their progress along certain dimensions and to illustrate points in their growth with specific works.
2. Ask students to include descriptions of activities outside class that reflect the growth illustrated in the portfolio.

Teach students how to create and use portfolios.

Examples

1. Keep models of very well done portfolios as examples, but stress that each portfolio is an individual statement.
2. Examine your students' portfolios frequently, especially early in the year when they are just getting used to the idea. Give constructive feedback.

---

the culminating experience of a whole program of study. Ted Sizer (1984) proposed that "exhibitions of mastery" replace traditional tests in determining graduation or course completion requirements. Grant Wiggins (1989) believes that an exhibition of mastery "is meant to be more than a better test. Like the thesis and oral examination in graduate school, it indicates whether a student has earned a diploma, is ready to leave high school" (p. 47). Figure 15.3 on page 568 is an example of a final exhibition required for graduation in a Racine, Wisconsin, high school. You can see that a portfolio, a research project, and oral work are elements of the exhibition.

Test Bank items
15.32–15.34, 15.87,
15.98, 15.104

Evaluating Portfolios and Performances

Checklists and rating scales are helpful when you assess performances, because assessments of performances, portfolios, and exhibitions are criterion-referenced, not norm-referenced. In other words, the students' products and

Background: For a description of one school's graduation exhibitions and a thoughtful analysis of the use of exhibitions in teaching, see McDonald, J. P. (1993). Three pictures of an exhibition: Warm, cool, and hard. *Phi Delta Kappan, 74,* 480–485.

Background: Dubert, L. A. (1989). Two ideas for grading simulation and higher level thinking activities. In *Annual editions: Educational psychology 89/90* (pp. 206–209). Guilford, CT: Duskin.

FIGURE 15.3

A FINAL EXHIBITION FOR HIGH SCHOOL STUDENTS

In this example of an exhibition, students must complete an eight-part portfolio, a research project, oral tests, and oral presentations.

**The Rite of Passage Experience (R.O.P.E.) at Walden III,
Racine, Wisconsin**

All seniors must complete a portfolio, a study project on U.S. history, and 15 oral and written presentations before a R.O.P.E. committee composed of staff, students, and an outside adult. Nine of the presentations are based on the materials in the portfolio and the project; the remaining six are developed for presentation before the committee. All seniors must enroll in a yearlong course designed to help them meet these requirements.

The eight-part *portfolio*, developed in the first semester, is intended to be "a reflection and analysis of the senior's own life and times." The requirements include:
•a written autobiography,
•a reflection on work (including a resume),
•an essay on ethics,
•a written summary of coursework in science,
•an artistic product or a written report on art (including an essay on artistic standards used in judging artwork).
The *project* is a research paper on a topic of the student's choosing in American history. The student is orally questioned on the paper in the presentations before the committee during the second semester.
The *presentations* include oral tests on the previous work, as well as six additional presentations on the essential subject areas and "personal proficiency" (life skills, setting and realizing personal goals, etc.). The presentations before the committee usually last an hour, with most students averaging about 6 separate appearances to complete all 15.

A diploma is awarded to those passing 12 of the 15 presentations and meeting district requirements in math, government, reading, and English.

Note: This summary is paraphrased from both the R.O.P.E. Student Handbook and an earlier draft of Archbald and Newmann's (1988) *Beyond Standardized Testing*.

Source: G. Wiggins (1989). "Teaching to the authentic test." *Educational Leadership*, 46 (7), p. 42. Reprinted with permission of the Association for Supervision and Curriculum Development. Copyright 1989 by ASCD. All rights reserved.

performances are compared to established public standards, not ranked in relation to other students' work (Cambourne & Turbill, 1990; Wiggins, 1991). For example, Figure 15.4 is a form for assessing student performance in conducting an experiment and to link performance to grades (Shavelson & Baxter, 1992).

Performance assessment requires careful judgment on the part of teachers and clear communication to students about what is good and what needs improving. In some ways the approach is similar to the clinical method first introduced by Binet to assess intelligence: it is based on observing the student

FIGURE 15.4

A SAMPLE HANDS-ON SCORE FORM FOR ASSESSING STUDENT PERFORMANCE IN A LABORARORY EXPERIMENT

This form allows the teacher to assess the process of experimentation and provide feedback to the student. The research question: Which of three paper towels holds the most water? An outstanding performance involves careful and systematic procedures applied consistently to all towels, complete saturation of each towel, and using a method that is consistent with the way the towel was wetted to determine the amount of water each towel held. Carelessness, using inconsistent methods to wet the towels, failing to saturate towels, and irrelevent methods result in lowered scores.

Paper Towels Investigation: Hands-on Score Form

Student _____   Observer _____   Score _____   Script _____

1. **Method**   A. Container   B. Drops   C. Tray (surface)
Pour water in/put towel in   towel on tray/pour water on
Put towel in/pour water in   pour water on tray/wipe up
1 pitcher or 3 beakers/glasses

2. **Saturation**   A. Yes   B. No   C. Controlled

3. **Determine Result**
A. Weigh towel   E. No measurement
B. Squeeze towel/measure water (weight or volume)   F. Count # drops until saturated
C. Measure water in/out   G. See how far drops spread out
D. Time to soak up water   H. Other

4. **Care in measuring**   Yes   No

5. **Correct Result**   Yes   No

Grade	Method	Saturate	Determine Result	Care in Measuring	Correct Answer
A	Yes	Yes	Yes	Yes	Yes
B	Yes	Yes	Yes	No	Yes/No
C	Yes	Yes/Controlled	Error		Yes/No
D	Yes	No	Missing		Yes/No
F			No Attempt		

Source: R. J. Shavelson and G. P. Baxter (1992). "What we've learned about assessing hands-on science."*Educational Leadership, 49*(8), p. 21. Reprinted with permission of the Association for Supervision and Curriculum Development. Copyright 1992 by ASCD. All rights reserved.

perform a variety of tasks and comparing his or her performance to a standard. Just as Binet never wanted to assign a single number to represent the child's intelligence, teachers who use authentic assessments do not try to assign one score to the student's performance. Even if rankings, ratings, and grades

Focus on . . . **Authentic Assessment**

- Summarize the characteristics of authentic assessment.
- How can checklists and rating scales be used to assess student portfolios and exhibitions? What should be included in the assessment?
- How would you assure reliability, validity, and equity in your use of authentic assessment tasks?

Objective 15.5: Discuss the potential positive and negative effects of grades on students.

Casebook: See the Teachers' Casebook for practicing teachers' ideas about how to handle the reactions of students and their parents when the students receive low grades.

Discussion: Classroom evaluation is frequently referred to as the "grading game." What aspects of grading resemble a game from the student's point of view?

Multicultural Awareness: According to the data collected by the U.S. Department of Education National Center for Education Statistics (*The Condition of Education 1991, Vol. 1*, p. 21), most students do progress through school on schedule. However, a consistently high number of African-American and Hispanic males fall below modal grade, which may put them at risk of dropping out. Dropout rates for most groups, however, are declining. In addition, the high school completion rate of whites and African Americans (but not Hispanics) is increasing. However, fewer Hispanics are enrolling in pre-K, almost half of 13-year-old male Hispanics have fallen below modal grade, and fewer than 60 percent of the 28- to 29-year-olds complete high school.

have to be given, these judgments are not the ultimate goals—improvement of learning is. If you look back to Table 15.4 you will see other grading characteristics of performance tests.

Because judgment plays such a central role in evaluating performances, issues of reliability, validity, and equity are critical considerations. As we saw in the previous chapter, judges assessing the Vermont Portfolios often have not agreed on ratings, so reliability is not adequate. And with a public performance there could be bias effects based on a student's appearance and speech or the student's access to expensive audio, video, or graphic resources. Performance assessments have the same potential as other tests to discriminate unfairly against students who are not wealthy or who are culturally different (McDonald, 1993).

Effects of Grades and Grading on Students

Test Bank items 15.35, 15.36, 15.38, 15.41

There is some evidence that high standards, a competitive class atmosphere, and a large percentage of lower grades are associated with increased absenteeism and dropout rates (Moos & Moos, 1978; Trickett & Moos, 1974). This seems especially likely with disadvantaged students (Wessman, 1972). Highly competitive classes may be particularly hard on anxious students or students who lack self-confidence. So while high standards and competition do tend generally to be related to increased academic learning, it is clear that a balance must be struck between high standards and a reasonable chance to succeed.

It may sound as though low grades and failure should be avoided in school. But the situation is not that simple. After reviewing many years of research on the effects of failure from several perspectives, Margaret Clifford (1990, 1991) concluded that failure can have both positive and negative effects on subsequent performance, depending on the situation and the personality of the students involved.

For example, one study required subjects to complete three sets of problems. On the first set, the experimenters arranged for subjects to experience either zero, 50, or 100 percent success. On the second set, it was arranged for all subjects to fail completely. On the third set of problems, the experimenters merely recorded how well the subjects performed. Those who had succeeded only 50 percent of the time before the failure experience performed the best. It appears that a history of complete failure or 100 percent success may be bad preparation for learning to cope with failure, something we must all learn. Some level of failure may be helpful for most students, especially if teachers help the students see connections between hard work and improvement. Efforts to protect students from failure and guarantee success may be counterproductive. Clifford (1990) gives this advice to teachers:

It is time for educators to replace easy success with challenge. We must encourage students to reach beyond their intellectual grasp and allow them the privilege of learning from mistakes. There must be a tolerance for error-making in every classroom, and gradual success rather than continual success must become the yardstick by which learning is judged. (p. 23)

The more able your students, the more challenging and important it will be to help them learn to "fail successfully" (Foster, 1981).

So far, we have been talking about the effects of failing a test or perhaps a course. But what about the effect of failing an entire grade—that is, of being "held back"? Some researchers believe that being held back injures students' self-esteem and increases the chances that they will drop out of school (Grissom & Shepard, 1989; Holmes, 1989). In their view, students generally do better academically when promoted. Other researchers have found some advantage for children who are retained in first, second, or third grade (Pierson & Connell, 1992), but the advantage may not last. In one study that followed many students for several years, children who could have been retained, but who were promoted, did about as well as similar children who were held back. No matter what, students who have trouble should get help, whether they are promoted or retained. Just covering the same material again in the same way won't solve the students' academic or social problems. The best approach may be to promote the students along with their peers, but to give them special remediation during the summer or the next year (Mantzicopoulos & Morrison, 1992; Shepard & Smith, 1989).

Effects of Feedback   Test Bank items 15.37, 15.39, 15.40

The results of several studies of feedback fit well with the notion of "successful" or constructive failure. These studies have concluded that it is more helpful to tell students when they are wrong than to tell them when they are right, but that the most productive approach is to tell them *why* they are wrong so they can learn more appropriate strategies (Bangert-Drowns, Kulik, Kulik, & Morgan, 1991). Students often need help in figuring out why their answers are incorrect. Without such feedback, they are likely to make the same mistakes again. Yet this type of feedback is rarely given. In one study, only about 8 percent of the teachers noticed a consistent type of error in a student's arithmetic computation and informed the student (Bloom & Bourdon, 1980).

Early research indicated that teachers' written comments on completed assignments can lead to improved performance in the future (Page, 1958). In more recent work the emphasis has been on identifying characteristics of effective written feedback. With older students (late elementary through high school), written comments are most helpful when they are personalized and when they provide constructive criticism. This means the teacher should make specific comments on errors or faulty strategies, but balance this criticism with suggestions about how to improve, and with comments on the positive aspects of the work (Butler & Nisan, 1986; Elawar & Corno, 1985). Working with sixth-grade teachers, Elawar and Corno (1985) found that feedback was dramatically improved when the teachers used these four questions as a guide: "What is the key error? What is the probable reason the student made this error? How can I guide the student to avoid the error in the future? What did the student do

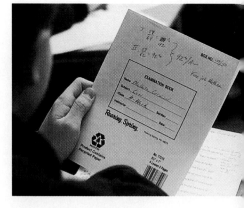

While high standards and competition may encourage high levels of performance, grading systems must offer a reasonable chance to succeed.

Discussion: Assign Harvard Graduate School of Education (1991, May/June). Retention: Can we stop failing kids? *Harvard Education Newsletter, 7*(3), 1–3. *Focus Question:* Ask your students to summarize the effects of retention on students and propose alternatives.

Research: Two studies and a synthesis of research on grade retention: Mantzicopolous, P., & Morrison, D. (1992). Kindergarten retention: Academic and behavioral outcomes through the end of second grade. *American Educational Research Journal, 29*, 182–198. Pierson, L. H., & Connell, J. P. (1992). Effect of grade retention on self-system processes, school engagement, and academic performance. *Journal of Educational Psychology, 84*, 300–307. Shepard, L. A., & Smith, M. L. (1990). Synthesis of research on grade retention. *Educational Leadership, 47*(8), 84–88.

Connections: See chapter 6 for a discussion of how to use praise effectively. These guidelines apply to written feedback as well.

Focus on . . . **Feedback**

- Summarize the characteristics of effective feedback.
- How can grading support student learning? Can authentic assessment play a role? How?

well that could be noted?" (p. 166). Here are some examples of teachers' written comments that proved helpful (Elawar & Corno, 1985, p. 164):

> Juan, you know how to get a percent, but the computation is wrong in this instance. . . . Can you see where? (Teacher has underlined the location of errors.)

> You know how to solve the problem—the formula is correct—but you have not demonstrated that you understand how one fraction multiplied by another can give an answer that is smaller than either ($1/2 \times 1/2 = 1/4$).

Extensive written comments may be inappropriate for younger students, but brief written comments are a different matter. These comments should help students correct errors and should recognize good work, progress, and increasing skill.

Grades and Motivation

Is there really a difference between working for a grade and working to learn? The answer depends in part on how a grade is determined. If grades are based on tests that require detailed memorization of facts, dates, and definitions, the students' study time will probably be spent learning these details. There will be little opportunity to explore the thought questions that may be found at the end of the chapter. But would students actually explore these questions if their work were not graded?

As a teacher, you can use grades to motivate the kind of learning you intend students to achieve in your course. If you test only at a simple but detailed level of knowledge, you may force students to choose between higher aspects of learning and a good grade. But when a grade reflects meaningful learning, working for a grade and working to learn become the same thing. The Guidelines summarize the effects grades can have on students.

Grading and Reporting: Nuts and Bolts

In determining a final grade, the teacher must make a major decision. Should a student's grade reflect the amount of material learned and how well it has been learned, or should the grade reflect the student's status in comparison with the rest of the class? In other words, should grading be criterion-referenced or norm-referenced?

Criterion-Referenced versus Norm-Referenced Grading

In **criterion-referenced grading,** the grade represents a list of accomplishments. If clear objectives have been set for the course, the grade may represent a certain number of objectives met satisfactorily. When a criterion-referenced sys-

Guidelines

Minimizing the Detrimental Effects of Grading

Avoid reserving high grades and high praise for answers that conform to your ideas or to those in the textbook.

Examples

1. Give extra points for correct and creative answers.
2. Withhold your opinions until all sides of an issue have been explored.
3. Reinforce students for disagreeing in a rational, productive manner.
4. Give partial credit for partially correct answers.

Make sure each student has a reasonable chance to be successful, especially at the beginning of a new task.

Examples

1. Pretest students to make sure they have prerequisite abilities.
2. Individualize instruction based on pretest results.
3. When appropriate, provide opportunities for students to retest to raise their grades, but make sure the retest is as difficult as the original.

Balance written and oral feedback.

Examples

1. Consider giving short, lively written comments with younger students and more extensive written comments with older students.
2. When the grade on a paper is lower than the student might have expected, be sure the reason for the lower grade is clear.
3. Tailor comments to the individual student's performance; avoid writing the same phrases over and over.
4. Note specific errors, possible reasons for errors, ideas for improvement, and work done well.

Make grades as meaningful as possible.

Examples

1. Tie grades to the mastery of important objectives.
2. Give ungraded assignments to encourage exploration.
3. Experiment with performances and portfolios.

Base grades on more than just one criterion.

Examples

1. Use essay questions as well as multiple-choice items on a test.
2. Grade oral reports and class participation.

Discussion: Can grades be used as motivators for all students? What determines whether a grade is motivating? How can a teacher use grades so that they tend to be motivating instead of discouraging?

Discussion: What would school be like for students if all testing were eliminated? Would most students still be motivated to learn and complete assignments?

Background: Hills, J. R. (1991). Apathy concerning grading and testing. *Phi Delta Kappan, 72*(7), 540–545.

Casebook: See the "Teachers' Casebook" for practicing teachers' descriptions of their ideal grading system.

Objective 15.6: Give examples of criterion-referenced and norm-referenced grading systems.

Activity 15.6: See the separate *Instructor's Resource Manual* for Grading Students, a mini-case study requiring students to decide on a grading system for a class. **Handout Master 15.2** provides needed information about the hypothetical class.

Norm-Referenced Grading Assessment of students' achievement in relation to one another.

tem is used, criteria for each grade generally are spelled out in advance. It is then up to the student to earn the grade she or he wants to receive. Theoretically, in this system all students can achieve an A if they reach the criteria.

In **norm-referenced grading,** the major influence on a grade is the student's standing in comparison with others who also took the course. If a student studies very hard and almost everyone else does too, the student may receive a disappointing grade, perhaps a C.

Activity 15.7: Reflection/Journal Writing. See the separate *Instructor's Resource Manual* for Should Teachers Grade Everything?, a journal-writing activity that encourages your students to anticipate what work they will grade and why.

Background: See the separate *Instructor's Resource Manual* for Classroom Standard Setting and Grading Practices, excerpts from Terwillinger, J. (1989). Classroom standard setting and grading practices. *Educational Measurement: Issues in Measurement, 8*(2), 15–19.

Background: For a summary of the considerations in developing a grading plan, see Frisbie, D. A., & Waltmen, K.K. (1992). Developing a personal grading plan. *Educational Measurement: Issues and practices* (pp. 35–42). Washington, DC: National Council on Measurement in Education. This module is reprinted in Cauley, K. M., Linder, F., & McMillan, J. H. (1993). *Annual Editions: Educational Psychology 93/94,* Guilford, CT: Duskin.

Application: A useful way of increasing the frequency of testing and students' motivation to study is by giving "pop quizzes." But how can pop quizzes be given in a way that is not overly anxiety producing? One answer: make them count as special incentives or bonus points.

Activity 15.8: Application. See the *Instructor's Resource Manual* for Dealing with a Student Who Refuses to Work.

Activity 15.9: Background. See the *Instructor's Resource Manual* for Classroom Standard Setting and Grading Practices.

Criterion-Referenced Systems. Criterion-referenced grading has the advantage of relating judgments about a student to the achievement of clearly defined instructional goals. Some school districts have developed reporting systems where report cards list objectives along with judgments about the student's attainment of each. Reporting is done at the end of each unit of instruction. The junior high report card shown in Figure 15.5 demonstrates the relationship between assessment and the goals of the unit.

FIGURE 15.5

CRITERION-REFERENCED GRADES AT THE SECONDARY LEVEL
This is one example of a criterion-referenced report card. Other forms are possible, but all criterion-referenced reports indicate a student's progress toward specific goals.

JERICHO JUNIOR HIGH SCHOOL
JERICHO, NEW YORK

EVALUATION

Teacher _____ Student _____
Counselor _____ Dates (from) _____ (to) _____
Unit: Analogy as a Thought Process Grade _____ Subject: English

Code: 1 The student has met the objective.
      2 The student has demonstrated progress toward meeting the objective.
      3 The student has not at this time met the objective.
      4 The student has not demonstrated whether or not the objective has been met.
      5 The objective does not apply at this time.

BASIC INFORMATION:
____a. The student can identify comparisons that use *like, as, than,* and *is.*
____b. The student can identify comparisons that do not use *like, as, than,* or *is.* (*The teacher threw the student out of class. Student = ball.*)
____c. The student can recognize the similarity in two unlike items.

UNDERSTANDING:
____a. The student can distinguish between the *is* of identity and the *is* of comparison. (*I am John. I am a block of wood.*)
____b. The student can distinguish between the literal sense of a poem and the meaning suggested by its imagery.

APPLICATION:
____a. The student can compose original sentences that make a comparison without using words such as *like, as,* or *than.*
____b. Given a comparison, the student can extend it into a paragraph.

In practice, many school systems would look askance at a teacher who turned in a roster filled with A's and explained that all the students had reached the class objectives. Administrators might say that if all the objectives could be so easily attained by all the students, then more or tougher objectives were needed. Nevertheless, a criterion-referenced system may be acceptable in some schools.

Norm-Referenced Systems. One very popular type of norm-referenced grading is called **grading on the curve.** As noted in the previous chapter, the characteristics of the normal curve, or normal distribution, are well known. For example, we know that two-thirds of the distribution (68 percent) are clustered within 1 standard deviation of the mean. In grading on the curve, the middle of the normal distribution or "average" performance becomes the anchor on which grading is based. In other words, teachers look at the average level of performance, assign what they consider an "average grade" for this performance, and then grade superior performances higher and inferior performances lower.

If grading were done strictly on the normal curve, there would be an equal number of A's and F's, a larger number of B's and D's, and an even larger number of C's. The grades would have to form a bell-shaped curve. For example, a teacher might decide to give 10 percent A's and F's, 20 percent B's and D's, and 40 percent C's. This is a very strict interpretation of grading on the curve, and it makes sense only if achievement in the class follows the normal curve.

Grading on the curve can be done with varying levels of precision. The simplest approach is to rank-order the students' raw scores on a test and use this ranked list of scores as the basis for assigning grades. Such a distribution might look like this: 92 91 91 90 83 80 78 76 72 68 65 61 57 54 53 49 48 47 46 43 38 36 29 29. Knowing that two-thirds of the scores in a normal distribution should be in the middle, you might bracket off the middle two-thirds of the scores and plan to give those students C's (or B's, if you believed B was an average grade for the class in question). Some people prefer to use the middle one-third of the students rather than the middle two-thirds as the basis for the average grade. Based on these two approaches, grades might be assigned as follows:

Transparency: An "Example of Grading on the Curve" is given in acetate transparency T 114.

Activity 15.10: See the separate *Instructor's Resource Manual* for Norm-Referenced Grading, a class activity that asks students to assign and justify grades for two students on two tests.

Middle Two-Thirds Assigned C's

A	B	C	D	F
92	91 91 90	83 80 78 76 72 68 65 61 57 54 53 49 48 47 46 43	38 36	29 29

Middle One-Third Assigned C's

A	B	C	D	F
92	91 91 90 83 80 78 76	72 68 65 61 57 54 53 49	48 47 46 43 38 36	29 29

This approximation to grading on the curve is very rough indeed. In these examples the distance between one letter grade and another is sometimes one point! Given the amount of error in testing, this assignment of grades is probably not fair. You can correct some of these problems by introducing common sense into the process. For example, you may believe the following grade assignment is fairer:

Grading on the Curve Norm-referenced grading that compares students' performance to an average level.

TABLE 15.5	Comparing Norm-Referenced and Criterion-Referenced Standards for Grading

Norm-referenced systems use the performance of the rest of the class as the standard for determining grades. Criterion-referenced systems use standards of subject mastery and learning to determine grades.

Grade	Criterion-referenced	Norm-referenced
A	Firm command of knowledge domain High level of skill development Exceptional preparation for later learning	Far above class average
B	Command of knowledge beyond the minimum Advanced development of most skills Has prerequisites for later learning	Above class average
C	Command of only the basic concepts of knowledge Demonstrated ability to use basic skills Lacks a few prerequisites for later learning	At the class average
D	Lacks knowledge of some fundamental ideas Some important skills not attained Deficient in many of the prerequisites for later learning	Below class average
F	Most of the basic concepts and principles not learned Most essential skills cannot be demonstrated Lacks most prerequisites needed for later learning	Far below class average

Source: D. A. Frisbie and K. K. Waltmen (1992). Developing a personal grading plan. *Educational Measurement: Issues and practices*, p. 37. Copyright 1992 by the National Council on Measurement in Education. Reprinted by permission of the publisher.

Adjusted Grades

A	B	C	D	F
92 91 91 90	83 80 78 76 72	68 65 61 57 54 53	49 48 47 46 43 38 36	29 29

In this case the instructor has used the natural gaps in the range of scores to locate boundaries between grades. Between the A and B categories are 7 points, between the B and C, 4 points, and so on.

Table 15.5 compares descriptions of a student's performance using criterion-referenced and norm-referenced standards and suggests a way to translate these descriptions into grades.

Preparing Report Cards

Whatever grading system you use, you will undoubtedly give several tests and you will probably assign homework or projects. Let's assume your unit assessment plan includes two short tests (mostly multiple-choice questions with

Transparency: An activity in which students "Assign and Justify Grades" is provided in acetate transparency T 125.

one essay), homework, a portfolio, and a unit test. If you use a criterion-referenced system for testing and grading, how will you convert scores on these individual performances to the overall indications of mastery on a report card such as that in Figure 15.4? What about using a norm-referenced system? How do you combine results from individual tests and assignments to yield a final distribution of scores for the unit grade?

Let us consider criterion-referenced grading first. If you adopt this system, you cannot average or combine test scores or homework grades mathematically. Since each test and assignment measures the mastery of a particular objective (or set of objectives), it would be meaningless to average, say, the students' mastery of addition of two-digit numbers with their mastery of measurement with a ruler, although both might be objectives in arithmetic. On the report card, the various objectives are listed and the student's level of proficiency in each is indicated.

Norm-referenced grading is a different story. In order to assign grades, the teacher must merge all the scores from tests and other assignments into one final score. Final grades are based on how each student's final score compares with that of the rest of the students. But the usual procedure of simply adding up all the scores and averaging the total is often not appropriate, and it can be misleading. For example, assume two students took two tests. The tests are equally important in the overall unit. The students' scores are shown below (from Chase, 1978, p. 328).

Discussion: What type of grading orientation, norm-referenced or criterion-referenced, would be best understood by parents? Which would parents generally favor? Would the choices vary depending on the grade level concerned?

	Test 1 Class mean = 30 Standard deviation = 8	Test 2 Class mean = 50 Standard deviation = 16	Total Raw score
Leslie	38	50	88
Jason	30	66	96

If we compute an average or if we rank the students based on their totals, Jason will be ahead of Leslie. But if we look at the class mean and standard deviation for each test, we see a different picture. On one test, Leslie's score was 1 standard deviation above the mean, and on the other her score was at the mean; Jason's record is exactly the same.

	Test 1	Test 2
Leslie	+1 SD	Mean
Jason	Mean	+1 SD

If these two tests are really equally important, Jason and Leslie have identical records in relation to the rest of the class on these tests. To compare students' performances on several tests, the scores for each must be converted to a standard scale like a *T* score. As you may recall from chapter 14, a *T* mean is automatically 50 and the standard deviation is 10. Most teachers do not calculate *T* scores for all their students, but the example illustrates the importance of using common sense in grading. Gross totals do not always reflect how well one student is doing in relation to others in the class.

The Point System

Activity 15.11: See the separate *Instructor's Resource Manual* for Determining Grades, an activity that asks your students to consider how they would grade the work of a youngster who is trying harder and improving.

Activity 15.12: Critical Thinking. See the separate *Instructor's Resource Manual* for Evaluation Decisions, an analysis of the grades of seven students. Handout Master 15.1 gives the rationale for the grades assigned. Your students are asked to decide if they agree with the grade assignments and to give reason for their decisions.

One popular system for combining grades from many assignments is a point system. Each test or assignment is given a certain number of total points, depending on its importance. A test worth 40 percent of the grade could be worth 40 points. A paper worth 20 percent could be worth 20 points. Points are then awarded on the test or paper based upon specific criteria. An A+ paper, one that meets all the criteria, could be given the full 20 points; an average paper might be given 10 points. If tests of comparable importance are worth the same number of points, are equally difficult, and cover a similar amount of material, we can expect to avoid some of the problems encountered with Jason and Leslie, when the means and standard deviations of two supposedly comparable tests varied so greatly.

Let us assume a grade book indicates the scores shown in Table 15.6. How would you assign grades to students for this unit of work? Here are several possibilities:

1. Find the total number of points for each student and rank the students. Assign grades by looking for natural gaps of several points or imposing a curve (a certain percentage of A's, B's, and so on).

Teaching Tip: Divide your class into groups and have them determine grades for the students in Table 15.6 using these three approaches, then compare the grades assigned. Do the groups assign the same grades using different methods? Using the same methods?

TABLE 15.6   Points Earned on Five Assignments

Student	Test 1 20% 20 points	Test 2 20% 20 points	Unit Test 30% 30 points	Homework 15% 15 points	Portfolio 15% 15 points	Total
Amy	10	12	16	6	7	___
Lee	12	10	14	7	6	___
Luis	20	19	30	15	13	___
Wayne	18	20	25	15	15	___
Étienne	6	5	12	4	10	___
Frieda	10	12	18	10	9	___
Grace	13	11	22	11	10	___
Houston	7	9	12	5	6	___
Isaac	14	16	26	12	12	___
Liz	20	18	28	10	15	___
Keith	19	20	25	11	12	___
Linda	14	12	20	13	9	___
Melody	15	13	24	8	10	___
Ned	8	7	12	8	6	___
Olivia	11	12	16	9	10	___
Peter	7	8	11	4	8	___

2. Convert each score to a percentage and average the percentages. Rank the students on percentages; proceed as above to look for gaps or impose a curve. Compare the results of this approach with the results of the one above.

3. Rank the students on each assignment, then calculate each student's average rank for all five assignments. (If two students tie for one rank, they split the difference between that rank and the one below. For example, if two students tie for third place, they each get 3.5 and there is no fourth place.) Use the average rankings to determine overall ranks, then look for gaps or impose a curve on the overall ranks.

Percentage Grading

There is another approach to assigning grades to a group of students like those in Table 15.6. Using **percentage grading** the teacher can assign grades based on how much knowledge each student has mastered—what percentage of the total knowledge he or she understands. To do this, the teacher might score tests and other classwork with percentage scores (based on how much is correct—50 percent, 85 percent, etc.) and then average these scores to reach a course score. These scores can then be converted into letter grades according to predetermined cutoff points. Any number of students can earn any grade. This procedure is very common; you may have experienced it yourself as a student. Let us look at it more closely, because it has some frequently overlooked problems.

The grading symbols of A, B, C, D, and F are probably the most popular means of reporting at the present time. School systems often establish equivalent percentage categories for each of these symbols. The percentages vary from school district to school district, but two typical ones are as follows:

> 90–100% = A; 80–89% = B; 70–79% = C; 60–69% = D; below 60% = F

> 94–100% = A; 85–93% = B; 76–83% = C; 70–75% = D; below 70% = F

As you can see, although both districts have an A to F five-point grading system, the average achievement required for each grade is different.

But can we really say what is the total amount of knowledge available in, for example, eighth-grade science? Are we sure we can accurately measure what percentage of this body of knowledge each student has attained? To use percentage grading appropriately, we would have to know exactly what there was to learn and exactly how much of that each student had learned. These conditions are seldom met, even though teachers use the cutoff points to assign grades as if measurement were so accurate that a one-point difference was meaningful: "In spite of decades of research in educational and psychological measurement, which has produced more defensible methods, the concept [of percentage grading], once established, has proved remarkably resistant to change" (Zimmerman, 1981, p. 178).

Any grading system prescribed or suggested by the school can be influenced by particular concerns of the teacher. So don't be fooled by the seeming security of absolute percentages. Your own grading philosophy will continue to operate, even in this system. Because there is more concern today with specifying objectives and criterion-referenced assessment, especially at the elementary-grade levels, several alternative methods for evaluating student progress against predetermined criteria have evolved. We will look at one: the contract system.

Objective 15.7: Assign grades to a hypothetical group of students, and defend these decisions in a class debate.

Percentage Grading System of converting class performances to percentage scores and assigning grades based on predetermined cutoff points.

Activity 15.13: See the separate *Instructor's Resource Manual* for Contracting, a set of questions that asks your students to consider how they would structure a contract system to improve the quality of their pupils' work.

Application: Ask your students the following. You are using a contract system in one of your classes. One of the requirements for an A is "to write a book report." However, some students are reporting on books that you think they read last year, and some are handing in short, superficial reports. How can you structure the contract system so that the students will do a better quality of work?

Connections: See chapter 11 for a discussion of behavior management contracts.

Discussion: Often, teachers tend to blame certain students for classroom disturbances even though they may not be guilty. Is this an example of the halo effect? Can your students think of other examples?

Contract System System in which each student works for a particular grade according to agreed-upon standards.

Revise Option In a contract system, the chance to revise and improve work.

The Contract System

When applied to the whole class, the **contract system** indicates the type, quantity, and quality of work required for each number or letter grade in the system. Students agree, or "contract," to work for particular grades by meeting the specified requirements. For example, the following standards might be established:

F: Not coming to class regularly or not turning in the required work.

D: Coming to class regularly and turning in the required work on time.

C: Coming to class regularly, turning in the required work on time, and receiving a check mark on all assignments to indicate they are satisfactory.

B: Coming to class regularly, turning in the required work on time, and receiving a check mark on all assignments except at least three that achieve a check-plus, indicating superior achievement.

A: As above, plus a successful oral or written report on one of the books listed for supplementary reading.

This example calls for more subjective judgment than would be ideal. However, contract systems reduce student anxiety about grades. They can also eliminate subjective judgment to whatever extent the teacher wants by specifying the quantity and quality required for various grades. The contract system can be applied to individual students, in which case it functions much like an independent study plan.

Unfortunately, the system can lead to overemphasis on the quantity of work. Teachers may be too vague about the standards that differentiate acceptable from unacceptable work. It is sometimes difficult to tell a student that a particular assignment is completely unsatisfactory ("Is it that bad?"), so many teachers accept almost every piece of work. In addition, if a school system requires a five-point grading system and all students contract for and achieve the highest grade, the teacher will wish that the principal had been consulted about the system before the grades came out.

A teacher can modify the contract system by including a **revise option**. For example, a check mark might be worth 75 points and a check-plus 90 points; a check-plus earned after revision could be worth 85 points—more than a check, but less than a check-plus earned the first time around. This system allows students to improve their work but also rewards getting it right the first time. Some quality control is possible, since students earn points not just for quantity but also for quality. In addition, the teacher may be less reluctant to judge a project unsatisfactory since students can improve their work (King, 1979).

Grading on Effort and Improvement

Grading on effort and improvement is not really a complete grading system but rather a theme that can run through most grading methods. Should teachers grade students based on how much they learn or on the final level of learning? One problem with using improvement as a standard for grading is that the best students improve the least, since they are already the most competent.

Do you want to penalize these students because they knew quite a bit initially, and the teaching and testing have limited how much learning they can demonstrate? After all, unless you assign extra work, these students will run out of things to do.

One solution is to use the **individual learning expectation (ILE)** system. With this system students earn improvement points on tests or assignments for scoring above their personal base (average) score or for making a perfect score. The teacher can count these improvement points when figuring a final grade or simply use them as a basis for giving other classroom rewards.

Many teachers try to include some judgment of effort in final grades, but effort is difficult to assess. Are you certain your perception of each student's effort is correct? Clement (1978) suggests a system for including a judgment about effort in the final grade called the **dual marking system**. Students are assigned two grades. One, usually a letter, indicates the actual level of achievement. The other, a number, indicates the relationship of the achievement to the student's ability and effort. For example, a grade of B could be qualified as follows (Clement, 1978, p. 51):

B1: Outstanding effort, better achievement than expected, good attitude

B2: Average effort, satisfactory in terms of ability

B3: Lower achievement than ability would indicate, poor attitude

Of course, this system assumes that the teacher can adequately judge true ability and effort. A grade of D1, D2, or F2 could be quite insulting. A grade of A3 or F1 should not be possible. But the system does have the advantage of recognizing hard work and giving feedback about a seeming lack of effort. An A2 or B2 might tell very bright students: "You're doing well, but I know you could do better." This could help the students to expect more of themselves and not slip by on high ability. The overall grade—A, B, C—still reflects achievement and is not changed (or biased) by teachers' subjective judgment of effort.

Cautions: Being Fair

The attributions a teacher makes about the causes of student successes or failures can affect the grades that students receive. Teachers are more likely to give higher grades for effort (a controllable factor) than for ability (an uncontrollable factor). Lower grades are more likely when teachers attribute a student's failure to lack of effort instead of lack of ability (Weiner, 1979). It is also possible that grades can be influenced by a **halo effect**—that is, by the tendency to view particular aspects of a student based on a general impression, either positive or negative. As a teacher, you may find it difficult to avoid being affected by positive and negative halos. A very pleasant student who seems to work hard and causes little trouble may be given the benefit of the doubt (B– instead of C+), whereas a very difficult student who seems to refuse to try might be a loser at grading time (D instead of C–). The Guidelines give ideas for using any grading system in a fair and reasonable way.

"I HOPE THIS ISN'T ANOTHER PLOY TO UP YOUR GRADE, HASKELL."

(© Art Bouthillier)

How would you evaluate Haskell's "effort"?

Transparency: Use acetate transparency T 120, "Halo Effects: Their Basic Nature."

Focus on . . . **Grading Systems**

- What grading systems are you experiencing right now in your college classes?
- What are the advantages and disadvantages of contract grading?
- What are the advantages and disadvantages of percentage grading?
- What are the advantages and disadvantages of grading on the curve?

Individual Learning Expectation (ILE) Personal average score.

Dual Marking System System of assigning two grades, one reflecting achievement, the other effort, attitude, and actual ability.

Halo Effect The tendency for a general impression of a person to influence our perception of any aspect of that person.

Guidelines

Using Any Grading System

Explain your grading policies to students early in the course and remind them of the policies regularly.

Examples

1. Give older students a handout describing the assignments, tests, grading criteria, and schedule.
2. Explain to younger students in a low-pressure manner how their work will be evaluated.

Set reasonable standards.

Examples

1. Discuss workload and grading standards with more experienced teachers.
2. Give a few formative tests to get a sense of your students' abilities before you give a graded test.
3. Take tests yourself first to gauge the difficulty of the test and to estimate the time your students will need.

Base your grades on as much objective evidence as possible.

Examples

1. Plan in advance how and when you will test.
2. Keep a portfolio of student work. This may be useful in student or parent conferences.

Be sure students understand test directions.

Examples

1. Outline the directions on the board.
2. Ask several students to explain the directions.
3. Go over a sample question first.

Correct, return, and discuss test questions as soon as possible.

Examples

1. Have students who wrote good answers read their responses for the class; make sure they are not the same students each time.
2. Discuss why wrong answers, especially popular wrong choices, are incorrect.
3. As soon as students finish a test, give them the answers to questions and the page numbers where answers are discussed in the text.

As a rule, do not change a grade.

Examples

1. Make sure you can defend the grade in the first place.
2. DO change any clerical or calculation errors.

Guard against bias in grading.

Examples

1. Ask students to put their names on the backs of their papers.
2. Use an objective point system or model papers when grading essays.

Keep pupils informed of their standing in the class.

Examples

1. Write the distribution of scores on the board after tests.
2. Schedule periodic conferences to go over work from previous weeks.

Give students the benefit of the doubt. All measurement techniques involve error.

Examples

1. Unless there is a very good reason not to, give the higher grade in borderline cases.
2. If a large number of students miss the same question in the same way, revise the question for the future and consider throwing it out for that test.

Source: Adapted by permission of the author and publisher from A. M. Drayer (1979), *Problems in middle and high school teaching: A handbook for student teachers and beginning teachers,* pp. 182–187. Boston: Allyn and Bacon.

Beyond Grading: Communication

No number or letter grade conveys the totality of a student's experience in a class or course. Both students and teachers sometimes become too focused on the end point—the grade. But children and adolescents spend the majority of their waking hours for many months of the year in school, where teachers are the relevant adults. This gives teachers the opportunity and the responsibility to know their students as people.

Conferences with parents are often expected of teachers in elementary school and can be equally important in junior high and high school. At every level, the success of the conference depends on a number of factors. At the simplest level, both parties must be present. Schedule conferences at a time convenient for parents; confirm appointments in writing or by phone.

Clearly, the more skilled teachers are at communicating, the more effective they will be at conducting these conferences. Listening and problem-solving skills such as those discussed in chapter 11 can be particularly important. When you are dealing with parents or students who are angry or upset, make sure you really hear the concerns of the participants, not just their words.

The conference should not be a time for lecturing parents or students. As the professional, the teacher needs to take a leadership role and yet remain sensitive to the needs of the other participants. The atmosphere should be friendly and unrushed. Any observations about the student should be as factual as possible, based on observation or information from assignments. Information gained from a student or a parent should be kept confidential. Table 15.7 on page 584 offers some helpful ideas for planning and conducting conferences.

An important federal law, the Buckley Amendment, may affect you as a teacher. Also called the Family Educational Rights and Privacy Act of 1974 and the Educational Amendments Act of 1974, this law states that all educational agencies must make test results and any other information in students' records available to the students and/or their parents. If the records contain information students or parents believe is incorrect, they can challenge such entries and have the information removed if they win the challenge. This means

The success of parent-teacher conferences depends largely on the teacher's skill as a communicator.

TABLE 15.7   Conducting a Successful Parent-Teacher Conference

Plan ahead.
What are your goals?
Problem solving?
Sharing test results?
Asking questions that you want answered?
Providing information you want to share?
Emphasize the positive.
Describing your "next steps" in the classroom?
Making suggestions for use at home?

Being with a positive statement.
"Howard has a great sense of humor."
"Giselle really enjoys materials that deal with animals."
"Sandy is sympathetic when somebody has a problem."

Listen actively.
Empathize with the parents.
Accept their feelings: "You seem to feel frustrated
when Lee doesn't listen."

Establish a partnership.
Ask parents to follow through on class goals at home:
"If you ask to see the homework checklist
and go over it at home with Iris, I'll review it and
chart her progress at school."

Plan follow-up contacts.
Write notes or make phone calls to share successes.
Keep parents informed *before* problems develop.

End with a positive statement.
"José has made several friends this year."
"Courtney should be a big help in the social studies
play that her group is developing."

Source: Adapted by permission from D. P. Fromberg & M. Driscoll (1985). *The successful classroom: Management strategies for regular and special education teachers,* p. 181. New York: Teachers College Press.

Objective 15.8: Role-play a conference with parents who do not understand the grading system or their child's grades.

that the information in a student's records must be based on firm, defensible evidence. Tests must be valid and reliable. Your grades must be justified by thorough testing and observation. Comments and anecdotes about students must be accurate and fair.

SUMMARY

Formative and Summative Assessment

Two important and challenging tasks for teachers are assessing students and assigning grades. Many schools have established policies about testing and grading practices, but individual teachers decide how these practices will be carried out. In the classroom, assessment may be formative (ungraded, diagnostic) or summative (graded). Formative assessment helps form instruction, and summative assessment summarizes students' accomplishments.

Getting the Most from Traditional Assessment Approaches

Assessment requires planning. Teachers can use a behavior-content matrix to plan tests so that test questions match course objectives. With the goals of assessment in mind, teachers are in a better position to design their own tests or evaluate the tests provided by textbook publishers.

Two traditional formats for testing are the objective test and the essay test. Objective tests, which can include multiple-choice, true-false, fill-in, and matching items, should be written with specific guidelines in mind. Writing and scoring essay questions requires careful planning plus criteria to discourage bias in scoring.

Innovations in Assessment

Critics of traditional testing believe that teachers should use authentic tests and other authentic assessment procedures. This approach requires students to perform tasks and solve problems that are similar to the real-life performances that will be expected of students outside of school. Portfolios and exhibitions are two examples of authentic assessment. With portfolios and exhibitions there is an emphasis on performing real-life tasks in meaningful contexts. Evaluating alternative assessments requires judgment and attention to validity, reliability, and equity, just as with all assessment.

Effects of Grades and Grading on Students

Students need experience in coping with failure, so standards must be high enough to encourage effort. Occasional failure can be positive if appropriate feedback is provided. Grades can encourage students' motivation to learn if grades are tied to meaningful learning.

Grading and Reporting: Nuts and Bolts

Grading can be either criterion-referenced or norm-referenced. Criterion-referenced report cards usually indicate how well each of several objectives has been met by the individual student. One popular norm-referenced system is grading on the curve, based on a ranking of students in relation to the average performance level.

Tests and papers are often scored on a point system. Many schools use percentage grading systems, but the difficulty of the tests and the scoring criteria often influence the results. The difference between a B and a C may only be a matter of one or two points on paper, but the effect of the difference can be large for a student.

Alternatives to traditional grading are the contract, ILE, and dual marking approaches. Whatever system you use, you will have to decide whether you want to grade on effort, improvement, or some combination and whether you want to limit the number of good grades available.

Many factors besides quality of work can influence grades: the teacher's beliefs about the student's ability or effort or the student's general classroom behavior, for example.

Beyond Grading: Communication

Not every communication from the teacher needs to be tied to a grade. Communication with students and parents can be important in helping a teacher understand students and create effective instruction. Students and parents have a legal right to see all the information in the students' records.

KEY TERMS

authentic tests, p. 562
contract system, p. 580
criterion-referenced grading, p. 572
curriculum-based assessment, p. 550
data-based instruction, p. 550
diagnostic test, p. 550
distractors, p. 555
dual marking system, p. 581

exhibition, p. 565
formative assessment, p. 550
grading on the curve, p. 575
halo effect, p. 581
holistic scoring, p. 561
individual learning expectation (ILE), p. 581
norm-referenced grading, p. 573

objective testing, p. 553
percentage grading, p. 579
portfolio, p. 565
pretest, p. 550
revise option, p. 580
stem, p. 555
summative assessment, p. 551

WHAT WOULD YOU DO?

Preschool and Kindergarten

The parents of several children in your class want a report about how their daughters and sons are "progressing" in preschool. How would you respond to their requests? What kind of assessment and reporting would be helpful for your young students?

Elementary and Middle School

Your school requires that you give letter grades to your fourth-grade students. How would you determine these letter grades?

During a parent-teacher conference, a mother and father accuse you of playing favorites and giving their child low grades "just because he's different." How would you respond?

Junior High and High School

Several students are very unhappy with the grades on their term projects. They come to you for an explanation and to try to get you to raise their grades. What would you do?

Your school requires percentage grading, but you would prefer a different system. How would you make a case for your alternative?

Cooperative Learning Activity

With four or five other members of your educational psychology class, plan how you would use portfolios in your teaching. What would be the content? How would you evaluate the work and give students feedback?

TEACHERS' CASEBOOK

Grades or Feedback?

If you could choose any method of grading your students or giving feedback on their performance, what would you do?

INFORMAL FEEDBACK

Students thrive on positive input from respected adults. Therefore, analyzing an assignment and discussing it would result in the greatest achievement. Unfortunately, we do not provide resources in public education that permit such intensive evaluation techniques.

Many times informal feedback can be very effective. Too often we assign a grade but fail to really communicate a genuine interest in the work submitted. Taking time to recognize extended effort or a particularly good thought process may create more incentive to excel. Simply assigning letter grades or numerical values can hinder academic growth and probably never has more than a neutral effect on student achievement.

Marc Gray, *Science Teacher*
Highland Middle School, Louisville, Kentucky

A BLESSING AND A CURSE

Evaluating student performance is both the blessing and the curse of teaching. Evaluation allows a teacher to measure the progress his/her class has made, to quantify the growth in their development, and to publicize the results of their labors. However, teacher evaluation can also shatter egos, stunt intellectual curiosity, and promote unnatural competition among students. Although grading is a pitfall-filled process for even veteran teachers, it is also a necessary component of education. My dream evaluation system would allow me to offer my students individual feedback based on each one's unique abilities, competencies, and needs. Sometimes the feedback would be oral, sometimes written. Both would rely heavily on close observation of the student's performance in independent and group work. Instead of arbitrary grades, anecdotal entries would allow me to comment on individual progress. However, human beings do not seem to work well in a vacuum. For this reason, I believe some group evaluation measures in which all students attempt to demonstrate the same task or exhibit the same knowledge in a competitive manner is also necessary. Students need to measure their progress against each other in order to ascertain growth. Letter grades, although useful in classifying students and awarding scholarships, are not really adequate indicators of student achievement. If students are to assume responsibility for their own learning, they must feel that they are viewed as individuals, not just as letters in a gradebook.

Jane C. Dusell, *English Teacher*
Medford Area Senior High School, Medford, Wisconsin

CONFERENCE AND PROGRESS REPORTS

I would use frequent individual student conferences as well as in-depth written progress reports. In both cases students are made aware of the areas in which they are doing well and those in which they are having difficulty. A plan is developed between student and teacher to specify ways to improve. Parents receive a copy of the progress report and the improvement plan. Advantages include student involvement, especially in the designing of improvement plans, and parental notification in a form more detailed than just a letter grade.

Carol Gibbs, *Sixth-Grade Teacher*
Happy Valley School, Rossville, Georgia

BE HONEST, BE FAIR

I'm not sure there is an ideal grading system. Children are very sharp. They know how they are doing before we ever try to evaluate them. The best way to evaluate children is to be honest and fair with them.

In the primary grades, I evaluate children on their performance at their levels of ability and maturity. I let parents know that "at this level (above, below, or at grade level), your child is doing this." This way, even the child who is performing below grade level can be acknowledged for effort and progress.

In the upper grades, you need a more sophisticated and formal grading system, but one that the students understand. It must be one that does not defeat them before they start. Since we all have good days and bad days, perhaps we could give students an option of selecting five of their best pieces of work in a unit or eliminating the lowest grade on one or two out of five papers.

Carolyn R. Cook, *Kindergarten Teacher*
Ramona Elementary School, Ramona, California

Communicating with Parents

What is the best way to prevent negative experiences with parents over your evaluation of their child's performance?

ENLIST PARENT SUPPORT

Enlist the support of parents prior to the beginning of the school year by calling each one. This is especially important for the parents of any students who have lower test scores, special education eligibility, and attendance problems. Many parents will not initiate such contact with the school, but when approached are very grateful for our interest and jump at the opportunity to share their concerns. After making this early contact, I continue to call parents, more often with positive comments than with negative, and I send positive notes home as frequently as I can.

You have just given a 50-item final exam. One of your students gets only 35 items correct—a score well below the average for the class. On your scale the 35 is a D, but the student and the student's parents are upset. They argue that 35 out of 50 is 70 percent and should be a C. What do you say to them?

STANDARDS ARE IMPORTANT

Parents need to feel confident that the teacher is concerned for the best interest of their child. Confrontation and strong words never bring consensus; thus, the classroom teacher must maintain her/his composure and explain that mastery of skills and concepts is vital. The teacher should explain that she or he cannot change the test grade without lowering her/his expectations and standards.

Perhaps a schedule of activities could be set up to help the student practice skills and review concepts, so that mastery might be achieved. Parents need to understand that grades mean nothing unless they represent some meaningful standard.

Darlene A. Walsh, *Rhode Island 1991 Teacher of the Year*
Greenbush Elementary School, West Warwick, Rhode Island

SHOWING THE EVIDENCE

I would show all the scores in the class—numbers only, without any names—to the parents and student. I would explain which scores are A's, B's, C's, and so on and point out that 35 right answers out of a possible 50 was just not an average grade or C on this particular test. I think the parents and student need to *see* the scores of the entire class. In this case, a picture is worth a thousand words.

Louise Harrold Melucci, *Fourth-Grade Teacher*
Greenwood School, Warwick, Rhode Island

Research in Educational Psychology

In order to achieve a better understanding of educational psychology, you must know how information in the field is created and how to judge the information you encounter. In this appendix we will explore the value and limitations of research, the major road to knowledge in educational psychology. Then we will examine a specific problem to determine how research might answer questions posed by teachers. Finally, we will describe how to judge a research study by evaluating a real experiment.

Asking and Answering Questions

To get a better understanding of a few of the basic methods for asking and answering questions in educational psychology, we will examine a question that may interest you: Do students' expectations about the competence of a new teacher influence the way the students behave toward the teacher? More specifically, do students pay more attention to a teacher they expect to be good? Suppose, for our purposes here, that an educational psychologist decided to look for an answer to this question. What methods might be used to gather information?

Forming a Research Question

The first step might be to frame a clear and specific question. In this case, we might begin with something like this: Do students' beliefs about a teacher's competence affect the amount of attention they pay to the teacher? Note how specific the wording is. We will [ ] the question is too vague, as in: Do [ ] about a teacher affect the way they be[ ] [ ]ere is too much territory to cover in [ ]estion. We need to be specific about [ ]efs—beliefs about the teacher's *com-*

petence, not age, intelligence, or marital status. And we need to be specific about what kind of behavior—attention to the teacher, not enthusiasm for the subject or anxiety about a new year.

Choosing Variables and Selecting Measurement Techniques

At this point we are ready to identify the variables to be studied. A **variable** is any characteristic of a person or environment that can change under different conditions or that can differ from one person to the next. In our hypothetical study, we have decided to examine two variables—student beliefs about the teacher's competence and student attention to the teacher.

The next thing we must do is decide how we will define what we mean by *beliefs* and *attention.* This question leads to the issue of measurement, because our definitions will be useful only if they give us something we can measure.

To study any variable systematically, there must be a way to measure changes or compare different levels of the variable. To simplify matters, let us concentrate at this point on just one of the variables: student attention. We will need to find a way to measure the degree of attention shown by the students. The method chosen will depend in part on the design of the study and on the limitations imposed by the situation. Here we will look at four basic approaches to measurement: (1) self-report, (2) direct observation, (3) testing, and (4) teacher or peer ratings.

Using the **self-report** method, we could ask the students questions about how attentive they thought they were being. Answers could be given in writing or face to face, in an interview with the students.

If we decided instead to use **direct observation,** we could send researchers into the classroom to watch the students and assess their attention. These investigators might simply rate the students (on a scale of one to five, perhaps, from very attentive to very inattentive), or they could use a stopwatch to count the number of seconds each student watched the teacher. Observers could also work from a videotape of the class, replaying the tape several times so that each student could be observed and his or her level of attention rechecked. These are only a few of the systems that could be designed using observers to measure attention.

A **test** would be a little more difficult to construct in this case. Many variables are measured with tests, especially those involving learning or achievement. But since attention is a process rather than a product, it is difficult to design a test to measure it. One approach, however, would be to use a "vigilance task." We could see if the students were paying attention by having the teacher give an unpredictable signal, such as saying "Stand up," during the lesson. The measure of attention in this case would be the number of people who stood up immediately (Woolfolk & Woolfolk, 1974).

Finally, we might decide to use **teacher ratings** or **peer ratings.** We could measure attention by asking the teacher or the students to rate the attention of every student in the class.

Clearly, each of these approaches has advantages and disadvantages. Using self-reports or ratings of teachers or peers means relying on the judgments of the participants themselves. Using observers or tests can be disruptive to the class, at least initially. Videotaping is difficult and expensive. Let us assume, however, that we have chosen direct observation from videotapes. We will train the observers to time student attention with a stopwatch to determine how many seconds each student looks at the teacher during a 10-minute lesson. Note that our system of measurement has given us our definition of *attention:* the number of seconds each student looks at the teacher during a 10-minute lesson. This seems to offer a reasonably good definition. If the measurement system did not offer a good definition, we would need to find another way of measuring.

To define and measure our first variable—students' beliefs about the teacher's competence—we could also choose from a number of methods. Let us assume, at least for the time being, that we have selected a rating system. Students' answers to the question "How competent do you think this teacher is?" should give us a good idea of student opinion.

One other definition may be in order here, although in this particular study it seems rather obvious. Since we will be studying student beliefs and student attentiveness, the subjects in our investigation will be stu-dents. As you probably know, **subjects** is the term for the people (or animals) whose behavior is being measured. We would want to specify the grade, sex, and type of student to be studied. For our hypothetical study, we will select male and female sixth graders in a predominantly middle-class school.

Stating a Hypothesis and Choosing an Approach

At this point we have our research question, the variables to be studied, the definition of these variables, the system for measuring them, and the subjects to be studied. We are now ready to add two new details: a **hypothesis** or guess about the relationship between the two variables, and a decision about what kind of approach we will use in our study. To some extent, the hypothesis will dictate the approach.

At the most general level, there are two approaches to answering research questions. The first is to describe the events and relationships in a particular situation as they take place in real life. The second approach is to change one aspect of a situation and note the effects of the change. These two approaches are generally called descriptive and experimental.

A Descriptive Approach. One hypothesis we might establish in our study of student beliefs and attention is that students pay more attention to a teacher they believe to be competent. To test this hypothesis, we could go into several sixth-grade classrooms and ask students to rate their teachers on competence. Ideally, we would conduct the study in a middle school where sixth graders usually have more than one teacher each day. We could then observe the students and measure their level of attention to each teacher. At this point we could get some idea about whether the two variables— believing that a teacher is competent and paying attention to that teacher—go together.

Let's assume, for the sake of the argument, that the two variables do go together. What we have now is a **correlation.** If two variables tend to occur together, they are correlated. We have just assumed such a correlation between beliefs and attention. Other variables that are often correlated are height and weight, income and education, and colder temperatures and falling leaves. A taller person, for example, is likely to weigh more than a shorter person. A richer person is likely to have completed more years of education than a poorer perso~~n~~ And, for the sake of the argument, we are now as~~~~

ing that a student who believes a teacher to be competent is more likely to pay attention to that teacher.

But what does this correlation give us? If educational psychologists know that two variables are correlated, they can then make predictions about one of the variables based on knowledge of the other variable. For example, because the IQ scores of parents and children are correlated, educators can predict a child's IQ based on that of the mother or father. The prediction may not be correct every time, because the correlation between parents' IQs and children's IQs is not perfect. But the prediction is likely to be correct or nearly correct much more than a prediction based on no information at all. Several studies have found a correlation between a teacher's enthusiasm and student learning. If we have information about a teacher's enthusiasm, we can make a prediction about the achievement level of the students in his or her class.

This last example brings us to a very important point about correlation and prediction, mentioned briefly in chapter 1. Knowing that two variables tend to occur together does not tell us that one variable is actually causing the other. Although enthusiastic teachers may tend to have students who achieve more than the students of unenthusiastic teachers, we cannot say that teacher enthusiasm leads to or causes student achievement. We know only that teacher enthusiasm and student achievement tend to occur together. Perhaps teaching students who are achieving more makes a teacher more enthusiastic. Perhaps a third factor—the interesting materials a teacher has chosen to work with, for example—causes both the teacher enthusiasm and student achievement.

Although being able to predict levels of one variable from information about levels of another is useful, teachers are often interested in finding out what factors actually will cause a desired change in behavior. For this, they would need a different kind of research—research based on experimental manipulation.

An Experimental Approach. Returning to our original question about student beliefs and attention, suppose we made a different hypothesis. Rather than just hypothesizing that student attention and beliefs mpetence go together, we could hy- e of the factors actually causing stu- ntion is the belief that a teacher is case, the hypothesis states a causal st this hypothesis, we must change s to see if this change actually causes

changes in the other variable. In our study, this assumed cause, known as the **independent variable,** is the belief that the teacher is competent. The purpose of our experiment will be to see if changes in this variable really cause changes in the other variable—the **dependent variable** of student attention to the teacher.

Assume that we create three comparable groups of students by randomly assigning the students to the groups. Since the selection and assignment of students to groups is totally **random**—by chance, based on no particular plan—the three groups should be very similar.

We then tell one group of students that the teacher they are about to meet is a "very good" teacher; we tell the second group that the teacher they will have is "not a very good" teacher; and we tell the third group nothing about the teacher they are going to have. This final group serves as the **control group.** It will give us information about what happens when there is no experimental manipulation. At some point in the experiment we would ask the students what they believed about the teacher to make sure they had accepted the description they were given.

Next, the teacher, actually the same person in all three cases, teaches the same lesson to each group. Of course the teacher should not be told about the experimental manipulation. We videotape the students in each group as they listen to the teacher. Later, raters viewing the tapes measure the number of seconds each student in the three groups has looked at the teacher. (You may have noticed that although the definition and measurement of the attention variable remain the same as they were in the descriptive study, the definition and measurement of the belief variable have changed. As you can see, such a change is necessary to turn the study into an experiment.)

What kind of results can we expect? If we find that students who believed the teacher was competent paid attention most of the time, students who believed the teacher was not very good paid very little attention, and students who were given no information paid a moderate amount of attention, have we proved our hypothesis? No! In psychology and in educational psychology it is assumed that hypotheses are never really proven by one study, because each study tests the hypothesis in only one specific situation. Hypotheses are "supported" but never proven by the positive results of a single study. Have we supported the hypothesis that student beliefs affect student attention? The answer to this question depends on how well we designed and carried out the study.

Since this is just a hypothetical study, we can assume, once again for the sake of argument, that we did everything just right. If you read the following list of requirements for a "true experiment," set forth by Van Mondrans, Black, Keysor, Olsen, Shelley, and Williams (1977), you will see that we were indeed on the right track:

> The "true experiment" is usually defined as one in which the investigator can (a) manipulate at least one independent variable; (b) randomly select and assign subjects to experimental treatments; and (c) compare the treatment group(s) with one or more control groups on at least one dependent variable. (p. 51)

With a real experiment, however, we would need to know more about exactly how every step of the investigation was conducted. And we would also want to know whether other researchers could come up with the same results if they did the same experiment.

Is the Research Valid?

Being able to evaluate research studies has a dual payoff. The kind of thinking needed is in and of itself valuable. It is the same kind of thinking required to evaluate any complex idea, plan, argument, or project. In all these cases, you need to search for errors, oversights, inconsistencies, or alternative explanations. The analytical ability necessary to evaluate research is useful in any occupation, from law to business to motorcycle maintenance. The second payoff is more specifically valuable for teachers. As an educator, you will have to evaluate research done in your school district or reported in professional journals to determine if the findings are relevant to your own situation.

To be valid, the results of an experiment must pass several tests. Changes in the dependent variable must be due solely to the manipulation of the independent variable. In the following pages, we will look at eight questions that can be asked in an evaluation of a research experiment.

1. *Were the groups to be studied reasonably equal before the experiment began?* If the subjects vary greatly from group to group, any changes found at the end of the experiment may be the results of the original differences in the groups and not of changes in the independent variable. Random assignment of subjects to groups usually takes care of this problem. If instead of randomly selecting the subjects in our own study we had used three different sixth-grade classes, our results would be questionable. Maybe one class already had more generally attentive students. Had they been given the teacher labeled "very good" in the experiment, their high degree of attention would have been relatively meaningless. With random selection from a number of sixth-grade classes, however, each group is likely to have gotten an equal share of the generally attentive and generally inattentive students.

2. *Were all the variables except the independent variable controlled so that the only real difference in the treatment of each group was the change in the independent variable?* We have just seen that the subjects in each group must be equivalent. This principle is equally true of everything else in the experiment. If different procedures were used with each group, it would be difficult to determine which of the differences caused the results. In our study, for example, if we had used different teachers or different lessons in each group, we would have run into this problem in evaluating the results. The students' attention to the teacher could have been based on many things other than the initial statement given by the experimenter about the teacher's competence (the independent variable).

3. *Were the measurement procedures applied consistently to each group?* Unreliable results may at times be caused by an inconsistent measurement system. In our study, if we had used a different videotape rater for each group, we could not have trusted our results. Perhaps one rater would give credit for student attention when students had their faces pointed toward the teacher even if their bodies were turned away. Perhaps another rater would give credit only if the students' entire bodies were directed toward the teacher. Ideally, one rater should make all the measurements. If more are used, there must be some test of the raters' ability to agree on the results. One way to check this would be to see if they agreed when measuring the same students' behaviors.

4. *Are the results of the study due to the experimental procedures rather than to the novelty of the situation?* It is always possible that subjects will respond in some special way to any change, at least temporarily. This possibility was pointed out dramatically by studies conducted at the Western Electric Plant in Hawthorne, Illinois. Investigators were trying to determine which changes in the plant environment

lead to greater worker productivity. As it turned out, everything they tried, every change in the working conditions, seemed to lead to greater productivity, at least for a while (Roethlisberger & Dickson, 1939). In other words, the workers were reacting not to the actual changes but to something new happening. Because the experiment took place in Hawthorne, Illinois, such results are now said to be examples of the **Hawthorne effect.** Our control group helped us avoid this problem. Although the independent variable of a "good" or "bad" teacher label was not applied to the control group, these students were given the special treatment of being in an experiment. If their attention ratings had been particularly high, we might have suspected the Hawthorne effect for all three groups.

5. *Has the investigator who designed the study biased the results in any way?* There are numerous obvious and subtle ways in which an investigator can influence the participants in an experiment. The investigator may have no intention of doing so but may still communicate to the subjects what he or she expects them to do in a given situation (Rosenthal, 1976). In our study, for example, if the investigator had told the teacher involved what the purpose of the experiment was, the teacher might have expected less attention from one of the groups and unintentionally done something to increase or decrease the attention actually given. If the investigator had told the videotape raters the purpose of the experiment, the same thing might have happened. Without meaning to, they might have looked harder for attention in one of the groups. In order to eliminate these problems, both teacher and raters would have to be unaware of the independent variable that was being studied.

6. *Is it reasonably certain that the results did not occur simply by chance?* To answer this question, researchers use statistics. The general agreement is that differences among the groups can be considered "significant" if these differences could have occurred by chance only 5 times out of 100. In reading a research report, you might see the results stated in the following manner: "The difference between the groups was significant ($p < .05$)." Unless you are planning to do your own scien~~tif~~ ~~rese~~arch, the most important part of this ~~~~ ~~w~~ord *significant*. The mathematical ~~~~ ~~t~~hat the probability (p) of such a dif~~~~ ~~b~~y chance factors alone is less than

~~~~*ings in this particular study be likely* ~~~~*situations?* This is really a question

of generalization. How similar to the research situation does a new situation have to be to get the same results? Consider our own experiment. Would we get similar results (a) with much older or younger students? (b) with students who are more or less intelligent? (c) with students who already know the teacher? (d) with different teachers or different lessons? (e) with the removal of videotape cameras? (f) with a lesson that lasts more than 10 minutes?

We cannot answer these questions until the study has been repeated with many different subjects in many different situations. This brings us to the question of **replication.**

8. *Has the study been replicated?* A study has been replicated if it has been repeated and the same results are found. Replication may involve exactly the same study conditions, or it may involve changes in conditions that will give us a better idea of the extent to which the findings can be applied to other situations. If results have been replicated in well-designed studies, the findings form the basis for principles and laws.

Since our own study was only hypothetical, we cannot get a replication of it. But we can look at a similar study done by Feldman and Prohaska (1979). Analyzing this study should be useful to you in two ways. First, it will provide a model for considering other research articles you will find in textbooks and in professional journals. Second, the results of the study itself will probably be of interest because they suggest ways in which student expectations may cause teachers to be more or less effective.

A Sample Study: The Effect of Student Expectations

Feldman and Prohaska's 1979 study concerns student expectations about a teacher's competence and the effect of these expectations on the students' and the teacher's behavior. (Remember that we are looking only at student behavior in our hypothetical study.) You may want to read the study in *Journal of Educational Psychology* (vol. 71, no. 4, 1979). At the beginning of the article you will find specific information: the names of the authors, the university where they work, the name of the article, the name of the journal, and the basic facts about the study. The basic facts describing the design and results of the study are usually included in a brief summary called an **abstract,** found at the beginning of such an article.

Essential Data

The subjects in Feldman and Prohaska's first experiment were undergraduate female volunteers from an introductory psychology class. Each subject was randomly assigned to a positive-expectation group or a negative-expectation group, but was not told which group she was in.

Each subject arrived separately at the experimental center and was told she would have to wait a few minutes before she could see the teacher. While she waited, she met another student who had supposedly just been working with the teacher and was now completing a questionnaire evaluating the teacher. Actually, this student, a male, was a **confederate** of the experimenter—an assistant pretending to be one of the subjects. The confederate played one of two roles, depending on whether he was meeting a subject from the positive-expectation group or the negative-expectation group. (The subjects, of course, did not know what group they were in.) When the confederate met a subject from the positive group, he told her the teacher had been really good, effective, and friendly. He then gave her a completed questionnaire (which also said good things about the teacher) and asked her to turn it in for him, since he had to leave. When the confederate met a subject from the negative group, he said very uncomplimentary things about the teacher and gave the subject a questionnaire with very negative comments on it.

The subject then went into a room and met the teacher, who was the same person for both groups. The teacher did not know the subject had been given any expectations at all. While she was teaching two mini-lessons, she and the subject were secretly videotaped. After the two lessons, the subject took a short quiz on the material and filled out a questionnaire just like the one she had seen the confederate completing. The same procedure was repeated for each subject.

Finally, the videotapes of all the subjects were shown to trained coders who were unaware of the actual experimental conditions. These coders measured three things: (1) percentage of time each subject looked at the teacher, (2) each subject's forward body lean toward the teacher, and (3) each subject's general body orientation toward the teacher. Taken together, these student behaviors could be called *paying attention.* When the coders rated the same subject's videotape, their ratings of the three behaviors were highly correlated. Thus we can assume that the coders agreed about how to use the measurement technique.

Results showed that the subjects who expected the teacher to be "bad" rated the lesson as significantly more difficult, less interesting, and less effective than the subjects who expected the teacher to be "good." They also found the teacher to be less competent, less intelligent, less likable, and less enthusiastic than the other subjects did. Furthermore, the subjects who expected the teacher to be "bad" learned significantly less as measured by the short quiz. They also leaned forward less often and looked at the teacher less frequently than the subjects who expected the teacher to be good.

How would you evaluate this study? The full report (Feldman & Prohaska, 1979) gives many more details, but based on our summary alone, what can you tell about the validity of the findings?

Judging Validity

If you look back at the eight questions for evaluating a research study, it appears that numbers 1, 3, 5, and 6 have been met. (Do you agree?) We cannot yet be certain about question 2—equal treatment of the subjects—because in this first experiment we have no detailed information about the way the teacher behaved toward the subjects. We know only that the teacher was instructed to give the same lesson, in the same way, to each subject. But what if the differences in the subjects' behavior toward the teacher—the differences that were found in the study—caused the teacher to give the lesson in different ways to different students? Perhaps after the first minute or so, subjects were reacting to real differences in the way the teacher delivered the lesson.

Feldman and Prohaska looked at this very real possibility in their second experiment. They found that students' nonverbal behavior (leaning forward or looking at the teacher) actually could affect how well the teacher taught the lesson. Although this may, to some extent, lessen the validity of their first experiment, it is a worthy finding in and of itself.

You may have noticed that we have not yet discussed conditions 4, 7, and 8. Feldman and Prohaska did not include a control group. The fact that the two experimental groups reacted in significantly different ways, however, shows that they were not simply reacting to the novelty of the situation. If both groups had been particularly eager or bored, we might have had good reason to expect the Hawthorne effect.

We can't know anything about conditions 7 a[...] or course, until further research has been co[...]

We can say, however, that two respected educational psychologists have reported findings that seem to support our initial hypothesis. In some cases, at least, student expectations about a teacher's competence do have an effect, not only on the students' behavior but also on the teacher's behavior.

The last two questions are equally difficult to answer. It is almost always possible to offer alternative explanations for the findings of any study. In a well-controlled study, an attempt is made to eliminate as many of these alternative explanations as possible. The question of educational versus statistical significance is also one on which reasonable people might easily differ. How large a difference between the test scores of the two groups is large enough to warrant a change in educational practice? This question must be answered in part by the individual teacher. Do the potential gains offered by the findings seem worthwhile enough to make whatever change is called for?

REFERENCES

(Blue bullets indicate references new to this edition.)

AAMD Ad Hoc Committee on Terminology and Classification. (1992). *Mental retardation: Definition, classification, and systems of support* (9th ed.). Washington, DC: American Association on Mental Retardation.

Abi-Nader, J. (1991). Creating a vision of the future: Strategies for motivating minority students. *Phi Delta Kappan, 72,* 546–549.

• Abruscato, J. (1993). Early results and tentative implications from the Vermont Portfolio Project. *Phi Delta Kappan, 74,* 474–477.

Adams, A., Carnine, D., & Gersten, R. (1982). Instructional strategies for studying content area texts in the intermediate grades. *Reading Research Quarterly, 18,* 27–53.

Adams, G. R., & Fitch, S. A. (1982). Ego stage and identity status development: A cross-sectional analysis. *Journal of Personality and Social Psychology, 43,* 574–583.

Adams, R. S., & Biddle, B. J. (1970). *Realities of teaching: Explorations with video tape.* New York: Holt, Rinehart & Winston.

• Airasian, P. W. (1994). *Classroom assessment* (2nd ed.). New York: McGraw-Hill.

Alberto, P., & Troutman, A. C. (1990). *Applied behavior analysis for teachers: Influencing student performance* (3rd ed.). Columbus, OH: Merrill.

Alderman, M. K. (1985). Achievement motivation and the preservice teacher. In M. Alderman & M. Cohen (Eds.), *Motivation theory and practice for preservice teachers* (pp. 37–49). Washington, DC: ERIC Clearinghouse on Teacher Education.

• Alessi, S. M., & Trollip, S. R. (1991). *Computer-based instruction: Methods and development* (2nd ed.). Boston: Allyn and Bacon.

• Alexander, P. A. (1992). Domain knowledge: Evolving themes and emerging concerns. *Educational Psychologist, 27,* 33–51.

Allington, R. (1980). Teacher interruption behaviors during primary-grade oral reading. *Journal of Educational Psychology, 71,* 371–377.

Alloway, N. (1984). *Teacher expectations.* Paper presented at the meetings of the Australian Association for Research in Education, Perth.

• Alloy, L. B., & Seligman, M. E. P. (1979). On the cognitive component of learned helplessness and depression. *The Journal of Learning and Motivation, 13,* 219–276.

Alwin, D., & Thornton, A. (1984). Family origins and schooling processes: Early versus late influence of parental characteristics. *American Sociological Review, 49,* 784–802.

• American Association of University Women (1991). *Shortchanging girls, shortchanging America.* Washington, DC: AAUW.

American Psychological Association. (1976). *Preliminary report of the commission on behavior modification: Case study issues raised by behavior modification in the schools.* Washington, DC: American Psychological Association.

• Ames, C. (1985). Attributions and cognition in motivation theory. In M. Alderman & M. Cohen (Eds.), *Motivation theory and practice for preservice teachers* (pp. 16–21). Washington, DC: ERIC Clearinghouse on Teacher Education.

• Ames, C. (1990). Motivation: What teachers need to know. *Teachers College Record, 91,* 409–421.

• Ames, C. (1992). Classrooms: Goals, structures, and student motivation. *Journal of Educational Psychology, 84,* 261–271.

Ames, R., & Lau, S. (1982). An attributional analysis of student help-seeking in academic settings. *Journal of Educational Psychology, 74,* 414–423.

Anastasi, A. (1988). *Psychological testing* (6th ed.). New York: Macmillan.

• Anderson, C. (1989). The role of education in the academic disciplines in teacher education. In A. Woolfolk (Ed.), *Research bases for the graduate preparation of teachers* (pp. 88–107). Boston: Allyn and Bacon.

Anderson, C. W., & Smith, E. L. (1983, April). *Children's conceptions of light and color: Developing the concept of unseen rays.* Paper presented at the annual meeting of the American Educational Research Association, Montreal.

Anderson, C. W., & Smith, E. L. (1987). Teaching science. In V. Richardson-Koehler (Ed.), *Educators' handbook: A research perspective* (pp. 84–111). New York: Longman.

Anderson, J. R. (1985). *Cognitive psychology and its implications* (2nd ed.). San Francisco: Freeman.

Anderson, J. R. (1990). *Cognitive psychology and its implications* (3rd ed.). New York: Freeman.

• Anderson, J. R. (1993). *Problem solving and learning. American Psychologist, 48,* 35–44.

Anderson, L. M. (1985). What are students doing when they do all that seatwork? In C. Fisher & D. Berliner (Eds.), *Perspectives on instructional time.* New York: Longman.

Anderson, L. M. (1989a). Learners and learning. In M. Reynolds (Ed.), *Knowledge base for beginning teachers* (pp. 85–100). New York: Pergamon.

Anderson, L. M. (1989b). Classroom instruction. In M. Reynolds (Ed.), *Knowledge base for beginning teachers* (pp. 101–116). New York: Pergamon.

Anderson, L. M., Brubaker, N. L., Alleman-Brooks, J., & Duffy, G. G. (1985). A qualitative study of seatwork in first-grade classrooms. *Elementary School Journal, 86,* 123–140.

Anderson, R., Hiebert, E., Scott, J., & Wilkinson, I. (1985). *Becoming a nation of readers: The report of the commission on reading.* Washington, DC: National Institute of Education.

• Anderson, S. M. Klatzky, R. L., & Murray, J. (1990). Traits a[...] cial stereotypes: Efficiency differences in social inform[...]

cessing. *Journal of Personality and Social Psychology, 59,* 192–201.

Anyon, J. (1980). Social class and the hidden curriculum of work. *Journal of Education, 162,* 67–92.

Archer, S. L. (1982). The lower age boundaries of identity development. *Child Development, 53,* 1551.

Archer, S. L., & Waterman, A. S. (1990). Varieties of identity diffusions and foreclosures: An exploration of the subcategories of the identity statuses. *Journal of Adolescent Research, 5,* 96–111.

Arlin, M. (1984). Time, equality, and mastery learning. *Review of Educational Research, 54,* 65–86.

Armbruster, B. B., & Anderson, T. H. (1981). Research synthesis on study skills. *Educational Leadership, 39,* 154–156.

Armstrong, L. S. (1991, January 16). Racial, ethnic prejudice still prevalent, survey finds. *Education Week,* p. 7.

ASCD Panel on Moral Education. (1988). Moral education in the life of the school. *Educational Leadership, 45*(8), 4–8.

Ashton, P. T. (1978). Cross-cultural Piagetian research: An experimental perspective. *Harvard Educational Review* (Reprint Series No. 13).

Ashton, P. T., & Webb, R. B. (1986). *Making a difference: Teachers' sense of efficacy and student achievement.* New York: Longman.

Ashton-Warner, S. (1963). *Teacher.* New York: Simon & Schuster.

Association for Supervision and Curriculum Development. (1990). Effective teaching redux. *ASCD Update, 32*(6), 5.

Association for Supervision and Curriculum Development. (1991). Issue. *ASCD Update, 33*(3), 7.

Atkinson, J. W. (1964). *An introduction to motivation.* Princeton, NJ: Van Nostrand.

Atkinson, R. C., (1975). Mnemotechnics in second-language learning. *American Psychologist, 30,* 821–828.

Atkinson, R. C., & Raugh, M. R. (1975). An application of the mnemonic keyword method to the acquisition of Russian vocabulary. *Journal of Experimental Psychology: Human Learning and Memory, 104,* 126–133.

Atkinson, R. C., & Shiffrin, R. M. (1968). Human memory: A proposed system and its control processes. In K. Spence & J. Spence (Eds.), *The psychology of learning and motivation* (Vol. 2). New York: Academic Press.

Au, K. H. (1980). Participation structures in a reading lesson with Hawaiian children: Analysis of a culturally appropriate instructional event. *Anthropology and Education Quarterly, 11,* 91–115.

Ausubel, D. P. (1963). *The psychology of meaningful verbal learning.* New York: Grune and Stratton.

Ausubel, D. P. (1977). The facilitation of meaningful verbal learning in the classroom. *Educational Psychologist, 12,* 162–178.

Babad, E. (1990) Measuring and changing teachers' differential behavior as perceived by students and teachers. *Journal of Educational Psychology, 82,* 683–690.

Babad, E. Y., Inbar, J., & Rosenthal, R. (1982). Pygmalion, Galatea, and the Golem: Investigations of biased and unbiased teachers. *l Psychology, 74,* 459–474.

nan memory: Theory and practice. Boston:

current status of gender equity research in *cational Psychologist, 28,* 321–339.

fferences in classroom interaction in sec- of *Classroom Interaction, 22,* 212–218.

Baker, L., & Brown, A. L. (1984a). Metacognitive skills and reading. In P. D. Pearson, M. Kamil, R. Barr, & P. Mosenthal (Eds.), *Handbook of reading research* (pp. 353–394). New York: Longman.

Baker, L., & Brown, A. L. (1984b). Cognitive monitoring in reading. In J. Flood (Ed.), *Understanding reading comprehension* (pp. 21–44). Newark, DE: International Reading Association.

Bakerman, R., Adamson, L. B., Koner, M., & Barr, R. G. (1990). !Kung infancy: The social context of object exploration. *Child Development, 61,* 794–809.

Baldwin, J. D., & Baldwin, J. I. (1986). *Behavioral principles in everyday life* (2nd ed.). Englewood Cliffs, NJ: Prentice-Hall.

Bandura, A. (1977). *Social learning theory.* Englewood Cliffs, NJ: Prentice-Hall.

Bandura, A. (1978). The self-system in reciprocal determinism. *American Psychologist, 33,* 344–358.

Bandura, A. (1986). *Social foundations of thought and action.* Englewood Cliffs, NJ: Prentice-Hall.

Bandura, A. (1993). Perceived self-efficacy in cognitive development and functioning. *Educational Psychologist, 28,* 117–148.

Bandura, A., Ross, D., & Ross, S. A. (1963). Vicarious reinforcement and imitative learning. *Journal of Abnormal and Social Psychology, 67,* 601–607.

Bangert, R., Kulik, J., & Kulik, C. (1983). Individualized systems of instruction in secondary schools. *Review of Educational Research, 53,* 143–158.

Bangert-Drowns, R. L., Kulik, C. C., Kulik, J. A., & Morgan, M. (1991). The instructional effect of feedback in test-like events. *Review of Educational Research, 61,* 213–238.

Banks, J. A. (1993). Multicultural education: Development, dimensions, and challenges. *Phi Delta Kappan, 75,* 22–28.

Banks, J. A. (1993). Multicultural education: Characteristics and goals. In J. Banks & C. McGee Banks (Eds.), *Multicultural education: Issues and perspectives* (2nd ed.) (pp. 2–26). Boston: Allyn and Bacon.

Banks, J. A. (1994). *Multiethnic education: Theory and practice.* Boston: Allyn and Bacon.

Banks, J. A. (1991). Teaching strategies for ethnic studies (5th ed.). Boston: Allyn and Bacon.

Baron, J. (1985). *Rationality and intelligence.* New York: Cambridge University Press.

Baron, J. (1990, July). *Blurring the edges of assessment, curriculum, and instruction.* Paper presented at the Institute on New Modes of Assessment, Cambridge, MA.

Baron, R. A. (1992). *Psychology* (2nd ed.) Boston: Allyn and Bacon.

Baroody, A. R., & Ginsburg, H. P. (1990). Children's learning: A cognitive view. In R. Davis, C. Maher, & N. Noddings (Eds.), *Constructivist views on the teaching and learning of mathematics* (pp. 51–64). Monograph 4 of the National Council of Teachers of Mathematics, Reston, VA.

Bartlett, F. C. (1932). *Remembering: A study in experimental and social psychology.* New York: Macmillan.

Barton, E. J. (1981). Developing sharing: An analysis of modeling and other behavioral techniques. *Behavior Modification, 5,* 386–398.

Baumeister, R. F. (1990). Identity crisis. In R. Lerner, A. Petersen, & J. Brooks-Gunn (Eds.), *The encyclopedia of adolescence* (Vol. 1, pp. 518–521). New York: Garland.

Baumrind, D. (1973). The development of instrumental competence through socialization. In A. Pick (Ed.), *Minnesota symposium on child psychology* (Vol. 7). Minneapolis: University of Minnesota Press.

Baumrind, D. (1983). Rejoinder to Lewis's reinterpretation of parental control effects: Are authoritative families really harmonious? *Psychological Bulletin, 94,* 132–142.

Beane, J. A. (1991). Sorting out the self-esteem controversy. *Educational Leadership, 49*(1), 25–30.

•Bear, T., Schenk, S., & Buckner, L. (1993). Supporting victims of child abuse. *Educational Leadership, 50*(4), 44.

Becker, W. C., Engelmann, S., & Thomas, D. R. (1975). *Teaching 1: Classroom management.* Chicago: Science Research Associates.

Bee, H. (1981). *The developing child* (3rd ed.). New York: Harper and Row.

•Bee, H. (1992). *The developing child* (6th ed.). New York: Harper & Row.

Beezer, B. (1985). Reporting child abuse and neglect: Your responsibilities and your protections. *Phi Delta Kappan, 66,* 434–436.

Belanoff, P., & Dickson, M. (1991). *Portfolios: Process and product.* Portsmouth, NH: Heinemann, Boynton/Cook.

•Belsky, J., & Braungart, J. M. (1991). Are insecure-avoidant infants with extensive day-care experience less stressed by and more independent in the Strange Situation? *Child Development, 62,* 567–571.

Bell, R. (1980). *Changing bodies, changing lives: A book for teens on sex and relationships.* New York: Random House.

•Bem, S. L. (1974). The measurement of psychological androgyny. *Journal of Consulting and Clinical Psychology, 42,* 155–162.

Benbow, C. P., & Minor, L. L. (1986). Mathematically talented males and females and achievement in the high school sciences. *American Educational Research Journal, 23,* 425–436.

Benbow, C. P., & Stanley, J. C. (1980). Sex differences in mathematical ability: Fact or artifact? *Science, 210,* 1262–1264.

Benbow, C. P., & Stanley, J. C. (1983a). Sex differences in mathematical abilities: More facts. *Science, 222,* 1029–1031.

Benbow, C. P., & Stanley, J. C. (1983b). Differential course-taking hypothesis revisited. *American Educational Research Journal, 20,* 469–473.

Benjafield, J. G. (1992). *Cognition.* Englewood Cliffs, NJ: Prentice-Hall.

•Bennett, C. I. (1995). *Comprehensive multicultural education: Theory and practice* (3nd ed.). Boston: Allyn and Bacon.

•Bereiter, C. (1991). Implications of connectionism for thinking about rules. *Educational Researcher, 20*(3), 1016.

Berg, C. A., & Clough, M. (1991). Hunter lesson design: The wrong one for science teaching. *Educational Leadership, 48*(4), 73–78.

Berger, K. S. (1986). *The developing person through childhood and adolescence* (2nd ed.). New York: Worth.

•Berk, L. E. (1993). *Infants, children, and adolescents.* Boston: Allyn and Bacon.

•Berk, L. E. (1994). *Child development* (3nd ed.). Boston: Allyn and Bacon.

Berk, L. E., & Garvin, R. A. (1984). Development of private speech among low-income Appalachian children. *Developmental Psychology, 20,* 272.

Berliner, D. (1983). Developing concepts of classroom environments: Some light on the T in studies of ATI. *Educational Psychologist, 18,* 1–13.

Berliner, D. (1987). But do they understand? In V. Richardson-Koehler (Ed.), *Educators' handbook: A research perspective* (pp. 259–293). New York: Longman.

Berliner, D. (1988). Simple views of effective teaching and a simple theory of classroom instruction. In D. Berliner & B. Rosenshine (Eds.), *Talks to teachers* (pp. 93–110). New York: Random House.

•Berliner, D. (1992).Telling the stories of educational psychology. *Educational Psychologist, 27,* 143–152.

•Berndt, T. J. (1986). Children's comments about their friendships. In M. Perlmutter (Ed.), *Cognitive perspectives on children's behavioral development* (pp. 189–212). Hillside, NJ: Erlbaum.

Berndt, T. J., & Perry, T. B. (1986). Children's perceptions of friendships as supportive relationships. *Developmental Psychology, 22,* 640–648.

•Berndt, T. J., & Perry, T. B. (1990). Distinctive features and effects of early adolescent friendships. In R. Montemayor, G. Adams, & T. Gullotta (Eds.), *From childhood to adolescence: A transitional period?* (pp. 269–287). Newbury Park, CA: Sage.

Berrueta-Clement, J. R., Schweinhart, L. J., Barnett, W. S., Epstein, A. S., & Weikart, D. P. (1984). *Changed lives: The effects of the Perry Preschool Program on youths through age nineteen.* Ypsilanti, MI: High Scope Press.

•Betancourt, H., & Lopez, S. R. (1993). The study of culture, ethnicity, and race in American psychology. *American Psychologist, 48,* 629–637.

•Beyer, B. K. (1985). Practical strategies for the direct teaching of thinking skills. In A. Costa (Ed.), *Developing minds: A resource book for teaching thinking* (pp. 145–150). Alexandria, VA: Association for Supervision and Curriculum Development.

Bigge, J., & Sirvis, B. (1982). Physical and multiple handicaps. In N. Haring (Ed.), *Exceptional children and youth.* Columbus, OH: Charles E. Merrill.

•Bivens, J. A., & Berk, L. E. (1990). A longitudinal study of elementary school children's private speech. *Merrill-Palmer Quarterly, 36,* 443–463.

Bjorklund, D. F. (1989). *Children's thinking: Developmental function and individual differences.* Pacific Grove, CA: Brooks/Cole.

Blackham, G., & Silberman, A. (1979). *Modification of child and adolescent behavior* (3rd ed.), Belmont, CA: Wadsworth.

Block, J. (1983). Differential premises arising from differential socialization of the sexes: Some conjectures. *Child Development, 54,* 1335–1354.

Bloom, B. S. (1968). *Learning for mastery. Evaluation Comment, 1*(2). Los Angeles: University of California, Center for the Study of Evaluation of Instructional Programs.

Bloom, B. S., Engelhart, M. D., Frost, E. J., Hill, W. H., & Krathwohl, D. R. (1956). *Taxonomy of educational objectives. Handbook I: Cognitive domain.* New York: David McKay.

Bloom, B. S., Hastings, J. T., & Madaus, G. F. (1971). *Handbook on formative and summarized evaluation of student learning.* New York: McGraw-Hill.

Bloom, R., & Bourdon, L. (1980). Types and frequencies of teachers' written instructional feedback. *Journal of Educational Research, 74,* 13–15.

•Blumenfeld, P. C. (1992). Classroom learning and motivation: Clarifying and expending goal theory. *Journal of Educational Psychology, 84,* 272–281.

•Blumenfeld, P. C., Puro, P. & Mergendoiller, J. R. (1992).Transla motivation into thoughtfulness. In H. Marshall (Ed.) *Red student learning: Roots of educational change* (pp. 207–240). Norwood, NJ: Ablex.

Boggiano, A. K., Flink, C., Shields, A., Seelbach, A., & Barrett, M. (in press). Use of techniques promoting students' self-determination: Effects on students' analytic problem-solving skills. *Motivation and Education.*

Bohannon, J. N., III, & Warren-Leubecker, A. (1989). Theoretical approaches to language acquisition. In J. Berko Gleason (Ed.), *The development of language* (pp. 167–223). Columbus, OH: Merrill.

Boldizar, J. P. (1991). Assessing sex typing and androgyny in children: The children's sex inventory. *Developmental Psychology, 27,* 505–515.

Borko, H. (1989). Research on learning to teach: Implications for graduate teacher preparation. In A. Woolfolk (Ed.), *Research perspectives on the graduate preparation of teachers* (pp. 69–87). Boston: Allyn and Bacon.

Borko, H., & Livingston, C. (1989). Cognition and improvisation: Differences in mathematics instruction by expert and novice teachers. *American Educational Research Journal, 26,* 473–498.

Borkowski, J. G., Johnston, M. B., & Reid, M. K. (1986). Metacognition, motivation, and the transfer of control processes. In S. J. Ceci (Ed.), *Handbook of cognition: Social and neurological aspects of learning disabilities.* Hillsdale, NJ: Erlbaum.

Bornstein, P. H. (1985). Self-instructional training: A commentary and state-of-the-art. *Journal of Applied Behavior Analysis, 18,* 69–72.

Boykin, A. W. (1986). The triple quandary and the schooling of Afro-American children. In U. Neisser (Ed.), *The school achievement of minority children.* Hillsdale, NJ: Erlbaum.

Brandt, R. On teaching for understanding: A conversation with Howard Gardner. *Educational Leadership, 50*(7), 4–7.

Bransford, J. D., & Stein, B. S. (1984). *The IDEAL problem solver.* New York: Freeman.

Bransford, J. D., Stein, B. S., Shelton, T. S., & Owings, R. A. (1981). Cognition and adaptation: The importance of learning to learn. In J. Harvey (Ed.), *Cognition, social behavior, and the environment* (pp. 93–110). Hillsdale, NJ: Erlbaum.

Bransford, J. D., Stein, B. S., Vye, N. J., Franks, J. J., Auble, P. M., Mezynski, K. J., & Perfetto, G. A. (1982). Differences in approaches to learning: An overview. *Journal of Experimental Psychology: General, 111,* 390–398.

Brantlinger, E. A., & Guskin, S. L. (1987). Ethnocultural and social-psychological effects on learning characteristics of handicapped children. In M. Wang, M. Reynolds, & H. Walberg (eds.), *Handbook of special education: Research and practice. Vol. 1 Learner characteristics and adaptive education* (pp. 7–34). New York: Pergamon Press.

Braun, C. (1976). Teacher expectation: Sociopsychological dynamics. *Review of Educational Research, 46*(2), 185–212.

Bredekemp, S. (1986). *Developmentally appropriate practice in early childhood programs ~~serving~~ children from birth through age 8.* ~~Nati~~onal Association for the Education of

~~____~~E. (1985). Growing points of attachment ~~M~~onographs of the Society for Research in ~~___~~1, 2, Serial No. 209).

The relationship between cognitive style ~~____~~t: A two-year longitudinal study. *Devel-~~___~~*, 617–626.

Brolyer, C. R., Thorndike, E. L., & Woodyard, E. R. (1927). A second study of mental discipline in high school students. *Journal of Educational Psychology, 18,* 377–404.

Brooks, D. (1985). Beginning the year in junior high: The first day of school. *Educational Leadership, 42,* 76–78.

Brooks, D., & Woolfolk, A. (1987). Students' effects on their teachers: The role of nonverbal behavior. *Elementary School Journal, 88,* 51–64.

Brooks, J. G. (1990, February). Teachers and students: Constructivists forging new connections. *Educational Leadership,* 68–71.

Brooks-Gunn, J. (1988). The impact of puberty and sexual activity upon the health and education of adolescent boys and girls. *Peabody Journal of Education, 64,* 88–113.

Brooks-Gunn, J., & Furstenberg, F. F., Jr. (1989). Adolescent sexual behavior. *American Psychologist, 44,* 2249–2257.

Brophy, J. E. (1981). Teacher praise: A functional analysis. *Review of Educational Research, 51,* 5–21.

Brophy, J. E. (1982, March). *Research on the self-fulfilling prophecy and teacher expectations.* Paper presented at the annual meeting of the American Educational Research Association, New York.

Brophy, J. E. (1983). Conceptualizing student motivation to learn. *Educational Psychologist, 18,* 200–215.

Brophy J. E. (1985). Teacher-student interaction. In J. Dusek (Ed.), *Teacher expectancies.* Hillsdale, NJ: Erlbaum.

Brophy, J. E. (1988). On motivating students. In D. Berliner & B. Rosenshine (Eds.), *Talks to teachers* (pp. 201–245). New York: Random House.

Brophy, J. E., & Evertson, C. (1976). *Learning from teaching: A developmental perspective.* Boston: Allyn and Bacon.

Brophy, J. E., & Evertson, C. (1978). Context variables in teaching. *Educational Psychologist, 12,* 310–316.

Brophy, J. E., & Good, T. (1986). Teacher behavior and student achievement. In M. Wittrock (Ed.), *Handbook of research on teaching* (3rd ed., pp. 328–375). New York: Macmillan.

Brophy, J. E., & Kher, N. (1986). Teacher socialization as a mechanism for developing student motivation to learn. In R. Feldman (Ed.), *Social psychology applied to education* (pp. 256–288). New York: Cambridge University Press.

Brough, J. A. (1990). Changing conditions for young adolescents: Reminiscences and realities. *Educational Horizons, 68*(2), 78–81.

Brown, A. L., Campione, J. C., & Day, J. D. (1981). Learning to learn: On training students to learn from tests. *Educational Researcher, 9,* 14–21.

Brown, A. L., & Smiley, S. S. (1977). Rating the importance of structural units of prose passages: A problem of metacognitive development. *Child Development, 48,* 1–8.

Brown, J. S., & Burton, R. R. (1979). Diagnostic models for procedural bugs in basic mathematical skills. *Cognitive Science, 2,* 155–192.

Brown, R. (1973). *A first language: The early stages.* Cambridge, MA: Harvard University Press.

Brown, R., & Hanlon, C. (1970). Derivational complexity and order of acquisition in child speech. In J. M. Hays (Ed.), *Cognition and the development of language.* New York: Wiley.

Brown, R., & McNeill, D. (1966). The "tip-of-the-tongue" phenomenon. *Journal of Verbal Learning and Verbal Behavior, 5,* 325–337.

Bruner, J. S. (1960). *The process of education.* New York: Vintage Books.

Bruner, J. S. (1962). *The process of education.* Cambridge, MA: Harvard University Press.

Bruner, J. S. (1966). *Toward a theory of instruction*. New York: Norton.

Bruner, J. S. (1971). *The relevance of education*. New York: Norton.

Bruner, J. S. (1973). *Beyond the information given: Studies in the psychology of knowing*. New York: Norton.

Bruner, J. S., Goodnow, J. J., & Austin, G. A. (1956). *A study of thinking*. New York: Wiley.

Buenning, M., & Tollefson, N. (1987). The cultural gap hypothesis as an explanation for the achievement patterns of Mexican-American students. *Psychology in the Schools, 14,* 264–271.

Burton, N. W., & Jones, L. V. (1982). Recent trends in achievement levels of black and white youth. *Educational Research, 11,* 10–14.

Burton, R. V. (1963). The generality of honesty reconsidered. *Psychological Review, 70,* 481–499.

Butler, R., & Nisan, M. (1986). Effects of no feedback, task-related comments, and grades on intrinsic motivation and performance. *Journal of Educational Psychology, 78,* 210–224.

Byrne, B. M., & Shavelson, R. J. (1986). On the structure of adolescent self-concept. *Journal of Educational Psychology, 78,* 474–481.

Caine, R. N., & Caine, G. (1991). *Making connections: Teaching and the human brain*. Alexandria, VA: Association for Supervision and Curriculum Development.

Calderhead, J., & Robson, M. (1991). Images of teaching: Student teachers' early conceptions of classroom practice. *Teaching and Teacher Education, 7,* 1–8.

Calmore, J. A. (1986). National housing policy and black America: Trends, issues, and implications. In *The state of black America 1986* (pp. 115–149). New York: National Urban League.

Cambourne, B., & Turbill, J. (1990). Assessment in whole-language classrooms: Theory into practice. *Elementary School Journal, 90,* 337–349.

Camp, R. (1990, Spring). Thinking together about portfolios. *The Quarterly of the National Writing Project, 27,* 8–14.

Canfield, J. (1990). Improving students' self-concepts. *Educational Leadership, 48*(1), 48–50.

Cangelosi, J. S. (1990). *Designing tests for evaluating student achievement*. New York: Longman.

Canter, L. (1988). Let the educator beware: A response to Curwin and Mendler. *Educational Leadership, 46*(2), 71–73.

Canter, L. (1989). Assertive discipline—More than names on the board and marbles in a jar. *Phi Delta Kappan, 71*(1), 41–56.

○ Canter, L., & Canter, M. (1992). *Lee Canter's Assertive Discipline: Positive behavior management for today's classroom*. Santa Monica: Lee Canter and Associates.

○ Carey, L. M. (1994). *Measuring and evaluating school learning* (2nd ed.). Boston: Allyn and Bacon.

Carnegie Forum on Education and the Economy. (1986). *A nation prepared: Teachers for the 21st century*. Washington, DC: Carnegie Forum on Education and the Economy.

Carnegie Foundation for the Advancement of Teaching (1987). *1987 national survey of public school teachers*. Princeton, NJ.

Carter, K. (1984). Do teachers understand principles of writing tests? *Journal of Teacher Education, 35,* 57–60.

Cartwright, G. P., Cartwright, C. A., & Ward, M. E. (1981). *Educating special learners*. Belmont, CA: Wadsworth.

Casanova, U. (1987). Ethnic and cultural differences. In V. Richardson-Koehler (Ed.), *Educators' handbook: A research perspective* (pp. 370–393). New York: Longman.

Case, R. (1978a). Piaget and beyond: Toward a developmentally-based theory and technology of instruction. In R. Glaser (Ed.), *Advances in instructional psychology (Vol. 1)*. Hillsdale, NJ: Erlbaum.

Case, R. (1978b). Developmentally-based theory and technology of instruction. *Review of Educational Research, 48,* 439–463.

Case, R. (1985a). *Intellectual development: Birth to adulthood*. New York: Academic Press.

Case, R. (1985b). A developmentally-based approach to the problem of instructional design. In R. Glaser, S. Chipman, & J. Segal (Eds.), *Teaching thinking skills* (Vol. 2, pp. 545–562). Hillsdale, NJ: Erlbaum.

Case, R. (1988, August). *The mind's staircase: Stages in the development of human intelligence*. Paper presented at the American Psychological Association, Atlanta.

Cauley, K., & Tyler, B. (1989). The relationship of self-concept to prosocial behavior in children. *Early Childhood Research Quarterly, 4,* 51–60.

Cazden, C. B. (1988). *Classroom discourse: The language of teaching and learning*. Portsmouth, NH: Heinemann.

○ Ceci, S. J. (1991). How much does schooling influence intelligence and its cognitive components? A reassessment of the evidence. *Developmental Psychology, 27,* 703–720.

Chambers, B., & Abrami, P. C. (1991). The relationship between student team learning outcomes and achievement, causal attributions, and affect. *Journal of Educational Psychology, 83,* 140–146.

○ Chance, P. (1991). Backtalk: a gross injustice. *Phi Delta Kappan, 72,* 803.

○ Chance, P. (1992). The rewards of learning. *Phi Delta Kappan, 73,* 200–207.

○ Chance, P. (1993). Sticking up for rewards. *Phi Delta Kappan, 74,* 787–790.

Chapman, M., Zahn-Waxler, C., Cooperman, G., & Iannotti, R. (1987). Empathy and responsibility in the motivation of children's helping. *Developmental Psychology, 23,* 140–145.

Charles, C. M. (1985). *Building classroom discipline: From models to practice* (2nd ed.). New York: Longman.

Charles, C. M. (1989). *Building classroom discipline: From models to practice* (3rd ed.). New York: Longman.

Chase, C. I. (1978). *Measurement for educational evaluation* (2nd ed.). Reading, MA: Addison-Wesley.

○ Chi, M. T. H. (1978). Knowledge structures and memory development. In R. Siegler (Ed.), *Children's thinking: What develops?* (pp. 73–96). Hillsdale, NJ: Erlbaum.

○ Chi, M. T. H., & Glaser, R. (1985). Problem-solving ability. In R. Sternberg (Ed.), *Human abilities: An information-processing approach* (pp. 227–250). New York: Freeman.

○ Chi, M. T. H., Glaser, R., & Farr, M. (Eds.) (1988). *The nature of expertise*. Hillsdale, NJ: Earlbaum.

○ Chi, M. T. H., & Koeske, R. D. (1983). Network representation of a child's dinosaur knowledge. *Development Psychology, 19,* 29–39.

○ Childs, C. P., & Greenfield, P. M. (1982). Informal modes of learning and teaching: The case of Zinacanteco weaving. In N. Warren (Ed.), *Advances in cross-cultural psychology* (Vol. 2, pp. 269–316). London: Academic Press.

Chomsky, N. (1965). *Aspects of a theory of syntax*. Cambridge, MA: MIT Press.

○ Chomsky, N. (1980). *Rules and representations*. New York: Columbia University Press.

○ Chomsky, N. (1986). *Knowledge of language: Its nature, origin, and use*. New York: Praeger.

Christy, P. R. (1975). Does use of tangible rewards with individual children affect peer observers? *Journal of Applied Behavior Analysis, 8,* 187–196.

Civil Rights Commission. (1973). *Teacher and students: Differences in teacher interactions with Mexican-American and Anglo students.* Washington, DC: Government Printing Office.

Cizek, G. J. (1991). Innovation or enervation: Performance assessment in perspective. *Phi Delta Kappan, 72*(9), 695–699.

Claiborn, W. L. (1969). Expectancy effects in the classroom: A failure to replicate. *Journal of Education Psychology, 60,* 377–383.

Clark, C. M. (1983). Personal communication.

Clark, C. M., Gage, N. L., Marx, R. W., Peterson, P. L., Staybrook, N. G., & Winnie, P. H. (1979). A factorial experiment on teacher structuring, soliciting, and reacting. *Journal of Educational Psychology, 71,* 534–550.

Clark, C. M., & Peterson, P. L. (1986). Teachers' thought processes. In M. Wittrock (Ed.), *Handbook of research on teaching* (3rd ed.) (pp. 255–296). New York: Macmillan.

Clark, C. M., & Yinger, R. (1988). Teacher planning. In D. Berliner & B. Rosenshine (Eds.), *Talks to teachers* (pp. 342–365). New York: Random House.

Clark, D. L., & Astuto, T. A. (1994). Redirecting reform: Challenges to popular assumptions about teachers and students. *Phi Delta Kappan, 75,* 512–520.

Clark, J. M., & Paivio, A. (1991). Dual coding theory and education. *Educational Psychology Review, 3,* 149–210.

Clarke-Stewart, K. A. (1989). Infant day care: Maligned or malignant? *American Psychologist, 44,* 266–273.

Clarke-Stewart, K. A., & Fein, G. G. (1983). Early childhood programs. In P. Mussen (Ed.), *Handbook of child development* (Vol. 2). New York: Wiley.

Clement, S. L. (1978). Dual marking system: Simple and effective. *American Secondary Education, 8,* 49–52.

Clements, D. H. (1991). Enhancement of creativity in computer environments. *American Educational Research Journal, 28,* 173–188.

Clifford, M. M. (1984a). Educational psychology. In *Encyclopedia of Education* (pp. 413–416). New York: Macmillan.

Clifford, M. M. (1984b). Thoughts on a theory of constructive failure. *Educational Psychologist, 19,* 108–120.

Clifford, M. M. (1990). Students need challenge, not easy success. *Educational Leadership, 48*(1), 22–26.

Clifford, M. M. (1991). Risk taking: Empirical and educational considerations. *Educational Psychologist, 26,* 263–298.

Cobbett, W. (1824, November 20). *Political Register,* L11.

Coburn, J. (1993). Opening new technological horizons for middle and high school. *Technology & Learning* (Special Supplement).

Cognition Technology Group at Vanderbilt. (1991). Some thoughts about constructivism and instructional design. *Educational Technology, 31* (5), 16–18.

Colby, A., Kohlberg, L., Gibbs, J., & Lieberman, M. (1983). A longitudinal study of moral judgment. *Monographs of the Society for Research in Child Development, 48* (1–2, Serial No. 200).

[...] in testing. *American Psychologist, 36,*

[...]r). Teachers who made a difference. *In-*

[...], Wood, A. M., Weinfeld, F. D., & York, [...] *f educational opportunity.* Washington, [...]tment of Health, Education and Welfare,

Collins, J. L. (1982, March). *Self-efficacy and ability in achievement behavior.* Paper presented at the Annual meeting of the American Educational Research Association, New York.

Collins, A., Brown, J. S., & Newman, S. E. (1989). Cognitive apprenticeship: Teaching the crafts of reading, writing, and mathematics. In L. B. Resnick (Ed.), *Knowing, learning, and instruction: Essays in honor of Robert Galser.* Hillsdale, NJ: Lawrence Earlbaum.

Collins, A., & Ferguson, W. (1993). Epistemic forms and epistemic games: Structures and strategies to guide inquiry. *Educational Psychologist, 28,* 35.

Collins, A., & Smith, E. (1980). *Teaching the process of reading comprehension* (Tech. Rep. No. 182). Urbana-Champaign: University of Illinois, Center for the Study of Reading.

Collins, A., & Smith, E. (1982). Teaching the process of reading. In D. K. Detterman & R. J. Sternberg (Eds.), *How and how much can intelligence be increased* (Table 1, p. 175). Norwood, NJ: Ablex.

Combs, A. W. (1984). *A personal approach to teaching: Beliefs that make a difference.* Boston: Allyn and Bacon.

Confrey, J. (1990a). A review of the research on students' conceptions in mathematics, science, and programming. *Review of Research in Education, 16,* 3–56.

Confrey, J. (1990b). What constructivism implies for teaching. In R. Davis, C. Maher, & N. Noddings (Eds.), *Constructivist views on the teaching and learning of mathematics* (pp. 107–122). Monograph 4 of the National Council of Teachers of Mathematics, Reston, VA.

Conklin, N. F., & Lourie, M. A. (1983). *A host of tongues.* New York: Free Press.

Conley, S. (1991). Review of research on teacher participation in school decision making. *Review of Research in Education, 17,* 225–266.

Cooke, B. L., & Pang, K. C. (1991). Recent research on beginning teachers: Studies of trained and untrained novices. *Teaching and Teacher Education, 7,* 93–110.

Cooper, G., & Sweller, J. (1987). Effects of schema acquisition and rule automation on mathematical problem-solving transfer. *Journal of Educational Psychology, 79,* 347–362.

Cooper, H. (1979). Pygmalion grows up: A model for teacher expectation communication and performance influence. *Review of Educational Research, 49,* 389–410.

Cooper, H. M., & Good, T. (1983). *Pygmalion grows up: Studies in the expectation communication process.* New York: Longman.

Copi, I. M. (1961). *Introduction to logic.* New York: Macmillan.

Corkill, A. J. (1992). Advance organizers: Facilitators of recall. *Educational Psychology Review, 4,* 33–67.

Corno, L. (1980). Individual and class level effects of parent-assisted instruction in classroom memory support systems. *Journal of Educational Psychology, 72,* 278–292.

Corno, L. (1987). Teaching and self-regulated learning. In D. Berliner & B. Rosenshine (Eds.), *Talks to teachers* (pp. 249–266). New York: Random House.

Corno, L. (1992). Encouraging students to take responsibility for learning and performance. *The Elementary School Journal, 93,* 69–84.

Corno, L., & Snow, R. E. (1986). Adapting teaching to individual differences in learners. In M. Wittrock (Ed.), *Handbook of research on teaching* (3rd ed.) (pp. 605–629). New York: Macmillan.

Corwin, R. (1981). Patterns of organizational control and teacher militancy: Theoretical continuities in the idea of "loose coupling."

In A. Kerckhoff (Ed.), *Research in the sociology of education and socialization* (Vol. 2, pp. 261–291). Greenwich, CT: JAI Press.

Costa, A. L. (Ed.). (1985). *Developing minds: A resource book for teaching thinking.* Alexandria, VA: Association for Supervision and Curriculum Development.

• Covaleskie, J. F. (1992). Discipline and morality: Beyond rules and consequences. *The Educational Forum, 56*(2), 56–60.

Covington, M. (1984). The self-worth theory of achievement motivation. *Elementary School Journal, 85,* 5–20.

Covington, M., & Omelich, C. L. (1984). An empirical examination of Weiner's critique of attribution research. *Journal of Educational Psychology, 76,* 1214–1225.

Covington, M., & Omelich, C. (1987). "I knew it cold before the exam": A test of the anxiety-blockage hypothesis. *Journal of Educational Psychology, 79,* 393–400.

Cox, W. F., & Dunn, T. G. (1979). Mastery learning: A psychological trap? *Educational Psychologist, 14,* 24–29.

Craig, G. (1986). *Human development* (4th ed.). Englewood Cliffs, NJ: Prentice-Hall.

Craik, F. I. M. (1979). Human memory. *Annual Review of Psychology, 30,* 63–102.

Craik, F. I. M., & Lockhart, R. S. (1972). Levels of processing: A framework for memory research. *Journal of Verbal Learning and Verbal Behavior, 11,* 671–684.

Crisci, P. E. (1986). The Quest National Center: A focus on prevention of alienation. *Phi Delta Kappan, 67,* 440–442.

Cronbach, L., & Snow, R. (1977). *Aptitudes and instructional methods.* New York: Irvington.

• Cronin, J. F. (1993). Four misconceptions about authentic learning. *Educational Leadership, 50*(7), 78–80.

Crouse, J. M. (1971). Retroactive interference in reading prose materials. *Journal of Educational Psychology, 62,* 39–44.

Cummins, D. D. (1991). Children's interpretation of arithmetic word problems. *Cognition and Instruction, 8,* 261–289.

Cummins, J. (1984). *Bilingualism and special education.* San Diego: College Hill Press.

• Cunningham, D. J. (1992) Beyond educational psychology: Steps toward an educational semiotic. *Educational Psychology Review, 4,* 165–194.

• *Current Directions in Psychological Science.* (1993). Special Section: Controversies, 2, 1–12.

Curwin, R. L., & Mendler, A. N. (1988). Packaged discipline programs: Let the buyer beware. *Educational Leadership, 46*(2), 68–71.

Damon, W. (1977). *The social world of the child.* San Francisco: Jossey-Bass.

Danner, F. W. (1976). Children's understanding of intersentence organization in the recall of short descriptive passages. *Journal of Educational Psychology, 68,* 174–183.

Dansereau, D. F. (1985). Learning strategy research. In J. Segal, S. Chipman, & R. Glaser (Eds.), *Thinking and learning skills. Vol. I: Relating instruction to research.* Hillsdale, NJ: Erlbaum.

Dark, V. J., & Benbow, C. P. (1991). Differential enhancement of working memory with mathematical versus verbal precocity. *Journal of Educational Psychology, 83,* 48–60.

Darley, J. M., Glucksberg, S., & Kinchla, R. (1991). *Psychology* (5th ed.). Englewood Cliffs, NJ: Prentice-Hall.

Davidson, J. (1982). The group mapping activity for instruction in reading and thinking. *Journal of Reading, 26,* 52–56.

Davis, R. B., Maher, C. A., & Noddings, N. (Eds.) (1990). Constructivist views on the teaching and learning of mathematics.

Monograph 4 of the National Council of Teachers of Mathematics, Reston, VA.

• Deaux, K. (1993). Commentary: Sorry, wrong number: A reply to Gentile's call. *Psychological Science, 4,* 125–126.

deCharms, R. (1976). *Enhancing motivation.* New York: Irvington.

deCharms, R. (1983). Intrinsic motivation, peer tutoring, and cooperative learning: Practical maxims. In J. Levine & M. Wang (Eds.), *Teacher and student perceptions: Implications for learning* (pp. 391–398). Hillsdale, NJ: Erlbaum.

Deci, E. (1975). *Intrinsic motivation.* New York: Plenum.

Deci, E., & Ryan, R. M. (1985). *Intrinsic motivation and self-determination in human behavior.* New York: Plenum.

Deci, E., Vallerand, R. J., Pelletier, L. G., & Ryan, R. M. (1991). Motivation and education: The self-determination perspective. *Educational Psychologist, 26,* 325–346.

De Corte, E., & Verschaffel, L. (1985). Beginning first graders' initial representation of arithmetic word problems. *Journal of Mathematical Behavior, 4,* 3021.

Delclos, V. R., & Harrington, C. (1991). Effects of strategy monitoring and proactive instruction on children's problem-solving performance. *Journal of Educational Psychology, 83,* 35–42.

De Lisi, R., & Staudt, J. (1980). Individual differences in college students' performance on formal operations tasks. *Journal of Applied Developmental Psychology, 1,* 201–208.

De Mott, R. M. (1982). Visual impairments. In N. Haring (Ed.), *Exceptional children and youth.* Columbus, OH: Charles E. Merrill.

• Demetras, M. J. , & Post, K. N. (1985, April). *Negative feedback in mother-child dialogues.* Paper presented at the biennial meeting of the Society for Research in Child Development, Toronto.

Dempster, F. N. (1981). Memory span: Sources of individual and developmental differences. *Psychological Bulletin, 89,* 63–100.

Dempster, F. N. (1991). Synthesis of research on reviews and tests. *Educational Leadership, 48*(7), 71–76.

• Dempster, F. N. (1993). Exposing our students to less should help them learn more. *Phi Delta Kappan, 74,* 432–437.

• Deno, S. L. (1987). Curriculum-based measurement. *Teaching Exceptional Children, 20,* 41.

• DeRidder, L. M. (1993). Teenage pregnancy: Etiology and educational interventions. *Educational Psychology Review, 5,* 87–107.

Derry, S. J. (1989). Putting learning strategies to work. *Educational Leadership, 47*(5) 4–10.

Derry, S. J. (1991). Strategy and expertise in solving word problems. In C. McCormick, G. Miller, & M. Pressley (Eds.), *Cognitive strategies research: From basic research to educational applications.* New York: Springer-Verlag.

Derry, S. J. (1992). Beyond symbolic processing: Expanding horizons for educational psychology. *Journal of Educational Psychology, 84,* 413–419.

Derry, S. J., & Murphy, D. A. (1986). Designing systems that train learning ability: From theory to practice. *Review of Educational Research, 56,* 1–39.

Deshler, D. D., & Schumaker, J. B. (1986). Learning strategies: An instructional alternative for low-achieving adolescents. *Exceptional Children, 52,* 583–590.

Dias, R. M. (1983). Thought and two languages: The impact of bilingualism on cognitive development. *Review of Research in Education, 10,* 23–54.

Dinnel, D., & Glover, J. A. (1985). Advance organizers: Enc manipulations. *Journal of Educational Psycholo* 514–522.

Doctorow, M., Wittrock, M. C., & Marks, C. (1978). Generative processes in reading comprehension. *Journal of Educational Psychology, 70,* 109–118.

Dodge, K. A., & Somberg, D. RR. (1987). Hostile attributional biases among aggressive boys are exacerbated under conditions of threats to the self. *Child Development, 58,* 213–224.

Donaldson, M. (1985). The mismatch between school and children's minds. In N. Entwistle (Ed.), *New directions in educational psychology. Vol. I: Learning and teaching.* Philadelphia: Falmer Press.

Dorans, N. J., & Livingston, S. A. (1987). Male-female differences in SAT Verbal ability among students of high SAT Mathematical ability. *Journal of Educational Measurement, 24,* 65–71.

Dorval, R., & Eckerman, C. O. (1984). Developmental trends in the quality of conversation achieved by small groups of acquainted peers. *Monographs of the Society for Research in Child Development, 49* (2, Serial No. 206).

Doyle, W. (1977). The uses of nonverbal behaviors: Toward an ecological model of classrooms. *Merrill-Palmer Quarterly, 23,* 179–192.

Doyle, W. (1983). Academic work. *Review of Educational Research, 53,* 159–200.

Doyle, W. (1985, May/June). Recent research on classroom management: Implications for teacher preparation. *Journal of Teacher Education,* pp. 31–35.

Doyle, W. (1986). Classroom organization and management. In M. Wittrock (Ed.), *Handbook of research on teaching* (3rd ed., pp. 392–431). New York: Macmillan.

Drayer, A. M. (1979). *Problems in middle and high school training: A handbook for student teachers and beginning teachers.* Boston: Allyn and Bacon.

Driscoll, M. P. (1994). *Psychology of learning for instruction.* Boston: Allyn and Bacon.

Duchastel, P. (1979). Learning objectives and the organization of prose. *Journal of Educational Psychology, 71,* 100–106.

Duffy, G., Roehler, L. R., Meloth, M. S., & Vavrus, L. G. (1986). Conceptualizing instructional explanation. *Teaching and Teacher Education, 2,* 197–214.

Duncker, K. (1945). On solving problems. *Psychological Monographs, 58* (5, Whole No. 270).

Dunkin, M. J., & Biddle, B. J. (1974). *The study of teaching.* New York: Holt, Rinehart & Winston.

Dunn, K., & Dunn, R. (1978). *Teaching students through their individual learning styles.* Reston, VA: National Council of Principals.

Dunn, K., & Dunn, R. (1987). Dispelling outmoded beliefs about student learning. *Educational Leadership, 44*(6), 55–63.

Dunn, R. (1987). Research on instructional environments: Implications for student achievement and attitudes. *Professional School Psychology, 2,* 43–52.

Dunn, R., Beaudry, J. S., & Klavas, A. (1989). Survey of research on learning styles. *Educational Leadership, 47*(7), 50–58.

Du_____ , G. E. (1984). *Learning Style Inventory.*
_____ms.

_____ Schroeder, H. (1983). Self-management _____A meta-analysis. *Psychological Bulletin,*

_____ivational processes affecting learning. _____, 1040–1047.

_____ J. (1983). Children's theories on intelli-_____learning. In S. Paris, G. Olson, & W.

Stevenson (Eds.), *Learning and motivation in the classroom* (pp. 239–256). Hillsdale, NJ: Erlbaum.

Dwyer, C. A., & Villegas, A. M. (1993, January). *Guiding conceptions and assessment principles for the Praxis Series: Professional assessments for beginning teachers.* Princeton, NJ: Educational Testing Service.

Dyer, H. S. (1967). *The discovery and development of educational goals.* Proceedings of the 1966 Invitational Conference on Testing Problems. Princeton, NJ: Educational Testing Service.

Eaton, J. F., Anderson, C. W., & Smith, E. L. (1984). Students' misconceptions interfere with science learning: Case studies of fifth-graders. *Elementary School Journal, 84,* 365–379.

Eaton, S., & Olson, J. (1986). "Doing computers?" The micro in the elementary curriculum. *Journal of Curriculum Studies, 18*(3), 342–344.

Ebbinghaus, H. (1913). *Memory.* New York: Teachers College, Columbia University.

Ebmeier, H. H., & Ziomek, R. L. (1982, March). *Increasing engagement rates of low and high achievers.* Paper presented at the annual meeting of the American Educational Research Association, New York.

Eccles, J., & Wigfield, A. (1985). Teacher expectations and student motivation. In J. Dusek (Ed.), *Teacher expectancies* (pp. 185–226). Hillsdale, NJ: Erlbaum.

Educational Testing Service (1962). *Hidden Figures Test* (Cf-1). Princeton, NJ.

Educational Testing Service. (1992). *The second international assessment of educational progress.* Princeton, NJ: ETS.

Eimas, P. D. (1985). The perception of speech in early infancy. *Scientific American, 252,* 46–52.

Eiseman, J. W. (1981). What criteria should public school moral education programs meet? *The Review of Education, 7,* 213–230.

Eisenberg, N., & Miller, P. A. (1987). The relation of empathy to prosocial and related behaviors. *Psychological Bulletin, 101,* 91–119.

Eisenberg, N., Shell, R., Pasernack, J., Lennon, R., Beller, R., & Mathy, R. M. (1987). Prosocial development in middle childhood: A longitudinal study. *Developmental Psychology, 23,* 712–718.

Eisner, E. (1986). A secretary in the classroom. *Teaching and Teacher Education, 2,* 325–328.

Elam, S. E., Rose, L. C., & Gallup, A. M. (1992). The 23rd annual Gallup Poll of the public's attitudes toward the public schools. *Phi Delta Kappan, 73*(1) 41–56.

Elam, S. E., Rose, L. C., & Gallup, A. M. (1993). The 25th annual Gallup Poll of the public's attitudes toward the public schools. *Phi Delta Kappan, 75*(2) 137–157.

Elashoff, J. D., & Snow, R. E. (1971). *Pygmalion reconsidered.* Worthington, OH: Charles A. Jones.

Elawar, M. C., & Corno, L. (1985). A factorial experiment in teachers' written feedback on student homework: Changing teacher behavior a little rather than a lot. *Journal of Educational Psychology, 77,* 162–173.

Electronic Learning (1987). Educational technology 1987: A report on EL's seventh annual survey of the states. *Electronic Learning, 7*(2), 39–44, 53–57, 83.

Elkind, D. (1981). Obituary—Jean Piaget (1896–1980). *American Psychologist, 36,* 911–913.

Elkind, D. (1986). *The miseducation of children: Superkids at risk.* New York: Knopf.

Elkind, D. (1989). Developmentally appropriate education for 4-year-olds. *Theory Into Practice, 28*(1), 47–52.

Elkind, D. (1991). Formal education and early childhood education: An essential difference. In K. M. Cauley, F. Linder, & J. H. MacMillan (Eds.), *Annual Editions: Educational Psychology 91/92* (pp. 27–37). Guilford, CN: Duskin.

Emery, R. E. (1989). Family violence. *American Psychologist, 44,* 321–328.

Emmer, E. T., & Evertson, C. M. (1981). Synthesis of research on classroom management. *Educational Leadership, 38,* 342–345.

Emmer, E. T., & Evertson, C. M. (1982). Effective classroom management at the beginning of the school year in junior high school classes. *Journal of Educational Psychology, 74,* 485–498.

Emmer, E. T., Evertson, C. M., & Anderson, L. M. (1980). Effective classroom management at the beginning of the school year. *Elementary School Journal, 80,* 219–231.

Emmer, E. T., Evertson, C., Clements, B., & Worsham, M. (1994). *Classroom management for secondary teachers* (3rd ed.). Boston: Allyn & Bacon.

Emmer, E. T., & Millett, G. (1970). *Improving teaching through experimentation: A laboratory approach.* Englewood Cliffs, NJ: Prentice-Hall.

Engel, P. (1991). Tracking progress toward the school readiness goal. *Educational Leadership, 48*(5), 39–42.

Engelmann, S., & Englemann, T. (1981). *Give your child a superior mind.* New York: Simon & Schuster.

Epstein, H. (1978). Growth spurts during brain development: Implications for educational policy and practice. In J. Chall & A. Mirsky (Eds.), *Education and the brain. The seventy-seventh yearbook of the National Society for the Study of Education, Part II.* Chicago: University of Chicago Press.

Epstein, H. (1980). EEG developmental stages. *Developmental Psychobiology, 13,* 629–631.

Epstein, J. L. (1989). Family structure and student motivation. In R. E. Ames & C. Ames (Eds.), *Research on motivation in education: Vol 3. Goals and cognitions* (pp. 259–295). New York: Academic Press.

Erez, M., & Zidon, I. (1984). Effects of goal acceptance on the relationship of goal difficulty to performance. *Journal of Applied Psychology, 69,* 69–78.

Erickson, F., & Shultz, J. (1982). *The counselor as gatekeeper: Social interaction in interviews.* New York: Academic Press.

Erikson, E. (1963). *Childhood and society* (2nd ed.). New York: Norton.

Erikson, E. H. (1968). *Identity, youth, and crisis.* New York: Norton.

Erikson, E. H. (1980). *Identity and the life cycle* (2nd ed.). New York: Norton.

Espe, C., Worner, C., & Hotkevich, M. (1990). Whole language—What a bargain. *Educational Leadership, 47*(6), 45.

Estes, W. K. (1988). Toward a framework for combining connectionist and symbol processing models. *Journal of Memory and Language, 27,* 196–212.

Estes, W. K. (1993). Concepts, categories, and psychological science. *Psychological Science, 4,* 143–153.

Evertson, C. M. (1982). Differences in instructional activities in high and low achieving junior high classes. *Elementary School Journal, 82,* 329–350.

Evertson, C. M. (1988). Managing classrooms: A framework for teachers. In D. Berliner & B. Rosenshine (Eds.), *Talks to teachers* (pp. 54–74). New York: Random House.

Evertson, C. M., Emmer, E. T., Clements, B. S., & Worsham, M. E. (1994). *Classroom management for elementary teachers* (3rd ed.). Boston: Allyn and Bacon.

Evertson, C. M., & Green, J. (1986). Observation as inquiry and method. In M. Wittrock (Ed.), *Handbook of research on teaching* (3rd ed., pp. 162–213). New York: Macmillan.

Fagot, B. I., & Hagan, R. (1991). Observations of parent reactions to sex-stereotyped behaviors: Age and sex effects. *Child Development, 62,* 617–628.

Fagot, B. I., Hagan, R., Leinbach, M. D., & Kronsberg, S. (1985). Differential reactions to assertive and communicative acts of toddler boys and girls. *Child Development, 56,* 1499–1505.

Faw, H. W., & Waller, T. G. (1976). Mathemagenic behaviors and efficiency in learning from prose. *Review of Educational Research, 46,* 691–720.

Federal Register (1977, December 29). *Procedures for evaluating specific learning disabilities.* Washington, DC: Department of Health, Education, and Welfare.

Feiman-Nemser, S. (1983). Learning to teach. In L. Shulman & G. Sykes (Eds.), *Handbook of teaching and policy* (pp. 150–170). New York: Longman.

Fein, G. (1978). *Child development.* Englewood Cliffs, NJ: Prentice-Hall.

Feitler, F., & Tokar, E. (1982). Getting a handle on teacher stress: How bad is the problem? *Educational Leadership, 39,* 456–458.

Feldman, R., & Prohaska, T. (1979). The student as Pygmalion: Effects of student expectancy of the teacher. *Journal of Educational Psychology, 71,* 485–493.

Fennema, E., & Peterson, P. (1988). Effective teaching for boys and girls: The same or different? In D. Berliner & B. Rosenshine (Eds.), *Talks to teachers* (pp. 111–127). New York: Random House.

Fennema, E., & Sherman, J. (1977). Sex-related differences in mathematics achievement, spatial visualization and affective factors. *American Educational Research Journal, 14*(1), 51–71.

Ferguson, D. L., Ferguson, P. M., & Bogdan, R. C. (1987). If mainstreaming is the answer, what is the question? In V. Richardson-Koehler (Ed.), *Educators' handbook: A research perspective* (pp. 394–419). New York: Longman.

Fetterman, N., & Rohrkemper, M. (1986, April). *The utilization of failure: A look at one social/instructional environment.* Paper presented at the annual meeting of the American Educational Research Association, San Francisco.

Feuerstein, R. (1979). *The dynamic assessment of retarded performers: The Learning Potential Assessment Device, theory, instruments, and techniques.* Baltimore: University Park Press.

Finn, J. (1972). Expectations and the educational environment. *Review of Educational Research, 42,* 387–410.

Fischer, K. W. (1980). A theory of cognitive development: The control and construction of hierarchies of skills. *Psychological Review, 87,* 477–531.

Fischer, K. W., & Knight, C. C. (1990). Cognitive development in real children: Levels and variations. In R. McClure (Ed.), *Learning and thinking styles: Classroom interactions* (pp. 43–67). Washington, DC: National Education Association.

Fiske, E. B. (1981, October 27). Teachers reward muddy prose, study finds. *New York Times,* p. C1.

Fiske, E. B. (1988, April 10). America's test mania. *New York Times* (Education Life Section), pp. 16–20.

Fitts, P. M., & Posner, M. I. (1967). *Human performance.* Belmont, CA: Brooks Cole.

Flavell, J. H. (1985). *Cognitive development* (2nd ed.). Englewood Cliffs, NJ: Prentice-Hall.

Flavell, J. H., Friedrichs, A. G., & Hoyt, J. D. (1970). Developmental changes in memorization processes. *Cognitive Psychology, 1,* 324–340.

Flecter, J. D., Hawley, D. E., & Piele, P. K. (1990). Costs, effects, and utility of microcomputer assisted instruction in the classroom. *American Educational Research Journal, 27,* 783–806.

*Flink, C. F., Boggiano, A. K., & Barrett, M. (1990). Controlling teaching strategies: Undermining children's self-determination and performance. *Journal of Personality and Social Psychology, 59,* 916–924.

Floden, R. E., & Klinzing, H. G. (1990). What can research on teacher thinking contribute to teacher preparation? A second opinion. *Educational Researcher, 19*(4), 15–20.

Forest, M. (1991). It's about relationships. In L. Meyer, C. Peck, & L. Brown (Eds.), *Critical issues in the lives of people with disabilities* (pp. 399–408). Baltimore: Paul H. Brookes.

Forrest, D. L., & Waller, T. G. (1980, April). *What do children know about their reading and study skills?* Paper presented at the annual meeting of the American Educational Research Association, Boston.

Foster, J. D. (1991). The role of accountability in Kentucky's Educational Reform Act of 1990. *Educational Leadership, 48*(5), 34–36.

Foster, W. (1981, August). *Social and emotional development in gifted individuals.* Paper presented at the Fourth World Conference on Gifted and Talented, Montreal.

Fox, L. H. (1981). Identification of the academically gifted. *American Psychologist, 36,* 1103–1111.

*Frank, S. J., Pirsch, L. A., & Wright, V. C. (1990). Late adolescents' perceptions of their parents: Relationships among deidealization, autonomy, relatedness, and insecurity and implications for adolescent adjustment and ego identity status. *Journal of Youth and Adolescence, 19,* 571–588.

Frederiksen, N. (1984). Implications of cognitive theory for instruction in problem solving. *Review of Educational Research 54,* 363–407.

*Freud, S. (1959). Creative writers and daydreaming. In J. Strachey (ed.), *The standard edition of the complete psychological works of Sigmund Freud* (vol. 9). London: Hogarth Press.

Frick, T. W. (1990). Analysis of patterns in time: A method of recording and quantifying temporal relations in education. *American Educational Research Journal, 27,* 180–204.

*Frisbie, D. A., & Waltmen, K. K. (1992). Developing a personal grading plan. *Educational Measurement: Issues and practices* (pp. 35–42). Washington, DC: National Council on Measurement in Education.

Fromberg, D. P., & Driscoll, M. (1985). *The successful classroom: Management strategies for regular and special education teachers.* New York: Teachers College Press.

Frymier, J. (1988). Understanding and preventing teen suicide: An interview with Barry Garfinkel. *Phi Delta Kappan, 70,* 290–293.

Fuller, F. G. (1969). Concerns of teachers: A developmental conceptualization. *American Educational Research Journal, 6,* 207–226.

Furman, W., & Bierman, K. L. (1984). Children's conceptions of friendship: A multimethod study of developmental changes. *Developmental Psychology, 20,* 925–931.

Furst, E. J. (1981). Bloom's taxonomy of educational objectives for the cognitive domain: Philosophical and educational issues. *Review of Educational Research, 51,* 441–454.

Furth, H., & Wachs, H. (1974). *Thinking goes to school: Piaget's theory in practice.* New York: Oxford University Press.

Gage, N. L. (1991). The obviousness of social and educational research results. *Educational Researcher, 20*(A), 10–16.

Gagne, E. D. (1985). *The psychology of school learning.* Boston: Little Brown.

*Gagne, E. D., Yekovich, C. W., & Yekovich, F. R. (1993). *The cognitive psychology of school learning* (2nd ed.). New York: HarperCollins.

Gagne, R. M. (1977). *The conditions of learning* (3rd ed.). New York: Holt, Rinehart & Winston.

Gagne, R. M. (1985). *The conditions of learning and theory of instruction* (4th ed.). New York: Holt, Rinehart & Winston.

Gagne, R. M., & Driscoll, M. P. (1988). *Essentials of learning for instruction* (2nd ed.). Englewood Cliffs, NJ: Prentice-Hall.

Gagne, R. M., & Smith, E. (1962). A study of the effects of verbalization on problem solving. *Journal of Experimental Psychology, 63,* 12–18.

Galambos, S. J., & Goldin-Meadow, S. (1990). The effects of learning two languages on metalinguistic development. *Cognition, 34,* 1–56.

*Galbraith, J. (1985). The eight great gripes of gifted kids: Responding to special needs. *Roeper Review, 7,* 15–18.

Gall, M. D. (1970). The use of questions in teaching. *Review of Educational Research, 40,* 707–721.

Gall, M. D. (1984). Synthesis of research on teachers' questioning. *Educational Leadership, 41,* 40–47.

Gallini, J. K. (1991). Schema-based strategies and implications for instructional design in strategy training. In C. McCormick, G. Miller, & M. Pressley (Eds.), *Cognitive strategies research: From basic research to educational applications.* New York: Springer-Verlag.

Gallup, A. M. (1984). Gallup Poll of teachers' attitudes toward the public schools. *Phi Delta Kappan, 66,* 97–107.

Gallup, A. M. (1985). The 17th annual Gallup Poll of the public's attitudes toward the public schools. *Phi Delta Kappan, 67,* 35–47.

Gallup, A. M. (1986). The 18th annual Gallup Poll of the public's attitudes toward the public schools. *Phi Delta Kappan, 68*(1), 43–59.

Gallup, A. M., & Clark, D. L. (1987). The 19th annual Gallup Poll of the public's attitudes toward the public schools. *Phi Delta Kappan, 69*(1), 17–30.

Gallup, A. M., & Elam, S. M. (1988). The 20th annual Gallup Poll of the public's attitudes toward the public schools. *Phi Delta Kappan, 70*(1), 33–46.

Gallup, G. (1982). Fifteenth annual Gallup Poll of public attitudes toward the public schools. *Phi Delta Kappan, 64*(1), 34–46.

*Garcia, E. E. (1992). "Hispanic" children: Theoretical, empirical, and related policy issues. Educational Psychology Review, 4, 69–94.

Garcia, R. L. (1991). *Teaching in a pluralistic society: Concepts, models, and strategies.* New York: HarperCollins.

Gardner, H. (1982a). *Art, mind, and brain: A cognitive approach to creativity.* New York: Basic Books.

Gardner, H. (1982b). *Developmental psychology* (2nd ed.). Boston: Little, Brown.

Gardner, H. (1983). *Frames of mind: The theory of multiple intelligences.* New York: Basic Books.

*Gardner, H. (1991). *The unschooled mind: How children think and how schools should teach.* New York: Basic Books.

*Gardner, H. (1993a). *Creating minds: An anatomy of creativity seen through the lives of Freud, Einstein, Picasso, Stravinsky, Elliot, Graham, and Gandhi.* New York: Basic Books.

*Gardner, H. (1993b). *Educating the unschooled mind: A science and public policy seminar.* Washington, DC: American Educational Research Association.

*Gardner, H. (1993c). *Multiple intelligences: The theory in practice.* New York: Basic Books.

*Gardner, H., & Hatch, T. (1989). Multiple intelligences go to school. *Educational Researcher, 18*(8), 4–10.

Garger, S., & Guild, P. (1984). Learning styles: The crucial differences. *Curriculum Review, 23,* 9–12.

Garner, R. (1990). When children and adults do not use learning strategies: Toward a theory of settings. *Review of Educational Psychology, 60,* 517–530.

Garner, R., & Kruas, C. (1982). Monitoring of understanding among 7th graders: An investigation of good comprehender–poor comprehender differences on knowing and regulating reading behaviors. *Educational Research Quarterly, 6,* 5–12.

Garrett, S. S., Sadker, M., & Sadker, D. (1986). Interpersonal communication skills. In J. Cooper (Ed.), *Classroom teaching skills* (3rd ed.). Lexington, MA: D. C. Heath.

*Garrod, A., Beal, C., & Shin, P. (1990). The development of moral orientation in elementary school children. *Sex Roles, 22,* 13–27.

Gartner, A., & Lipsky, D. K. (1987). Beyond special education: Toward a quality system for all students. *Harvard Educational Review, 57,* 367–395.

Gelman, R. (1979). Preschool thought. *American Psychologist, 34,* 900–905.

Gelman, R., & Baillargeon, R. (1983). A review of some Piagetian concepts. In P. Mussen (Ed.), *Carmichael's manual of child psychology. Vol. 3: Cognitive development* (E. Markman & J. Flavell, Volume Eds.). New York: Wiley.

Gelman, R., Meck, E., & Merkin, S. (1986). Young children's numerical competence. *Cognitive Development, 1,* 1–29.

Gelman, S. A., & Ebeling, K. S. (1989). Children's use of nonegocentric standards in judgments of size. *Child Development, 60,* 920–932.

Gentner, D. (1975). Evidence for the psychological reality of semantic components: The verbs of possession. In D. Norman & D. Rumelhart (Eds.), *Explorations in cognition.* San Francisco: Freeman.

*Gerbner, G., Gross, L. Signorelli, N., & Morgan, M. (1986). *Television's mean world: Violence Profile No. 14–15.* Philadelphia: Annenberg School of Communication, University of Pennsylvania.

*Giaconia, R. M., & Hedges, L. V. (1982). Identifying features of effective open education. *Review of Educational Research, 52,* 579–602.

Gibbs, J. W., & Luyben, P. D. (1985). Treatment of self-injurious behavior: Contingent versus noncontingent positive practice overcorrection. *Behavior Modification, 9,* 3–21.

Gick, M. L. (1986). Problem-solving strategies. *Educational Psychologist, 21,* 99–120.

Gick, M. L., & Holyoak, K. L. (1983). Schema induction and analogical transfer. *Cognitive Psychology, 15,* 1–38.

Gillett, M., & Gall, M. (1982, March). *The effects of teacher enthusiasm on the at-task behavior of students in the elementary grades.* Paper presented at the annual meeting of the American Educational Research Association, New York.

Gilligan, C. (1982). *In a different voice: Psychological theory and women's development.* Cambridge, MA: Harvard University Press.

Gilligan, C., & Attanucci, J. (1988). Two moral orientations: Gender differences and similarities. *Merrill-Palmer Quarterly, 34,* 223–237.

Gilstrap, R. L., & Martin, W. R. (1975). *Current strategies for teachers: A resource for personalizing education.* Pacific Palisades, CA: Goodyear.

Ginsburg, H. (1985). Piaget and education. In N. Entwistle (Ed.), *New directions in educational psychology. Vol. 1: Learning and teaching* (pp. 45–60). Philadelphia: Falmer Press.

Ginsburg, H., & Opper, S. (1988). *Piaget's theory of intellectual development* (3rd ed.). Englewood Cliffs, NJ: Prentice-Hall.

Glaser, R. (1981). The future of testing: A research agenda for cognitive psychology and psychometrics. *American Psychologist, 36,* 923–936.

Gleitman, H. (1987). *Basic psychology* (2nd ed.). New York: Norton.

Gleitman, H. (1991). *Psychology* (3rd ed.). New York: Norton.

Glover, J. A., Ronning, R. R., & Bruning, R. H. (1990). *Cognitive psychology for teachers.* New York: Macmillan.

Goin, M. T., Peters, E. E., & Levin, J. R. (1986, April). *Effects of pictorial mnemonic strategies on the reading performance of students classified as learning disabled.* Paper presented at the annual meeting of the Council for Exceptional Children, New Orleans.

Goleman, D. (1988, April 10). An emerging theory on blacks' I.Q. scores. *New York Times* (Education Life Section), 22–24.

Good, T. L. (1983a). Classroom research: A decade of progress. *Educational Psychologist, 18,* 127–144.

Good, T. L. (1983b). Research on classroom teaching. In L. Shulman & G. Sykes (Eds.), *Handbook of teaching and policy* (pp. 42–80). New York: Longman.

Good, T. L. (1988). Teacher expectations. In D. Berliner & B. Rosenshine (Eds.), *Talks to teachers* (pp. 159–200). New York: Random House.

Good, T. L., & Brophy, J. E. (1984). *Looking in classrooms* (3rd ed.). New York: Harper and Row.

Good, T. L., & Brophy, J. E. (1991). *Looking in classrooms* (5th ed.). New York: Harper Collins.

Good, T. L., & Grouws, D. (1979). The Missouri mathematics effectiveness project: An experimental study in fourth grade classrooms. *Journal of Educational Psychology, 71,* 355–362.

Good, T. L., Grouws, D., & Ebmeier, H. (1983). *Active mathematics teaching.* New York: Longman.

Good, T. L., & Marshall, S. (1984). Do students learn more in heterogeneous or homogeneous groups? In P. Peterson, L. C. Wilkinson, & M. Hallinan (Eds.), *The social context of instruction: Group organization and group processes* (pp. 15–38). Orlando, FL: Academic Press.

Good, T. L., & Stipek, D. J. (1983). Individual differences in the classroom: A psychological perspective. In G. Fenstermacher & J. Goodlad (Eds.), *1983 National Society for the Study of Education Yearbook.* Chicago: University of Chicago Press.

Good, T., & Weinstein, R. (1986). Schools make a difference: Evidence, criticisms, and new directions. *American Psychologist, 41,* 1090–1097.

Goodman, K. S. (1986). *What's whole in whole language: A parent-teacher guide.* Portsmouth, NH: Heinemann.

Goodman, Y. M., & Goodman, K. S. (1990). Vygotsky in a whole-language perspective. In L. Moll (Ed.), *Vygotsky and education: Instructional implications and applications of sociohistorical psychology* (pp. 223–250). New York: Cambridge University Press.

Goodspeed, J. (1988). Two million microcomputers now used in U.S. schools. *Electronic Learning, 7*(8), 16.

Gordon, E. W. (1991). Human diversity and pluralism. *Educational Psychologist, 26,* 99–108.

Gordon, S. (1986). What kids need to know: Most parents and school systems fail to provide teenagers with relevant sex education. *Psychology Today, 20*(10), 22–26, 74.

Gordon, T. (1974). *Teacher effectiveness training.* New York: Peter H. Wyden.

Gordon, T. (1981). Crippling our children with discipline. *Journal of Education, 163,* 228–243.

Grabe, M., & Latta, R. M. (1981). Cumulative achievement in a mastery instructional system: The impact of differences in resultant achievement motivation and persistence. *American Educational Research Journal, 18,* 7–14.

Graham, S. (1991). A review of attribution theory in achievement contexts. *Educational Psychology Review, 3,* 5–39.

Graham, S., & Barker, G. (1990). The downside of help: An attributional-developmental analysis of helping behavior as a low ability cue. *Journal of Educational Psychology, 82,* 7–14.

Graham, S., & Golan, S. (1991). Motivational influences on cognition: Task involvement, ego involvement, and depth of information processing. *Journal of Educational Psychology, 83,* 187–194.

Grant, C. A., & Sleeter, C. E. (1989). Race, class, gender, exceptionality, and educational reform. In J. Banks & C. McGee Banks (Eds.), *Multicultural education: Issues and perspectives* (pp. 49–66). Boston: Allyn and Bacon.

Green, B. F. (1981). A primer of testing. *American Psychologist, 36,* 1001–1012.

Green, J., & Weade, R. (1985). Reading between the lines: Social cues to lesson participation. *Theory into Practice, 24,* 14–21.

Gregorc, A. F. (1982). *Gregorc Style Delineator: Development, technical, and administrative manual.* Maynard, MA: Gabriel Systems.

Gresham, F. (1981). Social skills training with handicapped children. *Review of Educational Research, 51,* 139–176.

Grinder, R. E. (1981). The "new" science of education: Educational psychology in search of a mission. In F. H. Farley & N. J. Gordon (Eds.), *Psychology and education: The state of the union.* Berkeley, CA: McCutchan.

Grissom, J. B., & Smith, L. A. (1989). Repeating and dropping out of school. In L. Shepard & M. Smith (Eds.), *Flunking grades: Research and policies on retention* (pp. 34–63). Philadelphia: Falmer Press.

Grolnick, W. S., & Ryan, R. M. (1989). Parent styles associated with children's self-regulation and competence in school. *Journal of Educational Psychology, 81,* 143–154.

Grolnick, W. S., Ryan, R. M., & Deci, E. L. (1991) Inner resources for school achievement: Motivational mediators of children's perceptions of their parents. *Journal of Educational Psychology, 83,* 508–517.

Gronlund, N. E. (1985). *Measurement and evaluation in teaching* (5th ed.). New York: Macmillan.

Gronlund, N. E. (1993). *How to make achievement tests and assessments* (5th ed.). Boston: Allyn and Bacon.

Gronlund, N. E. (1991). *How to write and use instructional objectives* (4th ed.). New York: Macmillan.

Gross, M. U. M. (1992). The use of radical acceleration in cases of extreme intellectual precocity. *Gifted Child Quarterly, 36,* 91–99.

Grossman, H. G. (Ed.). (1983). *Classification in mental retardation.* Washington, DC: American Association on Mental Deficiency.

Grossman, H., & Grossman, S. H. (1994). *Gender issues in education.* Boston: Allyn and Bacon.

Guilford, J. P. (1988). Some changes in the Structure-of-Intellect model. *Educational and Psychological Measurement, 48,* 1–4.

Guskey, T. R., & Gates, S. L. (1986). Synthesis of research on mastery learning. *Education Leadership, 43,* 73–81.

Guitierrez, R., & Slavin, R. E. (1992). Achievement effects of the nongraded elementary school: A best evidence synthesis. *Review of Educational Research, 62,* 333–376.

Guttmacher (Alan) Institute (1984). *Issues in brief* (Vol. 4, No. 2). Washington, DC: Alan Guttmacher Institute.

Guttmacher (Alan) Institute (1991). *Issues in brief* (Vol. 11, No. 2). Washington, DC: Alan Guttmacher Institute.

Haertel, E. H. (1991). New forms of teacher assessment. *Review of Research in Education, 17,* 3–30.

Hakuta, K. (1986). *Mirror of language: The debate on bilingualism.* New York: Basic Books.

Hakuta, K., & Garcia, E. E. (1989). Bilingualism and education. *American Psychologist, 44,* 374–379.

Hale-Benson, J. E. (1986). *Black children: Their roots, culture, and learning styles* (rev. ed.). Baltimore: Johns Hopkins University Press.

Hall, J. W. (1991). More on the utility of the keyword method. *Journal of Educational Psychology, 83,* 171–172.

Hallahan, D. P., & Kauffman, J. M. (1994). *Exceptional children: Introduction to special education* (6th ed.). Boston: Allyn & Bacon.

Hamilton, R. J. (1985). A framework for the evaluation of the effectiveness of adjunct questions and objectives. *Review of Educational Research, 55,* 47–86.

Haney, W. (1981). Validity, vaudeville, and values: A short history of social concerns over standardized testing. *American Psychologist, 36,* 1021–1034.

Hansen, R. A. (1977). Anxiety. In S. Ball (Ed.), *Motivation in education.* New York: Academic Press.

Hansford, B. C., & Hattie, J. A. (1982). The relationship between self and achievement/performance measures. *Review of Educational Research, 52,* 123–142.

Hardman, M. L. (1994). *Inclusion: Issues of educating students with disabilities in regular educational settings.* A booklet to accompany Hardman, M. L., Drew, C. J., Egan, M. W., & Wolf, B. (1993). *Human exceptionality: Society, school, and family* (4th ed.). Boston: Allyn and Bacon.

Hardman, M. L., Drew, C. J., Egan, M. W., & Wolf, B. (1993). *Human exceptionality: Society, school, and family* (4th ed.). Boston: Allyn & Bacon.

Haring, N. G., & McCormick, L. (Eds.), *Exceptional children and youth* (4th ed.). Columbus, OH: Merrill.

Harris, K. R. (1990). Developing self-regulated learners: The role of private speech and self-instruction. *Educational Psychologist, 25,* 35–50.

Harris, K. R., Graham, S., & Pressley, M. (in press). Cognitive strategies in reading and written language. In N. Singhh & I. Beale (Eds.), *Current perspectives in learning disabilities: Nature, theory, and treatment.* New York: Springer-Verlag.

Harris, K. R., & Pressley, M. (in press). The nature of cognitive strategy instruction: Interactive strategy construction. *Exceptional Children.*

Harris, L. (1989, June). *The ICD survey III: A report card on special education.* New York: Louis Harris & Associates.

Harris, R. T. (1991). Anorexia nervosa and bulimia nervosa in female adolescents. *Nutrition Today, 26*(2), 30–34.

Harrison, A. O., Wilson, M. N., Pine, C. J., & Buriel, R. (1990). Family ecologies of ethnic minority children. *Child Development, 61*, 347–362.

Harrow, A. J. (1972). *A taxonomy of the psychomotor domain: A guide for developing behavior objectives.* New York: David McKay.

Hartup, W. W. (1989). Social relationships and their developmental significance. *American Psychologist, 44*, 120–126.

Harter, S. (1990). Issues in the assessment of self-concept of children and adolescents. In A. LaGreca (Ed.), *Through the eyes of a child* (pp. 292–325). Boston: Allyn & Bacon.

Harvard University (1985, June). Preschool: It does make a difference. *Harvard Education Letter, 1*(6), 1–3.

Harvard University (1986, January). Girls' math achievement: What we do and don't know. *Harvard Education Letter, 2*(1), 1–5.

Harvard University (1986, March). When the student becomes the teacher. *Harvard Education Letter, 2*(3), 5–6.

Harvard University (1988, March). Cultural differences in the classroom. *Harvard Education Letter, 4*(2), 1–4.

Haskins, R. (1989). Beyond metaphor: The efficacy of early childhood education. *American Psychologist, 44*, 274–282.

Hayes, J. R., Waterman, D. A., & Robinson, C. S. (1977). Identifying relevant aspects of a problem text. *Cognitive Science, 1*, 297–313.

Hayes, S. C., Rosenfarb, I., Wulfert, E., Munt, E. D., Korn, Z., & Zettle, R. D. (1985). Self-reinforcement effects: An artifact of social standard setting? *Journal of Applied Behavior Analysis, 18*, 201–214.

Herman, J. (1988, April). The faces of meaning: Teachers', administrators', and students' views of the effect of ACOT. Paper presented at the annual meeting of the American Educational Research Association and the International Association for Computing in Education, New Orleans.

• Herman, J. L., Aschbacher, P. R., & Winters, L. (1992). *A practical guide to alternative assessment.* Alexandria, VA: Association for Supervision and Curriculum Development.

• Hernshaw, L. S. (1987). *The shaping of modern psychology: A historical introduction from dawn to present day.* London: Routledge & Kegan Paul.

Hess, R., Chih-Mei, C., & McDevitt, T. M. (1987). Cultural variation in family beliefs about children's performance in mathematics: Comparisons among People's Republic of China, Chinese-American, and Caucasian-American families. *Journal of Educational Psychology, 79*, 179–188.

Hess, R., & McDevitt, T. (1984). Some cognitive consequences of maternal intervention techniques. A longitudinal study. *Child Development, 55*, 1902–1912.

Hess, R. D., & Shipman, V. C. (1965). Early experience and the socialization of cognitive modes in children. *Child Development, 36*, 869–886.

Hetherington, E. M. (1989). Coping with family transitions: Winners, losers, and survivors. *Child Development, 60*, 1–14.

Heward, W. L., & Orlansky, M. D. (1992). *Exceptional children* (4th ed.). Columbus, OH: Charles E. Merrill.

Hilgard, E. R., Atkinson, R. L., & Atkinson, R. C. (1979). *Introduction to psychology* (7th ed.). New York: Harcourt Brace Jovanovich.

Hill, K. T., & Eaton, W. O. (1977). The interaction of test anxiety and success-failure experiences in determining children's arithmetic performance. *Developmental Psychology, 13*, 205–211.

Hill, K. T., & Wigfield, A. (1984). Test anxiety: A major educational problem and what can be done about it. *Elementary School Journal, 85*, 105–126.

Hill, W. E. (1990). *Learning: A survey of psychological interpretations* (5th ed.). New York: Harper & Row.

Hiller, J. J. (1971). Verbal response indicators of conceptual vagueness. *American Educational Research Journal, 8*, 151–161.

Hills, J. R. (1976). *Measurement and evaluation in the classroom.* Columbus, OH: Charles E. Merrill.

Hines, C. V., Cruickshank, D. R., & Kennedy, J. J. (1982, March). *Measures of teacher clarity and their relationships to student achievement and satisfaction.* Paper presented at the annual meeting of the American Educational Research Association, New York.

Hines, C. V., Cruickshank, D. R., & Kennedy, J. J. (1985). Teacher clarity and its relation to student achievement and satisfaction. *American Educational Research Journal, 22*, 87–99.

Hinsley, D., Hayes, J. R., & Simon, H. A. (1977). From words to equations. In P. Carpenter & M. Just (Eds.), *Cognitive processes in comprehension.* Hillsdale, NJ: Erlbaum.

• Hiroto, D. S., & Seligmen, M. E. P. (1975). Generality of learned helplessness in man. *Journal of Personality and Social Psychology, 31*, 311–327.

Hodgkinson, H. L. (1985). *All one system: Demographics of education, kindergarten through graduate school.* Washington, DC: Institute of Educational Leadership.

Hoffman, L. W. (1977). Changes in family roles, socialization, and sex differences. *American Psychologist, 32*(8), 644–657.

• Hoffman, L. W. (1984). Work, family, and the socialization of the child. In R. Parke (Ed.), *Review of child development research* (Vol. 7, pp. 223–282). Chicago: University of Chicago Press.

Hoffman, M. L. (1978). Empathy: Its development and prosocial implications. In C. B. Keasey, (Ed.), *Nebraska Symposium on Motivation, 1977.* Lincoln, NE: University of Nebraska Press.

Hoffman, M. L. (1979). Development of moral thought, feeling, and behavior. *American Psychologist, 34*, 958–966.

Hoffman, M. L. (1983). Affective and cognitive processes in moral internal moralization. In T. Higgins, D. Ruble, & W. Hartup (Eds.), *Social cognition and social development.* Cambridge: Cambridge University Press.

Hoffman, M. L. (1984). Empathy, its limitations and its role in a comprehensive moral theory. In W. Kurtines & J. Gewirtz (Eds.), *Morality, moral behavior, and moral development.* New York: Wiley.

Hoge, D. R., Smit, E. K., & Hanson, S. L. (1990). School experiences predicting changes in self-esteem of sixth- and seventh-grade students. *Journal of Educational Psychology, 82*, 117–126.

• Holden, G. W., & Ritchie, K. L. (1991). Linking extreme marital discord, child rearing practices, and child behavior problems: Evidence from battered women. *Child Development, 62*, 311–327.

• Holmes, C. T., (1989). Grade-level retention effects: A meta analysis of research studies. In L. Shepard & M. Smith (Eds.) *Flunking grades: Research and policies on retention* (pp. 16–33). Philadelphia: Falmer Press.

Houston, J. P. (1991). *Fundamentals of learning of memory* (4th ed.). New York. Harcourt Brace Jovanovich.

Howard, K. (1990, spring). Making the writing portfolio real. *The Quarterly of the National Writing Project, 27*, 4–8.

Hoy, W. K., & Woolfolk, A. E. (1990). Organizational socialization of student teachers. *American Educational Research Journal, 27*, 279–300.

Hoy, W. K., & Woolfolk, A. E. (1993). Teachers' sense of efficacy and the organizational health of schools. *Elementary School Journal, 93,* 355–372.

Huessman, L. R., Eron, L. D., Klein, R., Brice, P., & Fischer, P. (1983). Mitigating the imitation of aggressive behaviors by changing children's attitudes about media violence. *Journal of Personality and Social Psychology, 44,* 899–910.

Huessman, L. R., Lagarspetz, K., & Eron, L. (1984). Intervening variables in the TV violence-aggression relation: Evidence from two countries. *Developmental Psychology, 20,* 746–775.

Hundert, J., & Bucher, B. (1978). Pupil's self-scored arithmetic performance: A practical procedure for maintaining accuracy. *Journal of Applied Behavior Analysis, 11,* 304.

Hunt, J. McV. (1961). *Intelligence and experience.* New York: Ronald.

Hunter, M. (1982). *Mastery teaching.* El Segundo, CA: TIP Publications.

Hunter, M. (1991). Hunter design helps achieve the goals of science instruction. *Educational Leadership, 48*(4), 79–81.

Hyde, J. (1981). How large are cognitive gender differences? *American Psychologist, 36,* 292–301.

Hyde, J. S., Fennema, E., & Lamon, S. J. (1990). Gender differences in mathematical performance: A meta-analysis. *Psychological Bulletin, 107,* 139–155.

IIS Report (1990). Water Mill, NY: Educational Products Information Exchange Institute.

Inclusive Education Programs. (1994, February). AFT President calls inclusion "Fad." *Inclusive Education Programs: Advice on Educating Students with Disabilities in Regular Settings.* LRP Publications, 1+.

Iran-Nejad, A. (1990). Active and dynamic self-regulation of learning processes. *Review of Educational Research, 60,* 573–602.

Iran-Nejad, A., Marsh, G. E., & Clements, A. C. (1992). The figure and ground of constructive brain functioning: Beyond explicit memory processes. *Educational Psychologist, 27,* 473–492.

Iran-Najad, A., Wittrock, M., & Hidi, S. (Eds.) (1992). Special Issue: Brain and Education: *Educational Psychologist, 27*(4), Washington, DC: American Psychological Association.

Irving, O., & Martin, J. (1982). Withitness: The confusing variable. *American Educational Research Journal, 19,* 313–319.

Irwin, J. W. (1991). *Teaching reading comprehension* (2nd ed.). Boston: Allyn and Bacon.

Isabella, R., & Belsky, J. (1991). Interactional synchrony and the origins of infant-mother attachment: A replication study. *Child Development, 62,* 373–384.

Isenberg, J. (1991). Societal influences on children. In K. M. Cauley, F. Linder, & J. H. MacMillan (Eds.), *Annual Editions: Educational Psychology 91/92* (pp. 38–44). Guilford, CN: Duskin.

Jacklin, C. N., Dipietro, J. A., & Maccoby, E. E. (1984). Sex-typing behavior and sex-typing pressure in child-parent interactions. *Sex Roles, 13,* 413–425.

Jacklin, C. N., & Maccoby, E. E. (1972, April). *Sex differences in intellectual abilities: A reassessment and a look at some new explanations.* Paper presented at the annual meeting of the American Educational Research Association, Chicago.

Jagacinski, C. M., & Nicholls, J. G. (1987). Competence and affect in task involvement and ego involvement: The impact of social comparison information. *Journal of Educational Psychology, 76,* 107–114.

James, W. (1912). *Talks to teachers on psychology: And to students on some of life's ideals.* New York: Holt.

Jencks, C., Smith, M., Acland, H., Bane, M., Cohen, D., Gintis, H., Heyns, B., & Michelson, S. (1972). *Inequality: A reassessment of the effect of family and schooling in America.* New York: Basic Books.

Jenson, W. R., Sloane, H. N., & Young, K. R. (1988). *Applied behavior analysis in education: A structured teaching approach.* Englewood Cliffs, NJ: Prentice-Hall.

Johnson, D., & Johnson, R. (1994). *Learning together and alone: Cooperation, competition, and individualization* (4th ed.). Boston: Allyn and Bacon.

Johnson, D., & Johnson, R. (1985). Motivational processes in cooperative, competitive, and individualistic learning situations. In C. Ames & R. Ames (Eds.), *Research on motivation in education. Vol. 2: The classroom milieu* (pp. 249–286). New York: Academic Press.

Johnson, D. W. (1993). *Reaching out: Interpersonal effectiveness and self-actualization* (5th ed.) Boston: Allyn and Bacon.

Johnson, J. S., & Newport, E. L. (1989). Critical period effects in second language learning: The influence of maturational state on the acquisition of English as a second language. *Cognitive Psychology, 21,* 60–69.

Jones, E. D., & Southern, W. T. (1991). Conclusions about acceleration: Echoes of a debate. In W. Southern & E. Jones (Eds.), *The academic acceleration of gifted children* (pp. 223–228). New York: Teachers College Press.

Jones, V. F., & Jones, L. S. (1995). *Comprehensive classroom management: Creating positive learning environments* (4th ed.). Boston: Allyn and Bacon.

Jordan, N., & Goldsmith-Phillips, J. (1994). *Assessment of learning disabilities.* Boston: Allyn and Bacon.

Joshua, S., & Dupin, J. J. (1987). Taking into account students conceptions in instructional strategy: An example in physics. *Cognition and Instruction, 4,* 117–135.

Joyce, B., & Weil, M. (1992). *Models of teaching.* Englewood Cliffs, NJ: Prentice-Hall.

Jussim, L. (1986). Self-fulfilling prophecies: A theoretical and integrative review. *Psychological Review, 93,* 429–445.

Kagan, S. (1983). Social orientation among Mexican-American children: A challenge to traditional classroom structures. In E. Garcia (Ed.), *The Mexican-American child: Language, cognition, and social development.* Tempe, AZ: Center for Bilingual Education.

Kanfer, F. H., & Gaelick, L. (1986). Self-management methods. In F. Kanfer & A. Goldstein (Eds.), *Helping people change: A textbook of methods* (3rd ed.). New York: Pergamon.

Kaplan, B. (1984). *Development and growth.* Hillsdale, NJ: Erlbaum.

Kaplan, J. S. (1991). *Beyond behavior modification* (2nd ed.). Austin, TX: Pro-Ed.

Karweit, N. (1989). Time and learning: A review. In R. E. Slavin (Ed.), *School and classroom organization.* Hillsdale, NJ: Erlbaum.

Karweit, N., & Slavin, R. (1981). Measurement and modeling choices in studies of time and learning. *American Educational Research Journal, 18,* 157–171.

Kash, M. M., & Borich, G. (1978). *Teacher behavior and pupil self-concept.* Reading, MA: Addison-Wesley.

Kaufman, P. (1976). The effects of nonverbal behavior on performance and attitudes in a college classroom. *Dissertation Abstracts International, 37* (1-A), 235.

Kazdin, A. E. (1984). *Behavior modification in applied settings.* Homewood, IL: Dorsey Press.

Keefe, J. W. (1982). Assessing student learning styles: An overview. In *Student learning styles and brain behavior.* Reston, VA: National Association of Secondary School Principals.

Keefe, J. W., & Languis, M. L. (1983). *Operational definitions.* Paper presented to the NASSP Learning Styles Task Force. Reston, VA: National Association of Secondary School Principals.

Keefe, J. W., & Monk, J. S. (1986). *Learning style profile examiner's manual.* Reston, VA: National Association of Secondary School Principals.

Keith, T. Z. (1982). Time spent on homework and high school grades: A large-sample path analysis. *Journal of Educational Psychology, 74,* 248–253.

Kiewra, K. A. (1988). Cognitive aspects of autonomous note taking: Control processes, learning strategies, and prior knowledge. *Educational Psychologist, 23,* 39–56.

Kindsvatter, R., Wilen, W., & Ishler, M. (1988). *Dynamics of effective teaching.* New York: Longman.

King, A. (1990). Enhancing peer interaction and learning in the classroom through reciprocal questioning. *American Educational Research Journal, 27,* 664–687.

King, G. (1979, June). Personal communication. University of Texas at Austin.

*Kirk, S., & Gallagher, J. J., & Anastasiow, N. J. (1993). *Educating exceptional children* (7th ed.). Boston: Houghton Mifflin.

*Kirschenbaum, H. (1992). A comprehensive model for values education and morals education. *Phi Delta Kappan, 73,* 771–776.

Kirst, M. (1991a). Interview on assessment issues with Lorrie Shepard. *Educational Researcher, 20*(2), 21–23.

Kirst, M. (1991b). Interview on assessment issues with James Popham. *Educational Researcher, 20*(2), 24–27.

Klatzky, R. L. (1980). *Human memory: Structures and processes* (2nd ed.). San Francisco: Freeman.

Klausmeier, H. J. (1976). Instructional design and the teaching of concepts. In J. Levin & V. Allen (Eds.), *Cognitive learning in children: Theories and strategies.* New York: Academic Press.

Knapp, M., Turnbull, B. J., & Shields, P. M. (1990). New directions for educating children of poverty. *Educational Leadership, 48*(1), 4–9.

Kneedler, P. (1985). California assesses critical thinking. In A. Costa (Ed.), *Developing minds: A resource book for teaching thinking.* Alexandria, VA: Association for Supervision and Curriculum Development.

Kneedler, R. (1984). *Special education for today.* Englewood Cliffs, NJ: Prentice-Hall.

Knight, S. L., & Waxman, H. C. (1991). Students' cognitions and classroom instruction. In H. Waxman & H. Walberg (Eds.), *Effective teaching: Current research.* Berkeley, CA: McCutchan.

Knupfer, N. (1988, April). *Providing teacher guidance for instructional computing: A model for implementation.* Paper presented at the annual meeting of the American Educational Research Association, New Orleans.

Kogan, N. (1983). Stylistic variation in childhood and adolescence: Creativity, metaphor, and cognitive style. In P. Mussen (Ed.), *Handbook of child psychology* (4th ed.), (Vol. 3, pp. 630–706). New York: Wiley.

Kohlberg, L. (1963). The development of children's orientations toward moral order: Sequence in the development of moral thought. *Vita Humana, 6,* 11–33.

Kohlberg, L. (1975). The cognitive-developmental approach to moral education. *Phi Delta Kappan, 56,* 670–677.

Kohlberg, L. (1981). *The philosophy of moral development.* New York: Harper and Row.

Kohlberg, L. (1984). *Essays on moral development.* San Francisco: Harper and Row.

Kohlberg, L., Yaeger, J., & Hjertholm, E. (1969). Private speech: Four studies and a review of theories. *Child Development, 39,* 691–736.

*Kohn, A. (1991). Caring kids; The role of the schools. *Phi Delta Kappan, 72,* 496–506.

*Kohn, A. (1993). Rewards versus learning: A response to Paul Chance. Phi Delta Kappan, 74, 783–787.

Kolata, G. B. (1980). Math and sex; Are girls born with less ability? *Science, 210,* 1234–1235.

*Kotrez, D., Stecher, B., & Diebert, E. (1993). *The reliability of scores from the 1992 Vermont Portfolio Assessment Program.* CSE Technical Report 355. Los Angeles: UCLA Center for the Study of Evaluation.

Kounin, J. (1970). *Discipline and group management in classrooms.* New York: Holt, Rinehart & Winston.

Kounin, J. S., & Doyle, P. H. (1975). Degree of continuity of a lesson's signal system and task involvement of children. *Journal of Educational Psychology, 67,* 159–164.

Kozulin, A. (1990). *Vygotsky's psychology: A biography of ideas.* Cambridge, MA: Harvard University Press.

Krathwohl, D. R., Bloom, B. S., & Masia, B. B. (1964). *Taxonomy of educational objectives. Handbook II: Affective domain.* New York: David McKay.

Kroger, J. (1989). *Identity in adolescence: The balance between self and other.* New York: Routledge.

Krumboltz, J. D., & Krumboltz, H. B. (1972). *Changing children's behavior.* Englewood Cliffs, NJ: Prentice-Hall.

Kulik, C. C., & Kulik, J. A. (1982). Effects of ability grouping on secondary school students: A meta-analysis of evaluation findings. *American Educational Research Journal, 19,* 415–428.

Kulik, J. A., & Kulik, C. C. (1984). Effects of accelerated instruction on students. *Review of Educational Research, 54,* 409–425.

Kulik, J. A., Kulik, C. C., & Bangert, R. L. (1984, April). Effects of practice on aptitude and achievement test scores. *American Educational Research Journal, 21,* 435–447.

Kupersmidt, J. B., Coie, J. D., & Dodge, K. A. (1990). The role of poor peer relations in the development of disorder. In S. Asher & J. Coie (Eds.), *Peer rejection in childhood* (pp. 274–305). New York: Cambridge.

Kutz, R. E. (1991). *Teaching elementary mathematics.* Boston: Allyn and Bacon.

*Laboratory of Comparative Human Cognition (1983). Culture and cognitive development. In W. Kessen (Ed.), *Handbook of child psychology, Vol. 1. History, theory, and methods* (4th ed., pp. 295–356). New York: Wiley.

Lamb, M. E. (1982). Parent-infant interaction, attachment, and socioemotional development in infancy. In R. Emde & R. Harmon (Eds.), *The development of attachment and affiliative systems.* New York: Plenum.

Land, M. L. (1987). Vagueness and clarity. In M. Dunkin (Ed.), *The international encyclopedia of teaching and teacher education* (pp. 392–397). New York: Pergamon.

*Langer, E. J. (1993). A mindful education. *Educational Psychologist, 28,* 43–51.

*Language Development and Hypermedia Group (1992). "Open" software design: A case study. *Educational Technology, 32,* 43–55.

*Languis, M. L., & Miller, D. C. (1992). Luria's theory of brain functioning: A model for research in cognitive psychophysiology. *Educational Psychologist, 27,* 493–512.

Laosa, L. (1984). Ethnic, socioeconomic, and home language influences on early performance on measures of ability. *Journal of Educational Psychology, 76,* 1178–1198.

Larrivee, B. (1985). *Effective teaching behaviors for successful mainstreaming.* New York: Longman.

Lefcourt, H. (1966). Internal versus external control of reinforcement: A review. *Psychological Bulletin, 65,* 206–220.

*Lefton, L. A. (1994). *Psychology* (5th ed.). Boston: Allyn and Bacon.

Leinhardt, G. (1986). Expertise in mathematics teaching. *Educational Leadership, 43,* 28–33.

Leinhardt, G. (1988). Situated knowledge and expertise in teaching. In J. Calderhead (Ed.), *Teachers' professional learning.* London: Farmer Press.

Leinhardt, G., & Greeno, J. D. (1986). The cognitive skill of teaching. *Journal of Educational Psychology, 78,* 75–95.

Leinhardt, G., & Smith, D. (1985). Expertise in mathematics instruction: Subject matter knowledge. *Journal of Educational Psychology, 77,* 247–271.

Leming, J. S. (1981). Curriculum effectiveness in value/moral education. *Journal of Moral Education, 10,* 147–164.

Lepper, M. R. (1988). Motivational considerations in the study of instruction. *Cognition and Instruction, 5,* 289–309.

Lepper, M. R., & Greene, D. (1978). *The hidden costs of rewards: New perspectives on the psychology of human motivation.* Hillsdale, NJ: Erlbaum.

Lerner, B. (1981). The minimum competency testing movement: Social, scientific, and legal implications. *American Psychologist, 36,* 1057–1066.

Lever, J. (1978). Sex differences in the complexity of children's play and games. *American Sociologist Review, 43,* 471–483.

Levin, J. R. (1985). Educational applications of mnemonic pictures: Possibilities beyond your wildest imagination. In A. A. Sheikh (Ed.), *Imagery in the educational process.* Farmingdale, NY: Baywood.

*Levin, J. R. Mnemonic strategies and classroom learning: A twenty-year report card. *Elementary School Journal, 94,* 235–254.

Levin, J. R., McCormick, C. B., Miller, G. E., Kessler, J., & Pressley, M. (1981). *Mnemonic versus nonmnemonic vocabulary learning strategies for children.* Report from the Project on Studies in Language: Reading and Communication. University of Wisconsin.

Lieber, J., & Semmel, M. (1988, April). *The relationship of group configuration to educational outcomes using microcomputers.* Paper presented at the annual meeting of the American Educational Research Association, New Orleans.

Linden, K. (1992). *Cooperative learning and problem solving.* Prospect Heights, IL: Waveland Press.

Lindsay, P. H., & Norman, D. A. (1977). *Human information processing: An introduction to psychology* (2nd ed.). New York: Academic Press.

Linn, M. C., & Hyde, J. S. (1989). Gender, mathematics, and science. *Educational Researcher, 18,* 17–27.

Linn, R. L. (1986). Educational testing and assessment: Research needs and policy issues. *American Psychologist, 41,* 1153–1160.

Linn, R., Klein, S., & Hart, F. (1972). The nature and correlates of law school essay grades. *Educational and Psychological Measurement, 32,* 267–279.

Lipscomb, T. J., MacAllister, H. A., & Bregman, N. J. (1985). A developmental inquiry into the effects of multiple models on children's generosity. *Merrill-Palmer Quarterly, 31,* 335–344.

*Locke, E. A., & Latham, G. P. (1990). *A theory of goal setting and task performance.* Englewood Cliffs, NJ: Prentice-Hall.

Lohman, D. L. (1989). Human intelligence: An introduction to advances in theory and research. *Review of Educational Research, 59,* 333–374.

Lortie, D. (1977). The balance of control and autonomy in elementary school teaching. In D. Erickson (Ed.), *Educational organization and administration* (pp. 335–371). Berkeley, CA: McCutchan.

Lovitt, T. C. (1977). *In spite of my resistance, I've learned from children.* Columbus, OH: Charles E. Merrill.

Luiten, J., Ames, W., & Ackerson, G. (1980). A meta-analysis of the effects of advance organizers on learning and retention. *American Educational Research Journal, 17,* 211–218.

Lyman, H. B. (1986). *Test scores and what they mean* (4th ed.). Englewood Cliffs, NJ: Prentice-Hall.

*Lytton, H., & Romney, D. M. (1991). Parents' sex-related differential socialization of boys and girls: A meta-analysis. *Psychological Bulletin, 109,* 267–296.

McClelland, D. (1973). Testing for competence rather than for intelligence. *American Psychologist, 28,* 1–14.

McClelland, D. (1985). *Human motivation.* Glenview, IL: Scott, Foresman.

McClelland, D. C. (1993). Intelligence is not the best predictor of job performance. *Current Directions in Psychological Science, 2,* 5–6.

McClelland, D., Atkinson, J. W., Clark, R. W., & Lowell, E. L. (1953). *The achievement motive.* New York: Appleton-Century-Crofts.

McClelland, D., & Pilon, D. (1983). Sources of adult motives in patterns of parent behavior in early childhood. *Journal of Personality and Social Psychology, 44,* 564–574.

McCombs, B. L., & Marzano, R. J. (1990). Putting the self in self-regulated learning: The self as agent in integrating skill and will. *Educational Psychologist, 25,* 51–70.

McCormack, S. (1989). Response to Render, Padilla, and Krank: But practitioners say it works! *Educational Leadership, 46*(6), 77–79.

McCormick, C. B., & Levin, J. R. (1987). Mnemonic prose-learning strategies. In M. Pressley & M. McDaniel (Eds.), *Imaginary and related mnemonic processes.* New York: Springer-Verlag.

*McDonald, J. P. (1993). Three pictures of an exhibition: Warm, cool, and hard. *Phi Delta Kappan, 6,* 480–485.

McGinley, P., & McGinley, H. (1970). Reading groups as psychological groups. *Journal of Experimental Education, 39,* 36–42.

McGuire, J. (1988). Gender stereotypes of parents with two-year-olds and beliefs about gender differences in behavior. *Sex Roles, 19,* 233–240.

McKenzie, T. L., & Rushall, B. S. (1974). Effects of self-recording on attendance and performance in a competitive swimming training environment. *Journal of Applied Behavior Analysis, 7,* 199–206.

McLaughlin, T. F., & Gnagey, W. J. (1981, April). *Self-management and pupil self-control.* Paper presented at the annual meeting of the American Educational Research Association, Los Angeles.

MacMillan, D. L. (1982). *Mental retardation in school and society.* Boston: Little, Brown.

McNemar, Q. (1964). Lost: Our intelligence? Why? *American Psychologist, 19,* 871–882.

Macionis, J. J. (1991). *Sociology* (3rd ed.). Englewood Cliffs, NJ: Prentice-Hall.

•Macionis, J. J. (1994). *Sociology* (4th ed.). Englewood Cliffs, NJ: Prentice-Hall.

•Madaus, G. F., & Kellaghan, T. (1993). Testing as a mechanism of public policy: A brief history. *Measurement and Evaluation in Counseling and Development, 26,* 6–10.

Madsen, C. H., Becker, W. C., & Thomas, D. R. (1968). Rules, praise, and ignoring: Elements of elementary classroom control. *Journal of Applied Behavior Analysis, 1,* 139–150.

Madsen, C. H., Becker, W. C., Thomas, D. R., Koser, L., & Plager, E. (1968). An analysis of the reinforcing function of "sit down" commands. In R. K. Parker (Ed.), *Readings in educational psychology.* Boston: Allyn and Bacon.

Maehr, M. L. (1974). *Sociocultural origins of achievement.* Monterey, CA: Brooks/Cole.

•Maehr, M. L., & Anderman, E.M. (1993). Reinventing schools for early adolescents: Emphasizing task goals. *The Elementary School Journal, 93,* 593–610.

Mager, R. (1975). *Preparing instructional objectives* (2nd ed.). Palo Alto, CA: Fearon.

Mahoney, M. J., & Thoresen, C. E. (1974). *Self-control: Power to the person.* Monterey, CA: Brooks/Cole.

Maier, N. R. F. (1933). An aspect of human reasoning. *British Journal of Psychology, 24,* 144–155.

Maker, C. J. (1987). Gifted and talented. In V. Richardson-Koehler (Ed.), *Educators' handbook: A research perspective* (pp. 420–455). New York: Longman.

Manaster, G. (1989). *Adolescent development: A psychological interpretation.* Itasca, IL: F. E. Peacock.

Mandlebaum, L. H., Russell, S. C., Krouse, J., & Gonter, M. (1983). Assertive discipline: An effective classwide behavior management program. *Behavior Disorders, 8*(4), 258–264.

Manning, B. H. (1991). *Cognitive self-instruction of classroom processes.* Albany, NY: State University of New York Press.

•Mantzicopolos, P., & Morrison, D. (1992). Kindergarten retention: Academic and behavioral outcomes through the end of second grade. *American Educational Research Journal, 29,* 182–198.

Maratsos, M. P. (1989). Innateness and plasticity in language acquisition. In M. L. Rice & R. L. Schiefelbusch (Eds.), *The teachability of language* (pp. 105–125). Baltimore, MD: Brooks/Cole.

Marcia, J. (1980). Ego identity development. In J. Adelson (Ed.), *The handbook of adolescent psychology.* New York: Wiley.

Marcia, J. (1987). The identity status approach to the study of ego identity development. In T. Honess & K. Yardley (Eds.), *Self and identity: Perspectives across the life span.* London: Routledge & Kagan Paul.

Markman, E. M. (1977). Realizing that you don't understand: A preliminary investigation. *Child Development, 48,* 986–992.

Markman, E. M. (1979). Realizing that you don't understand: Elementary school children's awareness of inconsistencies. *Child Development, 50,* 643–655.

•Markman, E. M. (1990). Constraints children place on word meanings. *Cognitive Science, 14,* 57–77.

Marsh, H. W. (1987). The big-fish-little-pond effect on academic self-concept. *Journal of Educational Psychology, 79,* 280–295.

Marsh, H. W. (1990). Influences of internal and external frames of reference on the formation of math and English self-concepts. *Journal of Educational Psychology, 82,* 107–116.

Marsh, H. W., & Holmes, I. W. M. (1990). Multidimensional self-concepts: Construct validation of responses by children. *American Educational Research Journal, 27,* 89–118.

Marsh, H. W., & Shavelson, R. (1985). Self-concept: Its multifaceted, hierarchical structure. *Educational Psychologist, 20,* 107–123.

Marshall, H. H. (1987). Motivational strategies of three fifth-grade teachers. *Elementary School Journal, 88,* 135–150.

Marshall, H. H. (1989). The development of self-concept. *Young Children, 44*(5), 44–51.

•Marshall, H. H. (Ed.) (1992). *Redefining student learning: Roots of educational change.* Norwood, NJ: Ablex.

Marshall, S. (1984). Sex differences in children's mathematics achievement: Solving computations and story problems. *Journal of Educational Psychology, 76,* 194–204.

•Martin, C. L. (1989). Children's use of gender-related information in making social judgments. *Developmental Psychology, 25,* 80–88.

•Martin, C. L., & Little, J. K. (1990). The relation of gender understanding to children's sex-typed preferences and gender stereotypes. *Child Development, 61,* 1427–1439.

Martin, G., & Pear, J. (1992). *Behavior modification: What it is and how to do it* (4th ed.). Englewood Cliffs, NJ: Prentice-Hall.

Martindale, C. (1991). *Cognitive psychology: A neural-network approach.* Pacific Grove, CA: Brooks/Cole.

Maslow, A. H. (1970). *Motivation and personality* (2nd ed.). New York: Harper and Row.

Maslow, A. H. (1968). *Toward a psychology of being* (2nd ed.). New York: Van Nostrand.

•Mason, D. A., & Good, T. L. (1993). Effects of two-group and whole-class teaching on regrouped elementary students' mathematics achievement. *American Educational Research Journal, 30,* 328–360.

Mathinos, D., & Woodward, A. (1991). Instructional computing in an elementary school: The rhetoric and reality of an innovation. *Journal of Curriculum Studies.*

Mayer, R. E. (1979). Can advance organizers influence meaningful learning? *Review of Educational Research, 49,* 371–383.

Mayer, R. E. (1982). Memory for algebra story problems. *Journal of Educational Psychology, 74,* 199–216.

Mayer, R. E. (1983a). Can you repeat that? Qualitative and quantitative effects of repetition and advance organizers on learning from science prose. *Journal of Educational Psychology, 75,* 40–49.

Mayer, R. E. (1983b). *Thinking, problem solving, cognition.* San Francisco: Freeman.

Mayer, R. E. (1984). Twenty-five years of research on advance organizers. *Instructional Science, 8,* 133–169.

Mayer, R. E. (1992). *Thinking, problem solving, cognition* (2nd ed.). New York: Freeman.

•Mayer, R. E. (1992). Cognition and instruction: Their historic meeting within educational psychology. *Journal of Educational Psychology, 84,* 405–412.

Means, B., & Knapp, M. S. (1991). Cognitive approaches to teaching advanced skills to educationally disadvantaged students. *Phi Delta Kappan, 73,* 282–289.

Mecklenburger, J. A. (1990). Educational technology is not enough. *Phi Delta Kappan, 72,* 105–108.

Medley, D. M. (1979). The effectiveness of teachers. In P. Peterson & H. Walberg (Eds.), *Research on teaching: Concepts, findings, and implications* (pp. 11–27). Berkeley, CA: McCutchan.

Meek, A. (1991). On thinking about teaching: A conversation with Eleanor Duckworth. *Educational Leadership, 48*(6), 30–34.

Meichenbaum, D. (1977). *Cognitive behavior modification: An integrative approach.* New York: Plenum.

Meichenbaum, D. (1986). Cognitive behavior modification. In F. Kanfer & A. Goldstein (Eds.), *Helping people change: A textbook of methods* (3rd ed., pp. 346–380). New York: Pergamon.

Meichenbaum, D., Burland, S., Gruson, L., & Cameron, R. (1985). Metacognitive assessment. In S. Yussen (Ed.), *The growth of reflection in children.* Orlando, FL: Academic Press.

Meisels, S. J. (1989). High-stakes testing in kindergarten. *Educational Leadership, 46*(7), 16–22.

Mendell, P. R. (1971). Retrieval and representation in long-term memory. *Psychonomic Science, 23,* 295–296.

Mendels, G. E., & Flanders, J. P. (1973). Teacher's expectations and pupil performance. *American Educational Research Journal, 10,* 203–212.

Mercer, C. (1992). *Students with learning disabilities* (4th ed.), Columbus: Merrill.

Merseth, K. K. (1993). How old is the shepherd? An essay about mathematics education. *Phi Delta Kappan, 74,* 548–554.

Messick, S. (1975). The standard problem: Meaning and values in measurement and evaluation. *American Psychologist, 35,* 1012–1027.

Metcalfe, B. (1981). Self-concept and attitude toward school. *British Journal of Educational Psychology, 51,* 66–76.

Meyer, B. J. F., Brandt, D. M., & Bluth, G. J. (1980). Use of top-level structure in text: Key for reading comprehension of ninth-graders. *Reading Research Quarterly, 15,* 72–103.

Miller, G. A. (1956). The magical number seven, plus or minus two: Some limits on our capacity for processing information. *Psychological Review, 63,* 81–97.

Miller, G. A., Galanter, E., & Pribram, K. H. (1960). *Plans and the structure of behavior.* New York: Holt, Rinehart & Winston.

Miller, K., & Gelman, R. (1983). The child's representation of number: A multidimensional scaling analysis. *Child Development, 54,* 1470–1479.

Miller, R. B. (1962). Analysis and specification of behavior for training. In R. Glaser (Ed.), *Training research and education: Science edition.* New York: Wiley.

Milliken math sequences. (1980). (Computer program.) St. Louis, MO: Milliken Publishing.

Mills, C. J., Ablard, K. E., & Stumpf, H. (1993). Gender differences in academically talented young students' mathematical reasoning: Patterns across age and subskills. *Journal of Educational Psychology, 85,* 340–346.

Mills, J. R., & Jackson, N. E. (1990). Predictive significance of early giftedness: The case of precocious reading. *Journal of Educational Psychology, 82,* 410–419.

Mitchell, B. M. (1984). An update on gifted and talented education in the U.S. *Roeper Review, 6,* 161–163.

Moely, B. E., Hart, S. S., Santulli, K., Leal, L., Johnson, T., Rao, N., & Burney, L. (1986). How do teachers teach memory skills? In J. Levin & M. Pressley (Eds.), *Educational Psychologist, 21* (Special issue on learning strategies), 55–72.

Moos, R. H., & Moos, B. S. (1978). Classroom social climate and student absences and grades. *Journal of Educational Psychology, 70,* 263–269.

Morgan, M. (1985). Self-monitoring of attained subgoals in private study. *Journal of Educational Psychology, 77,* 623–630.

Morris, C. G. (1988). *Psychology: An introduction* (6th ed.). Englewood Cliffs, NJ: Prentice-Hall.

Morris, C. G. (1991). *Psychology: An introduction* (7th ed.). Englewood Cliffs, NJ: Prentice-Hall.

Morrow, L. (1983). Home and school correlates of early interest in literature. *Journal of Educational Research, 76,* 221–230.

Morrow, L., & Weinstein, C. (1986). Encouraging voluntary reading: The impact of a literature. *Reading Research Quarterly, 21,* 330–346.

Moshman, D., Glover, J. A., & Bruning, R. H. (1987). *Developmental psychology.* Boston: Little, Brown.

Moskowitz, B. A. (1978). The acquisition of language. *Scientific American, 239,* 92–108.

Moskowitz, G., & Hayman, M. L. (1976). Successful strategies of inner-city teachers; A year-long study. *Journal of Educational Research, 69,* 283–289.

Moss, P. A. (1992). Shifting conceptions of validity in educational measurement: Implications for performance assessment. *Review of Educational Research, 62,* 229–258.

Murray, H. G. (1983). Low inference classroom teaching behavior and student ratings of college teaching effectiveness. *Journal of Educational Psychology, 75,* 138–149.

Musgrave, G. R. (1975). *Individualized instruction: Teaching strategies focusing on the learner.* Boston, MA: Allyn and Bacon.

Mussen, P., Conger, J. J., & Kagan, J. (1984). *Child development and personality* (6th ed.). New York: Harper and Row.

National Center for Education Statistics. (1990). *Digest of Education Statistics.* Washington, DC: Center for Education Statistics.

National Center for Research on Cultural Diversity and Second Language Learning, Center for Applied Linguistics (1992). *Instructional conversations.* Washington, DC: ERIC Document #EDO-FL-92-01.

National Commission on Excellence in Education. (1983). *A nation at risk: The imperative for educational reform.* Washington, DC: U.S. Government Printing Office.

National Governors Association (1989). *Results in education: 1989.* Washington, DC: NGA.

National Joint Committee on Learning Disabilities (1989). *Letter from NJCLD to member organizations. Topic: Modifications to the NJCLD definition of learning disabilities.*

National Organization for Victims' Assistance. (1989, March). *Newsletter*

National Science Foundation (1988). *Women and minorities in science and engineering* (NSF 88–301). Washington, DC: National Science Foundation.

Naveh-Benjamin, M. (1991). A comparison of training programs intended for different types of test-anxious students: Further support for an information-processing model. *Journal of Educational Psychology, 83,* 134–139.

Naveh-Benjamin, M., McKeachie, W. J., & Lin, Y. (1987). Two types of test-anxious students: Support for an information processing model. *Journal of Educational Psychology, 79,* 131–136.

Neimark, E. (1975). Intellectual development during adolescence. In F. D. Horowitz (Ed.), *Review of child development research* (Vol. 4). Chicago: University of Chicago Press.

Neisser, U. (1979). The concept of intelligence. In R. Sternberg & D. Detterman (Eds.), *Human intelligence: Perspectives on its theory and measurement* (pp. 179–190). Norwood, NJ: Ablex.

Nelson, K. (1981). Individual differences in language development: Implications for development and language. *Developmental Psychology, 17,* 170–187.

Nelson, K. (1986). *Event knowledge.* Hillsdale, NJ: Erlbaum.

Newby, T. J. (1991). Classroom motivation: Strategies of first-year teachers. *Journal of Educational Psychology, 83,* 195–200.

Newcomb, M. D., & Bentler, P. M. (1989). Substance use and abuse among children and teenagers. *American Psychologist, 44,* 242–248.

Newcombe, N., & Baenninger, M. (1990). The role of expectations in spatial test performance: A meta-analysis. *Sex Roles, 16,* 25–37.

• Newmann, F. M., & Wehlage, G. G. (1993). Five standards of authentic instruction. *Educational Leadership, 50*(7), 8–12.

Newsweek (1984, September 24). Why teachers fail, pp. 64–70.

Newsweek (Summer, 1991). *The end of innocence,* pp. 62–64. Special Edition: How Kids Grow.

Nicholls, J. G., & Miller, A. (1984). Conceptions of ability and achievement motivation. In R. Ames & C. Ames (Eds.), *Research on motivation in education. Vol. 1: Student Motivation* (pp. 39–73). New York: Academic Press.

• Nielsen, L. (1993). Students from divorced and blended families. *Educational Psychology Review, 5,* 177–199.

Niemiec, R., & Walberg, H. J. (1987). Comparative effects of computer-assisted instruction: A synthesis of reviews. *Journal of Educational Computing Research, 3,* 19–37.

Noddings, N. (1990). Constructivism in mathematics education. In R. Davis, C. Maher, & N. Noddings (Eds.), *Constructivist views on the teaching and learning of mathematics* (pp. 7–18). Monograph 4 of the National Council of Teachers of Mathematics, Reston, VA.

Norman, D. P. (1982). *Learning and memory.* San Francisco: Freeman.

Novak, J. D., & Musonda, D. (1991). A twelve-year longitudinal study of science concept learning. *American Educational Research Journal, 28,* 117–154.

Nucci, L. (1987). Synthesis of research on moral development. *Educational Leadership, 44*(5), 86–92.

Nungester, R. J., & Duchastel, P. C. (1982). Testing versus review: Effects on retention. *Journal of Educational Psychology, 74,* 18–22.

• Nuthall, G., & Alton-Lee, A. (1992). Understanding how students learn in classrooms. In M. Pressley, K. Harris, & J. Guthrie (Eds.), *Promoting academic competence and literacy in school* (pp. 57–87). San Diego: Academic Press.

• Nuthall, G., & Alton-Lee, A. (1993). Predicting learning from student experience of teaching: A theory of student knowledge in classrooms. *American Educational Research Journal, 30,* 799–840.

Nuthall, G., & Alton-Lee, A. (1990). Research on teaching and learning: Thirty years of change. *Elementary School Journal, 90,* 546–570.

Oakes, J. (1990). Opportunities, achievement, and choice: Women and minority students in science and math. *Review of Research in Education, 16,* 153–222.

Ogbu, J. (1987). Variability in minority school performance: A problem in search of an explanation. *Anthropology and Education Quarterly, 18,* 312–334.

Ogden, J. E., Brophy, J. E., & Evertson, C. M. (1977, April). *An experimental investigation of organization and management techniques in first-grade reading groups.* Paper presented at the annual meeting of the American Educational Research Association, New York.

O'Leary, K. D. (1980). Pills or skills for hyperactive children? *Journal of Applied Behavior Analysis, 13,* 191–204.

O'Leary, K. D., Kaufman, K. F., Kass, R. E., & Drabman, R. S. (1970). The effects of loud and soft reprimands on the behavior of disruptive students. *Exceptional Children, 37,* 145–155.

O'Leary, K. D., & O'Leary, S. (Eds.). (1977). *Classroom management: The successful use of behavior modification* (2nd ed.). Elmsford, NY: Pergamon.

O'Leary, K. D., & Wilson, G. T. (1987). *Behavior therapy: Application and outcome.* Englewood Cliffs, NJ: Prentice-Hall.

O'Leary, S. G., & O'Leary, K. D. (1976). Behavior modification in the schools. In H. Leitenberg (Ed.), *Handbook of behavior modification and behavior therapy.* Englewood Cliffs, NJ: Prentice-Hall.

Ollendick, T. H., Dailey, D., & Shapiro, E. S. (1983). Vicarious reinforcement: Expected and unexpected effects. *Journal of Applied Behavior Analysis, 16,* 485–491.

Olsen, L. (1988). *Crossing the schoolhouse border: Immigrant students and the California public schools.* San Francisco: California Tomorrow.

O'Neil, J. (1990a). Link between style, culture proves divisive. *Educational Leadership, 48*(2), 8.

O'Neil, J. (1990b). Piecing together the restructuring puzzle. *Educational Leadership, 47*(7), 4–10.

O'Neil, J. (1991). Drive for national standards picking up steam. *Educational Leadership, 48*(5), 4–8.

• O'Neil, J. (1993). Can national standards make a difference?. *Educational Leadership, 50*(5), 4–8.

• Onslow, M. (1992). Choosing a treatment program for early stuttering: Issues and future directions. *Journal of Speech and Hearing Research, 35,* 983–993.

• Ortony, A., Clore, G. L., & Collins, A. (1988). *The cognitive structure of emotions.* Cambridge: Cambridge University Press.

Osborn, A. F. (1963). *Applied imagination* (3rd ed.). New York: Scribner's.

Ovando, C. J. (1989). Language diversity and education. In J. Banks & C. McGee Banks (Eds.), *Multicultural education: Issues and perspectives* (pp. 208–228). Boston: Allyn and Bacon.

Owen, L. (1985). *None of the above: Behind the myth of scholastic aptitude.* Boston: Houghton Mifflin.

Page, E. B. (1958). Teacher comments and student performances: A 74-classroom experiment in school motivation. *Journal of Educational Psychology, 49,* 173–181.

Paivio, A. (1971). *Imagery and verbal processes.* New York: Holt, Rinehart & Winston.

Paivio, A. (1986). *Mental representations: A dual-coding approach.* New York: Oxford University Press.

Palincsar, A. S. (1986). The role of dialogue in providing scaffolded instruction. In J. Levin & M. Pressley (Eds.), *Educational Psychologist, 21* (Special issue on learning strategies), 73–98.

Palincsar, A. S., & Brown, A. L. (1984). Reciprocal teaching of comprehension-fostering and monitoring activities. *Cognition and Instruction, 1,* 117–175.

Pallas, A. M., & Alexander, K. (1983). Sex differences in quantitative SAT performance: New evidence on the differential coursework hypothesis. *American Educational Research Journal, 20,* 165–182.

Pallas, A. M., Natriello, G., & McDill, E. L. (1989). The changing nature of the disadvantaged population: Current dimensions and future trends. *Educational Researcher, 18*(5), 16–22.

• Papert, S. (1980). *Mindstorms: Children, computers, and powerful ideas.* New York: Basic Books.

Papert, S. (1993). *The children's machine: Rethinking school in the age of the computer.* New York: Basic Books.

Paris, S. (1988, April). *Fusing skill and will: The integration of cognitive and motivational psychology.* Paper presented at the annual meeting of the American Educational Research Association, New Orleans.

Paris, S. G., Lipson, M. Y., & Wixson, K. K. (1983). Becoming a strategic reader. *Contemporary Educational Psychology, 8,* 293–316.

Pasch, M., Sparks-Langer, G., Gardner, T. G., Starko, A. J., & Moody, C. D. (1991). *Teaching as decision making: Instructional practices for the successful teacher.* New York: Longman.

Pauk, W. (1989). *How to study in college* (4th ed.). Boston: Houghton Mifflin.

Paulman, R. G., & Kennelly, K. J. (1984). Test anxiety and ineffective test taking: Different names, same construct? *Journal of Educational Psychology, 76,* 279–288.

Paulson, F. L., Paulson, P. R., & Meyer, C. A. (1991). What makes a portfolio a portfolio? *Educational Leadership, 48*(5), 60–63.

Pearson, P. D. (1989). Commentary: Reading the whole language movement. *Elementary School Journal, 90,* 231–241.

Peeck, J., van den Bosch, A. B., & Kreupeling, W. J. (1982). Effect of mobilizing prior knowledge on learning from text. *Journal of Educational Psychology, 74,* 771–777.

Pelham, W. E. (1981). Attention deficits in hyperactive and learning-disabled children. *Exceptional Education Quarterly, 2,* 13–23.

Pelham, W. E., & Murphy, H. A. (1986). Attention deficit and conduct disorders. In M. Hersen (Ed.), *Pharmacological and behavioral treatment: An integrative approach* (pp. 108–148). New York: Wiley.

Penfield, W. (1969). Consciousness, memory, and man's conditioned reflexes. In K. Pribram (Ed.), *On the biology of learning.* New York: Harcourt Brace Jovanovich.

*Peng, S. & Lee, R. (1992, April). *Home variables, parent-child activities, and academic achievement: A study of 1988 eighth graders.* Paper presented at the annual meeting of the American Educational Research Association, San Francisco.

Peper, R. J., & Mayer, R. E. (1986). Generative effects of note taking during science lectures. *Journal of Educational Psychology, 78,* 34–38.

Perkins, D. N. (1986). Thinking frames. *Educational Leadership, 43,* 4–11.

Perkins, D. N. (1987). Thinking frames: An integrative perspective on teaching cognitive skills. In J. B. Baron & R. J. Sternberg (Eds.), *Teaching thinking skills: Theory and practice* (pp. 41–85). New York: Freeman.

*Perkins, D. N. (1991, May). Technology meets constructivism: Do they make a marriage? *Educational Technology, 31,* 18–23.

Perkins, D. N., & Salomon, G. (1989). Are cognitive skills context-bound? *Educational Researcher, 18,* 16–25.

*Perkins, D., Jay, E., & Tishman, S. (1993). New conceptions of thinking: From ontology to education. *Educational Psychologist, 28,* 67–85.

*Perrone, V. (1994). How to engage students in learning. *Educational Leadership, 51*(5), 11–13.

Peters, E. E., & Levin, J. R. (1986). Effects of a mnemonic imagery strategy on good and poor reader's prose recall. *Reading Research Quarterly, 21,* 179–192.

Peterson, C., & Barrett, L. C. (1987). Explanatory style and academic performance among university freshmen. *Journal of Personality and Social Psychology, 53,* 603–607.

*Peterson, M. P. (1993). Physical and sexual abuse among school children: Prevalence and prevention. *Educational Psychology Review, 5,* 63–86.

*Peterson, P. L. (1992). Revising their thinking: Keisha Coleman and her third-grade mathematics class. In H. Marshall (Ed.) *Redefining student learning: Roots of educational change* (pp. 151–176). Norwood, NJ: Ablex.

Peterson, P. (1979). Direct instruction reconsidered. In P. Peterson & H. Walberg (Eds.), *Research on teaching: Concepts, findings, and implications* (pp. 57–69). Berkeley, CA: McCutchan.

Peterson, P. L., & Comeaux, M. A. (1989). Assessing the teacher as a reflective professional: New perspectives on teacher evaluation. In A. Woolfolk (Ed.), *Research perspectives on the graduate preparation of teachers* (pp. 132–152). Englewood Cliffs, NJ: Prentice-Hall.

Peterson, P., Fennema, E., & Carpenter, T. (1989). Using knowledge of how students think about mathematics. *Educational Leadership, 46*(4), 42–46.

Peterson, P., Janicki, T. C., & Swing, S. R. (1980). Aptitude-treatment interaction effects of three social studies teaching approaches. *American Educational Research Journal, 17,* 339–360.

Peterson, S. E., DeGracie, J. S., & Ayabe, C. R. (1987). A longitudinal study of the effects of retention/promotion on academic achievement. *American Educational Research Journal, 24,* 107–118.

Pfeffer, C. R. (1981). Developmental issues among children of separation and divorce. In I. Stuart & L. Abt (Eds.), *Children of separation and divorce.* New York: Van Nostrand Reinhold.

Pfeffer, C. R. (1986). *The suicidal child.* New York: Guilford Press.

Pfiffner, L. J., Rosen, L. A., & O'Leary, S. G. (1985). The efficacy of an all-positive approach to classroom management. *Journal of Applied Behavior Analysis, 18,* 257–261.

*Phinney, J., & Alipiria, L. (1990). Ethnic identity in college students from four ethnic groups. *Journal of Adolescence, 13,* 171–183.

Piaget, J. (1954). *The construction of reality in the child* (M. Cook, Trans.). New York: Basic Books.

Piaget, J. (1963). *Origins of intelligence in children.* New York: Norton.

Piaget, J. (1965). *The moral judgment of the child.* New York: Free Press.

Piaget, J. (1970a). Piaget's theory. In P. Mussen (Ed.), *Handbook of child psychology* (3rd ed.). New York: Wiley.

Piaget, J. (1970b). *The science of education and the psychology of the child.* New York: Orion Press.

Piaget, J. (1974). *Understanding causality* (D. Miles and M. Miles, Trans.). New York: Norton.

*Pierson, L. H., & Connell, J. P. (1992). Effect of grade retention on self-system processes, school engagement. and academic performance. *Journal of Educational Psychology, 84,* 300–307.

Pine, G. J., & Hilliard, A. G., III (1990). Rx for racism: Imperatives for America's schools. *Phi Delta Kappan, 71,* 593–600.

*Pintrich, P. R., Marx, R. W., & Boyle, R. A. (1993). Beyond cold conceptual change: The role of motivational beliefs and classroom contextual factors in the process of conceptual change. *Review of Educational Research, 63,* 167–199.

*Pitts, J. M. (1992). Constructivism: Learning rethought. In J. B. Smith & J. C. Coleman, Jr. (Eds.), *School Library Media Annual* (Vol. 10, pp. 14–25). Englewood, CO: Libraries Unlimited.

*Popham, W. J. (1993). *Educational evaluation* (3rd ed.). Boston: Allyn and Bacon.

Posner, M. I. (1973). *Cognition: An introduction*. Glenview, IL: Scott, Foresman.

Powell, R. R., Garcia, J., & Denton, J. J. (1985, March). *The portrayal of minorities and women in selected elementary science series*. Paper presented at the annual meeting of the American Educational Research Association, Chicago.

Powers, S. I., Hauser, S. T., & Kilner, L. A. (1989). Adolescent mental health. *American Psychologist, 44*, 200–208.

Prawat, R. S. (1991). The value of ideas: The immersion approach to the development of thinking. *Educational Researcher, 20*, 3–10.

Prawat, R. S. (1992). Teachers beliefs about teaching and learning: A constructivist perspective. *American Journal of Education, 100*, 354–395.

Prawat, R. S., Anderson, A., Diamond, B., McKeague, D., & Whitmer, S. (1981, April). *Teacher thinking about the affective domain: An interview study*. Paper presented at the annual meeting of the American Educational Research Association, Los Angeles.

Premack, D. (1965). Reinforcement theory. In D. Levine (Ed.), *Nebraska symposium on motivation* (Vol. 13). Lincoln, NE: University of Nebraska Press.

Presidential Task Force on Psychology in Education. (1993). *Learner-Centered Psychological Principles: Guidelines for School Redesign and Reform*. Washington, DC: American Psychological Association.

Pressley, M. (1982). Elaboration and memory development. *Child Development, 53*, 296–309.

Pressley, M. (1986). The relevance of the good strategy user model to the teaching of mathematics. In J. Levin & M. Pressley (Eds.), *Educational Psychologist, 21* (Special issue on learning strategies), 139–161.

Pressley, M. (1991). Comparing Hall (1988) with related research on elaborative mnemonics. *Journal of Educational Psychology, 83*, 165–170.

Pressley, M., Barkowski, J. G., & Schneider, W. (1987). Cognitive strategies: Good strategy users coordinate metacognition and knowledge. In R. Vasta & G. Whitehurst (Eds.), *Annals of Child Development. Vol. 4*. Greenwich, CT: JAI Press.

Pressley, M., Levin, J., & Delaney, H. D. (1982). The mnemonic keyword method. *Review of Research in Education, 52*, 61–91.

Price, G., & O'Leary, K. D. (1974). *Teaching children to develop high performance standards*. Unpublished manuscript. State University of New York at Stony Brook.

Pring, R. (1971). Bloom's taxonomy: A philosophical critique. *Cambridge Journal of Education, 1*, 83–91.

Purcell, P., & Stewart, L. (1990). Dick and Jane in 1989. *Sex Roles, 22*, 177–185.

Purkey, W. W., & Novak, J. M. (1984). *Inviting school success: A self-concept approach to teaching and learning*. Belmont, CA: Wadsworth.

Quality Education Data (1988). *Microcomputer and VCR usage in schools, 1987–1988*. Denver: Quality Education Data.

Quay, H. C., & Peterson, D. R. (1987). *Manual for the revised behavior problem checklist*. Coral Cables, FL: Author.

Rachlin, H. (1991). *Introduction to modern behaviorism* (3rd ed.), New York: W. H. Freeman.

Ramirez, J., Yuen, S., & Ramey, D. (1991). *Executive summary: Longitudinal study of structured English immersion strategy, early-exit, late-exit transitional bilingual education programs for language minority children*. San Mateo, CA: Aguirre International.

Range, L. M. (1993). Suicide prevention: Guidelines for schools. *Educational Psychology Review, 5*, 135–154.

Rathus, S. A. (1988). *Understanding child development*. New York: Holt, Rinehart & Winston.

Raudenbush, S. (1984). Magnitude of teacher expectancy effects on pupil IQ as a function of the credibility of expectancy induction: A synthesis of findings from 18 experiments. *Journal of Educational Psychology, 76*, 85–97.

Raudsepp, E., & Haugh, G. P. (1977). *Creative growth games*. New York: Harcourt Brace Jovanovich.

Recht, D. R., & Leslie, L. (1988). Effect of prior knowledge on good and poor readers' memory of text. *Journal of Educational Psychology, 80*, 16–20.

Redfield, D. L., & Rousseau, E. W. (1981). A meta-analysis of experimental research on teacher questioning behavior. *Review of Educational Research, 51*, 181–193.

Reed, S. K. (1992). *Cognition* (3rd ed.). Pacific Grove, CA: Brooks/Cole.

Reed, S., & Sautter, R. C. (1990). Children of poverty: The status of 12 million Americans. *Phi Delta Kappan, 71*(10), K1–K12.

Reich, P. A. (1986). *Language development*. Englewood Cliffs, NJ: Prentice-Hall.

Reid, D. K., Hresko, W. P., & Swanson, H. L. (1991). *A cognitive approach to learning disabilities* (2nd ed.). Austin, TX: Pro-Ed.

Reid, M. K., & Borkowski, J. G. (1987). Causal attributions of hyperactive children: Implications for teaching strategies and self control. *Journal of Educational Psychology, 79*, 296–307.

Render, G. F., Padilla, J. N. M., & Krank, H. M. (1989). What research really shows about assertive discipline. *Educational Leadership, 46*(6), 72–75.

Rennie, L. J., & Parker, L. H. (1987). Detecting and accounting for gender differences in mixed-sex and single-sex groupings in science lessons. *Educational Review, 39*(1), 65–73.

Renzulli, J. S. (1982). Dear Mr. and Mrs. Copernicus: We regret to inform you . . . *Gifted Child Quarterly, 26*, 11–14.

Renzulli, J. S., & Reis, S. M. (1991). The schoolwide enrichment model: A comprehensive plan for the development of creative productivity. In N. Colangelo & G. Davis (Eds.), *Handbook of gifted education* (pp. 111–141). Boston: Allyn and Bacon.

Renzulli, J. S., & Smith, L. H. (1978). *The Learning Styles Inventory: A measure of student preferences for instructional techniques*. Mansfield Center, CT: Creative Learning Press.

Resnick, L. B. (1981). Instructional psychology. *Annual Review of Psychology, 32*, 659–704.

Resnick, L. B., & Klopfer, L. E. (1989). Toward the thinking curriculum: An overview. In *Toward the thinking curriculum: Current cognitive research* (pp. 1–18). Alexandria, VA: Association for Supervision and Curriculum Development.

Reynolds, M. C., & Birch, J. W. (1988). *Adaptive mainstreaming: A primer for teachers and principals* (3rd ed.). New York: Longman.

Reynolds, W. M. (1980). Self-esteem and classroom behavior in elementary school children. *Psychology in the Schools, 17*, 273–277.

Rhode, G., Morgan, D. P., & Young, K. R. (1983). Generalization and maintenance of treatment gains of behaviorally handicapped students from resource rooms to regular classrooms using self-evaluation procedures. *Journal of Applied Behavior Analysis, 16*, 171–188.

Rice, M. L. (1984). Cognitive aspects of communicative development. In R. Schiefelbusch & J. Pickar (Eds.), *The acquisition of communicative competence*. Baltimore: University Park Press.

Rice, M. L. (1989). Children's language acquisition. *American Psychologist, 44,* 149–156.

Richardson, T. M., & Benbow, C. P. (1990). Long-term effects of acceleration on the social-emotional adjustment of mathematically precocious youths. *Journal of Educational Psychology, 82,* 464–470.

Riley, M. S., & Greeno, J. G. (1991). Developmental analysis of understanding language about quantities and of solving problems. *Cognition and Instruction, 5,* 49–101.

Rist, R. (1970). Student social class and teacher expectations: The self-fulfilling prophecy in ghetto education. *Harvard Educational Review, 40,* 411–451.

Robbins, P. A. (1990). Implementing whole language: Bridging children and books. *Educational Leadership, 47*(6), 50–55.

Robert Wood Johnson (1988). *Serving handicapped children: A special report.* Princeton, NJ: Robert Wood Johnson Foundation.

Robinson, C. S., & Hayes, J. R. (1978). Making inferences about relevance in understanding problems. In R. Revlin & R. E. Mayer (Eds.), *Human reasoning.* Washington, DC: Winston.

Robinson, F. P. (1961). *Effective study.* New York: Harper and Row.

Robinson, S., Depascale, C., & Deno, S. (1988, April). *Technology and group instruction: An investigation of enhanced teacher monitoring, correction and student feedback.* Paper presented at the annual meeting of the American Educational Research Association, New Orleans.

Rodriguez, R. (1987, September 9). What is an American education? *Education Week, 7*(1).

Roethlisberger, F. J., & Dickson, W. J. (1939). *Management and the worker.* Cambridge, MA: Harvard University Press.

Rogers, C. R. (1969). *Freedom to learn.* Columbus, OH: Charles E. Merrill.

Rogers, C. R., & Freiberg, H. J. (1994). *Freedom to learn* (3rd ed.). Columbus, OH: Charles E. Merrill.

Rogers, D. (1985). *Adolescents and youth* (5th ed.). Englewood Cliffs, NJ: Prentice-Hall.

Rogoff, B. (1990). *Apprenticeship in thinking: Cognitive development in social context.* New York: Oxford University Press.

Rogoff, B., & Morelii, G. (1989). Perspectives on children's development from cultural psychology. *American Psychologist, 44,* 343–348.

Rogoff, B., & Wertsch, J. V. (Eds.). (1984). *Children's learning in the "zone of proximal development."* San Francisco: Jossey-Bass.

Rosch, E. H. (1973). On the internal structure of perceptual and semantic categories. In T. Moore (Ed.), *Cognitive development and the acquisition of language.* New York: Academic Press.

Rosch, E. H. (1975). Cognitive representations of semantic categories. *Journal of Experimental Psychology: General, 104,* 192–233.

Roschelle, J. (1991). *Students' construction of qualitative physics knowledge: Learning about velocity and acceleration in a computer microworld.* Unpublished Doctoral Dissertation, University of California, Berkeley.

Roschelle, J., & Clancey, W. J. (1992). Learning as social and neural. *Educational Psychologist, 27,* 435–454.

Rose, A. (1962). The causes of prejudice. In I. M. Barron (Ed.), *American cultural minorities: A textbook in intergroup relations.* New York: Alfred A. Knopf.

Rosen, L. A., O'Leary, S. G., Joyce, S. A., Conway, G., & Pfiffner, L. J. (1984). The importance of prudent negative consequences for maintaining the appropriate behavior of hyperactive students. *Journal of Abnormal Child Psychology, 12,* 581–604.

Rosenman, A. A. (1987, November 11). The value of multicultural curricula. *Education Week, 7*(10).

Rosenshine, B. (1977, April). *Primary grades instruction and student achievement.* Paper presented at the annual meeting of the American Educational Research Association, New York.

Rosenshine, B. (1979). Content, time, and direct instruction. In P. Peterson & H. Walberg (Eds.), *Research on teaching: Concepts, findings, and implications* (pp. 28–56). Berkeley, CA: McCutchan.

Rosenshine, B. (1986). Synthesis of research on explicit teaching. *Educational Leadership, 43*(7), 60–69.

Rosenshine, B. (1988). Explicit teaching. In D. Berliner & B. Rosenshine (eds.), *Talks to teachers* (pp. 75–92). New York: Random House.

Rosenshine, B., & Furst, N. (1973). The use of direct observation to study teaching. In R. Travers (Ed.), *Second handbook of research on teaching.* Chicago: Rand McNally.

Rosenshine, B., & Meister, C. (1992, April). *The uses of scaffolds for teaching less structured academic tasks.* Paper presented at the annual meeting of the American Educational Research Association, San Francisco.

Rosenshine, B., & Stevens, R. (1986). Teaching functions. In M. Wittrock (Ed.), *Handbook of research on teaching* (3rd ed., pp. 376–391). New York: Macmillan.

Rosenthal, R. (1973). The Pygmalion effect lives. *Psychology Today,* pp. 56–63.

Rosenthal, R. (1976). *Experimenter effects in behavioral research* (enlarged ed.). New York: Halsted Press.

Rosenthal, R. (1987). Pygmalion effects: Existence, magnitude and social importance. A reply to Wineburg. *Educational Researcher, 16,* 37–41.

Rosenthal, R., and Jacobson, L. (1968). *Pygmalion in the classroom.* New York: Holt, Rinehart, Winston.

Ross, S. M. (1986). *BASIC programming for educators.* Englewood Cliffs, NJ: Prentice-Hall.

Ross, S. M., McCormick, D., Krisak, N., & Anand, P. (1985). Personalizing context in teaching mathematical concepts: Teacher-managed and computer-managed models. *Educational Communication Technology Journal, 33,* 169–178.

Rosser, R. (1994). *Cognitive development: Psychological and biological perspectives.* Boston: Allyn and Bacon.

Rothenberg, J. (1989), The open classroom reconsidered. *Elementary School Journal, 90,* 68–86.

Rotherham-Borus, M. J. (1994). Bicultural reference group orientations and adjustment. In M. Bernal & G. Knight (Eds.), *Ethnic identity.* Albany, NY: State University of New York Press.

Rothman, R. (1988, April 1). "Computer competence" still rare among students, assessment finds. *Education Week,* p. 20.

Rotter, J. (1954). *Social learning and clinical psychology.* Englewood Cliffs, NJ: Prentice-Hall.

Rowe, M. B. (1974). Wait-time and rewards as instructional variables: Their influence on language, logic, and fate control. Part 1: Wait-time. *Journal of Research in Science Teaching, 11,* 81–94.

Rumelhart, D. & Ortony, A. (1977). The representation of knowledge in memory. In R. Anderson, R. Spiro, & W. Montague (Eds.), *Schooling and the acquisition of knowledge.* Hillsdale, NJ: Erlbaum.

Ruopp, F., & Driscoll, M. (1990, January/February). Access to algebra. *Harvard Education Letter, 6*(A), 4–5.

Ryan, R. M. (1991). The nature of the self in autonomy and relatedness. In G. R. Goethals & J. Strauss (Eds.), *Multidisciplinary perspectives on the self*. New York: Springer-Verlag.

Ryan, R. M., & Grolnick, W. S. (1986). Origins and pawns in the classroom: Self-report and projective assessments of individual differences in the children's perceptions. *Journal of Personality and Social Psychology, 50*, 550–558.

Ryans, D. G. (1960). *Characteristics of effective teachers, their descriptions, comparisons and appraisal: A research study*. Washington, DC: American Council on Education.

Sabers, D. S., Cushing, K. S., & Berliner, D. C. (1991). Differences among teachers in a task characterized by simultaneity, multidimensionality, and immediacy. *American Educational Research Journal, 28*, 68–87.

Sadker, M., & Sadker, D. (1985, March). Sexism in the schoolroom of the '80s. *Psychology Today*, 54–57.

Sadker, M., & Sadker, D. (1986a). Questioning skills. In J. Cooper (Ed.), *Classroom teaching skills* (3rd ed., pp. 143–180). Lexington, MA: D. C. Heath.

Sadker, M., & Sadker, D. (1986b). Sexism in the classroom: From grade school to graduate school. *Phi Delta Kappan, 68*, 512.

Sadker, M., Sadker, D., & Klein, S. (1991). The issue of gender in elementary and secondary education. *Review of Research in Education, 17*, 269–334.

Salili, F., Maehr, M. L., Sorensen, R. L., & Fyans, L. J. (1976). A further consideration of the effect of evaluation on motivation. *American Educational Research Journal, 13*(2), 85–102.

Salomon, G., & Perkins, D. N. (1989). Rocky roads to transfer: Rethinking mechanisms of a neglected phenomenon. *Educational Psychologist, 24*, 113–142.

Sandefur, J. T. (1985). Competency assessment of teachers. *Action in Teacher Education, 7*, (1–2), 1–6.

Sattler, J. (1992). *Assessment of children* (3rd ed. revised). San Diego: Jerome M. Sattler.

Sawyer, R. J., Graham, S., & Harris, K. R. (1992). Direct teaching, strategy instruction, and strategy instruction with explicit self-regulation: Effects on the composition skills and self-efficacy of learning disabled students. *Journal of Educational Psychology, 84*, 340–352.

Saxe, G. B. (1988). Candy selling and math learning. *Educational Researcher, 17*(6), 14–21.

Scarr, S., & Carter-Saltzman, L. (1982). Genetics and intelligence. In R. Sternberg (Ed.), *Handbook of human intelligence*. New York: Cambridge University Press.

Scarr, S., Weinberg, R. A., & Levine, A. (1986). *Understanding development*. New York: Harcourt Brace Jovanovich.

Schab, F. (1980). Cheating in high school: Differences between the sexes (revisited). *Adolescence, 15*, 959–965.

Scherer, M. (1993). On savage inequalities: A conversation with Jonathan Kozol. *Educational Leadership, 50*(4), 4–9.

Schiedel, D., & Marcia, J. (1985). Ego integrity, intimacy, sex role orientation, and gender. *Developmental Psychology, 21*, 149–160.

Schiefele, U. (1991). Interest, learning, and motivation. *Educational Psychologist, 26*, 299–324.

Schneider, W., & Bjorklund, D. F. (1992). Expertise, aptitude, and strategic remembering. *Child Development, 63*, 416–473.

Schoenfeld, A. H. (1979). Explicit heuristic training as a variable in problem solving performance. *Journal for Research in Mathematics Education, 10*, 173–187.

Schofield, J. W. (1991). School desegregation and intergroup relations. *Review of Research in Education, 17*, 235–412.

Schon, D. (1983). *The reflective practitioner*. New York: Basic Books.

Schuder, T. The genesis of transactional strategies for at-risk students. *Elementary School Journal, 94*, 235–254.

Schunk, D. H. (1987). Peer models and children's behavioral change. *Review of Educational Research, 57*, 149–174.

Schunk, D. H. (1991a). *Learning theories: An educational perspective*. New York: Merrill.

Schunk, D. H. (1991b). Self-efficacy and academic motivation. *Educational Psychologist, 26*, 207–232.

Schunk, D. H., & Hanson, A. R. (1985). Peer models: Influence on children's self-efficacy and achievement. *Journal of Educational Psychology, 77*, 313–322.

Schwartz, B., & Reisberg, D. (1991). *Learning and memory*. New York: Norton.

Schwartz, J. C., Scarr, S., & McCartney, K. (1983, August). *Center, sitter, and home care before age two: A report on the first Bermuda infant care study*. Paper presented at the annual meeting of the American Psychological Association, Los Angeles.

Science (1986). Obese children: A growing problem. *Science, 232*, 20–21.

Scruggs, T. E., Mastropieri, M. A., McLoone, B., Levin, J. R., & Morrison, C. R. (1985). *Mnemonic facilitation of learning-disabled students' memory for expository prose*. Unpublished manuscript, Utah State University, Logan.

Seddon, G. M. (1978). The properties of Bloom's taxonomy of educational objectives for the cognitive domain. *Review of Educational Research, 48*, 303–323.

Seiber, J. E., O'Neil, H. F., & Tobias, S. (1977). *Anxiety, learning, and instruction*. Hillsdale, NJ: Erlbaum.

Seifert, K. L., & Hoffnung, R. J. (1991). *Child and adolescent development*. Boston: Houghton-Mifflin.

Seligman, M. E. P. (1975). *Helplessness: On depression, development, and death*. San Francisco: Freeman.

Selman, R. L. (1981). The child as a friendship philosopher. In S. Asher & J. Gottman (Eds.), *The development of children's friendships*. Cambridge: Cambridge University Press.

Selman, R. L., & Byrne, D. F. (1974). A structural-developmental analysis of levels of role taking in middle childhood. *Child Development, 45*, 803–806.

Serbin, L., & O'Leary, D. (1975, January). How nursery schools teach girls to shut up. *Psychology Today*, pp. 56–58.

Shantz, C. (1975). The development of social cognition. In E. M. Hetherington (Ed.), *Review of child development research* (Vol. 5). Chicago: University of Chicago Press.

Shapiro, E. S., & Ager, C. (1992). Assessment of special education students in regular education programs: Linking assessment to instruction. *The Elementary School Journal, 92*, 283–296.

Shavelson, R. J. (1987). Planning. In M. Dunkin (Ed.), *The international encyclopedia of teaching and teacher education* (pp. 483–486). New York: Pergamon Press.

Shavelson, R. J., & Bolus, R. (1982). Self-concept: The interplay of theory and methods. *Psychology, 74*, 3–17.

Shavelson, R. J., Gao, X., & Baxter, G. (1993). *Sampling variability of performance assessments*. CSE Technical Report 361. Los Angeles: UCLA Center for the Study of Evaluation.

Shavelson, R. J., Hubner, J. J., & Stanton, G. C. (1976). Self-concept: Validation of construct interpretations. *Review of Educational Research, 46*, 407, 442.

Shepard, L. A., & Smith, M. L. (1989). Academic and emotional effects of kindergarten retention. In L. Shepard & M. Smith (Eds.),

Flunking grades: Research and policies on retention (pp. 79–107). Philadelphia: Falmer Press.

Sherman, J. G., Ruskin, R. S., & Semb, G. B. (Eds.) (1982). *The Personalized System of Instruction: 48 seminal papers.* Lawrence, KS: TRI Publications.

Sherry, M. (1990). Implementing an integrated instructional system: Critical issues. *Phi Delta Kappan, 72,* 118–120.

Shields, P., Gordon, J., & Dupree, D. (1983). Influence of parent practices upon the reading achievement of good and poor readers. *Journal of Negro Education, 52,* 436–445.

Shostak, R. (1986). Lesson presentation skills. In J. Cooper (Ed.), *Classroom teaching skills* (3rd ed., pp. 114–138). Lexington, MA: D. C. Heath.

Shuell, T. J. (1981a). Dimensions of individual differences. In F. H. Farley & N. J. Gordon (Eds.), *Psychology and education: The state of the union* (pp. 32–59). Berkeley, CA: McCutchan.

Shuell, T. J. (1981b, April). *Toward a model of learning from instruction.* Paper presented at a meeting of the American Educational Research Association, Los Angeles.

Shuell, T. J. (1986). Cognitive conceptions of learning. *Review of Educational Research, 56,* 411–436.

Shuell, T. J. (1990). Phases of meaningful learning. *Review of Educational Psychology, 60,* 531–548.

Shulman, L. S. (1987). Knowledge and teaching: Foundations of the new reform. *Harvard Educational Review, 19*(2), 4–14.

Shultz, J., & Florio, S. (1979). Stop and freeze: The negotiation of social and physical space in a kindergarten/first grade classroom. *Anthropology and Education Quarterly, 10,* 166–181.

*Siedenberg, M. S. (1993). Connectionist models and cognitive theory. *Psychological Science, 4,* 228–235.

*Siegel, J., & Shaughnessy, M. F. (1994). Educating for understanding: An interview with Howard Gardner. *Phi Delta Kappan, 75,* 536–566.

Siegel, L. J. (1983). Psychosomatic and psychophysiological disorders. In R. J. Morris & T. R. Kratochwill (Eds.), *The practice of child therapy.* New York: Pergamon.

Siegler, R. S. (1986). *Children's thinking.* Englewood Cliffs: NJ: Prentice-Hall.

Siegler, R. S. (1991). *Children's thinking* (2nd ed.). Englewood Cliffs, NJ: Prentice-Hall.

Silberman, C. (1966). Technology is knocking at the schoolhouse door. *Fortune, 74,* 120–125.

*Simmons, R. G. , & Blyth, D. A. (1987). *Moving into adolescence.* New York: Aldine De Gruyter.

Simon, D. P., & Chase, W. G. (1973). Skill in chess. *American Scientist, 61,* 394–403.

Simon, P. (1980). *The tongue-tied American: Confronting the foreign language crisis.* New York: Continuum.

Simpson, E. J. (1972). "The classification of educational objectives in the psychomotor domain." *The Psychomotor Domain. Vol 3.* Washington, Gryphon House.

*Singley, K., & Anderson, J. R. (1989). *The transfer of cognitive skill.* Cambridge, MA: Harvard University Press.

Sisk, D. A. (1988). Children at risk: The identification of the gifted among the minority. *Gifted Education International, 5,* 138–141.

Sizer, T. (1984). *Horace's compromise: The dilemma of the American high school* (updated ed.). Princeton, NJ: Houghton Mifflin.

Skinner, B. F. (1953). *Science and human behavior.* New York: Macmillan.

Skinner, B. F. (1950). Are theories of learning necessary? *Psychological Review, 57,* 193–216.

*Skinner, B. F. (1989). The origins of cognitive thought. *American Psychologist, 44,* 13–18.

Slavin, R. E. (1983). *Cooperative learning.* New York: Longman.

Slavin, R. E. (1984). Students motivating students to excel: Cooperative incentives, cooperative tasks, and student achievement. *Elementary School Journal, 85,* 53–64.

Slavin, R. E. (1987). Ability grouping and student achievement in elementary schools: A best-evidence synthesis. *Review of Educational Research, 57,* 293–336.

Slavin, R. E. (1990a). Achievement effects of ability grouping in secondary schools: A best-evidence synthesis. *Review of Educational Research, 60,* 471–500.

*Slavin, R. E. (1994). *Educational psychology: Theory and practice* (4th ed.). Boston: Allyn and Bacon.

*Slavin, R. E. (1995). *Cooperative learning* (2nd ed.). Boston: Allyn & Bacon.

Slavin, R. E., & Karweit, N. (1985). Effects of whole class, ability grouped, and individualized instruction on mathematics achievement. *American Educational Research Journal, 22,* 351–368.

Slavin, R. E., Karweit, N. L., & Madden, N. A. (1989). *Effective programs for students at risk.* Boston: Allyn and Bacon.

Sleeter, C. E., & Grant, C. A. (1987). An analysis of multicultural education in the United States. *Harvard Educational Review, 57,* 421–444.

*Smetana, J. G., & Braeges, J. L. (1990). The development of toddlers' moral and conventional judgments. *Merrill-Palmer Quarterly, 36,* 329–346.

Smith, F. (1975). *Comprehension and learning: A conceptual framework for teachers.* New York: Holt, Rinehart & Winston.

*Smith, F. (1992). Learning to read: The never-ending debate. *Phi Delta Kappan, 73,* 432–442.

Smith, J. (1991). What will the new SAT look like? An interview with Lawrence Hecht. *d'News: The Newsletter of Division D, American Educational Research Association, 1*(2), 1–4.

Smith, J. D., & Caplan, J. (1988). Cultural differences in cognitive style development. *Developmental Psychology, 24,* 46–52.

Smith, M. L. (1991). Put to the test: The effects of external testing on teachers. *Educational Researcher, 20*(5), 8–11.

Smith, S. M., Glenberg, A., & Bjork, R. A. (1978). Environmental context and human memory. *Memory and Cognition, 6,* 342–353.

Smith, S. M., & Neisworth, J. T. (1975). *The exceptional child: A functional approach.* New York: McGraw Hill.

Snider, V. E. (1990). What we know about learning styles from research in special education. *Educational Leadership, 48*(2), 53.

Snow, C. E. (1987). Beyond conversation: Second language learners' acquisition of description and explanation. In J. P. Lantolf & A. Labarca (Eds.), *Research in second language learning: Focus on the classroom* (pp. 3–16). Norwood, NJ: Ablex.

Snow, M. A. (1986). *Innovative second language education: Bilingual immersion programs* (Education Report 1). Los Angeles: Center of Language Education and Research, University of California.

Snow, R. E. (1977). Research on aptitude for learning: A progress report. In L. Shulman (Ed.), *Review of research in education.* Itasca, IL: F. E. Peacock.

Snowman, J. (1984). Learning tactics and strategies. In G. Phye & T. Andre (Eds.), *Cognitive instructional psychology.* Orlando, FL: Academic Press.

Snyderman, M., & Rothman, S. (1987). Survey of expert opinion of intelligence and aptitude testing. *American Psychologist, 42,* 137–144.

Soar, R. S. (1973). *Follow-through classroom process measurement and pupil growth 1970–1971: Final report.* Gainesville, FL: University of Florida.

Soar, R. S., & Soar, R. M. (1979). Emotional climate and management. In P. Peterson & H. Walberg (Eds.), *Research on teaching: Concepts, findings, and implications.* Berkeley, CA: McCutchan.

• Sobesky, W. E. (1983). The effects of situational factors on moral judgment. *Child Development, 54,* 575–584.

Sokolove, S., Garrett, J., Sadker, D., & Sadker, M. (1986). Interpersonal communications skills. In J. Cooper (Ed.), *Classroom teaching skills: A handbook.* Lexington, MA: D. C. Heath.

Soloway, E., Lockhead, J., & Clement, J. (1982). Does computer programming enhance problem solving ability? Some positive evidence on algebra word problems. In R. J. Seidel, R. E. Anderson, & S. B. Hunter (Eds.), *Computer literacy.* New York: Academic Press.

Spearman, C. (1927). *The abilities of man: Their nature and measurement.* New York: Macmillan.

Spencer, M. B., & Markstrom-Adams, C. (1990). Identity processes among racial and ethnic-minority children in America. *Child Development, 61,* 290–310.

• Spiro, R. J., Feltovich, P. J., Jacobson, M. L., & Coulson, R. L. (1991). Cognitive flexibility, constructivism, and hypertext: Random access instruction for advanced knowledge acquisition in ill-structured domains. *Educational Technology, 31*(5), 24–33.

Sroufe, L. A., Fox, N. E., & Pancake, V. R. (1983). Attachment and dependency in developmental perspective. *Child Development 54,* 1615–1627.

Stallings, J. A., & Kaskowitz, D. H. (1975, April). *A study of follow-through implementation.* Paper presented at the annual meeting of the American Educational Research Association, Washington, DC.

• Stainback, S., & Stainback, W. (1992). Schools as inclusive communities. In W. Stainback & S. Stainback (Eds.), *Controversial issues confronting special education: Divergent perspectives* (pp. 29–43). Boston: Allyn & Bacon.

• Stanovich, K. E. (1991). Reading disability: Assessment issues. In H. Swanson (Ed.), *Handbook of assessment of learning disabilities: Theory, research, and practice* (pp. 147–175). Austin, TX: Pro-Ed.

Stanovich, K. E. (1992). *How to think straight about psychology* (3rd ed.). Glenview, IL: Scott, Foresman.

Starch, D., & Elliot, E. C. (1912). Reliability of grading high school work in English. *Scholastic Review, 20,* 442–457.

Starch, D., & Elliot, E. C. (1913a). Reliability of grading work in history. *Scholastic Review, 21,* 676–681.

Starch, D., & Elliot, E. C. (1913b). Reliability of grading work in mathematics. *Scholastic Review, 21,* 254–259.

Starr, R. H., Jr. (1979). Child abuse. *American Psychologist, 34,* 872–878.

Stein, B. S., Littlefield, J., Bransford, J. D., & Persampieri, M. (1984). Elaboration and knowledge acquisition. *Memory and Cognition, 12,* 522–529.

Steinberg, L., Elmen, J. D., & Mounts, N. S. (1989). Authoritative parenting, psychosocial maturity, and academic success among adolescents. *Child Development, 60,* 1424–1436.

• Stepien, W., & Gallagher, S. (1993). Problem-based learning: As authentic as it gets. *Educational Leadership, 50*(7), 25–28.

Sternberg, R. (1985). *Beyond IQ: A triarchic theory of human intelligence.* New York: Cambridge University Press.

Sternberg, R. (1986). *Intelligence applied: Understanding and increasing your own intellectual skills.* New York: Harcourt Brace Jovanovich.

Sternberg, R. (1990). *Metaphors of mind: Conceptions of the nature of intelligence.* New York: Cambridge University Press.

Sternberg, R., & Davidson, J. (1982, June). The mind of the puzzler. *Psychology Today,* pp. 37–44.

Sternberg, R. J., & Detterman, D. L. (Eds.). (1986). *What is intelligence? Contemporary viewpoints on its nature and definition.* Norwood, NJ: Ablex.

• Sternberg, R. J., & Wagner, R. K. (1993). The *g*-ocentric view of intelligence and job performance is wrong. *Current Directions in Psychological Science, 2,* 1–5.

Stigler, J. W., Lee, S., & Stevenson, H. W. (1987). Mathematics classrooms in Japan, Taiwan, and the United States. *Child Development, 58,* 1272–1285.

• Stipek, D. J. (1993). *Motivation to learn* (2nd ed.). Boston: Allyn and Bacon.

• Stoddart, T., Connell, M, Stofflett, R., & Peck, D. (1993). Reconstructing elementary teacher candidates' understanding of mathematics and science content. *Teaching and Teacher Education, 9,* 229–241.

Stodolsky, S. S. (1988). *The subject matters: Classroom activity in math and social studies.* Chicago: University of Chicago Press.

Straus, M. A., Gelles, R. J., & Steinmetz, S. K. (1980). *Behind closed doors: Violence in the American family.* New York: Doubleday.

Strike, K. (1975). The logic of discovery. *Review of Educational Research, 45,* 461–483.

Sulzer-Azaroff, B., & Mayer, G. R. (1986). *Achieving educational excellence using behavioral strategies.* New York: Holt, Rinehart & Winston.

Suzuki, B. H. (1983). The education of Asian and Pacific Americans: An introductory overview. In D. Nakanishi & M. Hirano-Nakanishi (Eds.), *The education of Asian and Pacific Americans: Historical perspectives and prescriptions for the future.* Phoenix, AZ: Oryx Press.

Swanson, H. L., O'Conner, J. E., & Cooney, J. B. (1990). An information processing analysis of expert and novice teachers' problem solving. *American Educational Research Journal, 27,* 533–556.

Tal, Z., & Babad, E. (1990). The teachers' pet phenomenon: Rate of occurrence, correlates, and psychological costs. *Journal of Educational Psychology, 82,* 637–645.

Tanner, J. (1970). Physical growth. In P. Mussen (Ed.), *Carmichael's manual of child psychology* (3rd ed., Vol. 1). New York: Wiley.

Task Force on Pediatric AIDS: American Psychological Association. (1989). Pediatric AIDS and human immunodeficiency virus infection: Psychological issues. *American Psychologist, 44,* 258–264.

Taylor, J. B. (1983). Influence of speech variety on teachers' evaluation of reading comprehension. *Journal of Educational Psychology, 75,* 662–667.

Taylor, R. P. (Ed.) (1980). *The computer in the school: Tutor, tool, tutee.* New York: Teachers College Press.

Teacher Magazine (1991, April). *You and the system: Who you will teach,* p. 32H.

TenBrink, T. D. (1986). Writing instructional objectives. In J. Cooper (Ed.), *Classroom teaching skills* (3rd ed., pp. 71–110). Lexington, MA: D. C. Heath.

Tennyson, R. D. (1981, April). *Concept learning effectiveness using prototype and skill development presentation forms.* Paper presented at the annual meeting of the American Educational Research Association, Los Angeles.

Tennyson, R. D., & Cocchiarella, M. J. (1986). An empirically based instructional design theory for teaching concepts. *Review of Educational Research, 56,* 40–71.

Terman, L. M., Baldwin, B. T., & Bronson, E. (1925). Mental and physical traits of a thousand gifted children. In L. M. Terman (Ed.), *Genetic studies of genius* (Vol. 1). Stanford, CA: Stanford University Press.

Terman, L. M., & Oden, M. H. (1947). The gifted child grows up. In L. M. Terman (Ed.), *Genetic studies of genius* (Vol. 4). Stanford, CA: Stanford University Press.

Terman, L. M., & Oden, M. H. (1959). The gifted group in mid-life. In L. M. Terman (Ed.), *Genetic studies of genius* (Vol. 5). Stanford, CA: Stanford University Press.

Tharp, R. C., & Gallimore, R. (1988). *Rousing minds to life: Teaching, learning, and schooling in social context.* New York: Cambridge University Press.

Tharp, R. G., & Gallimore, R. (1991). *The instructional conversation: Teaching and learning in social activity.* Washington, DC: National Center for Research on Cultural Diversity and Second Language Learning.

Tharp, R. G. (1989). Psychocultural variables and constants: Effects on teaching and learning in schools. *American Psychologist, 44,* 349–359.

Thoma, S. J. (1986). Estimating gender differences in the comprehension and preference of moral issues. *Developmental Review, 6,* 165–180.

Thomas, E. L., & Robinson, H. A. (1972). *Improving reading in every class: A sourcebook for teachers.* Boston: Allyn and Bacon.

Thorndike, E. L. (1913). Educational psychology. In *The psychology of learning* (Vol. 2). New York: Teachers College, Columbia University.

Thorndike, R., Hagen, E., & Sattler, J. (1986). *The Stanford-Binet Intelligence Scale* (4th ed.). Chicago: Riverside.

Thurstone, L. L. (1938). Primary mental abilities. *Psychometric Monographs,* No. 1.

Tiedt, P. L., & Tiedt, I. M. (1990). *Multicultural education: A handbook of activities, information, and resources.* Boston: Allyn and Bacon.

Tierney, R. J., Readence, J. E., & Dishner, E. K. (1990). *Reading strategies and practices: A compendium,* (3rd ed.). Boston: Allyn and Bacon.

Timmer, S. G., Eccles, J., & O'Brien, K. (1988). How children use time. In F. Juster & F. Stafford (Eds.), *Time, goods, and well-being.* Ann Arbor, MI: Institute for Social Research, University of Michigan.

Tishman, S., Perkins, D., & Jay, E., (1995). *The thinking classroom: Creating a culture of thinking.* Boston: Allyn & Bacon.

Tobias, Sheila. (1982, January). Sexist equations. *Psychology Today,* pp. 14–17.

Tobias, Sigmund. (1979). Anxiety research in educational psychology. *Journal of Educational Psychology, 71,* 573–582.

Tobias, Sigmund. (1981). Adaptation to individual differences. In F. Farley & N. Gordon (Eds.), *Psychology and education: The state of the union* (pp. 60–80). Berkeley, CA: McCutchan.

Tobias, Sigmund. (1982). When do instructional methods make a difference? *Educational Researcher, 11*(4), 4–10.

Tobias, Sigmund. (1985). Text anxiety: Interference, defective skills, and cognitive capacity. *Educational Psychologist, 20,* 135–142.

Tobias, Sigmund, & Duchastel, P. (1974). Behavioral objectives, sequence, and anxiety in CAI. *Instructional Science, 3,* 232–242.

Tobin, K. (1987). The role of wait time in higher cognitive learning. *Review of Educational Research, 56,* 69–95.

Tobin, (1990, April). *Metaphors in the construction of teacher knowledge.* Paper presented at the Annual Meeting of the American Educational Research Association, Boston.

Tobin, K., & Dawson, G. (1992). Constraints to curriculum reform: Teachers and the myths of schooling. *Educational Technology Research and Development, 40*(1), 81–92.

Tochon, F., & Munby, H. (1993). Novice and expert teachers' time epistemology: A wave function from didactics to pedagogy. *Teaching and Teacher Education, 9,* 205–218.

Tomlinson-Keasey, C. (1990). Developing our intellectual resources for the 21st century: Educating the gifted. *Journal of Educational Psychology, 82,* 399–403.

Tomlinson-Keasey, C., & Little, T. D. (1990). Predicting educational attainment, occupational achievement intellectual skill, and personal adjustment among gifted men and women. *Journal of Educational Psychology, 82,* 442–455.

Torrance, E. P. (1972). Predictive validity of the Torrance tests of creative thinking. *Journal of Creative Behavior, 6,* 236–262.

Torrance, E. P. (1986). Teaching creative and gifted learners. In M. Wittrock (Ed.), *Handbook of research on teaching* (3rd ed.) (pp. 630–647). New York: Macmillan.

Torrance, E. P., & Hall, L. K. (1980). Assessing the future reaches of creative potential. *Journal of Creative Behavior, 14,* 1–19.

Travers, R. M. W. (1977). *Essentials of learning* (4th ed.). New York: Macmillan.

Trickett, E., & Moos, R. (1974). Personal correlates of contrasting environments: Student satisfaction with high school classrooms. *American Journal of Community Psychology, 2,* 1–12.

Turiel E. (1983). *The development of social knowledge: Morality and convention.* New York: Cambridge University Press.

Ure, A. (1861). *The philosophy of manufactures: Or an exposition of the scientific, moral, and commercial economy of the factory system of Great Britain* (3rd ed.). London: H. G. Bohn.

U.S. Bureau of the Census (1990). *Current Population Reports. Series P-20.* Washington, DC: U.S. Government Printing Office.

U.S. Bureau of the Census (1991). *Current Population Reports. Series P-20.* Washington, DC: U.S. Government Printing Office.

Vacc, N. N. (1989). Writing evaluation: Examining four teachers' holistic and analytic scores. *Elementary School Journal, 90,* 88–95.

Vaillant, G. E., & Vaillant, C. O. (1981). Natural history of male psychological health, X: Work as a predictor of positive mental health. *The American Journal of Psychiatry, 138,* 1433–1440.

Van Houten, R., & Doleys, D. M. (1983). Are social reprimands effective? In S. Axelrod & J. Apsche (Eds.), *The effects of punishment on human behavior.* San Diego: Academic Press.

Van Mondrans, A. P., Black, H. G., Keysor, R. E., Olsen, J. B., Shelley, M. F., & Williams, D. D. (1977). Methods of inquiry in educational psychology. In D. Treffinger, J. Davis, & R. R. Ripple (Eds.), *Handbook on teaching educational psychology.* New York: Academic Press.

Vargas, J. (1986). Instructional design flaws in computer-assisted instruction. *Phi Delta Kappan, 67,* 738–744.

Vasquez, J. A. (1990). Teaching to the distinctive traits of minority students. *The Clearing House, 63,* 299–304.

Veenman, S. (1984). Perceived problems of beginning teachers. *Review of Educational Research, 54,* 143–178.

*Vellutino, F. R. (1992). Introduction to three studies on reading acquisition: Convergent findings on theoretical foundations of code-oriented versus whole-language approaches to reading instruction. *Journal of Educational Psychology, 83,* 437–443.

Viadero, D. (1990). Battle over multicultural education rises in intensity. *Education Week, 10*(13), 1, 11, 13, 14.

*von Glaserfeld (1990). An Exposition of constructivism: Why some like it radical. In R. Davis, C. Maher, & N. Noddings (Eds.). *Constructivist views on the teaching and learning of mathematics* (pp. 19–30). Monograph 4 of the National Council of Teachers of Mathematics, Reston, VA.

*Vroom, V. (1964). *Work and motivation.* New York: Wiley.

Vygotsky, L. S. (1978). *Mind in society: The development of higher mental process.* Cambridge, MA: Harvard University Press.

Vygotsky, L. S. (1986). *Thought and language.* Cambridge, MA: MIT Press.

Wadsworth, B. J. (1978). *Piaget for the classroom teacher.* New York: Longman.

Wadsworth, B. J. (1989). *Piaget's theory of cognitive development: An introduction for students of psychology and education* (4th ed.). New York: Longman.

Walberg, H. J. (1990). Productive teaching and instruction: Assessing the knowledge base. *Phi Delta Kappan, 72,* 470–478.

Walberg, H. J., Pascal, R. A., & Weinstein, T. (1985). Homework's powerful effects on learning. *Educational Leadership, 42*(7), 76–79.

Walden, E. L., & Thompson, S. A. (1981). A review of some alternative approaches to drug management of hyperactive children. *Journal of Learning Disabilities, 14,* 213–217.

Walker, C., & Shaw, W. (1988). Assessment of eating and elimination disorders. In P. Karoly (Ed.), *Handbook of child health assessment: Biosocial perspectives.* New York: Wiley.

Walker, L. J. (1989). A longitudinal study of moral reasoning. *Child Development, 60,* 157–166.

Walker, L. J., & de Vries, B. (1985, August). *Moral stages/moral orientations: Do the sexes really differ?* Paper presented at the annual meeting of the American Psychological Association, Los Angeles.

Walker, L. J., de Vries, B., & Trevarthan, S. D. (1987). Moral stages and moral orientations in real-life and hypothetical dilemmas. *Child Development, 58,* 842–858.

*Wallerstein, J. S. (1991). The long-term effects of divorce on children: A review. *Journal of the American Academy of Child and Adolescent Psychiatry, 30,* 349–360.

Wallerstein, J., & Blakeslee, S. (1989). *Second chances: Men, women, and children a decade after divorce.* New York: Ticknor & Fields.

Walton, G. *Identification of the intellectually gifted children in the public school kindergarten.* Unpublished doctoral dissertation, University of California, Los Angeles, 1961.

*Wang, A. Y., Thomas, M. H., & Ouellette, J. A. (1992). Keyword mnemonic and retention of second-language vocabulary words. *Journal of Educational Psychology, 84,* 520–528.

Wang, M. C., & Palincsar, A. S. (1989). Teaching students to assume an active role in their learning. In M. Reynolds (Ed.), *Knowledge base for the beginning teacher* (pp. 71–84). New York: Pergamon.

Ward, M., & Sweller, J. (1990). Structuring effective worked examples. *Cognition and Instruction, 7,* 1–40.

Waterman, A. S. (Ed.). (1985). *Identity in adolescence: Processes and contents.* San Francisco: Jossey Bass.

Watson, B. (1990). The wired classroom: American education goes on-line. *Phi Delta Kappan, 72,* 109–112.

Webb, N. (1980). A process-outcome analysis of learners in group and individual settings. *Educational Psychology, 15,* 69–83.

Webb, N. (1982). Student interaction and learning in small groups. *Review of Educational Research, 52,* 421–445.

Webb, N. (1985). Verbal interaction and learning in peer-directed groups. *Theory into Practice, 24,* 32–39.

Webb, N. (1989). Peer interaction and learning in small groups. *International Journal of Educational Research, 23,* 253–261.

Weinberg, R. A. (1989). Intelligence and IQ. *American Psychologist, 44,* 98–104.

Weiner, B. (1979). A theory of motivation for some classroom experiences. *Journal of Educational Psychology, 71,* 3–25.

Weiner, B. (1980). The role of affect in rational (attributional) approaches to human motivation. *Educational Researcher, 9,* 4–11.

Weiner, B. (1984). Principles for a theory of student motivation and their application within an attributional framework. In R. Ames & C. Ames (Eds.), *Research on motivation in education* (Vol. 1). Orlando, FL: Academic Press.

Weiner, B. (1990). History of motivational research in education. *Journal of Educational Psychology, 82,* 616–622.

*Weiner, B. (1992). *Human motivation: Metaphors, theories, and research.* Newbury Park, CA: Sage.

Weiner, B., & Graham, S. (1989). Understanding the motivational role of affect: Lifespan research from an attributional perspective. *Cognition and Emotion, 4,* 401–419.

Weiner, B., Russell, D., & Lerman, D. (1978). Affective consequences of causal ascriptions. In J. H. Harvey, W. J. Ickes, & R. F. Kidd (Eds.). *New directions in attribution research* (Vol. 2). Hillsdale, NJ: Erlbaum.

*Weinstein, C. E. (1994). Learning strategies and learning to learn. *Encyclopedia of Education.*

*Weinstein, C. E., & McCombs, B. (in press). A model of strategic learning. In C. Weinstein & B. McCombs (Eds.), *Strategic learning: Skill, will, and self-regulation.* Hillsdale, NJ: Erlbaum.

Weinstein, C. E., & Mayer, R. E. (1985). The teaching of learning strategies. In M. C. Wittrock (Ed.), *Handbook of research on teaching* (3rd ed.). New York: Macmillan.

Weinstein, C. S. (1977). Modifying student behavior in an open classroom through changes in the physical design. *American Educational Research Journal, 14,* 249–262.

Weinstein, C. S., & Mignano, A. (1993). *Elementary classroom management: Lessons from research and practice.* New York: McGraw-Hill.

*Weisberg, R. W. (1993). *Creativity: Beyond the myth of genius.* New York: W. H. Freemen.

Wertsch, J. V. (1985). Adult-child interaction as a source of self-regulation in children. In S. Yussen (Ed.), *The growth of reflection in children.* Orlando, FL: Academic Press.

Wertsch, J. V. (1991). *Voices of the mind: A sociocultural approach to mediated action.* Cambridge, MA: Harvard University Press.

Wessells, M. G. (1982). *Cognitive psychology.* New York: Harper and Row.

Wessman, A. (1972). Scholastic and psychological effects of a compensatory education program for disadvantaged high school students: Project A B C. *American Educational Research Journal, 9,* 361–372.

*White, B. Y. (1993). TinkerTools: Causal models, conceptual change, and science education. *Cognition and Instruction, 10,* 1–100.

White, E. M. (1984). Holisticism. *College Composition and Communication, 35,* 400–409.

White, H. (1986). Damsels in distress: Dependency themes in fiction for children and adolescents. *Adolescence, 21,* 251–256.

White, K. R. (1982). The relation between socioeconomic status and academic achievement. *Psychological Bulletin, 91*(3), 461–481.

White, R. W. (1959). Motivation reconsidered: The concept of competence. *Psychological Review, 66,* 297–333.

White, S., & Tharp, R. G. (1988, April). *Questioning and wait-time: A cross cultural analysis.* Paper presented at the annual meeting of the American Educational Research Association, New Orleans.

Wigfield, A., & Eccles, J. (1989). Test anxiety in elementary and secondary school students. *Educational Psychologist, 24,* 159–183.

Wiggins, G. (1989). Teaching to the authentic test. *Educational Leadership, 46*(7), 41–47.

Wiggins, G. (1991). Standards, not standardization: Evoking quality student work. *Educational Leadership, 48*(5), 18–25.

Wiggins, G. (1991). Assessment, authenticity, context, and validity. *Phi Delta Kappan, 75,* 200–214.

Wiggins, G. (1993). Assessment, authenticity, context, and validity. *Phi Delta Kappan, 75,* 200–214.

Wiig, E. H. (1982). Communication disorders. In H. Haring (Ed.), *Exceptional children and youth.* Columbus, OH: Charles E. Merrill.

Wilen, W. (1990). Forms and phases of discussion. In W. Wilen (Ed.), *Teaching and learning through discussion* (pp. 3–24). Springfield, IL: Charles C. Thomas.

Wilkins, W. E., & Glock, M. D. (1973). *Teacher expectations and student achievement: A replication and extension.* Ithaca, NY: Cornell University Press.

Williams, G. C., Wiener, M. W., Markakis, K. M., Reeve, J., & Deci, E. L. (1993). Medical student motivation for internal medicine. *Annals of Internal Medicine.*

Willerman, L. (1979). *The psychology of individual and group differences.* San Francisco: Freeman.

Williams, J. P. (1976). *Individual differences in achievement test presentation and evaluation anxiety.* Unpublished doctoral dissertation, University of Illinois, Urbana-Champaign.

Williams, M. D. (1991). Observations in Pittsburgh ghetto schools. *Anthropology and Education Quarterly, 12,* 211–220.

Willis, P. (1977). *Learning to labor.* Lexington, MA: D. C. Heath.

Wilson, C. W., & Hopkins, B. L. (1973). The effects of contingent music on the intensity of noise in junior high home economics classes. *Journal of Applied Behavior Analysis, 6,* 269–275.

Wilson, S. M., Shulman, L. S., & Richert, A. R. (1987). 150 different ways of knowing: Representations of knowledge in teaching. In J. Calderhead (Ed.), *Exploring teacher thinking* (pp. 104–124). London: Cassell.

Wineburg, S. S. (1987). The self-fulfillment of the self-fulfilling prophecy: A critical appraisal. *Educational Researcher, 16,* 28–37.

Winett, R. A., & Winkler, R. C. (1972). Current behavior modification in the classroom: Be still, be quiet, be docile. *Journal of Applied Behavior Analysis, 15,* 499–504.

Wingate, N. (1986). Sexism in the classroom. *Equity and Excellence, 22,* 105–110.

Winograd, P., & Johnston, P. (1982). Comprehension monitoring and the error-detection paradigm. *Journal of Reading Behavior, 14,* 61–76.

Witkin, H. A., Moore, C. A., Goodenough, D. R., & Cox, R. W. (1977). Field-dependent and field-independent cognitive styles and their educational implications. *Review of Educational Research, 47,* 1–64.

Wittrock, M. C. (1978). The cognitive movement in instruction. *Educational Psychologist, 13,* 15–30.

Wittrock, M. C. (1982, March). *Educational implications of recent research on learning and memory.* Paper presented at the annual meeting of the American Educational Research Association, New York.

Wittrock, M. C. (1992). Generative learning processes of the brain. *Educational Psychologist, 27,* 531–542.

Wittrock, M. C. (1992). An empowering conception of educational psychology. *Educational Psychologist, 27,* 129–142.

Wlodkowski, R. J. (1981). Making sense out of motivation: A systematic model to consolidate motivational constructs across theories. *Educational Psychologist, 16,* 101–110.

Wolf, D. (in press). *Presence of minds, performances of thought.* New York: College Entrance Examination Board.

Wolf, D., Bixby, J., Glenn, J., III, & Gardner, H. (1991). To use their minds well: New forms of student assessment. *Review of Research in Education, 17,* 31–74.

Women on Words and Images. (1975). *Dick and Jane as victims: Sex stereotyping in children's readers* (expanded ed.). Available from author, P. O. Box 2163, Princeton, NJ.

Wong, L. (1987). Reaction to research findings: Is the feeling of obviousness warranted? *Dissertation Abstracts International, 48/12,* 3709B (University Microfilms #DA 8801059).

Wood, D., Bruner, J., & Ross, S. (1976). The role of tutoring in problem solving. *British Journal of Psychology, 66,* 181–191.

Wood, E. R. G., & Wood, S. E. (1993). *The world of psychology.* Boston: Allyn and Bacon.

Woolfolk, A. E., & Brooks, D. (1983). Nonverbal communication in teaching. In E. Gordon (Ed.), *Review of research in education* (Vol. 10 pp. 103–150). Washington, DC: American Educational Research Association.

Woolfolk, A. E., & Brooks, D. (1985). The influence of teachers' nonverbal behaviors on students' perceptions and performance. *Elementary School Journal, 85,* 514–528.

Woolfolk, A. E., & Hoy, W. K. (1988, April). *Efficacy, belief, and control orientations of prospective teachers.* Paper presented at the Annual Meeting of the American Educational Research Association, New Orleans.

Woolfolk, A. E., & Hoy, W. K. (1990). Prospective teachers' sense of efficacy and beliefs about control. *Journal of Educational Psychology, 82,* 81–91.

Woolfolk, A. E., Rosoff, B., & Hoy, W. K. (1990). Teachers' sense of efficacy and their beliefs about managing students. *Teaching and Teacher Education, 6,* 137–148.

Woolfolk, A. E., & Woolfolk, R. L. (1974). A contingency management technique for increasing student attention in a small group. *Journal of School Psychology, 12,* 204–212.

Workman, E. (1982). *Teaching behavioral self-control to students.* Austin, TX: PRO-ED.

Worthen, B. R. (1993). Critical issues that will determine the future of alternative assessment. *Phi Delta Kappan, 74,* 444–457.

Worthen, B. R., & Spandel, V. (1991). Putting the standardized text debate in perspective. *Educational Leadership, 48*(5), 65–70.

Wyler, R. S. (1988). Social memory and social judgment. In P. Solomon, G. Goethals, C. Kelly, & B. Stephans (Eds.), *Perspectives on memory research.* New York: Springer-Verlag.

•Wynne E. A. (1986). The great tradition in education: Transmitting moral values. *Educational Leadership, 43*(4), 4–9.

•Yee, A. H. (1992). Asians as stereotypes and students: Misperceptions that persist. *Educational Psychology Review, 4,* 95–132.

Yerkes, R. M., & Dodson, J. D. (1908). The relation of strength of stimulus to rapidity of habit formation. *Journal of Comparative Neurology, 18,* 459–482.

Youniss, J. (1980). *Parents and peers in social development.* Chicago: University of Chicago Press.

Yussen, S. R. (Ed.). (1985). *The growth of reflection in children.* Orlando, FL: Academic Press.

Zimmerman, B. J. (1990). Self-regulated learning and academic achievement: An overview. *Educational Psychologist, 21,* 3–18.

•Zimmerman, B. J., Bandura, A., & Martinez-Pons, M. (1992). Self-motivation for academic attainment: The role of self-efficacy beliefs and goal-setting. *American Educational Research Journal, 29,* 663–676.

Zimmerman, B. J., & Schunk, D. H. (Eds.). (1989). *Self-regulated learning and academic achievement: Theory, research, and practice.* New York: Springer-Verlag.

Zimmerman, D. W. (1981). On the perennial argument about grading "on the curve" in college courses. *Educational Psychologist, 16,* 175–178.

•Ziomek, R. L., & Maxey, J. M. (1993). To nationally test or not to nationally test: That is the question! *Measurement and Evaluation in Counseling and Development, 26,* 64–68.

INDEX OF KEY TERMS

This index gives the page or pages in the text where each key term is defined or explained. I encourage you not only to read the definitions but also to study and understand the terms in their larger context.

NAME INDEX

SUBJECT INDEX

Boldface page numbers indicate pages on which key terms and concepts are defined.

Photo Credits: